MW00450683

THE SLOW FOOD DICTIONARY TO
ITALIAN
REGIONAL
COOKING

edited by Paola Gho

adapted by John Irving

Slow Food Editore

Edited by
Paola Gho

Adapdet by
John Irving

Contributors
Antonio Attorre, Elisa Azzimondi,
Daniela Battaglio, Bianca Minerdo,
Grazia Novellini, Giovanni Ruffa,
Angelo Surrusca

Watercolors
Maria de Ferrari

Design
Maurizio Burdese

Printed on september 2010 by
Rotolito Lombarda,
Seggiano di Pioltello (Mi) - Italy

Copyright © 2010
© All rights reserved Slow Food® Editore

Slow Food® Editore
Via della Mendicità Istruita, 14
12042 Bra (Cn)
Tel. 0172 419611
Fax 0172 411218
www.slowfood.it
editorinfo@slowfood.it

Editor-in-Chief
Marco Bolasco

Managing Editor
Olivia Reviglio

ISBN 978-88-8499-240-6

FSC
Mixed Sources
Product group from well-managed
forests and other controlled sources

Cert no. SW-COC-002295
www.fsc.org
© 1996 Forest Stewardship Council

Editor's Introduction

This book is a dictionary. Not an encyclopedia, not a recipe book, but a dictionary. The entries are not always exhaustive, but brief and descriptive. Each definition seeks to capture the essence of a dish, of a product, of an animal or botanic breed or species or variety, sometimes adding relevant historical and cultural information with an eye to the past, to the present and sometimes to the future.

The subjects the book embraces or touches upon are: the dishes of Italian regional cooking as prepared in homes, osterias and restaurants; "raw materials"—from vegetables to legumes, from herbs to fruit, from meat to fish—and their standard Italian, regional and dialect names; the products of human culinary skill and imagination, from bread to cured meats, from cheese to pasta, from condiments to preserves; tools and techniques; biodiversity as it manifests itself though breeds, varieties, cultivars and ecotypes; associations between food and religion, history and social life.

Our main sources were: the archives of the Slow Food association and the books and magazines of its publishing company, Slow Food Editore; the oral accounts of experts, cooks, farmers, food producers and Slow Food members in every Italian region; the pasta and herb atlases published by the Italian National Institute of Rural Sociology; the websites of Italian regional, provincial and municipal authorities; and the Italian Ministry of Agriculture's database of native and/or traditional food products.

The book seeks to convey something of the complex reality that is Italian regional cooking, and is thus aimed primarily at food lovers. More generally, however, we hope and believe that it will also contain elements of interest for anyone curious to find out more about Italy in general, its people, its language, its history and its culture.

Useful Information

S low Food was founded in Bra, in the northwestern Italian region of Piedmont, in July 1986, to promote conviviality and the right to pleasure by safeguarding the country's food and agricultural heritage. The Slow Food presidia, frequently mentioned in this Dictionary, are small-scale projects designed to safeguard biodiversity and traditional food products at risk of extinction. There are currently 177 presidia in Italy and 121 in another 46 countries, all geared to saving quality food products that are: good to eat and typical; clean, made using sustainable techniques and with respect for the environment; and fair, made in conditions respectful of workers, their rights and their cultures, and with a decent guaranteed wage.

Frequently used acronyms in the dictionary are PDO and PGI. Both are geographical indications granted under European Union law to protect the names of regional foods.
PDO means Protected Designation of Origin (in Italian DOP, Denominazione di origine protetta)
PGI means Protected Geographical Denomination (in Italian, IGP, Indicazione geografica protetta).

Cross references in the dictionary are signaled by the ➤ symbol.

AUSTRIA

SWITZERLAND

SLOVENIA

Trentino
Alto Adige

Friuli
Venezia Giulia

Val d'Aosta

Lombardy

Veneto

Piedmont

France

Liguria

Emilia-Romagna

Tuscany

Marche

Umbria

Abruzzo

Lazio

Molise

Campania

Puglia

Basilicata

Sardinia

Calabria

Sicily

Italy
by Regions

Italy is divided into 20 regions (*regioni*), which are subdivided into 110 provinces (*province*), which are further divided into 8,100 municipalities or communes (*comuni*).

ITALIAN REGIONS AND PROVINCES

VAL D'AOSTA

PIEDMONT Turin, Alessandria, Asti, Biella, Cuneo, Novara, Verbano-Cusio-Ossola, Vercelli.

LOMBARDY Milan, Bergamo, Brescia, Como, Cremona, Lecco, Lodi, Mantua, Monza e Brianza, Pavia, Sondrio, Varese.

TRENTINO-ALTO ADIGE Trento, Bolzano.

VENETO Venice, Belluno, Padua, Rovigo, Treviso, Verona, Vicenza.

FRIULI-VENEZIA GIULIA Trieste, Gorizia, Pordenone, Udine.

LIGURIA Genoa, Imperia, La Spezia, Savona.

EMILIA-ROMAGNA Bologna, Ferrara, Forlì-Cesena, Modena, Parma, Piacenza, Ravenna, Reggio Emilia, Rimini.

TUSCANY Florence, Arezzo, Grosseto, Livorno, Lucca, Massa e Carrara, Pisa, Pistoia, Prato, Siena.

MARCHE Ancona, Ascoli Piceno, Fermo, Macerata, Pesaro e Urbino.

UMBRIA Perugia, Terni.

LAZIO Rome, Frosinone, Latina, Rieti, Viterbo.

ABRUZZO L'Aquila, Chieti, Pescara, Teramo.

MOLISE Campobasso, Isernia.

CAMPANIA Naples, Avellino, Benevento, Caserta, Salerno.

PUGLIA Bari, Barletta-Andria -Trani, Brindisi, Foggia, Lecce, Taranto.

BASILICATA Potenza, Matera.

CALABRIA Catanzaro, Cosenza Crotone, Reggio Calabria, Vibo Valentia.

SICILY Palermo, Agrigento, Caltanissetta, Catania, Enna, Messina, Ragusa, Siracusa, Trapani.

SARDINIA Cagliari, Carbonia-Iglesias, Medio Campidano, Nuoro, Ogliastra, Olbia-Tempio, Oristano, Sassari.

aA

abba ardente another name for ➤ **filu 'e ferru**, Sardinian grappa.

abbacchio Lazio name for an unweaned baby lamb butchered at the age of about six weeks or, according to more recent usage, when it has only just started to graze. Its tender, tasty meat is pale pink in color and features in a number of traditional recipes, especially in Rome (➤ **cotolette a scottadito**, ➤ **abbacchio alla romana**). Abbacchio used to be available only in the springtime, but is now sold all year round. The name derives from *bacchio*, the stick traditionally used to butcher lambs, but also the post to which lambs used to be tethered. Lazio.

abbacchio al forno roast baby lamb. A single piece or chunks of meat, perfumed with rosemary and garlic, marinated in extra virgin olive oil, white wine, salt and pepper and roasted in a slow oven with chopped potatoes. A typical springtime delicacy. Lazio.

abbacchio alla romana aka **abbacchio alla cacciatore** lamb stew. The meat is chopped into small pieces and stewed in extra virgin olive oil and white wine. When it is almost cooked, it is covered with a sauce of rosemary, garlic, red chili and mashed anchovy fillets. Lazio.

abbacchio brodettato. The meat is cut into chunks and browned in extra virgin olive oil to which salt, pepper and finely chopped onions and ham fat are added. White wine is then poured over the meat and allowed to evaporate. When the meat is well cooked, it is covered with a sauce made of beaten eggs, lemon juice, parsley and marjoram. A traditional Easter dish. Lazio.

abbattu honey and pollen boiled in water to which orange zest and, sometimes, slices of quince are added. The resulting liquid is preserved in hermetically sealed glass jars, and used to flavor desserts, cream cheese and baked fruit. Sardinia.

abbòjeli Lazio dialect name for ➤ **tamaro**, black bryony tips.

abbrustolire (1) to toast. Used in Italian in "rustic contexts" referred, for example, to country bread or polenta. Its synonym, ➤ **tostare**, is more urban and is more commonly used to describe the making of toast.

abbrustolire (2) to singe. An obsolete verb now largely replaced by ➤ **fiammeggiare** or ➤ **strinare**.

abbuoti baby lamb's intestines. Recipes and names vary according to place. The intestines are usually opened and washed, browned in oil, and barbecued. In the area round Benevento, they are seasoned with pepper and parsley, rolled up and barbecued, stewed or roasted (➤ **'ntrugliatielli al forno con patate**). The term **abbuoti** is common in Campania and southern Lazio (where ➤ **abbuoti alla fressor** are baby lamb's intestines browned in oil). In Campania dialect, the terms ➤ **'ntrugliatielli** and ➤ **stentenielli** also mean lamb's intestines. Lazio, Campania.

abbuoti alla fressor ➤ **abbuoti**, baby lamb's intestines browned in oil (➤ **abbuoti**). Lazio.

abburattamento sifting. Passing flour through a sieve to remove lumps.

abissini another name for ➤ **conchiglie**, pasta shells.

abomaso abomasum or vell, a ruminant's fourth stomach (➤ **trippa**, tripe) in the gastric glands of which food is digested. On account of its appearance when cleaned and washed for cooking, it is known popularly in Italian as *trippa riccia* (curly tripe) or *trippa frangiata/franciata* (fringed tripe), the latter adjective often being corrupted into ➤ **francese** (*frazeisa* in the dialect of Milan, where this type of tripe is an ingredient of ➤ **buseca**, tripe soup). Known in English as reed tripe.

acacia aka **robinia** acacia (*Robinia pseudo-acacia*). A small tree, popularly known as the black locust. Especially in northern Italy (where it is also known as ➤ **gaggìa** and ➤ **cassia**), its flowers are dipped in batter and fried. The resulting fritters can be either savory or sweet.

Accasciato cheese made with 100% ewe's milk from January to late spring and with a mixture of ewe's and cow's milk in the summer. It is usually eaten fresh, but may be aged for 40-60 days. Typical of the Garfagnana district (province of Lucca) and Apuan Alps (provinces of Massa-Carrara and Lucca). Tuscany.

accio aka **accia** word used in Campania, Calabria, Sicily and Puglia for ➤ **sedano**, celery (➤ **minestra di accio e baccalà**, ➤ **zuppa di accia**).

accirotta Sicilian dialect word for ➤ **beccaccino**, woodcock.

acciuga anchovy (*Engraulis enchrasicholaus*). The term is used mainly in northern Italy: in the center and south, the term ➤ **alice** is more common. It has fatty, tasty flesh, which may be marinated briefly in olive oil and lemon juice and eaten raw, or fried or grilled. Also available salted, preserved in oil or reduced to a paste. Native and/or traditional varieties include the ➤ **acciuga di Monterosso** and ➤ **alice di menaica**. Most Italian coastal regions have recipes for fresh anchovies, while the salted version is common as an ingredient and condiment all over the North. Common and regional names: ➤ **aliccia**, ➤ **alice**, ➤ **amplova**, ➤ **ancioa**, ➤ **anciova**, ➤ **lilla**, ➤ **magnana**, ➤ **masculinu**, ➤ **sardela**, ➤ **sardòn**, ➤ **speronara**.

acciugata creamy sauce made of anchovies melted in warm oil. Used to dress pasta, fish, eggs and boiled vegetables. Liguria.

acciughe all'ammiraglia another name for ➤ **acciughe marinate**, marinated anchovies.

acciughe col bagnet ross anchovies with "red sauce." Boned and filleted anchovies smothered in tomato sauce diluted with oil and vinegar and flavored with capers, garlic, bay leaf or basil, red chili and sugar. Piedmont.

acciughe col bagnet verd, anchovies with "green sauce." Boned, filleted anchovies smothered in a sauce of parsley, minced garlic, chili (➤ **spagnolin** in Piedmontese dialect), crushed hard-boiled egg yolks, vinegar and olive oil. Once a classic in osterias or as part of the ➤ **marenda sinoira** (late afternoon snack), today the recipe is served as an antipasto, or hors d'oeuvre. The salted anchovy (➤ **ancioa** in dialect) is of great historical importance in Piedmont: the Maira, Gesso, Stura and Vermegnana valleys, in the province of Cuneo, were stages on the "anchovy route" from the Ligurian coast, via Provence, to the markets of the Golfe du Lion on the Franco-Spanish border. The wandering anchovy sellers of the valleys used to sell the salted fish all over the region and sometimes traveled as far as Lombardy. Piedmont.

acciughe di Monterosso the celebrated anchovies of Monterosso, a village in the Cinque Terre stretch of Liguria, are still caught by night, as they always have been, using special fishing lanterns. Due to the difficulties involved in preserving such delicate fish in salt, local production of salted anchovies is limited. Liguria.

acciughe in salamoia aka **acciughe sotto sale** anchovies preserved in brine or salt. In Liguria, anchovies are decapitated and gutted, and placed in glass jars, alternated with layers of sea salt, to release excess water. The latter is gradually drained off and the jars filled to the brim with salted boiling water. The salted anchovies of the Ligurian Sea (*acciughe sotto sale del mar Ligure*) have been granted the PGI designation. In Sicily, anchovies are pressed between layers of sea salt without brine. Large salting and canning plants are to be found in the province of Agrigento at Sciacca, in the province of Trapani at Mazara del Vallo, and in Palermo.

acciughe in tortiera layers of anchovies, cleaned and opened out flat, alternated with layers of mixed herbs on a bed of finely chopped fresh tomato and baked in the oven. In a more complex version two layers of anchovies are filled, sandwich-style, with a mixture of tuna fish, breadcrumbs, Parmigiano, eggs and herbs. Liguria.

acciughe marinate marinated anchovies. Very fresh, larger than average anchovies decapitated, boned and marinated for 36 hours in white wine, white wine vinegar and salt, then drained and served dressed with olive oil, minced parsley and garlic, oregano and lemon wedges. (The dish is also common in other regions. In some, such as Lazio, it is known as ➤ **acciughe all'ammiraglia**, literally "flagship anchovies"). Liguria.

acciughe ripiene stuffed anchovies. A dish typical of coastal towns, especially in Liguria. Many variations exist, though flat-leaved parsley, garlic, eggs, breadcrumbs and herbs are ever-present ingredients in the stuffing. In some places they fry the anchovies, in others they bake them.

acciughe sotto pesto antipasto of rinsed, boned anchovies dressed with minced flat-leaved parsley and garlic, and seasoned with pepper. Tuscany.

acciughe tartufate anchovies with truffles. Antipasto typical of the Langa and Monferrato hills, both areas renowned for their white truffles. Salted anchovies are rubbed with a cloth and scraped clean, then placed in alternate layers with slivers of truffle, pressed down, and anointed with oil. The recipe was created by the families of truffle hunters as a way of using up odd bits and pieces of the fungus. Piedmont.

acciuleddhi fried cookies similar to ➤ **pinos**, traditionally made during the Carnival period. The paste (one of the ingredients of which is lard) is stretched into 10-inch spaghetti, which are wound and weaved together, fried in oil, dipped in hot honey and coated with refined sugar. Sardinia.

aceto vinegar. Clear liquid produced by transforming the ethylic alcohol in wine, cider or malt vinegar into acetic acid. The traditional way of making wine vinegar is the so-called "Orléans method," whereby small quantities of vinegar are added to wine for up to three quarters of the height of a wood barrel that has bungholes drilled into the upper part of its sides.

aceto balsamico di Modena balsamic vinegar of Modena, made from cooked grape must (20%), wine vinegar and caramel. The *affinato* (refined) version is aged for a minimum of 60 days, the *invecchia-*

to (aged) for a minimun of three years. Emilia-Romagna.

aceto balsamico tradizionale traditional balsamic vinegar, produced with analogous methods in the provinces of Modena and Reggio Emilia. Both versions have been PDO-protected since 2000, and are regulated by a strict protocol. Trebbiano di Spagna and lambrusco grape must is cooked until its volume is reduced by half, then aged in a battery of casks (*vaselli*) made of different woods and progressively smaller in size. The content of each cask is gradually transferred to the next in size. The vinegar may be bottled after 12 years (*affinato*, refined) and 25 years (*extra vecchio*, extra old). Emilia-Romagna.

aceto di frutta fruit vinegar (➤ **aceto**, vinegar). Following a production process similar to the one used for wine vinegar, vinegar can be made from fermented fruit, cereal, malt and honey alcohols. It can be made, for example, from cider (apples) and hydromel (honey).

acetosa sorrel, dock (*Rumex acetosa, R. acetosella, R. scutatus*). Spontaneous herbaceous plants widespread throughout Italy, but gathered for edible purposes mainly in the central and northern regions. The tender aerial parts, rich in oxalic acid with an acidulous, astringent flavor, are eaten raw in salads. Common and regional names: ➤ **erba brusca**, ➤ **erba agretta**, ➤ **erba salina**, ➤ **erba cucca**, ➤ **salsarella**.

acetosella *Oxalis acetosella*, wood sorrel. A spontaneous herb that grows in damp woody areas in mountains and foothills throughout Italy. Gathered and used in the kitchen mostly in the center and north of Italy. Acidulous in taste, it is used sparingly in salads, but also cooked with other herbs (➤ **acquacotta con le**

erbarelle). Common and regional names: ➤ **agretta**, ➤ **pancuculo**, ➤ **sugamele**, ➤ **trifoglio acetoso**, ➤ **zanzarella**.

acidulare to acidulate. To add lemon juice, vinegar, or ➤ **agresto**, verjuice, to a liquid. It is common in cookery to acidulate water to prevent certain vegetables (artichokes, cardoons) from discoloring. It is also common to acidulate cream.

aciughete agre small anchovies marinated in vinegar, usually with sliced onions. Veneto.

acqua di fiori d'arancio orange blossom water. Made by macerating and distilling bitter orange, also known as Seville orange, sour orange, bigarade orange or marmalade orange (*Citrus aurantium*, var. *bigardia*). The resulting highly scented essence is available both as an essential oil and as a "water." The latter is used as a flavoring in confectionery (➤ **pastiera napoletana**, shortcrust pastry tart).

acquacotta rustic soup of vegetables, herbs, water, olive oil, day-old bread and beaten eggs. It is traditionally associated with the Tuscan Maremma, but other, richer versions exist elsewhere in Tuscany and throughout central Italy. In the Casentino valley, in the province of Arezzo, porcini mushrooms and ➤ **nepitella**, calamint, are added. In the same valley, in the village of Moggiona, a soup of the same name is made with broth, tomatoes, onions, sausage and grated Pecorino cheese.

acquacotta alla viterbese another name for ➤ **acquacotta con le erbarelle**, a vegetable soup.

acquacotta con le erbarelle herb and vegetable soup. As in all recipes involving wild herbs (➤ **erbarelle**), ingredients vary according to season, but the following should always be included: ➤ **pastinache** (➤ **carota selvatica**, wild carrot), **su-**

gamele (➤ **acetosella**, wood sorrel) and wild fennel. The other basic ingredients are garlic, red chili, tomato, extra virgin olive oil, day-old bread and, of course, water. Some people add salt cod or beaten eggs, plus, according to season, spinach, asparagus, artichoke, legumes, turnip, cabbage and/or broccoli. Typical of the province of Viterbo. Lazio.

acquacotta di abbòjeli soup flavored with the sprouts of ➤ **tamaro**, black bryony (*abbòjeli* or *rafani* in the local dialect), gently fried in oil with garlic and red chili. When the soup is ready, beaten eggs are added. The resulting mixture is poured over slices of toasted bread and served. Recipe typical of the Tuscia area, in the province of Viterbo. Lazio.

acquacotta di Gubbio a variation on ➤ **acquacotta** in which slices of bread are soaked in chicory cooking water then heated with strips of ➤ **guanciale**, cheek bacon, and onions. Umbria.

acquacotta di patate soup made by gently frying cubed potatoes in olive oil with garlic, onion and chopped skinned tomatoes or tomato paste, then adding sliced celery and water. Served with slices of toasted bread and sprinkled with chopped parsley and grated Pecorino cheese. Umbria.

acquadella (*Atherino mochon*) silverside, another name for ➤ **latterino** in the Polesine area of the province of Rovigo, in the province of Ravenna and in the Valli di Comacchio lagoon, in the province of Ferrara. Veneto, Emilia-Romagna.

acquafrescai vendors of cool water and thirst-quenching, non-alcoholic drinks in central and southern Italy. They used to sell their wares from painted shacks and carts, now they have permanent kiosks where it is possible to buy commercial soft drinks, ➤ **granita** (ice slush), ➤ **grat-**

tachecca (Rome, Lazio), ➤ **zammù**, aniseed liqueur (Sicily), and homemade lemonade of water and lemon rendered fizzy by the addition of a pinch of bicarbonate of soda (Naples, Campania).

acquapazza, all' method of stewing fish in garlic, oil, tomato and water (in the old days, sea water was used). Today spices and herbs may also be added.

acquasala sliced day-old bread softened in water, rubbed with very ripe plum tomatoes, topped with chopped onion and oregano, and drizzled with extra virgin olive oil. In some versions, the bread is rubbed with garlic, and roughly torn basil, chopped chili, anchovies and the like are added to the topping. Puglia.

acquasale farmhouse soup of gently fried onion and chili to which boiling water and beaten eggs are added. Served in bowls with fresh breadcrumbs and sprinkled with grated salted ricotta. Basilicata.

acquatici arrosto an old wildfowl dish. Young mallards (or musk ducks or coots) are plucked, larded and wrapped in slices of ➤ **rigatino** (Tuscan flat pancetta), then cooked in a large skillet with olive oil, salt, pepper, onion, celery, bay leaf and white wine. Typical of the provinces of Pisa and Livorno. Tuscany.

acsenti leavened cookies made of cornflour, butter and sugar. In the past, they were baked specially for religious feasts, today they are commonly eaten for breakfast. A specialty of Sandigliano, in the province of Biella. Piedmont.

addensare to thicken. A liquid (a sauce or a gravy) may be thickened by: i) reducing it over a high heat; ii) adding flour or potato flour, partly diluted in the liquid itself. To bind a sauce, a ➤ **roux** is prepared.

affettare to slice meat, cured meats, bread or vegetables.

affettati literally "sliced." General term to

describe mixed sliced cure meats, especially when served as an antipasto.

affioramento afflorescence. Physiological process whereby the fatty emulsion in milk rises to the surface spontaneously.

affogagatti literally "cat drowners" (➤ **'nfocagatti**). Spiral-shaped candies.

affogato literally "drowned." Term used in different ways for different culinary preparations. In confectionery, it refers to an ice cream or ➤ **semifreddo** immersed in a warm or cold liquid (coffee or liqueur, for example). It is also an alternative way (➤ **in camicia**) for describing poached eggs. See also regional recipes, mostly involving stewing, such as ➤ **purpetielle affucate** (stewed octopus).

affumicare to smoke meat, fish, cured meats or cheeses.

affumicato (pl. **affumicati**) smoked. Used as a noun, the plural refers to a platter of mixed smoked meats (beef, goose breast, tongue, horsemeat) or fish (trout, salmon, sturgeon, tuna, swordfish), usually served finely sliced.

affumicatura smoking. A food preservation technique common all over Italy. Used for sea and freshwater fish (gray mullet in Sardinia, trout in Friuli and Trentino, eel in Veneto and Romagna, whitefish on Lake Garda), for meat (shin of pork in Friuli and Trentino-Alto Adige, goose breast in Lombardy), and for various regional cheeses and cured meats.

africani (1) buns made of eggs, sugar and creamed butter baked in fluted paper cases and sprinkled with cinnamon or grated lemon zest. Typical of the small town of Greve in Chianti, in the province of Florence. The odd name derives from the dark color of the cake on baking. Tuscany.

africani (2) long, tapered biscuits made of egg whites whisked to a stiff peak and

sugar. Typical of the small town of Galatina, in the province of Lecce. Puglia.

agarico delizioso another name for ➤ **sanguinello**, saffron milk-cap mushroom.

agarico imbutiforme another name for ➤ **imbutino**, common funnel mushroom.

agarico ostreato another name for ➤ **gelone**, oyster mushroom.

agghia pistata cold soup made by pounding garlic, basil, tomato, extra virgin olive oil, salt and pepper in a mortar and adding water. Served with slices of toasted bread. Sicily.

agghiata (1) a sweet and sour condiment made of garlic, vinegar and sugar, and served with fish. Calabria, Sicily.

agghiata (2) a sauce, similar to ➤ **aggiada**, made of garlic, oil, mint, parsley and vinegar. Sicily.

agghiotta (1) a technique for cooking fresh or preserved fish. The fish is cut into pieces and stewed with fresh or canned tomatoes, onions, celery, green olives and capers. In some of the many variations, the fish is pre-fried and raisins and pine kernels are added to the sauce. The most famous recipes are: *agghiotta di pescestocco alla messinese*, made with stockfish, and, in the province of Siracusa, *ghiotta di tonno fresco/salato*, made with fresh or salted tuna fish. Sicily.

agghiotta (2) type of fish stew. Sicily.

agghiotta (3) less commonly, mixed vegetables. Sicily.

aggiada sauce made of creamed, pounded garlic and breadcrumbs soaked in vinegar and oil, and seasoned with salt. Served with meat (especially liver and rabbit) and fried salt cod. Liguria.

agglassato aka **aggrassat)** Sicilian term derived from the French *glacer* ("to freeze," but also, in ancient usage, "to veil"). It refers to a leg of lamb or kid gently stewed in dry white wine with chopped skinned tomatoes. When the meat is cooked, the sauce is put through a sieve, and used to cover the sliced meat, and may also be used to dress pasta, in which case we would speak of ➤ **pasta aggrassata** or *pasta con la glassa*.

aggrassato Sicilian dialect term for ➤ **agglassato**.

agliata canavesana mixture of lardo, walnuts, white pepper and garlic, crushed to a smooth paste with a pestle and mortar. Spread on toast or used to dress tagliatelle. Specialty of the Canavese area, in the province of Turin. Piedmont.

agliata monferrina a delicate green creamy sauce made by blending ➤ **seirass**, ricotta, and fresh ➤ **Toma** cheese—preferably ➤ **Robiola di Roccaverano**—with finely minced garlic, parsley, sage, mint and basil. Lemon juice and oil are then folded in, and the resulting cream is spread on toasted bread. Typical of the Monferrato hills. Piedmont.

aglietto term used to refer both to cultivated spring garlic and to a number of herbs with a garlicky flavor, such as ➤ **aglio ursino** (*Allium ursinum*), wild garlic. Both are cut finely and added to salads.

aglio garlic (*Allium sativum*). A species whose numerous cultivars are mostly the result of selection and hybridization with local populations, which differ by the color of their skin, white or red. The Italian Ministry of Agriculture database recognizes the following varieties as native and/or traditional: *aglio rosso di Sulmona* (Abruzzo); *aglio dell'Ufita* (Campania); *aglio di Voghiera* (Emilia-Romagna); ➤ **aglio di Resia** (Friuli-Venezia Giulia); *aglio rosso di Castelliri* and *aglio rosso di Proceno* (Lazio); ➤ **aglio bianco di Vessalico** (Liguria); *aglio di Molino dei Torti* (Piedmont); ➤ **aglio rosso di Nubia** (Sicily); *aglio massese* and *aglio rosso*

maremmano (Tuscany); *aglio bianco polesano* and *aglio del medio Adige* (Veneto). Few savory dishes in Italy are made without garlic, and it is the main ingredient in some. They include: ➤ **aggiada** (Liguria), ➤ **agghia pistata** (Sicily), ➤ **aiòn** (Modena, Emilia-Romagna) and ➤ **bagna caoda** (Piedmont). In some parts of central Italy, garlic cloves are preserved in oil.

aglio bianco di Vessalico ancient handgrown garlic variety with a delicate aroma and an intense, slightly piquant flavor. Grown in and around the village of Vessalico in the Valle Arroscia, in the province of Imperia. Used to make the sauce known as ➤ **ajè**. A Slow Food presidium is seeking to promote its cultivation and marketing in traditional long plaits (*reste* in dialect). Liguria.

aglio cipollino another word for ➤ **erba cipollina**, chives.

aglio delle vigne another word for ➤ **porraccio**, wild garlic.

aglio di Resia garlic native to the isolated Val di Resia in the foothills of the Julian Alps, in the province of Udine, an area which has conserved a paleo-Slav culture and language, not to mention unique biodiversity. Known locally as *strock*, it has a medium-sized bulb and a skin with pinkish streaks. Inside, the white cloves are firmly joined together in a circular formation. In the olden days, the trade in Resia garlic flourished, and was sold on markets as far away as Llubljana and Vienna. Protected by a Slow Food presidium. Friuli-Venezia Giulia.

aglio rosso di Nubia garlic named for its color (red) and origin, in a small village in the province of Trapani (area of production: communes of Paceco, Trapani, Erice and part of the areas of Marsala and Salemi). Traditionally tied in large plaits of about 100 heads each and stored in cellars or warehouses. The principal ingredient in recipes such as the pasta sauce ➤ **pesto trapanese**. Protected by a Slow Food. Sicily.

aglio triangolare another name for ➤ **porraccio**, wild leek.

aglio ursino another word for ➤ **aglietto**, baby or green garlic.

aglione (1) traditional sauce for ➤ **pici**, a type of pasta. A number of garlic cloves are gently fried in olive oil and finished with chopped ripe tomatoes. Tuscany.

aglione (2) a mixture of finely chopped garlic, sage, rosemary, bay leaf, lemon zest and a generous amount of salt, used to flavor roast and broiled meats (➤ **castrato alla griglia**). Emilia-Romagna.

agnello lamb. Under Italian law, a lamb is a young sheep weighing no more than 10 kilos, which lives on an exclusively milk diet. Carcasses are normally halved into sides (➤ **mezzene**), one of which includes the head and the other the offal (➤ **coratella**), then into quarters, Outside the major sheep-rearing areas, the consumption of lamb in Italy is largely limited to the Easter period. The loin and leg are generally roasted, the shoulder (whole or chopped) stewed, cutlets grilled or fried. Sardinian lamb (➤ **agnello di Sardegna**) has had PGI recognition since 2001. The Italian Ministry of Agriculture's database of native and/or typical products includes the following varieties: in Piedmont, ➤ **agnello sambucano** and *agnello biellese*; in Emilia-Romagna, *agnello delle razze sarda e massese*; in Friuli-Venezia Giulia, *agnello istriano*; in Lombardy, *agnello di razza brianzola*; in Tuscany, ➤ **agnello di Zeri** (aka *agnello zerasco*), *agnello massese, agnello appenninico* and *agnello del Parco di Migliarino-San Rossore*. Slow Food presidia protect the following breeds: ➤ **agnello di Zeri**,

➤ **agnello sambucano**, and ➤ **agnello d'Alpago**.

agnello a scottadito literally "burn your fingers" lamb. A dish born of the pastoral tradition of the regions of central Italy. In Umbria it consists of grilled lamb cutlets served with a condiment of chopped ham fat, garlic, rosemary and marjoram. The same condiment is used to accompany roast lamb or mutton. Umbria.

agnello abbottonato literally "buttoned-up lamb." Shoulder of lamb, boned and stuffed with a mixture of bread, eggs, almonds, ➤ **Parmigiano-Reggiano** cheese and parsley. Similar but now hard to find is ➤ **agnello ammandorlato**, a 19th-century L'Aquila recipe made preferably with almonds from the Navelli plateau. Abruzzo.

agnello ai cardoncelli large pieces of lamb roast in the oven with mushrooms (➤ **cardoncello**, king trumpet mushroom), oil, garlic and chili. Basilicata.

agnello al calderotto lamb stew with onion, flat-leaved parsley, fresh tomatoes and olive oil with the addition, halfway through the cooking process, of wild endives or chard. Served with a sprinkling of grated Pecorino. The recipe takes its name from the *calderotto*, the clay pot in which it is cooked. Puglia.

agnello al limone lamb with lemon. Pieces of lamb are browned in olive oil with onion and parsley, then gently stewed with the addition of a little water. When the meat is almost tender, it is smothered with beaten eggs, lemon juice and salt. The dish is served piping hot when the eggs have scrambled. A typical Easter recipe. Sardinia.

agnello al testo lamb, cut into pieces and cooked with mountain potatoes in a ➤ **testo**, a sort of wrought iron (once earthenware) griddle pan with a lid (the technique is halfway between over-roasting, which makes the surface of the meat crisp, and steaming, which keeps the inside soft and tasty). Traditional recipe of the Lunigiana area, typically made with the local lamb breed (➤ agnello di Zeri). Tuscany.

agnello alla Carbonara whole lamb rubbed with salt, placed on baking paper in an oven dish, and roasted. Christmas dish named for Carbonara, a suburb of Bari. Puglia.

agnello alla coriglianese recipe for roast lamb typical of Corigliano Calabro, in the province of Cosenza. Before roasting, the meat is larded with pancetta, perfumed with minced garlic and oregano, and drizzled with vinegar. Calabria

agnello alla piacentina lamb stew typical of the province of Piacenza. The meat is cooked in white wine, broth and tomato. Its distinctive feature is the addition of ➤ **pista 'd gras**, mixture of finely chopped lardo, garlic and flat-leaved parsley Traditionally made at Easter. Emilia-Romagna.

agnello allo squero lamb flavored with thyme and other aromatic herbs, and roasted on a skewer over a brushwood fire. Puglia.

agnello ammandorlato old version of ➤ **agnello abbottonato**.

agnello cac' e ova, lamb cut into pieces, cooked in an earthenware pot with onion and white wine, then finished with a mixture of eggs, grated Pecorino and breadcrumbs. In Puglia and Basilicata, the recipe is sometimes enhanced by fresh peas (➤ **cac' e ova**). Abruzzo, Basilicata, Puglia.

agnello con pomodori secchi lamb with sun-dried tomatoes. Pieces of lamb browned in olive oil and finished with finely sliced onions, chopped sun-dried tomatoes and wild fennel. A specialty of

the province of Nuoro. Sardinia.

agnello d'Alpago Alpago lamb. An area of meadows and pastures, the Alpago valley, in the Alpine foothills in the province of Belluno, gives its name to a small- to medium-sized sheep breed (no horns, tiny ears, thick fleece with fine, wavy wool), raised almost exclusively for its meat, extremely tender, with just the right balance of fat and lean, and distinct notes of aromatic herbs. Unfortunately, numbers dropped drastically in the last century and a Slow Food presidium has now been set up to promote the breed. Veneto.

agnello di Sardinia Sardinian lamb. Lambs born, raised on the range (except in winter and at night), fed only on their mothers' milk, and butchered in Sardinia. Has enjoyed PGI recognition since 2001. Sardinia.

agnello di sfoglia Easter cake typical of the provinces of Pavia and Lodi. Baked in the shape of a lamb from ➤ **pasta sfoglia** (puff pastry dough), then cut into three layers and filled with confectioner's custard and chocolate cream. Lombardy.

agnello di Zeri Zeri sheep. Sheep breed with a white fleece, native to the village of Zeri, in the province of Massa-Carrara, where it grazes in pastures at an altitude of more than 2000 feet. Its milk is rich in nutritional elements (in particular proteins) and its meat tender and perfumed. Protected by a Slow Food presidium. The most traditional recipe for its meat is ➤ **agnello al testo**. Tuscany.

agnello in buglione Tuscan lamb stew, originally made with inferior cuts of meat, according to the ➤ **buglione** method. Typical of the Chianti and Monte Amiata areas, today it involves browning pieces of lamb in oil with finely chopped onion, garlic, chili and flat pancetta (➤ **rigati-**

no) in an earthenware pot. Red wine, tomato passata and hot broth are then added. When the meat is tender, the stew is served on toasted bread. Tuscany.

agnello in fricassea fricaséed lamb. In Liguria they cut the meat into small pieces and stew it with garlic, onion, carrot and artichoke. At the end of the cooking process, they stir in eggs and lemon juice (➤ **fricassea**, fricasée). In Umbria, the procedure is the similar, only that tomato is added and the artichokes are eliminated. Liguria, Umbria.

agnello pasquale Easter cake typical of the Salento peninsula (province of Lecce), made with a mixture of flour, sugar, almonds, eggs, orange zest and liqueur, which is placed in a special lamb-shaped mold and filled with jam, ➤ **faldacchiera** (a sort of zabaglione) and chocolate. Puglia.

agnello sambucano sheep breed which first appeared in the mountains of the Valle Stura, in the province of Cuneo, in the 18th century. In the 1980s the breed risked extinction, but today, thanks to the efforts of the Lou Barmaset cooperative and L'Escaroun consortium, supported by a Slow Food presidium, which run a ram selection center in the village of Pietraporzio, 10,000 lambs are born every year in the valley. The Sambucano sheep is medium- large in size with a straw-white fleece, a hornless head and a long, thin tail. The meat is firm, sapid and lean, and is usually eaten roasted in the oven, sometimes in a bread crust. The offal is also excellent. Piedmont.

agnello sambucano al forno roast lamb. The meat of the ➤ **agnello sambucano**, sambucano lamb, roast in the oven in an earthenware pot, flavored with aromatic herbs and bathed with grappa. Recipe typical of the Alpine valleys of the province of Cuneo. Piedmont.

agnello sotto la coppa lamb cut into pieces and cooked in the hearth in a pot covered by an iron or earthenware dome lid (*coppa*). Abruzzo, Molise.

agnellone commercial term for a weaned lamb butchered before it is a year old (normally from the sixth month to the tenth).

agnellotti word used in some central Italian dialects to refer to ➤ **agnolotti**, a type of pasta.

agneso another name for ➤ **aneto**, dill.

agnoli a pasta shape similar to ➤ **agnolini**, reminiscent of ➤ **cappelletti**. Stuffed with a mixture of boiled capon, beef marrow, eggs, cheese, cinnamon, cloves and spices, normally served in capon broth. In the second half of the 17th century, Bartolomeo Stefani, cook to the Gonzagas, cited the **agnoli** "of his most serene Highness." Typical of Mantua and surrounds. Lombardy.

agnolotti pasta (classically squares with sides of about an inch with serrated edges, though size and shape vary) stuffed with mixed meats, which may be cooked in different ways (roast, braised or stewed), bound with eggs and mixed with a vegetable (usually escarole, chard, cabbage or spinach) or with rice as a softening element. The pasta is made with a small amount of water, flour, salt and eggs, and is traditionally so fine as to be almost transparent. Boiled briefly in water or broth, **agnolotti**, known in southern Piedmont as ➤ **ravioli** or ➤ **raviole**, are normally served with ➤ **sugo di arrosto** (meat gravy) or butter, sage and grated Parmigiano-Reggiano. In the Langa and Monferrato areas, it is a custom to serve **agnolotti** on their own, wrapped in a canvas cloth. Piedmont.

agnolotti alessandrini di stufato the meat

for the stuffing (today neck of beef, in the old days horse or donkey) is marinated and stewed in red Barbera wine with aromatics and spices (➤ **stufato all'alessandrina**, beef stew). The pasta is served with the meat gravy. Recipe typical of the plain lands round Alessandria. Piedmont.

agnolotti astigiani ai tre arrosti the stuffing, softened with cabbage or spinach or escarole, is made of "three roasts": veal, rabbit and pork. Served either with ➤ **sugo di arrosto**, meat gravy, or butter melted in an earthenware pot with sage, rosemary, and unpeeled garlic. Typical of the Monferrato hills, in the province of Asti. Piedmont.

agnolotti canavesani the filling consists of veal and pork stewed in red wine and mixed with eggs, grated Grana cheese and rice boiled in beef broth and blended with butter and cheese. Typical of the Canavese area, northwest of Turin. Piedmont.

agnolotti casalesi the stuffing consists of beef and veal, ham, cabbage or escarole, eggs, Parmigiano and porcini mushrooms or truffles. Usually served with butter, cheese and meat sauce. Recipe typical of the Monferrato hills south of Casale. Piedmont.

agnolotti dal plin very fine pasta bundles pinched (*plin* or *pëssià* in dialect) round the edges. Typical of the southern Langa hills. Piedmont.

agnolotti del basso Monferrato the stuffing consists of cow's offal (marrow, brains, sweetbreads) mixed with braised beef and roast pork, eggs and Parmigiano. Boiled in broth with the addition of a glass of Barbera wine and served with meat sauce. Typical of the northwest part of the province of Asti. Piedmont.

agnolotti della Val Cerrina tiny pasta bundles filled with roast veal and rabbit, boiled salami, raw ham and a small amount of boiled cabbage. Typical of the Monferrato hills south of Casale. Piedmont.

agnolotti delle valli di Lanzo the stuffing consists of boiled meat (beef) and roast meat (veal, pork), calf's and pig's liver, eggs and Parmigiano. The vegetables used in the making of the beef broth in which the pasta is cooked may also be added. Served with the gravy from the roast meat or with melted butter and truffle. Typical of the Canavese area, north of Turin. Piedmont.

agnolotti di asino filled with ground donkey meat. Traditionally made in the village of Calliano (province of Asti) during the Carnival period. Piedmont.

agnolotti di fonduta stuffed with ➤ **fonduta**, cheese fondue, and cooked in either water or broth. Served with butter and Parmigiano and, in season, slivers of white truffle. A relatively recent creation, typical of the Alba area (province of Cuneo). Piedmont.

agnolotti di Fubine the recipe, typical of Fubine (province of Alessandria) since the 19th century, differs from ➤ **agnolotti del basso Monferrato** on account of the addition of cabbage leaves to the stuffing and the condiment of chicken giblets and mushrooms. Piedmont.

agnolotti di Gavi Italianization of ➤ **ravieu di Gavi**, a type of Piedmontese ravioli.

agnolotti di Langa in this version, typical of the Langa hills in southern Piedmont, the pasta dough contains more eggs (especially yolks) than normal, and the filling is made of veal and pork roast with broth or wine and mixed with cabbage or escarole or spinach, eggs and Parmigiano. The pasta, often shaped like ➤ **agnolotti dal plin**, is served with the gravy from the roast meat.

agnolotti di Torre Pellice the meat for the stuffing (breast of veal cooked in white wine) is softened with spinach or chard and fresh ricotta (➤ **seirass**). Traditionally served with melted butter and sage leaves. Recipe typical of the Val Pellice, southwest of Turin. Piedmont.

agnolotti di verdure vegetable stuffing of rice creamed with butter and cheese, chard, escarole, cabbage, leek and borage. Typical of the Langa hills in the province of Cuneo. Piedmont.

àgole salàe another dialect term for ➤ **àole sale**, bleak preserve.

agone (1) (pl. **agoni**) freshwater sardine *(Alosa fallax lacustris)*. Member of the Clupeidae which lives in Italy's subalpine lakes, on whose shores it used to be at the center of a thriving preserving industry. Like ➤ **alborella**, bleak, it may be sun-dried and salted. On Lakes Garda, Como and Iseo, it is, or was, also wind-dried (➤ **missoltini**, ➤ **pesce secco di Monte Isola e del lago d'Iseo**). Known in Veneto as ➤ **sardena** (Italianized as ➤ **sardella**). Lombardy, Trentino-Alto Adige, Veneto.

agone (2) Marche regional word for ➤ **latterino**, silverside.

agoni alla comasca fillets of freshwater sardine marinated in olive oil and lemon, fried, dressed with a small amount of the marinade liquid, vinegar, and anchovy fillets, and served cold with warm polenta. Recipe typical of Lake Como. Lombardy.

agresto verjuice. Juice from unripe *(agresto)* grapes used to give a sour flavor to sauces, condiments and gravies. The name also applies to a sauce made with sugar, vinegar, garlic, unripe grapes, walnuts and almonds, served warm with roast and boiled meats. The preparation dates back to the Middle Ages, and verjuice is still made in the village of Serra de' Conti, in the province of Ancona (Marche), with unripe white grapes boiled and reduced and supplemented with ➤ **sapa**, must, from the same grapes.

agretta another name for ➤ **acetosella**, wood sorrel.

agretti another name for ➤ **barba di frate**, oppositeleaf Russian thistle.

agretto another name for ➤ **crescione**, watercress.

Agrì di Valtorta cow's milk cream cheese inoculated with rennet and a little soured whey. Typical of the Valtorta, a small valley off the Val Brembana, in the province of Bergamo. Lombardy.

agro sour. Expression used to refer to dishes in which the flavor or lemon predominates. Such dishes generally involve stewed or baked fruit, but in regional cuisines also extend to other ingredients, such as tongue or calf's head.

agrodolce sweet and sour. This combination of flavors, typical of medieval and Renaissance cuisine, still survives in traditional regional dishes, such as ➤ **saor**, ➤ **lepre in dolceforte** and ➤ **caponata**, in preserved vegetables (onions, peppers), in some sauces in which balsamic vinegar and raisins feature: ➤ **salsa san Bernardo** (Sicily) and ➤ **salsa agrodolce alla parmigiana** and ➤ **duls e brusc** (Emilia).

agrume (pl. **agrumi**) citrus fruit. Members of the Citrus family, originally from southeast Asia, are cultivated to be eaten fresh, for industrial processing, or for ornamental purposes. Now common in many parts of the world, from the Mediterranean to the Americas to South Africa, in Italy they are grown principally in the southern regions, where the most cultivated variety of all is the lemon. The Italian name derives from the word ➤

agro, sour.

agrumi del Gargano Gargano citrus fruits. On the Gargano peninsula, in the province of Foggia, citrus groves are called *giardini*, or gardens, because they are traditionally clustered around farmhouses, protected from the wind by dry-stone walls or reed, holm oak or laurel fences. Fruits ripen all year round: *duretta* oranges at Christmas, *bionda* oranges from April to May, *femminello* lemons all year round. They are promoted by a Slow Food presidium whose members use their oranges and lemons to make excellent marmalades, candied fruits and limoncello liqueur. Puglia.

aguglia garfish, garpike (*Belone belone*). Boneless saltwater fish with tasty flesh. Cooked in the same way as ➤ **grongo**, conger-eel.

ahtufa de coi Piedmontese dialect word for ➤ **supa 'd còi**, cabbage soup.

aidos another name for ➤ **malloreddos**, tiny Sardinian gnocchi.

aion condiment made by mixing minced garlic cloves, sage and basil leaves with crushed sea salt. Used to flavor roasts and steaks. Typical of the province of Modena. Emilia-Romagna.

ajà walnut sauce made by pounding walnuts, garlic cloves, salt, and fresh breadcrumbs soaked in water. Typical of the province of Piacenza, where it is served on Christmas Eve and Good Friday with lasagne or tagliatelle. Emilia-Romagna.

ajè (1) garlic sauce. An evident relative of Provençal *aioli*. Made by crushing garlic cloves in a mortar and slowly incorporating egg yolks, oil, salt and pepper. Common in the valleys of the province of Imperia, the sauce is served with vegetables, fish and white meats. Liguria.

ajè (2) creamed boiled potatoes, garlic, egg yolks and oil. Excellent for dipping raw vegetables. Typical of the Alpine valleys of the province of Cuneo. Piedmont.

ajòli term used in the Provencal valleys of the province of Cuneo for *aïoli*, a sort of garlic mayonnaise (➤ **ajè**). Piedmont.

ajucca spiked rampion (*Phyteuma spicatum*). Like ➤ **raperonzolo**, rampion, a member of the bellflower family. A spontaneous edible plant with a bitterish flavor, widespread in subalpine environments in the Canavese district, northwest of Turin, it is used to make a soup: ➤ **zuppa di ajucche**. Also served on its own with polenta. Piedmont.

ajvar aka **haivar** fiery sauce made of chili, tomato, garlic and onion. Usually spread on bread or served as a condiment with ➤ **cevapcici**, sausages. Friuli-Venezia Giulia.

alaccia shad. Member of the Clupeidae family, similar to ➤ **sardina** (sardine), albeit larger, and cooked in the same way.

alalunga albacore tuna (*Thunnus alalunga*).

alalunga in agrodolce slices of albacore tuna coated in flour, fried, smothered with onions softened in butter, sugar and vinegar, and served cold. Calabria.

albatro another name for ➤ **corbezzolo**, arbutus.

albicocca apricot (*Prunus armeniaca*). Fruit of Chinese origin which arrived in the Mediterranean via Armenia, and was widely used in the Middle Ages during Arab domination. The flesh of the fruit is firm and, despite its high sugar content, has a slightly acid flavor. Italian production is concentrated mainly in Campania and Emilia-Romagna, and, thanks to the vast range of different varieties, the season lasts from early June to the second half of August. The Italian Ministry of Agriculture's database of native and/or traditional varieties include: *marille della Val Venosta* (Trentino-Alto Adige); *al-*

bicocca vesuviana (Campania); *Valsanterno di Imola* (Emilia-Romagna); *albicocca tigrata* and *albicocca valleggia* (Liguria); *tonda di Costigliole* (Piedmont); *albicocca di Galatone* (Puglia); *albicocca di Scillato* (Sicily). In Italy apricots are mostly eaten fresh, but the fruit is also dried, preserved in alcohol, and used to make jams, syrups and juices. In the kitchen, it is used to fill cakes, either in jam form or in pieces (➤ **struccolo**, sweet dumplings). Also an ingredient in savory dishes (➤ **gnocchi di susine**, plum gnocchi, but also made with apricots). Apricot jelly is often spread on cakes, hence the verb *apricottare* (from the French *abricot*, apricot).

alborella bleak (*Alburnus alburnus*), small freshwater fish of the Cyprinidae family. Also known, depending on place, as ➤ **àola**, ➤ **àvola** or ➤ **alburno**, it is common above all in the northern Italian lakes: Maggiore, Como, Garda and Iseo. Like ➤ **agone**, freshwater sardine, it may be fried, grilled, or pickled in ➤ **carpione**, with onion and vinegar. On Lake Garda it is also dried and preserved in brine. The increasingly rare technique of sun-drying provides the base for ➤ **sisam**, preserved dried bleak. Bleak pickled in brine (➤ **àole salè**), broken up into small bits and gently fried in oil, is a classic condiment for ➤ **bigoi** or **bigoli**, a type of pasta. Lombardy, Trentino-Alto Adige, Veneto.

alborelle fritte aka **àole fritte** fried bleak. The fish are coated in flour and fried in extra virgin olive oil. They may also be fried with abundant onions, coated in cornflour and broiled, pickled with onions and vinegar, preserved in brine with sea salt flavored with garlic, rosemary and bay leaves, preserved in white wine vinegar, oil, minced parsley and garlic, or dried in canvas bags with bay leaves.

Lombardy.

alburno another name for ➤ **alborella**, bleak.

alchechengi Peruvian cherry or Cape gooseberry (*Physalis alchechengi*). Plant with erect stalks that grow up to 20 inches in height and oval leaves that are sharp at the ends. Given its decorative appearance, it is often cultivated in orchards and gardens. The fruit, the only edible part of the plant, is a small round berry covered by a single parchment-like pod. It has a pleasantly sour flavor and is used in confectionery, often coated with chocolate. Common and regional names: ➤ **chichingero**, ➤ **ciliegine**, ➤ **fiasche de corai**, ➤ **lanterne**.

alchermes alkermes. Sweet, bright red liqueur supposedly invented by the friars of Santa Maria Novella in Florence. Produced from an infusion of various spices (cinnamon, cloves, vanilla, nutmeg), aromatic herbs and essences (rose, jasmine) in alcohol, it was originally colored with cochineal. Today it is used almost exclusively in confectionery to soak sponge cake or *savoiardi* sponge fingers (➤ **zuppa inglese**), as a coloring agent or to flavor fruit (➤ **pesche all'alchermes**). Tuscany.

algerini round flat baked cookies of flour, sugar eggs, lard and ➤ **ammonium carbonate**, sprinkled with icing sugar, very popular in the Palermo area. Sicily.

aliccia Sicilian word for ➤ **acciuga**, anchovy.

alice ➤ another word for ➤ **acciuga**, anchovy.

alicetta Lazio word for ➤ **latterino**, silverside.

alici a beccafico fried stuffed anchovies. The fish are opened out flat, dipped in dry white wine, coated with a mixture of fresh breadcrumbs, grated Pecorino, minced garlic and parsley, salt, pepper, oregano and other anchovies. They are then rolled up, coated in flour and fried in olive oil. The word *beccafico* means "garden warbler," and the dish is so-named because, presented in this way, the fish look like small birds. Calabria.

alici 'a piattella aka **alici in tortiera** anchovy "pie." Boned and filleted anchovies arranged in alternate layers in a pie dish with fresh breadcrumbs flavored with minced mint and parsley, and baked in the oven. Served anointed with extra virgin olive oil and sprinkled with lemon juice. Campania.

alici alla fuscaldese anchovies layered with fresh breadcrumbs, olive oil, lemon juice, salt, oregano, black pepper and chili, and baked in the oven. A specialty of Fuscaldo (province of Cosenza). Calabria.

alici alla reggina anchovies layered with fresh breadcrumbs, olive oil, black pepper, capers, green olives, garlic and parsley, and baked in the oven. A specialty of Reggio Calabria. Calabria.

alici all'aceto anchovies in vinegar. Anchovies boned, coated in flour, fried in boiling olive oil, transferred to an earthenware bowl and marinated in boiled vinegar, garlic and fried onions. Puglia.

alici ammollicate anchovies flavored with garlic, oil, parsley, white wine or lemon juice and breadcrumbs, and baked in the oven, sometimes with the addition of sliced tomatoes. Campania.

alici arracanate anchovies dressed with breadcrumbs, garlic, capers, oregano, mint and olive oil. Puglia.

alici arreganate anchovies dressed with oil, garlic, oregano, pepper and vinegar. Campania.

alici di menaica anchovies with pale pink flesh and an intense, delicate aroma, fished using an ancient technique that was once widespread throughout the Mediterranean, but now continues in a few isolated places on the Cilento coast. A group of fishermen go out at night with their boats and nets (known as *menaica* or *menaide*). Once landed, the anchovies are immediately washed in brine, then layered with salt in earthenware jars and left to rest for at least three months. The fish and fishing technique are promoted by a Slow Food presidium. Campania.

alici 'nchiappate aka **alici impaccate** anchovies opened flat and stuffed with fresh goat's cheese, egg, garlic and parsley, coated in flour, fried in olive oil, then finished in tomato sauce. Eaten immediately or preserved in oil. Calabria.

aliciotti con indivia anchovies with Belgian endive. A sort of mold made by alternating layers of tender Belgian endive leaves, and boned and opened anchovies, flavored with pieces of garlic, oil, salt and pepper. The mold is topped with a final layer of endive leaves and baked until golden brown, then sprinkled with finely minced flat-leaved parsley. In one traditional Roman-Jewish variant, artichoke replaces Belgian endive. Lazio.

aliotide aka **patella reale** green ormer or sea-ear (*Haliotis tubercolata*). Ear-shaped abalone eaten raw or cooked, according to size. Common in the spring and summer among the rocks along the eastern coast of Sicily, where it is known as ➤ **occhio di bue** (in dialect, **occhiu di voi**), which means "bull's eye," and eaten broiled. Other regional names: ➤ **orecchio di mare**, ➤ **orecchio di Venere**, ➤ **orecchio di san Pietro.** All evoke the mollusk's shape, *orecchio* meaning "ear" in Italian.

alivi 'a puddastredda olives flavored for a few minutes with garlic, oil, mint leaves and a drop of vinegar. Sicily.

alivi acciurati another name for ➤ **passuluna (2)**, pathogen-infected olives.

alivi cunzati olives squashed and boiled in water and vinegar for no longer than five minutes, drained and dressed with minced garlic, mint leaves and oregano. Transferred to a glass jar and covered with extra virgin olive oil, they can be preserved for several months. Sicily.

allardiato regional term used to refer to dishes involving the use of chopped lard (➤ **zite allardiate**). Campania.

alletterato another name for ➤ **tonnetto**, little tunny.

allievo dialect word for a tiny ➤ **seppia**, cuttlefish, to be eaten raw. Puglia.

alloro bay leaf (*Laurus nobilis*). Evergreen shrub that sometimes grows as high as a tree in woodland and scrub all over Italy. The glossy leaves are gathered all year round and eaten both fresh and dried. Used in all manner of recipes, bay leaf is especially suitable for flavoring meat and fatty fish. Common and regional names: ➤ **lauro**.

allulur bundles of lamb's tripe perfumed with herbs and wrapped in a rumen. After being boiled, they are cut into slices and dressed with oil and lemon. Molise.

almkäse one of the oldest mountain cheeses in the Val Venosta, in the province of Bolzano. Made from semi-skimmed raw cow's milk and aged at least three months. The name derives from *Alm*, German for "Alpine pasture." Trentino-Alto Adige.

alosa a clupeid (**Alosa alosa**) similar to the ➤ **agone (2)**, silverside, and ➤ **cheppia**, Mediterranean shad. Common in the northeast Atlantic and western Mediterranean, relatively rare round Italy.

alpeggio piece of land in the mountains used for summer grazing, and usually including a dairy for cheesemaking.

aluzzetiello dialect word for ➤ **cicerello**, Mediterranean sand eel. Campania.

alzavola teal (*Anas crecca*). Migrant duck that sometimes nests in Italy on moors, marshes and damp meadows. The male has a dark brown head with a green patch round the eye, a silvery gray back and a black-spotted whitish breast. The female is brown.

amalgamare to amalgamate. To mix different ingredients to achieve a homogeneous whole.

amareddi another name for ➤ **mazzareddi**, wild mustard leaves.

amareddu dialect term for ➤ **senape selvatica**, wild mustard.

amareggiola another name for ➤ **partenio**, feverfew.

amarella another name for ➤ **erba di San Pietro**, costmary.

amarelli another name for ➤ **cime di rapa**, broccoli rabe.

amarene in conserva preserved sour cherries. The tradition of preserving sour cherries (➤ **ciliegia**, cherry) to make jams is common, above all, in central and southern Italy. In Cantiano, in the province of Pesaro (Marche), the fleshy local sour cherries are pitted and boiled in their own juices with sugar. In the Marche and Campania regions, pitted cherries are also sweetened with sugar and sun-dried in jars. The fruit, finally, may be dried on large sieves and preserved in canvas bags or cans (a method still common in the Marche), though probably the most common practice is to process it into syrup.

amaretto (pl. **amaretti**) (1) semispherical almond cookie, the consistency of which depends on the amount of almonds used to make it. It probably came into being in Venice during the Renaissance and has since been adopted in many Italian regions, artisanally and commercially. The basic recipe envisages a paste of crushed sweet and bitter almonds (➤ **armellina**, peach or apricot stone), egg whites and sugar, sometimes with the addition of flavorings and cocoa. Commercial recipes may also include milk and milk proteins, leavening agents and honey. The most noteworthy artisan products are made in Sassello (province of Savona), Mombaruzzo (province of Asti), Gavi, Ovada and Voltaggio (province of Alessandria), Saronno and Gallarate (province of Varese), Barzanò (province of Lecco), Spilamberto (province of Modena) and Reggio Emilia, flavored with lemon, San Gimignano (province of Siena), Guarcino (province of Frosinone), Marino (province of Rome), Carloforte (province of Carbonia-Iglesias) and Oristano (➤ **amarettos**). Whole or crumbled, **amaretti** are used to flavor or garnish ice creams, cakes, and pastries (➤ **torta di amaretti**, amaretti cake; ➤ **bonet**, rum and chocolate dessert; ➤ **pesche ripiene**, stuffed peaches), and also feature in savory dishes such as ➤ **fritto misto piemontese**, ➤ **tortelli di zucca mantovani** and ➤ **tortelli cremaschi**.

amaretto (2) almond liqueur now famous all over the world. Recipes vary according to place, but the drink is generally made by infusing almonds (the main ingredient), cherries, plums, cocoa, herbs and up to 17 other aromatic ingredients in alcohol, to which a sugar and water syrup is added. Produced mostly in Lombardy and Liguria, it is used mainly in cocktails and to flavor confectionery.

amarettos popular Sardinian dry cookie made of chopped sweet and bitter almonds, egg whites, refined sugar and plain flour. Similar to but larger than Ligurian ➤ **amaretti (1)**. Sardinia.

amatriciana, all' term to describe a sauce for pasta (preferably ➤ **bucatini**) named for the town of Amatrice, in the province of Rieti. The modern recipe envisages ➤ **guanciale** (cheek bacon), onion, skinned tomatoes, grated Pecorino cheese and pepper or chili, though originally it was made without tomato (➤ **gricia**). **ambariegl** dialect term in the province of Latina for crayfish (➤ **gambero**). Lazio.

ambolina Piacenza term for ➤ **arborella**, bleak. Emilia-Romagna.

Ambra di Talamello a cheese (➤ **Formaggio di fossa**) made by leaving Pecorino and soft Caciotta cheese to mature in the pits at Talamello, in the Montefeltro district of the province of Pesaro-Urbino. The name, which refers to the color of the rind (*ambra* means "amber"), was coined by the poet Tonino Guerra. Marche.

ambulau soup of barley semolina flavored with onions gently fried in olive oil with the addition, towards the end of the cooking process, of a glass of white wine vinegar. Sardinia.

amiasc another name for **ronditt**, a griddle scone.

amido starch. Carbohydrate obtained from cereals and potatoes.

ammazzacaffè literally "coffee killer." Jokey, colloquial term for an alcoholic beverage or spirit drunk at the end of a meal after coffee.

ammogghiu r'agghia another name for ➤ **agghia pistata,** garlic soup.

ammogghiu Trapani dialect name for ➤ **pesto pantesco** sauce.

ammollare to soak or to soften. Usually referred to the soaking of dried food items (stockfish, legumes, day-old bread) in a liquid, usually water or milk, to rehydrate them, but also to the soaking or dipping (➤ **inzuppare,** to dip) of a fresh food item (bread, for example) in milk or another liquid before squeezing it dry and mixing it with other ingredients (a common practice for stuffings and fillings). Sicily.

ammollicare Italianization of ➤ **ammuddicare**, to sprinkle with dried breadcrumbs.

ammorbidire to soften.

ammuddicare (past part. **ammuddicate**) to sprinkle with dried breadcrumbs: a southern dialect term usually referred to recipes involving anchovy, pasta and vegetables, such as chard, chicory, spinach, borage, potatoes and artichokes.

ammugliatielli aka **mugliatielli** lamb's offal (lung, liver and sweetbreads) wrappped in the intestines and round a wood stick. Perfumed with garlic, parsley, cheese and chili, the resulting bundles may be roasted or stewed with potatoes and grated Pecorino. Recipe typical of inland areas. Campania.

amol Veneto dialect term for wild plum (➤ **bisato coi amoi**). Veneto.

amor sweet polenta made by whipping butter and confectioner's sugar and folding in plain and cornflour, eggs, peeled and minced almonds and amaretto or maraschino liqueur. The resulting soft, coarse mixture is baked in the oven and served with ➤ **zabaglione** or ➤ **crema inglese**. Typical of the province of Varese. Lombardy.

amplova Ligurian term for ➤ **acciuga**, anchovy.

anaci Tuscan term for the seeds (actually fruits) of ➤ **anice verde**, anise or aniseed.

anacioni aniseed cookies made by kneading plain flour, yeast, eggs, sugar and butter with anise seeds (➤ **anaci**) and liqueur. The mixture is allowed to rest, then shaped into long fingers, which are baked twice in the oven and cut obliquely into slices. Tuscany.

anara col pien duck stuffed with crumbled salami (➤ **soppressa**), ground pork and veal, egg yolks, fresh breadcrumbs and mushrooms, wrapped in canvas and boiled. Traditionally cooked in Venice on the third Sunday in July, the feast of the Redeemer. Veneto.

anara aka **arna** Venetian dialect term for ➤ **anatra**, duck.

anatra aka **anitra** duck. Name for various species of aquatic birds of the Anatidae family with webbed feet, flat beak and thick, virtually waterproof plumage. The covers both wild breeds (➤ **germano reale**, mallard, ➤ **alzavola**, teal, ➤ **marzaiola**, gargany, ➤ **canapiglia**, gadwall, ➤ **codone** pintail, ➤ **fischione**, widgeon) and domestic breeds, such as the musk dusk (*Chairina moschata*), a native of Amazonia. The Italian Ministry of Agriculture's database of native and/or traditional food products includes *anatra di corte padovana*, *anatra germanata* and *anatra mignon*, all raised in the Veneto region. Duck is popular in a number of Italian regions: in Tuscany (where it is known as *nana*) and in Marche (where it is known as *papera*), it is cooked with wild fennel (➤ **porchetta, in**). In Veneto (where it is known as *anara*) it is stuffed (➤ **anara col pien**) or used to make pasta sauces. In general, young birds are roasted, whereas adults are stewed, cooked in ➤ **salmì** or used to make patés.

anatra al sale duck flavored internally with sage, rosemary and cognac, coated with sea salt and roast in the oven. Typical of Piacenza. Emilia-Romagna.

anatra all'arancia duck with orange sauce. The duck, plucked and cut into small pieces is browned in a skillet with strips of orange zest, butter, salt and pepper, then bathed with brandy. Orange juice is gradually added to the pan until the meat is well cooked. The pan juices, with the addition of sugar, are thickened over a high heat and poured over the meat, which is usually served with potato purée. According to some culinary scholars, inasmuch as it has been mentioned in Tuscan recipe collections since the 15th century, the dish, usually associated with France, could be of Florentine origin. Tuscany.

anatra con le verze duck with cabbage. Duck stuffed with ground pork and chicken, sausage, grated cheese, eggs, breadcrumbs, minced garlic and parsley and spices, cooked with Savoy cabbage and served with polenta. Sometimes duck is replaced by chicken. Typical of the Valcamonica, in the provinces of Brescia and Bergamo. Lombardy.

anatra frasenà duck first boiled, then boned, then broiled until golden brown. A specialty of the province of Padua, the recipe first came into being as a way of using up leftover boiled poultry. Served with new potatoes, horseradish and grilled polenta. Veneto.

anatra muta a porchetta musk duck served with a condiment similar to that used for ➤ **porchetta**, roast pork. The bird is stuffed with chopped giblets flavored with wild fennel and olive oil, then roast in the oven and jointed. The meat is served with the stuffing and roast potatoes. The recipe is Umbrian, but the dish may also be found in the Marche and in Tuscany (see ➤ **nana in porchetta**).

anatra ripiena duck with a stuffing of soaked fresh breadcrumbs, egg yolks, chicken livers, butter, sage and rosemary, barded with slices of lardo, and cooked with white wine and broth. Friuli-Venezia Giulia

anatra ripiena alla novarese stuffed duck Novara-style. The province of Novara is famous for rice growing and the use of rice characterizes the stuffing for this dish. Boiled rice is amalgamated with chopped roast beef, sausage, lardo, eggs, garlic, parsley and nutmeg, and stuffed into the cavity of the bird, which is then cooked in a casserole with the addition of broth. The same stuffing is also used for chicken. Piedmont.

ancioa dialect term for ➤ **acciuga**, anchovy. Usually refers to salted anchovies or anchovies preserved in oil. Piedmont.

ancioada salad of winter vegetables (cabbage, beetroot) and cooked meats (beef, calf's tongue) with a sauce of anchovies, vinegar, wine and butter. Typical of the Monferrato area. Piedmont.

anciova Sicilian term for ➤ **acciuga**, anchovy.

anciti another word for ➤ **bietola selvatica**, chard.

anelli another word for ➤ **anellini**, a type of pasta.

anellini small durum wheat pasta rings. Cooked in broth or baked in the oven, especially in southern Italy. Other names: ➤ **anelli**, ➤ **occhialini**.

anellini alla pecorara ring-shaped pasta served with a sauce of ➤ **guanciale** (cheek bacon), beef, mushrooms, spring vegetables, Pecorino cheese and ricotta. Abruzzo, Molise.

anello di monaco cake made from a similar mixture to ➤ **panettone**, which, apart from a hole in the middle, it also resembles in shape. Topped with sugar icing, it is filled with a cream of toasted hazelnuts and almonds, sugar and Marsala. A Christmas specialty in the Mantua area. Lombardy.

anemone di mare sea anemone (*Anemonia sulcata*). A member of the Anthozoa class ("flower animals," from the Greek *anthos*, "flower," and *zoon*, "animal") of aquatic organisms named for the anemone, a terrestrial flower, which clings to stones and shells. In the Mediterranean, it is fished mostly off Sicily and Sardinia, where it is dipped in an egg and flour batter, and made into fritters, or served with pasta or other fish or seafood (➤ **cozze e orziadas**, mussels and anemones). Sicily, Sardinia.

aneto dill (*Anethum graveolens*). Aromatic herb spontaneous in the Mediterranean area, now cultivatd, especially in northern Italy. Its fresh leaves are chopped to perfume fish dishes, and its seeds are used to aromatize vinegar, wines and liqueurs. Common and regional names: ➤ **agneso**, ➤ **finocchio fetido**, ➤ **finocchio bastardo**.

anginetti sweet ring cookies covered with an icing of sugar aromatized with small quantities of aniseed liqueur or lemon juice. Campania.

angiolottos another word for ➤ **anzelottos**, Sardinian ravioli.

anguela ➤ word used in Venezia-Giulia for **latterino**, silverside.

anguidda Sardinian term for ➤ **anguilla**, eel.

anguidda chunks of eel, or small baby eels, impaled on skewers, alternated with bay leaves, and roasted over a fire. Sardinia.

anguidda incasada (aka **incasata anguilla**) eel boiled with garlic, onion, parsley and sun-dried tomatoes and finished in the oven with a sprinkling of grated Pecorino cheese. Sardinia.

anguilla eel (*Anguilla anguilla*). Begins life in the Atlantic Ocean, grows up in fresh water and returns to the sea to spawn. The fishing season lasts from the second half of the summer to late fall. In the marshes of the Po delta, in Comacchio (province of Ferrara, Emilia-Romagna) and the Venice lagoons, eels are farmed in freshwater ponds (*valli*), and fished late in the year in time for Christmas. The Italian Ministry of Agriculture's database of native and/or traditional food products lists the following eel varieties: *anguilla del delta del Po* (Veneto, Emilia-Romagna), *anguilla delle valli da pesca venete*, aka *bisat*, *bisato* or *bisatto* (Veneto), *anguilla del lago di Bolsena* (Lazio), *anguilla del Livenza* (Veneto) and *anguilla del Trasimeno* (Umbria). Particularly renowned are the eels of Lake Garda, especially on the Verona side, of the lagoons of Orbetello (province of Grosseto, Tuscany), and of Lesina (➤ **anguilla di Lesina**, province of Foggia, Puglia). The eel has fat, very delicate meat with only a few bones, and is cooked roast, spit-roast, stewed or in soups. It can also be smoked and marinated in vinegar (➤ **anguilla marinata tradizionale delle valli di Comacchio**, ➤ **anguilla scavecciata**, ➤ **anguilla sfumata**). See also ➤ **capitone**.

anguilla al verde the eel is cut into chunks and browned in a skillet, covered with a ➤ **bagna**, or sauce, of minced flat-leaved parsley, sage, garlic or spring onions, and chard or spinach leaves, and cooked in oil and butter. The dish is finished off with aromatic herbs, a little tomato sauce and anchovy fillets, and served with polenta. Recipe typical of the Monferrato hills in the province of Asti. Piedmont.

anguilla alla bisentina the eel is cut into pieces and browned in an earthenware pot with mixed dried herbs (sage, rosemary, bay leaf), to which tomato passata, salt, pepper and chopped chili are added to form a rich stew. Recipe typical of Lake Bolsena, in the province of Viterbo. Lazio.

anguilla alla borghigiana eel in the manner of Borgo Ticino, a neighborhood of Pavia on the right bank of the Ticino. The eel

anguilla in umido

is cut into pieces, gently fried in butter and onions, then finished off in red wine, to which flat-leaved parsley, bay leaves and other herbs are added. Lombardy.

anguilla alla fiorentina the eel is skinned and gutted and marinated for a couple of hours in olive oil seasoned with salt and pepper. It is then lightly breaded and baked in the oven with oil, crushed garlic, sage leaves and white wine. In one variation on the recipe, plum tomatoes and fresh peas are added. Tuscany.

anguilla alla lariana eel cooked in the manner of Lake Como. The fish is cut into pieces, coated in flour and browned in a mixture of finely chopped celery, carrot and onion. Soaked dried mushrooms are then added, together with tomatoes, red wine and herbs. The fish is left to simmer until cooked. Lombardy.

anguilla alla trentina eel cooked in the manner of Trento. The fish is cut into pieces and browned in butter with onion and herbs, flavored with cinnamon and lubricated with white wine. In some places they add beaten eggs and vinegar to the cooking juices and pour the resulting sauce over the fish. Trentino-Alto Adige.

anguilla alla veneziana Italianization of the Venetian dialect → **bisato a la veneziana**, eel Venice-style.

anguilla alla Vernaccia eels cleaned, skinned and macerated in Vernaccia wine for half a day, then stewed in a pot with onion, bay leaves, garlic, a little of the marinade and hot broth. An ancient dish cited by Dante in his *Divine Comedy*. Tuscany.

anguilla con le verze eel and cabbage stew. Large eels (→ **capitone**) first broiled, then stewed with rolled Savoy cabbage leaves, vinegar and tomato. A typical Christmas dish in Comacchio (province of Ferrara). In the province of Reggio,

the same name is used for a pie filled with small eels boiled with Savoy cabbage. Emilia-Romagna.

anguilla di Lesina in the lagoon of Lesina, in the province of Foggia, eels are still fished using traditional methods and the hundred or so surviving fishermen, organized in cooperatives, "share out the waters" among themselves every year (the season last four months). The most traditional local dishes are → **minestra di anguilla** (eel soup) and *anguilla alla brace*, broiled eel. Puglia.

anguilla dorata fillets of eel cut into small pieces, dipped in beaten egg, coated in breadcrumbs and deep-fried in olive oil. Typical of the province of Piacenza, the dish is served with vegetables dressed with balsamic vinegar and lemon wedges. Emilia-Romagna.

anguilla in carpione soused eel. The fish is cut into pieces, coated with flour, fried and steeped in a warm marinade of water, vinegar, garlic, onion, carrot, sage, rosemary, bay leaves, cinnamon and cloves. A dish common throughout northern Italy, especially round lakes, along the major rivers, in lagoon areas and in the Po delta. In Ferrara, they marinate fillets of eel in a simple liquid of vinegar, garlic, sage and bay leaves. On the northern shores of Lake Garda (province of Trento), lake eel is perfumed with aromatic herbs (marjoram, dill, chervil), coated in flour, fried, boiled for a few minutes and left to cool in a marinade of Nosiola white wine and grappa flavored with lightly fried aromatics, coriander and cloves.

anguilla in umido stewed eel. A dish common, with variations, throughout northern and central Italy. In Umbria and Veneto, for example, they skin the fish, cut it into pieces, stew it in oil, onion, garlic, tomato passata, water and white wine, and serve it with slices of toasted bread. In Emilia, they add lemon zest and replace the white wine with a few tablespoons of vinegar.

anguilla in umido alla napoletana small eels with fine skins cut into pieces, cooked in a mixture of tomato passata, extra virgin olive oil, onion, parsley, basil and white wine, and garnished with croutons. Campania.

anguilla marinata another name for **anguilla in carpione**, soused eel.

anguilla marinata tradizionale delle valli di Comacchio in the waterlands of the Valli di Comacchio and the Delta del Po National Park (Emilia-Romagna), wild eels are spit-roast or barbecued over fires of holm-oak and other woods from the Boscone della Mesola forest, then preserved in a brine of white wine vinegar, sea salt (➤ **sale marino di Cervia**), water and bay leaf) in wooden tubs (*zangolini*), today largely replaced by tin cans. A Slow Food presidium has been set up to revive the traditional 18th-century technique. Emilia-Romagna.

anguilla ripiena stuffed eeel. In a recipe typical of the province of Ferrara, the fish, boned and gutted, is stuffed with a mixture of its own flesh, capers, gherkins, parsley, thyme, marjoram, eggs and a few drops of cognac. Secured with a fine string, it is stewed with aromatic vegetables and white wine. On Lake Iseo, in the province of Brescia, eel used to be stuffed with breadcrumbs, cheese, garlic, and spices and baked in the oven, but the dish is hard to find today. Emilia-Romagna, Lombardy.

anguilla scavecciata opened from the abdominal cavity to the head, eels impaled on a skewer and dried in the open air. Cut into chunks, they are then fried and marinated (*scaveccio* is a dialect word for ➤ **scapece**) in vinegar, white wine and herbs. A specialty of the lagoon of Orbetello, in the province of Grosseto. Tuscany.

anguilla sfumata eel marinated briefly in vinegar and salt, brushed with chili sauce, and smoked. Typical of the lagoon of Orbetello, in the province of Grosseto. Tuscany.

anguille all'acqua marina eels (➤ **anguilla di Lesina**) placed in bowls, covered with sea water, left in the sun until the water evaporates, then served dressed with oil and vinegar. A popular recipe in the area round the lagoon of Lesina. Puglia.

anguille alla maniera di Cascia the fish is cleaned, skinned and marinated in olive oil, vinegar, bay leaves, rosemary and garlic. It is then seared in a skillet with breadcrumbs to form a crust, and finished in the oven, covered by the marinade liquid. Umbria.

anguille con cicoria di campo eel and wild chicory. The chicory (➤ **cicoria selvatica**) is boiled, then finished off in a skillet with onion, suet and tomato sauce. The eel, skin on, is cut into pieces and cooked in the mixture, seasoned with salt and chili. A recipe typical of Capua, in the province of Caserta. Campania.

anguilletta another name for ➤ **ciriola romana**, a Roman bread roll.

angulas another name for ➤ **pardulas**, Sardinian Easter cakes.

anguria another name for ➤ **cocomero**, water melon.

anice dei Vosgi another name for ➤ **cumino dei prati,** caraway.

anice stellato star anise (*Illicium verum*). Star-shaped fruit of an oriental plant of the Illiciaceae family, the source of the highest percentage of aniseed essence for industrial purposes.

anice verde anise (*Pimpinella anisum*). Herbaceous plant, a member of the Umbelliferae family, native to the Middle East but well acclimatized in Italy, where it grows spontaneously. Its flowers produce fruits (aniseed) that are rich in aromatic essences and are preserved and used dried. Anise is widely used in confectionery and in the liqueur industry (➤ **anice**, ➤ **anicione**, ➤ **anisetta**, ➤ **mistrà**, ➤ **sassolino**, ➤ **sambuca**) and in baking (➤ **anacioni**, ➤ **anicini**).

anicini cookies made from a mixture of eggs, flour, sugar, orange blossom water and anise seeds, first baked in a long loaf shape, then cut into slices which are subsequently twice-baked. Liguria.

anicione aka **anesone** aniseed liqueur. The aniseed liqueur family has always been one of the most prolific. The procedure for extracting the flavor was introduced to Italy by the Arabs and later spread with great success to France and Spain. Numerous anise liqueurs are produced in Italy, sometimes flavored with aromatic essences, such as fennel seeds and citrus fruit zest. Examples are: ➤ **sassolino** (Emilia-Romagna), ➤ **anisetta** (Marche) and ➤ **sambuca** (Lazio).

anime beate "happy souls" aka ➤ **vecchiarelle** "old women". Doughnut-like cakes made of plain flour, brewer's yeast and eggs, typical of the Christmas period. First fried, then soaked in honey or garnished with jam. Calabria.

animella (pl. **animelle**) sweetbreads. The white, spongy thymus, a gland located near the stomach, of calves, lambs or kids. Much exploited by classic French and Italian regional cuisine alike. Today the use of sweetbreads is in decline, but they still figure as ingredients in favorites such as ➤ **finanziera** (Piedmont) and ➤ **fritto misto all'italiana**.

animelle con carciofi e piselli stew of calf's sweetbreads wth artichokes and peas. The sweetbreads (➤ **animella**) are poached and cleaned and cooked in a skillet with chopped onion, prosciutto, lard and oil, plus an occasional small glass of Marsala. The artichokes and peas are boiled separately, then added to the stew. Lazio.

animelle in agrodolce sweet and sour sweetbreads. Sweetbreads (➤ **animella**) boiled and finely sliced, browned in a mixture of chopped carrot, onion, celery, lardo and prosciutto, and finished off in the oven. Served with a sweet and sour sauce (➤ **agrodolce**) of olive oil, sugar and capers. Lombardy.

anisetta mildly alcoholic member of the aniseed liqueur family (➤ **anicione**). The chief ingredient is ➤ **anice verde**, anise or aniseed (*Pimpinella anisum*). Others vary according to recipes, but invariably include star anise, fennel seeds and lemon zest. In 1870 Silvio Meletti perfected the liqueur using a very slow system of distillation and evaporation, and thereby associated his name with the product. His recipe is made today using traditional methods, the liqueur being left to rest in iron vats after distillation to allow the aromas to blend prior to bottling. Anisetta is used in the kitchen to flavor simple cakes and creams and drunk as a digestif or to lace coffee. Marche.

anlòti type of ➤ **agnolotti** typical of the area of Novi Ligure, in the province of Alessandria. Very similar to ➤ **ravieu di Gavi**, but with more sausage in the filling. Piedmont.

annecchia Neapolitan term for a cow of one year of age.

annoglia salami made of pig's intestines seasoned with salt and pepper and flavored with wild fennel. Served raw or, after a couple of months of aging, boiled in vegetable and legume soups (➤ **minestra maritata**). Campania.

annoia pig's stomach and intestine cleaned with water and cornflour, boiled for two hours, and cut into strips, which are then cured with salt, chili, garlic, fennel seeds and orange zest. The mixture is pressed into a pig's intestine and hung for a few days in a room warmed by a fire. Eaten fresh, either roast or cooked in white wine. A specialty of the province of Chieti. Abruzzo.

annutolo a buffalo of 13 to 24 months of age.

anolini stuffed pasta typical, in differing versions, of the provinces of Parma and Piacenza. In Parma they have a half-moon shape, in Piacenza they are round. The filling is made of ➤ **stracotto di manzo**, braised beef (though in Parma they only use the gravy). In some parts of the province of Piacenza (Castell'Arquato, Val d'Arda), where they are known as ➤ **anvein, anolini** are stuffed with dry breadcrumbs soaked in broth, eggs, mature Grana cheese and nutmeg. Traditionally served in beef or capon broth or, better still, in ➤ **brodo di terza**, beef, capon and pork broth. Emilia-Romagna.

antipasto cold or hot hors d'oeuvre, entrée or starter. The custom of beginning the meal with dishes designed to "open" the stomach and whet the appetite has enjoyed varying success from era to era. In the Roman period and the Middle Ages, the starter was characterized by unripe fruit and salads dressed with oil and vinegar, in the Renaissance by morsels of fruit, cakes, ricotta and preserved or soused fish. Since then classic cuisine has institutionalized the hors d'oeuvre, a succession of cold tidbits (cured meats, preserved fish, pâtés, terrines, ➤ **vitel tonné**, seafood, bruschettas and so on) and hot (molds, turnovers, frittatas and many more besides) served buffet-style or on a trolley. Today, despite the "destructuring" of the traditional meal, consolidated Italian regional antipasto habits die hard. In Piedmont they follow the classical model of many, varied cold and hot dishes; in Puglia they serve up a medley of the fruits of land and sea (vegetables galore, seafood, crustaceans, dairy produce); in Calabria they show a preference for pickles and vegetables; in Sicily they opt for stuffed olives, flatbreads and fresh cheeses. In central Italy, cured meats have pride of place: from *battilarda*, a trayful of mixed cold cuts (Emilia-Romagna) to ➤ **fellata** (Marche, Abruzzo, but also Campania, Molise), to the various specialties of Umbria and Abruzzo, often served with ➤ **torta fritta**, a fried pastry that changes name according to area.

antipast ross Piedmontese dialect name for ➤ **giardiniera**, mixed pickled vegetables.

antipasto campagnolo another name for ➤ **giardiniera**, mixed pickled vegetables.

antunna Sardinian dialect term for ➤ **cardoncello**, king trumpet mushroom.

anvein Piacenza dialect term for ➤ **anolini**, a type of pasta.

anzelottos aka **anzollotos** durum wheat ravioli filled with fresh sheep's cheese, eggs, chard or spinach and saffron or pennyroyal. Typically dressed with tomato or meat sauce. Sardinia.

àola Veneto and Trentino dialect term for ➤ **alborella**, bleak.

àole salè bleak (➤ **alborella**) partially sun-dried and preserved in glass jars with a generous amount of sea salt, rosemary, garlic and bay leaves. Mashed and gently fried in oil, they are used to dress ➤ **bi-**

goi aka ➤ **bigoli**, a local pasta. A condiment typical of Lake Garda. Lombardy, Trentino, Veneto.

ape nera sicula (*Apis mellifera sicula*) Sicilian black bee, similar to the African black bee, but less aggressive. Very dark, almost black, in color, it is very productive even at high temperatures and consumes less honey than its African cousin. When apiculturists began to import breeds from northern Italy, the Sicilian black risked extinction, and was only saved by the research of an entomologist who passed on his passion to a student, today the only possessor of 100% Sicilian bees. With them he produces thyme, orange blossom, medlar, mandarin, strawberry tree, cardoon and European milk vetch honey—European milk vetch (*Astragalus nebrodensis*) being a unique flower native to the Nebrodi mountains. A Slow Food presidium is seeking to reintroduce the black bee to the parts of the island, particularly the northwest, in which honey production is least common (hence where chances of contamination with other species are less probable). Sicily.

Apfelbrot flat oval loaf baked from a dough of dark rye and all-purpose flour (70%-30%), enriched with pieces of dried apple, water, sourdough, salt, fennel seeds, caraway seeds, fenugreek, cinnamon and lemon. Typical of the Val Venosta, in the province of Bolzano. Trentino-Alto Adige.

Apfelschmarn form of ➤ **Kaiserschmarn**, a sweet omelet, made with apples. Trentino-Alto Adige.

apio another name for ➤ **prezzemolo**, parsley.

appassire (1) to soften. Used in the kitchen usually with reference to onions.

appassire (2) to wither, to wilt. To cause a plant to become less fresh, to go wrinkled and to start to die, or (of a plant) to become less fresh, to go wrinkled and to start to die.

appassire (3) to dry or to desiccate.

appertizzazione technique of food preservation whereby foods are sterilized in hermetically sealed jars.

appiattire to flatten. Verb used to refer to the pounding, hence tenderizing, of meat.

appio montano another name for ➤ **sedano di monte**, mountain celery.

aquila di mare another name for ➤ **matàn**, eagle ray.

arachide peanut (*Arachis hipogea*). Native to South America, subsequently transported to Africa, cultivated to make oil or for direct consumption, toasted with or without the shell. Salted peanuts are a common snack in Italy with aperitifs. Local names include: ➤ **bagigi**, ➤ **giapponi**, ➤ **spagnolette**.

aragosta lobster. Marine crustacean of the Palinuridae family. Cannot be farmed but, after being caught, is immersed in tanks to keep it alive for the market. Usually eaten whole, boiled in a ➤ **court-bouillon** and served cold with mayonnaise (➤ **maionese**) or a sauce of olive oil and lemon beaten with minced parsley, salt and pepper, or roast in the oven or broiled. Cooked with tomato, it is an excellent accompaniment for pasta or rice.

aragosta alla bosana boiled lobster anointed with olive oil and served with hard-boiled eggs and vegetables. Typical of Bosa, in the province of Oristano. Sardinia.

aragosta alla catalana lobster cooked with tomatoes, peppers, garlic, onion, minced parsley, brandy and a pinch of saffron. Traditionally prepared for the Ferragosto national vacation (August 15), which coincides with the feast of the Assumption of the Virgin Mary. Sardinia.

aragosta arrosto roast lobster. The crustacean is shelled, placed in an oven dish, sprinkled with olive oil and lemon juice, covered with minced flat-leaved parsley and dried breadcrumbs, and baked in the oven. Sardinia.

aragostelle another word for ➤ **sfogliatelle**, sweet pastries.

arancia orange (*Citrus sinensis*). The fruit, available in a number of varieties, reached the Mediterranean in around the 9th century, and has been cultivated in Italy since the 18th, notably in Sicily and Calabria. It is harvested from October to July. Two quality varieties are: ➤ **arancia del Gargano** and ➤ **arancia rossa di Sicily**, both recognized with PGI status. The Italian Ministry of Agriculture database of native and/or traditional food products lists: *arancia della Costa dei Trabocchi* (Abruzzo); *arancia bionda tardiva di Trebisacce, arancia di Villa San Giuseppe* (Calabria); *arancia di Pagani e di Sorrento* (Campania); *arancia bionda di Fondi* (Lazio); *arancia pernabucco* or *arancia portugallo* (Liguria); *arancia dolce del Golfo di Taranto* (Puglia); *arancia massese* (Tuscany); *arancia di Muravera* (Sardinia); *arancia bionda di Scillato, arancia di Ribera, arancia ovaletto di Calatafimi* (Sicily). The orange features in a number of traditional savory recipes: ➤ **anatra all'arancia** (duck with orange sauce), ➤ **insalata di arance** (orange salad) ➤ **olive all'arancia** (olives with orange), ➤ **palomba alla todina** (pigeon with orange). Oranges are used widely in confectionery, especially candied. Sicilian confectionery is packed with recipes involving candied orange zest, which also appears in the spiced cakes of Tuscany and the rest of central Italy. A tradition of candied zest also exists in northern Italy (➤ **zest di Carignano**).

arancia amara another name for ➤ **melangolo**, bitter orange.

arancia del Gargano smallish sweet PGI orange. Prized since antiquity, the fruit is at the center of an annual procession in honor of San Valentino, the protector of citrus groves. Eaten fresh but also much used in cookery, not to mention in the preparation of juices and syrups. Puglia.

arancia rossa di Sicilia red Sicilian orange cultivated in the provinces of Enna, Catania, Siracusa and Ragusa. The *moro*, *tarocco* and *sanguinello* varieties are protected by PGI status. Very sweet in flavor, the flesh varies from orange to dark red in color. Sicily

arancino (pl. **arancini**), in Palermo aka, **arancina** (pl. **arancine**) small ball of rice filled with either meat sauce or chicken giblets (though variations exist), dipped in beaten eggs, coated in breadcrumbs and deep-fried. Usually spherical, but also pyramidal in shape. Sicily.

aranzada orange zest washed and cooked in honey with the addition of peeled and toasted almonds. The resulting compôte is rolled out on a marble surface and left to cool. It is then cut into pieces and served either as it is, decorated with confetti sugar or with ➤ **traggera**, colored sprinkles. Also available commercially in individual portions or boxes. A candy typical of Nuoro. Sardinia.

arbada soft polenta made by cooking together polenta flour, winter vegetables (potatoes, cabbage and so on), pork rind, chopped herbs and lardo. Typical of the province of Reggio Emilia. Emilia-Romagna.

arbadela savory pie popular in the Massa-Carrara and Lunigiana areas. Made with a mixture of onions, wild fennel, wild herbs, salt, polenta flour, Pecorino cheese, milk, pepper, ricotta and olive oil, which is spread out in a baking tin and baked in the oven. Tuscany.

Arbëreshë Albanian-speaking population (*arbereschi* in Italian) which, after waves of emigration, settled centuries ago in southern Italy. Its various colonies—most numerous in Calabria and Sicily—have managed to cling on to their cultural identity, though not all of them have conserved their language. Their typical dishes include ➤ **capretto alla civitese,** ➤ **drömsat,** ➤ **rrashkatjel,** ➤**strangulet.**

arca di Noè Noah's ark or arkshell (*Arca noae*). Bivalve mollusk of a family closely related to that of the mussel (➤ **cozza,** ➤ **mitilo**). Its unusually shaped shell resembles an ancient wooden boat, hence the Noah's ark connection. Clings to sea cliffs and has tasty flesh, generally eaten raw. Common and regional names: ➤ **arsella pelosa,** ➤ **brazzoleddu de mari,** ➤ **coffano di pietra,** ➤ **mussolo,** ➤ **mussolo di scoglio,** ➤ **zampa di vacca.** Listed in the Italian Ministry of Agriculture's database of native and/or traditional food products.

arcella niura Sicilian dialect term for ➤ **cozza,** mussel (➤ **mitilo**).

arcera southern dialect term for ➤ **beccaccia,** woodcock.

arciciòch aka **articioco** northern dialect terms for ➤ **carciofo,** artichoke.

arcigghiola southern dialect term for ➤ **beccaccino,** woodcock.

ardielut dialect term for ➤ **valerianella,** corn salad.

arganello dialect term for ➤ **scampo,** scampi. Marche.

argentina argentine (*Argentina sphyraena*). Tiny fish of the Argentinidae family, present in the Mediterranean, though not in the Adriatic. Mostly eaten fried.

aringa (pl. **aringhe**) herring (*Clupea harengus*). A member of the Clupeidae family, much loved in northern Europe for its tasty, nutritious flesh. So much so that it was once used as a means of exchange, even as a currency. In Italy it is only available preserved: salted–referred to as ➤ **scopetòn** throughout the Veneto region–salted and smoked (➤ **peclìn** in Trentino), in brine and marinated and aromatized in various ways. It is nonetheless used in Italian cooking in a number of popular dishes: ➤ **renghe e rati,** ➤ **aringa e ceci in insalata.**

aringa e ceci in insalata herring and chickpea salad. Tasty popular Tuscan dish, today served as an antipasto. The chickpeas are boiled and mixed with fillets of herring, and dressed with chopped baby onions, extra virgin olive oil, vinegar, salt and pepper. Served warm with toasted bread. In a Piedmontese version of the dish, boiled beans are mixed with baked onions and dressed with a ➤ **vinaigrette.** Piedmont, Tuscany.

arista term used (in Greek it means "excellent", "the best") since the 14th century for pork loin (➤ **carré di maiale**) on the bone, larded with garlic cloves and rosemary or fennel seeds, and spit or oven-roast.

arista di maiale al forno the meat (➤ **arista**) is partly boned, perfumed with minced garlic, rosemary and sage and seasoned with salt and pepper, before being roasted in the oven with new potatoes. Tuscany.

arista di maiale in porchetta pork seasoned with salt, pepper, crushed garlic, rosemary and juniper berries, rolled and baked in the oven. One of the many dishes cooked with the same ingredients used to cure ➤ **porchetta,** roast pork. Tuscany.

ariula Sicilian term for ➤ **donzella,** Mediterranean rainbow wrasse.

armelette another name for → **lasagne matte**, chestnut flour pasta.

armellina the stone of the peach or apricot, commonly known as *mandorla amara*, or bitter almond. Much used in the confectionery industry, especially as an ingredient of → **amaretto (2)**.

armidda Sardinian term for → **serpillo**, wild thyme.

aromi literally "aromas." Term used in recipes for mixed herbs (rosemary, sage, bay leaf, thyme) and aromatics (garlic, onion, celery, carrot).

arrabbiata, all' term used to describe a dish with a pungent, fiery condiment. Normally applied to meat (eg, *bistecca di manzo all'arrabbiata*: minute steaks cooked in oil with garlic and chili) and pasta (*penne all'arrabbiata*: pasta with a sauce of tomato, garlic or onion and chili).

arracanato aka **arraganato** term (which derives from → **origano**, oregano) for a baked layered casserole with dried breadcrumbs and herbs, including oregano, among the ingredients.

arrasojas dialect term for → **cannolicchio**, razor clam. Sardinia.

arriminari Sicilian verb meaning "to mix," "to blend," "to amalgamate," hence sometimes a synonym of → **ripassare**. Its past participle is used in the names of a number of recipes, often involving pasta (→ **bucatini con i broccoli arriminati**).

arrobiòlos pastries made with the same dough as → **brugnulusos de arrescottu**. Small cylinders joined at the ends to form rings. Sardinia.

arrosticini, in dialect aka **'rrustelle** small cubes of mutton or lamb impaled on wooden skewers and barbecued. Abruzzo.

arrostire to roast.

arrostita literally "roast" or "roasted." Word used, especially on the Adriatic coast, to refer to mixed fish cooked on a barbecue.

arrosto alle acciughe aka **arrosto alla casalese** literally "roast veal with anchovies," but actually a stew. A piece of not over-lean veal cooked in a mixture of powdered mustard diluted with water, vinegar, anchovies, chopped onion, bay leaf and oil or beef fat. The pan juices are filtered and served with the sliced meat. Recipe typical of the Monferrato hills in the province of Asti. Piedmont.

arrosto alle nocciole roast veal with hazelnuts. As it roasts, a piece of best end of veal, previously browned in butter, is bathed with Marsala and served with the pan juices blended with milk, a little toasted flour and very finely chopped toasted hazelnuts (→ **nocciola del Piedmont**). Typical of the Langa hills in the province of Cuneo. Piedmont.

arrosto della vena another word for → **copertina di sopra**, boneless chuck.

arrosto misto al forno mixed roast. Mixed meats (rabbit, chicken, goose, duck, pigeon and lamb) served with toasted bread topped with fried offal. A typical holiday dish all over the region. Umbria.

arrosto misto toscano mixed spit-roast of pork fillet and thrushes (or quails). The birds, gutted and stuffed with sage, salt and pepper, and the fillet, seasoned with salt and cut into chunks, are impaled on a spit, alternated with pieces of bread, brushed with oil and barbecued or roast in the oven. Lean sausage and pig's liver flavored with fennel seeds may also be added. The original recipe calls exclusively for various species of fowl, large and small. Tuscany.

arrosto morto literally "dead roast." Veal or beef browned in butter or oil, then slowly braised with the addition of broth, wine or water.

arrosto ripieno stuffed roast. A slice of veal stuffed with pancetta, frittata ad spinach, rolled up, secured with string and cooked following the ➤ **arrosto morto** technique. Recipe typical of the province of Reggio Emilia. Emilia-Romagna.

arrotolato ground beef mixed with eggs, grated Parmigiano, salt and pepper, stuffed with buttered spinach, and wrapped with slices of mortadella like a large meat loaf. Cooked in the pan, the loaf is allowed to cool, then served sliced. A recipe typical of the province of Florence. Tuscany.

arrusti e mancia aka **'rrusti e mancia** literally "roast and eat." Broiled or barbecued meat or fish to be eaten straightaway without tarrying. Sicily.

arsella (pl. **arselle**) another word for ➤ **vongola verace**, carpet shell clam, in Liguria, ➤ **vongola commune**, common clam, in Sardinia, and ➤ **tellina**, tellin, in Tuscany.

arsella pelosa Tuscan term for ➤ **arca di Noè**, Noah's ark.

arselle another term for ➤ **conchiglie**, "shells," a type of pasta.

arsomà cream of eggs and sugar diluted with wine, similar to ➤ **rusumada** in Lombardy, and a possible ancestor of ➤ **zabaglione**. Typical of the Biella area. Piedmont.

arvoltolo disks of bread dough fried in olive oil. Either seasoned with salt and served with cured meats as a snack, or coated with sugar, honey or jam as a dessert. In Gubbio they are known as ➤ **brustenghi**, in Orvieto as ➤ **tortucce**, elsewhere as ➤ **fregnacce**. Modern descendant of ➤ **bracalaccio**, a traditional bread dough fritter. Umbria.

arzdora aka **azdora** Romagna dialect term for ➤ **rezdora**, farmer's wife.

arzdoura Bologna dialect term for ➤ **rezdora**, farmer's wife.

arzedda Sicilian dialect term for ➤ **cuore di mare**, common cockle.

arzilla dialect term for ➤ **razza**, skate. The fish's broth is mixed with skinned tomatoes to make a sauce for crushed spaghetti (a Christmas recipe) and to make the traditional soup, ➤ **pasta e broccoli in brodo di arzilla**. Lazio.

asfodelo aka **bacchetta di re** asphodel (*Asphodelus albus, A. microcarpus, Asphodeline lutea*). Melliferous spontaneous herbs with linear leaves and dense inflorescences, which grow in mountain pastures or on dry, stony ground. Found in central and southern Italy (Abruzzo, Molise, Puglia, Sardinia, Sicily).

Asiago PDO raw cow's milk cheese from the Asiago plateau for which it is named. There are two versions: i) *d'allevo*, from *allevato* (literally "raised"), matured in mountain dairies with milk from two milkings, and aged at least three months (*mezzano*) and over nine months (*vecchio*); ii) *pressato*, made in low-lying areas from pasteurized milk and aged at least 20 days. Veneto.

Asiago stravecchio rare ➤ **Asiago** *d'allevo*, made from semi-skimmed and aged 19 months and more. The body is hard and grainy, and the rind is brownish yellow. A Slow Food presidium has been set up to promote its currently limited production. Veneto.

asianòt shortcrust pastry cookies. A specialty of Asigliano Vercellese, in the province of Vercelli. Piedmont.

Asìno cheese made in two versions: i) traditional, with raw or heat-treated cow's milk, the forms being immersed in wooden vats, or ➤ **salmueries**, preserving liquid of salt, milk and high-fat cream, for three to six months; ii) soft, with pasteurized milk, matured for 20 days. Produced in the Carnia area (province of Udine) and the Val d'Arzino (province of Pordenone). Friuli-Venezia Giulia.

asino donkey. Descendant of *Equus asinus,* the African wild donkey, which first appeared in Europe in the Neolithic age. Bred in Europe today especially in the Balkans and Turkey. Italian breeds, some of which close to extinction, are: *Grigia siciliana* (Sicily) *Pantesca* (island of Pantelleria, province of Trapani, Sicily), *Martinese* (Martina Franca province of Taranto, Puglia), *Romagnola* (Emilia-Romagna), *Amiatina* (Monte Amiata, province of Grosseto, Tuscany) and *Sarda* (Sardinia). On the island of Asinara (province of Sassari) live 120 native white-coated donkeys. The Ragusa donkey (➤ **asino ragusano**) is promoted by a Slow Food presidium. The meat of young donkeys is suitable for the same recipes as beef. In the old days, however, it was mainly old donkeys, no longer fit for work, that were butchered, and Italian regional gastronomy is full of recipes that demand long, slow cooking: eg, ➤ **stracotto di asinina**, ➤ **pastizzà de musso**, ➤ **tapulone**, ➤ **stufato di asino**, ➤ **agnolotti di asino**.

asino ragusano Ragusa donkey. Dark bay with a pale belly, gray muzzle, black mane and tail, white circles round eyes and straight ears. It can reach an age of 45, but is now on the verge of extinction. A Slow Food presidium has been set up to promote the breed and its milk. Native to the province of Ragusa. Sicily.

asparagina di monte another name for ➤ **barba di capra**, goat's beard.

asparagina (1) term used on some Italian regional markets for inferior quality asparagus (though the turions are still excellent for risottos, omelets and soups) from an asparagus patch at the end of its production cycle or season.

asparagina (2) popular name for ➤ **asparago pungente**, wild asparagus.

asparago (pl. **asparagi**) asparagus (*Asparagus officinalis*). Numerous varieties are cultivated all over southern Europe; in Italy the main growing regions are Piedmont, Lombardy, Veneto, Emilia-Romagna, Tuscany and Lazio. The Italian Ministry of Agriculture's database of native and/or traditional food products lists: ➤ **asparago di Terlano-Terlaner** (Alto Adige); *asparago verde di Altedo* (Emilia-Romagna); *asparago bianco* (Friuli-Venezia Giulia); *asparago verde di Canino e Montalto di Castro* (Lazio); ➤ **asparago violetto d'Albenga** (Liguria); *asparago di Cilavegna, di Mezzago* (Lombardy); *asparago di Borgo D'Ale, asparago di Poirino, asparago di Santena, asparago di Valmacca, asparago saraceno di Vinchio* (Piedmont); *asparago viola d'Argenteuil* and *asparago nostrale* (Tuscany); *asparago di Zambana* (Trentino); *asparago bianco del Sile,* ➤ **asparago bianco di Bassano**, *asparago bianco di Bibione,* ➤ **asparago bianco di Cimadolmo**, *asparago della Mambrotta, asparago di Arcole, asparago di Giare, asparago di Padova, asparago di Palazzetto, asparago di Rivoli Veronese, asparago verde amaro Montine* (Veneto). Asparagus is very popular in Italian cuisine, and the spears are used in soups, creams, frittatas, molds, pies and risottos, or simply boiled or steamed and dressed with extra virgin olive oil, or finished off in butter with eggs and Parmigiano. In some regions its flavor is heightened by special sauces (➤ **asparagi alla bolzanina**, ➤ **asparagi alla bassanese**).

asparago bastardo another word for ➤ **pungitopo**, butcher's broom.

asparago bianco di Bassano in this PDO variety, the turion, the edible part of the asparagus, is kept white by continually raising the soil to shelter the sprouts from the light. The result is a delicate aroma and less stringiness than other varieties. Cultivated in villages round the town of Bassano del Grappa, in the province of Vicenza. Veneto.

asparago bianco di Cimaldomo aka **oro bianco di Cimaldomo** PGI asparagus grown in the province of Treviso with tender non-fibrous turions and an exceptionally delicate flavor. Harvested from March to May. Veneto.

asparago di bosco another name for ➤ **asparago pungente**, wild asparagus.

asparago di mare another name for ➤ **salicornia**, samphire.

asparago pungente wild asparagus (*Asparagus acutifolius, A. tenuifolius*). Shrub-like plant typical of Mediterranean woodland. Gathered all over Italy, its tips are used in pasta sauces, risottos, frittatas and fillings. Common and regional names: ➤ **asparagina**, ➤ **asparago di bosco**, ➤ **corruda**, ➤ **sparacane**, ➤ **sparacogne**, ➤ **sparagnella**. The Italian Ministry of Agriculture's database of native and/or traditional food products lists: *asparago selvatico della Calabria* (Calabria), ➤ **asparagina** aka ➤ **sparazena** (Emilia- Romagna), ➤ **asparago selvatico** (Sardinia).

asparago selvatico (*Asparagus tenuifolius*) another name for ➤ **asparago pungente**, wild asparagus.

asparago verde di Altedo PGI green asparagus cultivated in a number of communes in the provinces of Bologna and Ferrara. Gathered in the spring and early summer until June 20. Emilia-Romagna.

asparago violetto di Albenga Albenga violet asparagus. The large spears are deep purple in color, fading to cream at the base of the stalk. This unique variety is cultivated completely by hand on the plain of Albenga, in the province of Savona, and harvested from mid-March to early June.

Soft and buttery, it lacks the stringiness of other varieties. A Slow Food presidium has brought growers together to relaunch the varity. Liguria

asparagi alla bassanese local asparagus boiled and served with a sauce of hard-boiled egg yolks, anchovies, capers, vinegar and oil. A delicacy in Bassano del Grappa, in the province of Vicenza. Veneto.

asparagi alla bolzanina asparagus boiled in water flavored with white wine, and served with ➤ **Boznersauce**, a sauce of hard-boiled eggs, oil, vinegar, chives, mustard, broth, salt and pepper. Recipe typical of the province of Bolzano. Trentino-Alto Adige.

asparagi alla milanese steamed asparagus tips dressed with grated Parmigiano-Reggiano and covered with eggs fried in butter. Recipe typical of Milan. Lombardy.

asparagi e uova basocche asparagus boiled in acidulated water with coddled eggs. Veneto.

asparedda Sicilian regional term for ➤ **aspraggine**, bristly oxtongue.

aspic clear jelly made from the cooked juices of meat, chicken or fish in which meat, chicken, fish, vegetables or fruit may be served cold.

aspraggine bristly oxtongue (*Picris echioides* and *P. pieracioides*). Spontaneous herbaceous plant with bristly leaves common all over Italy, save for the Po Valley. The rosetta base is gathered to be eaten raw in salads (to attenuate the bitter taste of wild chicor and radish), or cooked and flavored in the pan. Common and regional names: ➤ **asparedda**, ➤ **radicchio peloso**.

asseccaticcio weaned buffalo of 12 months or younger.

astracio Sicilian term for ➤ **scampo**, scampi.

astrea Sicilian term for ➤ **canocchia**, mantis shrimp.

asulette soup of rye flour cooked in water and butter and served with slices of bread and fontina. Val d'Aosta.

atreplice rare variety of cultivated ➤ **spinacio**, spinach.

attorta another name for ➤ **rocciata,** an Umbrian baked cake.

attuppateddi another Sicilian dialect name for ➤ **'ntuppateddi,** snails.

auciato (pl. **auciati**) small ring cookies (➤ **tarallo**) flavored with oil, white wine, and pepper, typical of the village of Sessa Aurunca, in the province of Caserta. Often eaten dipped in sweet wine. Campania.

avannotto newborn fish. (➤ **novellame di pesce**, fry).

avemarie tiny durum wheat pasta tubes, suitable for cooking in broth. Other names: ➤ **corallini**, ➤ **grandine**, ➤ **paternostri**.

avena oats (*Avena sativa*). Cereal (➤ **cereali**) similar to wheat but with longer, thinner ears. Culivated mainly in northern Europe, though wild varieties also thrive. Hard to decorticate and store, oats are used in Italy mainly in the form of flakes or flour for confectionery and baby foods.

àvola another name for ➤ **alborella**, bleak.

axelle name given in the Cinque Terre district on the eastern Ligurian coast (Riviera di Levante) to a dish made with the intestines of baby calves. The intestines are cleaned, impaled on a skewer, served seasoned with salt and pepper and anointed with extra virgin olive oil. Liguria.

azzada aka **agliata da sugo** garlic and parsley sauce, to which chopped sun-dried tomatoes, tomato passata and vinegar are sometimes added. Typical of the town of Bosa in the province of Nuoro, it is used to dress fish such as skate and dogfish. Sardinia.

azzau Sardinian regional name for ➤ **frue,** sheep's or goat's milk curd.

azzeruola another name for ➤ **lazzeruola,** hawthorn.

bB

babà small leavened mushroom-shaped cake made with a baked mixture of eggs, flour, milk, grated lemon zest, vanilla, yeast and butter, soaked in a syrup of sugar and rum. A symbol of Neapolitan confectionery, it is said to have been brought to the Kingdom of Naples by French cooks from the court of Stanislaus I of Poland. Campania.

babagnei al vino finely chopped snails stewed in red wine and broth flavored with onions and bay leaves, thickened with breadcrumbs, grated cheese and diced potatoes. Served with polenta or mushrooms sautéed in oil with garlic and parsley. Typical of the Val di Fassa, in the province of Trento. Trentino-Alto Adige.

babagnel Trento dialect term for ➤ **lumaca di terra**, earth snail.

babbaluci aka **vavaluci** dialect name in Palermo (in Catania they say ➤ **vaccaredde**) for a small white land snail with pale brown stripes (*Helix (Theba) pisana*). In Palermo, on the feast of Santa Rosalia, the patron saint, the snails (cooked in their shells with oil, garlic and parsley) are sold at stalls all over the city. Included in the Italian Ministry of Agricuture's database of traditional/native food products. Sicily.

babi, alla term used to describe the flattening of fowl (especially chicken) during the cooking process. The resulting shape is reminiscent of that of a toad (*babi* in Piedmontese dialect). Piedmont.

baccagliari recipe typical of Cagliari. Boiled ➤ **baccalà** (salt cod) drained, dressed with lemon juice and covered with toma-

to sauce. Sardinia.

baccalà salt cod. Northeastern Italy (where they say ➤ **stoccafisso**) apart, this word of Spanish origin refers to ➤ **merluzzo**, cod, preserved by salting, a technique developed in the mid 17th century as an alternative to drying. Salted and packed into bails in the fishing grounds of the North Sea, the fish is sold either encrusted in salt and opened out flat, or presoaked. It is necessary to soak the fish for another 48 hours in a plastic bowl either in running water or changing the water often. The fish is then boned and skinned according to the recipe.

baccalà a ciauredda stew of salt cod, tomato and spring onions served with toasted bread. Basilicata.

baccalà a foco morto old rural cooking method whereby soaked salt cod is cut into pieces, wrapped in paper and cooked in ash covered with burning embers. Once cooked, the fish is served with garlic, oil, parsley, salt and pepper (➤ **salmoriglio**). Umbria.

baccalà a sfincione fillets of salt cod cut into pieces, covered with sliced onion, minced garlic, parsley, wild fennel seeds, oregano, salt, pepper, extra virgin olive oil and breadcrumbs, then baked in the oven. Recipe typical of the provinces of Palermo and Trapani. Sicily.

baccalà al latte stockfish in milk. The milk may be used to soak the fish or cook it, or both. In one recipe the fish is soaked in milk, then cooked slowly in oil with butter, onions, flat-leaved parsley, breadcrumbs, lemon zest and crushed anchovies. In another, it is soaked in water, cut into large squares, sautéed in oil with garlic and celery, covered with milk, left to simmer on a low heat, then finished off with flat-leaved parsley and Trentin-grana cheese. Trentino-Alto Adige.

baccalà alla barcarola stockfish soaked, boned and cut into slices, poached, sautéed in oil and butter with finely chopped onions and anchovy fillets and finished off with a splash of vinegar and minced garlic and parsley. Veneto, Trentino-Alto Adige.

baccalà alla cappuccina pieces of stockfish gently fried with raisins, pine kernels, cinnamon and nutmeg, sprinkled with sugar and then cooked on a low heat with the addition of desalted anchovies and white wine. Veneto, Friuli-Venezia Giulia.

baccalà alla fiorentina slices of salt cod coated in flour and gently fried with potatoes cut into rounds. Finished off with tomato passata and slivers of garlic. Recipe typical of Florence. Tuscany.

baccalà alla lucana codfish soaked in water and fried in oil with pickled peppers. Basilicata.

baccalà alla napoletana slices of fried salt cod stewed with tomato, onion and roasted peppers. A recipe of Spanish origin, common in Naples. Campania.

baccalà alla perticaregna slices of fried salt cod briefly stewed in a mixture of tomatoes, onion, peppers and crushed chili. Named after the plow (*perticaro*), guided by a long board (*pertica*), on which chilis were hung to dry. Campania.

baccalà alla potentina stockfish fried to golden brown in olive oil and onions, then stewed in tomato sauce with the addition of black olives and raisins. Often served with fried peppers. Basilicata.

baccalà alla trainiera another term for →

baccalà con peperoni cruschi, salt cod with sun-dried red peppers. Basilicata.

baccalà alla trentina stockfish poached and stewed or baked with potatoes, onions and celeriac. Typical of the province of Trento. Trentino-Alto Adige.

baccalà alla trevigiana stockfish first poached in milk, then baked with oil and grated cheese. In mushroom season in the Montello area, stewed porcini are added as a final touch. Recipe typical of the province of Treviso. Veneto.

baccalà alla triestina salt cod coated in breadcrumbs and fried in butter with the addition of anchovies and pepper. Served dressed with oil, often accompanied by potatoes. Friuli-Venezia Giulia.

baccalà alla veneziana stockfish stewed with onions, raisins, pine kernels and cinnamon. Veneto.

baccalà alla verbicarese chopped salt cod baked in the oven with potatoes and peppers. A speciality of Verbicaro, in the province of Cosenza. Calabria.

baccalà alla vicentina the most celebrated stockfish recipe in the Veneto region. The dried fish is soaked in water, cut into slices and left to simmer for at least four hours in a mixture of onion, garlic, parsley, desalted anchovies, milk, grated Grana cheese, salt, pepper and oil. Served with fresh or grilled polenta. Veneto.

baccalà con i porri salt cod with leeks. The fish is cut into slices and boned, first lightly fried in olive oil, then baked in the oven with the pan juices, tomato passata, leeks and roughly torn basil. Tuscany.

baccalà con le acciughe stockfish with anchovies. The fish is cut into pieces, fried in oil with garlic and flat-leaved parsley, and finished with desalted anchovies and capers. In Friuli-Venezia Giulia, the fish is cut into squares, coated with flour, sautéed with onion, garlic, parsley and anchovies, then covered with milk and baked in the oven. Trentino-Alto Adige, Friuli-Venezia Giulia.

baccalà con le sarde stockfish with sardines. The fish is cut into pieces and boiled in milk, then lightly fried, dusted with breadcrumbs and cooked with crushed fillets of sardine, slices of onion, minced flat-leaved parsley and lemon zest. Trentino-Alto Adige.

baccalà con peperoni cruschi salt cod with sun-dried red peppers. The fish is boiled and served with ➤ **peperoni cruschi** fried in olive oil with garlic and parsley. Basilicata.

baccalà con pupazzelle a cumposta baked salt cod, potatoes, anchovies, fresh breadcrumbs, parsley, garlic and ➤ **pupazzelle a cumposta** (red peppers). A typical Christmas dish. Basilicata.

baccalà conzo stockfish boiled, flaked, mixed with minced flat-leaved parsley and garlic, oil, salt and pepper and left to cool. Served with polenta. Veneto, Friuli-Venezia Giulia.

baccalà dei frati literally "friars' stockfish." The fish is cut into small pieces and baked in the oven with aromatics, sautéed potatoes, milk, anchovy fillets, garlic and flat-leaved parsley. The recipe has been attributed to monks in Dominican monasteries, but was actually created by helpers in monastery kitchens who sold it at markets. Trentino-Alto Adige.

baccalà farcito stockfish covered with chopped anchovies, garlic, parsley and onion, rolled up, secured and cooked with water, milk, and raisins. Friuli-Venezia Giulia.

baccalà fritto fried salt cod (➤ **filetti di baccalà fritti**, fried fillets of salt cod, ➤ **frittelle di baccalà**) salt cod fritters).

baccalà in agrodolce sweet and sour salt cod. The fish is lightly fried in extra virgin olive with shallot, skinned plum tomatoes, prunes, honey and raisins. Recipe typical of the province of Terni, possibly of Arab origin. Umbria.

baccalà in bianco ➤ boiled stockfish dressed with oil, garlic, flat-leaved parsley and salted sardines. Friuli-Venezia Giulia.

baccalà in cassuola salt cod coated in flour and fried in oil, then finished in the oven in a thick sauce of tomatoes, raisins, capers, pine kernels, black olives and, sometimes, potatoes. A recipe of probable Sicilian origin. Campania.

baccalà in guazzetto aka **baccalà alla romana** fillets of salt cod coated in flour, fried and finished in the pan with tomato sauce, salt, pepper, pine kernels, onion, extra virgin olive oil, raisins and, sometimes, anchovy fillets. Lazio.

baccalà in rosso stockfish layered with potatoes and skinned tomatoes, and cooked on a very low heat with oil, garlic and bay leaves. Recipe typical of Trieste. Friuli-Venezia Giulia.

baccalà mantecato alla ferrarese salt cod coated in flour and cooked for an hour in milk with onion, flat-leaved parsley, nutmeg and a generous amount of Parmigiano. As it absorbs the milk, the fish breaks up to form a cream. Recipe typical of Ferrara. Emilia-Romagna.

baccalà mantecato alla veneziana stockfish broken up into small pieces, steamed with garlic, lemon and bay leaves, mashed with a wooden spoon and blended with extra virgin olive oil. Once made in a *zangola*, or butter churn. Often served on toasted bread as a ➤ **stuzzichino**, snack (➤ **cicheti**). Veneto, Friuli-Venezia Giulia.

baccalà ripieno stuffed salt cod. Fillet of salt cod shaped into a pouch, stuffed with fresh breadcrumbs soaked in milk, dried breadcrumbs, egg yolk, garlic, flat-leaved parsley and lemon zest, and cooked in oil and white wine. Umbria.

baccalà sotto il pesto salt cod soaked and cut into pieces, coated in flour and fried in olive oil, then covered with a warm marinade of chopped garlic, olive oil, chopped chilis or peppers, vinegar, salt, and pepper. Tuscany.

bacchetta di re another name for ➤ **asfode-lo**, asphodel.

baci al cioccolato balls of crumbled cookies, chopped walnuts, butter, dark chocolate, espresso coffee and Marsala bound with beaten egg yolks, coated with cocoa powder and hazelnut chips, and chilled in the refrigerator. Piedmont.

baci di dama literally "lady's kisses." Semispherical shortcrust pastry cookies enriched with chopped almonds or hazelnuts joined together sandwich-style by a thin layer of dark chocolate cream. Said to have come into being in Tortona, in the province of Alessandria, in the mid-19th century, they are produced throughout the south of the region and in the province of Turin. Piedmont.

baci di fichi al cioccolato ripe figs baked in the oven, chopped, mixed with sweet liqueur, shaped into balls and coated with melted chocolate. Sometimes chopped almonds are added to the mixture. Campania.

baci panteschi ricotta pastries. Typical of the island of Pantelleria, in the province of Trapani. Sicily.

bacicci another name for ➤ **finocchio marino**, samphire.

baciocca savory pie of sliced *quarantina* potatoes (➤ **patata**, potato), lardo and Parmigiano, cooked on a bed of chestnut leaves and, traditionally, covered with a wrought iron or earthenware dome lid. Typical of the province of Genoa. Liguria.

baffa name of the slice of leg of pork used to make speck.

baffo pig's cheek (➤ **guanciale**) gently fried in vinegar. Recipe common in the area round Lake Trasimeno. Umbria.

baggiana (1) aka **bagiana** soup of fresh fava beans, tomato and basil, sometimes with the addition of sausage and Swiss chard. Typical of the province of Perugia. Umbria.

baggiana (2) aka **bagiana** dialect terms in Lombardy and Veneto for ➤ **taccola**, mangetout.

baggianata sort of ➤ **ratatoia**, vegetable stew, made with mangetouts or green beans. Typical of the Val d'Ossola. Piedmont.

bagigi northern word for peanuts (➤ **semi e legumi tostati**, toasted seeds and legumes).

bagna aka **bagnet** northern dialect words for sauce or dip.

bagna brusca sourish sauce made with white wine, numerous aromatic herbs and vinegar, emulsified with ➤ **bagna caoda**. Served warm or cold with roast peppers, boiled vegetables, ➤ **nervetti**, pickled tongue and so on. The summer version of ➤ **bagnet**. Typical of the Monferrato hills in the province of Alessandria. Piedmont.

bagna caoda aka **bagna cauda** warm dip of garlic, anchovies, and olive oil served with raw vegetables—peppers, celery, cabbage, Jerusalem artichoke, and cardoons (➤ **cardo gobbo di Nizza Monferrato**)—or boiled (potatoes, beetroot, cauliflower). The dip was once eaten from a large communal earthenware bowl placed at the center of the table; today it is often served in individual spirit stoves (*dianet* or *fojòt* in dialect). It is also common these days to accompany vegetables, flans or molds with a tablespoonful of the dip. Another modern trend, looked down upon by purists, is to "sweeten" the garlic by pre-cooking it in water or milk. Dish typical of the Langhe and Monferrato hills. Piedmont.

bagna d'arbion a sort of sauce (➤ **bagna**) of peas (*arbion*), coddled eggs, chopped onion and parsley. Typical of the Monferrato district, in the province of Asti. Served warm, sometimes with canned tuna. Piedmont.

bagna del diavolo aka **bagna dl'inferno** literally "devil's sauce"or "hell sauce." A warm sauce of garlic, anchovies, oil, chili and tomato passata used to accompany polenta or poached eggs. The name may refer either to the color or to the inclusion of chili. In some areas, they add red wine and omit the chili. Piedmont.

bagna del pòvr'òm literally "poor man's sauce." Meat gravy diluted with broth and vinegar and blended with onion or garlic, breadcrumbs and capers. Served with boiled meats. Piedmont.

bagna dl'infern dialect name for ➤ **bagna del diavolo**.

bagna fèrgia summer version of ➤ **bagna caoda** (**fèrgia** means "cold"). An emulsion of extra virgin olive oil and finely chopped anchovies. Used in the province of Asti to dress raw vegetables, from peppers to Savoy cabbage leaves. Piedmont.

bagna grisa literally "gray sauce." Traditional condiment (onions, garlic, milk, cream and cheese) for ➤ **corset**, small gnocchi typical of the mountains of the province of Cuneo. Piedmont.

bagnarola, alla method of cooking fish with olives, capers, parsley, dried breadcrumbs, Parmigiano-Reggiano, lemon juice and black pepper. Calabria.

bagné 'nt l'euli literally "to dip in oil." Piedmontese dialect expression to refer to the use of vegetables in ➤ **pinzimonio**. Ac-cording to season, the rite involves dipping radishes, peppers, tomatoes, fennel, artichokes, leeks and celery in top quality extra virgin olive oil. *Siolòt* (spring onions) and *ajet* (fresh garlic) are especially popular in the springtime.

bagnet aka **bagnetto**. The second term is the Italianization of the first, a Piedmontese dialect word for a sauce used: to accompany ➤ **bollito misto alla Piemontese**; to smother anchovies (➤ **acciughe col bagnet**); to stuff tomatoes as an antipasto. There are two types of **bagnet**: *verd* (green) and *ross* (red). Both contain garlic, red pepper (*spagnolin* in dialect), desalted anchovies, vinegar and oil. The green version is enhanced by abundant chopped flat-leaf parsley, chopped hard-boiled egg yolk, breadcrumbs soaked in vinegar, capers and, sometimes, mashed tuna fish in oil, the red version by tomato sauce and, in some recipes, sliced peppers.

bagnomaria bain-marie. Cooking method normally used for sauces and recipes involving eggs or other food items unsuited to very high temperatures. Two techniques are possible: i) in a large pan of hot water, or "bath," in which a smaller pan is placed to cook the contents or keep them warm, or; ii) in a double saucepan with water in the lower half.

bagnone soup made with sun-dried tomatoes, garlic, dried wild fennel and chopped salt cod. Served with toasted bread. Typical of Vallerano, in the province of Viterbo. Lazio.

bagnun de anciue anchovy stew. Fresh anchovies stewed with tomato, gently fried garlic and onion and served on toasted bread. In Sestri Levante and Riva Trigoso (province of Genoa), it is served over crumbled ship's biscuits (➤ **gallette del marinaio**). Liguria.

Bagòss di Bagolino uncooked raw milk cheese. Distinctive for the size of its wheels (eight to ten pounds) and the frequent addition of a pinch of saffron to the rennet. Made in the summer in mountain dairies with milk from cattle fed exclusively on local hay in the winter. Ages anything from 10-12 to 24-36 months. A Slow Food presidium promotes production according to traditional artisan methods. Named for the local dialect nickname for the inhabitants of Bagolino, a village in the province of Brescia. Lombardy.

bagozia traditionally a purée of beans and potatoes, flavored with lard or bacon. A more modern version consists of a potato polenta served as a side dish with game or lamb. Typical of the mountains of the province of Belluno, especially of the valley of Alpago. Veneto.

baìcoli twice-baked cookies made of butter, brewer's yeast, salt and orange juice. Available commercially in cardboard boxes or tins, they are eaten as an accompaniment to coffee, tea, passito wines and ➤ **Vin Santo**. Said to have been invented in Venice in the 18th century. Veneto.

baldino Tuscan regional term for ➤ **castagnaccio**, chestnut cake.

baldonazzo another name for ➤ **brusto**, a blood sausage typical of the Trentino region.

bale 'd luc Piedmontese dialect name for ➤ **bale d'aso**, a cured meat.

bale d'aso round boiled cured meat. Donkey meat, today mixed with pork and beef, coarsely ground and flavored with salt, pepper, nutmeg, aromatic herbs and red wine. The mixture is pushed into cow skin and shaped into balls, which are cooked for about two hours and usually served with mashed potatoes or boiled legumes. Typical of Mondovì, in the province of Cuneo. Piedmont.

bales Ladin name for ➤ **knödel**, dumpling.

balin balls of grated cold polenta, ricotta, eggs, sugar, cinnamon and lemon zest, coated in flour and fried. Typical of the province of Belluno. Veneto.

balletti Ligurian dialect term for fresh chestnuts boiled in their skins.

ballotte popular term for chestnuts boiled in their skins in water flavored with fennel seeds. In some regions, they are known as ➤ **caldallesse**.

balocchi soft, friable cookies made of flour, sugar, white wine, sambuca, olive oil, cinnamon, chopped toasted almonds, pine kernels and raisins. The mixture is shaped into balls and baked in the oven until golden brown. Lazio.

balosecc Bergamo dialect word for ➤ **nervetti**, ligaments, sinew and cartilage of a calf's hock and shin.

balòta Piedmontese dialect name for a boiled chestnut.

balote slices of cold polenta covered with slices of fatty mountain cheese, rolled into balls and broiled. Veneto.

balòtte di seirass balls of ricotta, egg yolk, flour, sugar and cinnamon, coated with crushed ➤ **savoiardi** sponge fingers and fried in oil. Typical of the mountains of the province of Cuneo. Piedmont.

balsamella regional name for ➤ **besciamella**, béchamel sauce.

banana (1) a richer version of ➤ **toponin**, a round bread roll. Piedmont, Lombardy, Veneto.

banane (2) (pl. banane) banana. Asian in origin and cultivated in tropical countries. The United States and European Union import bananas mainly from Ecuador, Costa Rica and Colombia. They made their first appearance in Italy at the time of the first colonial wars and their consumption rose in the 1930s following the invasion of Abyssinia. Now so common a part of the everyday Italian diet as to have lost all exotic connotations.

banane commercial durum wheat pasta similar in shape and size to ➤ **rigatoni**. Served with light vegetable or tomato sauces.

bandiera Umbrian name for a side dish, common in many regions, of peppers stewed with onions, ripe tomatoes and basil.

barattiere another word for ➤ **melone immature**, unripe melon.

barba di becco salsify (*Tragopogon leeksfolius*). Long, thin edible root which grows in damp pastures and meadows. Found mostly in central and southern Italy. The related yellow goatsbeard (*Tragopogon pratensis*) is very popular in northern Italy (the Piedmontese version, known in dialect as ➤ **barbabuch**, is included in the Italian Ministry of Agriculture's database of native and/or traditional food products) and also in central regions, where the tender parts of the plant are boiled briefly in water and finished in the frying pan with butter or lardo. The *sativus* variety of salsify (➤ **scorzobianca**) has a sweet, fleshy white root and is much used—boiled, fried in butter or battered and fried in oil— in Liguria, Piedmont, Lombardy and Veneto. Common and regional names: ➤ **barba di prete**, ➤ **barbetta**, ➤ **basapret**, ➤ **papalina**, ➤ **salsefica**, ➤ **sassefica**.

barba di capra goat's beard (*Aruncus dioicus*). Spontaneous border plant which grows with straight stalks in bushy clumps. Used in the kitchen mainly in northern Italy (Piedmont, Friuli, Trentino-Alto Adige), where the reddish sprouts are cooked in stuffings and frittatas or preserved in oil. Common and regional names: ➤ **asparagina di monte**, ➤

barba di Giove, ➤ **coda di volpe**, ➤ **erba cannona**.

barba di frate oppositeleaf Russian thistle (*Salsola soda*). Spontaneous plant resembling grass or chives, with a delicate, slightly acid flavor. Eaten sautéed in butter, in risottos or boiled and served with oil and herbs (➤ **roscani all'anconetana**). Known in Romagna as ➤ **lischi** and listed in the Italian Ministry of Agriculture's database of native and/or traditional food products. In some Italian regions, the term **barba di frate** also refers to ➤ **crescione inglese**, garden cress. Common and regional names: ➤ **agretti**, ➤ **roscano**, ➤ **salsola**.

barba di Giove another name for ➤ **barba di capra**, goat's beard.

barba di prete another name for ➤ **barba di becco**, salsify.

barba gentile another name for ➤ **cardogna**, Spanish salsify.

barbabietola aka **rapa rossa**) beetroot (*Beta vulgaris* var. *conditiva*). A close relative of sugar beet, cultivated mainly in the Po Valley, Lazio, Puglia and Campania. The Italian Ministry of Agriculture's database of native and/or traditional food products lists the following two varieties: *bietola rossa di Castellazzo Bormida* (Piedmont) and *bietola rossa di Chioggia* (Veneto). The roundish roots are normally eaten oven-roasted, steamed or boiled, peeled and sliced. Beetroot's sweet flavor marries well with savory or sour condiments (➤ **barbabietole in agrodolce**, ➤ **bagna caoda**). In northeast Italy, it is an ingredient in the filling of stuffed pastas (➤ **casunziei**, ➤ **schlutzkrapfen**) and in dumpling mixes (➤ **canederli**, ➤ **knödel**). In the Val d'Aosta, beetroot replaces pig's blood in ➤ **boudin**.

barbabietole in agrodolce diced boiled beetroot bathed in a warm mixture of vinegar, sugar, bay leaves and peppercorns and finished in melted butter or dressed with oil, salt and pepper. Excellent side dish with roast pork. Trentino-Alto Adige, Friuli-Venezia Giulia.

barbabuch Piedmontese dialect word for ➤ **barba di becco,** salsify or yellow goatsbeard.

barbaforte regional name for ➤ **cren,** horseradish.

barbagiuai fried ravioli filled with pumpkin, rice, eggs, chard, Parmigiano (or, occcasionally ➤ **bruzzu,** fermented sheep's milk ricotta) and aromatic herbs. Eaten hot as an antipasto or cold as a snack between meals. Liguria.

barbagliata aka **barbajada** beverage, typical of Milan, made with bitter cocoa, milk, coffee and sugar to taste. Served hot, topped with cream, or cold. Invented by the theatrical impresario Domenico Barbaja, hence the name. Lombardy.

barbaja regional term for pig's cheek. Commonly preserved in salt. Marche.

barbani another name for ➤ **crastuna,** a type of snail.

barbazio e peladei pasta and beans. Soup of boiled borlotti beans (➤ **borlotto**) cooked with toasted flour, diced potatoes and ➤ **peladei,** a local egg pasta. Recipe typical of the province of Trento. Trentino-Alto Adige.

barbein dialect term for ➤ **nespola comune,** medlar.

barbetta another name for ➤ **barba di becco,** salsify.

barbo barbel. Freshwater fish of the Barbus genus, a member of the Cipronidae family, diverse species of which (*B. plebejus, B. tyberinus, B. caninus, B. barbus*) are common in rivers and deep lakes all over Italy, islands excepted. The flesh is delicate but very bony. The smallest specimens are mostly fried or broiled, the largest boiled and stewed.

barbo al vino barbel in wine. Barbel gently fried with onion softened in butter, walnuts, honey armillary mushrooms and red wine. Piedmont.

barbon Veneto and Venezia Giulia term for ➤ **triglia,** mullet, and ➤ **pesce gatto,** catfish.

barbon de porto Veneto and Venezia Giulia term for ➤ **triglia di fango,** striped red mullet.

barbon in tecia catfish, coated in flour and fried, and finished with onion, celery, tomato and spices. In the Polesine district, they sprinkle the fried fish with vinegar and bake it in the oven with tomatoes. Veneto.

barbone di scoglio Marche name for ➤ **triglia di scoglio,** red mullet.

barbotla another name for ➤ **barbotta (2),** a sort of focaccia.

barbotta (1) aka **puticiana** or, in Pontremoli, **erbadèla.** A sort of focaccia made by mixing finely chopped onions with cornflour, milk, grated Parmigiano, olive oil and salt. Baked or cooked on a ➤ **testo,** a sort of griddle pan. Typical of the area of Massa-Carrara. Tuscany.

barbotta (2) aka **barbotla** focaccia made from a dough of flour, water, oil and zucchini flowers. Typical of the Val Magra, in the province of La Spezia. Liguria.

barbozza cured meat made from local pork. The cheek is rubbed with minced fresh garlic, black pepper and sea salt, and left for a week. It is then hung for a few days in a warm environment and aged for at least two or three weeks. In certain areas it is one of the ingredients of the mixture for ➤ **mazzafegato.** Umbria.

barbozzo aka **barbazza** regional term for pig's cheek preserved in salt and pepper. Umbria.

barcarola, alla name for any recipe in which

fresh fish (perch) or preserved fish (salt cod) or offal (liver) are cooked in vinegar with onions. Typical of Lombardy, Veneto, Friuli-Venezia Giulia.

barchetta (pl. **barchette**) small shortcrust or brisée pastry "boats" baked in special oval-shaped molds. Fillings may be sweet (jam, cream, melted chocolate) or savory (pâté, mousse, cream cheese). Served at cold buffets or with aperitifs.

barchiglia cake consisting of a shortcrust pastry base spread with pear jam, topped with a mixture of egg yolks, sugar, chopped almonds, cinnamon and grated lemon zest and, once baked, decorated with chocolate icing. Traditional in the Easter period. Puglia.

barciùll Piacenza dialect term for ➤ **frutta secca**, dried fruit.

bardare to bard. To cover lean meat, game, poultry and fish with thin slices of lardo, pancetta, bacon or pork fat to prevent flesh from drying out during roasting, baking or broiling.

bardele coi marai broad green fettuccine made from a dough of plain flour, eggs and borage (➤ **borragine**, *marai* in dialect), served with butter and a generous amount of grated Parmigiano-Reggiano. Lombardy.

bardiccio fiorentino sausage of pork and beef scraps (in the past, offal as well) ground and cured with salt, pepper, garlic and wild fennel. Cased in a natural intestine and secured with string, the sausage is eaten broiled. Produced from September to May in the Val di Sieve, Mugello, Rufina and Valdarno areas. Tuscany.

bardotto hinny. Whereas the mule (➤ **mulo**) is the offspring of a cross between a male donkey and a female horse, or mare, a hinny is the offspring of a cross between a male horse and a female donkey. Both animals are infertile. The hinny is bred exclusively in Sicily and its meat has only a very limited use in the kitchen.

barlanda regional name for ➤ **cascellore**, crested wartycabbage.

barlocca cake of all-purpose flour and cornflour halfway between ➤ **tortionata** and ➤ **sbrisolona**. Lombardy.

barone cut of rabbit comprising legs and ➤ **sella**, saddle.

bartolaccio quadrangular stuffed pastry (➤ **tortello**), similar to ➤ **cassone**. Made from a flour and water dough, it is stuffed with boiled potatoes, fried bacon and Parmigiano, and cooked on a griddle or hot-plate. Like ➤ **piadina**, it is a classic street food, popular at country festivals and fêtes. Typical of the Apennines in the province of Forlì. Emilia-Romagna.

barzellana another name for ➤ **porcellana**, little hogweed.

barzigole sheep's or lamb's bone marrow marinated, seasoned, cut into slices and broiled. Typical of the province of Reggio Emilia. Emilia-Romagna.

Barzotto (1) mixed sheep's and cow's cheese made in the spring, matured briefly and traditionally eaten with fava beans. Marche.

barzotto (2) coddled (➤ **bazzotto**).

basapret another name for ➤ **barba di becco**, salsify.

base (1) concentrated meat, fish or vegetable stock or broth (➤ **fondo**).

base (2) aka **salsa base** base sauce derived directly from the so-called mother sauces (➤ **salse madri**).

base di cucina concentrated meat, fish or vegetable stock or broth (➤ **fondo**).

basilico aka **ocimo** basil (*Ocimum basilicum*). Aromatic herb which originated in tropical Asia and is now widespread in Europe with different varieties (cinnamon, dark opal, minimum, crispum, anise, purple ruffles). Thanks to its adaptability, it can be seen in pots in summer on balconies all over Italy and is now an irreplaceable ingredient in Mediterranean cooking. Genoa (➤ **basilico genovese**) and Naples are the places that boast the most varieties, while in Tuscany they grow an outsize *basilico gigante*.

basilico genovese broad-leaved PDO basil variety produced from native ecotypes or selections. Stands out for its fragrant flavor, totally devoid of notes of mint. Originally grown only in and around the Genoa suburb of Prà, it is now to be found all along the Ligurian coast. Sold in bunches, it is ideal for making ➤ **pesto genovese**. Liguria.

basilisco aka **tartufo delle Madonie** aka **porcino bianco** white ferula mushroom (*Pleurotus nebrodensis*), a member of the Pleurotus genus. Its white flesh is particularly good in sauces or raw in salads. It takes its Latin name from the Nebrodi mountains, where it is very common and popular. Sicily.

basini amari small round baked cookies made from a paste of egg whites, sugar and bitter almonds. One early 19th century recipe suggests that they should be flavored in spring with violet petals. A specialty of the province of Trento. Trentino-Alto Adige.

bassiga regional term for ➤ **finocchio marino**, samphire.

bastardello small pork and/or beef salami, sometimes lightly smoked. Typical of the Chiavenna area, in the province of Sondrio. Lombardy.

bastoncino, tagliare a to cut into matchsticks, to julienne.

batata aka **patata dolce** aka **patata americana** sweet potato (*Ipomoea batatas*). Native to the tropical Americas, cultivated for its tuberous roots, which may be boiled, fried or roasted. In Italy the sweet potato is grown mainly in the Polesine area (Veneto), where it is an ingredient in local confectionery (➤ **pinza mula**) and in some parts of the Salento area (Puglia). The *batata dell'Agro leccese* is listed in the Italian Ministry of Agriculture database of native and/or traditional food products.

batiur cured meat made of pork seasoned with spices and wine, and cased in a pig's bladder. May be eaten raw or boiled and served cold in its own broth. Created in the Po Regional Park, in the province of Cuneo, to celebrate christenings, it is now made by only one pork butcher in Cavour, in the province of Turin. Piedmont.

batoi mixture of boiled potatoes, flour, yeast, sugar, raisins and rum, shaped into balls, fried in oil and dusted with sugar. Veneto.

batsoà pigs' trotters boiled in water and vinegar, boned, breaded and fried. The dialect name may derive from the French (*bas de soie*, silk stockings), a reference to the soft texture of the dish. Typical of the Monferrato and Langhe districts of Piedmont.

battere (1) to pound or to flatten a food (meat, octopus, stockfish) to break up its fibers and tenderize it.

battere (2) to hand-cut and crush a food (vegetables, herbs lardo) to make a ➤ **battuto**.

battere (3) to beat (eg, eggs), a synonym of ➤ **sbattere**.

battolli fresh tagliatelle of plain and chestnut flour traditionally served with pesto, diced potatoes and *naun*, a local white turnip. A delicacy in Uscio, inland of Genoa. Liguria.

battuta term used to refer to hand-chopped dressed raw beef (➤ **carne cruda in insalata**). Piedmont.

battuto mixture of lardo (or pancetta) and

aromatic vegetables (garlic or shallot, carrot, onion or leek, celery and parsley in variable proportions), finely cut and pounded with a knife blade to a creamy texture. Used to flavor and thicken concentrated meat, fish or vegetable stock or broth (➤ **fondo di cottura**), especially in Lombardy and Emilia-Romagna (➤ **gras pistà**, ➤ **pista 'd gras**), Rome (where they invariably use it as a base for soups) and Umbria (where they sometimes even use it to dress pasta).

batù d'oca goose meat preserved in its own fat. The leanest meat is cut into pieces, left to rest in a mixture of minced garlic, salt and pepper, wrapped and hung in a kitchen cloth. It is then transferred to earthenware jars and covered with its own melted fat. Served with toasted polenta or used as an ingredient in soups and pasta sauces. One recipe, typical of Piacenza, consists of ➤ **maltagliati** cooked, drained and served with a sauce of **batù d'oca** mixed with crushed walnuts. Emilia-Romagna.

batuda Friuli-Venezia Giulia term for acidulated milk or ➤ **laticello**, buttermilk.

Bauernkäse another name for ➤ **Lagundo**, a cheese typical of the Alto Adige region.

Bauernpaarl pairs of round loaves made of rye flour, sourdough, salt, fennel seeds, cumin (➤ **cumino**) and fenugreek (➤ **fieno greco**), joined together as one. Sometimes dried and toasted. Typical of the Val d'Ultimo, in the province of Bolzano. Trentino-Alto Adige.

Bauernschmaus boiled mixed meats. Smoked pork loin, pickled tongue, liver sausage, blood sausage and ➤ **würstel**, served on a bed of ➤ **crauti** (sauerkraut), sometimes with ➤ **canederli**, dumplings. The name means "farmer's feast" and the dish is typical of the Dolomites. Trentino-Alto Adige.

bàule balls of polenta filled with fresh ➤ **Toma**, cooked in the fireplace or on the stove until the cheese melts. Typical of the mountain valleys of the Canavese area, north of Turin. Piedmont.

bàule bread made from a dough of all-purpose flour, water, sourdough and salt. The dough is scratched and cut on the top to create a crest effect after baking. Typical of Mantua. Lombardy.

bauletti general term to describe ➤ **involtini**, rolls or bundles of pasta and meat.

bavarese (1) bavarois. Dessert of French origin and very popular in Italy. Made of ➤ **crema inglese** or fruit purée and whipped cream bound by gelatin and set in the refrigerator.

bavarese (2) hot beverage of tea, milk and alcohol.

bavarese al Moscato cream dessert made with sweet Moscato d'Asti wine (➤ **bavarese**). Egg yolks are beaten over a low heat with sugar and Moscato, thickened with isinglass and whipped cream, poured into molds and left to set in the refrigerator. A relatively recent restaurant creation that has already entered household kitchens.

bavette commercial durum wheat semolina pasta reminiscent of rectangular flat spaghetti. Served with sauces of aromatic herbs, ➤ **pesto genovese** or sauces involving fish and/or mollusks. Other names: ➤ **lingue di passero**, ➤ **linguine**, ➤ **trenette**.

bavosa aka **blennio** blenny. Sea fish of the Blennidae family reminiscent of the goby (➤ **ghiozzo**). A freshwater variety (*Blennius fluvialis*) also exists. In the kitchen, blennies may be fried or mixed with other fish in stews or soups.

baxin d'Albenga quadrangular cookie made of all-purpose flour, water, sugar, chopped almonds and anise seeds. The recipe dates from the 19th century and is the property of a pastry shop in Albenga, in the province of Savona. Liguria.

bazott aka **basotti** fresh egg tagliolini cooked in broth (traditionally of pork bones), served with butter and Parmigiano, then baked in the oven. Emilia-Romagna.

bazzoffia rich soup of chard, or escarole, and quartered artichokes cooked in a pan with peas, fava beans and spring onion, with the addition, at the end of the cooking process, of beaten eggs, extra virgin olive oil and grated Pecorino. Served with slices of day-old bread. Typical of the Agro Pontino area, the soup was traditionally eaten by field workers, who often added snails to it. Lazio.

bazzotto aka **barzotto** coddled. Refers to the method of briefly boiling eggs (around five minutes) to keep the yolk soft.

béarnaise French term Italianized as ➤ **salsa bernese**.

becadeli aka **becanoto** northern Italian dialect terms for ➤ **beccaccino**, snipe.

beccaccia woodcock (*Scolopax rusticola*). Wading bird with a long beak, present in Italy from mid-October to November and from February to April. Lives in damp mountain and hillside woodland and is much prized by hunters (partly because it is impossible to farm). After hanging and removing the giblets, gizzard excepted, the bird is cooked briefly and traditionally served on toasted bread (➤ **crostini toscani**).

beccacce alla lucana woodcocks cleaned, gutted, flavored internally with bay leaves, salt and pepper, barded with slices of prosciutto and cooked in white wine. In the meantime, the giblets are cleaned and cooked in oil with capers, anchovies and a final splash of Marsa-la. The cooked woodcocks are served accompanied by slices of toasted bread spread with the giblet sauce. A specialty of the province of Potenza. Basilicata.

beccacce alla norcina woodcocks Norcia-style. Woodcocks roast on a spit stuffed with a mixture of their own giblets, sausage, thyme, marjoram and black truffle. Typical of Norcia, in the province of Perugia. Umbria.

beccacce in salmì quartered woodcocks coated in flour and browned in butter, covered with chopped pancetta and herbs, lubricated with Madeira and rum, with the addition of broth aromatized with crushed juniper berries. Served with the chopped giblets and grilled or fried polenta. Lombardy.

beccacce in tegame woodcocks barded with slices of lardo, cooked in butter with crushed lardo and sage and lubricated with white wine. Friuli-Venezia Giulia.

beccaccino common snipe (*Capella gallinago*). Smaller relative of the woodcock (➤ **beccaccia**), but even harder to hunt. Winters and sometimes nests in wetlands in northern Italy. Before land reclamation, it used to be common in the Agro Pontino and Tuscan Maremma areas. Its meat is as highly prized as the woodcock's and is cooked in the same ways.

beccafico garden warbler (*Sylvia borin*). Lives on fruit, especially grapes and figs. A traditional ingredient of mixed spit roasts, like the Orphean warbler (*S. hortensis*) and the barred warbler (*S. nisoria*), the garden warbler cannot be hunted.

beccute sweet irregularly shaped baked buns made from a dough of corn flour, pine kernels, dried figs, walnuts and almonds. Common throughout the region, especially in the cold months, at Christmas and Lent (in Fano in particular). Marche.

béchamel béchamel sauce → **besciamella**.

bechi-panzalini boat-shaped bread of various sizes made from a dough of plain flour (sometimes mixed with malt flour), water, natural yeast and salt. Baked in a steam oven. Typical of the province of Trento. Trentino-Alto Adige.

Beddo disk-shaped cow's milk cheese produced in the Valle Cervo, in the province of Biella. Fresh, it has a strong milky flavor; matured for a couple of weeks, it develops a characteristic wrinkly, white rind and a pronounced, persistent flavor. Piedmont.

bédui dialect term for slices of dried apple or pear (→ **frutta secca**).

befanini cookies made from a mixture of plain flour, butter, sugar, eggs, yeast, grated lemon or orange zest and liqueur (anise or rum), bathed with milk and left to rest. Rolled out with a pin, the mixture is cut into various shapes, brushed with beaten egg and baked in the oven. A specialty of the area of Lucca and Prato made every year for Epiphany. In Italian folklore, *La Befana* is an old woman who delivers presents to children on Epiphany Eve, hence the name of the cookies. In Barga (province of Lucca), where the tradition of *La Befana* is especially strong, a special rich marzipan version is made. The same cookies may be found in the province of Ancona, aromatized with → **mistrà**, anise liqueur. Tuscany, Marche.

beignet French term Italianized as → **bignè**.

belecauda aka **belicada** name (meaning *bell'e calda*, "nice and hot") used for → **farinata** in southern Piedmont (Nizza Monferrato, Ovada and Novi Ligure, in the provinces of Asti and Alessandria). Here, where the plainer → **panizza** already existed, this type of chickpea batter was introduced from Liguria. Piedmont.

belecot a sort of → **cotechino** (boiling sausage) made with fat and lean pork aromatized with cloves, pepper, cinnamon, sugar and nutmeg. The name (which means "nice and cooked") refers to the fact that the meat is cooked and ready to be eaten. A specialty of the province of Ravenna. Emilia-Romagna.

bella della Daunia large fleshy PDO table olive (→ **oliva da mensa**). Color varies from green to black as the harvest progresses. The green olive harvest commences on October 1, the black olive harvest last from October to December. Sold preserved in brine. Puglia.

bella di Garbagna bright red cherry with crisp flesh, particularly suitable for preserving in alcohol. Until 20 years ago, in Garbagna and other villages of the Valle Grue, in the province of Alessandria, the cherry used to be picked by the ton. Today it has been largely replaced by better known, more resistant varieties. A Slow Food presidium is seeking to revive the cherry, which is also ideal as a filling for chocolates (→ **boero**) and for making jam and liqueurs. Piedmont.

bellavista, in term used to describe a presentation technique, typical of international cuisine, whereby cold foodstuffs (usually large crustaceans, such as lobster, fish, such as salmon or trout, and game) are covered in aspic and decorated with artistically cut raw vegetables, wedges of hard-boiled egg, shaved or diced black truffle and so on.

belle bimbe regional term for → **papavero (2)** corn poppy.

bellide regional term for → **margheritina dei prati,** English daisy.

belommu dialect term for → **boccione maggiore,** golden fleece.

belu aka **trippa di tonno** tuna tripe. The stomach of the fish is opened, cleaned and covered with salt for a day. It is then washed with sea water, left to dry on racks of ivy or other branches and dried in a cellar. A delicacy of the coastal strip of the Sulcis Iglesiente area in the province of Carbonia-Iglesias, it serves as an ingredient in many local dishes. Sardinia.

benardi bread made from a dough of equal amounts of plain and corn flour, water, milk, brewer's yeast, olive oil, raisins and fennel seeds. Typical of the western Riviera. Liguria.

benedetto Easter dish of hard-boiled eggs (blessed during the Easter mass), ➤ **soppressata** or salami, ricotta and slices of orange. Puglia.

bensone spindle- or "S"-shaped cake made of leavened dough and decorated with sugar chips. Typical of Modena, in some provinces it is ring-shaped, like a ➤ **ciambella**. Emilia-Romagna.

beretta aka **berretta** term used in some northern dialects for ➤ **reticolo**, reticulum.

bergamotto bergamot (*Citrus bergamia Risso*). Tree with white flowers and fruits similar to thin-skinned oranges. Rich in essential oils, the fruits are inedible, but are used to make perfumes, liqueurs and confectionery. The region is the world's major producer and the essence of Reggio Calabria bergamot has been granted PDO status. Calabria.

Bergkäse cheese made with full-cream or semi-skimmed pasteurized cow's milk. Ages for about ten weeks. Typical of the upper Val Pusteria, in the province of Bolzano. Trentino-Alto Adige.

bericuocoli aka **beriquoccoli** Tuscan names for a type of ➤ **cavallucci (1)**, spicy cookies.

berlingozzo cake of Renaissance origin made from a mixture of plain flour, eggs, sugar, grated lemon or orange zest, olive oil, vanilla, yeast and anise seeds. Baked in the oven in a ring-shaped mold. Typical of the province of Pistoia, it used to be made in the Carnival period. Today it is commonly eaten for breakfast or at the end of a meal with a glass of Vin Santo.

Bernardo creamy summer cheese made from cow's and goat's milk with a postcurdling pinch of powdered saffron. Typical of the Clusone area, in the province of Bergamo. Lombardy.

berodo Ligurian term for ➤ **sanguinaccio**, blood sausage.

bersaglieri a variation of ➤ **biscotti regina** with chocolate icing. Delicacy of Catania. Sicily.

bertagnì Brescia dialect name for ➤ **bertagnino**, salt cod, still cooked and sold by street vendors.

bertagnino aka **bertagnin** name used in parts of Veneto and Lombardy for salt cod (➤ **baccalà**).

bertolina cake made with plain and corn flour, yeast, grapes, sugar and olive oil. Typical of the Crema area. One variation, typical of Cremona, now almost forgotten, consists of a sort of flatbread made with two types of flour, olive oil or lard, onions and grated lemon zest, dusted with refined sugar. Lombardy.

besciamella béchamel sauce. One of the "mother sauces" (➤ **salse madri**), used as a base for other sauces, to bind meats and vegetables in molds and soufflés, or to cover baked pasta dishes. Made of flour, butter and milk, flavored with nutmeg and seasoned with salt and pepper.

Bettelmatt highly prized ➤ **Toma della montagna ossolana** made with full-cream raw cow's milk. Produced only in the summer months on the Bettelmatt Alp on the border with Switzerland, it ages at least two months. Piedmont

bevarassa aka **biberassa** Veneto dialect

terms for → **vongola commune**, common clam.

beverelli another name for → **rete**, caul.

bevr'in vin beef and chicken broth mixed with Lambrusco red wine and served with → **agnoli** (→ **sorbir d'agnoli**), fine tagliatelle or rice. In Mantua, the tradition is to enjoy the broth in front of the fireplace before sitting down to dine. Lombardy.

bianchetto a variety of truffle (→ **tartufo**).

bianchetti Ligurian term for newborn fish of the Clupeidae family such as anchovies, sardines and pilchards (→ **novellame di pesce**, fry).

bianchetti con l'uovo numerous regional recipes feature → **novellame di pesce**, fry. In Tuscany they wash the newborn fish in salted cold water, dip them in beaten egg and stir-fry them in olive oil with chopped onions. Sometimes the fish are added directly to beaten eggs and cooked as a frittata.

bianchini another name for → **bianchittos**, meringues.

bianchittos a sort of meringue enriched with toasted and chopped almonds and hazelnuts and grated lemon zest. Sardinia.

bianco costato aka **biancostato** aka **scaramella** cut of beef comprising the side rib muscles, from the fifth or sixth thoracic vertebra to the breast, roughly the equivalent of plate. A fatty, tasty piece of meat, excellent for stews and as a component of → **bollito misto**.

bianco e nero d'agnelletto mixture (the name means "black and white" and refers to the contrasting colors of the offal parts used) of baby lamb's lung, intestines, liver and spleen sautéed in oil with bay leaves and lemon juice. A traditional dish of the Genoa area, now hard to find. On the western Riviera, they add garlic, parsley and white wine to the flavoring. Liguria.

bianco, in (1) way to describe a condiment for pasta, meat, fish or vegetables that does not contain tomatoes.

bianco, in (2) way of serving foods "naturally" with light condiments and without too many spices or fats.

biancomangiare (1) dish of medieval origin consisting only of "white" ingredients: namely boiled chicken breasts, rice flour with goat's or ewe's or almond milk, ginger, lardo, sugar and so on.

biancomangiare (2) blancmange. A cream dessert made by boiling almond milk (→ **latte di mandorla**) with starch and sugar (and often lemon zest). The mixture is poured into molds and allowed to set in a refrigerator for a few hours. In one version, melted chocolate is added to the mixture. Sicily.

biancomangiare (3) Italianization of → **blancmanger**, a cream dessert with almonds. Val d'Aosta.

biancomangiare (4) in contemporary usage, a "white" milk or cream dessert with or without almonds.

biaveta hand-stretched variation of → **bechi-panzalini**, a bread loaf.

biavetta fresh egg pastina for cooking and serving in broth. It used to be made in homes by twisting tiny pieces of dough between thumb and index finger to form "grains." Today some companies produce it commercially as a dried durum wheat semolina pasta. Typical of the province of Asti. Piedmont.

bibanesi friable, crispy crackers prepared by a company in Bibano, near the village of Godega di Sant'Urbano, in the province of Treviso. Made by leavening a mixture of plain flour and extra virgin olive oil, hand-kneaded, coated with sesame seeds and baked in the oven. Veneto.

bicciolani dry, spicy artisan biscuits. The recipe has been documented since the 19th century, but it probably goes even further back in time. A soft mixture of plain flour, potato flour, eggs, butter, sugar and honey is blended with cinnamon, cloves and other spices, such as nutmeg, mace, coriander and white pepper, sometimes also vanilla, cocoa and lemon zest. Using a confectioner's poche, it is then squeezed onto a baking tray to form three-inch fingers. A specialty of Vercelli. Piedmont.

bicerin hot layered beverage of chocolate, coffee and milk, served in a *bicerin*, "small glass" in dialect. Popular in the drawing rooms and cafés of Turin since the mid 19th century. Piedmont.

bichi long pasta shape similar to ➤ **maccheroni alla chitarra**. Lazio.

biechi Italianization of ➤ **blecs**, a type of pasta (➤ **maltagliati**).

Bienenstichtorte cake of Austrian origin made of leavened dough filled with confectioner's custard and whipped cream and garnished with almonds. Trentino-Alto Adige.

bieta aka **bietola** chard (*Beta vulgaris* var. *cycla*). Grows well in temperate climates where its numerous cultivars may be subdivided between those cultivated for their ribs and those cultivated for their leaves. The Italian Ministry of Agriculture's database of native and/or traditional food products lists: *bietola a coste sottili* (Tuscany) and *bietola di Bassano* (Veneto). The leaves are usually cleaned and boiled, then dressed in olive oil and lemon juice or vinaigrette; sautéed with butter or olive oil; baked in the oven; cooked in soups or stews. Mostly used in regional cuisines as an ingredient in the fillings for savory pies (➤ **erbazzone**) and stuffed pastas (➤ **tortelli di erbette**). In Tuscany

and Liguria, chard is the principal ingredient of ➤ **zemino** recipes.

bietola selvatica aka **bietolina** wild chard (*Beta vulgaris*). Spontaneous plant with heart-shaped, fleshy leaves. Occurs along sea shores and on sedimentary terrains. Popular in southern Italy and the islands (dialect names include ➤ **anciti**, (➤ **geri**, **sechilli**, ➤ **zarche**) as a filling for savory pies and pastries (➤ **calzone**) and as an ingredient for soup. *Beta vulgaris* has spawned a number of cultivated varieties (➤ **bieta**).

bietolone another name for ➤ **lapazio**, munk's rhubarb, and the common name for ➤ **atreplice**, a rare variety of cultivated spinach (➤ **spinaci**).

biga type of sourdough starter similar to ➤ **poolish**, though ensuring a longer fermentation.

biga a mano aka **biga servolana** sourdough bread from Trieste consisting of two rolls joined together. Friuli-Venezia Giulia.

bigarani flat ring-shaped cookies made with all-purpose or cake flour, brewer's yeast or ammonium bicarbonate, milk, butter, oil and sugar, and twice-baked in the oven. Typical of the area of Bassano del Grappa (province of Vicenza). Veneto.

bigarani mori "black" variation of ➤ **bigarani** ring cookies with cocoa and grated chocolate added to the mix. A specialty of Venice. Veneto.

bigarano stick- or banana-shaped loaf made from the same dough as ➤ **ciopa**. Veneto.

bigia willow tit or barred warbler. Birds of the Sylvia genus, the same as the blackcap and ➤ **beccafico**, garden warbler.

bignè (1) small choux pastry bun usually filled with confectioner's custard, chantilly cream, zabaglione or chocolate cream, and iced or dusted with confectioner's sugar. Savory versions also exist.

bignè (2) in many regions a fried Carnival

pastry made from a dough of flour, eggs, sugar, milk, butter and liqueur.

bignè (3) Roman name for the ➤ **rosetta** bread roll.

bignè di san Giuseppe fritter traditionally made on the feast of San Giuseppe (March 19) with butter, sugar and salt thickened with plain flour and, as a final touch, egg yolks. The mixture is shaped into small walnut-sized balls (sometimes filled with confectioner's custard or chocolate), which are fried and dusted with confectioner's sugar. Lazio.

bignëtte apple fritters of the province of Cuneo. Piedmont.

bignola Piedmontese name for ➤ **bignè (1)**. By extension the term is used throughout the region to refer to *petite patisserie*. Piedmont.

bigolaro domestic press for the making of ➤ **bigoli**, a type of pasta.

bigoli aka **bigoi** soft wheat or durum wholemeal wheat pasta (*bigoli scuri*) made by pulling the dough through a special press (➤ **bigolaro**) to create a rough, sauce-retaining surface. Popular throughout the northeast of Italy, especially in Veneto and bordering areas (provinces of Mantua and Cremona). Veneto, Lombardy.

bigoli alla torbolana the pasta is boiled, drained and served with chopped bleak (➤ **àole**, ➤ **alborella**), mixed with rosemary and tossed in a skillet with garlic and oil. Typical of Nago-Torbole, on the northern shore of Lake Garda. Trentino-Alto Adige.

bigoli coi rovinassi bigoli with chicken giblets. Sauce of chicken giblets (*rovinassi*) browned in butter with sage, sprinkled with wine and cooked through. Popular in the province of Padua. Veneto.

bigoli col pocio bigoli with a thick sauce (*pocio*) of either ground beef and pork or of meat from a goose slow-cooked whole with vegetables and herbs until it falls off the bone. Veneto.

bigoli con l'arna bigoli with a sauce of musk duck slow-cooked with onion or shallot, celery, garlic and aromatic herbs, served with grated Parmigiano. Veneto.

bigoli con le àole aka **bigoli con le sardelle** bigoli with freshwater sardine or bleak, sometimes dried. The recipe is analogous to that of ➤ **bigoli in salsa**. In the Mantua area, they pour a drop of vinegar into the onions. Lombardy, Veneto.

bigoli in salsa bigoli with a sauce of stewed white onions mixed with boned chopped anchovies, oil and, sometimes, minced parsley. In the Vicenza area, they perfume the sauce with the herb feverfew (➤ **maresina**). Veneto.

bina type of bread consisting of four oblong loaves (all-purpose flour, water, yeast, salt and olive oil) joined together and baked in a steam oven. A sweet version exists with sugar in the dough, brushed with egg yolk straight after baking. Typical of the province of Trento. Trentino-Alto Adige.

bina badiota braid of leavened dough dotted with raisins. A delicacy of the Val Badia, in the province of Bolzano. Trentino-Alto Adige.

bindone horse's colon used as a casing for cured meats.

biova oblong bread roll made of all-purpose or cake flour. Piedmont.

birbanti sweet balls made from a mixture of plain flour, sugar, pine kernels, grated lemon and orange zest, egg whites and cinnamon. Umbria.

biroldo della Garfagnana cured meat made with pig's head (boiled and boned), heart, tongue, and blood mixed with wild fennel, nutmeg, cloves, cinnamon, star anise, salt, pepper and, sometimes, garlic, cased in an intestine and boiled for three hours. A specialty of the province of Lucca. A Slow Food presidium protects the last producers still in business and is striving to distribute this traditional product beyond its prevalently local market. Tuscany.

bisat aka **bisato** aka **bisatto** Veneto dialect term for ➤ **anguilla**, eel.

bisato a la veneziana chunks of eel coated with flour and cooked in minced onion and garlic with a few drops of vinegar. Veneto.

bisato coi àmoi eel with wild plums. Chunks of eel (➤ **bisato**) are cooked in oil with minced garlic and parsley, bathed with white wine and aromatized with bay leaves. Wild plums (➤ **àmoi**) are then added and the dish is finished in the oven. A specialty of the village of San Polo on the left bank of the Piave, in the province of Treviso. Veneto.

bisato in tecia eel cut into pieces, flavored with minced onion, garlic, bay leaf and parsley, splashed with vinegar and red wine, covered with tomato sauce and baked in the oven. Veneto.

bisato inverzà slices of eel and Savoy cabbage leaves layered in a pan with chopped lardo, drizzled with oil and cooked over a low heat, occasionally splashing with wine. Veneto.

bisato su l'ara eel baked in the oven, perfumed with bay leaves. A specialty of Murano, in the Venice lagoon, where fish used to be cooked on the red-hot stone used to temper the island's famous glass. Veneto.

biscette "S"-shaped crumbly shortcrust cookies dusted with confectioner's sugar. The name means "little snakes" in Italian. A specialty of the province of Savona, on the western Riviera. Liguria.

bischeuit dialect term for ➤ **viette**, dried chestnuts.

bisciöla aka **bisoela** oblong panettone made from a mixture of sourdough dotted with chopped walnuts, raisins and dried figs. Once baked, the cake is glazed with a water and sugar syrup. Typical of the Valtellina. Lombardy.

biscione cake made of almond paste, sugar and egg whites, decorated with candied fruits in the shape of a snake, hence the name (*biscia* means "snake" in Italian). A traditional Christmas favorite in Reggio Emilia. Emilia-Romagna.

biscotìn de Prost round thin cookies made of plain flour, butter and sugar. Typical of Prosto, a small village near Piuro, in the Val Chiavenna, where they are baked by the Del Curto family according to the traditional recipe. Lombardy.

biscoto term used in some areas for ➤ **caldarrosta,** chestnut (➤ **castagna**). Veneto.

biscottare to bake twice. The method used to make cookies ➤ (**biscotto (1)**).

biscotto (1) cookie.

biscotto (2) bread twice baked to make it less perishable (➤ **galletta del marinaio**, ship's biscuit).

biscotti dei morti literally "cookies of the dead." Almost all regional cuisines feature cookies and pastries baked or fried to commemorate the dead on All Souls' Day. These cookies are made with plain flour, boiled and crumbled chestnuts, sugar, honey, toasted and chopped almonds, raisins, cinnamon and yeast. The mixture is shaped into fingers, left to rest, then baked in the oven.

biscotti della cresima, in the patois of Carnia, aka **colaz** literally "Communion cookies." Ring cookies made of flour, sugar, lard, milk, ammonium bicarbonate, powdered vanilla, cinnamon and cloves. After baking in the oven, they are brushed with beaten egg yolks, decorated with sugar chips and sugared almonds and tied together with pink or blue ribbons. The resulting "necklaces" are used to decorate the clothes of communion candidates. Friuli-Venezia Giulia.

biscotti della sposa "bride's cookies." A mixture of flour, lard, sugar, almonds, walnuts, salt and eggs is shaped into long, narrow loaves, which are brushed with beaten egg yolks and baked in the oven. After being left to cool, they are cut crosswise to form cookies, which are then "re-baked." The recipe dates to two centuries ago, when poor families distributed cookies in lieu of bonbonnières at wedding ceremonies. Lazio.

biscotti di Fonni cookies similar to → **savoiardi** sponge fingers. Sardinia.

biscotti di Moiano lemon-flavored cookies made of eggs, sugar and flour. Typical of the village of the same name in the province of Benevento. Campania.

biscotti di Monreale "S"-shaped cookies made from a mixture of flour, egg yolks, milk, vanilla and, sometimes, ammonium carbonate. Decorated with curlicues of white icing made by mixing sugar, egg white and lemon. The recipe was created at the Benedictine monastery of San Castrenze in Monreale, in the province of Palermo, Sicily.

biscotti di Quaresima Lent cookies. The original ingredients were flour, milk, sugar, lemon zest and ammonium carbonate, so simple that the cookies could be eaten even during Lent. Their "penitential" character has since been attenuated, and today the mixture includes butter and eggs. Shaped into lozenges, after baking they are dusted with confectioner's sugar. Friuli-Venezia Giulia.

biscotti di san Martino crunchy, crumbly cookies made from a mixture of flour, sugar, fennel seeds, butter, cinnamon,

powdered yeast and water. Cut into spiral cylinders, they are often decorated with icing, chocolate drops, sugared almonds or → **pasta reale** (almond paste). Sometimes they are hollowed out, dipped in rum and filled with ricotta cream, candied fruit and chocolate shavings. Sicily.

biscotti di Taggia rectangular cookies with rounded edges made from a mixture of cake flour, sugar, olive oil, anise seeds and water. Typical of Taggia, in the province of Imperia, on the western Riviera. Liguria.

biscotti regina name for two small cookies, one typical of the province of Palermo, the other of the province of Catania. The former are made from a paste of flour, sugar, lard, baking powder, sugar, cinnamon, egg yolks, vanilla and milk and, after baking, are dipped in egg white and coated with sesame seeds. The latter are made from a paste without eggs and, once baked, coated in a sugar and lemon juice icing. Sicily.

biscotti sardi baked finger cookies made of plain flour, brewer's yeast, lard, refined sugar, cinnamon and anise seeds, and stored in hermetically-sealed glass jars. Sardinia.

biscottini alla mandorla aka **biscotti di Prato** aka **cantucci** aka **cantuccini** small almond cookies, popular throughout Tuscany. They originated in Prato and in traditional recipe collections are also referred to as *biscotti duri co' le mandorle*, → **pratesi** and → **chiantigiani**. The paste is made of plain flour, eggs, sugar and almonds (in Massa Marittima, in the province of Grosseto, they add grated lemon zest; in San Miniato, in the province of Pisa, they add raisins, aniseed and yeast) and rolled into lengths. After baking in the oven, these are sliced obliquely and allowed to cool. The resulting crunchy, scented, cookies are traditionally eaten dunked in ➤ **Vin Santo**. Tuscany.

biscottini di Novara cookies made from a thin mixture of plain flour, sugar and eggs. After baking in the oven, they are transferred to a desiccation chamber. Light, crumbly and spongy, they are ideal for dunking in wine or milk. The recipe was most likely created by monks. Piedmont.

biscotto a otto "8"-shaped savory pastry made of cake flour, olive oil, salt, eggs, natural yeast and water. Typical of the province of Potenza. Basilicata.

biscotto cegliese cookie made of chopped almonds mixed with sugar, eggs and ➤ **vincotto**, cooked wine must (or cherry jam), baked in a wood oven and iced. Known in local dialect as ➤ **pescuettele** and produced exclusively in the village of Ceglie Messapica, in the province of Brindisi. Puglia.

biscotto del Lagaccio twice-leavened baked breakfast rusk, typical of the city of Genoa, nowadays available commercially. Liguria.

biscotto di Agerola fennel seed-flavored savory ring biscuit of the ➤ **tarallo** family, first boiled, then baked in the oven. A specialty of Agerola, in the province of Naples. Campania.

biscotto ferrarese "S"-shaped baked cookie made from a paste of flour, sugar, lots of eggs and grated lemon zest. A specialty of Ferrara. Emilia-Romagna.

biscottu i granu name used in the Aspromonte mountains of Calabria for ➤ **fresa**, twice-baked bread.

biscuit term borrowed from French gastronomy to describe an ice-cream (*biscotto ghiacciato*), usually cut into slices from a block.

biscuteli tiny square cookies made from a paste of cake flour, brewer's yeast, sugar, butter, sunflower seed oil, eggs, honey, fennel seeds, pine kernels and raisins. Produced in Bordighera and environs, in the province of Imperia, on the western Riviera. Liguria.

biscuttina word used in the province of Enna (Sicily) for ➤ **firrincozza**, a sponge cookie.

biseca southern Piedmontese version of the Milanese tripe stew ➤ **buseca**, from which it differs for its spiciness (➤ **saporita**) and the variety of vegetables it contains: onions, onions, potatoes, carrots, celery, leeks, Savoy cabbage, beans and a little tomato paste. The final consistency is that of a minestrone. Piedmont.

bisecon a now rare version of boiled salami (➤ **salame cotto**). The meat mixture is aromatized with celery and carrots and cased in a pig's stomach. A specialty of Santo Stefano Belbo, in the province of Cuneo. Piedmont.

bisi Veneto dialect term for baby peas (➤ **risi e bisi**).

Bismarck, alla term to describe dishes topped with fried eggs. It used to refer only to meat dishes (eg, *bistecca alla Bismarck*), but is now also applied to asparagus and pizza.

bisna hearty mountain dish of polenta with beans and ➤ **crauti** (sauerkraut) or ➤ **brovade** (fermented turnips), flavored with lightly fried lardo and onion. Friuli-Venezia Giulia.

biso regional term for ➤ **tambarello**, frigate tuna.

bisque crustaceans sautéed in butter with herbs and flambéed with cognac, puréed and enriched with cream and potato flour. According to density, this French classic may be served as a soup or as a condiment for pasta.

bisse degli ebrei literally "Jews' eels." "S"-shaped cookies made from an unleavened paste of flour, sugar, eggs, olive oil, butter and lemon zest. Veneto.

bissetta soused eel. The fish is cut into chunks, which are coated in flour and fried, then covered with a warm marinade of vinegar, garlic, onion, carrot, celery and sage, or bay leaf. A traditional dish of the province of Milan and environs, where eels used to be fished in stream and dykes. Lombardy.

bistecca steak. The term, derived from the English "beefteak," entered the Italian language in the course of the 19th century. Today it is used generically to refer to a slice of meat, without reference to cut, with the bone or without, which is generally broiled or fried.

bistecca alla cacciatora slice of veal or beef lightly coated in flour and cooked with lemon zest, skinned tomatoes, finely chopped dried mushrooms and red wine. Many variations exist, and in some recipes onions are added. Another regional dish with the same name consists of pork chops cooked with rosemary, garlic and tomato. Tuscany.

bistecca alla fiorentina huge T-bone steak, at least an inch and a half thick, preferably from Chianina or Maremmana cattle. Broiled *al sangue* (➤ **sangue, al**), it is served with oil, salt and pepper. Tuscany.

bistecca panata alla palermitana veal chop dipped in oil, coated with breadcrumbs (sometimes with the addition of grated Caciocavallo cheese), flavored with salt, pepper, oregano and minced flat-leaf parsley, and broiled on a hot grill. Sicily.

bistecchine alla napoletana minute steaks baked in the oven over a layer of finely chopped prosciutto and another of finely sliced mushrooms flavored with oil and flat-leaf parsley. The dish is served in the oven dish itself with a generous sprinkling of lemon juice. Campania.

bistecchine di maiale in padella pork chops cooked in extra virgin olive oil, garlic, sage and white wine. Umbria.

bisulàan dialect term for ➤ **bossolano**, a type of ring-shaped cake.

Bitto PDO cheese made from fresh drawn cow's milk with the addition of a maximum of 10% goat's milk. Dry-salted with coarse kitchen salt to form a more delicate rind, hence improved maturation. Named for the Bitto river and produced in the valleys of the provinces of Sondrio and Bergamo. The Bitto valli del Bitto version, made in the valleys of Albradeo and Gerola, in the province of Sondrio, is protected and promoted by a Slow Food presidium. Lombardy.

blancmanger blancmange. Cream dessert similar to the Sicilian ➤ **biancomangiare (2)**, made with sugar, ininglass, milk, and crushed sweet and bitter almonds. Val d'Aosta.

blanquette French gastronomic term. Cubed veal, poultry or rabbit in a creamy sauce.

blecs aka **bleki** large homemade ➤ **maltagliati** made with mixed plain and buckwheat flour and, traditionally, curly at the edges. Typical of the Carnia, Isonzo and Natisone areas of Friuli-Venezia Giulia.

blecs cul gial homemade pasta (➤ **blecs**) served with a sauce of pieces of rooster browned in a lightly fried mixture of lardo, herbs and aromatic vegetables and cooked slowly in white wine, tomato passata and broth. Recipe typical of the Carso area, in the province of Gorizia. Friuli-Venezia Giulia.

blecs di Cjanal di Guart homemade pasta (➤ **blecs**) boiled, drained, mixed with cornflour toasted in butter and served with grated cheese. Typical of the Valle di Gorto and Val Pesarina, in the Carnia area. Friuli.

blennio another name for ➤ **bavosa**, blenny.

blò blò flour and water fettuccine served with a sauce of tomato flavored with lightly fried lardo, garlic, marjoram and flat-leafed parsley. The odd onomatopeic name evokes the bubbling of the water for the pasta. Umbria.

blu, al blue. Italianization of **al bleu**. Technique for cooking fish (usually trout) in a ➤ **court-bouillon** flavored with vinegar. **blutnudeln** tagliatelle made from a dough of plain and rye flour, eggs and pig's blood, boiled and served with melted butter, sage and grated cheese. Trentino-Alto Adige.

bobici Venezia Giulia for corn on the cob and corn kernels. **boboli da vida** Veneto word for sea snails (➤ **lumaca di mare**) served with oil, garlic and parsley.

boca in cao northeast Italian dialect term for ➤ **pesce lucerna**, stargazer.

bocca di dama (1) cake of peeled, toasted and crushed almonds, candied fruit, eggs, plain flour and grated lemon zest. The mixture is left to rest and baked in a greased tin lined with flour. Tuscany.

bocca di dama (2) bun made with flour, potato flour, eggs and sugar, soaked in liqueur, filled with confectioner's custard and garnished with a candied cherry. Typical of the province of Lecce. Puglia.

bocca in cava Marche regional name for ➤ **pesce lucerna**, stargazer.

bocca in cielo Abruzzo and Campania regional name for ➤ **pesce lucerna**, stargazer.

boccione maggiore golden fleece (*Urospermum dalechampii*). Large spontaneous herbaceous plant with a prickly stalk; grows in fields, on uncultivated land and meadows up to an altitude of 1,200 meters. Common in the western Mediterranean, it is gathered in northern and central Italy and used to add a bitterish taste to boiled mixed greens and vegetable fillings (➤ **gattafin**). Common and regional names: ➤ **cicoria amara**, ➤ **ingrassaporci**.

bocconata cured meat made of coarsely ground lean pork cased in a cow's intestine and aged for at least four months. Typical especially of the province of Vicenza. Veneto.

bocconcello small ring-shaped savory of bread dough dressed with olive oil, diced Pecorino cheese and prosciutto. Often served as an antipasto. Umbria.

bocconcini alla panna di bufala dairy product made by coating tiny mozzarellas (➤ **mozzarella di bufala campana**) with the cream from the centrifuging of buffalo's or cow's milk. Campania.

bocconcini del cardinale small mozzarellas immersed in whey and preserved in clay pitchers. Campania.

bocconcino (pl. **bocconcini**) word for a food or dish served or cooked in small, bite-sized portions: eg, ➤ **spezzatino**, ➤ **polpette** etc.

boccone del prete Italianization of ➤ **bocon del preivi,** parson's nose.

bocconotto small shortcrust pastry filled (according to the original recipe, typical of the province of Chieti) with chopped almonds, cinnamon, bitter cocoa and lemon zest, popular in many regions of central and southern Italy. In other versions, the filling consists of apples, pine kernels and cooked wine must. In the province of Teramo, they fill the pastry with grape jam, plums and sour cherries, oil, eggs, almonds and lemon. In the province of Cosenza, the pastry is round, oval or ring-shaped and filled with ➤ **mostarda**, grape jam and almonds. In Puglia, the favorite filling is a mixture of sour cherries and confectioner's custard, though some local recipes envisage the use of quince or ricotta and candied fruit. The Lazio version is filled with ➤ **ricotta romana** perfumed with cinnamon, lemon zest and candied lime.

bocon del preivi "priest's tidbit," the Piedmontese dialect equivalent of the English "parson's nose:" namely, the undertail) of a chicken or other fowl, thus named because it was a prized part of the bird and, as such, traditionally given as a present to the clergy (*preivi*, or *previ*, means "priest" in dialect). The Italianization ➤ **boccone del prete** is used in a number of Italian regions.

bocon du diable "Devil's tidbit." A dish consisting of ➤ **mocetta**, a cured meat, served with thin slices of rye bread, toasted, rubbed with garlic, buttered and spread with honey. Val d'Aosta.

bòdi Provençal word for "potatoes."

bòdi e ajòli potatoes and garlic mayonnaise. Potatoes boiled and halved and served with ➤ **ajòli** (*aïoli*), a sauce of finely minced garlic blended with egg yolk and olive oil. A very popular dish in the mountain valleys of the province of Cuneo, where links with Provençal cuisine are still strong. Piedmont.

bòdi succ potato purée flavored with lightly fried onion and flat-leafed parsley, sometimes used to stuff ravioli. Specialty typical of the mountains of the province of Cuneo. Piedmont.

boero dark chocolate with a liqueur cherry filling sold in a paper wrapping.

boga bogue (*Boops boops*). General name for different species of bream of the Sparidae family, abundant in the Mediterranean, especially in the Tyrrhenian. The most common is known as ➤ **buga** in Liguria and ➤ **vopa** or ➤ **opa** in the regions of central and southern Italy, and is usually fried.

boghe con la nepitella Italianization of ➤

opi ca' nipitedda, bogues with lesser calamint.

bogone (pl. **bogoni** aka **bovoloni**) Veronese term for ➤ **lumaca vignaiola** Roman snail (*Helix pomatia*). Other names: ➤ **corgnòi** (Vicenza), ➤ **s'ciosi** (Treviso). These snails are so popular in the region that one village in the province of Verona has erected a *monumento al bogon*. Most of the snail recipes recorded in northern and central Italy use this variety. Veneto.

boldrò Ligurian term for ➤ **rana pescatrice**, monkfish.

bolé dialect term for ➤ **porcino**, porcini mushroom.

bolé dij fò dialect term for ➤ **porcino**, porcini mushroom.

bolé real dialect term for ➤ **ovolo**, royal agaric mushroom.

bollento another name for ➤ **neccio**, a type of waffle.

bollire to boil. To cook a food item in a liquid (water, broth or wine, sometimes aromatized) at a temperature of 100°C.

bollito affumicato smoked boiled meats. Pork (loin, rump, shin, cured meats such as ➤ **servelade**), beef (head, tongue), all smoked, cooked—some together, some separately— in boiling water aromatized with onion, celery, garlic, shallot and leek. Served with boiled potatoes, onions, spinach or other vegetables, grated ➤ **cren**, horseradish and crushed sea salt. Veneto, Friuli-Venezia Giulia.

bollito alla ligure sliced boiled beef, crumbled ship's biscuits and red wine amalgamated over a medium heat. The meat is served cold with a sauce of oil, anchovies, capers, hard-boiled egg, mustard and vinegar. One of the many ways of using leftover boiled meat. Liguria.

bollito ammudicatu breast of veal breaded and roasted. Sicily.

bollito misto, in some regions aka **lesso**

misto mixed boiled meats. A traditional dish comprising a variable number of meats and cuts and, sometimes, cooked cured meats. Common not only in Italy, but also in Spain, France and the United States. In Italy, the dish is to be found in the traditional beef-producing regions (Piedmont, Lombardy, Friuli-Venezia Giulia, Veneto and Emilia-Romagna). Though it arose from the need to exploit every food resource available (in the case in question adult, often overworked animals), it has always been seen as a rich, holiday recipe. Normally the cooking liquid, flavored with aromatics such as celery, carrot and onion (sometimes with the addition of a bouquet garni, ➤ **mazzetto odoroso**) is heated to boiling point and the various cuts of meat are added progressively, according to size and texture. The resulting boiled meats are usually served with suitable sauces.

bollito misto alla bolognese a mixture of boiled capon, boiling sausage (➤ **cotechino**), ➤ **zampone** and various cuts of beef and veal, bones and their marrow, pork ribs and pig's udders. Often a meat loaf (ground beef, dried breadcrumbs, grated Parmigiano, eggs and minced flatleaf parsley and garlic) is also added. The meats are served with parsley sauce, pepper sauce, ➤ **mostarda** (made with quince and preserved fruit flavored with mustard), stewed beans, sweet and sour onions, potato purée, buttered spinach, boiled potatoes and the traditional cream of onion and tomatoes cooked in lard (➤ **friggione**). The recipe was registered at the Bologna Chamber of Commerce in 2006. Emilia-Romagna.

bollito misto alla piemontese traditionally composed of seven cuts of meat: boneless blade, round, tip, head and tail (preferably of a fattened ox), chicken or capon and ➤ **cotechino**. Sometimes tongue is also included. The chicken and beef cuts, save for the head, are cooked in same pan; the **cotechino** and head are cooked separately. The meats are either served with ➤ **bagnet**, ➤ **cognà**, ➤ **saossa d'avie** and, sometimes, horseradish sauce (➤ **cren**) or ➤ **mostarda di Cremona**, or simply dipped in salt. Piedmont.

bollito misto alla triestina various cuts of pork, including ➤ **porcina** (aka **porzina**) for which the dish used to be named. In Trieste the dish is served in specific restaurants (➤ **buffet**). The classic composition envisages **porcina** (from the back of the head or the shoulder), smoked loin (➤ **Kaiserfleisch**), pancetta, picked tongue, head, ears, trotters, ➤ **cotechino** and ➤ **würstel**. In the buffets, the meats are cooked in large cauldrons, in which the water is kept constantly just below boiling point, and served sliced with ➤ **crauti** (sauerkraut) perfumed with cumin seeds or mustard and horseradish (➤ **cren**). Typical of Trieste. Friuli-Venezia Giulia.

bollito misto alla veronese a couple of cuts of beef (usually the equivalent of hip sirloin and brisket), calf's head, pickled tongue, chicken and ➤ **cotechino** (or ➤ **musetto**), the latter two being boiled apart. According to season, duck, goose or guinea fowl may also be included in the assortment. The meats are accompanied by ➤ **pearà** sauce and, on occasion, horseradish sauce (➤ **cren**). Veneto.

bollito misto lombardo especially in the Milan area, the cuts used are roughly the equivalent of socket, hip sirloin, shoulder clod, brisket and plate, calf's head and trotters, capon and ➤ **cotechino**, which is cooked separately. Once cooked, the meat is cut into thickish slices, sprinkled with sea salt and covered with a few tablespoons of boiling broth. Traditionally served with buttered spinach, potato purée, pickles, ➤ **mostarda di Cremona** and, often, ➤ **salsa verde**. Lombardy.

bollito rifatto alla vicentina a slice of veal spread with crushed salt and pepper, cinnamon and cloves, sewn to form a "pouch," stuffed with boiled calf's head and tongue and ➤ **cotechino**, and cooked in meat broth with aromatic vegetables. This elaborate specialty owes its name (*rifatto* means "repeated") to the double-boiling of the meats. Veneto.

bollito toscano fat and lean ribs of beef boiled in water with onion, carrot, celery and skinned tomatoes. Served with ➤ **salsa verde** and pickles.

bollo antico sweet compact bun of Jewish origin with a brown crust, originally unleavened and eaten on religious holidays. Imported by Jews fleeing from Spain in the 15th century. Today, after centuries of proximity with *goyim* (Gentile) cooking, the bun is made of leavened dough, eggs, sugar, anise and lemon zest, and brushed with egg yolk before baking in the oven. Traditionally made on Ferrgosto (August 15) in the towns of Pitigliano and Sorano, in the province of Grosseto. Tuscany.

bologna another name for ➤ **mortadella Bologna**.

bomba (1) word for a round cake or pastry, fried (➤ **bombolone**) or baked, soaked in liqueur and filled with cream or custard.

bomba (2) sponge cake soaked in liqueur, filled with layers of custard and ice-cream and shaped into a ball in a special mold known as a *bomba*.

bomba (3) a "shell" or casing that contains a filling. A well known known example is ➤ **bomba di riso**.

bomba (4) sauce of vegetables and chili used to dress pasta or to spread on bread. Calabria.

bomba di Canossa a sort of ➤ **zuccotto** made in a mold by alternating ➤ **savoiardi** sponge fingers soaked in egg liqueur and zabaglione. Invented in the early 20th century by a confectioner in Reggio Emilia. Emilia-Romagna.

bomba di riso timbale of rice filled with stewed pigeon and baked in the oven. The original recipe included giblets, porcini mushrooms and truffle in the filling. Typical of Parma, but also common in the province of Piacenza. Emilia-Romagna.

bombardoni another name for ➤ **rigatoni**, a type of pasta.

bombas meatballs made of a mixture of ground beef, minced garlic and parsley, beaten eggs, salt and breadcrumbs cooked in tomato sauce or in broth. Sardinia.

bombetta roll of pork (➤ **capocollo**) stuffed with a mixture of Pecorino cheese, parsley, salt and pepper. Sometimes breaded and fried or broiled. Often cooked in the butcher's oven (➤ **fornello**). Puglia.

bombinati chocolate pralines containing a coffee bean and coated with white ➤ **diavolicchi**, confetti sugar. Campania.

bomboletti aka **bombetti** Marche word for sea snail (➤ **lumaca di mare**). Often stewed with wild fennel.

bombolone fried doughnut-like cake (though not always with a hole in the middle) similar to ➤ **krapfen**. Sometimes filled with confectioner's custard, jam or chocolate. Eaten piping hot and dusted with sugar for breakfast. A symbol of summer seaside vacations for whole generations of Italians.

Bonassai cheese developed relatively recently, but already considered traditional. Made from pasteurized ewe's milk and matured for 20-30 days. Sardinia.

bonbon French term for sweet or candy. In Italian it refers to dainty cookies, sugared almonds, pralines and so on. In a gastronomic sense, it can also be used for any tiny round-shaped food item, sweet or savory.

bondeana cow's or pig's large, or caecum, intestine. Virtually impermeable and very thick, it is used to case numerous cured meats.

bondella another name for ➤ **coregone**, chub.

bondiola (1) another name for ➤ **bondòla**, a smoked cured meat.

bondiola (2) another name for ➤ **saùc**, a sort of boiling sausage.

bondiola lombarda round boiling sausage made with a similar mixture to ➤ **cotechino**. The word *bondiola* (*bundiöla* in dialect) also refers to ➤ **coppa piacentina**. Lombardy.

bondòla smoked cured meat made from coarsely ground fat and lean pork mixed with salt, crushed peppercorns, garlic and red wine. Cased in a pig's bladder or a turkey's neck, it is lightly smoked for 30 days, then aged for four to five months. Typical of the lower Polesine area. Veneto.

bondòla co'l lengual cured meat made from pig's head, pork rind and cheek, ground and flavored with salt, pepper, bay leaf, juniper berries and Marsala. The mixture is cased in calf's bladder containing a pickled pig's tongue. After maturing for a fortnight, the meat ages for four to five months. Typical of the provinces of Padua, Vicenza and Venice. Veneto.

bondòla di Adria cured meat similar to ➤ **salama da sugo**. Made from a mixture of lardo and lean pork or veal cured with salt, pepper and red wine and cased in a pig's bladder. Aged for four months, it is eaten steamed or boiled. A specialty of Adria, in the province of Rovigo. Veneto.

boné liquid produced by souring the whey and/or ricotta from spontaneous lactic fermentation. Used to make ➤ **brossa**. Val d'Aosta.

bonet aka **bunèt** cream dessert made with milk, eggs, sugar, cacao, amaretti cookies, rum and, in some cases, coffee powder. In one version, chopped walnuts are added. Typical of the Langhe hills, in the province of Cuneo, it is named for its round, flat shape (*bunèt* means "bonnet" in dialect). Piedmont.

bonetto northern Italian dialect term for ➤ **reticolo,** reticulum.

bonissima aka **sarzenta** shortcrust pastry tart filled with honey, walnuts and rum and coated with chocolate or white icing. Typical of Modena. Emilia-Romagna.

bonita another name for ➤ **tonnetto**, striped bellied bonito.

boraggine alternative spelling of ➤ **borragine**, borage.

borana selvatica another word for ➤ **consolida maggiore**, comfrey.

bordatino thick soup of red beans, polenta flour, olive oil, "black cabbage" (➤ **cavolo nero**), red onions, celery, carrots, garlic, parsley (or basil), salt, and pepper. Once a way of using up leftovers on board ships and boats, now common in the provinces of Livorno and Pisa. Tuscany.

bordura the word means a crown-shaped garnish. More specifically, today it refers to a dish (such as ➤ **cibreo**, ➤ **fricassea**, ➤ **finanziera**) served with or in a crown of semolina, potatoes or, more often, rice, cooked together with the dish or separately in a ring-shaped mold. The final appearance is similar to that of a ➤ **savarin**.

boreto term used in some northern Adriatic lagoon areas for ➤ **brodetto**, fish stew.

borlengo soft, crumbly pancake made of water, eggs and all-purpose flour cooked in a beaten copper pan. Eaten with ➤ **cun-**

za, chopped raw lardo mixed with finely minced garlic and rosemary and grated Parmigiano-Reggiano. Typical of the Modena hills. Emilia-Romagna.

borlotto (pl. **borlotti**) type of ➤ **fagiolo**, bean. Oval and rounded in shape, creamy in color with red streaks. Cultivated mainly in central and northern Italy. The name is believed to derive from the Lombard verb *borlare*, "to tumble," and evokes the way the oldest plants grow. Noteworthy among the varieties present on the Italian market are *borlotto lingua di fuoco* and *borlotto di Lamon* (province of Belluno, Veneto). More local varieties are *borlotti di Vigevano* (province of Pavia, Lombardy), *borlotti di Mangia* (Sesta Godano, province of La Spezia, Liguria) and *borlotti di Sorano* (province of Grosseto, Tuscany). Marketed fresh or dried, borlotti beans have a strong flavor, suitable for long, slow cooking. They are an essential ingredient in recipes in Veneto (➤ **fasoi in potacin**), Lombardy (➤ **risòtt coi borlott**, **risòtt rustì**, **tortelli sguassaròt**) and Piedmont (➤ **paniscia**, ➤ **panissa**).

borola Italianization of the Lombard ➤ **borroeûla**.

borraggine borage (*Borago officinalis*). Herbaceous plant with hairy leaves and blue flowers common throughout Italy. The leaves are used for fillings and soups, especially in Liguria, where they are an ingredient in ➤ **preboggion**, and also appear in savory pies and mixed fries. Common and regional names: ➤ **boraggine**, ➤ **borrana**, ➤ **erba pelosa**.

borragine selvatica another word for ➤ **consolida maggiore**, comfrey.

borrana dialect term for ➤ **borragine**, borage.

borrana selvatica another term for ➤ **polmonaria**, common lungwort.

borroeûla Brianza term for salami meat cooked in ash with potatoes. The word also refers to the meat mixture itself, which is traditionally spread on toasted bread or served with pasta. Lombardy.

borsa del pastore shepherd's purse (*Capsella bursa-pastoris*). Spontaneous herbaceous plant so named on account of its purse-like pods. Especially in northern and central Italy, its basal rosettes are gathered and used in mixed salads and soups (it is one of the ➤ **erbucci versiliesi**). Common and regional names: ➤ **borsette**, ➤ **cassetta**, ➤ **erba borsa**, ➤ **scarsellina**.

borsette regional term for ➤ **borsa del pastore**, shepherd's purse.

bortellina Italianization of ➤ **burtlèina**, a sort of fritter.

borzillo ground wild boar meat mixed with ➤ **peperone di Senise**, salt, chili and a mixture of aromatic herbs, cased in a natural intestine (in the past, the bladder was used), secured by hand and aged for five to six months. The production of this old cured meat has now been revived by a pork butcher's shop in Pietragalla, a village in the province of Potenza. Basilicata.

bosa word used in Lombardy and Veneto for ➤ **bottatrice**, burbot.

boscaiola, alla generic term (literally "woodland-style") to describe recipes featuring mushrooms (preserved, fresh, wild or cultivated) and tomato sauce. Usually refers to sauces for pasta and meat.

bosega Veneto term for ➤ **cefalo**, mullet.

bosine tiny burbots (➤ **bosa**, ➤ **bottatrice**).

bossolà (1) Brescia dialect name for ➤ **bossolano**, a traditional cake.

bossolà (2) crisp savory ring pastry (➤ **tarallo**). It stays fragrant for weeks and is used as a substitute for bread. The dough is made of all-purpose flour, water, extra virgin olive oil, brewer's yeast, lard and salt. Typical of Chioggia, in the province of Venice. Veneto.

bossolà (3) sweet ring cookie made of all-purpose flour, eggs and a generous amount of butter. Typical of the island of Burano, in the province of Venice. Veneto.

bossolano baked leavened ring-shaped cake made from a mixture of plain flour, yeast, sugar, salt, eggs, grated lemon or orange zest, melted butter, yeast and powdered vanilla. Common all over the Po Valley, especially in Lombardy and Veneto, from Cremona and Mantua up to Brescia and Vicenza, and down across the Po to Piacenza, with a consequent variety of dialect names and small differences in measures, flavorings and toppings: ➤ **bussolano** in Soresina, in the province di Cremona; ➤ **buslan**, ➤ **bussolan**, ➤ **buzilan** in the province di Piacenza (where they put almonds on the top); ➤ **bossolà** in Brescia (where the cake is yellow on account of the generous amount of eggs used in the mixture); ➤ **bussolà**, ➤ **busolà**, ➤ **buzolà** in Vicenza (where they add Marsala or grappa or aniseed liqueur). Lombardy, Veneto.

bostrengo rectangular or round cook made with plain flour, milk (sometimes with cooked rice), eggs and sugar. Typical of the Montefeltro area (Carpegna, Macerata Feltria and San Leo). Not to be confused with ➤ **frustingo**, typical of the south of the region. Marche.

botìro di malga di Primiero soft, spreadable raw milk butter (*botìro* in dialect), straw-yellow to golden in color, aromatic with notes of flowers and herbs. Once considered the best in Italy, ten years ago on the verge of extinction, now promoted by a Slow Food presidium, which supports the local dairy in Primiero (province of Trento) and is seeking to increase the number of mountain dairies involved in production. Trentino-Alto Adige.

bottaggio term of French origin for ➤ **casoeûla**, Milanese pork and cabbage stew.

bottarga botargo. Gray mullet (➤ **muggine**) or tuna roe, salted, cured and matured for four to five months. Its color varies from amber to pink, depending on the variety of the fish used and time of aging. It is eaten in thin slices dressed with or marinated in oil and lemon juice or grated over pasta. The Italian producer regions are Sardinia (where it is made with the roe of gray mullet, tuna and ling, a member of the cod family, respectively in the province of Oristano, the Sulcis area and Alghero), Tuscany (➤ **bottarga di Orbetello**, made with gray mullet roe), Calabria (where it is made with tuna roe in the province di Vibo Valentia) and Sicily (➤ **bottarga di Favignana**, made with tuna roe).

bottarga di Favignana botargo of tuna roe with a stronger flavor to that made with gray mullet roe. Today the ancient fish preserving tradition of the island of Favignana off the western Sicilian coast (province of Trapani) is carried on by a single artisan company.

bottarga di luccio botargo made with the ovarian sacs of female pike fished in December, a period in which 30% of the fish's weight is made up of roe. The latter is placed in brine, covered with a mixture of sea salt, sugar, juniper berries, black pepper and coriander, pressed for four to seven days, then lightly smoked. The resulting botargo is served in thin slices on fresh or toasted bread, spread on hot croutons, or used to dress tomato and onion salads or spaghetti. Lombardy.

bottarga di Orbetello the art of preserving

fish was probably introduced to the lagoon of Orbetello (province of Grosseto) by the Spanish. The local gray mullet roe botargo is protected by a Slow Food presidium and produced by a fishing cooperative, complete with shop, market and restaurant. Soft in texture and amber in color, it is cut into very thin slices and dressed with extra virgin olive oil and lemon juice.

bottatrice burbot (*Lota lota* or *Lota vulgaris*). The only freshwater gadiform (cod-like fish) common in lakes and rivers in northern Italy. Its delicate, tasty, boneless white flesh is suitable for recipes similar to those adopted for eel (➤ **anguilla**). Excellent broiled, stewed, stuffed and baked. Its fried fillets may be served on their own or with other fishes in ➤ **frittura di lago**, mixed fry of lake fish. The fatty, tasty liver is also cooked in butter and served sliced.

botticella spicy boiled salami made with the poorer parts of the pig. Emilia-Romagna.

boudin aka **budeun** cured meat made from a mixture of pig's or cow's blood, boiled potatoes, lardo, salt, pepper, garlic, cinnamon, nutmeg, sage, rosemary, juniper and, sometimes, wine or powdered milk. Cased in a thin intestine, it is hung to dry for a couple of weeks. Fresh, it is eaten raw; briefly aged, it is broiled, fried or boiled. Today, due to legal restrictions, the blood is partly or totally replaced by beetroot.

bovina piemontese, razza Piedmontese cattle breed. A very ancient breed, like all those with white coats. It was only in 1886, however, that spontaneous variation led to the birth of a bull with huge haunches and extremely muscular thighs on a farm in Guarene (Cuneo). This was the progenitor of the so-called *vitello della coscia* (*coscia* means "thigh" in Italian) or *fassone*, the quality of whose meat is so outstanding that it is now common to eat it raw. The heads marketed by the La Granda producers' association are raised exclusively on natural feed (corn, barley, bran, fava beans, hay). The butchers' shops that have adhered to the presidium sell the meat specially labeled to ensure its traceability. The cattle are bred in the area between Fossano, Cuneo and Mondovì. Piedmont.

bovina romagnola, razza Romagna cow breed. Traditionally raised in a number of valleys in the Romagna Apennines. The cattle are recognizable by their whitish to pale gray coats, and are impressively muscular with sturdy robust limbs. The females have black, lyre-shaped horns, while the males' horns are crescent-shaped. The Romagna is more resistant to the elements than any other white breed and adapts well to pasture. Its meat is also excellent, particularly the fatty and flavorful rib steaks, just as good as those from the more famous Chianina breed. Emilia-Romagna.

bovino bovine. The term refers to the domestic cow, the bison and the bufalo. Descendants of the urus (*Bos primigenius*), a large wild bull which became extinct in the 17th century, they have been raised as meat, dairy and work animals since the Neolithic era. The most important species is *Bos taurus*, which boasts many native breeds in Italy and others that have lived in the country for centuries: Chianina, Piemontese, Marchigiana, Romagnola for meat, *Bruno Alpina* and *Pezzata Nera* for milk, not to mention the recently introduced Friesian). Italian legislation classifies beef cattle into three categories: ➤ **vitello** (an animal slaughtered before the age of eight months), ➤ **vitellone** (eight to 12 months), and *bo-*

vino adulto (which refers to oxen, bulls and adult cattle). European legislation has introduced a system of identification and registration that allows the consumer to trace the meat's history. The Italian Ministry of Agriculture's database of native and/or traditional food products lists: ➤ **bovina piemontese**, *vacca cabannina* (typical of Cabanne, near Rezzoaglio in the Val d'Aveto, Liguria), ➤ **bovina romagnola**, *maremmana, calvana, marchigiana, podolica pugliese, podolica calabrese, sardo-modicana* and *sardo-bruna* raised in the regions of origin and the meat of the *mucca pisana* (aka *mucco pisano*), the Pisan cow, raised in the Parco di Migliarino-San Rossore, near Pisa, in Tuscany.

bovoeto aka **bovoleto** Veneto names for ➤ **lumaca di mare**, sea snail. In the province di Vicenza, instead, **bovoeto** refers to the small land snail *Helix theba pisana* (➤ **babbaluci** in Sicily, ➤ **ciogga minudda** in Sardinia), lightly fried in oil with garlic and parsley, bathed with dry white wine and stewed on a medium heat in a covered earthenware pot. Veneto.

bovoloni another name for ➤ **bogoni**, Roman snails.

Boznersauce "Bolzano sauce." Hard-boiled egg yolks mixed with chopped parsley and chives, mustard, broth, vinegar, oil, salt and pepper. Trentino-Alto Adige.

bozza pratese rectangular loaf with a dark brown, flour-dusted crust. Made from a dough of soft wheat flour, water and natural yeast, and baked in a wood oven. Typical of Prato. Tuscany.

Bra PDO cow's milk cheese (with the occasional addition of small percentages of ewe's or goat's milk) named after the city of Bra, in the province of Cuneo. Comes in three versions: *tenero* (soft), *duro* (hard) or *d'alpeggio* (produced in the mountains in the summer and non-PDO). Piedmont.

bracalaccio old version of ➤ **arvoltolo**, fried bread dough. Umbria.

bracciatelli traditional pastries used to form garlands (or rings or wheels). Made from a simple dough, aromatized with nutmeg and aniseed liqueur, brushed with egg white and sugar prior to baking in the oven. Emilia-Romagna.

braciolata in modern Italian, an alternative term for ➤ **grigliata mista**, mixed broil, though it originally referred to only one type of meat. The word is also used to describe the rite of the open-air barbecue among friends and relatives.

braciole alla napoletana boneless pork chops covered with finely chopped raisins, ham, capers, and pine kernels, rolled up and stewed in tomato sauce. Recipe typical of Naples. Campania.

braciole di alici anchovies opened flat, central backbone and head removed, dipped in white wine, coated with a mixture of fresh breadcrumbs, Pecorino, garlic, parsley, salt, oregano, rolled up, floured and fried. Calabria.

braciole di maiale slices of pork fillet, well flattened, covered with Pecorino, garlic, parsley and black pepper, rolled up and fried in lard. Eaten immediately or preserved in pottery jars in their own cooking fat and more lard. Recipe typical of the Cosenza area, but also to be found elsewhere in the south. Basilicata, Puglia, Calabria.

braciole di manzo rifatte thin slices of beef breaded and fried in olive oil, covered with chopped garlic and parsley and a sauce of skinned tomatoes, broth, salt and pepper, and baked in the oven. Tuscany.

braciolette patties made from a mixture of ground beef and pork, raisins, prosciut-

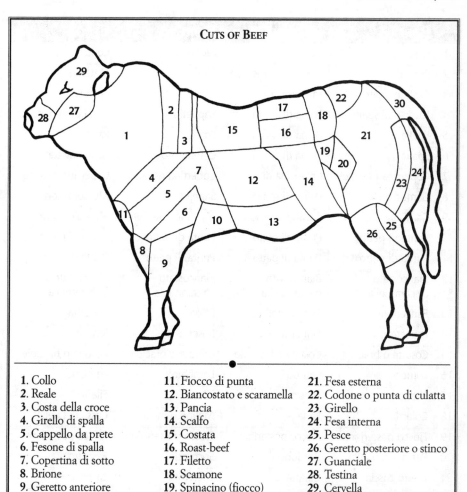

CUTS OF BEEF

1. Collo
2. Reale
3. Costa della croce
4. Girello di spalla
5. Cappello da prete
6. Fesone di spalla
7. Copertina di sotto
8. Brione
9. Geretto anteriore
10. Petto
11. Fiocco di punta
12. Biancostato e scaramella
13. Pancia
14. Scalfo
15. Costata
16. Roast-beef
17. Filetto
18. Scamone
19. Spinacino (fiocco)
20. Noce
21. Fesa esterna
22. Codone o punta di culatta
23. Girello
24. Fesa interna
25. Pesce
26. Geretto posteriore o stinco
27. Guanciale
28. Testina
29. Cervella
30. Coda

to and pine kernels molded into spindle shapes and cooked in extra virgin olive oil with sage and white wine. Sometimes the patties are put on skewers alternated with croutons and baked in the oven or broiled. A traditional Neapolitan dish. Campania.

braciolette di spada swordfish rolls. Recipe common, with variations, throughout Sicily. Slices of swordfish spread with a mixture of chopped swordfish, dried breadcrumbs, pine kernels, raisins and grated lemon zest, rolled up, dipped in breadcrumbs and baked in the oven. In the province of Messina, the stuffing is made with toasted breadcrumbs, extra virgin olive oil and minced garlic. Other possible ingredients are capers, basil and grated Pecorino or other strong cheeses. Sometimes the dish is given a sweet and

	BARI	BOLOGNA	FLORENCE	GENOA
1	Rosciale	Guido	Giogo	Collo
2	Rosciale	Costa di sottospalla	Polso	Matamà
3	Costate rigate	Fallata di lombo	Polso	Costola
4	Lacerto di spalla	Polpa di spalla	Soppello	Rotondino di spalla
5	Spalla	Polpa di spalla	Sorra	Paletta
6	Spalla	Polpa di spalla	Cotennotto	Soprapaletta
7	Copertina di sotto	Copertina di sotto	Copertina di sotto	Copertina di sotto
8	Gamboncello	Polpa di spalla	Sapello	Muscolo storto
9	Gamboncello	Gamba anteriore	Muscolo anteriore	Muscolo diritto
10	Punta di petto	Punta di petto	Punta di petto	Punta di petto
11	Punta di petto	Punta di petto	Punta di petto	Punta di petto
12	Biancostato o scaramella	Biancostato o scaramella	Biancostato o scaramella	Biancostato o scaramella
13	Pancettone	Finta cartella	Falda	Panzetta
14	Pancettone	Finta cartella	Rosetta	Scalfo
15	Costate o braciole	Costate o braciole	Costate o braciole	Costate o braciole
16	Lombo	Lombo	Lombata	Lombata
17	Filetto	Filetto	Filetto	Filetto
18	Colarda	Fetta	Melino o mela	Cassa del belin
19	Fiocco posteriore	Fiocco posteriore	Fiocco posteriore	Fiocco posteriore
20	Pezza a cannello	Bordone	Soccoscio	Pescetto
21	Dietro coscia	Culatta	Lucertolo	Lacerto
22	Punta di culatta	Punta di culatta	Punta di culatta	Punta di culatta
23	Sfasciatura	Scannello	Scannello	Schenello
24	Girello	Girello	Girello	Rotondino
25	Pesce	Gamba	Callo del campanello	Muscolo posteriore
26	Gamboncello	Lanterna	Muscolo posteriore	Muscolo posteriore

sour touch with a final splash of sugared lemon juice.

braciolone alla partenopea a large slice of veal spread with prosciutto, hard-boiled eggs, spinach, parsley, garlic, oregano, raisins and pine kernels, sewn up to form a "pouch" and stewed with vegetables in white wine and tomato sauce. Campania.

braciulittini Sicilian dialect term for meat or fish rolls (➤ **braciola (2)**).

	MANTUA	MILAN	NAPLES	PALERMO
1	Collo	Collo	Locena	Spinello
2	Ropracosta	Reale	Locena	Spinello
3	Coste delle prime	Coste della croce	Locena	Spinello
4	Girello	Fusello	Lacertiello	Ovo di spadda
5	Fettone di spalla	Cappello da prete	Spalla	Pieno di spadda
6	Fettone di spalla	Fesone di spalla	Spalla	Pieno di spadda
7	Copertina di sotto	Pernice	Copertina di sotto	Copertina di sotto
8	Zoia di spalla	Brione	Spalla	Sfasciaturedda
9	Muscolo anteriore	Geretto anteriore	Gamboncello	Manuzza
10	Punta di petto	Punta di petto	Punta di petto	Bruschetto
11	Fiocco	Fiocco anteriore	Fiocco anteriore	Fiocco anteriore
12	Biancostato o scaramella	Biancostato	Corazza	Gabbia
13	Pancia	Scalfo	Pancettone	Pancia
14	Scalfo	Scalfo	Pancettone	Pancia
15	Costate o braciole	Roast-beef	Costale o coverta	Costata
16	Roast-beef	Roast-beef	Biffo	Trinca
17	Filetto	Filetto	Filetto	Filetto
18	Scannello	Scamone	Colarda	Sotto codata
19	Spinacino o fiocco posteriore	Fiocco posteriore	Fiocco posteriore	Fiocco posteriore
20	Noce o spola	Noce	Pezza a cannella	Bausa
21	Coscia magra	Fetta di mezzo	Dietro coscia	Dietro coscia
22	Punta di culatta	Codone	Codone	Codone
23	Part-grasa	Rosa	Natica	Sfasciatura
24	Rotolo di coscia	Magatello	Lacerto	Lacertu
25	Muscolo posteriore	Pesce	Colarda	Pisciuni di dietro
26	Muscolo posteriore	Geretto posteriore	Gamboncello	Pisciuni

bramesc a blend of milk, buttermilk, cream (*brama* in Ladin) and butter, heated with honey, poppy seeds, raisins and a pinch of salt. Served cold as a dessert with cubes of rye bread and apple softened in butter with sugar and cinnamon. Typical of the Fassa and Fiemme valleys, in the province of Trento. Trentino-Alto Adige.

	Parma	Reggio C.	Rome	Turin
1	Collo	Coddu	Collo	Collo
2	Sottospalla	Scorcia di coddu	Fracosta	Sottospalla
3	Sottospalla	Scorcia di coddu	Fracosta	Sottospalla
4	Girello di spalla	Ovu di spadda	Sbordone	Rollino
5	Copertina	Spadda	Polpa di spalla	Spalla
6	Polpone	Spadda	Polpa di spalla	Spalla
7	Copertina di sotto	Copertina di sotto	Copertina di sotto	Copertina di sotto o foglia
8	Muscolo di spalla	Spasciatura	Pulcio	Nocetta di spalla
9	Geretto anteriore	Manuzza	Muscolo anteriore	Muscolo anteriore
10	Punta di petto	Punta di pettu	Petto grosso	Punta di petto
11	Fiocco anteriore	Fiocco anteriore	Petto grosso	Punta di petto
12	Taglio reale	Gabbia	Spuntatura	Spezzato
13	Pancia	Pettu	Spuntatura di lombo	Spezzato
14	Pancia	Bollito	Scalfo	Scalfo
15	Braciole	Scorcia di spadda	Costa	Costola
16	Controfiletto	Trinca	Lombo	Sottofiletto o lonza
17	Filetto	Filetto	Filetto	Filetto
18	Culatello	A codata	Pezza	Sottofiletto spesso
19	Fiocco posteriore	Fiocco posteriore	Fiocco posteriore	Fiocco posteriore
20	Noce	Bausa	Tracoscio	Boccia grande
21	Sottofesa	Dietro a codata	Controgirello	Coscia infuori
22	Codone	Codone		
23	Fesa interna	Entrocoscia	Scanello	Fesa
24	Girello	Lacerto	Girello	Coscia rotonda
25	Muscolo	Pisciuni	Piccione campanello	Pesce
26	Geretto posteriore	Pisciuni	Muscolo posteriore pulcio	Giaret muscolo posteriore

brandacujun stockfish and mashed potatoes amalgamated vigorously, flavored with minced garlic, flat-leaved parsley and pine kernels, and blended with an emulsion of oil, lemon juice and egg yolks. Served as an antipasto. Typical of the western Riviera di Ponente. Liguria.

branzi variant on ➛ **formai de mut** cheese.

	TREVISO	VENICE	VERONA	VICENZA
1	Collo	Modegal	Collo	Collo
2	Fondo di schiena	Fondo di schiena	Sottospalla	Sottocoperta o sottospalla
3	Braciola reale	Fondo di schiena	Sottospalla	Sottospalla
4	Muscolo di spalla	Zogia	Girello di spalla	Spalla
5		Zogia	Copertina di spalla	Spalla
6	Taglio lungo di spalla	Taglio lungo di spalla o scapin	Fesone di spalla	Spalla
7	Copertina di sotto	Copertina di sotto	Copertina di sotto	Copertina di sotto
8		Zogia	Muscolo di spalla	
9	Muscolo di spalla	Muscolo anteriore	Geretto anteriore	Muscolo di spalla
10	Fiocco o zoia	Petto	Punta di petto	Punta di petto
11	Fiocco o zoia	Petto	Fiocco	Petto
12	Stecca o fracosta	Bongiolo	Taglio reale	Biancostao o oriada
13	Tasto	Tasto	Pancia o tasto	Pancia o bognigolo
14	Scalfo	Scalfo	Scalfo	Scalfo
15	Costate o braciole	Schiena	Braciole	Costate o braciole
16	Roast-beef	Lai sottile	Lombata	Lombata
17	Filetto	Filetto	Filetto	Filetto
18	Sottofiletto	Taglio di nombolo	Scamone	Straculo
19	Fiocco posteriore	Fiocco posteriore	Fiocco posteriore	Fiocco posteriore
20	Noce	Culatta	Noce	Noce
21	Codino	Lai di fuori	Fesa	Controfesa
22	Punta di codino			Punta di controfesa
23	Fesa	Lai di dietro	Fesa	Fesa
24	Girello	Lai di fuori	Girello	Girello
25	Muscolo	Muscolo posteriore	Pesce	Muscolo
26	Muscolo	Muscolo posteriore	Geretto	Muscolo

Takes its name from Branzi, in the province of Bergamo, where it is produced. Lombardy.

branzino northern Italian word for → **spig-ola**, sea bass.

brasadé sweet ring cookies made of flour, ammonium carbonate, olive oil or lard, butter and sugar. A specialty of the village of Staghiglione, in the Oltrepò area of the province of Pavia. Linked together to form necklaces, the cookies were traditionally given to children as Confirmation gifts. Lombardy.

brasadele broè boiled ring-shaped cookies. Small rings of leavened sweet dough plunged into boiling salted water, dried and baked in the oven. Trentino-Alto Adige, Veneto.

brasare to braise. To brown in hot fat, then to cook slowly in a covered pot with vegetables and a little liquid, usually wine.

brasato "braised" (➤ **brasare**). As a noun, the word designates a precise northern Italian dish, typical in particular of Lombardy and Piedmont. After browning in butter or oil or both, a piece of appropriately chosen meat, usually beef, is cooked slowly in wine and herbs and, if it has been marinated, with the marinade liquid (➤ **marinata**). The wine should be a full-bodied red: eg, Barolo or a Barbaresco in Piedmontese recipes. In other regions, the same cooking procedure is called ➤ **stracotto**.

brasato al Barolo a soft cut of beef marinated in Barolo wine, then braised slowly in a covered pan (➤ **brasare**). A classic of Piedmontese cuisine, especially in the Langhe hills, in the province of Cuneo. Elsewhere in the region, other wines might be used: in the province of Asti Barbera, in the north Gattinara, in parts of the Langhe hills Barbaresco. When the season comes, the meat of the fattened ox (➤ **bue**) is used.

brasciola Puglia term for a meat roll (➤ **involtino**), generally of horsemeat or veal, filled with lardo, Pecorino, flat-leaved parsley, garlic, pepper and salt. Lightly stewed with tomato and herbs, it one of the typical condiments for ➤ **orecchiette** and other traditional pastas.

brasola aged loin of pork. Lombardy.

brasolara rare and prized cured meat. Pork fillet cured with salt, cinnamon and cloves, set aside to rest, then cased in a large intestine and completely covered in the mixture used to make ➤ **sopressa vicentina**. The meat is immersed in hot water and massaged, secured with string, dried and aged for at least ten months. Typical of the Alpine foothills. Veneto.

brassadela leavened dough (flour, eggs, sugar, butter, milk, grappa) kneaded into a large ring or S" shape and baked in the oven. Traditional Easter cake in the province of Vicenza, but also made in the province of Rovigo and, without grappa, in the province of Verona. Veneto.

bratte aka **jette** figs stuck on skewers and baked in the oven. Calabria.

brazadel traditional ring-shaped Christmas cake made of bread dough, eggs, butter and sugar. Trentino-Alto Adige.

brazadèla sweet ring-shaped cake made of leavened dough, scented with lemon zest and decorated with sugar chips. Traditionally given to children as a Confirmation gift. Typical of Bologna and Ferrara, but popular throughout the region. In Modena known as ➤ **bensone**. Emilia-Romagna.

brazzadelle ring-shaped cake made of wheat and rye flour, brewer's yeast, eggs, milk, and sugar. Typical of the Valtellina. Lombardy.

brazzoleddu de mari Sardinian dialect term for ➤ **arca di Noè**, Noah's ark or arkshell.

Breatl bread loaf typical of the province of Bolzano. In Val Pusteria it is made with rye flour (75%) and durum wheat flour (25%), fennel seeds (➤ **finocchio selvatico**), cumin, fenugreek (➤ **trigonella**) and coriander. In the Valle Isarco they eliminate the coriander, in the Val d'Ultimo they use only rye flour. Trentino-Alto Adige.

Brennsuppe Tyrolese soup made of toasted flour, similar to ➤ **brö brüsà**, in the province of Trento. Trentino-Alto Adige.

brent'e sanguni Sardinian dialect term for ➤ **zurrette**, an offal dish.

bresaola beef cured in brine, dried and aged. The meat originates from and is traditional to the Valtellina and Valchiavenna. Also produced in limited quantities with horsemeat. Lombardy.

bresaola (aka **brisaola**) **della Valtellina** PGI cured meat documented since the 15th century. Made from one of five cuts of beef, including fillet, cured with salt, coarsely ground pepper, potassium nitrate and a mixture of woodland herbs inside wood or steel tubs, and layered with more salt. After ten days, the meat is washed, dried, cased in a calf's caecum intestine and aged for two to three months. Lombardy.

bresaola della Val d'Ossola made from prized cuts of veal, aromatized with pepper, cinnamon, nutmeg, thyme, rosemary, cloves, bay leaves, sugar and white wine. Dry-salted for a few days, it is cased in a calf's caecum intestine and aged for two to three months. Piedmont.

bresaola di cavallo horsemeat bresaola producd in Lombardy and, less so, in Veneto. In the Valchiavenna and Valtellina, a horse's leg is cured for eight to twelve days in a mixture of red wine, salt, pepper, finely crushed garlic, cinnamon and coarsely ground cloves. After two periods of maturation (for 48 hours, then for ten days), it ages for one to three months. In the provinces of Padua, Venice and Treviso, prized cuts of horsemeat are cured in a secret mixture, which varies from butcher to butcher, for 20 days. They are then secured with string,

wrapped in canvas to dry and aged for three to five months. Lombardy, Veneto.

bresaola di cervo a type of ➤ **slinzega** (bresaola by-product) made with red deer venison.

bretzel or **brezel** or **brezen** baked figure "8"-shaped savory cookies made of flour, malt, water, lard and salt. In Friuli, they add ➤ **papavero**, poppy seeds. Trentino-Alto Adige, Friuli-Venezia Giulia.

briciolata simple condiment of coarsely grated day-old bread fried with extra virgin olive oil, sometimes flavored with chili, used to dress ➤ **pici**, a type of pasta. Tuscany.

brigaldo traditional blood sausage. Pig's blood is cooked over a low heat with grappa, eggs, orange juice, pine kernels, breadcrumbs, raisins, grated Grana cheese, sugar and salt. Recioto della Valpolicella is then poured into the mixture, which, when thick, is cased in a pig's intestine and divided into short "sausages," which are boiled at 90°C for ten minutes. Served with polenta or cut into slices and sautéed with pounded lardo. Typical of the province of Trento and the Lake Garda area, in the province of Verona. Trentino-Alto Adige, Veneto.

brigidini di Lamporecchio thin wafer-like confections made of plain flour, eggs, aniseed essence and sugar. The batter is divided into small portions and cooked in a utensil similar to a waffle iron. The resulting wafers, round in shape, orange-yellow in color and curly at the edges, are sold in paper bags or directly at kiosks. Typical of Lamporecchio, in the province of Pistoia. Tuscany.

brillantatura frosting. Coating candied fruit, jellied fruit and candies with sugar to give them an inviting, glossy appearance.

brinare to frost. The technique of brushing small fruits, such as strawberries and grapes, with lightly beaten egg whites, then dipping them in refined sugar.

bringoli aka **brigoli** large spaghetti made of flour, salt, water and, nowadays, eggs. Similar to ➤ **pici senesi** (in Umbria they used the same word to refer to ➤ **umbricelli**). Typical of the province of Arezzo. Tuscany.

brioche soft bread made from a dough of plain flour, butter, eggs, milk qnd yeast, with or without sugar. In some regions, Italianized as ➤ **brioscia**.

brioche rustica soft leavened dough made from flour, Parmigiano and eggs, stuffed with cured meats and cheese, baked in the oven in a ring-shaped mold, then filled with buttered peas or eggplants (➤ **melanzane a fungitielli**). Campania.

brioscia Italianized regional term for ➤ **brioche**.

brisa aka **briza (1)** sour-flavored warm soup of ➤ **batuda** (buttermilk), potatoes, fresh beans and pumpkin, which originated in the Balkans. Friuli-Venezia Giulia.

brisa aka **briza (2)** Trentino and Veneto term for ➤ **porcino**, porcini mushroom.

brisaola da brisa cured meat which differs from ➤ **bresaola della Valtellina** insofar as it is made from different cuts of beef (➤ **sottofesa**, socket, and, ever more rarely, **noce intera (2)**, top surloin), and because it is often smoked before being aged. Traditionally made in the Valchiavenna (Lombardy).

brö brüsà literally "burnt broth". Soup of flour toasted in the oven, mixed with butter and diluted with meat broth, to which boiled beans, stewed mushrooms and pasta may be added. Typical of the Lake Garda area of the province of Trento. Trentino-Alto-Adige.

broàde aka **brovade** turnips fermented for months in wine must, then cut in-

to strips. Usually eaten cooked in lardo and served with boiled sausage (➤ **muset**) or used to flavor soups. Friuli-Venezia Giulia.

broccoletti regional name for the florets of broccoli (➤ **broccolo**) or broccoli rabe (➤ **cime di rapa**).

broccoletti di rapa another name for ➤ **cime di rapa**, broccoli rabe.

broccolo broccoli. A member of the Brassica oleracea species, it comes in two varieties: *cavolo broccolo* (*B. oleracea italica forma caput*) and *cavolo broccolo ramoso* (*B. oleracea italica forma cimosa*). The first has a stumpy stalk, bright green leaves and florest similar to those of a cauliflower. The second is dark green in color with small clusters of florets or flower heads (*broccoletti*) which grow on their own on lateral stems; it is particularly common and popular in Calabria, hence its alternative name of *broccolo calabrese*. The Italian Ministry of Agriculture's database of native and/or traditional food products lists: *broccolo ramoso* aka *broccolo di rapa* (Calabria); *broccolo del Vallo di Diano* (Campania); *broccolo romanesco* (Lazio); *cavolo broccolo* aka *sparacello palermitano* (Sicily); *broccolo di Bassano, fiolaro di Creazzo, broccolo di Torbole e Santa Massenza* (Veneto). Broccoli is widely used in the kitchen. As a side dish, it is boiled or steamed and dressed with oil and lemon juice or vinegar, finished in a skillet (➤ **broccoli affogati**) or cooked in a timbale (➤ **broccolo in crosta**). It is also an important ingredient in many traditional soups and pasta dishes : ➤ **friscatuli**, ➤ **minestra di broccoli alla romana**, ➤ **pancotto**, ➤ **pasta e broccoli in brodo di arzilla**, ➤ **pasta rò malutempu**. It is worth pointing out, however, that terminology is confusing and that in regional recipes the words *broccoli* and *brocco-*

letti may refer to other vegetables. In Sicily *broccolo* means "cauliflower;" in Lazio *broccoletti* and *broccoli* are either "broccoli rabe" or *cavolo broccolo ramoso*, and *cavolbroccolo* or *broccolo romano* mean *broccoletti*. In Naples, *broccoletti* are, botanically speaking, ➤ **cime di rapa** (broccoli rabe), but are universally known as ➤ **friarielli**. Brocoletti are also known as ➤ **sparacelli** (Sicily), ➤ **broccoleit** (Puglia), ➤ **mignluch** (Basilicata).

broccoli affogati broccoletti (➤ **sparacelli**) cut into pieces and cooked in oil with sliced onion and seasoned with salt and pepper. Water is poured into the pan in small quantities until it evaporates. When the vegetables are half-cooked they are splashed with white wine, and when they are ready they are topped with shavings of Pecorino and, sometimes, anchovy fillets and black olives. Specialty of Catania. Sicily.

broccoli strascinati in padella broccoli rabe slow-cooked in oil with garlic cloves and seasoned with salt and pepper and, according to taste, powdered chilli.

broccolo in crosta blanched broccoli hearts, eggs, breadcrumbs, cream and nutmeg baked in a pie. A relatively recent recipe which exploits the beautifully delicate flavor of the *broccolo di Torbole e Santa Massenza*, an ecotype imported to the Lake Garda area of the Trentino from Verona in the 18th century. Trentino-Alto Adige.

broccolo ramoso broccoli (*B. oleracea italica forma cimosa*), ➤ **broccolo**.

brochat cream made by thickening equal parts of sugar, milk and red wine over a low heat. Traditionally spread on rye bread. Val d'Aosta.

brôd Asti variant on ➤ **marzapane (2)**. The mixture is made of fresh blood, milk, chopped onion fried in oil, pig's or calf's brains and raisins soaked in Marsala, aromatized with salt, black pepper, powdered cinnamon and nutmeg. After being cased in an intestine, it is boiled for ten minutes and traditionally served with polenta and onions. Piedmont.

brodera rice cooked in a broth of pork ribs to which pig's blood is added. The meat from the ribs may also be added to the dish. A recipe developed in conjunction with the slaughtering of the pig in the provinces of Vercelli and Novara. Piedmont.

brodeto aka **broeto** terms used in some north Adriatic lagoon areas for ➤ **brodetto**, fish stew.

brodeto de bisato ala valesana lagoon eel cooked with garlic, onion, water and vinegar. Traditional dish of the fishermen of Cavallino, Jesolo and Cortellazzo, in the province of Venice. Veneto.

brodettare literally "to cook with broth," though today the term has come to refer to a meat cooking technique, reminiscent of ➤ **fricassea**, common throughout central Italy, in especial in Lazio, Marche and Umbria. Meat is browned in finely chopped fat and lean ham, onions, salt and pepper, then slow-cooked in wine and water. At the end of the process, a mixture of egg yolks beaten with lemon juice is poured into the pan and allowed to set on a low heat. Baby lamb, rabbit, lamb and kid are all cooked in this way.

brodetto fish soup or stew. A symbol of the fish cuisine of the Adriatic coast from Trieste, in Venezia-Giulia, to Termoli, in Molise (further south, in Puglia fish soups are known as *zuppe* or *guazzetti*). Recipes vary from one place to the next so as to almost tell the story of each single local community. The dish originated among sailors who would cook their meals at sea with part of their catch—

usually fish of poor commercial value or others damaged by the nets—and the few condiments available on board.

brodetti dell'alto Adriatico the fish soups of the northern Adriatic are characterized by the use not only of sea fish but also of fish from the area's lagoons and rivers and by the large number of recipes featuring a single species. Typical of the Venice lagoon and the coast just east of Venice itself is *brodeto de gô*, a soup of gobies (➤ **ghiozzo**), fish which are still caught by hand in the fall and winter. Decapitated, gutted and soused in vinegar, the fish are put in an earthenware pot, cooked in oil with garlic cloves (subsequently removed) and minced flat-leaved parsley and seasoned with salt and pepper. They are then splashed with half a glass of white wine and half a glass of vinegar, covered with water and immered for half an hour before serving. *Boreto a la graisana*, a speciality of Grado, in the province of Gorizia (Friuli-Venezia Giulia) is also made with a single fish: sometimes goby, more often turbot (➤ **rombo**) or gray mullet (➤ **cefalo**). The fish is lightly fried in oil with garlic and cooked for 15-20 minutes in water and vinegar. In another version cuttlefish are cooked for about an hour in the same way with the addition of tomato paste and, sometimes, a little of the mollusk's ink. In another still, different species of fish (monkfish, scorpion fish, gray mullet and so on) are poached in water and vinegar (and, sometimes, white wine) for no longer than half an hour, after which the resulting sauce is thickened with plain or potato flour, if necessary. In Veneto and Friuli-Venezia Giulia, cooking times tend to be briefer than in the middle Adriatic. The *boreto* of Marano Lagunare, in the province of Udine (Friuli), follows the same procedures as Grado's, but the unboned fish is pushed through a sieve. A relative of lagoon soups in terms of flavorings (garlic or onion, parsley, vinegar, white wine) is *brodeto ciosoto* (aka *brodeto a la ciosota*), typical of Chioggia, in the province of Venice. The difference is that it comprises different fish species, preferably scorpionfish, goby, John Dory, small monkfish, gray mullet, English whiting, stargazer, weever and eel. The chief ingredient in the *brodeto polesano* of the Po delta (province of Rovigo) is eel: it and other fish (gobies, gray mullet, gilthead bream and sardines) are cut into pieces and added to pieces of squid in a mixture of lightly fried onion, carrot, celery, garlic and parsley diluted with boiling water and served with fried bread. In lagoon areas the accompaniment to soups is more likely to be polenta. The *brodetto dalmata* (Venezia-Giulia), in which monkfish, conger eel, weever and, in modern versions, crustaceans are lightly fried with garlic and parsley, and cooked in tomato, water and vinegar, is often served with rice. In Trieste, finally, they tend to use very small fish and add fresh tomato to their *brodetto*.

brodetti del medio Adriatico the fish soups of the Middle Adriatic are characterized by the presence of a certain variety of firm-fleshed fish, mollusks (cuttlefish, in particular) and crustaceans (mantis shrimp), though soups made with single varieties (red mullet, for example) do exist. Another common feature is the use of fresh tomato and onion (and, sometimes, garlic). Green peppers, pepper, chili (from San Benedetto del Tronto southwards), saffron (only in Porto Recanati) and vinegar— these are the ingredients that, from Pesaro to Pescara, from San Benedetto del Tronto to Vasto, are mixed and matched in local takes on the *brodetto*. Cooking times vary, but normally range from 45 minutes to two hours. In Fano, for example, they take about 45 minute to cook their simple *brodetto* of onion, garlic, tomatoes and cuttlefish supplemented with varieties such as monkfish, smooth hound, scorpion fish and red mullet. In one Pesaro recipe, white wine vinegar is splashed over fresh tomatoes as they cook and the resulting sauce is poured over fish arranged carefully in a pan without being superimposed. The soup takes half an hour to cook and is served with toasted bread. As is the Ancona version of the dish, in which chili may replace peppers, and tomato passata and paste diluted with water provide the base for cuttlefish and other fish, which are gradually introduced according to size and consistency. Different in color and flavor is the *brodetto* of San Benedetto del Tronto, in which onion, garlic and flat-leaved parsley are joined by green and red tomatoes and yellow and green peppers, a generous amount of vinegar and chili. Southwards into the Abruzzo region, chili is a permanent ingredient, even in the delicate *brodetto* of Giulianova, where they also add a few strips of sweet yellow pepper. Gurnard, weever, smooth hound, and monkfish are the fish varieties that appear most in the soups of Abruzzo, including that of Pescara and → **brodetto vastese**, one of the most famous.

brodetti romagnoli Romagna fish soups. In Romagna the tradition is to add vinegar, black pepper, lightly fried onion and tomato paste to fish stews, though nowadays fresh tomato and aromatic herbs may be used instead. The only crustacean which appears with any frequency is the mantis shrimp and, bar for a handful of clams or mussels, mollusks are conspicuous by their absence. Ingredients that almost always feature are the ones to be found in Rimini's *brodetto riminese*: scorpion fish, gurnard, weever, stargazer, smooth hound, blenny, turbot, red mullet, cuttlefish, *rospetti* (small monkfish), sea eels and mantis shrimp. The latter, together with cuttlefish, are the main ingredient in Ravenna's *brodetto alla ravennate*. Moving north to Ferrara, the eel predominates (→ **brodetto a becco d'asino**).

brodetto a becco d'asino aka **brodetto alla vallante** soup of eel cut into chunks and cooked with onion, tomato preserve, vinegar, lemon zest and water, and served with grilled polenta. Typical of the province of Comacchio, in the province of Ferrara. Emilia-Romagna.

brodetto di seppie e piselli cuttlefish and peas stewed in lightly fried garlic and onion, white wine, tomato and flat-leaved parsley, and served with polenta or toasted bread. A dish made in late spring, when the peas are tender and cuttlefish cluster along the Po delta to spawn. A specialty of the province di Ferrara. Emilia-Romagna.

brodetto pasquale soup of beef or lamb broth thickened with eggs beaten with lemon juice, flavored with marjoram and Parmigiano, and served over slices of toasted bread. Lazio.

brodetto vastese celebrated fish soup typical of Vasto, in the province of Pescara, made with the following varieties (head left on): cod, red mullet, sole, weever, gurnard, gray mullet, octopus or small cuttlefish, conger eel and scorpion fish, plus a small skate and mantis shrimp. The fish are arranged in a broad, low earthenware pot (*tijelle*), according to consistency, and cooked with the lid on for 15-20 minutes with tomatoes, garlic, fresh red pepper, flat-leaved parsley, extra virgin olive oil and salt. Abruzzo.

brodo broth. The cooking liquid of meat, fish or vegetables (➤ **court-bouillon**, ➤ **fumetto**). To produce a rich, tasty broth, meat should be placed in the pan before heating the water so that the nutritional and aromatic substances that it contains go into the water before the heat coagulates them. Consumed on its own (➤ **bevr'in vin**) or as a cooking liquid for risottos, sauces, stews and a base for vegetable and pasta soups (➤ **agnoli**, ➤ **agnolini**, ➤ **anolini**, ➤ **cappelletti**, ➤ **tortellini**), broth plays an important role in regional cooking.

brodo alla sciabicota stew of "poor" fish (shark meat, umbrine, goby etc.), flat-leaved parsley, pepper and olive oil, to which a couple of tablespoons of ➤ **ricotta forte** is added. The broth may be used to cook short pasta or snapped spaghetti. A recipe popular in Brindisi, the name of which derives from a fishing technique (*sciabica*) once common along the Adriatic coast. Puglia.

brodo brustolà literally "toasted broth." Flour toasted in butter or oil and diluted with water. Often flavored with cumin and marjoram, sometimes thickened with eggs and cheese. Friuli-Venezia Giulia.

brodo chinu soup of beaten eggs with grated Pecorino, breadcrumbs and minced parsley mixed into boiling beef broth. A typical Easter recipe. Calabria.

brodo di giuggiole lightly alcoholic syrup made by stewing ➤ **giuggiole** (jujubes), quince, lemon zest, grapes and other fruit in water and sugar, with the addition of red wine. Mainly used as a cake filling. Typical of the Lake Garda area. Lombardy, Veneto.

brodo di pesce fish broth. Made of fish heads, bones and so on, flavored with finely chopped vegetables and cooked in water. After being carefully filtered, the broth is used to cook ➤ **passatelli** or homemade tagliolini. A soup typical of the Romagna Riviera. Emilia-Romagna

brodo di terza term to describe a broth made from three different meats. The classic combination is capon, beef, and lean pork. Used to cook ➤ **cappelletti**, ➤ **tortellini**, and ➤**anolini**. Emilia-Romagna.

brofadei in brodo a Milanese recipe in which flour, eggs, Parmigiano-Reggiano and nutmeg are mixed together, pushed through a potato ricer to make vermicelli-like strings and cooked in meat broth. In the province of Brescia and in Veneto, Parmigiano is replaced by milk and butter, and the mixture is cooked in a skillet and cut into squares. On Lake Garda they use wheat flour and cornflour, in the province of Bergamo (where they call the dishf *sbrofadei*), they use cornflour and cook it in salted milk. Lombardy, Veneto.

bronzino regional name for ➤ **porcino**, porcini mushroom.

Bross aka **Brusso** whitish cheese spread with a strong, tangy flavor. Made by fermenting pieces of different cheeses in earthenware jars, sometimes with the addition of milk. The fermentation is eventually interrupted after about 20 days with a measure of grappa. Eaten with toasted bread or polenta. Piedmont, Lombardy, Liguria.

brossa cream made by mixing whey left over from cheesemaking with ➤ **boné**. Eaten within two or three days of production. Val d'Aosta.

bruciata another term for➤ **caldarrosta**, roast chestnut.

bruciatini fresh diced pancetta browned

in oil and finished with vinegar. Used to garnish salads of mixed leaves. Emilia-Romagna.

bruciuluni large meat roll. A finely chopped mixture of ground beef, beaten eggs, breadcrumbs, grated Pecorino, shavings of → **Ragusano** cheese, carrot, rosemary, parsley, nutmeg, salt and pepper and, sometimes, a few chopped hard-boiled eggs is spread over large slice of fillet of beef, which is rolled up and secured with kitchen string. The roll is splashed with white wine, which is allowed to evaporate, covered with water and tomato paste and cooked in the oven. The dish is also known as → **falsomagro** (in dialect **farsumagru** aka **farsumauru**). Sicily.

brugnolusos de arrescottu walnut-sized balls of soft ewe's ricotta cream or grated fresh Pecorino, sugar, eggs, durum grain semolina, grated orange zest, grappa (→ **filo e ferru**), vanilla, saffron fried in olive oil. Sardinia.

brunello another name for → **russola**, russula mushroom.

Bruno Alpina Alpine brown. German-Swiss cattle breed which originated from the Caucasian *Bos brachyceros* and spread throughout Europe, even south of the Alps, in the mid 19th century. It has a uniform brown coat and a darker muzzle. A mainly dairy cow, it is also used for beef production. In the last few decades, it has suffered the aggressive competition of the more productive Friesian.

brunoise a cutting technique (→ **tagliare**).

brusa Veneto term for a gridiron, grill or griddle.

brusarol balls of firm polenta filled with mountain cheese and broiled. Typical of the Valli Ossolane. Piedmont.

bruscandoli regional term for → **luppolo**, hops.

bruscansi regional term for → **pungitopo**, butcher's broom.

bruscare regional term for → **abbrustolire**, to toast.

brüsch Piedmontese adjective for *acido*, "sour," used to refer to dishes that include vinegar among their ingredients. Often Italianized as *brusco*.

bruschetta a slice of toasted bread dressed with garlic, salt and oil. Today the range of possible ingredients has been extended to include chopped tomatoes, sautéed mushrooms, black truffle and so on.

bruscitt stew of finely chopped or ground meat first browned in butter and lardo with fennel seeds, then finished in red wine and served with polenta flavored with garlic or potato purée. A traditional dish of the area north of Milan and the province of Varese, it is also to be found in the province of Novara, where it is made using horsemeat. Lombardy, Piedmont.

brusco regional term for → **pungitopo**, butcher's broom.

bruscolini salted pumpkin seeds (→ **semi e legumi tostati**, toasted seeds and legumes).

brusso Italianization of → **bruzzu**, fermented sheep's ricotta.

brustengo (1) name used in the area round Gubbio, in the province of Perugia, for → **arvoltolo**, a fried pastry.

brustengo (2) another Umbrian name for → **bustrengolo**, a cake.

brustico term to describe a way of cooking fish on the shores of Lake Trasimeno, where fishermen used to barbecue tench and pike over a fire of lake rushes and dress them with oil and vinegar. Umbria.

brusto a blood pudding which used to made in the Trentino countryside on the day of the killing of the pig. The tradition was revived in the 1960s in the form of a mixture of pig's or, sometimes, cow's blood, milk and flour, and perfumed with summer savory (➤ **santoreggia**) and other herbs and spices. The mixture is heated, cased in natural intestines and tied to form sausages, which are immersed for half an hour in boiling water. After cooling, the sausages are ready to be eaten as they are or broiled.

brustolini salted pumpkin seeds (➤ **semi e legumi tostati**, toasted seeds and legumes).

brut e bon Piedmontese expression for ➤ **brutti e buoni**, dry cookies.

brutti boni Tuscan expression for ➤ **brutti e buoni**, dry cookies.

brutti e buoni literally "ugly but good." Dry cookies named for their irregular shape. Born in Piedmont (where they are known as ➤ **brut e bon**), they are produced virtually everywhere in the region, especially in Borgomanero, in the province of Novara. They spread to Tuscany (➤ **brutti boni**), especially to Prato and Pistoia, thanks to the arrival of Piedmontese pastry chefs when the capital of Italy was transferred from Turin to Florence. The Piedmontese recipe envisages a mixture of almonds and/or hazelnuts, sugar, egg white and vanilla, and some versions are aromatized with cinnamon or cocoa. The mixture is cooked in a pan on a low heat, then subdivided into small "lumps," which are baked on a hot plate. In Tuscany, small portions of a mixture of chopped almonds, plain flour, eggs and sugar are baked directly in the oven. A version also exists in Lazio (➤ **brutti ma buoni**) made with eggs, sugar, hazelnuts and chopped bitter almonds.

brutti ma buoni Lazio name for ➤ **brutti e buoni**.

bruzzu aka **brusso** dairy product made with sheep's milk ricotta fermented in wood barrels. Creamy in texture with a sharp flavor, it is eaten with polenta or spread on toast. Used in the filling of ➤ **barbagiuai**, fried ravioli, and ➤ **sanguinelli ripieni**, stuffed saffron milk-cap mushrooms. Typical of the mountain valleys on the border between Piedmont and Liguria.

buatto Marche term for **ghiozzo**, goby.

bubbola maggiore another name for ➤ **mazza di tamburo**, parasol mushroom.

bubbolini regional name for ➤ **silene rigonfia**, bladder campion.

bucatini dried durum wheat, hollow, spaghetti-like pasta of Neapolitan origin, now common in Lazio. Served with rich sauces made of butter, eggs, pancetta, vegetables and cheese (➤ **amatriciana, alla**). Also known as ➤ **perciatellini**.

bucatini con i broccoli arriminati bucatini with a sauce of cauliflower, lightly fried onion, anchovies, raisins, pine kernels, tomato paste and chili, sprinkled with toasted breadcrumbs. Sicily.

bucatini con la mollica bucatini dressed first with breadcrumbs toasted in olive oil, then anchovies dissolved in oil and a sprinkling of black pepper. In some places, anchovies, olives and capers are also added. A dish traditionally made on Christmas Eve. Calabria.

buccellato calabrese another name for ➤ **muccellato**, an Easter cake.

buccellato di Serra San Bruno baked ring-shaped cake made of flour and natural yeast. Produced in the province of Vibo Valentia. Calabria.

buccellato siciliano Christmas cake made in different shapes and sizes. The pastry is made by rolling out a dough of flour, butter, sugar and Marsala. The filling consists of a mixture of chopped dried figs and/or walnuts, almonds and pine kernels, raisins, orange zest, chocolate shavings, candied pumpkin (➤ **zuccata**), cinnamon, cloves, sugar and pepper. The filling is spread over the dough, which is usually rolled up and joined at the ends to form a ring. Small incisions are made in the surface, which is brushed with egg yolk. After baking in the oven, the cake is decorated with candied fruit and chopped pistachio nuts. Sicily.

buccellato toscano cake made from a mixture of flour, water, milk, sugar, butter, anise seeds, zibibbo grapes, yeast and, sometimes, grated orange or lemon zest, candied citron and Marsala, hand-shaped and allowed to leaven before being brushed with egg yolk and baked in the oven. Either loaf- or ring-shaped, the cake comes in different sizes. Fresh from the oven, it is soft and fragrant and is commonly eaten dunked in milk. It can also be left for a few days and twice-baked. The cake originated in the province of Lucca, but is now common all over the north of Tuscany. A variant exists in La Spezia with pine kernels and walnuts instead of candied fruit. Tuscany, Liguria.

buccuna Sicilian term for sea snail (➤ **lumaca di mare**).

buccuni (1) Sicilian and Sardinian specialty of rock snails (➤ **murice**) boiled in ➤ **court-bouillon** aromatized with thyme and bay leaf, allowed to cool, removed from their shells and served cold, dressed with extra virgin olive oil and lemon. In Sicily also known as ➤ **vuccuni**. Sicily, Sardinia.

buccuni (2) Calabrian term for stargazer (➤ **pesce prete**, ➤ **pesce lucerna**).

Buchteln balls of leavened dough, baked in the oven, filled with fruit jam, vanilla cream or ricotta. Trentino-Alto Adige, Friuli-Venezia Giulia.

Buchweizentorte regional term for ➤ **torta di grano saraceno**, buckwheat cake.

bùdego aka **budegasso** Ligurian term for ➤ **rana pescatrice**, monkfish.

budella intestines. Bovine intestines may only be used to case cured meat if they come from animals in countries unaffected by BSE.

budelletti di stoccafisso stockfish tripe. The dried intestines of the preserved fish stewed in white wine, *taggiasca* olives and chopped potatoes. A hard dish to find these days. Liguria.

budelli salati aka **budellacci** pig's intestines washed and flavored with salt, chilli and wild fennel seeds, rolled and left to dry, traditionally smoked in the fireplace. They are then stewed with beans or broiled. In the past, a non-aromatized, more smoked version was made to be broiled and dressed with extra virgin olive oil. Umbria.

budellina pig's or sheep's small intestine used to case cured meats with a narrow diameter.

budelline agnellate the name derives from a method used to stew lamb (*agnello* in Italian). Lamb's intestines cooked with chopped herbs (or garlic, onion and chili) and skinned, puréed tomatoes. Still to be found on the stalls of tripe-sellers (➤ **trippaio**) in Florence. Tuscany.

budello artificiale artificial casing (usually made of textile fibers, synthetic materials or animal skins) used instead of animal intestines.

budello cieco pork butcher's term for caecum intestine.

budello culare another name for ➤ **budello gentile**, large intestine.

budello diritto aka **budello dritto** name used by pork butchers for a pig's colon.

budello gentile cow's or pig's large intestine. Used whole as a casing, it endows cured meats with a characteristic pear shape. Its exceptionally fatty walls keep the meat mixture soft even after long aging.

budello grasso di vitello ripieno a pig's caecum intestine (➤ **budello pappone**) washed with warm water, dried and filled with a soft, smooth mixture of beaten eggs, grated Pecorino, chopped boiled potatoes, diced pancetta (or prosciutto) and sausage, wild fennel seeds, chopped tomatoes, salt and pepper. Secured with string at both ends, it is either boiled or, albeit rarely, fried in boiling oil. Recipe typical of the Madonie mountains. Sicily

budello pappone old Sicilian term for the pig's large intestine.

budello torto small intestine, used wholly or in part to case cured meats.

budino cream dessert. The name of a series of soft desserts, etymologically related to the English "pudding" and the French *boudin*, which, in turn, derive from the Latin *botellus*, intestine. (➤ **budello**) perhaps because **budino** started out life as an aromatized blood sausage. In Italian regional cookery today, it consists of a mixture of milk and sugar bound with all-purpose flour, potato flour, semolina, rice, eggs or isinglass, and flavored with ingredients such as fresh or dried fruits, custards, bread and cookies: eg, vanilla and nougat in Piedmont, pumpkin in the province of Mantua, plums and red wine in Trentino, walnuts in Friuli. Poured into a greased mold dusted with flour, breadcrumbs or crushed cookies, the mixture is either baked in the oven or cooked in a bain-marie (➤ **bagnomaria**). It may be served warm or cold, on its own or accompanied by a sweet sauce.

budino di albicocche apricot dessert. The apricots are stoned, stewed slowly with sugar, rum, Moscato d'Asti, cinnamon and vanilla to form a purée, blended with eggs, crushed amaretti cookies, sugar, rum and Fernet, poured into a mold lined with caramel and baked in the oven in a bain-marie. Piedmont.

budino di avena a cream of milk, eggs, sugar and toasted and boiled oats, thickened over the heat, then left to set in the refrigerator. Friuli-Venezia Giulia.

budino di carne alla ligure potted meat. Chopped cooked veal and raw ham mixed with béchamel sauce, eggs and nutmeg, pressed into a mold and left to set in the refrigerator. Liguria.

budino di castagne chestnut dessert. Various versions exist in the north of Italy. In Piedmont, they cook a mixture of milk, dried chestnuts or chestnut flour, sugar, cocoa and, sometimes, eggs in a bain-marie. In Trentino, they blend boiled chestnuts, sugar, dark chocolate, melted butter and crushed almonds and allow the mixture to set in the refrigerator. In Veneto, more simply, they purée the boiled, sugared chestnuts and serve them with chocolate melted in milk.

budino di lemon lemon dessert. The name refers to two very different confections. The first is an old Ferrara recipe in which lemon juice, sugar, beaten eggs and alkermes (➤ **alchermes**) are cooked in a bain-marie, allowed to cool and served cold. The second, typical of Trentino-Alto Adige, is made by incorporating sugar, eggs, chopped almonds and grappa to boiled and puréed lemons, and baking the resulting mixture in the oven. Emilia-Romagna, Trentino-Alto Adige.

budino di mosto dessert of croatina grape must cooked with all-purpose flour and, if necessary, sugar to the consistency of thick chocolate. Typical of the Oltrepò Pavese area (province of Pavia), it is a close relative of Lombard ➤ **suc** and Emilian ➤ **sughi**. Lombardy.

budino di pane bread dessert. To a ➤ **panada** (breadcrumbs or roughly torn pieces of bread heated in milk) are added sugar, egg yolks, egg whites whipped to a peak, chopped almonds and grated lemon zest or, more traditionally, cinnamon and nutmeg, and the resulting mixture is cooked in a bain-marie (➤ **bagnomaria**). A Friulian versions involves baking a mixture of bread soaked in milk and squeezed dry, sugar, eggs, grated apples, pine kernels and raisins. Emilia-Romagna, Friuli-Venezia Giulia.

budino di potatoes potato mold. Boiled puréed potatoes mixed with egg whites whipped to a peak, softened butter, salt and pepper and baked in the oven. A sweet version also exists in which cream, sugar, pine kernels and raisins are added to the purée. Friuli-Venezia Giulia.

budino di puina a Venetian variant on ➤ **budino di semolina**, semolina dessert.

budino di ricotta ricotta dessert. Local ewe's milk ricotta mixed with eggs, all-purpose flour, sugar, powdered cinnamon, candied citron, grated lemon zest and rum, slow-baked in the oven and dusted with sugar and cinnamon. Lazio.

budino di riso semifino rice cooked in milk with butter and sugar and left to cool. Egg yolks, egg whites whipped to a peak, orange zest, raisins, candied citron and rum are then added, and the mixture is cooked in the oven in a bain-marie. Friuli-Venezia Giulia.

budino di semolino semolina dessert. Semolina boiled in milk mixed with vanilla, sugar, egg whites whisked to a peak, crushed almonds and sponge cake soaked in rum, then cooked in the oven in a bain-marie (➤ **bagnomaria**). In a richer version, butter, candied fruits, raisins and pine kernels are added to the mixture. More typically Venetian is ➤ **budino di puina**, which consists of an oven-baked mixture of semolina thickened in boiling milk, ricotta, egg whites whisked to a peak, feverfew (➤ **maresina**) and lemon zest. Veneto, Friuli-Venezia Giulia.

bue ox. Castrated male of the *Bos Taurus* species. A draught animal, in the past it was the main source of energy for work in the fields. Today it is raised in small numbers in small areas of Italy (the Langhe and Monferrato districts of Piedmont, the Tuscan Maremma) exclusively for its beef. To the so-called fattened ox (*bue grasso*) are dedicated traditional pre-Christmas fairs in Carrù, in the province of Cuneo, and Moncalvo, in the province of Asti (Piedmont) and the animal's meat is much prized, especially for boiling and braising. Legally, insofar as it is slaughtered at an age of no younger than four years, the ox is considered an adult bovine. Its prolonged fattening is expensive but, carried out correctly, it ensures exceptionally sapid meat. The *bue di Carrù* is listed in the Italian Ministry of Agriculture's database of native and/or traditional food products.

bue rosso the ox of the ➤ **sardo modicana** cattle breed.

bufalo buffalo (*Bubalus bubalis*). Domesticated in India, it possibly arrived in southern Europe in Roman times and is now raised in a number of countries as a draught-animal—especially in the rice fields of Asia—but also for its milk and meat. In Italy, the western country with most buffaloes, herds are concentrated mainly on the plains of the provinces of Salerno, Caserta, Latina and Frosinone, where the milk is used chiefly to produce ➤ **mozzarella**. The consumption of buffalo meat, suitable for the same recipes as beef and veal, is limited in Italy, despite a recent trend to relaunch it (with the production of cured meats, for example). The meat of buffaloes raised in Campania and that of the female raised in Amaseno, in the province of Frosinone (Lazio) are listed in the Italian Ministry of Agriculture's database of native and/or traditional food products. Lazio, Campania.

buffa cured meat named for its shape, which vaguely resembles a frog (*buffa* in Sicilian dialect). The mixture is obtained by macerating pork shoulder, leg and pancetta in a mixture of spices, for a few hours, grinding and mixing the meats and casing them in a pig's large intestine (➤ **budello pappone**). The meat is dried for 15-20 days and aged for two months. Typical of Castelbuono (Palermo), this delicacy is now produced by a single pork butcher. Sicily.

buffet a gastronomic institution in Trieste (Venezia-Giulia). A trattoria specialized in cuts of pork boiled in cauldrons: ➤ **cotechino**, ➤ **zampone**, ➤ **pancetta**, corned tongue, ➤ **würstel**, smoked pork loin (which the locals call ➤ **Kaiserfleisch**) and ➤ **porcina** (aka **porzina**), a shoulder or head cut. Sometimes pig's head and trotters are also served. The meat is invariably accompanied by ➤ **crauti** (sauerkraut), mustard and grated horseradish (➤ **cren**). Today other dishes, such as hot boiled ham, fried fish, stockfish and ➤ **jota** soup are also on offer.

buffetta a sort of ➤ **chisola** (flatbread) to which grapes are added during the wine harvest. A traditional Mantuan recipe. Lombardy.

buffulitu small round or triangular ➤ **panforte** made with all-purpose flour, yeast, sugar, walnuts, hazelnuts, orange zest, wild fennel seeds, raisins, milk, honey and vanilla. The mixture is slow-baked and decorated with a thin veil of honey over which walnuts, hazelnuts and confetti sugar (➤ **traggera**) are scattered. Sardinia.

buga Ligurian word for ➤ **boga**, bogue.

bughe a scabeccio marinated bogues (➤ **scapece**). The fish are fried in oil, marinated in vinegar and white wine, and flavored with garlic, shallot or onion, sage and bay leaf. Some recipe also call for raisins. Liguria.

bugie regional name for fried pastries equivalent to ➤ **cenci**.

buglione Tuscan term for the long, slow stewing of meat, perfumed with aromatic herbs, which is then served on toasted bread. The method originates from the old peasant tradition of boiling together the feudal lord's leftover scraps of meat (rabbit, chicken, pig's trotters, tripe, kid, goose). Today the dish is normally made with a single type of meat (➤ **agnello in buglione**). Vegetable versions also exist, reminiscent of ➤ **ratatuia**.

buglossa regional name for ➤ **echio**, viper's bugloss.

bugnoletti di patate sweet potato fritters. A mixture of boiled potatoes, all-purpose flour, yeast, eggs, refined sugar and grated lemon zest, shaped into rounds, fried in oil and dusted with confectioner's sugar. Sardinia.

buiadnik aka **buiarnik** leavened cake of cornflour and wheat flour, eggs, sugar, cream, fresh fruit, fennel seeds and cinnamon, cooked on a hotplate. Typical of the Valle di Resia, in the province of Udine, where it used to be cooked in the hearth wrapped in cabbage leaves. Friuli-Venezia Giulia.

buida lumps of cold polenta boiled for a few minues in salted milk. Specialty of the province of Bergamo. Lombardy.

bukë giant loaf made from a dough of durum wheat semolina, water, salt and natural and/or brewer's yeast. The crust, sprinkled with sesame seeds (➤ **sesamo**), is crunchy, and the crumb is compact with tiny eyes. Baked in Santa Cristina Gela and Piana degli Albanesi (province of Palermo). Sicily.

bulasi Ligurian term for ➤ **rossetto**, transparent goby.

bulbo castano another word for ➤ **casciomaci**, pignut.

bulide Friulian term for "boiled." Used to refer to two restorative drinks, one similar to ➤ **vin brulé** (mulled wine), the other a sort of ➤ **zabaglione** made with egg yolks, honey, milk and wine. Friuli.

bummalitt' Abruzzo term for sea snail (➤ **lumaca di mare**). **bunettu** Ligurian dialect term for ➤ **budino** (note the linguistic affinity with the Piedmontese dialect ➤ **bonet**). Usually made with milk, eggs, sugar and baked in the oven (*bunettu de laete*). Sometimes flavored with lemon zest, caramel or cocoa.

buon enrico or **buonenrico** good King Henry (*Chenopodium bonus-Henricus*), also known as poor-man's asparagus, perennial goosefoot, Lincolnshire spinach or markery. A spontaneous herb with a long stem that grows in mountain areas. The leaves and tops are used in the kitchen before flowering: boiled and buttered, in omelets and focaccias, and as an ingredient in fillings. Very popular in Abruzzo (➤ **orapa**) where whole recipes and festivals are dedicated to it. Common and regional names: ➤ **colubrina**, ➤ **erba sana**, ➤ **farinello**, ➤ **spinacio di montagna**, ➤ **spinacio selvatico**, ➤ **tutta buona**.

buranella, alla name applied, in the Venice lagoon, to pasta dishes dressed with fish and béchamel sauces. Veneto.

buranelli cookies with a similar shape to ➤ **esse**, but not grooved or coated with sugar. Typical of Burano, an island in the Venice lagoon. The dough is made of flour, egg yolks, butter, sugar, powdered vanilla, salt and grated lemon zest. Veneto.

burda a soup of rice and beans cooked in chicken broth and thickened with cornflour. It is served with extra virgin olive oil, pepper and grated Grana Padano grattugiato. The dialect name means "mist" and refers to the appearance the soup assumes when the flour is poured in. Typical of Crema, in the province of Cremona. Lombardy.

buricco a large raviolo filled with cooked chicken, bread soaked in broth and eggs. The ingredients and the fat used in the pasta dough (veal or goose) evoke the Jewish tradition, strong in Ferrara and Reggio. Emilia-Romagna

buridda today the term refers to a soup of fish cut into pieces, stewed with herbs, tomato, white wine and a mixture of chopped anchovies, dried mushrooms and walnuts, served with slices of toasted bread. According to old recipes, the soup was made with stockfish and diced potatoes. In the Savona area, tomato is omitted and aromatic vegetables, capers and taggiasca olives added. Liguria.

buridda, a term for a method of of stewing fresh fish, cuttlefish, squid or stockfish cut into pieces. Liguria.

burischio another name for ➤ **buristo senese**, a cured meat.

buristo senese cured meat typical of the Chianti area of the province of Siena, produced from November to March. The meat from a pig's head is coarsely ground with pork rind and mixed with fried lardons of fat and filtered pig's blood. The mixture is cured with salt, pepper, lemon zest, parsley, garlic, pine kernels ad raisins, and is cased, still warm, in the pig's stomach. The meat is conserved for no more than ten days and is normally eaten sliced, lightly fried and finished in wine. Tuscany.

Burlina, razza a cattle breed brought to Veneto by drivers from Morlakia, in the Balkans or, according to a second hypothesis, by German speaking peoples of Cambric stock. Only about 300 head of the breed (small- to medium-sized cows with black and white spotted coats) survive today, and a Slow Food presidium has been set up to protect ➤ **Morlacco del Grappa** cheese, traditionally made from their milk. Veneto.

buro Veneto term for ➤ **murice**, a sea snail.

burrata stretched curd cow's milk cheese envelope filled with strings of stretched curd and whey. Puglia.

burrida traditional marinade used to dress fish of the shark family (especially ➤ **gattuccio**, lesser spotted dogfish) and skate (➤ **razza**). The fish is boiled in water aromatized with onion, carrots, celery, parsley and lemon, allowed to cool and covered with a sauce of garlic lightly fried in olive oil, white wine vinegar and crushed walnuts or pine kernels. Traditionally, the preparation should contain the lesser spotted dogfish's liver, by many considered to be toxic. A specialty of Cagliari. Sardinia.

burrielli another name for ➤ **bocconcini di cardinale**, small mozzarellas.

Burrino cheese with an outer layer of soft spring cheese and an inside layer of butter from the whey. The most prized version is made with milk from the Podolica cow. Basilicata

Burrino di bufala type of ➤ **burrino** made with buffalo's milk. May be smoked, and must be eaten within eight days of production. Campania.

burro butter. A fat made by churning milk (a "churn" is *zangola* in Italian) and its natural cream. Historically, butter has been widely used in the northern areas of Europe. Whereas the Romans did not eat it but used it exclusively as an ointment or unguent, it was an essential ingredient in the diet of the Gauls, Longobards, Goths and Normans. Until the Middle Ages and the assertion of Christian doctrine and its dietary rules (including the imposition of many days in which it was necessary to abstain from meat), butter and lardo had been the prerogative of "barbarian" nomads and herders. At a certain point, the Church classified butter as a non-meat food, suitable for consumption on days of abstinence. Today, after centuries of migration and exchange, the Po Valley is recognizable as an appendix of the butter culture of northwest Europe in contrast to the oil culture of the Mediterranean. Most of the butter sold today is centrifuged from pasteurized creams. Naturally churned butter made from raw milk is more aromatic but, unless properly refrigerated, tends to go rancid quickly. In the Trentino area, an excellent butter, ➤ **botìro di malga di Primiero**, is protected by a Slow Food presidium.

burro aromatizzato aka **burro composto** aromatized butter. Butter into which herbs such as tarragon and parsley, garlic or anchovy fillets have been blended. If the aromatization takes place on the heat with vinegar and shallot, the result is known as *burro bianco* (*beurre blanc*). Aromatized butter is used to accompany broiled meat and fish.

burro chiarificato clarified butter is made by melting butter in a bain-marie (➤ **bagnomaria**) to get rid of the casein and water and make the fat more suitable for frying and keeping. Clarified butter has the color and consistency of a pale oil and can be easily separated using a strainer and a damp gauze. It may be stored in glass jars.

burro composto another term for ➤ **butter aromatizzato**, aromatized butter.

burro di cacao cocoa butter. Fat extracted by pressing ground cocoa (➤ **cacao**) beans. It is used to enrich chocolate (➤ **cioccolato**).

burro maneggiato *beurre manié*. Blend of flour and butter in equal parts, used to thicken sauces and gravies.

burro rosso, nocciola, nero red, hazel, black butter. As butter cooks, it changes color, from red to hazel (at this stage it is used to fry ➤ **cotoletta alla milanese** and ➤ **cotoletta alla bolognese**), to black (at this stage it is used as a condiment: eg, in *razza al burronero*, skate in black butter).

burtlèina fritter made from a fluid batter of flour, water (or milk) and eggs fried in lard or oil. Traditionally made with the leftovers from soups and risottos, in some areas (the Val Tidone and Val Luretta) it is now flavored with spring onions. Served with cured meats, like ➤ **crescentina fritta** (➤ **gnocco fritto** in Bologna and Modena, **torta fritta** in Parma, **pinzin** in Ferrara), of which it is the Piacenza equivalent. Emilia-Romagna.

burzill Basilicata dialect term for ➤ **borzillo**, cured wild boar meat.

busara, alla aka **alla buzara**, **alla busera** method of Istrian origin for cooking scampi and other crustaceans, but also fish such as scorpion fish, in a strong-flavored, fiery sauce. In ancient Venetian dialect, *busara* meant "tangle" or "concoction", though some believe it also meant the covered pot in which fishermen cooked meals on board their boats. Many recipes are described as **alla busara**: their common denominators are a ➤ **soffritto** of garlic or garlic and onion, the pouring in of wine and sprinkling

with dried breadcrumbs and paprika or chili. In Trieste, **alla busara** refers to fish stewed with tomato. Veneto, Friuli-Venezia Giulia.

busbana fish similar to ➤ **merlano**, English whiting.

busecca aka **pancia** aka **trippa liscia** regional name (Lombardy, Piedmont) for rumen (➤ **rumine**). Nowadays the term commonly refers to tripe in general, and also to a traditional soup in which it is an ingredient (➤ **biseca**, ➤ **buseca**).

buseca winter soup of veal or beef tripe (➤ **trippa**) cut into strips, butter, onion, chopped lardo, sage or bay leaf, carrots and celery, all slowly cooked in beef broth, and seasoned with salt. Served poured over toasted bread sprinkled with grated Parmigiano-Reggiano. A specialty of Milan. Lombardy.

busecca matta aka **trippa finta** very thin frittatas rolled up and finely sliced, heated in butter with onion, sage and pancetta, and subsequently flavored with tomato salsa or paste. The final appearance of the dish is reminiscent of ➤ **busecca**. Lombardy.

busecca matta in brodo soup made by replacing ➤ **busecca** with Savoy cabbage and served with breads made with various types of flours. In the Milan area, frog meat and livers are sometimes added. Lombardy.

busecchin mixture of pig's blood, cream, butter, Grana Padano, onions and spices, boiled and spread on bread. Lombardy.

busecchina cake made by boiling dried chestnuts in water aromatized with fennel seeds, peeling them and boiling them a second time in dry white wine and sugar, sometimes mixed with milk. Typical of Milan. Lombardy.

busella bread loaf with a curiously flat, rolled up appearance made with ➤

strong flour, all-purpose flour, water, yeast, salt and lard.

busiate aka **busiati** fresh durum wheat pasta (→ **bucatini**) typical of the province of Trapani, but common all over Sicily. The name derives from *busa*, the dried reed once used to shape the pasta, now replaced by a darning needle.

buslan aka **bussolan** aka **buzilan** Piacenza dialect names for → **bossolano**. A type of ring cake.

buslanein simple ring-shaped cookies, plunged into boiling water, coated in flour and baked. Traditionally presented to candidates for confirmation or sold at fairs, though now rare. Typical of the province di Piacenza. Emilia-Romagna.

busolà aka **bussolà** aka **buzolà** Vicenza dialect names for → **bossolano**, a type of ring cake. Veneto.

bussolai aka **buzolai** ring-shaped pastries made from a leavened dough of flour, butter, sugar, white wine or grappa and lemon zest, and baked in the oven. As in the case of → **buslanein** (Piacenza) and → **colaz** (Friuli), a necklace of **bussolai** was what a godfather gave as a present to a candidate for confirmation. The custom was typical of the island of Burano, in the province of Venice, and in the city of Trieste. Veneto, Friuli-Venezia Giulia.

bussolano dialect term for → **bossolano**, a type of ring cake.

busto commercial term for the front quarter of a calf or sheep, as well as for poultry without head and legs.

bustrengh a rich cake made of many ingredients, among which all-purpose and cornflour, honey, dried fruit, raisins, citrus fruit zest and wine. A traditional specialty of the village of Borghi in the province of Forlì-Cesena, where a festival is held in its honor. Emilia-Romagna.

bustrengolo aka **pan giallo** sweet baked bread made from a dough of corn flour mixed with water, or milk, flavored with grated lemon zest, pine kernels, walnuts, raisins, *mistrà* (anise liqueur), wild fennel, sugar and apple slices. It used to be made only in the fall, but is now available all year round. In alternative recipes it is cooked in extra virgin olive oil or melted lard. Umbria.

Butirro type of → **Burrino**, a cheese. Calabria.

butoon de pajaas literally "clown's button." Stew made with pork sausages cut into rounds like buttons. Served with toasted polenta. Lombardy.

buttariga another name for → **bottarga**, botargo.

buzzega bean, potato and lardo soup, typical of Pesaro. Marche.

buzzillan another name for → **ciambella**, a ring-shaped cake.

buzzonaglia meat from the darkest parts— the least prized but also the tastiest—and the innards of tuna or other fish, such as grouper. Preserved in oil and often used in southern Italy, Sicily in particular, to dress pasta dishes.

cC

Cabannina mainly dairy cattle breed native to Cabanne, a hamlet near the village of Rezzoaglio in the Val d'Aveto, in the province of Genoa. It has a brown coat with a long pale stripe down the back. No more than 300 head survive today, hence fears that the breed is on the verge of extinction. Liguria.

cabbucio bread roll typical of the province of Trapani. The dough is made by kneading durum wheat flour, cake flour, water, full-cream milk, oregano, aniseed, brewer's yeast and salt, then divided into rolls. After baking, the rolls are cut in half and filled with rinsed and boned anchovies, tomato slices, mature Pecorino, salt, pepper, oil and oregano. Sicily.

cac north-eastern dialect term for → **pesce lucerna**, stargazer.

cac' e ova Abruzzo dialect term to describe dishes finished off with eggs and grated Pecorino. The best known is → **agnello cac' e ova**.

cacao cocoa (*Theobroma cacao*). A tree of the Sterculiacee family common in Amazzonia and cultivated mainly in Central and South America and in Africa (especially the Ivory Coast, Togo, Nigeria and Ghana), where its berries are used to make → **cioccolato**, chocolate. The tree produces pod-like berries full of a sour pulp dotted with bitter seeds or beans. Fermented, dried, toasted and ground, the beans produce cocoa liquor from which cocoa butter is separated by pressing. The residue from the operation, known as cocoa solids, is processed into cocoa powder. It was Hernan Cortés who brought cocoa beans to Europe from Mexico and Central America, and they were used to prepare a chocolate drink that was much appreciated for its restorative and energy-giving properties. The three main varieties of cocoa are: *criollo*, *forastero* and *trinitario*. *Criollo* was how the conquistadors called the cocoa produced by the Aztecs. *Forastero* was the name given by Central American peasants to cocoa from the Amazon basin, now cultivated in Brazil, Venezuela and Ecuador, as well as in Asia, in Java and Sri Lanka. *Trinitario* is probably a hybrid of a *criollo* from Trinidad and *forastero*. The continent where most coffee is grown is Africa : the principal producing countries are the Ivory Coast, Togo, Nigeria and Ghana.

cacca del Bambino literally "Baby's shit." Christmas soup made with capon broth, chopped chicken livers, day-old bread, saffron and Parmesan. Once cooked, the soup is removed from heat and well beaten eggs are stirred into it. The recipe originated in the province of Alessandria and signifies devotion to the Baby Jesus. Piedmont.

cacchi another word for → **ciambelle zagarolesi**, ring-shaped cookies.

cacchiatella name given to small loaves of → **pane di Velletri** joined together. Lazio.

caccia 'nnanza thicker Ascoli Piceno variation of → **crescia maceratese**. The name, which means "put in first," derives from the fact that the → **crescia** was and is baked in a wood oven before the bread as a way of testing the temperature. Marche.

cacciagione game. Generic term often used as a synonym of → **selvaggina**.

caccialepre another name for → **grattalingua**, common brighteyes.

cacciatora, alla name of a cooking method that encompasses diverse recipes and ingredients. It refers generally to dishes with simple, robust flavors, usually involving chicken or rabbit, sometimes lamb. Northern Italian variations tend to include tomato, onion and lardo or pancetta and, sometimes, mushrooms. Central Italian versions feature garlic, rosemary and vinegar.

cacciatorino another name for → **salamino italiano alla cacciatore**, small pork salami.

cacciatorino di cavallo small salami made of scraps of horsemeat from the leg or breast of the animal, plus 30% pancetta and lardo. The mixture is seasoned with salt and pepper, flavored with spices and piped into pig's intestines. After resting for 24 hours, salamis are aged for 15-20 days. Typical of the Valchiavenna and Valtellina. Lombardy.

cacciucco alla livornese fish stew typical of Livorno but common, with variations, all along the Tuscan coast. The Livorno recipe uses bony fish (scorpion fish, smooth hound, cappone, gurnard), mollusks (cuttlefish, octopus, mussels and clams), crustaceans (mantis shrimp, nowadays also prawns, shrimps and scampi), tomato paste, garlic, sage, chili, salt and white (or young red) wine. It is served with slices of bread, rubbed with garlic and toasted. In Viareggio, in the province of Lucca, they use less chili and add other fish, such as mullet and monkfish, as well as finely chopped aromatics (onion, celery, carrot). The original meaning of the word *caciucco* was probably "mixture." Tuscany.

cacciucco di ceci chickpea and chard soup cooked in an earthenware pot with the addition of finely chopped onion, garlic and salted anchovies dissolved in olive oil. Served on sliced toast sprinkled with grated Pecorino. Tuscany.

cacciucco di funghi mushroom stew typical of the hills inland from Livorno. Mixed mushrooms are cut into pieces and gently fried in oil with garlic and chili. Broth and chopped tomatoes are then added and the stew is cooked through and served on slices of toasted bread rubbed with garlic. The dish's only connection with the famous Livornese fish stew is through the original meaning of the word *cacciucco*, "mixture." Tuscany.

Cachat milk and goat's cheese spread flavored with juniper liqueur (and sometimes leeks), similar to → **Bross**. Typical of the Valle Stura, in the province of Cuneo. Piedmont.

cacigno Abruzzo name for → **grespigno**, field sowthistle.

cacio all'argentiera warm antipasto consisting of thin slices of Caciocavallo cheese melted in a pan with garlic and oil, flavored with vinegar and dusted with pepper and oregano. Typical of the, Madonie mountains, in the province of Palermo. Sicily.

cacio e pepe "cheese and pepper." Condiment for pasta obtained by shaking the pasta (generally → **tonnarelli**) on a high heat with garlic, pepper and a little cooking water. The pan is then removed from the flame and grated → **Pecorino Romano** cheese is stirred in vigorously. Served with a further sprinkling of Pecorino and a twist of the peppermill. Lazio.

Cacio in asse recently invented large stretched curd cow's milk cheese. Hung to mature in natural caves for more than a year. Produced in the village of Casacalenda (province of Campobasso). Molise.

Cacio in forma di limone sheep's cheese flavored with lemon zest. Typical of the Vallata del Metauro, in the province of Pesaro-Urbino. Marche.

cacio marcetto fiery fermented sheep's cheese spread. Similar to ➤ **bross**. Abruzzo/Molise.

Caciocavallo mature sretched curd cheese typical of southern Italy. Made from cow's (sometimes buffalo's) milk in the shape of a bag, twisted at the top into the so-called *testa*, or head. The name would appear to derive from the Turkish *qasqawal*, a similar type of cheese.

Caciocavallo affumicato smoked ➤ **Caciocavallo**. Aged for 60 days after smoking. Campania.

Caciocavallo di Agnone stretched curd cow's cheese. The pear-shaped forms are tied together and aged in natural caves for three months to a year. Molise.

Caciocavallo di bufala raw or heat-treated stretched curd cow's milk cheese, made mainly in winter. May also be smoked. Ages up to 60 days. Campania.

Caciocavallo di Castelfranco in Miscano cheese produced in the Benevento area with milk from the Podolica cattle breed. Aged for three months. Campania.

Caciocavallo palermitano raw cow's milk cheese produced in northwest Sicily. Has the same parallelepiped form as ➤ **Ragusano**, but is slightly smaller. After long stretching and working by hand, it is kept in brine for one day per two pounds in weight. Aged for two to six months. Sicily.

Caciocavallo podolico Alburni cheese with milk of Podolica cattle using an ancient production technique in the province of Salerno. May be eaten fresh or mature. Campania.

Caciocavallo podolico del Gargano stretched curd cheese made with the milk of Podolica cattle. May be matured for a few months or for a number of years. A Slow Food presidium promotes the Podolica breed and is seeking to reactivate local production traditions. Puglia.

Caciocavallo podolico della Basilicata stretched curd cheese made with the milk of Podolica cattle. Matures for up to four-five years and has an extraordinarily complex flavor. A Slow Food presidium promotes the Podiolica breed and is seeking to strengthen the production chain. Basilicata.

Caciocavallo podolico picentino cheese produced in the province of Avellino. Made from the whole milk of Podolica cattle. May be eaten fresh or mature. Campania.

Caciocavallo silano PDO cheese produced in some parts of Molise, Puglia, Campania, Basilicata and Calabria at both artisan and industrial level. The mature raw milk version is particularly good.

Caciofiore buttery pasteurized sheep's milk cheese from the province of Foggia. Eaten after a brief period of maturation. Puglia.

Caciofiore aquilano fresh, creamy cheese made from full raw ewe's milk and coagulated with rennet extracted from the flowers of a wild cardoon. Matures for 20 to 40 days. Abruzzo.

Caciofiore della campagna romana ewe's milk cheese made by coagulating the milk with rennet extracted from the flowers of a wild cardoon. Matures for 35-40 days. The rind is yellowish and thin, the paste moist, soft, compact and friable. The flavor is lightly astringent and pungent. Lazio.

Cacioforte cow's, goat's or, most likely, sheep's cheese produced exclusively in the Roccaromana and Statigliano areas in the province of Caserta from September until the end of the winter. Each form has a gray-red rind and matures for six months to 12 years, during which time it acquires a strong, aromatic flavor. Also known as ➤ **Saticulano**. Campania.

Cacioricotta goat's cheese produced in Puglia, Basilicata and the Cilento area of Campania. May be eaten fresh or matured for grating.

Cacioricotta del capra cilentana cheese made from the milk of the Cilentana goat, a breed native to the Cilento national park and the Valle di Diano. The black sub-breed is bred for its meat, the tawny and gray for their milk, which is protected by a Slow Food presidium. Campania.

Caciotta cheese typical of central and southern Italy, flat and cylindrical in shape with rounded edges, made of cow's, ewe's, goat's or mixed milk. Produced both by artisans and by industry, Caciotta is an often generic typology and name, much exploited by commercial dairies.

Caciotta caprina semi-hard raw or pasteurized cow's milk cheese. Ages about 30 days. Friuli.

Caciotta del Fermano cheese produced in the hill country inland from Fermo using varying proportions of local cow's and ewe's milk. Sold fresh after ten to 15 days or aged for a month and a half. Marche.

Caciotta di bufala di Amaseno buffalo's raw whole milk cheese typical of the small village of Amaseno, in the province of Frosinone. Aged for up to 24 months in glass containers. Lazio.

Caciotta romana pasteurized sheep's milk cheese. Eaten after 15 days or aged longer, in which case forms are washed once a month. Lazio.

Caciotta toscana one of the commonest cheeses in the region. Made from mixed,

usually pasteurized, cow's and sheep's milk, it is eaten after maturing for 20 days. Tuscany.

Caciottella di Sorrento ewe's milk cream cheese for immediate consumption. Traditionally wrapped in fig or vine leaves. Campania.

Caciottina canestrata di Sorrento raw cow's milk cheese. Cylindrical in shape with a soft paste, it is eaten fresh. Campania.

caciù another name for ➤ **calcione**, sweet fried raviolo.

caciuf polenta, solidified and fried, mixed with beans, pancetta, sausage and Parmesan. Typical of Ferrara. Emilia-Romagna.

caciuni another name for ➤ **calcione**, sweet fried raviolo.

caciunitti another name for ➤ **calcione**, sweet fried raviolo.

caco (pl. **cachi**) persimmon, sharon fruit (*Diospyros kaki*), introduced to Europe from Asia at the start of the 19th century. Eaten in October-November, when the fruit is completely ripe (though the so-called *caco-mela* variety may be eaten straight from the tree). The Italian Ministry of Agricutlure database of native/traditional food products lists the following varieties: *cachi di vaniglia napoletano* (Campania); *loto di Romagna* (Emilia-Romagna); *cachi di Misilmeri* (Sicily). Mostly eaten fresh, persimmons are also used to make jam, especially in Puglia.

cacocciuliddi spinusi Sicilian name for spiny, wild artichokes. Also known as *cacocciuliddi d'a chiana* (Catania) and *cacocciuli passatempu* (Siracusa). Cooked in salt and water, they are nibbled leaf by leaf. Used to be sold by street vendors and still are, but much less so than in the past. Sicily.

caffè coffee (*Coffea arabica, Coffea canephora, Coffea iberica*). The coffee plant originated in Ethiopia and spread to the Yemen, Arabia and Egypt, where the partaking of the beverage became a daily feature of Arab-Islamic civilization. It arrived in Europe in the 16th century and went on to conquer the world. Coffee entered Italy for the first time in 1570 through Venice, where the first coffee shop was opened in 1683. The fashion soon spread to France, Britain and The Netherlands. In Northern Europe this bourgeois stimulant beverage was seen as perfectly functional to the Protestant work ethic, unlike chocolate, which was considered a symbol of decadence. In the 19th century the domestic consumption of coffee was consolidated throughout Italy as a pleasure, a ritual and an element of national identity. In those days only well-off families could afford coffee machines, others having to make do with boiling water and coffee in pans or pots. Then *caffettiere napoletane*, Neapolitan coffeepots, appeared on the scene, followed, in 1933, by the alluminium Moka Express was created by Alfonso Bialetti (the first espresso machine to make coffee expressly for the customer by steam extraction invented by the Milanese engineer Luigi Bezzera). In 1948 Achille Gaggia presented the first piston-operated espresso machine, an important development in that the extraction of coffee powder by water under pressure gives a concentrated texture and a thick, smooth *crema*. In the early 1960s, the Pavoni company came up with Europiccola, the first electric coffee machine for domestic use. A cup of espresso coffee is the classic conclusion to a meal in every Italian region, where variations, such as → **moretta marchigiana**, → **ponce alla livornese**, → **caffè alla valdostana** have been created. Recently the Catalan chef Ferrán Adriá combined with Lavazza of

Turin to create Espesso, a solid soufflé-like espresso made with coffee, sugar and gelatin and to be eaten with a teaspoon. In times of hardship (though sometimes also for health reasons) coffee surrogates have been invented, made with barley, chicory, oats, spelt and rye. Of the many, worthy of mention is the lupin coffee of Anterivo, a small village in the Val di Fiemme, in the province of Bolzano, popular in the 1950s and 1960s.

caffè alla valdostana a mixture of coffee, red wine, grappa, sugar and lemon zest. Traditionally drunk boiling hot from the many-spouted, communal *coppa dell'amicizia*, "cup of friendship." Val d'Aosta.

cagliata curd. The clotted portion of coagulated milk, which has transformed from the colloidal solution of casein in sol phase into a gel after inoculation with rennet, or the curdling of the milk. Curd is essentially casein in a gelatinous phase that has been separated from the whey. This separation is the first stage in cheesemaking.

caglio rennet. An extract of animal origin containing proteolytic enzymes (chymosin and pepsin) that coagulate casein. Generally obtained from the abomasum, or fourth stomach, of unweaned ruminants (calves, kids or lambs). Some rennets also contain lipases, enzymes that can catalyse the hydrolosis of fats and contribute to the sensory profile of a cheese. Commercially, rennets are available in liquid, pellet, paste or, more rarely, fungal and vegetable form.

cagnetto freshwater blenny (→ **bavosa**).

cai aka **caj** Friulian term for → **lumaca di terra**, earth snail.

caicc large ravioli typical of the village of Breno, in the Valcamonica, in the province of Brescia, filled with braised beef and Parmigiano and served with melted butter and Parmigiano. Lombardy.

caiet boiled cured pork today produced by a single pork butcher in Valdieri, in the province of Cuneo. Pig's throat, liver and spleen are cut into pieces, cured with spices and herbs, and wrapped in an omentum. The mixture is then pressed and boiled inside a square or cylindrical mold. Eaten sliced, on its own or with polenta. Piedmont.

caillettes boiled Savoy cabbage leaves stuffed with chopped calf's liver and lung, renetta apple, cinnamon, salt, pepper, nutmeg and cooked in red wine. A dish traditionally made to mark the ritual killing of the pig. Piedmont.

cajincì aka **cajoncìe** aka **ciaroncìe** ravioli of the Ladin area of the Dolomites. Filled with spinach fried in butter and fresh cheese (like ➤ **schlutzer** or ➤ **schlutzkrapfen**, with which they share the same half-moon shape) or with boiled potatoes, egg yolks, and ➤ **Puzzone di Moena** cheese. Either boiled and served with melted butter, mature cheese and poppy seeds, or fried (*cajincì arestis*). Veneto, Friuli-Venezia Giulia.

cajoncìe da Moena pasta (made of wheat and rye flour, whole egs and yolks, and olive oil) filled with wild spinach fried with butter and onion mixed with mascarpone or another fresh creamy cheese, and nutmeg. Served with smoked ricotta, poppy seeds and melted butter. Recipe typical of the Val di Fassa. Trentino-Alto Adige.

calacausi peanuts (➤ **semi e legumi tostati**, toasted seeds and legumes).

calamàr tòdero Veneto term for ➤ **totano**, squid.

calamarata dry durum wheat pasta, usually bronze-drawn. Ring-shaped like large calamari sliced for frying, hence the name. Popular mainly in southern Italy, it originates from Gragnano, in the province of Naples. Best enjoyed with fish sauces. Campania.

calamaretto baby squid (➤ **calamaro**) of up to two inches in length.

calamaretti affogati baby squid (or cuttlefish) cooked in a skillet until they have thrown out all their water, then finished with a splash of vinegar and a squirt of lemon juice. Lazio.

calamaretti alla sanremese baby squid lightly stewed with garlic, parsley, taggiasca olives, potatoes and artichokes. A recipe typical of the western Riviera. Liguria.

calamaro (pl. **calamari**) squid. A cephalopod mollusk with a cigar-shaped body of a few inchs to three feet in length. Two of its ten tentacles, longer and thinner than the others, have fleshy tips. The common squid (*Loligo vulgaris*) inhabits the waters of Sicily and the Adriatic and is available all year round, fresh or frozen. May be confused with ➤ **totano**, European flying squid which, though smaller, has lateral fins and larger tentacles, and ➤ **seppia**, cuttlefish. The Italian Ministry of Agriculture's database of native/traditional food products includes *calamaro di saccaleva*, typical of Trieste. Baby **calamari** (➤ **calamaretto**), may be cooked without gutting, whereas larger specimens need to be gutted and skinned. **Calamari** are best boiled and cut into rings, breaded or battered, and fried, grilled or stuffed and baked. Large **calamari** should be cut into pieces and fried or grilled like cuttlefish. Common and regional names: ➤ **totano del riso**, ➤ **totanu**, ➤ **toutinus**, ➤ **toutineddus**.

calamari imbottiti stuffed squid. A recipe common, with numerous variations, all round the Italian coast. In Campania, the squid is stuffed with a mixture either of ground shrimp, scampi, mussels and swordfish, or with a mixture of the head of the mollusk, breadcrumbs, Caciocavallo, pine kernels, raisins and eggs, and cooked in white wine. Not dissimilar are the recipes commonly used in Puglia and Sardinia, where they make the filling with the chopped tentacles of the mollusk, dried breadcrumbs, minced garlic and, sometimes, capers, olives and anchovies. The term *imbottito* ("stuffed" or "filled") is typical of the south of Italy.

calamari ripieni stuffed calamari. In the coastal areas of Veneto, they stuff squid with a chopped mixture of onion, garlic, parsley, salted anchovies, dried breadcrumbs and wine, then cook them on a high heat with white wine. In Friuli-Venezia Giulia, they make the stuffing with the chopped tentacles of the mollusk, minced parsley and garlic, dried breadcrumbs and oil, then broil or bake them. The term ➤ **ripieno** ("stuffed" or "filled") is typical of the north of Italy.

calamento aka **calaminta** other names for ➤ **nepetella**, lesser calamint.

calandraca boiled beef, cut into pieces and reheated in wine, broth, tomato sauce and diced potatoes. Recipe typical of Trieste, said to have been invented by sailors to use up leftover galley meat. Friuli-Venezia Giulia.

calariddhe, u lamb cooked in ewe's milk with olive oil, garlic, onion, parsley and wild fennel. Served with bread soaked in the cooking juices. Typical of Gravina, in the province of Bari, where it was traditionally made by shepherds, the dish is now very rare. Puglia.

calascioni a sort of large ➤ **panzerotto**. A thin sheet of pastry (made from a dough of eggs, flour, salt, suet and olive oil) and filled with ricotta and field greens or grated Parmigiano and Pecorino, eggs, parsley and sausage. A typical Roman snack or antipasto, probably of Neapolitan origin. Lazio.

calcione (pl. **calcioni**) in the Marche and Abruzzo regions, the term refers, with variations in ingredients, to a large pastry raviolo filled with fava bean purée flavored with lemon zest, sugar and cinnamon, fried and dusted with more powdered cinnamon. In the period between Carnival and Easter, the pastry dough is made of flour, butter, eggs, lard, egg yolks and grated lemon zest, the filling of Pecorino flavored with lemon. The pastry is turned over into a half-moon shape and pricked with a knife and the resulting ravioli are brushed with egg yolk and baked in the oven. In the provinces of Chieti and Pescara, in the Abruzzo, where they are known as ➤ **calgiunitti**, the ravioli are filled with a mixture of cooked wine must, chickpeas and candied fruit, or jam and chopped almonds, pine kernels and walnuts flavored with rum or anisette, and fried. Other dialect names: ➤ **caciù**, **a caciuni**, ➤ **caciunitti**, ➤ **calgiunitti**, ➤ **piconi**.

caldaia popular name for ➤ **bollito misto alla triestina**, mixed boiled meats.

caldallessa regional term for ➤ **ballotta**, boiled chestnut.

caldariello another name for ➤ **calariddhe, u**, a lamb dish.

caldarrosta chestnut roasted with its skin over coals or a wood fire in a perforated pan. The outer skin of the chestnut is nicked with a knife to prevent it exploding. The traveling or seasonal roast chestnut vendor is still a common sight all over Italy.

caldidolci soft cookies made of cornflour, milk, sugar, butter, pine kernels, mulled wine, cinnamon, cloves and grated lemon zest, traditionally eaten in the province of Mantua on November 2, All Souls' Day. Lombardy.

caldo, a term to describe the cooking of food in a hot liquid (usually water or broth).

calendula English or pot marigold (*Calendula officinalis*). Spontaneous or cultivated perennial plant with erect stems and yellow-orange flowers, which open in the morning and close at night, common in all Italian regions. The leaves are used to add flavor to spring salads, the petals to color risottos in lieu of saffron. The fruits may be pickled in vinegar of preserved in brine like capers. Common and regional names: ➤ **cappuccina**, ➤ **fior d'ogni mese**, ➤ **fiorrancio**.

calgiunitti another word for ➤ **calcione**, sweet fried raviolo.

calhettas aka **calhiettes** gnocchi made of day-old bread, grated raw potatoes, milk and aromatic herbs, served with melted butter and ➤ **Toma** cheese. Typical of the Susa Valley, in the province of Turin. Piedmont.

calia toasted chickpeas (➤ **semi e legumi tostati**, toasted seeds and legumes).

callariedde soup of chicory or wild fennel broth enriched with mozzarella, slices of salami, beaten eggs and pieces of lamb. Traditionally cooked on Easter Monday. Puglia.

Callu de cabreddu cheese made by filling an emptied, washed kid's vell, or fourth stomach, with raw goat's milk. Smoked during aging (four months), it has a creamy texture, tangy taste and pungent smell. Sardinia.

calsù curious stocking-shaped ➤ **casoncelli** obtained by pinching the edges of the dough. Fillings vary from place to place; favorites include potatoes, ground veal, beef and pork, and grated Grana Padano, herbs and cotechino, and salami, Savoy cabbage and potatoes. Lombardy.

calzagatti aka **calzagàtt** aka **cassagài** polenta cooked with bean stew and sprinkled with Parmigiano. Eaten either hot and "wet" or, once solidified, cut into lozenge shapes and fried. The ironic name, literally "good for cats," refers to the fact that this is a humble dish without meat. Emilia-Romagna.

calzengiiddhe dialect term for ➤ **panzerotto**. A fried or baked turnover usually filled with ground pork and herbs, Provola and eggs, or ricotta, anchovies and tomatoes. Puglia.

calzoncelli crumbly wafer cakes filled with chopped almonds, sugar, dark chocolate, chestnut flour, cooked wine must (➤ **vincotto**) and grated orange zest. A specialty of Melfi, in the province of Potenza. Basilicata.

calzoncini lucani halfmoon pasta filled with ricotta, sugar, cinnamon and nutmeg, served with lamb sauce. A typical Carnival recipe. Basilicata.

calzone (pl. **calzoni**) half-moon pastry made of pizza dough, filled with various ingredients and baked in the oven. Typical of many southern cuisines. The traditional *calzone napoletano* (Campania) is filled with ricotta, Parmigiano, mozzarella, pieces of salami or ham and, sometimes, eggs. The *calzone barese* (Puglia) is filled with fried onions, cherry tomatoes, black olives, capers and anchovies, bound with salted ricotta and Pecorino. The *calzone di verdura alla lucana* (Basilicata) is filled with chard, black olives or raisins and chili. In southern Italy they also make sweet **calzoni**, almost always fried (➤ **calzone di castagne**).

calzone con lo spunzale typical of the Gargano peninsula. Two disks of bread dough filled with gently fried leeks (➤

spunzali) anchovies, olives, pepper and oil, and baked in a wood oven. Puglia.

calzone di Carnevale Carnival pie made from a dough of flour, eggs and sugar and filled with ground veal, eggs, grated cheese, ricotta and Scamorza. Puglia.

calzone di castagne a purée of chestnuts and chickpeas, sprinkled with cocoa, cinnamon, sugar and maraschino liqueur is spread over squares of pasta dough (flour, suet, sugar, eggs and Marsala), which are then folded over and sealed. The resulting *calzoni* are fried in oil and covered with honey and sugar. Basilicata.

calzonicchi type of tortelli filled with brains, boiled and served with simple condiments. A traditionally Jewish dish, like many in Roman cuisine. Lazio.

calzuncieddhi aka **panzerotti** small half-moon focaccias made with risen pastry dough and filled with onions, cherry tomatoes, black olives, capers, anchovies and Pecorino, or other combinations of ingredients (fried onion and ricotta; ham and cheese; mozzarella, eggs, grated cheese and parsley; anchovies). Fried in oil and eaten piping hot dusted with salt. Puglia.

camadia Campania dialect word for ➤ **tartufo di mare**, clam (➤ **vongola**). Campania.

camarezza regional term for ➤ **valeriana rossa**, red valerian.

càmbara de fangu Sardinian term for ➤ **canocchia**, mantis shrimp.

camicia, in (1) literally "in its shirt." Term used to refer to the poaching of eggs. *Uova in camicia* = poached eggs.

camicia, in (2) literally "in its shirt." Term used to refer to unpeeled garlic.

camicia, in (3) literally "in its shirt." Emilia cotechino recipe (➤ **cotechino in camicia**).

càmmaro old Neapolitan term for a dish containing meat, as opposed to ➤ **scàmmaro**, a dish without meat. Campania.

camomilla bastarda common name for ➤ **partenio**, feverfew.

camoscio chamois (*Rupicapra rupicapra*). Horned ruminant of the goat family. The horns are hooked at the tip and the coat is reddish brown in summer, brownish black in winter. Lives in herds at altitudes of over 4-5,000 feet. In the Abruzzo the chamois is a protected species, but elsewhere, in protected areas such as the Gran Paradiso national park, it may be hunted according to selective culling projects. It may also be farmed. The sapid red meat needs to be hung and marinated for longer than other game and is mainly stewed or cooked in wine. The loin and saddle of young specimens may also be roasted. Leg of chamois preserved in salt provides the basis for traditional cured meats such as ➤ **mocetta**. Val d'Aosta.

camoscio al civé aka **camoscio al civet** chunks of chamois venison marinated in red wine with herbs and spices (garlic, onion, parsley, rosemary, bay leaves, juniper berries, cloves, cinnamon, nutmeg), lightly coated with flour, browned in butter and chopped lardo, and slowly cooked in the marinade liquid. Served with polenta and the reduced pan juices (in the 19th century the animal's blood was added). Val d'Aosta/Piedmont.

camoscio al ginepro chamois with juniper berries. Boned leg of chamois stuffed with mushrooms and juniper berries, roast in the oven with vegetables and served with a sauce made of the pan juices blended with cream, juniper berries and juniper liqueur. Trentino-Alto Adige.

camoscio alla tirolese chamois venison marinated in wine with vinegar and herbs, cooked in red wine and buttermilk. Trentino-Alto Adige.

camoscio in umido stewed chamois. Recipe similar to ➤ **camoscio al civé**. In the Val d'Aosta they marinate a leg of chamois in red wine flavored with garlic, onion, carrot, celery, parsley, sage, rosemary, bay leaves, peppercorns and a glass of grappa, cut it into pieces, brown them in butter with chopped onion, coat them in flour, and cook them slowly in the filtered marinade wine. In Friuli-Venezia Giulia, chamois venison is cut into pieces and immersed in water, vinegar, wine, garlic, onion, sage, pepper and cinnamon, browned in lardo and cooked with part of the marinade liquid.

camoscio stufato chamois stewed in white wine. Pieces of chamois shoulder marinated in vinegar with vegetables and herbs, dried, coated with flour, browned in butter with onions and slowly cooked in white wine and broth. Served with the filtered pan juices. Valle d'Aosta, Piedmont.

campanello another name for ➤ **pesce (2)**, end cut round, a cut of beef.

campanula selvatica common name for ➤ **raperonzolo**, rampion.

campigliese baked cake made of eggs, sugar, lard, crushed walnuts, pine kernels, grated lemon zest and flour, garnished with lardo and sugar. Typical of Campiglia Marittima, in the province of Livorno. Tuscany.

campofiloni very thin egg tagliolini, not much thicker than ➤ **capelli d'angelo**. Also known as ➤ **maccheroncini di Campofilone**, they originate from and are named for the village of Campofilone, in the province of Ascoli Piceno. Marche.

canapiglia gadwall (*Anas strepera*). Similar to the ➤ **germano reale**, mallard, but with more pointed wings and more uniform plumage. Bird of passage in Italy from September to November. Inhabits shallow inland ponds and lakes and occasionally nests in the Po delta.

canarino (1) hot digestive drink made with boiling water and lemon zest sweetened with sugar.

canarino (2) name for *radicchio rosa di Gorizia*, a type of radicchio with yellow-green leaves (➤ **radicchio**).

canata viterbese cold antipasto, very similar to ➤ **panzanella**. Day-old bread roughly torn into pieces, dressed with oil and mixed with chopped tomatoes, celery, anchovies, tuna, spring onions, pickles and so on. Lazio.

canavera abbreviated name for ➤ **cappone alla canavera**, steamed capon.

cancarillo dialect term for ➤ **peperoncino**, chili.

cancelle name for ➤ **scaldatelle**, ring-shaped pastries, in Matera (Basilicata).

candelaos cakes made with small cupfuls of almond paste baked in the oven, impermeabilized with sugar, filled with sliced almonds and coated with a sugar icing. Aromatized with orange blossom water, they are embellished with fine decorations. Made for weddings in a few villages west of Cagliari (Quartu Sant'Elena, Selargius, Monserrato, Settimo San Pietro, Maracalagonis, Sinnai). Sardinia.

candele another name for ➤ **ziti**, a type of pasta.

candire to candy. The slow boiling of fruit in a sugar and water solution whereby internal water is replaced by sugar and the fruit becomes firm and preservable for a long period of time. Fruit for candying must not be fully ripe; if it is, it must be cut into pieces (in the case of citrus fruits, only the zest must be used). Using more elaborate techniques, it is also possible to candy flower petals (rose, violet, rose geranium etc.). It is also common in Italian households to candy chestnuts (➤

marron glacé) and orange zest (➤ **zest di Carignano**).

canditi candied fruits. Whole fruits or pieces of fruit that have undergone the candying process (➤ **candire**). Candied fruit is the main ingredient of ➤ **mostarda di Cremona**.

canditi di Carignano another name for ➤ **zest di Carignano**.

canederli bread dumplings. The Italian version, typical of Trentino and Veneto, of the ➤ **knödel** of the Alto Adige. Made in different sizes with different flavorings they are served in broth, as a side-dish or on their own. The classic version is flavored with liver like ➤ **leberknödel**, but a rye bread version (*canederli neri*) also exists, usually flavored with speck or smoked pancetta. Trentino-Alto Adige, Veneto.

canederli al formaggio dumplings of fresh breadcrumbs, grated cheese, eggs, butter, spices cooked in boiling broth. Trentino-Alto Adige.

canederli allo speck dumplings of diced bread, salami and speck lightly fried in butter with onions, eggs, flour and chives, poached in water and served with broth. Trentino-Alto Adige.

canederli di magro dumplings of day-old bread, flour, eggs, milk, butter, onion and parsley, boiled in salted water and dressed with melted butter and grated cheese. Trentino-Alto Adige.

canederli dolci aka **gnocchi boemi** dumplings of boiled potatoes, flour and egg yolks with a plum (or an apricot) at the center, boiled briefly in salted water, coated with dried breadcrumbs and finished in butter with sugar and cinnamon. Trentino-Alto Adige, Friuli-Venezia Giulia.

canello aka **cannella** regional terms for ➤ **matterello**, rolling pin.

Canestrato goat's and cow's milk cheese typical of the south of Italy. Owes its name (*canestro* means basket in Italian) to the fact that the curd is put into traditional woven-rushes molds.

Canestrato crotonese cheese with a salty, tangy flavor, made with ewe's and goat's milk from two milkings in the province of Crotone and on the Sila plateau (Calabria). Calabria.

Canestrato di Castel del Monte cheese made in the mountain pastures of the province of L'Aquila from the raw milk of mainly Sopravvissana sheep, a cross between ewes of the Vissana breed, native to the Marche, and Merino or Gentili di Puglia rams from the province of Foggia. It is aged for two to 12 months, and is regularly rubbed with oil. A Slow Food presidium has been set up to preserve the cheese, its environment and its production techniques. Abruzzo.

Canestrato pugliese PDO raw sheep's milk cheese typical of the province of Foggia. Used mainly for grating, it ages for up to ten months. Puglia.

canestrelli liguri crumbly flower- or star-shaped cookies made of flour, a generous amount of butter, sugar and eggs, sometimes dusted with confectioner's sugar. Typical of inland Liguria and southern Piedmont (province of Alessandria), they are a specialty in especial of Torriglia, in the upper Val Trebbia (province of Genoa). At Easter they traditionally contained colored hard-boiled eggs. Piedmont, Liguria.

canestrelli piemontesi small warm wafers once made in the fireplace using a utensil similar to a waffle iron, which left a weave design (*canestro* means "basket" in Italian) on the surface. Today a mixture of flour, hazelnuts, butter, sugar and vanilla is divided into balls and pressed between irons that imprint the producer's trademark or some other design on the wafer. In Borgofranco d'Ivrea, in the Canavese area north of Turin, *canestrelli* contain cocoa; in Biella, they are made with cocoa, almonds and hazelnuts; in Crevacuore, near Biella, chocolate-flavored *canestrej'd na vira* are cooked between red-hot irons according to a 17th-century recipe. Chocolate-coated ➤ **cavagnolesi** are yet another variant.

canestrello (pl. **canestrelli**) collective name for a number of mollusks (*Pecten maximus*, *Chlamys opercularis* and *Chlama varia*), common in the Adriatic. Similar to the greater Mediterranean scallop (➤ **conchiglia di San Giacomo**), but smaller. In Venice they fry them and use them as an ingredient in risottos. In the Marche region, they call them ➤ **cuore di mare**.

canestrello di Brugnato risen ring-shaped cake made of flour, water, sugar, eggs, honey, vegetable fat and aniseeed. Specialty of the Val di Vara, in the province of La Spezia. Liguria.

canestrello di Taggia crumbly, crunchy savory ring- or horseshoe-shaped biscuit made of flour, water, salt, yeast and extra-virgin olive oil. A specialty of Taggia, in the province of Imperia. Liguria.

canestrelo Veneto term for ➤ **canestrello**, ring-shaped cookie.

canestri another name for ➤ **farfalline**, butterfly-shaped pasta.

cannaca cured meat of coarsely chopped pork and pork fat cured with salt, pepper, fennel and spices. Cased in a pig's or bull's intestine washed with vinegar or Vernaccia di Oristano wine. Tied into 12-15 inch sausages and bent into a "U" shape, it is ready after 15 days and may age for a month. Typical of the province of Nuoro and Gallura.

cannarìculi sweet sticks of flour and cooked wine must, coated first in honey, then in ➤ **diavolina**, confetti sugar. A Christmas specialty. Calabria.

cannaruozzoli egg pasta squares cheese served with lamb, mushroom, pork, anchovy or tuna sauce and sprinkled with grated Pecorino cheese. Calabria.

cannaruta salt cod baked in the oven with oil, garlic, lemon juice and breadcrumbs. Typical of Naples. Campania.

cannella aka **cinnamomo** cinnamon. One of the spices most exploited in the kitchen, made from the bark of two evergreen shrubs, one (*Cinnamomun zeylanicum*) native to Sri Lanka and cultivated throughout tropical Asia, the other, known as cassia (*C. aromaticum*), native to China and southeast Asia, the former being more prized, in terms of subtlety aroma and texture. Both are dried and sold rolled up in "quills" or powdered. Cinnamon is one of the spices used to cure meats (➤ **concia**) and is a major ingredient in any number of spicy regional cakes and pastries (➤ **spongata**, ➤ **mostaccioli**, ➤ **cartellata**, ➤ **panpepato**), in apple cakes and pies (➤ **strudel**), in the stuffings and condiments of traditional fresh pastas (➤ **cjalsons**). *Cannellini di Sulmona* are a unique candy: long, thin sugared almonds (➤ **confetto**) with a heart of cinnamon. Likewise, in Campania, *cannellini* are made with sugar and vanilla and aromatized with cinnamon, sugar and vanilla.

cannellini type of sugared almond (➤ **canella**, cinnamon, and ➤ **confetto**, sugared almond).

cannellino (pl. **cannellini**) type of ➤ **fagiolo**, bean. The pod is green and about three inches long, the bean itself is whitish in color and small, flat and cylindrical with rounded ends. Cultivated mainly in central Italy (well known ecotypes are ➤ **fagiolo di Sorana**, near Pescia in the province of Pistoia, *fagiolo di Atina*, in the Valle di Comino in the province of Frosinone), it is regarded as one of the best beans for drying and conserving. The beans feature in many Tuscan recipes: from soups and local versions of ➤ **pasta e fagioli** (pasta and beans) to ➤ **fagioli al fiasco** and ➤ **fagioli all'uccelletto**.

cannello Marche term for ➤ **cannolicchio**, European razor clam.

cannelloni large commercial dried durum wheat pasta tubes suitable for stuffing and baking. The surface may be smooth or ridged. In Emilia-Romagna, a fresh version exists (➤ **canoli**) consisting of egg pasta rectangles rolled up to form cylinders.

canneroni ➤ another name for **cannaruozzoli**, egg pasta squares.

cannoli calabresi wafers made with wheat flour, sugar and wine, rolled up, fried and smothered in honey. Calabria

cannoli di eggplants slices of eggplant coated in flour, fried, covered with slices of boiled ham and pieces of Provola cheese, and rolled up. Covered with a little tomato sauce and grated Parmigiano-Reggiano and baked in the oven. Calabria.

cannolicchio (pl. **cannolicchi**) European razor clam (*Solen vagina*). Tubular bivalve mollusks which lives buried in sandy sea beds near the coast. The *cannolicchio del Molise* features in the Italian Ministry of Agriculture's database of native and/or traditional food products. Sold in sealed nets labeled with indication of provenance. Sometimes available shelled, the mollusk may be eaten raw. Most specific recipes belong to the Veneto tradition, but *cannolicchi* can also be cooked like mussels (➤ **gratin**). Common and regional names: ➤ **arrasojas**, ➤ **cannello**, ➤ **capalonga**, ➤ **cappalunga**, ➤ **coltellaccio**, ➤ **manego de cutelo**, ➤ **manico di coltello**.

cannolicchio femmina Campania name for bean razor clam (*Pharus legumen*), similar to the European razor clam (➤ **cannolicchio**), but with a shorter, wider, rounder shell.

cannolo siciliano pastry cylinder, baked or fried, filled with ricotta cream dotted with candied fruits and/or chocolate drops. The *cannolo* of Piana degli Albanesi (province of Palermo) is famous for its size. The pastry is of Arab-Sicilian origin, but can now be found all over Italy.

cannoncino puff pastry spiral filled with confectioner's custard or cream, chocolate and ➤ **zabaglione**. Piedmont.

canocchia (pl. canocchie) mantis shrimp (*Squilla mantis*). Crustacean which lives in muddy, sandy sea beds close to the shore. It can survive for a long time out of the water and it is not uncommon to find it live at the market. The Italian Ministry of Agriculture's database of native and/or traditional food products lists the *canocchia di nassa* (Friuli-Venezia Giulia) variety. Used in soups, served with pasta, or boiled, shelled and marinated in olive oil, lemon juice, minced parsley, salt and pepper. Common and regional names: ➤ **astrea**, ➤ **càmbara de fangu**, ➤ **canocia**, ➤ **caraviedde**, ➤ **cicala di mare**, ➤ **pannocchia**, ➤ **schirifizu**, ➤ **sparnocchia**, ➤ **stracciavocc**, ➤ **strappabocca**.

canocchie ripiene mantis shrimp (fished in the cold months, when the flesh is at its best) stuffed with a mixture of grated dried bread and Parmigiano, garlic, parsley and chopped anchovy fillets, and baked or broiled. Emilia-Romagna.

canocia Veneto term for ➤ **canocchia**, mantis shrimp.

canoli aka **cannelloni** egg pasta rectangles rolled up into cylinders, stuffed with ground meat and grated Parmigiano, covered with béchamel sauce and meat sauce and baked in the oven. Emilia-Romagna.

Cansiglio cheese produced on the plateau of the same name from the raw milk of the ➤ **Bruno Alpina** cow. Ready to eat after a month, it may also be aged for six months and more. Veneto.

cantarella regional term for ➤ **tanuta**, black sea bream.

cantarello chanterelle, mushroom of the *Cantharellus cibarius* genus (the *lutescens* and *tubaeformis* species may also be called ➤ **finferla**), very common in clusters all over Italy. Golden yellow in color, with a small, funnel-shaped cap. Other names include: ➤ **galletto**, ➤ **gallinaccio**, ➤ **galluzzo**, ➤ **gialletto**, ➤ **galitola**, ➤ **garitola**, and ➤ **finferlo**. The chanterelle is usually stewed and served with meat (➤ **guancia di manzo con potatoes e finferli**) and is suitable for preserving. The *gallinaccio del Molise* is included in the Italian Ministry of Agriculture's list of traditional food products.

cantaro regional name for ➤ **tanuta**, black sea bream.

cantucci aka **cantuccini** another name for ➤ **biscottini alla mandorla**, almond cookies.

cantucci di San Miniato a variation on ➤ **biscottini alla mandorla**, almond cookies.

cao cream on the top of fresh milk. Friuli-Venezia Giulia.

capaccia another name for ➤ **soppressata Toscana**, a cured meat.

capalonga Veneto term for ➤ **cannolicchio**, European razor clam.

caparello regional term for ➤ **cefalo**, mullet.

caparòn Veneto term for ➤ **vongola**, clam.

caparossolo aka **caperozzolo** Veneto term for ➤ **vongola verace**, carpet shell clam.

capasanta Veneto term for ➤ **conchiglia di San Giacomo**, great Mediterranean scallop.

capatonda Veneto term for ➤ **cuore di mare**, common cockle.

capelli d'angelo literally "angel's hair." Commercial durum wheat pasta. Long very thin strands gathered into small "nests." Eaten in light broths or with butter and Parmigiano or cream. In southen Italy they are used to make baked pasta dishes. Other names: ➤ **capellini**, ➤ **fedelini**, ➤ **fidelini**.

capellini another name for ➤ **capelli d'angelo**, a type of pasta.

capelonghe in padella European razor clams (➤ **cannolicchio**) lightly fried with minced parsley, bathed with white wine and sautéed. Veneto, Friuli-Venezia Giulia.

capetroccole aka **teste di chiodo** tiny octopuses that are either fried or used to dress pasta or rice. Lazio.

capicollo azze anca grecanico cured meat made from boned leg pork, chopped, sprinkled with chili, wild fennel seeds and black pepper, and cased in the animal's bladder. Aged for at least 180 days in *catoi*, typical cellars of the rural areas of the province of Reggio Calabria. Breeders who are members of the Slow Food presidium set up to promote the delicacy raise free-range pigs from the Grecanica district of the province on a natural diet. Calabria.

capicollo lucano a whole piece of pork fillet, cured with salt, pepper and natural flavorings for two weeks, rubbed with finely minced dried chili and cased in the animal's intestine. Wrapped in caul or secured with kitchen string, it is aged for 90-150 days. Basilicata.

capiler coffee laced with liqueur and syrup

of *capelvenere* or *barba di Giove* (*Adiantum capillus Veneris*), black maidenhead fern, a herb believed to have medicinal properties. A beverage popular in the 19th century Piedmont/Lombardy.

capitone a mature female eel, traditionally eaten fried in Naples on New's Year's Eve. Campania.

capitone allo spiedo eel on a skewer. The eel is cut into pieces and marinated for a couple of hours in vinegar, olive oil, salt and pepper. It is then cooked on a skewer, basted with the marinade liquid. Basilicata.

capitone marinato marinated eel. Popular throughout central and southern Italy, traditionally at Christmas, but now throughout the year. In Lazio, the fish is skinned, rolled into a spiral, stuck on a skewer, placed in a pot and covered with olive oil, bay leaves, salt, pepper and vinegar. It is then left to stand for 48 hours so that the meat soaks up all the flavor of the marinade.

caplet Piedmontese dialect term for ➤ **porcino**, porcini mushroom.

capocollo al vino fresh pork cured with salt, garlic, pepper and nutmeg, left to rest for a day, washed with red wine to eliminate excess salt, baked in the oven, sliced and served with the pan juices. Umbria.

capocollo di Calabria PDO salami, made all over the region from boned pork loin, preserved in salt for 4-8 days. Washed with water and bathed in vinegar, the meat is massaged, cured with black peppercorns, wrapped in a pig's parietal diaphragm, and aged for at least 100 days. Calabria

capocollo di Martina Franca cured meat consisting of pork loin macerated in salt for 15-20 days, washed with cooked wine and spices and cased in a pig's intestine. Wrapped in a cloth to dry, it rests for 10 days before being smoked over a Macedonian oak fire and aged for up to 90 days. A Slow Food presidium is encouraging local pig breeders to use natural practices. A specialty of Martina Franca, in the province of Taranto. Puglia.

capocollo umbro cured meat made from the top of the pig's neck and shoulder. Cured with pepper, garlic, coriander and, in some places, fennel seeds, it is cased in the pig's large intestine and aged for a period of four months to a year. Umbria.

capofreddo another name for ➤ **soppressata toscana**, a cured meat.

capomazzo (1) term used in the province of Viterbo for a baby lamb's intestines (➤ **pajata**). Eaten broiled, roast with potatoes, or stewed with onion. Lazio.

capomazzo (2) regional word for ➤ **capone**, gurnard (➤ **gallinella di mare**). Marche.

caponata in historical recipe collections, the term (which probably derives from the Latin *caupona*, "tavern") defines a stew of various vegetables, sometimes with the addition of fish. Today it is served as an antipasto or side dish, often cold.

caponata di melanzane one of the most popular dishes in Sicilian cooking. Eggplants, complete with skin, are diced and fried in oil. Finely sliced onions are fried separately, while pitted olives, capers and diced celery sticks are boiled in water and vinegar. The olives, capers, celery and fried eggplants are then transferred sticks the skillet with the onions together with tomato paste, vinegar and sugar. The resulting mixture is served warm. There are many variations on the theme. For example, the eggplants may be roasted in the oven, fresh tomatoes may replace tomato paste, and raisins and pine kernels may also be added. Finally, in the Catania area, the fried eggplants are mixed with ➤ **salsa san Bernardo**.

caponata di scampi e molluschi original, richer version, nowadays rare, of → **caponata di eggplants**, with the addition of scampi, octopus and lobster, and garnished with → **salsa san Bernardo**. Sicily.

caponata napoletana salad of pickles, → **papaccella** (round sweet pepper) escarole, lettuce, capers, Gaeta olives and salted anchovies, mixed with crumbled *friselle* (→ **fresa**) and mackerel fillets dressed with oil and lemon juice. A typical Christmas dish.

capone aka **cappone** gurnard. Sea fish of the Triglidae family, which includes a number of different varieties. The most common at Italian fish markets are *capone coccio* (aka *capone imperiale*), red or cuckoo gurnard (*Trigla pini*), *capone lira* (aka *capone organo*), piper (*T. lyra*), *capone ubriaco* (aka *capone lineato*), streaked gurnard (*T. lineata*), and *capone gallinella*, gray gurnard (*T. lucerna*). Common and regional names: → **mazzolina** (*capone lira*); → **pesce briaco** (*capone ubriaco*); → **capomazzo**, → **cuoccio riale**, → **gallinella**, → **luserna**, → **mazzola**, → **testa grossa** (*capone gallinella*). Note, however, that in Puglia and Sicily the name *capone imperiale* refers to → **lampuga**, dolphin fish, while in Liguria and Tuscany they use the word **cappone** to mean → **scorfano rosso**, red scorpion fish.

caponet aka **capuneit** zucchini flowers or Savoy cabbage leaves stuffed with chopped boiled or roast meat, boiled salami, parsley, garlic, eggs and Parmigiano, fried or baked. Dish typical of the Langhe and Monferrato areas. In the Valsesia district, *capuneit valsesiani* are leaves of → **lavassa**, monk's rhubarb, or → **rabarbaro alpino**, Chinese rhubarb, stuffed with chopped roast beef, boiled chard, chicory, borage, garlic, amaretti cookies and pine kernels or walnuts. Piedmont.

cappa santa another name for → **conchiglia di San Giacomo**, great Mediterranean scallop.

cappa verrucosa another name for → **tartufo di mare** (→ **vongola**, clam).

cappalunga Veneto term for → **cannolicchio**, European razor clam.

cappasanta Veneto term for → **conchiglia di san Giacomo**, great Mediterranean scallop.

cappatartufo Tuscan term for → **tartufo di mare** (→ **vongola**, clam).

cappellacci large tricorne-shaped egg pasta filled with a variety of ingredients. The most famous are → **cappellacci ferraresi** filled with pumpkin. An old Molise dish, *cappellacci del brigante*, unfilled pasta triangles, would now appear to be extinct. **cappellacci ferraresi** aka **cappellacci di zucca** large round → **cappellacci** (in dialect *caplaz*) with a filling of pumpkin, grated Parmigiano and nutmeg. The sweet and sour flavor (redolent of the cooking of the courts of the D'Estes and the Gonzagas) is accentuated by crushed amaretti cookies and → **mostarda di frutta** in areas of the province of Ferrara that border with the provinces of Mantua and Cremona. Traditionally served with mixed meat sauces or melted butter, sage and Parmigiano. A specialty of Ferrara, but present also in the provinces of Reggio and Parma, where they are rectangular in shape. Emilia-Romagna.

cappellaccio regional term for the → **prataiolo** mushroom.

cappelle di porcini al forno baked porcini mushroom caps. The caps are cleaned, arranged in a terrine, covered with olive oil and a mixture of minced parsley, garlic, breadcrumbs and chili, anointed with extra virgin olive oil and baked in the oven. Basilicata.

cappelle di porcini in frasca porcini mushroom caps dressed with thyme, salt and pepper, wrapped in vine leaves and cooked on a red-hot granite slab. Lombardy.

cappelletti (1) stuffed egg pasta typical of Emilia-Romagna, but now popular—and produced industrially—all over the country. The most traditional versions are to be found in Reggio Emilia and in Romagna: identical shapes but different fillings. In Reggio the typical filling consists of a mixture of lean meat, raw ham, breadcrumbs and Parmigiano. In Romagna, they eschew meat for a mixture of Parmigiano, spinach or chard and ricotta or ➤ **Raviggiolo** cheese. In the province of Ferrara, *caplìt* (**cappelletti** in dialect), filled with meat, raw ham, sausage and/or mortadella and Parmigiano, are larger than the others. All are served in broth. Emlia-Romagna

cappelletti (2) name used on the south bank of the Po in the province of Mantua for ➤ **agnolini** filled with raw ham, pancetta, boiled sausage, breadcrumbs and grated Parmigiano-Reggiano. Lombardy

cappello da gendarme literally "gendarme's hat," named for its felucca-like shape. A type of ➤ **calzone** made with shortcrust pastry or pizza dough reinforced with olive oil, and filled with eggplant, zucchini, hard-boiled eggs, mozzarella, prosciutto, pork, turkey breast and cheese. A classic street food (➤ **cibo di strada**). Puglia.

cappello da prete another name for ➤ **copertina di sopra**, a cut of beef roughly equivalent to shoulder clod.

cappello del prete traditional boiling sausage stitched into the shape of a tricorne hat. Scraps of lean pork and pancetta, pork rind and fat are coarsely ground and cured with salt, pepper and garlic crushed in white wine. The mixture is cased in the skin from the pig's leg, which is sewn into a triangular shape. After drying for four to five days and aging for two to four months, it is cooked like ➤ **zampone**. Produced in the southern part of the province of Parma and in the provinces of Modena and Reggio Emilia. Emilia-Romagna.

cappelloni huge ➤ **cappelletti** filled with chopped stewed beef, salami and other ingredients which differ from place to place. Typical of the Lomellina area. Lombardy.

cappero caper (*Capparis spinosa*). The flower bud of a shrub that grows on south-facing walls and cliffs in all the Italian coastal regions. Picked and preserved in brine or pickled in vinegar on both domestically and commercially. The buds (aka ➤ **cetriolini** and, in Sicily, ➤ **cucunci**) are listed on the Italian Ministry of Agriculture's database of native and/or traditional food products: ➤ **cappero di Salina**, ➤ **cappero di Pantelleria**, *cappero del Gargano, cappero di Mattinata* (Puglia), *capperone di Selargius* (Sardinia). Larger capers have less flavor, smaller ones are more prized gastronomically. Most capers come from the Italian islands (the Aeolian Islands, the Egadi Islands, Pantelleria, the Tremiti Islands, Ustica, Sardinia). They feature as an ingredient in an infinite number of recipes.

cappero di Pantelleria the warm, dry climate of the island (province of Trapani), its volcanic terrain and a long tradition of cultivating and gathering (local farmers have now set up a cooperative of caper producers) have earned this caper PGI recognition. The capers are hand-picked from May to September and preserved in brine. According to an old island recipe, fresh capers are boiled, dressed with oil and vinegar and served as a side-dish. Sicily.

cappero di Salina the caper bush is an integral part of the landscape on the island of Salina (province of Messina). Until the advent of tourism, capers were the cornerstone of the island's economy, but the industry is now in crisis because of competition from cheaper North African products. The capers are picked individually by hand and placed in wooden barrels in layers alternated with coarse salt. They are ready to eat after about a month and can be stored for up to three years. Salina capers, known for their firmness, fragrance and uniformity, are promoted by a Slow Food presidium. Sicily.

cappesante al forno baked scallops. Scallops flavored with garlic, parsley and oil or butter, and baked in the oven for a few minutes. Veneto, Friuli-Venezia Giulia.

cappidduzzo sweet fried raviolo filled with sheep's milk ricotta flavored with lemon zest and cinnamon. Typical of Trapani. Sicily.

cappieddi 'i prievidi "priest's hats." Tricorne-shaped egg pasta squares. Traditionally dressed with lamb sauce, though mushroom and anchovy sauces are also used. Calabria.

cappon magro elaborate holiday dish composed of layers of fish (preferably → **capone**, gurnard, crustaceans, mollusks and → **mosciame**, dried fillet of tuna) and vegetables: → **scorzonera** (black salsify), celery hearts, cauliflower, beetroot, artichoke, potatoes, carrots and runner beans. All the ingredients are boiled separately, mixed and covered with a sauce of eggs, parsley, fresh breadcrumbs, vinegar, garlic, capers, olives and anchovies. Traditionally served on a bed of ship's biscuits (→ **galletta del marinaio,**). Typical of the province of Genoa. Liguria.

capponada aka **capponadda** aka **capponalda** a bed of ship's biscuits (→ **galletta del marinaio**) softened in water topped with anchovy fillets, dried tuna fillets (→ **mosciame**), olives, capers in brine, garlic, oregano and oil. Richer modern versions add tuna preserved in oil, hard-boiled eggs and tomatoes. Liguria.

cappone capon. Cockerel (Gallus domesticus) surgically castrated at the age of 60-70 days, fattened for at least 77 days, and slaughtered at the age of six to seven months. Castration increases surface and intramuscular fat, which makes the meat soft and tasty. Capons are generally commercialized as partially gutted carcasses (→ **pollame**, poultry), complete with neck and tail feathers. Boiled, roasted or stuffed, capon is a classic Christmas meat, and production, some of which still artisan, is limited and geared to the end-of-year demand. There are many recipes for cooking capons: particularly worthy of note are → **cappone ripieno**, stuffed capon, typical of Piedmont and Lombardy, and → **cappone alla canavera** steamed capon, typical of Veneto. In Emilia and in the province of Mantua (Lombardy), anolini, cappelletti, tortellini, agnolini are cooked in a broth, → **brodo di terza**, in which capon is an important ingredient. Capon meat is also used in the stuffings of certain pastas. Of the capons listed in the Italian Ministry of Agriculture's database of native and/or traditional food products, four are Piedmontese (→ **cappone di Morozzo**, *cappone di Monasterolo di Savigliano*, *cappone di San Damiano d'Asti*, *cappone di Vesime*), one is Friulian, and one (known as the *rustico* or *nostrale*) is typical of the Marche.

cappone alla canavera aka **cappone alla canevera** aka **cappone in prigione** pieces of capon meat, aromatized with spices, onion, carrot, celery and garlic, steamed in a pig's bladder connected to a piece of bamboo (*canavera* in Veneto) which acts as an airhole. A popular recipe in Venice and Vicenza. Veneto.

cappone alla Stefani sweet and sour capon recipe devised by the head cook at the court of the Gonzagas in the second half of the 17th century, for whom it is named. Capon breasts boiled in water aromatized with onion, celery and carrot, cut into strips, seasoned with salt and pepper and served with a sauce of olive oil, vinegar, white wine and raisins. Lombardy.

cappone di Morozzo In Morozzo, capons are traditionally of the Bionda Piemontese breed. When they are adult, they have a long metallic black tail and glossy brick-red feathers trimmed with blue or green. They are recognizable by their lack of crest and wattle. Women do the castrating, an operation that requires a deft touch. The Morozzo capon has soft, tender and delicate meat. Purists prefer it boiled and dipped in salt. The bird is protected by a Slow Food presidium. Piedmont.

cappone in gelatina capon in aspic. The aspic is prepared by slow-boiling beef, pig's trotters and chicken bones in water with herbs. The fat is skimmed from the surface and the broth is drained and clarified with egg whites beaten with Marsala. After being strained through muslin, it is poured over pieces of boiled capon and left to set in the refrigerator. Piedmont.

cappone in prigione "capon in prison." Another name for ➤ **cappone alla canavera,** steamed capon.

cappone incapponato another name for ➤ **cappone ripieno,** stuffed capon.

cappone ripieno stuffed capon, a traditional Christmas dish. The bird is stuffed with ground veal or pork, sausage, fresh breadcrumbs, eggs, cheese, onion, garlic,

parsley and rosemary, and either boiled in vegetable broth or roast in the oven. In the areas of Bra and Mondovì in the province of Cuneo, the dish is traditionally made with ➤ **cappone di Morozzo.** In Tuscany, they bone the capon, stuff it with a mixture of finely ground chicken, turkey, veal and pork, nutmeg, eggs, diced boiled ham and tongue, black olives and chopped pistachio nuts, wrap it in canvas and poach it slowly in water. The cooked bird is left to cool with a weight on top, then served cut into very thin slices.

cappone ripieno di noci capons stuffed with walnuts. The bird is stuffed with a mixture of chopped walnuts, day-old bread soaked in milk, eggs, butter, Parmigiano-Reggiano, salt, pepper, cinnamon and nutmeg, boiled and served cut into pieces with slices of the stuffing. Lombardy.

cappuccetto aka **capputteddi** Sicilian term for a baby cuttlefish (➤ **seppia**).

cappucci e cicorie stew of pig's trotter, pork rind, field chicory, white cabbage and fennel seeds. Basilicata.

cappuccina common name for ➤ **calendula,** English or pot marigold.

cappuccino another name for ➤ **budello cieco,** caecum intestine.

cappuccio ➤ **cavolo cappuccio,** white cabbage.

cappuliato aka **capuliatu** Sicilian dialect term for i) ground beef; ii) pasta condiment whose main ingredient is sun-dried tomatoes.

capra goat (*Capra aegagrus hircus*). Domesticated ruminant descended from the wild goat of central and western Asia, similar to the ibex. In Italy, the most common species are *capra alpina*, *capra pugliese*, *capra sarda*, ➤ **capra garganica** and ➤ **capra girgentana.** Goat milk (closer to human milk than cow's) is used mainly for cheesemaking. Meat production is of secondary importance and regards almost exclusively kid (➤ **capretto**), though recipes featuring adult goat meat do exist: in Liguria ➤ **capra e fagioli**, in Abruzzo ➤ **capra alla neretese**. The Italian Ministry of Agriculture's database of native and/or traditional food products lists the *primaticcio*, *corvesco* and *mulattio* goat meats of the province of Foggia (Puglia). Salted and dried goat meats include ➤ **mocetta**, ➤ **muscisca**, ➤ **violino di capra della Valchiavenna**.

capra alla neretese pieces of goat's leg stewed slowly with herbs, tomato and chili in an earthenware pot and finished off with fried sweet peppers. Recipe typical of Nereto, in the province of Teramo. Abruzzo.

capra e fagioli goat meat and bean stew. Peasant dish typical of western Liguria made preferably with local bean varieties (➤ **fagioli di Badalucco, Conio e Pigna**. Liguria.

capra garganica a particularly hardy goat breed well adapted to grazing in the arid pastures and stubble of the Gargano peninsula. It has a long, jet-black coat and a large head with a small tuft on the top and a long beard. The horns are prominent and the ends bend outward slightly to form an arc. Both meat and milk are excellent, the milk being used to make cheeses such as Cacioricotta and Canestrato and a very delicate ricotta. Only 15 years ago there were still 30,000 animals, but numbers have now fallen to fewer than 3,000. A Slow Food presidium aims to promote the breed's meat and cheese. Puglia.

capra girgentana goat breed probably taken to Sicily from Asia by the Moors, who colonized the island in the 9th century. The goat, whose name comes from Girgenti (modern-day Agrigento), has distinctive long, spiral horns and resembles some Asian breeds. Medium-sized with long, thick, white and occasionally dappled fleece, it has a short beard and a thick tuft of hair over its eyes. A Slow Food presidium is seeking to make its farming more economically viable by promoting its cheese and increasing its numbers. The breed is to be found in the provinces of Agrigento, Caltanissetta, Catania, Enna, Messina and Palermo. Sicily.

capra murata goat meat cooked with potatoes and tomatoes. Sicily.

caprese (1) popular salad of tomatoes, ➤ **Fior di latte** (or buffalo milk mozarella), basil and extra virgin olive oil, named for the island of Capri. Campania.

caprese (2) cake of shelled almonds, dark chocolate, crumbled ➤ **frollini** cookies or rusks, eggs and sugar (without flour). Often served with iced lemon liqueur. Created in Sorrento in the 1920s. Campania.

capretto kid or baby goat. The meat is very delicate before the kid begins to graze, when it immediately becomes stronger. Suitable for all the same recipes as lamb, it is popular in most Italian regions, where it is cooked in numerous different recipes in as many different ways: spit-roast, oven-roast, fried, with cheese and eggs, in pies and so on. The Italian Ministry of Agriculture's database of native and/or traditional breeds lists the following varieties: *capretto della Val Vigezzo* (Piedmont), *capretto da latte pesante* (Lombardy), *capretto delle Apuane* (Tuscany), *crabittu* (Sardinia).

capretto al forno con muscari oven-roast kid with grape hyacinth bulbs. Casserole of chunks of kid with boiled grape hyacinth bulbs (➤ **lampascioni**, ➤ **musca-**

ri), garlic and parsley covered with bread-crumbs and grated Pecorino. Basilicata.

capretto all'agordino roll of kid meat spread with butter aromatized with garlic and rosemary baked in the oven, basting frequently with the pan juices. A specialty of Agordo, a village in the province of Belluno. Veneto.

capretto alla civitese: pieces of kid browned in olive oil with garlic and chili, finished with tomatoes, aromatic herbs and red wine. Named for Civita, an → **Arbëreshë** enclave at the foot of Monte Pollino. Calabria.

capretto alla silana stew of kid, olive oil, potatoes, onions and tomatoes, flavored with grated Pecorino, oregano, salt and black pepper. Typical of the Sila plateau. Calabria.

capretto allo spiedo spit-roast kid. In Vicenza (Veneto), they flavor a whole kid internally with garlic, rosemary, bay leaves and sage and marinate it in oil and lemon juice prior to roasting. In Friuli-Venezia Giulia, they slow-roast a whole animal or leg rubbed with garlic, barded with pancetta and rosemary and bathed with white wine or oil and vinegar. Veneto, Friuli-Venezia Giulia.

capretto con asparagi di fiume kid with river asparagus. Partly boned kid flavored with butter and parsley slow-cooked in white wine and served with polenta, river asparagus (cultivated in the Valle dell'Adige) and hard-boiled eggs. A traditional Easter dish in the Trento area. Trentino-Alto Adige.

capretto in tegame a stew of chopped kid, butter, minced rosemary and white wine. Served with polenta and, in the Easter period, river asparagus. Typical of the Valle dell'Adige, in the province of Trento. Trentino-Alto Adige.

capretto in umido kid stew. In the Val-le Colla, in the province of Cuneo, pieces of kid are browned with herbs, lubricated with vinegar and white wine and stewed in broth over a low heat with diced potatoes. In Friuli-Venezia Giulia, they cook pieces of kid in an earthenware pot with parsley, basil, diced prosciutto, nutmeg and broth. Piedmont, Friuli-Venezia Giulia.

capretto marinato allo spiedo marinated spit-roast kid. A whole kid is rubbed with a mixture of minced garlic, rosemary and sage, and marinated in an earthenware pot with oil, lemon juice, bay leaves and peppercorns. After 48 hours, it is spit-roast, basting frequently with the marinade liquid. A specialty of Gambellara in the province of Vicenza. Veneto.

capretto ripieno stuffed kid. The animal is stuffed with boiled → **vermicelli**, dressed with a sauce of lamb's intestines and aromatic herbs, and baked in the oven. The same recipe may be made with rabbit. Calabria.

capretto stufato pieces of kid browned in butter and lardo, splashed with red wine and slow-cooked in broth with boiled beans. Piedmont.

capriata legumes and cereals slow-cooked in an earthenware pot and anointed with extra virgin olive oil. Basilicata.

capricciosa (1) "capricious" salad of julienned raw vegetables, boiled ham (and/or cooked chicken breast) and cheese bound with mayonnaise, and served as an antipasto.

capricciosa (2) "capricious." Word used to describe a pizza topping of baby artichokes, mushrooms preserved in oil and black and green olives.

Caprino (pl. **Caprini**) cheese made entirely or partly of goat's milk.

Caprino a latte crudo smoked goat's milk cheese, aged for 3-6 months. Eaten as a table cheese or as an ingredient in a number of recipes. Sardinia.

Caprino dell'Aspromonte goat's cheese eaten fresh as a table cheese or matured on rush or wood racks for grating. Typical of the Aspromonte mountains inland from Reggio. Calabria.

Caprino della Limina Rare mountain cheese produced on the slopes of Monte Limina. During aging (from eight months to a year), the rind is brushed periodically with olive oil. Calabria.

Caprino della Valbrevenna raw whole goat's milk cheese made in the province of Genoa from Easter to October. Usually eaten fresh, it can be matured for about a month. Liguria.

Caprino di Cavalese raw goat's milk cheese. Once produced throughout the Val di Fiemme, but today only at the cooperative dairy in Cavalese, in the province of Trento. Cheeses are round, weigh three to four kilos and age for 45-90 days.

Caprino di Montefalcone nel Sannio cheese made with raw milk from the native local breed of goat in the province of Campobasso from April to September. Pressed into rush baskets, which are then immersed in the hot whey from ricotta making, it ages for at least two months. Molise.

Caprino di Rimella typical cheese of the Valsesia, in the province of Vercelli, eaten fresh if made with calf's rennet, mature if made with lamb's rennet. Piedmont.

Caprino lattico small cheese made with whole goat's milk by rennet or the lactic coagulation thereof. Piedmont.

Caprino ossolano raw goat's milk cheese typical of Domodossola, Varzo and the Val Vigezzo (province of Verbano-Cusio-Ossola). Produced from March to November and eaten three days after production. Piedmont.

Caprino stagionato whole or part-skimmed raw goat's milk cheese. Typical of the Valsassina (province of Lecco) and some communes of the Val d'Intelvi (province of Como), where it is aged for 30 days. Some versions are flavored with parsley, garlic, chives and pepper. Lombardy.

capriolo roe deer. A member of the Cervidae family which lives in herds, mainly in Alpine woodland. It has a red-brown coat in summer, gray-brown in winter, and the male has small antlers with three points on either side. Roe deer venison on sale in shops and markets is mostly farmed or imported. It may be cooked in the same ways as chamois (→ **camoscio**).

capriolo al vino roe deer venison in red wine. In the province of Trento, the meat is cut into pieces and marinated in Teroldego or another full-bodied red wine aromatized with a mixture of finely chopped vegetables, bay leaves, juniper berries and peppercorns. It is then drained, sprinkled with flour, flambéed with grappa, browned in oil and butter with pancetta and onion and cooked—first in a pot, then in the oven—with the marinade liquid. In Friuli, the meat is marinated for some days in white wine with sage, bay leaves, rosemary, cloves and cinnamon, browned in butter and oil, and cooked in the reduced marinade liquid. Both versions are served with polenta. Trentino-Alto Adige, Friuli-Venezia Giulia.

capriolo alla tirolese leg of roe deer venison, first browned with diced vegetables, then soaked with red wine and roast in the oven. According to Tyrolean tradition, the dish is served with redcurrant jam or jelly. Trentino-Alto Adige.

capriolo con i funghi roe deer venison with mushrooms. The meat is boned, soaked in water for a day and cooked in red wine with a mixture of chopped onion, celery, carrot and crushed juniper berries. The recipe is completed with skinned tomatoes, salt, pepper, dried mushrooms and finely minced garlic, sage and rosemary. Tuscany.

capriolo in salsa al ginepro roe deer venison with juniper sauce. Roe deer bones are boiled in a small amount of water with aromatic vegetables. The liquid is reduced on a high heat with red wine and crushed juniper berries. The resulting sauce is served with sliced roast roe deer venison. Trentino-Alto Adige.

capriolo ripieno stuffed roe deer venison. Cutlets of saddle of roe deer stuffed with chopped roe deer venison mixed with sausage and dusted with paprika, fried in butter and flambéed with kirsch. Trentino-Alto Adige.

capro aka **caprone** buck or billy goat.

Caprone old name for → **Scacione** cheese.

capù di romice monk's rhubarb (→ **lapazio**) leaf stuffed with a mixture of ground beef, salami, grated Parmigiano-Reggiano, fresh bread and eggs. The original name of the recipe, typical of the Val Brembana, in the province of Bergamo was *capù màgher*, "capon for days of abstinence for meat," and the stuffing consisted of bread, Grana Padano and spices. Lombardy

capuc aka **capus** aka **capuss** a mixture of dried breadcrumbs, mature → **Spressa** cheese, eggs, mountain herbs, or chard heated in butter, then wrapped in vine leaves, which are slowly boiled in salted water, allowed to cool and served cold. A summer recipe typical of the Val Rendena and the Valle del Chiese. In the Giudicarie area they make a similar roll with Savoy cabbage leaves, adding fresh sausage or pancetta to the stuffing and removing the raisins. These are stewed

and served hot with polenta or potatoes. Trentino.

capuneit another name for → **caponet**, stuffed cabbage or zucchini leaves.

capunsei small gnocchi flavored with lardo, garlic, salt, pepper and nutmeg, and served with melted butter, sage and Parmigiano-Reggiano. Typical of the province of Mantua. Lombardy.

capunti Basilicata term for → **cavatelli**, type of pasta.

capus de verza type of → **capuc** made with Savoy cabbage leaves.

capuzi garbi boiled sauerkraut (→ **crauti**), sautéed in lardo and stewed. Friuli-Venezia Giulia.

capuzi in dolzegarbo sauerkraut (→ **crauti**) cooked in lard and caramelized sugar, perfumed with cumin and drizzled with vinegar. Friuli-Venezia Giulia.

capuzi in tecia white cabbage lightly fried with smoked pancetta with garlic and cumin. A specialty of Trieste. Friuli-Venezia Giulia.

capuzzelle sheep's or goat's head, split in two and baked in the oven with olive oil, garlic, parsley and potatoes. Puglia, Basilicata.

carabaccia traditional onion soup that used to be flavored with peeled, crushed almonds, verjuice vinegar (→ **agresto**), cinnamon and sugar. Today it is made with finely sliced onions cooked in oil and broth (sometimes with pancetta and aromatics), with the addition of fresh fava beans and peas, a splash of white wine and salt and pepper. Served with slices of toasted bread. A specialty of Florence since at least the 16th century. Tuscany.

caragol Veneto term for → **lumaca di mare**, sea snail.

caragol longo Veneto term for → **torricella**, turret shell.

caramella candy. Popular sweet confection,

it owes its name to the Spanish corruption of *canna mellis*. The first rudimentary candies, which arrived in Europe from the Near East shortly after the Crusades, were nothing other than bars of sugar cane. Today candy production is almost exclusively industrial, though in Italy quality artisan production still manages to survive in a number of areas. Candies may be hard (with a percentage of humidity of less than 3%) and soft (with a percentage of humidity of 8% and a higher quantity of fats). The first are made by adding glucose syrup to sugar dissolved in water and raising the temperature to 110°C. The second are made by adding butter (hydrogenated vegetable fats in industrial products) to the same mixture and cooking at a temperature of about 126°C. In both cases, coloring agents, flavorings and gelatin (in some soft candies) are added. Molded into shape, the candies are allowed to cool and packaged. The Italian regions produce a huge number of hard candies with digestive properties, mostly made with herbs and herb liqueurs. In Bormio (province of Sondrio, Lombardy) and at the monastery of Camaldoli (province of Arezzo, Tuscany), they make candies flavored with essence of dwarf mountain pine, in Sicily, with an infusion of carobs (➤ **carruba**), according to a late 19th-century recipe.

caramella, a "candy-style." Way of closing a stuffed pasta by pinching and twisting the edges. An example is ➤ **tortelli con la coda**.

caramellare (1) to caramelize. To slowly heat sugar until it dissolves, assuming a characteristic dark amber color and a sticky texture (➤ **caramello**).

caramellare (2) to caramelize. In the language of confectionery, to cover fresh, dried or candied fruit or other preparations with caramelized sugar. The fruit is washed and dried, plunged into the caramelized sugar and allowed to cool on a marble surface.

caramellare (3) to caramelize. Expression also used to refer to foods which have been given the appearance and color of caramel. Eg, baby onions, carrots or turnips, cooked briefly on a high heat with butter and a sprinkling of sugar (➤ **glassare**).

caramelle di limone e arancio candies typical of the Gargano Peninsula, made by macerating shredded lemon and orange zest in water for four days, then cooking it in sugar. Puglia

caramellizzazione caramelization. As associated with the roasting of meats (➤ **arrosto morto**), fish or vegetables, the process whereby, at a temperature higher than 130°C, the surface of a foodstuff browns (like caramel) and hardens to a crispy texture. As associated with confectionery, the process consists of heating sugar slowly to around 170°C. As the sugar melts, it assumes a characteristic dark amber color and a sticky texture (➤ **caramellare**).

caramello caramel. A sticky confection made by slowly heating refined sugar with a small amount of water. Used to coat fresh, dried and candied fruit, to flavor desserts and candies and to line molds for cream deserts.

caranciuli aka **riccetti di Gesù Bambino** ("Baby Jesus's curls") traditional Christmas cookies, fried, dipped in honey, and decorated with colored sprinkles. Puglia.

caraviedde Puglia term for ➤ **canocchia**, mantis shrimp.

carbonade aka **carbonata** thin slices of beef browned in butter with onions and stewed in red or white wine with herbs and spices. Used to be made with salted beef. Val d'Aosta.

carbonara, alla condiment for various shapes of pasta consisting of ➤ **guanciale** (cheek bacon), eggs and grated Pecorino cheese. Said to have been created in Rome after World War II. Lazio.

carbonaretti sui sarmenti small ➤ **pesce persico**, perch (fished mainly in Lake Piediluco), barbecued over a fire of vine shoots. The technique makes the fish black, like coal (*carbone* in Italian). Umbria.

carbonato di ammonio ammonium carbonate. Also known as cake ammonium, a chemical agent with a leavening function. Makes make mixtures soft and friable.

carcagnola pig's trotter (➤ **insalata di mussu e carcagnola**).

carcassa carcass. The whole body of a butchered animal after bleeding, gutting, skinning or plucking and, in some cases, the removal of the head and legs.

carcerato calf's innards, trotters, tail and head boiled with aromatics and reduced to a broth, which is thickened with slices of day-old bread. The resulting "porridge" is served piping hot with the addition of salt, pepper and a generous amount of grated Pecorino. The word *carcerato* means "prisoner" in Italian. According to tradition, the dish is so-named because in Pistoia, where it originated, the city slaughterhouse is close to the prison, separated only by a rivulet into which uncommercializable offal used to be thrown. Apparently the prison inmates applied for and were granted the use of the discarded offal to make soup. Tuscany.

carcino another name for ➤ **granchio marino commune**, Mediterranean green crab.

carciofo artichoke (*Cynara cardunculus scolymus*). Many varieties exist, with spines or without, and all prefer temperate, sunny climes. The bracts, often wrongly referred to as leaves, are thicker and more fibrous towards the outside, and may be green or purple in color, according to the variety. The chief cultivars in Italy are *catanese*, *spinoso* and *romanesco* aka *cimarolo*, and the finest varieties are: ➤ **carciofo di Paestum** (Campania) and ➤ **carciofo romanesco del Lazio**, which have both been granted PGI status. The Italian Ministry of Agriculture's database of native and/or traditional food products lists the following varieties: *carciofo vastese* (Abruzzo); *carciofo bianco*, ➤ **carciofo bianco di Pertosa**, *capuanella*, *carciofo di Castellammare*, ➤ **carciofo violetto di Castellamare**, *carciofo di Montoro*, *carciofo di Pietrelcina*, *carciofo di Procida*, *pignatella* (Campania); *carciofo di Orte*, *carciofo di Sezze*, *carciofo di Tarquinia* (Lazio); *violet di Provenza* (➤ **carciofo di Perinaldo**), *carciofo violetto spinoso di Albenga*, *carciofo spinoso di Pompeiana* (Liguria); *carciofo monteluponese*, *carciofo violetto precoce di Jesi* (Marche); *carciofo violetto di Brindisi*, *carciofo di San Ferdinando* (Puglia); *carciofo spinoso* (Sardinia); *carciofo spinoso di Palermo o Menfi*, *carciofo violetto catanese* (Sicily); *carciofo del litorale livornese*, *carciofo di Chiusure*, *carciofo di Pian di Rocca*, *mamma di San Miniato*, *mamma empolese* (Tuscany); *mame d'Alpago*, *mamma bianca di Bassano*, ➤ **carciofo violetto di Sant'Erasmo** (Veneto). In the kitchen, the artichoke appears in numerous recipes; in stews, sauces, pies (➤ **torta pasqualina**), and is the main ingredient in several famous traditional dishes: ➤ **carciofi alla giudia**, ➤ **carciofi alla matticella**, ➤ **carciofi alla romana**, ➤ **carciofi attuppati**, ➤ **carciofi ritti**, ➤ **cilele in tecia**, ➤ **mamme ripiene**. It is also eaten raw in salads or dipped in oil, boiled (➤ **cacocciuliddi spinusi**) and preserved in oil. The shoots and sprouts are edible too (➤ **carducci**, ➤ **castraure**).

carciofi al tegame stewed artichoke. Side dish of artichokes sliced into wedges, stewed in olive oil with minced garlic and parsley, and mixed with beaten eggs towards the end of the cooking process. Sardinia.

carciofi all'inferno artichokes stuffed with a mixture of garlic, parsley and mint leaves. Liguria.

carciofi alla Cavour artichokes parboiled, baked in the oven with butter and cheese, and served with a sauce of anchovies, hard-boiled eggs and parsley. Piedmont.

carciofi alla giudia globe artichokes turned with a sharp knife and pressed into a flower shape, seasoned with salt and pepper, and fried in a generous amount of olive oil. One of the many Jewish recipes assimilated by Roman cuisine. Lazio.

carciofi alla matticella artichokes pressed on a hard surface to open the leaves, then filled with a mixture of minced fresh garlic, pennyflower, salt and extra virgin olive oil, broiled over a fire of dried vine shoots (*matticelle*). Traditionally served with fresh fava beans, toasted bread and Pecorino. A specialty of Velletri, in the province of Rome. Lazio.

carciofi alla romana globe artichokes cleaned and filled with breadrcrumbs mixed with oil, minced garlic and parsley, arranged upright and closely packed in a tall, narrow casserole dish. They are then almost covered with water and extra virgin oil, and cooked in the oven until the liquid has almost evaporated. Lazio.

carciofi attuppati large artichokes stuffed with a mixture of grated Pecorino, dry breadcrumbs, boned anchovies, finely minced garlic and parsley, pepper and extra virgin olive oil, and cooked in water and lemon juice. Sometimes the anchovy and Pecorino may be replaced by pork sausage. Sicily.

carciofi con i piselli artichokes with peas. Popular spring side dish of fresh peas and artichoke hearts sautéed with onion, strips of prosciutto and extra virgin olive oil or lard, and finished off with broth. Lazio.

carciofi in tortiera layers of artichokes, potatoes, Pecorino and garlic lubricated with olive oil and sprinkled with dry breadcrumbs, and baked in the oven. Excellent warm or cold. Calabria.

carciofi ripieni stuffed artichoke. In Puglia, they stuff the artichokes of Rutigliano (province of Bari) with a mixture of breadcrumbs, grated Pecorino and finely minced capers, parsley and garlic, and cook them slowly in water with oil and sliced potatoes. In Sardinia, thorny artichokes are stuffed with sausage, eggs, breadcrumbs and chopped sun-dried tomatoes, and cooked slowly in water with onion and parsley.

carciofi ripieni al sugo stuffed artichokes in sauce. Side dish of artichokes stuffed with a mixture of beaten eggs and Parmigiano, fried in olive oil and finished in a skillet with tomato sauce. Campania.

carciofi ritti literally "upright artichokes." Artichokes stuffed with ground beef amalgamated with grated Parmigiano, parsley, salt, pepper and fresh breadcrumbs. The artichoke hearts and stalks, chopped and lightly fried in olive oil with smoked pancetta and skinned plum tomatoes, are used as a serving sauce. Tuscany.

carciofo bianco di Pertosa During the 1920s, the Pertosa artichoke was much sought after in all the markets in the area, but today it has almost disappeared. Only a few farmers still grow it on small plots of land among their olive trees. Many traits set the variety apart, among which its resistance to low temperatures and its very light green, almost white, color. Its sweet flavor and the extraordinary tenderness of its inner leaves make it an excellent artichoke for eating raw, dressed with nothing more than a drizzle of extra-virgin olive oil. Protected by a Slow Food presidum, it is grown around villages in the Valle del Basso Tanagro, in the province of Salerno. Campania.

carciofo di Paestum aka **tondo di Paestum** PGI artichoke grown in the province of Salerno. Green to purple in color, its flesh is tender in texture and delicate in flavor. Harvested from February to May. Campania.

carciofo di Perinaldo aka **violet francese** artichoke cultivated in the mountains of Provence and round the village of Perinaldo, in the province of Imperia. Spineless and purple in color, it has very tender flesh. A Slow Food presidium promotes its cultivation using organic methods. Liguria.

carciofo di Schito another name for ➤ **carciofo violetto di Castellammare.**

carciofo piccolo regional term for ➤ **cardogna**, common or spotted goldenthistle.

carciofo romanesco del Lazio PGI spineless globe artichoke grown in the provinces of Viterbo, Rome and Latina. Sweet and delicate in flavor, it has a tender heart that features in numerous recipes. Harvested from August to September, it is normally sold in bunches. Other names: ➤ **cimarolo**, ➤**mamma**, ➤ **mammola.**

carciofo violetto di Castellammare aka **carciofo di Schito**, Artichoke with green bracts with hints of purple. The first inflorescence (*mamma* or *mammolella*) is traditionally protected by an earthenware pot to make the plant tender and pale. Traditionally served on Easter Monday, broiled over charcoal and seasoned with salt, pepper, parsley, fresh wild garlic and olive oil, or stuffed (*m'buttunata*) with cheese, chopped salami, eggs, salt, pepper, parsley and day-old bread. Grown in and around a number of towns and villages in the province of Naples and protected by a Slow Food presidium. Campania.

carciofo violetto di Sant'Erasmo spiny artichoke with purple bracts, cultivated for centuries in the kitchen gardens of the island of Sant'Erasmo and other small islands of the Venice lagoon. Tender and fleshy, it is eaten raw (its young shoots, known as ➤ **castraure**, are a real delicacy) or boiled and dressed with garlic, parsley, oil and pepper, fried in batter, *alla grega* (quartered, sautéed and served cold with lemon juice), or stewed with shrimp (➤ **schia**), anchovies and sardines. A Slow Food presidium has brought growers together to promote the cultivation of the variety and fetch more remunerative prices. Veneto.

carcioppola Neapolitan word for ➤ **carciofo**, artichoke.

carcotto Roman recipe of breast of veal stewed with the same herbs and spices as ➤ **porchetta**, with the addition of red wine. Lazio.

cardamomo cardamom (*Elettaria cardamomum*) Spice native to India, cultivated in Sri Lanka and Malaysia. It has a sweet-sour lemony aroma and is used in medicine and perfumery. In the kitchen it is widely used in the Far East and the English-speaking world, less so in Italy. It features, though, in ➤ **spicchitedda**, a traditional cake of the Aeolian Islands (Sicily).

cardarella aka **cardarello** regional terms for ⇀ **cardoncello**, king oyster mushroom.

cardedda dialect term for ⇀ **grespigno**, field sowthistle.

cardella regional term for ⇀ **gelone**, oyster mushroom.

cardi acidi cardoons scraped clean, cut into pieces, immersed in acidulated water overnight, poached in olive oil and water, then sprinkled with lemon juice. Originally a Jewish recipe, now an integral part of Roman cuisine. Lazio.

cardi all'uovo cardoons cut into pieces and boiled, sautéed with chili and mixed with beaten eggs and grated Pecorino. Basilicata.

cardi con le acciughe cardoons with anchovies. Cardoons (⇀ **gobbi**) cut into pieces, boiled and finished in a skillet with butter, garlic, bay leaves and anchovies. Piedmont.

cardi e uova sode cardoons and hard-boiled eggs. Cardoons arranged in a baking tin, covered with a cream of minced parsley, crushed hard-boiled eggs, fried breadcrumbs and lemon juice, and baked in a very hot oven. Sardinia.

cardi in tegame cardoons coated in flour and fried until golden in oil and butter, to which bone marrow dissolved in broth, spices, and herbs are added. Veneto.

cardi ripieni stuffed cardoons. Cardoons (⇀ **gobbi**) sliced in half, filled with ground veal, sausage, ham, grated cheese, eggs, garlic and parsley, joined together, breaded, fried, and finished in butter and broth. Piedmont.

cardi selvatici sott'olio, in dialect aka **gureu aresti cunfittau** wild cardoons preserved in oil. Tender young shoots (⇀ **carducci**), cleaned, acidulated, cut into chunks, parboiled and preserved in hermetically sealed glass jars (sometimes aromatized with garlic and parsley). Sardinia.

cardo (pl. **cardi**) cardoon (*Cynara cardunculus* var. *altilis*). At its sweetest and crispest best when bleached: ie, covered with mounds of soil, straw or canvas to protect it from the sun. In Umbria, a cardoon grown in this way is called a *cardo incartato*. In some regions, especially in Piedmont and Tuscany, when the plant is tall and healthy, they bend it back and cover it with soil. As it seeks the sunlight, the cardoon swells and curves, and the stems lose all their chlorophyll to become white and tender. At this point, they are called *gobbi*, or "hunchbacks" (⇀ **gobbi**). The Italian Ministry of Agriculture's database of native and/or traditional food products lists the following varieties: *cardone* (Campania); *gigante di Romagna* (Emilia-Romagna); *gobbo di Trodica* (Marche); *cardo avorio di Isola d'Asti, cardo bianco avorio di Andezeno*, ⇀ **cardo gobbo di Nizza Monferrato** (Piedmont); *cardo* (aka *gobbo*) *della Val di Cornia, cardo massese* (aka *cardone* aka *gobbo*) (Tuscany). At the table, cardoons are mostly eaten cooked (though in Piedmont they are also eaten raw, dipped in ⇀ **bagna caoda** or oil), after first parboiling them in acidulated water. They may be baked, fried, stewed, stuffed, finished in the pan with sausage or anchovies or used as an ingredient in soups (⇀ **cardone**), purées, pies, flans, molds and casseroles.

cardo asinino milk thistle (*Silybum marianum* sinon. *Onopordum Illyricum, Cirsium vulgare*) Herbaceous plants of the Asteraceae family. Tall, spiny with thorny pinkish flowers. Their pungent inflorescences, roots, heads and stems are cleaned and eaten boiled and fried in most of the south of Italy, some species also in Abruzzo and Lazio. Common and regional names: ⇀ **cardo campestre**, ⇀ **cardone**, ⇀ **spina bianca**, ⇀ **scardic-**

cione; ➤ **cardo santo** (*Silybum*); ➤ **ono-pordo** (*Onopordum*), ➤ **stoppione** (*Cirsium*). *Cardone della Campania* is listed in the Italian Ministry of Agriculture's database of native and/or traditional food products.

cardo campestre another name for ➤ **cardo asinino**, milk thistle.

cardo gobbo di Nizza Monferrato "hunchback cardoon." In the sandy terrains between Nizza, Incisa Scapaccino and Castelnuovo Belbo (province of Asti), cardoons are sowed in May and harvested in October. They are neither irrigated nor fertilized, but they are "bleached." In September they are bent back and covered with soil; as they try to look for light, they swell and bend, and the stalks lose every trace of chlorophyll to become white and tender. Protected by a Slow Food presidium, the "hunchback" of Nizza Monferrato is the only cardoon to be eaten raw and is an essential ingredient of ➤ **bagna caoda**. It may also be fried, baked, stuffed or used in soup. Piedmont.

cardo santo another name for ➤ **cardo asinine**, milk thistle.

cardo selvatico wild cardoon (*Cynara cardunculus sylvestris*). Large wild and naturalized herbaceous plant. A member of the same family as the artichoke (➤ **carciofo**), it is commonly called *cardo* in southern Italy and the islands. The gem is eaten fried, baked and preserved in oil. Popular in the Madonie mountains in Sicily (➤ **napruddi**) and in Sardinia (➤ **gureu**), where they preserve the shoots and heads in oil (➤ **cugutzula**), and also make a liqueur with the plant.

cardogna common goldenthistle, spotted goldenthistle (*Scolymus hispanicus* and *S. grandiflorus*). Spiny, cardoon-like herbaceous plants common along Mediterranean sea shores. Used in the kitchen in southern Italy (and also in an area of Lazio), where the heads are trimmed, boiled and dressed or fried in batter. Common and regional names: ➤ **barba gentile**, ➤ **carciofo piccolo**, ➤ **cardoncello**, ➤ **guardabue**, ➤ **scardiccione**, ➤ **scolino**.

cardolino della ferula regional term for ➤ **cardoncello**, king oyster mushroom.

cardoncello (pl. **cardoncelli**) name used in Puglia and other southern Italian regions for ➤ **Carducci**, artichoke shoots, but also for the young tips of ➤ **cardogna**, common goldenthistle.

cardoncello (pl. **cardoncelli**) king oyster mushroom (*Pleurotus eryngii*, sinon. *P. fuscus*, *Agaricus eryngii*). Mushroom renowned since antiquity for the excellent flavor of its firm white flesh. Eaten stewed with tomato, in soups, baked (➤ **tiella di cardoncelli**), broiled and with meat (➤ **agnello ai cardoncelli**). The cap is broad and flat, the stalk thick and elastic. It grows in the vicinity of wild cardoons, hence its name. Much loved in southern Italy, especially in Puglia and Basilicata. Common and dialect names: ➤ **cardarello**, ➤ **cardarella**, ➤ **cardolino della ferula**, ➤ **ferlengo**, ➤ **fungo del cardo**, ➤ **fungo di carne**, ➤ **fungo di ferla**, ➤ **antunna**, ➤ **cardulinu 'e petza**, ➤ **feurazzu**, ➤ **tunniu biancu**. The *ferlengo* (aka *finferlo*) *di Tarquinia* (Lazio) and ➤ **cardoncello** (Puglia) are listed in the Italian Ministry of Agriculture's database of native and/or traditional food products.

cardone (1) thick winter soup consisting of cardoons arranged in a pot and covered with chicken broth, mixed veal and pork meatballs, eggs, breadcrumbs, flat-leaved parsley and Parmigiano. When the soup is ready, more eggs are beaten in with grated Parmigiano and pine kernels.

Campania.

cardone (2) regional name for → **cardo asinino**, milk thistle.

cardone in brodo rich Christmas soup of cardoon ribs, eggs, chicken livers and meatballs cooked in capon or turkey broth and sprinkled with grated Pecorino cheese. Typical of the province of Chieti. Abruzzo.

cardoni another name for → **carducci**, artichoke shoots.

carducci artichoke shoots. Having been bent back and buried in the soil, hence bleached by lack of sunlight, they are dug up, cleaned, cut into pieces, which are parboiled in acidulated water, they are cooked in the same way as cultivated cardoons. They are particularly popular in Puglia, where they are known as → **cardoni** or → **cardoncelli**, not to be confused with the mushrooms of the same name.

cardulinu 'e petza Sardinian dialect term for → **cardoncello**, king oyster mushroom.

carduncieddhi baby goldenthistles (→ **cardogna**). Mostly eaten boiled and dressed with oil and vinegar. In Brindisi they cook them with black olives, capers, anchovies, grated Pecorino and breadcrumbs. In Foggia and Bari, as a traditional Easter dish, they are mixed with eggs beaten with cheese and pepper and baked in the oven. Puglia.

carej dialect term for → **porcino**, porcini mushroom.

carfogn fried sweet ravioli prepared for weddings, Carnival and village festivals. The dough is made from flour, butter, sugar, whole eggs and egg yolks, lemon zest, wine or beer and grappa. The stuffing consists of toasted poppy seeds mixed with crumbled dry cookies, sugar, fruit jams, grappa and milk. Typical

of the Valle del Biois, in the province of Belluno. Veneto.

carletti regional term for → **silene rigonfia**, bladder campion.

carlina, alla method of cooking fish (John Dory, sole, turbot) and crustaceans (scampi) typical of the Venice area. The fish is lightly coated in flour, briefly fried in butter, then baked in the oven with diced skinned tomatoes, chopped capers and curls of butter. A specialty at the Locanda Cipriani in Torcello, in the province of Venice is *sampietro alla carlina*: fillets of John Dory briefly fried in oil, butter and parsley, covered with capers, gherkins, skinned tomatoes, lemon juice and Worcestershire sauce. Veneto.

carnacotta traditional Neapolitan street food (→ **cibo di strada**). Calf's offal, tripe and muzzle, sheep's and pig's heads, boiled and dressed with salt and lemon juice, or stewed with tomatoes or boiled in broth. That of the *carnacottaro* selling the dish at the side of the road used to be a familiar sight in Naples, but the trade has now virtually disappeared. The dish can still be found in the odd traditional *tripperia*, or tripe restaurant. Campania.

carnasecca aka **carnesecca** old Tuscan word still used in the region to refer to salted pork pancetta.

carne meat.

carne 'ncantarata pork dressed with chili and fennel seeds and aged for a few months. Soaked overnight in cold water prior to use, the pork is stewed with tomato flavored with wild fennel or chicory. The name derives from that of the earthenware jars (*kantaros* in Greek) in which the meat used to be preserved in salt. Calabria.

carne alla genovese another term for → **genovese**, beef and onions.

carne alla pecorara pork marinated in olive oil, garlic and pepper, then browned in oil and basted with the marinade liquid. Covered with onions lightly fried in lard and grated Pecorino, it is finished in the oven. The dish can also be made with veal, chicken or lamb. Calabria.

carne cruda raw veal or beef. Highly popular antipasto made with the hand-chopped or ground meat from the leg of the ➤ **fassone** calf and dressed like a salad. Sometimes grated white truffles, finely sliced royal argaric mushrooms, slivers of Parmigiano or slices of celery are also added. In the 1970s, restaurants in Alba, in the province of Cuneo, began to use the same dressings on very thin slices of beef: a sort of simplified ➤ **carpaccio** often presented as ➤ **carne cruda all'albese**. Piedmont.

carne cruda all'albese another name for ➤ **carne cruda**, raw beef.

carne di cavallo horsemeat. Smoked cured meat produced by a single butcher's shop in Rovereto (province of Trento). Cuts of horsemeat (fillet or shoulder) are layered in tubs and aromatized with salt, garlic, juniper berries, aromatic herbs and spices. The barrel is covered with a lid and a weight is placed on top to press the meat. After 25 days, the pieces of meat are rolled, tied up with string and cased in intestines, then smoked for 15-16 hours and aged for seven to 30 days.

carne di cavallo alla pignata another term for ➤ **pignata di cavallo** horsemeat casserole.

carne ferrata "meat with horseshoes." Name used in areas of the Salento peninsula for horsemeat. Puglia

carne fumada Veneto dialect for smoked meat.

carne maritata stew of veal, pork and sweetbreads (➤ **animelle**) cooked using the same technique as ➤ **arrosto morto**. The meat is first lightly fried in oil with garlic and onion, then cooked with tomatoes, parsley and sometimes, quartered artichokes. Campania.

carne salada chunks of beef are placed in a stainless steel container (in the past, in a wood tub or earthenware pot) and covered with a mixture of salt, pepper, garlic, rosemary, bay leaves, juniper berries and, on occasion, lemon, onion and cinnamon. The container is then covered with a lid and a weight is placed on top to press the meat, which is ready for consumption after two weeks. It is served raw, dressed with oil and lemon juice and seared in butter or stewed with beans. Typical of the province of Trento. Trentino-Alto Adige.

carne sfilata aka **carne sfilacciata** prime quality horsemeat cut into very thin slices and covered with salt for ten to 15 days. Smoked in chimneys for a month, it is pounded with a hammer and shredded. A specialty of the province of Padua, produced in limited quantities. Veneto.

carnesecca another name for ➤ **carnasecca**.

Carnia (1) cow's milk similar to Montasio. Produced all over the Carnia area in the province of Udine. Friuli.

Carnia (2) partly pasteurized Bruno Alpina cow's milk cheese produced in Padola, a village in the province of Belluno. Veneto.

carosella soft wheat used to make a very white flour. Widespread in the south of Italy and used for cooking purposes mainly in the Cilento area. Campania, Basilicata.

caroselle sott'aceto inflorescences of the wild fennel plant preserved in vinegar. Left to pickle for 20 days or so before eating. Puglia.

carosello an unripe melon (➤ **melone**).

carota carrot (*Daucus carota* var. *sativus*). Many varieties are cultivated all over Italy. The Italian Ministry of Agriculture's database of native and/or traditional food products lists: ➤ **carota dell'Altopiano del Fucino** (Abruzzo); *carota di Albenga* (Liguria); *carota di San Rocco Castagnaretta* (Piedmont); *carota di Zapponeta, carota giallo-viola di Tiggiano* (Puglia); *carota di Ispica* (Sicily); *carota della Val di Gresta* (Trentino); *carota di Chioggia* (Veneto). Carrots are used in many dishes: to flavor boiled, stewed and braised meats; chopped with celery and onion to flavor sauces and stuffings; cut into rounds or julienned, boiled, sautéed or puréed as side dishes for meat and fish; grated raw to be eaten on their own or in mixed salads; to make molds, pies and cakes, such as ➤ **torta di carote**, typical of the province of Trento. In rare occasions, they are also preserved (➤ **carote di Viterbo in bagno aromatico**).**carota dell'Altopiano del Fucino** PGI carrot produced in the province of L'Aquila. Bright orange in color, it is eaten fresh, but also, thanks to its high vitamin content, processed to make juices. Abruzzo.

carota selvatica wild carrot or Queen Anne's lace (*Daucus carota*). Spontaneous herbaceous plant with an erect hairy stem, umbrels and edible roots. Common all over Italy especially in the central regions, where the tips and roots are used as ingredients for vegetable soups (➤ **acquacotta con le erbarelle**). Domesticated varieties are cultivars of the wild carrot. *Pastinocello toscano* is included in the Italian Ministry of Agriculture's database of native and/or traditional food products. Common and regional names: ➤ **gallinaccio**, ➤ **pastinaca**, ➤ **pastinello**, ➤ **pastinocello**.

carote di Viterbo in bagno aromatico a sort of jam traditionally served in Viterbo with boiled meats and local cured meats. Carrots are cut into strips, sun-dried and immersed in vinegar for a few days. The vinegar, minus the carrots, is then mixed with sugar, cloves, nutmeg, cinnamon and, in some recipes, raisins, pine kernels, chocolate, candied fruits and anise seeds. Lazio.

carote in agrodolce sweet and sour carrots. Carrots sliced into rounds and cooked in oil (in the past, goose fat was used) and mixed with raisins, pine kernels and vinegar. A recipe of the Jewish tradition. Veneto.

carozzi Lazio dialect term for slices of dried apples and pears (➤ **frutta secca**).

carpa carp. A member of the Cyprinidae family, introduced to Italy by the Romans from Asia, and today common in lakes and rivers all over the world. The numerous varieties of the fish enjoy stagnant, muddy water, and can be farmed in artificial ponds (in the past, they used to be raised in rice fields). The Italian Ministry of Agriculture's database of native and/or traditional food products lists the *carpa del Trasimeno* (Perugia, Umbria). Any unpleasant muddy smells can be eliminated by plunging the fish into water and vinegar. Small specimens are fried or served in ➤ **carpione** or used as an ingredient in risottos, whereas larger ones are baked.

carpa in bianco alla tremezzina carp cut into chunks, cooked in a pot with baby onions, bay leaves, white wine, vinegar, salt and water, then left to cool so that the cooking liquid sets to a jelly. Served with olive oil and lemon juice. A specialty of Tremezzo, in the province of Como. Lombardy.

carpa in carpione fillets of carp coated in flour, fried and steeped in a warm marinade of water, vinegar and aromatic herbs and spices. Piedmont.

carpa regina a porchetta the fine *carpa regina*, queen carp, is a symbol of Lake Trasimeno, in the province of Perugia. This recipe takes a pounded mixture of garlic, rosemary, pepper and wild fennel (the same used for → **porchetta**, hence the name) and spreads it over gashes in the fish's back and into the fish's stomach (innards removed). The fish is then baked in a wood oven and basted frequently with the cooking juices, which are collected in a dripping pan (→ **leccarda**). Umbria.

carpaccio recipe devised and made famous by Giuseppe Cipriani of Harry's Bar in Venice. Wafer-thin slices of prime raw beef dressed with a mixture oil, salt, pepper and lemon or with a light mustard mayonnaise. In the wake of its success, the term now refers to any dish of similarly dressed sliced raw meat, fish or vegetables.

carpasinn-a aka **carpascina** barley bread soaked in water and vinegar, squeezed dry and topped with tomato, anchovies, oil and basil. Typical of Badalucco, in the province of Imperia. Liguria.

carpendù dialect term for *carpendola*, an apple variety with a sourish flavor. Piedmont.

carpionata variable mixture of zucchini, eggs and breaded veal cutlets served in → **carpione (2)** (hence the name of the dish): ie, fried and marinated in vinegar, oil, garlic and sage. Served in the summer as an antipasto, as a main course or as a meal in one. Piedmont.

carpione (1) brown trout (*Salmo trutta carpio*). Freshwater member of the salmon family (Salmonidae) and a subspecies of the trout, endemic to Lake Garda. Cooked either broiled or boiled, dressed with extra virgin olive oil. Its flesh is del-

icate and it was traditionally preserved in a marinade of vinegar and herbs, hence the preparation named for it (→ **carpione (2)**). Lombardy.

carpione (2) named for the fish of the same name (→ **carpione (1)**, brown trout), a technique for marinating freshwater fish (tench, eel, carp, freshwater sardines, bleak, smelt), after previously coating it with flour and frying it in oil. The marinade liquid, which must cover the fish entirely, is made with lightly fried sliced onion, sage (or bay leaf) and, sometimes, celery and carrot, salt, water and vinegar. The marinade, common especially in northwest Italy (similar methods elsewhere in Italy include → **saor** and → **scapece**), is also used with sea fish, meat, eggs and vegetables, such as pumpkin and zucchini. Piedmont.

carraginu → Sardinian term for → **pesce castagna**, pomfret.

carrargiu, a literally "buried," a cooking technique typical of the Barbagia area, in the province of Nuoro. A pit is dug to contain a whole animal—kid, wild boar, lamb, turkey, calf—stuffed with various herbs and, in some cases, another smaller animal, and lined with aromatic branches. The walls of the pit are dried by burning dry branches, the resulting ash is removed and the animal is lowered in. The pit is then covered with stones and a fire is lit on top. Sardegna.

carrati flour and water gnocchi served with Pecorino cheese, fried pancetta and beaten eggs. The same name is sometimes applied to → **maccheroni alla chitarra**. Abruzzo.

carré term for a cut of meat roughly corresponding to rib (beef, lamb) and loin (pork).

carrettiera, alla name for a pasta sauce which varies according to local recipes, mainly in central and southern Italy, the common denominator of which is the inclusion among the ingredients of ground beef, tomatoes, pepper and chili. In Campania, the name refers to a pasta sauce (normally served with ➤ **vermicelli**) made with breadcrumbs, garlic, parsley, oil, onion and oregano.

carruba carob (*Ceratonia siliqua*). Brown-purplish fruit-pod of an evergreen shrub native to the southern Mediterranean. Common chiefly in Sicily and Sardinia, an important source of animal and human nourishment in times of poverty. The pleasantly sweet seeds and flesh of the fruit were once used to make cocoa substitutes, flours, syrups and candies (still produced in Sicily according to a recipe dating from the late 19th century). Small artisan firms in Sicily (where the carob dessert, ➤ **gelo di carrube**, is also a traditional favorite) and in Puglia make a carob cream for spreading on bread and carob syrup. Today the carob is enjoying something of a revival as an ingredient in low-fat foods.

carsenta (1) leavened flatbread typical of the Lunigiana area, made with all-purpose flour, oil, milk and water and served with cheese or filled, sandwich-like, with cured meats. Baked in the oven (in the past, in a ➤ **testo**, griddle pan) in a tin lined with chestnut leaves. Tuscany.

carsenta (2) oven-baked flatbread typical of the Monferrato area made with bread dough, butter, eggs and a pinch of sugar. May be either savory (anointed with oil and seasoned with salt) or sweet (brushed with beaten egg whites and sprinkled with sugar). Piedmont.

carteddate Puglia dialect term for ➤ **cartellate**, fried pastries.

cartellate fried pastries made with flour, olive oil and dry white wine. The mixture is shaped into corollas, which are fried, repeatedly dipped in ➤ **vincotto** (cooked grape must) or ➤ **cotto di fichi** (fig syrup) and sometimes dipped in powdered cinnamon and chopped cloves. Traditionally made at Christmas, they can be stored in earthenware jars until Easter. Dialect names: ➤ **crustoli**, ➤ **frìnzele**, ➤ **krustuli**, ➤ **scartagghiate**, ➤ **carteddate**.

carteretu the front quarter of a kid, boned and sewn to form a pouch, stuffed with a mixture of chard, eggs and grated Parmigiano, boiled and served hot, cut into slices. Typical of the western Riviera, but now rare. Liguria.

cartoccio, al *en papillote* ("in parchment"). The technique of sealing fish, meat or vegetables in a sheet of greaseproof paper or tin foil and baking it in the oven.

cartufules cuinzades potatoes boiled and baked in the oven with milk and grated smoked ricotta. Friuli-Venezia Giulia.

carvi another name for ➤ **cumino dei prati**, caraway.

casada, de northeast Italian expression for a small farmyard animal.

casadello aka **latteruolo** aka **coppo** custard of sugar, eggs, nutmeg or vanilla flavoring baked in a flour and water crust (➤ **pasta matta**). In Romagna, a peasant dessert traditionally given to the landlord at the end of the harvest. In Emilia, a custard of milk and eggs flavored with cinnamon, cloves and lemon baked without the pastry crust. Emilia-Romagna.

casadinas semolina pastry baskets filled with ricotta or cream cheese, similar to ➤ **pardulas**, but larger. May be sweet, often with raisins in the filling, or savory, the cheese flavored with mint leaves. Sardinia.

Casalina cheese typical of the Marca Trevigiana area made with pasteurized cow's milk. May be eaten fresh or after a few months of aging. On the palate, it has a dominant sourish note. Veneto.

casalinga, alla "homemade." Expression fashionable a few years ago to add a positive connotation to simple home cooking, made in an unadulterated way with cheap ingredients. The analogous term *casereccia*, referred to a style of cooking or a trattoria, now has a dual meaning: on the one hand, the memory of homemade, family recipes tied to tradition; on the other, stereotyped cooking generated by everyday routine.

Casatella Romagnola fresh cheese made with pasteurized cow's milk, ripened in a cold chamber for a week. Emilia-Romagna.

Casatella Trevigiana rindless PDO fresh cheese made with pasteurized cow's milk. The milky-white body is creamy with a buttery consistency. Its mild flavor reveals a characteristic note of acidity. Should be eaten within ten to 15 days of production. Veneto.

casatiello (1) Sorrentino version of ➤ **tortano (1)**, savory ring-shaped pastry. The recipe is the same, only that the eggs are not included in the filling, but arranged to form a crown on top, held on by criss-cross pastry strips. A typical Easter recipe.

casatiello (2) Easter cake of leavened dough aromatized with orange blossom water or limoncello, decorated with hard-boiled eggs held on by criss-cross pastry strips. A recent offshoot of the savory ➤ **casatiello (1)**. Campania.

cascà couscous made with durum wheat semolina, extra virgin olive oil and salt, served with vegetables (peas, white cabbage, cauliflower, eggplant, onions, carrots, fava beans, artichoke), flavored with spices. Typical of Carloforte on the island of San Pietro, in the province of Carbonia-Iglesias, where an annual festival is held in honor of the dish. Sardinia.

cascà alla calasettana aka **cascà alla maniera di Calasetta** couscous served with a sauce of squid, cuttlefish, shrimp and other crustaceans, mollusks and fish, flavored with onion, chili and cherry tomatoes. Typical of Calasetta, in the province of Carbonia-Iglesias. Sardinia.

cascasa another name for ➤ **cascà**, vegetable couscous.

cascella another name for ➤ **cascellore**, crested wartycabbage.

cascellone another name for ➤ **cascellore**, crested wartycabbage.

cascellore crested wartycabbage (*Bunias erucago*). Spontaneous herbaceous plant whose leaves are gathered all over Italy. Eaten raw or cooked, sautéed or in soups (➤ **ris e barland**). Common and regional names: ➤ **barlanda**, ➤ **cascella**, ➤ **cascellone**, ➤ **cassella**.

caschettas name which refers to two distinct Sardinian sweet confections. In the province of Nuoro, where they are also known as ➤ **tiliccas** or ➤ **pistiddos**, they are made for the feast of Sant'Antonio Abate, and are obtained by thickening honey, chopped almonds, citrus fruit zest and saffron over a low heat and shaping the resulting mixture into three-inch cylinders, which are then partially wrapped in very fine pastry in the form of half-moons, hearts, figure "8"s and so on. In Belvì, in the Barbagia area, the same word means wedding pastries filled with hazelnuts and honey. Sardinia.

cascigno Abruzzo word for ➤ **grespigno**, field sowthistle.

casciomaci great pignut (*Bunium bulbocastanum*). Small brown bulb of a spontaneous herbaceous plant that grows to almost three feet in height in cultivated fields, especially barley fields, in subalpine areas. Gathered in Piedmont, Marche, Abruzzo and Basilicata, the bulbs are eaten raw or used to make rustic cakes (in the Monti Sibillini area a sort of ➤ **castagnaccio**). The bulbs are now risking extinction since, unable to find acorns, wild boars have taken to eating them instead. Common and regional names: ➤ **bulbo castano**, ➤ **castagna nera**, ➤ **ceci di terra**, ➤ **noce di terra**, ➤ **pan casciolo**.

Casciotta d'Urbino ancient PDO cheese produced all over the province of Pesaro e Urbino with raw and filtered ewe's and cow's milk from two milkings. Aged for 15 to 30 days, it has a fatty body and a mild, lingering flavor. Marche.

Casecc creamy square cow's cheese, made from October to March in the province of Pesaro e Urbino, especially in the Montefeltro area. It is aged for one to 12 months, first on walnut leaves, then in traditional terracotta jars. Marche.

casera generic name, used in the province of Sondrio, for dairies in which cheese is made and matured. Also the name of a commercial semi-fat cheese matured for four to six months. Lombardy.

caserecce short, slightly twisted commercial durum wheat pasta. Generally served with fish and vegetable sauces or ➤ **pesto alla genovese**.

casgiatini dialect term for ➤ **pardulas**, sweet pastries, in some areas of the provinces of Sassari and Nuoro. Sardinia.

Casieddu di Moliterno ball-shaped traditional variation on ➤ **Cacioricotta** produced in the summer months in Val d'Agri, in the province of Potenza, with goat's milk from two milkings filtered with fern leaves and aromatized with calamint (➤ **nepetella**). Garnished with fern leaves, it is eaten fresh or aged for up to 60 days. Basilicata.

Casizolu rare stretched curd cow's milk cheese traditionally made by hand by the womenfolk of Montiferru, in the province of Oristano, a long job that requires effort and patience. The cheese is pear-shaped and is aged for 30 days to 15 months. When the curd has been stretched, the *s'abbagasu*, or white whey, is not discarded but set aside to make a tasty broth for fragrant cheese soups. A Slow Food presidium aims to guarantee the entire production chain: from the milk of ➤ **Sardo Modicana** or ➤ **Bruno Sarda** cattle that graze in the wild to the delicate and complex final processing. Sardinia.

Caso di Elva aka **Toma di Elva** cow's, ewe's and goat's milk cheese produced in the village of Elva, in the province of Cuneo. Eaten fresh or aged. In the latter case, it may develop a blue-green mold reminiscent of that on ➤ Castelmagno. Piedmont.

casoeûla aka **cassoeûla** winter stew made with Savoy cabbage, various cuts of pork (ribs, rind, head, trotters) boiling sausage (*salamino* or ➤ **luganega**), traditionally served with polenta. Excellent freshly made, but, according to connoisseurs, even better the day after. Many variations exist: in some the cabbage is cooked until it falls apart, in others it is kept crisp, in others still tomato paste is added. The dish, typical of Milan takes its name from the pot in which it is made. Lombardy.

casoeûla aka **ragò d'oca** similar to ➤ **cassola novarese**, made like Milanese ➤ **casoeûla** but with pieces of goose in place of the various cuts of pork. Lombardy.

Casolèt della Val di Sole, Rabbi e Pejo typical whole-milk, uncooked mountain cheese made in wheels weighing about two pounds with a diameter of three inches. Usually eaten after 20 days but more mature versions also exist. A Slow Food presidium encourages production of the cheese with raw milk. Trentino-Alto Adige.

casonsei aka **casoncelli** stuffed pasta filled not with fresh meat but a mixture of cured meats, bread, eggs, cheese and, sometimes, potatoes, field greens or spinach, parsley, costmary (➤ **erba di san Pietro**) and other herbs. In most places the shape of the pasta is *a caramella* (➤ **caramella, a)**, but in the province of Brescia the pasta is a curved tube filled stuffed with crumbled amaretti cookies and raisins, while in the Valcamonica it takes the form of a small bundle. Lombardy.

casonsei de la Bergamasca type of ➤ **casonsei** which includes meat in the stuffing. The other ingredients are ground salami, eggs, Grana Padano, breadcrumbs or dry bread soaked in milk, amaretti cookies, raisins, pears, lemon zest, garlic and flat-leaved parsley. Served with butter, sage and pancetta. Lombardy.

Casoperuto traditional pungent goat's cheese made from January to July in the province of Caserta. Coagulates with dried vegetable rennet and matures for 10-12 months in clay or glass jars, moistened with vinegar and a little oil aromatized with thyme leaves. Campania.

cassagài dialect term for ➤ **calzagatti**, polenta and bean stew.

cassata al forno lighter, less baroque, baked version of ➤ **cassata siciliana**, in appearance and composition similar to ➤ **sfogghiu**, (the only difference is that ➤ **Tuma** cheese is used in lieu of ewe's milk ricotta. Sicily.

cassata napoletana sponge cake filled with ricotta blended with sugar and maraschino (or another sweet liqueur), pieces of dark chocolate and candied fruits, covered with ricotta and decorated with can-

died fruits. A Neapolitan variation on the famous Sicilian delicacy. Campania.

cassata siciliana one of Sicily's most famous cakes. Many scholars believe it is of Arab origin, arguing that the name derives from the Arabic *quas'at*, the bowl in which the cake took its shape. According to others, the name is older and derives from the Latin *caseus* (cheese), a reference to the use of sweetened ricotta. Whatever, the contemporary cassata is the result of the evolution of a cake to which new ingredients have gradually been added, some of which, such as sponge cake, chocolate and refined sugar, have only been adopted since the 18th century. The cake was probably elaborated by nuns in Sicilian convents, and was traditionally eaten only at Easter. According to one of the classic recipes, a disk of sponge cake is placed in the base of a mold, and the walls of the latter are lined with pieces of sponge cake and almond paste (➤ **pasta reale**). The mold is then filled to the brim with a cream made of ricotta, sugar, vanilla and chocolate drops. The cake is then turned out and glazed with white icing and decorated with candied fruit, whole and in pieces. Sicily.

cassateddi ri Pasqua disks of puff pastry filled with ricotta, honey, sugar and cinnamon. Typical of Ragusa. Sicily.

cassatele fritte aka **cassatelle** large fried sweet ravioli. The dough is made by amalgamating durum wheat flour, olive oil, sugar, cinnamon and Marsala. The filling is a cream of ricotta with chocolate shavings, powdered vanilla and cinnamon. Served dusted with sugar (sometimes, confectioner's sugar) mixed with cinnamon. Typical of Trapani. Sicily.

cassatella dessert made by filling a mold lined with cookies soaked in anise liqueur (➤ **sassolino**) and alkermes with a mixture of eggs, sugar, butter, chocolate, liqueur and crushed amaretti and dry cookies, refrigerated and served cold. A specialty of Reggio Emilia. Emilia-Romagna.

cassatelle di Ferla shortcrust pastry baskets filled with a cream of ricotta, sugar, eggs and cinnamon. Typical of a village in the province of Siracusa. Sicily.

cassella regional name for a number of wild herbs: common chicory (➤ **cicoria selvatica**), crested wartycabbage (➤ **cascellore**), rush skeletonweed (➤ **lattugaccio**).

casseruola di polpetti ragout of baby octopuses, lightly fried onions, tomatoes, parsley and white wine. Used to dress pasta or as a dipping sauce. Puglia.

cassetta regional term for ➤ **borsa del pastore**, shepherd's purse.

cassia word for ➤ **canella** (cinnamon), but also for ➤ **acacia** (acacia).

cassola novarese winter stew of pork (ribs, trotters) and pieces of goose. The meat is first browned, then slow-cooked in water to which garlic and Savoy cabbage are subsequently added. The equivalent, in the province of Novara, of Lombard ➤ **casoeûla**. Piedmont.

cassòla (1) soup made of various types of fish, tomato sauce aromatized with garlic, onion, basil and chili. Served poured over day-old bread fried in lard. Sardinia.

cassòla (2) mountain stew of mutton aromatized with vegetables and cooked with Savoy cabbage leaves, lardo and tomato. A specialty of the province of Reggio Emilia. Emilia-Romagna.

cassone flatbread (➤ **piada**) with a filling of buttered wild herbs and lardo, pancetta or sausage, and pork scratchings (➤ **ciccioli**), garlic and onion. Flipped over into a half-moon shape, it is cooked on a ➤ **testo**, or griddle pan. May also be fried

in lard. A popular street food (➤ **cibo di strada**), eaten as an antipasto or snack. Emilia-Romagna.

cassopipa, in a technique of slow cooking (➤ **pipare**) in a covered earthenware pot (*casso* in dialect). Used to cook shellfish, such as carpet shell clams (➤**caparossolo**), common clams (➤ **bevarasse** aka **pevarasse**), mussels (➤ **peoci**), razor clams (➤ **capelonghe**), which are heated in oil with onion or garlic until they are all open, then sprinkled with pepper and minced parsley tritato. Veneto.

cassuola term used in the southern regions of Italy for a pot suitable for making stews and, by extension, the stew made in it. In Campania, for example, it refers to a stew of meat, tomatoes, minced garlic and chili.

castagna chestnut. Fruit of the sweet chestnut tree (*Castanea sativa*), once known as *albero del pane*, or bread tree, on account of its importance as a source of nourishment in poor mountain areas. Native to the Mediterranean, it is common in Italy, especially in the Apennines, in numerous varieties whose fruits are divided generically into **castagna** and ➤ **marrone**. The former is dark brown in color and flat on one side, the latter is larger with a streaked pale brown outer skin. Chestnuts are still dried (➤ **castagne secche**) to make flour (➤ **farina di castagne**). Fresh chestnuts are eaten in the fall, when they also feature in confectionery (➤ **budino di castagne**, ➤ **busecchina**, ➤ **calzone di castagne**, ➤ **kastanientorte**, ➤ **mohrenkopfe**, ➤ **montebianco**, ➤ **salame di castagne**, ➤ **tortellini dolci**) and in stuffings for roast pheasant, goose, turkey and so on. Other delicacies are ➤ **marron glacé** and boiled and roast chestnuts (➤ **caldarroste**), which have a colorful variety of regional and dialect names all over Italy: ➤ **allesse**, ➤ **balletti**, ➤ **ballotte**, ➤ **brusè**, ➤ **caldallesse**, ➤ **palluotte**, ➤ **rostìe**, ➤ **vallàne**, ➤ **veròle**. Deforestation, the exodus of people from the mountains and disease have decimated chestnut woods. The finest varieties still common are: ➤ **castagna Cuneo**, ➤ **castagna del Monte Amiata**, ➤ **castagna di Montella**, ➤ **marrone del Mugello**, ➤ **marrone di Castel del Rio**, ➤ **marrone di Roccadaspide**, ➤ **marrone di San Zeno**. The Italian Ministry of Agriculture's database of native and/or traditional food products also lists: *castagna roscetta Valle Roveto, marrone di Valle Castellana* (Abruzzo); *kastanien von Suedtirol* (Alto Adige); *castagne di Calabria* (Calabria); *castagna del monte Faito, castagna del prete, castagna di Acerno, castagna di Serino, castagna paccuta, castagna tempestiva del vulcano di Roccamonfina, castagna di Santa Cristina, castagna di Scala* (Campania); *antiche varietà di castagne piacentine, castagna di Granaglione, marrone di Campora* (Emilia-Romagna); *castagna canalutta, castagna marrone di Vito d'Asio, castagna obiacco* (Friuli); *castagna di Terelle, marrone di Arcinazzo Romano, marrone dei monti Cimini, marrone di Latera* (Lazio); *castagna bodrasca, castagna gabbiana* (Liguria); *marrone di Santa Croce* (Lombardy); *marrone del Montefeltro, marrone di Acquasanta Terme, marrone di Roccafluvione* (Marche); *castagna molisana* (Molise); *castagna della Val Borbera, castagna delle valli di Lanzo, marrone della Val Pellice, marrone della valle di Susa* (Piedmont); *castagna carpinese, castagna mondigiana e perella del Pratomagno, castagna pistolesa, castagne e marroni della Toscana* (Tuscany); *marone trentino* (Trentino); *marrone umbro* (Umbria); *castagna del Baldo, castagne e marroni dei Colli Euganei, marrone di San Mauro, marrone* feltrino, *marrone di Combai, marrone del Monfenera, marrone di Valrovina* (Veneto).

castagna Cuneo PGI chestnut with a distinctive sweet flavor and crisp texture. The dried fruit may be ground to make flour. Piedmont.

castagna d'acqua water chestnut (*Trapa natans*). A native of Asia, long present in Europe, it consists of a floating rosette of leaves beneath which the roots are anchored into the underwater mud. It produces small white flowers which, in summer, turn into nuts whose flavor is redolent of chestnuts. Much loved in oriental cuisine, in Italy it is hardly ever eaten, except in the Mantua area, where lakes and streams abound (➤ **risotto e trigoi**).

castagna del Monte Amiata the PGI denomination embraces three varieties, known locally as *marrone, bastarda rossa* and *cecio*. Reddish in color with dark streaks, their pale cream-colored flesh has a sweet, delicate flavor. Only commercialized fresh. Tuscany.

castagna di Montella PGI chestnut with a brown outer skin and sweet, crisp white flesh. Commercialized fresh or dried, with or without the outer skin. The flavor is redolent of caramelized sugar. Grown in the province of Avellino. Campania.

castagna essiccata nei tecci di Calizzano e Murialdo chestnut dried in *tecci*, small stone huts with pine thatches. The technique used to be common throughout the Ligurian Apennines and Piedmontese Alpine valleys, but now only survives in the Val Bormida, in the province of Savona. The chestnuts, mostly of the *gabbina* or *gabbiana* variety, are smoked for about two months over low fires. They are eaten either as they are or used to make cookies, preserves and ice cream.

Protected by a Slow Food presidium. Piedmont, Liguria.

castagna nera another name for ➤ **casciomaci**, great pignut.

castagnaccio sweet chestnut flatbread or cake popular in the Tuscan, Ligurian, Emilian and Piedmontese Apennines, where chestnuts were once a staple, in Lazio (province of Rieti), Lombardy (provinces of Cremona and Mantua), and some areas of the Marche. Probably of north Tuscan origin, it is made by baking a mixture of chestnut flour, water and olive oil in a rectangular tin. Nowadays the surface may be sprinkled with pine kernels, rosemary needles, raisins, crushed hazelnuts or candied orange peel. Regional and dialect names: ➤ **baldino**, ➤ **castagnun**, ➤ **ghirighio**, ➤ **ghiriglio**, ➤ **migliaccio**, ➤ **migliaccio dolce**, ➤ **patona**, ➤ **patuna**, ➤ **pattona**).

castagne con il burro dried chestnuts (see ➤ **castagne secche**) boiled and served, hot or warm, with ➤ **lardo di Arnad**, mountain butter, chestnut honey and rye bread. Served as an antipasto or snack. Val d'Aosta.

castagne d'o prevete "priest's chestnuts." Oven-roast chestnuts splashed with grappa and white wine and tightly wrapped in a cloth to rest before being skinned and eaten. The technique, typical of Campania, is also to be found in some regions of northern Italy. Campania.

castagne e verze a sort of ➤ **casoeûla**, in which the meat is replaced by fresh or dried chestnuts. Lombardy.

castagne secche dried chestnuts. Also known as *castagne bianche* (white chestnuts) inasmuch as they are commercialized skinned. The product of subsistence agriculture in the Alps and Apennines, they are still dried using traditional methods in some areas (➤ **castagna essiccata nei tecci di Calizzano e Murialdo**). Used to make cakes and cookies, but, above all, polentas and soups: ➤ **minestra di castagne**, ➤ **minestrone con castagne**, ➤ **minestra di ceci e castagne**, ➤ **riso e castagne**.

castagneddhe baked chestnut-shaped cakes made with all-purpose flour, almonds, sugar, cinnamon, vanilla and grated lemon zest, and coated with dark chocolate. Typical of the Murgia area. Puglia, Basilicata.

castagnole (1) small round Carnival fritters aromatized with lemon zest or liqueur (aniseed in Romagna and the Marche, where they use ➤ **mistrà**, grappa in Friuli). Fried in oil or lard, they are dusted with sugar, though in the Monti Lepini (Lazio) they also smother them with honey.

castagnole (2) small rectangular buns made of flour, sugar, bitter cocoa, coffee, orange blossom water, cinnamon and ground cloves. Only made nowadays in holiday periods. Typical of Ventimiglia on the western Riviera. Liguria.

castagnun Ligurian term for ➤ **castagnaccio**, chestnut cake or flatbread.

Castelmagno PDO blue cheese (though mostly white these days) produced since the 13th century in the village of the same name and in those of Pradleves and Monterosso Grana, in the province of Cuneo, with cow's milk and small amounts of ewe's and goat's milk. It is aged in caves for four months. Castelmagno d'alpeggio, protected by a Slow Food presidium, is made from June to September in mountain dairies at an altitude of over 5,000 feet. No ferments are used and the milk comes from two consecutive milkings of cows raised in the wild. Piedmont.

castradina traditionally, smoked, dried castrated lamb (➤ **castrato**), nowadays fresh leg of lamb, simmered for hours with onion, carrot, celery, bay leaves and juniper berries. The recipe, which originated in the Balkans, is cooked in Venice every year on November 21 for the feast of the Madonna della Salute (Blessed Virgin Mary), and served with blanched Savoy cabbage, sardines preserved in salt, capers, garlic and chili. Veneto.

castratello con le potatoes castrated lamb (➤ **castrato**) stewed with herbs, seasonal vegetables and chopped potatoes. Many variations on the recipe exist all over the region, especially in mountain areas. Umbria.

castrato castrated sheep slaughtered at the age of 18 to 30 months of age. The Italian Ministry of Agriculture's database of native and/or traditional food products includes: *castrato biellese* (Piedmont) and *castrè* aka *castròn* (Romagna).

castrato alla griglia wood-roast castrated lamb (➤ **castrato**) flavored with ➤ **aglione**, a mixture of finely minced garlic, sage, rosemary, bay leaf, lemon zest and a generous amount of salt. Emilia-Romagna.

castrato con patate castrated lamb (➤ **castrato**) or kid browned in onions, splashed with red wine and stewed with tomatoes and potatoes. Puglia.

castrato marinato marinated castrated lamb. In Trentino-Alto Adige, pieces of castrated lamb (➤ **castrato**) are marinated in white wine and herbs, browned in lardo with sardine fillets and slowly stewed in the marinade liquid. In Friuli-Venezia Giulia, the meat is steeped in a warm marinade of wine, vinegar and herbs, then cooked in an earthenware pot with lardo, cloves, cinnamon, white wine and broth. Trentino-Alto Adige, Friuli-Venezia Giulia.

castraure small tender young sprouts of artichokes grown in the kitchen gardens of the Venice lagoon. Eaten raw, dressed with oil, salt and pepper, cooked in an earthenware pot (➤ **tecia**), or dipped in batter and fried. Excellent with shrimp (➤ **schia**). Veneto.

Casu Axedu fresh, slightly acidic ewe's and goat's milk cheese. In some places, the curd is left to drain for 48 hours and then steeped in brine, in which case the cheese is called Fiscidu. Sardinia.

Casu cottu literally "cooked cheese." Stretched goat's milk curd cooked four times (in the final phase it is fried), then coated in honey. Made only in Fluminimaggiore, a village in the province of Carbonia-Iglesias. In some areas, the name simply means boiled fresh cheese. Sardinia.

Casu de 'acca another name for ➤ **Murutzulu** cheese.

Casu marzu cheese made from sheep's cheese, chiefly ➤ **Fiore Sardo**, that has gone off on account of infestation by the maggots of the cheese fly *Piophila casei*. The result is a tangy, aromatic cream which can be kept for up to four months. Theoretically, the cheese is considered spoiled and cannot be sold commercially. Sardinia.

casunziei ravioli stuffed with pumpkin or spinach, boiled ham and a pinch of cinnamon, boiled, drained, and served with melted butter and smoked ricotta. In Cortina d'Ampezzo, they stuff them with beetroot, ricotta, dried breadcrumbs and eggs, and serve them with melted butter, grated Pecorino and poppy seeds. The classic shape is semi-circular with pinched braiding round the edges. Typical of the province of Belluno. Veneto.

catalani flat, oval ➤ **tatù**, a type of cookie, glazed with white icing. Typical of the village of Collesano, in the province of Palermo. Sicily.

catalogna endive. A member of the *Cichorium intybus* species of the chicory family with long, narrow leaves with serrated edges. The edible parts are the leaves themselves, the ribs and the sprouts. The Italian Ministry of Agricuture's database of native and/or traditional food products lists the following varieties: *cicoria verde di Napoli* (Campania); *cicoria di catalogna frastagliata di Gaeta* (Lazio); *cicoria pan di zucchero casalese* (Piedmont); *catalogna gigante di Chioggia* (Veneto). In the kitchen it is generally boiled and finished in a skillet with oil and garlic, like common chicory (➤ **cicoria selvatica**), but also appears in a number of regional specialties (➤ **cicoria in brodo**, ➤ **puntarelle**).

cattas type of ➤ **zippulas**, Carnival fritters, in which mandarin juice is used in lieu of orange juice and the saffron is eliminated.

caulada aka **cavolata** soup of cabbage, fava beans, lardo, sausage, veal and pork, flavored with garlic, wild fennel, mint and, sometimes, chilli and tomato. Sardinia.

cauliceddu Sicilian dialect word for ➤ **cavolicello**, Mediterranean cabbage.

cauraro tasty soup of potatoes, anchovies, fava beans, wild herbs and wild fennel. Campania.

cautarogne another name for ➤ **cavatelli**, a type of pasta.

cauzuni ravioli stuffed with ricotta, eggs and mint and served with meat sauce. Basilicata.

cavaddistr type of ➤ **pucciatidd**, sweet ring cookies.

cavagnolesi type of ➤ **canestrelli** cookie coated with chocolate specialty. A specialty of Cavagnolo, in the province of Turin, since 1911. Piedmont.

cavallo horse. Descendant of the wild animals that live in the steppes of Siberia and China, where they are believed to have gone from America prior to the formation of the Bering Strait. The first humans to domesticate horses were nomad shepherds in Turkmenistan in around 4000 BC. The animal was subsequently bred first for food and religious purposes, then for transport and farming work in Asia Minor and Europe. In modern times, horsemeat was always been limited to times of need (sieges, famines) or as a way of exploiting the carcasses of animals put down for health reasons or because they were at the end of their working lives. Today, however, horses are bred for consumption in certain areas, hence a series of traditional dishes: ➤ **pastisada de caval** (province of Verona), ➤ **pìcula ad cavàl**, ➤ **faldìa** (Emilia), ➤ **braciola**, ➤ **pezzetti** (Puglia). The Italian Ministry of Agriculture's database of native and/ or traditional food products lists *puledro di Comano* (Massa-Carrara, Tuscany) and *cavallo del Catria* (Pesaro e Urbino, Marche).

cavallucci (1) spicy pastries made by dissolving honey and sugar in water, and kneading the resulting syrup with flour, candied orange and lime, honey, aniseed (or coriander) and yeast. The dough is then shaped into small balls, which are baked in the oven. Once known as *morsetti* or *morselletti*, they may be enriched with walnuts, almonds and spices, in which case they are called ➤ **bericuocoli** (aka **berriquoccoli**). Sienese in origin, they have been popular since the 16th century when they were offered at post stations, hence the name (*cavallo* means horse in Italian). Tuscany.

cavallucci (2) horse-shaped cookies made from a paste of flour, yeast, eggs, butter and sugar and filled with a mixture dried fruit, sugar, ➤ **sapa**, breadcrumbs, coffee, grated citrus fruit zest and liqueur. Traditionally baked at Christmas in the area of Jesi (province of Ancona) and the northern part of the province of Macerata. Marche.

cavasì a squaquaciò chub with peas. Slices of chub coated in flour, fried and covered with peas stewed with herbs and tomato paste diluted with white wine, baked in the oven and sprinkled with parsley. Typical of the Lake Garda area in the province of Verona. Veneto.

cavateddri Calabrian dialect word for ➤ **cavatelli**, type of pasta.

cavatelli traditional durum wheat pasta (in Puglia also made with ➤ **grano arso**, "burnt wheat," in Calabria with boiled potatoes, in Campania with eggs). A member of the ➤ **strascinati** pasta family. Roughly shaped cylinders about alf an inch thick, hollowed (*cavati*) by rolling on a wooden board and applying pressure with the fingers or the rounded edge of a knife. In Campania, they add eggs to the dough and shape the pasta into oval shells. Other relatives of **cavatelli** are short pastas grooved with a needle: eg, ➤ **minuich** aka **minnicchi** (Basilicata) and ➤ **rascatieddi** (Calabria). **Cavatelli** are popular in Calabria, Campania, Basilicata, Puglia, Molise and, to a lesser degree, in Sicily. Regional and dialect names: ➤ **cazzarille**, ➤ **ciufele** (Molise); ➤ **cecatelli** (Campania); ➤ **cavatielli**, ➤ **cavatieddi**, ➤ **cecatidde**, ➤ **cecatielle**, ➤ **strascinati chiusi**, to differentiate them from ➤ **orecchiette** (Puglia); ➤ **capunti**, ➤ **cautarogne**, ➤ **minuich**, ➤ **raskatelli** (Basilicata); ➤ **cavateddri**, ➤ **rascatielli**, ➤ **rascatieddi** (Calabria); ➤ **cavatiddi**, ➤ **gnocculi**, ➤ **gnucchitti** (Sicily). Accompanying sauces vary according to region. Dried and vacuum-packed fresh **cavatelli** are available commercially.

cavatiddi aka **cavatieddi** aka **cavatielli** dialect terms for ➤ **cavatelli**

cavedano chub (*Leuciscus cephalus*) freshwater fish of the Ciprinidae family. Lives in most Italian lakes and rivers, except those in Sardinia, Sicily and parts of southern Italy. Its tasty white, though bony, flesh is ideal for broiling. Finely chopped it is also used as an ingredient in fish cakes and stuffings (➤ **cavedano con piselli**, ➤ **cavasì a squaquaciò**).

cavolata another name for ➤ **caulada**.

cavolbroccolo broccoli (➤ **broccolo**) of the *Brassica oleracea italica forma caput* variety.

cavolfiore (pl. **cavolfiori**) cauliflower (*Brassica olerecea* var. *botrytis*). Mostly grown in the south of Italy, where climate and terrains are most suitable. Cultivated for its florets (*cima*, *testa* or *palla* in Italian) which vary in color, from white to cream to purple, according to variety. Genetic research and hybridizations have produced cultivars that are on the market from November to April. The Italian Ministry of Agriculture's database of native and/or traditional food products lists the following varieties: *cavolfiore gigante di Napoli* (Campania); *cavolfiore precoce di Jesi, cavolfiore tardivo di Fano* (Marche); *cavolfiore di Moncalieri* (Piedmont); *cavolfiore violetto natalino* (Sicily); *cavolfiore fiorentino tardivo con il cappuccio, cavolfiore precoce toscano con il cartoccio* (Tuscany). Cauliflower is much used in the regional kitchen but there is some confusion over its name. In Sicily and other southern regions, for example, it is called not **cavolfiore** but *broccolo*. It is normally boiled and its florets divided. It is then cooked in a variety of ways: ➤ **cavolfiore a vastedda**, ➤ **cavolfiore in umido**, ➤ **cavolfiore rifatto**, ➤ **cavolfiore soffocato**, ➤ **bucatini con i broccoli ar-**

riminati, ➤ **frittelle di sant'Antonio**, ➤ **pasta 'ncaciata**.

cavolfiore a vastedda boiled cauliflower florets dipped in batter flavored with chopped anchovies and fried. Sicily.

cavolfiore in umido cauliflower cooked in a skillet in a sauce of oil, garlic, chili, tomato pasta and pitted olives. Much loved as the ideal side dish for fatty meats and liver sausage (➤ **fegatelli**). Tuscany.

cavolfiore rifatto cauliflower sliced, coated in a batter of milk, eggs and flour, fried, then covered with abundant tomato sauce. Tuscany.

cavolfiore soffocato cauliflower florets and black olives stewed with onion and sun-dried tomatoes. Sardinia.

cavoli della comare regional term for ➤ **silene rigonfia**, bladder campion.

cavoli ripieni stuffed cabbage. Savoy cabbage leaves first boiled, then stuffed and rolled up. In Umbria, they stuff the rolls with a mixture of ground beef or pork, eggs, fresh breadcrumbs, Pecorino and spices and bake them in the oven; they cover them with meat sauce in winter and tomato sauce in summer. The recipe is common, with variants, in many regional cuisines: eg, ➤ **polpette di verza** (Lombardy) and ➤ **capunet** (Piedmont).

cavoli strascinati cabbage first boiled, then finished in a skillet with extra virgin olive oil, garlic, diced bread and, sometimes, potatoes. This "poor" country dish was often served with tasty meats such as pork chops or sausages. Umbria.

cavolicello aka **cavolo rapiciolla** Mediterranean cabbage (*Brassica fruticulosa*). Wild plant found on uncultivated land and in vineyards, almost exclusively in the center and south of Italy, especially in eastern Sicily, where it is extremely popular (➤ **cauliceddu**, ➤ **qualiceddu**). The young leaves are boiled and dressed with oil or finished in the pan as a side dish for broiled sausage. Sometimes confused with the numerous varieties of ➤ **senape selvatica**, wild mustard.

cavollat aka **caulat** custard of egg yolks, sugar, cream and, sometimes, lemon zest, thickened on the heat and served with ➤ **sbrisolona** or other cakes or cookies. Traditionally made in Milan and Mantua. Lombardy.

cavolo cabbage (*Brassica oleracea*). This member of the Brassica family comes in many shapes and sizes and also grows wild in Europe on the Atlantic and Mediterranean coastlines (➤ **cavolicello**, Mediterranean cabbage). The main Italian varieties are : Savoy cabbage (➤ **cavolo verza**), white cabbage (➤ **cavolo cappuccio**), kohlrabi (➤ **cavolo rapa**) and the loose-leaved "black cabbage" (➤ **cavolo nero**).

cavolo cappuccio white cabbage (*Brassica oleracea* var. *capitata*). Headed brassica with smooth, close-packed leaves, usually greenish-white, though color varies according to cultivars (which also include red cabbage). The Italian Ministry of Agriculture's database of native and/or traditional food products lists the following: *cavolo gaggetta, cavolo lavagnino* (Liguria); *cavoli cappucci della Val di Gresta* (Trentino); *cavolo dell'Adige* (Veneto). In the kitchen, it is eaten shredded in salads (➤ **ancioada**, in soups (➤ **tognaque**), boiled (➤ *cavolo rosso stufato*, ➤ *pecora e cavoli*, ➤ *piedini di maiale con cavolo*, sautéed (➤ **capuzi in tecia**, ➤ **cappucci e cicorie**), stuffed (➤ **gaggette pinn-e**) and used, in Trentino-Alto Adige, to make sauerkraut (➤ **crauti**).

cavolo di Bruxelles Brussels sprout (*Brassica oleracea* var. *gemmifera*). Despite its name, a native of Italy. Relatively popular in the country, boiled and dressed with oil and lemon juice or vinegar, sautéed with butter and Parmigiano, or baked in the oven covered with béchamel sauce.

cavolo nero "black cabbage" (*Brassica oleracea* var. *acefala* subvar. *viridis serotina*). Produces long, dark green leaves with curly tips from a heartless base. The most important varieties come from Tuscany (*cavolo nero riccio di Toscana* aka *braschetta*, and *cavolo riccio nero di Lucca*), as do the most popular recipes: ➤ **fetta col cavolo nero**, ➤ **riso e cavolo sul lampredotto**, ➤ **minestra di bread per la ribollita**, ➤ **zuppa frantoiana**, ➤ **arbada**, ➤ **bordatino**, ➤ **farinata con le leghe**.

cavolo rapa aka **cavolo torso** kohlrabi (*Brassica oleracea* var. *gongyloides*). Hearted brassica eaten in much the same way as the turnip (➤ **rapa**). Cultivated in both northern and southern Italy, it only has one native variety: *cavolo rapa di Acireale*, known in dialect as *trunzu di Aci*. Its consumption in Italy is limited, and most of the production is exported to northern Europe. It appears in one specific recipe in Alto Adige (➤ **cavolo rapa soffocato**), and is eaten raw in salads in Puglia, where it is known as ➤ **verruch**.

cavolo rapa soffocato the swollen stem of the kohlrabi (➤ **cavolo rapa**) diced, sautéed in butter and sugar, stewed in water and finished with cream. Trentino-Alto Adige.

cavolo rapiciolla another name for ➤ **cavolicello**, Mediterranean cabbage.

cavolo ripieno stuffed Savoy cabbage. In the province of Piacenza (Emilia-Romagna), they stuff a small boiled cabbage with a mixture of ground boiled beef, eggs, bread and grated cheese, and cook it in oil and butter: an alternative to ➤ **verzolini**. In Piedmont, they stuff the cabbage with boiled rice, sausage, boil it wrapped in a canvas cloth and flavor it

with sage fried in butter, grated Grana and chopped hard-boiled egg yolks.

cavolo rosso stufato stewed red cabbage. The julienned leaves are marinated in red wine, vinegar and orange juice, and cooked slowly with onion softened in butter and broth. Served as a side dish with smoked roast pork. Trentino-Alto Adige; Friuli-Venezia Giulia.

cavolo verza Savoy cabbage (*Brassica oleracea* var. *bullata* subvar. *sabauda*). Cabbage with loose, wrinkled green leaves, cultivated mostly in northern Italy. Much appreciated in the kitchen thanks to its delicate flavor; especially prized are so-called *verze gelate*, "frozen cabbages," with outside leaves hardened by the frost and soft tender hearts. The Italian Ministry of Agriculture's database of native and/or traditional food products lists the following varieties: *cavolo verza di Montalto Dora*, *cavolo verza di Settimo Torinese* (Piedmont). Sometimes eaten raw in salads, Savoy cabbage is mostly cooked: ➤ **casoeûla**, ➤ **castagne e verze**, ➤ **coda alla valdostana**, ➤ **oca con le verze**, ➤ **trippa con le verze**, ➤ **sancrao**, ➤ **verze e luganega**. It is also the prime ingredient in many northern Italian soups (➤ **riso e verze**, ➤ **seupa vapellenentze**, ➤ **supa 'd coi**, ➤ **zuppa di cavoli alla canavesana**), served as a side dish (➤ **verze imbracate**, ➤ **verze sofegae**, ➤ **pipeto**) and stuffed (➤ **caponet**, ➤ **nosecc**, ➤ **valigini**).

Cavour, alla term applied to two Piedmontese-style dishes: i) veal chops or sweetbreads served with slices of fried or baked polenta; ii) large cuts of meat served with fried semolina gnocchi.

cavret in tecia Veneto and Venezia-Giulia dialect term for stuffed kid.

cavuluciuri Sicilian dialect word for ➤ **cavolfiore** (cauliflower).

cazini ➤ Basilicata word for ➤ **calzoncini**,

half-moon pasta shape.

cazòle dialect term used in the southern Marche to refer to cod roe, much loved by fishermen partly on account of its significant symbolic value. After the last fishing trip before Christmas, **cazòle** was the only part of the catch to be divided equally among all the members of the crew, whereas the rest was assigned according to hierarchical order. The roe is simply boiled, roasted or stewed with tomato. Given its creamy consistency, it also goes very well with pasta. Marche.

cazzamarru wild herbs and vegetables (➤ **amarelli**, ➤ **senape selvatica**, ➤ **asparagi**, ➤ **broccoletti**, ➤ **cipolline novelle** and so on) cut lengthwise into uniform strips. Dressed with oil, garlic, salt and black and red pepper, they are wrapped in tin foil and cooked on the stove or in hot ash. A specialty of Sortino, in the province of Siracusa. Sicily.

cazzaregli aka **cazzarieglie** aka **cazzarej** small durum wheat (or corn) flour and water pasta made by rubbing a small cylinder of dough in the palm of the hand. Traditionally served with beans. Molise.

cazzareji another name for ➤ **cazzaregli**, a type of pasta.

cazzarele dialect term for ➤ **peperoncino**, chili.

cazzarieglie another name for ➤ **cazzaregli**, a type of pasta.

cazzarille Molise term for ➤ **cavatelli**, a type of pasta.

cazzilli potatoes boiled and mashed, flavored with mint and parsley, shaped into cylinders and deep-fried in oil. In the province of Palermo, they often accompany ➤ **panelle**, chickpea fritters in a classic combination of street foods (➤ **cibo di strada**). In the province of Catania, they use garlic in lieu of mint and dip the cylinders in beaten egg whites and bread-crumbs before frying. Sicily.

cazzimperio central-southern Italian term for ➤ **pinzimonio**, oil, salt and pepper into which raw vegetables are dipped.

cazzmarr rolls of lamb's or kid's offal wrapped in the animal's caul and secured with its intestines. In Puglia they are flavored with semi-mature Pecorino cheese, in Basilicata with prosciutto. Puglia/Basilicata.

cazzoeûla aka **cazzola** other names for ➤ **casoeûla**, pork and cabbage stew.

cecamariti a sort of ➤ **pancotto** soup made of crumbled ➤ **friselle** (➤ **fresa**) or pieces of day-old bread, fried and covered with boiled broccoli rabe and puréed peas. A traditional dish of the Salento peninsula (province of Lecce). Puglia.

cecatelli aka **cecatidde** aka **cecatielle** dialect terms for ➤ **cavatelli**, a type of pasta.

cecc du bambine disks of bread dough fried in oil. Basilicata.

cece chickpea (*Cicer arietinum*). Legume which adapts easily to different climatic and soil conditions (though it prefers warm, dry areas). Its cream-colored peas possess great nutritional properties and may be eaten fresh or dried. A great many varieties grow in Italy. The Italian Ministry of Agriculture's database of native and/or traditional food products lists the following varieties: *cece abruzzese* (Abruzzo); *cece di Cicerale* (Campania); *cece del solco dritto di Valentano, ceci laziali* (Lazio); *cece di Merella* (Piedmont); *cece siciliano* (Sicily); *cece di Grosseto, cece nostrale* (Tuscany). Chickpeas are on sale canned, ground into flour (➤ **farina di ceci**) or dried. Italy's numerous chickpea recipes include soups and stews (➤ **caciucco di ceci**, ➤ **ciceri e tria**, ➤ **cisrà**, ➤ **lagane e ceci**, ➤ **mes-ciùa**, ➤ **zemin di ceci**, ➤ **maccu di san Giuseppe**), main courses (➤ **ceci con la tempia di maiale**) and some sweet confections (➤ **calzone di castagne, cicirata (2)**).

ceci con la tempia di maiale soup of chickpeas, parts of the pig's head (ears and temple in particular) and aromatic herbs. Cooked in Milan every year on November 2, All Saints' Day. Lombardy.

ceci di terra common name for ➤ **casciomaci**, great pignut.

ceci e costine another name for ➤ **cisrà**, pork and chickpea stew.

ceci e farro chickpea and emmer soup. The chickpeas are boiled and stewed in a pan with a mixture of chopped carrots, onions and celery, to which their cooking water and emmer are added. The resulting soup is seasoned with pepper and drizzled with extra virgin olive oil. The recipe combines two of the most characteristic ingredients of a region in which legume and cereal soups abound. Umbria.

ceciliani fresh flour and water pasta very similar to Calabrian ➤ **fileja**, made by rolling strips of pasta round a needle. Traditionally served with meat and mushroom sauces. Typical of the province of Viterbo. In the Sabina area, in the province of Rieti, the same type of pasta is called ➤ **ciufulitti**, and is served with lamb sauce and grated Pecorino. Lazio.

cecina aka **torta di ceci** chickpea focaccia. A close relative of Ligurian ➤ **farinata** but made from a more liquid dough (water and chickpeas). A specialty of Livorno, it may be found in the city's pizzerias and cake shops. People still ask for a *cinque e cinque*, "five and five," which now means 50 cents' worth of focaccia and 50 cents' worth of bread. Tuscany.

cedrina lemon verbena (*Lippia triphylla, L. citriodora*). Shrubs whose fragrant leaves, when squeezed, give off an intense lemony scent. Brought to Europe from South America, they are cultivated as ingredients for the perfume and alcohol industries. In the kitchen, their fresh or dried leaves add aroma to jams, jellies, sorbets, fruit salads and vinegars. Common and regional names: ➤ **erba luigia**, ➤ **erba luisa**, ➤ **limoncina**, ➤ **verbena odorosa**.

cedro citron (*Citrus medica* var. *macrocarpa*). Large citrus fruit which came to Europe from Persia, and is now cultivated especially in the south of Italy. The citron, fresh or candied, is, together with chili, a staple product on the Tyrrhenian coast of Calabria, *La Riviera dei Cedri*. Round in shape with thick peel, smooth or lumpy according to variety, it has fleshy, aromatic fruit. Much used in confectionery for the preparation of desserts (including ➤ **cassata siciliana**), citron is also an important ingredient in meat dishes such as ➤ **cinghiale in agrodolce**, sweet and sour wild boar.

cedronella common name for ➤ **melissa**, lemon balm.

cèe literally "blind." In Tuscan dialect, the term refers to newborn eels that have still to open their eyes. In the late winter they swim down rivers towards lagoons, but their fishing has long since been prohibited. They used to be a delicacy, especially in the province of Pisa, but the relevant recipes now use the fry of other fish (➤ **novellame di pesce**). Tuscany.

cefalo (pl. **cefali**) gray mullet. The name applies to various sea and freshwater species, all members of the Mugilidae family. From a gastronomic point of view, the most important are: *cefalo volpina*, striped mullet (*Mugil cephalus*), *cefalo dorato*, golden gray mullet (*M. auratus*) and *cefalo bòsega*, bluespot gray mullet. (*M. chelo*). The Italian Ministry of Agriculture's database of native and/or traditional food products lists the following varieties: *cefali delle valli da pesca venete, cefali del Polesine* (Veneto) and *calamita del lago di Fondi* (Lazio). Gray mullet may be bought fresh, frozen, dried and smoked. The firm and flavorsome flesh is excellent baked in the oven, broiled, *en papillote*, boiled, stewed, in soup (➤ **brodetti dell'alto Adriatico**, ➤ **cassola sarda**). The roe, especially of the *volpina*, which is common in the lagoon of Orbetello (province of Grosseto, Tuscany) and in brackish ponds in Sardinia, is used to make an excellent botargo (➤ **bottarga**). Common and regional names: ➤ **caparello**, ➤ **muggine comune**, ➤ **muggine cefalo**, ➤ **mussau**.

cefali alla comacchiese in the areas of Comacchio, the Lidi Ferraresi and the Po delta (province of Ferrara), they fish, farm and cook the bluespot gray mullet (*cefalo bòsega* ➤ **cefalo**). The fish is first marinated in oil, sea salt, rosemary and lemon juice, then broiled and basted with the marinade liquid. If the fish is very fresh and of certain provenance, the innards are left in the fish to add flavor. The fish is served with polenta and barbecued onions. Emilia-Romagna.

cefali alla muranese gray mullet baked in the oven with bay leaves, vinegar and oil. A recent revisitation of a cooking technique once common on the island of Murano (province of Venice) where they used to roast fish on red-hot plates in glass factories (➤ **bisato su l'ara**). Veneto.

celidonia minore another name for➤ **favagello**, fig buttercup.

cellentani short, corkscrew-shaped commercial durum wheat pasta with a ridged surface and hollow in the middle. Served with light, often vegetable, sauces.

celli pieni small pastries (moon- or ring-shaped, made of shortcrust dough or from a simple mixture of flour, eggs, sug-ar and oil) filled with jam (grape, fig or mixed fruits), sometimes with the addition of other ingredients (cooked grape must, crushed almonds, cinnamon, chocolate) baked in the oven and covered with confectioner's sugar. They originated in Teramo, but are now common all over the region. They owe their name to the fact that they were originally shaped like little birds (*uccelli* in Italian). Other regional names: ➤ **cellitti**, ➤ **cellucci**, ➤ **ciell' rechiene**. Abruzzo.

cellitti (1) fresh flour and water pasta. Stick-like shapes hollowed at the center by applying pressure with the fingers. Ideal with meat, tomato, mushroom and seasonal vegetable sauces. Lazio. **cellitti (2)** another name, in Abruzzo and Molise, for➤ **celli pieni**.

cellucci another name for ➤ **celli pieni**, filled pastries.

celteno Italianization of ➤ **zelten**, a rich ➤ **pandolce**.

cena de lacc soup of milk diluted with water (sometimes sweetened with sugar), potatoes, good King Henry (➤ **buon enrico**), wild greens, spinach, runner beans and rice or pasta. Typical of the Valtellina, in the province of Sondrio. Lombardy.

cenci little deep-fried Carnival pastries made from a rich dough of wheat flour, butter, sugar, eggs, salt, flavored with grappa, brandy, rum or anise liqueur, rolled out, cut into strips and knotted, into lozenges or rectangles, fried in olive oil and dusted with refined or confectioner's sugar. Common all over Italy under different names: ➤ **gale** in Bergamo, ➤ **galani** in Veneto, ➤ **crostoli** in Trentino, ➤ **lattughe** in Mantua, ➤ **bugie** in Piedmont and parts of Liguria, ➤ **sprelle**, ➤ **frappe** aka **sfrappole** and ➤ **intrigoni** in Emilia-Romagna, ➤ **frappe** aka **sfrappe** in Marche and Lazio, ➤ **cenci** or

stracci in Tuscany, **pampuglie** or **chiacchiere** in Campania, and so on. The term **chiacchiere** is also used in parts of northern Italy and sometimes refers to the same pastries oven-baked not fried.

cencioni fava bean flour tagliatelle. Lombardy.

centime coarse-grained polenta flavored with wild fennel and **broccoletti**. A delicacy of Messina, Sicily.

centopelli aka **centopezzi** (in southern Italian dialects) aka **cientepella** aka **cientepelle**, (in Sardinian dialect) aka **centupilloni**) for **omaso**, omasum.

centrifugare (1) to juice.

centrifugare (2) to dry lettuce and greens using a salad dryer. **cepola** red band fish (*Cepola rubescens*). Long orange-red sea fish which lives in small shoals on muddy and sandy sea beds. Common throughout the Mediterranean, it has beautifully flavored flesh, which is best enjoyed fried (in Liguria, it features in mixed fries, **fritto misto di pesce**), stewed or in soups (**brodetti dell'alto Adriatico**). Common and dialect names: **ciapudda**, **fettuccia**, **galera**, **lanspada**, **pesce cordela**, **scuriazno**, **signorina**, **spada rossa**, **zigarella**.

ceppaluna dry cookies glazed with a lemon icing known locally as **naspro**. Campania.

ceppe bucatini made by wrapping the pasta dough round thin wooden sticks. Traditionally served with meat sauce and grated Pecorino. Typical of Civitella del Tronto, in the province of Teramo. Abruzzo.

cerasa Campanian dialect term for **ciliegia**, cherry.

cerasella regional term for **peperoncino**,

cerasiello fiery cherry-shaped chili much used in the Neapolitan kitchen. Campania.

cerasiola regional term for **tamaro**, black brony.

ceré another name for **sérac**, a type of ricotta.

cereali cereals. General term derived from Ceres, the Roman goddess of agriculture, for various grasses, mostly members of the Graminacee o Poaceae families, cultivated all over the world to produce grains to be used as they are or ground (**farina**, **semola**) for human or animal nourishment. Cereals have a high nutritional value thanks to the presence in their seeds of proteins, sugars and starch (**amido**). The most important cereals are: soft and durum wheat (**frumento**), corn (**granoturco**, **mais**), rice and barley, and, to a lesser degree, emmer (**farro**), rye and buckwheat, the latter a member of Poligonaceae. The use of oats (**avena**) and millet is negligible.

cerfoglio aka **erba stella** chervil (*Anthriscus cerefolium*). Aromatic herb with a delicate scent of anise and parsley, at its best when fresh. One of the traditional French *fines herbes*, it is used to flavor salads, soups, sauces, fish, white meat and fresh cheeses.

ceriole (1) small eels, usually cooked with fresh peas or with garlic, capers, anchovies and white wine (*ceriole alla fiumarola*). Lazio

ceriole (2) another name for **ciriole**, a type of pasta. Umbria.

cernia grouper. A sea fish, a member of the same family as the sea bass (**spigola**), it has firm, delicately flavored, boneless flesh. Several varieties exist, the most common in the Mediterranean being the brown grouper (**Epinephelus guaza**). A big fish normally cooked in slices: roasted, *en papillote* or boiled and served with mayonnaise (**maionese**) of other sauces. Stewed with tomato it may be used to dress pasta or as a main course.

certosino aka **panspeziale** dome-shaped Christmas cake of ancient origin made of flour, butter, yeast, candied fruit (➤ **mostarda bolognese**), dried fruit, chocolate, cinnamon and wine syrup. The traditional recipe has been registered at the Bologna Chamber of Commerce. Emilia-Romagna.

cervella alla napoletana baby lamb's brains (= **abbacchio**) baked in the oven and covered with minced capers, Gaeta olives, breadcrumbs and a twist of black pepper. Campania.

cervella finta spoonfuls of a mixture of scrambled eggs and béchamel sauce coated first in flour, then in breadcrumbs and fried in butter. A specialty of Cremona. Lombardy.

cervellata fine-grained fresh sausage, typical of the south of Italy (a version that used to be made in Milan has now virtually disappeared). In Calabria it is made with mixed cuts of pork and flavored with chili and dry white wine, in Puglia with a mixture of beef, kid and lamb, aromatized with garlic, basil or parsley, Pecorino cheese, salt and ground black pepper. In Martina Franca, in the province of Taranto, they make the sausage with mixed pork and beef, or pork alone, flavored with salt, ground pepper, fennel seeds and red wine. It is eaten cooked. Calabria, Puglia.

cervellatine thin pork sausages often served with broccoli rabe (➤ **friarielli**), or as a stuffing in traditional recipes, such as ➤ **lasagna napoletana**. Typical of Naples. Campania.

cervello brain. In Italy, lamb's, kid's and calf's brains are the most used in the kitchen (though the sale and consumption of calf's brains was limited following the mad cow disease outbreak a few years ago), first blanched, then coated in flour or dipped in egg and breadcrumbs or in batter, and fried. An essential ingredient in Piedmontese ➤ **finanziera** and in many a regional ➤ **fritto misto**. Other recipes include ➤ **cervella alla napoletana** (Campania) and ➤ **Hirn profesen** (Alto Adige).

cervo red deer (*Cervis elaphus*). Though huntable on the Italian mainland (the Sardinian red deer is, instead, a protected species), the animal has never been a common prey for hunters and appears in few recipes. Due to the difficulties involved in farming red deer, the venison on sale (fresh, frozen, preserved or in the form of hams and other cured varieties) is almost all imported.

cervo in salsa red deer venison in sauce. Fillets of red deer venison larded, coated in flour, browned in butter and served with the pan juices mixed with brandy, broth and butter. Trentino-Alto Adige.

cervo nel coccio pieces of red deer venison marinated and cooked in an earthenware pot with wine, lardo, herbs and cinnamon. Friuli-Venezia Giulia.

cesena regional term for ➤ **tordo**, thrush.

cestino (pl. **cestini**) small shortcrust, brisée or puff pastry "basket" or case, made using a small mold or a bowl turned upside down, served with a sweet or savory filling.

cetriolini caper buds (➤ **cappero**).

cetriolo (pl. **cetrioli**) cucumber (*Cocumis sativus*). In Italy, cultivated mainly in Campania, Puglia and Sicily. The varieties grown have knobbly or smooth skins which vary in color from bright green (with or without streaks) to yellow and white. The flesh is firmy and dotted with seeds. Cucumbers are harvested when the cucurbit is still unripe to retain its flavor and aroma. A few hundred cultivars and varieties have been recorded in Italy, some suitable for eating fresh, others for pickling. Fresh cucumbers are eaten raw in salads (➤ **panzanella**, ➤ **condiggiun**), cooked in soups (➤ **zuppa di cetrioli**) or as an ingredient in certain fillings. Pickled, they are served with aperitifs and used as an ingredient in a number of antipasti and side dishes.

ceusi ianchi aka **ceusi niùri** Sicilian dialect names for the white (*ianca*) and black (*niùra*) berries of the mulberry tree (➤ **mora di gelso**, (*ceusu* in dialect). A granita is made with black mulberries.

cevapcici sausages of mixed ground meats (veal, pork, mutton or lamb). Usually eaten grilled, common all along the Italian border with Slovenia. Friuli-Venezia Giulia.

Cevrin di Coazze goat's milk cheese (made from the milk of the hardy Camosciata delle Alpi breed) to which a small amount of cow's milk is also added. It ages for three months in shepherd's huts or natural cellars, where it is turned and cleaned every day. The rind is coarse and damp and amber yellow in color, the paste is slightly grainy. A Slow Food presidium is seeking to relaunch the breeding of the goats and production of the cheese, which is now rare. Typical of the Val Sangone, in the province of Turin. Piedmont.

champignon another term for the ➤ **prataiolo** mushroom.

chantilly (1) cream and sugar whipped to double their volume. Much used in confectionery, the cream base may be flavored according to taste and necessity.

chantilly (2) mousseline sauce. Mayonnaise (➤ **maionese**) into which cream is incorporated.

chardé a sort of ➤ **panforte** of almonds, honey, candied lime and grappa. Val d'Aosta.

charlotte French term, sometimes Italianized as *carlotta*, for a cold molded dessert, shaped like a truncated cone, made of sponge fingers or sponge cake soaked in liqueur and vanilla, chocolate or fruit cream. The most famous and elementary version is *charlotte alle mele*, apple charlotte, made with slices of buttered bread.

charlotte alla milanese dessert made by lining a mold with buttered day-old bread and filling it with apples and pears, sugar, raisins, candied fruits, lemon zest and white wine. Lombardy.

checca, alla condiment for pasta, usually spaghetti, made by mixing raw ripe tomatoes, salt, pepper, roughly torn basil and, sometimes, flat-leaved parsley, wild fennel and/or roughy chopped black olives. Typical of the city of Rome. Lazio.

Chega ancient Novara term for ➤ Gorgonzola, possibly derived from the Celtic *cagios*, "of or pertaining to a barn or fenced enclosure." Piedmont.

chenella (pl. **chenelle**) Italianization of the French ➤ **quenelle**, a sort of oblong dumpling made of creamed meat or with an egg binding poached in water or cooked in béchamel sauce. Served as an entrée or a garnish, or in broth. Also used in more complex recipes as a ➤ **farcia**, stuffing.

cheppia aka **salacca** Mediterranean shad (*Alosa fallax milotica*). A member of the Clupeidae family, which enters rivers during the mating season. Similar to the freshwater sardine (➤ **agone**), it used to be an important source of nourishment, especially in poor Alpine areas such as Carnia (province of Udine, Friuli-Venezia Giulia) and the district round Belluno (Veneto). According to oral tradition, like the smoked herring (➤ **aringa affu-**

micata), the fish used to dangle from the ceiling on a string in mountain huts, and diners would take turns at rubbing their polenta on it for flavor (➤ **salacca abbrustolita**). Before the war, many peasant and mountain communites used to eat shad and herring (➤ **aringa**) with polenta during Lent.

chiacchiere regional name for fried pastries similar to ➤ **cenci**.

chiachia ➤ northeast Italian term for ➤ **pesce lucerna**, stargazer.

chiancarelle another name for ➤ **orecchiette**, a type of pasta.

Chianina, razza ancient cattle breed named for the Val di Chiana, in Tuscany, whence it probably originated. Also raised in Umbria and Marche. Tall, powerful with a white coat, it is the largest cattle breed in the world. Sturdy and good for grazing, it is now raised in wild or semi-wild conditions.

chiantigiani another name for ➤ **biscottini alla mandorla**, almond cookies.

chiarificare to clarify. To make a cloudy liquid, normally broth or wine, clear. To clarify broth, egg white is added and the mixture is heated for about 40 minutes, then strained. For the clarification of butter ➤ **burro chiarificato**.

chibuddadu Sardinian term for ➤ **zuppa di cipolle**, onion soup.

chicche della nonna literally "granny's tidbits." Small gnocchi made of potatoes, spinach or chard, flour and ricotta, served with butter and Parmigiano or melted cheese. Recipe typical of Piacenza. Emilia-Romagna.

chicculiata half-moon pastry (➤ **calzone**) filled with fresh tomato flavored with olive oil, garlic, parsley and chili, sometimes also with anchovies, capers, olives and tuna. Calabria.

chichì focaccia made from a dough similar to that for bread, enriched with a little lard. The filling consists of red and yellow peppers, anchovies, tuna, baby artichokes and green olives. Typical of the town of Offida, in the province of Ascoli Piceno, and said to be of Ottoman origin (though it is also very similar to the Armenian *lahmagiun*). The name means pizza in the local dialect. Marche.

chichingero dialect term for ➤ **alchechengi**, Peruvian groundcherry.

chiciòla warm slab of leftover polenta mixed with milk, oil, egg yolk and flour, and fried in oil. Typical of the Monferrato hills in the province of Asti. Piedmont.

chifeleti aka **chifeletti** aka **chifelini** by analogy with the appearance of ➤ **chiffel** (small croissant), in northeastern Italian the term refers a number of specialties with half-moon shapes. In Trieste, **chifeletti** are either buns, which used to be eaten as a snack by children with a bar of chocolate, or shortcrust pastry cookies aromatized with vanilla or almonds. Again in Trieste, but also in Valcanale (province of Udine) and some parts of the province of Trento, **chifeletti** (or ➤ **kiffel**) are half-moon pastries of potatoes and flour (the mixture is similar to that of gnocchi), fried in oil and served as a side dish with main courses or coated with sugar and served as a dessert. Friuli-Venezia Giulia, Trentino.

chiffel aka **kiffel** small sweet croissant of Austrian origin. Made of brioche pastry and filled with a tablespoon of confectioner's custard or fruit jam. The term **chiffel** (from the German **Kipfel**, "half-moon") is used in some areas of the north for ➤ **croissant**, whereas in the rest of Italy the term ➤ **cornetto** prevails.

chifferi commercial dry durum wheat pasta invented in northern Italy. Hollow smooth or ridged curved pasta shells.

Served in broth or with light tomato or cheese sauces. Other names: ➤ **gobbetti**, ➤ **mezzi gomiti**.

chiffero half-moon cookie made of crushed sweet almonds, sugar and egg whites, coated with sliced almonds. Typical of the province of Savona. Liguria.

chifferotti another name for ➤ **gomiti rigati**, a type of pasta.

chiffonade a method of cutting leafy green vegetables and herbs into long, thin strips (➤ **tagliare**, to cut).

chinotto citrus fruit of the bitter orange (*Citrus aurantium*), species. A native of China, hence its name. Cultivated chiefly in Liguria (➤ **chinotto di Savona**), Calabria and Sicily. Similar to a tiny orange but with a sharp, bitter flavor. Used exclusively to make syrups, candied fruit, and the soft drink of the same name.

chinotto di Savona name of the evergreen citrus tree of Chinese origin that has grown on the Ligurian Riviera from Varazze to Finale Ligure since the 17th century, and which bears the ➤ **chinotto** fruit. A Slow Food presidium promotes the tree, the fruit and the related candying industry. Liguria.

chinulille aka **chinuchille** aka **chinule** sweet fried ravioli typical of Diamante, in the province of Cosenza, traditionally prepared at Christmas. Square or round in shape, they are filled with ricotta, eggs, sugar, and lemon zest. They may also be filled with boiled chestnuts, sugar, dark chocolate, candied fruit, nougat, vanilla, cinnamon, and cloves, and dipped in honey after frying. Calabria.

chiocciola another word for ➤ **lumaca**, snail.

chiocciole alla paesana after being purged and deslimed, the snails are cooked in their shells in a skillet with minced aromatics, thyme (preferably the wild variety: ➤ **serpillo**, known in Tuscany as ➤ **pepolino**, and chilli, bathed with white wine and finished with chopped ripe tomatoes. Tuscany.

chiodi di garofano cloves (*Eugenia caryophyllata*). The dried flower buds of a tree that originated in Indonesia, and is now cultivated in all the tropical regions. Noted for their sweet yet pungent aroma, they are used whole to aromatize mulled wine (➤ **vin brulé**) and broth (onions stuck with cloves often appear), marinades for meat and game, vegetables pickled in vinegar or preserved in oil, stewed fruit (with cinnamon), fruit loaves and, above all, meat sauces and stews (➤ **garofolato**).

chiodino honey armillary mushroom (*Armillariella mellea*). Nail-shaped mushroom (*chiodo* means "nail" in Italian) with a semisperical cap, that grows in the fall on tree stumps. Best enjoyed stewed with tomatoes or with garlic and parsley. In Lombardy, they cook it with duck, rice, guinea fowl, pork ribs or preserve it in oil, and it is also popular in Veneto. Common and dialect names: ➤ **famigliola buona**, ➤ **sementino**, ➤ **ciudin**, ➤ **ciuet**. Lombardy.

chioppetta ancient name for ➤ **salamella di Mantova** a type of salami.

chisciöl a type of ➤ **sciatt**. A sort of large fritter made of buckwheat flour, a dash of grappa and semi-fat cheese, typically ➤ **Latteria**, and traditionally fried in lard. Recent recipes suggest a blend of buckwheat and wheat flour, though the proportions of the two vary from place to place. Typical of the Valtellina, in the province of Sondrio. Lombardy.

chisoi Carnival fritters typical of the Crema area made with flour, yeast, apples, raisins, lemon zest, lemon zest and cognac, which, on frying, take on a round, bloated shape. Lombardy.

chisol scone made with wheat flour, water, salt and a pinch of bicarbonate of soda. Cooked in a griddle pan (➤ **testo**) or in a covered baking tray in the hearth it used to be a bread substitute. Sprinkled with sugar, it could also be transformed into a cake for children. Typical of the province of Mantua. Lombardy.

chisola flatbread (all-purpose flour, natural yeast, lemon zest, salt and lard) baked in the oven and dusted with refined sugar. Sometimes the lard is replaced by the fat skimmed from the surface of ➤ **cotechino** cooking water. A specialty of Mantua but common elsewhere in Lombardy, sometimes with the name of ➤ **schissoeula**, and also in Emilia, in the province of Piacenza, where the fat element is provided by ➤ **ciccioli di maiale**, pork scratchings. Lombardy, Emilia-Romagna.

chisolini aka **chisulin (1)** fritters of wheat flour, yeast, milk, butter and salt, generally served with cured meats. A specialty of Mantua. Lombardy.

chisolini aka **chisulin (2)** scones made with the same dough as the flatbread ➤ **chisola mantovana**, without the yeast and lemon zest. They used to be cooked directly in the fireplace. A specialty of Mantua. Lombardy.

chisolini aka **chisulin (3)** small fritters made of leftover buckwheat polenta, sweetened with sugar and often aromatized with anise, and fried in butter. A specialty of Cremona. Lombardy.

chitarra wood utensil with metal strings used to make ➤ **maccheroni alla chitarra**.

chiurchiarole dialect expression for red peppers pickled in vinegar. Campania.

chivalzu another name for ➤ **civraxiu**, a type of bread.

chizze aka **chezzi**, similar to ➤ **crescentina fritta**. Fritters made of a dough of flour, butter, lard, salt, water and a dash of verjuice (➤ **agresto**), stuffed with slivers of Parmigiano, fried in oil or, better still, lard, and eaten piping hot. A specialty of Reggio Emilia. The recipe is said to have been invented by a baker in the city's Jewish ghetto, hence the dough is unleavened. Emilia-Romagna.

chjusoni small durum wheat gnocchi served with meat sauce and generous amounts of grated Pecorino. Typical of the Gallura area, where they are traditionally served on August 1 to mark the end of the threshing period. Sardinia.

christollen irregularly cylindrical Christmas cake consisting of a case of leavened dough without eggs and a filling made by incorporating almonds, pistachio nuts, raisins, candied citron and rum into the dough itself. After baking in the oven, it is brushed with melted butter and sprinkled with confectioner's sugar. Trentino-Alto Adige.

ciabatta bread of Lombard origin now common in other regions. The dough is similar to but softer than that of ➤ **michetta** and is stretched over and over again to make the loaf flat and crisp.

ciabatta Italia a new-style ➤ **ciabatta** created by a certain Arnaldo Cavallari in 1982 and made with high-gluten wholemeal flour known as *tipo 1 Italia*, suitable for long periods of leavening. **ciabattoni (1)** aka **ciavattoni** giant ➤ **rigatoni** best enjoyed with rich sauces made—in the case of the Marche, for example—with stockfish or lamb.

ciabattoni (2) Lazio word for ➤ **fagiolo bianco di Spagna**, scarlet runner bean.

ciabbotto aka **ciabotta** summer vegetable stew whose ingredients include zucchini, peppers, tomatoes, runner beans, carrots and so on, perfumed with basil and chili and served with toasted bread. A close relative of ➤ **ciambotta**. Abruzzo.

ciabuscolo another name for ➤ **ciauscolo**, a cured meat.

ciacchetegli a variety of broccoli with small purple inflorescences cultivated solely in the area round Priverno, in the province of Latina. Used to make a soup, which is poured over slices or pieces of day-old bread. Lazio.

ciacci di ricotta pancakes of wheat flour, ewe's ricotta, milk salt and a pinch of yeast, made in a special iron. A specialty of Modena. Emilia-Romagna.

ciaccia another name for ➤ **schiaccia maremmana** (Tuscany) and ➤ **torta al testo** (Umbria).

ciaccino flat dark brown loaf made from a dough of soft wheat flour, water, yeast, salt, pepper, oil, lard, chopped walnuts and raisins. Nowadays made in only one bakery in Civitella Marittima, in the province of Grosseto. Available all year round but typical of November 2, All Souls' Day. Tuscany.

ciaccio a variation on ➤ **borlengo**, a sort of pancake. Cooked with special irons (*cottole*) and usually eaten with cream cheese and ricotta, which is sometimes mixed into the batter. A specialty of the Apennines, in the provinces of Bologna and Modena. Emilia-Romagna.

ciacer Lombard regional name for fried pastries identical to ➤ **cenci**.

ciakiciuka variation on ➤ **caponata di melanzane** made with stewed vegetables. Typical of the island of Pantelleria, in the province of Trapani. Sicily.

cialda a thin layer of unleavened, kneaded dough cooked in special hinged irons (*ferri*). In the Italian regional tradition they are sweet and crisp, made from a dough of flour, sugar, eggs, oil or but-

ter, flavored with anything from anise to hazelnut, from wine to cocoa. Sometimes the irons are engraved with designs, which leave an imprint on the surface of the wafer. The confection is often associated with popular fairs and festivals, where the *cialdonaro*, the wafer seller, was and is a familiar figure. Similar specialties include: ➤ **brigidini, cialde di Montecatini** (Tuscany), ➤ **canestrelli**, ➤ **miacce** (Piedmont), ➤ **panicocoli** (Umbria), ➤ **tegole** (Val d'Aosta).

cialda di Montecatini round sandwich of two wafers made from a batter of milk, egg yolks and cake flour, filled with almonds and sugar and packaged in fine yellow parchment. The 1920s creation of a Jewish pastry chef in Montecatini, in the province of Pistoia. Tuscany.

cialdedda aka **cialledda** peasant dish of slices of day-old bread soaked in broth in which chopped tomato, onion, oregano or flat-leaved parsley have been cooked. Puglia, Basilicata.

cialdoni (pl. **cialdoni**) pancake-like confection made from a batter made by amalgamating wheat flour, sugar, milk, butter, eggs and orange essence (or liqueur). The batter is cooked in red-hot hinged irons until it takes on a pleasant pale hazelnut color, then served rolled up. Tuscany.

cialicurda a mush of day-old bread, legumes, oregano and olive oil. A typical peasant dish. Puglia.

ciamballella dialect term for ➤ **imbutino**, common funnel mushroom.

ciambella (1) leavened baked ring- or loaf-shaped cake made from a mixture of flour, sugar, eggs, butter, lemon zest and, according to place, a little lard and a glass of milk. In Emilia-Romagna, where it is very popular, it is the custom to dunk the cake in sweet wine. Regional dialect names (➤ **buslan**, ➤ **busilan**,

➤ **buzzillan**, ➤ **bussolan**) reveal its close relationship with ➤ **buccellato** (Tuscany), and also evoke the ➤ **bensone** of Modena and the ➤ **bossolano** (Lombardy, Veneto).

ciambella (2) flat, soft, ring-shaped loaf made with twice-ground durum wheat bran, traditionally baked in a wood oven. Basilicata.

ciambella al mosto twice-leavened ring-shaped cake made from a mixture of wheat flour, sugar, olive oil, grape must and raisins. Brushed with sugar syrup, the cake comes out of the oven with a crispy glaze. The recipe is believed to date to the 15th century and traditionally made after the grape harvest. This would explain why it is common especially round Marino and the Castelli Romani, in the province of Rome, both major wine-producing areas. Lazio.

ciambella di Quaresima unleavened ring-shaped cake made from a dough of flour, sugar, butter, lots of eggs and lemon juice and zest. After baking in the oven in a bain-marie (➤ **bagnomaria**), it is coated with caramelized sugar and rolled in a mixture of sugar and lemon zest. Traditionally made in Reggio Emilia during Lent (*Quaresima*). Emilia-Romagna.

ciambella pugliese cake made of bread dough, mashed potatoes, sugar, lard, eggs, wheat flour and butter. The mixture is left to rest for a day before baking. Fresh from the oven, the cake is sprinkled with refined sugar. Puglia.

ciambella sorana aka **ciammella** bread made from a well-kneaded dough of flour, brewer's yeast, water, salt, aniseed and, sometimes, eggs, which is first boiled, then baked in a wood oven. Typical of the province of Frosinone. Lazio.

ciambella strozzosa. Ring-shaped cake with jagged edges made from a mixture of flour, sugar, a pinch of salt, eggs, olive oil and a small glass of anise liqueur (➤ **mistrà**). Named for its dense texture and dryness (*strozzare* means "to throttle"), it is ideal for dipping in a glass of mulled wine or milk. The cake is traditionally baked at Easter, especially on Maundy Thursday and Easter Monday, when it is eaten as part of the classic picnic in the country. Marche.

ciambellas ring cookies made from a paste of wheat flour, eggs, sugar, lard and lemon zest (sometimes with the addition of a glass of Marsala or liqueur), briefly leavened and baked in the oven. Either shaped like daisies with a candied fruit at the center or transformed, two at a time, into sandwiches sprinkled with confectioner's sugar with a jam filling.

ciambelle al vino bianco ring cookies baked in a number of different ways. The most common recipe is made from a paste of plain flour, olive oil, sugar, dry white wine, and a pinch of salt, shaped into thin fingers, formed into rings, baked in the oven, and coated with sugar. In the area of Arsoli (province of Rome), the cookie takes the name of ➤ **ciammellette de magru**, in Affile (province of Rome) ➤ **risichelle**. Lazio.

ciambelle sweet potato cakes. Mashed potatoes are amalgamated with melted butter and yeast diluted in water and the resulting mixture is shaped into rings. After leavening, these are fried in oil or lard and coated in confectioner's sugar. The cakes are made preferably with the red potatoes of Colfiorito, in the province of Perugia. Umbria.

ciambelle scottolate sweet ring-shaped cookies scalded in boiling water before being baked in the oven. Ingredients vary from one place to another but normally include flour, ammonium bicarbonate, eggs, sugar and olive oil. In some recipes, the eggs are omitted, in which case the cookies are called ➤ **scutturniate** or ➤ **marturiate**. In other versions (eg, the heart-shaped *ciammelle* of Velletri, in the province of Rome, traditional at the Fair of San Clemente), they are flavored with aniseed. Lazio.

ciambelle zagarolesi aka **cacchi** ring-shaped cookies made of leavened bread dough and aniseed, traditionally served at weddings. Typical of the town of Zagarolo, in the province of Rome. Lazio.

ciambelline con il vino rings of dough (soft and durum wheat flour, yeast, sugar, red or white wine, anise liqueur, olive oil and grated lemon zest) baked in the oven. Calabria.

ciambelline salate fritte ring-shaped savories made from a mixture of wheat flour, salt, brewer's yeast and eggs and fried in extra virgin olive oil. Traditionally served in the Ciociaria area as an antipasto with cured meats on Christmas Eve. Lazio.

ciambellone soft leavened cake found in numerous regional cuisines. In the Marche, where it is traditionally made at postgrape harvest weddings, the mixture consists of butter, eggs, sugar, flour, grated lemon zest, yeast and milk. The Tuscan version is more aromatic, the ingredients being wheat flour, eggs, sugar, milk, butter, yeast, vanilla, grated lemon zest and anise or orange liqueur. If chopped walnuts are added to the mixture and whole walnuts used as a decoration, the cake takes the name of ➤ **serpentone**. Again in Tuscany, sometimes they fill the cake with a cream of ricotta, egg yolks and sugar.

ciambotta the term is used in southern Italy to refer to stews of mixed varieties of vegetables and, sometimes, fish. Variations on the theme are numerous, as are regional names: ➤ **ciabbotto abruzzese**, ➤ **ciambotto pugliese**, ➤ **ciambrotta calabrese**, ➤ **ciammotta lucana**, ➤ **cianfotta campana**.

ciambotto fluid stew of tiny fish (varieties depend on the catch of the day) cooked in water with tomatoes and peppers. Served with croutons or crushed pasta, and sometimes used to dress pasta. Puglia.

ciambrotta stew of mixed vegetables (potatoes, peppers, zucchini, eggplants, tomatoes, garlic, onions, celery, olives), into which eggs are sometimes scrambled, flavored with parsley, basil, oregano and saffron. The region's version of ➤ **ciambotta**. Calabria.

ciambudeo a variation on ➤ **ciarimbolo**, a cured meat, made with leftover pig's intestine not used to case other cured meats. Washed with wine and cut into pieces, it is seasoned with salt and pepper and left to dry. A specialty of the province of Pesaro. Marche.

ciammariche aka **ciammaruche** dialect word for earth snails (➤ **lumaca**). Popular regional recipes are a "salad" of snails dressed with lemon juice, garlic, mint and chlli, and snails stewed with liberal amounts of aromatic herbs. Abruzzo.

ciammaruchedd dialect word for earth snails (➤ **lumaca**). Usually sautéed with garlic, chili, mint and skinned tomatoes. Basilicata.

ciammella Lazio term for ➤ **ciambella sorana**, a type of bread.

ciammelle (1) long twisted hand-worked breadsticks, first boiled, then baked in the oven. Typical of the Ciociaria area. Lazio.

ciammelle (2) knot-shaped caked coated with julep (➤ **giulebbe**). Lazio.

ciammellette de magru dialect term for ➤ **ciambelle al vino bianco**, ring cookies.

ciammellone soft elastic baked cake made by amalgamating soft flour, butter, eggs, milk, yeast and, sometimes, aniseed. Possibly of 16th-century origin, the cake was traditionally made for the feast of Sant'Antonio Abate in the small town of Tivoli, in the province of Rome. Now available all year round, it is eaten for breakfast with tea. Lazio.

ciammotta (1)) regional version of ➤ **ciambotta**, in which the vegetables (peppers, eggplants, potatoes) are fried separately in olive oil, mixed together in a pot with garlic and tomatoes, and slow-cooked for about an hour. Sometimes eggs are scrambled in at the end. Basilicata.

ciammotta (2) central and southern Italian word for the common snail (*Helix aspersa*).

ciammotte ammuccate snails cooked with pennyroyal and wild herbs, which give the dish a distinctly green color. Lazio.

cian another name for ➤ **neccio**, type of waffle.

cianchetta regional term for ➤ **suacia**, scaldfish.

cianfotta regional version of ➤ **ciambotta** made with eggplants, peppers, potatoes, ripe tomatoes, onions, parsley and basil. In some variations, zucchini, capers and olives are also added. Campania.

ciapa northern dialect term for ➤ **reticolo**, reticulum.

ciapazoi pasta squares made from a dough of flour, water and chopped chard (or borage leaves, or even grated potatoes), boiled and served with mushroom sauce. An old specialty of the upper Valle Argentina, inland from the western Riviera, they are named for their resemblance to slates (*ardesia* in Italian, *ciappa* in the local dialect). The quarrying and working of slate are, incidentally, the main industries in the valley. Liguria.

ciape 'd nòna dialect term for dried pears and plums (➤ **frutta secca**).

ciapilaia horsemeat stew. The meat is cut into thin strips (in the local dialect, *ciapilé* means "to chop" or "to grind"), marinated for 12 hours in red wine and mixed minced herbs, sautéed in a generous amount of sliced onion, and slow-cooked in the marinade liquid. Served with polenta or boiled potatoes, or used to dress tagliatelle. Typical of the province of Alessandria, the dish is closely related to ➤ **tapulon** (province of Novara). Piedmont.

ciapinabò Piedmontese dialect term for ➤ **topinambur**, Jerusalem artichoke.

ciapini horseshoe-shaped shortcrust pastry cookies. The recipe first appeared in a document signed by a Piedmontese notary public, Lorenzo Porini, in 1797. Typical of the province of Cuneo. Piedmont.

ciapòle dialect term for dried peaches and plums (➤ **frutta secca**).

ciappa Sicilian term for ➤ **pomodoro secco**, sun-dried tomato.

ciapudda dialect term for ➤ **cepola**, red band fish.

ciaramicola ring-shaped cake made with wheat flour, sugar, eggs, grated lemon zest and lard, covered at the center with two strips of pastry in the form of a cross. After baking, it is brushed with egg whites whipped to a peak and covered with confetti sugar. It is then baked again to allow the meringue topping to set. A specialty of ancient origin, once offered as a gift to betrothed brides. Umbria.

ciardedda another word for ➤ **cialdedda**, a bread soup.

ciarimbolo aka **ciaringolo** rare regional cured meat. In the province of Macerata, a pig's large intestine (➤ **budello gentile**) is washed with vinegar, rinsed with wine and lemon juice and filled with a mixture of hand-chopped sausage or lean pork seasoned with salt, aromatized with pepper and wild fennel flowers, secured with string at either end and smoked over a juniper wood fire. In the province of Ancona, the outside protective membrane is eased from a pig's intestine, cured for 24 hours with salt, pepper, garlic and rosemary, then left to dry. Ready to eat after two weeks, the meat can be aged for a few months. Usually eaten barbecued in a sandwich.

ciarla a type of round flatbread made with bread dough, baked in the oven, sliced and filled with ham, ricotta or fresh Pecorino cheese. Used to be served fresh from the oven, spread with honey as a snack, now served as an antipasto or savory snack. Lazio.

ciaroncie another name for ➤ **cajincì**, a type of ravioli.

ciascuna word for ➤ **nucatili**, a type of pastry, in Palazzolo Acreide, in the province of Siracusa. Derives from *ciascu*, a dialect term for "flask."

ciaudedda Basilicata version of ➤ **ciaudella**, vegetable stew.

ciaudella aka **ciaurella** vegetable stew popular throughout southern Italy and Sicily with numerous variants. In Campania, it is made with fresh fava beans sautéed in oil with onion and pieces of sausage or pancetta. In Basilicata, they add artichokes and potatoes to the mixture and call the soup ➤ **ciaudedda**.

ciauscolo cured meat made of pancetta, shoulder and loin pork and trimmings and 30-50% fat, cured with salt, pepper, orange zest, fennel seeds or dried fennel flowers, garlic and white wine. The mixture is chopped finely and cased in a pig's intestine. The meat is ready to eat after 30 (or, more rarely, 60) days. Produced in the provinces of Ascoli Piceno, Macerata and Ancona. Marche.

ciauscolo di fegato another name for ➤ **fegatino (2)**, a cured meat.

ciavàr sausage made from a mixture of pork and pig's offal cured with salt, pepper, garlic and Sangiovese red wine. Cased in a pig's intestine, it may be eaten fresh (broiled or roast), aged or preserved in oil. Emilia-Romagna.

ciavarro soup, vaguely reminiscent of ➤ **virtù**, of fresh peas, cereals (sweet corn and pearl barley) and legumes from the pantry (lentils, chickpeas, fava beans, beans), flavored with onion, garlic, chili and tomato. Prepared, like ➤ **virtù**, every year on May 1. A specialty of the village of Ripatransone, in the province of Ascoli Piceno. Marche.

ciavattoni another name for ➤ **ciabattoni (1)**, giant rigatoni.

ciavuscolo another name for ➤ **ciauscolo**, a cured meat.

ciballo simple nougat made of peanuts, glucose and sugar, thus named in Cremona. Used to be popular among those who could not afford the genuine article. Lombardy.

cibo di strada street food. Italians have a long tradition of buying local delicacies from specific vendors and eating them in the streets. Classic regional street foods are: ➤ **frisceu**, ➤ **panizze**, ➤ **cuculli**, ➤ **cartocci di pesce** (Genoa); ➤ **crocchè di potatoes**, ➤ **pasta cresciuta**, ➤ **sciurilli**, ➤ **scagliuzzi** (Naples); ➤ **filetti di baccalà**, ➤ **supplì** (Rome); ➤ **arancine**, ➤ **cazzilli**, ➤ **panelle** (Palermo); ➤ **calzone**, ➤ **panzerotto (1)**, ➤ **tomasine** (elsewhere in the south). Italian street foods also comprise a whole range of focaccias, flatbreads and the like: ➤ **piadina**, ➤ **sfincione**, ➤ **pizza**, ➤ **puccia**, ➤ **farinata**, ➤ **scacciata**. Offal and boiled meats also figure, on their own or in sandwiches: ➤ **lampredotto**, ➤ **carna-**

cotta, ➤ **pani ca' meusa**, ➤ **quarume**, ➤ **insalata di musso e carcagnola**. Fish and mollusks are popular too, dishes ranging from the boiled octopus of the Vucciria market in Palermo (Sicily) to that on sale in special kiosks in Padua ➤ **folpeto** (Veneto).

cibreo chicken livers, kidneys, crests and testicles (known locally as *fagioli*, "beans"), lightly floured (the crests and testicles are blanched beforehand), sautéed in butter with minced onions and garlic, and cooked in white wine. When the dish is ready, egg yolks beaten with lemon juice are poured into the pan and allowed to scramble slightly. The dish is Florentine in origin and probably dates from the Renaissance. Tuscany.

cicala di mare (1) Ligurian and Tuscan term for ➤ **canocchia**, mantis shrimp.

cicala di mare (2) term used in some Italian regions for ➤ **magnosella**, slipper lobster.

cicc flatbread made by frying thin slices of buckwheat polenta mixed with cheese, or (in the savory version) mixed with milk, sugar and vanilla. Typical of the Valtellina, in the province of Sondrio. Lombardy.

cicci e baine side dish of cannellini (➤ **cannellino**) or round beans (*cicci*) and runner beans (*baine*), first boiled, then cooked in the pan for a few minutes in a sauce of garlic, onion, basil and crushed ripe tomatoes. Served with slices of toasted bread. Campania.

cicci maritati soup made with mixed legumes (including round beans, *cicci*) and cereals, traditionally cooked in the fireplace. Used to be made on May 1 to celebrate the end of the winter. Campania.

cicciarelli di Noli (sing. **cicciarello**), locally aka **lussi** aka **lussotti**. Tiny sand eels traditionally fished just off the coast using a kind of trawl net called a *sciabica*: one boat floats over the fish, while another surrounds them with the horseshoe-shaped net. Small, tapered in shape and silvery in color, the fish, protected by a Slow Food presidium, are excellent marinated in vinegar or fried. The historical fishing village of Noli is situated in the province of Savona, west of Genoa. Liguria.

cicciarello Ligurian name for ➤ **cicerello**, Mediterranean sand eel.

cicciolata di Parma cured meat halfway between ➤ **ciccioli**, pork scratchings, and ➤ **testa in cassetta**. The scratchings are wrapped in a canvas and pressed for a week to obtain a "cake," which is subsequently crumbled and mixed with the hand-chopped meat of a boned pig's head. The mixture is aromatized with salt, pepper, cinnamon, cloves and, sometimes, minced bay leaves, then rewrapped in canvas and pressed until it reaches the right compact texture. Eaten fresh with polenta or ➤ **torta fritta**, a type of fritter. Emilia-Romagna.

ciccioli scratchings. The crispy, crunchy bits left over from the rendering down of fat from an animal's carcass, a pig's or goose's in particular (➤ **strutto**, lard). The term, derived from *ciccia*, fat. has numerous regional synonyms: ➤ **cicoli**, ➤ **cigoli**, ➤ **cicines**, ➤ **siccioli**, ➤ **grasei**, ➤ **graso**, ➤ **grasul**, ➤ **garisoli**, ➤ **greppole**, ➤ **sgriscioli**, ➤ **lardinzi**, ➤ **frittula**, ➤ **frizze**, ➤ **sfrizzoli**, ➤ **frinzuli**, ➤ **sprinzuli**, ➤ **friccioli**, ➤ **scriccioli**, ➤ **scarafuagli**, ➤ **risimoglie**, ➤ **gelda**, ➤ **gigiole** etc. By themselves or aromatized with pepper, bay leaf or cinnamon, scratchings have a very strong flavor and are full of calories. They are eaten as they are with aperitifs, or as an antipasto, or used as an ingredient in more elaborate dishes (➤ **cicciolata di Parma**) or to add flavor to frittatas, savory pies and polentas (➤ **polenta e ciccioli**), focaccias and breads (➤ **pizza con ciccioli**, ➤ **farinella con i ciccioli**, ➤ **migliaccio campano**, ➤ **chisola**, ➤ **pane con gerda**, ➤ **pane con i cicoli**, ➤ **pan de frizze**, ➤ **spianata**).

ciccioli d'oca pieces of goose fat and skin to which a little meat is still attached lightly fried with salt and pepper and transferred to canvas bags to dry. Typical of Mortara, in the province of Pavia, and the southern part of the province of Lodi. Lombardy.

ciccioneddas tiny pastries filled with cherry or apricot jam, hazelnut cream or confectioner's custard. Sardinia.

cicerbita common alternative name for ➤ **grespigno**, field sowthistle.

cicerbita alpina another name for ➤ **radicchio di monte**, alpine blue sowthistle.

cicerchia grass pea (*Lathyrus sativus*). Flat, irregularly shaped, yellowish legume, native to the Mediterranean. Rich in protein, it has been cultivated since ancient times. Long neglected, partly thanks to the discovery of traditional foods, it is now enjoying a revival, especially in Umbria, Marche, Abruzzo, Campania, Puglia and Lazio. The Italian Ministry of Agriculture's database of native and/or traditional food products lists the following varieties: *cicerchia commune, cicerchia di Campodimele* (Lazio), ➤ **cicerchia di Serra de' Conti** (Marche), *cicerchia del Molise, cicerchia della Puglia* (where the legume is also known as *cicercola, dente di vecchia* and *pisello quadrato*). After being soaked (or, sometimes, boiled), it may be prepared in the same manner as chickpeas, in soups, stews and purées (➤ **sfricugliata di cicerchie**, ➤ **zuppa di cicerchie**).

cicerchia di Serra de' Conti grass pea very common in the Marche region until the mid 20th century, grown among rows of corn with beans and chickpeas. The Serra de'Conti cicerchia is tiny and irregular in shape and ranges in color from gray to speckled pale brown. It has a delicate skin and a less bitter flavor than other varieties. It was once on the brink of extinction, but, with the help of a Slow Food presidium, young farmers in the village of Serra de' Conti, in the province of Ancona, continue to cultivate it in their kitchen gardens, thereby saving it from oblivion. Marche.

cicerchia e zampetti grass pea and pig's trotter soup. Dish popular inland of Ancona and Pesaro. Marche.

cicerchiata dolce a cake made with a mixture of wheat flour, sugar, eggs, grated lemon zest and liqueur, shaped into balls, blanched in water and fried in lard. After cooling, the balls are smothered in honey and built into a ring or a pyramid. Umbria and Abruzzo contend the paternity of the cake. In the latter region, they garnish it with candied fruit and colored sugared almonds. In the Marche, they aromatize the mixture with anise liqueur (➤ **mistrà**). The name refers to the balls' resemblance to grass peas (➤ **cicerchie**). An analogous cake in Calabria and Basilicata, ➤ **cicirata**, is compared to chickpeas (➤ **cece**).

cicerchie in umido stewed grass peas. The peas are soaked overnight, boiled in salted water, drained, sautéed in extra virgin olive oil with finely minced garlic, flat-leaved parsley and pennyroyal, then stewed in tomato passata and water. Umbria.

cicerello Mediterranean sand eel (*Gymnammodytes cicerellus*). Tiny fish which live on sand banks close to shore and are fished in the spring. Until the 1970s, they were very common, but have now become a rarity. The Ministry of Agriculture's database of native and/or traditional food products lists ➤ **cicciarello di Noli**. Common and regional names: ➤ **aluzzetiello**, ➤ **cicciarello**, ➤ **cicirello**, ➤ **cicirieddu**, ➤ **cixireddu**, ➤ **lusso**, ➤ **lussotto**.

ciceri e tria pasta and chickpeas. The chickpeas are soaked overnight, then cooked in an earthenware pot covered with water aromatized with garlic, cherry tomatoes, bay leaf, flat-leaved parsley, celery, spring onion and a small potato. The pasta (*tria*) is a dried homemade broad flour and water ribbon. Following a custom of Arab origin, a portion of the pasta is cooked in the chickpea soup, another is fried. The dish is then assembled, anointed with extra virgin olive oil and sprinkled with chili. A classic dish of the southern Salento peninsula, in the province of Lecce. Puglia.

cichet Piedmontese dialect for a small glass or shot of liquor.

cicheti Venetian word for savories served with an ➤ **ombra** (glass of wine). The counters of traditional osterias in Veneto are spread with a vast assortment of tidbits, among which small fried fish, boiled mollusks and crustaceans, marinated anchovies and sardines, salt cod on toast or with polenta, cow's offal (tripe, spleen), boiling sausage (➤ **cotechino**), meatballs, fried artichokes, hard-boiled eggs and pickles.

cicines Friulian term for ➤ **ciccioli**, pork scratchings.

cicinielli Campania term for newborn smelt (➤ **novellame di pesce**, fry).

ciciniello veraco Campania term for ➤ **rossetto**, transparent goby.

cicio aka **ciciu** sweet pastry doll which a godfather gives as a present to his godson on the day of the latter's christening. Typical of the province of Cuneo and other area. Piedmont.

ciciones Sassari dialect from for ➤ **malloreddos**, a typical pasta shape. Sardinia.

cicirata (1) Christmas cake similar to ➤ **struffoli** (Campania) and to ➤ **cicerchiata** (Umbria). Basilicata, Puglia.

cicirata (2) half-moon-shaped ravioli, filled with puréed chickpeas mixed with honey or cooked wine must, liqueur, cloves, cinnamon and lemon zest, and fried in butter until golden brown. Calabria.

cicirello Calabrian dialect name for ➤ **cicerello**, European sand eel.

cicirieddu Sicilian dialect name for ➤ **cicerello**, European sand eel.

cicitt long, thin 100% goat meat sausage (➤ **luganiega**), dark red in color with a tangy smell. Made with cheaper cuts of meat mixed with fat, the animal's stomach (pre-blanched in water) and heart, and cured with minced garlic, salt, pepper, cinnamon, nutmeg, cloves and red and white wine. A specialty of the Maggia and Verzasca in the Swiss Cantone Ticino, on the border with Italy. The sausage is promoted by a Slow Food presidium.

cicoli Campania term for ➤ **ciccioli di maiale**, pork scratchings.

cicoria chicory (*Cichorium intybus*). Many cultivated and wild varieties grow in Italy. The two most important groups in the family are ➤ **radicchio** and ➤ **catalogna**, endive; others are Belgian endive and cutting chicory (*ceriolo*). Wild varieties are much used in southern Italy (➤ **cicoria selvatica**, wild chicory).

cicoria amara common name for ➤ **boccione maggiore**, golden fleece.

cicoria di campo another name for ➤ **cicoria selvatica**, wild chicory, but also ➤ **dente di leone**, bristly hawkbit.

cicoria di campo in brodo wild chicory and

other greens (➤ **cicorielle**) boiled and drained and steeped in meat broth with tomatoes (of the type hung in bunches in cool environments, hence dried and very sweet). Puglia.

cicoria e annoglia chicory and salami. Wild chicory (➤ **cicoria selvatica**) boiled and turned in a skillet in olive oil with garlic and slices of ➤ **annoglia** salami. A soupier, more liquid version is also made with the addition of a ladleful or two of the chicory cooking broth. Campania.

cicoria in brodo chicory in broth. Boiled chicory turned in a skillet with lard and diced ham, then cooked in meat broth. Served with grated Pecorino. Basilicata.

cicoria pazza cooked chicory turned in a skillet with oil, garlic and chili. A delicacy in Rome. Lazio.

cicoria selvatica wild chicory (*Cichorium intybus*). Herbaceous plant with unmistakable blue flowers, which grows wild in uncultivated fields and meadows, common throughout Italy. In the north of the country it is eaten mostly raw, mixed with other leaves in salads. In the center and south, it is extremely popular, and the Calabrian and Campanian varieties are included in the Ministry of Agriculture's database of native and/or traditional food products. It is cooked and turned in a skillet with beans and chili, or sausages, or fava bean purée (➤ **'ncapriata**). It is an ingredient in soups (➤ **cicoria di campo in brodo**, ➤ **cicorielle a'zise**), goes well with ➤ **polenta macafana**, with pasta (in Lazio, traditionally with ➤ **frascarelli**) and meat (➤ **agnello al calderotto**), and is also preserved in oil. Common and regional names: ➤ **cassella**, ➤ **cicorina**, ➤ **cicoria di campo**, ➤ **cicoriella**, ➤ **grugno**, ➤ **radicchio di campo**, ➤ **radicetta**.

cicoria strascinata a recipe common to many central and southern Italian regions. In Lazio, the unseparated leaves are turned in a skillet with lard, or extra virgin olive oil, crushed garlic and minced chili. Broccoletti and endive may be cooked in the same way, sometimes with the addition of chopped anchovy and a little tomato passata.

cicoriella another word for ➤ **cicoria selvatica**, wild chicory, or ➤ **radicchiella**, beaked hawksbeard.

cicorielle, in dialect aka **cicureddhe**, term for wild chicory (➤ **cicoria selvatica**) the main ingredient in many dishes, from ➤ **timballo di cicorielle** to ➤ **'ncapriata**. In some areas, it also refers to wild edible herbs and greens of other varieties: field sowthistle ➤ **grespigno**, common brighteyes ➤ **latticrepolo**, cat's ear ➤ **costolina**, beaked hawksbeard ➤ **radicchiella**, wild mustard ➤ **senape selvatica**. Puglia.

cicorielle a'zise aka **azzise** wild chicory (➤ **cicoria**) first sautéed with cherry tomatoes, garlic and bay leaves, then cooked in chicken broth and served with grated Pecorino, sometimes with small meatballs. Puglia.

cicorietta amara common name for ➤ **radicchiella**, beaked hawksbeard.

cicorina regional term ➤ for ➤ **cicoria selvatica**, wild chicory.

cicureddhe dialect term for ➤ **cicorielle**, wild chicory and other greens.

ciell' rechiene another name for ➤ **celli pieni**, pastries.

cientefigliole aka **cientopoglione** aka **cientopognone** dialect words for ➤ **omaso**, omasum.

cif e ciaf aka **ciffe ciaffe** lean pork stew with onion, garlic, parsley and chili (a version also exists with lamb offal as the main ingredient). In the past, the dish was made on the day of the killing of the pig with the fattier parts of the animal, including the ribs and cheek, and the onomatopeic name evokes their sizzling in the pot. Abruzzo.

cigoli regional term for → **ciccioli**, pork scratchings.

cilele in tecia the bases of artichokes (*cilele* in dialect) opened and sautéed with garlic and parsley, then simmered in vegetable or meat broth. Veneto.

ciliegia cherry (*Prunus avium*). Fruit enjoyed for its sweetness since Roman times. Italy is one of the world's major producers, the fruit being cultivated intensively in four regions (Veneto, Emilia-Romagna, Campania and Puglia). Two varieties in particular are grown: *Prunus juliana*, with soft flesh, known as *ciliegia tenerina*, and *Prunus duracina*, with firmer flesh, known as *durone*. Color varies from bright red to blackish, and the fruit is on sale at markets from May to the start of August. Other varieties are → **marasca**, → **visciola** and → **amarena,** all characterized by a sourish flavor. Albeit appearing in a few regional recipes, they are used mainly to make syrups, preserves, jams, soft drinks and liqueurs (→ **maraschino**, → **vino di visciole**). Besides being eaten fresh, the cherry is used in confectionery, often candied, and to make jams and liqueurs. Many cakes, cookies and pastries make use of fresh cherries (→ **strudel**) or cherry jam (→ **crostata di visciole**, → **rufioi (2)**). It also features in some savory dishes (eg, → **cinghiale in agrodolce**, sweet and sour boar). In some regions cherries are preserved in alcohol both industrially and in households. The Italian Ministry of Agriculture's database of native and/or traditional food products lists the following varieties: *ciliegie di Raiano e Giuliano Teatino* (Abruzzo); *ciliegia del monte, ciliegia della recca, ciliegia di Bracigliano, ciliegia di Siano, ciliegia maiatica, ciliegia melella, ciliegia san Pasquale* (Campania); *antiche varietà di ciliegia piacentina, ciliegia di Cesena* (varieties: *moretta, durona, durella, duroncina, del fiore, primaticcia, corniola*), *ciliegia di Vignola* (Emilia-Romagna); *ciliegia di Celleno, ciliegia ravenna della Sabina, visciolo dei Monti Lepini* (Lazio); *durone sarzanese* (Liguria); *ciliegia duracina di Tarcento* (Friuli), *amarena d'Uschione* (Lombardy); *visciole e amarene di Cantiano* (Marche); *amarena di Trofarello*, → **bella di Garbagna**, *precoce di Rivarone, ciliegia di Pecetto* (Piedmont); *cerase di Puglia* (Puglia); *ciliegia furistera, ciliegia tardiva* aka *ciliegia carrufale* (Sardinia); *mastrantoni* (Sicily); *ciliegia di Lari* (Tuscany); → **ciliegia di Marostica**, *ciliegia delle colline veronesi, ciliegia dei Colli asolani, ciliegia dei Colli Euganei, durona del Chiampo, durone/mora di Cazzano* (Veneto).

ciliegia di Marostica sweet PGI cherry grown in the hills round Marostica, in the province of Vicenza. Firm skin and flesh, pink-dark red in color, high vitamin and mineral salt content. Veneto.

ciliegia marina regional term for → **corbezzolo**, strawberry tree or arbutus.

ciliegine regional term for → **alchechengi**, Peruvian groundcherry.

ciliegino term often used for **pomodorino a ciliegia**, cherry tomato (→ **pomodorino al piennolo**).

cima breast of veal opened up like a pouch, filled with a mixture of ground veal, sweetbreads or brains and marrow, eggs, peas, and Parmigiano, boiled, cooled, and served sliced. A specialty of Genoa, though variations exist all over Liguria and in the valleys on the border with the province of Piacenza. Liguria.

cimaredda Puglia dialect term for → **senape selvatica**, wild mustard.

cimarolo Lazio dialect word for → **carciofo**

romanesco, globe artichoke.

cimballo regional term for ➤ **imbutino**, common funnel mushroom.

Cimbro cow's milk cheese of the Lessinia area, suitable for aging. Often flavored with herbs, spices and marc, and matured in pits. Veneto.

cime di rapa broccoli rabe (*Brassica rapa*, subsp. *sylvestris* var. *esculenta*). Plant of Mediterranean origin available all year long. Develops a rosette of spiked leaves that surround a fleshy green bud with edible yellow flowers. The inflorescences, leaves, and the tender part of the stalk are eaten boiled and sautéed (➤ **rape e ciccioli**, ➤ **rape 'infucate**, ➤ **broccoli strascinati**), or as an accompaniment to pasta (➤ **orecchiette con le cime di rapa**), and as an ingredient in ➤ **pancotto** (➤ **cecamariti**). The vegetable is eaten mostly in the central and southern regions of Italy: Puglia, Calabria, Campania (➤ **friarielli**), Lazio (*broccoletti sezzesi* and *broccoletti di Anguillara*), Tuscany (*rapini di Bergiola Foscalino* and *rapo del Valdarno*), Umbria (*pulezze del Lago Trasimeno*). Common and regional names: ➤ **amarelli**, ➤ **broccoletti**, ➤ **broccoletti di rapa**, ➤ **friarielli**, ➤ **mugnoli**, ➤ **pulezze**, ➤ **rapini**, ➤ **rapi**, ➤ **spigatelli**, ➤ **tanni**.

cime di rapa stufate stewed broccoli rabe with sliced onions, salt, pepper and oil, served as a side dish with meat and cheese. Puglia.

cimieri another name for ➤ **creste di gallo**, a type of pasta.

cimino (1) another name for ➤ **cumino dei prati**, caraway.

cimino (2) Palermo term for ➤ **sesamo**, sesame.

cin filling of potatoes and vegetables used to make a type of ➤ **tortei**, fried and coated with sugar. Typical of Ormea, in the province of Cuneo. Piedmont.

cinciacotte dialect term for dried apple and pear slices (➤ **frutta secca**, dried fruit).

cinestrata aka **ginestrata** egg yolks beaten with Marsala, broth and cinnamon, thickened over a low heat with the addition of small pieces of butter and a sprinkling of nutmeg and sugar. Possibly of Renaissance origin, the dish is served as a first course in the Chianti area (though it is now rare). Tuscany.

Cingherlino another name for ➤ **Zincarlin**, type of cheese.

cinghiale wild boar (*Sus scrofa*). An ancestor of the domestic pig, this hirsute mammal used to inhabit deciduous and mixed forests, marshland and meadows. Today, on account of the abandonment of the countryside and the introduction of hybrids, small herds roam the land almost everywhere, causing untold damage. Hunting boars is difficult and, though the animal is common in the wild, the meat sold in shops and served in restaurants, is mostly farmed. The meat of young animals, up to the age of one year, may be used in the same recipes as pork. Older animals tend to be marinated and strongly flavored with herbs and spices (➤ **cinghiale in agrodolce**). Wild boar meat is also used in various cured meats.

cinghiale al cioccolato wild boar with chocolate (➤ **cinghiale in agrodolce**, sweet and sour wild boar).

cinghiale al civé a whole piece of wild boat meat is marinated, browned and slowly cooked in Nebbiolo red wine aromatized with minced onion, carrot and celery, rosemary, bay leaf, cloves and cinnamon. Piedmont.

cinghiale all'Aspromonte after being suitably hung, the meat, usually the saddle, is flavored with bay leaves and roast on a spit. Calabria.

cinghiale alla cacciatora generally pieces of wild boar stewed in tomato. In an alternative recipe from the Emilian Apennines, the pieces of meat are marinated briefly in wine, browned in chopped herbs and spices (cinnamon, coriander, aniseed, cloves, black pepper), covered with wine, which is allowed to evaporate, and finished in broth mixed with white flour. Emilia-Romagna.

cinghiale alla maremmana chopped meat from the leg of a wild boar marinated for 24 hours in red wine, vinegar and aromatic vegetables, browned, then stewed with herbs, wine, tomato purée and black olives. Tuscany.

cinghiale alle erbe wild boar stew flavored with garlic, bay leaves, oregano, rosemary, juniper berries, fennel seeds, cloves, and chili. Typical of the Alpine valleys of the province of Cuneo. Piedmont.

cinghiale in agrodolce sweet and sour wild boar. The meat (normally from the leg) is marinated in wine, aromatic herbs and spices, brownedand cooked slowly in wine and water (or in the marinade liquid). It is served with a sauce made from the pan juices, sugar, vinegar, grated dark chocolate, raisins, pine kernels, prunes, dried cherries, citron zest and candied orange. The recipe may also be used with hare and is very similar to ➤ **dolceforte** sauce (➤ **lingua in dolceforte**). The recipe is typical of the Lazio Maremma and evokes the Renaissance taste for ➤ **agrodolce**, sweet and sour flavors. Lazio.

cinghiale in umido wild boar stew. In the Monferrato area (Piedmont), meat from the neck or shoulder of the animal is browned with herbs, covered with Barbera wine, cooked slowly over a medium heat and served with a sauce made with the pan juices mixed with potato flour and warm water. In Friuli-Venezia Giulia, pieces of meat are marinated in red wine, garlic and rosemary, coated in flour and cooked in wine, tomato passata and broth.

cingoli grape harvest pastries made from a flour and water dough, molded into a variety of shapes (matchsticks, bows, cubes and so on), first cooked in ➤ **vincotto**, cooked wine must, then left to cool in it. Basilicata.

cininieje dialect name for fritters made of ➤ **bianchetti**, newborn fish, locally known as *cicinelli*. The tiny fish are dipped in a batter of eggs, minced parsley and garlic, flour, salt and lemon juice, then fried, a tablespoonful at a time, in boiling olive oil. Lazio.

cinnamomo another word for ➤ **cannella**, cinnamon.

Cinta senese native pig breed raised in the province of Siena in the area of Monteriggioni, Sovicille and Poggibonsi. It has a black to slate-gray coat with a pale stripe round the shoulder. One of the first black pig breeds to be saved from extinction and raised in a semi-wild state. Today its pork, eaten fresh or used to make cured meats, is much prized. Tuscany.

cioccolata hot chocolate. Hot or, more rarely, cold beverage made of cocoa (➤ **cacao**), milk or water and sugar. Believed to have been introduced to the French court by the Spanish wife of Louis XIII, the habit of sipping hot chocolate spread among the upper classes and became fashionable until well into the 18th century. For a long time the beverage was identified with Catholic southern Europe, hence the old order, whereas coffee (➤ **caffè**), more popular in Protestant northern Europe came to represent the advent of a new age and new customs. Today hot chocolate is available in all Italian bars, mostly in the form of commercial blends containing potato flour (➤ **fecola di patate**).

cioccolatino chocolate. A small candy made or coated with chocolate (➤ **cioccolato**). Chocolate fillings include chopped, crushed or whole hazelnuts or almonds, variously aromatized creams, marzipan, liqueur, cherries preserved in alcohol, fruit preserves and candied fruit, but chocolate must constitute at least 25% of the product. Artisan- or industrially-made, variously shaped (square, round, heart-shaped), chocolates are generally sold wrapped in tin foil or packaged in boxes in pleated paper cups Typical Italian regional chocolates: ➤ **gianduiotto**, ➤ **boero**, ➤ **tartufo,** and all the various liqueur-filled and hazelnut or almond-flavored ➤ **baci** (every town and city in Piedmont alone has a version of its own).

cioccolato chocolate. In solid form, composed of ➤ **cacao**, cocoa (a minimum 35% according to European legislation), and sugar, with or without the addition of other substances such as cocoa butter (➤ **burro di cacao**), vanilla, milk, honey and dried fruits. Bars of chocolate first appeared in Turin in the late 18th century, when cocoa was beginning to be solidified. Just years later, pioneers chocolatiers began working in Genoa (Romanengo, from 1780) and Bologna (Majani, from 1796). In Turin, Caffarel built a chocolate factory to exploit the hydraulic power of the Pellerina river, and in 1802 Bozelli created the blender, based on the olive oil press, in Genoa. From then on chocolatiers flocked from all over Europe to Turin (where in the early 19th century, responding to Napoleon's trade restrictions, Michele Prochet created ➤ **gianduia**, a blend of choco-

late and hazelnuts) to learn solidification techniques. In 1875, the Swiss artisan Cailler, who had learned his trade in Turin, invented milk chocolate. Chocolate is currently enjoying a boom in Italy thanks to the efforts of artisan chocolatiers. Hence the birth of chocolate crus and the fashion of combining different types of chocolate with foods, wines and spirits. In the Italian kitchen, chocolate is an ingredient in cakes and pastries, fillings, creams, custards and ice creams. Grated bitter chocolate also features in savory dishes: in ➤ **salmì**, game stews, meat dishes such as ➤ **agrodolce** and ➤ **dolceforte**, ➤ **coda alla vaccinara**, ➤ **cinghiale in agrodolce**, ➤ **lingua in dolceforte**.

ciociole Neapolitan dialect word for the dried fruit and nuts exchanged at Christmas. Campania.

ciof aka **ciuf** mixture of boiled potatoes, day-old bread, milk and strong cheese, with the texture of a soft polenta. Typical of the mountains of the province of Cuneo. Piedmont.

ciogga minudda Sassari dialect name for the Roman snail (*Helix theba pisana*), otherwise known as ➤ **lumachella** and, in Sicily, ➤ **babbaluci**. Very small and pale in color, it is to be found clinging to plants and trees. Cooked in its shell in oil with garlic, parsley or chili. Sardinia.

cioncia calf's head meat boiled, cut into strips, then browned with finely chopped onion, carrot, celery, calamint and garlic, lubricated with red wine and finished with ripe tomatoes, salt and pepper. Served on slices of toasted bread. The name (a dialect word for the Italian *concia*, meaning "tanning") refers to the fact that the dish used to be made from cheaper cuts of veal, stripped from the hides which were to be sent off for tanning. This very humble recipe originated in the small town of Pescia, in the province of Pistoia. Tuscany.

ciopa compact-crumbed, crisp-crusted bread made by joining together two long loaves. Veneto.

ciopa de pan taià aka **ciopa mantovana** Trentino terms for ➤ **gramolato**, double loaf.

ciota Cremona name for ➤ **mariola cotta**, boiling sausage.

cipolla onion (*Allium cepa*). Cultivated for millennia, onions of countless varieties of diverse sizes and colors are grown all over Italy, especially in Emilia-Romagna, Campania, Puglia and Sicily. The Italian Ministry of Agriculture's database of native and/or traditional food products lists the following varieties: ➤ **cipolla rossa di Tropea** (Calabria); *cipolla bianca di Pompei* and *cipolla ramata di Montoro* (Campania); *cipolla di Medicina* (Emilia-Romagna); *cipolla di Pignone, cipolla rossa genovese* (Liguria); *cipolla rossa della Val Cosa, cipolla di Castelnovo del Friuli e* Cavasso (Friuli); *cipolla rossa di Sermide* (Lombardy); *cipolla di Suasa* (Marche); *cipolla di Isernia* (Molise); *cipolla bionda e rossa astigiana, cipolla dorata e rossa di Castelnuovo Scrivia, cipolla di Andezeno* (Piedmont); ➤ **cipolla rossa di Acquaviva**, *cipolla di Zapponeta* (Puglia); ➤ **cipolla di Certaldo**, *cipolla di Bassone, cipolla di Ripola, cipolla di Tercetoli, cipolla di Treschietto, cipolla lucchese, cipolla massese, cipolla rossa toscana, cipolla sagonese, cipolla vernina* (Tuscany); *cipolla di Cannara* (Umbria); *cipolla rossa* (Sardinia); ➤ **Giarratana** (Sicily); *cipolla bianca di Chioggia, rosa di Bassano* (Veneto). The onion appears in countless recipes as an aromatic and also features in its own right in many traditional dishes (eg, ➤ **cipollata**).

cipolla di Certaldo onion cultivated in two varieties: *statina*, round, pale purple, juicy and sweet; *vernina*, red flat at the ends, with a tangy flavor. Grown round the town of Certaldo, in the province of Florence, listed in the Ministry of Agriculture's database of native and/or traditional food products, and supported by a Slow Food presidium. Used in Tuscan classics such ➤ **lesso rifatto** or ➤ **francesina**. Tuscany.

cipolla di Giarratana flat onion with a brownish-white skin and sapid, white flesh. It weighs an average four to five ounces but can reach a pound. Cultivated on a plateau in the province of Ragusa, Sicily. Harvested from late July to the end of August, given its size it is often stuffed or filled, locally with Modica fava beans. A Slow Food presidium is helping growers to improve preservation techniques and launch production of pickles and other specialties. Sicily.

cipolla porraia southern Italian name for ➤ **cipollotto**, spring onion or ➤ **porro**, leek.

cipolla porrata another name for ➤ **erba cipollina**, chives.

cipolla rossa di Acquaviva flat purplish-red onion with a distinctively fresh, sweet flavor, grown in Acquaviva delle Fonti, in the province of Bari, Puglia. Following a decline in cultivation, a Slow Food presidium was set up a few years ago to relaunch the onion, which can be eaten raw in salads, baked in the oven and used as an ingredient in pies, flatbreads, roasts and stews. Puglia.

cipolla rossa di Tropea PGI red onion with sweet white flesh, cultivated in Tropea, in the province of Vibo Valentia, where, thanks to the mild climate, it is available all year round. Calabria.

cipollaccio col fiocco another name for ➤ **lampascione**, grape hyacinth bulb.

cipollata (1) onion soup, traditional in all

Italy's central regions. In Tuscany, onions are softened with chopped ➤ **rigatino** bacon and sausage and covered with a broth made with pork ribs, the meat of which is cut into strips and added to the pot. The finished soup is served with toasted bread rubbed with garlic. In Umbria, onions are sautéed in chopped lardo, aromatized with basil and puréed tomatoes and, when cooked, amalgamated with a mixture of grated Parmigiano and beaten eggs and served with toasted bread. In Abruzzo, they add generous amounts of chili to the soup.

cipollata (2) mounds of sliced onion fried to golden and finished with white wine and vinegar. The preparation is used as a cooking base for fish, especially slices of tuna coated in flour and fried. Sicily.

cipolle ripiene stuffed onions. Side dish or antipasto common in many Italian regions. In Liguria they are one of the traditional ➤ **ripieni** (stuffed vegetables), in Piedmont they are prepared in many ways, stuffed with ground veal or pork or both, with eggs, cheese and breadcrumbs, or with mixed herbs and vegetables, and baked in the oven. In the Provencal valleys in the province of Cuneo, the stuffing consisst of a risotto cooked al dente and mixed with eggs, grated Grana cheese and nutmeg, and the onions (*sebos*) are baked upside down (*abausos*). In the Canavese area, north of Turin, they make a sweet and sour version with crushed amaretti cookies and raisins in the stuffing. In the province of Alessandria, on the border with Lombardy, onions are stuffed with a mixture of pumpkin, crushed amaretti cookies and ➤ **mostarda**. In Veneto, onions are baked in salt, hollowed out and filled with their own flesh mixed with breadcrumbs, grated Grana and ➤ **Latteria** cheese.

cipolle sott'aceto pickled onions. Small white onions (preferably of the *brianzola* variety) boiled in red vinegar aromatized with garlic, bay leaf, pepper, cloves, thyme and cinnamon, drained, allowed to cool, transferred to glass jars and covered with vinegar, salt and the flavorings used for the cooking, except for the garlic. Covered with olive oil, they should rest for at least a week. Typical of the province of Lodi and the Brianza area. Lombardy.

cipollina (pl. **cipolline**) Small onion, often harvested early. The variety most cultivated for the pickling industry is the *borettana*, which originated in Emilia. Another noteworthy variety is the *cipollina d'Ivrea* (now grown only round the villages of Quincinetto and Tavagnasco, in the province of Turin, Piedmont), which stewed or glazed are traditionally served with the region's renowned roast and braised meats (➤ **cipolline in agrodolce**).

cipolline in agrodolce sweet and sour onions. Side dish served in many regions with roasts and stews, especially popular in Lazio. Small onions (➤ **cipollina**) softened in a mixture of lard, ham fat, minced garlic, sugar and salt, covered with water and vinegar. The dish is ready when the liquid has evaporated completely. In Piedmont and Tuscany, the sweet and sour flavor is obtained simply by glazing the onions with a mixture of white wine and sugar caramelized in butter (➤ **glassare**).

cipollino another name for➤ **lampascione**, grape hyacinth bulb.

cipollotto (1) spring onion or scallion (*Allium cepa*). Small onion harvested early when the bulb has just formed. Depending on variety, may be white (➤ **cipollotto nocerino**), or red, usually sweeter. Used in the spring sliced raw in salads, frittatas and stuffings, it is especially popular in Puglia (➤ **sponzala** aka **sponsale** aka **spunzali**). The Italian Ministry of Agriculture's database of native and/or traditional food products lists *cipollotto del Molise*.

cipollotto (2) in some regions of central Italy, such as Abruzzo, the name used for ➤ **lampascione**, grape hyacinth bulb.

cipollotto nocerino all-white (skin and flesh) PDO spring onion famous for its sweetness and digestibility. Typical of Nocera, in the province of Salerno. Campania.

cipuddata soup of salt cod, leeks, eels and chili. Basilicata.

cipuddata Sicilian term for ➤ **cipollata**, onion soup.

cipuddazza Sicilian term, the pejorative form of *cipudda* (dialect for "onion"), used in fishermen's slang for ➤ **scorfano rosso**, red scorpion fish. Like the ➤ **scorfano nero** (*scrofanu niuru*), the **cipuddazza** is best enjoyed in fish soups.

ciriola romana traditional long bread roll. Lazio.

ciriole fresh pasta common in Umbria (especially in the province of Terni). Made from a dough of flour and water (nowadays sometimes olive oil) and shaped like large quadrangular spaghetti. Traditionally served with garlic, oil and chili or parsley (*ciriole alla ternana*), but also popular with black poplar mushrooms (➤ **pioppino**) and Norcia black truffle. Tuscany, Umbria.

cisi (aka **cise**) Piedmontese dialect term for ➤ **ceci**, chickpeas.

cisrà chickpea soup of prepared on All Souls' Day and eaten by the "living" the day after in honor of the dead. The chickpeas are soaked overnight and cooked in water with oil, sage and gar-

lic cloves. Strips of fresh pork rind are added to the pot, and, when it is cooked, the soup is served sprinkled with pepper and anointed with a "cross" of extra virgin olive oil. This is the traditional recipe in the Monferrato and Langhe areas, though other cuts of pork, such as ribs, may be added. In southeast Piedmont, potatoes, aromatics and, sometimes, beans are added. In the province of Alessandria, they serve the soup with pasta or croutons. Piedmont.

ciudin aka **ciuet** dialect term for ➤ **chiodino**, honey armillary mushroom.

ciufele Molise dialect term for ➤ **cavatelli**, a type of pasta.

ciufulitti dialect term in the Sabina area for ➤ **ceciliani**. Lazio.

ciui fritti dialect term for small snails (➤ **lumaca**) of the *Helix vermiculata* variety, purged, boiled, coated with flour and fried.

ciuiga del Banale ancient cured meat typical of the Giudicarie Esteriori district of Trento. Produced from October to April by only one pork butcher. The mixture includes prime and cheap cuts of pork and boiled turnips. Cured with table salt, black pepper, and minced garlic, it is pressed into a pig's intestine and smoked for eight days. After three or four days it is eaten boiled. After ten days, it can be eaten raw. A Slow Food presidium has been set up to increase production with the traditional technique. Trentino-Alto Adige.

ciuliri sieve made of fine reeds and used to make ➤ **malloreddos**, a type of pasta. The pasta dough is pressed against the base of the sieve using pressure with the thumbs. A fine wicker basket may also be used. Sardinia.

ciupeta dialect term for ➤ **coppia ferrarese**, a type of bread. Emilia-Romagna.

ciuppin semi-liquid fish soup (➤ **zuppa di pesce**) consisting of puréed mixed fish, vegetables and tomatoes poured over slices of toasted bread. Typical of the whole region, in particular of the area of Lavagna, Chiavari and Sestri, in the province of Genoa. Liguria.

civé aka **civet** aka **sivé, al** technique for cooking game (especially hare, but also chamois and roe deer venison) or rabbit. The chosen meat is first marinated in wine, herbs and spices, then cooked in the marinade liquid with the addition of the animal's blood and finely minced liver. Not to be confused with ➤ **salmì**, the method is typical of Piedmont, Val d'Aosta and Lombardy, and derives from the medieval French hare recipe, *civet de lièvre.*

civraxiu aka **chivalzu** aka **crivatzu** bread made from a dough of durum wheat meal, or mixed semolina and flour, and starter yeast. Once shaped into large oblong loaves weighing up to a pound, the dough is allowed to rest in baskets lined with linen or canvas before baking in the oven for one hour at 300°C. Typical of the Campidano area. Sardinia.

cixireddu Sardinian term for ➤ **cicerello**, Mediterranean sand eel.

cjalsons aka **cjalzons** aka **cjarsons** sweet-savory half-moon ravioli typical of the Carnia, usually served with butter, grated smoked ricotta, cinnamon and a little sugar. Fillings vary from one village to another. In Timau, they use mashed potatoes, onion fried in butter, powdered cinnamon, raisins, sugar, lemon zest and dried mint. In Piedim, they add walnuts and candied fruit to the mixture, in Rualp dried figs, in Paular chocolate and bitter cocoa, in the Valle del But a variety of aromatic herbs. As a dish without meat, **cjalsons** were traditionally cooked on Christmas Eve, though a version also exists with a filling of raisins, pine kernels, mustard-flavored quince ➤ **mostarda**, and ground meat fried in lard. Friuli.

clementina clementine (➤ **mandarino**, mandarin).

clementine del golfo di Taranto round, seedless PGI clementines with a smooth peel. Used in confectionery and for the production of juices, syrups, sorbets, and marmalades. Also widely use in cosmetics by virtue of its tonic, refreshing properties. Puglia.

clementine di Calabria PGI clementines grown in various communes in the provinces of Reggio Calabria, Catanzaro, Cosenza, Vibo Valentia and Crotone. Almost or totally seedless, they mature early and are picked at the start of October. Calabria.

coagulare to coagulate, to curdle. To change from a liquid to a solid state. The fundamental transformation in cheesemaking.

coareti lozenge- or horn-shaped cuttings of leftover polenta reheated with ➤ **ciccioli**, pork scratchings, raisins, and lemon zest. Typical of the Polesine area. Veneto.

coari pieces of bread dough fried in lard. Once a treat for children when bread was baked at home. Typical of the Polesine area. Veneto.

cobeletti aka **cubeletti** regional names for ➤ **gobeletti**, jam tarts. Liguria.

coccetti Lazio term for small fish for use in soups and stews.

cocciua Sardinian term for ➤ **arsella** (see ➤ **vongola commune**, clam), of which different varieties exist. The most common are the *niedda* (black), to be found in clayey sea beds, and the *pintada* (black and white), typical of sandy sea beds. Sardinia.

cocciuaconca de moru literally "moor's head," a typical sweet Carnival fritter. Sardinia.

cocciue a schiscionera clams (→ **arsella** and → **vongola comune**) cooked with olive oil, garlic and parsley, and sprinkled with breadcrumbs. Named after the typical *schiscionera* skillet. Sardinia.

còcciula Sardinian and Sicilian term for → **vongola**, clam.

còcciule riccia Sicilan term for → **vongola**, clam.

cocco aka **cocco giallo** regional terms for → **ovolo**, royal argaric mushroom.

coccoeddu common snails (*Helix aspersa*), known as *boveri* in other parts of the region, stewed with tomato flavored with garlic, onion, basil and parsley. In another recipe (→ **coccoeddu prenu**), the snails are boiled, returned to their shells, filled with a mixture of minced garlic and parsley and grated Pecorino, bound with beaten eggs and Vernaccia and baked in the oven. A specialty of the province of Sassari. Sardinia.

coccoeddu prenu another word for → **coccoeddu**, a Sardinian snail recipe.

coccoi decorative bread, worked and engraved by hand, made with fine semolina, starter yeast, salt and water. Typically made for weddings (*coccoi de is sposus*) and at Easter time (*coccoi de anguli*). Forty shapes exist, each representing a different locality. Sardinia.

coccois cun gerda flatbread perfumed with mint leaves, dotted with pork scratchings (→ **ciccioli**) or lardo, and flavored with cheese and, sometimes, raisins. Baked to celebrate the killing of the pig. Sardinia.

coccola regional term for → **ovolo**, royal argaric mushroom.

coccoli savory fritters of leavened dough (plain flour, brewer's yeast and water) enriched with beaten eggs and fried in small portions. A classic street food, also eaten with cured meats and antipasti. Tuscany.

coch aka **cock** aka **koch** a dessert of Austrian origin made of cookies, rice, semolina, almonds or fresh fruit. Savory versions also exist. Friuli-Venezia Giulia.

cocomerazzo Puglia term for → **barattiere** and → **carosello** (→ **melone immaturo**, unripe melon).

cocomero aka **anguria** watermelon (*Citrullus lanatus*). Popular summer fruit of African origin, cultivated in Italy mostly in Puglia, Lazio and the plains of Lombardy and Emilia. On sale from June to August, it has sweet red, thirst-quenching flesh. The Italian Ministry of Agriculture's database of native and/or traditional food products lists the following varieties: *cocomero tipico di San Matteo Decima* (Emilia-Romagna); *anguria di Siracusa* (Sicily); *cocomero della Val di Cornia*, *cocomero gigante* (Tuscany). In Italy, watermelon is eaten almost exclusively fresh, though in confectionery it is used to make sorbets and ice creams. In Sicily it features in → **gelo**, in Tuscany in → **vettaioli**.

cocon dialect term for → **ovolo**, royal argaric mushroom.

cocozza aka **cucuzza** term used in central and southern Italy for pumpkin or, on occasion, zucchini.

cocule small balls of potatoes, Pecorino, breadcrumbs and eggs cooked and served in broth. The potatoes may be replaced by eggplants, and one version exists in which fresh breadcrumbs substitute vegetables altogether. A traditional Easter Saturday dish in the Salento area. Puglia.

coda tail. Gastronomically speaking, usually referred to bovines. The tail is normally removed from the carcass of an animal during the butchering process. A pig's tail is known as a → **codino**, while the tails of sheep and goats and large game animals are not used in the kitchen. Like offal (→ **frattaglie**), tails form part of the fifth quarter (→ **quinto quarto**) of butchered cattle. At one time it was a custom to gave the tail as a gift to cowherds and slaughterhouse workers. This is probably when the recipe for → **coda alla vaccinara** was created. Other recipes include: → **coda di bue al vino** (Piedmont) and → **coda alla valdostana** (Val d'Aosta),

coda alla vaccinara stewed oxtail. One of the classic dishes of Roman cuisine, which came into being in an area of the city whose livelihood depended on the local slaughterhouse. The modern recipe involves cutting a calf's tail into chunks and browning them in chopped lardo, bathing them with white wine and slowly stewing them in tomato sauce. About 15 minutes before the end of the cooking process, large pieces of celery are added to the sauce, part of which is traditionally used to dress pasta. In the old days, an oxtail was used, together with an ox cheek (→ **gaffo**), and the sauce was enriched with bitter cocoa or crumbled dark chocolate, pine kernels and raisins. Lazio.

coda alla valdostana oxtail cut into pieces and stewed with broth, crumbled sausage meat and Savoy cabbage leaves. Val d'Aosta.

coda di bue al vino oxtail cut into pieces, browned in oil with herbs, covered with red wine, finished with broth and supplemented with dried mushrooms rehydrated in warm water. Piedmont.

coda di maiale in padella skinned pig's tail and ears boiled in water, browned in oil and garlic, stewed with roughly chopped potatoes and seasoned with salt and pepper and wild fennel. A recipe typical of the province of Viterbo. Lazio.

coda di rospo another name for → **rana pescatrice**, monkfish.

coda di volpe regional term for → **barba di capra**, goat's beard.

coda ripiena salt cod tail stuffed with chard, egg, parsley, Parmigiano and dried breadcrumbs. The flesh hollowed from the tail is used in the sauce made to accompany the fish. A dish rarely found in restaurants. Liguria.

coddu virdi Sicilan term for → **germano reale**, mallard.

coddura another word for → **cuzzupa**, Easter cake.

codeghe cui fazuleen de l'oc black-eyed peas and pork rind, stewed in tomato and broth with a dash of Marsala, served with a sprinkling of grated Grana Padana cheese. Traditionally prepared in the province of Cremona on November 2, All Saints' Day. Lombardy.

codeghin northern dialect word for → **cotechino** (boiling sausage), more specifically, in Emilia, for → **cotechino Modena**.

codegotto regional term for → **cotechino** (boiling sausage).

codino pig's tail. Rarely used on its own (one exception is → **coda di maiale in padella**), it appears as an ingredient in recipes such as → **casoeûla**.

codone (1) cut of meat roughly equivalent to tenderloin. Eaten roast, cut into steaks or raw.

codone (2) pintail (*Anas acuta*). Partial migrant duck with a chocolate-colored head and neck, so named for its pointed tail. Lives on inland and coastal ponds and occasionally nests in some areas of northern Italy.

codriga Veneto and Friuli term for → **cotenna di maiale** (pork rind).

coffano de pietra Friuli-Venezia Giulia term for → **arca di Noè**, Noah's ark or arkshell.

cognà condiment similar to → **mostarda d'uva**, made during the wine harvest by slow-cooking grape must (mostly, barbera, dolcetto, nebbiolo and moscato) and adding pieces of seasonal fruit (quinces, figs, pears and, sometimes, plums and pumpkin), walnuts and toasted hazelnuts to the mix. The final consistency should be as thick as jam. Transferred to glass jars, it may be stored for a long time. It is served as an accompaniment to ➤ **polenta**, ➤ **bollito misto** and cheeses. Produced in the Langhe hills and elsewhere in the province of Cuneo. Piedmont.

cognotti shucked mussels coated in flour, fried and stirred into a warm mixture of honey and vinegar. Once cool, they are transferred to glass jars and stored. An old recipe, now virtually forgotten. A specialty of Taranto. Puglia.

còi Piedmontese dialect word for ➤ **cavolo**, cabbage.

coietas (1) slices of beef covered with a mixture of finely chopped lardo, garlic and parsley, rolled and slowly browned in olive oil and broth. Sardinia.

coietas (2) Savoy cabbage leaves stuffed with meat sauce. Sardinia.

cojëtte aka **cojëtte al seirass** aka **coujette** potato gnocchi typical of the mountains in the province of Cuneo. Served with ricotta, butter softened with garlic and ground pepper. Traditionally made in the Valle Gesso on December 8, the feast of the Immaculate Conception. Piedmont.

colare to strain, to filter. To separate liquids from solids by passing them through a sieve or through muslin (➤ **filtrare**).

colas aka **colaz** aka **kolac** Confirmation cookies ➤ **biscotti della cresima**.

colascione faggot of bread dough with fresh Pecorino, prosciutto and pancetta. Delicacy of Sezze, in the province of Latina. Lazio.

colatura di alici anchovy extract typical of Cetara, on the Costiera Amalfitana, in the province of Salerno. An amber-colored liquid made from anchovies fished in the Gulf of Salerno between March and early July. Immediately after they are caught, the anchovies are cleaned by hand and salted, then layered in wooden tubs. After four or five months, the liquid that drips from a small hole in the base of the tub is collected and used as a condiment, best enjoyed with spaghetti or linguine. This traditional product is now protected and promoted by a Slow Food presidium.

colla di pesce isinglass. Substance obtained from the dried swim bladders of fish. Sold in the form of transparent odorless, flavorless sheets, it is used as a gelatinizing agent (➤ **gelatina**) in cooking and confectionery and as a clarifier in winemaking.

collaccio cookie made of flour, yeast, suet and eggs, shaped like animals and flours, glazed with icing and dusted with confetti sugar. Calabria.

collo neck. Neck of beef is excellent stewed, braised, boiled and raw, hand-chopped. The necks of poultry (chicken, goose, turkey) also play a role in popular cooking, usually stuffed (➤ **collo di pollo ripieno**).

collo d'oca ripieno stuffed neck of goose. The bird's neck is stuffed with its own ground meat, eggs, day-old bread softened in milk, parsley, nutmeg, salt and pepper. A recipe typical of southern Lombardy and the Lomellina area, where geese have always been bred. In one Lomellina variant, the stuffing is made of goose liver, very finely minced garlic and grated Grana Padano, and the goose is cooked in tomato sauce. Similar recipes are to be found in Piedmont, where they stuff the neck with ground goose meat and pork, and serve it sliced with diced aspic. Lombardy, Piedmont.

collo di cappone farcito stuffed neck of capon. Recipe similar to ➤ **collo d'oca ripieno**, stuffed neck of goose. Traditionally cooked on Christmas Day to enrich the capon broth served at the start of lunch, sometimes with ➤ **raviolini di carne**. Lombardy.

collo di pollo ripieno stuffed neck of chicken. A recipe present in a number of regional cuisines. In Tuscany the boned necks are stuffed with a mixture of ground beef, eggs, fresh breadcrumbs soaked in milk, grated lemon zest, salt and pepper. Boiled in broth, the necks are sliced and served cold. In Umbria the same dish is served warm or hot in tomato sauce.

collo di tacchino farcito stuffed neck of turkey. The neck is hollowed out and stuffed with a mixture of chopped beef and pork, calf's liver, egg yolks, marjoram and a couple of hard-boiled eggs. After securing the two ends with string, the neck is cooked in boiling water or broth, allowed to cool and served cold in slices. Friuli-Venezia Giulia.

colomb sweet pastry doll similar to the ➤ **cicio**. Given to children as a present at Christmas. A typical custom in the area round Saluzzo, in the province of Cuneo. Piedmont.

colomba dove-shaped leavened Easter cake made from a dough of wheat flour, sourdough, eggs, sugar, milk, butter and candied citrus zest, glazed with a sugar and almond icing. Believed to have been created in Pavia (Lombardy), now popular throughout Italy.

colombaccio common wood pigeon (*Columba palumbus*). A partial migrant with a slate-gray plumage and a white patch on the side of its neck. Larger than urban pigeons, it lives in woods, meadows and gardens, feeding on seeds, berries, roots and larvae. Its meat is bright red, firmer and more aromatic than that of the common pigeon (➤ **piccione**). Cooked spit- or oven-roast or, if the bird is over a year old, in ➤ **salmì**. Classic Umbrian recipes are ➤ **palomba alla ghiotta**, ➤ **palomba alla todina**, ➤ **palomba all'umido nero**.

colombina another name for ➤ **titola**, an Easter cake.

colombina dorata aka **colombina verde** another name for ➤ **russola**, russula mushroom.

colombo al pentolo wood pigeon plucked and gutted (leaving the liver), stuffed with ➤ **rigatino** bacon, garlic, salt and pepper, and stewed on an earthenware pot with onion, oil, red wine and cloves and, occasionally, grappa, lardo, myrtle and juniper berries.

coltellaccio Tuscan word for ➤ **cannolicchio**, European razor clam.

coltello, al term to describe chopping by hand with a knife. Typically associated with the preparation of the Piedmontese antipasto ➤ **carne cruda in insalata**.

colubrina another name for ➤ **buon enrico**, good King Henry.

comaut soup of potatoes, onions and carrots cooked in water, then puréed, blended with milk and garnished with sage fried in butter. Recipe typical of the Provencal valleys of the province of Cuneo. Piedmont.

Comelico whole raw milk produced in Santo Stefano in Cadore, in the province of Belluno, from Bruno Alpina cows (rich in fat and protein, and particularly suitable for cheesemaking. Dry-salted or bathed in brine, it is aged for 60 days and has a markedly sweet flavor. Veneto.

composta compôte. Dessert of fresh or dried fruit cooked in sugar and water syrup and served cold, sometimes also as an accompaniment to meat. More liquid than traditional jams and preserves (→ **confettura**), sometimes scented with liqueur, citrus zest and spices.

concentrare to concentrate. To thicken broth, sauce or condiment by making part of its water content evaporate through prolonged cooking or cooking on a high heat.

concentrato concentrate. Usually referred to a tomato sauce condensed and partly dehydrated to a paste.

conchiglia del pellegrino another name for → **conchiglia di san Giacomo**, great Mediterranean scallop.

conchiglia di san Giacomo great Mediterranean scallop (*Pecten jacobaeus*). Mollusk which lives in sandy sea beds in the Mediterranean and Atlantic. Many of its popular names—→ **cappasanta**, → **cappa santa**, → **conchiglia del pellegrino**, → **jacopo**, → **pellegrina** (*santo* means "holy" in Italian, *pellegrino* "pilgrim," *Jacopo* "James") refer to its beautiful valves, abundant on the beaches of Galicia, in northwestern Spain, with which wayfarers returning from the sanctuary of Santiago (St James) of Compostela used to decorate their walking sticks. Eaten fried, baked in the oven or steamed.

conchiglie (1) commercial dried pasta made of durum wheat semolina and popular in central and southern Italy. Shaped like a shell (*conchiglia* means "shell" in Italian), it comes in various sizes. The larger versions go well with tomato or herb sauces, the smaller ones are generally served in broth. Other names: → **abissini**, → **arselle**, → **tofettine**.

conchiglie (2) another name for → **dolci di riposto**, marzipan cakes.

conchigliette another name for → **lumachine**, a type of pasta.

concia cure. Blend of aromas and spices used to cure meats.

conciare (1) to cure, to pickle, to dress. To preserve a foodstuff (generally olives or meats) in a "cure" (a blend of salt and aromas).

conciare (2) to make a preserved foodstuff (fish, dried meats, vegetables) more appetizing: eg, in Sicily, → **alivi cunzati**, → **olive conciate**.

Conciato romano ewe's and/or goat's and/or cow's milk cheese produced in the province of Caserta, allegedly since the time of the Samnites. The cheese is washed in the cooking water from a kind of homemade pasta called *pettole*, coated in a mixture of oil, vinegar, wild thyme and ground chili, and matured in earthenware pitchers. A Slow Food presidium is seeking to revive production of the cheese. Campania.

condiggiun aka **condiggion** aka **cundiggiun** salad of raw summer vegetables (tomatoes, cucumbers, peppers, spring onions), ship's biscuits (→ **galletta del marinaio**) and olives in brine and basil. If tuna fillets (→ **mosciame**), desalted anchovies and hard-boiled eggs are added, the dish comes to resemble → **capponada**. Liguria.

condiglione Italianization of → **condiggiun**, vegetable salad.

condimento (pl. **condimenti**) condiment. Ingredient or set of ingredients used to flavor a foodstuff. The principal categories are: fats (oil, butter, lard and so on), spices, aromatic herbs, aromatic vegetables (garlic, onion, celery, carrot, shallot, all essential ingredients of a broth or cooking base), vinegar, wine and sugar. Today cream is used ever more frequently.

condrilla another name for → **lattugaccio**, rush skeletonweed.

confetto (pl. confetti) sugar-coated candy. The most famous Italian producers are Pelino, in Sulmona (province of L'Aquila, Abruzzo), and Mucci in Andria (Puglia), each of which boast a dedicated *Museo del confetto*. The classic candy has an almond at the center, others are filled with pistachio nuts, hazelnuts, chocolate or cinnamon (➤ cannellini). Tiny colored confetti (➤ diavolina) are used to decorate traditional cakes and pastries.

confettura jam or conserve. Gelatinized mixture of fruit and sugar.

confortini Piedmontese sponge fingers similar to ➤ lingue di gatto.

congelare to deep-feeze.

congelazione deep-freezing.

conglufi hollow brioche dough cylinders filled with béchamel sauce, strips of prosciutto, buttered mushrooms and peas, small chicken patties, Parmigiano and eggs. Leftover scraps of dough are used to make lids to cover the cylinders, which are then baked in the oven.

coniglio rabbit (*Oryctolagus cuniculus*). Rodent common throughout the Mediterranean, domesticated and wild. Until a few decades ago rabbits were mainly raised and eaten by farming families, but are now bred intensively (Italy is the world's number one producer and consumer of the animal). The domestic rabbit's meat is considered to be "white" and, if the animal has been properly raised and fed, is tender and tasty, suitable for many regional recipes (➤ civé, ➤ cacciatora, ➤ agrodolce). The Italian Ministry of Agriculture's database of native and/or traditional food products lists the following varieties: **coniglio grigio di Carmagnola** (Piedmont), ➤ **coniglio da fossa di Ischia** (Campania), *coniglio veneto* (Veneto), and *coniglio leprino viterbese* (Lazio).

coniglio a bujone rabbit, jointed, stewed in oil and broth flavored with garlic, salt, pepper, rosemary, and tomato, and finished with vinegar and minced rosemary and sage. Recipe typical of Viterbo. The term *a bujone*, the Lazio equivalent of the Tuscan ➤ buglione, may derive from the French *bouillon*, broth. Lazio.

coniglio a purtuisa rabbit, jointed, marinated in red wine and vinegar, fried and served with eggplant or potatoes, peppers, olives, capers, celery, pine kernels and raisins, with the addition of more vinegar. Many variations on the recipe exist. Sicily.

coniglio al civé (or al civet) rabbit cooked in the same manner as hare in ➤ lepre al civé, the animal being jointed and marinated in Nebbiolo or another robust red wine. Piedmont.

coniglio al ginepro rabbit with juniper berries. The rabbit is jointed, browned with lightly fried onion, juniper berries and diced pancetta and finished with broth and a few drops of grappa. Recipe typical of the mountain valleys of the province of Cuneo. Piedmont.

coniglio al rosmarino rabbit with rosemary. Pan-roasted rabbit with lardo, garlic and rosemary, served with polenta. Recipe typical of the province of Bergamo. Lombardy.

coniglio all'aceto balsamico rabbit with balsamic vinegar. The animal is jointed and marinated in white wine, browned in oil and flavored with salt, garlic and rosemary. Towards the end of the cooking process, traditional balsamic vinegar (➤ aceto balsamico tradizionale di Modena) is poured over the meat. The recipe is typical of the province of Modena. Emilia-Romagna.

coniglio all'aggiada rabbit in ➤ aggiada, garlic sauce. Liguria.

coniglio all'Arneis rabbit cut into pieces

171

and browned in a mixture of chopped vegetables and herbs, lubricated with Arneis white wine and stewed with the addition of broth. A relatively recent creation now on the menu, especially in the summer, in many restaurants in the Langhe and Roero areas. Piedmont.

coniglio all'astigiana rabbit, jointed, browned in a mixture of chopped pancetta and herbs (parsley, thyme, sage, rosemary, bay leaf), and lubricated with a light red wine, such as Grignolino or Freisa. When the meat is almost ready, a mixture of its chopped liver, parsley, sage, and garlic (sometimes a couple of desalted, filetted anchovies) is added. Recipe typical of the Monferrato area. Piedmont.

coniglio all'ischitana small pieces of rabbit stewed with tomatoes, white wine, garlic, and aromatic herbs (rosemary, thyme, basil, and chili). The recipe originally envisaged the rabbit's innards. Typical of the island of Ischia (province of Naples). Campania.

coniglio alla cacciatora classic Italian rabbit stew with many regional variations. In Emilia-Romagna, especially in the province of Modena, they marinate the jointed rabbit in water and vinegar, flavored with garlic, onion and salt, brown it in oil with herbs and white wine, and stew it in a sauce of tomato, onion and peppers. In Tuscany, they joint the rabbit, coat it in flour, brown it in oil with rosemary and garlic, flavor it with chopped herbs, stew it in red wine and tomato sauce with black olives, and finally sprinkle it with minced parsley.

coniglio alla canavesana rabbit jointed, marinated in vinegar, oil, onion, sage and cloves, and cooked in an earthenware pot with the marinade liquid. Piedmont.

coniglio alla carlona pieces of rabbit stewed with mixed herbs, white wine and finished with a mixture of finely chopped black olives, capers and pine kernels. For a simplified version: → **coniglio alla ligure**.

coniglio alla cassanese rabbit stewed in olive oil, butter, white wine and lemon juice, and flavored with garlic, parsley, salt and pepper. Typical of the village of Cassano d'Adda, in the province of Milan. Lombardy.

coniglio alla ligure pieces of rabbit cooked in Vermentino wine and taggiasca olives. Popular, with some variations, throughout the region. Liguria.

coniglio alla stimpirata jointed rabbit first fried in oil with garlic and capers, then finished with strips of pepper, carrots, chopped boiled potatoes and celery, vinegar, mint and chili. Traditional recipe of the provinces of Siracusa and Ragusa. Sicily.

coniglio alla trentina pieces of rabbit marinated in water, vinegar and white wine aromatized with an onion stuck with cloves, browned in oil and butter with chopped lardo, garlic, onion and rosemary, covered with water and white wine and cooked in the oven. The cooking juices are thickened with the animal's finely chopped liver to make a sauce. Recipe typical of Trento and its province. Trentino-Alto Adige.

coniglio alla Valle d'Itria pieces of rabbit coated in four, cooked in Locorotondo white wine with the addition of onion, celery and tomatoes, and finished in the oven with grape hyacinth bulbs (→ **lampascione**). Puglia.

coniglio alla valleogrina pieces of rabbit marinated in water and vinegar, browned with onion softened in butter and oil, and cooked in white wine and broth. Accompanied by a sauce made by simmering the animal's chopped liver, sausage, salted sardines, raisins, pine kernels, vinegar and sugar. An old sweet and sour rabbit recipe (similar ones are to be found in 17th-century documents), traditional in the Val Leogra, in the province of Vicenza, but common also on the border with the provinces of Padua, Venice and Treviso. Veneto.

coniglio arrosto alla reggiana rabbit marinated for 12 hours in a mixture of sage, rosemary, juniper berries, salt, pepper, vinegar and white wine, then cooked in a pot. Typical of the city of Reggio. Emilia-Romagna.

coniglio arrotolato aka **coniglio ripieno** aka **coniglio in porchetta** stuffed rabbit roll. A rabbit is boned and opened flat, then spread with a variety of ingredients, rolled, barded with lardo to keep it soft, and cooked in a pot or roast in the oven. In Piedmont, they spread the rabbit with slices of prosciutto, pancetta and minced vegetables and herbs, sew it up and cook it in a pot. In Veneto, they cover the meat with aromatic herbs, raisins and pine kernels, roll it up and cook it in the oven with white wine and lemon juice. In Friuli-Venezia Giulia, the rabbit is stuffed with slices of pancetta and frittata, or with its finely chopped entrails mixed with ground pork, prosciutto and herbs, and cooked in the oven with white wine. In one Tuscan recipe, a frittata of eggs, crushed almonds, garlic, parsley, rosemary and the animal's innards is used to stuff a rabbit flavored with nutmeg, salt, pepper and fennel seeds, which is then rolled up and roast in the oven covered with a mixture of olive oil, bay leaf, rosemary, salt, pepper and nutmeg.

coniglio con i peperoni rabbit with peppers. Pieces of rabbit cooked with herbs, pancetta, red and yellow peppers, tomatoes,

Barbera red wine and, at the end, a dash of vinegar. Recipe typical of the Langhe hills in the province of Cuneo and of the Monferrato area in the provinces of Asti and Alessandria. Piedmont.

coniglio da fossa di Ischia Ischia pit rabbit. Raised on the island of Ischia (province of Naples) in pits ten to 12 feet deep, where it burrows long warrens, this rabbit, has firmer, tastier meat than cage-raised rabbits. The meat is a symbol of the cooking of the island, where it was traditional to organize a *conigliata*, or rabbit feast, to inaugurate every new *casa a carusiello*, a typical local domed house. The rabbit is protected by a Slow Food presidium, Campania.

coniglio 'dla bagna neira jointed rabbit browned with onion and rosemary, then cooked with tomato, vinegar, red wine and peppers. Partly thanks to the caramelization (→ **caramellizzazione**) of the sugar, the resulting sauce is almost black (*bagna neira*). A rustic version of the bourgeois → **salmì**, typical of the province of Asti. Piedmont.

coniglio fritto fried rabbit. The rabbit is first heated for a few minutes in a pan on its own to dry out, then cut into pieces, which are breaded and fried. In Veneto, they marinate pieces of rabbit in oil, lemon juice and herbs, dip them in beaten egg, coat them in breadcrumbs and fry them in oil with chopped onions. Small morsels of fried rabbit and chicken are also popular in Tuscany where they form part of the → **fritto misto**.

coniglio grigio di Carmagnola gray Carmagnola rabbit. The Carmagnola gray rabbit is the only native Piedmontese rabbit breed still in existence. Although it was quite popular up to the end of the 1950s, later it virtually disappeared until genetic recovery work was carried out by the

University of Turin and the Institute for Agriculture in Verzuolo, in the province of Cuneo. A center to promote the breed has now been set up in Carmagnola itself (province of Turin) and a Slow Food presidium supports a breeders' consortium. The breed probably descends from a cross with the chinchilla and does not adapt to intensive breeding. The rabbits of the Presidium live in enclosures where they are free to move and are raised only on grass and natural feed. Their meat is fine, tasty and tender. Piedmont.

coniglio in porchetta like the duck and the goose, in central Italy the rabbit is another farm animal whose meat is cooked *in porchetta* (➤ **porchetta, in**). The Tuscan recipe involves gutting a whole rabbit (without the head), stuffing it with slices of pancetta, salt, pepper, garlic and wild fennel, then roasting it in the oven with aromatic herbs. In another version, *alla senese*, the stuffing is made with wild fennel blanched in water and garlic cloves, then lightly fried with crumbled sausage meat and the rabbit's liver. In Umbria, they bone the rabbit and make the stuffing with its entrails cooked with potatoes, aromatic herbs and, sometimes, a slice of prosciutto to line the inside of the animal, before oven-roasting with olives.

coniglio in tegame, in Veneto aka **cunicio in tecia.** The term signifies a rabbit stewed in wine and broth, preferably in an earthenware pot. In Valsugana, between Trentino and Veneto, pieces of rabbit are cooked slowly, alternated with thin slices of lardo and aromatic herbs, and covered with white wine. They are served with a sauce made with the animal's entrails, salted sardines and onion. In the rest of the Trentino and in Alto Adige, pieces of rabbit are stewed in a sauce made with the animal's entrails, browned

with herbs and mixed with flour, tomato passata and broth. In the Vicenza area (Veneto), they often brown rabbit in oil with garlic, pancetta and rosemary, and proceed to cook it in wine and vinegar, before adding chopped liver and onion. In one variant, pieces of rabbit are cooked in oil with garlic, sage and rosemary, bathed in white wine, transferred to a pot and covered with broth. In the Polesine area, in the province of Rovigo (Veneto), the rabbit is marinated in water and vinegar, turned in a mixture of finely minced aromatic vegetables, lardo and spices (cinnamon, nutmeg, cloves), and cooked partly in the marinade liquid diluted with water, and partly in a separate pan with wine. In a simpler recipe popular in Venezia-Giulia, the rabbit is marinated in red wine, herbs and spices, cooked in the same liquid, and served with polenta. Trentino-Alto Adige, Veneto, Friuli-Venezia Giulia.

conillu a succhittu wild or home-raised rabbit, cut into pieces and marinated overnight in water, vinegar and salt, browned in olive oil with chopped garlic and parsley, and served with rounds of carrot and celery, sliced onion, capers, green olives, walnuts, pine kernels and raisins. Sardinia.

conserva (1) conserve. Generic term to describe a food product conserved using one of the various domestic or industrial methods of conservation (➤ **conservare**)

conserva (2) in Campania and other southern Italian regions, the word refers to the concentrated paste obtained by crushing tomatoes and drying them in the sun.

conserva (3) conserve of tomatoes cooked, seasoned with salt, flavored and stored in sterilized glass jars.

conservare to conserve, to preserve. To render a foodstuff suitable for long-term storage. The most widely used techniques are drying, salting, preserving in brine, oil or alcohol, pickling in vinegar and mixing with sugar (➤ **candire**), as well as those that exploit modern technology, such as vacuum-packing (➤ **sottovuoto**), dehydration, freeze-drying, sterilization, deep-freezing and freezing.

consiero aka **conzier** meat or offal, without tomato, but with the addition of seasonal vegetables, such as ➤ **radicchio** (*conzier rustego*). Traditional sauce for ➤ **gargati**, a regional pasta. Veneto.

consolida maggiore common comfrey and tuberous comfrey (*Symphytum officinale* and *S. tuberosum*). Wild herbaceous plants with rough oval leaves and coblike inflorescences. The tips are picked in mountain areas (in the province of Biella, in Piedmont, in the Garfagnana area, in the province of Lucca, in Tuscany) and used in much the same way as borage, whose family they belong to. Common and regional names: ➤ **borana selvatica**, ➤ **borragine selvatica**, ➤ **erba di san Lorenzo**, ➤ **orecchie d'asino**, ➤ **salosso**.

consommé concentrated meat broth (reduced by a third by slow boiling), clarified and served at the start of a meal, as it is, aromatized (usually with a wine such as port or sherry) or with the addition of pasta, vegetables or meat.

contadina, alla literally "peasant-style." Expression used to describe traditional dishes featuring "humble" vegetables, legumes, potatoes and meat. Often referred to soups and stewed.

contorno side dish.

controfiletto term used in some regions for ➤ **lombata**, short loin of beef.

conza Sicilian term for ➤ **ripieno**, filling or stuffing.

coperchiole another name for ➤ **ferratelle**, sweet wafer sandwiches.

copertina di sopra name used in some regions for ➤ **cappello da prete** or ➤ **arrosto della vena**, a cut of beef roughly equivalent to shoulder clod, perfect for roasting and braising.

copertina di sotto name of a cut of beef, roughly equivalent to shoulder clod.

copete dessert of a blend of minced almonds, sugar, egg whites and a pinch of cinnamon spread on wafers and baked in the oven for about ten minutes. Basilicata.

coppa raw salami made from pork from the back of the pig's neck and the top of its shoulder.

coppa al Marsala before being baked in the oven with Marsala, fresh ➤ **capocollo** is rubbed with salt and minced sage, rosemary and juniper berries. When cooked, the meat is sliced and served with the pan juices as a main course. Emilia-Romagna.

coppa di Ceglie Messapica cured meat produced by a group of restaurateurs in the province of Brindisi from the pork of black Calabrian pigs raised in a semi-wild state. Rubbed with salt and pepper, the meat is steeped in Verdeca, the local white wine, for 10-12 days, dried in the open air, pressed into a pig's intestine, and aged for six to eight months. Puglia.

coppa di Parma the neck muscles of the pig cured with salt, crushed peppercorns, garlic and wine and, after two weeks, cased in a large intestine (➤ **bondeana**). Well secured with kitchen string, it is aged for four to six months. Emilia-Romagna.

coppa di seirass another name for ➤ **coppa sabauda**, a dessert.

coppa di testa salami typical of central Italy. In the Marche region, the meaty parts of a pig's snout, ears and tongue, the meat attached to the spine, pork rind, fat and lean cuttings left over from the processing of other cured meats are boiled for two hours. Once cooked, they are roughly chopped and cured with salt, pepper, pistachio nuts or shelled almonds, green olives, grated orange zest, cinnamon, crushed garlic and nutmeg. The mixture is cased in a bladder (or a cow's or artificial intestine) and simmered for another hour. In Lazio, a whole pig's head is boiled for at least three hours in salted water, aromatized with garlic, pepper, and chili. Boned and hand-chopped with cuttings from the shoulder and cheek, the meat is cured with salt, garlic, pepper, chili and orange and lemon peel. In Abruzzo, the edible parts of the head are boiled for four hours with the cartilage of the shin, roughly cut into pieces, dressed with lemon juice, grated lemon zest and (in a particularly fiery version) red chili. In all cases, the **coppa** is pushed into canvas sacks, pressed and eaten fresh.

coppa mantovana cured meat made from the pork of pigs of over a year in age with a weight of at least 80 pounds. Shaped into a flat cylinder, it is cured with salt and a dash of pepper and cased in a pig's bladder or a calf's intestine. Tied very tightly with string, it is left to dry for three to four days. It is then aged for four to five months, sometimes for up to a year. Typical of the central and southern part of the province of Mantua. Lombardy.

coppa piacentina PDO cured meat made with pork from pigs on farms which produce → **prosciutto di Parma**. The cervical muscle is cured with sodium chloride, potassium nitrate, crushed peppercorns and a mixture of spices, aromatics, and preservatives (including sugar, cloves, bay seeds and powdered cinnamon). After refrigerating for a week, the meat is wrapped in the peritoneum, the lining of the pig's abdomen, and tied up with string. It then dried for a another week and aged for at least six months. Produced throughout the province of Piacenza. Emilia-Romagna.

coppa sabauda aka **coppa di seirass** a popular dessert made by blending Piedmontese ricotta (→ **Seirass** aka → **Seras** aka → **Siras**) with egg yolks, sugar, raisins, lemon zest, whipped Marsala and rum. Best enjoyed briefly refrigerated. Piedmont.

coppa senese fresh cured meat traditionally made on the day of the killing of the pig with the leftovers from butchering operations (pork rind, ears, trotters, head and so on). These are boiled, roughly chopped and cured with salt, pepper, garlic, lemon or orange zest, mixed spices, cinnamon and fennel seeds. The mixture is pressed into cloth sacks and hung to dry. It is then kept in a refrigerator and consumed in the space of a few days. A specialty of the province of Siena. Tuscany.

coppia ferrarese traditional crisp, almost crumbless, bread now with PGI recognition. Made with soft wheat flour and sourdough starter (→ **biga**), it is characterized by its unusual shape: two sets of spiral horns joined together. Typical of Ferrara. Emilia-Romagna.

coppiette loin of pork, left to rest in salt for a few days, cut into ten inch strips, which are flavored with white wine, garlic and chili or wine and dried fennel flowers and hung to dry, to at a time, for ten days. Once typical of the pastoral tradition of the northern part of the province of Macerata, the delicacy used to be made with mutton. Marche.

coppiette dei Castelli Romani ten-inch

strips of pork fillet or leg cured with salt, pepper, a little garlic, fennel flowers and chili. After a brief marinade, the strips are dried in a warm environment, stretched over small boards or in the oven in tins for at least 48 hours. **Coppiette** used to be made with horsemeat (and still are in Marino and Albano Laziale, in the province of Rome) and were a favorite food of shepherds. Lazio.

coppo another name for ➤ **casadello,** cake typical of Emilia-Romagna.

coppone al forno neck of pork bathed with white wine and broth and roast in the oven. Emilia-Romagna.

coprire to cover, to cover with a lid.

copuletas very fine layers of pastry made of flour, lard, water and salt, with a filling of a mixture of sponge cake, grated lemon zest, toasted, chopped almonds and, sometimes, a splash of lemon juice. Cake typical of the province of Sassari, in especial the villages of Ozieri and Goceano, traditionally baked for patron saints' feasts, weddings and baptisms. Sardinia.

coque, alla (1) French term used to describe the soft-boiling of eggs. *Uova alla cocque* = soft-boiled eggs.

coque, alla (2) by extension, the term refers to any foodstuff cooked in is own natural shell, skin or protection. *Rognoni alla coque,* for example, are kidneys cooked in their own fat.

corada aka **corata** aka **coreda** northern and central Italian dialect terms for the lungs of butchered animals. A traditional Lombard recipe is ➤ **ris e corada.**

coralli another name for ➤ **ditalini,** a type of pasta.

corallina short cylindrical dried pasta similar to ➤ **ditalini,** but smaller. Very popular in Sicily.

corallina di Norcia very long salami made from a mixture of very finely ground pork shoulder and prosciutto and diced fat. Cured with salt, whole and crushed peppercorns and garlic macerated in wine, the mixture is cased in a large intestine. Dried for a few days (and usually smoked slightly with juniper berries), it is aged for three to five months. The most famous Umbrian cured meat outside the region, it was created in Norcia, in the province of Perugia, and is now also produced in the province of Terni. Umbria.

corallina romana cured meat made of roughly chopped rib, neck, shoulder and leg pork, cured with sea salt and black pepper, sometimes with the addition of garlic and wild fennel. After being cased and hand-tied with string, it is dried and aged for at least two weeks. Traditionally produced in the Agro Romano and Frosinone areas at Easter. Lazio.

corallini another name for ➤ **avemarie,** a type of pasta.

corata name for the offal group composed of lungs (trachea and esophagus included), heart and liver (➤ **frattaglie**).

coratella the diminutive of ➤ **corata,** the word (which originated in Lazio) refers to lamb and kid offal. In central Italy, that of baby lamb (➤ **abbacchio**) is the most readily available, and is very popular in Lazio (➤ **coratella con i carciofi**) and Sardinia.

coratella alla barbaricina lamb's offal (➤ **coratella**) cut into tiny pieces and served with fava beans and new carrots. Sardinia.

coratella alla perugina lamb's offal stewed with tomatoes and onions and, in the Easter period, thickened with beaten eggs. Umbria.

coratella con i carciofi lamb's offal with artichokes. The lamb's offal (➤ **coratella**) is cleaned, cut into pieces and stewed with extra virgin olive oil, broth and white wine, with the subsequent addition of globe artichokes. The combination of lamb's offal (also sweetbreads and brains) is a common feature of Lazio cuisine. Lazio.

coratella di agnello brodettata lamb's lung, heart, liver and spleen (➤ **coratella**) slow-cooked with finely minced onion, garlic and lardo. In the Marche, they scramble eggs into the dish (➤ **brodettare**), in Abruzzo, they simply add tomato and fresh or dried chili. Marche, Abruzzo.

coratella di agnello in umido stewed lamb's offal. Diced offal (➤ **coratella**) browned in a skillet with a generous amount of chopped onion and bathed with white wine. Excellent spread on slices of toasted bread, the mixture is often enriched with wedges of artichoke (in Umbria, perfumed with garlic and marjoram) and served as a sauce with pasta. In one variant (which, in Tuscany, takes the name of *coratella alla cacciatore*) the offal (usually lamb's, but also calf's or chicken giblets are used) is browned in extra virgin olive oil with garlic and rosemary (or sage), bathed with white wine and seasoned with salt and pepper.

corbezzolo strawberry tree or arbutus (*Arbutus unedo*). Small evergreen melliferous shrubby tree, a native of the Mediterranean, bearing edible globular fruits with fleshy pulp and many seeds. Rarely eaten fresh, the fruits are generally processed into jams, jellies, syrups, juices, creams, sauces and candied fruits. Fermented, they are made into wine. Common and regional names: ➤ **albatro**, ➤ **ciliegia marina**, ➤ **pomino rosso**.

corda aka **cordedda** other words for ➤ **cordula**, braided kid's or lamb's tripe.

cordula braided kid's or lamb's tripe. The tripe is washed and secured inside braids made with the animal's intestines. Eaten broiled, cooked on the spit, baked in the oven with potatoes or stewed with tomatoes and fresh peas. Sardinia.

coregone chub. Two species live in Italy: *Coregonus lavaretus*, common in prealpine lakes in the north and volcanic lakes in Lazio; the smaller *Coreganus macrophthalmus* (aka **bondella**), recorded in Lakes Como, Lugano and Maggiore. The latter, together with *coregone del lago di Bolsena* (Lazio), is listed in the Italian Ministry of Agriculture's database of native and/or traditional food products. The flesh of the chub is white, lean and boneless, and may be cooked whole (broiled, baked, *en papillote*, boiled) or minced to make fish cakes and stuffings, or to dress pasta and rice, or transformed into mousses and served as an antipasto with seasonal vegetables and mushrooms.

coregone alla bolsenese Lake Bolsena chub baked whole or filleted, flavored with garlic, wild fennel or sage, salt, pepper and vinegar. Lazio.

corgnòi Veneto term for large earth snails (➤ **bogoni**).

coriandolo coriander (*Coriandrum sativum*). Herbaceous plant of the Umbrelliferae family, which produces tiny roundish fruits, erroneously referred to as seeds, much used in extra-European cuisines. In Italy they are used, in combination with other spices, to aromatize cured meats, such as ➤ **mortadella classica**, ➤ **mortadella di Prato**, ➤ **salsiccia di Monte San Biagio**. Common and regional names: ➤ **erba cimicina**, ➤ **prezzemolo cinese**.

corifena regional term for ➤ **lampuga**, dolphin fish.

corigheddos small baked tarts consisting of a mixture of grated orange, chopped almonds and honey wrapped in very fine puff pastry and sometimes sprinkled with confetti sugar (➤ **momperiglia**). Used to be heart-shaped and given to brides as an omen of good luck and prosperity. Sardinia.

cornabusa regional term for ➤ **origano**, oregano.

cornaletti Puglia term for curved green chili peppers.

cornetti smooth or ridged commercial durum wheat pasta shaped like small curved tubes. Served with simple tomato or vegetable sauces, in broth or in vegetable soups.

cornetti in salsa boiled runner beans turned in a skillet with oil, garlic and desalted anchovies. Veneto.

cornetto (1) half-moon brioche or puff pastry confection commonly eaten in Italy for breakfast in bars. Empty or filled (with jam, chocolate or confectioner's custard), it is a close relative both of the French ➤ **croissant** and the Austrian ➤ **chiffel**.

cornetto (2) another name for ➤ **fagiolino**, runner bean.

cornetto (3) Veneto term for ➤ **torricella**, turret shell.

cornetto de ma Ligurian term for ➤ **murice**, murex or rock snail.

cornetto istriano bow-shaped bread loaf made with cake flour and ➤ **biga**, starter yeast. Typical of Trieste. Friuli-Venezia Giuli.

corniello another name for ➤ **corniolo**, cornelian cherry.

corniolo cornelian cherry (**Cornus mas**). Small melliferous tree or shrub native to southern Europe and very common in Italy. Its bright red fruits (oval drupes) are eaten fresh, but may also be processed to make soft drinks, liqueurs, cakes, jellies, sauces (➤ **salsa di corniole**) and jams. They are also preserved in alcohol, like cherries, and in brine, like olives. Common and regional names: ➤ **corniello**, ➤ **crognale**.

corno a type of **torciglione (1)** made with the same dough as ➤ **ciopa**. Typical of Asolo, in the province of Treviso. Veneto.

corno dell'abbondanza aka **cornucopia** alternative names for ➤ **trombetta dei morti**, horn of plenty or black trumpet mushroom.

corolli cookies made with wheat flour, yeast, honey, sugar, olive oil and aniseed. After leavening, the mixture is shaped into rings, brushed with egg yolk and baked in the oven. In the province of Livorno, ➤ **corolli incesi** (*incesi* being a Tuscan word for *incisi*, "engraved") are a finger-shaped variation on the theme, in which eggs are included in the paste and honey omitted, and the surface is covered with small slashes, hence the name. Another difference is that the cookies are briefly boiled in water before baking. Tuscany.

corolli incesi finger-shaped version of ➤ **corolli**, ring cookies.

coroniello Campania slang for fillet of stockfish (➤ **stoccafisso**).

corruda regional term for ➤ **asparago pungente**, wild asparagus.

corseti di Novi Ligure another name for ➤ **corzetti**, type of pasta.

corsetin aka **crosetin** small ➤ **croset** made with barley or rye flour mixed with wheat flour, generally served with boiled potatoes, melted butter and sliced Toma. Typical of the mountain valleys of the province of Cuneo. Piedmont.

cortecce commercial durum wheat pasta shaped like a bean pod. Very popular in Campania.

corvina croaker (*Micropogonius undulates*). Small fish similar to the ➤ **ombrina**, umbrine. Its delicate white flesh is boiled or fried in butter with vegetables and white wine, or used in soups.

corzetti aka **corsetti** aka **crosetti** fresh pasta made in two versions. The first, typical of Valpolcevera, in the province of Genova, is made from small balls of flour and water dough, stretched and pressed at the ends to create an "8" shape (in dialect they are called *tiae co-e dïe*, in Italian *tirate con le dita*, "pulled with the fingers"), and served with meat and pea or mushroom sauce (➤ **tocco**). The second, common throughout Liguria and also in neighboring areas of Piedmont (eg, ➤ **corseti di Novi Ligure**, province of Alessandria) consists of disks of dough on which the family or the pasta maker would stamp their symbols or coats-of-arms. Usually served with pesto or meat, mushroom or sausage sauce (Novi Ligure), or simply with oil, pine kernels and marjoram. Piedmont, Liguria.

cosciotto d'agnello in cieramida aka **cosciotto d'agnello nella creta** boned leg of lamb stuffed with a mixture of minced garlic, rosemary, sage, oregano and pork rind, coated with clay to retain the flavor and aroma of the herbs, and baked in the oven. Calabria.

cosi chini small cakes made with the same pastry and filling as ➤ **buccellato**. Sicily.

costa (pl. **coste**) aka **costola** (pl. **costole**) rib, ribs. Ruminants have 13 pairs of ribs, pigs 14-15, horses and donkeys 18. See individual entries for gastronomic uses.

costardella aka **costardello** aka **luccio sauro** needlefish (*Scomberesox saurus*). Marine fish similar to the ➤ **aguglia** (garfish), very popular in the south of Italy, especially Sicily and Calabria.

costardelle ripiene needlefish (➤ **costardella**) with heads and tails removed, boned and stuffed with minced garlic and parsley, oregano, breadcrumbs, olive oil and pepper, and stewed with tomato.

Calabria.

costarella another word for ➤ **costoletta**, cutlet or chop.

costarelle di abbacchio a scottadito another name for ➤ **scottadito**, fried or broiled lamb chops.

costarelle di maiale con la panuntella pork spare ribs (known locally as *costarelle*), rubbed with a mixture of olive, oil, salt and pepper. When the meat starts to release its fat, it is placed over slices of bread, which soak up its juices and are served with it. Lazio.

costata "L" shaped rib steak barbecued or broiled with or without the bone (but tastier with it).

costata di maiale ripiena a pork chop, cut lengthwise on the bone, stuffed with a slice of pancetta and a slice of fresh Caciocavallo, coated in breadcrumbs on both sides, flavored with flat-leaved parsley, garlic, chili and salt, and baked in the oven. A sweet and sour version exists in which the stuffing consists of salami, grated and diced cheese, beaten eggs, dried breadcrumbs, raisins and pine kernels. Sicily.

coste al brusch beet stalks (➤ **bietola**) boiled, drained and baked in a batter of eggs, flour, vinegar and water. Piedmont.

coste alla veneziana beet stalks (➤ **bietola**) cut into pieces and boiled in water with the addition of oil, garlic and minced flat-leaved parsley. When all the liquid has been consumed, the stalks are drizzled with vinegar, which is allowed to evaporate, then served. Veneto.

coste della croce Lombard term for a cut beef comprising the third to the fifth ribs, equivalent to second cut rib. Tender and tasty, used for steaks on the bone.

costina pork or lamb rib. Pork spare ribs are much loved in popular cooking, in stews and soups such as ➤ **casoeûla** and ➤ **cis-**

rà, or roasted or broiled (➤ **costoleccio,** ➤ **rosticciana**).

costine di maiale con verze e chiodini pork spare ribs with Savoy cabbage and honey armillary mushrooms. Fall recipe associated with the killing of the pig and the picking of honey armillary mushrooms (➤ **chiodini**). A typical combination of ingredients in Italian regions north of the Po.

costine in umido pork spare ribs browned in an earthenware pot with oil and onion, sprinkled with vinegar and stewed with roughly chopped Savoy cabbage leaves. Veneto.

costole d'asino regional term for ➤ **costolina,** cat's ear.

costoleccio term used in various parts of Tuscany for pork rib.

costoletta veal cutlet or chop.

costoletta alla valdostana a veal chop sliced to form a pouch, stuffed with Fontina cheese, breaded and fried. Typical restaurant fare of the postwar years, created to raise the profile of the valley's most celebrated cheese. Val d'Aosta.

costolina cat's ear, swine's chicory (*Hypochoeris radicata* and *H. neapolitana*). Wild herbs common throughout Italy, the second mostly in the south. Usually cooked mixed with other herbs. Common and regional names: ➤ **costole d'asino,** ➤ **ingrassaporci,** ➤ **piattello.**

cotechinata rolls of pork rind stuffed with minced lardo, garlic, flat-leaved parsley and chili , browned in lard and finished off in tomato sauce. Served with homemade pasta or as a main course with lentils. Basilicata.

cotechino boiling sausage named for the presence in its mixture of pork rind (➤ **cotenna di maiale,** ➤ **a cotica**). The percentage used to be 50%, now it never exceeds 30%. The rind is supplemented by cuts of neck and head pork and lardo or, preferably, the thicker ➤ **golato.** Common, with variants, in Piedmont, Val d'Aosta, Lombardy and Emilia-Romagna.

cotechino alla vaniglia type of ➤ **cotechino cremonese** which includes a small amount of vanilla in the cure. Typical of the small town of Villastrada, in the province of Mantua. Lombardy.

cotechino cremonese type of ➤ **cotechino** made by grinding lean pork left over from other cured meats, thick fat and pork rind, and curing the mixture with salt, sugar, Barbera red wine, ground pepper or peppercorns, spices and natural aromas infused in red wine, saltpeter and soy lecithin. Cased in a bladder or an intestine, it dries for two days and ages for 30-40, before being eaten boiled. A specialty of Cremona, it is also produced in the province of Piacenza, south of Milan and in the mountains of the province of Bergamo. Lombardy, Emilia-Romagna.

cotechino cremonese vaniglia leaner, sweeter variation of ➤ **cotechino cremonese** made with a much lower percentage of pork rind, only 240 hours' drying and no aging. Should be eaten within a week of production. Lombardy.

cotechino in camicia aka **cotechino in galera** literally "cotechino in a shirt" and "cotechino in jail." The ➤ **cotechino** is first boiled and skinned, then wrapped in slices of boiled ham and a large slice of veal, and baked in the oven. In some versions, spinach is inserted between the ham and the veal, in others the sausage is wrapped in tin foil before baking, in others still it is cooked in a skillet with Lambrusco red wine. In the province of Cremona, instead of pre-boiling the sausage, they skin it raw, wrap it in a large slice of veal or beef, cook it in broth, and serve it sliced with saffron-flavored risotto and covered with mushrooms. Emilia-Romagna, Lombardy.

cotechino Modena PGI boiling sausage made of streaky pork, pork fat and pork rind ground and cured with salt and pepper, wine, water, natural aromas, spices and aromatic herbs, sugar, sodium and/or potassium nitrite, ascorbic acid and monosodium glutamate, cased in natural or artificial intestines. Once dried, it is sold fresh or cooked. Produced in the provinces of Modena, Ferrara, Ravenna, Rimini, Forlì-Cesena, Bologna, Reggio Emilia, Parma, Piacenza, Cremona, Lodi, Pavia, Milan, Varese, Como, Lecco, Bergamo, Brescia, Mantua, Verona and Rovigo. Lombardy, Veneto, Emilia-Romagna.

cotechino piemontese neck and head pork, coarsely chopped and cured with kitchen salt, cloves, pepper and cinnamon and cased in calf's intestines previously steeped in water and dry white wine. An ingredient in ➤ **bollito misto**. Piedmont.

cotenna di maiale aka **cotica** pork rind or skin. The skin of the pig, bristly, fat and rich in jelly. Used by pork butchers in the mixture of ➤ **cotechino**, ➤ **musetto**, ➤ **cappello da prete** and ➤ **zampone** (and also for the casing of the latter two). Rolled spiced pork rind is used to make ➤ **previ (2)**, a Piedmontese specialty. Cleaned, scraped and blanched, pork rind features in many popular regional dishes: ➤ **cisrà**, ➤ **paniscia** (Piedmont), ➤ **casoeûla** (Lombardy). Also stewed with tomato and beans, boiled and garnished (➤ **cotica 'bbiturata**), and made into rolls (➤ **involtini**, ➤ **braciole**), all preparations that evoke the ancient rite of the butchering of the pig. In Calabria they also use pork rind to make ➤ **frittole**.

cotica regional term for ➤ **cotenna di maiale**, pork rind.

cotica 'bbiturata strips of pork rind boiled and formed into rings with Pecorino, tomato and marjoram. Recipe typical of the province of Ascoli. Marche.

cotiche con fagioli pork rind cut into strips and cooked with minced aromatic herbs, tomatoes and broth with the subsequent addition of boiled beans. Piedmont, Emilia-Romagna, Friuli-Venezia Giulia, Lazio.

cotizza aka **cutizza** aka **cutizzit** thin sweet flatbread made from a dough of flour, milk, eggs, grated lemon zest, fried in olive oil and served sprinkled with sugar. Typical of the province of Como. Lombardy.

cotogna quince (*Cydonia oblonga Miller*). Member of the Rosaceae family, common in China and the western Mediterranean. Indigenous in many Italian regions, after years of oblivion it is now returning to family orchards. It comprises numerous varieties which produce irregularly round fruits. The flesh can only be eaten after cooking and has an astringent flavor. Rich in gelatinizing substances, it is used in all sorts of jams, relishes and preserves: ➤ **mostarda**, ➤ **cotognata**, ➤ **savor**. In the province of Parma (Emilia-Romagna), they traditionally use quince to make a liqueur, *sburlon*.

cotognata preserve of stewed quinces pushed through a sieve and slow-cooked with the same weight of sugar until amber in color. The mixture is allowed to cool and set, then cut into cubes. It is stored in glass jars or wood or tin boxes. Common all over Italy, in some regions it has been a specialty for centuries: in Puglia and Abruzzo, where they aromatize the fruit with lemon juice and zest, and in Veneto, where it is called ➤ **persegada** and perfumed with crushed cloves and cinnamon.

cotoletta alla bolognese breaded veal chop browned in butter, covered with prosciutto, slivers of Parmigiano and, in season, grated white truffle, and finished in a covered skillet with a drop of broth and meat sauce. The recipe has been registered as "typical" at the Bologna Chamber of Commerce. Emilia-Romagna.

cotoletta alla milanese veal chop half an inch thick, dipped in beaten egg, coated with breadcrumbs and fried, preferably in clarified butter (➤ **burro chiarificato**). Lombardy.

cotoletta alla petroniana another name for ➤ cotoletta alla bolognese.

cotoletta alla triestina another name for ➤ cotoletta alla Viennese.

cotoletta alla viennese aka **Wienerschnitzel** veal escalope coated in flour, dipped in beaten egg and breadcrumbs and fried in oil or lard. Served with melted butter and decorated with desalted anchovies and olives or capers. Sometimes appears on menus as *cotoletta alla triestina*. Friuli-Venezia Giulia.

cotoletta di melina breaded oyster mushrooms. Common in the Po Valley, the oyster mushroom (➤ **melina**, ➤ **gelone**) was one of the first to be cultivated, and its ear-shaped caps are frequently used in the kitchen. This traditional Cremona recipe consists of boiling the mushrooms, coating them with flour, dipping them in beaten eggs and breadcrumbs, then frying them in butter. Lombardy.

cotolette alla pontremolese fried breaded veal escalopes transferred to a baking tin over a sauce of tomatoes, onion, butter and olive oil, covered with a mixture of finely chopped parsley, garlic, anchovy, dried mushrooms (revived in warm water), capers and walnuts, baked in the oven and garnished with a handful of whole capers. Typical of Pontremoli, in the province of Massa-Carrara). Tuscany.

cotolette dus in brüsc sweet and sour antipasto (➤ **agrodolce**). First sugar is caramelized with butter, then white wine vinegar, raisins and pine kernels are added and the mixture is brought to the boil and reduced. The resulting sauce is poured over slices of fried breaded guinea fowl or chicken. Lombardy.

cotto d'oca cured meat consisting of a boned goose stuffed with its own boned, salted legs, sewn up by hand, baked in the oven for at least ten hours, then lightly smoked. May be stored for 90 days. Typical of the province of Udine. Friuli.

cotto di fichi thick syrup obtained by slow boiling and filtration of figs picked in the last fortnight of August. The resulting concentrate is stored in hermetically sealed jars. Locally known as **miele di fichi** (fig honey), it is used to coat ➤ **cartellate**, fried pastries, and in the dough or mixture of a number of other regional cakes and pastries. Served in certain restaurants with filleted and boiled meats. Calabria and Puglia.

cotto di vino another word for ➤ **vincotto**, cooked grape must.

cottura in bianco blind baking. Technique used to bake pastry, especially tartlets and flan cases, before the filling is put in. It consists of pricking the base and sides of a pastry case and weighing it down with dried beans to prevent swelling, then baking it in the oven.

coturnice Greek rock partridge (*Alectoris graeca*). Very similar to the red-legged partridge, but slightly larger. Cooked in the same way as other partridges (➤ **pernice**).

court-bouillon broth for boiling fish and crustaceans made of salted water, dry white wine, onion, celery and carrot.

coviglia foamy dessert of confectioner's custard aromatized with coffee or chocolate and served ice-cold in individual coupes topped with whipped cream. Very popular in Naples, it takes its name from the silver-plated coupe in which it is served. Campania.

cozza mussel (➤ **mitilo**).

cozza 'e schiave aka **cozza scarpara** Puglia and Campania dialect words for ➤ **piè d'asino**, a type of mussel.

cozze alla leccese shelled mussels dressed with extra virgin olive oil, lemon juice, minced parsley and pepper. Lecce recipe very similar to the classic ➤ **'mpepata** of Naples. Puglia.

cozze alla pugliese shelled muscles stewed in oil and garlic with the addition of white wine and tomato passata, then browned in the oven with a topping of grated Pecorino and breadcrumbs. Puglia.

cozze, cocozze e ove first sliced zucchini (*cocozze*) are sautéed in oil with onions, then mussels (*cozze*) are added to the pan. When the mussels open, eggs (*ove*) beaten with grated Pecorino are poured in and scrambled. Recipe typical of Molfetta, in the province of Bari. Puglia.

cozze e orziadas mussels and sea anemones. Shelled mussels and ➤ **orziadas**, sea anemones, coated in plain flour and durum wheat semolina and deep-fried in olive oil until golden. Sardinia.

cozze fritte fried mussels. Mussels dipped in flour and beaten eggs, deep-fried and eaten piping hot. Puglia.

cozze piccinne dialect name used on the Salento peninsula (province of Lecce) for the small Roman (*Helix theba pisana*) and garden (*Helix hortensis*) snails that appear on tree trunks or in meadows after rainfall. Purged and washed, they are boiled and dressed with extra virgin olive oil, oregano, minced garlic, black pepper and salt. Puglia.

cozze ripiene al forno baked stuffed mussels. Shucked mussels stuffed with a mixture of tomato, chili, dried breadcrumbs, grated Pecorino and a little of their own liquid, and baked in the oven. Sardinia.

cozze ripiene al sugo stuffed mussels in sauce. Shucked mussels stuffed with a mixture of breadcrumbs, eggs, flat-leaved parsley and garlic, closed again and stewed in tomato sauce. Puglia.

cozzica Neapolitan term for ➤ **cozza**, mussel (➤ **mitilo**).

cozzola Sicilian term for ➤ **tellina**, tellin or wedge shell clam.

cozzola riale Puglia term for ➤ **cuore di mare**, common cockle.

cozzolo regional term for ➤ **pesce lucerna**, stargazer.

cozzulas de regottu Sardinian term for ➤ **pane con ricotta**.

crafen Italianization of ➤ **krapfen**, a type of doughnut.

crafen di potatoes flour and potato pastry bundles stuffed with ham, cheese or mushrooms and fried. Friuli-Venezia Giulia.

crafun môre savory doughnut (➤ **krapfen**), often filled with game sauce. A recipe of the Ladins, a linguistic minority who live in five valleys in the Dolomites. Trentino-Alto Adige, Veneto.

crafus sausage made of ground pig's liver mixed with grated bread, raisins, citrus zest, salt and spices. Eaten fried in lard within ten days of production. Typical of villages round the town of Gemona, in the province of Udine. Friuli-Venezia Giulia.

crapiata soup of wheat berries and legumes (chickpeas, beans, lentils, grass peas, fava beans) soaked and boiled in salted water with new potatoes. After cooking for two hours or so, it is served on slices of toasted bread and anointed with extra virgin olive oil. Typical of Matera, where it is eaten ritually every year in a sort of harvest festival. Basilicata.

crastatelli aka **tirignole** Lazio regional names for the common snail (➤ **lumaca**).

crastuna aka **crastuni** aka **barbani** Sicilian regional terms for a type of a large green-brown common snail (*Helix aspersa*) which lives in vineyards. Traditionally cooked sprinkled with dried breadcrumbs in the province of Siracusa and the Aeolian islands.

crauti sauerkraut, literally "sour herb." A dish of German origin, but now common all over Europe, in some German-speaking areas still made at home. Shredded white cabbage is squashed into wooden tubs or large jars and layered with salt and flavorings (juniper berries, caraway seeds, coriander, wild fennel). It is ready to eat after four to five weeks and has a long shelf life. Heated in a skillet it is a classic side dish with fresh or cured pork, especially if smoked. In the Trentino area, they crush the cabbage and call the dish *verdòle*. Trentino-Alto Adige, Friuli-Venezia Giulia.

crauti rostidi sauerkraut heated in lard and mixed with boiled borlotti beans. Trentino.

crava aka **cravetta** alternative names for the birch bolete mushroom (➤ **porcinello**).

crema (1) custard. Divided into two categories. Milk or liquid cream and sugar bound with eggs, flour or potato flour, well mixed and thickened over a heat.

crema (2) cream. Uncooked cream of butter, sugar and eggs.

crema (3) cream soup of puréed vegetables, meat or fish and béchamel sauce (➤ **besciamella**) or (➤ **roux**), thickened with flour or cornflour and finished with concentrated broth (➤ **fondo**) and cream.

crema (4) a component of some regional mixed fries (➤ **fritto misto all'ascolana** ff.), also known as ➤ **crema fritta** (Lombardy, Emilia-Romagna) or ➤ **cremino** (Marche).

crema al burro uncooked butter cream used to fill cakes and pastries, made by amalgamating butter, sugar and eggs and folding in egg whites whisked to a peak.

crema del Lario whipped cream blended with refined sugar, liqueur, lemon juice and zest, refrigerated and served with shortcrust pastries or dry cookies. Lombardy.

crema di asparagi alla milanese cream of asparagus soup. Spring soup thickened with egg yolks and served with croutons. Lombardy.

crema di castagne chestnut custard. Compôte of boiled, skinned, puréed chestnuts, cooked in milk with egg yolks and cream, perfumed with cinnamon. Served with diced rye bread fried in butter. Typical of the province of Trento. Trentino-Alto Adige.

crema di ciliegie cherry cream. Dessert of ripe cherries, stoned and boiled with red wine, sugar, lemon zest and cloves. The resulting mixture is allowed to cool and refrigerated for at least 24 hours. Piedmont.

crema di Cogne semiliquid custard made by simmering (without boiling) milk, cream, egg yolks, sugar and bitter cocoa. Served with dry biscuits or ➤ **tegole** (wafers). Typical of the village of Cogne. Val d'Aosta.

crema di Courmayeur custard dessert made by blending eggs, sugar, milk, red wine, spices, walnuts and crushed breadsticks and cooking until creamy. Val d'Aosta.

crema di mascarpone dessert made by whipping mascarpone, refined sugar, eggs and Marsala or liqueur. Generally served with dry biscuits. Lombardy, Emilia-Romagna..

crema di mirto myrtle custard. Made by folding myrtle liqueur and fresh cream into milk brought to the boil with sugar. After cooling, the liquid is refrigerated for a few hours before serving. Sardinia.

crema di zucca agli amaretti pumpkin cream. Made by blending pumpkin flesh, shallot, crushed amaretti cookies, milk and butter. The cream, typical of the province of Cremona, is a classic combination of the sweetish flavor of pumpkin with the bitterness of the almonds in the cookies. Lombardy.

crema frangipane a blend of confectioner's custard and crushed almonds or amaretti cookies, used to fill tarts and cakes and flavor butter cream (➤ **crema al burro**) and chocolate cakes.

crema fritta "fried custard." Cooked lozenges or cubes of custard (flour, milk, butter, sugar, eggs) allowed to set, breaded and fried in oil. One of the ingredients of some of Italy's many mixed fries (eg, ➤ **fritto misto alla bolognese and** ➤ **fritto misto all'ascolana**). The same name is used in Trentino, where they sometimes dust the custard with confectioner's sugar.

crema gallurese using a skimmer, egg whites whisked to a peak are plunged, a little at a time, in milk warmed with lemon zest, then set aside. The pan is then removed from the heat and a mixture of egg yolks, flour and sugar is rapidly whisked into the milk to form a sort of confectioner's custard. The cooked egg whites are covered with the custard and topped with caramel. Sardinia.

crema ganache aka **crema parigina** French confection of dark chocolate, butter and liquid cream often used to fill and decorate cakes.

crema inglese literally "English custard." Delicate, light custard made with milk, sugar, egg yolks and flavorings (vanilla pod, lemon zest, caramel, coffee, chocolate or liqueur) served with dried biscuits or used in confectionery.

crema parigina another name for ➤ **crema ganache**, chocolate cream.

crema pasticciera confectioner's custard. One of the most common fillings for cakes and pastries. Made with egg yolks, milk, sugar, wheat flour and lemon zest.

crema reggina pinkish rum-flavored ice cream. A specialty of Reggio Calabria. Calabria.

crème brûlée baked dessert made with egg yolk, sugar, cream and lemon zest. Now fashionable in Italian restaurants, where it is also called *crema bruciata* or *crema cassonade*.

crème caramel dessert made by cooking together milk, sugar, vanilla, lemon zest and beaten eggs, pouring the mixture into a mold or individual ramekins lined with caramelized sugar, and allowing it to set. The French term is used everywhere, but similar desserts using the same ingredients are to be found in many Italian regional cuisines: ➤ **fiordilatte**, ➤ **lattaiolo** aka **latteruolo**, ➤ **latte alla portoghese**, ➤ **latte in piedi**. Some of these are baked.

cremino dolce another name for ➤ **crema fritta**, "fried custard."

cremolato di frutta cremosa type of ➤ **granita** dessert made with fruit juices or other aromatized liquids (eg, coffee), adopting the same system used for sorbets (➤ **sorbetto**). The liquid, sweetened with a little sugar and frozen, is stirred frequently to obtain small ice crystals. The dessert is served in bowls, often garnished with whipped cream. Lazio.

cremortartaro cream of tartar. Added to

baked cakes, on its own or with bicarbonate of soda, to make them softer. Today often replaced by chemical yeast.

cren horseradish (*Armoracia rusticana*). Subspontaneous herbaceous plant whose root, when grated, releases a strong pungent aroma. The root is eaten fresh as an accompaniment to boiled meats (➤ **porcina**) and smoked fish, or transformed into a sauce (➤ **salsa di cren**) to attenuate its piquancy. In Italy, horseradish is most used in areas that have undergone Germanic or Slav influence: Friuli-Venezia Giulia and Trentino-Alto Adige in the north and, by virtue of Swabian domination during the Middle Ages, Basilicata in the south (➤ **rafanata**). Common and regional names: ➤ **barbaforte**, ➤ **erba da scorbuto**, ➤ **pizzicalingua**, ➤ **rafano** (an improper usage which creates confusion with ➤ **rapastrello** (*Rapahanus raphanistrum*), wild radish. The Italian Ministry of Agriculture's database of native and/or traditional food products lists the *cren del Veneto* and *kren dell'Alto Adige* varieties.

crepada another word for ➤ **suc**, grape dessert.

crêpe French for ➤ **crespella**.

crepinetta popular Lombard term for meatball.

cresc' tajat northern Marche dialect term for ➤ **maltagliati**, a type of pasta, made with cornflour.

crescenta A Ferrara variation on ➤ **gnocco al forno** in which lardo is used in lieu of prosciutto.

crescentina flatbread made from a dough of wholemeal or cake flour, milk, natural yeast and sugar, rolled into a thin sheet and cut into disks, which are cooked in a griddle pan (➤ **tigella**, ➤ **testo**). A specialty of the Apennines in the province of Modena. Emilia-Romagna.

crescentina fritta pastry made by frying small lozenges of a leavened dough of cake flour, brewer's yeast, water, olive oil and salt (in the Modena hills they also make an unleavened wholemeal version). The same pastry is called ➤ **gnocco fritto** in Bologna, ➤ **pinzin** in Ferrara, and ➤ **torta fritta** in Parma. Emilia-Romagna.

Crescenza fresh pasteurized cow's milk cheese, a member of the ➤ **Stracchino** family. Produced in two versions: in winter, soft and creamy; in summer, firmer. Matured for five or six days, it has a sweet, delicate, milky flavor. Lombardy.

crescia the term refers to various types of flatbread typical of Marche and Umbria. In the latter region, it is identical to ➤ **torta al testo**, the term **crescia** being used almost exclusively in the area round Gubbio, in the province of Perugia. In the Marche, depenning on locality, it can be a thickish focaccia made with leavened dough (➤ **crescia maceratese**) or puff pastry (➤ **crescia sfogliata di Urbino**), or with other ingredients (➤ **crescia sul panaro**). It came into being as a bread to accompany other warm or cold dishes, but has now developed into a dish in its own right, enhanced by various types of fillings. In the Marche, they make an exceptionally thick ➤ **crescia di Pasqua** during the Easter period. Marche, Umbria.

crescia di Pasqua aka **pizza di Pasqua** aka **pizza al formaggio** flatbread made in two versions, one savory, the other sweet. The first is made with starter yeast, flour, oil, eggs, salt, pepper and grated Pecorino. The second is made with the same dough, dotted with raisins and grated lemon or citron zest in lieu of the savory ingredients, which, after resting, is brushed with beaten egg yolk, baked in the oven, and coated with egg whites whisked to a peak and sugar. Both versions are made all over the region at Easter. Marche.

crescia maceratese soft, round flatbread usually topped with salt and oil (it has dimples on the surface to retain the oil), or rosemary and onions. Other possible toppings are wild field greens or pork scratchings (➤ **ciccioli,** known locally as *sgriscioli*). Used to be made with the leftover dough from breadmaking. A specialty of the province of Macerata. Marche.

crescia sfogliata di Urbino puff pastry flatbread. A round, flat disk of dough made of soft wheat flour kneaded with eggs and lard. Stretched and greased with lard, the dough is rolled up, cut into pieces and rolled out a second time. A specialty of Urbino, like ➤ **crostolo del Montefeltro**. Both are close relatives of the ➤ **piadina**, typical of nearby Romagna. Marche.

crescia sul panaro round flatbread made with leftover polenta kneaded with wheat flour cooked on a metal hot plate, known locally as a *panaro*. A specialty of the Castelli di Jesi area. Marche.

crescionda traditional baked cake made from a mixture of eggs, sugar, amaretti cookies, milk, crushed rusks and lemon zest. The outside hazel-colored crust contrasts with the paler interior, which looks like a filling but isn't. Umbria

crescione (1) watercress (*Nasturtium officinale*). Plant with reclining stems and round, fleshy, peppery-tasting leaves. Occurs mainly in running water. Eaten raw in salads, on its own or mixed with other leaves. Also popular as a garnish or as an ingredient for cream soups.

crescione (2) name used in the provinces of Ravenna and Forlì-Cesena to refer to ➤ **cassone**, a stuffed flatbread. Emilia-Romagna.

Crescione inglese, garden cress (*Lepidium sativum*), also known as **agretto** or **agretto d'orto**, and **crescione dei prati** (*Cardamine pratensis*), lady's smock, are also used in the kitchen. Lady's smock, in particular, is parboiled and used to flavor and color butter (*burro di crescione*). Common and regional names: ➤ **agretto**, ➤ **nasturzio**.

cresenzin fruit loaf made with a leavened dough of mixed rye and wheat flour (like ➤ **pane nero di Coimo**), worked with sugar, raisins, walnuts (and, sometimes, dried figs, more rarely hazelnuts and almonds). The surface may be decorated with walnuts and sugar, the crust is hard and irregular, dark brown in color with gold streaks. Typical of the Antrona and Vigezzo valleys (province of Verbano-Cusio-Ossola), where it used to be shaped like a baby and baked at Christmas. Piedmont.

crespella (1) Italian version of the French savory crêpe, or pancake. The basic recipe consists of a batter of flour, eggs, milk, salt and butter which, after resting for a few minutes, is dropped to cook on a hotplate or in a hot skillet. Innumerable variations exist, stuffed with cured meats, cheeses and so on. In Abruzzo, the pancakes are called ➤ **scrippelle** and feature in soups and timbales: ➤ **scrippelle 'mbusse**, ➤ **timballo di scrippelle**. In Campania and Florence, they are stuffed and baked.

crespella (2) a smaller, square version of ➤ **vastedda**, a Sicilian bread loaf.

crespella alla valdostana a very thin crêpe filled with ham and Fontina cheese, covered with cheese fondue. A creation of the 1960s. Val d'Aosta.

crespelle alla fiorentina very thin crêpes

(made of flour, eggs, milk and butter) filled with ricotta and spinach, arranged in a baking tin, smothered with béchamel sauce, sprinkled with grated Parmigiano, and baked in a hot oven, In international gastronomic language, the term *alla fiorentina* is applied to dishes containing spinach.

crespelle ripiene stuffed pancakes. Thin pancakes made from a batter of wheat flour, eggs and Parmigiano, covered with ricotta, Parmigiano, diced mozzarella, eggs and flat-leaved parsley, rolled up, baked in the oven and served with tomato sauce. Campania.

crespellitti small disks of batter fried in oil. Cornflour is often added to achieve a crisper effect. Abruzzo.

crespignolo Ligurian term for ➤ **grespigno**, field sowthistle.

crespone part of the pig's ➤ **budello**, intestine. By analogy, the name also applies to the cured meats for which it is used as a casing. The most common of these is ➤ **salame Milano**.

cresponetto part of the pig's ➤ **budello**, intestine.

creste another name for ➤ **creste di gallo**, a type of pasta.

creste di gallo commercial durum wheat pasta consisting of ➤ **chifferi** with a crenellated ribbon along the top. Served with light tomato and vegetable sauces. Other names: ➤ **creste**, ➤ **cimieri**.

crestine another name for ➤ **farfalline**, a type of pasta.

creta, alla term for a cooking technique, said to have been brought to Italy by the Longobards, whereby a foodstuff is coated in clay, then baked in the oven or on a barbecue. Regional recipes that adopt the method include: ➤ **cosciotto di agnello in cieramida**, ➤ **faraona alla creta**.

cretamo another name for ➤ **finocchio ma-rino**, samphire.

crisommola another name for ➤ **albicocca**, apricot, especially the variety that grows on the slopes of Mount Vesuvius. Campania.

crispella a binidittina a variation on ➤ **crispella di riso**, sweet rice crêpe cum pancake coated in flour and fried.

crispella di riso sweet crêpe popular in eastern Sicily. Made by cooking rice in milk with sugar and vanilla, then incorporating egg yolks. The mixture is shaped into small balls, which are dipped in a batter of flour, eggs and milk, fried until golden and dusted with confectioner's sugar. In Catania and Siracusa, the eggs are left out of the mixture, but brewer's yeast diluted in warm water and orange and lemon zest are added (another difference is that, in the province of Siracusa, the rice is not cooked in milk but in salted water). In both cases, the fritters are served covered with honey diluted in water. Sicily.

critmo another name for ➤ **finocchio marino**, samphire.

crivatzu another name for ➤ **civraxiu**, a type of bread.

croccante brittle. Confection of almonds or hazelnuts, peanuts, sesame or other dried fruits, whole or cut into pieces, bound with caramelized sugar. Popular all over Italy, though ingredients and aroma may change from place to place. In Lazio and Campania, for example, it is perfumed with vanilla, in southern Italy with pieces of lemon or orange zest. Finely or coarsely chopped, it is used as an ingredient in sauces, custards and cream desserts, to coat or fill pralines, truffles and ice creams. The most famous local recipes are: ➤ **cupeta** (Puglia), ➤ **cumpittu** (Calabria), ➤ **giuggiulena** (Sicily), ➤ **gattò (2)** (Sardinia). In the Abruzzo version, the almonds are bound with honey. In

Tuscany, pine kernels are the main ingredient, aromatized with grated orange zest and garnished with confetti sugar.

croccantini almond and aniseed Carnival candies, typical of the province of Ancona. Marche.

crocchè di potatoes croquette potatoes. Boiled potatoes mashed and mixed with butter, eggs, cheese and grated lemon zest, shaped into small cylinders, breaded and fried. Made according to different recipes throughout Italy. In Sicily they are known as ➤ **cazzilli**. Street food (see ➤ **cucina di strada**) common throughout the south of Italy. In Naples, popular combined with ➤ **pasta cresciuta**.

crocchetta (pl. **crochette**) spherical, oval, or cylindrical patty made of a mixture of potatoes or rice, or meat or fish, bound with beaten eggs or a fluid sauce. Breaded and fried, they are a common feature in a number of regonal cuisines (➤ **arancina**, ➤ **cazzilli**, ➤ **crocchè di potatoes**).

croccolone great snipe (*Capella media*). Wading bird similar to, but slightly larger than the common snipe (➤ **beccaccino**).

croce aka **crocetta** other names for ➤ **rumine**, rumen.

crocetta name used in the area round Ancona for the sea snail knwn ➤ **piè di pellicano**, pellican's foot, commonly known as ➤ **garagolo**. Marche.

crocetta bolognese Bologna variation on ➤ **coppia ferrarese** with a ribbon-like central part. Emilia-Romagna.

crocetta piacentina naturally leavened, star-shaped bread loaf. Emilia-Romagna.

crocette another name for ➤ **crucette**, baked sun-dried figs.

crognale regional term for ➤ **corniolo**, cornelian cherry.

cropa buckwheat polenta cooked with cream and mixed with potatoes and cheese. Traditional dish of the area round Arigna, in the Valtellina, in the province of Sondrio. Lombardy.

croset aka **crouzet** small flour and egg gnocchi with slightly crenellated edges. Traditionally served (in the Valle Stura) with *bagna grisa* ("gray sauce"), made with onion, garlic, milk, cream and cheese, or with leeks. A typical recipe of the Provencal communities in the mountains of the province of Cuneo. Piedmont.

crosetti another name for ➤ **corzetti**, a type of pasta. Liguria.

crosta fiorita bloomy rind. Term used to describe a cheese whose rind is covered by a gray-white mold caused by surface micloflora (Mucor and Penicillium).

crosta, in *en croûte*. Term used to describe a foodstuff (fish or meat) wrapped in a thin layer of pastry.

crosta lavata washed rind. Term used to describe a cheese whose rind is periodically washed with water and salt or solutions of water and alcohol during the aging process.

crostaceo crustacean.

crostata tart. Cake baked in a special mold and constituted by a shortcust pastry base (➤ **pasta frolla**), covered before or after baking, with jam or marmalade, custard or fresh fruit. The surface may be criss-crossed with strips of pastry. Popular in all Italian regions, often making use of local ingredients, dairy products included.

crostata chiusa pie. A tart (➤ **crostata**) with a pastry lid.

crostata del diavolo ➤ literally "devil's tart." Consists of a base of shortcrust pastry spread with one layer of orange marmalade and another of chili preserve, sprinkled with crushed peeled almonds and topped with strips of shortcrust pastry. Calabria.

crostata di ricotta ricotta tart. A disk of

shortcrust pastry spread with a mixture of ricotta, sugar, eggs, grated lemon and orange zest, raisins, cinnamon, pine kernels and candied citron and orange. In one variation, typical of Sermoneta, in the province of Latina, the ricotta is perfumed with an aromatic liqueur. Lazio.

crostata di tortelli cremaschi tart made by spreading boiled, dressed tortelli, crumbled amaretti cookies, egg yolks beaten with grated parmesan over a dough base of flour, egg yolks, butter and salt, and baking in the oven. A way of using up leftover tortelli. Lombardy.

crostata di visciole sour cherry tart. The cherries are cooked in a large pan with sugar and cinnamon to obtain a homogeneous, jam-like consistency. The mixture is spread over a shortcrust pastry base and the surface is criss-crossed with strips of leftover pastry. The resulting tart is baked in the oven. In some recipes, mostly of Jewish origin, a layer of almond paste may also be added. The tart is popular in several regions, especially in Lazio and Marche where the sour or morello cherry (➤ **visciola**) grows abundantly. A version also exists in the Trentino, where they alternate the fruit in layers with cinnamon and breadcrumbs.

crostata di zucca pumpkin tart. A shortcrust pastry base covered with a mixture of over-roast pumpkin, melted butter, cornflour, crumbled amaretti cookies, minced toasted almonds, candied fruit and cinnamon. The tart is topped with criss-crossed pastry strips and baked in the oven. Veneto.

croste con midollo di bue al vino rosso fried, hollowed out bread loaf (➤ **pan carré**), filled with diced, poached ox spleen mixed with a sauce of red wine and chopped parsley. Lombardy.

crostini alla napoletana sliced bread (the classic ➤ **palata**), topped with mozzarella, butter, anchovy fillets, fresh tomato and oregano, then toasted. A classic antipasto. Campania.

crostini alla norcina another name for ➤ **crostini umbri**,

crostini alla ponticiana slices of bread fried in butter until golden, topped with prosciutto, diced ➤ **mozzarella di bufala** or ➤ **Provatura** cheese and a spoonful of mushrooms, and baked in the oven. Popular antipasto named for an old quarter of Rome. Lazio.

crostini alla provatura skewers of pieces of ➤ **provatura** (or ➤ **fiordilatte** or ➤ **Provola**), alternated with pieces of bread, baked in the oven and covered with butter flavored with anchovy fillets. Lazio, Campania.

crostini con il merollo traditional antipasto consisting of toasted bread topped with ox bone marrow (*merollo* in dialetto), fried in a skillet and seasoned with salt. Lazio.

crostini di provatura another name for ➤ **crostini alla provatura**.

crostini toscani hugely popular antipasto consisting of slices of toasted bread with various toppings, among which classics are: woodcock (➤ **beccaccia**), now hard to find, calf's spleen and chicken livers. In the latter two cases, the spleen or livers are browned in butter with onion and herbs, bathed with white wine or ➤ **Vin Santo**, flavored with anchovies and capers and chopped finely to a paste (sometimes the bread is dipped in Vin Santo before being spread with the mixture. Simple variations on the **crostino** theme are ➤ **fettunta** and, in winter, ➤ **fetta col cavolo nero**. Restaurants also serve **crostini** topped with beans, tomato (➤ **bruschetta**) and mushrooms, cooked in a mixture of minced pine kernels, garlic, flat-leaved parsley and chili. In the Maremma area, **crostini** used to constitute the only antipasto at holiday lunches, and the offal of farm animal and game was set aside to make them. Tuscany.

crostini ubriachi slices of day-old bread soaked in a mixture of alkermes, coffee and rum, then coated with chocolate and finely minced sweet almonds bound with the alkermes and rum used to soak the bread. A traditional Carnival treat in Città di Castello, in the province of Perugia. Umbria.

crostini umbri slices of toasted bread spread with a sauce of chopped Norcia truffles, anchovy fillets and extra virgin olive oil. Another version, *crostini alla norcina*, consist of day-old farmhouse bread dressed with chicken livers sautéed with garlic, sage, rosemary, wild fennel, capers, anchovy and vinegar. Umbria.

crostino (1) crouton. Piece of diced bread fried in butter or toasted and used to garnish broths, soups and creams.

crostino (2) slice of toasted bread spread with any of a variety of ingredients and sauces and eaten as an antipasto or snack: ➤ **crostini toscani**, ➤ **crostini umbri**, ➤ **fettunta**, ➤ **bruschetta**.

crostino (3) in international cuisine almost a synonym of canapé. A slice of crustless white bread spread with any of a variety of savory mixtures.

crostol aka **crostole** shell-like pastries made with durum wheat semolina and eggs, fried in boiling oil, smothered with honey and sprinkled with refined sugar. Basilicata

crostoli Emilia-Romagna regional name for fried pastries similar to ➤ **cenci**.

crostoli di potatoes lozenges of a very fine dough of potatoes, flour, eggs and butter, fried in boiling. Friuli-Venezia Giulia.

crostoli aka **grostoi** fried Carnival pastries similar to ➤ **cenci**, often aromatized with grappa and filled with sweet custards or fruit jams. Savory versions also exist known as ➤ **grastoi**. Veneto, Tentino-Alto Adige, Friuli-Venezia Giulia.

crostolo del Montefeltro puff pastry flatbread made with a dough of soft wheat flour, eggs, salt, pepper, lard, water, milk, bicarbonate of soda and, sometimes, curd left over from cheesemaking, worked in the same way as that for ➤ **crescia sfogliata di Urbino.** Typical of the Montefeltro district in the northwest of the region. Marche.

crostone grossa slice of fried, toasted or plain bread topped with meats in sauce: eg, ➤ **salmì di cacciagione**, ➤ **buglione**, ➤ **palomba alla ghiotta**.

crucelle ➤ dialect word for **piè di pellicano**, pelican's foot. Campania.

crucette aka **crocette** baked sun-dried figs filled with almonds, walnuts and candied citrus zest. Calabria.

crudità from the French *crudité*. Sliced raw vegetables (carrots, celery, fennel, artichokes, peppers, radishes, tomatoes) dressed with a ➤ **vinaigrette** and served at the start of a meal, or julienned to garnish a dish. The first usage coincides with the rite of the ➤ **pinzimonio**, in some areas of southern Italy known as *sopratavola* (➤ **spingituro**).

crumiri alternative spelling of ➤ **krumiri**, baked cookies.

crusca bran. The hard outer layer of grain, the principal by-product of the grinding of soft wheat or other cereals into flour (➤ **frumento**).

cruschello bran flakes, a residue of the grinding and sifting of cereals.

crusciot dialect term for ➤ **silene rigonfia**, bladder campion.

crustoli dialect term for ➤ **cartellate**, fried pastries.

cubaite sandwich of wafers (flour, water, egg white) filled with a crisp mixture of toasted hazelnuts, honey, sugar and finely minced orange zest). Typical of the western Riviera, reminiscent of the southern Italian ➤ **cubbaita**. Liguria.

cubbaita another name for nougat (➤ **giuggiulena (2)**), from the Arabic *qubbayt*, a word used for similar sweetmeats in Algeria, Egypt and Tunisia. Traditional in Sicily and Calabria, where it is also called ➤ **giurgiulena** or ➤ **cumpittu**.

Cuc another name for ➤ **Carnia (1)** cheese.

cucamela dialect term for ➤ **mazza di tamburo**, parasol mushroom.

cucchiaio, al literally "suitable for a spoon," the term is used to describe desserts of a not entirely solid consistency that need to be eaten with a spoon: ie, custards, bavarois, frozen mousses and so on.

cuccìa (1) cream dessert made by boiling wheat berries, allowing them to cool, and mixing them with a custard of sugar, ricotta, candied orange zest, dark chocolate shavings, cinnamon-flavored oil and vanilla. Made on December 13, the feast of Santa Lucia, who, according to legend, saved the citizens of Siracusa from famine by having ships laden with grain moor in the city's port. In the past, the devotional rite involved boiling the wheat berries (*cuocci* in dialect) and eating them hot with milk, ricotta, honey or cooked wine must (➤ **vincotto**) or simply sprinkled with sugar. Typical of Siracusa. Sicily.

cuccìa (2) baked goat and pork with wheat berries. The three ingredients are boiled separately (the wheat berries after soaking in water for two days), then layered in an earthenware casserole dish and baked in the oven. The dish originated in the village of Pedace, in the province of Cosenza. Calabria, Basilicata.

cucciddata di Natali type of ➤ **buccellato** with a beautifully decorated crust. Typical of Salaparuta, in the province of Trapani. Sicily.

cucciddatu (1) ring-shaped bread loaf made with a dough of durum wheat flour, natural and/or brewer's yeast, water and salt, and baked in the oven. Typical of Catania. Sicily.

cucciddatu (2) Sicilian term for ➤ **buccellato**, a ring-shaped cake.

cucciddatu di carrozza large ring-shaped bread loaf made from a dough of durum wheat semolina, natural yeast, water, salt and lard with numerous regular slashes round the edges. Typical of some villages of the province of Trapani, where it is used to decorate floats and standards during religious processions. Sicily.

cucciddatu scaniatu left over bread dough kneaded again with grated Caciocavallo cheese, pepper, lard, ricotta and sausage, leavened for an hour and a half, and baked in the oven. Typical of Scicli, in the province of Ragusa. Sicily.

cucciole Marche term for ➤ **lumache di terra**, earth snails.

cuciarolli word used in the Romagna Apennines for skinned dried chestnuts.

cucina expression used in the province of Massa-Carrara to describe a selection of wild herbs (bristly ox tongue ➤ **aspraggine**, borage ➤ **borragine**, Mediterranean cabbage ➤ **cavolicello**, wild chicory ➤ **cicoria selvatica**, wild fennel ➤ **finocchio selvatico**, bristly hawkbit ➤ **dente di leone**, field sowthistle ➤ **grespigno** aka ➤ **cicerbita**, high mallow ➤ **malva**, cat's ear ➤ **piattello** aka ➤ **costolina**, ribwort plantain ➤ **piantaggine**, small burnet ➤ **pimpinella**) from February to April. Eaten fresh or cooked in soups and pies, **cucina** is still sold in that period at the fruit and vegetable market in Massa. Tuscany.

cucine delle minoranze minority cuisines. Over the millennia, Italy has been home to the most diverse peoples, sometimes invaders, sometimes on the run themselves from conflict and invasion. Hence the existence in some areas of small isolated communities (Provencals, Waldensians, Walsers, South Tyroleans, Ladins, Slovenes and so on in the Alps, Albanians, Greeks, Catalans and so on in the south and the islands), some of which preserve part of their cultural, linguistic and gastronomic heritage. Some of their dishes, such as ➤ **mnestro de ris e erbetes**, ➤ **bodi e ajòli** (Provencals), ➤ **tirtlen** (South Tyroleans), ➤ **crafuns** (Ladins), ➤ **jota** (Slovenes), ➤ **drömsat** (Albanians) and others besides are recorded in this book.

cucina di strada street food. Another term for ➤ **cibo di strada**.

cucina ebraica Jewish cuisine. The cuisine developed by Jews as they came into contact with the eating habits of the places in which they settled. Jews of diverse provenance have settled in waves in different parts of Italy over the centuries, enriching the cooking of every region. The biggest influx (ever since ancient times) has always been in Rome, where dishes of certain Jewish origin, such as ➤ **carciofi alla giudia**, ➤ **cardi acidi**, ➤ **aliciotti con indivia** and ➤ **polpettone di pollo** are part and parcel of the city's culinary tradition. In some places, aspects of local cuisines compatible with Jewish dietary precepts have been accentuated (the consumption of goose and the use of goose fat in the Po Valley, for example); in others, Jewish habits have been assimilated (the taste for sweet and sour of Ashkenazis arriving from central and eastern Europe or the use of olive oil and spices typical of the Sephardic Jews expelled from Spain in the late 15th century). Veneto dishes such as ➤ **carote in agrodolce**, ➤ **verze sofegae** and perhaps even ➤ **tortelli di zucca** typical of Mantua and Ferrara, can be traced to a Jewish matrix, while the mullet dish, ➤ **triglie alla livornese**, still appears as **triglie al pomodoro** in the Sephardic New Year's Eve menu. Cakes and pastries of Jewish origin include ➤ **bisse degli ebrei**, ➤ **bollo** and ➤ **orecchie di Amman**.

cucinidd lamb cooked with pancetta, sausage, cardoons, eggs, tomatoes, parsley and cheese. A typical Easter dish. Basilicata.

cucire to sew. Certain large pieces of meat need to be sewn with kitchen string to retain their stuffing.

cuculli fritters of mashed potatoes, pine kernels, marjoram, eggs and grated Parmigiano. In some areas the term also means chickpea fritters. Liguria.

cuculu type of ➤ **muccellato** decorated with fresh eggs, as a token of good luck and prosperity, before being baked in the oven. Calabria.

cucunci the small oval berries that constitute the fruits of the caper plant. May be preserved in salt, used as an ingredient in salad or to flavor certain pasta dishes. The island of Salina's **cucunci** are listed in the Italian Ministry of Agriculture's database of native and/or traditional food products. Sicily.

cuddhura aka **scarcella** Easter bread made with leavened dough, shaped in the form of doves, lambs, rings, roosters, baskets and so on, and dotted with hard-boiled eggs. Typical of the province of Lecce (Puglia). Today the name also refers to an Easter cake made from a dough of flour, oil, lard, sugar, eggs, lemon zest, anise liqueur, milk and salt with a hard-boiled egg at the center, secured by strips of pastry. Once baked, the cake is glazed with sugar icing and decorated with anise-flavored confetti sugar. Puglia.

cuddrireddra di Delia elaborate, crown-shaped pastry roll made of durum wheat flour, fresh eggs, sugar, lard, red wine, cinnamon and orange zest. Originally home-baked during the Carnival period and grooved with a weaver's "comb." Said to have been created as a tribute to the châtelaines who lived in the village of Delia, in the province of Caltanissetta, during the Sicilian Vespers, the pastry is protected by a Slow Food presidium. Sicily.

cuddura special holiday bread made in Reggio Calabria from a dough of water, natural yeast, sourdough starter (➤ **biga**), durum wheat meal and sea salt. Shaped into a ring, it is patterned with reliefs and slashes and sprinkled with sesame seeds. In the provinces of Ragusa and Siracusa, the same word refers to a type of ➤ **cucciddatu (1)**, a ring-shaped loaf, with a firmer, smoother crumb. Calabria, Sicily.

cudduruni type of ➤ **calzone** with a variety of fillings, which include onions, broccoletti with anchovies, and wild chard (➤ **bietola selvatica**, known in dialect as *anciti*) with diced mortadella and Pecorino and black olives. Sicily.

cuffia another name for ➤ **reticolo**, reticulum.

cugnitti earthenware jars, enameled on the inside and fitted with a ➤ **timpagnu**, or wooden lid. Used to store foods over long periods. Calabria.

cuguluf aka **kugeluf** from the German *Gugel*, hood. The *kugelhupf* is a sponge cake of Austrian and Alsatian origin, dotted with raisins and baked in a special ring mold. **Cuguluf** is a variant typical of Trieste, normally dusted with confectioner's sugar. Friuli-Venezia Giulia.

cugutzula wild cardoon (➤ **cardo selvatico**) preserved in oil.

cuincîr simple dairy product made of ricotta mixed with salt and pepper (and sometimes other spices), aged for 45-60 days in large glass or plastic containers. White in color, it has a creamy consistency and a tangy smell. Typical of the Canal del Ferro and Val Canale areas of the province of Udine. Friuli.

cularino southern Italian term for ➤ **budello gentile**, large intestine.

culatello di Zibello one of Italy's finest PDO cured meats, made from a muscle detached from the heart of a ham. Cured with salt, it is washed with wine and massage with salt and coarsely ground pepper. Cased in the pig's bladder or intestine in a pear-shape, it is loosely tied up with string and aged for ten to 12 months. A consortium brings together producers from the eight communes in which the PDO cured meat can be produced and ensures the application of production protocols: namely that the meat can only be made by hand in winter, that the ham has to come from pigs raised in Emilia-Romagna and Lombardy, and that aging has to take place naturally. A Slow Food presidium protects this quality product from industrialization. A presidium culatello has to be prepared from November to January, aged for at least 18 months and weighing at least two pounds.

culingiones another name for ➤ **culurjones**, Sardinian savory or sweet ravioli.

cullurielli sweet or savory rings made with mashed potatoes, wheat flour and yeast. Calabria.

culurgiones another name for ➤ **culurjones**, Sardinian savory or sweet ravioli.

culurjones (1) handmade pear-shaped egg and durum wheat ravioli, usually stuffed with potatoes and cheese or dried cheese curd preserved in brine (➤ **merca**), and served with tomato sauce and grated Pecorino. Typical of the Ogliastra area, but now common all over the island.

culurjones (2) sweet ravioli made from a dough of durum wheat flour, soft wheat flour and lard, stuffed with a mixture of almonds, orange blossom water, powdered vanilla, refined sugar and lemon zest, and deep-fried. Other names: ➤ **culingiones**, ➤ **culurgiones**, ➤ **culurzones**, ➤ **gurigliones**. Sardinia.

culurzones another name for ➤ **culurjones**, Sardinian savory or sweet ravioli.

cumino dei prati caraway (*Carum carvi*). Dried fruit, not seeds, of a wild herbaceous plant with an intense aroma redolent of anise (➤ **anice**). In regional Italian cooking, caraway is used to flavor meat, bread, cheese and cakes. Black cumin (*Cuminum cyminum*) is also widely used in Mediterranean and oriental cuisine. Common and regional names: ➤ **anice dei Vosgi**, ➤ **carvi**, ➤ **cimino**, ➤ **cumino tedesco**, ➤ **kümmel**.

cumino tedesco another name for ➤ **cumino dei prati**, caraway.

cumpittu soft nougat made of almonds, sesame seeds and honey. Calabria.

cunicio in tecia Veneto term for rabbit stew (see ➤ **coniglio in tegame**).

cunza chopped raw lardo mixed with finely minced garlic and rosemary and grated Parmigiano-Reggiano. Used to fill the ➤ **crescentina** roll, which, warm from the oven, softens the fat. A richer variation with the addition of pancetta and ground sausage is used, warmed over the fire, to fill the ➤ **borlengo** roll. A specialty of Modena. Emilia-Romagna.

cuoccio Campania term for *capone coccio*, red or cuckoo gurnard (➤ **capone**).

cuoccio riale Campania term for ➤ **capone gallinella**, gurnard

cuore heart. The most easily available hearts for cooking in Italy are those of cows and calves. The hearts of lambs and kids are generally cooked with other offal (➤ **coratella**), and the same often applies to the heart of the pig. The hearts of fowl, domestic and wild, are considered as giblets (➤ **rigaglie**). Calf's heart may be cooked roast, fried or broiled. An adult animal's needs to be cooked longer, braised or stewed.

cuore di mare literally "sea heart." Common cockle (*Cardium edule*), so named because, viewed sideways, it looks like a small heart. Albeit not one of the tastiest mollusks, it is often eaten raw. Common and regional names: ➤ **arzedda**, ➤ **canestrello**, ➤ **capatonda**, ➤ **còzzola riale**.

cuore di tonno tuna heart. The heart of the fish is opened and trimmed of all fat, covered in salt for at least one day, washed in sea water, left to dry on wooden frames and hung in cellars to age. Best enjoyed as an antipasto. Sardinia.

cuoricini flat heart-shaped commercial durum wheat pasta available in various sizes. Usually cooked in broth.

cuoricino term for the heart of the chicken and other fowl, domestic and wild. Considered part of the bird's giblets (➤ **rigaglie**).

cuosta china Sicilian term for ➤ **costata di maiale ripiena**, stuffed pork chop.

cupa cured meat made from the flesh of the head of the pig cured with salt, pepper, nutmeg, wine and grappa. Eaten fresh. Typical of the Valli Ossolane (province of Verbano-Cusio-Ossola). Piedmont.

cupeta (1) caramelized sugar and crushed sweet almond brittle (in the Salento area of Puglia, they use whole almonds), cut into rectangles, strips and lozenge shapes. Bars of the candy are still to be found at fairs in Puglia where vendors (*cupitari*) make them with the old techniques. The name is of Arab-Sicilian derivation (➤ **cubbaita**).

cupeta (2) aka **copeta** (in Italian, *coppette*, "little cups." Wafer sandwiches with a filling of whole walnuts warmed in honey. Traditionally prepared in the Tortona area, in the province of Alessandria, on January 17 for the feast of Sant'Antonio Abate. Piedmont.

cupett dessert made with honey, walnuts, candied orange and citron zest and wafers. Typical of Busto Arsizio, in the province of Varese, and similar to ➤ **cupeta (2)**. Lombardy.

curabié term of Greek origin used to refer to small shortcrust pastry half-moon cookies, probably of Bosnian origin (➤ **chilefeti**). Specialty of Trieste. Friuli-Venezia Giulia.

curacchie another name for ➤ **frittole**, an offal dish.

curadduzzu Sicilian term for ➤ **corallina**, a type of pasta.

curadura the innards of freshwater sardines (➤ **agone**) cooked in olive oil with breadcrumbs, lemon zest and herbs, and served with polenta. A specialty of Lake Como but also to be found on both sides of Lake Maggiore. Lombardy, Piedmont.

curcùci the fat and cheaper parts of the pig cooked in a cauldron and rendered to ➤ **ciccioli** (pork scratchings) used to flavor polenta and a special ➤ **pitta** bread (together with ricotta and eggs) traditionally eaten on Easter Monday picnics. Other names: ➤ **frisuli**, **risimogli**, **risulimiti**. Calabria.

curiuli southern name for a pasta similar to ➤ **tagliatelle**.

currioli zucchini cut into strips and dried in the sun. Revived in warm water, they are fried in olive oil perfumed with garlic and oregano, as they are or dipped in batter. Calabria.

curritholata bean soup flavored with lardo, sausage, potatoes and wild fennel. A specialty of the province of Nuoro. Sardinia.

currucolo Easter cake made with flour, olive oil, refined sugar, sugar chips, milk and eggs. Ring-shaped with a hard-boiled egg at the center. Puglia.

curzul broad homemade flour and egg tagliolini typically served with lamb or shallot sauce. A specialty of Faenza. Emilia-Romagna.

cuscus couscous. Of Arab origin, the dish is eaten across the Mediterranean from Morocco to Egypt. Its presence in Italy is mainly limited to the provinces of Trapani and Sardinia (➤ **cuscus alla trapanese**, ➤ **cascà**, ➤ **fregula**), but has echoes in Livorno and Liguria (➤ **scucuzzu**). Sweet versions also exist (➤ **cuscus duci**).

cuscus alla trapanese or **cuscusu** couscous Trapani-style. Durum grain semolina kneaded by hand with water in a large earthenware bowl (*mafaradda* in dialect) to form small grains. Dressed with salt, pepper, extra virgin olive oil and a chopped onion, it is poured into a *couscoussière* (a special perforated earthenware pot), which is rested over a pan containing boiling water aromatized with bay leaf, parsley, onion and salt. To prevent the steam from escaping, the space between *couscoussière* and pan is sealed with a strip of dough. When ready, the couscous is served with fish stew (➤ **agghiotta di pesce**) after first resting for half an hour soaked in the broth. In San Vito Lo Capo (province of Trapani), a town which stages an annual festival in honor of the dish, they say that the couscous has "to sleep." The dish was brought to the island more than a century ago by Tunisians and Algerians. Sicily.

cuscus duci sweet couscous, a specialty of the nuns of the convent of Santo Spirito in Agrigento. The couscous is served with a cream of pistachio nuts, toasted almonds, chocolate shavings, candied fruit, cinnamon and confectioner's sugar. Sicily.

cuscussiera *couscoussière*. Perforated pan used for cooking couscous (➤ **cuscus**).

cushot Reggio Emilia term for ➤ **violino di pecora**, a cured meat.

cutizza another name for ➤ **cotizza**, a sweet flatbread.

cutturidde aka **cutturiddi** pieces of lamb stewed slowly in an earthenware pot with celery, onion, rosemary, bay leaves, olive oil, chili, tomato and Pecorino cheese. Basilicata, Puglia.

cutumè small fried choux pastry bun made with a dough of flour, ricotta and eggs. Served with warm honey and a sprinkling of powdered cinnamon. The name probably derives from Greek and means "small bundle." Catania, Sicily.

cuz mutton cooked in its own fat and flavored with sage, parsley, and other aromatic herbs. Served immediately or preserved in salt in an earthenware or wood bowl. Typical of Corteno Golgi, in the upper Valacamonica. Lombardy.

cuzzedde aka **cuzzieddi** dialect words for ➤ **cozze piccinne**, snails.

cuzzupa classic Easter cake of lamb- or ring-shaped leavened dough, often garnished with unshelled hard-boiled eggs. In the Catanzaro area, it is also known as ➤ **tortano** or ➤ **piccillato**. A savory version also exists made with pasta dough enriched with suet. Calabria.

dD

dadetti al vincotto another term for ➤ **stuezzi**, almond cakes.

dado bouillon cube.

dadolata diced vegetables, cheese, ham or tongue.

daino fallow deer (*Dama dama*). Deer with a brown coat (grayer in winter) with white spots; the buck has palmate antlers. Common especially in the woods of central Italy and Sardinia. The meat, red in color with a very gamey flavor, cooked in the same ways as chamois, roe deer and red deer venison.

daino in umido fallow deer venison stew. The meat is browned with onions, pancetta, bay leaf and black peppercorns, then cooked slowly in red wine and water with the addition of rosemary, tomato paste and garlic. Umbria.

darmassin another word for ➤ **ramassin**, damson.

dattero word used in Livorno for ➤ **mitilo**, mussel. **decorticare** to decorticate. To remove a hard husk, rind or shell. The term refers in particular to crustaceans.

deglassare *to deglaze, déglacer.* To dilute pan juices by adding wine, broth or cream.

delizie al limone traditional Neapolitan dessert consisting of balls of sponge cake flavored with lemon juice and filled with lemon cream and whipped cream. Campania.

dente, al cooked but firm to the bite. Term used of pasta and rice.

dente di carne another name for ➤ **tarassaco**, dandelion.

dente di leone bristly hawkbit (*Leontodon hispidus*). Spontaneous herb with hairy,

serrated basal leaves. Like spinach, common and popular mainly in northern and central Italy, especially in Liguria and Marche. The term **dente di leone** is also commonly, though improperly, used for ➤ **tarassaco**, dandelion. Common and regional names: ➤ **cicoria di campo**, ➤ **grugno peloso**, ➤ **radicchio di campo**.

dentice Mediterranean dentex (*Dentex dentex*). The member of the Sparidae family most commonly found in Italian waters. May reach a meter in length and five to six pounds in weight. Sold fresh or frozen, whole or in slices, it is cooked whole or filleted like ➤ **orata**, gilthead seabream, and ➤ **cernia**, grouper. Broiled, roast or boiled, it is served with lemon sauce or mayonnaise.

dentice al forno oven-baked dentex. A dish common, with many variations, all round Italy. In Campania they stuff the fish with garlic, parsley, thyme and garden savory and coat it with breadcrumbs, in Puglia they cover it with oil, vinegar and black olives.

dessert the Greeks and Romans were wont to "close" a meal with the likes of pomegranates, chestnuts, walnuts, fava beans, pistachio nuts and dried fruit, and the same custom was revived in the Middle Ages. The sweet dessert first appeared in the 17th century and was codified in France in the 19th (the word derives from the French *desservir*, "to clear the table") as the last important part of any meal, consisting of cheese, fresh fruit and cake or ice-cream. Today a whole range of sweet confections (bavarois, mousses, molds, semifreddi, parfaits, tarts) featuring the most disparate ingredients appear as desserts . The Italian regional repertoire is endless, ranging from the simple ➤ **ciambella** for dipping in sweet wine to the refined and elaborate ➤ **cassata siciliana**.

di centro ➤ term used to describe the production of ➤ **Parmigiano-Reggiano** in the summer, more precisely from July to August.

di coda ➤ term used to describe the production of ➤ **Parmigiano-Reggiano** in the late summer and fall, more precisely from September to November 11. During thw inter, production is described as *invernenga*.

di testa term used to describe the production of ➤ **Parmigiano-Reggiano** in the spring and summer, more precisely from April to June. Also described as *maggese*.

diaframma diaphragm. The large flat muscle that separates the thoracic from the abdominal cavity. The cow's diaphragm—dark red in color and excellent broiled—is popular in Sardinia, where it is known as ➤ **parasangue** or ➤ **parasambene**.

dianet dialect term for earthenware pot, especially of the type used to serve ➤ **bagna caoda**. Piedmont.

diavola, alla in the popular imagination, the term conjures up the punishment of sinners by burning them on red-hot grills and fires of Hell (*diavolo* means "devil in Italian"). It refers to two methods of cooking: i) roasting meat on a red-hot grill to make it crisp (➤ **pollo alla diavola**); ii) the liberal use of red chili to set the diner's mouth "on fire": pizza alla diavola, for example, is topped with abundant fiery chilli-flavored salami or sausage.

diavoletti another word for ➤ **sedani**, type of pasta.

diavolicchi aka **diavolilli** ➤ other words for ➤ **diavolina**.

diavolina colored sprinkles. Tiny multicolored sugar chips used in southern Italian confectionery to decorate cakes.

diavolo di mare literally "sea devil." Term used for ➤ **rana pescatrice**, monkfish, in Veneto and Sicily.

diavulicchi ripieni stuffed chilis. Chilis (➤ **diavulicchi**) macerated in vinegar for one day, filled with a mixture of tuna, anchovies, and capers and preserved in jars in extra virgin olive oil. Puglia.

diavulicchio (aka **diavulicchiu**, **diavulillo**, **diavulillu**) southern dialect words for ➤ **peperoncino**, chili.

diliscare to bone a raw, cooked or dried fish. To bone a raw fish, it is necessary, using a very sharp knife, to slit the belly, remove the entrails and separate the flesh to uncover the backbone (if the fish is large it is easier to cut along the backbone and leave the belly intact). With cooked fish, the task is easier, part and parcel of normal cleaning operations. With dried fish it is necessary to proceed by hand as the blade of the knife would break the dehydrated flesh.

diluire to dilute. To make a liquid less thick. In the kitchen sauces are diluted with gravies and pan juices to make them more fluid, with syrup in sweet confections and with vinegar to control their aroma.

dindo term used in some regions for ➤ **tacchino**, turkey.

diomeneguardi sweet pizza. A thick batter of corn flour, water and salt is spread on a hot plate and baked in the oven. Typical of the province of Viterbo. Lazio.

dischi volanti commercial durum wheat pasta shaped like buttons with a dent in the center. Served in broth or with light meat and tomato sauces.

disidratazione dehydration. Procedure whose results are identical to those of desiccation (➤ **essiccamento**), but achieved quicker thanks to the use of modern tunnels at a temperature of 80°C.

disossare to bone. To remove the bones of meat, poultry, game or fish.

dissalare to desalt. To remove excess preserving salt from a food by prolonged rinsing or immersion in cold water or milk. Water is used to desalt salt cod, stockfish and capers and oil in brine. Milk is widely used to desalt salted, smoked fish inasmuch as it removes the pungent note in the aroma resulting from the smoking process. Some meats, such as salted lardo, are desalted by blanching in water. An exception to the general rule is the salted anchovy whose special aromas are worth not losing entirely: hence the method of removing excess salt from the fish without washing.

dissanguare to bleed. To remove excess blood from an animal during the butchering process. Blood is released by cutting through one of the most important arteries, either the jugular or the arteries that flow to the heart. Pig's blood is gathered immediately and used to make savory and sweet dishes (➤ **sangue**, blood).

dita degli apostoli literally "apostles' fingers." Light egg and water crêpes fried in olive oil, spread with ricotta blended with sugar, dark chocolate chips or candied lime and maraschino or aniseed liqueur, and rolled up. Served dusted with confectioner's sugar and powdered cinnamon. Dessert originally made at Easter, now common all year round. The name refers to its tapered, finger-like shape. Puglia.

ditaletti another name for ➤ **ditalini**, a type of pasta.

ditali short durum wheat pasta tubes with a smooth or grooved surface. The diameter varies from one and a half to three inches. The smaller ones (➤ **ditalini**) are best cooked in broth, whereas larger may be served with light sauces. Also known as ➤ **gnocchetti di ziti**.

ditalini small durum wheat pasta cylinders, either smooth or ridged, similar to ➤ **avemarie**. Other names: ➤ **coralli**, ➤ **ditaletti**, ➤ **gnocchettini**.

ditalini con cozze e patate thick soup of mussels with the addition of garlic, parsley, chilli, potatoes, and pasta such as ➤ **ditalini**. Puglia.

diuneddi southern dialect term for ➤ **frattaglie**, offal.

dòba stew made of large chunks of beef with chopped vegetables, orange zest, nutmeg, tomato and red wine. A specialty of the Provencal valleys of the province of Cuneo. The name derives from the French *daube*. Piedmont.

dobostorte another name for ➤ **torta Dobos**, type of cake.

doganeghin Piedmontese name for ➤ **cotechino**, boiling sausage.

doil container for the aging of cured meats. Once made of chestnut wood, now mostly of steel or plastic. Val d'Aosta.

dolce al torrone semifreddo of nougat, ➤ **mascarpone**, eggs, sugar and dark chocolate, decorated with chocolate shavings. Typical of Cremona. Lombardy.

dolce dei morti baked fingers of flour, yeast, cinnamon, crumbled boiled chestnuts, chopped almonds and pine kernels, vanilla and raisins. Typical of the Casentino area, they used to be made in the fall and sold at stalls in late October and early November. Tuscany.

dolce di carne another name for ➤ **'mpanatigghia**, Sicilian cake.

dolce di pane bread cake. Mixture of day-old bread softened in milk, squeezed and crumbled, amalgamated with yeast, sugar, eggs, orange or lemon zest and raisins soaked in grappa, then baked in the oven. Tuscany.

dolce salame another name for ➤ **salame dolce**, chocolate "salami."

dolceforte, in name given in Tuscany to certain sweet and sour (➤ **agrodolce**) meat dishes (usually wild boar or hare) in which vinegar and wine are mixed with sultanas, pine kernels, dark chocolate and pieces of candied fruit. Tongue is also prepared in the same way: ➤ **lingua in dolceforte**.

dolcetta another name for ➤ **valerianella**, common corn salad.

dolcetto della sposa almond paste cookie filled with ➤ **faldacchiera**, a sort of zabaglione, and iced. Puglia.

dolci di riposto cakes made of almond paste (➤ **pasta reale**), filled with citron preserve, candied pumpkin (➤ **zuccata**) or jam, and decorated with an icing of water, sugar and coloring agents. First baked in convents and monasteries (*riposto* is an archaic term for "pantry" or "sideboard"). Sicily

dolcificare to sweeten.

dolico another word for ➤ **fagiolo dall'occhio**, black-eyed pea.

Dolomiti full-cream cow's milk cheese from one or two milkings. Produced in the province of Trento, it ages 15 days. Trentino-Alto Adige.

dolzegarbo aka **garbodolze** Veneto version of ➤ **agrodolce**, sweet and sour. Mixture of vinegar, onion, spices (cinnamon, cloves, nutmeg, aniseed, cumin, ginger) often with the addition of pine kernels and sultanas (➤ **saor**). Veneto.

donderet occitani tapered gnocchi made from a thick batter of flour, milk, eggs and salt. Served with melted butter and sage. Typical of the Provencal valleys, especially of the Valle Colla, in the province of Cuneo. Piedmont.

dondolo aka ➤ **tartufo di mare** (➤ **vongola**, clam). Clam listed in the Italian Ministry of Agriculture's database of native and/or traditional food products. Friuli-Venezia Giulia.

donzella (1) Mediterranean rainbow wrasse (*Coris julis*), a sea fish of the Labridae family, commonly used in soups and stews. Common and regional names: ➤ **ariula**, ➤ **iriula**, ➤ **viriola**.

donzella (2) another word for ➤ **ficattola**, a small, sweet focaccia. Tuscany.

dorare (1) to brown or bake until golden. Used to refer to baked pasta dishes topped with béchamel or dried breadcrumbs, or meat cooked briefly in a skillet with a knob of butter.

dorare (2) to fry until golden. Refers to the frying of an ingredient previously coated in flour and dipped in beaten eggs. **dorare (3)** to glaze. In confectionery, to give a cake or cookie a glossy finish by brushing with beaten egg or egg white, sometimes mixed with other liquids.

doratura frying technique suitable for various foodstuffs—including vegetables such as zucchini flowers—whereby the ingredient is first coated in flour and dipped in beaten eggs, then fried.

dose dose, amount. In Emilia-Romagna they also use the word to mean a sachet of powdered yeast.

dragoncello tarragon or dragon's wort (*Artemisia dracunculus*), an aromatic herb with fine leaves and a subtle pungent flavor. Widely used in France, in Italy it tends to be reserved to haute cuisine as a flavoring ingredient for sauces, white meats, fish, eggs and vinegar. Also known as ➤ **estragone** and ➤ **serpentaria**.

dragone another word for ➤ **tracina**, greater weever.

dreierle name given to ➤ **pindl** in the Valle Isarco. Trentino-Alto Adige.

droghe synonym of ➤ **spezie**, spices.

drömsat balls of wheat flour served with tomato sauce flavored with basil, pork ribs, mature Pecorino or salted ricotta and, sometimes, chili. A recipe of the ➤ **Arbëreshë** tradition. Calabria.

duchesse small cake consisting of two wafers made of hazelnuts, cocoa, eggs and butter stuck together with a cream of chopped almonds, dark chocolate, sugar and liqueur. Created in the early 20th century by the confectioner Giuseppe Gallarato on his return to his native Canale (province of Cuneo) from a sojourn on the Côte d'Azure. Piedmont.

dudola dialect term for ➤ **giuggiola**, jujube.

duls e brusc sweet and sour (➤ **agrodolce**) sauce made with wine vinegar, sugar, raisins, pine kernels and grated chocolate. Served with stewed meats, especially game. Typical of the province of Piacenza. Emilia-Romagna.

dumega local barley variety used in the area round the village of Teglio, in the Valtellina. Used to make a soup at the start of the week, which was then reheated and enriched day by day with the addition of new ingredients (pig's trotters, pork rind and so on). Lombardy.

durello (pl. **durelli**) aka **durone** (pl. **duroni**) name for the stomachs of poultry (➤ **rigaglie**, giblets).

duroc domestic pig of American origin, the most widely raised in the USA, the result of crosses between Iberian, African and English (Berkshire) breeds. Red or black-and-red and large-framed, it is used mainly to create mixed-breed commercial hogs for the production of cured meats.

eE

e pica sö literally "hit it." Polenta typical of the Bergamo area flavored simply by rubbing it with a smoked herring. A throwback to times of great poverty. Lombardy.

echio viper's bugloss (*Echium vulgare*). Spontaneous herb similar in appearance and flavor (delicate and aromatic) to borage (➤ **borragine**), which it sometimes replaces in the kitchen (in pasta fillings, for example). Gathered and eaten mostly in central Italy, where some dialect and popular names are based on the belief that the herb healed snake bites. Common and regional names include: ➤ **buglossa**, ➤ **erba pelosa**, ➤ **erba serpentina**, ➤ **erba viperina**, ➤ **lingua di bove**.

eliche literally "helixes," a commercial short dry durum wheat pasta. Of northern origin, it is shaped like a double helix. Goes well with various sauces, especially those made with tomato, aromatic herbs and ricotta. Also known as ➤ **fusilli a elica**.

elicoidali literally "helicoids." A commercial short dried durum wheat pasta. Slightly curved ridged tubes with a diameter of about three inches, reminiscent of ➤ **tortiglioni**. Served with rich tomato and meat sauces.

elvezia literally "Helvetia," a cake that combines Swiss tradition with the art of Mantuan confectionery. Three disks of almond paste, egg whites and sugar are baked in the oven until golden. They are then cooled and placed on top of each other with layers of creamed butter, zabaglione and dark chocolate chips in between. The top is coated with almond chips. Lombardy.

emulsionare to emulsify (➤ **emulsione**, emulsion).

emulsione emulsion. Blend of two or more liquids that tend to separate, created by mixing vigorously. To stabilize an emulsion it is necessary to add a binding agent such as an egg yolk, as in the case of mayonnaise (➤ **maionese**).

entrecôte the French term, sometimes referred to as ➤ **fracosta** in Italian, refers not only to a slice of meat cut between one rib and another of the loin of a cow, but also to a rib steak on the bone.

eporediesi small finger cookies, hard on the outside and soft on the inside, made of chopped hazelnuts, sugar, cocoa and egg whites, and liberally dusted with sugar. A specialty of Ivrea. The name derives from Eporedia, the Roman name for the town, and also refers to its inhabitants. Piedmont.

equino equine. Refers to the horse (*Equus caballus*), the donkey (*Equus asinus*) and their hybrids (the mule and the hinny).

erba acciuga regional term for ➤ **origano**, oregano.

erba agretta regional term for ➤ **acetosa**, sorrel.

erba amara another term for ➤ **erba di san Pietro**, costmary. In Veneto, the term (➤ **erba maresina** in dialect) also refers to ➤ **partenio**, feverfew.

erba borsa regional term for ➤ **borsa del pastore**, shepherd's purse.

erba brusca dialect term for ➤ **acetosa**, sorrel.

erba buona regional term for ➤ **erba di san Pietro**, costmary.

erba caciola Marche term for ➤ **erba di san Pietro**, costmary.

erba cannona regional term for ➤ **barba di capra**, goatsbeard.

erba cedrina common name for ➤ **melissa**, lemon balm.

erba cerea Piedmontese term for ➤ **santoreggia**, garden savory.

erba cimicina regional term for ➤ **coriandolo**, coriander.

erba cipollina chives (*Allium schoenoprasum*). A subspontaneous herb, one of the essential French *fines herbes*. In Italy used chopped in omelets, salads, butter and cream cheeses, and whole as a garnish. Common and regional names: ➤ **aglio cipollino**, ➤ **cipolla porrata**, ➤ **erba di Provenza**, ➤ **porro sottile**.

erba cucca regional term for ➤ **acetosa**, sorrel.

erba da scorbuto regional term for ➤ **cren**, horseradish.

erba dei cinque nervi regional term for ➤ **piantaggine**, ribwort plantain.

erba dei porci regional term for ➤ **porcellana**, little hogweed.

erba del cucco regional term for ➤ **silene rigonfia**, bladder campion.

erba di mare regional term for ➤ **finocchio marino**, sea fennel.

erba di Provenza regional term for ➤ **erba cipollina**, chives.

erba di san Lorenzo regional term for ➤ **consolida maggiore**, comfrey.

erba di san Pietro costmary (*Balsamita major* synon. *Chrysanthemum balsamita*). Perennial herb with tall stems and long, broad leaves, commonly cultivated in kitchen gardens or vases. Thanks to its intensely aromatic, minty flavor, a popular ingredient in omelets, frittatas (➤ **frittata di balsamita**) and vegetable pies and pastries (➤ **casoncelli**, ➤ **tortelli amari di Castelgoffredo**). In the area of Jesi, in the Marche, where it is traditionally used to mature Pecorino, it is called ➤ **erba caciola**, literally "cheese grass." Common and regional names: ➤ **amarella**, ➤ **erba amara**, ➤ **erba buona**, ➤ **erba caciola**, ➤ **erba di santa Maria**.

erba di santa Maria regional term for ➤ **erba di san Pietro**, costmary.

erba grassa regional term for ➤ **porcellana**, little hogweed.

erba limonina regional term for ➤ **melissa**, lemon balm.

erba luigia aka **erba luisa** common name for ➤ **melissa**, lemon balm.

erba macchiata regional term for ➤ **polmonaria**, common lungwort.

erba maresina Veneto term for ➤ **partenio**, feverfew.

erba pelosa regional term for ➤ **borragine**, borage, but also for ➤ **echio**, viper's bugloss.

erba pepe regional term for ➤ **santoreggia**, garden savory.

erba rugo regional term for ➤ **rucola selvatica**, perennial wallrocket.

erba sacra regional term for ➤ **salvia**, sage.

erba salina regional term for ➤ **acetosa**, sorrel.

erba sana regional term for ➤ **buon enrico**, good King Henry.

erba savia regional term for ➤ **salvia**, sage.

erba serpentina regional term for ➤ **echio**, viper's bugloss.

erba spezia regional term for ➤ **salvastrella**, small burnet.

erba stella depending on the region, another name for ➤ **cerfoglio**, chervil, ➤ **ioseride**, perennial hyoseris, or ➤ **salvastrella**, small burnet.

erba striscia regional term for ➤ **silene rigonfia**, bladder campion.

erba viperina regional term for ➤ **echio**, viper's bugloss.

erbadèla another name for ➤ **barbotta (2)**, a sort of focaccia.

erbarelle term used to describe a mixture of spontaneous herbs (including wild chicory, field sowthistle, dandelion leaves, rampion, common brighteyes, ribwort plantain and common cornsalad) used to make soups (➤ **acquacotta con le erbarelle**), but also eaten raw in salads (➤ **misticanza**). Lazio.

erbazzone a flagship recipe of the province of Reggio Emilia. A savory pie consisting of two thin layers of pastry filled with a mixture of chard, Parmigiano and herbs (sometimes rice too), bound with egg. Usually baked in the oven, but fried versions also exist. The senior citizens of Reggio call the pie ➤ **scarpazzoun**. Emilia-Romagna.

erbe aromatiche aromatic herbs. Cultivated and wild herbs used in the kitchen to heighten and enhance the flavors of dishes. The most common are included in the bouquet garni (➤ **mazzetto odoroso**), others are essential for single dishes or recipes, which often include them in their names. Many can be dried or frozen, most change their aroma during the cooking process. Save for the most common (parsley, sage, rosemary, basil, bay leaf), the use of aromatic herbs is closely tied to local tradition. Thyme, for example, grows all over Italy but is hard to find in recipes, though wild thyme (➤ **serpillo**) is popular in Tuscany, where it is known as ➤ **pepolino**. For a long time, marjoram was used almost exclusively in Liguria, and myrtle is hardly known outside Sardinia. Many Lazio recipes, finally, feature pennyroyal.

erbe fini Italian translation of *fines herbes*, the fine herbs—parsley, chervil, chives, and tarragon—used in French cuisine to flavor omelets and other dishes.

erbe selvatiche wild herbs. Herbaceous plants that grow spontaneously and have always been gathered and used for gastronomic purposes. In Italy, the choice of varieties varies from place to place. Some species (field sowthistle, common brighteyes, wild and bladder campion, for example) are universal, others, such as black bryony, wild mustard, feverfew and nettles are limited to specific, well-defined geographical areas. Many Italian regions have words to describe wild herbs in general or certain combinations thereof: ➤ **cucina**, ➤ **erbi**, ➤ **erbi boni**, ➤ **erbucci**, ➤ **erbarelle**, ➤ **fogghie**, ➤ **gattafin**, ➤ **litump**, ➤ **misticanza**, ➤ **preboggion**.

erbetta (pl. **erbette**) generic northern Italian word for > **bietola**, chard.

erbi aka **erbetti** aka **erbi boni** terms used in the Garfagnana and Lunigiana areas (and eastern Liguria) for a number of spontaneous herbs used in the spring in a variety of soups, pies, omelets and pasta fillings (➤ **minestrella di Gallicano**, spring vegetable soup). Tuscany.

erborinatura process whereby the body of a cheese is streaked with blue or gray-green veining due to the presence of mold. The term is derived from the Lombard dialect word *erborin*, meaning "parsley," with obvious reference to the color of the streaks. In Italian, a blue or veined cheese is known as a *formaggio erborinato*.

erbucci wild herbs. Term used in the Versilia area for a mixture of spontaneous summer herbs (including dandelion, wild chicory, borage, bladder campion, field sowthistle and so on) eaten raw in salads, boiled and finished in the frying pan with oil or butter, and in soups. Tuscany.

erbuzzu another name for ➤ **ministru**, Sardinian potato and bean soup.

Erdäpfelblattln potato fritters, generally served with ➤ **crauti**, sauerkraut. Trentino-Alto Adige.

ericini name given to > **dolci di riposto**, marzipan cakes, typical of Erice, in the province of Trapani. Sicily.

ertuti stew of beans, chickpeas, lentils, fava beans and spelt, with the addition of finely chopped prosciutto and pancetta, pieces of salami and tomato. Served with slices of brown bread. In Alatri, in the province of Frosinone, it used to be served to pilgrims attending the feast of the town's patron saint, San Sisto. Lazio.

Escarun sheep's or goat's cheese of Provençal origin, produced in the village of Farigliano, in the province of Cuneo, using techniques similar to those used to make ➤ **Castelmagno**. Piedmont

esofago oesophagus. Channel which permits the passage of food from the upper portion of the digestive apparatus to the the stomach (in the case of ruminants, to the prestomachs). It is situated behind the trachea and both are included in the offal known as ➤ **corata** and ➤ **coratella**. May be eaten on its own, boiled and sliced or together with certain types of tripe (➤ **trippa**).

esse large crumbly "S"-shaped cookies, made from a paste of flour, yeast, eggs, sugar, butter, milk and aniseed liqueur, grooved on the surface and coated with sugar. Traditionally baked in families at Easter and Christmas. Today they can be bought in confectionery shops and bakeries in the Lessinia, Bassa veronese, Polesine (especially in the town of Adria) and Venice lagoon areas. Veneto.

esse di Raveo vanilla-flavored shortcrust pastry cookies baked for the last century or so in the village of Raveo, in the Carnia district. Albeit "S"-shaped too, they are finer than the Veneto cookies of the same name and are not grooved on the surface. Friuli.

essiccamento desiccation. Technique for preserving fresh foodstuffs by exposing them to the sun and/or air. Already adopted in ancient times, today it is used to for artisan preparations, such as sun-dried tomatoes, and the domestic preservation of seasonal fruits, such as peaches, plums, apricots, figs, apples and pears, which are sun-dried over grates. The most obvious example of desiccation is that of stockfish (➤ **stoccafisso**). The flavor and aroma of desiccated foods changes as a result of oxidization and loss of water.

estragone common name for ➤ **dragoncello**, tarragon.

estratto extract. Concentrate of animal or vegetable susbtances classified and regulated by law. In the kitchen, meat extract (discovered by the German Liebig) must be obtained from beef through processes of extraction (with hot water or steam) of the nutritional principles, filtration and concentration. The resulting brown paste is seasoned with salt and stored in jars.

fF

facci i vecchia coarse-grained focaccia topped with oil and oregano. Sicily.

facciuni one of the many Sicilian cakes that originated in the island's convents. It owes its odd name (literally "large face") to its colored wrapping paper, which bears the face of an angel. The cake itself consists of two sponge disks, one spread with citron marmalade, the other with orange marmalade, coated with almond paste (➤ **pasta reale (1)**), glazed with chocolate icing, and decorated with confetti sugar (➤ **diavolina**). Typical of the provinces of Ragusa and Siracusa. Sicily.

facioli in greppa soup of wild fennel and beans with tomato, garlic and toasted bread, anointed with extra virgin olive oil. Typical of Viterbo and surrounds. The term *greppa* derives from the Latin *grippus*, meaning a "pile" or "mound," and in this case refers to the way the beans are ladled over the bread and the thick texture of the soup. Lazio.

fae e fogghie Puglia dialect term for ➤ **'ncapriata**, fava bean purée and wild chicory.

fagiano pheasant (*Phasianus colchicus*). Large bird of the Galliformes with a small head and long tail; the plumage of the male is particularly beautiful. The bird arrived in Europe from the Caucasus in ancient times and was subsequently crossed with the Chinese ring-necked pheasant (*Phasianus torquatus*). The commonest and most popular game bird, it is also one of the most easily domesticated. Wild birds should be gutted, hung for three to five days, then plucked. Males, whose meat is drier than that of females, should be barded with slices of lardo or bacon before roasting. For older birds the best method of cooking is ➤ **salmì**. The meat of the pheasant is also used to make mousses and pâtés.

fagiano alla ghiotta pheasant and its giblets stewed in a casserole with sage and rosemary, thin strips of prosciutto, red wine and broth. When the bird is tender, it is jointed and divided into portions. In the meantime, the innards are minced and amalgamated with the cooking juices to form a thick sauce, which is then poured over the meat. The dish is served with slices of toasted bread. The same recipe is used for ➤ **faraona**, guinea fowl. Umbria.

fagiano con l'uvetta pheasant with raisins. The bird is cut into pieces and cooked in a thick mixture of breadcrumbs, broth and raisins. Piedmont.

fagiano di monte another name for ➤ **gallo forcello**, black grouse.

fagiano in salmì roast pheasant. First the cavity is flavored with garlic, rosemary, sage and bay leaf, then the bird is wrapped in slices of pancetta, browned whole with other herbs and roast in the oven. The chopped liver, gently fried with herbs and flambéed with brandy, is added to the cooking juices, and the mixture is then pushed through a sieve to form a thick sauce, which is poured over the jointed pheasant. Piedmont.

fagiano lardellato larded pheasant. After being plucked and gutted, the bird is stuffed with a mixture of finely chopped pancetta, prosciutto, sage, salt and pepper. It is then wrapped in slices of fatty prosciutto or lardo. Tuscany.

fagiano ripieno stuffed pheasant. The bird is stuffed with chopped sausage meat, ground lean veal, chicken livers, aromatic herbs, eggs and breadcrumbs soaked in grappa, wrapped in slices of pancetta or fatty prosciutto and roast in the oven. Veneto, Friuli-Venezia Giulia.

fagiola aka **fagiolana** names for traditional bean varieties: *fagiola garfagnina, fagiola schiacciona* (Tuscany), *fagiolana della Val Borbera* (Piedmont), *fagiolana di Torza* (Liguria).

fagiolata fresh beans boiled with pork rind and onion, then left to simmer with tomatoes and herbs. Piedmont.

fagiolina del Lago Trasimeno small brown, black, salmon-pink or white oval bean with a soft texture and buttery taste. Protected by a Slow Food presidium and cultivated exclusively on small plots of land round Lake Trasimeno. Umbria.

fagiolino (pl. **fagiolini**) (1) runner bean (*Phaseolus vulgaris*). Also known as ➤ **cornetto**. Yellow varieties also exist, such as *meraviglia di Venezia*, included in the Italian Ministry of Agriculture's database of native and/or traditional products, together with the *stortino* and the *fagiolo stringa* (or *serpente*) *di Lucca*. Another variety is the large, flat, yellowish *fagiolino a corallo*, which is very popular in Lazio, in Rome in particular (➤ **fagioli a corallo**). Traditional dishes include ➤ **fagiolini al pomodoro** (runner beans with tomato), the Campania side dish ➤ **cicci e baine** (cannellini and runner beans), the Venetian ➤ **cornetti in salsa** (runner beans with anchovy), and the ➤ **polpettone genovese** (vegetable loaf) of Liguria, a region where ➤ **trenette** are traditionally served with ➤ **pesto**, potatoes and

runner beans. The Italian regions that grow most runner beans are: Campania, Emilia-Romagna, Veneto, Lazio and Piedmont.

fagiolini another name for ➤ **sedani**, a type of pasta.

fagiolini al pomodoro runner beans with tomato. The beans are stewed for an hour or so with chopped vegetables (tomato, celery, carrot, onion, garlic, parsley, basil), olive oil, salt and pepper, and generally served as a side dish. Various regional variations exist. In Tuscany, they cook long, thin *fagiolini di sant'Anna*, also known as *serpenti* or *stringhe*, in tomato with garlic and oil; in the Marche, they flavor the beans with pennyroyal; in Friuli-Venezia Giulia, they add paprika; in Lazio and Puglia, finally, they pre-boil the beans and stew them in tomato, garlic, parsley, pennyroyal and chili.

fagiolini alla genovese boiled runner beans flavored with crushed garlic, parsley, and anchovy fillets dissolved in olive oil. Liguria.

fagiolo (pl. **fagioli**) bean (*Phaseolus vulgaris*). Legume brought to Europe from Central America. The varieties most used in Italian belong to the ➤ **borlotto** and ➤ **cannellino** groups, and are eaten fresh, harvested during the summer, or dried, harvested in the fall. Fresh beans are sold in their pods, dried beans are sold loose or in sealed packages (and like other legumes have to be soaked in water for at least half a day before use). Beans are also commercialized in cans, jars and cartons. Since its arrival in Italy, the bean has played a leading role in popular cooking in every region, especially Tuscany and Veneto. One dish in particular, ➤ **pasta e fagioli**, pasta and beans, is found all over the country, naturally with regional variations. Italy's PGI varieties are: ➤ **fagiolo di Lamon** (Belluno, Veneto), ➤ **fagiolo di Sorana** (near Pescia, province of Pistoia, Tuscany), ➤ **fagiolo di Sarconi** (province of Potenza, Basilicata). A hundred or so beans are listed in the Italian Ministry of Agriculture's database of native and/or traditional food products. They are: *fagioli a olio, fagioli a pane, tondino del Tavo* (Abruzzo); *fagiolo di Caria, poverello bianco* (Calabria); *fagioli lardari, fagioli quarantini, fagioli tabacchini, fagiolo a formella, fagiolo di Controne, fagiolo di Villaricca, fagiolo di Volturara Irpinia, fagiolo striato del Vallo di Diano, tondino bianco del Vallo di Diano* (Campania); *borlotti di Carnia, borlotto di Pesariis, cesarins, fagiolo del santisim, fagiolo dal voglut, fagiolo laurons, militons* (Friuli-Venezia Giulia); *fagiolina arsolana, fagiolo a pisello, borbontino, cannellino di Atina, cappellette di Vallepietra, ciavattone piccolo, cioncone, fagiolo del purgatorio di Gradoli, fagiolo di Sutri, gentile di Labro, fagiolo giallo, regina di Marano Equo, solfarino, verdolino, fagiolone di Vallepietra* (Lazio); *fagiolana di Torza, borlotto di Mangia, cannellino della Val di Vara, cenerino della Val di Vara, fagioli bianchi,* ➤ **fagioli di Badalucco, Conio e Pigna,** *gianetto, lupinaro, rampicante basso di Pignone* (Liguria); *fagiolo borlotto di Gambolò, fasolo gnoco borlotto lingua di fuoco* (Lombardy); *fagioli di Riccia, fagiolo bianco, fagiolo scuro* (Molise); *fagiolana della Val Borbera, fagioli di Cuneo, fagiolo di Saluggia* (Piedmont); *fagiolo dei Monti Dauni meridionali* (Puglia); ➤ **fagiolo badda di Polizzi** (Sicily); *fagiola garfagnina, schiacciona, fagiolo aquila, borlotto di Maremma, borlotto nano di Sorano, borlotto nostrale, burro toscano, cannellino del San Ginese-Compitese, cannellino di Sorano, cappone, coco nano, decimino, fagiolo dell'Amiata, fagiolo di Bigliolo, fa-*

giolo di Zeri, fico di Gallicano, giallorino della Garfagnana, fagiolo malato, marconi a seme nero, mascherino, massese, piattella frisona, pievarino, romano, rosso di Lucca, schiaccione, scritto della Garfagnana, scritto di Lucca, turco di Castello, fagiolo zolfino (Tuscany); *fagiolo giallo e verdino di Cave,* ➤ **fagiolina del Lago Trasimeno** (Umbria); *borlotto nano di Levada, fagiolo scalda di Posina, fasol del lago, fasol gialet, fasola posenata, fasolo gnoco borlotto lingua di fuoco* (Veneto).

fagioli a corallo side dish of broad flat runner beans (➤ **fagiolino**) stewed in a skillet in extra virgin olive oil with garlic and chopped tomatoes and garnished with minced parsley. Lazio.

fagioli al fiasco an old peasant dish. A large wine flask or carafe with a woven straw base is filled with unsoaked cannellini beans, peeled garlic cloves, sage leaves, extra virgin olive oil and water, sealed with a cap and string, and placed in hot ashes on the edge of the fireplace for an hour, then moved to the hot embers. The beans are ready when they start to break up and all the liquid has been absorbed. Tuscany.

fagioli all'uccelletto cannellini (➤ **cannellino**) or round white toscanelli beans simmered in salted water aromatized with rosemary and garlic, then finished off in an earthenware pot with crushed garlic, sage, rosemary, puréed tomatoes, salt and pepper. Drizzled with extra virgin olive oil, the dish often accompanies meat dishes and sausage. A classic of the region's cuisine. Tuscany.

fagioli alla maruzzara soup of cannellini or ➤ **spollichini** beans, celery, ripe tomatoes, garlic, oregano and chili. Served with toasted bread (➤**palata abbrustolito al forno**), the soup owes its name to the fact that, in the past, it also included earth snails (*maruzze* in dialect). Campania.

fagioli alla smolz beans (➤ **borlotto** or similar) boiled and flavored with a mixture of lardo and onion gently fried in butter butter and a dash of vinegar, and bound with flour. Friuli-Venezia Giulia.

fagioli di Badalucco, Conio e Pigna beans of different shapes and sizes, but all soft and fleshy, cultivated on hill terraces in the west of the region. Excellent both fresh and dried, they are best enjoyed with the classic goat dish of the area ➤ **capra e fagioli**. A Slow Food presidium is working to improve their distribution. Liguria.

fagioli grassi soup of beans and pork leftovers, flavored with cinnamon and cloves. Typical of the Canavese district. Piedmont.

fagioli in inzimino boiled beans and shredded, trimmed Swiss chard gently stewed with garlic, oil and chopped skinned tomatoes. Typical of the Chianti area. Tuscany.

fagioli in salsa fresh ➤ **borlotto** beans boiled and dressed with a hot mixture of desalted anchovies, onion and aromatic herbs, gently fried in lardo with cinnamon and pepper, and diluted with vinegar. Veneto.

fagioli in umido bean stew. Beans stewed with lightly fried onions, diced prosciutto (or sausage or strips of pork rind), wine (in Friuli-Venezia Giulia and Umbria) and skinned tomatoes. A classic peasant dish common, with variations, all over Italy.

fagioli nel tiano dried beans soaked overnight and cooked slowly with celery, onion and salt in a traditional earthenware pot (➤ **tiana**, ➤ **tiano**) by the fire. Served anointed with extra virgin olive oil and the addition of a sauce of cherry tomatoes, pancetta and chili or, in season, porcini mushrooms. Calabria.

fagioli rifatti nell'unto di arista boiled beans finished off in the juices from pork loin (➤ **arista**) browned in the pan with crushed garlic, sage and bay leaves. A simple, traditional way of flavoring the legume. Tuscany.

fagioli zolfini sul pane beans on toast. The small, round yellow *zolfino* bean (aka *burrino*) is traditionally cultivated in the provinces of Florence and Arezzo, between the Arno and Pratomagno rivers. Its thin skin and thick, creamy flesh make it ideal for eating fresh or puréed. In this recipe, it is simply boiled, spooned over slices of toasted bread and anointed with extra virgin olive oil. Tuscany.

fagiolo a formella flat button-like bean with a delicate flavor. Campania.

fagiolo badda di Polizzi small round bean (hence the name, *badda* meaning "small ball" in Sicilian dialect), white with pink-orange or purple streaks. The beans are sowed in the first half of June in domestic kitchen gardens in the Madonie mountains; at lower altitudes, sowing is postponed to the second half of July, when the summer heat begins to abate. Beans to be eaten fresh are harvested after a couple of months, whereas those to be dried are only picked when their pods are about to open naturally. Cooked in stews and soups, the beans have a distinctive flavor with notes of almond and chestnut. Production is very limited and is protected by a Slow Food presidium. Sicily.

fagiolo bianco di Spagna scarlet runner bean (*Phaseolus coccineus*). Produces large flat green pods with kidney-shaped white beans. Well acclimatized in Italy, especially in the north, thanks to its resistance to rigid temperatures. Widely used in soups, salads and purées.

fagiolo dall'occhio aka **fagiolo dell'occhio** aka **fagiolo dolico** black-eyed pea. Legume introduced to Europe from Africa in ancient times. Thus named for its characteristic black spot, similar to the pupil of an eye. The Ministry of Agriculture's database of native and/or traditional food products lists the following varieties: *fagiolo dall'occhio* aka *fagiolo gentile* aka *cornetto* (Tuscany), *fagiolo dall'occhio* (Campania), *fagiolo dell'aquila di Pignone* and *fagiolo dall'occhio rosso* (Liguria). Whiter, smaller and more bitter than common beans, the black-eyed pea is harvested in the fall. If it is harvested in the summer, it is possible to eat the whole pod.

fagiolo di Lamon della vallata bellunese PGI bean produced in 21 communes of the province of Belluno. Four varieties are covered by the denomination: *spagnolo*, oval-shaped with red stripes; *colonega*, oval and flat in shape; *canalino*, with a thick skin; *spagnolit*, round with a thin skin. Veneto.

fagiolo di Sarconi name that applies to PGI ➤ **cannellino** and ➤ **borlotto** beans cultivated in some areas of the province of Potenza. Eaten both fresh and dried, they have a delicate flavor and cook very quickly. Basilicata.

fagiolo di Sorana small, flat PGI bean with a very thin skin. Tasty and easy to digest, it is cultivated on a few acres of land reclaimed by the Medici on the banks of the river Pescia in the province of Pistoia. After being hand-picked, it is dried in the sun for three to four days. Stored in special containers with the addition of peppercorns and valerian roots or bay leaves, it is protected by a Slow Food presidium. Tuscany.

fagiolo mangiatutto another name for ➤ **fagiolino**, runner bean.

fagopiro synonym of ➤ **grano saraceno**, buckwheat.

fagottino bundle or parcel. Term to describe pastas or crêpes that contain a stuffing. Slices of meat that contain a stuffing are called ➤ **involtini**.

fagottino di melanzane eggplant faggots. Fried slices of egg plant, filled with linguine or spaghetti in a sauce of tomato, ricotta and mozzarella, folded over and baked in the oven topped with tomato sauce, basil and mozzarella. Campania.

fainâ Ligurian term for ➤ **farinata**, chickpea focaccia.

faldacchiera a sort of ➤ **zabaglione** of egg yolk and sugar cooked in a bain-marie. Used to fill ➤ **pesce natalizio** and ➤ **agnello pasquale**. Puglia.

faldìa breaded horsemeat chop, typical of Piacenza. Emilia-Romagna.

falia large loaf typical of the province of Latina. Made with sourdough, ➤ **biga** (raising flour), water, and extra virgin olive oil. Lazio.

Fallone di Gravina cheese typical of Gravina, in the province of Bari. Made with ewe's milk (85-90%) and goat's milk (10-15%). Highly perishable, it has to be eaten on the day of production. Puglia.

falloppe Puglia term for ➤ **novellame di pesce**, fry.

falsomagro another word for ➤ **bruciuluni**, Sicilian meat roll.

famigliola buona common name for ➤ **chiodino**, honey armillary mushroom.

famiòla Piedmontese dialect word for ➤ **chiodino**, honey armillary mushroom.

famiole al verde small honey armillary mushrooms first boiled, then finished with oil, garlic and abundant minced parsley. Typical of the Monferrato hills, in the province of Asti. Piedmont.

famiòle fritte fried honey armillary mushrooms. The mushroom caps are first boiled, then coated in corn flour and fried. Piedmont.

fanfolo Sicilian term for ➤ **pesce pilota**, pilot fish.

fantoccia holiday cake made of wheat flour, yeast, eggs, sugar, butter and grated lemon zest. The mixture is left to rest for a couple of hours, rolled out, shaped like a Befana, decorated with colored sugared almonds and baked in the oven. Tuscany.

faòlo Ligurian dialect term for ➤ **grancevola**, spider crab.

faraona aka **gallina faraona** aka **gallina di Numidia** guinea fowl, a descendant of wild African species. The first domestic varieties, bred by the Greeks and Romans, became extinct at the beginning of the Christian era. The bird reappeared in Europe in the era of the great voyages of exploration, when Portuguese navigators brought new specimens back from Guinea, in Africa. Today the bird is bred intensively, both in the open and in battery farms. Its meat can be adapted to the same recipes as chicken and pheasant. The most famous exclusively guinea fowl recipe is the ancient ➤ **faraona alla creta**, but the bird can also be cooked ➤ **al cartoccio** (*en papillote*), ➤ **in umido** (stewed), or roast with special condiments, as in the case of the historic ➤ **faraona in salsa peverada** (➤ **pollame**, poultry). The Italian Ministry of Agriculture's list of native and/or traditional food products includes two varieties of guinea fowl bred in Veneto: *camosciata* and *faraona di corte padovana*.

faraona al coccio guinea fowl in the pot. The bird, its cavity stuffed with rosemary, sage, garlic cloves, salt pepper and slices of pancetta, is cooked whole in oil and lard in a traditional earthenware pot.

Specialty of the village of Fratte Rosa, in the Valle del Cesano, in the province of Pesaro e Urbino. Marche.

faraona alla creta guinea fowl baked in clay. The bird is seasoned with salt, flavored with rosemary, rubbed with butter or lard, wrapped in greaseproof paper, smothered with soft clay and baked in the oven. The clay crust is then broken and the bird cut into portions for serving. A specialty of the area between Piacenza and Cremona. In Valcuvia, in the Lombard province of Varese, they make the same dish using the same techniques, but flavor the bird with oregano, rosemary and sage. Emilia-Romagna, Lombardy.

faraona con le olive guinea fowl with olives. The bird is jointed and browned in oil, to which chopped onion, sage and pitted black olives are added. Finished with Marsala and tomato paste, the dish is served with slices of fried polenta. Tuscany.

faraona in salsa di fegatini guinea fowl with chicken liver sauce. The bird is stuffed with minced garlic and sage and barded with slices of pancetta before being cooked with its own giblets and chopped chicken livers. It is served with a sauce made of the pan residues diluted with lemon juice. Typical of the Langa hills. Piedmont.

faraona in salsa peverada jointed guinea fowl roast in the oven with herbs and white wine. Served with ➤ **peverada** sauce, amalgamated with the pan juices and white polenta. One of the region's flagship dishes. Veneto.

faraona ripiena stuffed guinea fowl. The bird is boned and stuffed with a mixture of sausage, cheese, eggs, herbs and nutmeg, browned in butter and oil, bathed with brandy and Marsala, and cooked through. Served with the pan juices, deglaced and thickened with flour, a little broth and brandy. Piedmont.

farcia Italianization of the French *farce*. A stuffing composed of various ingredients, amalgamated by chopping finely and puréeing, with a smoother, more homogeneous texture than a → **ripieno**, which also means "stuffing" or "filling."

farciò sweet fritters made from a batter of milk, eggs, flour, butter and salt, fried, a tablespoonful at a time, in hot oil, then coated in sugar. Typical of the province of Alessandria. Piedmont.

farcire (1) to stuff a foodstuff (meat, fish, vegetable) with a *farce* (→ **farcia**).

farcire (2) (in confectionery) to spread a custard, cream or jam on disks of sponge cake or similar (before placing the disks one on top of the other to create a sandwich cake).

farecchiata a thick porridge made by mixing the flour of wild peas (→ **roveja**) with water. Flavored with garlic and anchovies. Umbria.

farfalle "butterflies." Butterfly- or bow-shaped commercial dried durum wheat pasta with crenellated ends. Common in northern Italy and available in different sizes. The smallest (→ **farfalline**) are cooked and served in broth. Larger sizes are best enjoyed with tomato sauces or cream- and butter-based sauces. Other names: → **farfalline**, → **farfalloni**.

farfalle genovesi kind of → **farfalle**, a type of pasta, in which all the edges are crenellated.

farfalline "little butterflies." Dried egg dried pasta made of small oval disks pinched at the center with crenellated ends. Usually served in broth. Other names: → **canestri**, → **crestine**, → **nastrini**, → **tripolini**.

farfalloni large → **farfalle**, type of pasta.

farina (1) flour. Produced by grinding (→ **macinazione**) seeds or dried fruits (cereals, legumes such as chickpeas, peas or beans, chestnuts etc.) and, by extension, other substances such as meat, fish or bones. The word derives from the Latin *far* (→ **farro**), emmer wheat, much cultivated in pre-Roman and Roman times.

farina (2) aka **farina bianca** flour. In current Italian usage, the term refers to wheat flour. Other kinds of flour are specified by type: → **farina di mais** (corn flour), → **farina di ceci** (chickpea flour), → **farina di castagne** (chestnut flour) etc. Wheat flours or meals (**sfarinati**) are divided into two categories: durum wheat semolinas (→ **semola**), used mainly to make pasta, and soft wheat flours, used to make bread, cakes and pastries.

farina bramata coarse-grained corn flour (→ **farina di mais**).

farina di castagne chestnut flour. Made by grinding dried chestnuts, in poor mountain areas it used to be used in lieu of cereal flours, even to make bread (→ **marocca di Casola**). Still popular are homemade pastas prepared from variable percentages of wheat and chestnut flours (→ **pasta bastarda**), and a PDO chestnut flour is still produced in the province of Lucca (→ **farina di neccio della Garfagnana**). The Italian Ministry of Agriculture's database of native and/or traditional food products lists the following chestnut flours: *carpinese, della Lunigiana, dell'Amiata, del Pratomagno, di Antona, di Prato, pistoiese, di Villa Basilica* (Tuscany); *di Granaglione* (Emilia-Romagna); *farina di marroni* (Lazio), and those of Liguria and Calabria. The same regions boast numerous chestnut flour recipes: → **castagnaccio**, → **neccio**, → **pattona**, → **polenta di castagne**, plus a myriad of local cakes and pastries, baked or fried (→ **fritloc**,

➤ **menni**, ➤ **mietti**, ➤ **mistocchine**, ➤ **squadatieddri**, ➤ **tamplun**).

farina di ceci chickpea flour. Flour made by grinding dried chickpeas, used especially in Liguria, southern Piedmont and Tuscany to make flatbreads and purées ➤ **cecina**, ➤ **farinata**, ➤ **panizza**. In Puglia *farnedd* (dialect for *farinella*, which is also the name for the Carnival masque in Putignano, in the province of Bari) as a toasted flour of oats and chickpeas. In Sicily they use chickpea flour to make ➤ **panelle**, fritters.

farina di frumento aka **farina di grano** wheat flour (➤ **farina (2)**).

farina di grano duro durum wheat flour.

farina di granturco corn flour (➤ **farina di mais**).

farina di mais aka **farina gialla** cornflour. Flour made by grinding corn or maize to fine, medium and coarse consistencies (➤ **fioretto**). Flour is also made from white corn, especially in Veneto and Friuli. In Italy, the most common way of using cornflour is to make ➤ **polenta**, in particular in northern Italy. It is also used to make cakes and pastries. The Italian Ministry of Agriculture's database of native and/or traditional food products lists: *farina per polenta tradizionale di Langa, farine (di mais, grano tenero, grano saraceno, castagne) della Valle Vermenagna* (Piedmont); *farina per polenta della Bergamasca* (Lombardy); *farina per polenta di mais sponcio, rostrato, pignol* aka *pignol fiorentin, farina di* ➤ **mais biancoperla**, *farina di mais* ➤ **marano** (Veneto), *farina di granturco quarantino nostrano del Maceratese* (Marche).

farina di neccio della Garfagnana PDO chestnut flour traditionally produced in the Garfagnana district of northern Tuscany. The chestnuts (eight local varieties cultivated in and around 22 towns and villages in the province of Lucca) are dried for 40 days in small stone buildings known as *metati*, skinned and stoneground. The flour is white to dark ivory in color and the flavor is sweet with a bitterish aftertaste. Tuscany.

farina di segale rye flour. According to the degree of sifting or bolting, classified as dark, semi-white and white. Rye bread, now invariably made by blending rye and wheat flours, is brown in color and high in fibers. Very common in Alto Adige (➤ **apfelbrot**, ➤ **breatl**, ➤ **pearl**, ➤ **segalino**, to name but a few varieties), rye bread also survives in some Piedmontese mountain areas (➤ **pane barbarià**, ➤ **pane nero di Coimo**), and throughout the Val d'Aosta. In the same areas, fresh pastas are made with rye flour: ➤ **blutnudeln**, ➤ **cajoncìe de Moena**, ➤ **murbe**, ➤ **rofioi**, ➤ **tajadele smalzade**, ➤ **türteln**.

farina forte strong flour. Flour with a high content of proteins, gliadin and glutenin in particular, which combine to form gluten. Due to the presence of these elements, the flour absorbs a greater quantity of water and the dough is less conducive to rising and swelling.

farina gialla another name for ➤ **farina di mais**, cornflour.

farina integrale wholemeal flour. An unsifted flour (➤ **abburattamento**, ➤ **farine di grano tenero**).

farina manitoba Manitoba flour. Canadian, gluten-rich strong flour often blended with softer flours to make bread, cakes and pastries.

farina nera "black flour." Synonym of buckwheat flour (➤ **grano saraceno**).

farina rinforzata reinforced flour. All-purpose flour to which Manitoba flour (➤ **farina Manitoba**) or durum wheat semolina (➤ **semola di grano duro**) has been added.

farina speciale "special flour." Name for Manitoba flour (➤ **farina Manitoba**) or durum wheat semolina (➤ **semola di grano duro**).

farinacei farinaceous foods. Generic term for starch-rich foods such as pasta, rice and potatoes.

farinata, in dialect aka **fainâ** baked thin flatbread or focaccia made from a dough of chickpea flour, water and olive oil. Popular all over the region, it is sometimes flavored with rosemary, fresh spring onion or ➤ **bianchetti**, newborn fish. Liguria.

farinata con le leghe strips of ➤ **cavolo nero** (known locally as *leghe*) are boiled in salted water into which cornflour is gradually poured. When the dish is almost ready, it is flavored with minced garlic, salt, grated Parmigiano and extra virgin olive oil. Slightly more liquid than classic polenta, it is served in individual bowls. Tuscany.

farine di grano tenero soft wheat flours. Classified, according to grade of sifting (➤ **abburattamento**), into types 00, 0, 1, 2 and wholemeal. Type 00 (also known as ➤ **fior di farina**), the equivalent of cake flour, is the finest and is used to make cakes and delicate doughs. Type 0, all-purpose flour, is only slightly less fine, and is used to make most breads and fresh pastas, to thicken sauces, and to coat foods for frying and lining the inside of baking tins and molds. Types 1 and 2, which contain bran (➤ **crusca**) in percentages established by law, are, like wholemeal flour, used to make rough, rustic doughs. A distinction is also made between weak, medium and strong (➤ **farina forte**) flours on the basis of their *panificabilità*, their suitability for making bread, which is directly proportional to their gluten and protein content.

Weak flours are suitable for biscuits, wafers, grissini and crumbly cakes, medium flours for bread, pizza and pasta, strong flours for egg pasta and leavened cakes and pastries.

farinella con i cicoli liquid cornflour polenta soup cooked with pork scratchings (➤ **ciccioli di maiale**), flat-leaved parsley and grated cheese. Campania.

farinello common name for ➤ **buon enrico**, good King Henry.

farro emmer wheat (*Triticum dicoccum*). The name is also used for einkorn (*T. monococcum* and spelt (*T. spelta*). All three are "covered" wheats, thus named on account of the adherence of their outer husks to the tiny oval grains. To get rid of the husks, they have to be winnowed before threshing. Emmer wheat in particular appears to have been a staple grain since the dawn of agriculture, and is probably the progenitor of all the Graminaceae of the Triticum genus, hence also of wheat (➤ **frumento**). The name itself derives from the Latin *far*, which is also the root of the word Italian *farina*, "flour." Pounded grains of emmer wheat provided the base of *puls*, a sort of porridge that was a staple in the daily diet of legionaries and plebeians in ancient Rome. Over the centuries, emmer was gradually supplanted by wheat and corn, but has recently enjoyed a revival in the wake of the contemporary interest for poor, rustic, traditional foods. Especially worthy of mention is ➤ **farro della Garfagnana**, grown in the Valle del Serchio (province of Lucca, Tuscany). The Italian Ministry of Agriculture's database of native and/or traditional food products lists the following varieties: *farro di Monteleone* (Umbria), *farro dicocco delle Marche*, *farro dei Monti Lucretili* (Marche), *farro del pungolo di Acquapendente*, *farro del*

1 *chopping board*
2 *herb chopper*
3 *pestle and mortar*

1 *couscoussière*
2 *mixing bowl*

earthenware couscoussière

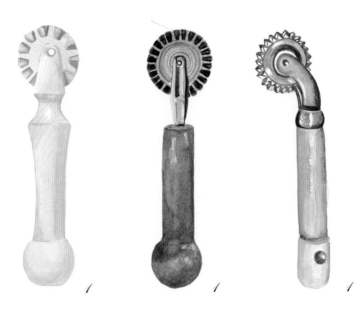

1 pasta or pastry wheels
2 tortelli cutters

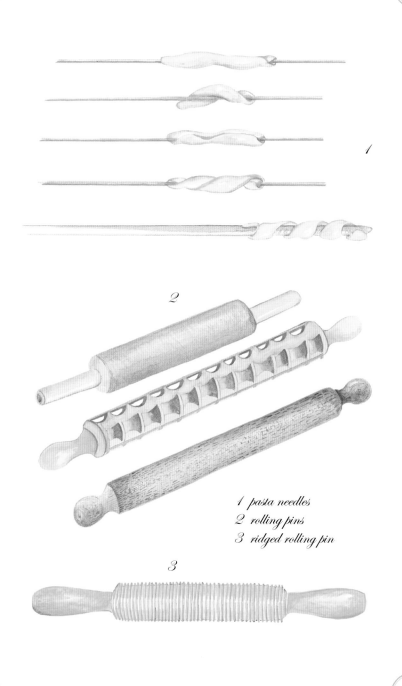

1 pasta needles
2 rolling pins
3 ridged rolling pin

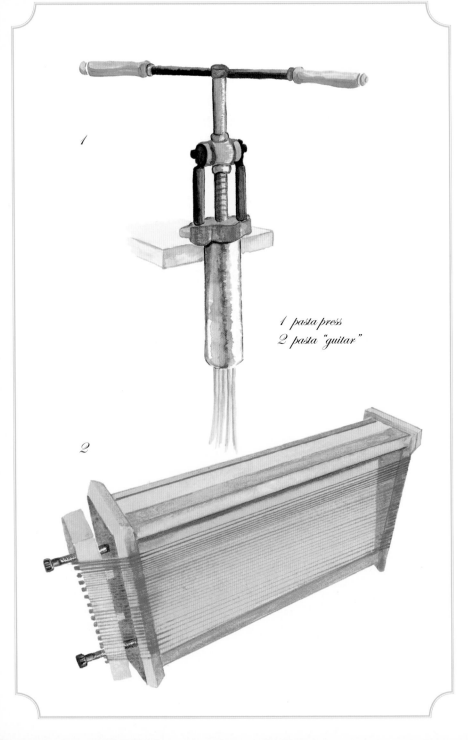

1 pasta press
2 pasta "guitar"

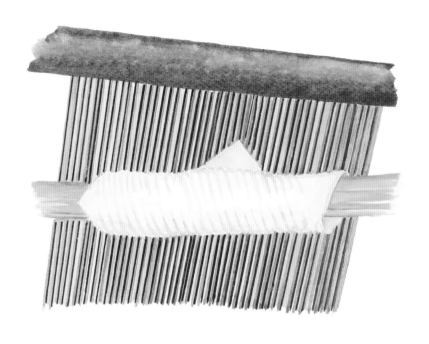

pasta combs

1   *hot plates for waffles and wafers*
2   *waffle iron*

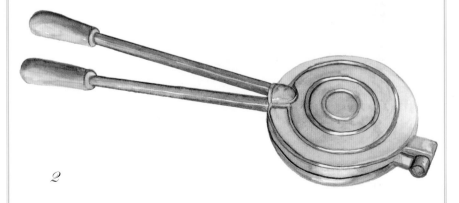

1 hot plates for crescentina and tigella
2 waffle iron

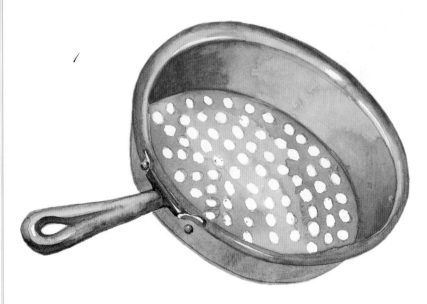

1 *chestnut pan*
2 *sieve*

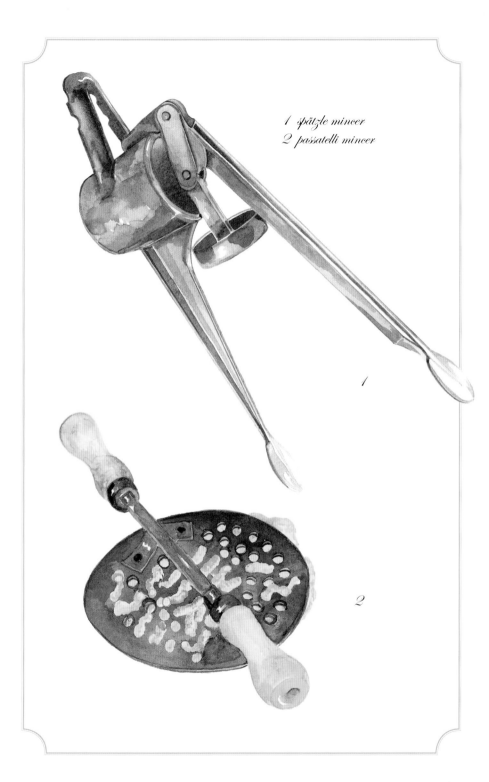

1 *spätzle mincer*
2 *passatelli mincer*

1

2

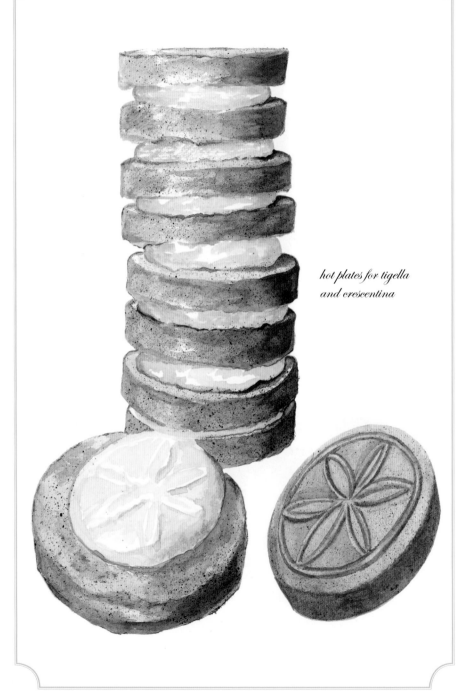

hot plates for tigella
and crescentina

1

1 sieve for malloreddus
2 testo, griddle pan for testaroli

2

1 testo, griddle pan for crescia or torta al testo
2 testi, griddle pans for piadina

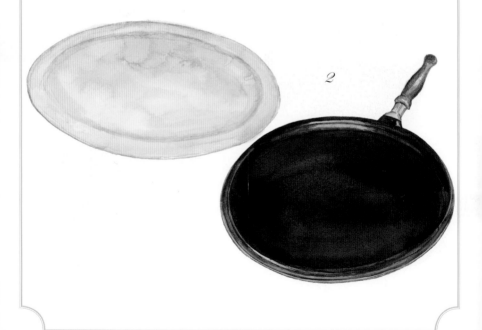

iron for necci, closed and open

dies for corzetti

Lazio (Lazio), *farro d'Abruzzo, farro dicocco* (Molise), *speuta* aka *speutone* (Campania). In central Italy, emmer is popular in soups and salads: ➤ **ceci e farro,** ➤ **gran farro,** ➤ **farro alla perugina,** ➤ **minestra di farro,** ➤ **zuppa di faro,** ➤ **farrotto,** ➤ **fracchiata.**

farro all'antica Pompei stew of emmer, ➤ **alici di menaica** (anchovies), garlic, and chili, flavored with ➤ **colatura di alici** and oregano, usually served with bread fried in the cooking pot. Campania.

farro alla perugina emmer soup. The original recipe involves boiling emmer with a ham bone, carrot, celery, onion and ripe tomatoes. When the soup is ready, it is supplemented with pieces of ham scraped from the bone and sprinkled with grated Pecorino. Richer versions envisage the addition of strips of ➤ **guanciale,** cheek bacon, fried with aromatic vegetables and rosemary. The soup is one of the region's most representative dishes. Umbria.

farro della Garfagnana PGI emmer cultivated naturally since time immemorial at an altitude of 900-2000 feet in the upper Valle del Serchio, in the Garfagnana district of the province of Lucca, and ground in stone mills. Tuscany.

farro di san Nicola simple soup of emmer boiled in a broth aromatized with onion, olive oil, minced celery, tomato sauce, salt and pepper. Made by and for the inhabitants of the village of Monteleone (province of Terni) on December 5, its patron saint's day, to commemorate the miraculous end of a terrible famine that hit the area centuries ago. Umbria.

farrotto emmer cooked risotto-style with mixed field greens (➤ **misticanza**) and their cooking water, and served with grated Pecorino. Abruzzo.

farsò sweet fritters of flour, eggs, milk, sug-ar and raisins, typical of the province of Pavia. Traditionally made for the feast of San Giuseppe or on All Saints' Day. Lombardy.

farsumagru aka **farsumauru** Sicilian dialect words for ➤ **falsomagro,** another name for ➤ **bruciuluni,** a large meat roll.

fasiola ➤ Lazio term for ➤ **tellina,** tellin or wedge shell clam.

fasoi en bronzon boiled ➤ **borlotto** beans mixed with lardo and butter, then baked in the oven with tomato sauce, fresh sausage (➤ **lucanica**) and warm water. The name of the recipe comes from the bronze tin in which the beans (which may be replaced by potatoes) were traditionally baked. Trentino-Alto Adige.

fasoi in potacin boiled ➤ **borlotto** beans slowly stewed to a creamy consistency with tomato passata or tomato paste dissolved in water. In some versions of the recipe, the tomato is left out and the beans are simply flavored with bay leaf or rosemary. Veneto.

fasoi in tocieto another name, especially in the Polesine area, for ➤ **fasoi in potacin.** Veneto.

fasoi sofegai literally "suffocated beans." Boiled beans stewed in tomato sauce or water. Veneto.

fasolaro another name for ➤ **vongola,** common clam.

fasolo (pl. **fasoi** or **fasioi**) aka **fasul** (pl. **fasui**) Veneto and Friulian dialect words for ➤ **fagiolo,** bean.

fassone calf with very pronounced upper haunches whose veal is highly prized (➤ **bovina piemontese, razza**). Piedmont.

fasui cul muset beans, usually dried, with ➤ **muset** (boiling sausage), which is either cooked with the beans or boiled separately and added later. Friuli-Venezia Giulia.

fasule e scarole bean and escarole soup. Beans boiled with garlic and celery, turned in a skillet with boiled escarole, lardo and chili, and covered with just enough water to obtain a thickish, soupy consistency. Popular throughout the region, especially in the Cilento area. Campania.

fattisù di verza pasta stuffed with cooked Savoy cabbage, salami, eggs and grated Parmigiano, similar in shape to ➤ **tortelli con la coda**. Typical of the province of Piacenza. Emilia-Romagna.

fatula Sicilian dialect term for ➤ **pesce castagna**, pomfret.

Fatulì della Val Saviore goat's cheese (*fatulì* means "small piece" in the local dialect) made from the milk of the native Bionda dell'Adamello goat in the Val Camonica, in the province of Brescia. Smoked with juniper branches and berries, it is aged for one to six months. Protected by a Slow Food presidium. Lombardy.

fava fava bean or broad bean (*Vicia faba maior*). Annual legume whose long pods contain two to ten kidney-shaped, pale green beans. The Italian Ministry of Agriculture's database of native and/or traditional food products lists the following varieties: *fava di Miliscola* (Campania); ➤ **fava di Carpino**, *fava di Zollino* (Puglia); ➤ *fava larga di Leonforte* (Sicily); *fava lunga delle Cascine* (Tuscany); *fava bellunese* (Veneto). Important in the history of human nutrition, fava beans, especially dried, long provided the main source of protein for whole communities, especially in the south of Italy. They are still a popular ingredient in regional cuisine in dishes such as: ➤ **favetta**, ➤ **frittella**, ➤ **scafata**, ➤ **minestrone di fave**, ➤**fave con i lolli**, ➤ **favò**, ➤ **fave 'ngrecciate**, ➤ **ciaudella**, ➤ **faixeddas a cassola**, ➤ **fave al guanciale**, ➤ **stufato di fave**, ➤ **macco**, ➤ **'ncapriata**, ➤ **calcione**. In Liguria, Lazio and Marche, fava beans are also

eaten raw, freshly picked, usually accompanied with salami and Pecorino cheese.

fava alessandrina a very thick, creamy soup of fava beans, preferably fresh, finely sliced potatoes, leek, garlic, butter, oil, a bouquet garni and homemade tagliatelle. The day after, the now solidified mixture can be fried, a spoonful at a time. The recipe is typical of the province of Alessandria, but similar preparations are to be found elsewhere in Piedmont. In the province of Asti, for example, *fava amnaja* is a soup of fava beans thickened with goat's cheese, pancetta and softened onions, while in some mountain valleys in the province of Cuneo they still make a crem of fava bean soup thickened with semolina. Piedmont.

fava di Carpino Carpino fava bean. The clayey, limestone soil of Carpino, in the province of Foggia, is perfect for the cultivation of fava beans The local variety is tiny with a dimple in the lower half. Green when harvested, it gradually turns a sandy white. It is protected by a Slow Food presidium. Puglia.

fava 'e lardu stew of fava beans sausage, pork ribs and rind, wild fennel garlic and chili, served piping hot over ➤ **pane carasau** or day-old farmhouse bread at Carnival celebrations, as of January 17, the feast of Sant'Antonio. A tradition of the province of Nuoro. Sardinia.

fava grassa regional term for ➤**valeriana rossa**, red valerian.

fava larga di Leonforte Leonfort fava bean. This fava variety was once very common and was cultivated in rotation with grain to enrich the soil. On account of its being labor-intensive and relatively unprofitable, the crop was beginning to disappear, hence the setting up of a Slow Food presidium to protect it. The bean is sowed in November and December and harvested when the plants start to wither, towards the end of March. The bean is eaten fresh or dried (long soaking is unnecessary) as an ingredient in soups and stews (➤ **macco**). Cultivated in the area of Leonforte, in the province of Enna, Sicily.

fava luina a common term for ➤ **lupino**, lupin.

favagello aka **celidonia minore** fig buttercup or lesser celandine (*Ranunculus ficaria*). Glossy, hairless wild herb with heart-shaped fleshy leaves and sparse yellow flowers. Common in fields, along hedgerows and on damp terrain. Gathered almost exclusively in northern and central Italy. The pleasantly tangy young shoots are eaten (in moderation, since they are somewhat indigestible) in salads.

favata soup of fava beans, pork ribs and rind, sausage, lardo, Savoy cabbage, garlic, onions, celery, carrots, sun-dried tomatoes and wild fennel, served piping hot with country bread.

fave dolci aka **favette dolci** aka **fave dei morti** cookies made from a paste of chopped almonds, flour, sugar, butter, eggs, cinnamon and lemon zest, baked in the oven a spoonful at a time. In some areas the term is synonymous with ➤ **cenci**, sweet fried pastries. Veneto, Friuli-Venezia Giulia.

fave al guanciale fava beans cooked in a skillet with chopped onion, salt, pepper, strips of ➤ **guanciale** (cheek bacon), white wine and water. Lazio.

fave alle sette insalate fava beans and "seven salads." Boiled fava beans placed at the center of a large plate, surrounded by seven small bowls containing boiled chicory, tendrils, rocket, olives, eggplants preserved in oil, raw onions and pickled peppers. Puglia.

fave bianche e loane pasta with fava beans. Fava bean purée with homemade flour and water fettuccine (*loane*), served with warm oil, chili and garlic. An old peasant dish of the province of Foggia. Puglia.

fave con i lolli soup of fava beans (preferably the local *cottoia* variety), broccoli, tomato, carrot, celery and onion and ➤ **lolli**, a type of local pasta. A specialty of Modica, in the province of Ragusa. Sicily.

fave con le animelle a stew of boiled fava beans turned in a skillet with oil, garlic and blanched, chopped pig's sweetbreads. Sometimes beans are used in lieu of fava beans. A dish traditionally prepared to mark the annual peasant ritual of the killing of the pig. Umbria.

fave dei morti crisp cookies made from a paste of chopped almonds, wheat flour, eggs and sugar, aromatized, depending on the region, with grated lemon, pine kernels, cinnamon or grappa. Popular all over Italy on the Day of the Dead (November 2), and usually shaped like fava bean pods, hence the name (➤**fave dolci**).

fave e canolicchi purée of fava beans with razor clams (➤ **cannolicchio**), boiled or raw. Puglia.

fave e cicoria another term for ➤ **'ncapriata**, fava bean purée and field greens. Puglia.

fave e Pecorino fresh raw fava beans served with ➤ **Pecorino Romano**. Served as an antipasto at home, but also popular on Easter Monday picnics. Lazio.

fave fritte fried fava beans. Boiled fava beans, dried in the oven for a few minutes, then deep-fried in extra virgin olive oil, seasoned with salt and served cold. Puglia.

fave 'ngrecciate a simple salad of boiled fresh or dried fava beans dressed with an emulsion of olive oil and minced garlic and mint (or marjoram). A specialty of Macerata, Marche.

fave scarfate dish made with leftover fava bean purée from ➤**'ncapriata**, mixed with fried onions and day-old bread. Puglia.

favetta (1) a sort of polenta of fava bean flour set aside to cool, then heated in a skillet with sautéed spring onions, or simply dressed with extra virgin olive oil and ground black pepper. Similar to → **panizza**. Liguria.

favetta (2) soup of fava beans, celery and tomato slow-cooked to a thick, creamy texture, served with boiled, snapped vermicelli and bread. Typical of Bari. Puglia.

favetta con le cicorielle another term for → 'ncapriata, fava bean purée and field greens. Puglia.

favi caliati toasted fava beans (→ **semi e legumi tostati**, toasted seeds and legumes).

favò short pasta mixed with boiled fresh fava beans, tomato sauce and diced Fontina cheese, and served with rye bread croutons fried in butter. A specialty of Cogne. Val d'Aosta.

favollo yellow shore crab (*Eriphia verrucosa*). Cooked in the same way as spider crab (→ **grancevola**).

fazzino aka **lisone** aka **lisotto** flatbread made from a leavened potato dough with a dimple at the center to retain the condiment, usually stewed onions or leeks. A specialty of the province of Savona. Liguria.

fecola potato flour. Used to thicken and/or bind sauces, cream soups and baby food (→ **tapioca**).

fegatazzo → sausage typical of Ortona, in the province of Chieti, made from the liver, belly and jowls of the pig. Abruzzo.

fegatelli di maiale sullo spiedo pig's livers cut into pieces (in one recipe marinated in red wine, olive oil and wild fennel), wrapped in caul, impaled on a skewer, alternated with bay leaves and pieces of bread, and barbecued. Umbria, Lazio.

fegatelli nella rete finely chopped pig's liver mixed with ground pork, seasoned with salt and pepper, flavored with fennel seeds, garlic, bay leaves and breadcrumbs, and bound with extra virgin olive oil. The mixture is shaped into balls, wrapped in caul, stuck with wild fennel stems, and fried in lard or olive oil. Alternatively, the balls are impaled on a skewer and alternated with diced →rigatino bacon, or reinforced with crumbled sausage meat and cooked in the pan with a dash of Vin Santo. Prepared in this way, the **fegatelli** can be covered with lard and preserved in glass or earthenware jars. A specialty of the central Italian regions (→ **fegatelli di maiale sullo spiedo**), especially Tuscany.

fegatello suino now rare cured meat consisting of a large ball of pig's liver, trimmings from various cuts of pork and fat, coarsely ground and cured with salt. Wrapped in caul and tied up with string, it is cooked in lard for three to four hours. Produced artisanally, it should be eaten within two weeks of production. Typical of the province of Pavia. Lombardy.

fegatini di pollo con l'uva chicken livers with grapes. The livers are cut into two or three pieces, browned in butter and bathed with Marsala. White grapes are then added to the pan. The livers are served on slices of toasted day-old Bread and covered with the sauce. Veneto, Friuli-Venezia Giulia.

fegatino (1) (pl. **fegatini**) the liver of any kind of farmyard poultry: chicken, turkey, guinea fowl and so on. Without specification, the term generally refers to chicken. Chicken livers have been enjoyed since Renaissance times and figure in countless recipes, often in sauces and mixed with other giblets (→ **rigaglie**). The livers of chicken and game birds are also among the main ingredients of →

crostini toscani and → crostini umbri. The only fish livers eaten in Italy, albeit rarely, are those of cod (smoked and preserved in oil) and monkfish, which are cooked fresh.

fegatino (2) pig's liver, pancetta and shoulder pork cured with kitchen salt, ground black pepper, chili, grated orange zest, crushed garlic, nutmeg and cinnamon, and cased in a natural intestine. After drying for 24 hours (often by smoking), it is aged for 15 days. A cured meat typical of the hills and mountains of Ascoli Piceno and Macerata. The Macerata version, similar to → ciauscolo, can be stored for a relatively long time, whereas the thinner Ascoli version is made from a more coarsely ground mixture and can be stored for two to three months. Marche.

fegato liver. Livers are the most consumed organs of edible animals, but also the most perishable. Their protein content is comparable to that of meat, their fat content is low and they contain vitamin B and iron. The livers of all edible domestic animals, with the exception of horses, are much used in the kitchen. The most prized is calf's liver (more delicate than cow's), but pig's is also popular, fresh (sometimes in specific recipes such as → fegatelli nella rete), in pâtés or as an ingredient in cured meats (→ mortadella di fegato). Lamb's and kid's livers tend to be cooked with other offal (→ coratella), while those of game birds and rabbit are often added to the sauces in which the respective sauces are cooked.

fegato all'aggiada calf's liver cut into thin strips and cooked briefly on a high heat, then covered with a sauce (→ aggiada) made by pounding garlic, fresh breadcrumbs and a little calf's spleen in a mortar and diluting the mixture with vinegar. A recipe typical of Genoa. Liguria.

fegato alla barcarola calf's liver cut into slices, coated with flour and cooked in butter with onion, vinegar (sometimes replaced by white wine) and minced flatleaved parsley. An analogous recipe in Alto Adige, made exclusively with white wine, is called fegato alla tirolese. Veneto, Friuli-Venezia Giulia.

fegato alla lodigiana slices of calf's liver covered with slices of prosciutto, flavored with fennel seeds, rolled up, wrapped in caul and fried. A specialty of the city of Lodi. Lombardy.

fegato alla milanese slices of liver sprinkled with minced flat-leaved parsley, seasoned with salt and pepper, coated in flour, dipped in beaten egg and fried in butter. Typical of Milan. Lombardy.

fegato alla triestina slices of pig's liver flavored with bay leaves and wrapped in caul, sprinkled with white wine or vinegar and baked in the oven. Venezia-Giulia.

fegato alla veneziana recipe common throughout the Mediterranean, where the combination of liver and onion dates from Roman times (reappearing later in Byzantine cuisine). In the oldest versions of the recipe, calf's liver is cut into thin slices, marinated in water and vinegar, cooked in oil, or a mixture of oil and butter, with an equal amount of sliced white onion (which has to soften without frying), seasoned with pepper, sprinkled with minced flat-leaved parsley and sometimes lemon juice, and served, frequently, with polenta. Veneto.

fegato di maiale alla lucana a barbecued bundle of pig's liver, bay leaves and garlic (or onion), wrapped in pig's caul. Basilicata.

fegato dolce a variant on → salsiccia di fegato made from a mixture of pig's liver, offal and belly pork, flavored with honey, candied citron and orange, pine kernels and pistachio nuts. A specialty of L'Aquila. Abruzzo.

fegato fritto all'emiliana slices of calf's or pig's liver coated in dried breadcrumbs and fried in butter or lard. An old country dish common throughout the region. Emilia-Romagna.

fegato grasso foie gras. The liver of a goose or duck fattened abnormally by forced feeding. Made almost everywhere in France, where it is subject to complex legal classification: *foie gras entier* (fresh whole liver), *cuit* (cooked), *mi-cuit*, (semi-cooked), *frais* (fresh), *foie gras* (reassembled pieces of livers), *bloc de foie gras* (cooked block), *pâté de foie gras, mousse de foie gras, parfait de foie gras* and so on). In some Italian regions, in especial Lombardy (in the Lomellina, area, in particular in the town of Mortara) and Friuli (in the area between Udine and Palmanova), small-scale breeders produce not only the cured meats of the local Jewish tradition, but also *torchons*, patés and terrines.

fegato in agrodolce sweet and sour liver. Slices of calf's liver dipped first in beaten egg, then in breadcrumbs, cooked briefly in butter and sprinkled with lemon juice sweetened with sugar. Typical of the province of Vicenza in particular. Veneto.

fela struzn horseshoe-shaped bread made with wheat flour and lard (no more than 25%). Trentino-Alto Adige.

Felciata another name for ➤ **Giuncata**, a type of cream cheese.

Felciata di Morano, in dialect aka **Filicèta**. A cream cheese of ancient origin which should be eaten very fresh. Produced in the summer in the province of Cosenza with goat's and ewe's milk. The curd is layered in wood tubs with ferns (*felce* in Italian, hence the name of the cheese).

Calabria.

fellata (1) in Campania an antipasto of sliced cured meats. At Easter, *fellata di Pasqua* is traditionally served in households supplemented by fresh fava beans, hard-boiled eggs and salted ricotta. In Abruzzo and Molise the same term refers to an antipasto of local cured meats and cheeses. Campania, Abruzzo, Molise.

fellata (2) cured meat consisting of coarsely chopped pork shoulder, leg, loin and pancetta cured with salt, pepper and chili, cased in a pig's large intestine and aged for two to three months. Typical of a number of towns and villages in the province of Messina. Sicily.

fellata (3) Lazio name for a sheep of two to three years of age. **fellette** aka **fillette** a variant of ➤ **firrincozza**, sponge fingers, with pistachio nuts in the mixture. Typical of Bronte, in the province of Catania. Sicily.

femminella name used in the lagoons of Orbetello and Burano (province of Grosseto) for the female crab (➤ **granchio**) in its mating period. Listed in the Italian Ministry of Agriculture's database of native and/or traditional food products. Fished only in the winter, it is excellent in soups. Tuscany.

fenecchiedde wild fennel boiled and sautéed in oil with garlic and anchovy fillets. Puglia.

fenocio Veneto term for ➤ **finocchio**, fennel.

ferdinandi rolls made with flour, yeast, milk and sugar, filled with a cream of butter, sugar and powdered vanilla baked in the oven, covered with boiling hot sugared milk, then returned to the oven. Veneto.

ferlengo regional term for ➤ **cardoncello**, king oyster mushroom.

fermenti lattici milk enzymes. Important micro-organisms (bacteria) for cheesemaking because they promote acidity and the precipitation of milk protein into a solid curd. They are mainly responsible for the taste profile of cheese. Since they are eliminated by pasteurization, it is necessary to inoculate pasteurized milk with a starter culture in order to turn it into cheese.

ferratelle sweet wafers made from flour, eggs, butter, white wine, sugar and, occasionally, aniseed made with a special utensil similar to a waffle iron. Sprinkled with sugar, they are joined together in sandwiches filled with Montepulciano grape jam. Otherwise they are rolled up and filled with ricotta, sugar and saffron, with confectioner's custard, with chocolate or with the same filling as → **bocconotto**, a small shortcrust pastry, in which case they are called → **neole** (aka **nevole**). Other local names are → **coperchiole** and → **pizzelle**. Abruzzo.

ferrazzuoli hollow egg pasta served with a sauce of tomato, lamb, pork, turkey and veal, browned in butter and onion. Made by wrapping strips of pasta dough round a needle or stick. Calabria.

ferretto needle-like tool traditionally used to make pasta (→ **maccheroni al ferretto**).

ferri, ai generic expression for "broiled" or "grilled" (→ **griglia**).

ferricieddi Campania dialect name for → **maccheroni al ferretto**, type of pasta.

fesa cut of beef from the rump roughly equivalent to tenderloin, used to make → **carpaccio** and → **tartara** or for steaks. In butchers' terminology, the word also refers to a boned breast of turkey.

fesa francese cut of veal that corresponds to the rump in the adult animal.

fesone di spalla shoulder clod. Cut of beef used for escalopes, steaks, chops and rolls. May also be marinated.

fessilsuppu rice and beans cooked together, layered in a baking tin with slices of Toma and baked in the oven. Typical of the Valle del Lys. Val d'Aosta.

fetta col cavolo nero "black cabbage" leaves (→ **cavolo nero**) stewed in salted water and served on slices of toasted bread rubbed with garlic, drizzled with extra virgin olive oil and sprinkled with black pepper. Traditionally served in winter as a snack or antipasto (→ **crostini toscani**). Tuscany

fettucce another name for → **fettuccine**, a type of pasta.

fettucce romane another name for → **tagliatelle**, a type of pasta.

fettuccelle another name for → **tagliatelle**, a type of pasta.

fettuccelle ricce another name for → **reginelle**, a type of pasta.

fettuccia regional term for → **cepola**, red band fish.

fettuccine broad egg pasta ribbons typical of central and southern Italy, especially Lazio. Best enjoyed with meat and giblet sauces and traditionally served in Roman households for Sunday lunch. Other names: → **fettucce**, → **lasagnette**, → **pappardelle**.

fettuccine alla ciociara fettuccine served with a sauce of lardo, chicken giblets and tomato with the addition of peas, mushrooms and lean pork. A specialty of the Ciociaria district in the province of Frosinone. Lazio.

fettuccine alla papalina fettuccine mixed with beaten eggs, grated Parmigiano and pepper and topped with a sauce of butter, onion, peas and prosciutto. Lazio.

fettuccine alla romana fettuccine with a rich sauce of tomato, ham fat, dried mushrooms softened in warm water and chicken giblets stewed in butter and white wine. Lazio.

fettuccine dolci dessert made with fresh fettuccine (made with wheat flour, water and salt, no eggs) mixed with breadcrumbs, minced walnuts and warm honey. Served at room temperature when the mixture has begun to set. Umbria.

fettunta aka **panunto** a slice of toasted Tuscan bread rubbed with garlic and dressed with salt, pepper and extra virgin olive oil. Once eaten as an afternoon snack, now considered one of the ➤ **crostini toscani**. Tuscany.

feurazzu Sardinian term for ➤ **cardoncello**, great oyster mushroom.

fiadone halfmoon pie typical in Abruzzo at Easter, but also made in Trentino. The Abruzzo version, which may also be savory, is filled with a mixture of cow's milk cheese or ricotta, eggs and lemon zest. The pastry crust is made of flour, eggs, oil or lard and sugar. The only feature which the Trentino version has in common is the shape. The pastry is enriched with butter and cream, and the filling is a mixture of minced almonds, cherry syrup and rum. After baking the crust is brushed with beaten egg whites sweetened with sugar. Abruzzo, Trentino.

fiamma, alla flambed (➤ **flambare**).

fiammeggiare (1) to singe. To pass fowl over a flame to remove the small feathers that may still remain after plucking. The same operation is performed to remove bristles from pork rind. **fiammeggiare (2)** improper Italianization of the French *flamber*, to flambé (➤ **flambare**).

fiamminga aka **fiammenghilla** "Flemish" oval earthenware serving dish.

fiandolein a sort of ➤ **zabaglione** made of milk, egg yolks, sugar, lemon zest and cognac (or rum), cooked in a bain-marie. Val d'Aosta.

fiapon fritters made of leftover polenta, wheat flour, sugar and grated lemon. Excellent hot or cold, typical of the Po Valley. Lombardy.

fiasche de corai dialect term for ➤ **alchechengi**, Peruvian cherry or Cape gooseberry.

fiazzin another word for ➤ **fazzino**, a type of flatbread.

ficarello aka **ficazzedda** a type of sweet ➤ **panzerotto** (turnover) made from a dough of wheat flour, olive oil and brewer's yeast filled with a mixture of cooked wine must (➤ **vincotto**), durum wheat semolina, lemon zest and pounded walnuts. Baked in the oven and glazed with icing. Puglia.

ficattola flatbread whose shape is reminiscent of the female sex organ (the Italian name has vulgar overtones). Made from a leavened pastry dough of soft wheat flour, olive oil, sugar, yeast, water and salt, broken into three-inch fingers slashed lengthwise. Used to be eaten as a dessert, now served with cured meats and cheese. Other regional names: ➤ **donzella**, ➤ **panzanella**, ➤ **zonzella**. Tuscany.

ficatu ri sette cannola Sicilian term for ➤ **zucca gialla all'agrodolce**, sweet and sour marrow. The name derives from the fact that, in olden days, Palermo street vendors used to set up their stalls near the Garraffello fountain, which has seven spouts (*cannelli*), and often sold this dish, in which the marrow is cooked as if it were liver (*ficatu*). Sicily.

ficazza "fish salami" made by casing tuna trimmings, cured with salt and pepper, in a pig's intestine. Sicily.

ficcanasi fried pastry, similar to ➤ **arvoltolo**, made from a dough of soft wheat meal, butter, sugar, eggs, salt, anise liqueur (➤ **mistrà**), wine, alkermes and vanilla. The dough is flattened, cut into pieces, aromatized with grated orange or lemon zest, rolled up and fried. A specialty of Spoleto, the province of Perugia. Umbria.

ficcilatidd a large savory cookie made with soft wheat, sourdough and fennel seeds. Baked in the province of Matera on December 7, the eve of the feast of the Immaculate Virgin. Basilicata.

fiche maschie a stocchetto salted dried fillets of ➤ **melù**, blue whiting. Tuscany.

fico (1) fig (*Ficus carica*). Typical of the Mediterranean, the fig originated in southwest Turkey, where it was known as *caria*, hence its Latin name. Of the many varieties, some produce one crop a year, others two or more. The calorie content of fresh figs is not high, but increases almost fivefold in dried fruits (➤ **fico secco**). Figs are grown all over Italy, especially in the Mediterranean regions. The Italian Ministry of Agriculture's database of native and/or traditional food products lists the following varieties: *fico del Cosentino* (Calabria); *fico di San Mango* (Campania); *antiche varietà di fichi piacentini* (Emilia- Romagna); *figo moro* (Friuli); *figalini neri*, *rondette* (Liguria); *dottato*, *san piero*, *verdino* (Tuscany). In the kitchen, figs are used to make tarts and cakes (➤ **panficato**, ➤ **torta di fichi**), jams and preserves and, in some regions, they are popular caramelized (➤ **fichi caramellati**). Another noteworthy recipe is the syrup of figs, known as ➤ **cotto di fichi**, traditional of Puglia and Calabria

fico (2) regional term for ➤ **mostella**, greater forkbeard.

fichi caramellati caramelized figs. A traditional specialty of Romagna, where it is served as a dessert, but also to accompany cream cheeses, such as ➤ **Squaquarone**. The figs are covered with sugar and sprinkled with water (or vinegar) and cooked slowly. Transferred to hermetically sealed glass jars, they can be kept for some time. Emilia-Romagna.

fichi imbottiti sun-dried figs stuffed with walnuts, almonds, candied fruit and chocolate, baked briefly in the oven, and steeped in syrup of figs (➤ **cotto di fichi**) or cooked wine must (➤ **vincotto**).

fico bianco del Cilento PDO dried local cultivar of the *dottato* fig variety. It is sometimes commercialized stuck on wooden skewers or stuffed with almonds, walnuts, hazelnuts and fennel seeds. A delicacy in the Cilento area. Campania.

fico d'India prickly pear (*Opuntia ficus-indica*). Cactus native to Latin America, naturalized in the south of Italy, especially Sicily (➤ **fico d'India dell'Etna**), where it is a common feature of the landscape. Its spiny fruits may be yellow, white and red and their flesh is firm and sweet. The Italian Ministry of Agriculture's database of native and/or traditional food products lists the following variety: *fichi d'India di Calabria* (Calabria); *fico d'India della Valle del Belice*, *fico d'India di San Cono*, *fico d'India della Valle del Torto* (Sicily). Prickly pears are eaten fresh or processed into jams, sauces (➤ **sapa di fichi d'India**), relishes (➤ **mostarda di fichi d'India**), granitas, ice creams and desserts (➤ **gelo**, ➤ **pani 'e sapa**). In Sicily, when prickly pears are in season in the late summer, it is common to find stalls selling them ready-peeled.

fico d'India dell'Etna egg-shaped prickly pear with sweet, juicy flesh. It is grown in a number of communes in the province of Catania and has received PDO recognition. It is mainly eaten fresh, though it also appears as an ingredient in traditional cakes and is used to make a liqueur called *rosolio di fico d'India dell'Etna*. Sicily.

fico dottato cosentino the dried *dottato fig*,

a variety common throughout the center and south of Italy, is the principal ingredient in this recipe. Overripe figs are picked and sun-dried on racks for a week. They are then cut in two, filled with walnuts or almonds, and baked in the oven until golden. The dried fruits are sometimes joined together to form crosses (➤ **crucette**) and aromatized with orange zest before going into the oven.

fico secco dried fig. Ripe figs (preferably the central and southern varieties *brogiotto* and *dottato*) may be dried naturally or artificially with hot air. In the traditional method, freshly harvested figs are sun-dried on racks by day and protected at night. They are then baked in the oven and stored in earthenware or glass jars with bay leaves. The main Italian producer regions are Calabria, Puglia, Campania (➤ **fico bianco del Cilento**), Sicily and Tuscany (➤ **fico secco di Carmignano**), followed by Lazio, Marche and Molise. In Calabria dried figs are stuffed with dried or candied fruit, sugar, spices and so on (➤ **bratte**, ➤ **crucette**, ➤ **padruni**), in Puglia with almonds, fennel seeds, walnuts, pieces of chocolate and lemon zest. Noteworthy recipes in the Marche region are ➤ **lonzino di fichi** and ➤ **panetto di fichi**. Dried figs appear in numerous cakes and pastries, from ➤ **pitta 'mpigliata** in Calabria to ➤ **frustingo** in the Marche, and a recent fashion is to coat them with chocolate.

fico secco di Carmignano *dottato* figs are opened, arranged on rush mats, smoked with sulphur, and sun-dried for four to five days. They are then transferred to a cool, dry room where they rest for 35-40 days until a sugar patina forms on the skin. The figs are superimposed on skewers in four pairs of two, and anise seeds are placed between each pair. They are

served with ➤ **mortadella di Prato** or with ➤ **Vin Santo**. The product, a specialty of Carmignano, in the province of Prato, is protected by a Slow Food presidium. Tuscany.

ficoccetti small unripe figs sautéed with broccoletti and served as a sauce with homemade pasta. In the Sabina district, in the province of Rieti, they are cooked with garlic, oil, salt, pepper and chili, and served with country bread. Lazio.

fidej very thin handmade pasta ribbons. Piedmont.

fidelini aka **fedelini** now synonyms of ➤ **capelli d'angelo**, the two terms are amongst the oldest to refer to long dried pasta. They derive from the Castilian Spanish *fideos*, in turn a transposition of the Arabic *fidaws*, "food of flour in the shape of threads." In Trabia in Sicily in 1154, the geographer Al-Idrisi saw pasta "in quantities such as to feed, beyond the towns and villages of Calabria, those of Muslim and Christian territories."

fidichella Lombard term for ➤ **mortadella di fegato di Novara**.

fidighin Piedmontese term for ➤ **mortadella di fegato di Novara**.

fidlin Piedmontese and Lombard term for ➤ **capelli d'angelo**, a type of pasta.

fieno greco common name for ➤ **trigonella**, fenugreek.

figà Veneto term for ➤ **fegato**, liver (generally bovine).

figadet rare sausage made from a mixture of calf's sweetbreads, pork and pig's liver, pancetta and lung, cured with salt, pepper, other spices and raisins (cinnamon and garlic in the Trentino), and cased in a natural intestine. Tied up and dried for a few hours, it is eaten fried or barbecued within days of production. Typical of the Dolomites in the province of Belluno (Veneto) and on the border with the

Trentino. Veneto, Trentino-Alto Adige.

figadin pieces of pig's liver wrapped in pig's omentum (➤ **omento**) and gently fried in lard. Emilia-Romagna.

figascia another name for ➤ **bisciöla**, an oblung panetone.

figatej liver patties. Pig's liver is cooked briefly with lardo and bone marrow, then ground with grated cheese and parsley, and shaped into balls. These are wrapped in pig's caul, impaled, two at a time, on skewers, alternated with sage leaves, and fried. A Milan recipe. Lombardy.

figatello Sicilian word for ➤ **lattume**, tuna sperm sac.

filacci synonym of ➤ **sfilacci**, shredded horsemeat.

filascetta focaccia made from rolled bread dough covered with finely sliced stewed red onions and Crescenza cheese. In some areas the cheese is avoided and the surface is sprinkled with sugar or salt. A specialty of the province of Como. Lombardy.

filatelli another name for ➤ **spaghettoni**, giant spaghetti .

filateddhi aka **filatieddi** Calabrian version of ➤ **maccheroni al ferretto**.

filatrota aka **filatrotta** large freshwater eel (➤ **anguilla**), very common in Sardinia, fished when it starts to move out to sea to reproduce. Similar to ➤ **capitone**, it is boiled and aromatized with ➤ **zibba**, samphire.

filazzuolo Siciliano dialect term for ➤ **peritoneo**, peritoneum.

file e daspe boiled potatoes cut in half and smothered with a warm cream of ➤ Montasio cheese, egg yolks, milk and apple vinegar, and garnished with chives. A specialty of the hamlet of Fielis, near the village of Zuglio in the Valle del But, north of Tolmezzo (province of Udine). The odd name (translatable in Italian as *filare e diraspare*, "weave and untangle," evokes the movements that have to be made with a fork to amalgamate the cheese sauce on the heat. A specialty of the Carnia area, in the province of Udine. Friuli.

fileja fresh long, twisted flour and water pasta. Made by "spinning" (*filando*) long five to ten inches strips of pasta round a wooden rod (➤ **maccheroni al ferretto**). Served, in season, with fresh tomato sauce, abundant basil and grated Pecorino, or classic ➤ **ragù calabrese**, meat sauce.

filetti di baccalà fritti fillets of salt cod dipped in a batter of water, flour, salt and brewer's yeast and deep-fried in oil. A typical street food (➤ **cibo di strada**) in Rome, where it is still made at kiosks by so-called *filettari*. Elsewhere—in Tuscany, Liguria and Piedmont, for example—salt cod is more likely to be coated in flour before frying. If and when it is battered (sometimes with the addition of other ingredients such as minced garlic and parsley), it is more common to speak in terms of ➤ **frittelle di baccalà**, salt cod fritters.

fillleto fillet. Very tender muscle virtually devoid of connective tissue situated under the lumbar vertebrae, usually of large bovines. Much used in international cuisine (often *en croûte*, *à la* Wellington or *à la* Stroganoff) and in Italian restaurants in simpler recipes: eg, broiled, with black, green or pink pepper, with Roquefort cheese and so on. Fillet of pork is also widely used, as are fillet of some game animals, such as red deer.

filetto baciato di Ponzone cured meat the size of an ostrich egg created in the 1950s. A whole fillet of pork is cased in a cow's large intestine inside a ground mixture of pork and pig's fat, salt, pepper, nutmeg, garlic, red wine and saltpeter. A specialty of the village of Ponzone Monferrato, in th province of Alessandria. Piedmont.

filetto controbaciato aka **filetto salamato** another name for ➤ **brasolara**, a rare and prized cured meat.

filiferru another name for ➤ **filu 'e ferru**, Sardinian grappa.

filindeu lliterally "God's hair." A pasta made from a dough of durum wheat flour, salt and water, shredded into very fine threads, and dried in three superimposed layers to create a gauze-like effect. The pasta is made exclusively by two women in Nuoro specifically for the feast of San Francesco di Lula, at the start of May. A soup of mutton broth, sour cheese and **filindeu** is offered to pilgrims arriving at the saint's sanctuary. Sardinia.

filon de purcel Friulian name for loin of pork (➤ **lonza suina**). In the province of Pordenone, the loin is boned and cured for 24 hours in salt, pepper and herbs, then smoked for three to four days over a fire of beech and juniper branches. Friuli-Venezia Giulia.

filone generic name for a long, French-style bread loaf weighing from four ounces to half a pound.

filoni a common name for ➤ **schienali**, bovine bone marrow.

filtrare to filter, to put a sauce or a marinade through a sieve. To separate the solid part from the liquid part.

filu 'e ferru aka **file e ferru** aka **filiferru** aka **abba ardente** (*acqua ardente*). A type of grappa. The dialect name corresponds to the Italian *filo di ferro*, "wire," and derives from the fact that in the past clandestine producers used to hide their bottles buried in the ground tied to long wires to retrieve them after police searches. The spirit is distilled from wines or

the dregs left from the pressing of grapes for wine (especially Vernaccia), aromatized with local essences, such as strawberry tree fruits or fennel seeds. After distillation, the spirit is aged in wood for a year before bottling. Sardinia.

filzetta part of a pig's colon (➤ **budello diritto**).

finanziera calf's sweetbreads, brains, testicles, bone marrow and fillet of veal, meatballs, cock's crests, wattle and hearts, cut into pieces, sautéed in butter (crests, wattle, brain and sweetbreads are blanched first) and stewed with pickled mushrooms, Marsala, vinegar or white wine and, in some variations, peas and other pickles. A historic bourgeois dish, once on the verge of extinction on account of the complexity of its preparation, now making a comeback in the region's better restaurants. Piedmont.

finferlo aka **finferla** common and regional terms for ➤ **cantarello**, chanterelle mushroom.

fini-fini very thin tagliatelle made from a dough of wheat flour and eggs, typical of the Ciociaria area, in the province of Frosinone. Usually served with oil, garlic and chili. Lazio.

finocchio fennel (*Foeniculum vulgare*, var. *sativum*). The bulbous base of the plant, cultivated chiefly in Campania and Puglia, is much used in Italian regional cooking. The Italian Ministry of Agriculture's database of native and/or traditional food products lists the following varieties: *finocchio di Isola Capo Rizzuto* (Calabria); *bianco palettone, finocchio di Sarno* (Campania); *finocchio della Maremma viterbese* (Lazio). Fennel's gastronomic fortunes are tied to a number of historical preparations: raw in salads or ➤ **pinzimonio**, boiled and sautéed in butter, breaded and fried, baked.

Regional recipes include: ➤ **finocchi al-la giudia**, ➤ **finocchi in tegame**, ➤ **risi coi fenoci**.

finocchi alla giudia Roman recipe of Jewish origin. Fennel cut into wedges and cooked in oil with vinegar, with the addition of water or broth, until tender and golden brown. Lazio.

finocchi in tegame fennel coated in flour, fried in oil and butter until golden, and finished off with beef marrow, herbs and spices. Veneto.

finocchietto aka **finocchiella** common and regional terms for ➤ **finocchio selvatico**, wild fennel.

finocchini cookies of flour, eggs, sugar and honey, aromatized with fennel seeds and anise essence. A specialty of Refrancore, in the province of Asti, but also produced in other areas of the provinces of Asti and Turin. Piedmont.

finocchio asinino regional term for ➤ **finocchio selvatico**, wild fennel.

finocchio bastardo aka **finocchio fetido**, regional terms for ➤ **aneto**, dill.

finocchio marino, samphire or rock samphire or sea fennel (*Crithmum maritimum*). Spontaneous aromatic herb that grows on sand dunes and sea cliffs. Its fleshy leaves are used to flavor sauces, soups, eggs and fish. In Liguria and Puglia it is pickled in vinegar or preserved in oil to dress bruschettas and tomato salads. The plant is common in all coastal areas, especially in Liguria, Tuscany, Marche, Abruzzo and Puglia. Common and regional names: ➤ **cretamo**, ➤ **critmo**, ➤ **bacicci**, ➤ **bassiga**, ➤ **erba di mare**, ➤ **paccasassi**.

finocchio selvatico wild fennel (*Foeniculum vulgare Mill* subsp. *piperitum*). Typically Mediterranean spontaneous herbaceous plant, which grows in sunny, dry, rocky environments. Highly aromatic on account of the essential oils it contains. The green herbaceous parts are used to dress pastas (➤ **pasta con le sarde**) and soups (➤ **macco**); the fruits, or seeds, to flavor fresh and cured meats (➤ **fegatelli**, ➤ **porchetta**, ➤ **finocchiona**, ➤ **salsiccia lucana**), fish (➤ **sardella**, ➤ **rosamarina**), breads, flatbreads and boiled chestnuts (➤ **ballotta**). In Puglia, the inflorescences are used to make a preserve (➤ **caroselle sott'aceto**) and in confectionery as an ingredient in the filling of tiny sugared almonds. The wild fennels of Calabria and Sardinia are listed in the Italian Ministry of Agriculture's database of native and/or traditional food products. Common and regional names: ➤ **finocchiella**, ➤ **finocchietto**, ➤ **finocchio asinino**.

finocchiona large cured meat typical mainly of the provinces of Florence and Siena. Pork shoulder and loin and prosciutto and pancetta scraps are cured with garlic crushed in wine, black or green pepper, wild fennel seeds, wild thyme and other natural flavorings. Cased in a natural bladder, the mixture is cooked for a week, then aged for 60-90 days. Tuscany.

fiocca dessert made of whipped cream, sugar and grappa. Often garnished with grated chocolate. Val d'Aosta.

fiocchetto cured meat prepared with leg of pork, minus the ➤ **culatello**. The meat is cured for two weeks in sea salt, saltpeter and ground spices. It is then steeped in wine or vinegar for three days, massaged, cased in a bladder and tied up with string. After maturing for eight to ten days, it ages for three to six months. More rarely, it may be aged for more than nine months. A specialty of the province of Parma, but also common in the Piacenza and Cremona areas. Lombardy, Emilia-Romagna.

fiocco name for two cuts of beef. In the front of the animal it corresponds to brisket and is used in a number of traditional dishes: ➤ **cima alla genovese**, ➤ **sacòcia**, ➤ **picaia**. In the rear it is roughly equivalent to top sirloin and is best enjoyed in roasts, escalopes and marinated carpaccio (➤ **spinacino**).

fiòco whipped cream sweetened with sugar, sometimes aromatized with cocoa or coffee powder. Typical of the mountain valleys of the province of Cuneo. Piedmont.

fior d'ogni mese common term for ➤ **calendula**, English or pot marigold.

fior di farina soft wheat meal with a very low grade of sifting (➤ **abburattamento**), comparable to cake flour.

Fior di latte a fresh, stretched curd cheese typical of south and central Italy. Worked exactly like ➤ **mozzarella**, it differs insofar as it is made exclusively with cow's milk. According to production controls, it may be made in Basilicata, Calabria, Campania, Puglia and in Lazio (though only in the provinces of Frosinone and Latina). The shape varies, depending on where the cheese is made, and can be a knot, a twist, rectangular or round, with or without a head. The curd is matured with the inoculation of a whey-based starter for a time varying from three to five hours. The version produced in the Monti Lattari (Campania) is made with raw milk from Agerola cattle, acidified for 12 hours, and stretched during the night.

fior di sole regional term for ➤ **topinambur**, Jerusalem artichoke.

fior gentile regional term for ➤ **margheritina dei prati**, English daisy.

fiordilatte (1) dessert of milk aromatized with vanilla and grated lemon zest, sugar, egg yolks and whole eggs cooked in a bain-marie in a mold lined with caramel. Common in Emilia, it is, with ➤ **latte alla portoghese** and ➤ **lattaiolo**, the traditional cream dessert that most resembles ➤ **crème caramel**.

fiordilatte (2) plain ice cream.

Fiore sardo PDO cheese of very ancient origin, manufactured industrially with mixed ewe's and cow's milk, by artisans with raw ewe's milk. Lightly smoked, it is aged for two to eight months. A Slow Food presidium protects traditional production techniques: the milk used comes from a single milking, the smoking takes place in *pinnette*, shepherds' huts in the mountains, and, during aging, the rind is greased with olive oil, sometimes mixed with mutton fat. Sardinia.

Fiore sicano, in dialect aka **Tumazzu ri vacca** whole raw cow's milk cheese produced in the Monti Sicani (in the provinces of Agrigento and Palermo, Sicily) from two milkings. Ready for the table after 60 days, it may be aged for up to a year. Thanks to the microclimate in the aging rooms, the body may develop native molds.

fiorentina abbreviation of ➤ **bistecca alla fiorentina**.

fioret sweet flatbread made with wheat flour, brewer's yeast, eggs, sugar, milk and butter, decorated with dried fennel flowers (*fioret* in the local dialect). Typical of the Valchiavenna, once prepared on the occasion of christenings, confirmation ceremonies and so on. Lombardy.

fioretto finely ground cornflour (➤ **farina di mais**) used as an ingredient in cookies and cakes, in some recipes to coat fish or other foodstuffs for frying.

fiori di zucca ripieni fritti fried stuffed zucchini flowers. Zucchini flowers are stuffed with matchsticks of mozzarella and anchovy fillets, dipped in a batter of wheat flour, brewer's yeast, warm water, vinegar, sugar, extra virgin olive oil and salt, deep-fried in olive oil, and served piping hot. A traditional Jewish antipasto that has long been adopted by Lazio cuisine. In Piedmont they make the same dish with a meat stuffing (ground beef, chopped boiled salami, beaten eggs, cheese, parsley and garlic) and they fry it in butter. In Liguria stuffed zucchini flowers are one of the group of stuffed vegetables known as ➤ **ripieni**.

fiorilli Campania dialect term for zucchini flowers.

fioroni di Morcone large egg pasta ravioli stuffed with a mixture of mature and fresh Pecorino, eggs and pieces of salami, and baked in the oven. Cut into smaller disks, they may be fried and served as an antipasto. The name may derive from the pasta's resemblance to the precocious fig (*fiorone* in Italian). A specialty of Morcone, in the province of Benevento. Campania.

fiorrancio regional term for ➤ **calendula**, English or pot marigold.

firrincozza aka **firringozza** sponge fingers made from a mixture identical to that of ➤ **savoiardi**. After baking until golden brown, the mixture is cut into long, wide strips and baked a second time for a few minutes. Sicily.

firzuli aka **frizzuli** Calabrian version of ➤ **fusilli** , a type of pasta (➤ **maccheroni al ferretto**).

fischietti Basilicata version of ➤ **maccheroni al ferretto**, a type of pasta.

fischione widgeon (*Anas penelope*). A dabbling duck with thin pointed wings, a short round tail and a bluish-gray beak with a black tip. The female has a brown back and a white stomach, the male (whose whistle, *fischio* in Italian, gives the breed its name) has a chestnut-red head with a vertical yellow band. A mi-gratory bird, it transits in Italy between the end of August and November and in February-March. Many specimens spend the winter in Italy, nesting on flooded ground and in marshes. The bird feeds mainly on vegetables, which it finds by "dabbling" on the surface of the water or on land.

fischirol aka **fisquirol** soup of flour and water lasagne cooked in milk and sprinkled with grated cheese. A delicacy in the Provencal valleys in the province of Cuneo. Piedmont.

Fiscidu name used for ➤ **Casu axedu** cheese preserved in brine (➤ **frue**).

fisola term used in Emilia for ➤ **budellina**, pig's or sheep's small intestine.

fisti regional term for ➤ **valeriana rossa**, red valerian.

fitascetta ➤ **filascetta**, a type of focaccia.

fitri buckwheat tortelli filled with cheese and fried, usually served with chicory salad. Typical of the Cantone Ticino, a Swiss Italian canton.

fiurit thick white yogurt-like dairy product made by extracting the first lumps from the coagulation of ricotta and cooling them rapidly. A specialty of the mountain valleys of the provinces of Brescia, Bergamo and Trento. Lombardy, Trentino-Alto Adige.

fladenbrot variant of ➤ **breatl**, made with wholemeal rye flour (80%) and all-purpose wheat flour (20%).

flambare Italianization of the French *flamber*, in English to flambé, to flame. To toss a food in a pan to which burning brandy or other alcohol has been added.

flan a term born in French cuisine (in ancient French the word *flaon* meant "cream") for a savory or sweet tart with a shortcrust pastry base and a soft filling. In Italy it is now the custom to use the word as a synonym of ➤ **sformato**, mold, possibly by analogy with ➤ **crème caramel**, basically a mixture of eggs and milk, which the French also refer to as a flan.

flan di asparagi asparagus mold (➤ **flan di ortaggi alla piemontese**, Piedmontese vegetable molds).

flan di cardi cardoon mold (➤ **flan di ortaggi alla piemontese**, Piedmontese vegetable molds).

flan di ortaggi alla piemontese, Piedmontese vegetable molds. Piedmontese cuisine boasts numerous vegetable molds (➤ **flan**), presumably on account of it geographical and historical contiguity with France. Such recipes became popular in the 18th and 19th centuries, and they are now cooked all over the region using seasonal vegetables of every type. The preparation method is always virtually the same with vegetables being boiled, squeezed dry and puréed, amalgamated with béchamel sauce eggs (sometimes the whites are whisked to a peak), and, in some cases, grated Grana and herbs and spices (such as nutmeg, flat-leaved parsley, pepper and so on). The mixture is then baked or cooked in a bain-marie in ring-shaped molds or individual ramekins. The resulting vegetable molds are served with savory sauces or creams such as ➤ **fonduta** and ➤ **bagna caoda**. The most traditional recipes are ➤ **flan di cardi** with cardoons, ➤ **flan di topinambur** with Jerusalem artichokes, ➤ **flan di spinaci** with spinach, ➤ flan di asparagi with asparagus, ➤ **flan di porri** with leeks, ➤ **flan di zucchine** with zucchini and ➤ **flan di patate** with potatoes, the latter typical of the Provencal valleys in the province of Cuneo. Another type of vegetable mold, ➤ **sformato di ortaggi**, differs insofar as the vegetables are chopped as opposed to puréed. Piedmont.

flan di patate potato mold (➤ **flan di ortaggi alla piemontese**, Piedmontese vegetable molds).

flan di porri leek mold (➤ **flan di ortaggi alla piemontese**, Piedmontese vegetable molds).

flan di spinaci spinach mold (➤ **flan di ortaggi alla piemontese**, Piedmontese vegetable molds).

flan di topinambur Jerusalem artichoke mold (➤ **flan di ortaggi alla piemontese**, Piedmontese vegetable molds.

flan di zucchine zucchini mold (➤ **flan di ortaggi alla piemontese**, Piedmontese vegetable molds).

flantze baked fruit loaf made of wheat and rye flour, yeast, eggs, butter, sugar, almonds, walnuts, cocoa and candied orange zest. Val d'Aosta.

flissa another name for ➤ **griva**, a meat and offal patty.

focaccetta di Aulla flatbread made from a dough of wheat flour, cornflour, salt, natural yeast and water, cut into portions then pressed into half-inch disks, which are piled up and cooked briefly in earthenware griddle pans. A specialty of Aulla, in the mountains inland from Massa and Carrara. Tuscany.

focaccia ai semi di sambuco rare ➤ **pitta** bread consisting of two disks of dough filled with elderberry seeds (➤ **sambuco**), olives, anchovies and, in some cases, onions. A delicacy in the village of Serra San Bruno (province of Vibo Valentia). Calabria.

focaccia al miele sweet pastry made from a dough of wheat flour, honey blended with milk, vanilla-flavored sugar, eggs, yeast, butter and grated lemon zest. The dough is given the shape of a rolled up snake, coated with honey, butter and egg white, and sprinkled with minced almonds and walnuts. Umbria.

focaccia alla materana "sandwich" of bread dough focaccia filled with mozzarella, tomatoes, olives, baby artichokes and mushrooms preserved in oil, chili and grated Pecorino. A specialty of Matera. Basilicata.

focaccia di Chieri twice-leavened focaccia made from a dough of water, flour, milk, butter and sugar, iced with sugar, typical of Chieri, in the hills near Turin. The recipe dates from the late 19th century. Until a few decades ago, the same dough was used to make ➤ **galucio**. Piedmont.

focaccia di Lerici cake made with a dough of cake flour, sugar, oil and brewer's yeast, perfumed with Marsala and dotted with almonds, raisins and candied fruit. Typical of the seaside town of Lerici on the eastern Riviera, it is reminiscent of the ➤ **pandolce** of Genoa. Liguria.

focaccia di Pasqua salata di Pitigliano soft loaf made with a dough of flour, ricotta, cinnamon, salt, pepper, olive oil and natural yeast, The surface is decorated with a check pattern, brushed with beaten egg and garnished with an olive leaf before being baked in the oven. A specialty of Pitigliano in the province of Grosseto. Tuscany.

focaccia di patate flatbread made with mashed potatoes, flour, salt, brewer's yeast dissolved in water and olive oil. Spread in an oven dish, it is dotted with pieces of chopped tomato and baked. Puglia.

focaccia di Recco traditional cheese focaccia. Two slices of focaccia dough with a soft cheese filling (mostly Stracchino these days) anointed with oil and baked in the oven. A symbol of the town of Recco, in the province of Genoa. Liguria.

focaccia di Voltri very thin focaccia made from a relatively liquid dough coated with corn flour, and baked on a hot plate. Typical of Voltri, a suburb of Genoa. Liguria.

focaccia dolce della nonna sweet flatbread (made from a dough of flour, brewer's yeast, sugar, milk, oil, lemon zest, raisins and pine kernels) topped with sugar, sprinkled with orange blossom water and decorated with pine kernels.

focaccia farcita two disks of dough filled with boiled vegetables (field greens, asparagus, artichokes, potatoes) and baked in the oven. Typical of Ascoli Piceno. Marche.

focaccia genovese aka **fugassa** traditional focaccia made from a dough of flour, extra virgin olive oil, water, sea salt and, sometimes, a dash of white wine from the valleys inland from Genoa. The crust is a glossy amber-yellow thanks to the oil, the crumb is ivory white with small "eyes." The dough is sometimes supplemented with onion, potatoes, sage or the leftover flesh of olives from the oil press. Liguria.

focaccia novese thin, soft, friable focaccia made by "stretching" by hand a dough of flour, water, lard, yeast, and extra virgin olive oil, and pricking the surface to create a honeycomb effect conducive to the absorption of the oil. Specialty of Novi Ligure, in the province of Alessandria, Piemonte.

focaccia pugliese another name for ➤ **focaccia di patate**, potato focaccia. Puglia.

foderare (1) to line the walls of a cooking recipient with ingredients to cover a food (eg, pastry for pies, gelatin for pâtés).

foderare (2) to wrap, to bard. To cover lean meat, game or poultry with pork fat, pork rind, pancetta or prosciutto to soften the flesh and prevent it drying out during roasting (➤ **bardare**).

Fodom cow's milk cheese with a sweetish flavor made since the 1980s in the village of Fodom, near Livinallongo, in the province of Belluno. Produced with part-skimmed milk from Bruno Alpina cattle. Ready for the table after maturing for at least two months. Veneto.

fogasa flatbread made with flour and grappa-flavored milk and cooked in a griddle pan. Typical of the province of Trento and the Lake Garda area of the province of Verona. Trentino-Alto Adige, Veneto.

fogassa simple oven-baked cake of flour, yeast, sugared white wine, oil (at one time, they used to use the cooking water of the ➤ **cotechino**, boiling sausage) and lemon zest. Veneto.

fogazza cun tamatica Sardinian term for ➤ **pane con pomodoro**, a stuffed bread "pouch."

fogghie dialect word used mainly in the Murge and Saletno areas term for edible wild herbs, such as chicory and mustard, essential for the preparation of ➤ **'ncapriata** (fava bean purée and wild greens). Puglia.

foglia crumbier version of ➤ **toponin**, a bread roll. Piedmont, Lombardy, Veneto.

foglietto aka **fogliolo** other names (Italianizations of the Milanese dialect word *fojoeu*) for ➤ **omaso**, omasum.

foiade broad tagliatelle made from a dough of wheat flour, eggs salt, and, often, dough left over from the preparation of ➤ **casonsei**, a type of stuffed pasta, typical of the provinces of Bergamo and Mantua. In the Val di Scalve, they are made with cornflour, in the Valle Brembana and Valle Seriana with buckwheat flour, according to a recipe identical to that of ➤ **pizzocheri**. Normally served with porcini mushrooms, with or without sausage, with salame softened in oil and red wine, with salame and amaretti cookies, with ➤ **Strachitund** cheese, walnuts and pears, ➤ **Formai de mut** cheese and smoked ➤ **guanciale**, cheek bacon, or es-

carole. A specialty of the provinces of Mantua and Bergamo. Lombardy.

foiolo, in dialect aka **fojoeu** Milanese terms for ➤ **omaso**, cooked locally with white beans and tomato paste. Lombardy.

fojòt Piedmontese dialect word for a small earthenware pot.

folaga coot (**Fulica atra**). A member of the rail and crake bird family, known as the Rallidae. The size of a small chicken, it has black and slate-gray plumage and an ivory white beak. An excellent swimmer, it lives in beds of rushes, ponds and lagoons, where it feeds on aquatic plants, insects, fish roe, small mollusks and crustaceans, and hence has flesh with a fishy flavor. A freshly killed coot should not be hung but plucked immediately, gutted and cooked within 24 hours. To attenuate its fishy smell, it can be browned in pieces without fats, bathed with wine or vinegar, or poached repeatedly in water and vinegar.

folpeto Veneto dialect term for ➤ **moscardino**, a small octopus-like mollusk. Boiled in water with bay leaves and lemon juice, oil, salt and pepper, it is one of the assortment of savories (➤ **cicheti**) served in traditional osterias with aperitifs. In some towns, such as Padua, it can be bought at special kiosks, known as *folpari*. In households, the mollusk is stewed in earthenware pots with oil, garlic, bay leaves, white wine and tomato passata. Veneto, Friuli-Venezia Giulia.

fondente Italianization of the French fondant, a white cream confection used in confectionery to fill or coat cakes, pastries and candies.

fondere to melt.

fondo concentrated meat, fish or vegetable stock or broth, specially made to form the basis or to flavor innumerable soups and sauces.

fondo di cottura the natural juices, fats, broth, spice, aromatics used to stew or braise meat. Normally they are filtered and used as a sauce. Sometimes they are served separately in a sauce or gravy boat.

fondue bourguignonne beef bourguignonne. Chunks of beef cooked at the table in a special pot filled with boiling oil. The dish is French in origin but has now become popular in Italy.

fonduta cheese fondue. A cream of Fontina cheese, milk and egg yolks. Cooked in a bain-marie, it is served with croutons, and, in season, sprinkled with flakes of white truffle. Today cheese fondue is also served as a sauce with vegetable molds, risotto, cotechino and boiled vegetables, and as a filling for fresh pasta. Piedmont, Val d'Aosta,

fongadina lamb's offal (heart, lung, liver, trachea) slowly stewed with wine, flour, onion and rosemary. Served as a savory snack with aperitifs (➤ **cicheti**) or with polenta. Veneto.

Fontal largely industrial semi-hard cow's milk cheese produced all year round throughout northern Italy. It has a delicate aroma and bland flavor.

fontana, a term used to refer to the making of a well in a mound of flour on a baking board prior to kneading in other ingredients to make a dough or cake mixture.

Fontina PDO washed rind (➤ **crosta lavata**) cheese made with raw milk from a single milking of Valdostana cattle. After complex processing, it matures in natural environments for at least 80 days. Best enjoyed as it is, but also used to make classic cheese fondue (➤ **fonduta**). Val d'Aosta.

foraguadole Mantua dialect term for the Italian *cobito*, spined loach (*Cobitis bilineatus*), tiny freshwater fish often used as bait, but also in the kitchen as an ingredient for frittatas and risottos. Once common, now on the verge of extinction in the Po.

forcello abbreviated name for ➤ **gallo forcello**, black grouse.

Formadi frant a typical dairy product from the Carnia area, in the province of Udine, protected by a Slow Food presidium, made from mountain cheeses unsuitable for aging. Flakes of the cheeses are mixed with milk, cream, salt and pepper, and the resulting mass is matured in wooden molds for 40 days. The fragrance is intense, the flavor mild yet tangy. Friuli.

Formadi salât salty cheese preserved in ➤ **salmuerie**, a preserving liquid of salt, milk and high-fat cream. Known in the Valle dell'Arzino as ➤ **Asìno**. Friuli-Venezia Giulia.

formagel cheese cooked with apples, butter, milk and, in some cases, onions. Lombardy.

Formaggella del Sannio recently conceived raw ewe's milk cheese that follows the traditional local Pecorino production processes. A small amount of rennet is used to coagulate the milk, and the curd is left to sour for a few hours. The cheese then matures in damp, cold cellars. Abruzzo, Molise.

Formaggella di monte cheese made with whole or slightly skimmed cow's milk with a technique similar to that used for ➤ **Scimudin**. Eaten fresh after 15-30 days' aging, it has a delicate flavor. Produced in the Adamello Regional Park, in the province of Brescia. Lombardy.

Formaggetta dell'Acquese cheese made with goat's and cow's milk (with the possible addition of a small amount of ewe's milk), in the province of Alessandria. Ready for the table after eight to twelve hours, it can also be aged for about a month. Piedmont.

Formaggetta della Valle Argentina produced in the valleys inland from the provinces of Savona and Imperia from goat's, ewe's or cow's milk, whole and raw. Its distinctive feature is the fact that the curd is put into molds without being broken. It is eaten fresh, but may also be aged and used for grating. Liguria.

Formaggetta di cabannina a cheese with a firmer body than others in the region. It is produced mainly in the Val d'Aveto and Valbrevenna with milk from the hardy ➤ **Cabannina cow**, supplemented with a little goat's milk. It ages for seven to 20 days, during which a white patina of mold may form on the rind. Liguria.

Formaggetta savonese cheese produced in a single dairy in the village of Stella, in the province of Savona, with 90% goat's milk and 10% cow's milk from one or two milkings on the same day. Usually eaten fresh, it may be aged for a month. Liguria.

Formaggina cream cheese. In northeast Piedmont and in the northern part of the province of Milan and the province of Varese (Lombardy), the term refers generically to a fresh cheese produced simply by leaving milk in a warm environment until it coagulates, adding the rennet and allowing the curd to drain. Delicate, slightly sour in flavor, normally served on its own with oil and pepper.

formaggino commercial processed cheese.

formaggio cheese. Italian cheeses are classified on the basis of their characteristics and production technologies, bearing in mind the following parameters: milk (cow's, sheep's, goat's, buffalo's, mixed); fat content (fat, semi-fat and low-fat cheeses); water content (hard, semi-hard, soft); production technology (uncooked, semi-cooked, cooked, stretched curd, pressed curd, blue or veined, bloomy rind, washed rind); maturing period (fresh, briefly, medium matured, slow matured).

Formaggio a crosta rossa aka **Rebruchon** fat-rich, creamy cow's milk, the Italian equivalent of the French Reblochon (hence its alternative name). Dry-salted and/or brine-salted, it matures for 20 days in increasingly cold rooms. Typical of the Valsusa area, west of Turin. Piedmont.

Formaggio a pasta pressata washed rind cheese (➤ **crosta lavata**), made with ewe's or goat's milk. Pressed with a weight, it is aged for at least two months in cool, damp cellars. Val d'Aosta.

Formaggio agordino di malga Slow Food presidium cheese made with raw whole or semi-skimmed Bruno Alpina cows' milk in the mountain pastures of Agordo, in the province of Belluno. After 48 hours in a brine bath, it is aged for two to eight months. Most of the cheese produced is sold directly at mountain dairies. Veneto.

formaggio conciato the term refers to the chiefly domestic habit of flavoring small fresh cheeses with herbs and spices and/or preserving them in oil.

Formaggio d'alpeggio di Triora cheese made with raw cow's milk, aged for three months to a year or more. Produced in the mountains round Triora, in the province of Imperia. Liguria.

Formaggio di capra a pasta molle washed rind cheese (➤ **crosta lavata**) produced both in the valley and at high altitudes in the mountains. Ready for the table after 20-25 days' aging. Val d'Aosta.

Formaggio di fossa literally "cave cheese." Cow's or ewe's milk cheese placed in canvas sacks sealed with chalk paste and aged, from the end of August until November 24 (Santa Caterina's day) in the caves at Sogliano, in the province of For-lì-Cesena, ancient grain stores hewn out of the tufaceous rock. Fermenting under these conditions, the cheese assumes bitterish flavors and an aroma of autumn leaves, mushroom and truffle. Emilia-Romagna

Formaggio di Pietracatella cheese made with raw milk from grazing animals (cows, sheep, goats), typical of the Fortore area, in the province of Campobasso. Matures for at least two months in tufa caves. Molise.

formaggio fritto fried cheese. Slices of sheep's and goat's cheese coated in butter and fried in oil. Abruzzo.

Formaggio misto literally "mixed cheese." Washed rind (➤ **crosta lavata**) cheese made of cow's, ewe's and goat's milk in variable proportions. Aged for 60-90 days. Val d'Aosta.

Formaggio puntato another name for ➤ **Marcetto**, a ewe's milk cheese.

Formaggio salato literally "salted cheese." Name used in the Carnia area (Friuli) for ➤ **Asìno**, a cow's milk cheese.

Formai dal cit an ancient and now rare tangy dairy product typical of the Val Tramontina, in the province of Pordenone. It is made by grinding up ➤ **Latteria** cheeses unsuitable for aging and mixing the pieces with milk, salt, pepper and local spices. It should be eaten immediately. Friuli-Venezia Giulia.

Formai de mut dell'alta Val Brembana PDO cheese made with cow's milk in the high Alpine pastures of the province of Bergamo. It is aged from 45 days to six months and more. The flavor is delicate and fragrant. Lombardy.

Formai parat another name for ➤ **Formagel**.

Formaio embriago literally "drunk cheese." Cow's milk cheese produced in the prov-

ince of Treviso. After maturing for 20 days, it is placed for two days under fresh pomace from red grapes (raboso, cabernet and merlot), continually sprinkled with wine from the press. It is ready for the table immediately, but may also be aged for one or two months. It has an aromatic, tangy flavor. Veneto.

formentazzo aka **frumentone** common words for ➤ **mais**, maize or corn.

formentin or **frumentin** northern Italian dialect words for ➤ **grano saraceno**, buckwheat.

formentino another word for ➤ **grano saraceno**, buckwheat.

formentone another word for ➤ **mais**, corn, and, in some regions, for ➤ **grano saraceno**, buckwheat.

fornello oven. In the Valle d'Itria and southeast Murgia areas, it is traditional for customers in butchers' shops to choose meat (normally pork, lamb and kid, sausages and offal) and have it cooked on a spit in the shop's oven. Puglia.

forno, al baked in the oven.

fortaes aka **fortaie** sweet fritters, similar to ➤ **kaiserschmarren**, made with a batter of flour, eggs, milk, cream and grappa squeezed in concentric circles into boiling oil using a poche. Due to their irregular, twisted appearance, the fritters are also known, respectively in Ladin and in German, as ➤ **straboi** or ➤ **strauben**, "curled," "frilled." Dusted with confectioner's sugar, they are generally served with redcurrant jam. A specialty of the Ladin Fiemme and Fassa valleys in the province of Trento. Trentino-Alto Adige.

fortaia aka **fortaja** Veneto terms for ➤ **frittata**.

forti duri cookies made with a paste of flour, crushed almonds or peanuts, treacle and pepper, typical of Bassano del

Grappa, in the province of Vicenza. Veneto.

fracassà d'articiocche fricassée (➤ **fricassea**) of artichokes in which the cooked vegetables are mixed with beaten eggs, lemon juice and grated Parmigiano. Liguria.

fracchiata polenta of grass pea and buckwheat (or chickpea) flour flavored with fava beans and ➤ **guanciale**, or with anchovies and fried sweet peppers. Abruzzo.

fracosta another word for ➤ **entrecôte**.

fragaglia (small) fry (➤ **frittura di fragaglia**); in Campania, Puglia and other southern regions ➤ **novellame di pesce**, fry.

fragola strawberry (*Fragaria vesca*). Today strawberries are cultivated mainly in Emilia-Romagna, Campania, Veneto and Piedmont. A wild variety exists, known as *fragolina*, with small aromatic fruits. The Italian Ministry of Agriculture's database of native and/or traditional food products lists the following varieties: *fragola di Romagna* (Emilia-Romagna); *fragolina di Nemi, fragola di Terracina* (Lazio); ➤ *fragola di Tortona, fragolina delle valli cuneesi, fragola di San Raffaele Cimena, fragola di San Mauro Torinese* (Piedmont); *fragola e fragolina di Naletto, fragolina di Ribera, fragolina di Sciacca* (Sicily); *fragolina delle montagne pistoiesi* (Tuscany); *fragola delle Dolomiti bellunesi e di Verona* (Veneto). Strawberries are mainly eaten fresh in fruit salads or on their own with wine. They are also widely used in confectionery as an ingredients in cakes, tarts, ice cream, jams, syrups and so on. Also used by creative cooks in risottos and other savory preparations.

fragola di Tortona references to the Tortona strawberry can be found in 16th-century texts, but it was only about a century ago that careful selection of wild species from the surrounding hills produced this excellent, highly perfumed cultivar, markedly different from others. Not much bigger than a raspberry, it has a heady fragrance and a sweet, delicate flavor. Only available for about 20 days between mid-May and mid-June, in the Tortona area, in the province of Alessandria, it is generally eaten on its own, sprinkled with sugar and good Barbera red wine. Production reached its peak in the 1930s, but declined in the postwar years. Now it is being relaunched by a Slow Food presidium. Piedmont.

fragolino liqueur typical of Pincara (Rovigo), though it is now homemade, with local variations, all over Italy, especially in the center and south of the country. To make it, strawberries and strawberry juice are infused in pure alcohol, filtered and mixed with water and sugar syrup, set aside to rest and bottled. Some recipes envisage the use of wild strawberries in lieu of cultivated varieties, others the addition of a vanilla pod during the maceration phase. Besides being enjoyed as it is, the liqueur is also used to garnish ice creams. Veneto.

fragolino regional name for ➤ **pagello**, sea bream.

fraina another name for ➤ **grano saraceno**, buckwheat.

francese regional name for ➤ **abomaso**, abomasum.

francesina Tuscan word for ➤ **lesso rifatto**, leftover boiled beef with onions.

francesine another name for ➤ **stricchetti**, an egg pasta.

fràndura a bake of finely sliced potatoes covered with batter and grated Grana cheese. Typical of the Valle Argentina, inland from the western Riviera. Liguria.

frangipane custard made with hazelnut

flour, almonds, cocoa, coffee, sugar and egg whites whisked to a peak, spread on puff pastry and baked in the oven (➤ **crema frangipane**). Piedmont.

frappe regional name for fried pastries similar to ➤ **cenci**.

frappé milk shake. Drink made of milk, sugar and ice, aromatized with coffee, chocolate, sweet liqueurs or fruit, and liquidized or whisked.

frascarelli aka **frascatelli** aka **frascarilli** flour and water pasta, sometimes enriched with eggs, popular mainly in central Italy. Named for the ancient custom of using a branch of wood (*frasca*) dipped in water to dampen the dough. Served in broth, preferably chicken, or with strong sauces, often made with ➤ **guanciale** (cheek bacon), onion and Pecorino (Marche), chicory and garlic (Lazio), or potatoes (Abruzzo). In the province of Viterbo, where it is also known as ➤ **'nsaccheragatti** or ➤ **'nsaccagnotti**, the pasta used to be recommended in the diet of women in childbirth insofar as it was believed to help of lactogenesis. Lazio, Marche, Umbria, Abruzzo.

frascariegl' molisani polenta of cornflour and potatoes dressed with oil and chili, and supplemented with beans (or vegetables) and, traditionally, pork rind. Molise.

frascarilli Abruzzo dialect word for ➤ **frascarelli**, a type of pasta.

frascatelli word used in some parts of Lazio for ➤ **frascarelli**, a type of pasta.

frascatole (aka **frascatula**) a sort of runny white polenta typical of central and eastern Sicily. In Modica (province of Ragusa), they cook durum wheat semolina in boiling water for 10 minutes and serve the resulting polenta with oil, salt, pepper and grated Pecorino or Caciocavallo. In the province of Enna, they add baby broccoli, wild fennel or other vegetables to the mixture. Sicily.

frattaglie offal. The innards (➤ **interiora**) of slaughtered quadrupeds. In a narrow sense, everything that is edible in the thoracic and abdominal cavities—heart, lungs, kidneys, liver, spleen, sweetbreads—stomachs (tripe), tenuous intestine, testicles and mammary glands (➤ **quinto quarto**, fifth quarter). Many traditional recipes use cow's, pig's and sheep's offal. Every Italian region has its own tripe recipes (➤ **trippa**), and dishes made from lamb's and kid's offal (➤ **coratella**) are popular all over central and southern Italy.

frattaglie di capriolo in umido stewed roe deer offal. The offal is washed in water and vinegar, browned in oil and butter with onion, carrot and celery, lubricated with white wine and finished in tomato sauce with cloves and cinnamon. Served with polenta. Friuli-Venezia Giulia.

fratto di fave traditional country soup of puréed fava beans and pasta. Basilicata, Calabria.

frecacha beef and potato hash. Val d'Aosta.

frecandò fresh vegetables (peppers, zucchini, eggplant, onions) stewed with tomatoes and vegetables. Marche.

freddo, a method of cooking in which a foodstuff is steeped in a liquid (broth or water) or mixed with other ingredients (sauces, vegetables, gravies) before being cooked or heated.

frega di pomodoro term used in some parts of Tuscany for ➤ **bruschetta**.

fregamài soup of small gnocchi, made by kneading and shaping flour, water and Parmigiano, cooked and served in meat broth. Liguria.

fregnacce small square or lozenge-shaped lasagne made from a dough of flour and eggs (in some versions of durum wheat and buckwheat flour without eggs). Traditionally served with tomato sauce and a generous amount of grated Pecorino, with mixed vegetable sauces, and, in the Sabina area, tomato sauce, garlic, oil and black olives. Sometimes the pasta is folded over and filled with meat sauce and Pecorino. Abruzzo, Marche, Lazio.

fregnaccia another name for → **arvoltolo**, Umbrian fried pastry.

fregola small irregular balls, reminiscent of couscous, made by rubbing semolina on the sides of an earthenware bowl. Cooked like a risotto, it is flavored in a variety of ways. The most traditional is with fresh tomato and grated Pecorino, but it is also often served with clams (→ **arselle**) and sea anemones (→**orziadas**). Sardinia.

fregolotta crumbly unleavened dry cake (in Veneto dialect the word *fregola* means "crumb") made with a mixture of flour, grated almonds, butter, sugar, powdered vanilla and a hard-boiled egg yolk. After resting in the refrigerator to lose elasticity, it is sprinkled with refined sugar and baked in the oven. Typical of the province of Treviso. Veneto.

fregula stufada tiny balls of semolina (→ **fregola**) boiled in salted boiling water, drained, layered in a heatproof eartheware dish with lightly fried lard, onion, flat-leaved parsley and grated Pecorino, and baked in the oven or in the heart covered with a lid. Sardinia.

fresa (or **frisella**) **(1)** twice-baked, often ring-shaped, bread typical of many regions of southern Italy. It may be kept for 15 days and more. Softened with a little water, it is topped with slices of fresh tomato, oil, salt and oregano.

Fresa (2) cow's or ewe's milk cream cheese, similar to → **Stracchino**. Eaten fresh or cooked in a skillet. Sardinia.

Fresa (3) another name for → **Murutzulu** cheese.

fresca Neapolitan word for tomato sauce made with chopped fresh tomatoes, oil, salt and minced garlic. Campania.

frese another name for → **mafalde**, a type of pasta.

fresine di quaresima long flat pasta with curly edges. Traditionally served with sauce of tomato, fresh anchovies and sardines and wild fennel. Abruzzo.

fresse meatballs (ground pork, onions, spices, egg and grated Parmigiano) enveloped in pig's caul, fried and serve either as an antipasto or as a main course with polenta. Similar to the Piedmontese → **griva** (or → **frissa**). Val d'Aosta.

friarelli another name for → **friggitelli**, sweet peppers.

friarielli exclusively Neapolitan word for → **cime di rapa**, broccoli rabe. Often stewed in oil with garlic and chili, and served with sausage. Campania.

fricandò stew of cubed beef first browned in butter with lardo, garlic and rosemary, splashed with wine (first white, then red) and finished off with finely minced aromatic vegetables, small Ivrea onions (→ **cipollina**) and diced potatoes. In the countryside they make a spicier version with generous amounts of onion, cloves, juniper berries and red wine (in some cases, using pork as well as beef). The dish is traditional in southern Piedmont, especially in the province of Asti. It is also made in the Val d'Aosta, where they serve it with polenta. Piedmont, Val d'Aosta.

fricassea fricassee. Pieces of mostly white meat (though some recipes use lamb, veal or sweetbreads) stewed with butter, herbs, spices and, in some cases, mushrooms, with the addition of egg yolks beaten with lemon juice when the dish is cooked. The term and the concept are derived from the French *fricassée* (→**brodettare**).

fricassea di pollo chicken fricasée. Pieces of chicken browned in butter and oil with garlic, sage and rosemary, bathed with white wine, covered with a lid and cooked through. The pan is then removed from the heat and a sauce of beaten egg yolks, lemon juice, salt and pepper is folded in. The recipe may be of distant French origin and is already documented in 18th-century recipe collections. Tuscany.

friccioli Tuscan term for → **ciccioli**, pork scratchings.

fricco' di pollo chicken cooked in wine and vinegar with herbs (thyme, bay leaves, rosemary, sage). A recipe also made with rabbit, lamb, duck or veal. Typical of Gubbio (province of Perugia). Umbria.

fricelli Puglia version of → **maccheroni al ferretto**, type of pasta.

frichetto mold of cheese (see → **frico**), potatoes e onions. Friuli-Venezia Giulia.

fricia Piedmontese dialect word for → **fritto misto**, mixed fry.

fricieu aka **friciula** Piedmontese dialect words for "fritter" or "fried pastry." In some provinces they are synonymous with and refer to leavened bread dough rolled out into a sheet, cut into lozenge shapes and fried. Today these are sometimes given invented names (*gonfiotti*, *sgonfiotti* etc.) and served with cured meats, as in other regions (→ **chisolini**, → **crescentina fritta**, → **gnocco fritto**, → **torta fritta**). In other areas, the province of Asti, for example, **friciula** is savory, whereas **fricieu** is sweet, made from a dough of flour, yeast, white wine or Marsala, eggs, butter, sugar, lemon zest and, at Carnival time, raisins and slices of apple. Piedmont.

friciolin diminutive of → **friciola** (fritter). In the province of Asti, it is the name of a fried meatball, usually made with beef, egg and an aromatic herb such as costmary (→ **erba di san Pietro**). In households it used to be the custom to make the meatballs with leftover agnolotti stuffing. Elsewhere in the region, **friciolin** may contain other ingredients, such as cod flesh, rice, spinach and potatoes (→ **subrich**). Piedmont.

fricis aka **frize** aka **frizzis** Venetian and Friulian terms for → **ciccioli**, pork scratchings.

frico a sort of "eggless" cheese frittata, an ancient peasant dish and a symbol of Friulian cooking. It comes in two versions, one soft, the other crisp. In the first case, coarsely grated potatoes are slowly fried in oil (or diced smoked bacon) with a little onion. When the potatoes are soft, pieces of medium aged → **Montasio** cheese are added to the pan. The mixture is browned on both sides and served. The crisp version is made by covering the base of a non-stick skillet with cornflour and adding grated supermature → **Latteria** cheese.

fricò another name for → **fricandò**, Piedmontese beef stew.

friggere to fry.

friggione cream of onion and tomatoes cooked in lard, traditionally served with boiled meats. Sometimes potatoes are also added. In the province of Piacenza (where it is known as → **rustisana**), it is served with horsemeat or eggs. In Modena (where it is known as → **frizon**), they add sweet green peppers and sausage. Emilia-Romagna.

friggione contadino onion, chopped tomatoes, boiled potatoes, rosemary, salt, ground pepper, wine and boiled beef cut into pieces, slowly cooked and finished off with beef broth. Served on slices of fried or toasted black bread. Tuscany.

friggitelli aka **friarelli** long, small, sweet green peppers, best enjoyed, as the name suggests, fried (➤ **friggere**) or stuffed. The term is typical of Campania (especially the Salerno and Cilento areas), but is also used in other regions of central and southern Italy.

frigulozzi pieces of bread worked by hand into braids of ten to twelve inches in length, cooked in salted water, and served with homemade tomato sauce and Pecorino. Specialty of Montopoli di Sabina, in the province of Rieti. Lazio.

frijenno e magnanno Neapolitan mixed fry in which the ingredients are prepared a few at a time, hence eaten constantly fresh (the dialect name translates into Italian as *friggendo e mangiando*, "frying and eating"). The traditional recipe envisages 36 ingredients, including anchovies, sardines, salt cod, polenta, zucchini flowers, artichokes, borage, brains, bone marrow, liver, sweetbreads and potatoes.

frinzele dialect term for ➤ **cartellate**, fried pastries.

frinzuli southern Italian term for ➤ **ciccioli**, pork scratchings.

friscalutu bread roll filled with mushrooms and slivers of Pecorino. A specialty of Buccheri, in the province of Siracusa. Sicily.

friscatuli polenta cooked with (➤ **broccolo ramoso**, wild cabbage, and finished with lard and ➤ **curcùci**, pork scratchings. Calabria.

frisceu aka **friscïöi** Ligurian terms for various types of fritter: sweet (flour, yeast, sugar, eggs, milk, raisins, grated lemon zest) and savory (flour, water, yeast, eggs, sometimes with the addition of herbs (➤ **preboggion**), vegetables cut into strips, larval newborn fish (➤ **bianchetti**) or salt

cod cut into pieces. Also called **frisceu** are chickpea flour fritters, not to be confused with ➤ **cuculli** and ➤ **panizza**. Liguria.

frisedda Puglia dialect word for ➤ **fresa**, twice-baked bread.

friselline word used in Potenza (Basilicata) for ➤ **stozze**, cookies.

frisjoli longhi classic Carnival fritters similar to ➤ **zippulas**, made with wheat flour, yeast, eggs, sugar and grated citrus fruit zest. Soft inside with a crisp surface, they are an inch wide and up to six feet long. They are served piping hot coated with bitter honey. Typical of the Gallura area. Sardinia.

frison di maiale chunks of lean pork stewed in olive oil with diced onion, carrots, eggplants, peppers, tomatoes, celery and zucchini. Lombardy.

frissa name used in the Langhe hills, in the province of Cuneo, for ➤ **griva** (meat and offal patty), typical of the Monferrato hills, in the province of Asti. Piedmont.

frisuli Calabrian pork scratchings (➤ **ciccioli di maiale**, ➤ **curcùci**).

frit gris literally "gray fries," a Franco-Provencal term from the northern part of the Canavese district in the province of Turin. A frittata made with onions, boiled potatoes, chard and grated Grana, but fried on one side only. Typical of the Valle Soana, in the province of Turin. Piedmont.

frite di prat wild herbs boiled and finished in the frying pan with butter or oil. Friuli-Venezia Giulia.

fritloc fritters made with a batter of chestnuts, milk, water and salt, typical of the mountains of the province of Reggio Emilia. A similar recipe is also made in the Romagna Apennines. Emilia-Apennines.

fritole di san Giovanni aka **frittole di san**

Giovanni potato, flour and oil matchsticks fried in butter and dusted with cinnamon. Or boiled, drained and served with melted butter, sugar and cinnamon. Traditionally prepared for the feast of San Giovanni on June 24. Friuli-Venezia Giulia.

fritole aka **fritule** Carnival fritters made with a batter, usually leavened, of flour, sugar, eggs, milk (in Istria, white wine), raisins and maraschino or another liqueur. *Fritole de pomi* and *fritole de risi* are the same fritters made with the addition, respectively, of slices of apple and rice cooked in milk. Veneto, Friuli-Venezia Giulia.

frittata beaten eggs, normally with the addition of other ingredients, fried in butter or other fats according to locality, similar to an omelet but cooked on both sides. Eaten as an antipasto or main course, hot or cold, sometimes dressed with a dash of vinegar.

frittata alla lodigiana a sort with pancake filled with ➤ **raspadura**, fine slices of local Grana cheese. Typical of Lodi. Lombardy.

frittata alle erbe frittata with boiled spinach, chard, leeks and onions flavored in the pan with basil and sage. The mixture is seasoned with salt and pepper and either fried or baked in the oven. Friuli.

frittata con fiori di zucca frittata with zucchini flowers. Veneto.

frittata con gli zoccoli frittata with diced salted pork pancetta (➤ **carnesecca**). The odd name may derive from the rough, rustic nature of the dish (in Florentine slang, the word *zoccolo* is used to describe someone who is distinctly unrefined). Tuscany.

frittata con i ciccioli frittata with pork scratchings (➤ **ciccioli**). Friuli-Venezia Giulia.

frittata con i germogli di luppolo frittata with hops shoots (➤ **luppolo**).

frittata con i tartufi frittata with black Norcia truffle. Umbria.

frittata con l'aceto frittata with grated Latteria cheese and drizzled with vinegar. Friuli-Venezia Giulia.

frittata con la balsamita frittata with costmary (➤ **erba di san Pietro** aka *balsamita* aka *erba caciola*). Piedmonte, Marche.

frittata con le ortiche frittata with nettles. Lombardy.

frittata con le rane frittata with frogs. Emilia-Romagna, Piedmont, Lombardy.

frittata con le vitabbie frittata with old man's joy (➤ **vitalba**), shoots of a creeper gathered in hedgerows in springtime. Umbria.

frittata con saltarelli frittata with fried pond shrimp (➤ **saltarèl**) Also made with frogs and ➤ **foraguadole**, spined loach. A specialty of the province of Mantua. Lombardy.

frittata di bianchetti frittata with newborn larval fish (➤ **novellame di pesce**, fry). Liguria.

frittata di bietole frittata (including egg whites whisked to a peak) with chard, dried mushrooms softened in water, desalted anchovies and grated cheese. Trentino-Alto Adige.

frittata di cipolle frittata with onions. A recipe with numerous regional variants.

frittata di coratella frittata with lamb's offal (➤ **coratella**). Umbria.

frittata di funghi frittata with mushrooms. Emilia-Romagna/Piedmont.

frittata di lampascioni frittata with grape hyacinth bulbs (➤ **lampascioni**), minced garlic and flat-leaved parsley. Puglia

frittata di mele frittata with apples. Valle d'Aosta, Trentino-Alto Adige.

frittata di moeche frittata with soft-shelled crabs (➤ **moeca**). Veneto.

frittata di patate (1) a frittata without eggs. The potatoes are boiled and puréed and mixed with finely sliced bacon and onions. The surface is leveled with a wooden spoon and the resulting potato cake is fried to golden on both sides, Typical of the province of Viterbo. Lazio.

frittata di patate (2) frittata of potatoes with eggs, often flavored with herbs or spices (flat-leaved parsley or cinnamon, for example). Piedmont.

frittata di riso frittata with rice cooked in milk, grated Parmigiano-Reggiano, egg whites whisked to a stiff peak and salt. Not fried but baked in the oven. Lombardy.

frittata di sarde frittata with sardine fillets. Friuli-Venezia Giulia.

frittata di scàmmaro another term for → **scàmmaro**, pasta frittata.

frittata di zucchine frittata with zucchini, often flavored with marjoram, flat-leaved parsley or lesser calamint. Liguria, Piedmont, Tuscany.

frittata rognosa frittata with pieces of leftover roast beef, sausage or salami. Piedmont, Lombardy, Veneto.

frittatensuppe thin frittatas made of eggs, flour, milk and herbs, cut into strips and served in meat broth. Trentino-Alto Adige.

frittatine di castagne frittatas made with beaten eggs, sweetened with sugar, and crumbled boiled chestnuts, served dusted with vanilla sugar (a savory version also exists). A specialty of the mountains of the province of Pistoia. Tuscany.

frittatine trippate small frittatas of eggs, flour and milk, rolled up, cut into strips and served with a light tomato sauce, sometimes flavored with grated cheese and marjoram. The appearance is that of a plate of tripe, hence the name. Similar recipes exist in other Italian regions: → **busecca matta**, → **trippa finta**, → **uova in trippa** . Tuscany, Marche.

frittedda soup of fresh fava beans, artichokes and peas. Specialty of Palermo, but common elsewhere in Sicily. In the Madonie mountains, it is flavored with wild fennel. Some serve it as a condiment for pasta. Sicily.

frittelle da sagra Italian name for → **Kirchtagskrapfen**, a type of doughnut.

frittelle di baccalà salt cod fritters. Pieces of salt cod (→ **baccalà**) dipped in batter and deep-fried in boiling oil. In Pontremoli (province of Pisa, Tuscany), the batter is made of flour, milk, eggs and oil. In Umbria, they use a similar batter and traditionally make the fritters on Christmas Eve together with fried cardoon, broccoli and other vegetables. In Veneto, they boil stockfish in milk and fry it coated with very soft bread dough. In Liguria, they break the fish up into small pieces to make → **frisceu**. In Naples, they coat the fish in → **pasta cresciuta** (→ **zeppulelle**).

frittelle di castagnaccio chestnut fritters. A soft batter of chestnut flour diluted with water, olive oil, raisin and powdered vanilla fried in oil, a tablespoon at a time. Emilia-Romagna, Tuscany.

frittelle di fagioli fritters of mashed boiled beans bound with flour and water and flavored with spring onions. Specialty of the Valle Argentina. Liguria.

frittelle di fiori di zucca zucchini flower fritters. Zucchini flowers coated in flour, dipped in beaten eggs and fried in oil. A recipe common, with regional variations, all over Italy.

frittelle di fontina croquettes made by frying in oil a mixture of flour, eggs and Fontina cheese dissolved in milk, a tablespoon at a time. Val d'Aosta.

frittelle di luccio fritters of pike flesh, bread soaked in milk and squeezed dry, grated cheese, eggs, salt, pepper and nutmeg. A recipe typical of the Valcamonica. Lombardy.

frittelle di mele apple fritters. Common all over Italy with regional variations. Generally they consist of slices of apple dipped in a light batter (in some regions flavored with white wine or rum or grappa) and fried in boiling oil. In Trentino-Alto Adige and the Cadore area of Veneto, they dust them with sugar and cinnamon, and serve them with a blackcurrant or raspberry sauce. In northern Italy, apple fritters often accompany roast pork and feature in a number of mixed fries. In Emilia instead they make them with a mixture of day-old bread soaked in hot milk, chunks of apple, grated lemon zest, anise liqueur, beaten eggs and sugar, fried a tablespoon at a time and dusted with refined sugar.

frittelle di patate potato fritters, which may be either savory or sweet. In the first case, a mixture of mashed potatoes, wheat flour, butter, beaten eggs and salt is rolled out, cut into circles or squares and fried in boiling oil. The sweet version is made the same way (but with only a pinch of salt in the mixture) and the shapes are joined together like "sandwiches," filled with blackcurrant or other jams and dusted with confectioner's sugar after frying. Trentino-Alto Adige.

frittelle di polenta polenta fritters. In Trentino they are made sweet with polenta, flour, yeast, sugar, milk, eggs and lemon zest. In Lombardy, *frittelle di polenta alla lodigiana*, typical of the city of Lodi, are savory, consisting of lumps of polenta stuffed with Fontina cheese and ham, and, in season, truffle, coated in breadcrumbs and fried.

frittelle di riso rice fritters. Common in many parts of Italy with regional variations, they may be savory or sweet. In the Crema area (Lombardy), they used to be made to use up leftover rice soup. Today they are made sweet with rice boiled in milk, beaten egg, wheat flour, sugar, crushed amaretti cookies, raisins and dried fruit. Also sweet are the rice fritters (*pallotte*) made in Umbria for the feast of San Giuseppe with rice, wheat flour, grated lemon zest and, in some cases, pine kernels and raisins soaked in wine and dusted with vanilla sugar. In Piacenza (Emilia), they make them savory with rice, flour, eggs and salt, while in Veneto they flavor their rice fritters with feverfew (→ **partenio**). Specific to Tuscany are the fritters known as → **sommommoli**.

frittelle di sambuco elder fritters. Elderflowers washed and dried, dipped in a batter of eggs, wheat flour, milk and grappa, fried and dusted with confectioner's sugar. Typical of the Valtellina (Lombardy), Friuli-Venezia Giulia (where a savory version also exists) and Piedmont.

frittelle di sant'Antonio fritters of parboiled cauliflower florets coated with flour aromatized with cinnamon, fried in oil and dusted with sugar. Traditionally made in Tuscania (province of Viterbo) for the feast of Sant'Antonio Abate on January 17. Lazio.

frittelle di zucca pumpkin fritters. Boiled or baked pumpkin flesh amalgamated with sultanas, sugar, flour, yeast and grated lemon zest (sometimes also ginger or cinnamon). The thick mixture is fried a tablespoon at a time in boiling oil, and the resulting fritters are dusted with confectioner's sugar.

frittelle giuseppine another name for → **sommommoli**, rice fritters.

fritti name used in some areas of the province of Piacenza (Emilia) for fritters made with mashed potatoes amalgamated with beaten eggs, coated with flour and fried in oil. Very similar to ➤ **subrich** (Piedmont) and ➤ **crocchè di patate** (Naples, Campania). Emilia-Romagna.

fritti nell'ostia patty made by sandwiching a mixture of finely ground bovine offal (sweetbreads, bone marrow, udder and testicles), cooked with artichoke hearts, between two dampened ostias, and frying in oil. An ancient Ligurian (more specifically, Genovese) recipe, now extremely rare. Liguria.

fritto di paranza mixed fry of small fish and seafood (mullet, anchovies, mackerel, soles, tiny mollusks and so on) from the daily catch of a *paranza*, a fishing boat typical of Italy's Tyrrhenian coast. The expression is common in central and southern Italy as an alternative to ➤ **fritto misto di pesce)**.

fritto di provatura Roman equivalent of ➤ **mozzarella in carrozza**. Lazio.

fritto misto all'ascolana mixed fry of mainly vegetables (artichokes, zucchini, or zucchini flowers, and stuffed olives, ➤ **olive ripiene all'ascolana**). The only meat used is lamb, and the dish is completed with "fried custard" (➤ **crema fritta**, ➤ **cremino**).

fritto misto all'italiana the composition of the grand Italian mixed fry (well documented in the menus of bourgeois families of the 17th century) varies from region to region. In general, the dish consists of fried meats (including offal), vegetables, pastries and, in some regions, cheeses and sweet items. Frying fats (oil, butter) and methods (battering, breading) depend on foodstuff and local tradition.

fritto misto alla bolognese mixed fry of meat (lamb chops, chunks of chicken, mortadella and sweetbreads), cheese (Emmenthaler and mozzarella), dipped in egg yolk, then in dried breadcrumbs; vegetables (zucchini, artichokes, croquette potatoes, cauliflower, zucchini flowers, eggplant, mushrooms, fennel, green tomatoes, acacia flowers); fruit (slices of apple); and sweet tidbits (confectioner's custard, semolina, ricotta, rice, amaretti cookies) coated in batter. The classic Bolognese ➤ **stecchi alla petroniana** (chopped offal skewers) are also part of the dish, though they can be served separately. The official recipe for **fritto misto alla bolognese** was registered at the Bologna Chamber of Commerce in 2004.

fritto misto alla ligure mixed fry of vegetables (artichokes, cauliflower, zucchini and their flowers, carrots, salsify, eggplants, fennel, mushrooms, sage, borage); meat (chunks or slices of veal, rabbit and chicken); offal (brain, sweetbreads, liver); sweetmeats (slices of apples or pears, and, in some areas, amaretti cookies, imported from Piedmont); and cubes of ➤ **latte brusco**. The various items (the vegetables coated in batter) are fried in separate skillets. Two traditional components of the dish, ➤ **stecchi** and ➤ **fritti nell'ostia**, are rarely included these days. The above description refers to the recipe typical of Genoa and the Golfo del Tigullio. Liguria.

fritto misto alla milanese calf's offal (sweetbreads, brains, bone marrow, liver and lung) quickly blanched, coated in breadcrumbs and fried in butter. Sometimes mushroom caps, slices of zucchini and eggplants and chicken and sausage patties may also be added to the fry. Recipe typical of Milan. Lombardy.

fritto misto alla piemontese aka **fritto misto alla alla langarola** aka **fritto misto all'astigiana**, in dialect aka **fricia** grand mixed savory and sweet fry of veal chops, chunks of pork sausage and bone marrow, sliced liver, sweetbreads, brains, → **griva** aka **frissa** (a meat patty), semolina (→ **frittura dolce**), slices of apple and, sometimes, amaretti cookies softened in Marsala, carrots, zucchini matchsticks, cauliflower florets and fennel wedges. Old recipes also call for calf's lung and bull's testicles (→ **granelli**). Modern versions may also include frogs, snails, porcini mushrooms, lamb cutlets, eggplants and artichokes. Piedmont.

fritto misto alla romana mixed fry featuring two of the staples of Roman cuisine: artichokes and offal. The ingredients generally include globe artichoke wedges, lamb's or calf's brain, plus calf's bone marrow, sweetbreads and liver. They are coated with flour, then dipped in beaten egg and fried in boiling oil (in the past, lard). The recipe used to include → **pandorato** (a miniature fried ham and cheese sandwich), today it embraces rice or potato croquettes, slices of mozzarella and zucchini flowers. Lazio.

fritto misto alla toscana mixed fry of mainly white meats (chicken and rabbit), first marinated in oil and lemon, then dipped in beaten egg, but also lamb chops and croquettes of leftover boiled beef and potatoes; offal (lamb's or calf's brains and sweetbreads, chicken livers and stomachs); and vegetables (onion rings, zucchini and their flowers, artichokes and sage (→ **salvia fritta**). The version described refers to the recipe typical of the province of Florence. Tuscany.

fritto misto di laguna mixed fry of small lagoon fish (anchovies, gobies, soles, eels etc.), crustaceans (gray and pink shrimp etc.) and mollusks (baby squid, cuttlefish etc.), the composition of which varies according to season and catch. Tra-

ditionally served with polenta. Veneto, Emilia-Romagna.

fritto misto di pesce mixed fried fish. In Liguria, the dish originated in restaurants on the Riviera, not in popular tradition. It should include baby squid, shrimp, anchovies, mullet, sea bream picarel and red band fish, though combinations vary according to locality. In the center and south of Italy, they call the same dish → **frittura** or → **fritto di paranza**. Liguria.

frittole aka **frittuli** aka **curacchie** pig's innards, snout, ears and pork rind flavored with salt and chili and cooked in their own fat in a copper pan (*caddàra*). The mixture, which can be kept for up to a year preserved in lard, is eaten cold or heated, or in soups and sauces. This dish is traditionally prepared on the day of the killing of the pig in areas of the Sila plateau (Calabria) and the province of Messina (Sicily).

frittula Sicilian term for → **ciccioli**, pork scratchings.

frittuli another name for → **frittole**.

frittura bianca Piedmontese expression for a cow's lung, once an ingredient of → **fritto misto alla piemontese**.

frittura di fragaglia tiny fish, the ones that stick to the bottom of nets, coated in wheat flour, and fried in boiling oil. In some areas of the south, the term *fragaglia* also refers to the fry of anchovies, mullet and other fish (→ **novellame**, fry).

frittura di lago mixed fry of bleak and freshwater sardines coated in flour and fillets of burbot and bleak dipped in beaten egg, then in breadcrumbs. The fish are fried in olive oil and in natural or clarified butter. A specialty of Laks Garda and Como.

frittura di pesce di fiume mixed fry of freshwater fish. In the province of Piacenza it is made with eel, catfish and bleak, in Piedmont with bleak, stroemling and barbel. The fish may be coated with flour or batter, depending on local custom.

frittura di rane e gamberi frogs and crayfish fried in oil and seasoned with salt. A dish typical of the southern part of the province of Milan, a great rice-growing area, now a recognized "agricultural park" (Parco Agricolo Sud Milano). Lombardy.

frittura di sangue di pollo now rare dish of slices of bread sprinkled with the blood of a recently slaughtered chicken, fried in butter and dusted with sugar or salt. Typical of the province of Pavia. Lombardy.

frittura dolce fried semolina. A cooked mixture of semolina, eggs and milk, seasoned with salt and aromatized with grated lemon zest, first allowed to cool and set, then rolled out and cut into lozenge shapes, dipped in egg, coated with breadcrumbs and fried in oil. Served as a side dish or garnish, and also an important component in ➤ **fritto misto alla piemontese**. Piedmont.

frittura piccata another name for ➤ **piccata**.

fritules di lops fritters made with a small, slightly sour-tasting apple variety typical of the Carnia area, in the province of Udine, sliced, dipped in a batter of eggs, flour, sugar, milk and yeast, fried in boiling oil and dusted with confectioner's sugar. Friuli-Venezia Giulia.

frizon another name for ➤ **friggione**, cream of onion and tomatoes

frizze Friulian term for ➤ **ciccioli**, pork scratchings.

frollatura the hanging of meat or game.

frollini di santa Lucia flat buttery cookies dusted with sugar and variously shaped: stars, halfmoons, butterflies, donkeys, dolls etc. Traditionally given as a gift to children on Santa Lucia's day (December 13) and still popular in Verona and its province around that period. Veneto.

frollino (pl. **frollini**) variously shaped shortcrust pastry cookie, sometimes garnished with candied fruits, dried fruit, chocolate and jam, often eaten for breakfast.

Fromadzo abbreviated name for ➤ **Valle d'Aosta fromadzo**.

fromadzo de cochon literally "pig's head cheese". A cured meat obtained by slow-cooking a pig's head. A specialty of the La Thuile area. Val d'Aosta.

frostenga another name for ➤ **frustingo**, a Christmas cake.

frue either the fresh curd of ewe's or goat's milk, also known in some areas as *fiscidu* or *viscidu*, or sour curd in brine (➤ **merca**). Sardinia.

frullare to blend. To combine different ingredients with a spoon, beater or electric liquidizer to achieve a uniform mixture.

frullato smoothie. Fruit or vegetables puréed with an electric liquidizer. If ice is added, it becomes a ➤ **frappé**.

frullino half snipe (*Limnocryptes minima*). Wading bird similar to the snipe (➤ **beccaccino**), but smaller.

frumentin northern Italian dialect term for buckwheat (➤ **grano saraceno**).

wheat wheat. Common name for grasses of the Triticum genus of the Graminaceae family. Wheats for breadmaking are divided into two categories: soft *grano tenero* (*Triticum vulgare* or *aestivum*) and strong durum *grano duro* (*T. turgidum durum*). The former is cultivated mainly in the Po Valley, the latter in central and southern regions, especially Puglia and Sicily. Wheat is an annual crop, generally sowed in late autumn, and harvested in June-July., The durum wheat of Sicily, the "granary" of Italy since Roman times, is listed in the Italian Ministry of Agriculture's database of native and/or traditional food products, along with *senatore cap-*

pelli (Campania and Sardinia) and *sara-golla* (Campania).

frumento Vemento name for →**mais**, corn.

frusta long-lasting wholemeal bread, typical of Giulianello di Cori, in the province of Latina. Lazio.

frustingo Christmas cake once made with poor ingredients such as dried figs, walnuts and almonds, now with the addition of raisins, candied fruit, cocoa, rum, coffee and →**mistrà**, aniseed liqueur. There are two main recipes: in the first, extra virgin olive oil is used as the binding element; in the second, the ingredients are amalgamated with bread dough. The name of the cake derives from *frusto* (poor, humble). Other popular names: →**frostenga**, →**pistinco**, →**pistringo**. Marche.

frutta martorana another name for →**pasta reale (1)**, almond paste, derived from the fact that most almond past confections are shaped like fruits and that the nuns of the Martorana monastery in Palermo used to be particularly good at making them. Sicily.

frutta secca dried fruit. The term covers not only "nuts", such as walnuts, hazelnuts, almonds, pine kernels, pistachio nuts and peanuts, but also seasonal fruit, such as peaches, apricots, plums, pears, apricots, figs and grapes, dried and dehydrated. Also dried and widely used for culinary purposes, especially in mountain areas, are chestnuts (→ **castagne secche**). Piedmont dried apricots and plums are called → **ciapòle**, peaches → **ciape 'd nòna**. In Romagna dried apple and pear slices are called → **parsèch**, in Emilia → **bédui** or → **barciùll**. In the province of Belluno (Veneto), they are → **kodinze**, in the Sabina area → **carozzi** and → **cinciacotte**.

frutti del sottobosco aka **frutti di bosco** woodland fruits. Wild strawberries, rasp-berries, blackberries, redcurrants and so on. Also cultivated in Val d'Aosta, Piedmont (the mountain valleys of the provinces of Cuneo and Turin), Trentino-Alto Adige and Tuscany (especially in the mountains of the province of Pistoia). In Italy wild fruits are eaten fresh but more often processed into jams, juices, syrups and (in the case of raspberries) vinegars.

frutti di bosco another name for → **frutti del sottobosco**, woodland fruits.

frutti di mare seafood. Edible marine organisms, including mollusks, gastropods, crustaceans, echinoderms, tunicates and and so on.

fruttone a variation on → **pasticciotto** with almond paste in lieu of confectioner's custard and dark chocolate icing. A cake typical of the province of Lecce. Puglia.

fuazza crisp pizza filled with vegetables and rolled up. Sicily.

fügascia de Punt sweet flatbread made with wheat flour, sugar, yeast and abundant butter. Typical of the area round Ponte in Valtellin, in the province of Sondrio, and traditionally baked in a wood oven. Lombardy.

fugascina di Mergozzo leavened flatbread made with flour, butter, sugar, eggs, Marsala and lemon zest. Baked in the village of Mergozzo (province of Verbano-Cusio-Ossola) for the feast of Santa Elisabetta, and served cut into small squares. Piedmont.

fugassa (1) rich sweet Easter bread, not to be confused with →**fogassa veronese**. Leavened dough is mixed with butter, eggs, sugar, honey, raisins, vanilla and lemon zest and shaped into loaves. These are brushed with beaten egg white, covered with sugar chips, garnished with almonds, leavened a second time, then baked in the oven. A specialty of Vicenza. Veneto.

fugassa (2) Ligurian dialect term for ➤ **fo-caccia genovese**.

fugassin another name for ➤ **fazzino**, a type of flatbread.

fumetto (1) fumet. One of the cooking bases (➤ **fondo**) of international cuisine. A concentrated broth obtained from fish (bones, head and trimmings), vegetables and aromatic herbs, butter and pepper.

fumetto (2) very finely ground cornflour.

funciddi dried almond and hazelnut cookies. Specialty of Buccheri, in the province of Siracusa, Sicily.

funghetti di Offida mushroom-shaped Carnival pastries made of flour, water, sugar and aniseed. Typical of Offida, in the province of Ascoli Piceno. Marche.

funghetto, al technique for cooking diced vegetables with garlic, oil and parsley.

fungo mushroom. Common name for fungi, of which various species exist, differing in shape and color. They grow in symbiosis with the roots of some trees, especially in the mountain and hilly woodland and in meadows. Italy boasts a large variety of edible varieties, the cep or porcini and royal argaric, being the most prized, hence costly. In Tuscany numerous excellent varieties of Boletus are available all year round, while the porcini of the Sila plateau (Calabria), the volcano of Roccamonfina (Campania) and the mountain valleys of the province of Cuneo and Giaveno, in the province of Turin, are also highly regarded. The ➤ **fungo di Borgotaro** (Emilia-Romagna) has received the PGI seal. In other regions, honey, mousseron and morel mushrooms are very popular. In Puglia, the great oyster mushroom features in many recipes, as do St George's mushroom in Molise, mousserons in Campania and the white ferula mushroom in Sicily's Madonie mountains. In Piedmont,

they love the honey armillary mushroom, in Liguria chanterelles, ceps and saffron milk-caps, in Calabria red pine mushroom. In some cases minor mushroom varieties have long been cultivated in Montello, in the province of Treviso, and in Costozza, in the province of Vicenza. The domestic tradition of preserving mushrooms in oil and drying them has given rise to a large industrial sector, supported by small artisan firms in the various Italian regions.

funghi sott'olio mushrooms preserved in oil. A specialty in many regions. In most places, freshly picked mushrooms are cleaned and poached in boiling vinegar with a pinch of salt. They are then transferred to glass jars and covered with oil. Finally, the jars are hermetically sealed. Preserved in this way, the mushrooms are served as an antipasto.

funghi trifolati sautéed mushrooms. A dish common in many regions. The mushrooms are cut into slices or diced, sautéed in olive oil with garlic and chopped parsley. In Veneto and Piedmont the ➤ **chiodino** mushroom is popular, in Tuscany and Liguria they prefer mixed mushrooms and add fresh ➤ **nepitella** lesser calamint.

funghiascia another name for ➤ **fioret**, a flat sweetbread.

fungo de la saeta dialect term for ➤ **prugnolo**, mousseron mushroom.

fungo del cardo regional term for ➤ **car-doncello,** king oyster mushroom.

fungo del sangue regional term for ➤ **san-guinello**, saffron milk-cap mushroom.

fungo di Borgotaro the PGI seal protects four varieties of fleshy porcini mushrooms (*Boletus aestivalis, B. pinophilus, B. edulis* and *B. aereus*) in the valley of Borgataro, in the province of Parma (Emilia-Romagna).

fungo di carne regional term for → **cardoncello,** king oyster mushroom.

fungo di ferla regional term for → **cardoncello,** king oyster mushroom.

fungo di san Giorgio regional term for → **prugnolo,** mousseron mushroom.

fungo reale common name for → **ovolo,** royal argaric mushroom.

furbi Marche dialect word for baby octopus (→ **polpo**). Baby octopus cooked with chard, tomato, marjoram and chili, served with polenta is a popular dish in Civitanova Marche. Marche.

fusaglia regional term for → **lupino,** lupin.

fusidde Puglia term for → **fusilli,** → **maccheroni al (con il) ferretto,** a type of pasta.

fusilli spiral-shaped commercial durum wheat pasta of southern Italian origin, long or short, sometimes hollow. Served with → **ragù napoletano** or tomato sauce, sometimes with the addition of ricotta.

fusilli alla napoletana fusilli served with roast beef gravy strengthened with pancetta, aromatic vegetables, diced salami and ricotta. The roast beef is served after the pasta as the main course. Campania.

fusilli con la mollica simple pasta dish of →**maccheroni al ferretto** served with lightly fried oil, garlic and breadcrumbs. Basilicata.

gG

gabbespata dialect term for the smoked ricotta of the Sila mountains and the area round Crotone. Calabria.

gaccio another name for → **neccio**, a type of waffle.

gaffo Roman dialect name for the cow's cheek used as an ingredient in many local recipes, including → **coda alla vaccinara**. Lazio.

gaggette pinn-e white cabbage stuffed with fresh breadcrumbs, grated Parmigiano, eggs, marjoram and, sometimes, sausage or mortadella, then blanched. Liguria.

gaggìa common name for → **acacia**, acacia.

galani northeast Italian term for sweet fried pastries similar to → **cenci**. A savory version also exists.

galantina (1) galantine. A *farce* (→ **farcia**) of diced chicken or turkey garnished with boiled ham, tongue, truffle and pistachio nuts, wrapped in the bird's skin, caul or a thin slice of veal, and boiled. Served cold, often in aspic.

galantina (2) variation on → **testa in cassetta**, made with meat from the leg of the pig and pancetta as opposed to meat from the head and shoulder.

galantina di pesce galantine of fish. Eel, carp, perch and tench flesh covered with a mixture of gently fried butter, parsley, garlic, anchovy, salt, pepper, pistachio nuts and, on occasion, truffle, marinated for a day in white wine, boiled in fish or frog broth and left to cool. A specialty of Milan, but probably Mantuan in origin. Lombardy.

galantina di pollo aka **galantina di cappone** galantine of chicken or capon. The bird is boned, flattened, stuffed with mixed meats (veal, pork, the breast of the bird, prosciutto and corned tongue) marinated in Marsala, chopped, seasoned with salt and pepper and bound with eggs. Strips of prosciutto, tongue, mortadella, diced black truffle and pistachio nuts, arranged in alternate layers, complete the filling. The galantine is cooked in vegetable broth (in Tuscany in a broth made from the remains of the bird), then left to cool before being served sliced, garnished with diced aspic. A traditional specialty in a number of regions, where it is served as an antipasto or main course. Emilia-Romagna, Piedmont, Tuscany.

gale regional name for → **cenci**, fried pastries. Lombardy.

galera regional term for → **cepola**, red band fish.

galiti term used in the Polesine area for → **popcorn**. Veneto.

galitola dialect term for → **cantarello**, chanterelle mushroom.

galle durum wheat pasta with an oval section and serrated edges, pinched at the center to form a small bow. Smaller than → **farfalle**, it is served with tomato sauce or ham, cream and peas. Of northern Italian origin. Other names: → **francesine**, → **strichetti**.

galletta del marinaio ship's biscuit. Flat, round, long-lasting rusk once used in the military and merchant navy. Made from soft flour, sourdough, water, salt, olive oil and malt, today almost exclusively for certain Ligurian dishes, such as → **cappon magro**, → **capponada**, and → **con-**

diggiun. The same dough is used, with the addition of sugar and eggs, to make sweet cookies.

gallettinas crumbly cookies, oval in shape and about three inches long. Made from a dough of wheat flour, ammonium carbonate, eggs, refined sugar, lard and grated lemon zest. Dusted with icing sugar, baked in the oven and served with tea or milk, they are a classic part of the Sardinian breakfast. Sardinia.

galletto (1) a young cockerel or rooster (➤ **pollo**, chicken).

galletto (2) another name for ➤ **cantarello**, chanterelle mushroom.

galletto ripieno di ragù a free-range rooster or chicken stuffed with a mixture of its own giblets, chopped and fried with herbs, bread soaked in water and grated Pecorino, bound with beaten eggs and cooked in the pot with cherry tomatoes and white wine. A traditional holiday dish, served at Christmas, Easter and, above all, Ferragosto (August 15). Puglia.

gallina hen. Hens are raised mainly for their eggs, of which, from the age of five to 18-20 months, they lay 250 and more a a year. Free-range hens raised on varied, natural feed produce excellent broth and tasty meat, which figures in a number of important recipes. In northern Italy, boiled hen (**gallina bollita**) is an ingredient in ➤ **bollito misto**; in the south, stuffed hen (➤ **gallina ripiena**) is popular. The Italian Ministry of Agriculture's database of traditional and/or native food products includes the following hen breeds: in Piedmont, ➤ **gallina bianca di Saluzzo** and **gallina bionda piemontese**; in Veneto, ➤ **gallina padovana**, *gallina a collo nudo di corte padovana, gallina dorata di Lonigo, gallina ermellinata di Rovigo, gallina polverara, gallina robusta lionata* and *gallina robusta mac-*

ulata; in Tuscany, *gallina mugellese* (aka *gallina mugginese*).

gallina bianca di Saluzzo, gallina bionda piemontese traditional hen breeds supplanted over the last few decades by battery breeding. A Slow Food presidium has been established to protect them. The **gallina bianca**, or white hen, is bred in the Saluzzo area, in the province of Cuneo, and in villages nearby in the province of Turin. The **gallina bionda**, or blonde hen, is bred in the provinces of Cuneo, Asti and Turin. Piedmont.

gallina con il mirto chicken with myrtle. The bird is boiled in water flavored with onion, celery, carrot and parsley, drained and wrapped for a day in myrtle leaves. After which it is served cold. Sardinia.

gallina faraona another name for ➤ **faraona**, guinea fowl.

gallina in cialòta hen cut into pieces and served with a sauce of vegetables lightly fried in oil with vinegar and desalted anchovies. Served hot or cold. The dialect term ➤ **cialòta**, now rarely used, means sauce or delicacy. Recipe typical of the Langhe hills. Piedmont.

gallina padovana Paduan hen. Brought to the Veneto region in the 14th century, probably from Poland. Plumage can be black, white, gold, tan or silver, and the bird has a long beard and whiskers. Its most distinctive feature is the large tuft of long feathers which crowns its head and drops over its eyes. It scratches about in spaces of at least four square feet and eats mainly corn. On the verge of extinction, the breed was saved by a group of amateur breeders and a Slow Food presidium. In restaurants and poultry shops in and around Padua, the hen is now available with the presidium's seal of approval. The classic recipe for the breed is ➤ **cappone alla canavera**. Typical of the province of Padua and bordering areas of the province of Venice. Veneto.

gallina ripiena stuffed hen. A hen stuffed with a mixture of its own giblets, chicken livers and ground beef (or sausage) boiled rice, grated Caciocavallo cheese, breadcrumbs, beaten eggs and herbs, and slowly roasted in a casserole dish with broth and wine. In Sardinia, they stuff the fowl with a mixture of its own gizzard, sausage or lardo, eggs, fresh breadcrumbs, chopped sun-dried tomatoes, onion and parsley. In another version, the fowl is stuffed with fresh breadcrumbs, eggs, parsley, lard and sugar, slow-boiled for two to three hours, and served with the sliced stuffing (sometimes the latter even appears as a dessert at the end of the meal). A Christmas specialty, especially in the province of Ragusa. Sicily.

gallina ripiena di verze e amaretti hen stuffed with Savoy cabbage and amaretti cookies. Typical of the area round the town of Crema, the recipe is a throwback to Renaissance court cuisine based on the contrast between sweet and savory. The bird is stuffed with shredded Savoy cabbage (➤ **cavolo verza**), sautéed in butter with onions, crushed amaretti cookies, grated Grana Padano cheese, eggs, salt, pepper and nutmeg. Lombardy.

gallinaccio regional term for both ➤ **cantarello**, chanterelle mushroom, and ➤ **carota selvatica**, wild carrot.

gallinella (1) another name for ➤ **capone gallinella**, tub gurnard.

gallinella (2) another name for ➤ **pesce (2)**, a cut of beef.

gallinella (3) common regional term for ➤ **valerianella**, common cornsalad.

gallinetta common regional term for ➤ **valerianella**, common cornsalad.

gallo maschio rooster or cockerel (*Gallus domesticus*). Characterized by its bright-

colored plumage, fleshy red crest and curved beak. Now rare commercially, the market now being dominated by chickens (➤ **pollo**, chicken). Today the only roosters with meat of decent quality come from small family farms. *Gallo ruspante delle Marche* (Marche) and *galletto nano di corte padovana* (Veneto) are the only varieties listed in the Italian Ministry of Agriculture's database of traditional and/or native food products.

gallo alla babi chicken split open and flattened so that it assumes the shape of a toad (*babi*, in dialect). Cooked in a casserole dish with garlic, peppercorns, bay leaves, and juniper berries, and basted with boiling wine. A weight is placed on top to keep the shape. Typical of the province of Asti. Piedmont.

gallo cedrone capercaillie (*Tetrao urogallus*).

gallo d'India another name for ➤ **tacchino**, turkey.

gallo forcello, or ➤ **fagiano di monte**, black grouse (*Tetrao tetrix* or *Lyrurus tetrix*). The bird lives in the wild in the Alps, though it is also occasionally spotted in the Tuscan and Emilian Apennines. Unlike the ➤ **gallo cedrone**, capercaillie, and albeit rare, the black grouse may be hunted. It is cooked in the same ways as the common pheasant.

galluzzo regional name for the ➤ **cantarello**, chanterelle mushroom.

galucio cockerel-shaped sweet cookie, given to children as a Christmas gift. Piedmont.

gamberetto shrimp (➤ **gambero**), less than 10 centimeters long.

gamberetto di nassa red shrimp (*Plesionika narval*) with long and pointed rostrum. Lives in dark underwater caves and has particularly sweet, firm meat. Fished with the *nassa*, a hand-plaited rush and myrtle basket, on the southern side of the

Sorrento peninsula (province of Naples). Campania.

gambero shrimp, prawn, or crayfish. The shrimp typically fished and eaten off Italy are *gambero rosso mediteraneo*, red Mediterranean shrimp (*Aristeomorpha foliacea* and *Aristeus antennatus*), *gambero imperiale*, triple-grooved shrimp (*Penaeus kerathurus*)— not to be confused with the kuruma shrimp or prawn (*Penaeus japonicus*), imported frozen from the Pacific—, *gambero rosa*, deep water rose shrimp (*Parapenaeus longirostris*) and ➤ **gamberetto di nassa**, red shrimp (*Plesionika narval*). Small shrimp are eaten fried or briefly boiled and served with tomato sauce or finished in the pan with garlic and parsley, whereas larger species are broiled. Italian freshwater species are *gambero delle zampe*, white-clawed crayfish (*Austropotamobius pallipes*), to be found all over the peninsula, and *gambero di fiume*, European crayfish (*Astacus astacus*), which survives today only in the eastern part of Venezia Giulia. Delicate in flavor, they are broiled or used to flavor risottos and pasta sauces. The European crayfish and *gamberetto ligure*, Ligurian shrimp, are included in the Italian Ministry of Agriculture's database of native and/or traditional species.

gamberone Red Mediterranean shrimp (*Aristeomorpha foliacea* and *Aristeus antennatus*), over five inches in length (➤ **gambero**).

gamberone mediterraneo another name for *gambero imperiale*, triple-grooved shrimp (➤ **gambero**, shrimp, prawn, or crayfish).

gambetta dialect term for ➤ **porcinello**, type of mushroom.

gambòn Piacenza dialect name for *gambotto*, the leg of a young pig, boned, pressed between two boards and hung to age in a cool place. When the time comes, the leg is softened in water for half an hour, then boiled for hours. Served hot in slices with potato purée. Emilia-Romagna.

ganascino calf or pig's cheek, stewed, braised or boiled. Lombardy, Piedmont.

ganassino another word for ➤ **ganascino**, calf or pig's cheek.

garagolo dialect word for ➤ **piè di pellicano**, pelican's foot, a sea snail, along the Romagna coast and as far as Pesaro, in the Marche. Further south, in the province of Ancona, the name changes to ➤ **crocetta**. Mostly stewed, cooked ➤ **in porchetta** with wild fennel, or simply boiled with oil and lemon. In Romagna, it used to be sold at kiosks on seaside promenades. Emilia-Romagna, Marche.

garazze Calabrian term for ➤ **ciccioli**, pork scratchings.

garbo Veneto term for "acid," "vinegary," as in ➤ **dolzegarbo**, the regional equivalent of ➤ **agrodolce**, sweet and sour.

garbodolze another word, for ➤ **dolzegarbo**, sweet and sour. Veneto.

gardela aka **gratela** traditional grill for broiling meat, fish (➤ **rustida romagnola**), vegetables. Emilia-Romagna.

garessine dried chestnuts typical of the area round Garessio, a village in the Valle Tanaro, in the province of Cuneo. Piedmont.

garfagnino another name for ➤ **pane di patate della Garfagnana**, potato bread.

garganelli al pettine small hollow egg maccheroni enriched with Parmigiano and nutmeg. Made by cutting a sheet of pasta dough into small squares, wrapping them round a stick, and running them over a utensil known as a *pettine*, or comb. Traditionally served in broth, now also with a sauce of sausage and peas. Emilia-Romagna.

gargati con il consiero hollow, ridged fresh maccheroni made from a dough of flour, durum wheat semolina and eggs, drawn through a small press. The word *consiero* is the name of the traditional accompanying sauce of coarsely ground mixed meats (pork, chicken, veal, beef), browned in the pan and cooked in white wine with seasonal vegetables (eg, ➤ **radicchio rosso di Treviso**, ➤ **bruscandoli**, or hops, artichokes, asparagus, peas). The same type of pasta also goes well with pigeon or chicken giblet sauce. A specialty of the province of Vicenza. Veneto.

garisole aka **garisoli** northern Italian term for ➤ **ciccioli**, pork scratchings.

garmugia centuries-old spring soup of spring onions, artichokes, peas, fava beans, pancetta (or fatty prosciutto), ground beef, beef broth, salt and pepper, typical of the province of Lucca. Served poured over slices of toasted bread. Tuscany.

garofolato round of ox or beef (though in the Ciociaria area they use castrated lamb) stuck with rosemary-flavored lardons, aromatized with marjoram, seasoned with salt and pepper, tied up with kitchen string and slow-braised in a pot for three hours with wine, skinned tomatoes or tomato paste, nutmeg and a generous amount of cloves. The resulting sauce is excellent served with pasta. Lazio.

garunet word used in Tortona for lasagna (➤ **lasagne della vigilia**). Piedmont.

garusol Veneto word for ➤ **murice**, murex or rock snail.

garusoli in umido rock snails stewed with garlic, onion, parsley, desalted anchovies, white wine and tomato. Veneto, Friuli-Venezia Giulia.

gasse form of egg pasta created by taking a strip of pasta dough and tying it into a noose (the name refers to a Genovese sailors' knot). Liguria.

gattafin aka **gattafuin (1)** large fried ravioli filled with chard, herbs, ricotta and Parmigiano. A specialty of Levanto, in the province of La Spezia.

gattafin (2) ancient eastern Ligurian vegetable soup (similar to ➤ **preboggion**) consisting of a mixture of the following leaves and herbs: bristly hawkbit (➤ **dente di leone**), common brighteyes (➤ **grattalingua**), beaked hawksbeard (➤ **radicchiella**), poppy (➤ **rosolaccio**), golden fleece (➤ **boccione maggiore**), field sowthistle (➤ **grespigno**), dandelion (➤ **tarassaco**), red valerian (➤ **valeriana rossa**), wild fennel (➤ **finocchio selvatico**). The same mixture may originally have been used for the filling of **gattafin (1)**, fried ravioli. The name may derive from ➤ **gattafura**, mentioned in late Medieval and Renaissance recipe collections. Liguria.

gattafura two layers of pastry filled with cream cheese mixed with chopped chard and mint. The ancestor of modern Ligurian vegetable pies, cited by Mastro Martino in the 14th century and Bartolomeo Scappi in the 16th century. Liguria

gattò (1) aka **gattò Santa Chiara** mixture of puréed potato, suet, eggs, grated Pecorino and Parmigiano layered in a baking tin with slices of salami, Provola and ➤ **Fiordilatte** and baked in the oven. A specialty of Naples. The alternative name derives from the Monastery of Santa Chiara, where they used to make the dish. Campania.

gattò (2) a "brittle" made of peeled, crushed almonds, refined sugar and grated lemon zest, cut into lozenge shapes. Keeps for a long time in glass jars or tin boxes. Sardinia.

gattò aretino cake made with a mixture of wheat flour, eggs, sugar, potato flour, butter and yeast shaped into a thin, flat "loaf," baked in the oven, drizzled with alkermes and sugar syrup (or Vin Santo), filled with jam, vanilla custard or chocolate sauce (depending on the area), rolled up into a sausage shape and dusted with sugar. Traditionally made at country weddings. In the Chianti and other areas, the cake is known as → **salame dolce**. Tuscany.

gattuccio lesser spotted dogfish (*Scyliorhinus canicula*). One of the commonest sharks in the Mediterranean. Its rather tough meat is sold fresh or dried as pre-skinned steaks. Used in strong-flavored recipes with tomato, garlic, onion and herbs. Also used in soups and stews, especially in Sardinia (see → **azzada**, → **burrida**).

gedule regional term for → **rapastrello**, wild radish.

gelatina gelatin. Thickening agent which assumes a sticky texture when heated, solid when cooled. May be of vegetable or animal origin. In the former case, it is also known as pectin, and is derived from apple and citrus fruit peel. In the latter case, it is derived from animal bones, tendons, connective tissues, hooves and other parts, or from fish bones and heads. In the kitchen, it serves to thicken broths or gravies. It figures in regional recipes such as → **cappone in gelatina**, → **gelatina di maiale**, → **gelatina friulana**, → **zeraria**.

gelatina di frutta fruit jelly. Sweet, gelatinized condiment of sugar and the juice of a single or mixed fruits, especially those with a high pectin content, such as raspberries, blackcurrants, apples, quinces, redcurrants and gooseberry. Fluid and translucent, it is used in confectionery to fill cakes and pastries and to glaze cakes decorated with candied fruit. Wild berry and woodland fruit *gelées* (→ **gelée**) are still popular among the Waldensian populations of Piedmont, historically connected with Germany, France and the English-speaking world.

gelatina di maiale (1) pieces of pork (in the old days the cheapest cuts, now also blade, knuckle and hock) in water and vinegar with mixed herbs. After which they are boned, pressed in a mold and refrigerated for 12 hours. The day after they are cut into slices, which are covered with the filtered broth and refrigerated for another three hours to set. A traditional cold dish. Sicily.

gelatina di maiale (2) traditional, long-lasting cured meat consisting of boned pig's head, trotters and tail boiled and cut into pieces. The meat is then recooked in the filtered broth with vinegar, hot chili, garlic cloves and bay leaves. The mixture is allowed to cool, then transferred into glass or earthenware jars (→ **terzaluru**). Calabria.

gelatina di melagrana pomegranate jelly. Pomegranate juice cooked with sugar and grated orange zest until thick, and preserved in glass jars. Puglia.

gelatina friulana jelly made from a broth of calf's trotter and tongue and a pig's smoked shin and ears. Three quarters of the way through the cooking process, which lasts for six hours, a dash of vinegar is added. The warm broth is poured into dishes containing garlic, bay leaf, pepper and a sliced hard-boiled egg. It is then left to set completely and served. Traditional as an antipasto on Easter Sunday. Friuli-Venezia Giulia.

gelatinare to cover with → **gelatina**, gelatin or aspic.

gelato ice cream. The basic ingredients (sugar, milk, cream, egg yolks, fruit), flavored with vanilla, cocoa, coffee and so on, are blended to a homogeneous, velvety consistency (→**mantecare**) and refrigerated at between -14°C and-18°C. Ice creams may be divided into two main groups: cream (with a base of milk or cream, egg yolks and sugar thickened over a heat and cold-blended) and fruit (fresh or in the form of pulp, juice or syrup, mixed with water or milk). Related sweet confections are: ➤ **bomba (2)**, ➤ **soufflé gelati**, iced ➤ **parfait**, ➤ **spumone**, ➤ **cassata**, ➤ **semifreddo**, ➤ **granita**, ➤ **cremolato di frutta**, ➤ **sorbetto**. Sweet substances, fruit juices in particular, were already being frozen in antiquity, especially in Asia Minor. In modern times, however, the story of ice cream is entirely Italian. Created in the 16th century, its paternity is contended between two Florentines: a butcher and pastry chef by the name of Ruggeri and Bernardo Buontalenti, an architect whose hobby was cooking. A century later, a pioneer in the sorbet and granita business was a Sicilian, Francesco Procopio dei Coltelli (whose real name was probably Cutò), manager of the celebrated Café Procope in Paris in 1686. Ice creams were introduced to Britain and later to North America by emigrants from Genoa, Naples and, above all, Veneto. A capital of artisan ice cream making is the Cadore area, especially the Val Belluna and Val Zoldana, in the province of Belluno. Here the confection was made in tubs, frozen with ice and salt and carried off on carts to be sold in urban streets and piazzas. To this day, ice cream makers from the two valleys travel abroad, mainly to Germany, to sell their wares.

gelato di campagna dessert made by blending colored sugar syrup with cinnamon, pieces of candied fruit, almonds and pistachio nuts. Of Arab origin, it was elaborated in the island's monasteries and convents in the mid 19th century. Invariably on sale at stalls during popular festivals, it owes its name to the fact that it melts in the mouth just like an ice cream. Sicily.

gelato di ricotta frozen mousse made by whipping very fresh ➤ **ricotta romana**, sugar, eggs and rum or cognac, and refrigerating before serving. Typical of Rome. Lazio.

gelda aka **jelda** Sardinian terms for ➤ **ciccioli**, pork scratchings.

gelée French word for ➤ **gelatina di frutta**, fruit jelly.

gelo dessert that changes flavor according to place. The most popular **gelo** is *gelo di mellone*, in dialect, *jelu* aka *gelu 'i muluni*. The rind and the seeds are removed from the melon and the flesh is puréed, then cooked on a low heat with starch, sugar, cinnamon and an infusion of jasmine. Once the mixture has thickened, it is allowed to cool, then decorated with pieces of dark chocolate, chopped pistachio nuts and/or candied pumpkin. A delicacy in the provinces of Ragusa and Siracusa is **gelo** made with carob (➤ **carruba**). Chopped dried carobs are boiled in water, and the resulting infusion is filtered and thickened with starch on a high heat. The dessert is made in much the same way with cinnamon. Made with prickly pears, the juice of the fruit is used. To make coffee-flavored **gelo**, water and strong, bitter coffee are mixed in equal parts, then sweetened with sugar and cooked with starch to thicken. Sicily.

gelone oyster mushroom (*Plerotus ostreatus*). Common edible mushroom, much cultivated, hence available all year round. The cap is white, hazel or brown in color, its flesh white and elastic. Normally stewed (often with other varieties), broiled or preserved in oil. Common names: ➤ **orecchione**, ➤ **cardella**, ➤ **melina**, ➤ **peperona**, ➤ **agarico ostreato**.

gelsomino jasmine. All varieties of *Jasminum* are creepers with white, highly scented flowers. Jasmine essences are used in Sicilian and Sardinian confectionery. In Sardinia, ➤ **gesminos**, almond cakes, used to be aromatized with jasmine, now replaced by orange blossom water (➤ **acqua di fiori d'arancio**); in Sicily, ➤ **gelo di mellone** is perfumed with a jasmine infusion.

gemelli commercial spiral-shaped durum wheat pasta typical of central-southern Italy. Served with all manner of sauces, from meat to tomato, often with the addition of ricotta.

genepì aka **genepy** herb liqueur made by macerating wormwoods (*Artemisia mutellina*, *A. glacialis* and others), herbs common throughout the western Alps, especially in the Val Chisone, in the province of Turin. Now sometimes specially cultivated for the purpose, the herbs are left to infuse for about 40 days in alcohol to which a sugar and water syrup is added. The liquid is filtered repeatedly and, after aging for a certain period in the bottle, the final liqueur assumes a pale greenish-yellow color. With its sweet, complex taste, redolent of Alpine herbs, **genepì** is one of the basic ingredients of ➤ **caffè alla valdostana**.

genovese leftover boiled beef and pork reheated with abundant onions, lardo, aromatics, tomato paste, bay leaves and basil. The meat is served as a main course, the sauce is served with pastas such as ➤ **paccheri**, ➤ **ziti**, or ➤ **perciatelli**. Campania.

gensola regional term for ➤ **giuggiola**, jujube.

Gentile di Puglia sheep breed, first produced in the Foggia area in the 15th century by crossing Carfagna ewes from Puglia with Spanish Merino rams. In the past, it was raised mainly for its wool, nowadays for its meat. Medium-sized with spiral horns, a long trunk and a curly fleece, it has now spread from Foggia to the rest of Puglia, Basilicata and Calabria.

genuidde sweet ravioli made of flour, sugar, milk, extra virgin olive oil and grappa, filled with ➤ **mostarda** or unsweetened stewed grapes. Calabria.

geretto cut of beef roughly equivalent to shin and leg (➤ **ossobuco**). Boned, boiled and shredded, it is served in salads. The leg may also be used to make jelly.

geri dialect term for ➤ **bietola selvatica**, wild chard.

germano reale mallard (*Anas plathyrhynchos*). A native of Eurasia, the best known of wild ducks but easy to farm. Feeds on worms, insects, small fish and their roe and aquatic plants. Common in the wetlands of northern and central Italy from November to February. Albeit leaner and firmer than that of the common duck, mallard meat is prepared according to the same recipes.

germogli sprouts, shoots, tips. The new sprouts, shoots or tips of mainly spontaneous plants (hops, ➤ **luppolo**, and ➤ **pungitopo**, butcher's broom, for example). Edible varieties are cooked in many ways: boiled and dressed or turned in a skillet with other ingredients, as ingredients in stuffings, frittatas and risottos or mixed with other wild herbs (➤ **erbe selvatiche**) to make soups.

Gerstsuppe soup of barley, vegetables (onion, carrot, leek, potato, celery, flat-leaved parsley) and smoked meats (speck, pork). Trentino-Alto Adige.

gesminos baked cakes made with a mixture of almonds, confectioner's sugar, egg whites, lemon juice and orange blossom water. Named for the fact that they used to be flavored with jasmine essence. A specialty of Quartu Sant'Elena, in the province of Cagliari. Sardinia.

gherssa Piedmontese dialect word for ➤ **grissia**, a bread loaf.

ghiaccia an icing (➤ **glassa**) of egg white and sugar cooked to a white, flossy texture. Sardinia.

ghiaccia reale ➤ icing made of lemon juice, sugar and egg whites.

ghiacciolo popsicle. Thirst-quenching confection of ice and sugar, flavored with sweet fruit syrups, frozen round a stick. Introduced to Italy in the post-World War II years, it is still highly popular.

ghibaniza another word for ➤ **gibanica**, a type of cake.

ghiotta, alla in southern Italy a way of stewing fresh or preserved fish (➤ **agghiotta**). In Umbria and Tuscany, the term refers to dishes in which pigeon is served with the cooking juices collected in the ➤ **leccarda**, dripping pan.

ghiozzo goby. Three varieties —the giant goby (*Gobius cobitis*), the black goby (*G. niger*) and the rock goby (*G. paganellus*)—inhabit the northern Adriatic and the Venice lagoon, where they burrow in the shallow sea beds (➤ **gô**).

ghirighio term used in the provinces of Prato and Florence for ➤ **castagnaccio**, chestnut cake.

ghisadu stew of beef, tomato, potatoes, onions and red wine, typical of the province of Oristano. Sardinia.

giacinto delle vigne another name for ➤ **lampascione**, grape hyacinth bulb.

giaco rare, oddly crooked bread loaf made from a dough of soft wheat flour, water, sourdough and salt. Typical of Pinerolo, in the province of Turin. Piedmont.

giagiuela another name for ➤**cumpittu calabrese**, a type of nougat.

gialetti traditional cookies, typical of Ravenna and Bologna, made of wheat and cornflour (hence their color: *giallo* means "yellow" in Italian), raisins and pine kernels. Emilia-Romagna.

gialletti Lazio cookies similar to the ➤ **gialetti** of Emilia-Romagna.

gialletto regional term for ➤ **cantarello**, chanterelle mushroom.

giambone Italianization of the French *jambon*, ham, used exclusively in northern Italy. In Piedmontese restaurants, the diminutive *giambonetto* is sometimes used for fowl boned, stuffed and tied up with string like small hams.

giambonin de pollaster boned chicken legs stuffed with strips of pancetta, browned in butter with onions and finished off in white wine and broth. A specialty of Milan. Lombardy.

giancheti Ligurian term, often Italianized as **gianchetti**, for ➤ **bianchetti**, newborn larval fish, especially anchovies (➤ **novellame di pesce**, fry).

gianchetti Italianization of ➤ **giancheti**, newborn larval fish.

gianduia a fondant of dark chocolate, chopped toasted hazelnuts, sugar and vanilla, created in 1852 by the Turin confectioner Michele Prochet, who used it as the base for the ➤ **gianduiotto** chocolate. Named for Gianduia, *Gioan d'la duya*, John of the Flagon, a Turin Carnival masque, as is a related cake (➤ **torta gianduia**). Piedmont.

gianduiotto morbido a chocolate enriched with hazelnut cream and shaped like the hat of the Turin Carnival masque, Gianduia. First commercialzed by the Turin-based chocolatiers Caffarel-Prochet in 1865. Piedmont.

gianfottere another name for **ciambotta**, a vegetable stew.

giardinetto word used in gastronomy for a

brightly colored assortment of fruit and/or vegetables, and also of a many-flavored ice cream. The word is the diminutive of *giardino*, "garden," and conjures up a sense of colorful variety, like flowers in a garden. In Piedmont, it refers to a composition of raw or boiled vegetables.

giardiniera mixed vegetables (celery, carrots, runner beans, gherkins, cauliflower florets, baby onions, peppers), cooked, cut into pieces and pickled in vinegar. Produced industrially but also made in households to accompany boiled and cured meats in the winter months. In Piedmont, the same ingredients are covered with a sweet and sour tomato sauce (in dialect *antipast ross*) and served with tuna preserved in oil, olives and sliced hard-boiled eggs. In the northeast regions they also make a sweet and sour version by adding sugar to the pickling vinegar. In Calabria, they cut carrots, cauliflowers, gherkins, baby onions, fennel, eggplants, peppers and celery into small pieces, leave them in brine for a day, squeeze them dry, pickle them in vinegar for another day and, finally, preserve them in oil.

giardiniera agrodolce another word for ➤ **giardiniera**.

gibanica cake of Slovenian origin consisting of various layers of pastry (flour, eggs, oil, a hint of vinegar) filled with ricotta, sour cream, poppy seeds, raisins, and walnuts. Friuli-Venezia Giulia.

gigi aka **giggi** Carnival pastries typical of the Aeolian Islands (province of Messina). Small cylinders of pastry made from a sweet dough of flour, lard, egg yolks and sugar are fried until golden brown, plunged into cooked wine must (➤ **vincotto**) and warm Malvasia, and dusted with sugar. Sicily.

gigiole Sardinian term for ➤ **ciccioli**, pork scratchings.

giglietti lily-shaped cookies made with a paste of flour, sugar and eggs, baked in the oven for ten minutes at a high temperature. The recipe was introduced to Italy from France by the cooks of the Barberini family in the 17th century. Lazio.

ginepro juniper (*Juniperus communis*). Wild shrub that grows near the sea and in the mountains all over Italy. Its ripe black berries (preferably fresh and slightly crushed) are used to make spirits and liqueurs, to flavor game, fowl and pork, and as an ingredient (mixed with butter and pancetta) in stuffings for thrushes and woodcock.

ginestrata alternative name for ➤ **cinestrata**, a sweet and sour Renaissance soup.

ginestrella regional term for ➤ **lattugaccio**, rush skeletonweed.

ginetti ring cookies made of flour, eggs and olive oil, parboiled, baked and decorated with lemon-scented icing. Traditionally made on Palm Sunday. Calabria.

ginevrina (1) disk-shaped candy, made by blending sugar and essences (aniseed, mint, lemon, orange, jasmine, rose etc.), thickening the mixture over a low heat, then pouring it onto a marble surface to set. Recipe typical of the town of Pontremoli, in the povince of Pisa. Tuscany.

ginevrina (2) regional name for ➤ **russola**, russula mushrooms.

ginocchiello regional term for ➤ **murice**, murex or rock shell.

gioddu type of ➤ **yogurt** made by warming ewe's milk to 80-95°C, cooling it to 45°C, and adding milk enzymes. Sardinia.

gioga minuda common earth snails boiled, flavored with olive oil and garlic, and served with tomato sauce. Antipasto typical of Sassari. Sardinia.

giovenca heifer. A young cow that has yet to calve. The masculine form of the noun, *giovenco*, means steer.

giraffa braided loaf made from the same dough as ➤ **ciopa**. Typical of Treviso. Veneto.

girasole selvatico common name for ➤ **tarassaco**, dandelion.

girello a cut of veal or beef, roughly equivalent to tenderloin. Used to make ➤ **carpaccio** and ➤ **vitel tonné**.

girello di spalla cut of beef roughly equivalent to shoulder clod. Suitable for steaks.

giromette fortune cookies made of flour, water and sugar and shaped like knights (some with colored plumes) or animals. Typical of the province of Varese. Lombardy.

gittone regional term for ➤ **silene rossa**, red catchfly.

giubba e calzoni (literally "jacket and trousers") aka **zuppa di agnello** a hearty stew, a symbol of the region's pastoral tradition. Pieces of lamb are slowly cooked in chopped ham fat, aromatics, skinned tomatoes, white wine and water. Sprinkled with grated Pecorino and served with country bread. In the Maremma area, they add one artichoke per person and eliminating the cheese. Lazio.

giuggiola jujube (*Ziziphus zizyphus*). Small deciduous tree or shrub, originally from Asia. The fruit is an edible oval drupe with pale brown skin and firm green flesh with a slightly sour taste. Eaten above all in the Veneto (where the two main varieties are *giuggiola dei Colli Euganei* and *giuggiola del Cavallino*) and in the Lake Garda area of Lombardy. Used to make jams, candies, jellies, syrups and liqueurs (see ➤ **brodo di giuggiole**). Common and dialect names: ➤ **dùdola**, ➤ **gensola**, ➤ **sciscùla**, ➤ **zizola**.

giuggiulena (1) Sicilian term, from the Arabic *giolgiolan* or *giulgiulan*, for ➤ **sesamo**, sesame.

giuggiulena (2) nougat traditionally eaten at Christmas on the east of the island. Made by cooking honey in a copper pan and adding sesame, toasted chopped almonds, chopped orange zest and cinnamon. The mixture is poured onto a damp marble surface, shaped into a rectangle, cut into slices and set aside to cool. A similar nougat in Calabria is called ➤ **giurgiulena**, ➤ **giagiuela** or ➤ **cumpittu**. Sicily.

giulebbe julep. Pink beverage made from fruit juice boiled with sugar, diluted, and clarified. The name derives from the Persian *gulâb* (rose water).

Giuncata (1) fresh softy cheese made cow's milk (or sheep's or ewe's or mixed) coagulated with rennet and left to drain in rush baskets or wrapped in ferns. Eaten as it is or used as a kitchen ingredient. Made in Liguria, the Apennines between Emilia-Romagna and Tuscany and all over the south of Italy. Other names: ➤ **Felciata**, ➤ **Raviggiolo**.

Giuncata (2) cheese made with goat's milk, strained off and placed in rush baskets, then dry-salted and dried on rush racks. Eaten fresh or briefly aged, in which case it may be smoked. The mature cheese may also be use for grating on rice or pasta. Calabria

giuncata dell'Ascensione simple dessert of milk and rennet. When the milk sets, it is left to cool and sprinkled with sugar and, sometimes, cinnamon. Speciality of the Tuscia area. Lazio.

giuncata dolce dessert of fresh curdled milk with cream and a sprinkling of sugar. Val d'Aosta.

giuranna di mari Sardinian term for ➤ **rana pescatrice**, monkfish.

giurgiulena ➤ another name for **cumpittu**, a type of nougat.

glassa icing or glaze.

glassare to ice or to glaze.

gliu zeppolone chicory and other field greens boiled and turned in a skillet with oil, garlic, minced mint and flat-leaved parsley, chili and salt. A dash of vinegar is then added, together with buckwkeat flour. The surface of the mixture is leveled to give it the form of a large frittata, and it is browned on both sides. A delicacy of the village of Spigno Saturnia, in the province of Latina. Lazio.

gnaccheragatti pasta of semolina, chestnut flour and water much loved in the Castelli di Jesi area. Marche.

gnoc co la suca gnocchi made of pumpkin, milk, flour and eggs served with melted butter and grated Grana Padano. Typical of Mantua. Lombardy.

gnocarei chicken broth with shredded chicken and balls of leftover polenta dipped in beaten eggs. Typical of the province of Brescia. Lombardy.

gnocc de la cua aka **gnocchi della coda** gnocchi of flour, wild herbs (or spinach or beet) and potatoes. Served with boiled potatoes, grated mountain cheese, and onion fried in butter. Typical of the village of Pezzo, in the upper Valcamonica. Lombardy.

gnocchetti commercial durum wheat short dried pasta which originated in Campania. Resembles a hollow almond, open on one side with a ridged shell. Available in two sizes, it is served with light sauces or pesto.

gnocchetti a coda de soreca fresh rustic flour and water pasta, tapered like a mouse's tail (which is what the dialect term means). Known in the south of the region as **gnocchitti**, Lazio.

gnocchetti alla collescipolana small cylindrical gnocchi of wheat flour and breadcrumbs served with a sauce minced aromatic vegetables (onion, celery, carrot), crumbled sausage meat, diced pancetta, tomato passata and boiled beans. A traditional recipe in the province of Terni. Umbria.

gnocchetti di milza small gnocchi made from a mixture of calf's spleen, eggs, garlic, flat-leaved, parsley, breadcrumbs, ox's bone marrow and nutmeg and cooked in boiling broth. Trentino-Alto Adige.

gnocchetti di seirass small gnocchi made from a mixture of ricotta (in dialect → **seirass** aka **saras** aka **siras**) flour, eggs and grated Grana, served, in season, with mushrooms or white truffle. Piedmont.

gnocchetti di ziti another name for → **ditali**, short pasta tubes.

gnocchetti in salsa di nocciole small gnocchi made from a mixture of potatoes and baked pumpkin flesh, served with a sauce of hazelnuts, renetta apples, chicken broth and cream, and sprinkled with powderd cinnamon. A dish of Renaissance origin, typical of the city of Ferrara. Emilia-Romagna.

gnocchetti sardi another name for → **malloreddos**.

gnocchettini another name for → **ditalini**, short pasta tubes.

gnocchi, gnocchetti (1) (sing. **gnocco, gnocchetto**) the name, usually used in the plural, for the equivalent of round, tapered or cylindrical "dumplings," boiled in water and served with a variety of sauces and condiments. Common all over Italy, especially in mountain areas.

gnocchi, gnocchetti (2) (sing. **gnocco, gnocchetto**) the term is often used generically to refer to → **gnocchi di patate**, common all over Italy, especially in northern regions. In the northeast, cinnamon, cocoa, day-old bread, fruit (→ **gnocchi di susine**) are often added to the mixture, in Piedmont they add mountain cheese (→ **ravioles**) or chestnut flour and pumpkin (→ **gnocchi ossolani**). **Gnocchi** can also be made from semolina (→ **gnocchi alla romana**, → **gnoches de gries**), cornflour, polenta (→ **gnocchi di polenta**, → **matuffi**). Regional names for **gnocchi** are → **canerderli**, →**knödel**, → **strangolapreti** (Trentino-Alto Adige), → **rabaton** (Piedmont), → **malfatti** (Lombardy, Emilia-Romagna), all made without potatoes.

gnocchi, gnocchetti (3) (sing. **gnocco, gnocchetto**) the term also applies, on account of analogy of shape, to certain soft cakes and pastries: eg, → **maneghi**, → **turdiddri**.

gnocchi alla bava relatively recent creation of → **gnocchi di patate** served with a cream of Fontina cheese melted in milk. Val d'Aosta, Piedmont.

gnocchi alla lariana a dough of wheat flour, eggs, milk and herbs cooked, a tablespoon at a time, in boiling water and served with a meat or tomato sauce and sprinkled with grated cheese. Lombardy.

gnocchi alla romana disks of a mixture of semolina cooked in milk, salt, butter and grated Parmigiano, layered in a greased oven dish with grated Parmigiano, moistened with melted butter and baked. Lazio.

gnocchi alla sorrentina potato gnocchi (→ **gnocchi di patate**) layered with tomato sauce, slices of mozzarella, basil, oregano and grated Parmigiano and baked in the oven. Campania.

gnocchi boemi name for sweet → **canederli**, dumplings.

gnocchi con il cacao potato and flour gnocchi served with a mixture of smoked ricotta (→ **ricotta affumicata**), raisins, candied citron, cocoa, sugar and cinnamon. Friuli-Venezia Giulia.

gnocchi del Kyè potato and flour gnocchi served with a sauce of tomato, pancetta, onion and garlic. Typical of villages of the Kyè area in the Valle Corsaglia (province of Cuneo). Piedmont.

gnocchi del prete soft corn flour and semolina gnocchi served with butter and cheese. A specialty of the village of Raveo, in the Carnia area (province of Udine). Friuli.

gnocchi della vigilia homemade flour and water pasta formed into shell shapes using the thumb, served with tomato sauce and grated Parmigiano. Traditionally made in the province of Piacenza on Christmas Eve. Emilia-Romagna.

gnocchi di grano saraceno spindle-shaped gnocchi made from a dough of buckwheat and wheat flour, boiled potatoes and eggs, served with slices of Toma cheese and melted butter. Typical of the mountains in the province of Cuneo. Piedmont.

gnocchi di latte lozenge-shaped gnocchi made with egg yolks, sugar, milk, potato flour, butter, nutmeg and cinnamon, coated in flour, dipped in beaten eggs and breadcrumbs, and fried in butter. Served hot with a sprinkling of grated cheese. Lazio.

gnocchi di pane gnocchi made from a dough similar to that of → **canederli di magro**: day-old bread, flour, eggs, parsley, chives cipollina, or other seasonal shoots (in Veneto, especially in the province of Vicenza, caraway, → **cumino dei prati**, is popular). In Trentino, it is traditional to serve the gnocchi with melted butter and sage; in Veneto, they serve them with butter and chives or with sautéed spring onion or leek and smoked prosciutto. In modern versions, grated or melted cheese and diced speck or prosciutto may be added to the dough. Veneto, Friuli-Venezia Giulia.

gnocchi di patate potato gnocchi began to appear in recipe collections only in the 19th century. The dough consisted of one part of potato to two parts of breadcrumbs and flour, used to bind the mixture. In the classic recipe, floury potatoes are mashed, pushed through a special mincer and mixed with salt and flour to obtain a soft, elastic, non-stocky dough. This is shaped into long fingers which are cut into one-inch pieces. Each piece is ridged slightly by applying light pressure with the prongs of a fork, or by pressing on a special board (*rigagnocchi*). The resulting gnocchi are plunged into boiling salted water and drained when they come to the surface. Variations include: the addition to the dough of a handful of grated Grana (province of Piacenza) or a pinch of nutmeg; the use of coarsely grated raw potatoes (Trentino-Alto Adige: in the region's Val di Fassa they also add melted butter and diced lardo). Gnocchi can be served in many ways, the most popular being with: melted butter and grated Parmigiano (with or without sage), melted cheese and milk (➤**gnocchi alla bava**), sausage sauce (Piedmont), roast beef gravy, dried mushroom and tomato sauce (in the Apennines, in the province of Piacenza). Potato gnocchi are popular all over Italy today, especially in the north, Veneto in particular (a *Baccanale del gnocco* has been held in Verona for the last 400 years and more).

gnocchi di patate alla veronese classic ➤ **gnocchi di patate** are very popular in the city of Verona. In the Carnival period, a masque called *papà del gnoco* is elected, and on Fridays (*venèrdi gnocolar*), most families used to eat gnocchi for lunch, traditionally with melted butter, cinnamon, sugar and grated Grana, though nowadays tomato sauce seems to be taking over. Restaurants in the city have also recently taken to serving gnocchi with

a sauce made from ➤ **pastissada de caval**. Veneto.

gnocchi di poina e sgrizoi gnocchi of flour, mountain ricotta, eggs and bladder campion (➤ **silene rigonfia**) served with Trentingrana cheese and clarified butter. Sometimes scattered with sesame seeds. Trentino-Alto Adige.

gnocchi di polenta (1) gnocchi made of polenta, flour, potato flour, Grana cheese, eggs and chives. The same mixture can be used to make short pasta ribbons (*stracci*). Both gnocchi and *stracci* are served with fresh mountain cheese and mushrooms (➤ **porcino**, ➤ **finferlo**) sautéed in butter with flat-leaved parsley, or sausage (➤ **lucanica**) cooked in wine. Trentino-Alto Adige.

gnocchi di polenta (2) gnocchi made from day-old polenta, maybe mixed with a little flour, and served with clarified butter, sage, mature, strong-flavored cheese and a sprinkling of powdered cinnamon. Veneto.

gnocchi di polenta (3) name used in some areas for ➤ **matuffi**, actually more similar to ➤ **polenta pasticciata**, baked layered polenta. Tuscany.

gnocchi di ricotta gnocchi made with flour, eggs and breadcrumbs, served with butter and Grana cheese or smoked ricotta. A more complex sweet and sour version also exists made with butter whisked with sugar and egg yolks, egg whites, ricotta, flour, lemon zest and salt, sprinkled with breadcrumbs fried in butter and plum compôte. Veneto, Friuli-Vnezia Giulia.

gnocchi di susine stoned plums (in some recipes, stuffed with breadcrumbs fried in butter, sugar and cinnamon) covered with a mixture of mashed potatoes, flour, and eggs, served with breadcrumbs fried in butter, sugar and cinnamon. Sometimes apricots are used in lieu of plums. The dish, popular in Trieste and its province, is of clear Austrian origin. Friuli-Venezia Giulia.

gnocchi di zucca pumpkin gnocchi, common throughout the north, especially in Lombardy. In the province of Cremona, they are made with a mixture of oven-baked pumpkin flesh with wheat flour, eggs, amaretti cookies, salt, oil and nutmeg and served with melted butter, sage and grated Grana Padano. In the province of Brescia they simply mix pumpkin with wheat flour and egg whites and serve the resulting gnocchi with butter, garlic and rosemary. In Friuli, likewise, they make gnocchi from oven-baked pumpkin flesh, flour, egg yolks, grated Grana cheese, salt and pepper, cover them with dried breadcrumbs, Grana, melted butter and sage and bake them in the oven.

gnocchi dolci di Natale large square flour and water gnocchi (or maccheroni or tagliatelle) served with a mixture of crushed walnuts, sugar (or honey), dried breadcrumbs, dark chocolate or cocoa powder, grated lemon zest, cinnamon and alkermes (➤ **alchermes**). A dessert traditionally prepared on Christmas Eve. Umbria.

gnocchi 'ncotti cylindrical flour and water pasta similar to ➤ **strozzapreti** served, in the Tuscia area of the province of Viterbo, with a sauce of sausage, tomato, garlic, chili and mature Pecorino. Lazio, Abruzzo.

gnocchi ossolani gnocchi made from a mixture of pumpkin, potatoes and boiled chestnuts (today with chestnut flour, available all year round) and served with butter and mountain cheese. A specialty of the valleys of the north of the region. Piedmont.

gnocchi ricci curly-edged fresh pasta disks made from two separate doughs: one of flour and water, the other of flour and eggs. A specialty of Amatrice, in the province of Rieti. Lazio.

gnocchi verdi "green" gnocchi made of spinach, eggs, Parmigiano and ricotta, preferably ewe's. Common throughout Emilia-Romagna, with the exception of the Ferrara area, and in Tuscany, where they are called ➤ **ravioli gnudi**. Emilia-Romagna, Tuscany.

gnocchitti southern Lazio name for ➤ **gnocchetti a coda de soreca**.

gnocco al forno savory flatbread, no more than half an inch thick, made from leavened soft wheat dough dotted with diced prosciutto, lardo, mortadella or pork scratchings (➤ **ciccioli di maiale**). Common throughout Emilia, where it changes name according to province: ➤ **crescenta** (Ferrara), ➤ **gnocco ingrassato** or ➤ **spianata** (Modena), *gnocco cotto al forno* (Reggio). Served with meat stews and cured meats. Emilia-Romagna.

gnocco fritto Bolognese name for ➤ **crescentina fritta**.

gnocco ingrassato Modenese variation on ➤ **gnocco al forno**.

gnocculi Sicilian term for ➤ **cavatelli**.

gnoches de gries dumplings of fine semolina, butter, egg yolks, egg whites whisked to a peak, salt, pepper and nutmeg, cooked in meat broth. A sweet version exists in which the dumplings are fried in oil and dusted with sweet cocoa. Trentino-Alto Adige, Veneto, Friuli-Venezia Giulia.

gnochi sbatui aka **smalzai** gnocchi made with a mixture of flour and milk and served with butter and cheese or smoked ricotta. A dish typical of the Monti Lessini. Veneto.

gnucchitti Sicilian term for ➤ **cavatelli**.

gnucheit soft polenta mixed with butter and Toma. Typical of some mountain areas. Piedmont.

gnudi abbreviated name for ➤ ravioli gnudi, a type of "green" gnocco.

gnumerieddhi aka gnumarieddhi aka gnumereddhe dialect names for rolls of lamb's or kid's innards, flavored with salt, pepper, flat-leaved parsley, Pecorino and strips of lardo, wrapped in caul, softened in water and vinegar, secured with the animal's intestines. The rolls are generally stuck on a secure and barbecued. Together with sausages, mutton, lamb and pork, they are one of the specialties often cooked directly in the local butcher's oven (➤ fornello). Puglia.

gô Venetian term for ➤ ghiozzo, goby. Cooked fried, broiled, in ➤ saor, in risottos and in soups (➤ brodetti dell'alto Adriatico).

gobbetti (1) another name for ➤ chifferi, a type of pasta.

gobbetti (2) Lazio term for ➤ gamberetto, shrimp.

gobbi (1) literally "hunchbacks." Regional term (used chiefly in Piedmont, Tuscan and Umbria) for bleached cardoons (➤ cardo). Recipes include: ➤ gobbi al forno, ➤ gobbi trippati, ➤ parmigiana di gobbi.

gobbi e salsicce cardoons and sausage. The fleshy cardoons of Trodica, in the province of Macerata (➤ cardo), sautéed with sausage. Marche.

gobbi trippati side dish of boiled cardoons finished off in oil with garlic and tomato passata, and sprinkled with grated Pecorino. The cardoons may also be coated in flour, dipped in beaten eggs, fried, then turned in a skillet with meat sauce. Tuscany.

gobboni another name for ➤ gomiti rigati, a type of pasta.

gobein a dialect word for gobbi, "hunchbacks." Rectangular ➤ agnolotti filled with vegetables, pork and beef, cooked in broth, and served with meat sauce. A recipe typical of Tortona, in the province of Alessandria. Piedmont.

gobeletti aka gubelletti aka cobeletti aka cubeletti shortcrust pastry tarts filled with apricot or peach jam. Typical of the provinces of Genoa and Savona. Liguria.

goffri honeycomb waffles made from a dough of leavened flour, salt and water, cooked on both sides in special irons. Eaten crisp and hot filled with jam, honey and so on. Typical of the Waldensian valleys and the upper Valsusa, west of Turin. Piedmont.

golato type of fat, thicker than lardo, found at the base of the pig's head.

gomiti rigati small curved commercial durum wheat pasta with a hole at each end. Served with sauce or in broth. Typical of northern Italy. Other names: ➤ chifferotti, ➤ gobboni.

gomma arabica gum Arabic. Extract of some species of acacia, used in confectionery as a thickener.

Gorgonzola PDO blue cheese made with pasteurized cow's milk inoculated with *Penicillium roqueforti*, milk enzymes and liquid calf's rennet. A month after production, the cheese is perforated to encourage an even distribution of mold. A naturally fermented, tangier version is produced in very limited qualities. Piedmont, Lombardy.

gosa fer a sauce of sardines or herrings, butter, garlic, parsley, and vinegar, served with polenta. Typical of the province of Cremona. Lombardy.

gota (1) regional term for ➤ guanciale or ➤ pancetta.

gota (2) small triangular or trapezoidal cured meat. Pork cheek cured for five to seven days with salt, garlic, pepper, herbs and chili, brushed or washed and dried, seasoned with pepper and hung to age for at least a month. Typical of the Casentino area and some villages in the Apennines. Emilia-Romagna, Tuscany.

gota bollita di Colle di Val d'Elsa pork cheek massaged into a round shape, cured with a mixture of salt, pepper and other spices, and aged for a few days. Typical of the province of Siena. Tuscany.

goto Veronese dialect word for a glass of wine and, by extension, aperitif. The equivalent of ➤ **ombra** in Venice. Veneto.

graf small ring-shaped doughnut-like cake of wheat, potatoes and eggs, dusted with sugar. Campania.

grafion Piedmontese term for ➤ **ciliegia duracina**, a type of cherry.

grafons variety of ➤ **grostoi** (sweet fritters) filled with raisins or jam. A specialty of the Ladin valleys. Trentino-Alto Adige.

gramigna (1) short curved hollow egg pasta shaped with a special press. Traditionally served with a sauce of sausage, onion and tomato. Emilia-Romagna.

gramigna (2) tiny commercial durum wheat pasta suitable for serving in broths and soups.

gramignoni another name for ➤ **spaccatelle**, a type of pasta.

gramolaccio regional term for ➤ **rapastrello**, wild radish.

gramolata (1) Roman slang for ➤ **granita** and/or the finer ➤ **cremolato di frutta**. Lazio.

gramolata (2) condiment or "finishing touch" (➤ **gremolada**).

gramolato loaf formed by two flattened braids of bread. Named for a screwed wooden utensil devised for making pasta. Typical of the province of Trento. Trentino-Alto Adige.

gran farro soup common, with many variations, in the Garfagnana and Chianti areas. Fresh or canned tomatoes are cooked in olive oil with celery, onion, garlic, sage, marjoram and diced pork rind, and flavored with cloves, cinnamon and nutmeg. Boiled, puréed beans are then added, along with emmer wheat. Tuscany.

gran pistau soup of wheat berries slow-cooked with pork rind and finished with lightly fried leeks and grated cheese. A traditional dish of the western Riviera. Liguria.

gran premio Sardinian term for a horsemeat rib steak, usually broiled.

Grana Padano PDO part-skimmed raw cow's milk cheese made all year round (in winter it is also known as *Vernengo*) along the Po Valley as far as Trento. Ripening and aging take place in temperature- and humidity-controlled rooms for 12-36 months. The hard, smooth, thick rind must bear the mark of the Grana Padano Consortium. Only Grana Padano made in the province of Trento can be identified by its place of origin with the ➤**Trentingrana** mark. The body is straw-yellow, finely granular and breaks away in flakes.

granatina grenadine syrup. Bright red, slightly sharp syrup made by pressing pomegranate seeds. Used to make soft drinks and cocktails. In some regions, the same word means a ➤ **granita** flavored with any fruit syrup.

granatina di carne meatball of ground beef to which boiled ham, fresh breadcrumbs may be added, dipped in beaten egg, or simply in flour, and fried. Served with tomatoes and vegetables or aromatized with Marsala. Campania.

granatine di riso tapered croquettes of leftover rice, mixed with eggs and grated Parmigiano, and fried in oil. A richer version with ground roast meat resembles the Sicilian ➤ **arancina**. Liguria.

grancevola spider crab (*Maja squinado*). The females have the most meat and are at their fullest from December to February. They are normally cooked in a ➤ **court-bouillon** and shelled. The meat and any eggs are then dressed with minced garlic and parsley, olive oil, vinegar, salt and pepper, and served in the decorative upper part of the shell. In some recipes the meat is sprinkled with breadcrumbs and finished off in the oven. It may also be used as an ingredient in risottos, soups and sauces. Common and regional names: ➤ **faolo**, ➤ **granga**, ➤ **granseola**, ➤ **granzeola**, ➤ **granzo**, ➤ **granzòn**, ➤ **grittòn**, ➤ **maia**, ➤ **margherita**, ➤ **marmotta**, ➤ **musciarola**, ➤ **pilargiu**, ➤ **rancio 'e funno**, ➤ **rancio fellone**, ➤ **suenne**, ➤ **tarantula**.

granchio crab. The crabs used in the kitchen are the *granchio marino commune*, shore crab (*Carcinus mediterraneus*), called ➤ **moeca** in Veneto when its shell is about to break, small sand crabs (*Portunus bolsatus, P. deputatur, P. corrugatur*), ➤ **granciporro**, edible crab, ➤ **favollo**, yellow shore crab, and ➤ **grancevola**, spider crab. Smaller crabs are used in fumets, soups and sauces; larger meatier specimens are boiled in a ➤ **court-bouillon** and dressed in various ways, the simplest being with an emulsion of minced garlic and flat-leaved parsley, olive oil, vinegar, salt and pepper.

granchio poro another word for ➤ **granciporro**, edible crab.

granciporro edible crab (*Cancer pagurus*). Large crab found in the lagoons of the northern Adriatic in the fall and winter. Cooked in the same ways as spider crab (➤ **grancevola**). In some recipes the meat is dressed with sizzling-hot garlic butter and finely minced flat-leaved parsley and served raw. Common and regional names: ➤ **granchio poro**, ➤ **gransoporo**, ➤ **granzoporo**.

grandine another name for ➤ **avemarie**, a small pasta shape.

grandula Sardinian guanciale, or cheek bacon. The best is made with meat from pigs raised in the wild on the Gennargentu massif. The mixture, made with the fleshy part of the cheek, cheek fat and part of the neck, is trimmed to an almost triangular shape, cured with salt and pepper and set aside to rest for four to 15 days. After pressing, it may be smoked or hung to dry. It is aged for 30-60 days. Sardinia.

grane cuotte Puglia term for ➤ **grano dolce**, a dessert.

granella mixed finely minced dried fruit (hazelnuts, almonds, walnuts, pistachios) used to coat or decorate cakes and pastries. The term is also used, by extension, for sugar, chocolate or cookie chips.

granelli calf's testicles or calf fries. Skinned, sliced and breaded, they are used as an ingredient in mixed fries.

granerise e fafe rice, boiled fava beans, onion and tomato passata flavored with pepper, basil and extra virgin olive oil. Puglia.

granga Marche term for ➤ **grancevola**, spider crab.

granita a grainy ice slush made by freezing fruit juices, coffee, almond milk or other sweetened, aromatized liquids, stirring often during the freezing process. The name also refers to the domestic habit of flavoring crushed ice with fruit syrups, juices or other aromatized liquids.

granitte tiny lumps of egg, water and flour pasta served in broth with Pecorino. A member of the so-called *pasta "grattata"* ("grated" pasta) family (➤ **gratini**, ➤

malfattini, ➤ **pastaresa**, ➤ **tridarini**, ➤ **triddhe**). Abruzzo.

grano wheat, synonym of ➤ **frumento**. Used mostly to refer to the use in the kitchen of "wheat berries," common in the south of Italy: ➤ **cuccìa**, ➤ **grano dolce**, ➤ **pastiera**, ➤ **grano al sugo**, ➤ **grano stumpatu**, ➤ **gran pistau**, ➤ **insalata di grano**.

grano al sugo wheat berries soaked overnight, then boiled and served with meat sauce (traditionally with ➤ **ragù alla potentina**) and grated Pecorino. Basilicata.

grano arso literally "burnt wheat." In southern Italy, gleaners used to gather the few grains left lying in the fields after the threshing of the grain. The fields would then be burned to fertilize the soil. In times of extreme poverty, country dwellers would then seek out any burnt grain still remaining and use it to make a dark flour, which they mixed with others to produce a dough with a slightly smoky flavor. Pasta made with "burnt wheat" flour is still a specialty. Puglia.

grano cotto di santa Lucia wheat berries soaked overnight, transferred to a *pignatieddu*, a special earthenware pot, covered with water, slow-cooked and served with cooked wine must (➤ **vincotto**). Calabria.

grano dolce a dessert made with boiled wheat berries sweetened with sugar, chocolate shavings, pomegranate seeds, walnuts and cooked wine must (➤ **vincotto**), similar to the Sicilian ➤ **cuccìa**. In Puglia it is made on November 2, All Saints' Day, and called ➤ **grano dei morti**. Puglia, Basilicata.

grano duro another word for ➤ **frumento**, durum wheat.

grano, patate e carciofi layered oven-baked casserole of sliced potatoes, artichokes and wheat berries flavored with grated Pecorino, minced garlic and flat-leaved parsley, skinned tomatoes and chili. Puglia.

grano saraceno buckwheat (*Fagopyrum esculentum* or *sagittatum*). Classified commercially as a cereal (➤ **cereali**), it is a seed as opposed to a grain. Much used in the past in the Alps to make bread, polenta (➤ **polenta taragna**), pasta (➤ **pizzocheri**), frittatas and pancakes (➤ **chisciöl**, ➤ **cicc**, ➤ **manfrigole**, ➤ **sciatt**. Named for the fact that it may have been introduced into Italy by the Arabs, or maybe on account of its dark color. Thanks to the contemporary healthy eating trend, buckwheat is now enjoying something of a revival.

grano saraceno della Valtellina, in the pasta aka **furmentun** aka **farina negra** Until the 1970s this buckwheat variety was a staple in the Valtellina, in the province of Sondrio, but then risked extinction. A Slow Food presidium is collaborating with the local authorities to reintroduce it and to rebuild the stone terraces on which it is cultivated. Lombardy.

grano stumpatu pearl durum wheat grains pounded in a stone mortar (*stumpo*), soaked in water, sun-dried, cooked in salted water and served with ➤ **ricotta forte**, Pecorino and a generous amount of meat sauce, or legumes and vegetables, or tomato sauce and Pecorino. An old specialty of the Salento peninsula, in the province of Lecce. Puglia.

grano tenero another name for ➤ **frumento**, soft wheat

granone another name for ➤ **mais**, corn.

Granone lodigiano another name for ➤ **Tipico lodigiano** cheese.

granoturco aka **granturco** synonyms of ➤ **mais**, corn.

Gransardo recently created cheese produced in the province of Sassari following → **Grana Padano** processing techniques and using ewe's milk from two milkings. Aged for 20 to 42 months. Sardinia.

granseola Veneto and Venezia Giulia word for → **grancevola**, spider crab.

granseola alla triestina boiled spider crab meat (→ **grancevola**) lightly fried with garlic, parsley and breadcrumbs, dressed with oil and lemon juice and either stuffed back into the shell or spread on toasted bread. Typical of Trieste. Friuli-Venezia Giulia.

granseola alla veneziana boiled spider crab meat (→ **grancevola**) served in the shell, dressed with pepper, lemon juice, parsley, oil and, sometimes, diced tomato. Veneto.

gransoporo aka **granzoporo** Veneto and Venezia Giulia words for → **granciporro**, edible crab.

gransoporo in cassopipa edible crab (→ **granciporro**) slow-cooked according to the common regional → **cassopipa** method. Veneto.

granzeola aka **granzòn** aka **granzo** Veneto dialect terms for → **grancevola**, spider crab.

gras pistà a mixture of finely minced lardo, flat-leaved parsley and garlic, seasoned with salt and pepper, common in the Po Valley, where it is eaten spread on slices of toasted bread or polenta or used to thicken legume soups, or to flavor boiled or baked potatoes. In the province of Mantua they replace parsley with rosemary in the mixture, in the province of Cremona they call it → **pistaada**. Lombardy, Emilia-Romagna.

graso aka **grasei** aka **grasul** Emilia-Romagna terms for → **ciccioli**, pork scratchings.

Grasso d'alpe another name for → **Ossolano d'alpe** cheese.

grasso viniditto literally "blessed fat" in Macerata dialect. In local tradition, the capon broth prepared for Christmas Eve was left outside on the window ledge overnight and the solidified fat was separated the following morning and kept over long periods. Marche.

grastoi lozenges of dough filled with various stuffings (eg, desalted anchovies, sage and other herbs) and fried in boiling oil. Veneto, Friuli-Venezia Giulia.

gratin, al au gratin. Term used to refer to a cooked food, covered with a sauce, sprinkled with breadcrumbs or grated cheese, often dotted with butter, and browned under the grill or in the oven. **gratinare** to cook au gratin.

gratini homemade pasta of grated dried bread, cheese, eggs and nutmeg, traditionally served in soups. Similar to the → **pastaresa** aka **pasta rasa** of Emilia. Typical of the province of Trento. Trentino-Alto Adige.

grattachecca a sort of → **granita** (ice slush) made from roughly crushed ice sweetened with colored, flavored syrups, especially sour cherry and → **tamarindo**, tamarind. Popular in Rome, where it is sold at kiosks in the summer. Lazio.

grattalingua common brighteyes (*Reichardia picroides*). Spontaneous herbaceous plant with fleshy, serrated leaves. Common and popular throughout Italy on screes and fallow land, it is picked and eaten in Tuscany, Umbria, Marche and Campania, raw, boiled, and sautéed. In Liguria, it is know as → **talegua** and is an ingredient in → **preboggion**, vegetable pie. Common and regional names: → **caccialepre**, → **latticino**, → **latticrepolo**, → **lattughino**, → **paparrastello**, → **terracrepolo**.

grattata another name for → **tempestine**, egg pasta cubes.

grattini word used in Ferrara for → **malfattini**, a type of pasta.

grattonato ground lamb's tripe and offal mixed with Pecorino and eggs and cooked in meat broth. A traditional dish at wedding lunches. Basilicata.

Graukäse della Valle Aurina traditional Tyrolese cow's cheese made from the milk left over from butter making through long acid coagulation. It is either matured for two or three weeks at room temperature or transferred, after ten days or so, to a cooler place, where it ages for up to 12 weeks. Uneven in shape with gray-green rind mould, it is promoted by a Slow Food presidium. Typical of the province of Bolzano. Trentino-Alto Adige.

grecile aka **gricile** aka **grocile** Lazio dialect terms for the gizzards of fowl (➤ **rigaglie**, giblets).

gremolada aka **gramolata** condiment made by mixing and mincing anchovy, lemon zest and flat-leaved parsley, traditionally used to finish ➤ **ossobuco alla milanese**.

greppole Lombard and Emilian term for ➤ **ciccioli**, pork scratchings.

grespigno aka **grespino** field sowthistle (*Sonchus arvensis, asper,* and *oleraceus*). Prolific wild plant with fleshy leaves, found all over Italy. Eaten raw in ➤ **misticanza**, boiled and finished off in a skillet, with fava bean purée, stewed with pancetta, chili, cherry tomatoes and grated Pecorino, especially in the Murgia and Salento areas of Puglia. Regional names include ➤ **cacigni** aka **cascigni** (Abruzzo, Molise), ➤ **cardedda** (Sicily), ➤ **sivone**, ➤ **zangone** (Puglia). Others are: ➤ **cicerbita**, ➤ **crespignolo**, ➤ **grespino**, ➤ **lattarolo**, ➤ **riccetto**, ➤ **sonco**.

Greviera a cheese created in the second half of the 19th century in the province of Sassari. Made with cow's milk from two milkings, it is aged for at least three months. Sardinia.

gricia, alla sauce for pasta, usually bucatini or spaghetti, typical of some areas of the region and also popular in Rome. An ➤ **amatriciana** without tomato. Lazio.

gries or **griess** northeast Italian terms for ➤ **semolina**, semolina.

Griessuppe another name for ➤ **zuppetta di semolina**, semolina porridge.

grifi all'aretina the flagship dish of the city of Arezzo. *Grifi* (the lean, gelatinous parts of a calf's muzzle) are cut into pieces and stewed in an earthenware pot with water and onion. When the water has evaporated, a fresh onion stuck with cloves, thyme, salt, pepper, red wine and tomato conserve are added. The dish is currently enjoying a revival as a street food (➤ **cibo di strada**), served on slices of bread. Tuscany.

Grigio Alpina, razza dairy and beef cattle breed raised mostly in Alto Adige and the mountain areas of the provinces of Trento, Belluno and Treviso. Only a few thousand head of this sturdy, gray cow are left today, most of them in the province of Bolzano. A Slow Food presidium supports the initiatives of the breeders' association, which monitors the genealogical records of the breed, declared on the verge of extinction in 2004.

griglia, alla term to describe the broiling or grilling of a food.

grigliare to broil or grill.

grigliata mista mixed grill or broil.

grijòta Piedmontese dialect term for sour cherry.

grilet Piedmontese dialect term for salad bowl.

grisëtta Piedmontese dialect term for ➤ **raschietta**, a bread roll.

grispelle another name for ➤ **anime beate**, doughnut-like cakes.

grispolenta large friable breadsticks (➤ **grissino**) made with cornflour, all-purpose flour and natural yeast, sprinkled with cornflour before baking. Typical of the Carnia area, in the province of Udine. Friuli.

grissa di Dolceacqua bread made with well-kneaded dough in three different versions: rolls shaped like small open books (*libretti*), the most traditional; long soft loaves with a lengthwise crack; dry, crisp loaves. Typical of the town of Dolceacqua, in the province of Imperia. Liguria.

grissia aka **grizia** long bread loaf made from a dough of all-purpose or cake flour, sourdough starter (➤ **biga**), salt, malt, yeast and water. Piedmont.

grissino long stick made from bread dough, to which fats and malt are added to enhance its friability. Typical of Piedmont and, more specifically, the province of Turin (➤ **grissino stirato**, ➤ **robatà**). According to legend, it was invented the 17th century by a Turin baker named Brunero for the Savoy royal family. In reality, it seems to have come into being in the late 14th century when, due to inflation, bakers apparently started making the ➤ **grissia** loaf, then sold not be weight but by number, increasingly lighter and thinner. Piedmont.

grissino stirato "hand-stretched" breadstick made from a dough of all-purpose or cake flour, water, yeast, lard and salt. Piedmont.

grittòn Ligurian term for **grancevola**, spider crab.

griù unusual sweet half-moon ravioli filled with an elaborate stuffing of ground boiled chicken, celery, carrot, onion, grated Pecorino, day old-bread, egg yolks, cinnamon, anise liqueur (➤ **mistrà**) and chicken broth, and sprinkled with sugar, grated mature Pecorino and powdered cinnamon. A delicacy in Ascoli Piceno. Marche.

griva (1) aka **frissa** a patty of pig's offal wrapped in caul. Eaten on its own or as an ingredient in ➤ **fritto misto alla piemontese**. Piedmont.

griva (2) spit-roasted thrushes perfumed with myrtle, often preserved in oil. Sardinia.

grongo conger eeel (*Conger conger*). Sea fish caught mainly in the winter and normally cooked skinned and cut into chunks. Excellent in fish soups and as an ingredient for pasta sauces.

grostel di baccalà salt cod or stockfish boiled, cut into pieces, combined with sautéed potatoes in a mixture of lightly fried garlic and onion, and sprinkled with finely minced flat-leaved parsley. Trentino-Alto Adige.

gröstl slices of boiled beef, potatoes and onions turned in a skillet with aromatic herbs and a little broth. Trentino-Alto Adige.

grostoi dolci fried pastries similar to ➤ **cenci**.

grugno regional term for ➤ **cicoria selvatica**, wild chicory, or ➤ **radicchiella**, beaked hawksbeard.

grugno peloso regional term for ➤ **dente di leone**, bristly hawkbit.

guancia di manzo con patate e finferli cow's cheek boiled with herbs and served with boiled potatoes, sautéed mushrooms (➤ **cantarello**, chanterelle) and chives. Trentino-Alto Adige.

guanciale pig's cheek or jowl. Especially in central and southern regions of Italy, the term usually refers to the same cuts of meat cured as a bacon. An essential ingredient in pasta dishes such as ➤ **amatriciana**, ➤ **gricia** and ➤ **carbonara**.

guanciale amatriciano cured pig's cheek or jowl, once a staple in the diet of the shepherds on the Monti della Laga, a mountain range in the central Apennines, flavored with abundant pepper and chili, smoked and aged for 60 days. Lazio, Abruzzo.

guardabue regional term for → **cardogna**, common or spotted goldenthistle.

guastedda another name for → **muffoletta**, a Sicilian bread roll.

guastella another name for → **pè**, a Sicilian bread loaf.

guazzetto (1) a relatively fluid sauce, often including tomatoes, in which fish or meat are cooked ((→ **baccalà in guazzetto**, → **rane in guazzetto**).

guazzetto (2) a simplified, lighter version of the classic → **brodetto** (fish soup), cooked with only a few varieties of fish. Typical of the area round Recanati, in the province of Macerata. Marche

guazzetto di rane another name for → **rane in guazzetto**, frog stew.

guazzo Tuscan term for fruit preserved in glass jars with sugar and alcohol. The great Italian gastronome Pellegrino Artusi cites a recipe for mixed seasonal fruit with sugar and cognac or brandy.

gubana baked fruit loaf of Slovenian origin, similar to → **gibanica**, enclosed in a crust. In Gorizia and Trieste, the crust is made of shortcrust pastry, whereas in the Natisone valleys, in the province of Udine, it is made from a leavened dough of flour, milk, sugar, egg yolks and whole eggs. Friuli-Venezia Giulia.

gubeletti another name for → **gobeletti**, Ligurian jam tarts.

guccijata aka **guccidata** Calabrian term for → **buccellato di Serra San Bruno,** baked ring-shaped cake.

gueffos round, hazelnut-sized cookies made of almonds, sugar, lemon, orange blossom water and liqueur, coated in sugar, wrapped in paper and stored in glass jars or tins. Sardinia.

gugligliones Carnival pastries, reminiscent of → **acciuleddhi**, made of wheat flour, eggs, lard, sugar and salt, fried, covered with hot honey and dusted with refined sugar. Sardinia.

gulasch goulash. Beef, onion and paprika stew of Hungarian origin (*gulyas*), common, with variations, in some areas of northeast Italy. May also be made with pork, lamb, red deer venison and other game. Trentino-Alto Adige, Friuli-Venezia Giulia.

gulaschsuppe (1) soup derived from the preparation of → **gulasch**, goulash. Water, wheat flour and diced potato are added to the stew, and cooking is prolonged for at least an hour. Trentino-Alto Adige.

gulaschsuppe (2) chopped beef browned with garlic and onion, perfumed with marjoram, bay leaf, paprika and lemon zest and cooked with water and tomato passata. Typical of the Carnia area of the province of Udine. Friuli.

gureu Sardinian term for → **cardo selvatico**, wild cardoon.

gurgulestro aka **falso crescione** aka **sedano d'acqua** European marshwort (*Apium nodiflorum*). Wild herb, a relative of celery, which grows in spring water, lakes and rivers. Used in the preparation of → **misticanza** and as an ingredient in frittatas and sauces. The delicate taste is redolent of fennel. The name **gurgulestro** is typical of the province of Viterbo, where the herb is popular. Lazio.

gurigliones another name for → **culurjones**, Sardinian savory or sweet ravioli.

hi HI

haivar another word for ➤ **ajvar**, a fiery sauce.

halibut aka **ippoglosso** halibut (*Hippoglossus hippoglossus*) flatfish of the family of the Pleuronectidae, right-eye flounders. Excellent for cooking, it is imported to Italy and sold frozen. Sometimes used as an ingredient in place of ➤ **rombo**, turbot.

hirn profesen slices of bread topped with calf's brains, battered and fried in butter. Trentino-Alto Adige.

Hirtenbrot another name for ➤ **Fladenbrot**, a wholemeal bread. Trentino-Alto Adige.

Hoamatkas variation on ➤ **Malga Stelvio**, cheese wrapped in mountain hay and aged for a month and a half in wood casks. Trentino-Alto Adige.

imbalsadura stew of fresh peas and beans cooked with chopped pancetta, onion, tomato, garlic and parsley. In Reggio Emilia they use a tablespoon of the stew to dress ➤ **maltagliati**, a type of pasta, cooked in broth. Emilia-Romagna.

imbianchire to blanche. To boil meat and vegetables briefly to set their color.

imbiondire to brown, to fry until golden brown.

imbottire to stuff or fill. The term is used especially for sandwiches, focaccias, piadinas and the like. Also used for vegetables, mollusks and meat, albeit more commonly in central and southern Italy than in the north.

imbracata soup typical of the area round Viterbo. Dried beans are soaked overnight, boiled with chopped pork rind and flavored with chopped lardo (or belly pork), onion and basil. When all the ingredients are well cooked, corn flour and grated Pecorino are amalgamated to the soup to form a thickish polenta. Lazio.

imbrecciata soup made by cooking cereals and legumes separately (grain, spelt, barley, corn, lentils, pea, fava and other beans), then amalgamating them in a skillet with chopped lardo and onion and olive oil, and flavoring with marjoram, sage, parsley, rosemary and chopped tomatoes. A dish traditionally made in spring to clear out pantries in anticipation of the new harvest. Umbria.

imbrogliata di carciofi young tender spiny Ligurian artichokes sliced, gently fried in oil with garlic and parsley, smothered with scrambled eggs and sprinkled with grated Parmigiano. Liguria.

imburrare to grease or butter (a pan or another recipient).

imbutino common funnel mushroom (*Clitocybe gibba*) of the Clitocybe genus with characteristic funnel-shaped cap (the word *imbutino* means "small funnel" in Italian). Commonly used in soups and sauces. Common names: ➤ **cimballo**, ➤ **ciamballella**, ➤ **volterrano**, ➤ **agarico imbutiforme**. In some regions, especially in northern Italy, the name **imbutino** refers to ➤ **trombetta dei morti**, horn of plenty.

impanare to bread, to coat with breadcrumbs.

impanata di palombo smooth hound pie. A Ragusa version of ➤ **agghiotta**, fish stew,

made with ➤ **palombo**, smooth hound.
Fried zucchini are added to the mixture,
which is then baked in the oven with a
pastry crust. Sicily.

impastare to knead, to work. To amalgamate liquid and solid ingredients to obtain
a homogeneous mixture

impastellare to batter, to coat in a batter (➤
pastella).

impastoiata popular traditional dish of polenta to which beans stewed in tomato
are added towards the end of the cooking
process. Umbria.

impazzire to curdle, to separate

imperialine thin crispy wafers filled with
chocolate and hazelnut cream. Typical of Omegna and the Lake Orta area,
Piedmont.

inacidire to sour or acidify.

inchiostro ink. Used to refer to ➤ **nero di
seppia**, squid ink.

indivia endive (*Cichorium endivia*) a member of the same family as ➤ **cicoria**,
common chicory. The autumn and winter varieties are the ones most commonly eaten in Italy, though summer varieties also exist. Cultivated species can be
divided into two varieties: *indivia riccia*,
curly endive, easten mainly raw in salads, and **scarola**, escarole, eaten mainly boiled. Both varieties need fertile soil
and plenty of sunshine, but escarole
is more resistant to the cold. The Italian Ministry of Agriculture's list of native and/or traditional food products includes *scarola bianca riccia schiana* (Campania) and *scarola di Bassano* (Veneto).
Escarole is particularly popular in traditional Campanian cooking (➤ **fasule
e scarole**, beans and escarole ➤ **minestra di scarole e ceci neri**, escarole and
black chickpea soup, ➤ **pizza di scarola**, escarole pizza ➤ **scarola 'mbuttunata**, stuffed escarole ➤ **zuppa di scarole**

e **spollichini**), and also in Lazio (➤ **minestra di scarola**, escarole soup ➤ **aliciotti con indivia**, anchovies with Belgian endive).

indoradda Ligurian term for ➤ **lampuga**,
dolphin fish.

infanfolo Sicilian term for ➤ **pesce pilota**,
pilot fish.

infarinare to flour, to coat with flour.

infarinata casentinese polenta to which
a mixture of stewed beans, tomato,
chopped sausage and fried day-old bread
is added towards the end of the cooking
process. Tuscany.

infusione (1) infusion. Brew created by
steeping fragments of fresh or dried
herbs in boiling water.

infusione (2) the maceration of aromatic herbs or spices in alcohol to make a liqueur or digestif.

infusione (3) synonym of marinade (➤
marinare).

ingrassaporci regional name for the wild
herbs ➤ **boccione maggiore**, golden
fleece, and ➤ **costolina**, cat's ear.

insaccato general name for ➤ **salumi**, cured
meats, prepared by pressing a ground
meat mixture into a natural or artifical
intestine.

insalata salad. General term (from *insala-
re*, an archaic word meaning to add salt)
for cultivated or spontaneous leaves to
be eaten raw and dressed, or for dishes
in which single or mixed raw or cooked
vegetables are served with a certain condiment (in Italy, salt and/or oil and/or
vinegar, elsewhere ➤ **vinaigrette**). In traditional regional cuisines, the term may
also apply to other dishes served cold and
dressed with condiments.

insalata calabrese potatoes baked in their
jackets and cut into slices, peppers cut
into strips and finely chopped ➤ **cipolla
rossa di Tropea**, red onions. The ingre-

dients are mixed and dressed with extra virgin olive oil and salt. Calabria.

insalata di arance traditional orange salad used to accompany boiled and fatty meats. The oranges are peeled and cut into thick rounds, then dressed with chopped parsley, sliced onions, extra virgin olive oil, salt and pepper. Sicily.

insalata di cavolo e speck cabbage and speck salad. A spring cabbage is finely sliced and dressed with cumin seeds, vinegar, salt, pepper and diced speck gently fried in oil. Trentino-Alto Adige.

insalata di cavolo verza winter side dish in which shredded Savoy cabbage is dressed with a light ➤ **bagna caoda** (anchovy and garlic dip), to which a tablespoon of vinegar has been added. Piedmont.

insalata di fagioli salad of boiled beans, tuna in oil, onions and hard-boiled eggs. A dish once popular in old osterias. Piedmont.

insalata di grano boiled wheat berries dressed with pickled peppers, ➤ **lampascioni** (grape hyacinth bulbs), eggplant, cucumber, baby onions, capers and so on. Puglia.

insalata di melanzane antipasto of cubed eggplant, boiled and well drained, dressed with olive oil, salt, vinegar, chopped garlic and minced fresh mint. Calabria.

insalata di mussu e carcagnola "salad" of boiled, boned calf 's head, pig's trotters (➤ **carcagnola**) and snout (➤ **mussu**), chopped and dressed with lemon juice, oil, salt, pepper and flat-leaved parsley. A traditional ➤ **cibo di strada**, street food. Sicily.

insalata di ovoli salad of ➤ **ovolo** (royal agaric) mushrooms finely sliced and served raw with oil, parsley and lemon juice (sometimes with a hard-boiled egg yolk and a desalted anchovy). Piemonte.

insalata di Quaresima literally "Lent salad." Traditionally made with tuna in oil and salted filleted anchovies, herring and cod dressed with finely minced parsley and capers and mixed with boiled potatoes. Piedmont.

insalata di rinforzo traditional Christmas Eve side dish of cauliflower florets, green and black olives, ➤ **papaccelle** (round sweet peppers), mixed pickles, anchovy fillets, and extra virgin olive oil. The name seems to derive from the fact that an addition (*rinforzo*) of ingredients was made day by day to gradually assimilate the condiment. Campania.

insalata di trippa "salad" of tripe. In Tuscany they boil tripe and cut it into strips, then dress it with finely minced onion, celery, carrot, garlic and parsley, olive oil, salt, pepper, vinegar and a pinch of chili. In Piedmont they either dress finely sliced ➤ **tripa 'd Muncalé** (Moncalieri tripe salami) or boil tripe and cut it into strips, dress it and serve it with boiled beans and raw onion cut into rounds.

insalata di zampi calf's trotters boiled with aromatics and cloves, cut into small pieces or strips and served hot with boiled beans, olives and raw carrot matchsticks, salt, oil, vinegar and parsley and garlic sauce. Lazio.

insalata di zampetti salad of calf's or pig's trotters and gelatinous beef served with anchovies, capers, herbs and vinaigrette. Piedmont.

insalata matta regional term for ➤ **tarassaco**, dandelion.

insalata russa Russian salad. Mixed diced vegetables blended with mayonnaise, sometimes with the addition of tuna in oil, capers and pickles. The recipe, which originally contained prized ingredients such as truffle, lobster and caviar, is said to have been created in Paris during the

Belle Epoque, when the city was a favorite destination for wealthy, big-spending Russians. From France it was exported to Piedmont, where it soon became popular as an antipasto. Today it is common all over northern Italy.

insaporire to flavor.

interiora offal. The intestines and other organs contained in the thoracic and abdominal cavities of slaughtered animals. In Italian gastronomy, the offal of quadrupeds are referred to as ➤ **frattaglie**, those of poultry and game birds as ➤ **rigaglie**, giblets.

intingolo In the past the word simply referred to cooking juices into which bread was dipped. Today it means the gravy or sauce produced by the cooking of a food, or a meat or another type of sauce made to dress pasta or rice or legumes.

intoppo a sauce for pasta, usually ➤ **strascinati**, made of veal, pork, sausage and tomato. Common all over southern Italy.

intragli Lombard term for offal or giblets.

intridere to mix, to soak.

intrigoni Emilia-Romagna term for ➤ **cenci**, sweet fried pastries.

invernengo Parmigiano-Reggiano produced from mid November to February (see ➤ **di testa**).

inverzà verb used in the Polesine district of the province of Rovigo to describe the addition of Savoy cabbage to traditional ➤ **pasta e fagioli**, pasta and beans. Veneto.

involtino (pl. **involtini**) roulade or roll. A slice of meat or fish or a vegetable leaf spread with a filling or simply sprinkled with aromatic herbs, folded over and secured with a cocktail stick. Regional variations are as numerous as the dialect terms used to describe them. In the south, the most commonly used word is ➤ **braciola**.

involtini alla canavesana patties of calf's liver, sausage, grana cheese, raisins and juniper berries wrapped in pig's caul and cooked in tomato sauce. Typical of the Canavese district. Piedmont.

involtini alla palermitana thin slices of veal spread with breadcrumbs, raisins, cheese, bay leaves and onion, rolled up and fried or stewed. In many parts of Sicily, another name for **involtini** is **braciulittini** (see ➤ **braciola (2)**).

involtini di manzo beef rolls. A dish to be found in many regional recipes. In Rome, it consists of thin slices of veal stuffed with prosciutto, strips of celery and carrot, tied with kitchen string, secured with a cocktail stick, and cooked in a casserole dish with dry white wine and skinned tomatoes. Regional variations include ➤ **coietas** (Sardinia), **messicani** (Lombardy), **polpette di carne**, meatballs , **quaïette** (Piedmont), **stufato a rolò** (Emilia-Romagna), and **tomaxelle** (Liguria).

involtini di melanzane sott'olio antipasto of grilled eggplant slices spread with fresh breadcrumbs, capers, anchovy fillets, tuna fish (optional), oregano, pennyroyal, wild fennel and vinegar, rolled and anointed with extra virgin olive oil. Calabria.

involtini di peperoni alla pugliese pepper rolls. Roasted peppers skinned, filled with capers, anchovies, pine kernels, raisins, fresh breadcrumbs and flat-leaved parsley, and finished in the oven. Recipe typical of the province of Foggia. Puglia.

involtini fritti fried meat rolls. Slices of beef stuffed with prosciutto and a mixture of chopped garlic, capers (or juniper berries) and sage, dipped in beaten eggs, coated in breadcrumbs, and fried in oil. Umbria.

involtini nella rete slices of beef filled with

a mixture of chopped pork, chicken breast, prosciutto, garlic, fresh breadcrumbs, grated cheese, pepper, salt, nutmeg and marjoram, and rolled up. The rolls are wrapped in pig's caul, browned in the frying pan with chopped prosciutto and finished off with white wine. Served with the pan juices, often accompanied by potato purée. Umbria.

inzimino Tuscan regional name for ➤ **zimino**, a stew or soup which includes spinach or chard among the ingredients. The word refers both to the type of preparation and to the name of the recipe in which it is an ingredient (➤ **inzimino di lampredotto,** ➤ **fagioli in inzimino,** ➤ **seppie in inzimino**). Tuscany.

inzimino di lampredotto boiled cow's abomasum (➤ **abomaso,** ➤ **lampredotto**), a type of tripe, is added to a base of olive oil, onion, chili, chopped ripe tomatoes and shredded chard leaves. Served with slices of toasted bread rubbed with garlic. Tuscany.

inzuppare to dip.

ioseride perennial hyoseris (*Hyoseris radiata*). Spontaneous plant that grows in patches of scrubland and on ruins from the coastal strip to the Apennines. The heads and leaves are popular, especially in Liguria and Marche, in salads, or boiled and mixed with other wild herbs (see ➤ **preboggion,** mixture of herbs). Common and regional names: ➤ **erba stella,** ➤ **pissarella,** ➤ **radicchio selvatico,** ➤ **schiappagrotti,** ➤ **trinette**.

iota alternative spelling of ➤ **jota,** cabbage and bean soup.

ippoglosso Italian name for ➤ **halibut**.

Ircano fresh hexagonal-shaped pasteurized goat's milk cheese with a slightly acidic flavor. Ripened for two or three hours at 37-45°C. Produced in the province of Cagliari. Sardinia.

iriula Sicilian term for ➤ **donzella (1),** Mediterranean rainbow wrasse.

irrancidire to go rancid.

ispessire to thicken (➤ **addensare**).

jk JK

jacculi aka **jaccoli** homemade spaghetti, closely related by way of preparation technique to ➤ **maccheroni alla mulenàre** (Abruzzo) and ➤ **manate** (Basilicata region). In all three cases, pasta dough is spun and stretched round the hands and arms to create a tangle of spaghetti. The varieties almost certainly derive from ➤ **shtridhëlat**, traditional in the Italo-Albanian communities of central and southern Italy (see ➤ **Arbëreshë**). **Jacculi** are typical of the province of Reati, where they are also known as ➤ **maccaruni a cento**, ➤ **maccaruni a centinara**, ➤ **maccaruni a matassa**, ➤ **maccheroni a fezze**. Lazio.

jacopo regional term for ➤ **conchiglia di san Giacomo**, pilgrim's scallop. Lazio.

jaddazzu Sicilian term for ➤ **beccaccia**, woodcock.

jambarei Lazio term (province of Latina) for ➤ **gamberetti di lago**, crayfish.

janculilli Campania term for anchovy fry (➤ **novellame di pesce**, fry).

jancunedda Sicilian term for picarel fry (➤ **novellame di pesce**, fry).

jelu 'i muluni Sicilian term for ➤ **gelo** made with melons.

jeur Friulian term for ➤ **lepre**, hare.

jlatina Sicilian term for ➤ **gelatina di maiale**, pork jelly.

jomoglitto bread typical of Sezze (Latina) made of wheat flour, bran and starter yeast. Lazio.

jota a hearty soup of fermented cabbage, ➤ **borlotti** beans, potatoes and smoked pork. The dish is a symbol of the city of Trieste, but variations are also to be found in the Carso and Isonzo, valleys, in the first case with the addition of barley, in the second with the addition of ➤ **broàde**, fermented turnips. Friuli-Venezia Giulia.

jufa savory or sweet soup of milk and flour, originally a mush for small children. Typical of the Ladin valleys in the Dolomites. Trentino-Alto Adige.

julienne to cut vegetables (but also boiled ham, tongue chicken breast, truffles, lemon and orange zest and candied fruit) into matchsticks.

Kaiser Trieste name for ➤ **rosetta**, bread roll. Friuli-Venezia Giulia.

Kaiserfleisch smoked boiled pork loin. Dressed with grated ➤ **cren** (horseradish) or mustard, it is one of the components of ➤ **bollito misto alla triestina**, mixed boiled meats. Typical of Trieste and Gorizia. Friuli-Venezia Giulia.

Kaiserschmarrn (aka **Kaiserschmarren**) sweet omelet of Austrian origin. Once cooked, it is cut into pieces and served hot or warm, spread with fruit jam or jelly and dusted with confectioner's sugar. Sometimes raisins are added. Trentino-Alto Adige.

Kaminwurz thin six to eight inch smoked sausage. Made with pork or red meat venison (more rarely with mutton) and local spices and herbs, it is reddish in color or with a coarse texture. Eaten fresh or aged. Trentino-Alto Adige.

kamut commercial name, registered by a US company, for a high-protein durum wheat (➤ **frumento,** wheat) of the *Triticum turanicum turgidum* species. Its grains or berries are used in salads and soups and can replace rice in ➤ **pilaf**. They can also be processed into flakes and flours to make pasta, bread and other baked products.

Kastanientorte chestnut cake typical of Bolzano. Boiled chestnuts are puréed and amalgamated with flour, butter, sugar and eggs. The mixture is baked in the oven and topped with whipped cream. Trentino-Alto Adige.

kiffel aka **kipfel** other names for ➤ **chiffel** and ➤ **chifeleti**, sweet buns.

kinzica round cookies made of pine kernel paste, sugar, egg whites and honey, dusted with confectioner's sugar and coated with whole pine kernels. Typical of Pisa. According to a story bathed in legend, the name is that of a young Pisan noblewoman (Chinzica or Kinzica), who saved the city from a Saracen pirate raid. The citizens of Pisa hailed her as a heroine and dedicated these cookies to her. The pine kernels used should come from the pinewood in the nearby Migliarino-San Rossore Park. Tuscany.

Kirchtagskrapfen literally "festival fritters" (➤ **krapfen**, dougnuts), filled with redcurrant jam. Common on stalls at village fêtes in the Sudtirolo area. Trentino-Alto Adige.

Kirsch aka **Kirschwasser** liqueur typical of Central Europe (southern Germany, Switzerland, Austria: the name in German means "cherry water"). In Italy it is produced in the Alto Adige region. Cherries, pips included, are crushed and left to ferment, and sugar is added to increase the alcohol content. The mixture is then distilled into a delicate, aromatic white brandy with a fruity flavor. In the Sudtirolo area, it is used in the kitchen in cakes and game recipes (➤ **capriolo ripieno**, stuffed roe deer venison). Trentino-Alto Adige.

kiwi kiwifruit aka Chinese gooseberry (*Actinidia deliciosa*). Oval in shape, it has a rough brown-green skin and bright green flesh doted with edible black seeds. The flesh has a soft texture and a very pleasant flavor. The kiwifruit arrived in Italy from New Zealand and is now naturalized and grown commercially in many parts of the country, especially in the north and center (➤ **kiwi di Latina**). The Italian Ministry of Agriculture's database of native and/or traditional food products includes: *actinidia di Cuneo* (Piedmont), *actinidia del Lazio* (Lazio), *kiwi di Treviso* and *kiwi di Verona* (Veneto). Kiwifruit is now popular in Italy, and is eaten both fresh (on its own or in fruit salads) and as an ingredient in cakes and ice-creams. It is also widely used in the production of fruit juices and other drinks.

kiwi di Latina PGI kiwifruit grown mainly in the area round Cisterna, a village in the province of Latina. Lazio.

kizoa small leavened focaccia typical of Castelnuovo Magra, in the province of La Spezia. The surface of the dough is pressed with the fingers to create dimples, which are anointed with oil and filled with pieces of sausage. Liguria.

Knieküchel type of ➤ **krapfen**, doughnut, filled with blackcurrant jam. Trentino-Alto Adige.

knödel large dumplings typical of the Sudtirolo area. Made of day-old bread, flour, milk and eggs, flavored with cheese, spinach, mushrooms, speck, pancetta, liver or other ingredients. May be eaten on their own with sauce, in broth or as a side dish. Their Italian name is ➤ **canederli**. Sweet versions also exist made with ricotta, sugar and cinnamon (➤ **canederli dolci**). Trentino-Alto Adige.

knödel venostani dumplings made from a mixture of day-old bread, ➤ **Graukäse**

della Valle Aurina cheese, milk, eggs, fried onion and chives, boiled in water, drained, dressed with Grana cheese and melted butter, and served with cabbage salad and roasted → **speck**. Typical of the Valle Venosta. Trentino-Alto Adige.

Koch German name for → **coch**, a creamy dessert. Friuli-Venezia Giulia.

kodinze Belluno dialect word for dried apples (→ **frutta secca**, dried fruit). Veneto.

kraffi square egg ravioli of Istrian origin. Filled with grated → **Latteria** cheese, eggs, raisins, sugar and salt, served with melted butter and grated cheese. Friuli-Venezia Giulia.

krapfen fried doughnut-like cake of Austro-German origin, common in many Italian regions, where it is also known as → **bombolone**. Made from a mixture of flour, butter, milk, egg yolks and grappa or rum kneaded and shaped into small balls, half-moons or rings, which are then fried and sprinkled with sugar. Generally filled with confectioner's custard or fruit jam. In Trentino-Alto Adige they use rye flour for the dough and make a filling of ricotta, cubed pears, raisins, lemon juice, honey, rum and dried, grated sponge cake.

krasko pecivo cake of Slovenian origin made with wheat and hazelnut flour yeast, eggs, butter, sugar, chopped walnuts and almonds and rum. Served warm with → **amoi** (wild plums) or fox grape jam. Typical of the Valle dell'Isonzo. Friuli-Venezia Giulia.

krumiro (pl. **krumiri**) ridged, curved cookie typical of Casale Monferrato, in the province of Alessandria. Created in 1870 by confectioner Domenico Rossi, owner of the town's Caffè della Concordia. The name is said to derive from that of a confederation of Arab tribes (Kroumirs) whose marauding provided the pretext for the French occupation of Tunisia in 1881, though *crumiro* was also the name of a sweet liqueur into which the cookies were dipped. Piedmont.

krustuli dialect term for → **cartellate**, fried pastries. Puglia.

Kugeluf aka **Kugelhupf** alternative words for → **cuguluf**, a fruit cake typical of Trieste. Friuli-Venezia Giulia.

kuhani struklji boiled version of → **struccolo dolce**, a type of strudel. Friuli-Venezia Giulia.

Kümmel German word for → **cumino dei prati**, caraway, from which the liqueur of the same name is made.

IL

laane another name for➤ **làgane**, a type of pasta.

labritti co' li facioli old country recipe from the Terni area using a cut of meat hard to come by and hardly ever used these days: the inside serrated part of the cow's mouth, known locally as *labritti*. The meat, replaced nowadays by➤ **nervetti**, sinews, ligaments and cartilage from pig's or cow's trotters, is boiled and cut into pieces, then dressed with oil, vinegar, pepper and boiled beans. The dish used to be dressed with the juice of a ➤ **melangolo**, bitter orange. Umbria.

laccabone a hard honey and sugar stringy candy traditionally made in Alessandria for the feast of Santa Lucia. Eaten licked like a popsicle. Piedmont.

lacerto aka **laxerto** aka **axerto** Ligurian dialect word for ➤ **sgombro**, mackerel

lacerto coi piselli mackerel with peas. Stew flavored with chopped onion and parsley. Liguria.

lacèt Piedmontese dialect name for ➤ **animella**, sweetbread.

laciada dessert of egg, milk and sugar crêpes, spread with peach or apricolt jam, arranged in layers and baked in the oven. Lombardy.

laciaditt apple fritters served piping hot and sprinkled with sugar. Typical of Milan. Lombardy.

làgana chiapputa Christmas specialty of ➤ **làgane**, a type of pasta, cooked in boiling salted water and dressed with fresh breadcrumbs fried in oil, sugar, raisins, hazelnuts and cooked must. Typical of the Vulture area, Basilicata.

laganari another name for ➤ **làgane**, a type of pasta.

laganaro aka **laganaturo** southern regional term for➤ **matterello**, rolling pin, and, in some areas, for *spianatoia*, baking board.

làgane fresh pasta made of water and durum wheat meal or all-purose flour, common in central and southern Italy. Made from a roll of pasta dough (*lu lainàre*), cut into strips, reminiscent of ➤ **tagliatelle**, ➤ **pappardelle** or ➤ **maltagliati**. Width and length vary according to areas. **Làgane** can be dressed with sauce or served in legume soups (chickpeas, beans, lentils, grass beans) or vegetables (asparagus, Savoy cabbage or broccoli rape). The Latin term *laganum* is the same one from which ➤ **lasagna** is derived. Other dialect words: ➤ **lane**, ➤ **làine**, ➤ **laane**, ➤ **lahane**, ➤ **tria**, ➤ **lajanelle**, ➤ **laganedde**. In restaurants, the term ➤ **laganari** is also frequently used.

làgane al sugo di anguilla dish of ➤ **làgane** dressed with a sauce of tomatoes and ➤ **anguilla di Lesina**, Lesina eel, flavored with garlic, parsley and basil. Typical of the province of Foggia. Puglia.

làgane col latte simple dish of ➤ **làgane** boiled in salted milk. Traditionally made on Ascension Day. Calabria.

làgane di san Giuseppe homemade lasagne served with two sauces: tomato, basil and garlic, and anchovies, almonds and breadcrumbs. Specialty of Mola, in the province of Bari, where it is traditionally made for the feast of San Giuseppe on March 19. Puglia.

làgane e ceci common southern Italian soup

of boiled chickpeas (or beans or leeks), flavored with gently fried garlic, rosemary and chili.

laganedde another name for ➤ **làgane**, a type of pasta.

Lagundo aka **Bauernkäse** a mountain cheese made with semi-skimmed, pasteurized cow's milk. Ages two months. Trentino-Alto Adige.

lahane aka **laine** aka **lajanelle** another name for➤ **làgane**, a type of pasta.

lampagione regional term for ➤ **lampascione**, grape hyacinth bulb.

lampascione (pl. **lampascioni**) grape hyacinth bulb (*Leopoldia comosa*). Edible bulb of an onion-like plant, which grows wild (and in some places is cultivated) in the south of Italy. It is generally parboiled or soaked prior to serving or cooking to eliminate some of its characteristic bitterness. In the Murge area of Puglia and in Basilicata, it is often cooked in ash or, like onions, made into a jam. Common and regional names: ➤ **onionccio col fiocco**, ➤ **cipollino**, ➤ **cipollotto**, ➤ **giacinto delle vigne**, ➤ **lampagione**, ➤ **lampasciuolo**, ➤ **muscaro**, ➤ **pampascione**, ➤ **porrettaccio**. Puglia, Basilicata, Calabria.

lampascioni alla caprara typical dish of the Murge area in which ➤ **lampascioni**, grape hyacinth bulbs, are coated in flour and fried, then smothered with beaten eggs and grated Pecorino. Puglia.

lampascioni fritti fried grape hyacinth bulbs. The bulbs are boiled and drained, coated in flour and dipped in egg, then fried in boiling oil. When they come into contact with the oil, they open out to form little "roses." Attractive to the eye and tasty on the palate. Puglia.

lampascioni in purgatorio grape hyacinth bulbs gently stewed with diced pancetta (or lardo), mature Pecorino and tomatoes. Puglia.

lampascioni sott'olio grape hyacinth bulbs soaked in water for two days and boiled in water and vinegar, left to dry for a day, transferred to glass jars and covered with extra virgin olive oil, and flavored, depending on the area, with chili, parsley, mint and garlic. Puglia, Basilicata, Calabria

lampasciuolo regional term for ➤ **lampascione**, grape hyacinth bulb.

lampedusana, alla term used to describe fish baked with potatoes, wild fennel, garlic and parsley. Named for the island of Lampedusa. Sicily.

lampone European raspberry (*Rubus idaeus*). Edible fruit of a perennial shrub, typical of cold, temperate climates. A cultivated variety of blackberry with an unmistakable, delicious flavor, and a vitamin content comparable to that of citrus fruits. Eaten fresh on its own, in ice-creams, and in confectionery (jams, juices, essences, sauces and syrups, in the production of which Trentino-Alto Adige is particulary specialized). The Italian Ministry of Agriculture's database of native and/or traditional food products includes the raspberry varieties of the mountains of the province of Pistoia in Tuscany, of the province of Turin and of the mountains of the province of Cuneo in Piedmont.

lampreda lampern or river lamprey (*Lampetra fluviatilis*). Eel-shaped member of the Petromizonidae family of primitive acquatic vertebrates. Once common in the network of *bialere* (canals) that criss-cross the upper Po Valley round Turin, they are now very rare. Small specimens are fried and used to be a prized component of ➤ **fritto misto piemontese**, mixed fry. Larger ones are stewed or roasted. The lampern features in the Italian Ministry of Agriculture's database of native and/or traditional food products and is a great delicacy in the village of Cercenasco, in the province of Turin. Piedmont.

lampreda all'aceto slices of ➤ **lampreda**, lampern, first fried, then stewed in a sauce of aromatics, desalted anchovies, vinegar, lemon zest and nutmeg. Typical of Cercenasco, in the province of Turin. Piedmont.

lampredotto (1) Tuscan term for ➤ **abomaso**, abomasum, a tripe used in many regional dishes. Tuscany.

lampredotto (2) tripe boiled in broth with vegetables, dressed with olive oil and seasoned with black pepper. Typical Florentine street food (➤ **cibo di strada**), served in sandwiches (usually a ➤ **semelle** roll) by tripe sellers (➤ **trippaio**). Tuscany.

lampuca Sicilian term for ➤ **lampuga**, dolphin fish.

lampuga dolphin fish (*Coryphena hippurus*). Fish whose firm, tasty flesh is best enjoyed *en papillote*, broiled, and with ➤ **salmoriglio** sauce. Much loved in Puglia and Sicily, where it is known as *capone imperiale* (➤ **capone**). Other common and regional names: ➤ **corifena**, ➤ **indoradda**, ➤ **lampuca**, ➤ **piscicapuni**.

lanache rustic durum wheat tagliatelle, usually served with stuffed mussels. A specialty of Bari. Puglia.

lancette commercial dried egg pasta in the shape of small ellipses pinched in the middle. Available in two different sizes and served in broth.

landeires name used for ➤ **calhettas**, bread gnocchi, in the area round Bardonecchia, in the province of Turin. Piedmont.

landrace pig breed created in Denmark at the end of the 19th century by crossing local sows with ➤ **large white** hogs imported from England. In Italy two types of landrace are bred—the Italian and the Belgian—both with pink skin and white bristles. They provide excellent meat yield for the production of ➤ **suino pesante** and lean pork for direct consumption.

lane another name for ➤ **làgane**, a type of pasta.

lanspada Friuli-Venezia Giulia regional term for ➤ **cepola**, red band fish.

lanterne common and regional term for ➤ **alchechengi**, Peruvian groundcherry.

lapaccio regional term for ➤ **lapazio**, monk's rhubarb.

lapacendro buono common and regional term for ➤ **sanguinello**, saffron milk-cap.

lapazio aka **romice** monk's rhubarb. Not a rhubarb but the name for certain species of dock (*Rumex alpinus* and *Rumex crispus*) with erect stems and basal leaves up to 50 cm long. The species grows in damp Alpine pastures, on scree and among ruins. Picked mainly in the Alps and Apennines in Piedmont, Liguria and Tuscany, where the leaves are cooked in soups, omelets, pies and fillings: ➤ **caponet** (Piedmont), ➤ **capù di romice della Val Brembana** (Lombardy). Common and regional names: ➤ **bietolone**, ➤ **lapaccio**, ➤ **lavasso**, ➤ **rabarbaro alpino**.

lardare aka **lardellare** to lard. To thread strips of fat (➤**lardelli**, lardons) through lean meat, using a special needle. To prevent the meat from drying during roasting.

lardelli lardons. Strips of lardo, pancetta or prosciutto threaded through or stuck into lean meat.

lardiato Sicilian term for i) "larded" (➤ **lardare**), or ii) cooked in finly chopped lardo.

lardinzi Campania term for ➤ **ciccioli**, pork scratchings.

lardo (pl. **lardi**) cured pig's fat, usually from the back of the animal. Not to be confused with lard (➤ **strutto**). Salted and/ or smoked, it is used finely chopped as a condiment (➤ **battuto**), or, finely sliced, as an antipasto or savory snack. From Roman times at least until the 16th century, it was regarded, like butter (➤ **burro**), as the "barbarian" fat of the north in opposition to the nobler Mediterranean olive oil. Today ➤**Valle d'Aosta lard d'Arnad** (Val d'Aosta) is recognized as PDO, ➤ **lardo di Colonnata** (Tuscany) as PGI. Other noteworthy traditional **lardi** are produced in the southern part of the province of Vicenza (Veneto), the Montefeltro area (Marche), Leonessa and San Nicola (Lazio), and Faeto (Puglia).

lardo al rosmarino di Cavour produced by a single pork butcher using artisan techniques with fat from the top shoulder of heavy pigs bred in local farms. Cut into rectangular slabs and removed from the skin, it is then dry-spiced and rubbed with salt, powdered rosemary and pepper. It is aged in cold steel chambers for a month and a half. Typical of the provinces of Cuneo and Turin. Piedmont.

lardo di Arnad another name for ➤**Valle d'Aosta lard d'Arnad**.

lardo di Colonnata cured meat produced from September to May in the village of Colonnata, famous for its white marble, in the province of Massa-Carrara. Fat is removed from the skin of pigs from farms in north and central Italy and cut into even rectangular slabs, which are rubbed with sea salt and layered in marble *conche* (troughs or coffins) with a *mistura* (cure) of salt, black pepper, rosemary and fresh garlic, to which cinnamon, nutmeg, cloves, star anise, sage, bay leaf, oregano and thyme may also be added. Here it ages for anything from six months to two years. A Slow Food presidium has drawn up a production dis-

cipline and obtained PGI recognition to promote the product. Tuscany.

lardo di guanciale pieces of fat removed from the pig's throat, salted, rubbed and covered with a generous amount of salt and a mixture of spices. Piled on top of one another for at least 30 days, they are aged for one to five months (or even a year in ideal cellar conditions). Sometimes wrapped with splints or pressed into an ox's caecum (➤ **bondeana**) prior to aging. Specialty of the province of Parma. Emilia-Romagna.

lardo di schiena pig's back fat cured and aged in the same way as ➤ **lardo di guanciale**. Typical of the province of Parma. Emilia-Romagna.

lardo pesto lardo ground very finely with garlic, shallot, salt (and sometimes flat-leaved parsley and other aromatics). Preserved in jars or, less frequently, pressed into pig's intestines, it can be stored in a dark, cool place for up to six or seven months. Otherwise, it should be eaten within 20 days. Used in the kitchen as a flavoring, especially with polenta and in soups. Typical of the province of Parma. Emilia-Romagna.

lardone salted and smoked lardo.

large white pig breed native to Yorkshire, England. Characterized by pink skin and white bristles, it is particularly prolific and productive. At six months, pigs can weigh more than 50 pouns, after a year 80-100 pounds. In Italy the breed has been raised since the late 19th century in Emilia-Romagna and Lombardy. Its meat is ideal for curing but also excellent eaten fresh.

lasagna (pl. **lasagne**) one of the oldest Italian pastas (first mentioned in a document in 1282, but certainly made long before that in ancient Rome), now common virtually in every region, albeit with different doughs, cooking techniques, sauces and names. Generally **lasagne** are rectangular (about two inches by five) and very thin, made from a dough of all-purpose or cake flour and a variable percentage of eggs. Narrow versions are cooked and served like long pasta, broader versions are boiled, then baked in the oven layered with sauce.

lasagna beneventana casserole of broad tagliatelle layered with tiny fried meatballs, slices of mozzarella and grated Pecorino, lubricated with capon broth, and baked in the oven. Campania.

lasagna napoletana aka **lasagna di Carnevale** durum wheat pasta sheets layered in a baking tin with meat sauce, ricotta, diced→ **Fior di latte** (cow's milk mozzarella), fried beef or pork meatballs, sliced and browned → **cervellatine** sausages and grated Parmigiano. Sometimes sliced hard-boiled ggs are also added. Dish traditionally cooked in Naples on the Thursday before Lent. Campania.

lasagnasse egg pasta rectangles served with diced potatoes, fried onion and garlic, and slices of → **Raschera** cheese. Dish typical of the Valle Corsaglia, in the province of Cuneo. Piedmont.

lasagne rectangular dried egg pasta made all over Italy in different sizes. The commercial version may be baked directly in the oven without prior boiling.

lasagne ai semi di papavero broad egg and flour tagliatelle served with crushed poppy seeds, sugar and melted butter. Friuli-Venezia Giulia.

lasagne al sangue a now near extinct dish of homemade egg tagliatelle served with ground beef or sausage sauce, pig's offal and blood diluted with milk. Traditionally prepared in the Langa hills in the fall, to mark the annual killing of the pig. Piedmont.

lasagne alla bolognese classic Bologna dish, now popular all over Italy. Green pasta rectangles (made with spinach or nettles) layered with →**ragù alla bolognese**, béchamel, butter and a generous amount of grated Parmigiano, and baked in the oven. A classic Sunday lunch pasta dish for families in Bologna. Especially outside the city, chicken giblets and livers may be added to the sauce. Emilia-Romagna.

lasagne alle lenticchie layers of lasagne dressed with lentils puréed with oil, garlic, thyme and lardo, Parmigiano and whole boiled lentils, and baked in the oven. A dish typical of Viterbo. Lazio.

lasagne cacate a traditional New Year's Eve dish in Palermo and Modica, in the province of Ragusa. Broad, curly → **lasagnette** served with pork and veal (or beef) sauce and sprinkled with fresh sheep's ricotta and salted ricotta. Sicily.

lasagne della vigilia lasagne (known in Tortona as → **garunet** and lozenge-shaped) or tagliatelle served with a sauce of garlic, anchovies dissolved in oil (→ **bagna caoda leggera**), and leeks. A traditional recipe of the province of Alessandria. Piedmont.

lasagne doppio festone another name for → **lasagne ricce' lasagne matte** rectangles or lozenges of → **pasta bastarda** (made of chestnut and wheat flour), also known as → **armelette**. Usually layered with oil and Pecorino and/or ricotta or with lardo, leeks and tomato. Typical of the Lunigiana area. Tuscany.

lasagne ricce long commercial egg pasta ribbons with curly edges. Best with rich sauces, especially made of game. Other names: → **lasagne doppio festone**, → **sciabò** aka **sciablò**.

lasagne tordellate thin pasta squares layered with meat sauce, tomato, chard and eggs, but not baked in the oven. Liguria.

lasagnette another name for → **fettuccine**.

lasca roach (*Chondrostoma genei*). Small freshwater fish of the Cyprinidae family (→ **alborella**, bleak), common in northern Italy (Piedmont and Lombardy, where it is known as → **striscia**, *stricc* in dialect) and, until recently in the lakes, especially Trasimeno, in the central regions. Very bony but with delicate flesh, it is eaten coated in flour and fried, roast in the oven with dried breadcrumbs and herbs, or marinated in vinegar and sage (→ **stricc' in carpion**).

lati de sepa Veneto dialect term for → **latti di seppia**, female cuttlefish glands.

Laticauda sheep breed common in Campania, especially in the provinces of Benevento and Avellino. Bred both for its milk and its meat, it is large in size, hornless, with a hefty rump, long limbs and a thick tail. A descendant of the North African Barbaresca breed and subsequent crosses with local Apennine breeds. Campania.

lattaiola regional term for → **lattugaccio**, rush skeletonweed.

lattaiolo (1) dessert of milk, sugar, whole eggs, grated lemon zest and, in season, peach leaves, cooked in a bain-marie in a mold lined with caramel. Typical of Tuscany, the Apennines between Tuscany and Romagna and Marche, where it is flavored with cinnamon. Together with → **fiordilatte** and → **latte alla portoghese**, it is the traditional Italian cream dessert that most resembles → **crème caramel**. Once made with eggs, sugar, whey, breadcrumbs, salt and nutmeg. Emilia-Romagna, Tuscany, Marche.

lattaiolo (2) regional term for → **sanguinello**, saffron milk-cap.

lattarina term used in central Italy for **bianchetti**, larval newborn fish (→ **novellame di pesce**, fry).

lattarolo regional term for → **grespigno**, field sowthistle.

latte milk. In Italy, milk was a common ingredient in peasant cooking in soups such such as → **riso e latte**, → **minestra di castagne** and → **polenta al latte**, and in main courses such as → **maiale al latte** and → **baccalà alla vicentina**. In classic cuisine, it is an ingrdient in many sauces, béchamel first and foremost.

latte alla portoghese dessert of milk aromatized with a vanilla pod, sugar, egg yolks and whole eggs, cooked in a bain-marie in a mold lined with caramel. Popular in Tuscany, Emilia and other areas of central Italy. It is, with → **fiordilatte** and → **lattaiolo**, the Italian traditional cream dessert that most resembles → **crème caramel**.

latte brulé crème brulé. Cream, eggs, sugar and flour cooked in a mold lined with caramel, allowed to set and eaten cold. Popular in Piacenza, where the sugar is not allowed to caramelize and the cream is completed with layers of → **savoiardi** sponge fingers soaked in liqueur. Emilia-Romagna.

latte brusco mixture of flour, milk, eggs, salt, flat-leaved parsley and a generous amount of grated lemon zest. Once cooked and set, it is dipped in breadcrumbs and fried. A component of → **fritto misto alla ligure**. Liguria.

latte crudo raw milk. Milk that has not been heat-trated, used for cheesemaking. The microflora contribute to the taste profiles of cheeses.

latte di gallina restorative drink made by beating an egg yolk with sugar, diluting it with boiling milk and topping it up with cognac or rum. Also served as a dessert in Piacenza aromatized with lemon zest and vanilla. Emilia-Romagna.

latte di lepre tiny balls of egg whites

whisked to a peak, allowed to set in warm milk and served with a custard of egg yolks, sugar and milk. Typical of the Valle Stura, in the province of Cuneo. Piemonte.

latte di mandorla almond milk. Beverage made by filtering the water in which finely minced almonds have been soaked. Popular in the south of Italy, where it is also used in confectionery. Eg, in Puglia, to make a dessert of the same name, a thick cream obtained by boiling the "milk" with starch, sugar, and cinnamon, with the subsequent addition of rice or tiny pasta shapes or spaghetti broken up into small pieces. Served in individual dessert bowls.

latte dolce fritto custard of milk, eggs, sugar, flour, grated lemon zest and cinnamon, cooked until it sets, cut into lozenge-shapes, coated in breadcrumbs and fried. Liguria.

latte in piedi, in dialect aka **latt in pe** cream dessert of milk, sugar, eggs, crushed amaretti cookies, powdered chocolate, grated lemon zest and isinglass, served cold after resting for a day. A specialty of the province of Piacenza. Emilia-Romagna.

lattemiele, in dialect aka **latmel** term used, mainly in Modena, for whipped cream, named for the fact that honey (*miele* in Italian) used to be added. Emilia-Romagna.

Latteria generic name in northern Italy for cow's cheese produced in dairies on low-lying plainland. Production techniques are identical, but flavor varies according to breed and feed.

latterino smelt. Small fish of the Aterinidae or silverside family. Three species exist in Italy: *Atherina mochon* and *A. boyeri*, which live in coastal waters and in lakes in central and southern Italy and the islands, and *A. hepsetus* which lives almost exclusively in the sea. *Latterino del Trasimeno* (Umbria) and *latterino del lago di Bracciano* (Lazio) are listed in the Italian Ministry of Agricuture's database of native and/or traditional food products. Smelt are best enjoyed fried whole or marinated as an antipasto. Common and regional names: ➤ **acquadella**, ➤ **alicetta**, ➤ **anguela**, ➤ **ciciniello**, ➤ **muscione**.

latteruolo another name for ➤ **casadello**, a custard.

latti di seppia female cuttlefish glands. Boiled in a ➤ **court-bouillon**, they are dressed with flat-leaved parsley, oil and lemon and served with ➤ **cicheti**, aperitifs.

latticello buttermilk. By-product of the processing of milk into butter.

latticino (1) dairy product. Made from the acid fermentation of milk or cream or from whey, yogurt, ricotta and so on.

latticino (2) regional term for ➤ **grattalingua**, common brighteyes.

latticrepolo another name for ➤ **grattalingua**, common brighteyes.

lattone a horse less than a year old.

lattonzo aka **lattonzolo** suckling pig (➤ **maialino**).

lattuccio regional term for➤ **lattuga selvatica**, wild lettuce.

lattuchedda Sicilian term for cut of beef equivalent to navel. Once considered *il filetto dei poveri*, "the fillet of the poor," on account of its leaness and flavor.

lattuchina regional term for ➤ **lattuga selvatica**, wild lettuce.

lattuga lettuce (*Lactuca sativa*). A huge number of varieties are cultivated for the market. The Italian Ministry of Agriculture's database of native and/or traditional food products lists the following: *lattuga signorinella di Formia* (Lazio); *lattughino di Moncalieri* (Piedmont); *lattuga quattro stagioni* (Tuscany). Lettuce is generally eaten raw in salads, but examples exist of recipes in which it is cooked: eg, ➤ *lattughe ripiene in brood* (Liguria).

lattuga selvatica wild lettuce (*Lactuca serriola* and *L. viminea*). Wild herbaceous plants that grow on fallow land, in vineyards and in hedgerows. Their leaves are eaten young in spring salads in central and southern Italy. Common and regional names: ➤ **lattuccio**, ➤ **lattuchina**, ➤ **lattughella**.

lattugaccio rush skeletonweed (*Chondrilla juncea*). Wild herbaceous plant, which grows on cultivated and uncultivated land and in hedgerows. Its leaves are gathered and eaten in most Italian regions: raw in salads, with garlic and anchovies or mixed with other field greens; cooked and turned with oil or butter; as a pie filing or to dress pasta. Common and regional names: ➤ **condrilla**, ➤ **cassella**, ➤ **ginestrella**, ➤ **lattaiola**, ➤ **lattughiello**, ➤ **mastrici**.

lattughe sweet fried pastries similar to ➤ **cenci** or ➤ **orecchie di Amman**. A specialty of Mantua. Lombardy.

lattughe ripiene in brodo Roman lettuce hearts stuffed with a mixture of veal, sweetbreads and brain bound with eggs and Parmigiano and cooked in broth. Liguria.

lattughella regional term for both ➤ **lattuga selvatica**, wild lettuce, and ➤ **valerianella**, common cornsalad.

lattughiello regional term for ➤ **lattugaccio**, rush skeletonweed.

lattughino common term for both ➤ **valerianella**, common cornsalad, and ➤ **grattalingua**, common brighteyes, as well as for a kind of cultivated lettuce (➤ **lattuga**).

lattume the sperm sac of the tuna fish (➤ **tonno**), boiled, fried or dressed with oil, vinegar, lemon, salt and aromatic herbs. Also preserved in brine and dried for slicing like botargo (➤ **bottarga**). A traditional delicacy in Sicily and Sardinia (where it is known as ➤ **littume** or ➤ **figatello**).

lauro "laurel." Common name for ➤ **bay leaf**, bay leaf.

lausciera aka **lausciera** individual plate cum tray fitted with a slab of soapstone (*pietra ollare*) to cook meat. A tradition of the Val d'Ossola (province of Verbano-Cusio-Ossola). Piedmont.

lavanda lavander (*Lavanda angustifolia*). The culinary use of the blossoms, highly scented thanks to the presence of various essential oils, is more creative than traditional. They aromatize not only sorbets, creams, bavarois, semifreddi and so on, but also fish, fowl and rabbit. Common and regional names: ➤ **lavandula**, ➤ **spigo**, ➤ **spighetto**.

lavandula another name for ➤ **lavanda**, lavender.

lavarelli al vino bianco fillets of chub cooked in butter with chives, flat-leaved parsley and white wine. Typical of Lake Como. Lombardy.

lavarelli alla salvia fillets of chub coated in flour, and baked in the oven with butter and sage. Typical of Lake Como. Lombardy.

lavarello aka **lavareto** regional and dialect names for ➤ **coregone**, chub.

lavasso regional term for ➤ **lapazio**, monk's rhubarb.

lavertin Piedmontese dialect term for ➤ **luppolo**, hops.

lavorare synonym of ➤ **impastare**, to knead.

laxerto Ligurian word for ➤ **sgombro**, mackerel.

lazzarette Abruzzo dialect term for ➤ **peperoncino**, chili.

lazzeruola (or **azzeruola**) hawthorn (*Crataegus azarolus*). Native to Asia Minor, and common throughout the Mediterranean, both wild and cultivated. Its berries are used to make syrups, jams, jellies and liqueurs.

Leberknödel type of ➤ **knödel** made by kneading white bread soaked in milk, eggs, puréed calf's liver, and lightly fried onion, butter and minced parsley and shaping the resulting mixture into small balls. These are cooked in boiling water and served in broth. The dish is known as *Leberknödelsuppe* (➤ **zuppa di canederli di fegato** in Italian). Trentino-Alto Adige.

Lebkuchen Christmas cookies made, in various shapes, with flour, sugar, honey, cinnamon, cloves, lemon juice and, in some cases, almonds or walnuts. Trentino-Alto Adige.

leccarda aka **ghiotta** dripping pan. Long, flat metal recipient with a handle placed under a spit to catch juices dripping form cooking meat. The juices may be used to make sauces (➤ **palomba alla ghiotta**).

leccarda, alla another term for ➤ **ghiotta, alla**, a method for cooking pigeon.

leccia aka **leccia bastarda** regional terms for ➤ **ricciòla**, amberjack.

legante a binding agent. An ingredient (flour, potato flour, starch, egg, cream, butter and so on) used to bind or thicken sauces and gravies.

legare (1) to tie. (In gastronomy) to secure a food (fowl, large cuts of meat) with kitchen string to maintain its shape during the cooking process.

legare (2) to bind or thicken sauces and gravies.

leghe Tuscan term for the leaves of "black cabbage" (➤ **cavolo nero**).

legumi legumes. Beans, peas, fava beans, lentines, chickpeas, grass peas and so on.

lempete Puglia term for ➤ **totano**, squid.

lempitu di fangu Sicilian term for ➤ **scampo**, scampi.

lenga ponciu-a boiled calf's tongue in a fiery sauce preserved tuna and anchovies, capers, garlic, chili, tomato paste, oil, vinegar and sugar. Typical of the mountain valleys of the province of Cuneo. Piedmont.

lengua Ligurian term for ➤ **sogliola**, sole.

lenticchia lentil (*Lens esculenta*). Probably the legume of most ancient cultivation. Thanks to its high nutritional content, it was a precious staple for the poor for centuries. Today it is possible to buy lentils already decorticated to speed up cooking times. Especially prized for the fineness of its skin is ➤ **lenticchia di Castelluccio di Norcia**, protected by a PGI seal. The Italian Ministry of Agriculture's database of native and/or traditional food products lists the following varieties:➤ **lenticchia di Santo Stefano di Sessanio** (Abruzzo); lenticchia di Valle Agricola (Campania); ➤ **lenticchia di Onano**, *lenticchia di Rascino, lenticchia di Ventotene* (Lazio); *lenticchia* molisana (Molise); *lenticchia gialla* aka *lenticchia gigante di Altamura* (Puglia), ➤ **lenticchia di Ustica**, *lenticchia di Villalba* (Sicily); *lenticchie umbre* (Umbria). Lentils are traditionally served as a side dish with ➤ **zampone**, as well as in purées, stews, soups and with pasta: ➤ **purè di lenticchie**, ➤ **zuppa di lenticchie**, ➤ **lasagne alle lenticchie**.

lenticchia di Castelluccio di Norcia tiny, fragrant PGI lentil produced in the area of the Monti Sibillini national park. Cultivated in the uplands round the village of Castelluccio, it does not require soaking. Umbria.

lenticchia di Onano ancient lentil that grows in the sandy, vulcanic soil round the small town of Onano, in the province of Viterbo. Virtually extinct in the 1970s, it is now cultivated in family gardens and an organic producer is trying to return it to the market. A Slow Food presidium is striving to increase its cultivation. Lazio.

lenticchia di Santo Stefano di Sessanio native lentil variety that grows at altitudes of over 3,000 feet on the slopes of the Gran Sasso, in the province of L'Aquila. Protected by a Slow Food presidium. Abruzzo.

lenticchia di Ustica tiny, delicate lentil cultivated in the lava soil of the small island of Ustica, in the province of Palermo. Harvested in the middle of June, it does not require soaking. A Slow Food presidium assists the three growers still left on the island. Sicily.

lenticchie con salsicce boiled local lentils (➤ **lenticchia di Castelluccio di Norcia**) added to stewed mixed meats (sausages, ➤ **cotechino** and pig's snout, or ➤ **guanciale**, cheek bacon), flavored with garlic, celery, mixed herbs and tomato passata. Umbria.

lenzuolino del Bambino literally "Baby's sheet." The "sheet" is a combination of very broad and very thin egg lasagne, "crumpled" on the plate, covered with a sauce of crumbled sausage meat, dried mushrooms and tomatoes and sprinkled with grated Parmigiano-Reggiano. A traditional Christmas dish in the province of Alessandria. Piedmont.

lepericchio round cake decorated with a hard-boiled egg at the bottom and the initials of San Marco Evangelista at the center. Baked on the saint's day (April 25) in the village of Capena, in the province of Rome, it is the "male" version of ➤ **sposatella**. Lazio.

lepre hare (*Lepus europaeus*). The most common game animal in Italy. The meat, which is best from young animals, is hung and/or marinated in red wine with herbs and spices, or in water nd vinegar.

Cooked *al* ➤ **civé** or *in*➤ **salmì**, in Lombardy and Piedmont, in ➤ **dolceforte**, in Tuscany, and often as an ingredient in terrines.

lepre al civé aka **lepre al civet** hare cut into pieces and marinated for 36-48 hours in red wine with celery, carrot, onion, garlic, flat-leaved parsley, thyme, bay leaf, juniper berries, cinnamon and peppercorns (➤ **civé**). The meat is then browned in butter and oil, sprinkled with flour and cooked with the vegetables from the marinade and the marinade liquid (the hare's blood used to be used as a binding agent). The cooked chopped hare's liver is added towards the end of the cooking process, and the dish is served with the filtered pan juices and polenta and boiled potatoes. Piedmont, Val d'Aosta.

lepre al Vin Santo pieces of hare marinated in red wine with carrot, onion, celery, cinnamon, cloves, peppercorns, bay leaf, lemon zest, garlic and salt, browned in onion, lardo and prosciutto, bathed with Vin Santo and finished off with dried mushrooms. Tuscany.

lepre alla cacciatora pieces of hare first marinated, then cooked with aromatic vegetables, wine and tomato sauce.

lepre disossata alla piacentina pieces of hare marinated in full-bodied red wine with aromatic vegetables and herbs, browned in oil and butter with minced carrot and celery, sage, bay leaves and ➤ **pista 'd gras**, covered with the marinade wine and cooked very slowly until the meat comes away from the bones (which are removed with a fork). Typical of the province of Piacenza. Emilia-Romagna.

lepre in agrodolce sweet and sour hare. In Trentino-Alto Adige, pieces of hare are marinated in wine, grappa, herbs and spices, cooked in wine and broth and served with a sauce made with the animal's liver, some of the marinade liquid, raisins, pine kernels, cinnamon, sugar and lemon zest. In Friuli-Venezia Giulia, they marinate the meat in wine, vinegar and herbs, sprinkle it with sugar and bake it in the oven with vinegar and broth. Trentino-Alto Adige, Friuli-Venezia Giulia.

lepre in crostata a spit-roast hare, basted with cream and coated with salted crushed amaretti cookies to form a golden crust. Lombardy

lepre in salmì in Lombardy, in the provinces of Brescia and Mantua (where many use the term *alla* ➤ **cacciatora** in lieu of *in* **salmì**), they marinate pieces of hare in white wine with bay leaves, peppercorns and salt, brown it in a mixture of minced lardo and and finish it off with the marinade liquid. In Friuli-Venezia Giulia, chunks of hare are first marinated, browned in butter and oil and cooked with minced prosciutto, onion, garlic and white wine. In Tuscany, the marinade consists of vinegar, water, bay leaves, juniper berries and rosemary, the cooking liquid of white wine, broth and little tomato paste. In Reggio Emilia, the hare pieces are browned in a mixture of crushed lardo and aromatic herbs and finished in red wine with the addition of the animal's blood and chopped innards (a recipe more akin to a ➤ **civé**).

lepre in tegame hare stew. Pieces of hare browned with rosemary and sage, sprinkled with white wine and slow-cooked with the subsequent addition of a sauce made with the animal's liver, sausage, lemon juice, flat-leaved parsley, cinnamon and cloves. Veneto.

lepudrida thick soup of pork and beef, ham, lardo, onions, beans, peas, chickpeas and, in some cases, Savoy cabbage, chicory and lettuce, sprinkled with generous amounts of grated Pecorino. A popular recipe in the province of Cagliari, it came into being as a way of using up leftovers and is reminiscent of the Spanish *olla potrida*.

lessare to boil (➤**bollire**).

lesso "boiled." Adjective referred to fish, meat, and vegetables. As a noun, in some regions the word is used as a synonym of ➤ **bollito**, commonly with reference to meat, usually beef to make broth. Regional recipes include: ➤ **lesso fritto**, ➤ **lesso in castigo**, ➤ **lesso in insalata**, ➤ **lesso in tecia**, ➤ **lesso rifatto**.

lesso fritto typical Milanese dish in which leftover boiled beef is coated in Parmigiano, peppered beaten eggs and breadcrumbs, fried in butter, and seasoned with salt. Lombardy.

lesso in castigo leftover boiled beef fried with rosemary, garlic, and potatoes. Marche.

lesso in insalata diced leftover boiled beef dressed with finely sliced fried onions, white beans, extra virgin live oil, vinegar and salt. Lombardy.

lesso in tecia leftover boiled beef sautéed with gently fried onion, sprinkled with wine and vinegar, and garnished with minced parsley. Veneto.

lesso rifatto aka **francesina** leftover boiled beef diced and sautéed with onion, skinned tomatoes, broth and abundant ground black pepper. Tuscany.

lesso sporco recipe typical of the fishermen of Senigallia, in the province of Ancona. A casserole of mantis shrimp, soles, skate wings, spotted flounder, olive oil, garlic, salt, pepper, parsley and white wine. Marche.

letto bed. A base (eg, of raw or cooked vegetables, salad, rice, polenta, potato purée etc) over which a cooked food is served.

levadèi another name for➤ **ficattola**, a type of flatbread.

levistico another name for→ **sedano di monte**, lovage.

liberazza regional term for → **vongola**, common clam.

liberòn Veneto term for→ **vongola**, common clam.

libretto (1) "little book." Genoa bread roll scored down the middle with a wood quill to make it look like an open book. Liguria

libretto (2) another name for → **omaso**, omasum.

libro another name for → **omaso**, omasum.

licnide another name for → **silene rossa**, red catchfly.

licurdia (1) traditional soup of potatoes, carrots and chard, escarole or lettuce with the addition of Tropea onions. An all-onion version also exists, flavored with chili and grated mature Pecorino. Calabria.

licurdia (2) fiery garlic, onion and chili spread. Calabria.

lidric aka **radric cul poc** wild chicory (→ **cicoria selvatica**), roots included, dressed with strips of cooked lardo, salt and vinegar.

lievitare to leaven.

lievito chimico chemical yeast. Added to bread or pastry dough either dry or diluted in water.

lievito di birra brewer's yeast.

lievito madre starter yeast.

ligaboschi regional term for → **luppolo**, hops.

ligustico regional term for → **sedano di monte**, lovage.

lilla Marche term for→ **acciuga**, anchovy.

limetta aka **lima** aka **limone bergamotto** lime (*Citrus aurantiflia*). Tropical citrus fruit much used in the preparation of cocktails and soft drinks, domestically and commercially. *Limetta calabrese* is listed in the Italian Ministry of Agricul-

ture's database of native and/or traditional food products.

limoncello aka **limoncino** popular digestive liqueur made from the peel of lemons (→ **limone di Sorrento**, → **limone costa d'Amalfi**), immersed in alcohol and diluted with sugar and water. Also used in the kitchen to aromatize ice creams, sweet doughs (→ **pasticciotto**), and custards and creams.

limoncina regional name for → **cedrina**, lemon verbena.

limone lemon (*Citrus limonia*). Probably introduced to Italy during the Arab invasions from the 9th to the 11th century. The → **limone costa d'Amalfi**, → **limone femminello del Gargano**, → **limone di Sorrento** are all PGI-protected. The Italian Ministry of Agriculture's database of native and/or traditional food products lists the following varieties: *limone Costa dei Trabocchi* (Abruzzo), *limoni di Rocca Imperiale* (Calabria), *limone di Procida* (Campania), *limone massese* (Tuscany), *limone in seccagno di Pettineo*, *limone verdello* (Sicily). Slow Food presidia protect and promote → **agrumi del Gargano** (Puglia) and → **limone Interdonato** (Sicily).

limone bergamotto another name for → **limetta**, lime.

limone Costa d'Amalfi juicy PGI lemon cultivated on terraces along the Amalfi coast, in the province of Salerno, and harvested from February to October. Campania.

limone di mare another name for → **frutti di mare**, seafood.

limone di Sorrento beautifully scented, juicy PGI lemon, typical of the Sorrentine peninsula and the islands of Capri and Anacapri, in the province of Naples. Campania.

limone femminello del Gargano prized

PGI lemon cultivated in communes of the Gargano peninsula, in the province of Foggia. Puglia.

limone Interdonato a lemon obtained by crossing a citron with a local variety (*ariaddu*), named for the hybridizer Giovanni Interdonato, a follower of Garibaldi and former governor of Sicily. Grown on steep terraces from Messina to Letojanni and hard to harvest, surviving groves are protected by a Slow Food presidium. Sicily.

linarda Ligurian term for→ **molva**, ling.

lingua tongue. In Italy, calf's, ox's and pig's tongues are the most used in the kitchen. Lamb's and kid's tongues are normally sold with the head of the animal. In the Tuscan and Emilian Apennines, smoked wild boar's tongue is a specialty. Ox's and pig's tongues are available corned. Fresh ox tongue is usually braised or stewed, pig's tongue is best enjoyed boiled, served with sauerkraut (→ **crauti**). In traditional regional cookery, calf's tongue is the most used of all, usually boiled and served with parsley and garlic or horseradish sauce, but also as a component of → **bollito misto**, → **lingua in giardino** and → **lingua in dolceforte**.

lingua alla muranese boiled pig's tongue, cut into slices and served with a sauce of grated horseradish, vinegar, salt and pepper. A specialty of the island of Murano, in the province of Venice. Veneto.

lingua cotta di Carnia cured meat typical of the Valle del But in the Carnia area of the province of Udine. A pig's tongue is washed, dried and cured for three days in salt, pepper, garlic, juniper berries and bay leaf, then steeped for 15 to 20 days in a brine of water, salt and sugar. It is then left in running water for eight to ten hours and dried for three days. Finally, it is smoked for 72-96 hours and steamed

for 60-90 minutes. Friuli-Venezia Giulia.

lingua di bove regional term for→ **echio**, viper's bugloss.

lingua di cane regional term for→ **piantaggine**, ribwort plantain.

lingua di suocera baked thin, crisp cookie made from a thrice-leavened dough of water, flour and starter yeast. Sometimes 20 inches long and five inches wide. Typical of the province of Asti. Piedmont.

lingua in dolceforte sweet and sour tongue. The meat is poached and marinated in red wine and vinegar, then sliced and finished in the pan with mixed aromatic herbs and the marinade liquid. It is then smothered in a sauce of butter, dark chocolate, raisins, pine kernels, sugar and candied fruit. Sometimes even crumbled spicy cakes and cookies, such as →**panforte** or → **cavallucci**, are added (→**agrodolce**, sweet and sour). Tuscany.

lingua in giardino thin slices of boiled calf's tongue covered with a sauce of vegetables (finely minced stewed onion, carrot and celery), minced flat-leaved parsley and capers, tomato sauce, a piece of red chili (*spagnolin* in dialect), broth and vinegar. A common warm antipasto. Piedmont.

lingua in salsa slices of boiled calf's tongue covered either with a red sauce with a "green" sauce (flat-leaved parsley, garlic, hard-boiled egg yolk, anchovies, oil and vinegar) or a "red" sauce (tomato, peppers, anchovies, oil and vinegar): → **bagnet**. Piedmont.

lingua in umido stewed tongue. Calf's tongue, boiled or sautéed, cut into chunks or slices and finished in butter, wine, aromatic herbs and tomato sauce. Dish typical of northern Italy, especially of Piedmont and the eastern regions.

linguattola spotted flounder (*Citharus linguatula*). Sea fish much loved in the Marche region. Cooked in the same way as ➤ **sogliola**, sole. Common and regional names: ➤ **pataracia**, ➤ **zanchetta**, ➤ **zanchettone**.

lingue di gatto "cat's tongues." Crisp sponge fingers made of butter, confectioner's sugar, flour egg whites and vanilla served with tea, hot chocolate or, in Piedmont, Moscato or ➤ **zabaglione**.

lingue di passero "sparrow's tongues." Another name for ➤ **bavette**, a type of pasta.

linguette square cookies made of flour, sugar, cooked wine must (➤ **vincotto**), cocoa and yeast, originally made in the region's convents. Basilicata.

linguette ripiene sponge fingers filled with apricot jam and coated with chocolate. Trentino-Alto Adige.

linguine another name for ➤ **bavette**, a type of pasta.

Linztorte tart of shortcrust pastry dotted with almonds and topped with raspberry or blackcurrant jam. Typical of Linz, in Austria, but also common in the Sudtirolo area. Trentino-Alto Adige.

liptauer cream of ricotta, butter, onion, cumin, capers and paprika. Typical of Veneto. Friuli-Venezia Giulia.

liquirizia liquorice (*Glycyrrhiza glabra*). Herbaceous plant whose sweet roots are dried, cleaned and sold as sticks. Grows spontaneously along the coastline of Calabria, where noble families started to process it into sticks, pastilles and tablets in factories as early as the 18th century (the prestigious Amarelli company still survives).

liquori di tradizione traditional liqueurs. Drinks made by distilling fruit, spices, herbs and so on, or mixing them with alcoholic drinks or with ethylic alcohol or brandy. Many liqueurs made by adding spices or fruit to alcohol or spirits derive from ancient recipes, often invented in monasteries and convents. Anise liqueurs, rosolio, alkermes, ratafià and amaro belong to this typology, as do many domestic recipes made by infusing citrus fruit zest, fruit and berries in alcohol.

lisandros pasta similar to ➤ **fettuccine**. Sardinia.

lischi term used in Romagna for ➤ **barba di frate**, oppositeleaf Russian thistle.

lisone aka **lisotto** another name for ➤ **fazzino**, a type of flatbread.

littume Sardinian term for ➤ **lattume**, the sperm sac of the tuna.

litump aka **litum** mixture of spontaneous aromatic herbs which, according to tradition, should be picked before sunrise. Friuli-Venezia Giulia.

Livigno another name for ➤ **Semigrasso d'alpe** cheese.

loertis Lombard term for ➤ **luppolo**, hops.

lolli short fresh pasta typical of Modica, in the province of Ragusa, and the southern part of the province of Siracusa. In Frigintini, near Modica, they make *lolli di carruba*, cooking the pasta in carob syrup (➤ **carruba**) and coating it with minced toasted almonds. Sicily.

lombata cut of beef roughly equivalent to short loin, from which T-bone steaks (➤ **bistecca alla fiorentina**) are extracted. Also known as ➤ **controfiletto** or ➤ **roastbeef**. The equivalent cut of pork is called ➤ **lonza**.

lombello incamiciato pork fillet (known locally as *lombello*) flavored with bay leaves wrapped in pig caul (*ratta*) and roast on a spit. Umbria.

lombetto northern Marche name for ➤ **lonzino**, a cured meat.

lombrichi aka **lombrichelli** Lazio pasta similar to ➤ **umbricelli**.

longone regional term for *vongola gialla*, golden carpet shell (➤ **vongola**).

lonza loin. Cut of pork or, less frequently

veal. Corresponds to ➤ **lombata**, and is generally boned.

lonza aquilana a whole piece of loin of pork cured in sea salt for 24 to 36 hours, sprinkled generously with pepper and cased in a natural or artificial intestine. After maturing for two weeks, it is aged for five months. Abruzzo.

lonza marchigiana pork loin trimmed to a cylindrical shape, rubbed and covered with salt for thee to five days, then cleaned, washed with red or dry white wine, dried and covered with ground black pepper. Wrapped in the pig's large intestine, it is tied with kitchen string and smoked for three to four days. It is aged for six to seven months. Marche.

lonze di vitello alla mugellana dish typical of the Mugello district, in the province of Florence, where the word *lonza* means a calf's cheek. It consists of cheeks cut into strips like tripe, browned with a bouquet garni, stewed with tomato and served with boiled beans. Now very rare, the dish is comparable to ➤ **grifi all'aretina** and ➤ **cioncia pesciatina**. Tuscany.

lonzino cured meat made from a cut of pork that runs from the back to the tail. The production technique is identical to that of ➤ **lonza marchigiana**. Marche.

lonzino aperto cured meat made from the end of the pig's back complete with rind. The lean pork is cured with salt, pepper, crushed garlic, white or cooked wine and aromatic herbs, including rosemary, sage, juniper berries and fennel, cleaned and lightly smoked over sprigs of rosemary and wild fennel for 24 hours. Cured meat common in the provinces of Fermo and Macerata. Marche.

lonzino con cotenna another name for ➤ **lonzino aperto**, a cured meat.

lonzino di fichi A traditional rural cake made from dried figs mixed with al-monds, pieces of walnut and star anise, sometimes with a little ➤ **sapa** (slowly cooked grape must) or ➤ **mistrà** (aniseed liqueur), and wrapped in fig leaves. Best enjoyed with a medium-aged cheese and a glass of passito wine. Produced in some towns and villages in the province of Ancona (Marche), it is protected by a Slow Food presidium. Marche.

lorighittas handmade pasta spaghetti shaped like spiral spaghetti. Typical of Morgongiori, a village in the province of Oristano. Sardinia.

lose golose dry biscuits that look like local slates (*lose*), hence the name. A specialty of Susa, in the province of Turin. Piedmont.

luadei small bread rolls, once made to establish the exact temperature of the oven before baking, served as an antipasto with cured meats. Lombardy.

lubjanska breaded steak topped with ham and cheese. A dish of Slovenian origin. Friuli-Venezia Giulia.

lucanica traditional "U"-shaped sausage produced in different versions according to area of provenance. The finest is made with prime pork cured with salt, pepper, fennel seeds and a dash of powdered chili. Cased in a pig's intestine and hung to dry for 15 to 20 days. A fatter version is preserved in lard. Basilicata.

lucanica trentina cured meat of lean pork mixed with salt, ground pepper and garlic. The mixture is cased in natural intestines in ten-foot lengths divided into three to four inches "sausages," which are sometimes smoked. A Slow Food presidium has brought together producers, who now adhere to a strict production protocol. Trentino-Alto Adige.

luccio pike (*Esox lucius*). Lake and river fish with delicate flesh usually boiled, broiled, baked, fried and stewed. *Luc-*

cio del Trasimeno (Umbria) is listed in the Italian Ministry of Agriculture's database of native and/or traditional food products. **luccio alla barcaiola** aka **luccio alla barcarola** recipe derived from ➤ **luccio in consa**. Perch boiled and dressed with a mixture of oil, salted capers and desalted anchovies. Typical of Lake Garda. Lombardy, Trentino-Alto Adige, Veneto.

luccio alla gardesana fried balls of boiled pike boiled in white wine and lemon juice and mixed with day-old bread soaked in milk, garlic, flat-leaved parsley and desalted anchovies. A recipe of relatively recent creation, typical of Lake Garda. Lombardy, Trentino-Alto Adige, Veneto.

luccio in bianco pike cooked in a ➤ **court-bouillon** of white wine and vinegar, opened and flattened, boned and dressed with oil and minced flat-leaved parsley, or with oil and a sprinkling of black pepper. A recipe typical of Lake Garda. Lombardy, Trentino-Alto-Adige, Veneto.

luccio in concia di àole pike boiled in acidulated water with aromatic vegetables and herbs, served with crushed bleak (➤ **alborella**) in brine. Typical of the eastern side of Lake Garda. Trentino-Alto Adige, Veneto.

luccio in consa aka **luccio in salsa,** in dialect aka **luss in salsa** boiled fillets of pike layered with a sauce of olive oil, vinegar, capers, garlic, flat-leaved parsley and salted anchovies, and served with toasted polenta. A specialty of the province of Cremona, but also common in the provinces of Cremona, Brescia and Verona. Lombardy, Veneto.

luccio sauro another name for ➤ **costardella**, needlefish.

lucertolo Tuscan term for ➤ **sottofesa**, round, a cut of beef.

lucioperca aka **sandra** zander or pike-perch

(*Stizostedion lucioperca*). A fish similar to the perch (➤ **pesce persico**, but larger. Cooked in the same way as perch and pike (➤ **luccio**).

lucioperca in salsa zander (➤ **lucioperca**) boiled with vinegar and herbs, filleted and dressed with a cream of desalted anchovies, capers, lemon juice and oil. Served with slices of grilled polenta. Typical of the eastern shore of Lake Garda, in the province of Verona. Veneto.

luganega a type of long thin sausage, usually stewed or fried or barbecued. The term is used in Lombardy and Veneto and derives from ➤ **lucanica**, northern Italians having learned to make the sausage from the Lucanians, inhabitants of Basilicata (ex-Lucania).

luganega lombarda long, thin sausage made from finely ground fat and lean pork cured with salt, pepper and other spices. The mixture is cased in the small intestines of pigs or lambs. In Monza (province of Monza and Brianza), the mixture is flavored with chicken or beef broth and Grana Padano. The sausage is eaten cooked within two or three days of production. Lombardy.

luganega trevisana cured meat made with chicken and pork neck and jowl cured with peppers, cinnamon, cloves, mace and coriander, cased in a pig's intestine and twisted into four "sausages." Eaten fresh. Veneto.

luganeghe e fasoi sauasage and beans. Fresh sausage (➤ **luganega trevisana**) with beans flavored with garlic and onion and stewed in tomato passata and vegetable broth. Popular all over the region. Veneto.

luganeghette di passola traditional cured meat, also known as *salame di rape* (turnip salami) made from a mixture of lardo, lean pork and small dried turnips (*passole* in dialect). Produced exclusively in the area round Livigno, in the province of Sondrio. Lombardy.

lui regional term for ➤ **lupino**, hops.

lumaca snail. A gastropod mollusk of the Helix genus. Snails are easiest to find after rain in fields, orchards and gardens, but their collection is restricted by law and numerous varieties have been decimated by pesticides and chemical fertilizers. As a result, they are farmed in many places, with excellent results in terms of quality and safety. The most commonly farmed varieties are: *Helix pomatia* (Roman snail: ➤ **bogoni**, ➤ **bovoloni**, ➤ **corgnòi**) and *H. aspersa* (common snail: ➤ **cai**, ➤ **ciammotta**, ➤ **ciammariche** aka **ciammaruche**, ➤ **cucciole**, ➤ **crastuna**, ➤ **barbani**, ➤ **boveri**, ➤ **coccoeddu**), and to a lesser degree *H. aperta* (garden snail: ➤ **monacella**, ➤ **crastatelli**, ➤ **moniceddhi**, ➤ **monzetta**, ➤ **tappadas**, ➤ **tirignole**, ➤'**ntuppateddi**).

lumache another name for ➤ **pipe**, a type of pasta.

lumache al verde snails stewed with parsley and garlic (➤ **lumache trifolate**).

lumache all'ossolana boiled snails mixed with butter, egg yolks, garlic, flat-leaved parsley, walnuts and crushed amaretti cookies, returned to their shells and baked in the oven. Typical of the province of Verbano-Cusio-Ossola. Piedmont.

lumache alla bobbiese snails sautéed in a skillet with a little tomato sauce and finished off, the day after, with finely minced leek, celery and carrot, white wine and water. A delicacy typical of Bobbio, in the Val Trebbia, in the province of Piacenza. Emilia-Romagna.

lumache alla castellana boiled snails turned in olive oil with garlic and flat-leaved parsley and finished off with boned, boiled frogs' legs and, in season, truf-fle. A specialty of the province of Pavia. Lombardy.

lumache alla casumarese boiled snails, removed from their shells, stewed with red wine, tomato paste, spices (traditionally cinnamon, saffron, ginger and pepper), and sprinkled with grated mature Parmigiano. The recipe dates from the 18th century and is still made (albeit in a simplified manner) in the village of Casumaro, in the province of Ferrara, on the occasion of the feast of San Lorenzo (August 10), rechristened *Sagra della lumaca*, the Feast of the Snail. Emilia-Romagna.

lumache alla comacina snails cooked in butter, oil and vegetable broth flavored with minced walnuts. Lombardy.

lumache alla finalina small snails cooked in lightly fried onion, aromatic herbs (flat-leaved parsley, basil and marjoram), white wine and tomato. Before serving, the snails are flavored with crushed walnuts, hazelnuts, capers and grated cheese. A specialty of Finale Ligure, in the province of Savona. Liguria.

lumache alla meranese chopped snails lightly fried with lardo and herbs, cooked in white wine and broth and added to a pea purée. Trentino-Alto Adige.

lumache alla romana another name for ➤ **lumache di san Giovanni**, stewed snails.

lumache alla vignaiola shelled snails (*Helix pomatia*) sautéed in a base of salted anchovy, lardo and herbs and finished in red wine and tomato sauce. Piedmont.

lumaca di mare sea snail. Small marine gastropod that lives among sea rocks and brackish waters. Especially common in the Venice lagoons. Often served, dressed with oil and lemon, as an antipasto. Common and and regional names: ➤ **bombetto**, ➤ **bomboletto**, ➤ **bovoeto**, ➤ **bovoleto**, ➤ **caragol**, ➤ **maruzela**, ➤ **maruzza**, ➤ **maruzzella**, ➤ **uccuna**, ➤ **vuccuna**.

lumache di san Giovanni snails (*Helix pomatia* or *H. aspersa* or *H. Eobania*) boiled in water with salt and pennyroyal, removed from their shells and cooked with tomatoes, anchovies, garlic, onion, chili and pennyroyal leaves. Traditionally prepared in the popular neighborhoods of Rome on the night of San Giovanni, June 23-24 (*La ciumacata di San Giovanni*). Lazio.

lumache e funghi snails and mushrooms. Boiled snails cooked with bay leaves, juniper berries, skinned tomatoes, mushrooms and broth, and served with polenta. Trentino-Alto Adige

lumache fritte fried snails. Boiled snails dipped first in beaten, then in breadcrumbs, and fried in boiling oil. Piedmont.

lumache grandi another name for ➤ **lumaconi**, a type of pasta.

lumache in padella snails sautéed in oil and butter, splashed with white wine and cooked on a low heat with the addition of milk. Friuli-Venezia Giulia

lumache in porchetta garden snails (➤ **cucciole** in dialect) stewed with tomato, pennyroyal and wild fennel. A recipe typical of the province of Macerata. Marche.

lumache in umido stewed snails. Most recipes use large snails (*Helix pomatia* or *H. aspersa*) removed from their shells. In the province of Milan (Lombardy), they sauté the snails in olive oil with garlic, onion, flat-leaved parsley, anchovies, fennel seeds and wheat flour, and finish them with dry white wine, salt, pepper and nutmeg. In the Valdadige, in the province of Verona (Veneto), the snails are poached in broth and aromatized with garlic, flat-leaved parsley and mint. In Friuli, they cook snails with mixed minced herbs, white wine and broth and serve the resulting thick sauce with soft polenta. In Umbria, they turn them in a skillet with minced herbs, including wild fennel and pennyroyal, and finish them with white wine and skinned tomatoes.

lumache trifolate in Lombardy, snails are removed from their shells and sautéed in a base of olive oil or butter and garlic, and finished off with white wine and minced flat-leaved parsley. The same recipe in Piedmont is called *lumache al verde*. Lombardy, Piedmont.

lumachelle all'urbinate egg pasta, similar to fettuccine, rolled up to look like snails, served in broth with chicken giblets. Marche.

lumachelle di Orvieto baked spiral, snail-shaped savories made from a dough of flour, brewer's yeast, grated Pecorino and chopped cheek bacon (➤ **guanciale**). Umbria.

lumachine aka **lumache grandi** dry durum wheat pasta similar to small ➤**pipe**, generally cooked in broth. Another name for ➤ **conchigliette.**

lumaconi commercial smooth or ridged hollow, snail-shaped durum wheat pasta of Campanian and Ligurian origin. Suitable for stuffing and baking in the oven.

lumello another name for ➤ **salsicciotto di Guilmi**, a cured meat.

lupa Campanian term for ➤ **molva**, ling.

lupari Lazio term for ➤ **luppolo**, hops.

lupini tiny Carnival pastries made from dough aromatized with orange and lemon zest. Typical of the province of Ferrara. Emilia-Romagna.

lupino (1) lupin (*Lupinus albus*). A member of the pea family (➤ **pisello**) which grows wild and cultivated all over Italy and whose pods contain hard bitter seeds. The latter are washed in running water, boiled, briefly soaked in brine and eaten largely as a snack or as street food (in Lazio they are called ➤ **fusaglie** and street vendors, *fusagliari*, sell them in paper cones). Thanks to their high protein and fat content, lupins are now enjoying something of a revival, and a project is underway to reproduce a traditional lupin-based coffee surrogate, *caffè di Anterivo* (➤ **caffè**). The Italian Ministry of Agriculture's database of native and/or traditional food products include two varieties: *lupino dolce di Grosseto* (Tuscany) and *lupino gigante di Vairano* (Campania). Common and regional names: ➤ **fava luina**, ➤ **fusaglia**, ➤ **lui**.

lupino (2) Campania term for ➤ **vongola**, common clam, Sicilian term for *vongola gialla*, golden carpet shell, or *vongola grigia*, gray clam, in Sicily.

lupo word used in Calabria for ➤ **mostella**, greater forkbeard.

lupo alla marinara fillets of greater forkbeard (➤ **mostella**) stewed in tomato, thickened with the flesh from the head, and minced flat-leaved parsley. The sauce is also used to dress pasta. Calabria.

luppolo hops (*Humulus lupulus*). A climbing perennial that grows among hedgerows and on uncultivated ground, known for its use in the brewing industry. The young lateral shoots, which resemble wild asparagus, are used in risottos, frittatas, soups and fillings. Hops are particularly popular in the north of Italy: in Piedmont (➤ **lavertin**, ➤ **vartis**), in Lombardy (➤ **loertis**), in Veneto (➤ **bruscandoli**), in Friuli (➤ **urtizzon**, ➤ **urticions**), in the province of Ferrara (➤ **bruscandoli**), in Lazio (➤ **lupari**). Popular recipes include: ➤ **frittata di germogli di luppolo**, ➤ **minestra di riso e bruscandoli**, ➤ **risoto coi bruscandoli**. Other common names: ➤ **ligaboschi**, ➤ **orticaccio**.

lupu de mari central-southern Italian word for ➤ **spigola**, sea bass.

luserna Veneto term for➤ **capone gallinella**, tub gurnard.

luserna in guazzetto tub gurnard cooked with garlic, skinned tomatoes and flat-leaved parsley. The sauce is used to dress pasta and the fish are served as a main course. Veneto.

luserna incovercià tub gurnard marinated for half an hour in oil, garlic salt and pepper, broiled for a quarter of an hour, transferred to a pan and cooked in more oil and half a glass of vinegar for a few more minutes, covered with a lid (*incovercià* means "covered"). Served with polenta. Veneto.

lusso (pl. **lussi**) or **lussotto** (pl. **lussotti**) local names for ➤ **cicciarello di Noli**, sand eel.

luvaro term used in southern Italy for ➤ **pagello**, seabream, newborn larval specimens of which are used make a fiery condiment (*nonnata*), now rare. Scientifically, the name refers to *pesce imperatore*, angelfish.

mM

macafame sweet modern version of an old peasant pie made with flour, potatoes or breadcrumbs, sausage, lardo and → **Vezzena** cheese, popular in the Veneto region and bordering areas of the Trentino until a few decades ago. There are two variations on the sweet version: in the province of Vicenza the ingredients are wheat flour and cornflour, breadcrumbs, eggs, milk boiled with sugar and cinnamon, (or star anise), slices of apple cooked in lard, dried fruit (figs, raisins, walnuts or almonds, pine kernels); in the province of Belluno they use day-old bread soaked in milk, flour, yeast, eggs, apple slices, butter, vanilla and refined sugar, and grated lemon zest. Both are baked in the oven. Veneto.

Macagn mountain cheese produced twice a year with whole raw cow's milk from a single milking and aged for 4-6 months. It takes its name from the Maccagno Alp on the border with the Val d'Aosta. Produced today in the mountains round Biella and in the Valsesia, in the province of Vercelli. It has a fragrant delicate aroma with floral, grassy notes, and is promoted by a Slow Food presidium. Piedmont.

macagnani slices of day-old bread soaked in milk, spread with blackcurrant jam, joined together in a sandwich, soaked in a sweet batter and fried in lard. Typical of the Valle di Fiemme. Trentino-Alto Adige.

macaron del fret small hollow maccheroni (macaroni) made by rolling rectangles of egg pasta dough round a darning needle. A northern equivalent of the many southern pastas made with needles of various shapes and sizes. In the Langhe hills, in the province of Cuneo, some restaurants serve it with sausage or seasonal sauces. Piedmont.

macaron e triforas literally "pasta and potatoes." Pasta cooked with chopped potatoes and served with local cheese and mushrooms sautéed in milk with onion and parsley. A typical dish of the Provencal valleys of the province of Cuneo. Piedmont.

maccaronara all'uso di Montemarano a type of → **maccheroni alla chitarra** made from a flour and water dough rolled out with a *maccaronara*, a special grooved rolling pin. Served with a sauce of beef, bacon, tomato, basil, red wine and grated cheese. Typical of Montemarano, in the province of Avellino. Campania.

maccarrones a ferritus another name for → **maccarrones de busa**, type of pasta.

maccarrones cravaos dialect name in the province of Nuoro and the Logudoro district for → **malloreddos**. Sardinia.

maccarrones de busa ancient artisan durum wheat pasta traditionally made for feast days and holidays using a special iron utensil (*ferritus*) or a darning needle. Served with ricotta or fresh Pecorino and tomato or meat sauce. Sardinia.

maccarrones de ponzu durum wheat pasta made from dough pressed through wicker baskets (or → **ciuliri**, rush sieves) to make it coarser and better suited to soaking up the sauce it is served with. Sardinia.

maccarrones furriaos another name for ➤ **maccarrones de busa**, type of pasta.

maccaruni 'i casa another name for ➤ **maccheroni al ferretto**, type of pasta.

maccaruni a cento aka **maccaruni a centinara** or **maccaruni a matassa** other names for ➤ **jaccoli**, type of pasta.

maccheroncini another name for ➤ **perciatelli**, type of pasta.

maccheroncini di Campofilone another name for ➤ **campofiloni**, type of pasta.

maccheroni a fezze another name for ➤ **jaccoli**, type of pasta.

maccheroni (sing. **maccherone**) standardized Italian of the word corrupted into English as macaroni. A general term for a vast range of dried durum wheat pasta shapes, cylindrical, sometimes twisted (especially in northern Italy) and usually short, though occasionally long, with a smooth or ridged surface: rigatoni, sedani, ziti, mezzani, mezze maniche are just some of the names attributed to "modern" maccheroni. In southern Italy, the word has a broader meaning, referring to some fresh pasta and all sorts of dried pastas, long or short, hollow or otherwise, from spaghetti to linguine, from bucatini to penne. This is a legacy of the times in which the word **maccherone** meant pasta in general. In the 17th century **maccheroni** began to be associated with Naples, but earlier it was the Sicilians who were nicknamed *mangiamaccheroni* (maccheroni-eaters) and, thanks to Arab influence, it was most likely they who were responsible for spreading pasta through the south of Italy. The traditional fresh pasta shapes still referred to as **maccheroni** can be classified into a number of groups. Some are hollow, made with special metal utensils or knitting or darning needles (➤ **maccheroni al ferretto**), others have a square or rectangular section and are cut with tools such as the ➤ **chitarra** or grooved rolling pins (➤ **maccheroni alla chitarra**, ➤ **maccheroni a lu rentròcele**, ➤ **troccoli**). Maccheroni may be stretched and "spun" into balls (➤ **maccaruni a cento**, ➤ **maccheroni alla mulenàre**), in other cases they are little more than very fine tagliolini (➤ **campofiloni**). Dried **maccheroni** (or *maccheroncelli* or *maccheroncini*) are the equivalent of: ➤ **bucatini**, ➤ **perciatelli**, ➤ **sedani**, ➤ **tubetti**.

maccheroni al (con il) ferretto fresh homemade hollow pasta made by wrapping a rectangular sheet of dough round a specially made iron needle—in the past round reeds, canes, umbrella spokes, darning needles and so on. This type of pasta is made all over Italy and has a variety of regional names: ➤ **busiate**, ➤ **ceppe**, ➤ **ferrazzuoli**, ➤ **ferricieddi**, ➤ **fricelli**, ➤ **fusidde**, ➤ **fileja**, ➤ **filateddhi**, ➤ **fischietti**, ➤ **maccarones a ferritus**, ➤ **maccarones de busa**, ➤ **maccaron del fret**, ➤ **maccheroni bobbiesi**), ➤ **minchiareddhi**, ➤ **subioti**. Certain types of ➤ **scialatielli** and ➤ **strangolapreti** might also fit into this category.

maccheroni a lu rentròcele type of long pasta with an oval section which, like ➤ **maccheroni alla chitarra**, takes its name from the utensil used to make it, a special toothed rolling pin, known as a ➤ **rentròcele** (aka *rintròcilo* aka *ritròcilo*). According to some scholars, the ➤ **chitarra** is a descendant of the latter. In Lanciano and the upper Sangro valley, in the province of Chieti, the dish itself, served with a sauce of lamb and pork, a generous amount of chili and grated Pecorino cheese, is known as *rintròcilo*. In Basilicata and Puglia, the same pasta is known as ➤ **troccoli**, also named after a rolling pin, a *torcolo* or *troccolo*. All the various versions are made with durum wheat flour, cake flour and, sometimes, egg whites, which give them a very pale color. Abruzzo.

maccheroni al gratté a version of ➤ **timballo di maccheroni**, made with large pasta (eg, ➤ **paccheri**) boiled, layered in a casserole dish with butter, Parmigiano, béchamel sauce and ➤ **fior di latte**, then baked in the oven. Campania.

maccheroni alla calabrese maccheroni, or ➤ **ziti**, served with lard and freshly ground black pepper, arranged in a baking dish in layers, each covered with a sauce of tomato, prosciutto, parsley and basil, and liberally sprinkled with grated Pecorino, then baked. Calabria.

maccheroni alla chitarra aka **caratelle alla chitarra** square spaghetti made from a dough of durum wheat flour and eggs, using a ➤ **chitarra**, guitar (*carrature* in dialect), consisting of steel or copper strings stretched over a beechwood box. A sheet of the pasta dough is rolled out over the "guitar" to create strands of about ten inches in length. Traditionally served with tomato sauce and tiny meatballs. Known in Lazio as ➤ **tonnarelli**. Abruzzo.

maccheroni alla mulenàre aka **maccheroni alla molinara** a pasta made in flour mills (*mulini* in Italian), though nowadays very few people continue the tradition. A ring of pasta dough is progressively stretched to the desired thickness and wound up into a ball. The tangle is then cut in two and unwound. The resulting long spaghetti are served with a rich sauce of mixed meats (lamb, beef, pork) and a generous amount of grated Pecorino. Typical of Abruzzo, this type of pasta is also made in Basilicata, where it is known as ➤ **manate**, and in Lazio (province of Rieti), where it is known as

➤ **jacculi**. Abruzzo, Basilicata, Lazio.

maccheroni alla toranese pasta served with onion and pancetta, lightly fried in olive oil, and a generous sprinkling of grated Pecorino and chili. A specialty of Torano Castello, in the province of Cosenza. Calabria.

maccheroni bobbiesi homemade egg, flour and water pasta. The dough is rolled into a sheet which is cut first into strips, then into squares. The latter are rolled round a sort of knitting needle (*agùgia* in dialect) to form hollow ➤ **maccheroni**. Traditionally served with the sauce from ➤ **stracotto alla piacentina**, beef stew, or with dried mushrooms. A specialty of Bobbio, in the province of Piacenza. Emilia-Romagna.

maccheroni cape e code literally "heads and tails." Pasta (usually ➤ **ziti** or ➤ **mezzani**) served with a sauce made with the heads and tails of the *pesce cuoccio* (➤ **capone**, gurnard) with garlic and tomato. Campania.

maccheroni con la ricotta pasta served with a mixture of ➤ **ricotta romana**, cinnamon, confectioner's sugar and a few drops of the pasta cooking water. Lazio.

maccheroni con le sarde maccheroni served with a sauce of sardines, garlic, raisins and breadcrumbs. Calabria.

maccheroni dalmati flour and egg pasta lozenges served with meat sauce or grated Pecorino. A recipe of Dalmatian origin, as the name implies. Friuli-Venezia Giulia.

maccheroni del pettine aka **maccheroni dal pettine** aka **maccheroni sul pettine** another word for ➤ **garganelli**, a type of pasta.

maccheroni di fuoco pasta, usually ➤ **bucatini**, with a fiery sauce of dried chili and garlic.

maccheroni di Natale Christmas dish in

which ➤ **natalini** (long smooth ➤ **penne**) are cooked in capon broth thickened with boiled cardoon, tripe and chopped sausage. A recipe typical of Genoa. Liguria.

maccheroni di san Giovanni short pasta served with anchovies in oil, skinned tomatoes, capers and black olives. Puglia.

maccheroni natalizi con le noci another name for ➤ **nociata (2)**.

maccheroni strascinati coarse textured maccheroni, or often fettuccine, mixed with beaten eggs, grated Parmigiano, and broiled pork sausage. Umbria.

macchettu Sicilian term for newborn picarel (➤ **novellame di pesce**, fry).

macco southern Italian term for puréed dried fava beans. In Sicily they flavor the purée with wild fennel, in Calabria they add onion and tomato and serve it with crushed spaghetti, extra virgin olive oil, grated Pecorino, black pepper or chili. In Puglia the purée is known as ➤ **'ncapriata** and is one of the most popular dishes in the region. The etymology of the word **macco** is uncertain but maybe related to the verb *ammaccare*, "to crush."

maccu di san Giuseppe dried legume soup (fava beans, chickpeas, beans, peas, lentils), flavored with borage, wild fennel, chopped tomato and onion. In Siracusa they add dried chestnuts, and in some places they finish the soup with ➤ **corallina** pasta or squares of fried bread. The soup was traditionally cooked in rural villages on March 18 for the feast of San Giuseppe. Sicily.

macedonia fruit salad.

macerare (1) (in winemaking) to leach a grape's phenolic materials from its skins, seeds and stems into the must.

macerare (2) to soften food by soaking in liquid.

macerare (3) to macerate. Sometimes used incorrectly as a synonym of ➤ **marinare**, to marinate.

mach aka **machet** aka **machtabe** thick soup of rice, milk, and chestnuts, typical of the Biella mountains. Piedmont.

machettera another name for ➤ **sardenaira**, Ligurian pizza.

machetto condiment made of sardines, macerated for 40 days and more in sea salt, preserved in extra virgin olive oil and crushed to a paste. Liguria.

machettusa another name for ➤ **sardenaira**, Ligurian pizza.

machitt boiled Savoy cabbage, turnips and beans flavored with onions fried in butter. Side dish typical of the Val Travaglia. Lombardy.

macinazione aka **macinatura** aka **molitura** the crushing or milling of grain into flour.

macis mace (*Myristica fragrans*). The aromatic dried and powdered outer covering of nutmeg (➤ **noce moscata**). Used mainly to flavor cured meats.

mafalda type of ➤ **scaletta**, "beer bread." Sicily.

mafalde long, curly-edged commercial durum wheat pasta. Other names: ➤ **frese**, ➤ **tagliatelle nervate**.

mafrone Tuscan term for ➤ **pagello**, sea bream.

magatello another word for ➤ **girello**, tenderloin.

maggengo, **maggiolino** regional terms for ➤ **prugnolo**, mousseron mushroom.

maggiolino bread roll, a variation on the ➤ **michetta** with pointed ends.

maggiorana marjoram (*Origanum majorana*). Typically Mediterranean herbaceous plant cultivated as an aromatic. Especially popular as an ingredient in Liguria (➤ **torta pasqualina**, ➤ **cima alla genovese**) and in central Italy (➤ **persata dell'isola**

d'Elba). Common and regional names: ➤ **persa**, ➤ **persia**, ➤ **persica**.

maghetti name for chicken giblets (➤ **rigaglie**), much used throughout the region to make rich sauces for homemade tagliatelle at Sunday lunch. Marche.

maglione castrated buffalo.

magnana aka **papalina** Marche term for ➤ **novellame di pesce**, fry, especially tiny anchovies and sardines. Marche.

Magnocca semi-fat, part-skimmed, raw cow's milk cheese produced in the Valchiavenna (province of Sondrio) with techniques similar to those used for ➤ **casolet**. May age for up to a year. Lombardy.

magnosa aka **cicala grande** Mediterranean slipper lobster (*Scyllarides latus*). An edible but rare crustacean, it is cooked in the same ways as lobster (➤ **aragosta**).

magnosella slipper lobster (*Scyllarides arctus*). Small relative of ➤ **magnosa**, used in fish soups.

magra a mano ridged bread roll made with the same dough as ➤ **biova**. Typical of Pinerolo, in the province of Turin. Piedmont.

magro di piatta skimmed cow's milk cheese, one of the lowest fat cheeses in Italy. Ready to eat 60 days after production, it may also be aged for up to a year. Produced in Bormio, in the province of Sondrio. Lombardy.

magroncello a pig weighing no more than 30 pounds.

magrone young pig, prior to fattening, weighing no more than 50 pounds.

magu Sardinian term for ➤ **rana pescatrice**, monkfish.

maia Ligurian term for ➤ **grancevola**, spider crab.

maiale pig (*Sus scrofa*). Domestic mammal similar in form to the wild boar (➤**cinghiale**) from which it descends and with which it shares the same scientific name. Its Italian name is also of Latin origin and is said to derive from the custom of sacrificing a "fattened pig" to the goddess Maia. In the Latin, Greek and Celtic traditions, the pig was appreciated for its meat, but in others (Brahmanic, Jewish, Muslim) it is banned as impure. In the Middle Ages, pork became a staple in the peasant diet, mainly because pigs could be raised very cheaply and the meat could be eaten fresh in the fall and cured for the rest of the year. Pig fat (➤ **lardo**, ➤ **strutto**) was the main condiment at the time and continued to remain so, even in olive oil producing countries, well into the 20th century. The Italian Ministry of Agriculture's database of native and/or traditional food products list the following varieties: *suino di razza mora romagnola* and *suino pesante* (Emilia-Romagna), *razza casertana* (Campania), *maiale nero* (Calabria).

maiale al latte pork in milk. A recipe common in various regional cuisines, made with boned loin of pork or, as in Tuscany, loin on the bone (➤ **arista**). The meat is browned, sometimes stuck with garlic and rosemary (Piedmont) or on a bed of minced aromatic vegetables (Tuscany), covered with milk and cooked. The milk is filtered and served as a sauce. In Veneto, *mascio al late*, typical of the province of Verona, is loin of pork salted and covered with milk, cooked until it evaporates and served with slices of toasted bread.

maiale 'briaco scamerita chunks of shoulder pork (➤ **capocollo**) browned in oil with lardo and finely minced aromatic herbs and vegetables, covered with semifermented Sangiovese must (which may be replaced by young red wine). Wild fennel may also be added. Tuscany.

maiale casertano aka **maiale pelatello** relatively unprolific pig suited to raising in the open air. Campania.

maiale con i crauti pork with sauerkraut. The pork is cooked in broth with paprika, cumin seeds and tomato sauce, and served with sauerkraut. Friuli-Venezia Giulia, Trentino-Alto Adige.

maiale 'ndocca 'ndocca pork snout, rind and ribs blanched in water and vinegar and cooked in water aromatized with chili. The meats are served piping hot with a few spoonfuls of their broth and farmhouse bread, or cold covered with the jelly that has formed in the meantime. The second preparation is reminiscent of the Sicilian and Calabrian ➤ **gelatina di maiale**. Abruzzo.

maialino suckling pig of four to eight weeks in age. Usually cooked whole (➤**porcheddu, porchetta**). The Italian Ministry of Agriculture's dabase of native or traditional food products lists the following varieties: *porchetta di Ariccia, porchetta di Viterbo, porchetta di di Poggio Bustone* (Lazio), *porchetta dell'Abruzzo* (Abruzzo), *porchetta delle Marche* (Marche) *porchetta dell'Umbria* (Umbria), *porchetta di Monte San Savino* (Tuscany), *purcheta* (Emilia-Romagna), *porchetta trevigiana* (Veneto) and *porcetto* aka *porcheddu* (Sardinia).

maiassa fruit loaf of cornflour, sugar, milk, butter, dried figs, sultanas and apples, similar to ➤ **polenta di Marengo** (Alessandria, Piedmont) and ➤ **smegiassa** (Veneto). A specialty of the province of Bergamo. Lombardy.

Maioc aka **Maiocca** alternative names for ➤ **Magnocca** cheese.

maionese mayonnaise. Cold sauce of egg yolks, salt, pepper, oil and vinegar or lemon juice, one of the most common and best known in international gastronomy.

maiorca wheat variety ground very finely to an almost powdery consistency, suitable for certain cakes, pastries and other sweet confections, such as ➤ **pasta reale (1)**, almond paste. Today it has virtually disappeared and is often replaced by cake flour. **Maiorchino** rare old raw ewe's and goat's milk cheese produced in the province of Messina from February to June using traditional techniques and utensils. Dry-salted for 20-30 days, and aged for up 24 months. Cheeses are large in size and may weigh up to ten pounds. Promoted by a Slow Food presidium. Sicily.

maiorchino di Ostra Vetere loaf-shaped cake made with a mixture of beaten eggs, sugar, almonds, flour and ammonia. Marche.

mais maize or corn (*Zea mays*). The term "maize" derives from *mahiz*, a word spoken in Haiti at the time of of Columbus's arrival. The cereal is native to Central and South America whence it was introduced to Europe, and was being cultivated in Veneto as early as the mid 15th century. At the time it was deceivingly known, and still is, as ➤ **grano turco**, literally "Turkish grain," but in those days the adjective *turco*, "Turkish," was applied to anything of exotic or colonial origin. In the centuries that followed, maize passed from being mere fodder for livestock to a staple in the diet of northern Italian peasants. Today maize is ground into flour to make ➤ **polenta**, bread and cakes (➤ **macafame**, ➤ **pinza**, ➤ **putana**, ➤ **xaeti**), or eaten on or off the cob, its kernels are boiled or roasted or used as an ingredient in salads. A typical Venezia Giulia recipe is ➤ **menestra de bobici**. In Italy, especially in the Po Valley, hybrids of American origin now prevail, but in certain areas some ancient ecotypes still survive. The Italian Ministry's database of native and/or traditional ecotypes lists the following varieties: *spogna bianca* (Campania); *blave di Mortean, mais da polenta* (Friuli-Venezia Giulia); *mais agostinella* (Lazio); *granturco dell'asciutto* (Liguria); *granturco bianco massese, granturco formenton ottofile della Garfagnana, granturco nano di Luco e di Grezzano, mais quarantino, mais rustico per polenta aretino* (Tuscany); *mais spin o nostrano della Valsugana, mais nostrano di Storo* (Trento); ➤ **marano** (Veneto).

mais biancoperla maize ecotype with tapered cobs and large pearl-white kernels, used to make a white polenta, once common in the plains and hills of the region as an accompaniment to river and lagoon fish. Its cultivation has declined since the 1950s due to competition from more productive hybrids. A Slow Food presidium is helping surviving growers to improve the quality of their flour and to spread knowledge of the variety. Veneto.

maizena trademark registered in 1877 for a corn starch used as a an alternative to potato flour (➤ **fecola**) as a thickener in sauces, stews, cake mixes, soups and porridges.

majatica Messina term for Sardine fry (➤ **avannotti di sarda**, newborn sardines).

majatiche egg and wheat flour pancakes spread with syrup of figs ➤ **cotto di fichi**) and rolled up. Calabria.

malfatti irregular shaped gnocchi made of spinach or other leaf greens, wheat flour, eggs, grated Parmigiano-Reggiano and ricotta (or mascarpone or even bread soaked in milk and squeezed dry), boiled and served with melted butter. Lombard in origin, they are now common throughout northern Italy.

malfattini aka **manfrigoli** tiny pasta balls made from a dough of flour, eggs and nutmeg coked in meat or bean broth. In Romagna they are also known as *manfrigne*, in Ferrara as ➤ **grattini**. In inland areas of the province of Ancona, they are made with grated day-old bread mixed with flour and eggs. Emilia-Romagna, Marche.

malga another name for ➤ **alpeggio**, piece of land in the mountains used for summer grazing, and usually including a dairy for cheesemaking. By extension, in the north of Italy the word is also used generically for a cow's milk cheese produced in the mountains.

Malga fane part-skimmed cow's milk cheese produced for centuries in the Val Pusteria, in the province of Bolzano at altitudes of 1,700 to 2,600 meters. Aged for six to 12 months. Trentino-Alto Adige.

Malga mountain cheese matured in a mixture of wine and pomace for two to three days and aged for eight months. Trentino-Alto Adige.

Malga Stelvio cheese made from part-skimmed cow's milk from two milkings in one of the oldest mountain dairies in the Alto Adige. Aged for four to 12 months. Trentino Alto-Adige.

mallegato blood sausage (➤ **sanguinaccio**) typical of the province of Pisa, in particular of the town of San Miniato. Pig's blood is mixed with lardons, salt, nutmeg, cinnamon, pine kernels and raisins, cased and boiled. In a variation made in Volterra, the mixture is thickened with *pappa*, day-old bread soaked in milk and squeezed between the hands. The sausage is aromatic on the nose thanks to the spices and sweet on the palate thanks to the blood. It is protected and promoted by a Slow Food presidium. Tuscany.

mallo husk or hull, the outer shell of nuts. Green in color, sometimes fleshy, as it ripens it goes dark in color, dries up and breaks, thus releasing the fruit. Astringent in flavor, it is not edible, though the husk of the walnut is used to make ➤ **nocino** liqueur.

malloreddos Sardinian gnocchi (the name is the diminutive of *malloru*, which means "calf" in the dialect of the Campidano area) made, using a sieve (➤ **ciuliri**) with durum wheat meal, soft wheat flour, salt and a pinch of saffron. Served with tomato sauce or lamb or sausage sauce (in some areas flavored with minced parsley) and grated Pecorino. Sardinia.

malloreddos cun ghisadu Sardinian gnocchi (➤ **malloreddos**) served with ➤ **ghisadu**, beef sauce, or a sauce of meat picked from the bones of lamb and sheep. Sardinia.

malmaritati bean soup common in the province of Bologna and, with minor variations, also in that of Modena. It consists of fresh ➤ **maltagliati** cooked in a broth of borlotti beans (in some cases, puréed) flavored with garlic, parsley and tomato and sometimes, lightly fried lardo and onion. The soup is sprinkled, finally, with grated Parmigiano. Emilia-Romagna.

maltagliati literally "badly cut." Unevenly shaped fresh egg or flour and water pasta: lozenges, rectangles, long strips, short strips, often made with leftover dough from pasta-making. Served in vegetable and legume soups (➤**maltaià**, ➤ **maltagliati coi fagioli**, ➤ **sguazzabarbuz**, ➤ **straciamuus**) or with sauces that vary from region to region, where names may also differ: ➤ **blecs** (Friuli-Venezia Giulia), ➤ **maltaià** (Piedmont, Lombardy), **mantajà**, **malintaià** (Emilia-Romagna), **sagnette**, **pizzelle** (southern Italy).

maltagliati coi fagioli typical pasta and bean soup (➤ **pasta e fagioli**) of the Monferrato and Langhe areas. Dried borlotti and scarlet runner beans soaked overnight and cooked with potatoes in beef broth flavored with lightly fried minced lardo, onion and rosemary. Some of the potatoes and a portion of the beans are puréed and returned to the pan to thicken the soup, to which separately boiled homemade ➤ **maltagliati** are added. The soup, finally, is sprinkled with freshly ground black pepper and drizzled with extra virgin olive oil. Piedmont.

maltaià thick soup of beans, potatoes, carrots and tomatoes flavored with finely minced lardo, garlic, parsley, basil, celery and onion, and served with ➤ **maltagliati**. Lombardy.

malva high mallow (*Malva sylvestris*). Spontaneous plant, typical of hedgerows and uncultivated land, whose edible shoots and leaves are popular in Piedmont (➤ **ris e riondele**) and some regions of central Italy. The shoots are eaten raw in salads or fried, the flowers in salads and as a garnish.

mamme ripiene stuffed globe artichokes. Side dish of globe artichokes (*mamma* in Tuscan dialect) are cleaned, flattened and stuffed with a mixture of beaten eggs, ground pork, finely minced flat-leaved Parsley, grated Pecorino, salt and pepper, cooked in a saucepan. A specialty of the areas of Empoli (province of Florence) and San Miniato (province of Pisa). Tuscany.

mammella cured meat made from a salted, pressed, boiled cow's udder, eaten sliced as an antipasto. In Val d'Aosta it is called ➤ **teteun** and is listed in the Italian Ministry of Agriculture's database of native and/or traditional food products, as is *busecchia* (Campania). Fresh boiled cow's udder is sold by Florentine tripe vendors (➤ **trippaio**), who also use it to make a sort of pâté for spreading on ➤ **crostini**.

mammola another name for ➤ **violetta**, violet, and for ➤ **carciofo romanesco**, globe artichoke

manai aka **menai** other names for ➤ **marafanti**, cabbage and corn soup.

manata slice of day-old black bread softened in a mixture of heated ricotta and whey. Typical of Latina. Lazio.

manate aka **manatelle** spaghetti-like pasta made with durum wheat meal, water and salt (today eggs and oil or lard are also added) worked by hand into a cluster (similar to ➤ **maccheroni alla mulenàre,** made in Abruzzo and Molise). Usually served with meat sauce (➤**intoppo**, ➤ **'ntruppc**). Basilicata

mandagadas another name for ➤ **acciuleddhi**, fried cookies.

mandarancio tangor. A type of ➤ **mandarino**, mandarin.

mandarino mandarin (*Citrus nobilis*). A native of China, the fruit has undergone numerous hybridizations to limit the number of its seeds and standardize its size for marketing abroad. Hence the birth of the clementine and the *mandarancio* (tangor), sometimes considered varieties or synonyms of mandarin but actually hybrids: the first between a mandarin and a tangor, the second between a mandarin and an orange. All these various fruits share the same sweet flavor and aromatic scent. They are harvested from November to January, but since they store well, may be bought from December to February (the clementine until March). The main producer regions are Sicily, Calabria (➤ **clementine di Calabria**), Puglia (➤ **clementine del golfo di Taranto**) and Sardinia. The Italian Ministry of Agriculture's database of native and/or traditional food products lists ➤ **mandarino tardivo di Ciaculli** (Sicily) and *manda-*

rini della Costa dei Trabocchi (Abruzzo). In the kitchen, the mandarin is used as an ingredient in cakes, tarts, mousses, ice creams, bavarois and liqueurs.

mandarino tardivo di Ciaculli late Ciaculli mandarin. The city of Palermo used to be famous for its splendid gardens and terraces, many of which have been lost on account of neglect and property speculation. Ciaculli and Croceverde Giardina, recently recognized as an agricultural park, are two green areas in the heart of the city in which this late mandarin, born in the 1940s from the spontaneous mutation of the *avana* variety, is still cultivated. The fruit, which matures from January to March, has a thin skin and very sweet flesh with few seeds. It is used to make granitas, ice creams, juices and liqueurs. Small producers have set up a consortium to promote the product, which is also protected by a Slow Food consortium. Sicily.

mandilli de saèa literally "silk handkerchiefs." Very fine quadrangular lasagne usually served with ➤ **pesto** or ➤ **tocco di carne**, meat sauce. Liguria.

mandorla almond (*Prunus amygdalis, P. dulcis*). Common all over Asia and the Mediterranean, cultivated in the central and southern regions of Italy. The fruit consists of an oval drupe with an outer hull or husk (➤**mallo**) wich encloses a woody shell with a seed or nut inside. Almonds have a high protein and oil content and can be sweet or bitter. The latter contain a substance known as amigdalin and are slightly smaller than the former. Since they are slightly toxic, their use in the kitchen is limited, but they do constitute an indispensable ingredient for ➤ **amaretti** cookies. Almonds mature in the summer and are eaten fresh or, more often, dried. The Italian Ministry of native and/or traditional food products lists the following varieties: *mandorle di Navelli* (Abruzzo); *mandorla piacentina* (Emilia-Romagna); → **mandorla di Toritto** (Puglia); *mandorle sarde* (Sardinia); *mandorla di Avola* and → **mandorle di Noto** (Sicily). Almonds are widely used in Italian confectionery (→ **confetto**, → **mandorle atterrate**, → **mandorle confettate**, →**torrone**, → **croccante**, → **torta di mandorle**) and also appear in savory recipes, such as → **pesto trapanese** and → **agnello abbottonato**.

mandorla di Toritto in the province of Bari, almond growing was a very common activity, and it has had a profound influence on the landscape and on popular culture. Today the small town of Toritto and environs still grow a number of ancient cultivars and continue to withstand the invasion of more productive Californian varieties. Toritto almonds are protected by a Slow Food presidium. Puglia.

mandorlaccio rustic cake of almond flour, eggs and honey, coated with chopped almonds, and baked in the oven. Puglia.

mandorlata di peperoni side dish of peppers, almonds, tomatoes, raisins, sugar, vinegar and oil, typically served with boiled or roast meats. Basilicata.

mandorlato a type of → **torrone**, nougat, made with minced almonds, beaten egg yolks, egg whites whisked to a peak, sugar and wheat flour. The mixture is baked in the oven, dusted with more sugar and cut into squares. Tuscany.

mandorlato di Cologna Veneta a sort of friable nougat made by cooking honey, sugar and almonds in copper cauldrons. A specialty of Verona, Veneto.

mandorle atterrate "buried almonds." In Foggia, toasted almonds are added to a blend of sugar and water syrup and melted chocolate. The mixture is transferred, a spoonful at a time, to a marble working surface and allowed to set. In Abruzzo, toasted almonds are coated with cocoa powder and sugar to look like little stones covered with soil (*atterrate*). Puglia, Abruzzo.

mandorle confettate almonds coated with a paste made of sugar and spices (usually cinnamon and cloves). A specialty of the city of Isernia. Molise.

mandorle di Noto three ancient almond varieties are cultivated in the groves of Noto and another three communes in the province of Siracusa: *romana, pizzuta d'Avola* and *fascionello*. All have thick, woody shells that retain fats and preserve the flavor and perfume of the fruit. Yields are very low, however, and the market sometimes fails to appreciate the not always regular shape of these varieties. A Slow Food presidium has thus been set up to protect the cultivars and their producers. Almonds reign supreme in Sicilian confectionery in recipes such as → **latte di mandorla**, → **pasta reale**, → **frutta martorana**, → **dolci di riposto** and many more besides. Sicily.

mandorlini del ponte baked cookies similar to →**brutti e buoni** made with almonds, flour, egg whites and sugar worked in a bain-marie. A specialty of Pontelagoscuro, in the province of Ferrara. Emilia-Romagna.

maneghi (1) sweet dumplings made of cornflour cooked in milk, molasses, raisins and candied fruit, and served with butter, cheese, sugar and cinnamon. Traditionally made in the Carnival period in the Polesine area. Veneto.

maneghi (2) spindle-shaped potato gnocchi traditionally served with smoked ricotta, sugar and cinnamon. Friuli-Venezia Giulia.

manego de cutelo Ligurian term for ➤ **cannolicchio**, razor clam.

manene small risen focaccias reinforced with boiled potatoes or polenta and fried in oil. Liguria.

manfricoli another name for ➤ **ciriole,** a type of pasta.

manfrigola buckwheat ➤ **crespella** filled with cheese and butter. Typical of the village of Grosio, in the upper Valtellina (province of Sondrio). Lombardy.

manfrigoli aka **manfrigne** another name for ➤ **malfattini**, a type of pasta.

mangia e bei literally "eat and drink." Characteristic pastries made by frying squares of flour, water and sugar dough and slashing the inflated side to create small "phials." These are set aside to cool on kitchen paper. Just before serving, the cavity is filled with rosolio or alkermes. Typical of the province of Florence, now common also in the province of Pistoia. Tuscany.

mangiare di strada another way of saying ➤ **cibo di strada**, street food.

maniata a sort of pizza pie filled with Provola and ricotta, salami or ➤ **soppressata di Calabria**, hard-boiled eggs and chili. Calabria.

maniche rigate another name for ➤ **rigatoni**, a type of pasta.

manico di coltello term used in the Lazio and Abruzzo regions for ➤ **cannolicchio**, razor clam.

manicotto another name del ➤ **cappello del prete**, a boiling sausage.

manna delle Madonie by making a cut in the bark of the manna ash (*Fraxinus ornus*) in Castelbuono and Pollina, villages in the Madonie area (Sicily), it is possible to obtain a resinous, sugary extract which sets into a natural sweetener (manna) with a very low glucose and fructose content. Not all the substance is of high quality: only that which runs down the trunk of the tree stalactite-like is 100% pure (*manna eletta*). The gathering technique is very ancient and survives only in this corner of the Mediterranean. The product and the technique are protected by a Slow Food presidium. Sicily.

manteca dairy product consisting of a central nucleus of fat extracted from ricotta cased by stretched curd, both residues from the production of ➤ **Caciocavallo Podolico**. Campania, Puglia, Basilicata.

mantecare (1) to cream. To stir a food preparation of buttery consistency until homogeneous and velvety. Term used chiefly in confectionery (eg, with regard to ice creams).

mantecare (2) to bind. To mix a pasta, for example, with its sauce, gradually adding grated cheese or, in the case of a risotto, knobs of butter.

mantovana (1) light sponge cake (eggs mixed with eggs, sugar, butter, flour and vanilla) coated with minced almonds and topped with pine kernels and confectioner's sugar. Despite its name ("Mantuan"), it is a specialty of Prato, where it is said to have been introduced by Isabella d'Este, who became marquise of Mantua when she married Francesco Gonzaga. Or maybe the recipe was simply filched by a Prato confectioner. Tuscany.

mantovana (2) bread loaf made with the same dough as ➤ **ciopa** in two different sizes: one fist-sized, the other weighing four ounces or so. Typical of the Lake Garda area in the province of Verona. Veneto.

manzo bullock. The exact meaning of the word, devoid of any legal significance, varies from region to region. It refers generically to a castrated male bovine of three to four years of age. In Milan, however, it mean's a fully grown ox, and in central Italy an almost fully grown ox.

manzo al latte topside of beef, stuck with lardo and rosemary coated in flour, browned in butter, bathed with vinegar and finished off with milk and broth. Trentino-Alto Adige.

manzo all'olio a piece of shoulder clod (➤ **cappello da prete**), preferably from the oxen of Rovato, in the province of Brescia, cooked in olive oil with capers and anchovies, diced vegetables and white wine. Cut into slices, it is served with the filtered sauce thickened with breadcrumbs and Grana Padano, and sprinkled with finely minced parsley. A specialty of the province of Brescia. Lombardy.

manzo alla California beef larded with pancetta, coated in flour and braised for a few hours with vinegar, broth and milk (or cream in modern recipes). A recipe typical of California, a large farm near the village of Montevecchia in the Brianza area (province of Lecco). Lombardy.

manzo alla friulana spicy roast beef. The meat is browned in lardo with onions and herbs, flavored with crushed cumin seeds (➤ **cumino**), cloves, and grated ➤ **cren**, horseradish, and finished in the oven with a little broth. Friuli-Venezia Giulia.

manzo in teglia minute steaks spread with finely chopped ham and dried mushrooms (revived in warm water), cooked in a skillet and sprinkled with minced flatleaved parsley and lemon juice. Umbria.

manzole Umbrian regional name for fried pastries equivalent to ➤ **cenci**. Umbria.

mappina curly white lettuce dressed with pieces of sweet red chili and garlic, extra virgin olive oil and salt, then refrigerated for a few days with a weight on top to allow the flavors to mingle. A traditional Christmas salad in the province of Cosenza. Calabria.

maracucciata buckwheat polenta traditionally mixed with *maracuoccio*, an irregularly shaped legume, only slighty larger than a pea, cultivated mainly in Lentiscosa, a village near Camerota, in the province of Salerno. Today, given the rarity of the legume, variable amounts of flava, chickpea flour and cornflour are added to the polenta. Campania.

marafanti aka **menafanti** aka **menai** soup of finely ground cornflour, Savoy cabbage and, often, beans, cooked in a broth made with pig's bones. A recipe typical of the Polesine area, in the province of Rovigo, and the province of Padua, which takes a long time to make. In the broth are cooked first the beans (if used), then the cabbage. After removing the bones, the broth is passed through a sieve and deglazed. It is then returned to the heat and brought to the boil. At this point the flour is poured in, stirring all the time to prevent lumps from forming. In the version without beans, the Savoy cabbage is cooked separately with celery stalks, carrots, onions and potatoes. The dish is sometimes enriched with sausage or fresh pork browned in butter. The soup, which should have a soft, almost creamy consistency, is served with grated or flaked Pecorino and a twist of the peppermill. Its names are many and some of them mysterious: ➤ **marafanti**, ➤ **malafanti**, ➤ **menafanti**, ➤ **manai**, ➤ **menai**. Inhabitants of the Polesine area jokingly call it "smaltamuri," wall enamel, because the bones make a broth that resembles glue. Veneto.

maranin polenta made with ➤ **marano** corn, a variety grown in Veneto.

marano aka **maranelo** corn variety, the best for making polenta, selected in around

1890 by a farmer in Marano Vicentino (province of Vicenza) by crossing a local variety with the *pignoletto d'oro* cultivated in Caldogno, also in the province of Vicenza. The variety enjoyed great success, especially in the Veneto and the province of Bergamo, but its use declined in the post World War II years with the introduction of hybrids from America, mainly as livestock feed. Today its cultivation, concentrated Val Leogra, near Schio, in the province of Vicenza, is enjoying a revival. Veneto.

marasca sour cherry (→ **ciliegia**).

maraschino transparent liqueur with straw-yellow highlights made by infusing sour cherries, preferably those cultivated in the Euganean Hills, in the province of Padua (→ **marasca**, → **ciliegia**) in alcohol, aging in oak barrels, and distilling with sugar and water syrup. The liqueur, which originated in Dalmatia, is now used mostly in confectionery or to "lace" fruit salads.

marasciuoli wall rocket (*Diplotaxis erucoides*). Wild herb used to make sauces to spread on toasted bread, boiled and served as a side dish or mixed with garlic, oil and chili to dress pasta. Puglia.

Marcetto very strong ewe's milk cheese produced to salvage "bad" cheese that has gone off. It is characterized by the presence of the maggots of the cheese fly, *Piophila casei*, which grow inside the cheese itself. Abruzzo.

Marchigiana, razza medium-large cow breed with a grayish-white coat, the product of the crossing of animals of the → **Podolica** and → **Chianina** breeds in the middle of the 19th century and of a subsequent crossing, at the start of the 20th century, with the → **Romagnola**. It was once used for work in the fields, but is now bred mostly for its beef. Typical of the hills and mountains of the Marche region, but also reared in the rest of central Italy, Campania, Sicily, Latin America and the United States. Marche.

marcundela boiling sausage made by grinding together a pig's liver, spleen, kidneys, lungs, belly fat and bloodier meat and curing the mixture with salt, pepper and, sometimes, garlic and wine. The mixture is then shaped into balls, which are cased either in a small intestine or in an omentum (in which case they are sprinkled with cornflour and left to rest). Traditionally they were aged covered in lard, but today they are eaten within eight days of production, boiled in red wine or fried in a skillet. The specialty, of peasant origin, is popular all over the region. Friuli-Venezia Giulia.

Maremmana, razza a cow breed with a white coat and huge lyre-shaped horns, a descendant of animals that arrived in Italy from Asia via Hungary. Raised in the wild in the Tuscan and Lazio Maremma and in some areas of the Marche. Once used as a draught animal, it is now bred chiefly for its meat. Protected by a Slow Food presidium.

maren dialect word used in some areas of Piedmont for dried chestnuts boiled with their skins on.

marenda sinoira a late afternoon snack of cured meats, anchovies, frittatas, hard-boiled eggs and so on (*marenda* is the dialect word for the Italian *merenda*, snack; *sin-à* means *cena*, dinner). A traditional Piedmontese custom still carried on in a few old osterias in the Langhe and Monferrato hills. Piedmont.

maresina Veneto term for → **partenio**, feverfew.

margherita Tuscan term for → **grancevola**, spider crab.

margheritina dei prati English daisy (*Bellis perennis*). Very common spontaneous plant to be found in meadows and fields from the sea to the mountains. The leaves are eaten raw in salads such as ➤ **misticanza** or cooked in soups, while the pink-white petals are used to garnish salads. The plant was also certainly used in the old days in cooked mushes such as ➤ **minestrella**. Common and regional names: ➤ **bellide**, ➤ **fior gentile**, ➤ **pratolina**.

margheritine di Stresa buttery, crumbly cookies made from a paste of flour, potato flour, hard-boiled egg yolks, butter, sugar, vanilla and lemon zest shaped into small balls stamped with a flower petal pattern and liberally dusted with confectioner's sugar. Like many other gastronomic specialties, dedicated to the former Queen of Italy, Regina Margherita, daughter of the duke and duchess of Genoa, who owned a villa near Stresa on the eastern shore of Lake Maggiore. Created by a confectioner called Pietro Antonio Bolongaro. Piedmont.

margottini molds made by filling two layers of semolina polenta with slices of ➤ **Formai de mut**, Grana Padana or Stracchino, egg yolks and, in season, slices of truffle, baked in the oven and served hot. A specialty of the province of Bergamo. Lombardy.

mariconde small dumplings made of day-old bread, Parmigiano-Reggiano, eggs, milk, salt, pepper, nutmeg and, sometimes, meat (in the Cremona they used to be made when there were good broth and leftover meat in the house) and vegetables, in general served in meat broth. Chicken livers, cooked separately in butter or directly in the broth, may also be added. In the Mantua area, the same dish is known as ➤ **mericonda**, which is also a sort of cornflour soup thickened with stewed sausage and beans. In the up-

per Val Sabbia, in the province of Brescia, they make ➤ **mereconde** with breadcrumbs, grated ➤ **Bagòss**, eggs, parsley and broth. Lombardy

mariettina cold milk sweetened with sugar and diluted with a little red wine, into which bread is dunked. A traditional summer snack in the countryside round Milan. Lombardy.

marinà a sweet soup made by boiling pitted cherries with white wine, sugar and cinnamon and served poured over farmhouse bred. A specialty of the province of Piacenza. Emilia-Romagna.

marinara, alla term to describe a generic condiment for pasta, pizza and fish (usually salt cod), normally involving tomato and aromatic Mediterranean herbs, such as basil, garlic and oregano. In some versions, capers, olives and salted anchovies are added; this is the case of certain variations on pizza alla marinara (➤ **pizza napoletana marinara**).

marinare to marinade. To steep in a marinade in order to tenderize meat, game or fish.

marinata blend of oil wine or vinegar, herbs and spices used to tenderize meat, game or fish.

mariola broth (traditionally of castrated lamb) into which small lozenges of frittata (beaten eggs, grated Pecorino), parsley, basil and dried breadcrumbs or wheat flour) are plunged. Calabria.

mariola cotta large spherical or cylindrical cured meat made with cheap cuts of pork, plus tongue, cheek and rind, finely ground and cured with salt, pepper and wine aromatized with numerous spices. The mixture is then cased in the pig's caecum intestine. Cremonese in origin, the meat is now mostly produced in the southern part of the province of Parma. Emilia-Romagna.

mariola cruda cylindrical or spherical cured meat typical of the province of Piacenza. Ground pork from the back, shoulder and cheek of the pig is ground and cured with ground pepper and peppercorns, saltpeter, dry white wine and, sometimes, the juice from a crushed garlic clove. The mixture is cased in a pig's caecum intestine, which, thick and fat as it is, keeps the meat soft throughout a long period of aging. Protected and promoted by a Slow Food presidium. Emilia-Romagna.

maritozzo (pl. **maritozzi**) sweet oval bun typical of central Italy, in especial of Lazio. Made from a dough of flour, brewer's yeast, water, eggs, sugar and raisins (sometimes pine kernels and cubed candied citron). Today often filled with whipped cream. In Cerveteri and Capena (province of Rome), on the occasion of the feast of San Luca, a variation is made with wine must and grapes. In the Marche they make a naturally leavened, bobbin-shaped **maritozzo** dotted with anise seeds. Simple buns, ideal for snacks or breakfast, **maritazzi** have been viritually supplanted by the now seemingly universal ➤ **cornetto**.

mariur a version for ➤ **batiur**, a cured meat, once served by families to a future son-in-law on his first visit to the household.

markandela aka **markundela** alternative names for ➤ **marcundela**, a boiling sausage.

marmellata marmalade. According to European legislation, the term indicates the product of the blending of a sugary substance (refined sugar, brown sugar, honey, fructose etc) with a citrus fruit. The citrus fruits used to make marmalade are: sweet orange, bitter orange, lemon, mandarin, clementine, yellow grapefruit, pink grapefuit, citron, bergamot and chinotto. In idiomatic Italian, the word refers to a jam of any fruit.

marmotta Sardinian word for ➤ **grancevola**, spider crab.

marmotte Carnival fritters made of eggs, milk, sugar, apples and raisins. A specialty of Urbania, in the province of Pesaro e Urbino, Marche.

marò sauce made by pounding in a mortar fresh new fava beans, garlic and mint and binding with a little vinegar and olive oil. A specialty of the western Riviera. Liguria.

marocca di Casola ancient bread now made in only one bakery in Casola, a village in the Lunigiana area in the province of Massa-Carrara. The dough is made with chestnut flour and cornflour, mashed potatoes, extra virgin olive oil, yeast dissolved in milk, sourdough and very hot water. Dusted with cornflour, loaves are baked in the oven. The resulting crust is dark brown, the crumb spongy in texture. The bread is protected by a Slow Food presidium. Tuscany.

maroglia regional term for ➤ **radicchiella**, beaked hawksbeard.

marretto another word for ➤ **cazzmar**, offal bundle.

marro in Puglia and Calabria, lamb's offal wrapped in the animal's intestines with matchsticks of Pecorino (sometimes also mortadella), barbecued or baked in the oven. In Abruzzo lamb's innards are made into bundles with pancetta, garlic, salt and pepper, wrapped in the intestines, secured with a cocktail stick and barbecued. Abruzzo, Puglia, Calabria.

marrone a type of chestnut (➤ **castagna**).

marron glacé French term, now commonly used, for candied chestnuts, dried and coated with a sugary icing. The delicacy seems to have been created in the 16th century and its paternity is disputed between France and Piedmont.

marrone del Mugello medium-large chestnut with a reddish-brown skin. The fruit is smooth, sweet and delicate. It is derived from the Florentine chestnut variety and its cultivation in nine communes of the Florentine Apennines has received PGI revognition. In the village of Marradi it is used to make ➤ **torta di marroni**. Tuscany.

marrone di Castel del Rio a large PGI chestnut with a brown skin and an intensely flavored sweet fruit. Locally, it is roasted (*brusè*) or used to make soup. Cultivated in the Valle del Santerno, in the province of Bologna. Emilia-Romagna.

marrone di Roccadaspide medium-sized PGI chestnut with a brown skin and smooth, crisp fruit. Eaten roasted or used to make ➤ **marron glacé**, preserves and purées. Cultivated in the province of Salerno. Campania.

marrone di San Zeno PDO chestnut cultivated and harvested at an altitude of 750 to 3,000 in the area of Monte Baldo (province of Verona), between Lake Garda and the River Adige. Sold only fresh, it has a thin, glossy pale brown skin and sweet fruit. Veneto.

marrozza Calabrian term for ➤ **lumaca di terra**, earth snail.

Marsala fortified wine that takes its name from the town in the province of Trapani around which it is produced. For the production of Marsala, it is possible to add to the base wine (made mainly from *catarratto* and *grillo* grapes) alchol and must brandy, to Marsala Vergine concentrated must or *mistella* (must rendered unfermentable by the addition of alcohol). Golden yellow in color with orange highlights, the wine is classified according to typology and aging. Fine, Superiore and Superiore Riserva refer to Marsalas aged from four months to four years; Vergine and Vergine to Marsalas aged from five to ten years. Speciale refers to Marsalas obtained with the addition of other ingredients such as eggs (eg, Marsala all'uovo traditionally produced in Emilia-Romagna), cream and spices. The wine's gastronomic importance can be appreciated from the number of recipes in which it appears: from cakes and custards (eg, ➤ **buccellato**, ➤ **zabaglione**) to game and meat dishes (eg, ➤ **beccacce alla lucana**, ➤ **faraona ripiena**, ➤ **finanziera**, (➤ **piccata**). Sicily.

martin sec small pear variety with a rusty-colored skin and firm, grainy flesh. Probably introduced to Italy from France via the mountains of the valleys of the province of Cuneo, it is eaten stewed, on its own or as an ingredient in cakes and pastries (eg, ➤ **timballo di martin sec**). It is named for the period in which it is harvested, in the days leading up to the feast of San Martino. Piedmont.

martorana abbreviated term for ➤ **frutta martorana**, marzipan fruit.

martundela another name for ➤ **marcundela**, a boiling sausage.

marturiate another name for ➤ **ciambelle scottolate**, sweet ring cookies.

marubèn dolci sweet fried pastries traditional in the province of Piacenza, especially in areas on the border with the Oltrepò area of the province of Pavia. The dough is similar to that of ➤ **bignè (1)**, beignet, rich in eggs and lard. Emilia-Romagna

marubini ravioli with a stuffing of mixed meats (braised or roast beef and local sausage), eggs, breadcrumbs, Grana Padano and nutmeg and cooked in a broth of mixed meats (beef, chicken and boiling sausage). Depending on area, they may be square, round or half moon-shaped. Typical of the province of Cremona. Lombardy.

maruzela Veneto term for ➤ **lumaca di mare**, sea snail.

maruzze e maruzzelle Campania terms for sea (➤ **lumaca di mare**) and earth snails (*Helix aspersa*).

marzaiola gargany (*Anas querquedula*).Wild duck slightly larger than a teal (➤ **alzavola**). Nests in central and eastern Europe, and winters in Africa, stopping in Italian swamps and estuaries during its migration.

marzapane (1) marzipan. Paste of almond flour worked with sugar (or, in some cases, honey). The origin of the technique is certainly Arab, whether it arrived in Italy via Sicily or Venice (through its trade with the Hanseatic League) is unsure. A large part of Sicilian confectionery is based on ➤ **pasta reale**, almond paste, a marzipan in which almond flour is blended with vanilla and sugar dissolved in water.

marzapane (2) a blood sausage typical of the southern part of the province of Novara. A mixture of fresh blood, milk, minced lardo, spices, garlic, red wine and breadcrumbs is cased in a calf's or pig's colon. The sausage is eaten after two days, boiled, roasted or, more traditionally, sliced, breaded and fried. Piedmont.

marzapani crunchy lozenge-shaped cookies typical of the village of Minervino Murge (province of Bari) made from a paste of almonds, sugar, eggs and lemon zest, and decorated with sugar chips. Puglia.

marzapani quaresimali (aka **quaresimali**) ring-shaped almond cookies flavored with orange blossom water and fennel seeds. A specialty of Genoa. Liguria.

Marzolina a small cylindrical cheese made with goat's milk from two milkings on the Lazio side of the Abruzzo national park, in the province of Frosinone. It is eaten fresh or aged in glass jars, on its own (in which case it is tangier), or preserved in olive oil (in which case it is softer). A Slow Food presidium protects and promotes the production of the cheese that once looked as if it was about to disappear. Lazio.

Marzolino del Chianti cheese made between Florence and Siena with raw ewe's milk from two milkings, inoculated with a wild artichoke flower rennet. It matures in cellars for seven days and ages for no more than six months. Tuscany.

masaneta aka **mazaneta** aka **maseneta** Veneto names for the female crab (➤ **granchio**) in its fertile period, which lasts from the late summer until early December, when its ovaries, the most prized part, are mature and swollen. Listed, like ➤ **moeca** aka **moleca**, in the Italian Ministry of Agriculture's database of native and/or traditional food products. Veneto.

masanete alla barcarola the crab (➤ **masaneta**) is poached in water with lemon juice, allowed to cool and dressed with salt, pepper, garlic and parsley. The best time to eat it is from mid October to early November. Veneto.

masarà aka **meserà** a stew of ➤ **salam d'la doja**, onions, potatoes and zucchini, cooked with tomato sauce or conserve. Typical of the province of Novara. Piedmont.

masaro aka **masuro** aka **mazorin** Veneto and Friuli terms for ➤ **germano reale**, mallard.

mascarpone cheese produced all over the region from cream obtained by centrifuging or allowed to rise spontaneously and coagulated with organic acids. Thought to have come originally from the areas around Lodi and Abbiategrasso, in the province of Milan, and used in the preparation of custards and desserts. Lombardy.

Mascherpa word used in the Lombard Alps for ➤ **ricotta**, obtained by working the whey left over from cheesemaking. In the Valgerola (in the province of Sondrio), **Mascherpa** is a characteristic dairy product, strengthened with fresh goat's milk and smoked, used in the making of ➤ **Bitto**. All types of **Mascherpa** can be eaten fresh or, if dry-salted, aged for a year, in which case they can be grated. Lombardy.

masculina da magghia a type of anchovy. In the marine nature reserve of the Ciclopi islands, the stretch of sea between Capo Mulini and Capo Santa Croce in the gulf of Catania, small boats still fish for anchovies (*masculina*) with traditional *menaidi* (aka *tratte*), drift nets 900 feet long with a half-inch mesh (in Italian *maglia*, in dialect *magghia*). Only a few families still practice the technique, which is protected by a Slow Food presidium and is also to be found in limited areas in the Cilento district (Campania) and Liguria. The fish is particularly tasty and is sold fresh or salted. Locally a paste is made with the heads and discarded parts. Sicily.

masigott oval fruit loaf made from a blend of flours (wheat, buckwheat and corn), yeast, eggs, butter, confectioner's sugar, walnuts, sultanas, pine kernels and candied orange zest. The dialect name means a "clumsy" person and the albeit delicious loaf has a somewhat unappetizing appearance. A specialty of Erba, in the province of Como. Lombardy.

masìn Veneto dialect term for ➤ **prugnolo**, mousseron mushroom.

mastrici regional term for ➤ **lattugaccio**, rush skeletonweed.

masuro in tecia pieces of mallard sautéed in oil with onion, rosemary and cinnamon, or with garlic and desalted anchovies, and finished off with white wine and broth. Friuli-Venezia Giulia.

matafam apple fritters. Apples coated in a batter of flour, yeast, milk, sugar and eggs, fried in oil and dusted with sugar. Typical of the Val Soana in the Canavese district, northwest of Turin. Piedmont.

matafama literally "hunger killer." A soft polenta of cornflour and wheat flour into which fried onions are mixed. An ancient specialty of Portovenere, in the province of La Spezia. Liguria.

matalocch an ancestor of ➤ **resca**. A round sweet bun made with flour, butter, eggs, sugar, honey, raisins, candied fruit and anise. A specialty of the Lake Como area. Lombardy.

matalotta, alla term used to describe a Sicilian technique for cooking slightly fatty fish. The term derives from the French *matelote* (fish stew with wine), but the technique is very different. Cut into slices without removing the head, the fish is put in a pot with tomato paste dissolved in warm water (or tomato passata), garlic, basil flat-leaved parsley, pitted green olives and capers, covered with water and cooked, lid on, for half an hour. The sauce from the fish is used to dress pasta. Sicily.

matàn aka **aquila di mare** eagle ray (*Myliobatis aquila*). The Italian Ministry of Agriculture's database of native and/or traditional food products lists the fish under Friuli-Venezia Giulia, where it is also known as ➤ **pesce colombo**.

mataroccu Sicilian dialect term for ➤ **pesto trapanese**, a pasta sauce.

matassa, a term used to describe the presentation of various types of commercial dried egg pasta ribbons in tangled clusters.

mato savory pie filled with potatoes, pumpkin, leeks, costmary, rice, grated mountain cheese, cream, butter and nutmeg. Typical of the mountain valleys of the province of Cuneo, especially the Valle Maira. Piedmont.

matricale aka **matricaria** common names for ➤ **partenio**, feverfew.

matrice Tuscan term for a cow's uterus, boiled and sold at stalls by tripe vendors in Florence (➤ **trippaio**).

matriciana abbreviated slang name for ➤ **amatriciana** sauce.

matsafam aka **matzafam** cake made with slices of day-old bread soaked in sugared milk alternated with peaches or pears fried in butter. The dialect name, *ammazzafame* in Italia, means "hunger killer." A specialty of the Biella area. Piedmont.

matterello aka **mattarello** rolling pin. Regional names: ➤ **canello**, ➤ **cannella**, ➤ **laganaturo**, ➤ **rasagnolo**, ➤ **spianatoio**, ➤ **stenderello**. A special toothed rolling pin, *lu rentròcele*, is used in some parts of the Abruzzo region to make a traditional pasta, ➤ *maccheroni a lu rentròcele*. A similar pin, *troccolo*, is used to make a pasta of the same name, ➤ **troccoli**, in Puglia.

Mattone Italian name for the Alto Adige cheese ➤ **Ziegel**.

matuffi tablespoons of soft polenta layered with a sauce of ground beef cooked with aromatic vegetables and herbs, dried mushrooms, tomatoes, red wine and meat broth, and sprinkled with grated Parmigiano. A common dish in the north of Tuscany (especially in the Garfagnana and Versilia areas). In other parts of the region, a similar dish is ➤ **gnocchi di polenta**, in which the sauce, however, is made with chunks of lamb or pork. Another comparable recipe, in the province of Pisa, is ➤ **pallette**, balls of polenta served with mushrooms, rabbit, pork or duck sauce, or salt cod. In Friuli-Venezia Giulia instead the term **matuffi** refers to baked polenta layered with sausage, sage and ➤ **Montasio** cheese.

Maultaschen large ravioli with various stuffings, traditionally served with chives or poppy seeds. A specialty of the Dolomites, but Swabian in origin. Trentino-Alto Adige.

mauru sargasso (*Sargassum hornschhuchii*). Brown alga to be found at the same stalls that, in season, sell sea urchins in the province of Catania and elsewhere in eastern Sicily. Usually eaten raw drizzled with lemon juice. Sicily.

maüsc side dish made by lightly frying potatoes, onions and, according to availability, runner beans or mange-touts or borlotti beans in butter. Typical of the area round the village of Teglio, in the Valtellina, in the province of Sondrio. Round the city of Sondrio itself they make the dish, which the call ➤ **tarozz**, only with potatoes, runner beans and lightly fried onions, flavoring it with semi-fat cheese. Lombardy.

mazaresi al pistacchio oval cookies made from a paste of minced pistachio nuts, sugar, eggs, flour, potato flour and orange zest. A specialty of Mazara del Vallo, in the province of Trapani. Sicily.

mazza di tamburo parasol mushroom (*Macrolepiota procera*). Mushroom with a tall, rigid stipe and, when young, an egg-shaped cap, which makes it resemble a drum stick (hence its Italian name). The mature cap opens out like a parasol, hence the English name. Its white, tasty flesh is greatly prized and is best enjoyed in frittatas or stewed with tomato. Common and dialect names: ➤ **bubbola maggiore**, ➤ **ombrella**, ➤ **ombrellone**, ➤ **parasole**, ➤ **cucamela**.

mazzafegato pork sausage, of which two versions exist, made from meat scraps and 25% liver. The first version is sweet and is cured with salt, pepper, sugar, pine kernels, raisins and orange zest; the second is savory and is cured with salt, pepper and pine kernels. Cased in a natural intestine and separated with string, the sausages are dried for a few days in warm, ventilated environments. Eaten fresh or aged for two to seven months. Umbria.

mazzafrissa cream heated in a pan and thickened with plain flour. Used to dress pasta, to flavor boiled fresh fava beans, to accompany lettuce and as a dessert, smothered in honey. A specialty of the north of the island. Sardinia.

mazzamurru "soup" of slices of day-old bread dipped in salted boiling water and layered in a bowl with fresh tomato sauce and grated Pecorino cheese. When the bread has absorbed the condiment, the dish is ready. Typical of the south of the island. Sardinia.

mazzancolla common alternative name for ➤ **gamberone mediterraneo**, triple-grooved shrimp.

mazzareddi (aka **mazzareddri**) tops of wild greens mainly of the Brassicaceae family (*Brassica napus*, B. *nigra*, B. *fruticulosa*), generally referred to as wild mustards (➤ **senape selvatica**) or wild cabbages (➤ **cavolo rapiciolla**). Slightly bitter in flavor, they are eaten sautéed in the frying pan and in frittatas. Sicily.

mazzarelle lamb's innards cut into strips, gathered into bundles with herbs, wrapped in endive and browned in the frying pan. Abruzzo.

mazzetto odoroso aka **mazzetto aromatico** bouquet garni. Bunch of herbs (in Italy usually rosemary, bay leaf, flat-leaf parsley, thyme and basil) used to flavor soups, sauces and stews.

mazzi cured meat made by washing pig's intestines, whole and turned inside out, curing them with salt, finely ground black pepper, chopped chili, crushed garlic, wild fennel and white wine and immersing them in water and vinegar for 2-3 hours. The intestines are then covered with the herbs for another two or three hours, cut into 20-30 inch portions and laid out to dry or smoked. Eaten within a week. Recipe typical of Marino (province of Rome). Lazio.

mazzi ripieni traditional variation on ➤ **mazzi**. The intestines are filled with pieces of lean pork, secured with string and hung to dry for 20-25 days. Lazio.

mazzi sfumati name for smoked ➤ **mazzi**, Lazio.

mazzola another name for ➤ **capone gallinella**, gray gurnard.

mazzolina name for ➤ **capone lira**, piper, in the Marche and Abruzzo regions where it used in ➤ **brodetti del medio Adriatico**, fish soups, and baked in the oven with black olives. **mazzulara** Messina term for ➤ **novellame di pesce**, fry.

'mbuttunatu southern Italian dialect term for "filled" or "larded." **meascia** cake made from a mixture of day-old bread soaked in milk, corn and plain flour, eggs, pears, apples, grapes, raisins, pine kernels and grated lemon zest, topped with minced rosemary and sugar and baked in the oven. Lombardy.

mecoulen aka **mécoulin** leavened fruit loaf with raisins, rum, cream, butter, eggs and grated lemon zest. Similar to ➤ **panettone**, it used to be baked at Christmas, but is now available all year round. A specialty of Cogne. Val d'Aosta.

medaglione medallion. A term used in international cuisine for a round or oval slice obtained from a prime cut of meat (veal, beef, pork, lamb, chicken, turkey), from fish, a crustacean, ham, tongue or foie gras (➤ **bellavista, in**).

meddha Puglia dialect term for ➤ **nespola**, medlar.

meini Lombard dialect word for ➤ **pan de mei**, a type of cake.

mela apple (*Malus communis*). Apples are probably the most common fruit in Europe, where over 250 varieties exist. Fresh consumption is facilitated by the fact that they store well and are available all year round. The finest Italian varieties are those of the Trentino-Alto Adige (➤ **mela Alto Adige**, ➤ **mela Val di Non**) and Campania (➤ **mela annurca**), The Italian Ministry of Agriculture's database of native and/or traditional food products lists the following varieties: *mela della Valle del Giovengo* (Abruzzo); *mele di montagna* (Calabria); *capodiciuccio, chianella, chichedda, limoncella, limoncellona, sangiovanni, sergente, tubbiona, zitella* (Campania); *antiche varietà di mele piacentine, campanina* (Emilia- Romagna); *mela zeuka* (Friuli-Venezia Giulia); *belfiore, beverina, bianchetta, carla, musona, pipin, rugginin, stolla* (Liguria); *mele di Valtellina* (Lombardy); *mela rosa* (➤ **mele rosa dei Monti Sibillini**), *mela rozza* (Marche); *limoncella, zitella* (Molise); *carla della Val Borbera, renetta grigia di Torriana* (➤ **mele antiche piemontesi**), *golden di Cuneo, mele del Monferrato, mele della Val Curone, mele della Val Sangone, mele della Valle Bronda, mele della Valsusa, mele della Valle Grana, mele della Valsesia, mele della Valsessera, mele delle Valli di Lanzo, mele di Cavour, mele di San Marzano Oliveto, mele rosse delle valli cuneesi, mele autoctone del Biellese* (Piedmont); *limoncella dei Monti Dauni meridionali* (Puglia); *appicadorza, melappia, noi unci, miali, trempa orrubia* (Sardinia); *mele cola, mele gelate cola* (Sicily); *binotto,*

carla aretina, casciana, casolana, francesca aretina, muso di bue, nesta, panaia, roggiola, rosa del Casentino, rotella della Lunigiana, rugginosa della Valdichiana, stayman aretina (Tuscany); *mela renetta della Valle d'Aosta*; *mele del medio Adige, mela di Monfumo, mela di Verona, pom prussian* (Veneto). The apple is widely used in baking and confectionery (➤ **torta di mele**, ➤ **strudel**), but also in savory dishes such as ➤ **fritto misto all'italiana** or other northeast Italian recipes of central European origin. It is also used to produce spirits and liqueurs. Quince (➤ **mela cotogna**) contains pectins necessary for the production of jams, chutney and relishes (➤ **mostarda**, ➤ **cognà**, ➤ **cotognata**, ➤ **persegada**).

mela Alto Adige numerous apple varieties (*elstar, fuji, gala, golden delicious, granny smith, idared, jonagold, morgenduft, red delicious* and *stayman winesap*), are cultivated in the 72 communes of the autonomous province of Bolzano, all protected by the PGI seal and all with different scents, flavors and colors. Common qualities are glossy skins, compact, crisp sweet flesh and good storability.

mela annurca campana PGI apple with red-streaked yellow green peel and crisp, white, slightly sour flesh, produced in two varieties: *annurca* and *annurca rossa del Sud*. Grown in the provinces of Avellino, Benevento, Caserta, Naples and Salerno. Campania.

mela Val di Non three apple varieties of the Val di Non, in the province of Trento, are PGI-protected: *golden delicious, red delicious* and *renetta del Canada*. Trentino-Alto Adige.

melagrana aka **granata** pomegranate (*Punica granatum*). Round fruit with a thin leathery yellow to pink skin. The opened fruit is subdivided into segments of seeds covered with bright red sweetly astringent-flavored seeds. The pomegranate, much used in the kitchen in the Middle Ages, still figures in specific recipes. Albeit not intensively cultivated, it is found all over Italy. *Melagrana di Firenze* (Tuscany) is listed in the Italian Ministry of Agriculture's database of native and/or traditional food products. In confectionery, the fruit is used to flavor ice creams and decorate fruit cakes and tarts (➤ **gelatina di melagrana**). Fresh pomegranate seeds also appear in recipes such as ➤ **grano dolce** and ➤ **paeta rosta al malgaragno.**

melangolo aka **arancia amara** bitter orange. Citrus tree often used in gardens for ornamental purposes. Its fruit is a small orange which is inedible fresh, but which is used in confectionery for candying, for marmalades and for the preparation of essential oils. It is rarely used in the kitchen (its relative unavailability means that it is often replaced by oranges), but its juice was traditionally used in ➤ **anatra all'arancia** and for the old Umbrian specialty ➤ **labritti co' li facioli.**

melanzana eggplant or aubergine (*Solanum melogena*). Vegetable introduced to Europe by the Arabs, it was originally popular only in the south of Italy but is now common on tables all over the country. A member of the Solanaceae family, it originated in China or India. It is round or oval in shape and the color of its skin may vary from white to violet to dark purple to almost black. The flesh is tangy and bitterish in flavor and is often salted before cooking. Eggplants are harvested from June through to the winter. The Italian Ministry of Agriculture's database of native and/or traditional food products lists the following varieties: *melanzana cima di viola* (Campania); *melanzana*

tonda genovese (Liguria); *violetta casalese* (Piedmont); *violetta fiorentina* (Tuscany). A Slow Food presidium protects the ➤ **melanzana rossa di Rotonda** (Basilicata). The eggplant is one of the most used vegetables in southern Italian cuisine and is the principal ingredient in classics such as ➤ **parmigiana** and ➤ **caponata di melanzane.** Other eggplant-based recipes are: ➤ **melanzane a fungitielli,** ➤ **melanzane ammuttunate,** ➤ **melanzane a schibbeci,** ➤ **melanzana a mannella,** ➤ **melanzane Capodimonte,** ➤ **melanzane chine,** ➤ **quaglie.**

melanzana rossa di Rotonda eggplant brought to the village of Rotonda, in the Valle Mercure, in the province of Potenza, at the end of the 19th century by soldiers returning from Africa. Bright orange in color with green and reddish streaks, it is small and round like an apple. The pulp is fleshy and retains its creamy color even hours after being cut open. The aroma is intense and fruity and the flavor is slightly spicy with a pleasantly butter aftertaste. It is best enjoyed preserved in oil or pickled in vinegar, or stewed and even the leaves are good to eat. Basilicata.

melanzanata di sant'Oronzo slices of eggplant coated in flour, dipped in beaten egg, fried, layered in a baking tin with tomato, onion, basil and Pecorino. Served as a side dish in Lecce on its patron saint's day. Puglia.

melanzane a fungitielli chunks of eggplant cooked in a skillet with oil, garlic and flat-leaved parsley, to which capers and tomato sauce are sometimes added. The dish is served cold as an antipasto, but may also be preserved in oil. Campania.

melanzane a mannella eggplants cut into strips and fried, then layered in a tin with garlic and oregano, splashed with vinegar and baked in the oven. May be served hot or cold as an antipasto or side dish. A specialty of Naples. Campania.

melanzane a quaglia another name for ➙ **quaglie**, deep-fried eggplants.

melanzane a schibbeci slices of eggplant first fried, then cooked in vinegar and tomato sauce with mint leaves and cubes of Caciocavallo. Sicily.

melanzane al forno thick eggplant slices covered with a mixture of anchovies, olives, capers, parsley, garlic, oregano, day-old bread and tomato slices, and baked in the oven. Basilicata.

melanzane alla finitese "sandwiches" of eggplant slices filled with Caciocavallo cheese and basil, coated in flour, dipped in beaten egg and breadcrumbs and fried. A specialty of the village of of San Martino di Finita, in the province of Cosenza. Calabria.

melanzane alla parmigiana alternative name for ➙ **parmigiana di melanzane**, eggplant casserole.

melanzane alla siciliana slices of eggplant coated in flour, dipped in beaten egg and fried, then baked in the over layered with slices of mozzarella. A summer fish typically served with tomato sauce. Sicily.

melanzane ammuttunate eggplants slashed lengthwise and stuck with slices of garlic and mint leaves, cooked on a low heat for 20 minutes, then covered with tomato sauce aromatized with basil and parsley. In the Palermo area, the eggplants may be stuffed with garlic, basil leaves and small pieces of Caciocavallo, and baked in the oven. Sicily.

melanzane Capodimonte aka **melanzane alla partenopea** "sandwiches" of fried eggplant slices filled with Caciocavallo, covered with tomato sauce and grated Parmigiano and grated in the oven. Campania.

melanzane chine stuffed eggplants. Long small eggplants cut in half, flesh removed, fried, boiled or baked and filled with a variety of stuffings all involving ground meat of some sort. Other ingredients may include capers and black olives, anchovies and fresh breadcrumbs, grated Pecorino or pieces of Caciocavallo, eggs and aromatic herbs. The stuffed eggplants are usually baked in the oven with tomato sauce or dipped in egg and flour and fried. Calabria, Puglia, Sicily.

melanzane dorate in the Milan area they salt, wash and dry raw sliced eggplants, coat them with flour, dip them in beaten eggs and dried breadcrumbs, then fry them until golden. In other areas of the region they blanche and dry the slices, put them to macerate in milk for a couple of hours, dip them in beaten eggs and a mixture of breadcrumbs and grated Parmigiano, and then fry them. Lombardy.

melanzane fritte in umido fried eggplants with eggs. Pieces of eggplant are fried and mixed with chopped tomatoes fried in olive oil. The mixture is covered with eggs beaten with grated Pecorino and stirred until the eggs scramble. Calabria

melanzane in saor slices of eggplant browned in the oven with a little oil, allowed to cool and layered with ➙ **saor** with raisins and pine kernel. Veneto.

melanzane sott'olio eggplants preserved in oil. In Calabria they cut eggplants into strips or thin slices and put them in brine for a day with a weight on top. After drying them well, they transfer them to glass jars, covering each layer with extra virgin olive oil, minced chili, oregano and a little vinegar, and top up the finished jars with more oil. In Puglia, they sun-dry the eggplants, dip them in vinegar and cover them with oil. Calabria, Lazio, Puglia, Sicily.

melanzane sotto sale salted eggplants. Eggplants blanched in boiling water, drained, left for a day under a weight, layered in an earthenware pot with slices of garlic, pieces of pepper, salt, fennel seeds and covered with a lid (→ **timpagnu**). Served as an antipasto or as a side dish with meat dishes. Calabria.

melassa molasses, treacle. By-product of the processing of cane or beet sugar, used as a sweetener in confectionery.

melata honeydew (→ **miele di melata**).

mele antiche piemontesi heritage Piedmontese apples. At the start of the last century, thousands of apple varieties were still being cultivated in Piedmont. Since then the development of industrial agriculture has led to a cruel and drastic selection, with the market preferring foreign apple varieties, often larger, prettier and more suited to modern cultivation techniques. A Slow Food presidium is working to save varieties such as *grigia di Torriana*, *buras*, *runsè*, *gamba fin-a*, *magnana*, *dominici*, *carla*, *calvilla*, cultivated round Pinerolo, in the province of Turin, and Saluzzo, in the province of Cuneo. Piedmont.

mele ripiene svuotate stuffed apples. Apples stuffed with a mixture of ricotta, chopped walnuts, raisins and sugar, sprinkled with sugar and powdered cinnamon and baked in the oven. Piedmont.

mele rosa dei Monti Sibillini "pink" apples have always been grown in the Monti Sibllini, usually at altitudes of 1,500 to 3,000 feet. A Slow Food presidium promotes different typologies (eight ecotypes in particular), all with the same sweet, slightly acidic taste and intense aromatic scent. The apples are very small, irregularly shaped and rather flat with a short stem.

melia aka **melica** aka **meliga** northern dialect terms for → **mais**, corn or maize.

melichini cookies made with variable proportions of cornflour and wheat flour, egg yolks, sugar, butter, milk and grated lemon zest. Usually round in shape, they are filled with apricot jam and sprinkled with confectioner's sugar. A specialty of Piacenza. Emilia-Romagna.

melicotti cookies made with cornflour and wheat flour, sugar, butter, egg yolks and orange zest. Piedmont.

meligheddas cake composed of small balls of wheat flour, eggs and sugar, baked in the oven, soaked in alkermes, stuck together two at a time with jam, covered with refined sugar and decorated with cloves. Sardinia.

melina Lombard regional name for → **gelone**, oyster mushroom.

melissa lemon balm (*Melissa officinalis*). Wild herb which grows in cool, shaded places all over Italy from the Mediterranean to the mountains. Today it is cultivated as an aromatic on account of the intense lemony scent of its leaves. It is added fresh to salads, fruit salads and to stewed or baked fruit. It is also used to flavor stuffings for white meats. Common and regional names: **cedronella**, → **erba cedrina**, → **erba limonina**.

mellone Sicilian name for water melon (→ **anguria**), used to make → **gelo**, a dessert.

meloncello common name for → **salvastrella**, small burnet.

melone aka **popone** melon (*Cucumis melo*). Large fruit of Asian and African origin. Two main categories exist: winter melons, with a thin, smooth skin and whitish flesh, which can be kept throughout the season, and summer melons, which are divided into musk or netted varieties, sometimes with a grooved surface, and cantaloupe varieties, with a smooth, streaked skin and orange flesh. The producer regions are Sicily, Campania, Puglia, Lazio and Emilia-Romagna, and thanks, to the differences in climate from north to south, the fruits are available from July to October. The Italian Ministry of Agriculture's database of native and/or traditional food products list the following varieties: *melone di Altavilla, melone del Napoletano* (Campania); *melone tipico di San Matteo Decima* (Emilia-Romagna); *melone di Casteldidone, melone di Viadana* (Lombardy); *melone di Isola Sant'Antonio* (Piedmont); *melone della Val di Cornia* (Tuscany); *melone in asciutto* (aka *melone de jerru*) (Sardinia); *melone giallo* (aka *melone d'inverno di Paceco*), *melone invernale giallo cartucciaru, verde purceddu* (➤ **melone purceddu d'Alcamo**) (Sicily); *melone del Delta polesano, melone precoce veronese* (Veneto). Melon is mostly eaten fresh, as as an antipasto or main course with prosciutto, in fruit salads and in cakes and tarts. Candied melon is used to make ➤ **panforte** and its preserved sprouts (➤ **vettaioli**) are a specialty in Tuscany.

melone immaturo literally "unripe melon." The term refers to varieties of *Cucumis melo*, such as *carosello* and *barattiere*, cultivated and consumed in Puglia as an alternative to cucumber. They are eaten raw, as they are or seasoned with salt, in salads with tomato and oregano or with fresh onion, or as an accompaniment to fava bean purée and pasta with fresh tomato sauce and Cacioricotta. The fruit is listed in the Italian Ministry of Agriculture's database of native and/or traditional food products.

melone purceddu d'Alcamo winter melons (➤ **melone**) risk disappearing. This variety, typical of Alcamo, in the province of Trapani, is sowed in May and harvested in June and maintains its flavor and aroma until Christmas. The wrinkly green skin preserves white juicy flesh, which, thanks to its concentrated sugar content, increases in sweetness all the time. A Slow Food presidium has been set up to encourage and assist the few surviving growers. The melons are stored hung in nets in cool, dry environments. Sicily.

melù blue whiting (*Micromesistius poutassou*). Marine fish of the cod family (➤ **merluzzo**). It is fished mostly in the spring and summer and has delicate, albeit slightly insipid flesh. Not to be confused with the higher prized whiting (➤ **merlano**) and the hake (➤ **nasello**). Small specimens are fried, larger ones boiled. In Tuscany, the fillets are salted and sun-dried directly on fishing boats in the summer to make *fiche maschie a stocchetto*, a ➤ **mosciame** listed in the Italian Ministry of Agriculture's database of native and/or traditional food products. Common and regional names: ➤ **pesce morgano**, ➤ **potassolo**.

menacc puréed beans cooked with carrots, onion, celery and bay leaf, finished with butter, Grana Padano and garlic, and served with polenta. The name derives from the dialect verb *menare* to stir continuously. Typical of the area round the town of Crema, in the province of Cremona. Lombardy.

mendula Sardinian dialect term for ➤ **zerro**, picarel.

menestella a lighter version of ➤ **minestra maritata**. A meat broth with assorted vegetables served in Naples for Christmas lunch. In the province of Caserta the same name refers to a soup of beans and chickpeas cooked in an earthenware pot. Campania.

menestra de bisi spacai soup of dried peas (*bisi spacai* aka *spessati*) cooked in broth with garlic and aromatic herbs until they disintegrate. The resulting thick soup is served with croutons. Veneto, Venezia-Giulia.

menestra de bobici soup of corn kernels, beans and potatoes flavored with lardo, typical of the Carso area in the province of Trieste. Fresh corn cobs are boiled for about 45 minutes, after which the kernels are removed and put in a pot with the beans, a sausage and finely minced lardo, garlic and onion. The ingredients are covered with water and simmered. Diced potatoes, salt and pepper are added halfway through the cooking process. The soup is left to stand covered with a lid for half an hour before serving. Friuli-Venezia-Giulia.

menestra de brovade e fasui soup of puréed beans cooked with fermented turnips (➤ **broàde**) and lardo. Friuli-Venezia Giulia.

menestra de fregoloti pasta lumps made with flour, salted cold water (or water and milk) and, sometimes, eggs gradually poured into boiling broth (or water and milk), cooked and flavored at the end with butter and a pinch of salt. Trentino-Alto Adige.

menestra de grani soup of boiled corn kernels, diced potatoes sautéed in lard with onion and sage, covered with water and simmered in the pan. Trentino-Alto Adige.

menestra de piron Trieste and Gorizia dialect expression for a side dish of stewed vegetables. The expression means, in Italian *minestra da forchetta*, a soup fit for a fork, and refers to the thickness of the dish. Friuli-Venezia Giulia.

menietti small flakes of pasta, obtained by rubbing the dough between the hands (a variation on ➤ **fregamài**), cooked in a broth of diced vegetables (pumpkin, potato, leek, onion). Typical of the western Riviera. Liguria.

menni sweet fritters made of chestnut flour amalgamated with salted water, bicarbonate and raisins, served dusted with sugar. Tuscany.

menola blotched picarel (*Maena maena*), a close relative of the picarel (➤ **zerro**). Its flesh is tasty but full of bone. Much used in soups and mixed fries.

menta mint. The members of the Mentha genus (species, hybrids, varieties) are many and various. The most commonly used in the kitchen are *Mentha pulegium*, pennyroyal; *Mentha spicata*, spearmint; *Mentha piperita*, peppermint; *Mentha suaveolens*, applemint; *Mentha requienii*, Corsican mint. All these intensely scented varieties are used to make liqueurs, as an ingredient in frittatas, in marinades (➤ **scapece**), with some vegetables and meats (duck, lamb), in cold soups, in sorbets, in desserts and in some sauces, not always traditionally Italian.

menta strisciante a common name for ➤ **pulegio,** pennyroyal.

mentastro common name for ➤ **nepetella**, lesser calamint, but also for ➤ **pulegio**, pennyroyal.

mentuccia word used for ➤ **nepetella**, lesser calamint, in Tuscany, for ➤ **pulegio**, pennyroyal, in Lazio.

Meraner hauswurst sausage traditionally produced round Merano, in the province of Bolzano, but common throughout the Alto Adige. The mixture is made of lean cuts of beef and pork cured with salt, pepper, garlic, nutmeg, pimento, lardo, cheek bacon and ice. It is cased in a sheep's intestine, boiled and smoked. After being steeped in cold water, it is ready for the table, but it may also be kept for five days. Trentino-Alto Adige.

merca saturated preserving brine whose saltiness depends on the the time a food has to be preserved for. In Cabras (province of Oristano), it is called ➤ **mre-ca** and is used for boiled gray mullet (➤ **muggine**), which is then preserved wrapped in samphire, locally known as ➤ **zibba** (➤ **salicornia**, samphire). In the province of Nuoro, it is used to preserve sheep's or goat's curd, which subsequently becomes hard enough to grate. It is also used to add flavor to soups, as an ingredient in the filling of ➤ **culurjones**, and to dress tomatoes and boiled potatoes. Sardinia.

merdas de chan patties made with boiled or roast beef, wild spinach, eggs and cream, boiled in water, drained and served with melted butter and grated cheese. The name is unappetizing but the patties are delicious. Typical of the Valle Gesso, in the province of Cuneo. Piedmont.

mereconde aka **mericonda** dialect terms for ➤ **mariconde**, small dumplings.

mericanill Basilicata dialect term for ➤ **peperoncino**, chili.

meringa meringue. Whisked egg whites blended with refined or confectioner's sugar, sometimes with the addition of a drop or two of lemon juice, spooned or piped onto of sweet pies or tarts and baked crips at a low temperature. In Italian regional cooking, it appears under different guises: ➤ **bianchittos**, ➤ **poppe di monaca**, ➤ **schiumini**, ➤ **spumiglie**, ➤ **spumini**, ➤ **spumette**. Meringue is especially popular in Piedmont, where it is formed into round shapes which are used to make "sandwiches" filled with whipped or chantilly cream, sometimes mixed with chopped hazelnuts or almonds, candied fruits, pieces of marron glace and flakes of dark chocolate.

merlano aka **molo** whiting or English whiting (*Merlangius merlangus*). Common in the Atlantic but rare round Italy (at Italian fish markets it is easier to find blue whiting, ➤ **melù**). Its flesh is delicate, soft and flaky, and is often used in fish soups to to thicken the sauce.

merluzzo cod (*Gadus morhua callarias* or *G. morhua morhua*). Atlantic and Baltic fish much loved in its preserved states: ➤ **baccalà** (salt cod) and ➤ **stoccafisso** (stockfish). Confusingly, in many parts of Italy, the name **merluzzo** also means hake (➤ **nasello**).

merluzzo a la fior soaked salt cod (➤ **baccalà**), cut into pieces, coated with flour, fried then finished off in a pot with flat-leaved parsley, garlic and cream. A recipe typical of the mountain valleys of the province of Cuneo. Piedmont.

merluzzo al verde squares of soaked salt cod (➤ **baccalà**) coated in flour, fried and flavored with a sauce of finely minced garlic, sage, abundant flat-leaved parsley and (in the Langa hills) spinach or (in the Monferrato hills) chard. Traditionally served with polenta. Piedmont.

merluzzo alla palermitana cod Palermo-style. Two versions of the recipe exist. In the first, the fish is dressed with a sauce made by dissolving anchovies in oil, sprinkled with breadcrumbs and herbs and baked in the oven. In the second, the same sauce is used to dress cod coated in flour, beaten egg and breadcrumbs and fried in boiling oil. Sicily.

merluzzo argentato a common name for ➤ **nasello**, hake.

merluzzo comodà Piedmontese dialect name for ➤ **merluzzo in umido**, stewed cod.

merluzzo con le cipolle pieces of soaked salt cod (➤ **baccalà**) coated in flour and fried with abundant sliced onions. Piedmont.

merluzzo in umido stewed cod. Salted cod (➤ **baccalà**) or stockfish (➤ **stoccafisso**) stewed with or without tomato sauce, generally as an accompaniment to polenta or potatoes. In Piedmont, especially in the Monferrato hills, where it is known as ➤ **merluzzo comodà**, soaked salt cod is cooked with mixed minced herbs and vegetables (flat-leaved parsley, chard and spinach, spring onion, garlic), desalted anchovies and a little tomato sauce. In the province of Piacenza (Emilia), they also make the dish with tomato sauce and flat-leaved parsley, but they add a few potatoes too. In the Polesine area (Veneto), they sauté pieces of stockfish with onion, garlic and desalted sardines, cover them with white wine and milk (and maybe a little tomato sauce) and garnish them with finely minced flat-leaved parsley. In Friuli-Venezia Giulia, they bake stockfish in the oven, layered with potatoes sprinkled with finely minced garlic and parsley and flavored with desalted anchovies.

mes mànag da frà soup of ➤ **mezze maniche** stuffed with ground braised beef (➤ **stracotto alla piacentina**) amalgamated with its juices, breadcrumbs, grated Parmigiano and egg cooked in meat broth. A specialty of Piacenza. Emilia-Romagna.

mes-ciùa soup of cannellini beans (➤ **cannellino**), chickpeas , wheatberries (or emmer) boiled separately and mixed together. A dish typical of the region in general and La Spezia in particular. The name means "mixture" and may allude to the mixed grains women used to gather at the port of La Spezia after ships had landed their cargoes or at home after emptying their pantries. Liguria.

mesoro dialect term for ➤ **pesce lucerna**, stargazer.

messicani slices of veal or pork loin covered with sausage, eggs, grated Parmigiano-Reggiano, and herbs, secured with cocktail sticks and cooked in butter with sage and Marsala or tomato sauce. Specialty of Milan. Lombardy.

mesta aka **meste** polenta similar to ➤ **zuf**, but thicker, often served with boiled beans. Friuli-Venezia Giulia.

meuza 'mbuttunata cold dish of slices of calf's spleen stuffed with a mixture of minced garlic, flat-leaved parsley, chili and mint, browned in a skillet and covered with their own juices. Campania.

mezzanelli aka **mezzani** another name for ➤ **perciatelli**, a type of pasta.

mezzanielli al pesto cilentano short durum wheat pasta served with a sauce of cherry tomatoes, chili, oregano, garlic, basil and dry ricotta, all well minced and amalgamated with extra virgin olive oil and fresh ricotta. Campania.

Mezzapasta aka **Spress** cheese typical of the northern part of the province of Novara, especially of the Val Formazza and Valle Antigorio, similar to ➤ **Grasso d'Alpe** but more suitable for aging. Produced with part-skimmed cow's milk, it is pressed for a few hours and aged for three to 14 months. Typical of the province of Verbano-Cusio-Ossola. Piedmont.

mezze maniche commercial dried durum wheat pasta, slightly curved in shape and either smooth or ridged. Popular mostly in Campania, where smaller versions are served in broth, larger with slightly liquid sauces. Other names: ➤ **mezzi rigatoni**, ➤ **noccioloni**.

mezze penne short tubular commercial dried durum wheat pasta, either smoothed or ridged. Served with fresh vegetable or rich, spicy sauces. **mezze zite** another name for ➤ **perciatelli**, a type of pasta.

mezzena each of the two parts into which the carcass of slaughtered cow, pig, or sheep is divided.

mezzi gomiti another name for ➤ **chifferi**, a type of pasta.

mezzi rigatoni another name for ➤ **mezze maniche**, a type of pasta.

mezzi vermicelli another name for ➤ **spaghettini**, a type of pasta.

mezzina term used in the Versilia area of Tuscany for pork belly.

miaccia a round waffle cum pancake made from a batter of flour, milk, cream and egg whites cooked in a special hinged iron. Crisp, it is served as an accompaniment to savory dishes; soft, it is filled with sweet or savory ingredients. Typical of the Valsesia, in the province of Novara. Piedmont.

miaccitto a Marche variation on ➤ **migliaccio**, sweet blood sausage.

miascia aka **miassa** square or round sheet of puff pastry, very similar to the French *millas*. The classic dough consists of cornflour (plus, in some cases, a little wheat flour) and water; a richer version also includes eggs, milk, butter and salt. The mixture is cooked in a *millasseur,* a special hinged iron. Val d'Aosta, Piedmont.

miassa another name for ➤ **smegiassa**, a rustic fruit loaf.

mica aka **micca** aka **miccone** bread made with the same dough as ➤ **biova**, but oval in shape and larger. Piedmont.

miccone pavese large bread loaf at its best after a couple of days and fragrant for a week. Lombardy.

micete scientific term for ➤ **fungo**, mushroom.

michetta a small round bread loaf made with cake flour. A specialty of Milan. Lombardy.

michette oval, twice-leavened bun made from a dough similar to that used for ➤ **brioche**. Typical of Dolceacqua, in the province of Imperia. Liguria.

michittos nieddos broad durum wheat and bran fettuccine. Sardinia.

micischia another name for ➤ **muscisca**, preserved lamb's of goat's meat.

micotti savory buns made of mashed potatoes, cornflour, lardo, butter and onions, traditionally cooked in a wrought iron griddle pan. Typical of inland eastern Liguria.

micoula twice-leavened, home-baked sweet bun made with a dough of equal amounts of rye and soft wheat flour, eggs, butter, sugar and raisins (in the old days also dried chestnuts). Val d'Aosta.

midollo osseo bone marrow. In the kitchen only bovine marrow is used these days. It has a very delicate aroma and is an indispensable ingredient in many dishes: eg, ➤ **risotto alla milanese**, ➤ **ossobuco**.

miele honey. A liquid or thick mixture of fruit sugars produced as a result of the transformation of nectar from flowers by bees. Honeys vary according to the flowers they come from. Production is divided into monoflora honeys, made from the nectar of a single or predominant plant variety and millefiori honeys, made from nectars of diverse botanic provenance. Certain millefiori have exclusive and constant characteristics; this is the case of ➤ **mieli di alta montagna**, promoted by a Slow Food presidium and the acacia and chestnut PDO ➤ **mieli della Lunigiana**. Acacia and chestnut are the most common floral essences in Italy, though each region has its own specific varieties. In the Alps, rhododendron is common, in northeast Italy lime, dandelion and cherry prevail. In the south of Italy, eucalyptus, thyme, rosemary and citrus blossom honeys are widespread, while in Sicily and Sardinia flavors include asphodel, cardoon, carob, arbutus and French honeysuckle. Honey was more widely used in antiquity than today, but the product does appear a lot in traditional baking and confectionery. Many cakes in Sicily and Sardinia are coated with honey, the result of historical links with the Middle East, and honey is also an indispensable ingredient in many central Italian spiced cakes and in nougats.

miele di fichi another name for ➤ **cotto di fichi**, fig syrup.

miele di melata honeydew. Honeydew (*melata*) is a sugar-rich sticky substance secreted onto the bark of usually coniferous trees by aphids and ladybirds which live on the sap. Bees also use honeydew to make honey. The most prized variety is fir, which stands out for its dark amber color with petrol green nuances and a strong aroma of pine. Honeydew is normally darker and sweeter than nectar honey. It is produced in particular in Calabria and in Tuscany (fir) and Friuli-Venezia Giulia (*bosco del Carso*) and used in the same ways as nectar honeys (➤ **miele**).

mieli della Lunigiana two PDO honeys, acacia and chestnut. The first is liquid and pale in color with a delicate aroma with notes of vanilla. The second is dark amber in color and has a strong, pungent aroma. The Lunigiana area is traditionally a prolific producer of honey. Tuscany.

mieli di alta montagna high mountain honeys. Three honeys are made in the Alps at an altitude of more than 3,500 feet: fir honeydew, rhododendron and millefiori. The first is dark and very aromatic, the other two are pale in color with a fresh, delicate flavor. All three are promoted by a Slow Food presidium.

mietti thick cream of milk and chestnut flour typical of the peasant tradition of the western Riviera. Liguria.

migliaccetto fried small version of ➤ **migliaccio campano**, cornflour polenta. A specialty of Pozzuoli, in the province of Naples. Campania.

migliacci aka **migliecci** thin pancake-like fritters made with a simple batter of water, flour and salt and fried in oil or lard. Sometimes other ingredients such as eggs, sugar, anise seeds and liqueur and orange juice or zest are added to the mixture. In Volterra, in the province of Pisa, pork jelly is traditionally added to the mixture. Tuscany.

migliaccini another name for ➤ **frittelle di castagne**, chestnut fritters.

migliaccio (1) term used for various sweet and savory dishes whose original recipes envisaged the use of millet flour (➤ **miglio**), today replaced by wheat flour or, more often, cornflour (eg, ➤ **migliaccio giallo** in Tuscany or ➤ **migliaccio campano** in Campania).

migliaccio (2) in some central Italian regions the term refers to a sort of sweet ➤ **sanguinaccio**, or blood sausage. In Emilia-Romagna, for example, it consists of a baked shortcrust pastry tart filled with a mixture of pig's blood, milk, flour, chocolate, pine kernels, almonds, candied citron, nutmeg and orange and lemon zest. In the Marche too the term refers to a small oven-baked tart. In Fermignano (in the province of Pesaro e Urbino), the filling is a mixture of pig's blood, milk, sugar, bitter cocoa, grated orange zest, powdered vanilla, eggs and cinnamon. In the upper Valle dell'Esino, ➤ **miaccitto** is a baked mixture of lard, pig's blood, cornflour, cooked wine must (➤ **saba**), honey and breadcrumbs.

migliaccio (3) name in some areas of Tuscany for ➤ **castagnaccio**, chestnut cake or flatbread.

migliaccio campano cornflour polenta cooked with ➤ **ciccioli**, pork scratchings, and sausage and finished off in the oven with cheese (Parmigiano and Pecorino Romano) and flat-leaved parsley. A sweet version also exists consisting of durum wheat polenta mixed with eggs, butter, candied fruit, nutmeg and raisins and finished off in the oven. At Carnival time, in the hills between Praiano and Agerola (in the province of Salerno), they prepare *migliaccio salato*, a sort of rustic baked timbale (➤ **timballo**) of pasta, durum wheat meal, mozzarella and sausage. Campania. **migliaccio giallo** a dough of coarsely ground cornflour kneaded with water and raisins baked in the oven scattered with rosemary needles. Tuscany.

migliatello lamb's or goat's innards flavored with garlic and flat-leaved parsley, wrapped in a slice of pancetta or prosciutto and tied up with the animal's intestine. The resulting bundle is baked in the oven with oil, salt, rosemary and bay leaves. Basilicata.

migliecci another name for ➤ **migliacci**, fritters.

miglio millet (*Panicum miliaceum*). A cereal of Asian origin and much used by the Greeks and the Romans, it was a staple in Europe until the introduction of rice and corn, by which it was totally supplanted. In Italy today it is only used as seed for poultry and cage birds. Some specialties which used to be made with millet and conserve its name are now made with cornflour or chestnut flour (➤ **migliaccio giallo**, ➤ **pan de mei**).

mignaculis fluid batter of flour, water and salt. Friuli.

mignecci unleavened flatbread made from a batter of cornflour, salt and water, cooked in a griddle pan. A specialty of the Garfagnana area, in the province of Lucca. Tuscany.

milanese colloquial abbreviated term for ➤ **cotoletta alla milanese**.

milanisa, a term used to describe a food served with a condiment of sardines, wild fennel and, sometimes, grated day-old cooked in a skillet. Sicily.

milinciani Sicilian term for ➤ **melanzana**, eggplant.

millecosedde soup of legumes (chickpeas, grasspeas, beans, fava beans, lentils) with the addition of Savoy cabbage, celery, onions, fresh or dried porcini mushrooms and short pasta, flavored with grated Pecorino and pepper. Calabria.

millefogli aka **millefoglie** other terms for ➤ **omaso**, omasum.

millefoglie millefeuille. Cake composed of several wafer-thin sheets of puff pastry filled with confectioner's custard or Chantilly cream or zabaglione. Today creative chefs also make savory versions.

millefoglie strachin variation on millefeuille (➤ **millefoglie**), filled and coated with a very soft cream, which tends to go soggy (in dialect *se straca, si stanca* in Italian, means "it gets tired," hence the name). A specialty of Verona. Veneto.

millepieghe aka **millerighe** other terms for ➤ **omaso**, omasum.

milunciani Calabrian dialect term for ➤ **melanzana**, eggplant.

milza spleen. The organ which forms blood cells and performs other important functions. It is situated in the abdomen in contact with the diaphragm. It is soft and elastic and in meat animals is long in shape and gray-brown to dark red in color. It keeps for only a short time, so is used mainly in mixed fried offal dishes. It is very rich in vitamin B and iron, and its bitter taste can be easily attenuated by skinning. It is used in popular recipes such as: ➤ **crostini neri** (Tuscany), ➤ **pani ca' meusa** (Sicily), ➤ **zuppa di milza** (Veneto), ➤ **Milzschnittensuppe** and ➤ **gnocchetti di milza** (Trentino-Alto Adige). Some Roman recipes of Jewish origin feature spleen, one such being ➤ **milza di bue in padella**. The spleen can also be cut into "pouches" and filled with ricotta or other ingredients.

milza di bue in padella sliced ox spleen cooked in a skillet with garlic, oil, sage and vinegar. An ancient Roman dish of Jewish origin. Lazio.

milza ripiena calf's spleen cut to form a pouch and stuffed with a mixture of chopped spleen and veal, garlic, parsley, eggs and grated Parmigiano. Cooked in a skillet with herbs and spices and white wine, it is served warm or cold. A now rare dish, typical of the province of Alessandria. Piedmont.

milzera dialect term for ➤ **polmonaria**, common lungwort.

Milzschnittensuppe soup consisting of meat broth poured over slices of toasted bread spread with a mixture of spleen, eggs, garlic and herbs cooked in butter. Trentino-Alto Adige.

minchiareddhi short wholemeal and "burnt grain" (➤ **grano arso**) maccheroni made from a braid of dough hollowed with a needle (➤ **ferretto**). Often served on the Salento peninsula (province of Lecce) mixed with ➤ **orecchiette**. Puglia.

mindula aka **minula** dialect term for ➤ **zerro**, picarel.

minestra the word is usually translated as "soup" and does indeed mean a dish of vegetables, legumes, pasta, rice or cereals cooked in broth or water. *Minestra asciutta*, however, refers to a pasta or rice dish served as a first course (*asciutto* means "dry").

minestra acchiatizza soup of wild greens typical of the province of Avellino. Campania.

minestra al latte rice or pasta cooked in milk, perfumed with spices (cinnamon, cloves, nutmeg and bay leaf) and served with butter and grated ➤ **Toma**. Val d'Aosta.

minestra alla murese vegetables (chicory, fennel, potatoes and beans) boiled in salted water to which lightly fried lardo, suet, garlic and chili are added, and served with croutons. Typical of the province of Potenza. Basilicata.

minestra alla sangrina meat from the pig's head boiled in water with leek, cabbage, potatoes, broccoli rabe, lardo and previously boiled lentils. A specialty of the Val di Sangro, in the province of Val di Sangro, in the province of Chieti. Abruzzo.

minestra alla viterbese a soup of zucchini cut into strips, chopped tomatoes, potatoes and grated carrots to which semolina is gradually poured. When it is ready, it is creamed with butter and Parmigiano. A specialty of Viterbo. Lazio.

minestra bugiarda a type of ➤ **acquacotta** made by lightly frying onion and celery, then adding chopped tomatoes, wild asparagus tips and spinach. The mixed vegetables are covered with water and, when ithe soup is ready, eggs beaten with grated Parmigiano are added. The soup is served over slices of toasted bread. Tuscany.

minestra carsolina flour and egg mixture broken up into crumbs which are first fried in butter, then boiled in broth. Typical of the Carso area in the province of Trieste. Friuli-Venezia Giulia.

minestra chin frue soup of potatoes, zucchini and green beans. Typical of the province of Nuoro, enriched with ➤ **frue,** sour curd in brine. Sardinia

minestra co' lo pane sotto soup of seasonal vegetables, enriched with potatoes and beans, served hot or cold on day-old bread and anointed with extra virgin olive oil. Served with whole white spring onions for munching between spoonfuls. Typical of the Monti Lepini area. Lazio.

minestra con i pristi soup named for a type of homemade pasta typical of the inland part of the province of Savona. The *pristi* are made from a dough of flour, water, salt and eggs, which is cut up into small "grains." These are then cooked in a very simple broth of water, oil, salt and garlic cloves, and served sprinkled with grated cheese. Liguria.

minestra cun casu friscu vegetable soup thickened with fresh cheese. Sardinia.

minestra d'orzo dei Walser barley soup. First onion and pancetta are browned with sliced vegetables (potatoes, carrots, onions, celery). Barley and water are then added, and the soup is thickened with milk towards the end of the cooking process. The recipe belongs to the tradition of the Walsers, a Germanic people who settled in the Ossola valley and Monte Rosa centuries ago. Piedmont.

minestra di accio e baccalà celery and salt cod soup. In summer the recipe includes potatoes, in winter chopped walnuts, hazelnuts and pickled peppers are also added. Typical of the Irpinia area. Campania.

minestra di anguilla eel soup. The fish (➤ **anguilla di Lesina**) is boiled in water and a vegetable broth is prepared separately with field chicory, turnips, pumpkin, celery, onion and wild aromatic herbs. The fish is then added to the broth and served. Typical of Lesina, in the province of Foggia. Puglia.

minestra di broccoli alla romana Roman broccoli (➤ **broccolo**) cut into pieces and cooked with lardo, garlic, tomato sauce and pork rind cut into strips. The resulting mixture is traditionally served with broken up spaghetti. Lazio.

minestra di castagne chestnut soup. Traditional soup common in many Alpine and Apennine areas. In the Valle di Gressoney (Val d'Aosta), dried chestnuts (➤ **castagne secche**) are cooked first in water, then in milk with a piece of lardo. In

another version, the soup is thickened with cornflour and served in a bowl with ➤ **Toma** cheese and day-old rye bread. In some mountain areas in Piedmont, rice is cooked in the milk with the chestnuts, and the soup is flavored with butter, Fontina and cinnamon. In the Modena area (Emilia), the chestnuts are boiled in salted water flavored with cinnamon and cloves.

minestra di castagne fresche fresh chestnut soup. Onion, celery and parsley are lightly fried in olive oil, to which chopped tomato, salt and pepper are added. Peeled fresh chestnuts and wild fennel then go into the pot, and the whole mixture is covered with water. The soup takes about an hour to cook and is served piping hot. Sardinia.

minestra di cavolo (1) cabbage soup. Pre-boiled Savoy cabbage leaves are plunged into boiling lamb broth, sprinkled with a generous amount of grated Pecorino, and served over croutons fried in olive oil. Calabria.

minestra di cavolo (2) Savoy cabbbage leaves cooked in water to which potatoes flavored in lightly fried garlic and rosemary and tomato paste are added. Typical of the mountain valleys of the province of Cuneo. Piedmont.

minestra di ceci chickpea soup. A winter soup made with chickpeas (or beans), cardoons, celery and carrots flavored with a ➤ **soffritto** of olive oil, onion, parsley, pork rind and tomato conserve. Pasta may also be added, or, alternatively, the soup can be served with croutons. Sardinia.

minestra di ceci e castagne chickpea and chesnut soup. A dish made on Christmas Eve in L'Aquila (Abruzzo) and also very popular in the province of Viterbo (Lazio), where it consists of puréed chickpeas and chopped chestnuts mixed with lightly fried ham fat, garlic, rosemary and oil, covered with meat broth and chopped tomatoes. Abruzzo, Lazio.

minestra di ceci e costine Italian name for ➤ cisrà, pork and chickpea stew.

minestra di dumega barley soup (➤ dumega).

minestra di fagioli e cardoncelli bean and mushroom soup. Beans (➤ fagioli di Sarconi) cooked with pork rind and mixed with lightly fried onions and king oyster mushrooms (➤ cardoncello). The soup is garnished with chili and drizzled with extra virgin olive oil. Basilicata.

minestra di fagioli e castagne bean and chestnut soup, Thickish soup in which chestnuts and dried beans are first boiled in water then flavored in extra virgin olive oil with pepper, salt, saffron and flatleaved parsley, and covered with water to achieve the required density. Umbria.

minestra di farro soup of emmer cooked in a pot with minced celery, carrot, flatleaved parsley, onion and diced pancetta to which ham or vegetable broth is continually added. When it is ready, it is sprinkled with grated Pecorino and, if desired, pieces of ham scraped from the bone used to make the broth. Umbria.

minestra di fave bianche white fava bean soup. Dried white fava beans soaked overnight and simmered for a few hours in salted water. The resulting soup has the texture of a purée and should be drizzled with olive oil. In some places they add pasta (eg, ditalini) or rice cooked separately. Puglia.

minestra di frittatine small flour, milk, egg and parsley frittatas rolled up, cut into strips and cooked for a few minutes in boiling meat broth. Trentino-Ato Adige.

minestra di giancheti newborn fish or whitebait (➤ bianchetti) briefly cooked in vegetable broth (for the most part made with zucchini, together with pasta (➤ capelli d'angelo and eggs beaten with Parmigiano and marjoram. Liguria.

minestra di gulasch Italianization of ➤ gulaschsuppe.

minestra di orzo e potatoes barley and potato soup. First barley is boiled in water to which are added first lightly fried aromatic herbs and vegetables, then, in some cases, meat (fresh or smoked) or pork rind, then milk and diced potatoes. The soup is served with grated cheese. Trentino-Alto Adige, Friuli-Venezia Giulia.

minestra di orzo, fagioli e castagne barley, bean and chestnut soup. In an earthenware pot are cooked first the beans (soaked dried borlotti: ➤ borlotto), then the barley and the chestnuts. The mixture is then flavored with lightly fried garlic and onion, a pig's trotter and a piece of pork rind (potatoes and chopped tomatoes may also be added). This is how they make the soup in Italy's northeastern regions. In Valsusa, in the province of Turin (Piedmont), a soup of beans, dried chestnuts and barley simply simmered in milk has the same name.

minestra di pane per la ribollita a minestrone of roughly sliced onion, tomato, beans, Savoy cabbage, "black cabbage" (➤ cavolo nero), chard, carrot, celery and herbs poured over day-old Tuscan bread. The soup is either eaten immediately or the day after anointed with extra virgin olive oil and scattered with thinly sliced spring onions (➤ ribollita). In the old days soups were "reboiled" out of necessity, today similar dishes are to be found on menus at restaurants in the region. Tuscany.

minestra di pasta e patate pasta and potato soup. Diced potatoes are browned with finely chopped lard, herbs and chopped tomatoes, then covered with a generous amount of meat broth and pieces of egg pasta. The soup is served with a sprinkling of grated Pecorino. Lazio.

minestra di pasta reale beef stock garnished with tiny beignets (➤ **pasta reale (2)**) which are served separately and should not be allowed to go soggy. The soup is probably of French origin but is now part of Italian national cuisine, and is considered one of the most typical in Emilia-Romagna.

minestra di paternoster small pasta balls (eggs, wheat flour, olive oil, nutmeg and grated Parmigiano), shaped with a needle to look like the beads on a rosary, cooked in chicken broth. The soup is served with a generous sprinkling of grated Parmigiano. Umbria.

minestra di riso con il luppolo rice and hops soup. In Cremona (Lombardy), they cook the rice in a light meat broth with hops (➤ **loertis** in dialect, **luppolo in** Italian) and serve the soup with minced parsley and garlic, grated Grana Padano and butter. In Veneto, the hops (➤ **bruscandoli** in dialect) are sautéed in lardo or butter and added to rice cooked in broth. Lombardy, Veneto.

minestra di riso e fegatini rice and chicken liver soup. Rice cooked in meat broth with the addition of chicken livers browned in butter, grated cheese and, in the winter, Savoy cabbage made crisp by the frost. The same soup is made with pasta in lieu of the rice. Lombardy.

minestra di riso e latte rice and milk soup. A typical Piedmontese family dish, especially in the northeast province of Verbano-Cusio-Ossola, where it is the tradition to cook the rice in water and milk aromatized with onion, bay leaf and cloves. Served with knobs of butter. Piedmont.

minestra di riso e tinca rice and tench soup.

A broth made from the head and bones of the tench, carrot, celery, onion and garlic is filtered and used to cook the rice and the chopped fish fillets. Served with minced flat-leaved parsley and, according to taste, chopped tomato. Lombardy.

minestra di riso e verze rice and cabbage soup. Soup typical of the province of Milan (Lombardy) and of Friuli. It consists of rice cooked in a broth of Savoy cabbage lightly fried in pancetta (or lardo) and onions, and served with minced parsley. Lombardy and Friuli.

minestra di riso e zucca rice and pumpkin soup. A specialty of the province of Mantua (Lombardy), where they make it very thick with the addition of onion and no other vegetable. In Piedmont, instead, the soup is a fluid purée of pumpkin and potatoes cooked in milk, with the subsequent addition of rice. Lombardy, Piedmont.

minestra di scarola escarole soup. Escarole cut into pieces and cooked in broth or water. When cooked, one or more eggs and grated Parmigiano are mixed into the soup. Served poured over fried or toasted bread. Typical of the Ciociaria area, Lazio.

minestra di scarole e ceci neri escarole and black chickpea soup. Thickish soup made with the black chickpeas of Caposele, in the province of Avellino, sanmarzano tomatoes (➤ **pomodoro sanmarzano**), onion, guanciale (cheek bacon), and escarole, flavored with garlic, rosemary, and bay leaves. Served with toasted bread. Campania.

minestra di semola d'orzo very ancient soup of meat broth and barley meal flavored with chunks of fresh cheese and crushed mint leaves. Sardinia.

minestra di tinca con i tagliolini soup of tench cooked in broth or water flavored with aromatic herbs and chili to which tagliolini are added. A recipe typical of the lake areas of Lazio and Umbria.

minestra di trippe tripe soup. Boiled tripe cut into strips, browned in oil and herbs and diluted with broth to which breadcrumbs and diced potatoes are added. Trentino-Alto Adige.

minestra di zucca pumpkin soup. Many variations exist throughout Italy. In Umbria, a thick ➤ **velouté** of pumpkin cooked with slices of lard, gradually diluted with broth (preferably made with wood pigeon, ➤ **colombaccio**) and flavored with verjuice (➤ **agresto**), cinnamon, pepper, parsley and saffron. zafferano. Umbria. In Maniago, in the province of Pordenone, cream of pumpkin soup is flavored with ricotta, cheese, pepper and cinnamon.

minestra mariconda a soup with small dumplings (➤ **mariconde**).

minestra maritata hearty traditional soup lighter versions of which are now on the menu in many restaurants in Campania. A meal on its own, it "marries" (*maritata*) meat and vegetables. Similar soups are also made in Basilicata and Calabria (where Savoy cabbage, chicory, fennel, curly endive, spinach and chard, are parboiled and added to a broth made with a ham bone), but the Campania version is certainly the richest. The dish is traditionally eaten in the spring and records of it date from the late 16th century. It consists of a broth of veal, pork stuffed capon, pig's trotter, ➤ **pezzentelle**, ➤ **annoglia** and aromatic herbs. The vegetable used *de rigeur* are: ➤ **torzella** cabbage, borage, escarole, chard, chicory, broccoli and Savoy cabbage. The soup, which used to be known as *pignatto grasso*, is finished off with flakes of mature Caciocavallo. Campania.

minestra matta homemade egg tagliolini cooked in broth to which diced pancetta and tomato are added. Served with a generous sprinkling of Parmigiano-Reggiano. Emilia-Romagna.

minestra nel sacco a mixture of eggs, grated Parmigiano and dry bread, butter, salt, pepper, nutmeg and, if desired, grated lemon zest is wrapped in a cloth and cooked in capon broth. It is then allowed to cool and cut into cubes, which are served at the table in the cooking broth. A historic Bolognese recipe, now rare, recently registered at the city's Chamber of Commerce. A similar, lighter version of soup made in Romagna is known as *minestra nel sacchetto*. Emilia-Romagna.

minestra sfritta side dish of stewed chicory, cardoon, chard, wild fennel and diced potatoes tossed in extra virgin olive oil, garlic and chili. Typical of the Cilento area. Campania.

minestra spersa chopped escarole, wild greens, onions and potatoes cooked in salted water and flavored with lardo, garlic and chili. Basilicata.

minestra sullo scio rosemary, garlic and chopped tomato, seasoned in salt and pepper, gently fried in extra virgin olive oil and diluted with water, to which small short pasta is subsequently added and cooked. The resulting soup is sprinkled with grated Pecorino cheese. The dialect word *scio* means something which slides away, hence of little value, a reference to the simplicity of the soup. A recipe typical of Volterra, in the province of Pisa. Tuscany.

minestra verde "green soup" made by simmering vegetables (Savoy cabbage, celery, fennel, escarole, chicory, cauliflower, cardoon and so on) and mixed meats (beef on the bone, pork), and best enjoyed if left to rest for an hour or so, then reheated. The dish is traditionally eaten to settle the stomach after a day of merrymaking and excess. Puglia.

minestra virdi Palermo name for ➤ **maccu di san Giuseppe**, a dried legume soup.

minestredda Siracusa name for ➤ **maccu di san Giuseppe**, a dried legume soup.

minestrella di Gallicano spring vegetable soup made of spontaneous herbs (no fewer than 20-30). To a mixture of garlic, lardo, and a piece of pork rind, gently fried, are added the finely chopped herbs (➤ **erbi**), boiled puréed beans and water. The soup is served with small focaccias known as ➤ **mignecci**. Recipe typical of the village of Gallicano, in the Garfagna area of the province of Lucca. Tuscany.

minestrone soup of mixed vegetables with pasta or rice and oil, lardo or other parts of the pig, depending on the region. Recipe vary greatly from place to place, one of the most complex being ➤ **virtù** (Abruzzo).

minestrone alla genovese vegetable soup made, according to season, with beans, potatoes, runner beans, white cabbage, carrots, celery, leeks, tomatoes, zucchini, peas and so on, mixed herbs, oil and a piece of Parmigiano rind. When it is almost ready, short pasta (➤ **scucuzzu**) and ➤ **pesto Genovese** is added for extra flavor. Best enjoyed warm or cold. Liguria.

minestrone alla milanese rich soup made with a great variety of vegetables, rice and diced pancetta, sometimes flavored with pork rind, garlic, sage, basil and flat-leaved parsley. Lombardy.

minestrone alla napoletana vegetable soup in which pumpkin abounds and to which short dried pasta is added. Campania.

minestrone con castagne chestnut soup. In the northern part of the Lake Garda area, in the province of Verona, the typical chestnuts of Monte Baldo are peeled,

boiled with salt and sage and added to a soup of beans, potatoes, Savoy cabbage and aromatic vegetables.

minestrone con la zucca pumpkin and vegetable soup to which short pasta (tubettini or ditalini or snapped spaghetti) are added after a couple of hours' cooking. May be served with or without grated Parmigiano-Reggiano. Lombardy.

minestrone dauno soup made with eggplants, peppers, onion, potatoes, basil and dry-leaved parsley. Typical of the Foggia area, of which Daunia (hence the name *dauno*) is the ancient name. Puglia.

minestrone di castrato small pieces of castrated lamb cooked in water with zucchini, potatoes, celery, onion and tomatoes. The recipe is a specialty of Alessano, in the province of Lecce, and the lambs used come from the salt pastures of nearby Capo di Leuca. Puglia

minestrone di cicerchie grass pea soup. Grass peas, celery and carrots simmered with lightly fried onions and diced potatoes. When the soup is almost ready, sliced cherry tomatoes and pasta (➤ **quadrucci** or similar) are added. The final touch is a generous sprinkling of grated Parmigiano. Umbria.

minestrone di fave fava bean soup. An old Tuscan soup of shelled, boiled fresh fava beans stewed in a pan with onion, chopped skinned tomatoes and minced chili. Water is poured over the mixture and, when it boils, fresh tagliatelle are added. The soup is drizzled with extra virgin olive oil before serving. Tuscany.

minestrone di verdure alla piemontese diced or sliced seasonal vegetables (carrots, zucchini, potatoes, tomatoes, leeks, Savoy cabbage etc.) cooked for a couple of hours in water with lightly fried onion, garlic, lardo and, traditionally, a piece of Parmigiano rind. The soup is served with a sprinkling of minced flat-leaved parsley in winter and roughly torn basil in summer. Sometimes beans are also added, fresh or dried and soaked. Piedmont.

minghiale di scoglio another name for ➤ **musdea**, forkbeard.

Minglen small sweet dumplings made with a leavened dough of flour, milk, eggs, sugar, oil and brandy, and decorated with poppy seeds and confectioner's sugar. Trentini-Alto Adige.

ministeriale chocolate medallion filled with a liqueur cream made from a secret recipe, patented by the Scaturchio family of confectioners. Only the ingredients are known: dark chocolate, milk, sugar, pure alcohol, rum and hazelnuts. A variation on the praline, now a classic of Neapolitan confectionery, is made from shortcrust pastry filled with the same cream and lightly coated with chocolate. It too is patented and is known as a ➤ **sandomenico**. Campania.

ministru aka **erbuzzu** soup of potatoes, beans and wild herbs, which can be strengthened with other ingredients such as ➤ **ciccioli** (pork scratchings), sausage, ➤**merca** (brine) and grated cheese. Sardinia.

minni chini o minni di sant'Agata aka **minni 'i vergini** pastries shaped like small women's breasts (*minna* in dialect), created in the monastery of Montevergine in Palermo. Two disks of differing thickness are cut from a sheet of puff pastry (eggs, sugar, flour and minced almonds). The smallest is used to cover the base of a ramekin, the sides of which are lined with almond paste (➤ **pasta reale (1)**). The ramekin is then filled with a cream of ricotta mixed with candied fruit, cinnamon and vanilla liqueur and covered with the larger of the two pastry disks. The confection is turned out, coated with fondant sugar and topped with a cherry cum nipple. Palermo.

minoia aka **minoscia** terms used in Brindisi and Lecce for fish fry (➤ **novellame di pesce**). Puglia.

minuich durum wheat and water pasta similar to ➤ **cavatelli**. Traditionally served with cauliflower, tomato sauce or garlic, oil and chili. Basilicata.

minuli a' stimpirata small fish such as bogues (➤ **boga**), coated in flour, fried, sprinkled with vinegar and mixed with pitted olives, capers, minced garlic and mint, seasoned with salt and pepper. Delicious warm or cold. The recipe comes from the small town of Avola, in the province of Siracusa. Sicily.

miottini irregularly shaped balls made from a mixture of cornflour, butter, sugar, raisins and pine kernels, coated in white flour and fried in lard. An ancient specialty of the province of Ferrara. Emilia-Romagna.

mirabella small round green plum (➤ **prugna**) native to Alsace, but now well acclimatized in the Carnia area of the province of Udine. Friuli.

mirtillo bilberry (*Vaccinium myrtillus*). Fruit of the Vaccinium genus, which comprises more than a hundred species of different colors. It grows wild and cultivated and matures in the summer, though selected early and late varieties also exist. The Italian Ministry of Agriculture's database of native and/or traditional food products lists two wild varieties: *mirtillo nero della montagna pistoiese* (Tuscany) and *mirtilli e altri frutti del sottobosco delle valli cuneesi* (Piedmont). In Italy bilberry are eaten fresh with ice creams and semifreddi, and they are also widely used to make jams, jellies, juices and fermented beverages.

mirto aka **mortella** myrtle (*Myrtus commu-*

nis). An aromatic evergreen plant with pinkish-white flowers and black berries, typical of Mediterranean scrubland. In the kitchen the leaves are used to flavor stews and roasts, in Campania also to wrap mozzarella (➤ **mozzarella nella mortella**) and in Sardinia to perfume the fire for ➤ **porcheddu in Sardinia**. Myrtle is included in the Italian Ministry of Agriculture's database of natuve and/or traditional food products.

mirto di Sardegna popular liqueur made in Sardinia and Corsica since the 19th century by macerating ripe myrtle berries (and a few leaves) in alcohol for about 40 days. The filtered solution is blended with a syrup of water and sugar (or honey), which determines the liqueur's alcohol content and sweetness. Matured for one to two months, the liqueur has a sharp, tangy flavor, after 15 months it becomes soft and velvety. Sardinia.

mirtol baked cake similar to ➤ **chisola**, but richer, the basic mixture being supplemented with finely ground cornflour, milk, sugar, grated lemon zest, anise liqueur or grappa and powdered vanilla. A specialty of Mantua. Lombardy.

mischiglio aka **miskiglio** fresh pasta, often shaped like ➤ **cavatelli**, made of blended cereal and legume flours (durum wheat, barley, chickpea and fava bean) and served with various sauces. Traditional in the Pollino area, in the province of Potenza. Basilicata.

misciarolu dialect term for ➤ **prugnolo**, mousseron mushroom.

misciska another name for ➤ **muscisca**, preserved lamb's or goat's meat.

miseria bread made from a dough of soft wheat flour, brewer's yeast dissolved in salted water and melted refined lard. Typical of the province of Parma. Emilia-Romagna.

miserie de le femene soft flour and water gnocchi traditionally served with a sauce of ➤ **sopressa vicentina** salami, ➤ **Asiago stravecchio** cheese, dry white wine and tomato passata. A specialty of the province of Vicenza. Veneto.

missoltini freshwater sardines (➤ **agone**) salted, sun- and wind-dried, layered in tins and pressed. The oily liquid that the fish releases allows them to keep for a long time. The sardines thus preserved are broiled or fried, or skinned and served as an antipasto with a sprinkling of olive oil and vinegar and, often, polenta. Typical of Lake Como. Lombardy.

misticanza a mixture of wild herbs the composition of which depends on season and place. The term is used mainly in central Italy: in the Marche it refers to herbs to be cooked as an ingredient in the emmer dish ➤ **farrotto**, in Lazio to a mixed salad dressed with oil, salt, pepper and vinegar. The base of the mixture is composed of wild herbs (➤ **erbarelle**) which nowadays, especially out of season, are supplemented by greens such as endives, chicory, radicchio, rocket and so on.

mistocchine oval or lozenge-shaped wafers made by cooking a mixture of chestnuts and milk on a hot-plate or in a griddle pan. In the past they were sold on the streets in winter. In Ferrara, they may also be fried, in which case they are called ➤ **tamplun**). Emilia-Romagna.

mistrà aka **anice secco** anise liqueur whose name may derive from Mystras, the ancient name for Sparta, or from mistral, the east wind. It is made by macerating finely minced unripe aniseed (➤ **anice verde**) in alcohol for a week, then adding sugar and water syrup. In the countryside, where the liqueur is still made at home, fruit or herbs may be added. Since the second half of the 19th century, **mistrà** has been made industrially and is now distributed elsewhere in Italy. It may be drunk straight, used to lace coffee, diluted with water as a thirst-quenching drink, or used to flavor traditional regional cakes and pastries, ➤ **frustingo**, first and foremost. Marche.

mitilo aka **cozza** aka **muscolo** mussel. The first is the scientific name, the second two are the words used respectively in central and southern Italy and in Liguria. The commonest mussel in Italian seas is the bay or blue mussel (*Mytilus galloprovincialis*) followed by the bearded horse mussel (*Modiolus barbatus*). Consumer demand for mussels is very high and the mollusks are widely farmed (as they have been in Campania and the gulf of Taranto since ancient times). The Italian Ministry of Agriculture's database of native and/or traditional food products list the following varieties: *cozza di Scardovari* (Veneto), *cozza tarantina, cozza gnure* (Puglia), *muscolo del golfo di La Spezia* (Liguria), while ➤ **mosciolo selvatico di Portonovo** (Marche) is promoted by a Slow Food presidium. The habit of eating mussels raw dressed with lemon and pepper is gradually disappearing, but the mollusks are the principal ingredient in many regional recipes (eg, ➤ **cozze, cocozze e ove** in the north, **muscoli ripieni** in the south) provide the base for pasta and rice sauces and appear in some fish soups. Common and regional names: ➤ **arcella niura**, ➤ **dattero**, ➤ **modiola**, ➤ **mosciolo**, ➤ **musciolo**, ➤ **pedocio**, ➤ **peocio**.

mitonà abbreviated name for ➤ **supa mitonà**, a type of soup.

mizzurado another name for ➤ **gioddu**, a type of yogurt.

mlinci pasta baked in the oven. Typical of the Carso area, in the province of Gorizia. Friuli-Venezia Giulia.

mnestra del bate 'l gran a soup once made for farm workers during threshing work, now served in some restaurants. It consists of veal and chicken broth to which minced stewed chicken giblets, a little tomato concentrate and tiny homemade egg pasta are added. Typical of the Langhe hills in the province of Cuneo and the Monferrato hills in the province of Asti. Piedmont.

mnestra marià "married soup." A soup of rice, vegetables (spinach or chard) and meat broth into which grated Parmigiano and eggs are beaten. In season, wild herbs such as good King Henry (➤ **buon enrico**) may be added. A recipe typical of the Provencal valleys of the province of Cuneo. Piedmont.

mocetta aka **motsetta** aka **motzetta** a cured meat once made with the boned legs of ibex, now with those of goat, chamois or cow. The sinews and fat are trimmed from the meat, which is steeped in a ➤ **doil** with a cure of salt, pepper, garlic cloves, thyme, sage, bay leaf, rosemary and savory for two weeks. The meat is then hung for a week and aged for three to four months. Mocetta is typical of the Val d'Aosta, but is also to be found in the Valli di Lanzo (province of Turin) and the Val d'Ossola (province of Verbano-Cusio-Ossola) in Piedmont. Val d'Aosta.

moddizzosu aka **moddighina** bread loaf made with a dough of flour (and/or durum wheat meal), salt, water, sourdough and brewer's yeast. Typical of the Campidano area, where it has a crisp crust and a soft crumb, and the province of Nuoro, where they make it round, flat and soft and add ricotta or potatoes to the dough Sardinia.

Modicana, razza very ancient cattle breed, present in Sicily for millennia. It has a streaked red coat and lives in the wild, only returning to byres for milking. Its milk is of excellent quality, ideal for the production of the local → **Ragusano** cheese, but has very low yields (fewer than 1,500 pints a year). The meat is lean and tasty but is in low demand on account of its bright red color and pale yellow fat (produced by the carotene contained in the wild plants the cattle feed on). The breed is mainly raised in the provinces of Ragusa, Enna and Palermo. Sicily.

modiola another word for → **mitilo**, mussel.

moeca aka **moleca** small soft-shelled crab typical of the Venice lagoon. In spring and fall, from Venice to Chioggia, the crabs are caught in nets, selected and transferred to *vieri*, porous wood tubs, to monitor their growth. They are eaten coated in flour, sometimes dipped in beaten egg, and fried. A Slow Food presidium is engaged in protecting the environment from pollution and encouraging youngsters to continue the crab fishing/ farming tradition. Veneto.

mohnnudeln egg tagliatelle served with crushed poppy seeds, toasted in butter and mixed with sugar. A recipe of Austro-Hungaric origin. Trentino-Alto Adige, Friuli-Venezia Giulia.

mohnsamen Alto Adige word for poppy seed (**papavero (2)**).

Mohrenkopfe "Moor's head." Cake of boiled chestnuts, chocolate, sugar and rum topped with whipped cream. Typical of the Sudtirolo area. Trentino-Alto Adige.

moleche al vino soft-shelled crabs coated in flour, sautéed in butter and finished off with finely minced flat-leaved parsley and dry white wine. Veneto, Friuli.Venezia Giulia.

molignana Campania dialect term for → **melanzana**, eggplant.

mollame con fiori di zucca stew of baby squid, octopus and cuttlefish flavored with zucchini flowers (*fiorilli* in local dialect), oregano and pepper. Campania.

mollica Sicilian term for both dried and fresh breadcrumbs.

mollusco mollusk. Invertebrate aquatic or land animal with a soft body and with or without a shell.

molo regional term for → **merlano**, whiting.

molva ling (*Molva molva*). Long fish similar to hake (→ **nasello**), with tasty, firm flesh. It is sold, fresh, dried and smoked, and in Sardinia is used to make botargo (→ **bottarga**). Common and regional names: → **linarda**, → **lupa**, → **molva allungata**, → **ruonco 'e funnale**, → **pisci palu**, → **stoccofissu**, → **stoccopesce**.

momboli another word for → **mumbulì**, pork rolls.

mommolao aka **mommolo** Marche and Abuzzo terms for → **murices**, murex or rock shell.

momperiglia Sardinia term for → **diavolina**, confetti sugar.

mon Piedmontese dessert, also common in other Italian regions, composed of layers of dry cookies soaked in a mixture of Marsala and coffee alternated with a cream of butter worked with sugar, cocoa, egg yolks and strong black coffee. The resulting "brick" (*mon*) is served cut into slices.

monacella Calabrian word for → **lumaca**, snail.

monachelle Italianization of → **moniceddhi** aka → **monicedde**, earth snails.

Moncenisio another name for → **Murianengo**, a blue cheese.

mondaj Cuneo term for roast chestnuts.

mondare (in cookery) to clean a vegetable or fruit and prepare it for cooking..

mondeghili soft meatballs made from leftover boiled or roast beef mixed with eggs, cheese, sausage, liver mortadella, fresh breadcrumbs soaked in milk and herbs, breaded and fried. A specialty of the province of Milan. Lombardy.

mondiola della Garfagnana relatively lean pork salami produced in the Valle del Serchio and Garfagnana area in the province of Lucca. Ground meat from the cheek and belly is cured with salt, sugar, herbs and spices, sometimes with the addition of ascorbic acid and potassium nitrate. The mixture is cased in a natural intestine, aromatized externally with bay leaves and rolled up like a snail. It is aged for 45-90 days.

moneghete aka **muneghete** Veneto dialect words for popcorn.

monferrina aka **monfrina** twice-leavened bread loaf made with a dough of all-purpose or cake flour, salt, brewer's yeast, malt and water). Typical of the province of Alessandria and the eastern Monferrato hills. Piedmont.

monfettini in brodo di seppie soup typical of the Romagna Riviera consisting of a stew of cuttlefish, tomato and fish broth to which *monfettini*, a tiny homemade egg pasta similar to → malfattini) are added. Emilia-Romagna.

moniceddhi aka **monicedde** Puglia for brown earth snails (*Helix aperta*). The flesh is soft and delicate, and the snails are eaten simply roasted or cooked with onions and white wine (*monicedde di Otranto*). Puglia.

montare (1) to whisk (egg whites), to whip (cream).

montare (2) to fold in, to amalgamate ingredients homogeneously (→ **amalgamare**).

Montasio PDO cheese from the Carnia area, in the province of Udine. Now produced not only in Friuli but also in parts of Veneto with raw or, more often heat-treated, cow's milk cheese. It can be sold

fresh (after 60-120 days' aging), semi-mature (aged for five to or mature (after 12 months and more). Friuli-Venezia Giulia, Veneto.

montasù bread with a friable crust and a compact crumb. Made by crossing two long loaves. Made with all-purpose or, more rarely, wholemeal flour. Veneto, Piedmont, Lombardy, Emilia-Romagna.

monte amiata cake almost identical to → **montebianco**. Tuscany.

Monte Veronese PDO cow's milk cheese typical of the Monti Lessini range in the province of Verona. May be made of whole milk or part-skimmed mountain dairy milk (*Monte Veronese di malga*). The latter, rarer, variety is protected by a Slow Food presidium. Veneto.

montebianco cake made of puréed chestnuts aromatized with rum, spooned into a mountain shape, covered with whipped cream and decorated with *marrons glacés*. Probably French in origin, the recipe is typical of the Val d'Aosta and Piedmont, but is also to be found in other regions (eg, in Tuscany= → **monte amiata**).

Montebore raw cow's and ewe's milk cheese shaped like a wedding cake. It takes its name from the village of the same name in the province of Alessandria. It may be eaten fresh after 15 days or mature. Created by Benedictine monks in the 12th century, it had almost disappeared when, in 1999, it was revived by a Slow Food presidium. Piedmont.

montone ram, a male sheep (→ **ovino**).

monzetta aka **monzitta** names used in the province of Sassari for brown earth snails (*Helix aperta*). In the province of Cagliari, they are called → **tappadas**. Sardinia.

mora di gelso mulberry. The fruit of the mulberry tree which, in a not too remote past, was a common feature of the Italian rural landscape, especially in the Po Valley where the silk industry flourished and silk worms were farmed. Two varieties exist: the white mulberry (*Morus alba*), whose fruits are sweet but rarely eaten; the black mulberry (*M. nigra*), whose fruits are used to make syrups, granitas and jams, and are also eaten fresh.

mora di rovo blackberry (*Rubus fruticosus*). The fruit of the almost ubiquitous bramble, many varieties of which, derived from American species, are now cultivated. Like many other woodland fruits, blackberries are eaten fresh with sugar cream and ice cream, or used in baking and confectionery to fill tarts and sweet ravioli and dumplings. The Italian Ministry of Agriculture's database of native and/or traditional food products lists: *mora delle montagne pistoiesi* (Tuscany), *mora della provincia di Torino*, *mora delle valli cuneesi* (Piedmont),

moretta a *digestif* consisting of a blend of coffee, rum and other liqueurs made to an old sailors' recipe. A specialty of Fano, in the province of Pesaro e Urbino. Marche.

Morlacco del Grappa an uncooked cheese made from cow's milk from two milkings (that from the evening milking, skimmed by allowing the cream to rise to the top, and that from the following morning). Soft, low-fat and salty, it ages for two weeks to three months. The version made with raw mountain dairy milk is protected by a Slow Food presidium. Produced in the provinces of Belluno, Treviso and Vicenza (Veneto).

mormora striped sea bream (*Lithognathus mormyrus*). As its name implies, a fish similar to the sea bream (➤ **pagello**) with excellent meat. *Mormora di Miramare* (Friuli-Venezia Giulia) is listed in the Italian Ministry of Agriculture's database of native and/or traditional food products.

mòro a dessert (a type of ➤ **zuppa inglese**) of sponge fingers layered with zabaglione and covered with chocolate. Typical of the valleys of the province of Cuneo. Piedmont.

morselletti spiced cakes, most likely the progenitors of ➤ **cavallucci**. Honey and sugar are melted in a pan and, after turning off the heat, flour, bicarbonate of soda, minced almonds, chopped candied fruit, cinnamon, nutmeg, coriander and chopped walnuts are added. The mixture is spread out on a working surface, cut into lozenges and baked in the oven. In Subiaco, in the province of Rome, the same name refers to small lozenge-shaped cookies made from a paste of ground walnuts, flour, chestnut honey, grated orange zest and pepper. Tuscany, Lazio.

morsello Italianization of ➤ **morzeddu**, an offal dish.

morsetti in tegame calf's offal (heart, liver, lung) browned in extra virgin oil with onions and finished off in tomato sauce. Umbria.

mortadella bologna oval or cylindrical PGI cured meat now produced almost exclusively at an industrial level. It dates from the 14th century, and is made in Piedmont, Lombardy, Veneto, Emilia-Romagna, Tuscany, Marche and Lazio, and in the province of Trento. It is made from cheaper cuts of pork and fat from the throat, cubed, heated, washed in water and drained. The meat and fat are finely ground and seasoned with salt and whole and crushed peppercorns. Aromas, pistachio nuts, sugar, water, hard pork fat and washed pig's stomachs may also be added. The mixture is cased in natural or artificial intestines and cooked in dry-air ovens.

mortadella classica same given to a traditional, artisan ➤ **mortadella bologna** protected by a Slow Food presidium, made only with pork from heavy Italian pigs and a minimum amount of preservatives. Trimmed shoulder pork, fresh ham scraps, fat from the throat, intestines and meat from the cheek are cured with salt, ground white pepper, minced mace and coriander and garlic. Cased in a pig's bladder, the mortadella is cooked in stone ovens. It is ready to eat within 24-48 hours of production and can be kept for up to three months. A specialty of the city of Bologna. Emilia-Romagna.

mortadella della Val d'Ossola a mortadella produced in limited quantities by a few artisans and protected by a Slow Food presidium. The mixture is made up of pork, 5% liver (in the Val Vigezzo they make a variation with twice the amount) and, in some cases, warm wine flavored with spices, and is cased in a pig's intestine. The mortadella can be eaten fresh, boiled or baked, or after two months' aging. Typical of the mountains in the province of Verbano-Cusio-Ossola. Piedmont.

mortadella di Camaiore slightly curved cured pork, produced all year round. Meat from the back, head and shoulder, prosciutto and pancetta are ground with pieces of hard fat and cured with salt, pepper and other spices, among which fennel seeds, cinnamon and cloves. The mixture is cased in a natural intestine and secured tightly with string. The meat matures for a week and ages for a period that varies according to weight. A specialty of Camaiore, in the province of Lucca. Tuscany.

mortadella di fegato cured meat made from a finely ground mixture of liver, lean pork trimmings and pancetta, which is cured with salt, natural aromas, spices and ground pepper filtered in red wine, and cased in a pig's bladder or intestine. After maturing for three to four days, the meat is aged for a month. It keeps longer preserved in suet in earthenware jars. This recipe is typical of the provinces of Pavia, Mantua and Como. A more artisanal variety is made in the southern part of the province of Lodi, in the province of Milan, and the southern part of the province of Pavia: in this case, the cure is strengthened with mulled wine (➤ **vin brulé**), and finely ground lardo sometimes replaces the pork trimmings. Lombardy.

mortadella di fegato di Novara mixture of ham trimmings, pancetta and fat from the pig's throat, plus a variable percentage of liver (50% in the village of Fara Novarese and environs), and, in some cases, pickled tongue, cured with salt, sugar, lemon zest, saltpeter and ➤ **vin brulé**, mulled wine, and pushed into a pig's or cow's intestine, or, if the product exceeds two pounds in weight, a ➤ **bindone**, horse's colon. Aged for four or five months, it is eaten cooked, unless it is preserved in fat or smoked, in which case it is eaten raw. Typical of Novara, as the name suggests. Piedmont.

mortadella di Prato this cured meat was born of the need to use up scraps from the production of salami and cheap cuts of pork. It is made by casing the above, curing them with spices and liqueurs (alkermes in particular) and cooking them in water. Produced today in Prato and Agliana, in the province of Pistoia, the mortadella is pink in color with a spicy smell. A Slow Food presidium has brought together the few producers still active and drawn up a production protocol. Tuscany.

mortadelle di Campotosto old traditional cured meats made in the province of L'Aquila. Cuts of prime lean pork are finely ground and mixed with salt, pepper and other aromas. A three-inch lardon is inserted into the mixture, which is then cased like sausages and linked in strings of two. The little mortadellas are smoked for 15 days over oak and beech fires, and aged for three months. A Slow Food presidium seeks to protect the specialty from industrial imitations. Abruzzo.

mortandela della Val di Non ancient rare cured meat revived and protected by a Slow Food presidium. It is made from ground pork cured with mixed spices and shaped into small balls. These are dusted with buckwheat flour and smoked over a long period. After maturing for seven to 30 days, they can be eaten raw or cooked. A specialty of Trento. Trentino-Alto Adige.

Mortarat a family of cheeses made with whole or raw cow's milk, which age briefly covered or stuffed with aromatic spices. There are four main traditional types: Maccagnetta alle erbe, covered in black pepper and mountain herbs, Maccagnetta alle noci, stuffed with walnuts and covered with corn flour, Ciambella all'aglio, which contains garlic cloves, and Mattonella al rosmarino, which matures under sprigs of rosemary. The cheeses are typical of the mountains in the province of Biella. Piedmont.

mortella a common name for ➤ **mirto**, myrtle.

morto a roast made according to the ➤ **arrosto morto** technique.

morzeddu a street food (➤ **cibo di strada**) consisting of calf's offal (lung, liver, spleen) and omasum (➤ **omaso**) browned in oil with garlic, aromatic herbs and chili, then stewed in wine and tomato sauce. The dialect name means "little bite" and refers to the fact that the stew is traditionally used to fill ➤ **pitta** bread, and is thus eaten a bite at a time. A delicacy of Catanzaro. Calabria.

morzello Italianization of ➤ **morzeddu**, an offal dish.

morzi aka **muerzi** small pieces of day-old bread fried in oil with chili with the subsequent addition of legumes (mostly peas and beans) or boiled greens. A typical recipe of the Salento peninsula, in the province of Lecce. Puglia.

mosa (aka **mose** and **muas**) very soft polenta cooked in water and milk, sometimes sugar and cinnamon, served with cold milk. Trentino-Alto Adige, Veneto.

moscardino orthopod mollusk similar to an octopus (➤ **polpo**) but with single suckers as opposed to double. Lives on muddy sea beds and is fished mostly in spring, when it approaches the shore to lay its eggs. A particularly prized variety is the *moscardino muschiato* ➤ **folpeto**, musky octopus (*Eledone moschata*), cooked like other cephalopods, less so the *moscardino bianco*, lesser or curled octopus (*E. cirrosa*), which may be coated in flour and fried or stewed with tomato sauce. Common and regional names: ➤ **polpo asinisco**, ➤ **polpo di sabbia**, ➤ **purpu de sicco**. The *moscardino di Caorle* (Veneto) is listed in the Italian Ministry of Agriculture's database of native and/or traditional food products.

mosciame aka **mosciamme** aka **musciame** the term originally referred to fillet of dried dolphin, but since the prohibition of the hunting of dolphins, has come to mean fillet of dried tuna. Consists of a dark red bar which has to be sliced and softened in oil prior to consumption. In Sicily a similar product is made with swordfish. Liguria, Sardinia, Sicily.

mosciolo aka **musciolo** Marche word for mussel (➤ **mitilo**).

mosciolo selvatico di Portonovo local name for mussels (*Mytilus galloprovincialis*), which reproduce naturally and live clinging to the underwater rocks of the Conero peninsula. Until World War II, these mussels were fished from rowing boats (*batane*) by peasant-fishermen and, to supplement their wages, by port workers from Ancona. Today the competition of mussel farming has much reduced their market, which is why a Slow Food presidium is now seeking to relaunch the mollusks. Typical of the province of Ancona. Marche.

most Friulian word for cider or perry.

mostaccioli aka **mostacciuoli** small pastries traditional under different guises in a number of Italian regions. The common ingredients are: wheat flour, eggs, sugar, spices (frequently cinnamon, pepper and cloves), sometimes honey and cocoa, often cooked wine must (➤ **vincotto**) and almonds. In Molise (where they are perfumed with orange and mandarin zest), in Basilicata and in Campania (where they are known as *mustacciuoli*), the cakes are characterized their classic lozenge shape and dark color, the result of a generous use of cocoa and chocolate icing. The ➤ **mustazzola** popular in the provinces of Catania and Messina (Sicily) is a shell of pastry with a filling of cooked wine must, chopped walnuts and almonds, orange zest and cinnamon. In Puglia, the basic ingredients are supplemented by cinnamon, lemon zest and syrup of figs (➤ **cotto di fichi**), and the cakes are sometimes coated with a chocolate icing. In Umbria, the pastries are ring-shaped and flavored with white wine must and aniseed, in some area of Piedmont they are hard lozeng-

es, pink-colored due to the presence of red wine in the dough. See also ➤ **mostazzit** aka **mostaccini**, ➤ **'nzudde** and ➤ **mustazzolos**.

mostaccioli another word for ➤ **penne**, a type of pasta.

mostarda generally speaking, a relish or condiment of candied fruit in a syrup spiced with mustard (essence or powder; ➤ **senape**): ➤ **mostarda di Cremona**, ➤ **mostarda di Mantova** and, to an extent, ➤ **mostarda vicentina**, fit into this category. In some places, however, the word refers to preserves of cooked grape must, sometimes flavored with autumn fruits: ➤ **cognà**, ➤ **savor**, ➤ **mostarda di Carpi**, ➤ **mostarda piemontese**, ➤ **mostarda pugliese**, ➤ **mostarda siciliana**, ➤ **mostarda toscana**.

mostarda bolognese in reality a jam, popularly known as *marmellata nera*, made with sugar, plums and quinces, and used to fill traditional cakes and pastries, such as ➤ **pinza** and ➤ **raviole di san Giuseppe**. Emilia-Romagna.

mostarda d'uva di Carpi preserve made from grape must and pieces of apple, pear, quince, orange zest and slow-cooked until reduced to a very thick consistency. Made during the grape harvest, it is stored in hermetically sealed glass jars. Emilia-Romagna.

mostarda d'uva piemontese preserve made by cooking the juice of ripe grapes with pieces of quince and other fall fruits until reduced to a thick consistency. The name is used in the Monferrato hills, in the provinces of Asti and Alessandria. In the province of Cuneo, the same recipe is called ➤ **cognà**. Piedmont.

mostarda d'uva pugliese syrup made by slow-cooking local grapes (negroamaro and malvasia) and sugar, and stored in glass jars. This is the procedure in Lecce, but in the province of Foggia they add pieces of quince to the mixture and store it in earthenware jars greased with extra virgin olive oil. Puglia.

mostarda d'uva siciliana preserve made by boiling grape must mixed with corn starch until very thick. It is then aromatized, usually with vanilla, cinnamon and toasted almonds, put into molds and allowed to dry in the sun. Next it is transferred to jars and covered with bay leaves. The preserve was usually served during the grape harvest or at family parties. Sicily.

mostarda d'uva toscana red grape must simmered with citron and lemon zest and fruit (quinces, apples, pears and peaches). The resulting mixture is pushed through a sieve, thickened on a low heat, aromatized with cinnamon and cloves and preserved in hermetically sealed glass jars. Tuscany.

mostarda di Cremona a relish of candied fruits preserved in a syrup spiced with mustard. In households, each type of fruit (apples, peas, pumpkin, melons, figs) is cooked separately in sugar and water syrup. In the industrial version, whole ready-candied fruit (including clementines, cherries and citrons) is used. The relish is served with boiled meats and, nowadays, also with mature cheeses. Lombardy.

mostarda di fichi d'India the juice of prickly pears is blended with grape must and corn starch and boiled until very thick. The mixture is dried in the sun in terracotta molds and preserved in containers with bay leaves. A specialty of the province of Catania. Sicily.

mostarda di Mantova a relish of candied fruits preserved in a syrup spiced with mustard. It differs from ➤ **mostarda di Cremona** insofar as the fruit used (apples or quinces, unripe pears, pumpkin, melon) is sliced or cut into pieces. The preparation is virtually identical, and this version too is served with boiled meats and, nowadays, also with mature cheeses. Lombardy.

mostarda di mele a runny sweet and sour sauce typical of a few mountain valleys in the province of Biella. It is made with the filtered juice of local apple varieties, cooked for 15 hours and more and kept in hermetically sealed glass jars. It is eaten with polenta, mixed boiled meat, roast pork and local cheeses. Piedmont.

mostarda di Voghera a relish, similar to ➤ **mostarda di Cremona**, made with whole candied fruits (pears, figs, cherries, apricots, white pumpkin, plums, mandarins, peaches) in a syrup spiced with mustard (➤ **senape**). The recipe is said to date from the 14th century and is still reproduced by the Pianetta di Barbieri company. Lombardy.

mostarda vicentina fruit relish with the consistency of a purée. It is made with quinces (➤ **cotogna**), sweet white wine, apples and pears, cooked to a pulp with the addition of sugar, citron and orange zest and mustard essence or powder (➤ **senape**). Veneto.

mostardella a cured meat made from a mixture of lean beef and pork fat, salt, garlic and pepper cased in a natural intestine, lightly smoked and matured for a week. It is eaten in thick slices, raw or roasted. Cut into pieces, it is also used to flavor tomato sauce. It used to be made with leftover scraps from the production of ➤ **salame di Sant'Olcese** and was traditionally given to girls as an engagement present. A specialty of the area between Genoa and La Spezia. Liguria.

mostazzit aka **mostaccini** very hard, small lozenge-shaped cookies made with wheat flour, refined sugar, water and spices. Very popular in the province of Varese and in the area round Crema, in the province of Cremona, where they are sometimes an ingredient in ➤ **tortelli cremaschi**. Lombardy.

mostazzoli another word for ➤ **mostaccioli**, small cakes.

mostella greater forkbeard (*Phycis blennioides*). Marine fish of the Gadidae family, it lives over sandy, muddy sea beds, where it is fished mainly in the winter months. As in the case of the hake (➤ **nasello**), the youngest specimens are fried, whereas older fish are cooked in soups, stewed or filleted and baked *en papillote*. Common and regional names: ➤ **fico**, ➤ **lupo**, ➤ **pastenula bianca**.

mosto must. Non-fermented ripe grape juice. Other types of must exist—apple, cherry, plum, fig—all made by crushing or pressing the fruit in question. In traditional gastronomy, grape must provides the base for ➤ **mostarda d'uva**, various desserts, and ➤ **vino cotto**. Regional names include: ➤ **saba**, ➤ **sapa**, ➤ **vincotto**. In southern Italy, fig must is used to make ➤ **cotto di fichi**. In the province of Piacenza, the word **mosto** also refers to ➤ **sughi di mosto**, must sauces.

mosto cotto another term for ➤ **saba**, ➤ **vincotto**.

motella aka **pecorella** three-bearded rockling (*Motella tricirrata*). Fish similar to the greater forkbeard (➤ **mostella**). It lives in shallow water on rocky sea beds and has very delicate, easily perishable flesh. It is cooked in the same ways as hake (➤ **nasello**).

Mottarone cow's milk cheese, the modern reproduction of the ancient Faterel, which takes its name from the mountain of the same name, between Lakes Maggiore and Orta. It can be sold after 45 days but may be aged for two and a half months. Piedmont.

motzetta another name for ➤ **mocetta**, a cured meat.

mousse delicate soft sweet or savory confection made with whipped cream and other ingredients. The Italian translation of the French term is *spuma*, but it is rarely used in domestic kitchens or on restaurant menus.

mozzarella one of Italy's most famous and popular fresh cheeses, but only that made with buffalo's milk using traditional techniques is technically allowed to use the name. In reality, commercially and colloquially, the word is used to refer to fresh stretched curd cheeses made with any kind of milk. In Italy three types of buffalo's milk mozzarellas are available: ➤ **Mozzarella di bufala campana**, *mozzarella di latte di bufala* (made with buffalo's milk, but without geographical delimitations), *mozzarella tradizionale* (made with buffalo's or cow's or mixed milks, without geographical delimitations). The various production stages include: the inoculation of the milk with calf's rennet; the milling of the curd; the ripening of the curd; the stretching of the curd; the shaping and cutting into portions; and the cooling and salting.

Mozzarella di bufala campana PDO fresh cheese made with whole buffalo's milk in the provinces of Caserta and Salerno (Campania) and Latina and Frosinone (Lazio), and in some communes of the provinces of Naples, Benevento and Roma. Campania, Lazio.

mozzarella in carrozza snack which originated in Tuscany, but now common all over Italy. Sandwiches of white bread, crusts removed, filled with mozzarella, dipped in milk and beaten eggs, and deep-fried in olive oil.

Mozzarella nella mortella raw cow's milk mozzarella typical of the southern part of the Cilento area, in the province of Salerno, drier and more compact than ➤ **Mozzarella di bufala campana**. It ripens wrapped in myrtle leaves and thus develops a fragrant, aromatic aroma. Campania.

'mpanata (1) round or half moon focaccia made with bread dough with various fillings, traditionally salt cod and eel for Christmas dinner. In fishing villages in eastern Sicily, other types of fish are used. In Portopalo di Capo Passero (province of Siracusa), conger eel, skate, moray eel and smooth hound are popular. The name derives from the Spanish *empanada*, a pasty filled with meat, cheese and fish. Sicily.

'mpanata (2) another name for ➤ **manata**, black bread softened in a mixture of heated ricotta and whey.

'mpanatigghia a pastry typical of Modica, in the province of Ragusa, whose name derives from the Spanish *empanadilla*, but which is probably an elaboration of an ancient Arab recipe. Small baked half moon pasties (made with a dough of cake flour, egg yolks, sugar and melted lard) filled with a mixture of ground veal, sugar, minced toasted almonds, dark chocolate, egg whites, cinnamon and cloves. Sicily.

'mpepata shellfish heated in a skillet until they open, cooked briefly in their own broth, generously sprinkled with pepper (*pepe* in Italian, hence the name of the dish), drizzled with extra virgin oil and, according to taste, sprinkled with lemon juice. The most famous version of the recipe is made with mussels, but clams and other shellfish can also be used. Campania.

mreca Cabras (province of Oristano) dialect word for ➤ **merca**, brine.

mucatuli another name for ➤ **nucatili**, a type of pastry.

mucca synonym of ➤ **vacca**, cow, especially in the animal's dairy, milk-producing connotation.

muccellato baked Easter cake made from a mixture of durum or soft wheat flour, milk, sugar, extra virgin olive oil, lard and orange or lemon zest. Calabria.

muccu aka **muccu jancu** dialect terms used on the east coast of Sicily for newborn sardines (➤**novellame di pesce**).

muccunedda Sicilian dialect term for ➤ **dolci di riposto**, cakes made with almond paste.

Muchidu another name for ➤ **Casu marzu**, a sheep's cheese.

mucroncini long-lasting cookies typical of Oropa and the Mucrone area in the Alpine foothills of the province of Biella. Piedmont.

muffoletta aka **guastedda** round, soft, spongy bread roll made from a dough of durum wheat meal, brewer's yeast, salt and water. In the Palermo area, it is used to make ➤ **pani ca' meusa**. Oil-based versions also exist, sprinkled with sesame seeds and aromatized with anise or fennel. Sicily.

muffoletto ri parrini a type of ➤ **muffoletta**, bread roll, leavened with ➤ **biga**, a type of sourdough starter, and sprinkled with seame seeds. Typical of Partinico, in the province of Palermo. Sicily.

muffuittu another name for ➤ **moddizzosu**, a bread loaf.

mugella Marche term for ➤ **cefalo**, gray mullet.

muggine cefalo aka **muggine comune** other names for ➤ **cefalo**, gray mullet.

mugheddu dried and smoked gray mullet (➤**cefalo**) ressed with extra virgin olive oil, vinegar and minced garlic and parsley.

mugliatelli another word for ➤ **ammugliatielli**, a lamb's offal dish.

mugnaia, alla *à la meuniere*. A method of cooking white fish (sole, sea bass, sea bream, trout), brains (usually calf's) and sweetbreads. The food is coated in flour and cooked in butter, then sprinkled with finely minced parsley and serve with melted butter blended with lemon juice.

mugnuli greens cultivated on the Salento peninsula (Puglia). A member of the Brassicaceae family, they are similar to broccoli rabe and broccoletti, but have smaller purple inflorescences and a sweeter, more aromatic flavor. The inflorescences and the tender parts of the stalks are cooked with pasta (*tria*) or cooked in the same way as broccoli rabe or broccoletti. In the province of Caserta (Campania), they are cooked with chunks of salted pork belly, day-old farmhouse bread and chili. Puglia, Campania.

mula rare cured meat typical of the provinces of Novara and Vercelli. Made with lean pork from the head and cheek of the pig, the tongue and sausage meat, it is cured with salt, pepper, garlic, nutmeg, cloves and cinnamon and cased in a horse's intestine. Aged for two months, it is eaten boiled. Piedmont.

mule aka **mulze** cured meat made with pig's blood thickened in boiling water, scraps of pork, lardo, salt and pepper, with the addition of buckwheat or day-old bread and, sometimes, raisins or pine kernels. Friuli-Venezia Giulia.

muletta another name for ➤ **budello cieco**, caecum intestine.

muletta del Casalese cured meat made with a mixture of ground prine pork, and bacon fat cured with salt, ground white and black pepper, nutmeg and an infusion of garlic and wine. It use to be cased in an equine intestine, hence the name,

but today a cow's intestine is used. After maturing for ten days, it is aged for six months. Typical of the Casale area. Piedmont.

mulo mule. The offspring of a male donkey and a mare, a female horse. Still bred in some areas of southern Italy and Sicily, but rarely used in the kiychen.

mulun cake of dried chestnuts and cannellini beans (➤ **cannellino**) cooked in milk and flavored with sugar, chocolate, isinglass, whipped cream and vanilla. Typical of the Valtellina, in the province of Sondrio. Lombardy.

mumbulì rolls of pork stuffed with lardo and sage, fried and served with polenta, or alternated on skewers with song birds and spit-roast. Lombardy.

mungana cake of milk, eggs, lard, cocoa, sugar and a drop of anise liqueur (➤ **mistrà**). Marche.

munizione a bread load, a round flat version of ➤ **monferrina**.

munnezzaglia bits and pieces of leftover pasta once used by the Naples poor to supplement legume soups. Today dried fruit (walnuts, hazelnuts), capers, cherry tomatoes, olives and oregano might be added for flavor. Campania.

Murazzano PDO ewe's and cow's cheese, a member of the Robiola family. Produced in the province of Cuneo, it is aged for two months. A Slow Food presidium is engaged in relaunching the traditional version, made exclusively with ewe's milk from the upper Langhe hills, in the province of Cuneo. Piedmont.

murbe half moon sweet rye flour ravioli stuffed with jam and fried. Trentino-Alto Adige.

murena moray eel. Fish with delicate, tasty flesh, usually stewed with tomato, coated in flour and fried, spit-roast or baked in the oven. Sometimes it is also used as a substitute for conger eel (➤ **grongo**) in fish soups.

Murianengo blue cheese similar to ➤ **Gorgonzola**. After maturing for 20 day, forms are aged for at lest three months in cellars. Typical of the areas of Mont Cenis, Fréjus, and the plateau of Novalesa, in the Alpine valleys west of Turin. Piedmont.

murice murex or rock shell. Spiral-shaped shellfish that lives on sandy sea beds close to the coast, but moves closer to sea cliffs in the spring to spawn. Three varieties, *Murex brandaris, Murex trunculus* and *Murex erinaceus* are used in the kitchen, all boiled and served cold, shells removed, dressed with extra virgin olive oil and lemon juice. Common and regional names: ➤ **buro**, ➤ **cornetto de ma**, ➤ **garusol**, ➤ **mommola**, ➤ **mommolo**, ➤ **quecciulo**, ➤ **ragusa**, ➤ **ronseggio**, ➤ **sconciglio**.

murseddu baked pie with a bread dough crust and a filling of calf's liver, pig's liver and offal, tomato sauce, chili, salt and pepper. Calabria.

Murutzulu cheese made in the Montiferru area, in the province of Oristano, with raw milk from grazing Bruno Sarda and Sarda Modicana cows. Aged for three weeks to a year, it is cleaned periodically and greased with olive oil. Also known as **Casu de 'acca, Fresa, Pischeddu**. Sardinia.

mus polenta cooked in milk with aromatic herbs. Typical of the province of Verbano-Cusio-Ossola. Piedmont.

muscari common name in southern Italy, especially in Basilicata, for grape hyacinth bulb (➤ **lampascione**).

musciame another name del ➤ **mosciame**, dried tuna fillet.

musciarola Venezia Giulia term for ➤ **grancevola**, spider crab.

musciarone dialect term for ➤ **prugnolo**, mousseron mushroom.

musciolo Marche term for ➤ **mitilo**, mussel.

muscione another name for ➤ **latterino**, smelt.

muscisca an ancient system for preserving lamb, mutton, goat and kid meat that derives from the food traditions born of transhumance. Typical of the Gargano peninsula, in the province of Foggia (Puglia), it also used to be common in the Abruzzo, Molise and Marche Apennines. Lean meat is cut into pieces six to ten inches long and an inch thick. Cured with salt, chili, wild fennel and garlic, they are sun- or wind-dried. Particularly prized is the meat of Garganica goat (➤ **capra garganica**) preserved in this way.

muscoli ripieni stuffed mussels. Shucked mussels stuffed with a mixture of eggs, Parmigiano, aromas and chopped cuttlefish and other mussels cooked in tomato and served either as an antipasto or as a main course. Typical of the province of La Spezia. Liguria.

muscolo (1) muscle.

muscolo (2) term used in Liguria and some area of the Marche for ➤ **mitilo**, mussel.

muscolo di spalla cut of beef roughly equivalent to shoulder clod, suitable for stewing, boiling and braising.

musdea forkbeard (*Phycis phycis*). A gadid similar to the ➤ **mostella**, greater forkbeard. Common and regional names: ➤ **minghiale di scoglio**, ➤ **pastenula bruna**.

muset (aka **musetto**) boiling sausage made with various parts of the head of the pig, ears excluded. The meat and pork rind are cured with cinnamon, coriander, cloves, nutmeg and pepper and the resulting sausage is eaten fresh after cooking slowly on water. In the Carnia area, they smoke the sausage for 12 hours. Friuli-Venezia Giulia.

muss (aka **musso**) Veneto term for ➤ **asino**, donkey.

mussao Ligurian dialect term for ➤ **cefalo**, mullet.

mussillo Campania dialect term for the fleshier, relatively boneless dorsal part of ➤ **baccalà**, salt cod.

mussolo (aka **mussolo di scoglio**) Veneto and Friuli- Venezia Giulia word for ➤ **arca di Noè**, Noah's ark.

mussu ➤ **insalata di mussu e carcagnola**,

mustacciuoli ➤ mostaccioli

mustardela delle valli valdesi cured meat of Provencal origin produced in the Val Pellice, Val Chisone and Val Germanasca, west of Turin by a few pork butchers supported by a Slow Food presidium. A pig's boned head, throat, tongue and skin are ground and mixed with scratchings and onions and leeks softened in fat. The mixture is bound with blood and cured with salt, pepper, spices and, at times, red wine aromatized with cinnamon. Cased in a calf's small intestine and tied up, it is boiled fro 20 minutes. Piedmont

mustasì, variously shaped cookies made with wheat flour, eggs, sugar, butter and vanilla and covered with sugar and lemon juice icing. In the past they were baked round at Epiphany from a richer paste including walnuts, honey, cinnamon and cloves, and made to look like look little faces with pastry eyes, noses and mouths (in dialect the name means "crafty little face"). Typical of the province of Bergamo. Lombardy.

mustazzola ➤ **mostaccioli**.

mustazzolos pastries of durum wheat flour, sugar, cinnamom, sugar and lemon zest. After leavening (traditionally for more than 20 days), they are baked in the oven and glazed with white icing. They differ from ➤ **mostaccioli** of other regions for their shape and absence of cooked

wine must and liqueur. Typical of Oristano. Sardinia.

mustela aka **musteba** cured meat made from a single piece of meat from back of the pig's head and loin. The meat is dry-salted twice with salt, spices and aromas, the first time for three dats and the second for 15. Washed in cold running water, it is cased in natural or artificial intestines, wrapped in a elastic net, dried and put to age for at least 60 days. Sardinia.

mustica a conserve of newborn sardines, similar to ➤ **sardella (1)**. Calabria.

mut small balls of polenta filled with mountain cheese, cooked in hot ash or baked in the oven. A recipe typical of the mountains in the province of Cuneo. Piedmont.

mutun a la sau pieces of mutton broiled with oil, vinegar, parsley, garlic and spices. A traditional dish in the province of Verbano-Cusio-Ossola. Piedmont.

nN

nadalin Christmas cake typical of Verona. Ancestor of the ➤ **pandoro**, with which, albeit more compact and flatter, it shares the same star shape (said to represent the comet followed by the Magi). Made from a mixture of flour, butter, sugar, eggs and chocolate chips (optional), after baking it is coated with sugar chips. Veneto.

nana Tuscan term for ➤ **anatra muta**, musk duck.

nana in porchetta female musk dusk stuffed with unpleeled garlic, bay leaves, fennel seeds, pancetta, salt and pepper, bathed with white wine and baked in the oven. The bird is then jointed and served with the pan juices (➤ **porchetta, in**). Tuscany.

nappare to spoon a sauce or gravy onto a cooked food.

napruddi Sicilian dialect term for ➤ **cardo selvatico**, wild cardoon.

nasello argentato aka **merluzzo argentato** European hake. Member of the Merlucciidae family, common in the Mediterranean. Albeit also known as *merluzzo*, not to be confused with the real ➤ **merluzzo**, cod, a member of the Gadidae family. May be served marinated as an antipasto, boiled, baked or steamed, or minced for fish cakes. Common and regional names: ➤ **pesce lupo**, ➤ **pesce prete**.

nasello con salsa di acciughe another name for ➤ **merluzzo alla palermitana**, hake with anchovy sauce.

naspro icing made of a cooked mixture of sugar, water, lemon juice and lemon zest in which typical southern candies and cookies (especially sweet ➤ **taralli** ring cookies) are dipped or coated.

nastrini another name for ➤ **farfalline**, type of pasta.

nasturzio another name for ➤ **crescione (1)**, watercress.

natalini see ➤ **penne di Natale**, pasta dish.

natalini in brodo see ➤ **maccheroni di Natale**, pasta dish.

'ncapriata dried fava bean purée (➤ **macco**) accompanied, according to season and place, by chard, wild endives or wild chicory, boiled and dressed with extra virgin olive oil. Other accompaniments might be fried green peppers, broccoli rabe or boiled ➤ **lampascioni**, grape hyacinth bulbs. Local names: ➤ **fae e fogghie**, ➤ **fave e cicorie**, ➤ **favetta con le cicorielle**, ➤ **scurdijata**. Leftover purée is mixed with fried onions and day-old bread to make ➤ **fave scarfate**. Basilicata, Puglia.

'ncartellate dialect name for ➤ **cartellate**, fried pastries.

'nciminateddi (1) bread rolls flavored with cumin. Sicily.

'nciminateddi (2) small bread rolls baked in a wood oven and dressed with oil and oregano. Typical of the town of Modica. Sicily.

'nciminati Palermo dialect term for ➤ **biscotti regina**, iced cookie.

'nduja fiery sausage spread. Traditionally made with the inferior parts of the pig, but now also with the cheek and the belly. The meat is ground finely and cured with a small amount of salt and a huge amount of chili. It is then pressed into a caecum intestine (➤ **crespone**) and aged for a year or more. Calabria.

necci con la ricotta a ➤ **neccio**, type of waffle, filled with ricotta.

neccio soft brown waffle with a diameter of about 8 inches, made from a batter of chestnut flour water and salt (in Tuscany the word *neccio* also means chestnut tree) and cooked on a ➤ **testo**, griddle pan. Mainly eaten today rolled up and filled with ricotta (➤ **necci con la ricotta**). Typical of the mountain communities of the province of Pistoia and the Garfagnana and Lunigiana districts (➤ **pattona**, ➤ **castagnaccio**). Also known as ➤ **bollento**, ➤ **cian**, and ➤ **gaccio**. Tuscany.

neige mixture of gently cooked mixed meats, artichokes, and peas bound with egg, wrapped in bundles in unleavened bread, coated in breadcrumbs, and fried in boiling oil. Typical of the province of Genoa. Liguria

neole aka **nevole** ➤ **ferratelle**, sweet wafers.

neonata "newborn." Southern Italian term for ➤ **novellame di pesce**, fry.

nepetella lesser calamint (*Calamintha nepeta*). Spontaneous aromatic herb gathered and eaten mostly in central and southern Italy, especially in Tuscany. Its scent is vaguely reminiscent of that of mint and its leaves are used to flavor omelets, mushroom and zucchini dishes and snails. Common and regional names: ➤ **calamento**, ➤ **calaminta**, ➤ **mentastro**, ➤ **mentuccia**, ➤ **nepitella**.

nepitella another name for ➤ **nepetella**, lesser calamint.

nepitelle oven-baked square or round ravioli filled with chopped almonds, raisins, chocolate, cooked must, sugar, cinnamon and citrus fruit zest. Calabria.

nepitte dialect term for ➤ **nepitelle**, sweet ravioli.

nero di seppia squid ink.

nervett aka **nervitt** northwestern dialect terms for ➤**nervetti**, ligaments, sinew, cartilage of a calf's hock and shin.

nervetti ligaments, sinew and cartilage of a calf's hock and shin. Traditionally boiled, finely sliced and served with olive oil, vinegar, spring onions, salt and pepper and, in some places, garlic and minced parsley. In the province of Milan and Piedmont, they also add beans. Known in dialect as ➤ **nervett** or ➤ **nervitt**. Piedmont and Lombardy.

nespola aka **nespola comune** medlar (*Mespilus germanica*). Fruit from a tree of the Rosaceae family. It has a thick skin and pulpy flesh, which encloses five separate pips. The flesh is hard and astringent when picked (late October), but bletted in crates covered with straw, it becomes soft and sweet in the spring. Dialect names: ➤ **barbein**, ➤ **meddha**, ➤ **pocio**.

nespola del Giappone loquat or Japanese medlar (*Eriobotrya japonica*). Fruit naturalized in Europe at least three centuries ago. Cultivated for ornamental purposes but, thanks to its tangy, succulent flesh, also eaten fresh (the variety gown in Trabia, in the province of Palermo, is particularly renowned). Harvested in the late spring and early summer.

'nfanfulo Sicilian dialect term for ➤ **pesce pilota**, pilot fish.

'nfigghiulata stuffed focaccia. Long in shape and folded three times over it contains pork sausage, fresh Tuma cheese or ewe's milk ricotta, tomato sauce, wild fennel seeds, olive oil, salt and pepper. The most famous is made in Rosolini (province of Siracusa). In Sortino (also in the province of Siracusa), the same word refers to a small round focaccia flavored with figs and lesser calamint. Sicily.

'nfocagatti literally "cat drowners," spiral-shaped candies brushed with an icing of sugar, lemon juice and liqueur. Also known with the Italianized name of ➤ **affogagatti**. Typical of Lecce. Puglia.

'ngrìtoli flour and water polenta, now rare, served with a sauce of chopped sausage and Pecorino (the word *'ngrìtoli* means "lumps" and refers to the coarse texture of the dish). Lazio.

nicolotta Venetian cake of day-old bread, flour, milk, eggs, sugar, butter or lard, white wine, pine kernels, fennel seeds and, sometimes, candied lime. Named for the inhabitants of the parish of San Nicolò dei Mendicoli, who used to baked the cake for their saint's day. Veneto.

nido, a term used to described the rolling up of commercial dried pasta ribbons (tagliatelle, fettuccine etc) into "nests."

nido d'ape literally "bee's nest." Another name for ➤ **reticolo**, reticulum.

nigelen risen pastry fritters sprinkled with poppy seeds. Trentino-Alto Adige.

niuleddi dessert made by cooking toasted and chopped almonds, crushed cookies and lemon zest in honey aromatized with cinnamon and cloves. The resulting thick mixture is rolled into a sheet, sometimes decorated with colored sugared almonds, and cut into lozenge shapes. Sardinia.

nocchetedde pasta butterflies served in the same way as ➤ **cannaruozzoli**. Calabria.

nocchia Marche term for ➤ **canocchia**, mantis shrimp.

nocciola hazelnut (*Corylus avellana*). The fruit of a tree introduced to the Mediterranean for Asia Minor and now mostly cultivated. It becomes fully ripe at the end of the summer. Italy boasts two PGI hazelnuts: *tonda gentile del Piemonte* (➤ **nocciola del Piemonte**) and *tonda di Giffoni* (➤ **nocciola di Giffoni**). The Italian Ministry of Agriculture's database of native and/or traditional food products also lists the following varieties: *nocciola camponica, nocciola di san Giovanni, mortarel-*

la, riccia di Talanico (Campania); *nocciola tonda piacentina* (Emilia-Romagna); *nocciola dei Monti Cimini* (Lazio); *nocciola bianchetta, codina, nocciola dall'orto, nocciola del rosso, longhera, menoia, noscella, ronchetta, savreghetta, tapparona, trietta* (Liguria); *nocciole dei Nebrodi* (Sicily). By combining chocolate with hazelnut, Turinese confectionery created the popular ➤ **gianduia** mixture, (➤ **gianduiotto**), and the Alba area, in the province of Cuneo, exports nougat made with the *tonda e gentile* hazelnut all over the world. Not that the use of hazelnuts in confectionery is restricted to the north of the country (recipes abound nationwide: ➤ **brut e bon**, ➤ **nocciolini di Chivasso**, ➤ **rametti di nocciole**, ➤ **torta di nocciole**). They also appear in savory recipes, such as ➤ **arrosto alle nocciole**. Hazelnuts are also eaten toasted, sometimes salted, with aperitifs, and the use of hazelnut oil, traditional in Piedmont and northern Italy, is also enjoying a revival.

nocciola del Piemonte Piedmontese hazelnut. The PGI seal has been granted to the round, streaked *tonda gentile* variety produced in the provinces of Alessandria, Asti, Cuneo, Novara, Torino and Vercelli. After toasting, the fruit has a subtle, lingering flavor that makes it a perfect ingredient in ice creams, creams and custards and ➤ **gianduia** chocolate. Piedmont.

nocciola di Giffoni a PGI hazelnut cultivar grown in numerous communes of the province of Salerno. Subspherical in shape with firm, white pulp, it is sold whole with or without its shell, in packets, as a paste and as a cream in glass jars. Campania.

noccioloni another name for ➤ **mezze maniche**, a type of pasta.

nocciolini di Canzo candies similar to ➤

nocciolini di Chivasso, but slightly larger. A specialty of Canzo in the province of Como. Lombardy.

nocciolini di Chivasso tiny baked button-shaped candies made of toasted hazelnuts, sugar and egg whites. Created by confectioner Giovanni Podio in Chivasso, in the province of Turin, in the early 19th century, and made famous by Ernesto Nazzaro (who registered them under the dialect name of *noasetti* in 1904) and Luigi Bonfante. Still handmade using ➤ **nocciola del Piemonte** and sold in pale blue or pink bags. Piedmont.

noce (1) walnut (*Junglas regia*). Of Italy's many walnut varieties, the most widespread is the *noce di Sorrento*, Campania being the region where the fruit is most cultivated. The Italian Ministry of Agriculture's database of native and/or traditional food products lists the following varieties: *noce malizia, noce san martino, noci di Sorrento* (Campania); *noce di Motta* (Sicily); *noce del Bleggio* (Trentino); *noce aretina* (Toscany); *noce dei grandi fiumi, noce di Feltre* (Veneto). The walnut is used less in confectionery than the almond and the hazelnut, but it is nonetheless the principal ingredient in a number of delicacies: eg, ➤ **torta di noci** and ➤ **pan nociato**, highly popular in central Italy. Minced or chopped walnuts figure with other types of dried fruit in innumerable mixtures and fillings for traditional cakes and pastries, not to mention in sauces and condiments: ➤ **ajà**, ➤ **salsa di noci**, ➤ **saossa d'avije**. The walnut liqueur ➤ **nocino** (aka➤ **nocillo**) is also much loved by Italians. An oil used to be made from walnuts as a sort of surrogate of olive oil.

noce (2) cut of beef roughly equivalent to top surloin. Very tender, it is used for roasts.

(3) noce another name for ➤ **vongola**, clam.

noce di terra common and regional name for ➤ **casciomaci**, great pignut.

noce moscata nutmeg (*Myristica fragrans*). Fruit of an evergreen tropical plant, native to the Moluccan Islands, which bursts from a soft outer layer enclosed in a shell (its reddish membrane is used to produce ➤ **macis**, mace). As it dries, it takes on a brownish color. Of the "historical" spices, nutmeg, which is used grated, is still one of the best loved in Italian cooking, especially in northern Italy, where it is used to flavor traditional pastas (➤ **tortellini**, ➤ **anolini**), ➤ **passatelli**), béchamel sauce, and stewed meats. It is also a popular ingredient in spicy central Italian cakes.

nocellara del Belice PDO olive which may be either eaten at the table (➤ **oliva da mensa**) or to produce oil (➤ **oliva**). Bright green in color, it turns wine red when fully ripe. Typical of he province of Trapani, it is harvested by hand from September. Sicily.

nociata (1) type of nougat popular in central Italy, made by blending honey and chopped walnuts (in Umbria they also add egg white and citrus fruit zest) over a low heat. The resulting mixture is spread over a damp surface and cut into lozenge shapes, each wrapped in a bay leaf.

nociata (2). Mixture of chopped walnuts, refined sugar, grated lemon zest, crushed ring cookies used to dress short dried pasta or egg fettuccine. Grated chocolate, sugar and cinnamon may also be added. A typical Christmas dessert. Lazio.

nocino or **nocillo** old liqueur, recorded in Emilia as early as the 18th century, and renowned for its digestive properties. Popular in many regions and in other European countries. Made by macerating quartered unripe walnuts (traditionally picked by female hands on the night of the summer solstice), still attached to the ➤ **mallo** (husk), in ethylic alcohol (or, according to some recipes, in brandy) in a sealed recipient exposed to the sun for 25 days. A sugar and water syrup is then added, sometimes with spices (cloves, for example), and the liqueur is aged for a further month, before being filtered and bottled.

nodino cut of veal corresponding to ➤ **lombata**, short loin.

norcineria the curing of pork. In modern usage, the term has come to refer to the work of the pork butcher who makes, maybe just sells, cured meats of various origin. Historically, the ➤ **norcino** was the person who castrated or killed pigs to process their meat, traveling to breeders and peasant families to supervise proceedings on the day of the killing of the animal. The word derives from the town of Norcia, in the province of Perugia (Umbria), whose inhabitants were renowned ad much sought after, from Florence to Rome, for their meat-curing skills. In the Po Valley, where most of Italy's pigs are raised, the norcino's was a prestigious job, and numerous dialect words exist to describe it: ➤ **masacrin**, ➤ **masadur**, ➤ **masalen**, ➤ **mas-ciaro**, ➤ **masin**, ➤ **massalein**, ➤ **massalin**, ➤ **purcitar**.

norcino person skilled in ➤norcineria, the curing of pork.

nosecc stuffed Savoy cabbages typical of the Val Brembana, similar to ➤ **polpette di verza**, cabbage patties. The stuffing includes pancetta, mortadella and a pinch of nutmeg. Lombardy.

nostrale aka **nostrano** both terms mean native, local, non-imported, autochthonous and implicitly imply a value judgment: ie, genuine, non-artificial, unadulterated. In Piedmont, Veneto and Trentino, the adjectives designate precise dairy products: ➤ **Nostrale di Elva**, ➤ **Nostrano di malga**, ➤ **Nostrano fiavé**, ➤ **Nostrano Val di Fassa**.

Nostrale di Elva pasteurized full-cream cow's milk cheese produced in the mountain village of Elva alongside the now rare ➤ **Caso**. Aged for 1-6 months. Piedmont

Nostrano di malga washed rind cheese produced from June to September in the mountains round Belluno with raw milk from the Bruno Alpina cow breed. Aged for one to four months, when it becomes sharp in falvor. Veneto.

Nostrano fiavé part-skimmed cow's milk cheese produced in the area round the Massiccio del Lagorai mountains, in the province of Trento. Aged in damp rooms for four months, during which time the crust is washed with water and salt or whey. Trentino-Alto Adige.

Nostrano Val di Fassa part-skimmed raw cow's milk cheese produced with techniques similar to those used for ➤ **Puzzone di Moena**. Ages from 40 days to six months. The best forms are the ones produced in the mountains in summer. Typical of the Val di Fassa and Conca del Primiero, in the province of Trento. Trentino-Alto Adige.

novecento another name for ➤ **torta 900**.

novellame di pesce fry, newborn larval fish, especially anchovies, sardines and other Clupeids (➤ **bianchetti**), but also mullet and picarel. Part of the gastronomic traditions of many Italian coastal regions, they are eaten boiled, dressed with oil and lemon juice, or in fritters, frittatas and molds. European Union law now bans their fishing law, but exemptions have been made for some "special fish," including ➤ **rossetto**, transparent goby, which can be caught for no more than two months during the winter.

'nsaccagnotti aka **'nsaccheragatti** other names for ➤ **frascarelli**, a type of pasta.

'ntaccariello long bread loaf typical of Velletrano, in the province of Rome. Baked from a dough of three parts cornflour to one part wheat flour, salt, yeast and water. Lazio.

'ntreme de vicchie traditional dessert made by mixing boiled broad tagliatelle in cooked wine must (➤ **vincotto**), and flavoring them with crushed walnuts, raisins and orange zest. The unappetizing dialect name translates in Italian as *frattaglie di vecchia*, old woman's offal, and refers to the appearance of the tagliatelle, darkened by the **vincotto**. A specialty of Martina Franca in the province of Taranto. Puglia.

'ntrugliatelli al forno con patate lamb's intestines wrapped round celery stalks, boiled and finished in the oven with potatoes, cherry tomatoes, pepper and Pecorino. Other richer versions of the recipe exist. In the most noteworthy, really a type of ➤ **ammugliatelli**, *fritticello* (lamb's offal, such as lung, liver and sweetbreads) and *rezza* (caul) are closed in the *paratura* (intestines) to form faggots, which are first boiled, then finished in the oven with potatoes. Campania.

'ntruppc dialect word for ➤ **intoppo**, meat sauce.

'ntuppateddi dialect name for operculate snails (ie, with their snails "shut" by a white membrane) of the Helix aperta variety. In Floridia, in the province of Siracusa, they are cooked *a 'mbriaca* (drunk), stewed with onion, oil, black pepper, red chili, salt and red wine. Sicily.

nucatili aka **nucatula** aka **nucatuli** cylindrical pastries made from a dough of durum wheat flour, sugar and suet, and filled with a mixture of chopped dried figs, walnuts, almonds, orange zest and cinnamon amalgamated with honey. Common in various areas of the island, they date from the 15th century. Sicily.

nuce riale Puglia dialect term for ➤ **tartufo di mare** (➤ **vongola**, clam).

nudini term used in the Marche and Abruzzo regions for newborn anchovies (➤**novellame di pesce**, fry).

nunnata term used in Sicily for newborn sardines. See ➤ **novellame di pesce**, fry.

nusèt Lombard dialect term per ➤ **pipeto**, cabbage stuffing.

'nzudde aka **'nzudda** dialect words for the Calabrian version of **mostaccioli**. In Calabria, the pastries are larger than elsewhere and shaped to look like animals, famous people and mythological characters. Unlike the **mostaccioli** of other regions, they include honey, orange juice and liqueur among their ingredients. They are said to bring good luck. Calabria.

'nzuddi round cookies created by the nuns in the monastery of San Vincenzo in Catania (*'nzuddu* being a Sicilian diminutive of Vincenzo). The paste is made of flour, sugar, eggs, butter or lard, milk or water, ammonium carbonate, ground almonds and candied orange zest. In the province of Messina, the cookies are square and often flavored with vanilla and cinnamon (and contain whole almonds). Sicily.

oO

obara thick soup meat (beef, pork or chicken), beans, potatoes, peppers, other vegetables and red wine. Balcanic in origin. Friuli-Venezia Giulia.

oca (pl. **oche**) goose. Domestic varieties descend from the gray goose (*Anser anser*) and the swan goose (*Cygnopsis cygnoides*). Raised for their meat, livers, (➤ **fegato grasso**, foie gras) and feathers. Easy to breed, quick to grow, and highly marketable, the goose has been a popular source of meat since classical times. For centuries it replaced the pig in Jewish gastronomy all over Europe. In Italy the traditional goose breeding areas are —or were—Casale and environs (Piedmont), the Lomellina area and the provinces of Cremona and Mantua (Lombardy), and low-lying parts of Veneto and Friuli. Two typical goose dishes in the Veneto are ➤ **oca in onto**, preserved goose, typical of Padua and the Berici hills, and *falso arsuto*, a composition of smoked goose breast typical of the Montagnana area. In the village of Chiopris-Viscone, in Friuli, they smoke goose breasts. Typical of the province of Pavia, in Lombardy, are: aged goose breast ham, ➤ **fegato grasso in terrina** (terrine of foie gras), goose liver pâté, goose preserved in fat, marinated goose giblets, goose scratchings and melted goose fat. A specialty of the province of Piacenza, in Emilia, is ➤ **batù d'oca**, goose meat preserved in its own fat. Like the turkey and the capon, the goose is popular in festive recipes, some of which elaborate and rich:➤ **oca ripiena** (stuffed goose), ➤ **oca rosta** (roast goose), ➤ **oca con le castagne** (goose with chestnuts). A classic combination is goose and Savoy cabbage (➤ **cassola novarese**).

oca affumicata smoked goose. Pieces of goose preserved for a few days in a wood bowl with salt and pepper, smoked, and transferred to eartherware jars with cooked goose fat, after the manner of ➤ **oca in onto**, preserved goose. Friuli-Venezia Giulia.

oca al forno goose roast in the oven with garlic, rosemary, bay leaves and white wine. Umbria.

oca alle verdure goose with vegetables. The cavity of the bird is filled with wedges of lemon and the skin is lubricated with oil, broth and white wine. The bird is then covered with minced aromatics and herbs, baked in the oven, and bathed with cognac. Once cooked, it is jointed and served with the pan juices. Typical of the province of Parma but rare these days, the dish is probably of Jewish origin. Emilia-Romagna

oca con le castagne goose with chestnuts. The chestnuts are boiled and peeled and placed in the cavity of the goose, which is then browned in butter, bathed with white wine and roast in the oven for half an hour or so. It is then barded with slices of pancetta, sprinkled with water and roasted in the oven for another couple of hours. Served jointed and sliced with the roasting juices. Trentino-Alto Adige.

oca con le verze goose with Savoy cabbage. A traditional dish of the province of Cremona, but also made, with variations, in

Piedmont (➤ **cassola novarese**). Served with polenta. Lombardy, Piedmont.

oca conservata nel grasso goose preserved in fat. Goose meat is preserved for a few hours in a mixture of salt, garlic and spices, then transferred to glass jars and covered with the fat from the scratchings (➤ **ciccioli d'oca**). Excellent after a week, either as it is or fried. May be preserved for five-six months. Antipasto popular in the area south of Lodi. Lombardy.

oca in confit another name for **oca in onto**, preserved goose.

oca in onto lightly roasted goose meat, preserved in salt for a few days in earthenware or glass jars, and covered with melted goose fat and bay leaves. The meat may be kept like this for up to two years. When removed from the jars, it is used as an ingredient in casseroles, sauces and legume soups. Once a common dish all over the provinces of Padua, Treviso and Vicenza, today it is hard to find. A Slow Food presidium is currently striving to relaunch traditional Veneto goose breeds for the dish. Veneto.

oca in pignatto another name for➤ **oca in onto**, preserved goose.

oca ripiena stuffed goose. Typical of the northern regions of Piedmont and Lombardy, where it exists in at least two variations. In the province of Novara, the filling is made of ground veal, lardo, aromatics and rice. In the Oltrepò and Lomellina areas of the province of Pavia, they mix boiled or roast chestnuts, sausage or pancetta and the goose's liver, chopped, then cook the bird in white wine or broth. Piedmont, Lombardy.

oca rosta roast goose. The bird is roast in the oven with aromatic herbs and abundant celery for a few hours, lubricated first with wine, then with broth. At the end of the process, the giblets and liver are mixed with the cooking juices to make a serving sauce. One of the hallmark dishes of the region, of Treviso in particular, **oca rosta** can still be found in trattorias and village fêtes in the fall. Veneto.

occhi di passero "sparrow's eyes." Tiny durum wheat pasta rings cooked exclusively in broth.

occhi di santa Lucia small sweet ➤ **taralli**, ring-shaped cookies, made of flour, oil, wine and a pinch of salt. Once baked, they are dipped in icing and left to dry before serving. Puglia.

occhialini another name for **anellini**, pasta rings.

occhialone aka **occhione** regional terms for ➤ **pagello**, sea bream.

occhiata saddled bream (*Oblata melanura*). A member of the Sparidae family. Best eaten very fresh and broiled, or added to soups and stews. Small specimens may also be fried.

occhiatella similar to ➤ **razza**, skate, but smaller. Popular in the Marche region, where it is usually fried or stewed.

occhio di bue (1) literally "ox's eye," a regional term for ➤ **aliotide**, green ormer.

occhio di bue (2) literally "ox's eye," a common term to describe a fried egg: ie, *uovo all'occhio di bue*.

occhiu di voi literally "ox's eye," a Sicilian regional term for ➤ **aliotide**, green ormer.

ociada bastarda Venetian dialect name for ➤ **pesce castagna**, black bream.

ocimo Tuscan term, albeit now rare, for ➤ **basilico**, basil.

ocio Tuscan term for ➤ **oca**, goose.

odori another word for ➤ **aromi**, aromatic herbs.

ofelle square flour, potato and egg ravioli, filled with a mixture of ground beef, sausage, buttered spinach and onion, and served with melted butter and grated cheese. Typical of Trieste. Friuli-Venezia Giulia.

Ofengedörrtes paarl dried version of ➤ **paarl**, a type of bread.

offelle from the Latin *offa* (flatbread), small baked cookies of 15th-century origin made of flour, egg whites, raisins, cinnamon, ginger, and saffron. Popular throughout Italy, especially in the north, they differ region by region. In the province of Pavia, in Lombardy, *offelle di Parona* are oval cookies made of flour, yeast, eggs, sugar and butter. In Mantua, also in Lombardy, **offelle** are baked shortcrust pastry ravioli filled with eggs, butter, and sugar.

of in cereghin egg fried in butter. In Milan they leave the yolk runny, in the Brianza area they fold the white over the yolk. Lombardy.

ola thick winter soup of beans, potatoes, vegetables, and pork ribs cooked in the oven for at least six hours. Named for the earthenware pot in which it is cooked. Typical of the mountains of the province of Cuneo. Piedmont.

olio di oliva olive oil. A component, with bread and wine, of the famous "Mediterranean triad." Made by crushing olives, the fruits of *Olea europaea sativa*, the cultivated variety of a tree that invaded the Mediterranean from Asia Minor three or maybe four millennia ago. Olive oil was used as a cooking fat by Greeks and Romans but, insofar as it was relatively expensive, tended to be a prerogative of the better off. Others had to make do with seeking alternatives among animal fats (butter, lard, starch and so on) or other vegetable oils, walnut oil for example. This explains why the use of olive oil declined until the late Middle Ages. Production began to revive in the 17th century when production methods were rationalized, and reached its peak in 1795 with the invention of the hydraulic press. In the kitchen, classic French cuisine privileged animal fats (butter in particular) over olive oil for the whole of the 19th century and much of the 20th. In the 1960s, olive oil also had to withstand the competition of seed oils, which were advertised as light and healthy. In recent decades, however, thanks to the advent of cooking styles based on the enhancement of the quality of raw materials and to its own dietetic properties and flavor, olive oil has made a comeback. Today every Italian region, except for the Val d'Aosta, produces olive oil, albeit with obvious differences in quality and quantity, with a total output of around 700,000 tons a year. Dozens of varieties are produced, and thanks to the PDO seal of quality scheme (38 Italian oils have received it to date), average quality is improving all the time. At the time of writing, European legislation still had to be passed to allow consumers to recognize local products (it is compulsory to indicate place of bottling on labels, but not place of production). On the basis of acidity, number of peroxides and sensory analysis, olive oils are classified as *vergine extra* (commonly known as *extravergine*, the finest), *vergine*, *corrente* and *lampante* (defective).

olio santo literally "holy oil." Extra virgin olive oil flavored with chopped chili and used as a condiment on pasta, pizza, salad, and boiled vegetables. Puglia.

oliva (pl. **olive**) olive (*Olea europaea sativa*). The fruit of the olive tree has always been a precious source of nutrition in the Mediterranean and has left a deep mark on the area's different cultures. The olive is a drupe whose flesh is rich in oil and whose stone contains seeds that are also oily. The flesh is compact and firm and the color of the outer skin varies from green to purplish-black, depending on degree of ripeness. Olives are cultivated in Italy mostly in the coastal regions (especially Tuscany, Liguria and the center-south) and round Lake Garda. More than for direct consumption (➤ **oliva da mensa**), the olive is precious for its oil, an element fundamental for Italian cooking and diet. To make oil, olives are harvested before they ripen completely (from November to January), when their oil content is at its highest. The varieties most used are: *coratina* (Puglia), *frantoio* (Puglia, Tuscany, Umbria) and *leccino* (Tuscany), as well as *moraiolo, pendolino, cellina* and *rosciola*. Some varieties, such as *taggiasca* (Liguria) and ➤ **nocellara del Belice Dop** (Sicily) are equally good for oil and for eating.

oliva da mensa table olive. The process that makes the hard, bitter fruit of the olive tree edible is very different from the one used to turn it into oil. Black olives may be harvested fully ripe (in the winter), green olives early (at the end of the summer). They then have to undergo a series of treatments, if they are not to go rancid and to get rid of the bitter flavor that makes them impossible to eat freshly picked. In the course of time, the techniques adopted to overcome these problems have taken on a gastronomic value of their own and enhanced the prestige of the olives themselves. The most prized table olive cultivars are: *oliva ascolana del Piceno* (➤ **oliva tenera ascolana**), *cerignola, maiatica, nocellara* (➤ **nocellara del Belice**), *santagostino, santacaterina*, ➤ **bella della Daunia Dop**, and the Spanish varieties *bella di Spagna* and *manzanilla*. The Italian Ministry of Agriculture's database

of native and/or traditional food products lists the following varieties: *olive intosso* (Abruzzo); *caiazzara, masciatica* (Campania); *olive da mensa bianche e nere di Latina, di Frosinone e della provincia di Roma* (Lazio); *colombaia, lavagnina o taggiasca, mortina, pignola, razzola, rossese* (Liguria); *verdi pugliesi* (Puglia); *oliva nebba* (Sicily). Slow Food presidia protect ➤ **oliva infornata di Ferrandina** (Basilicata) and ➤ **oliva minuta** (Sicily). Olives are much used in the kitchen, in breads (➤ **pan de molche**, ➤ **pane del pescatore (1)**) and in a huge variety of focaccias, pizzas and turnovers. In central and southern Italy, olives are often served at the start of a meal as an *amuse-bouche* (➤ **alivi cunzati**, ➤ **alivi 'a puddastredda**, ➤ **olive conservate**). They appear in countless recipes to flavor other foods, from Liguria (where the *taggiasca* is frequently combined with rabbit and fish) to the south (➤ **agghiotta**, ➤ **bagnarola, alla**). In the Marche, the *oliva tenera ascolana* is stuffed and fried and is one of the main elements in ➤ **fritto misto all'ascolana.**

oliva infornata di Ferrandina baked olives. The first written documents about the baking of olives in Ferrandina, in the province of Matera, date from the 18th century. The olives (of the native *majatica* cultivar) are scalded, dry-salted, then baked at about 50°C. In this way, the natural sapidity of the fruits is heightened and their characteristic sweetness preserved. Promoted by a Slow Food presidium, the baked olives of Ferrandina are excellent on their own, with local cured meats and mature Pecorino, orange salad or stewed salt cod. Area of production: various communes in the province of Matera. Basilicata.

oliva minuta a very ancient Sicilian cultivar, grown mostly in the northeast of the island, sometimes at high altitude, often alternating with hazelnuts and chestnuts. The olives are harvested by hand from mid-October to mid-December and gathered in nets. Their oil is soft and fruity with a very low level of acidity. The olive is penalized by the fact that it is hard to harvest, has a low yield and that its oil more difficult to keep than that mixed with other olive oils. Hence a project, supported by a Slow Food presidium to protect the cultivar and promote the production of its oil. Sicily.

oliva tenera ascolana this olive, a symbol of the province of Ascoli Piceno, stands out for its size, its rich, sweet flesh and its straw-green color. Cultivated in a limited area of calcareous terrain (no more than 100 hectares mainly in the province of Ascoli Piceno and partly in the province of Teramo), these olives are ideal for direct consumption (➤ **olive da mensa**). They are preserved in brine and are famous for being stuffed and fried (➤ **olive ripiene all'ascolana**). The olive is recognized under the PDO **oliva ascolana del Piceno**. Marche.

olive all'arancia dried black olives marinated with orange zest, chopped garlic, oil and, sometimes, oregano or bay leaf. Served as an antipasto or with aperitifs. Umbria.

olive conservate preserved olives. Generally the production of table olives is divided into two major categories: green olives and black olives. The first are fermented and preserved in various ways: in brine, bleached (preserved in brine until they lose their color) or cured. The second are either bleached or cured; they may also be left to undergo a natural process of oxidization during maturation (➤ **passuluna (2)**). Black olives are available with different preservation treatments: *baresane* are sweetened with lime and caustic soda, *olive di Grecia* in brine with vinegar and oil. In Puglia, olives are sundried, transferred to jars and covered with sea salt, anise and fennel seeds, the ➤ **oliva infornata di Ferrandina** is sundried and baked. Gaeta olives are soaked in water, salted and preserved in brine. In the Marche, *olive strinate* are kept in a cool place and spiced with garlic cloves, wild fennel and orange or lemon zest. *Olive cazzate* are soaked in water and cured (Calabria and Puglia). In some paces, olives are reduced to a paste with oil and herbs, which is commonly referred to, improperly, as pâté.

olive fritte sweet black olives fried in oil for about 20 minutes with a few cloves of garlic. Puglia.

olive ripiene all'ascolana stuffed olives. Made with the PDO *oliva ascolana del Piceno* (➤ **oliva tenera ascolana**), big enough to contain a stuffing of mixed roast meats, ground and mixed with egg, grated Parmigiano and nutmeg. The pitted, stuffed olives are coated in flour, beaten egg and breadcrumbs, then fried. Ingredients and procedures are established by a specific protocol (the PDO recognition regards not only the olive itself, but also the recipe), which allows for variations in flavoring. The stuffed olives are served as an antipasto, as a snack or as an appetizer with aperitifs, and are also a traditional element in the ➤ **fritto misto all'ascolana**. Marche.

omaso omasum. The third stomach in ruminants (➤ **trippa**, tripe), where chewed food returns and starts to ferment: connected on one side with the ➤ **reticolo**, reticulum, and on the other with the ➤ **abomaso**, the abomasum or fourth stomach. Oval in shape it is also known as ➤ **centopelli**, ➤ **millefogli**, ➤ **foglietto** (aka **foiolo**), ➤ **libretto** (aka **libro**).

ombra literally "shadow." In northeastern Italy, in Veneto in particular, the term refers to a glass of wine and, by extension, the rite of drinking it. In traditional osterias and bottleshops, it is accompanied by ➤ **cicheti**, savory snacks. In the old days, it was common to drink simple white wine from the Veneto countryside, but today these have been replaced by finer wines, sometimes from other regions and even from abroad. Other names: ➤ **tajut** (Friuli) and ➤ **goto** (Verona).

ombrella aka **ombrellone** regional terms for ➤ **mazza di tamburo**, parasol mushroom.

ombrina bearded umbrine (*Umbrina cirrhosa*). A member of the Sciaenidae family, comparatively rare in the Mediterranean, it lives in brackish water near the mouths of rivers. Its delicate, boneless white flesh is highly prized and versatile in the kitchen. Often imported and sold fresh. Suitable for the same recipes as ➤ **spigola**, bass—from boiling to baking, from broiling to stewing—it can also be dried and smoked. Other members of the same family are the *ombrina boccadoro*, or meagre (*Argyrosomus regius*), and the ➤ **corvina**, or brown meagre (*Sciaena umbra*).

omelette omelet. French term for a savory or sweet preparation common all over the world consisting of lightly beaten eggs cooked in butter a skillet until the base sets. Unlike the Italian ➤ **frittata** which is flipped over and cooked on both sides and incorporates other ingredients (herbs, mushrooms, cheese, ham and so on), an **omelet** is cooked on one side only, stuffed with other ingredients and folded into a parcel or bundle.

omento a large fold of peritoneum that extends from one abdominal wall to another. Known in gastronomy as ➤ **rete**, caul.

onda, all' (aka **a risotto**) term used to describe the creamy effect produced when rice releases its starch, leaving the small grains well-defined to the palate, but creating a homogeneous whole that is neither too thick nor too liquid.

onopordo regional term for ➤ **cardo asinino**, lady's thistle.

ont Friulian term for ➤ **burro fuso**, melted butter or ➤ **burro chiarificato**, clarified butter.

opa Sicilian term for ➤ **boga**, bogue.

opi ca' nipitedda bream with lesser calamint. Traditional recipe of the fishing village of Ognina, in the province of Catania. The fish are stewed in a covered pot with oil, onion, garlic, potatoes, sprigs of calamint and water. Eaten with toasted day-old bread. Sicily

orapa Abruzzo dialect term for ➤ **spinacio selvatico** (➤ **buon enrico**, good King Henry).

orapi e fagioli good King Henry with beans. The beans and good King Henry (➤ **buon enrico**) are boiled separately, and the latter flavored in oil with garlic and chili. The ingredients are then amalgamated and served with pieces of bread and grated Pecorino. Recipe typical of Abruzzo, one of the many in the region to use good King Henry, common in the mountains and their foothills. The herb is also eaten in frittatas, sautéed or as a condiment for pasta. Abruzzo.

oraro Veneto term for ➤ **alloro**, bay leaf.

orata gilthead sea bream (*Spaurus aurata*). A member of the Sparidae family, much prized for its firm white flesh. Farmed in large tanks or in the open sea in large cages. Cooked broiled, baked, *en papillote*, or in a salt crust.

orata alla pugliese gilthead sea bream baked with sliced potatoes, garlic, minced parsley, grated Pecorino and oil. Puglia.

orata alla san Nicola marinated gilthead sea bream, garnished with field greens, oil, and lemon, and barbecued. A specialty of Bari. Puglia.

ordura egg-sized balls of boiled ➤ **tagliolini** mixed with butter, Parmigiano and beaten eggs, filled with pieces of ham and ➤ **Fior di latte**, dipped in beaten eggs and deep-fried in olive oil. Campania.

orecchie d'asino literally "donkey's ears." Regional term both for ➤ **consolida maggiore**, common comfrey, and for ➤ **piantaggine**, common plantain.

orecchie di Amman, in dialect aka **rècie de Aman** in dialect fritters made with the same dough as ➤ **crostoli**, and similar to other sweet fritters made in the Carnival period all over Italy with different names (➤ **cenci**). Strips of dough (flour, sugar, eggs, oil, grated lemon zest, liqueur, white wine) rolled up, fried and sprinkled with sugar or coated in honey and dusted with cinnamon. A pastry of Jewish origin that has become part of Venetian popular tradition. Veneto.

orecchie di lepre literally "hare's ears." Regional term for ➤ **silene rossa**, red catchfly.

orecchiette traditional ear-shaped fresh durum wheat or all-purpose flour pasta. Very popular throughout southern Italy, especially in Puglia, so much so that, from province to province, it has innumerable names: among others, ➤ **strascenate**, ➤ **chiancarelle**, ➤ **stagghiodde**, ➤ **recchietedde**, ➤ **recchie de prevete**, ➤ **fenescecchie**. Larger versions are known as ➤ **pociacche**, ➤ **pestazzuole**.

orecchiette alla materana served with a sauce of tomato, lamb, mozzarella and grated Pecorino. Basilicata.

orecchiette alla ricotta forte served with tomato sauce and finished in a skillet with onion, basil and a few tablespoons of ➤ ricotta forte. Puglia.

orecchiette alla rucola the tender leaves of ➤ **rucola selvatica** are boiled and the pasta is then cooked in the same water. The cooked pasta is served with lightly fried oil, garlic, chili, cherry tomatoes and the cooked rocket. Puglia.

orecchiette con cacioricotta served with skinned tomatoes and a generous sprinkling of fresh Cacioricotta. Puglia.

orecchiette con le brasciole served with rolls of horsemeat (➤ **brasciole**) and their sauce and a generous sprinkling of grated Pecorino. Puglia.

orecchiette con le cime di rapa served with broccoli rabe (➤ **cime di rapa**) mixed with desalted, boned anchovies dissolved in extra virgin olive oil. Puglia.

orecchio ear (pl. **orecchie** or **orcecchi**) pig's and calf's ears are generally cooked with the rest of the head (➤ **testina**) and/or parts such as the trotters and the tail (➤ **casoeûla**, ➤ **orion**).

orecchio di mare literally "sea ear." Regional term for ➤ **aliotide**, green ormer.

orecchio di san Pietro literally "St Peter's ear." Regional term for ➤ **aliotide**, green ormer.

orecchio di Venere literally "Venus's ear." Regional term for ➤ **aliotide**, green ormer.

orecchione common name for ➤ **gelone**, oyster mushroom.

orecchioni large half-moon ➤ **tortelli** stuffed with ricotta, Parmigiano and nutmeg. Served with meat or fresh tomato sauce. Emilia-Romagna.

organo regional term for *capone lira*, piper (➤ **capone**).

oriada (1) barley soup with milk, pancetta or lardo, onions, leeks, beans and potatoes. Typical of mounain areas. Lombardy.

oriada (2) Veneto regional term for a cut of beef.

origano oregano (*Origanum vulgare* and *O.*

heracleoticum). The first variety is gathered in central and northern Italy (Liguria, Lazio, Marche, Molise, but is less fragrant and common than the second, grown in the south and sold at markets in dried bunches. The Italian Ministry of Agriculture's database of native and/or traditional food products lists the following varieties: *origano del Molise, origano della Sicilia, origano selvatico della Calabria*. Oregano is widely used in the kitchen with vegetables and fish (anchovies), on ➤ **pizza** (Campania, ➤ **rianata** (Sicily) and ➤ **sardenaira** (Liguria), to dress salads (➤ **caprese**), with pickles and with tomatoes. Common and regional names: ➤ **cornabusa**, ➤ **erba acciuga**, ➤ **rigano**.

orilletas strips of fried pastry covered with honey. A typical Carnival treat. Sardinia.

orion aka **oriot** "pig's ears" in dialect. The two terms actually refer to a whole pig's head boned, boiled in water, cut into strips and dressed with a hot sauce of flat-leaved parsley, sage, onion, carrot, celery, red pepper, garlic, desalted anchovy and chili (➤ **spagnolin**), well minced, lightly fried and bathed with vinegar and white wine. A recipe typical of the Langhe hills in the province of Cuneo. Piedmont.

Ormea whole or part-skimmed raw cow's milk cheese, similar to ➤ **Bra**, produced in the southern part of the province of Cuneo. The fresh version is eaten after a month, the mature after eight months and more. Piedmont.

orobanca common name, derived from the scientific name, for ➤ **succiamele delle fave**, bean broomrape.

ortica nettle (*Urtica dioica*). The sweet young tips and leaves are excellent in risottos, frittatas (➤ **frittata di ortiche**), fillings for pasta and pies (Liguria, Lombardy,

Piedmont, Veneto). They are also used as an alternative to spinach for the making of green pasta (➤ **pasta aromatizzata**).

orticaccio regional term for ➤ **luppolo**, hops.

orzetto alla trentina pearl barley soaked in water and slow-cooked with carrots, potatoes, and, often, a ham bone or pig's trotter. Typical of the province of Trento. Trentino-Alto Adige.

orziada Sardinian term for ➤ **anemone di mare**, sea anemone.

orzo barley (*Hordeum vulgare*) cereal cultivated since the Neolithic age and at every latitude for the production of animal feed, of flour and bread, malt and fermented drinks. Decorticated barley and pearl barley are obtained from the grains with their husks removed. Pearl barley, which does not require prior soaking or long cooking, is at is best in soups and stews, decorticated barley is roast and used in infusions or as a coffee surrogate. The Italian Ministry of Agriculture's database of native and/or traditional food products lists the following varieties: *orzo agordino* (Veneto) and *orzo perlato dell'alto Lazio*, made from barleys grown round Acquapendente, in the province of Viterbo (Lazio). Pearl barley is used in the kitchen especially in northeast Italy and the Val d'Aosta. Recipes include: ➤ **gerstsuppe**, ➤ **orzetto alla trentina**, ➤ **peilà d'orzo**, ➤ **seupa a la ueca**, ➤ **seupa de gris**, ➤ **uardi e fasui**.

orzotto pearl barley cooked following the same technique as risotto.

osei aka **oseleti scapaa** aka **scapati** common or regional names for ➤ **uccelli scappati**.

oseleti a lo speo small birds (thrushes, larks, warblers, snipe), plucked but not gutted, alternated on a spit with slices of lardo and bay or sage leaves, cooked brushing with oil and basting with their own juices. May also be cooked in the pan on wooden skewers. Veneto.

oss de mord aka **ossa da mordere** "bones for biting." Very hard but crumbly cookies made of flour, butter, sugar, almonds, Marsala, cloves and cinnamon, usually served with Vin Santo or Moscato. Lombardy.

oss in bögia pork ribs, pig's trotters, head and tail are steeped in brine with salt, pepper, nutmeg, cloves, bay leaves, garlic cloves and red wine in an earthenware pitcher (*ola*). The various parts are then washed in running water and cooked, covered with water for a couple of hours. After one hour Savoy cabbage, potatoes and dried chestnuts are added to the pot. A specialty of the Swiss Cantone Ticino.

osso bone. Thanks to their connective tissue, rich in collagen, and their mineral salts, the bones of butchered animals, especially cows and pigs, are important in the kitchen. Collagen soluble in water, produces gelatin (➤ **gelatina**), and lightly roasted bones are used to make base sauces (➤ **fondi**). Pork butchers use bones to mature prosciutto, and bone marrow is an essential ingredient in dishes such as ➤ **risotto alla Milanese**, is extracted from long calf's bones. A cut of beef on the bone makes mixed boiled meats and their broth tastier.

ossobuco a slice of leg of veal (➤ **geretto**) cut through the bone with a central cavity full of marrow (➤ **midollo osseo**). Similar slices may also be cut from turkey legs.

ossobuco alla fiorentina slices of veal (➤ **ossobuco**), coated in flour and browned in a skillet. After softening finely minced aromatic vegetables and herbs are softened in the pan juices, tomato passata is added. The meat is covered in the sauce and finished off slowly with water

or broth. Before serving it is garnished with grated lemon zest and minced basil. A classic Sunday lunch dish. Tuscany.

ossobuco alla milanese one-inch slices of leg of veal complete with bone and marrow, coated in flour and browned in butter with onions, finished off with white wine or broth, and garnished with a mixture of anchovy, lemon zest and flat-leaved parsley (➤ **gremolada**). Usually served with ➤ **risotto alla milanese**, though some prefer it with plain risotto flavored only with butter and onion or with puréed potatoes. Lombardy.

ossobuco alla reggiana slices of veal (➤ **ossobuco**), coated in flour browned with finely minced aromatic vegetables and herbs and finished with white wine (some people use Marsala), broth and a little tomato pasta. Served with ➤ **risotto alla milanese** or with rice cooked in broth and dressed with the sauce from the meat. A recipe typical of Reggio Emilia. Emilia-Romagna.

ossocolo aka **ossocollo** cured meat made with lean pork from the back of the pig's neck, salted and aromatized with cinnamon and cloves and cased in large intestines, which are wrapped with the mixture used to make ➤ **sopressa vicentina**. The meat is then bathed in hot water and carefully massaged. Secured with string, it is dried and aged for at least ten months. This prized delicacy was once served on special occasions. Veneto.

Ossolano d'alpe large whole cow's milk cheese with a rough rind and compact body. Produced in the mountain pastures of the Valdossola (province of Verbano-Cusio-Ossola) in the summer and aged through the winter. A particularly prized version is ➤ **Bettelmatt**, produced in the area of the same name. Piedmont.

ostia paper-thin unleavened flour wafer

used in confectionery to cover certain confections: eg, ➤ **torrone**, ➤ **cupeta**, ➤ **panforte**, ➤ **ricciarelli**, ➤ **ostie piene**.

ostie piene ostia sandwiches. Confection created in the monastery of Monte Sant'Angelo, in the province of Foggia. A large, egg-shaped ostia is spread with a warm mixture of toasted almonds, honey, cinnamon and cloves and covered by a second ostia. Puglia

ostrica bivalve hermaphrodite mollusk with an irregularly-shaped shell. Lives on rocky sea beds and is sometimes farmed. In Italy oyster farming has been somewhat supplanted by mussel farming, even in traditional areas such as the gulfs of La Spezia and Taranto, the Venice lagoon and the central and northern Adriatico. The most prized species is the European or round or flat oyster or belon (*Ostrea edulis*), local varieties of which are the *adriatica* and the *tarantina*, whereas the most served in restaurants are the Portuguese (*Crassostrea angulata*) and the concave or Japanese (*Cassostrea gigas*). Today most oysters consumed in Italy come from France. They are sold in sealed nets with a label indicating provenance and sell-by date and certifying depuration for 24 hours in controlled plants. They are normally eaten raw with a sprinkling of pepper.

ostriche alla tarantina shucked raw oysters flavored with a mixture of breadcrumbs, finely minced parsley and oil and baked in the oven for about ten minutes. The finest Italian oysters (*Ostrea edulis*) are to be found in Taranto, where they are traditionally farmed by lowering the larvae into the water attached to bundles of mastic and moving them into fresh water after a couple of months. Puglia

ova col pien hard-boiled eggs filled with sardines or herrings, capers, onion and cinnamon. A traditional Ash Wednesday dish in the Polesine area. Veneto.

ova murina cake said to have been specially created at the Convento delle Giummare in Sciacca (province of Agrigento), on the occasion of a visit by the Holy Roman Emperor Charles V. Egg yolks are whisked with sugar and the whites with salt. The two mixtures are blended with the addition of minced toasted almonds, cocoa and cinnamon and the resulting batter is refrigerated for six hours. The batter is then cooked into pancakes, which are spread with a cream of milk, candied pumpkin (➤ **zuccata**) and flour, and flipped over to form a parcel. They are served hot with a sprinkling of confectioner's sugar and powdered cinnamon. Sicily.

ovino ovine. Generic name for ruminants belonging to five genera, two of which (*Capra* and *Ovis*) are farmed. The first comprises goats, the second sheep. Both have been raised for their wool, meat and milk since the earliest human societies

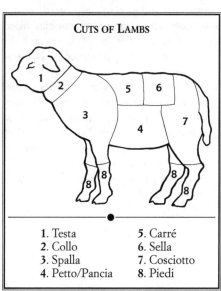

CUTS OF LAMBS

1. Testa
2. Collo
3. Spalla
4. Petto/Pancia
5. Carré
6. Sella
7. Cosciotto
8. Piedi

were formed, and in the Mediterranean goat- and sheep-rearing has given rise to the phenomenon of transhumance, important not only for economic reasons. In Italy, as in the rest of the industrialized west, this type of pastoral farming declined in the last century, but it is now enjoying certain revival in some areas. Sheep (*Ovis aries*) are mostly bred in Italy for their milk, which is used to make cheese. The most common breeds are the native ➤ **Sarda**, ➤ **Gentile di Puglia**, ➤ **Sopravvissana** and Leccese-Altamurana, followed well behind by the Massese, Bergamasca and Laticauda Campana. Sheep for meat are divided commercially into two categories: ➤ **agnello**, lamb, and *ovino adulto*, adult sheep, the second subdivided into ➤ **agnellone**, ➤ **castrato** and ➤**pecora**. The primal cuts are *coscia* aka *cosciotto*, leg; *spalla*, shoulder; *lombata*, loin and rib; *collo*, neck; and *pancia* aka *petto*, breast. Also important is sheep's and lamb's offal (➤ **frattaglie**), which in sheep-rearing areas is cooked regularly and used to make cured meats.

ovis molis shortcust pastry cookies filled with fruit jam. Typical of Arona on Lake Maggiore, in the province of Novara. Piedmont.

ovolo Caesar's mushroom (*Amanita caesarea*). A popular mushroom since antiquity on account of its delicate aroma. Best enjoyed raw in salads, but also excellent cooked (➤ **zuppa di cocchi**). Common and dialect names: ➤ **cocco**, ➤ **coccola**, ➤ **cocco giallo**, ➤ **fungo reale**, ➤ **bolé real**, ➤ **cocon**.

pP

Paarl loaf of bread created by joining two flat rolls together (the word **paarl** means "couple" in the local dialect). The dough is made of wholemeal rye flour (70%), all-purpose flour (30%), sourdough, water, salt, fennel seeds, cumin, fenugreek and sweet trefoil. Typical of the Val Venosta, in the province of Bolzano-Bozen. Trentino-Alto Adige.

pabassinas small cookies common, in numerous variations, all over the island. Traditionally made at the start of November for All Souls' Day, they are now available all year round. Made with a mixture of raisins, almonds, walnuts, wheat flour, orange zest, aniseed and nutmeg, they are baked in the oven, brushed with cooked wine must (➤ **mosto**, ➤ **vincotto**) and scattered with ➤ **traggera**, confetti sugar. Sardinia.

paccasassi dialect term for ➤ **finocchio marino**, samphire.

paccheri short durum wheat pasta shapes similar to ➤ **rigatoni**, though slightly shorter. Straight and either smooth or grooved, they go well with rich sauces or light summer sauces of cherry tomatoes and basil, and are also ideal for baking in the oven. Popular in the south of Italy.

paccheri al sugo di alici served with anchovy fillets, tomato, basil and fried and chopped sweet peppers (➤ **friarelli**). Campania.

paccheri allo scarpariello served with a simple sauce of cherry tomatoes, basil and chili. Some people add a sprinkling of Pecorino or Parmigiano, but not the purists. Campania.

pacciugo an ice cream of relatively recent invention (frozen cream, chocolate and fruit flavored ice-cream, chopped fresh fruit and cherries preserved in syrup), very popular in the province of Genoa. Liguria.

Paddaccio aka **Paddraccio** rare ewes's/goat's milk cheese, produced in summer in a few villages in the Pollino National Park, in the province of Potenza. Basilicata.

paddruni aka **pallone di fichi** boiled dried fig balls filled with walnuts and lime zest, soaked in fig syrup (➤ **cotto di fichi**), wrapped in orange leaves and dried in the oven. A specialty of Guardia Piemontese, in the province of Cosenza. Calabria.

padellaccia Umbrian dish traditionally associated with the day of the killing of the pig. Pieces of pork, pig's sweetbreads and other offal are cooked in oil with garlic, chopped onion and plenty of red wine, to which boiled beans and black pepper are added. Variations on the same recipe, generally associated with popular festivals, may be found in some inland areas of the Marche, of the Sabina area in Lazio, in Abruzzo, and in Campania (especially in the province of Benevento), where they add the pig's blood, replace the beans with potatoes or sweet peppers (➤ **papaccella**) and add aromatic herbs.

padellaccio all'ortica stew of pork loin cut into small pieces, browned with onion, garlic and sage, lubricated with white wine, and enriched with ripe tomatoes and boiled nettle tips. Traditionally served with chestnut flour polenta. Typical of the Monte Amiata area. Tuscany.

padellotto a dish of mixed calf's and cow's offal—heart, liver, sweetbreads, spleen, kidneys, intestines and so on—cut into pieces, browned in lard, and stewed in broth and white wine. Traditionally accompanied in Rome by a side dish of artichokes. Lazio.

paesana, alla literally "country-style." Term used to describe rustic, "authentic" dishes, generally soups, stews or omelets. Also used as a translation of the French *paysanne*: diced potatoes, carrots, cabbage, and turnips (→ **dadolata**, mixed diced vegetables) used as a garnish, in soups, or as a → **fondo di cottura**, or base, for braised meats (→ **brasare**, to braise).

paeta rosta al malgaragno turkey roast with pomegranate. The turkey is roast whole in the oven and basted with pomegranate juice. It is then cut into pieces and smothered in a sauce made from its chopped innards, fried in butter, and more pomegranate juice. A recipe typical of the city of Vicenza. Veneto.

pagello sea bream. The name may refer to any of the following: → **fragolino**, common pandora, (*Pagellus erythrinus*), → **occhialone** aka **occhione**, European seabream (*P. centrodontus and P. bogaraevo*), and → **pagello bastardo**, axillary seabream (*P. acarne*), all members of the Sparidae family. The first two may be baked in the oven, used as an ingredient in soups and stews, and, if large, broiled. The third has drier flesh and is unsuitable for broiling. Other common and/or regional names: → **luvaro**, → **mafrone**, → **parago**, → **pezzogna**.

paglia e fieno literally "straw and hay," fresh or dried egg fettuccine, tagliatelle or tagliolini, yellow and green in color, some of the strands being flavored with spinach. A relatively recent invention, also available commercially.

Paglierina fresh, flat cheese with or without a bloomy rind. Produced with mixed milks in the provinces of Cuneo and Turin, it has a firm rind and a soft, creamy center. Piedmont.

pagnotta del doge baked cake of bread dough, lard (nowadays butter), eggs, honey, treacle (nowadays sugar), walnuts, chopped dried figs, vanilla and orange or lemon essence, said to date from the dogeate of Silvestro Valier, 1694-1700). Typical of the village of Villadose, in the province of Rovigo. Veneto.

pagnotta pasquale leavened dome-shaped sweet loaf (made of flour, eggs, sugar, lard, vanilla and lemon zest), traditionally baked at Easter in Sarsina, in the province of Forlì-Cesena, now available all year round. Emilia-Romagna.

pagnottine santa Chiara small flour and potato flatbreads filled with anchovies sautéed in oil, vinegar and tomato. Typical of Naples. Campania.

pagro common sea bream (*Pagrus pagrus*). A member of the Sparidae family, reminiscent of the → **dentice**, dentex, and → **orata**, gilthead sea bream, and cooked in the same way.

pain des Salasses baked cake similar to a flattish → **panettone**, dotted with walnuts and chocolate. Val d'Aosta.

pain perdu sweet fried bread. Slices of white bread dipped in milk flavored with vanilla or cinnamon, egg and sugar, and fried in butter. Similar to Lombard → **panduls**. Val d'Aosta.

pais aka **paiz** marinade of wine or vinegar, onion, herbs and spices, suitable for game, red deer venison and hare in particular. Typical of the Carso area. Friuli-Venezia Giulia.

paisanotta di Druent bread shaped like an open book made with soft wheat flour, water and brewer's yeast. Specialty of

Druento (province of Turin). Piedmont.

paisel a variation on ➤ **sguazet di fratta-glie**, an offal stew. Calf's lungs, heart and spleen parboiled, finely chopped and stewed in water or meat broth flavored with bay leaves and thickened with toasted flour. Trentino-Alto Adige.

pajata aka **paiata** Roman dialect name for the fourth compartment (➤ **abo-maso**, abomasum) of the stomach of a calf, lamb or kid. The stomach is cut into three to six inch strips and tied at the ends to retain the chyme, partly digested milk. The strips may be broiled on their own, but are most famous as the main ingredient in the condiment for ➤ **rigatoni con la pajata**. Lazio.

palabirabrot flat oval fruit loaf made with a dough of bleached rye flour (70%), all-purpose flour (30%), pieces of dried pear, water, sourdough, salt, raisins, fennel seeds, cumin, fenugreek, cinnamon and lemon. Typical of the Val Venosta, in the province of Bolzano-Bozen. Trentino-Alto Adige.

palacinche aka **palacinke** crêpes filled with apricot jam or hazelnut cream. A dessert of Croatian and Slovenian origin. Friuli-Venezia Giulia.

palamida another name for ➤ **tonnetto**, skipjack tuna or little tunny.

palamita bonito (*Sarda sarda*). Similar to the ➤ **tonno**, tuna, and ➤ **sgombro**, mackerel, this member of the mackerel family reaches a maximum length of 25 inches and may weigh up to five pounds. Its compact, red meat may be broiled, fried, soused, stewed or preserved in oil. Included in the Italian Ministry of Agriculture's database of traditional and/or native food products.

palamita del mare di Toscana type of bonito fished off the islands of the Tuscan Archipelago in the late spring and early summer. At its best preserved in oil, flavored with bay leaves, pepper and chilli (➤ **zenzero (2)**). A Slow Food presidium has been set up to promote the technique. Tuscany.

palassiole Veneto name for newborn sardines (➤ **novellame di pesce**, fry).

palata popular long bread loaf with pointed ends weighing about a pound. Also available in a larger version, known as a *palatone*. Campania.

paletta di Coggiola rare ham promoted by a Slow Food presidium, produced today by only two pork butchers in Coggiola (province of Biella). Pork top shoulder is trimmed of fat, divided into two symmetrical parts and preserved in brine for 15-30 days. The parts are then cured with a mixture of local herbs and cracked black pepper, pressed into a natural intestine (or, more commonly, the bladder), secured and hung to age. May be eaten boiled after 20 days or raw, aged for at least four months. Piedmont.

pallette Pisan name for a polenta layered with sauce like ➤ **matuffi della Garfag-nana**. Tuscany

pallone di fichi another word for ➤ **paddru-ni**, boiled fig balls.

Pallone di Gravina spherical cow's cheese. Produced mainly in the province of Matera (once in the area round the town of Gravina, in the province of Bari, from which it takes its name) with techniques similar to those used for ➤ **Caciocavallo**. At its best after one year's aging. Basilicata, Puglia.

pallotte cac' e ova fritters of grated Pecorino, bread soaked in milk, eggs and herbs. Named from the "cheese-and-egg" cooking technique (➤ **cac' e ova**), typical of the Abruzzo region.

pallotte del pastore ricotta and Pecorino patties in tomato sauce. Abruzzo, Molise.

pallottoline di riso alla napoletana balls of rice bound with eggs, flavored with cheese and nutmeg, coated in flour, dipped in beaten eggs, fried in oil and served in chicken or beef broth. Campania.

pallottoline dolci di mascarpone balls of ➤ **mascarpone**, eggs, crushed amaretti cookies, breadcrumbs, grated Parmigiano-Reggiano, cinnamon and other spices, breaded and fried. In one variant, the Parmigiano-Reggiano is replaced with crushed cloves. Lombardy.

palomba aka **palombaccio** central Italian terms for ➤ **colombaccio**, wood pigeon.

palomba all'orvietana another name for ➤ **palomba all'umido nero,** a wood pigeon recipe probably of Renaissance origin.

palomba all'umido nero wood pigeon with black olives. An elaborate recipe probably of Renaissance origin. A sauce is made by crushing the heads and wings of the wood pigeons (➤ **colombaccio**), stirring in garlic, cloves, peppercorns, onion, sage and rosemary, and cooking the resulting mixture in extra virgin olive oil with vinegar, black olives and lemon zest. The wood pigeons themselves are roast on the spit, quartered and finished off in the pan with the filtered sauce mixed with the roasting juices from the ➤ **leccarda**, dripping pan. Umbria.

palomba alla ghiotta aka **palomba alla leccarda** wood pigeon (➤ **colombaccio**), plucked but not gutted, roast on a spit with bay leaves and prosciutto. The cooking operation takes place over a dripping pan (➤ **leccarda**), usually made of plated copper, in order to collect the roasting juices, which are then mixed with oil, wine, prosciutto, sage, garlic and capers. The resulting sauce, with the addition of a crushed boned anchovy, is used first to flavor the cooked bird, then pushed through a sieve and spread on slices of toasted bread to accompany the dish. Umbria.

palomba alla todina recipe similar to ➤ **palomba alla ghiotta**, from which it differs inasmuch as it is cooked in two stages using the ➤ **arrosto morto** technique. The pigeon is first roast on a spit, then gutted and quartered. It is finished off in an earthenware pot with extra virgin olive oil, its own entrails, white wine, onion, prosciutto, sage, black olives, capers and lemon and orange wedges. The pan juices are then pushed through a sieve and poured over the meat, which is served with slices of toasted bread.

palombo smooth hound. Name for the various sharks of the Triakidae family. Present in the Mediterranean are the common smooth hound (*Mustelus mustelus*), the starry smooth hound (*M. asterias*), and the black-spotted smooth hound (*M. punctulatus*). Common off Sicily, where they move in shoals over sandy and muddy sea beds, they should be marinated in oil and broiled or baked in the oven. In Sardinia, they boil the meat and serve it with ➤ **burrida**, a marinade.

palpiton traditional baked cake in some villages of the lower Valle dell'Elvo, especially Mongrando, in the province of Biella. Round in shape and dark brown in color, it is made with bread soaked in milk, crushed amaretti cookies, eggs, pears, sultanas, lemon zest, cocoa and Fernet. Piedmont.

pampapato skullcap-shaped cake. Dedicated to the Pope, created in 1580 from an idea of Alfonso II d'Este, and still produced both artisanally and commercially. Made from a mixture of cake flour, sugar, honey, sweetened bitter cocoa, toasted almonds, a mixture of spices (the composition is variable, but cinnamon and cloves are ever present), diced candied citron and orange and grated orange zest (today some people also add wine and/or coffee). Molded into the appropriate shape and baked in the oven, it is allowed to rest in a cool, damp place for two to three weeks (according to tradition, it used to be put outside on windowsills and balconies to keep it moist), and finally coated with melted chocolate. A specialty of Ferrara, the cake is not dissimilar from other types of ➤ **pan pepato**. What is special about it is its name (a cake worthy of Popes or for Popes), which has been registered at the city's Chamber of Commerce. Emilia-Romagna.

pampascione regional term for ➤ **lampascione**, grape hyacinth bulb.

pampavia slightly convex-shaped, small round cookies made of flour, eggs and sugar. Specialty of Ceresole d'Alba, in the province of Cuneo. The name is supposedly a contraction of *pan di Pavia*, "bread of Pavia," while the dialect name **pupe 'd monia**, "nun's breasts," refers to the shape of the cookies. Piedmont.

pampepato another name for ➤ **pan pepato**.

pampuglie regional name for ➤ **cenci**, fried pastries.

pan biscotto crumbly, crisp bread available in different shapes and sizes. The dough is made of flour, natural yeast, kitchen salt, water and, sometimes, extra virgin olive oil and lard, and is baked twice: the first time for 35-45 minutes at 210-240°C, the second for five to 40 hours at 140°C. Stored in a dry place, it stays fragrant for up to six months. Produced all over the region, especially in the southern part of the province of Vicenza and the Polesine area. Veneto.

pan brioche variously shaped bread made from brioche dough (➤ **pasta brioche**), often served, lightly toasted, with pâté and foie gras.

pan brodegh bread made from a dough of rye flour and a small percentage of wheat flour dotted with chopped dried figs and raisins. A specialty of the Valtellina, in the province of Sondrio. Lombardy.

pan caciato bread loaf made from a dough of soft wheat meal, water, salt, sourdough starter (➤ **biga**), extra virgin olive oil (or lard), pepper, walnuts and grated Parmigiano-Reggiano and Pecorino. Umbria.

pan carré soft white bread loaf (derived from the French *pain de mie*) made from a dough of cake flour, butter, milk and brewer's yeast. Baked in the oven in characteristic rectangular molds. Ideal for sandwiches, toast, toasted sandwiches and, crusts removed, for canapés.

pan casciolo regional term for ➤ **casciomaci**, great pignut.

pan co l'ua soft sweet raisin bread with a very thin crust. The loaf may be long, banana-shaped or round. Veneto.

pan co' santi aka **pane dei morti** fruit loaf made from bread dough to which chopped walnuts lightly fried in lard, raisins revived in hot water or wine, sugar (or honey) and black pepper are added. Today the lard is often replaced by olive oil, the walnuts by pine kernels, almonds and/or hazelnuts. Traditionally baked on All Saints' Day. A richer Christmas version (*pane dicembrino*) contains candied fruit and mixed spices. Tuscany.

pan coi fichi fruit loaf, now rare, made of all-purpose flour, yeast, sugar and chopped dried figs. Typical of the province of Milan and some parts of the province of Bergamo. Lombardy.

pan cor fenoceto aka **biscotto di Lerici** sweet loaf made of flour, sugar, aniseed and egg whites whisked to a peak. Typical of Lerici, in the province of La Spezia. Liguria.

pan d'Oropa sweet loaf of flour, potato flour, yeast, eggs, sugar and cocoa, baked in the oven in a plum cake mold. Typical of the Biella, it is believed to have been created in around 1935 by a group of women who wanted to send Italian soldiers engaged in the Ethiopian campaign foodstuffs that were nourishing and tasty, and whose fragrance would stay intact despite the long journey and change in climate. Named for the sanctuary of Oropa, dedicated to the Madonna Nera, or Black Madonna, a few miles from Biella itself. Piedmont.

pan d'orzu or **pan d'ordiu** another name for ➤ **carpasinn-a**, barley bread.

pan de fighi bread dough kneaded with dried figs and raisins and baked in the oven. Friuli-Venezia Giulia.

pan de frizze rare bread made from a dough of cake flour and rye flour dotted with ➤ **ciccioli**, pork scratchings.

pan de mei aka **pan meino** cake once made with millet flour, now with wheat and coarsely ground cornflour, eggs, sugar, butter and elder flowers (the same dough is also used to make the smaller *meini*). Traditionally eaten in the Milan area with *panera* (lightly whipped cream) on the day of San Giorgio, the patron saint of milkmen.

pan de molche traditional bitter-flavored, extremely nourishing bread loaf. Dark in color, it is made of bread dough enriched with ➤ **sansa**, the residues from the oil press (today often replaced by olive paste), and extra virgin olive oil. Typical of the Lake Garda area in the province of Trento. Trentino-Alto Adige.

pan de mort aka **pane dei morti** "bread of the dead." Flat sweet bread rolls, about three inches long, made of flour, yeast, egg whites, crushed cookies or amaretti, dried fruit, sugar and white wine, and baked on ostia wafers (➤ **ostia**). They resemble bones and are made on November 2, All Souls' Day. May be stored in metal boxes. Typical of Milan. Lombardy.

pan dei dogi oblong cookies made from a paste of flour, wine, almonds, raisins and pine kernels, and decorated with almonds. Veneto.

pan del lupo common name for ➤ **primavera**, cowslip.

pan dell'orso cake made from a mixture of almonds, honey, sugar, eggs and butter, coated with chocolate. Abruzzo.

pan di ramerino soft bread roll, typical of Prato and Florence, traditionally baked in the Easter period, now all year round, from a dough of tender wheat flour, natural yeast diluted in salt and water, rosemary and raisins (optional) and brushed with beaten egg yolks. Tuscany.

pan di Spagna sponge cake.

pan doss 'd Malgrà sponge cake made from a mixture of flour, yeast, sugar, butter and eggs, baked in a plum cake mold. A more rustic version is made with wholemeal flour and chestnuts. A specialty of Rivarolo Canavese, in the province of Turin, where Malgrà is the name of the local 14th-century castle. Piedmont.

pan duls slowly baked fruit loaf made from a mixture of day-old bread, amaretti cookies, milk, eggs, raisins, pine kernels, vanilla, lemon zest and cinnamon, Typical of the Valli Ossolane area (province of Verbano-Cusio-Ossola). Piedmont.

pan fritu or **pan fritto** sheet of bread dough cooked on a hot plate and sprinkled with salt or sugar. Liguria.

pan giallo another word for **pangiallo**, a Christmas cake.

pan martin black, sweetish bread made from a mixed dough of wheat and chestnut flour. Liguria.

pan molle another Tuscan name for ➤ **panzanella**.

pan negru Ligurian dialect term for ➤ **pane nero di Pigna**.

pan nociato aka **pannociato** one of the many sweetish breads typical of Marche and Umbria, made with normal bread dough enriched with yeast dissolved in milk, chopped walnuts, cooked grape must, lemon zest, chopped dried figs, fresh Pecorino, butter (or olive oil), eggs, salt and pepper. In the Marche, it is made in vive the province of Urbino e Pesaro, on and around November 2, All Souls' Day, the Day of the Dead; elsewhere in the province, it is popular throughout the winter. The Umbrian version, typical of Todi, in the province of Terni, is made from bread dough, walnuts, grated fresh Pecorino, extra virgin olive oil, salt and pepper. Local variants abound; they include the addition of raisins, chopped cloves, red wine (such as the local Sagrantino di Montefalco) and lard. The dough is shaped into small loaves, which are set aside to leaven before baking in the oven. Marche, Umbria.

pan pepato aka **pampepato** aka **panpepato** ancient baked cake present, with differences, in Tuscany and Umbria. According to popular tradition, the Tuscan version was created by Nicolò de Salimbeni of Siena in the 13th century. The recipe has undergone alterations over the centuries. For example, at the end of the 17th century, the number of ingredients was fixed at 17, like the contradas that compete in the Siena Palio. Today the mixture is made up of toasted hazelnuts, coarsely chopped almonds and walnuts, cubed candied citron and orange zest, pine kernels, raisins, bitter cocoa and mixed spices (including cinnamon, nutmeg, coriander and pepper, bound with flour and warm honey.

The version made in the province of Terni is simpler. Popular chiefly at Christmas, the mixture is made with cooked wine must, flour, cocoa, honey, candied fruits, black pepper, walnuts, almonds and raisins. Tuscany, Umbria.

pan pist crushed dry bread. The name also refers to a rustic soup made by cooking the crushed bread in meat or vegetable broth with the addition of butter. The soup is served with grated cheese, and sometimes an egg yolk is beaten in. Piedmont.

pan scafetò leaf-shaped twice-baked bread (➤ **pan biscotto**) named for the shelf in peasant houses on which it used to be stored. Veneto.

pan tajà another name for ➤ **gramolato**, a bread loaf.

pan zal aka **pan zalo** literally "yellow bread." Flatbread made of pumpkin flesh sweetened with molasses, at one time cooked in the hearth wrapped in Savoy cabbage leaves, like ➤ **pete** and ➤ **buiadnik**. Veneto/Friuli-Venezia Giulia.

panada aka **panata** a peasant dish that came into being to use up leftover bread, now often regarded as food for small children, the elderly and convalescents. In Emilia-Romagna, slices of bread are stirred into meat broth to form a porridge, to which chopped sage is added. The resulting thick soup (*panèda* in local dialect) is topped with butter and sprinkled with grated Parmigiano. The versions made in Piedmont and Lombardy (in the Milan area, the name is *pancott*) are similar. In Veneto, the same ingredients are used to make a creamier soup aromatized with cinnamon and drizzled with oil (in the past, dotted with butter).

panada sarda baked timbale or pie made with two sheets of pastry (durum wheat flour, salt and lard) with a variety of fillings: sun-dried tomatoes preserved in oil, pieces of eel with parsley; tomatoes, peas, lamb and parsley; chopped lamb and pork with parsley, garlic, sun-dried tomatoes and a pinch of saffron. Typical of the area east of Cagliari, especially in Assemini, and in the Montiferru area, in the province of Oristano. Sardinia.

panade dialect term in northeast Italy for ➤ **panada**, thick bread soup. In Friuli, the word also refers to a sort of soft frittata of day-old bread, cheese, bay leaf and fenel seeds.

panadina a small ➤ **panada sarda** pie. Sardinia.

panarda ritual, seemingly interminable lunch originally staged (especially in the province of L'Aquila) for weddings and local festivals, made up of at least 30 courses, including broth, boiled meat, pasta with mutton sauce (➤ **carrati al ragù di pecora**), stewed mutton (➤ **pecora alla callara**), boiled fava beans and fritters (➤ **ferratelle**). Abruzzo.

panata another name for ➤ **panada**, thick bread soup.

panatura breading. The coating of a food with breadcrumbs prior to frying.

pancetta cured meat made from belly pork and characterized by alternating fat and lean layers. Produced wherever pigs are bread, pancetta may be *tesa*, flat, or *arrotolata*, rolled, and is available in different typologies: with or without rind, natural, aged or smoked). The most common variety is the flat one, made in a slab, which is used above all as a condiment or cooking base as an alternative to lardo after aging for three weeks to two months. The PDO ➤ **pancetta di Calabria** and ➤ **pancetta piacentina** fit into this category, as do ➤ **rigatino** and ➤ **guanciale**, now popular outside their regions of origin, as well as the massive ➤ **tarese Valdarno**, a

Tuscan Slow Food presidium. Rolled pancetta, served at the table as a cured meat, is made from the leaner parts of the pig's abdomen, which are cut, trimmed, salted, cured with pepper and cloves, rolled, tied up, aged for variable periods and sometimes smoked. A member of the same category is *pancetta coppata*, wrapped around a piece of the pig's cervical muscle and aromatized with pepper and spices.

pancetta arrotolata dei Monti Nebrodi produced in winter in a number of villages in the Nebrodi mountains, in the province of Messina, from the bellies of pigs raised in the wild at a high altitude. The meat is lefty in a wood cupboard for 15 days in a cure of salt, wild fennel, garlic, oregano and vinegar. Rolled and tightly tied with string, it is dried, rubbed with more aromas such as pepper, chili, garlic and oregano, aged for three to four months. Especially prized is the pancetta made with pork from ➤ **suino nero dei Nebrodi**, the Nebrodi black pig. Sicily.

pancetta di Calabria PDO pancetta made throughout the region with belly pork from local pigs. The meat, skin on, is cut into a rectangle and salted for four to eight days. Washed with water and vinegar, it is sometimes coated with powdered chili. It is aged for at least a month. Calabria.

pancetta di Martina Franca pancetta made from boned back pork, salted and aromatized with pepper and a blend of Mediterranean herbs and spices. After steeping in brine for 20 days in brine, it is marinated in cooked wine for 24 hours. Rolled and tied up with string, it is hung up to dry for two weeks. Finally it is smoked over oak fires and aged for 60 to 100 days. Typical of the province of Taranto. Puglia.

pancetta di vitello arrotolata a common

dish in the Chianti area (province of Florence), made by covering a slice of belly pork with butter, salt, pepper and minced garlic, sage and rosemary, rolling it up and baking it in the oven with olive oil and white wine. Tuscany.

pancetta piacentina PDO cured meat made with belly fat from pigs on farms in Emilia and Lombardy authorized for the production of ➤ **prosciutto di Parma**. After trimming, the fat is cured with a mixture of sea salt, black pepper, cloves, sodium or potassium nitrates, sugar and ascorbate E 301. After 15 days in a refrigerated chamber, it is rolled, sometimes with the addition of lean pork, tied up, dried for a week and aged for at least 60 days. Emilia-Romagna.

pancetta steccata di Parma a pancetta produced almost everywhere in Emilia-Romagna since the 1960s as result of the virtual disappearance of native pig breeds, hence of increased difficulties in finding cheap rolled pancetta. The meat is rolled up, hand-sewn down the edges, pressed between two rods and secured with elastic strings. After drying for 24 to 36 hours, it is aged for five to six months (in ideal cellar conditions, for more than two years). Emilia-Romagna.

pancetta tesa lucana a pancetta, typical of the Pollino national park, produced with pork from pigs raised locally in the wild. The meat is cured in salt, pepper and natural aromas with a few preservatives for a couple of weeks (a fiery version made in the tiny village of Agromonte Magnano, near Latronico, in the province of Potenza, is coated with chili), then aged for 35 to 40 days. Basilicata.

pancia (1) cut of beef, roughly equivalent to plate.

pancia (2) name used in some regions for ➤ **rumine**, rumen.

pancott Lombard term for ➤ **pancotto** or ➤ **panada**, bread soups.

pancotto (pl. **pancotti**) literally "cooked bread." A soup developed all over Italy, with regional variations, to use up day-old or stale bread. The culture of butter, broth and Grana cheese on the one hand and that of water, oil and Pecorino cheese on the other mean that the dish can be classified into two groups: north and center-south. A northern example is ➤ **panada**, in all its various shapes and forms, a thick soup, almost a porridge. In the center-south, **pancotti** are flavored with different ingredients and are generally somewhat "dry," insofar as the bread used is usually "cooked" in aromatized water then drained. Members of the second group include: ➤ **pancotto calabrese**, ➤ **pancotto con l'olio**, ➤ **pancotto con i friarielli**, ➤ **pancotto con rucola e patate**, ➤ **pancotto pugliese e lucano**. Halfway between comes ➤ **pancöttu genovese**, sometimes made with meat broth, sometimes with water. The famous ➤ **pappa al pomodoro** (Tuscany) and ➤ **pancotto con i pomodori** (Umbria) can also be classified as "bread soups."

pancotto calabrese day-old bead rolls are lightly toasted and softened in vegetable broth (tomatoes, celery, garlic, parsley, bay leaf, olive oil, salt and pepper). They are then put into bowls and sprinkled with a generous amount of grated Pecorino (sometimes with the addition of eggs scrambled in the cooking broth). Calabria.

pancotto con i friarielli broccoli rabe (➤ **friarielli**) blanched and tossed in a skillet with oil, garlic and chili, to which day-old bread soaked in aromatized water is added. Campania.

pancotto con i pomodori diced tomatoes turned in a finely minced mixture of garlic and onion, bathed with white wine and cooked to a cream with pieces of day-old bread. The dish is served with roughly torn basil and a drizzle of extra virgin olive oil. Umbria.

pancotto con l'olio finely sliced garlic, tomatoes and day-old bread cooked in oil and water, then anointed with extra virgin olive oil and sprinkled with marjoram, pepper and/or grated cheese. Lazio.

pancotto con l'uvetta day-old bread broken up, simmered in water with raisins, and anointed with extra virgin olive oil. Popular recipe prepared as a snack for children. Umbria.

pancotto con rucola e patate sliced potatoes and rocket boiled in water with the addition of farmhouse bread. The water is drained off and the mixture is served in bowls with garlic cloves and pieces of chili. Puglia.

pancotto pugliese e lucano broccoli rabe, onions, wild chicory and cabbage boiled in water with cherry tomatoes, garlic, bay leaves and chili. The water is then drained off and the mixture is served anointed with extra virgin olive oil. Puglia, Basilicata.

pancöttu genovese pieces of day-old bread in meat broth flavored with garlic and oregano, drizzled with extra virgin olive oil and sprinkled with grated Grana. In another version the broth is replaced by water flavored with garlic, basil and tomatoes. Typical of Genoa. Liguria.

pancuculo regional term for ➤ **acetosella**, wood sorrel.

pandöçe dialect term for ➤ **pandolce genovese**.

pandolce typical of the Polesine area, in the province of Rovigo, a roll of leavened dough of flour, eggs, butter, sugar, raisins and lemon zest, baked in the oven. Veneto.

pandolce antica Genova a version of ➤ **pandolce Genovese**, a Christmas cake.

pandolce genovese, in dialect aka **pandöçe** traditional triangular Genoa Christmas cake, now available in bakeries and cake shops all year round. Over the course of time, its ingredients have increased in number and now include: pine kernels, raisins, candied citrus fruit zest, fennel seeds, orange blossom water, Marsala and vanilla. A more recent offshoot is ➤ **pandolce antica Genova**, which is flatter with a shortcrust pastry-like texture. Another relative is ➤ **pane del pescatore**, in the province of Savona. Liguria.

pandoli small rusks of flour, yeast, milk, eggs, sugar, and butter or lard. Typical of Schio and Malo, in the province of Vicenza. Veneto.

pandorato sandwich of two slices of white bread, crusts removed, filled with a slice of prosciutto and a slice of mozzarella or ➤ **Provatura**, dipped first in milk, then in four, then in beaten egg, deep-fried in oil and served as a warm antipasto. Typical of Rome. Lazio.

pandoro classico Christmas cake. Presumably created in the second half of the 19th century from the earlier ➤ **nadalin**, it has inherited some of the distinctive features and the name from the Venetian Renaissance *pan de oro veneziano* (once served in patrician dwellings coated with gold leaf). Another ancestor could be *pan di Vienna*, a French-inspired Hapsburgic cake rich in eggs and butter. The recipe for the cake, domestic and industrial, is extremely elaborate. The ingredients (flour, yeast, sugar, eggs, butter and powdered vanilla) are subdivided into three doughs, which are then kneaded and rolled out together repeatedly with the addition of small knobs of butter. The final dough is put into a mold, and when it swells to the brim, it is baked in the oven. The cake is served sprinkled with confectioner's sugar. A specialty of Verona. Veneto.

panduls snack, common until a few years ago, made with day-old bread soaked in milk and cinnamon, lightly coated in flour, and fried in foamy butter and sugar until caramelized. Lombardy.

pane bread. Bread was born with agriculture and humankind's transition to a more sedentary form of existence. Wild cereals seem to have been first used for nourishment (toasted, cracked, in infusions, as porridge) in around 10 000 BC. In the third and second millennia BC, the invention of millstones and ovens (in Egypt) led to the baking of bread. Proof of the fact is that remains of dough leavened by fermentation have been found dating from ancient Egypt and Neolithic Germany. Over the course of time, the consumption of bread has come to be a typically western, Mediterranean habit. Like wine, bread has assumed strong religious, not to mention political, connotations. As early as ancient Rome, the control of bread production constituted a political weapon (*panem et circenses*), and bread continued to be a tool of power at least until the *ancien régime*. Grain reserves were created, the price of bread was controlled, and important social figures such as the miller and the baker asserted themselves. Increases in the price of bread and bread famines were capable of triggering revolution and social upheaval. In the meantime, the 18th century also saw the invention of dough kneading machines and chemical powdered yeast. In Italy breads diversified to meet local customs and tastes, to the extent that the country now boasts hundreds of typologies definable as traditional. The shapes, sizes and textures of bread vary from north to south according to precise criteria. In northern regions, where polenta used to dominate and bread was a luxury, small, crisp, compact rolls now tend to prevail, along with well leavened, airy loaves. In the center and south of Italy, the preference is for larger, coaser-grained loaves, traditionally home-baked to last longer and more nourishing for peasants working in the fields. In Sicily they like to flavor bread with sesame seeds, in Alto Adige they are fond of "black" and wholemeal breads. In most southern regions, finally, they make wide use of durum wheat, well suited to the Mediterranean climate.

pane a birra "beer bread." Bread made in different shapes from a dough of all-purpose flour and brewer's yeast, common in most parts of Sicily.

pane a cassetta aka **pane in cassetta** Italian name for ➤ **pan carré**, sliced white bread.

pane a fittas day-old ➤ **spianata di Ozieri** (type of flatbread) cut into pieces and soaked for a few minutes in boiling salted water, drained and dressed with tomato sauce and a generous amount of grated Pecorino. Sardinia.

pane azzimo unleavened bread (from the Greek *ázymos*, yeast), baked by Jews during the Easter period. In Italy it is to be found mainly in the form of wafers (*mazzot*) in cities with large Jewish communities, such as Rome and Venice.

pane barbarià bread made from a dough of variable amounts of wheat and rye flour, yeast, water and salt. Typical of the Valle Maira, in the province of Cuneo. Piedmont.

pane bruno "brown bread." Used to be made from a variable mixture of flours of different cereals, now made with wholemeal flour. A typical product of the region's peasant tradition. Friuli.

pane cafone soft wheat bread produced in four different sizes: *cocchia* (long and flat), *pagnotta* (round and flat), *palatone* (a rounded parallelepiped), *palatella* (an eight-ounce loaf). Campania.

pane caliatu oven-baked rusk soaked in water before being dressed (*cunzatu*) with a variety of condiments. Used in the Aeolian Islands (province of Messina) to make a salad (reminiscent of → **panzanella**), with boiled potatoes, onions, capers, cucumbers, garlic and cherry tomatoes. Sicily.

pane carasau traditional durum wheat bread. After leavening, the yeast is shaped into very thin disks which are formed into a pile, divided by cloths, with a weight on top to prevent them from swelling. Baked singly they swell up like balloons, and each is split into two disks, which are, in turn, piled up one on top of another. They are then baked a second time one by one, at which point they release all their water and acquire color and crispiness. The total lack of water ensures the bread a long shelf life if kept in a dry place. Outside Sardinia the bread is often nicknamed *carta da musica*, "music paper," because it looks like the parchment on which sacred music used to be written. Sardinia.

pane casereccio di Genzano PGI bread made with a dough of all-purpose or cake flour leavened twice and sprinkled with bran flakes (→ **cruschello**) in between. Shaped into loaves and sticks, it has a thick brown crust and a soft, spongy crumb. Typical of the province of Genzano, in the province of Rome. Lazio.

pane co' bucu another name for → **cuccid-datu (1)**, a type of Sicilian bread.

pane con gerda triangular or oval bread roll made with a dough of cake flour, pork scratchings (→ **ciccioli**: in dialect, *gerda*, *edra* or *erda*), salt, water and natural and brewer's yeast, and baked in a wood oven. Sardinia.

pane con i cicoli twice-leavened soft wheat bread dotted with pork scratchings (→ **ciccioli**). Campania.

pane con la giuggiulena durum wheat bread covered with sesame seeds (→ **sesamo**), known as **giuggiolena** in local dialect. Typical of Reggio. Calabria.

pane con pomodoro, in dialect aka **pani cun tamatica** a sort of bread pouch stuffed with fresh tomato halves crushed and flavored with pepper, salt, garlic and olive oil. Created to use up leftover bread dough, it is baked in the oven. Typical of the southern part of the island, especially the Sulcis area. Sardinia.

pane con ricotta flat, triangular bread roll made of soft flour, ewe's ricotta, natural yeast and a pinch of brewer's yeast, and baked in the oven. Sardinia.

pane cottu dialect term for → **pancotto**, bread and vegetable soup.

pane del bollo soft wheat bread named for the ball of dough (*bollo*) placed at the center of each loaf after long leavening. Traditional specialty of Piacenza. Emilia-Romagna.

pane del pastore day-old bread softened with tomato, bay leaf, oregano and olive oil. Towards the end of the cooking process, eggs are added and left to poach whole. Basilicata.

pane del pescatore (1) rare bread made from a dough of durum wheat flour, water, salt, natural yeast, salted anchovies and black olives. The same dough is used to make → **frese**. A specialty of Sapri, in the province of Salerno. Campania.

pane del pescatore (2) a sort of flat, compact ➤ **panettone** typical of the western Riviera (province of Savona), based on ➤ **pandolce genovese**. Liguria.

pane di Altamura Italy's only PDO bread. Shaped like a broad-rimmed hat, a loaf weighs up to eight pounds. Made from twice-ground local durum wheat bran and sourdough. Twice-leavened, it it is baked in traditional wood-fired stone ovens. A Slow Food presidium is working to ensure the transparency of the production chain and to make a census of durum wheat producers and traditional flour mills in the northwestern Murgia area, where the town of Altamura is situated. Puglia.

pane di Carlo Alberto now rare traditional bread made from cake flour and a special gluten-rich flour, chopped walnuts and anchovies, water, salt, yeast, olive oil, lard and, sometimes, pepper. Baked in a wood-fired oven. Piedmont.

pane di castagne briefly leavened bread made of chestnut purée, wheat flour, water, sourdough, salt and sugar. A specialty of Cosenza. Calabria.

pane di Cerchiara giant loaf made of wheat flour (60%), bran, sourdough and water from mountain streams. Baked in a wood oven. A specialty of Cosenza. Calabria.

pane di Chiaserna slowly leavened bread made with soft wheat flour and sourdough. Typical of the province of Pesaro. Marche.

pane di Como renowned bread made from a well worked dough of all-purpose flour, water, natural yeast and salt. At its best baked in a wood-fired oven. Lombardy.

pane di Cutro bread produced in the village of Cutro, in the province of Crotone, with durum wheat bran, flour (25%), sourdough, water and sea salt. After a long, slow rising process, it is baked in a wood oven. Calabria.

pane di farina di neccio PDO long loaf made from chestnut flour (60%) (➤ **farina di neccio**), soft wheat flour (40%), water, salt and sourdough or ➤ **biga**, a type of sourdough starter. Typical of the Garfagnana area, in the province of Lucca. Tuscany.

pane di frutta another name for ➤ **zelten**, a rich ➤ **pandolce**.

pane di Lariano semi-wholemeal bread baked in wood-fired ovens, similar to ➤ **pane casereccio di Genzano**. Produced in the town of Lariano, in the province of Rome. Lazio.

pane di Laterza large loaf (it can weigh up to two pounds) made with twice-ground durum wheat flour and sourdough in Laterza, a town in the province of Taranto (Puglia). After six hours' leavening, it bakes for two hours in a stone oven. Puglia.

pane di mais al tartufo nero a sort of stiff polenta made of milk, cornflour, salt, Parmigiano and extra virgin olive oil. After cooling, it is supplemented with eggs (whites whisked to a peak), pepper and black pepper and baked in the oven. Umbria.

pane di Matera PGI bread made from durum wheat and natural yeasts obtained by fermenting local apricots. The rising process is long and slow, as is the baking in the oven. Can be kept for up to two weeks. Basilicata.

pane di Monreale long bread loaf made from a dough of durum wheat flour, natural yeast extracted from bran, water, milk and lemon juice (sometimes a small amount of brewer's yeast is also added), sprinkled with sesame seeds (➤ **sesamo**), and baked in a wood-fired oven. Typical of Monreale, in the province of Palermo (Sicily).

pane di Padula country bread made of a

blend of soft and durum wheat flours and baked in a wood-fired oven. Typical of the province of Salerno. Campania.

pane di patata potato bread. Made not only in northern Europe, but also in parts of the Mediterranean. In Italy, it is still baked in Emilia-Romagna, Tuscany, Puglia and Calabria by blending soft wheat or wholemeal flour, boiled potatoes and brewer's yeast.

pane di patate della Garfagnana aka **garfagnino** soft bread made with a dough of wheat flour, 15% mashed potatoes, a little bran and salt, kneaded with sourdough and baked in the oven. Cut into slices, it is served with local cured meats. A specialty of the Garfagnana area and the Valle del Serchio (province of Lucca). A Slow Food presidium plans to recreate the supply chain, linking farmers, stone mills and bakeries with wood-fired ovens. Tuscany.

pane di Pavullo bread with a crisp crust and soft crumb made from a dough of all-purpose and wholemeal flour, natural yeast (or sourdough) and lard. Produced in the province of Modena. Emilia-Romagna.

pane di riso rice bread. Made from a dough of equal amounts of rice and wheat flour, boiled rice, water and yeast. Typical of Pavia, though other versions exist elsewhere in Italy. Lombardy

pane di Rivello bread made from a dough of a mixture of three flours (wholemeal, all-purpose and cake) and traditional yeast. Produced in the province of Potenza. Basilicata

pane di Salisano large long unsalted loaf with three lengthwise surface slashes, baked in a wood oven. Typical of the province of Rieti. Lazio.

pane di san Martino a sweet raisin-enriched variant of ➤ **pan caciato**. Typically baked in the province of Perugia for the saint's day. Umbria.

pane di san Petronio twice-leavened flatbread made in Bologna from a yeast of flour, yeast, butter, oil, cream or milk, Parmigiano and ➤ **prosciutto crudo di Parma**. Served hot as a snack or with aperitifs. The recipe is registered at the Bologna Chamber of Commerce as one of the city's traditional specialties. Emilia-Romagna.

pane di san Siro sponge sandwich cake soaked in rum, filled with a cream of hazelnut-flavored butter and glazed with a chocolate and sugar icing. Traditionally baked in Pavia for the feast of San Siro (December 9). Lombardy.

pane di saragolla aka **pane saraolla** durum wheat bread made with the ancient *saraolla* cultivar. Typical of Benevento. Campania.

pane di senatore Cappelli bread made with the twice-ground grain of the prized Senatore Cappelli wheat cultivar. The variety, obtained by genealogical selection by Nazareno Strampelli in 1915, is named for the Abruzzo politician of the same name who promoted agrarian reform in his native region in the early 20th century. Typical of the province of Chieti. Abruzzo.

pane di Triora long-lasting bread made with all-purpose flour, water, salt and brewer's yeast, dusted with bran before baking. Typical of the village of Triora, in the province of Imperia. Liguria.

pane di Velletri bread typical of Velletri, in the province of Rome, made in loaves and characterized by "eyes" in the crumb. Lazio.

pane di zucca pumpkin bread. Made from a dough of all-purpose flour, boiled pumpkin flesh, brewer's yeast and salt. Emilia-Romagna.

pane frattau sheets of unleavened ➤ **pane carasau**, dipped in boiling water or beef stock and covered with tomato sauce, grated Pecorino and, often, topped with a poached egg. Sardinia.

pane frissu aka **pane indorau** bread dipped in beaten eggs, fried in lard and served with lardo and sausage. Sardinia.

pane giallo "yellow bread." Unsalted bread made with twice-ground durum wheat semolina and natural yeast. A specialty of Rome. Lazio.

pane guttiau sheets of unleavened ➤ **pane carasau** dressed with olive oil and salt, sometimes perfumed with garlic, and briefly heated in the oven. Sardinia.

pane indorau another name for ➤ **pane frissu.**

pane marocca rare homemade sweet version of ➤ **pane marocco di Montignoso**, in which the dough is dotted with raisins and aniseed. A delicacy of Massa-Carrara. Tuscany.

pane marocco di Montignoso bread made from a dough of soft wheat and buckwheat flour, yeast, water, oil, fresh black olives, minced rosemary and chili and salt, baked in a wood oven. Typical of the lowlands of the province of Massa-Carrara during the olive harvest, from November to March. Tuscany.

pane nero di Castelvetrano large round loaf made in the town of Castelvetrano, in the province of Trapani. Dark in color, sweet in flavor, made from a blend of stone-ground durum wheat wholemeal flour and ➤ **tumminìa**, an ancient Sicilian wheat variety. After leavening with a sourdough starter, loaves are baked in stone ovens fueled by olive branches. A Slow Food presidium supports the few remaining bakers, protects stone ovens and promotes the cultivation of the local wheat variety. Sicily.

pane nero di Coimo flat round loaf made with a dough of wholemeal rye flour (80-90%), soft wheat flour, water, salt, natural yeast and a pinch of brewer's yeast. Typical of the Val d'Ossola, in the province of Verbano-Cusio-Ossola. Piedmont.

pane nero di Pigna bread made with a dough of wholemeal flour, water, salt and brewer's yeast, sprinkled with bran before baking. Typical of the province of Imperia. Liguria.

pane pazzo similar to ➤ **schiacciata con l'uva**, a sweet flatbread.

pane pepato ring-shaped fruit loaf dotted with raisins, almonds, walnuts, candied fruit, nutmeg and pepper (*pepe* in Italian, hence the name), flavored with a glass of concentrated cooked wine must (➤ **sapa**). Marche.

pane purecasciu soft bread made from a dough dotted with onions and tomatoes. Typical of the province of Lecce. Puglia.

pane schiavone a type of ➤ **mostarda** of grape juice, toasted almonds and candied orange zest thickened with wheat flour. Calabria.

pane sciocco another name for ➤ **pane toscano**, Tuscan bread.

pane spiga well leavened bread made from a dough of soft wheat flour, sourdough and salted water. Typical of the province of Chieti. Named for the wheat ear (*spiga* in Italian) pattern on the crust. Abruzzo.

pane toscano Tuscan bread. Made from a dough of all-purpose flour and sourdough, famous for being totally unsalted, hence its nickname of *pane sciocco*, "stupid bread." The phenomenon dates from the 12th century, when the rivalry between Pisa and Florence reached its peak, and the Pisans blocked the trade in salt. Loaves are round or oval and the bread, when a day old or stale, is an important ingredient in many traditional regional recipes : ↣ **panzanella**, ↣ **ribollita**, ↣ **acquacotta**, ↣ **pappa col pomodoro**, ↣ **fettunta**, ↣ **minestra di cavolo nero**. Tuscany.

pane tradizionale di Lentini bread produced in the towns of Lentini and Carlentini, in the province of Siracusa. The crust is soft, hazel-brown in color and sprinkled with sesame seeds (↣ **sesamo**). The crumb is straw-yellow in color, compact, elastic and soft in texture. The classic loaf is "S"-shaped, but may also be ring-shaped or take the form of a cockerel. A Slow Food presidium has brought together bakers who still use traditional techniques. Sicily.

pane uddidu soup of mutton (or crushed lardo and parsley) broth with a generous amount of grated Pecorino cheese and day-old ↣ **spianata di Ozieri**, a flatbread. Sardinia.

panèda Emilia dialect term for ↣ **panada**, a bread soup.

panedda aglintesa grilled stretched curd cow's milk cheese. Sardinia.

panelle chickpea flour fritters often combined with ↣ **cazzilli**, potato fritters, as a panini filling. Chickpea flour (to which minced flat-leaved parsley or wild fennel may be added) is dissolved in water and mixed constantly until it achieves the required thickness. The batter is then poured into round or square molds and, once cooled, fried in hot oil. Sicily.

pànera coffee ice cream, cited in historical documents, made by bringing cream to the boil and folding in sugar, egg and ground coffe. Liguria.

panesiglio twice-leavened buns made with flour, milk, butter and eggs, enriched with raisins, and candied pumpkin and citron. The odd name would seem to derive from a Neapolitan dialect word for a slap violent enough to swell somebody's cheeks, a reference to the roundness of the bun. Campania.

panet rare mountain bread made with a dough of soft wheat flour, natural yeast, water and salt, baked in a wood oven. Typical of the Valle Maira, in the province of Cuneo. Piedmont.

panetto di fichi secchi fruit loaf made with dried figs, chopped toasted almonds, candied citron, cinnamon, cocoa, vanilla and candied orange zest. After drying, the mixture is pressed into a special tin and baked. A specialty of Monsampolo del Tronto, in the province of Ascoli Piceno. In the provinces of Ascoli Piceno (Marche) and Teramo (Abruzzo), it is the custom to eat the first loaves on November 11, San Martino's day. Marche, Abruzzo.

panettone a symbol of Milan and Italy's most popular Christmas cake. Made with a mixture of wheat flour, yeast, eggs, butter, sugar, sultanas and candied fruit. Tradtionally shaped like a cylinder with a domed top, the cake requires several lengthy risings. Historically, this yeasted cake is the most fortunate of a series of sweet and spiced breads which came into being in the Middle Ages as a result of the habit of celebrating important religious holidays with transfigured versions of daily bread: panettone is thus literally a "great big bread loaf." Easy to keep and transport, since the 1920s, it has been produced industrially with great success.

panettone basso a flatter panettone than the Milanese version, glazed with an icing of hazelnuts, egg whites, confectioner's sugar and vanilla. Created in Turin in around 1922 and produced all over the region. Piedmont.

panettone pasquale cake traditionally made during Easter week. A mixture of flour, yeast, milk, eggs and ↣ **Vin Santo** is allowed to leaven a little, then amalgamated with butter, olive oil, pine kernels, raisins, sugar, candied fruit, aniseed and lemon zest, and baked in the oven.

panficato a sort of rustic focaccia. The traditional version is made from a mixture of dried figs, bread dough and honey. A richer recipe adds walnuts, pine kernels, candied citrus fruit, dark chocolate, cinnamon, nutmeg and mixed spices. Tuscany.

panforte a cake typical of the province of Siena, where it is produced industrially and in households from October to December (to a lesser extent it is also made in Massa Marittima, in the province of Siena). It is believed to have been created in around the 13th century and derives from ➤ **pan pepato** and *melatello*, a focaccia enriched with honey and seasonal fruit. The dehydration of the fruit tended to give the cake an acidulous flavor, hence the name *pan forte*, "sour bread." Two typologies exist: black and white. The mixture of the first is older and is made by amalgamating chopped toasted almonds and walnuts, candied orange and melon, mixed spices (including cinnamon and coriander, flour and sugar). It is worked into a flat, round shape, dusted with flour and cinnamon, and baked in the oven on a tray covered with ostias. Il **panforte bianco** (aka **panforte margherita**, thus named in 1879 in honor of Margherita di Savoia) differs insofar as candied citron is used in lieu of melon and the cake is dusted with vanilla sugar. Also traditional is *panforte al cioccolato* (also known as *panforte delle dame*, panforte for ladies, on account of its more delicate flavor), created in 1820 by the confectioner Giovanni Parenti, which includes cocoa in the mixture and is covered with melted dark chocolate.

pangiallo aka **pan giallo** domed Christmas cake, yellow in color due to the presene of saffron. A mixture of warm honey, hazelnuts, pine kernels, almonds, candied citrus fruit, raisins, cinnamon, cloves and nutmeg (to which dark chocolate may also be added) is bound with flour, shaped and allowed to rest. Baked in the oven, it is covered with a water, sugar and saffron icing. In the past a flatter version was made, enriched with eggs and almond paste and glazed with chocolate and sugar icing. Lazio.

pangrattato fine breadcrumbs. Indispensable for breading (➤ **panatura**) and gratins (➤ **gratinare**) and also used to thicken sauces and soups, or to make a filling drier. In some regional traditions, it is used to dress pasta, vegetables and fish (➤ **pasta c'anciova e muddica atturrata**, ➤ **alici ammollicate**). An old family recipe in Piedmont is ➤ **pan pist**.

pani ca' meusa classic Palermo street food. A bread roll ➤ **muffoletta**) cut in half and filled with slices of boiled calf's lung and spleen turned in lard. Two versions exist: *schietta*, sprinkled with olive oil, and *maritata*, with the addition of strips of Caciocavallo cheese. Sicily.

pani cun arrescottu Sardinian term for ➤ **pane con ricotta**,

pani cun edra or **pani cun erda** another name for ➤ **pane con gerda**, a type of bread.

pani cun tamatica Sardinian term for ➤ **pane con pomodoro**, bread stuffed with tomatoes.

pani cunzato simple snack consisting of a freshly baked long bread roll, cut in half, filled with tomato slices, sardines, grated Sicilian Pecorino, seasoned with salt and pepper and anointed with extra virgin olive oil, then cut into slices. Sicily.

pani di Salemi votive bread loaves, made in

different shapes and sizes in the town of Salemi (province of Trapani) to decorate houses and churches during religious festivals. Sicily.

pani 'e saba small cakes whose shape changes from place to place. Once baked on All Saints' Day and Christmas Day with durum wheat flour, sour dough, cooked wine must or fig syrup (➤ **sapa** or ➤ **sapa di fichi d'India**, or, alternatively, ➤ **abbattu**), candied orange zest, raisins, honey, eggs, wild fennel, walnuts, almonds and pine kernels, brushed with a little ➤ **sapa**, and decorated with ➤ **traggera**, confetti sugar, or almonds. Sardinia.

pani nieddu traditional poor version of ➤ **civraxiu**, a type of bread made with bran flakes (➤ **cruschello**). In Italian, the name means "black bread." Sardinia.

pani ra Píana Sicilian term for ➤ **bukë**, a giant loaf. The name means "bread of Piana," the bread being a specialty of the town of Piana degli Albanesi, in the province of Palermo, where it is made.

paniccia another name for ➤ **panizza (1)**, chickpea polenta.

panicia a soup of vegetables, barley, beans and smoked pork. Typical of the Ladin valleys in the Dolomites. Trentino-Alto Adige.

panicielli baked bundles of citron leaves filled with sun-dried zibibbo grapes. Calabria.

panicocoli wafer made with a mixture of wheat flour, Vin Santo, aniseed, sugar, olive oil and anise liqueur, cooked with special red-hot irons. The latter are sometimes decorated with patterns (in the past with the coats-of-arms of noble families) that are stamped on the wafer. Today the wafers, which were traditionally made on Santa Lucia's day, are served with whipped cream. Umbria.

panigacci aka **panigazzi** thin disks of flour and water batter cooked in a griddle pan (➤ **testo**) and served with grated cheese and extra virgin olive oil. In Podenzana (Massa-Carrara), they are made in the same way with the same ingredients and eaten with cheese and cured meats. A specialty of the eastern Riviera and Lunigiana areas. Liguria, Tuscany.

panina gialla aretina a soft yellow bread loaf traditionally made at Easter in the Val di Chiana, the Casentino area and the Val Tiberina. The dough consists of wheat flour, brewer's yeast, saffron, warm water, raisins, oil and salt. Tuscany.

panino al lampredotto sandwich made with ➤ **lampredotto**, a type of tripe.

panino napoletano triangular bread roll made with a dough of soft wheat flour, water, milk, oil and brewer's yeast, filled with diced cured meats and cheese, rolled up strudel-like, brushed with beaten eggs and baked in the oven. Campania.

paniscia a risotto made by "toasting" rice in butter with onion, lardo and crumbled ➤ **salam d'la doja**. The mixture is bathed with red wine and, when this has evaporated, progressively supplemented with a soup made with strips of pork rind, beans, coarsely chopped celery, carrot, tomato and Savoy cabbage. A traditional dish in the province of Novara. Piedmont.

panissa (1) borlotti beans (➤ **borlotto**) boiled with pork rind, cut into strips, flavored with lighty fried lardo and crumbled ➤ **salam d'la doja**, to which rice is added. The mixture is lubricated with red wine and finished like a risotto with the occasional addition of broth and the bean cooking water. Unike ➤ **paniscia** of Novara, **panissa**, typical of the province of Vercelli, tends to be thick in texture;

it is said that a wooden spoon should be able to stand upright in it. Piedmont.

panissa (2) another name for ➤ **panizza (1)**, chickpea polenta.

panisse creamy soup of pumpkin, potatoes and leeks, thickened with flour. Recipe typical of the mountains of the province of Cuneo. Piedmont.

panizza aka **paniccia** aka **panissa** chickpea flour polenta. The polenta is allowed to cool and set and is eaten fried or cut into strips with spring onion, parsley and olive oil. A specialty of Liguria, but also of parts of southern Piedmont, such as the Valle Tanaro and Val Bormida, in the province of Cuneo, and the province of Alessandria. Piedmont.

panizza (2) a thick soup made with rice cooked in broth with wheat flour, grated Parmigiano, oil, butter and sausage. Typical of the province of Piacenza (Emilia-Romagna).

panmiz aka **panmuez** a mixture of day-old bread (rye or wheat, cubed and soaked in milk), eggs, sugar and raisins cooked in butter. Trentino-Alto Adige.

panna cream. The fat part which rises to the top of standing milk or is separated by skimming in a centrifuge. It is used mainly for making butter but has many other applications in the confectionery industry. Cream contains 25-40% fat but the proportions of its other constituents are almost identical to those of the original milk. It is used in the kitchen to bind condiments, sauces and veloutés. Cream-based condiments exist in regional traditions, but they are confined to mountain areas where the milk of native cow breeds was of prime quality. Italian confectionery boasts countless cakes and pastries *with* cream. Confections *of* cream are not so numerous, but certainly the most famous is ➤ **panna cotta**, now produced in-

dustrially as well as at home. Cream also features in numerous custards, such as ➤ **cavollat**, ➤ **crema del Lario**, ➤ **crema di Cogne**, ➤ **fiocca**, ➤ **fiòco**.

panna cotta the Piedmontese dessert that has most success outside the region's borders. It consists of liquid cream solidifed with isinglass and may be flavored with different ingredients, such as woodland fruits, chocolate and so on. Piedmont.

pannarella small Easter loaves made with a mixture of flour, water, eggs, oil and sugar, dipped in beaten egg and baked in the oven. A specialty of Matera. Basilicata.

Pannerone di Lodi full-cream, raw cow's milk cheese. Its distinguishing characteristic is the total absence of salting in any form, which makes for a complex, distinctive flavor. The maturing process lasts for about ten days in total. The cheese used to be common all over the Lombard flatlands, but now only one producer is left, supported by a Slow Food presidium. Lombardy.

pannicelli puff pastry dough, brushed with honey and egg yolks, cut into squares, fried and dusted with confectioner's sugar. Tuscany.

pannocchia Tuscan term for ➤ **canocchia**, mantis shrimp.

panocchia Marche term for ➤ **canocchia**, mantis shrimp.

pansarole fritters made from a dough of flour, milk, eggs, yeast, lemon zest and sugar, served piping hot sprinkled with aniseed liqueur and often accompanied by ➤ **zabaglione**. Typical of the western Riviera, in especial the small town of Apricale, in the province of Imperia. Liguria.

pansegla Piedmontese term for ➤ **pane nero di Coimo**, a black bread.

panseta de casada a home-cured pancetta (usually rolled). Veneto.

pansopà "bread soup." Dessert consisting of pieces of leavened flatbread steeped in a mixture of milk, eggs, sugar, vanilla and lemon zest, cooked in a baine-marie and served with confectioner's custard. Veneto.

pansoti aka **pansotti** traditional stuffed pasta with a filling of ricotta (originally ➤ **prescinsoea**), a mixture of wild and other herbs (➤ **preboggion**), grated Parmigiano and minced garlic. Triangular or rectangular in shape, generally served with walnut sauce (➤ **salsa di noci**). Liguria.

panspeziale another name for ➤ **certosino**, a Christmas cake.

pantasca veal flank stuffed with frittata, fried mushrooms, day-old bread, cheese, parsley and eggs. Campania.

pantrid maridàa a traditional Easter Sunday soup. A broth garnished with fried breadcrumbs in which beaten eggs mixed with Parmigiano-Reggiano are scrambled. On its own, *pantrid* is similar to ➤ **panada**, the only difference being that it uses breadcrumbs instead of day-old bread. Lombardy.

panun rounded fruit loaf typical of the Valtellina, in the province of Sondrio. The mixture consists of rye and wheat flour, brewer's yeast, refined sugar, walnuts, dried figs and raisins, and, once baked, the loaf is brushed with sugar and water syrup. Lombardy.

pan'untella a slice of bread (➤ **palata**) spread with a mixture of pancetta and herbs, topped with a sausage and baked in the oven. Campania.

panunto another name for ➤ **fettunta**.

panuozzo pizza bread. A specialty of the *maestri pizzaiuoli*, the master pizza makers of the province of Naples, in especial of Gragnano and Agerola. The appearance is that of a loaf of bread, but it is made with pizza dough and baked in a wood oven. It is filled mainly with mozzarella or Provola with cured meats, vegetables, mushrooms and the like. Campania.

panvinesco dessert made with wine must (➤ **vincotto**) boiled in a pan with very finely ground semolina, which is poured in gradually like polenta flour. After a few minutes, the mixture is poured into cake molds and allowed to cool. The individual molds are then turned out and sprinkled with powdered cinnamon and confetti sugar. Puglia.

panzanella (1) popular Tuscan summer salad made with lumps of day-old bread soaked in water, vinegar and olive oil mixed, according to place and availability, with ripe tomatoes, finely sliced onions, roughly torn basil and rounds of cucumber (to a similar salad in Campania they add green olives, peppers, anchovies and garlic). Tuscany.

panzanella (2) another Tuscan name for ➤ **ficattola**, a type of flatbread. Tuscany.

panzarotte fried or baked pastries (➤ **panzerotto**, turnover) stuffed with a variety of savory or sweet fillings, which range from fried chicken's giblets, grated Pecorino, parsley, egg and pepper to ricotta, confectioner's sugar, chocolate, powdered cinnamon and candied fruits. Calabria.

panzarotti napoletani fried turnovers made with a slightly sweet dough of flour, eggs, pepper, a pinch of salt and sugar, filled with pieces of mozzarella, dipped in beaten egg and fried. Sometimes made with bread dough filled with ricotta, fried onion and tomato, salami, Provola cheese and prosciutto. In Naples, the word *panzerotto* is also used for croquette potatoes (➤ **crocchè di patate**). Campania.

panzerotto (1) turnover made from pastry dough with a sweet or savory filling, fried in oil or lard or baked in the oven. Popular throughout the south of Italy.

panzerotto (2) half moon pasta shape stuffed with various ingredients.

papaccella napoletana round sweet pepper promoted by a Slow Food presidium. Pickled in vinegar or as a sweet and sour preserve, it is an ingredient in many recipes, as a side dish or stuffed with olives and day-old bread. It is also an essential ingredient in ➤ **insalata di rinforzo,** a rich Christmas salad. Campania.

papacei small flour and milk dumplings, the same size as ➤ **spätzle.** Typical of the Ladin valleys in the province of Trento. Trentino-Alto Adige.

papai biancu dessert made with milk, refined sugar, corn starch, orange blossom water and lemon zest, similar to ➤ **biancomangiare (2).** Sardinia.

papàina term used in the Irpinia area of Campania for a round red pepper pickled in vinegar.

papala dialect term for ➤ **papavero (1),** corn poppy.

papalina (1) brisling (*Clupea sprattus*). A small herring-type fish common off Italy's Adriatic coast and in the east Atlantic, from Portugal to Norway. Its flesh is easily perishable and is eaten mostly fried or preserved in oil or salt like the anchovy (➤ **acciuga**) and sardine (➤ **sardina**). Common and regional names: ➤ **saraghina,** ➤ **sarda papalina,** ➤ **spratto.**

papaina (2) name used in the Marche for ➤ **novellame di pesce,** fry.

papalina (3) regional term for ➤ **barba di becco,** salsify.

paparele Veneto term for tagliatelle, usually quite thin, handmade from a dough of flour, salt, water, eggs and a drop of oil. Normally served with traditional regional sauces: duck and fresh peas or pancetta, onion and parsley. Veneto.

paparele coi fegadini a soup of ➤ **paparele,** very thin tagliatelle, cooked in a broth to which fried, rosemary-flavored hen's giblets (liver, heart, stomach) are added. The dish used to be served for Sunday lunch in Verona, followed by the boiled beef used to make the broth. It is still served in traditional restaurants. Veneto.

paparina dialect term for ➤ **papavero (2),** corn poppy.

paparine 'nfucate a typical antipasto or side dish in the Salento area (province of Lecce) consisting of corn poppy leaves (➤ **papavero (1)**) lightly fried in oil with garlic, black olives and chili to taste.

paparolesse pickled peppers. Whole local red and green peppers pickled in wine vinegar in earthenware or glass jars for three months. Traditionally served at Christmas with salt cod. Molise.

paparot thick soup of cornflour and chard or spinach. Garlic cloves are lightly fried in butter with a handful of wheat flour, and when the mixture begins to brown, the boiled shredded greens are added to the pan. After about ten minutes, boiling water is poured over the mixture. The soup continues to cook for another quarter of an hour, at which point, stirring vigorously, cornflour is gradually sprinkled in. The soup is sometimes flavored with slices of lardo or pieces of sausage. Friuli-Venezia Giulia.

paparotta sweet polenta made with cooked wine must (➤ **vincotto**), sugar, wheat flour and cornflour. Cloves and cinnamon are sometimes added for extra flavor. Basilicata.

paparotte fava bean (or other legume) purée mixed with day-old bread and drizzled with extra virgin olive oil. A dish made by oil producers when they press the new olives. Puglia.

paparrastello regional term for ➤ **grattalingua,** beaked hawksbeard.

paparucia runny polenta cooked in bean

broth flavored with minced lardo and onion, served with a generous sprinkling of grated Parmigiano. Emilia-Romagna.

papasin chestnut flour cakes two inches thick and three inches long. Once a humble snack between meals, but extremely nourishing. Popular in the province of Mantua. Lombardy.

papassinas another Sardinian word for ➤ **pabassinas**, small cookies.

papavero (1) corn poppy (*Papaver rhoeas*). The plant's young leaves are gathered in spring and prepared, all over Italy from north to south, in the same ways as spinach: stewed, tossed in butter or oil (➤ **paparine 'nfucate**), in stuffings and in frittatas. Common and regional names: ➤ **belle bimbe**, ➤ **papala**, ➤ **paparina**, ➤ **rosola**, ➤ **rosolaccio**, ➤ **rosolina**.

papavero (2) poppy (*Papaver somniferum*). The ripe seeds, devoid of toxic substances, are used to garnish bread, sweet and savory pastries and cakes. The tradition is well rooted in the Trentino-Alto Adige region, whose ➤ **mohnsamen** is listed in the Italian Ministry of Agriculture's database of native and/or traditional food products.

papazoi aka **papazzoi** an old rustic soup of beans, barley, sweet corn or wheat berries simmered in water and flavored with fried lardo. Friuli.

papini sweet ring-shaped pastries, first boiled in salted water (like ➤ **brasadele broè**), then baked in the oven. A specialty of Chioggia, in the province of Venice. Veneto.

pappa al pomodoro a symbol of Tuscany in the kitchen. A mush of slices of Tuscan bread soaked in water, squeezed dry and stirred on a low heat into a sauce of minced onion, celery and carrot, puréed ripe tomatoes, salt and, if desired, ground chili. The heat is then turned off

and minced garlic cloves and roughly torn basil leaves are added. The mixture is left to stand for a while before serving. Tuscany.

pappa con l'olio an old dish, hard to find in restaurants these days, but still made by some families. Once considered to have restorative properties, it consists of day-old bread simmered in minced garlic, extra virgin olive oil and water. When the mixture is reduced to a creamy consistency, it is served sprinkled with roughly torn basil leaves, grated Parmigiano and extra virgin olive oil. Tuscany.

pappardelle typically Tuscan broad fresh egg pasta ribbons, now common also dried and industrially produced all over Italy, the name sometimes being used as a synonym of ➤ **fettuccine**. Genuine **pappardelle** are served mostly with meat and game sauces (beef, duck, goose, hare, rabbit, wild boar). Tuscany.

pappicci flour and water tagliatelle served with a sauce of tomato, lardo and onion. Abruzzo.

paprica aka **paprika** a spice made by grinding the dried fruits of peppers of the Capsicum genus. Flavor can range from mildly hot to fiery. The best paprika comes from Hungary and is used extensively in the cooking of the Balkans. In Italy, it is to be found in dishes of Austro-Hungaric origin, such as ➤ **gulasch**.

paradel sweet frittata of eggs, milk and flour, served dusted with sugar. Lombardy.

parago Tuscan term for ➤ **pagello,** sea bream.

paranzoli Marche term for newborn, larval anchovies (➤ **novellame di pesce**, fry).

parasambene slices of calf's diaphragm, flavored with minced garlic and parsley, salt and extra virgin olive oil, and broiled.

parasangue another name for ➤ **parasambene**, calf's diaphragm. Sardinia.

parasole regional term for → **mazza di tamburo**, parasol mushroom.

parazzole Marche term for newborn larval brisling (→ **papalina**, → **novellame di pesce**).

pardulas tarts popular all over Sardinia. In the past they were only made in the spring for Easter, the period in which most cheese and ricotta were produced. They consist of small pastry baskets of strong flour pastry filled with a custard made of fresh ricotta or cheese, eggs, sugar, lemon or orange zest and saffron, which swell up as they bake. Traditionally served with honey. Sardinia

parfait semifreddo or soft, foamy ice cream made with eggs, the whites whisked to a peak, sugar and whipped cream, aromatized as desired and frozen.

pariana Trentino term for → **diaframma**, diaphragm.

parigina a shorter, thicker version of the → **toponin** bread roll.

parigino long bread loaf, a member of the beer bread category (→ **pane a birra**), which stands out for the oblique slashes on its upper crust. Sicily.

parmigiana, alla expression used to describe a dish finished with butter and grated Parmigiano. Vegetables such as aparagus, cardoon and fennel, steaks and chops and truffle are cooked in this way. Emilia-Romagna.

parmigiana di gobbi peasant dish of fried, breaded boiled cardoons layered in a tin with tomato sauce, ground veal and, in some cases, chicken livers, and baked in the oven. Umbria

parmigiana di melanzane one of the most popular traditional dishes in the south of Italy, probably of Campanian origin. Fried eggplants layered in a tin with tomato sauce, grated Parmigiano, roughly torn basil leaves, and pieces of → **Fior di latte**, and baked in the oven. In Sicily, they add slices of hard-boiled egg to the tomato sauce, and elsewhere they add layers of onions or fried sliced potatoes.

parmigiana di zucchine a recipe identical to → **parmigiana di melanzane**, but with zucchini instead of eggplants. In some variants, slices of mozzarella or → **Scamorza** are among the ingredients. Campania.

Parmigiano-Reggiano PDO cheese produced with whole and part-skimmed cow's milk from two milkings. After a selection examination, it is aged for a minimum of 12 months or a maximum of 24 and more. A table and grating cheese, it has a hard, smooth, thick straw-yellow outer rind. The body is flaky and fine-grained. The characteristic Parmigiano-Regiano mark, with the producer's registration number and year and month of production, is punched onto the side of each wheel. The cheese is produced in the provinces of Parma, Reggio Emilia, Modena, communes on the left bank of the river Reno in the province of Bologna and those on the right bank of the Po in the province of Mantua. Emilia-Romagna, Lombardy.

parpagnachi walnut, honey and flour pastries aromatized with cinnamon, cloves and nutmeg. Veneto.

parrozzo the name of this famous cake originates, historically, from *pane rozzo*, "rough bread," the buckwheat flour bread of the poor as opposed to the refined white flour bread of the lords. It was created as a Christmas cake in the early 20th century by the Pescara confectioner Luigi D'Amico, and the poet and writer Gabriele D'Annunzio was among the first to taste it. These days it is available all year round. It is made with a mixture of wheat flour, milk, eggs, sugar, chopped almonds and orange zest, and glazed with a dark chocolate icing. Abruzzo.

parruozzo bread made with cornflour and sourdough, plunged into boiling salted water before being baked in the oven. A specialty of Benevento. Campania.

parsèch Romagna dialect name term for dried apple and pear slices (➤ **frutta secca**).

partenio feverfew (*Chrysanthemum parthenium*). An aromatic wild herb that grows on fallow ground, rocky slopes and among ruins with inflorescences reminiscent of those of chamomile. In the kitchen, it is used mostly in Veneto, especially in the province of Vicenza. Traditional recipes include: ➤ **frittelle di riso**, ➤ **budino di puina**, ➤ **torta con la maresina**,. Common and regional names: ➤ **amareggiola**, ➤ **camomilla bastarda**, ➤ **erba amara**, ➤ **erba maresina**, ➤ **maresina**, ➤ **matricale**, ➤ **matricaria**, ➤ **tanaceto**.

pasimata thrice-risen, oven-baked cake made with a mixture of wheat flour, yeast, salt, aniseed, grated lemon and orange zest, eggs, sugar, vermouth and raisins. Typical of the Garfagna area, in the province of Lucca. Tuscany.

passare (1) to filter a sauce, broth or gravy through a sieve.

passare (2) to purée a stuffing or a sauce.

passare (3) (in colloquial language) to finish, turn or toss cooked food, usually vegetables, in a skillet with oil or butter (➤ **ripassare**).

passata now universal term to describe tomato conserve or sauce.

passatelli "noodles" made with a mixture of grated dry white bread, Parmigiano, ox's bone marrow (or, alternatively, butter), eggs, nutmeg and lemon zest, pushed through a special perforated disk into boiling mixed meat broth. A new fashion is to serve them with tomato or white meat sauce. In inland Urbino, they add minced boiled spinach and ground beef to the mixture. In the seaside town of Pesaro, they add cuttlefish ink or hake flesh. Emilia-Romagna, Marche.

passato a purée of vegetables, legumes, fish or tomato.

passavulanti cookies made with toasted almonds, sugar, egg whites, cinnamon and vanilla. Sicily.

passera aka **passera pianuzza** flounder (*Platichthys flesus italicus*). Flatfish cooked like sole (➤ **sogliola**) and turbot (➤ **rombo**). Smaller specimens, known as ➤ **passerina** on the Adriatic, are eaten whole, coated in flour and fried. *Passera coi ovi*, "flounder with roe" (Friuli-Venezia Giulia), is listed in the Italian Ministry of Agriculture's database of native and/or traditional food products.

passerina name used on the Adriatic coast for small flounders (➤ **passera**).

passulate crisp square Christmas cake made with almonds, walnuts, raisins, wheat flour, honey, lemon zest and spices. A specialty of the village of Ardore, in the province of Reggio Calabria. Calabria.

passuluna (1) Sicilian term for dried figs.

passuluna (2) olives which, infected by *Camarosporium dalmaticum*, a pathogen widespread in southern Italy, sweeten as they rot. Harvested in October and November, they are eaten as they are. They are included in the Italian Ministry of Agriculture's database of native and/or traditional food products. Sicily.

pasta (1) (of bread, pizza, flatbread etc.) dough.

pasta (2) (of cakes and confectionery) pastry, mixture, paste.

pasta (3) pasta.

pasta (4) a synonym of ➤ **pasticcino**, a small cake.

pasta (5) the pulp or flesh of fruit or tubers.

pasta (6) the body or consistency of a cheese.

pasta a la paulota Sicilian term for ➤ **pasta alla paolina**, a pasta dish.

pasta a picchi pacchi aka **picchi pacchiu** pasta served with a sauce of fresh raw tomatoes marinated in oil, garlic, basil and chili and a sprinkling of grated Caciocavallo. Sicily.

pasta a ventu rare cake of noble origins. A mixture of wheat flour and durum wheat flour, eggs, warm salted water and saffron is rolled into a very thin sheet, which is then cut into strips. The latter are fried in boiling oil, dried, arranged in a pyramid and smothered with honey melted in orange blossom water, chopped pistachio nuts and pieces of candied fruit. A specialty of Catania. Sicily.

pasta acida sourdough. A piece of old dough saved from a prior leavening incorporated into a new dough to start fermentation.

pasta aggrassata a Sicilian pasta dish (➤ **agglassato**).

pasta al forno oven-baked pasta, a dish for major occasions and holidays. In the north of Italy, most recipes involve rectangular lasagne; in the south, they prefer medium- to large-sized dried pasta or broad tagliatelle pre-boiled and layered with all sorts of sauces and other ingredients. In northern Italy, béchamel sauce, Parmigiano and meat sauce; in central Italy, rich sauces involving calf offal and chicken giblets, béchamel sauce and Parmigiano; in southern Italy, meatballs, sausage, meat sauce, slices of Mozzarella or Caciocavallo, grated Pecorino, eggplant, tomato sauce and hard-boiled eggs. In some regions, **pasta al forno** is presented as a ➤ **pasticcio** or ➤ **timballo**, with or without a crust. Examples of

pasta al forno in this dictionary include: ➤ **lasagna beneventana**, ➤ **lasagna napoletana**, ➤ **lasagne alla bolognese**, ➤ **lasagne alle lenticchie**, ➤ **pasta al forno alla siciliana**, ➤ **pasta infornata**, ➤ **pasta 'ncaciata**, ➤ **sagne chine**, ➤ **taganu d'Aragona**, ➤ **vincisgrassi**.

pasta al forno alla siciliana first course common all over the island. Ingredients vary from place to place, but the most common are meat sauce, sausage, eggplant, hard-boiled eggs, tomato, cheese and mozzarella, and the pastas normally used are rigatoni or penne. One of the most characteristic versions is ➤ **timballo di anellini** in Palermo.

pasta alimentare generic term for pasta, the composition, processing techniques and storage of which are regulated by law. The various categories are dried pasta (➤ **pasta secca**), fresh pasta (➤ **pasta fresca**) and "special pasta," which includes egg pasta (➤ **pasta all'uovo**), stuffed pasta (➤ **pasta ripiena**) and flavored and colored pasta (➤ **pasta aromatizzata**).

pasta all'uovo egg pasta. For homemade egg pasta, the classic proportion is one egg per ounce of wheat flour, but some people (especially certain Piedmontese cooks when they make ➤ **tajarin**) use double the amount and even more. The flour is mounded into a well, which is filled with the eggs. The mixture is kneaded vigorously, pulled and punched into a smooth elastic dough. After resting for a quarter of an hour, the dough is rolled out into a thin sheet. After resting covered with a cloth for ten minutes, it is cut into the desired shapes or, in the case of ➤ **pasta ripiena**, stuffed.

pasta alla catalogna snapped ➤ **zite** boiled with endives and served with tomato sauce, garlic and Pecorino. Puglia.

pasta alla cuncimata pasta served with a

sauce of ground pork and wild fennel. Sicily.

pasta alla deficeira short pasta (maccheroni or penne) cooked in water, white wine and bay leaves served with grated Parmigiano or Pecorino and plenty of freshly pressed olive oil. *Deficeira* is the Italianization of *deficeu*, Ligurian dialect for "oil press." A popular dish on the western Riviera. Liguria.

pasta alla norma pasta with slices of fried eggplant, a generous sprinkling of grated smoked ricotta and roughly torn basil leaves. *Norma* is the title of a successful opera written in 1831 by the Catania-born composer Vincenzo Bellini. In those years it became common in local slang to describe anything perfect, hence comparable to Bellini's music, as "*Una Norma*." Pasta with eggplant was already a consolidated Sicilian recipe, but one day, eating a particularly tasty dish of it, the dramatist Nino Martoglio exclaimed, "*Chista è 'na vera Norma!*" (This is perfect!), and the name has stuck ever since. Sicily.

pasta alla paolina pasta served with a sauce of tomatoes, garlic, basil, olive oil, anchovies and powdered cinnamon and cloves. Ingredients in other versions include fresh or salted sardines, cauliflower, onions and wild fennel. The recipe seems to have been created in the monastery of San Francesco di Paola in Palermo. Sicily.

pasta ammiscata dialect name for ➤ **pasta e fagioli alla napoletana**, pasta and beans Neapolitan-style.

pasta aromatizzata flavored and colored pasta. Pasta of all shapes and sizes made with flour and water with the addition of herbs, vegetables and spices—spinach (➤ **lasagne alla bolognese**), nettles, borage (in Liguria), saffron (in Sardinia), tomato and so on—to flavor and color it.

pasta asciutta ➤ **pastasciutta**.

pasta asciutta 'nsulla palamita spaghetti (or another long pasta) tossed in a skillet with boned bonito (➤ **palamita del mare di Toscana**) onion, parsley, garlic, ripe tomatoes, white wine and a glass of brandy. A recipe to be found in the provinces of Livorno and Grosseto. Tuscany.

pasta bastarda (1) aka **pasta matta** lasagne, tagliatelle and tortelli made from mixed chestnut and wheat flour. Typical of the Levante and Lunigiana areas. Liguria, Tuscany.

pasta bastarda (2) (of cheese) Veneto expression for ➤ **pasta molle**, soft.

pasta biscotto soft sweet pastry dough made with well whisked eggs and sugar to which flour is added (sometimes mixed with potato flour). Used in traditional cooking to make rolled cakes and pastries (➤ **gattò aretino**, ➤ **tronco**).

pasta brioche French name for a very soft leavened dough of flour, butter, eggs, brewer's yeast, milk and salt, with or without sugar depending on use. Baked in the oven, it can be eaten on its own or used as a base for sweet and savory dishes.

pasta brisée French name for a light, delicate shortcrust pastry excellent for timbales, pie and tartlets, often used in lieu of puff pastry (➤ **pasta sfoglia**). It has a friable consistency and is made with two parts flour to one part butter and cold water. To give it a golden sheen, it may be brushed with milk or beaten egg yolk before baking.

pasta c'anciova e muddica atturrata first course common all over the island with variations from place to place. It consists of pasta with anchovies dissolved in a ➤ **soffritto** of garlic and onion, flavored with flat-leaved parsley and covered with

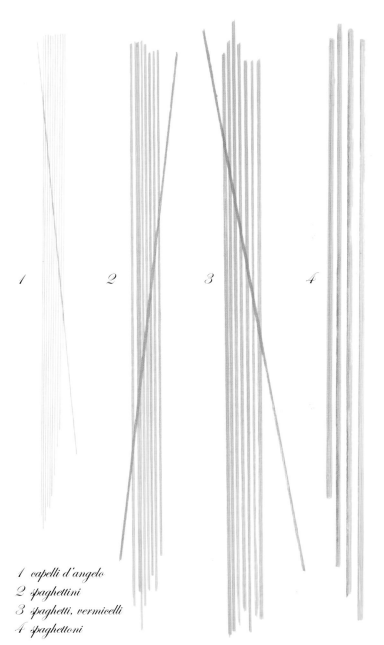

1

2

3

4

1 capelli d'angelo
2 spaghettini
3 spaghetti, vermicelli
4 spaghettoni

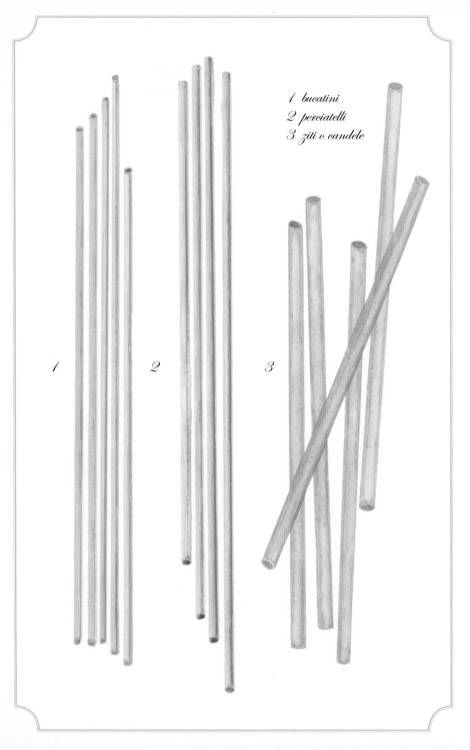

1 bucatini
2 perciatelli
3 ziti o candele

1   *2*   *3*

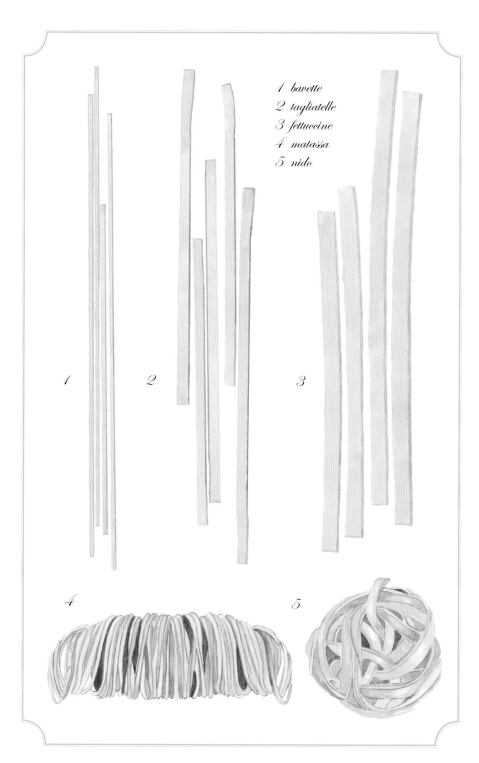

1 *bavette*
2 *tagliatelle*
3 *fettuccine*
4 *matassa*
5 *nido*

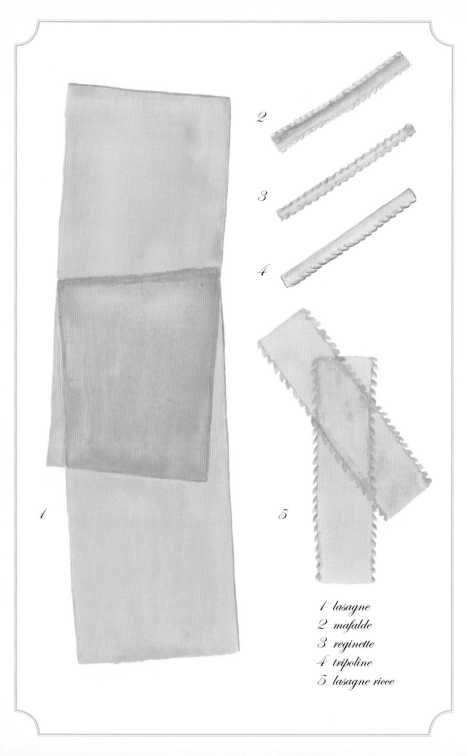

1 *lasagne*
2 *mafalde*
3 *reginette*
4 *tripoline*
5 *lasagne ricce*

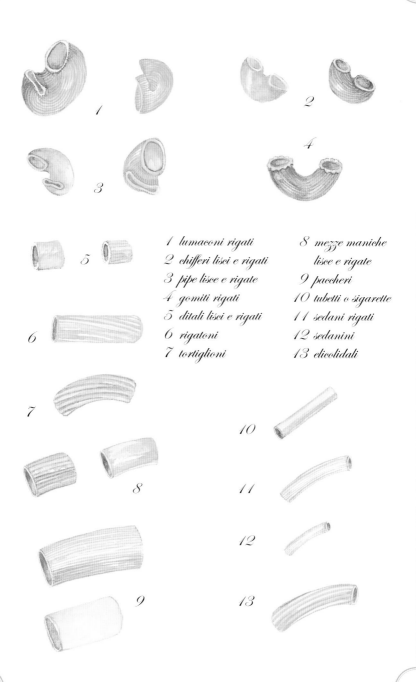

1 lumaconi rigati
2 chifferi lisci e rigati
3 pipe lisce e rigate
4 gomiti rigati
5 ditali lisci e rigati
6 rigatoni
7 tortiglioni
8 mezze maniche lisce e rigate
9 paccheri
10 tubetti o sigarette
11 sedani rigati
12 sedanini
13 elicoidali

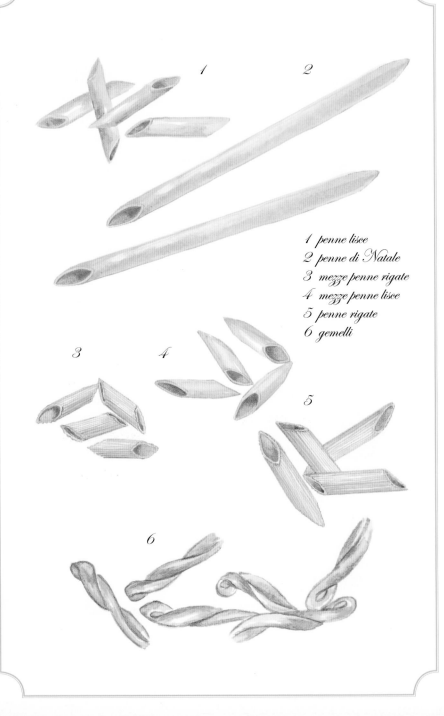

1 penne lisce
2 penne di Natale
3 mezze penne rigate
4 mezze penne lisce
5 penne rigate
6 gemelli

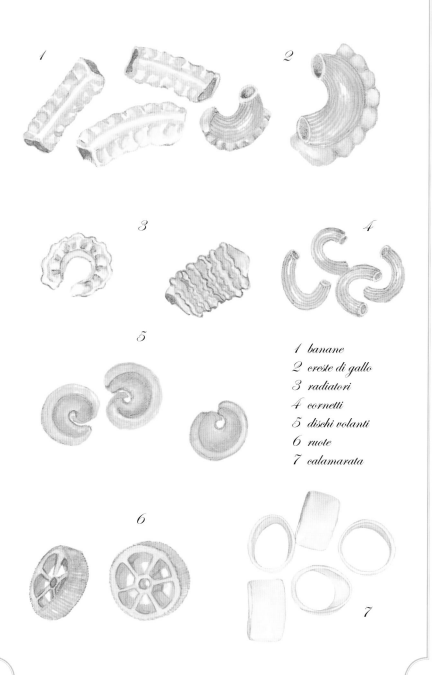

1 banane
2 creste di gallo
3 radiatori
4 cornetti
5 dischi volanti
6 ruote
7 calamarata

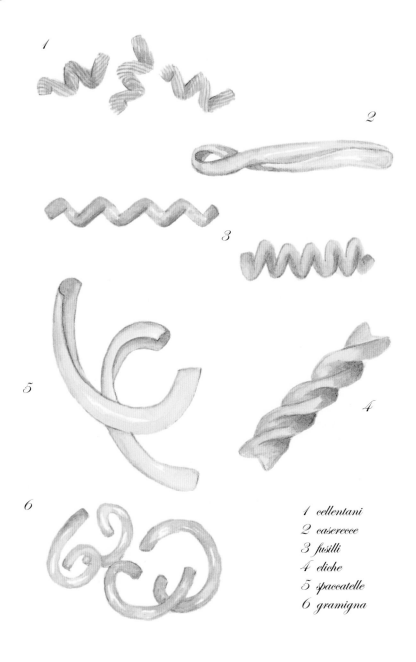

1 cellentani
2 caserecce
3 fusilli
4 eliche
5 spaccatelle
6 gramigna

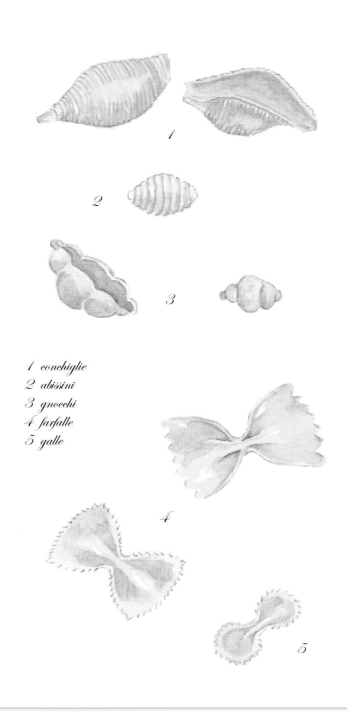

1 conchiglie
2 abissini
3 gnocchi
4 farfalle
5 galle

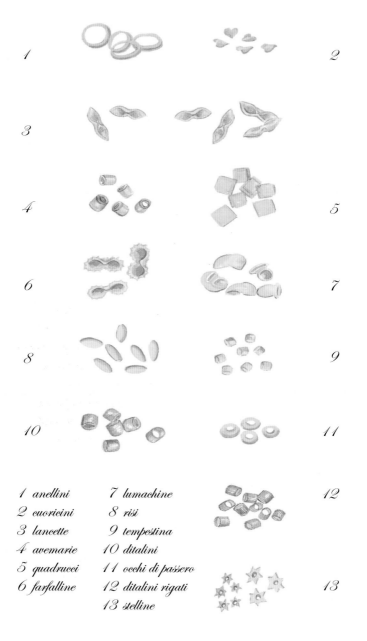

1

2

3

4

5

6

7

8

9

10

11

12

13

1 anellini
2 cuoricini
3 lancette
4 avemarie
5 quadrucci
6 farfalline
7 lumachine
8 risi
9 tempestina
10 ditalini
11 occhi di passero
12 ditalini rigati
13 stelline

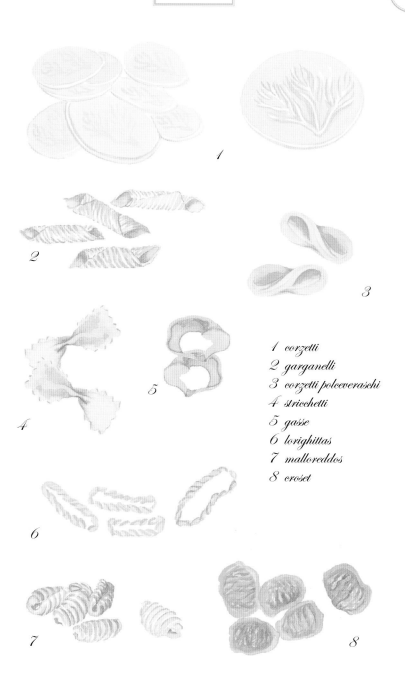

1 corzetti
2 garganelli
3 corzetti polceveraschi
4 stricchetti
5 gasse
6 lorighittas
7 malloreddos
8 croset

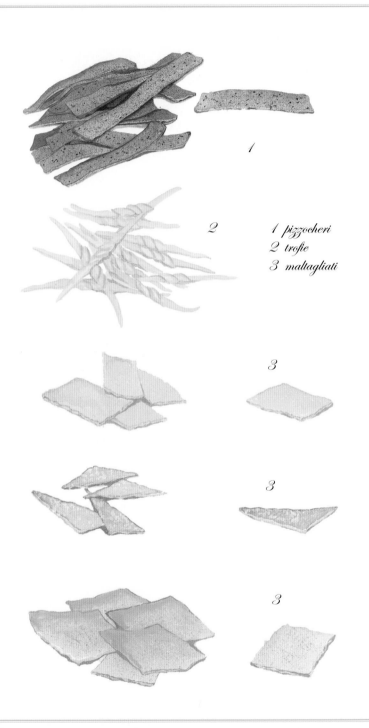

1 pizzocheri
2 trofie
3 maltagliati

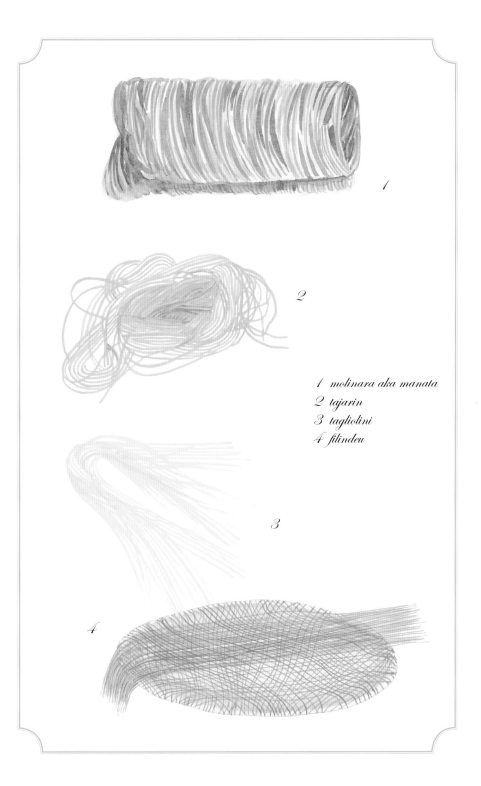

1 *molinara aka manata*
2 *tajarin*
3 *tagliolini*
4 *filindeu*

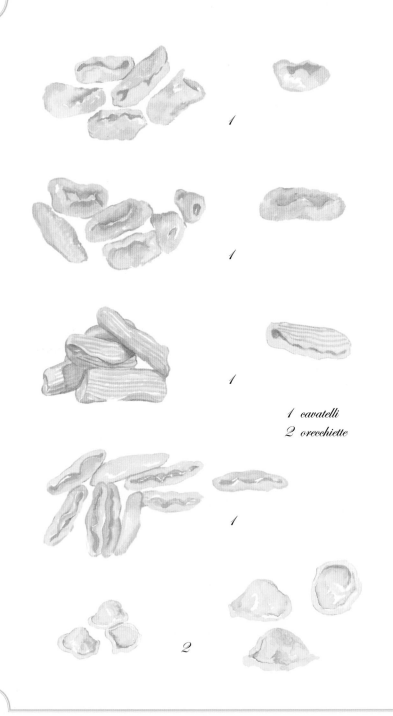

1 cavatelli
2 orecchiette

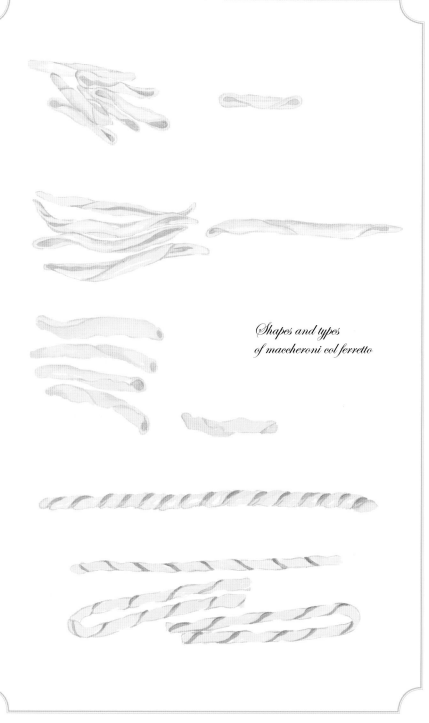

Shapes and types
of maccheroni col ferretto

1 mandilli de saèa
2 lasagne
3 lasagne verdi

1

2

3

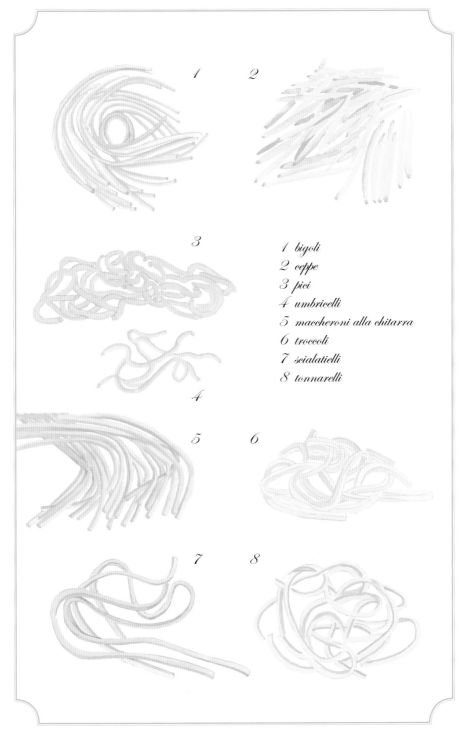

1 bigoli
2 ceppe
3 pici
4 umbricelli
5 maccheroni alla chitarra
6 troccoli
7 scialatielli
8 tonnarelli

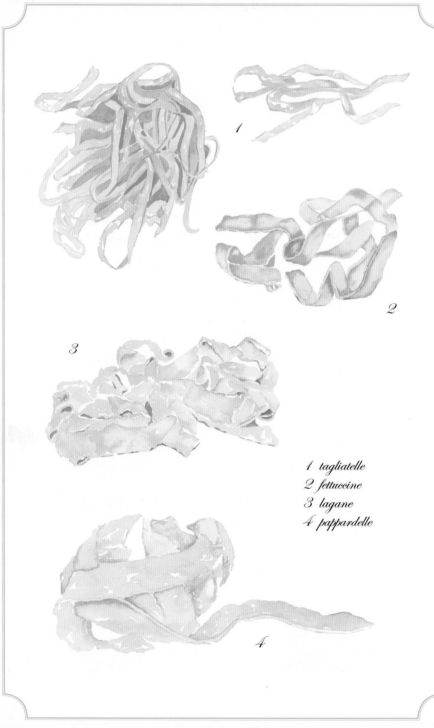

1 *tagliatelle*
2 *fettuccine*
3 *lagane*
4 *pappardelle*

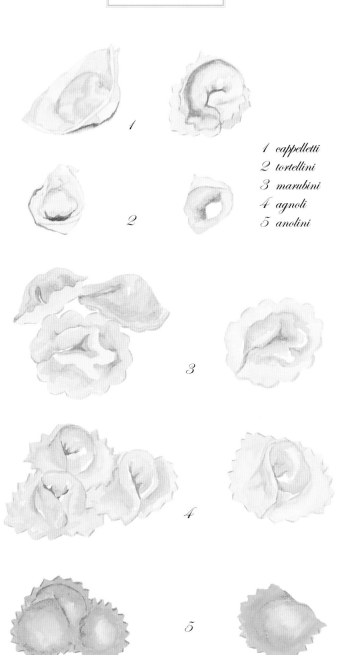

1 cappelletti
2 tortellini
3 marubini
4 agnoli
5 anolini

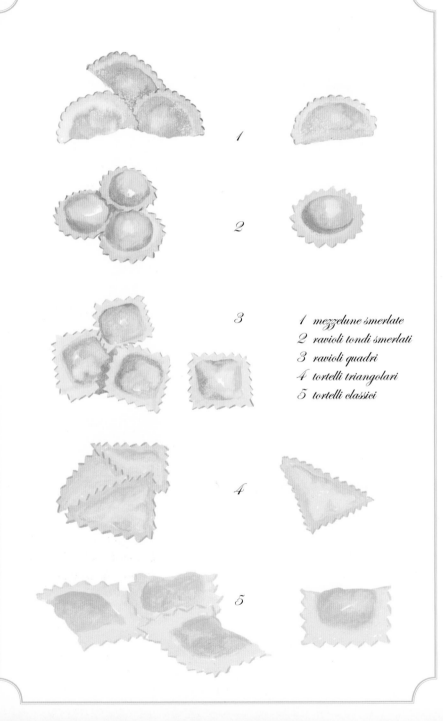

1 *mezzelune smerlate*
2 *ravioli tondi smerlati*
3 *ravioli quadri*
4 *tortelli triangolari*
5 *tortelli classici*

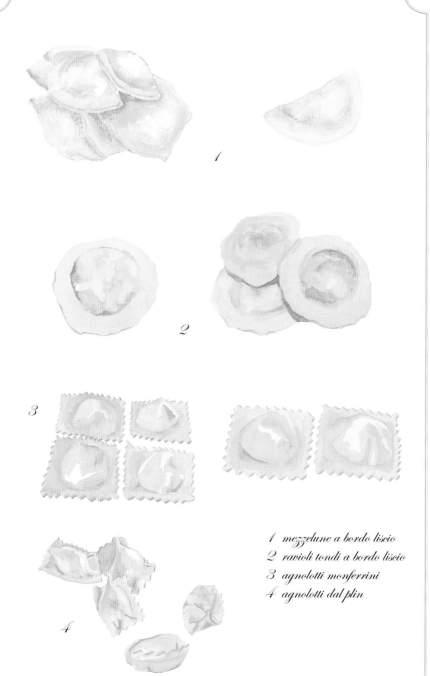

1 *mezzelune a bordo liscio*
2 *ravioli tondi a bordo liscio*
3 *agnolotti monferrini*
4 *agnolotti dal plin*

Shapes and types of casoncelli
del Bresciano
del Bergamasco
dell'Ampezzano

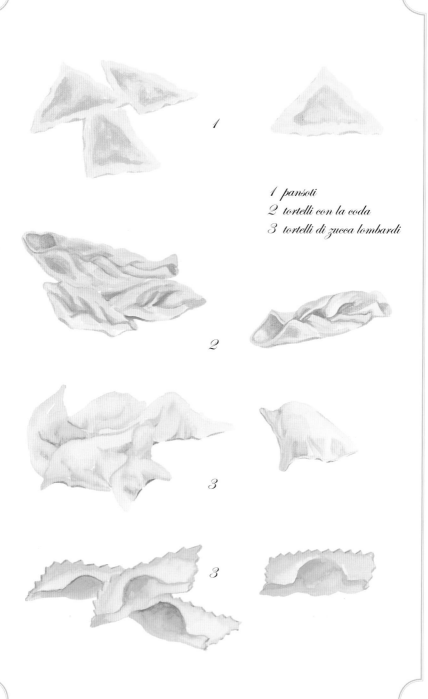

1 pansoti
2 tortelli con la coda
3 tortelli di zucca lombardi

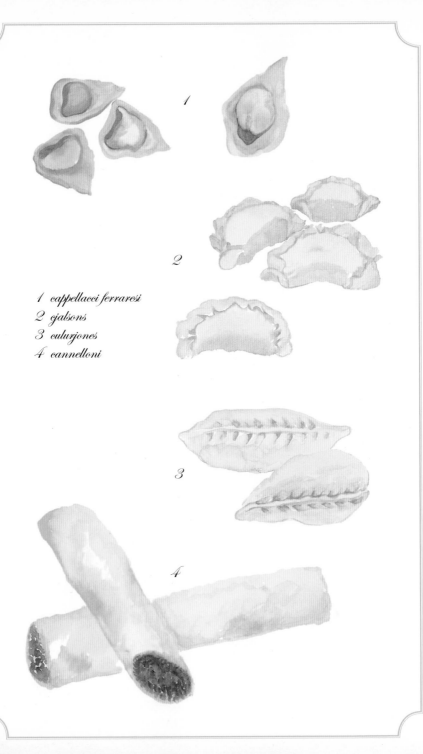

1 cappellacci ferraresi
2 cjalsons
3 culurjones
4 cannelloni

toasted breadcrumbs (sometimes mixed with grated Pecorino). Other ingredients may include tomato sauce, pine kernels and raisins. Sicily.

pasta ca' 'nnocca pasta served with a sauce of peas, sardines or anchovies, minced flat-leaved parsley, salt and pepper. In some recipes tomato is added. The dish is typical of the province of Catania. Sicily.

pasta china southern Italian term for stuffed pasta. In Calabria it refers to a sort of baked → **timballo** of short pasta layered with tomato, meatballs and cheese.

pasta co' riquagghiu pasta tossed with beaten eggs, grated Pecorino, minced parsley, salt and pepper. The name derives from the Sicilian verb *quagghiari*, which means "to set," and refers to the "scrambling" of the egg in the hot pasta. A specialty of Castellana Sicula, a village in the province of Palermo. Sicily.

pasta con i talli another name for → **pasta con i tenerumi**, pasta with zucchini shoots and leaves.

pasta con i tenerumi pasta with zucchini shoots and leaves. The shoots and leaves are first parboiled, then tossed with sundried tomatoes softened in warm water (or chopped fresh tomatoes) and a → **soffritto** of garlic, oil and chili. The cooked short pasta is mixed with the condiment for a couple of minutes before being served with a sprinkling of grated Caciocavallo or Pecorino. Sicily.

pasta con le castagne pasta with chestnuts. A poor dish typical of mountain villages. Originally made with rice, now with pasta, usually taglierini. The chestnuts are blanched, skinned and boiled in salted water until they start to fall apart. The resulting purée is used to cook the snapped pasta. The dish is dressed with olive oil and pepper. Sicily.

pasta con le sarde pasta, usually bucatini, with sardines. The sauce is made by cooking sardines with wild fennel, raisins, pine kernels, anchovies, black pepper and saffron. The dish, a specialty of Palermo, is normally sprinkled with toasted breadcrumbs. Sicily.

pasta con pomodori al forno pasta with baked tomatoes. The tomatoes are cut into thick slices, transferred to a baking tin, scattered with minced parsley and garlic, and sprinkled with oil salt and pepper. After baking for half an hour, they are mixed well with pasta cooked al dente and served. Puglia.

pasta con ricotta dolce pasta (→ **orecchiette** or rigatoni) served with fresh ricotta, grated lemon zest, sugar and a pinch of powdered cinnamon. Traditionally cooked on New Year's Eve. Puglia.

pasta cotta (of cheese) cooked. Category of cheeses in the production of which the curd is cut and cooked at 54-55°C.

pasta cresciuta leavened flour and water batter fried a tablespoonful at a time. Often filled with → **fiorilli**, chopped anchovies, salt cod, or → **cicinielli**. In Campania these tiny fritters are known as → **zeppulelle**: served today as an antipasto in restaurants, they are a traditional street food (→ **cibo di strada**), often accompanied by → **crocchè di patate**, croquette potatoes.

pasta cruda "raw curd." Category of soft cheeses produced with uncooked curd.

pasta cu a pumata dialect term for → **pizzalandrea** (→ **sardenaira**), Ligurian pizza.

pasta cu e erbe Ligurian dialect term for → **torta con le erbe**, vegetable pie.

pasta cull'àgghia Sicilian dialect term for → **pesto trapanese**.

pasta cumpettata sweet gnocchi similar to → **turdriddi**, but without wine and cooked must in the dough. A specialty of Corigliano, in the province of Cosenza. Calabria.

pasta cunscia pasta cooked with potatoes and served with tomato sauce. A specialty of the province of Como. Lombardy.

pasta cu' ra muddica, in Italian, aka **pasta con la mollica** pasta, usually ➤ **bucatini,** dressed with crumbled day-old bread fried in oil with garlic and oregano. Calabria.

pasta d'acciughe anchovy paste. The commercial version of Ligurian ➤ **machetto.**

pasta di mandorle almond paste (➤ **pasta reale (1)**).

pasta di polenta puff pastry pie filled with soft polenta, chopped spinach, grated Parmigiano, cream cheese and oil. A specialty of the western Riviera. Liguria.

pasta dura (of cheese) hard. Category of cheeses with a water content of less than 40%. It includes pressed curd, stretched curd and semi-cooked cheeses. **pasta e arrosto** pasta, usually ➤ **vermicelli,** served with pork (or kid or ➤ **porchetta**) and quails roasted with olive oil, rosemary, sage and the pan juices. Calabria.

pasta e broccoli in brodo d'arzilla skate (➤ **razza,** ➤ **arzilla**) cooked in water with carrot, celery, onion, parsley and sea salt to form a broth, which is filtered and used to cook a quartered head of broccoli. Once cooked, the broccoli is turned in a skillet with garlic, oil, chili, dry white wine and its own and the skate's cooking broths. Snapped spaghetti are added to the mixture halfway through the cooking process. Long forgotten, this dish, once a classic in Rome on Good Friday, is now reappearing on restaurant tables. Lazio.

pasta e fagioli pasta and beans. One of the most popular Italian soups, made in innumerable variations all over the country, especially in Veneto, Tuscany and the south, Naples in particular. Broadly speaking, it consists of dried or fresh beans cooked in water or broth on a base of oil or lardo and herbs, then mixed with snapped tagliatelle, maltagliati or spaghetti or short pasta such as ditalini or tubetti. Served with oil and pepper or grated cheese, pasta and bean soup may be eaten hot, warm or cold. In Veneto and Friuli they tend to use dried borlotti beans (➤ **borlotto**), half of which they usually purée, and they add lardo, pancetta or pork rind to the soup (➤ **alla lamonese,** ➤**pasta e fagioli alla padovana,** ➤**pasta e fagioli alla pordenonese**). Other variations exist, however, in which fresh beans are cooked in oil and butter (➤ **pasta e fagioli alla zoldana**). In Tuscany they use cannelloni beans (➤ **cannellino**), which they invariably boil and purée, flavoring them with garlic and chili (➤ **pasta e fagioli alla toscana**). A much thicker version is ➤ **pasta e fagioli alla napoletana,** characterized by the addition of fresh tomato and the use of mixed pasta shapes.

pasta e fagioli all'emiliana beans stewed with tomatoes and spooned over homemade egg pasta, usually maltagliati. Emilia-Romagna.

pasta e fagioli alla lamonese a soup of soaked dried Lamon beans (➤ **fagiolio di Lamon**), homemade tagliatelle, lardo, pork rind, potatoes and herbs, cooked in an earthenware pot. Before adding the pasta, half the beans are puréed and returned to the pot, and the pork rind is only added at the end. The soup is best enjoyed warm or reheated the day after. Veneto.

pasta e fagioli alla napoletana soup of boiled cannellini beans (➤ **cannellino**) flavored with garlic, chili, fresh tomato and oregano, thickened by puréeing half the beans and returning them to the pan. To the soup is added a mixture of different pasta shapes (*ammiscata*); once leftover pasta was used, now the pasta is available ready-mixed in packages. On the island of Ischia (province of Naples), the soup is made with fresh tomatoes, pancetta or crushed lard, and a handful of grated Parmigiano. A version also exists with fiery pork sausages, known as *muzzarielli* in Neapolitan dialect. Campania.

pasta e fagioli alla padovana soup of fresh or dried Lamon beans (➤ **fagiolo di Lamon**) boiled in water (thickened by puréeing half the beans) flavored with a ➤ **soffritto** of oil, pancetta, onion and a ladleful of broth. Egg pasta may be used and the soup is finished either with pepper or finely minced garlic and parsley. Veneto.

pasta e fagioli alla piemontese fresh or borlotti beans (➤ **borlotto**) boiled with potatoes, lardo (or salami preserved in fat) and lightly fried carrot, celery, onion, leek and garlic (when cooked, some of the potatoes are puréed with a ladleful of beans to thicken the soup). The pasta consists of broad egg tagliatelle snapped into one-inch pieces. Piedmont.

pasta e fagioli alla pordenonese soaked dried beans boiled with pig's trotters, partly puréed, cooked with pasta and flavored with garlic, rosemary, parsley and sage. Friuli.

pasta e fagioli alla toscana the classic version is made by a boiling cannellini beans (➤ **cannellino**) in a pan with water, garlic, sage and pepper, then finishing them in a pot with minced garlic, chili, salt and pepper. Short pasta is cooked directly in the soup, which is drizzled, finally, with oil aromatized with sage and rosemary. Tuscany.

pasta e fagioli alla zoldana preferably fresh Lamon beans (➤ **fagiolo di Lamon**) cooked in oil and butter with carrot, celery, tomatoes and pumpkin, covered with water. A few seconds before turning off the heat, homemade tagliatelle are added to the soup. Recipe typical of the Dolomites, in the province of Belluno. Veneto.

pasta e fasoi Veneto dialect for ➤ **pasta e fagioli**.

pasta e lenticchie soup of lentils boiled with celery, onion and garlic cloves. Separately cooked pasta, usually spaghetti snapped into one and a half inch pieces, is added at the end. Puglia.

pasta filata stretched curd. A cheesemaking technique involving the immersion of the curd in hot, acid whey for several hours to remove minerals from the body and render it elastic. The curd is then kneaded and stretched in warm water at 70-90°C until it acquires the required shape. Cheeses of this type include ➤ **mozzarella**, ➤ **Caciocavallo**, ➤ **Provola** , ➤ **Provolone**, ➤ **Scamorza**.

pasta fresca fresh pasta. Handmade fresh pasta is produced by kneading all-purpose or cake flour with salt and water. The use of strong flour is restricted to precise areas, mostly in the south, but blending with other flours is common: with wholemeal buckwheat flour (eg,➤ **pizzocheri**), with chestnut flour (eg, **pasta bastarda (1)** or ➤ **pasta matta**), or with barley flour. The use of eggs in the dough (➤ **pasta all'uovo**) depends very much on regional tradition. Roughly speaking, the oldest pastas are the simplest and most rustic: eg, pici and bigoli, lumps of dough tapered between the palms of the hands, or orecchiette and cavatelli, hollowed or ridged on a baking board. In central and northern areas, eggs are often added to the dough, though many flour and water versions are to be found in the Apennines. The dough is handmade by mounding the flour into a well (*fontana*) and rolling out the mass with a long thin rolling pin. Of course gadgets exist nowadays to do these jobs for you, but only the old methods give pasta the coarseness of texture needed to soak up sauce. The shapes and sizes of Italian fresh pasta are innumerable and a bewildering variety of names exist to describe them (sometimes changing within the space of a few miles).

pasta fritta leftover pasta mixed with eggs and fried like a ➤ **frittata**. Campania.

pasta fritta alla siracusana a simpler variation on ➤ **pasta a ventu**. Dried pasta (vermicelli or capelli d'angelo) briefly cooked, shaped into small balls using a fork, and fried in oil until golden outside and soft inside. Served smothered in warm honey. Sicily.

pasta frolla shortcrust pastry. Friable pastry used to make cookies and tarts (it may be pre-baked in a case before being filled), but also traditional savory dishes such as ➤ **pasticcio di maccheroni** (Lazio) and ➤ **pasticcio ferrarese** (Emilia-Romagna). The dough (wheat flour, butter, sugar, salt and egg yolks) has to be worked rapidly by hand to prevent the heat from making the pastry inelastic and hard to roll out.

pasta genovese sweet mold made of eggs whisked to a peak with sugar and cooked in a bain-marie into which flour and butter are folded. The mixture is baked in the oven, turned out, allowed to cool and usually filled and glazed with icing. Liguria.

pasta grataada Lombard term for ➤ **pasta trida**, a sort of noodle.

pasta infornata short pasta layered with a sauce of sausage, tomato and basil, meatballs (sometimes made with horsemeat),

slices of mozzarella and grated Pecorino, and baked in the oven. Puglia.

pasta lorda pasta with fried eggplants, shredded beef and pork cooked in red wine and tomato sauce, served with basil leaves and a sprinkling of Pecorino. Typical of the Madonie mountains. Sicily.

pasta maddalena aka **pasta viennese** a soft sweet cake mixture of wheat flour, potato flour, sugar, eggs, butter, grated lemon zest or powdered vanilla.

pasta margherita soft sweet mixture made of wheat flour, potato flour, confectioner's sugar, eggs and butter, baked in the oven and used to make the cake of the same name and as a base for sandwich cakes.

pasta matta (1) a friable baked pastry of flour, eggs, butter or oil and salt, used to make timbales, pies and tarts.

pasta matta (2) another name for ➤ **pasta bastarda**, chestnut flour pasta.

pasta molle, (of cheese) soft. A category of fresh and semi-mature cheeses with a water content of more than 40%.

pasta 'ncaciata a rich baked pasta dish. Cauliflower or broccoli boiled and turned in a ➤ **soffritto** of garlic and oil. Separately a sauce is prepared with onion, ground pork and sausage, wine and tomato. Cooked medium-large short pasta is tossed with the cauliflower or broccoli and the sauce, sprinkled with mature Pecorino, spooned into baking tin, covered with dry breadcrumbs and baked in the oven until a golden crust forms on the top. The dish may owe its name to the generous amount of cheese (*cacio*) used in the condiment. It originated in Messina but is now common all over the island. Sicily.

pasta ordinaria aka **pasta per pâté** plain pastry of flour, eggs, salt and butter used for making pies and tarts.

pasta per bignè choux paste. Light, fluffy paste made with water, butter, flour and eggs, used, with the help of a piping bag, to make sweet and savory puffs and beignets (→ **bignè**).

pasta rasa another word for → **pastaresa**, "grated" pasta.

pasta reale (1) almond paste. Marzipan made by blending sugar, ground almonds (sometimes with the addition of a little → **maiorca** wheat flour) and vanilla into a smooth paste. It can be shaped, decorated and colored as desired, and can also be given a glossy sheen with gum Arabic. In the Easter period, it is often shaped like a lamb.

pasta reale (2) small baked beignets which are added to meat broth. A soup usually served on important occasions, common mostly in the north of Italy (→ **minestra di pasta reale**).

pasta ripiena stuffed pasta. A popular way of using fresh pasta (→ **pasta fresca**). Every Italian region boasts at least ten different varieties, Emilia-Romagna, the capital of stuffed pasta for cooking in broth, many, many more. The dough is generally made of egg pasta (→ **pasta all'uovo**), while stuffings can be divided into two categories: meats (roast, braised, boiled, of one type only, or mixed), offal, sausage and cured meats such as prosciutto and mortadella, used on their own or, more frequently bound and softened with vegetables or rice; without meat (*magro*), hence with fresh cheese, such as ricotta or Raviggiolo, potatoes, mixed wild herbs and leafy cultivated greens such as chard, spinach and escarole. Eggs are used to bind, dried breadcrumbs to add firmness, grated nature cheese to strengthen and spices or herbs (nutmeg, cinnamon, aromatics) to flavor. Shapes can be classed as: square, rectangular, triangular, circular, semi-circular, half moon for the large ravioli and tortelli family; cylindrical for cannelloni and canoli; hat- or cap-like for cappelletti, cappellacci, agnoli, tortellini and tortelloni. Borders and cutting techniques also vary immensely. In recent years, Italian restaurants have successfully developed new stuffings for ravioli and tortelli, using fresh fish (though in Genoa a tradition of this kind already existed: → **zembi d'arzillo**) smoked fish, cheese fondue, eggplant, asparagus, artichokes, mushrooms, *foie gras*, duck, guinea fowl, pigeon and so on.

pasta ro' malutempu pasta with a sauce of broccoli, chopped pitted olives, boned anchovies, white wine and minced garlic and parsley, served with a sprinkling of fried breadcrumbs. A traditional dish among families of fisherfolk on the east coast of the island. It used to be made when the catch was disappointing due to bad weather (*malutempo* in Sicilian dialect, *maltempo* in Italian, hence the name). Sicily.

pasta rustida short pasta and boiled potatoes, mixed with butter and cheese and tossed with pancetta and more mountain dairy cheese. Typical of the Valle Vigezzo, in the province of Verbano-Cusio-Ossola. Piedmont.

pasta sablée baked paste of finely minced almonds which is added to shortcrust pastry (→ **pasta frolla**) to make it even more friable.

pasta sciancà roughly torn fresh pasta rectangles. Usually served with a sauce of vegetables, oil and Parmigiano. In the Valle del Tanaro, in the province of Cuneo, they are served with a sauce of leeks, cream, mushrooms and walnuts. Liguria, Piedmont.

pasta secca dried pasta. Pasta produced by

specialized companies (industrial or artisanal) normally available at corner shops and supermarkets. By law, it must consist of a blend of strong flour and water. A vital stage in the processing of pasta (which consists of the selection and blending of the grain, the mixing of the flour and water, the extrusion or drawing of the pasta, the drying of the pasta, cooling, packaging and storage) is the *trafilatura*, extrusion or drawing, which determines shape. Prime quality artisan dried pastas are drawn using bronze extruders which ensure a coarseness and porosity superior to that possible with plastic extruders.

pasta semicotta (of cheese) semi-cooked. A category of cheeses during the production of which the curd is cut and then cooked at a temperature of 44-45°C.

pasta sfoglia aka **sfogliata** puff pastry. A very light friable pastry used to make sweet and savory pies, pasties and so on.

pasta trida aka **rasida** aka **pasta grataada** the Mantua and Cremona version of the Emilian → **pastaresa** (→ **supa de tridarini**). Lombardy.

pasta viennese another name for → **pasta maddalena**, cake mixture.

pastafrolla a thin round buttery dry cake dusted with a little refined sugar. A specialty of the province of Verona, Veneto.

pastarella central-southern Italian name for a small cake or beignet.

pastaresa aka **pasta rasa**. The Reggio Emilia version of → **passatelli**. Parmigiano, eggs and dry bread worked into a compact mixture and grated to form small balls that are plunged into boiling mixed meat broth to cook. In dialect, **resa**, or **rasa**, means "grated." Emilia-Romagna.

pastasciutta aka **pasta asciutta** today the dish that, in the imagination of Italians, and of foreigners, most symbolizes Ital-*ianità*, or "Italianness." The ancient Romans made pasta (*lagana*) and cooked it either in the oven or on red-hot stone slabs. It was only in the Middle Ages that people began to boil it in water and model it into shapes. Of all pastas, the dried version is the one that identifies "Italianness" at the table. Cheap, easy to keep and easy to prepare, it is now produced in about 40 countries for a total of about 10 million tons a year. It was the Arabs who devised the pasta drying process (mentions of dried pasta first appeared in Arab recipe collections in the 9th century) and they too who brought pasta to Sicily in the 12th century. From that moment, Italy became a crossroads of different traditions. Genovese merchants shipped dried pasta to other countries and Liguria became one of its leading producers, along with Sicily and Puglia. Shapes multiplied, people gradually learnt not to overcook pasta but to prepare it al dente, and the most various sauces were created (until the 18th century, pasta had been simply sprinkled with cheese). Tomato began to be served with pasta in the 18th century. The first chapter in the story of pasta as the food of the people took place in the 17th century in Naples, where new production processes were developed to make it accessible to all, even to the city's poor masses, from then on nicknamed *mangiamaccheroni*, macaroni eaters. The subsequent conquest of the north by a food "born and bred" in the south was part and parcel of the process of Italian unification.

pastasciutta dolce dried pasta cooked al dente in salted water and dressed with grated mature ricotta, melted butter, cinnamon and sugar. Friuli-Venezia Giulia.

pastatelle half moon shortcrust pastry tarts filled with cherry or grape jam, minced walnuts, orange zest and a pinch of powdered cinnamon. Puglia.

paste butade a batter of flour, eggs and → **Montasio** cheese, plunged into boiling broth. Friuli-Venezia Giulia.

paste di meliga dry cookies made of cornflour blended with wheat flour, sugar, butter, eggs and, sometimes, vanilla or lemon zest. Served with → **zabaglione**, accompanied by passito wine or Moscato. Piedmont.

paste di meliga del Monregalese cornmeal cookies produced in the Mondovì area, in the province of Cuneo. A Slow Food presidium that has brought together eight producers to draw up a discipline to protect the composition of these traditional cookies: stone-ground flours, no preservatives, coloring agents or artificial aromas. The paste is formed into round, oblong or crescent shapes and the cookies are yellow and crunchy, melt-in-the-mouth without being greasy or cloying. Piedmont.

paste di Ormea handmade buttery ring-shaped cookies. Typical of the upper Valle Tanaro, in the province of Cuneo. Piedmont.

pastec a thick purée of potatoes and vegetables (Savoy cabbage, chard, runner beans, zucchini and so on). A typical mountain dish of the Valle di Cembra, in the province of Trento, it used to be eaten with bread. Trentino-Alto Adige.

pastella batter. A mixture of flour and water and sometimes other ingredients (egg, brewer's yeast, oil, beer, white wine and so on) used to coat foods before frying to preserve the right humidity inside and ensure a gold crust outside. Usually allowed to rest before being used.

pastenula bianca aka **pastenula bruna** alternative names for → **mostella**, greater forkbeard.

pasticca aka **pastiglia** pastille. Small round hard confection made of sugar cold-pressed and blended with gum arabic and aromatic extracts. Particularly famous in Italy are the pastilles of the Leone candy factory in Turin, created in 1857 and soon popular nationwide: thirst-quenching and digestive, they are available in many flavors in pretty tin boxes and cardboard packages.

pasticcelle star-shaped Christmas pastry made with a dough enriched with almonds, dried pears and pine kernels, filled with confectioner's custard and covered with honey. Typical of the Cilento area. Campania.

pasticcetti di gnocchi pastry sandwiches filled with a custard of sugar, egg yolks, starch, milk, flour, cinnamon, nutmeg and grated lemon zest thickened on the heat. After cooling it is spread between two shortcrust pastry disks, which are brushed with beaten egg and baked in the oven. The pastries are eaten cold, sprinkled with confectioner's sugar. A specialty of Rome. Lazio.

pasticciata term used to describe → **polenta** to which other ingredients are added during the cooking process or, already cooked and solidified, cut into slices, layered in a baking tin with butter, cheese or sauce (meat, sausage, mushrooms) and baked in the oven.

pasticciata alla pesarese ox braised in red wine with lardo, garlic, cinnamon, cloves and tomato sauce. Marche.

pasticcino miniature cakes, pastries and cookies (→ **cannoncini, bignè, babà, sfogliatelle,** → **meringhette,** → **africani,** → **petit four,** → **tartellette,** → **chifferi** etc.) usually made in cake shops and bakeries and served in restaurants at the end of a meal and in homes on festive occasions.

pasticcio pasta layered or stuffed with other ingredients and baked in the oven. This type of dish was popular in Renaissance times, since when, partly thanks to French influence, it has taken undergone many variations, while always maintaining a prestigious, upper-class aura. It is still a typical specialty in some regional cuisines (Abruzzo, Emilia-Romagna, Campania, Lazio, Sicily) sometimes under different names. Today, in gastronomic terminology, the term has a similar meaning to → **timballo**.

pasticcio di anguilla in dialect aka **pastiz di bisat** a timbale of puff pastry filled with sweet and sour eel. The cut is skinned, boned, cut into two inch chunks, coated in flour and turned in butter and oil with raisins, nutmeg, cinnamon, cloves, ginger and pepper. A pie dish is lined with a disk of puff pastry and filled with the eel, its cooking juices diluted with sugared vinegar, beaten eggs and minced walnuts. The dish is covered with a pastry lid pricked at the center, and baked in the oven for an hour or so. A delicacy in the lagoon areas of Marano and Grado. Friuli-Venezia Giulia.

pasticcio di cappelletti (tortellini) following in the wake of → **pasticcio ferrarese**, the cities of Emilia developed a tradition of sweet shortcrust pastry timbales filled with → **cappelletti** (Reggio Emilia) or → **tortellini** (Bologna). The pasta is cooked in salted boiling water and dressed with butter and grated Parmigiano, layered with more Parmigiano, sauce (→ **ragù alla bolognese** in Reggio, a sauce of meat, bone marrow, mushrooms and chicken livers in Bologna) and béchamel sauce. Emilia-Romagna.

pasticcio di fagiano strips of flour and egg pasta, chopped roast pheasant and béchamel sauce layered in a baking dish and baked in the oven. Friuli-Venezia Giulia.

pasticcio di maccheroni an ancient and elaborate sweet and savory Carnival recipe, now rare. In a pie tin, a mixture of finely chopped chicken giblets, calf's sweetbreads, porcini mushrooms and truffles sautéed in butter is arranged on a shortcrust pastry disk round → **maccheroni** cooked → **al dente** and mixed with meat sauce and grated Parmigiano. The pasticcio is topped with confectioner's custard and covered with a pastry lid. After baking in the oven, it is sprinkled with sugar and allowed to cool. Lazio.

pasticcio ferrarese pasta, preferably → **sedanini**, mixed with béchamel sauce, mushrooms, peas, truffle and a sauce of lean pork, chicken livers, and veal closed in a sweet shortcrust pastry pie. An old specialty of Ferrara which seems to have been created not at the court of the Estensi, but by papal delegates in the 18th century. Emilia-Romagna.

pasticciotto egg-shaped shortcrust pastry pie filled with confectioner's custard. Brushed with egg white, it is best enjoyed fresh from the oven. The original recipe is typical of the Salento peninsula, in the province of Lecce (Puglia), where variants have since been introduced: cocoa in the pastry and cherry jam in the filling. In Naples, they add cherries or strawberry to the confectioner's custard. In Sant'Anastasia, in the province of Napoli, a cake called *'o pasticciotto* is made by amalgamating very fresh ricotta, sugar, eggs, limoncello and lemon juice, folding in confectioner's custard and baking the mixture in the oven on a base of finely crushed cookies. Puglia, Campania.

pasticciotto di carni ca ciculatti another name for → **'mpanatigghia**, a type of pastry.

pastiddri aka **pastilli** dried, peeled chestnuts. Calabria.

pastiera shortcrust pastry tart with a filling of barley or corn or rice cooked in milk, ricotta, eggs, sugar, candied fruits (citron, orange and pumpkin) and spices and aromas (grated lemon zest, ➤ **acqua di fiori d'arancio**, orange blossom, water, and cinnamon), baked in a hot oven and dusted with confectioner's sugar. Sometimes ricotta is replaced with confectioner's custard in the filling. This traditional Neapolitan Easter tart is now a symbol of the city's confectionery and is available all year round. Campania.

pastieri di carne di agnello lamb pastry baskets. Thin puff pastry disks (made from a dough of durum wheat flour, brewer's yeast, water and salt) are spread, at the center, with a tablespoonful of a filling made of chopped lamb and lamb's innards, eggs and grated mature ➤ **Ragusano** cheese. The sides are raised to form small "baskets," and baked in the oven. An Easter delicacy in the province of Ragusa. In Modica, they fill the baskets with other meats. Sicily.

pastìn ground, salted and spiced pork (or, in some cases, veal or beef) for the making of raw salami. Typical of the province of Belluno, it is listed in the Italian Ministry of Agriculture's database of native and/or traditional food products (➤ **tastasal**). Veneto.

pastina (1) aka **pasticcino** a small cake. Known popularly in Rome and central-southern Italy as ➤ **pastarella**.

pastina (2) tiny pasta shape, usually cooked in broth.

pastinaca aka **pastinello** aka **pastinocello** regional terms for ➤ **carota selvatica**, wild carrot.

pastisada aka **pastissada de caval** marinated horsemeat, stewed with wine and tomato, a specialty of Verona. According to popular legend, the dish was born of the need to eat horse carcasses during a siege or a battle, possibly that between Verona and Padua, allied with the condottiero Ezzelino da Romano, on June 2 1207 (though some say the event might go back to the times of Theodoric). In Verona, the dish is cooked chiefly during the Carnival period, and is traditionally served with polenta. By extension, in northeast Italy the word *pastissada* is also used for a beef stew. Veneto.

pastiss, 'l like other cities in Emilia—Ferrara, **pasticcio ferrarese**; Reggio, **cappelletti**; Bologna ➤ **pasticcio di tortellini**— Piacenza too has a ➤ **pasticcio di maccheroni** all of its own. The common denominator with the others is the sweet shortcrust pastry casing, but the filling differs, being composed of preboiled ➤ **mezze maniche** and a sauce of boned pigeon, mushrooms, butter and Parmigiano.

pastizzà de musso a stew of chopped donkey simmered for a few hours with aromatic herbs, spices and a little tomato passata. Donkey (*musso* in dialect) is a common and popular meat in the province of Padua. Veneto.

pastone impagliato spiced ground sausage meat shaped into medium-sized cylinders, wrapped in damp parchment, and cooked until the latter starts to catch fire. At which point, the meat is cut into slices and served drizzled with extra virgin olive oil. One of the many dishes created in country villages in the days of the killing of the pig, it used to be cooked in hot embers, but is now baked in the oven. Umbria.

pastorale lamb or mutton stew with vegetables (potatoes, tomatoes, celery, carrot), bay leaf and chili, all covered with water and cooked until the latter evaporates. A dish born of the region's pastoral tradition. Basilicata.

pastorizzare to pasteurize.

pastorizzazione pasteurization.

patacche aka **pataccacce** strips of homemade pasta cut from a particularly thick sheet of dough. Lazio.

patacò a sort of polenta made with grass pea (➤ **cicerchia**) flour, which is gradually poured over a base of stewed crumbled sausage and chopped broccoli florets. The mixture is stirred constantly until thick, at which point it is served piping hot, generously anointed with extra virgin olive oil. It may also be served the day after, cut into slices, coated in flour and fried. Sicily.

patacucci large squares of wheat flour and cornflour dough cooked in a purée of beans, tomato and gently fried aromatics, accompanied by whole beans. Emilia-Romagna.

patao potato and runner bean purée dressed with pieces of ➤ **Spressa** cheese and grated ➤ **Trentingran**a, warmed in a skillet with minced lardo, onion and garlic sautéed in butter. A delicacy in the Trentino Dolomites. Trentino-Alto Adige.

pataracia Veneto word for ➤ **linguattola**, spotted flounder.

patata potato (*Solanum tuberosum*). A tuber of fundamental importance in the history of food and gastronomy. Many varieties exist, all round or oval, all with yellow or red skins, all with white or yellow bodies, all used in roughly similar recipes. The best potatoes for purées, croquettes, gnocchi, molds and the like are the white, floury varieties. Yellow ones, firmer and more compact, and those with red skins are better for cooking whole or fried. In Italy, almost half the potato yield comes from three regions, Campania, Emilia-Romagna and Abruzzo, but Puglia, Veneto, Calabria and Tuscany also make an important contribution to national production. Roast, mashed, fried, boiled steamed or cooked in ashes, potatoes are arguably the most popular side dish in the country, and are also the principal ingredient in any number of traditional recipes: ➤ **baciocca**, ➤ **bagozia**, ➤ **crocchè**, ➤ **frico**, ➤ **gattò**, ➤ **kiffel**, ➤ **patugol**, ➤ **subrich**. It is no exaggeration to say that, in the past, every mountain valley in Italy boasted a variety of its own. The Italian Ministry of Agriculture's database of native and/or traditional varieties lists: *patata di montagna del medio Sangro, patata degli altipiani* (Abruzzo); *patata della Sila* (Calabria); *patata novella* (Campania); *patata quarantina piacentina, patata di Montese* (Emilia-Romagna); *patata di Ribis e Godia, patatis cojonariis* (Friuli); *patata dell'alto Viterbese, patata di Leonessa* (Lazio); *cabannese, cannellina nera, patata di Pignone, prugnosa, quarantina bianca e gialla, morella, salamina* (Liguria); *patata di Campodolcino* (Lombardy); *patata lunga di San Biase* (Molise); *patata trentina di montagna* (Trentino); *patata quarantina bianca genovese, patata dell'alta Valle Belbo, patata di Castelnuovo Scrivia, patata di montagna di Cesana, patata di San Raffaele Cimena, trifulot del bur* (Piedmont); *patata novella sieglinde di Galatina, patata di Zapponeta* (Puglia); *patata novella di Messina, patata novella di Siracusa* (Sicily); *patata bianca del Melo, patata di Regnano, patata di Santa Maria a Monte, patata di Zeri, patata rossa di Cetica* (Tuscany); *patata rossa di Colfiorito* (Umbria); *patata americana di Anguillara e Stroppare, patata americana di Zero Branco, cornetta, patata del Montello, patata del Quartier del Piave, patata di Cesiomaggiore, patata di*

Chioggia, patata di *Montagnana, patata di Posina, patata dorata dei terreni rossi del Guà, patata di Rotzo* (Veneto).

patata americana aka **patata dolce** common names for ➤ **batata**, sweet potato.

patata selvatica another name for ➤ **topinambur**, Jerusalem artichoke.

patate alla contadina side dish of diced potatoes browned in oil with garlic and rosemary, then finished off with puréed tomatoes, salt and pepper. Tuscany.

patate alla parulana potatoes hollowed out, stuffed with zucchini flowers, mushrooms and anchovies, and baked in the oven. Campania.

patate alla pecurieddu scappatu an oven-baked casserole of onions, parsley, cherry tomatoes, rosemary and bay leaf, topped with thinly sliced potatoes sprinkled with dry breadcrumbs and grated Pecorino cheese. The richly flavored potatoes make up for the lack of meat (the ironic name refers to lamb, *pecurieddu,* that should be there, but isn't because it has run off somewhere else, *scappatu*). Puglia.

patate alla tarantina a mixture of mashed potatoes, grated Pecorino, eggs, a modicum of flour, salt and pepper, fried in extra virgin olive oil, a tablespoonful at a time. Puglia.

patate en bronzon a ➤ **battuto** of lardo softened in a little butter to which roughly cut potatoes are added, together with tomato concentrate, fresh ➤ **lucanica** sausage, bay leaves, sage, rosemary, salt and pepper. The stew is covered with warm water and finished off in the oven for at least half an hour. The whole operation takes place in an oven pan (*bronzon* in dialect). Trentino-Alto Adige.

patate in tecia boiled potatoes finished off in a skillet with onion, lardo and a ladleful or two of broth. Typical of Trieste and its province. Friuli-Venezia Giulia.

patate 'mpacchiate aka **patate 'mpacchiuse** thinly sliced potatoes fried in oil and finished off with onion and pancetta. In a simplified version of the recipe, the sliced potatoes are cooked until they develop a crisp outside crust but remain soft inside. Calabria.

patate raganate baked casserole of sliced potatoes layered with sliced onions and tomatoes, drizzled with oil and sprinkled with grated Pecorino, fried breadcrumbs and oregano. Basilicata.

patate ripiene stuffed or baked or jacket potatoes. Potatoes with their flesh scooped out, flavored with aromatized butter and baked in the oven with their jackets on. In one Friulian recipe, they are stuffed with ground pork or sausage, egg, parsley, salt and pepper.

patate rustì an Italian version of rösti. Boiled potatoes are allowed to cool, finely sliced, turned in a ➤ **soffritto** of onion and crushed lardo, flattened, topped with diced local cheese, cooked until a golden-brown crust forms on the surface, and flipped over like a frittata. A specialty of the province of Verbano-Cusio-Ossola. Piedmont.

pâté technically and historically, a *farce* (➤ **farcia**) of meat, fish or legumes enclosed in a pastry crust, cooked in a metal mold, and served cut into slices. Today the term is used, erroneously, to refers to terrines (➤ **terrine**), certain fish and liver mousses in aspic (➤ **mousse**), and artisan and commercial spreads, such as the black olive cream that is commercialized as *pâté di olive*.

pâté di carne meat pâté. Lean veal cooked with white wine and mushrooms, ground, mixed with isinglass and allowed to set in the refrigerator. Trentino-Alto Adige.

pâté di cavedano chub pâté. Fillets of chub

cooked in butter with garlic, salt, pepper and marjoram, puréed and amalgamated with butter, lardo and cognac. A specialty of the provinces of Como and Lecco. Lombardy.

pâté di fegato di vitello calf's liver pâté. A popular recipe, especially in the north of Italy, even though the end-product isn't a "pâté" at all. Often a ready-made dish such as ➤ **fegato alla veneziana** is finely ground, mixed with an equal amount of butter, and aromatized with dry Marsala (Veneto). In the province of Milan (Lombardy), the calf's liver is blanched in milk and cooked in the fat left over from thin slices of pork in butter with bay leaves. Liver and pork are subsequently pushed through a sieve and amalgamated with cold butter, port, salt and pepper. Both preparations and others like them are allowed to set and served in slices or spread on toasted bread.

pâté di lepre hare pâté. A mixture of ground hare meat and butter, perfumed with brandy and left to set in the refrigerator. Piedmont.

pâté di tonno tuna pâté. A mixture of tuna preserved in oil, desalted anchovy fillets and the flesh of black olives, puréed to a cream and left to set in the refrigerator. A popular antipasto in Piedmont, where a simpler version exists with the addition of mashed potatoes, known as *pesce di tonno* or *pesce di guerra*.

patedda a soup for important occasions. Egg tagliolini cooked in a broth of veal, wild boar, kid and mutton, aromatized with garlic, onion, carrot and celery.

patella limpet (*Patella coerulea, P. vulgata, P. tarentina* and other spices still). Marine gastropods that cling to rocks and are normally eaten raw.

patella reale common name for ➤ **aliotide**, green ormer or sea-ear.

paternostri regional name for ➤ **avemarie**, tiny durum wheat pasta tubes.

patora corn and legume soup. Typical of the mountains of the province of Belluno, in particular the Alpago valley. Veneto.

pattona today the word is used in some areas to refer to ➤ **castagnaccio**, a rustic chestnut cake. In the Lunigiana area of Tuscany, the word *patona* refers to bread made from a fluid mixture of chestnut flour and water cooked on a bed of chestnut leaves in a covered ➤ **testo**, a sort of griddle plan. On the other side of the Apennines, in Emilia and southern Lombardy, the word *patuna* again means ➤ **castagnaccio**. Oral sources record that Tuscan families used to sell the cake in Mantua first in markets, then in a couple of shops in the center of the city. Lombardy, Emilia-Romagna, Tuscany.

pattone di tagliatelle fritters made with leftover tagliatelle, butter, dry breadcrumbs, Parmigiano, eggs and pepper. A specialty of Reggio Emilia. Emilia-Romagna.

patugoi soft polenta served with cold milk (➤ **mosa**). Veneto.

patugol a sort of potato polenta flavored with onion, pancetta, butter and grated Grana. Traditionally served with a special local salami (➤ **ciuighe**). In some versions, Savoy cabbage, chard, runner beans, zucchini and other vegetables are added to the potatoes. Trentino.

pazientina sandwich cake consisting of two disks, one made with a mixture of flour, chopped almonds, butter and sugar, the other with a mixture similar to that of ➤ **polentina di Cittadella**, baked in the oven, filled with ➤ **zabaglione**, and coated with an icing of confectioner's sugar, flour and powdered vanilla. Stored in hermetically sealed tins. A specialty of Padua. Veneto.

pazientini quaresimali Lent cookies made

with a paste of sugar, egg whites, flour, caramel and a hint of vanilla, shaped into slightly flattened balls that are left to rest for a day, then baked in the oven. A specialty of Rome. Lazio.

pèa aka **guastella** bread load typical of Novara di Sicilia (province of Messina), made with a dough of strong flour and natural yeast and baked in a wood oven. When the crust starts to go brown, broom branches are thrown in to augment the smoke and steam, hence to stop the bread from leavening any further. Sicily.

pearà a sort of bread sauce made by beating to a cream grated day-old bread, ox bone marrow dissolved in butter and beef broth with the addition of generous amounts of freshly ground pepper and, in some recipes, grated Grana cheese. Traditionally served with ➤ **bollito misto alla Veronese**. Veneto.

pech cow's udder preserved in salt, like the Val d'Aosta delicacy ➤ **teteun**. Typical of the province of Biella. Piedmont.

peclin con polenta smoked herring fillets (➤ **aringa affumicata**) revived by steeping them for a week in oil aromatized with garlic, bay leaves and juniper berries. Warmed in the oven, they are served with potato polenta, wet or toasted, onion rings and a dash of the marinade liquid. Trentino-Alto Adige.

pecora generically sheep, specifically ewe. The domestic sheep is believed to descend from a cross between breeds now extinct with wild species still extant, among which the European mouflon, common in Sardinia. The animal's most important physical characteristic is its fleece, which covers most of its body. In general, the ram has horns, sometimes spiral-shaped, though there are some breeds which are hornless and others in which both sexes have horns. In Italy, the most important product of sheep rearing is milk, most of which is used to make cheese. The most used and popular meat is that of young animals (➤ **agnello**, ➤ **agnellone**). Mutton has never been as popular in Italy as in the Balkans and North Africa, but specific recipes do exist in sheep-rearing areas : eg, ➤ **pecora in cappotto sarda**, ➤ **pecora alla materana**, ➤ **pezzata**, ➤ **pecora alla callara**, ➤ **arrosticini**. The Italian Ministry of Agriculture's database of native and/or traditional food products lists: *pecora alpagota* (➤ **agnello d'Alpago**, Veneto), *brigasca* (Liguria), *sopravissana* (Marche), not to mention the meat of Calabrian and Campanian ➤ **Laticauda** sheep.

pecora alla callara aka **pecora a cotturo** chopped mutton cooked in water, white wine, tomato and herbs. Common in the provinces of Teramo and L'Aquila (Abruzzo), it is also to be found in the Apennines on the border with the Marche, especially in the provinces of Ascoli Piceno and Macerata, all areas with a long pastoral tradition. Marche, Abruzzo.

pecora alla materana chunks of mutton, tomatoes, potatoes, onions, ➤ **soppressata** and grated Pecorino slowly stewed over a medium heat. Typical of Matera. Basilicata.

pecora delle Langhe Langhe sheep. One of Italy's finest dairy breeds. Large in size and hornless, it has a narrow body and long, fine limbs. No more than 2,500 specimens survive today in 60 or so farms in southern Piedmont and Liguria.

pecora e cavoli mutton and cabbage. Mutton chops browned in oil with finely minced onion, garlic and rosemary, and stewed with shredded white cabbage, pepper, cinnamon and cumin seeds. Typical of the Valle Rendena. Trentino-Alto Adige.

pecora in cappotto literally "sheep in its coat." Chunks of mutton boiled in a generous amount of salted boiling water with potatoes and onions. In the Gallura area, the dish is supplemented with white cabbage, in other places with carrots, celery and parsley. The meat and vegetables are served on disks of unleavened bread (→ **pane carasau**) with a little of the cooking broth. Sardinia.

pecora in umido mutton stew. Cubed mutton browned in oil with aromatic herbs and chili, then stewed in red wine, tomato and, in some recipes, nutmeg and lemon zest. A winter dish of the Florentine countryside and the Pistoia mountains. Tuscany.

pecorella common name for → **motella**, three-bearded rockling a fish.

Pecorino abruzzese ewe's milk curd cooked in immersion in boiling whey, matured for 20 days in a warm, well-ventilated room and aged for a further month or more, then rubbed with oil.

Pecorino baccellone fresh sheep's cheese, usually made with pasteurized milk. Matured for two to five days in a cool damp environment. Tuscany.

Pecorino bagnolese cheese produced with the milk of the Bagnolese sheep, a native breed named for the village of Bagnoli Irpino, which lives in the wild in the Irpinia area, in the province of Avellino. The rind is firm-textured and the body is hard and fatty. Fresh, it should be eaten as it is; mature, it is tangy and best used for grating. A Slow Food presidium is encouraging breeders to produce the cheese with Bagnolese milk only. Campania.

Pecorino dei Monti Sibillini semi-cooked ewe's milk cheese produced in the Monti Sibillini national park. The freshly drawn milk is inoculated with lamb's rennet aromatized with wild thyme, marjoram, basil, bramble shoots, pepper, oil, cloves and even figs, honey and egg yolk. Ready to eat after 30 days, it may age for a few months. A Slow Food presidium protects this version of the cheese. A second fresh version is made from pasteurized milk by industrial dairies. Marche.

Pecorino del Beigua ewe's milk cheese produced by a family of Sardinian shepherds in the mountains of the Beigua nature park (between Genoa and Savona) with milk from two consecutive milkings. It is matured for at least 45 days and reaches its peak after six months. Liguria.

Pecorino del Matese cheese produced from April to September with milk from Pagliarola ewes (75%) mixed with goat's milk (25%), generally from grazing animals. It is aged for three months to a year or more, during which time it is periodically rubbed with oil and vinegar. Molise.

Pecorino del Monte Poro rare cheese produced in the province of Vibo Valentia from the milk of sheep raised in the wild on grazing land with a profusion of aromatic herbs. Before aging, forms are rubbed with olive oil and chili, which give the cheese a distinctive aromatic profile. The flavor is slightly tangy with an attractive hazelnut note in the finish. Calabria.

Pecorino del Parco cheese produced in the Abruzzo national park with organic raw ewe's milk. The curd is uncooked and the cheese is aged for at least 60 days. Abruzzo.

Pecorino del pastore ewe's milk cheese typical of the provinces of Rieti, Frosinone and Latina, which has to ripen for 20-30 days before it is ready for consumption, after which maturing may last for four to five months. Lazio.

Pecorino del Sannio cheese made with raw

milk from the Comisana shep. It is coagulated with a very small amount of rennet and after a slow acidification is aged for 50 to 90 days in damp, well-ventilated caves. Molise.

Pecorino dell'Appennino rare raw ewe's milk cheese made in the province of Reggio Emilia. Aged for three to ten months, it has excellent balance and outstanding elegance. Reggio Emilia.

Pecorino della Garfagnana cheese made with the milk of Massese sheep raised in the wild. Eaten fresh but can also be aged for three months. Tuscany.

Pecorino della montagna pistoiese cheese made with the raw milk of Massese breed ewes grazing in high-altitude pastures and natural rennet. Three types are produced: the *fresco* (fresh) version matures for only seven to 20 days; *abbucciato*, which means "with a wrinkly skin" for at least 35 days; *asserbo* (for conserving) for two to three months to a year. All three are round with an ivory white body. A Slow Food is seeking to protect the sheep's mountain pastures and support the 20 or so producers still remaining. Tuscany.

Pecorino della Vallata Stilaro Allaro a cheese produced from October to July with filtered ewe's and goat's milk. It is aged for four to ten months, during which the flavor develops from sweet to tangy. Typical of the upper Ionian area of the province of Reggio. Calabria.

Pecorino di Atri cheese made with filtered raw ewe's milk in the province of Teramo. It is aged for 40 days to two years, sometimes in bran, sometimes with oil flavored with spices. Abruzzo.

Pecorino di Capracotta ancient semi-cooked cheese with a very tangy flavor when aged. Particularly delicious dipped in egg and fried. Molise.

Pecorino di Carmasciano tangy ewe's milk cheese produced in the province of Avellino. Aged for three months, it may be eaten as a table cheese. Aged for longer, it is grated. Campania.

Pecorino di Farindola cheese produced in the provinces of Pescara and Teramo on the eastern side of the Gran Sasso massif with the raw milk of the Pagliarola sheep breed, raised in the wild. It is coagulated with pig's rennet, which gives it its characteristic aroma and flavor. It is aged for a period of 40 days to a year, during which time it is brushed periodically with a mixture of extra virgin olive oil and, sometimes, tomato conserve. A Slow Food presidium is seeking to safeguard and support the production of this unique cheese. Abruzzo.

Pecorino di Filiano ancient PDO cheese typical of the Vulture area, the lakes of Monticchio and a few small communes. The rind is golden yellow and the body is white to straw-yellow with a firm texture. Basilicata.

Pecorino di Garfagnina rare cheese produced with the raw milk of Garfagnina breed ewes. Aged for 60 to 180 days. Typical of the Garfagnana area, in the province of Lucca. Tuscany.

Pecorino di Moliterno cheese produced with raw ewe's milk in the Val d'Agri (province of Potenza). During aging it is periodically turned and brushed with oil and vinegar. Basilicata

Pecorino di montagna ewe's milk cheese which matures for at least 20 days, during which forms are turned and washed with water and whey. Tuscany, Marche.

Pecorino di montone the name given to ➤ **Pecorino del Sannio** preserved in extra virgin olive oil for six to eight months. Molise.

Pecorino di Norcia cheese made with pasteurized ewe's milk in the upper Val Nerina (Umbria). It is ready for the table after 30 days but may be aged for six months. Umbria.

Pecorino di Osilo smaller than other Sardinian Pecorinos, this cheese undergoes protracted pressing. This gives it a doughy texture that it conserves during maturation, which should last for five to six months. During this period the forms are periodically turned and washed with water and brine. A Slow Food presidium is seeking to organize producers and provide them with modern structures. Sardinia.

Pecorino di Pienza pasteurized ewe's milk produced in and around Pienza, in the province of Siena. During maturing (40-60 days), forms are treated with oil and tomato. Tuscany.

Pecorino dolce dei colli bolognesi semihard cheese made with pasteurized milk. It is aged for 20 days to four months. Emilia-Bologna.

Pecorino laticauda cheese produced in the province of Benevento with milk from the Laticauda cheese. It may be eaten fresh or aged, and when fully mature it is used as an ingredient in traditional regional dishes. Campania.

Pecorino romano PDO cheese produced in the Agro romano area, in the province of Grosseto and in Sardinia with filtered, heat-treated milk from two milkings. It is aged for five to eight months and wheels for export are encased in black plastic film. Lazio, Tuscany, Sardinia.

Pecorino salaprese soft, delicate cheese produced in the provinces of Avellino, Benevento, Caserta and Salerno. It is eaten fresh (*salaprese* means just "salted") after drying briefly. Campania.

Pecorino sardo PDO cheese produced with whole ewe's milk. It is eaten fresh after 20-60 days or mature after aging for up to 12 months, during which time it may also be smoked. Sardinia.

Pecorino senese ewe's milk cheese from the Valdelsa. Eaten fresh or after brief maturing, during which time forms are treated with oil, oil dregs and tomato. Tuscany.

Pecorino siciliano cheese produced with whole raw milk from two milkings, it may be eaten fresh from the dairy, when it is known as Tuma, after two week's maturing when it is known as Primo Sale, or semi-mature after aging for 50 days. A version staged for at least four months, with or without pepper, has received PDO recognition. Sicily.

Pecorino toscano PDO ewe's milk cheese, Tuscan by name but also produced in some areas of Umbria and Lazio. Made mostly with pasteurized milk. May be soft (20 days of maturing) or semi-hard (aged for at least four months). Tuscany, Umbria, Lazio.

Pecorino veneto rare cheese produced in the province of Padua mostly with the milk of the Massese sheep. An uncooked version is eaten fresh, a cooked version is aged. The flavor is mild without any tanginess. Veneto.

pectina pectin (→ **gelatina**, gelatin).

pedocio Friuli-Venezia Giulia term for → **mitilo**, mussel. The Italian Ministry of Agriculture's database of native and/or traditional food products lists the *pedocio di Trieste* variety.

peilà aka **péila** aka **peilò** term used to generically to describe a very fluid polenta of rye flour, buckwheat flour or barley flour cooked in milk (or broth or water) and served with butter and local cheese. *Peilà d'orzo* is a polenta of potatoes and barley and wheat flour mixed with cheese (→ **Fontina**, → **Toma**) and melted butter. Val d'Aosta.

peladei (1) Trentino dialect name for peeled boiled chestnuts.

peladei (2) traditional fresh pasta made from an egg and flour dough cut into small dice.

peladeo term used in some areas of Veneto for "boiled chestnut."

pelare to peel (→ **sbucciare**).

pelato (pl. **pelati**) used in the plural, the term refers to whole tomatoes, blanched, skinned, transferred to glass jars and sterilized. One of the best varieties for this preservation technique is → **pomodoro sanmarzano**.

pellegrina regional name for → **conchiglia di san Giacomo**, great Mediterranean scallop.

pencarelli di Antrodoco large fresh spaghetti, the equivalent of → **pincinelle marchigiane**, lengthened by hand on a baking board. Typical of the province of Rieti, in particular of the village of Antrodoco, the pasta is served with local sauces, especially with a mixture, reminiscent of → **carbonara**, of eggs, pancetta and crumbled sausage, Pecorino and black pepper. Lazio.

pence alle erbe tagliatelle (*pence*) made with bread dough served with crumbled sausages, garlic, chicory and mashed red Colfiorito potatoes. Umbria, Marche.

penchi broad egg tagliatelle usually served with → **guanciale** (cheek bacon), sausage, eggs, lemon juice, butter, pepper and nutmeg. Umbria.

penciarelle another name for → **pingiarelle**, small gnocchi.

pendolon a porridge-like mixture of potatoes and runner beans flavored with onion softened in butter or lard. It is allowed to set and eaten sliced, warm or cold. A food which mountain dwellers used to eat during their work in the field or pastures. The curious name might

derive from the haversack which shepherds used to sling over their shoulders and in which they carried their rations (hence from the verb *pendere*, to hang), or else from the fact that the porridge was cooked in a pot hanging from a hook in the fireplace. Veneto, Trentino-Alto Adige.

penne short, tubular, quill-shaped commercial durum wheat pasta with a ridged or smooth surface. According to size it comes in a whole range of other names. Smaller shapes may also be → **pennine** or → **pennette**, larger ones → **penne di ziti rigate**, → **pennoni**, → **ziti tagliati** or → **mostaccioli**. **Penne** originated in Campania, and may be served with different sauces according to size.

penne di Natale (aka → **natalini**). Long, tubular dried durum wheat pasta with a smooth surface. Usually broken up into two or three pieces before boiling. Served with rich sauces, baked or in broth. Liguria.

penne di ziti rigate a variety of → **penne**, type of pasta.

penne strascicate short durum wheat pasta very common in Tuscan cooking, often served with meat sauce. Once cooked, it is turned (*strascicata*) in the pan with the sauce, extra virgin olive oil and grated Parmigiano for a few minutes. Tuscany.

pennecciola regional name for → **sanguinello**, saffron milk-cap mushroom.

pennette aka **pennine** types of → **penne**.

pennoni type of → **penne**.

peocio aka **pedocio** Veneto terms for → **mitilo**, mussel.

peparuolo Campania term for → **peperoncino**, chili.

pepatelli aka **pepatielli** rectangular baked cakes. The name refers to the generous use of freshly ground black pepper (*pepe* in Italian) in the firm, elastic paste, the other ingredients of which are bran flour, whole almonds, grated orange and lemon zest and honey. Marche.

pepe common name for the different species of the Piperaceae, especially for *Piper nigrum*, from which the corns of one of the most famous spices of all are extracted. A native of southwest India, the plant is cultivated on the Malacca peninsula, in Thailand, Sumatra, Java, Borneo, the Philippines, Japan and along the Malabar coast in India, whence comes the most prized variety. The fruits are small drupes containing a single green seed which turns to yellow then, when ripe, to red. The different varieties (black ➤ **pepe nero**, white ➤ **pepe bianco**, green ➤ **pepe verde**, red ➤ **pepe rosso**) are tied to state of maturation and type of processing. In the kitchen, pepper is at its best freshly ground, though in many dishes whole peppercorns are used (➤ **peposo toscano**).

pepe bianco white pepper. The largest pods of the pepper plant are picked when they are fully ripe and macerated in water for about seven days. The darker colored skin is rubbed off (then ground and sold as powder), to release the peppercorns, which are then dried. White pepper is pungent and very aromatic.

pepedi Caienna Cayenne pepper. Powdered fiery chili pepper (*Capsicum annuum* cv *Caienna*) named for the city of Cayenne, the capital of French Guiana.

pepe garofanato another name for ➤ **quattro spezie**, allspice.

pepe nero black pepper. Made from the unripe drupes of the pepper plant. Yellow-green in color, after drying in the sun or in special chambers they turn black. Intense, tangy but harmonious in flavor and aroma, black pepper is the most common variety on the market.

pepper rosa pink pepper. Not a fruit of *Piper nigrum* (➤ **pepe**), but of *Schinus terebenthifolius*, a South American plant also known as "false pepper." It is very delicate and is often used mixed with other peppers for decorative purposes.

pepe rosso (1) red pepper. Made with the fully ripe fruits of the pepper plant (➤ **pepe**), then dried. Fruity and mild, it is rare in the West.

pepe rosso (2) term used in Tuscany for ➤ **peperoncino**, chili.

pepe verde green pepper. Extracted from the unripe fruit of the pepper plant (➤ **pepe**), it is treated with chemicals to fix its color, then dried or preserved in brine or vinegar. Less piquant than black pepper, it is much more aromatic, fresh and fruity, though the brine obviously attenuates its aroma.

pepentò piccante dialect term for ➤ **peperoncino**, chili.

peperati ring-shaped cakes made from a mixture of flour, sugar, cooked wine must (➤ **vincotto**), almonds, cocoa, orange zest and cloves. A delicacy in San Severo, in the province of Foggia. Puglia.

peperna regional term for ➤ **santoreggia**, savory.

peperona regional term for ➤ **gelone**, oyster mushroom.

peperonata stewed sweet or bell peppers. A dish common, with local variations and different names, all over the north of Italy. In Emilia it is called *rustisana* and *frizon* (Italianized as ➤ **friggione**, though the dish varies a lot round the region). In Piedmont, the classic **peperonata** (*povronà*) is made by softening finely sliced onions in a pan and adding yellow and red peppers, deseeded and cut into strips. When the peppers start to color, skinned, chopped tomatoes are added and the dish is cooked through with the occasional ladleful of broth. It is often served with sausage.

peperoncino chili pepper (*Capsicum annuum*). Only the Capsicum genus is common and cultivated in Italy, especially in Basilicata and, even more so, in Calabria, home to the Accademia italiana del peperoncino, the Italian Academy of the Red Chili. The most widespread varieties are: *abbreviatum* (small and cone-shaped), *acuminatum* (tapered and slightly curved), *fasciculatum* (thin and straight), *cerasiferum* (small, round and cherry-like), *bicolor* (tiny, violet and red), *christmas candle* (also used for ornamental purposes). Local names include: *povronin, spagnolin* (Piedmont), *pevium* (Liguria), *peverone* (Lombardy), *pevrum* (Emilia), *pepe rosso, zenzero* (Tuscany), *lazzarette, cazzarele, saitti, pepentò piccante* (Abruzzo), *diavulillu* (Molise), *peparuolo* (Campania), *diavulicchio* (Puglia), *cancarillo, pipazzu, pipi vruscente, diavulillo* (Calabria), *cerasella, mericanill, diavulicchiu* (Basilicata), *pipi addenti, pipi russi* (Sicilia), *pibiri moriscu* (Sardinia).

peperone sweet or bell pepper (Capsicum annuum). The types most common in Italy are large and square (*grosso* or *quadrato*) or long (*lungo*). The first group includes *california wonder* and *quadrato d'Asti*, the second *corno di bue, lungo marconi, calabrese verde, lombardo chiarissimo* and *sigaretta verde*. The *trottola* and *topego rosso* varieties are instead shaped like tomatoes. Yellow and red peppers predominate, but smaller cultivars exist which stay green even when ripe. The regions which cultivate most peppers are in the south of Italy (the Basilicata variety ➤ **peperone di Senise** has received PGI recognition), In the north, Piedmont is the most important producer region, renowned for its ➤ **peperone**

corno di bue di Carmagnola. The Italian Ministry of Agriculture's database of native and/or traditional food products lists the following varieties: *peperone rosso di Altino* (Abruzzo); *roggianese* (Calabria); ➤ **papaccella napoletana e quagliettano** (Campania); *corno di bue di Pontecorvo* (Lazio); *rosso* (Molise); *peperone di Capriglio, peperone di Cuneo, quadrato d'Asti* (Piedmont); *peperone di Zero Branco* (Veneto). In the kitchen peppers are eaten raw (➤ **pinzimonio**, ➤ **bagna caoda**), fried in olive oil (➤ **friggitelli**), stewed (➤ **peperonata**), roasted in the oven or barbecued. Sometimes they are left whole and, with their flesh scooped out, stuffed with other ingredients, in which case they become a meal-in-one (➤ **peperoni imbottiti**). Typical and traditional preserves include: ➤ **peperoni alla vinaccia**, ➤ **paparolesse**, ➤ **pupazzelle 'a cumposta**.

peperone corno di bue di Carmagnola long, cone-shaped "ox-horn" pepper, bright yellow or red in color with firm meaty flesh. It is one of the four varieties for which Carmagnola, a town on the plain south of Turin almost on the border with the province of Cuneo, is famous. Production is still sizable, but undermined by the habit of selling the peppers, often mixed with anonymous imported varieties, to the preserving and canning industry. A Slow Food presidium has been set up with the aim of creating a new market for this excellent vegetable, cultivated in 40 or so communes in the provinces of Turin and Cuneo. Piedmont.

peperone di Senise sweet PGI pepper, an ecotype native to the Sinni and Agri valleys in the provinces of Potenza and Matera, in Basilicata. Green or purple-red in color, it is small with a pointed, sometimes hooked end. The Senise is the best variety for drying (➤ **peperoni crusch**) Basilicata.

peperoni al brusco a summer antipasto or side dish in vegetable-growing areas. Sweet peppers are cut into pieces, softened in oil, sprinkled with finely minced garlic, parsley, basil, capers and desalted anchovies, simmered in vinegar (which gives them a sharp flavor, *brusco* in dialect), and served cold. Piedmont.

peperoni alla calabrese sweet peppers cut into strips and lightly fried in olive oil with the addition of chopped ripe tomatoes and salt. The peppers are used to make a frittata or as a side dish, while the sauce is served with pasta. Calabria.

peperoni alla vinaccia sweet peppers with pomace. In the province of Frosinone (Lazio), whole late sweet peppers are layered with pomace in small demijohns and covered with a solution of water, vinegar and salt. In Piedmont, in a similar recipe, *peperoni sotto raspa*, small peppers are covered with boiling water, vinegar, salt and salicylic acid and the top of the demijohn is sealed with pomace. Lazio, Piedmont.

peperoni con la bagna caoda classic antipasto in homes and restaurants, especially in vegetable-growing areas where they grow large, fleshy peppers suitable for roasting in the oven: eg, ➤ **quadrato d'Asti**, ➤ **peperone corno di bue di Carmagnola**. The roast peppers are skinned, cut into strips and topped with a spoonful of ➤ **bagna caoda**. Often they are dressed even more simply with salt, oil, vinegar and desalted anchovy fillets. Piedmont.

peperoni crusch aka **peperoni cruschi** sundried red peppers (ideally of the ➤ **peperone di Senise** variety). Used as an ingredient in a number of dishes and an excellent accompaniment for cheese and raw vegetables. In dialect ➤ **zafaran crusch**. Basilicata.

peperoni imbottiti stuffed peppers. Red and yellow sweet peppers, skinned and with their flesh scooped out, and stuffed with pieces of fried eggplant, olives, capers, anchovy fillets and breadcrumbs. In another recipe, *peperoni imbottiti alla caprese*, the peppers are stuffed with pasta, preferably bucatini, dressed with tomato, capers, olives and anchovies. Campania.

peperoni ripieni stuffed peppers. Recipes exist all over Italy. In Piedmont they stuff the vegetables with ➤ **seirass**, cheese and boiled rice. In the south of Italy ingredients such as breadcrumbs, anchovies, capers, green olives and tomato sauce tend to prevail.

peperoni secchi sun-dried peppers. A specialty of central and southern Italy since time immemorial. Dried peppers, fiery and sweet, can still be seen hanging in braids at the front of country cottages. The peppers used are small varieties. Cut into strips or left whole, they are sundried and kept for a long time. They can also be ground and sold in powder form. They are made in Calabria, Puglia, Lazio, Abruzzo and, above all, Basilicata, the capital of sun-dried peppers.

peperoni sotto raspa a Piedmontese version of ➤ **peperoni alla vinaccia**.

pepolino Tuscan term for ➤ **serpillo**, wild thyme.

peposo chunks of cheap cuts of beef stewed in wine with garlic and lots of peppercorns. This ancient dish is believed to have been created by the potters of the town of Impruneta, in the province of Florence, who used to use the residual heat from their ovens to cook the stew. Tuscany.

pera pear (*Pirus communis*). One of the most ancient fruit-bearing trees, it is to be found in numerous varieties, many of which no longer cultivated. According to species, the fruit is available from summer to fall. Italy is the major producer country in Europe and its ➤ **pera dell'Emilia Romagna** (Emilia-Romagna) and ➤ **pera mantovana** (Lombardy) both have PGI recognition. The Italian Ministry of Agriculture's database of native and/or traditional food products lists the following varieties: *pera del rosario, mastantuono, pennata, sant'anna, sorba, spadona di Salerno, spina* (Campania); *antiche varietà di pera piacentina* (Emilia-Romagna); *angelica* (Marche); *pera delle valli di Lanzo, madernassa del Cuneese* (Piedmont); *pera bianca e camusina di Bonarcado, brutta e buona, pera del duca, pera limone, pira ruspu* (Sardinia); *butirra d'estate, spinelli, ucciardona, virgola* (Sicily); *coscia aretina, coscia di Firenze, pera del curato, pera gentile, rusé* (Tuscany); *pere antiche trentine* (Trentino); *pere del medio Adige, pera del Veneziano, pera del Veronese* (Veneto). The ➤ **pera cocomerina** is promoted by a Slow Food. Pears are used extensively in jams and preserves, fresh in tarts, cakes and desserts (➤ **barchiglia,** ➤ **charlotte alla milanese**), chopped into pieces in the fillings of traditional stuffed pastas (➤ **casonsei de la Bergamasca**), or as an accompaniment to cheese. Domestic favorites include baked pears, with or without wine, and ➤ **pere madernassa al vino.** Pears are used, finally, to make juices and perries, like the Friulian ➤ **most,** produced with the klotzen variety.

pera cocomerina aka **perabriaca** aka **peracocomero** aka **pera cocomerina** a small pear which grows in the upper Valle del Savio and in other areas round the towns of Verghereto and Bagno di Romagna (in the province of Forlì-Cesena). It is named for its flesh, which, in the late harvest,

takes on a bright red color reminiscent of that of a watermelon (*cocomero*). Aromatic, fragile and relatively perishable, it is good for processing, but only a few trees survive, some of them left untended. An association, supported by a Slow Food presidium, has been set up to produce jams and preserves and thereby save this ancient variety. Emilia-Romagna.

pera dell'Emilia Romagna PGI pear varieties cultivated in communes in the provinces of Bologna, Modena, Ravenna, Ferrara and Reggio Emilia: *abate fetel, conference, decana del comizio, kaiser, william, max red barlett, cascade* and *passa crassana*. All different in appearance and aroma, they share the same juiciness and sweetness. Emilia-Romagna.

pera mantovana PGI pear varieties cultivated in a number of communes in the province of Mantua: *william* and *red barlett*, bright red in color; *conference*, green or yellow; *decana del comizio*, pale green or pinkish; *abate fetel*, pale green or yellowish; *kaiser*, rusty red. A protocol establishes the soil in which trees can be grown and imposes the use of traditional cultivation techniques. Lombardy.

pera martina a Piedmontese pear variety (➤ **martin sec**).

perbureira a pasta and bean soup typical of the Ovada area, in the eastern Monferrato hills (province of Alessandria). Piedmont.

perca regional name for ➤ **pesce persico,** perch.

perciatelli dried durum wheat pasta, similar to large hollow spaghetti with a diameter of one and a half to two inches. Served with rich meat sauces. Other names: ➤ **maccheroncini,** ➤ **mezzani,** ➤ **mezzanelli,** ➤ **mezze zite.** Campania

perciatelli con le lumache pasta with snails. A dish of ➤ **perciatelli** or ➤ **bucatini**

with snails stewed in garlic, onion, chili, tomatoes and parsley. Calabria.

perciatellini another name for ➤ **bucatini**, a type of pasta.

percoca clingstone peach. A variety of yellow peach (➤ **pesca**) with very firm flesh.

pere e musso a street food (➤ **cibo di strada**) still to be found at street vendors' stalls, kiosks and fairs. It consists of pig's head (**musso**) and trotters (**pere**), boiled and served with salt and lemon juice. Campania.

pere madernassa al vino a dessert very common especially in the provinces of Cuneo and Asti, where they grow the madernassa pear, a medium-sized variety with rusty red skin and firm, crisp, sugary flesh. It can be eaten raw, but it is best enjoyed stewed in a full-bodied red wine with sugar, cinnamon and cloves. The thick, caramelized cooking liquid is poured over the pears to serve. The same recipe is made with ➤ **pere martine** (➤ **martin sec**).

Peretta pear-shaped stretched curd cheese made with heat-treated cow's milk. It is matured for 15 days and eaten fresh. It is also used to stuff ➤ **seadas**, large sweet ravioli. Sardinia.

peritoneo peritoneum. The membrane that lines the abdominal cavity.

pernice partridge. Name common to various members of the Fasianidae family which live in the Alps and Sardinia: *pernice rossa*, red-legged partridge (*Alectoris rufa*), *pernice grigia*, gray partridge (*Perdix perdix*), the one most farmed for gastronomic purposes, *pernice bianca*, ptarmigan (*Lagopus mutus*), and *pernice sarda*, Barbary partridge (*Alectoris barbara*). Their meat is much prized: specimens of less than a year in age should be roast, older birds should be stewed or made into pâté.

pernici al sugo d'uva partridges with grape sauce. The cavities are filled with sage and juniper berries and the birds are barded with lard. They are roast in the oven and covered with a sauce made by heating aromatic white grapes in butter with blanched chestnuts, mushrooms, strips of speck and a little white wine. They are served with slices of apple coated in breadcrumbs and fried. Trentino-Alto Adige.

pernici alla cacciatora jointed partridge browned in oil and butter and finished off with breadcrumbs, lemon juice, desalted anchovies and red wine or broth. The sauce is filtered and served with the cooked partridge meats. Piedmont.

perrazza word used along the Abruzzo and Molise coast for ➤ **vongola comune**, clam.

persa aka **persia** Ligurian terms for ➤ **marjoram**.

persata soup (➤ **acquacotta**) typical of the island of Elba made with marjoram (➤ **maggiorana**), *persa* in dialect, garlic, chili pepper, olive oil, day-old bread and eggs. Tuscany.

persegada solid preserve of cooked quinces highly aromatized with cinnamon and powdered cloves. The mixture is cooled in ramekins, turned out and dusted with crystallized sugar. The recipe is typical of the province of Treviso where, for the feast of San Martino they decorate the desserts with small silver sugared almonds bearing the image of the saint. Veneto.

perseghini crisp ring-shaped pastries made with leavened dough (without eggs). A specialty of Cividale del Friuli (Udine).

persica dialect term for ➤ **maggiorana**, marjoram.

persicata a solid preserve of peaches and sugar, cut into small triangles and dusted with sugar. Typical of the province of Brescia. Lombardy.

persico reale another name for ➤ **pesce persico**, perch.

persucc d'la paletta Piedmontese term for ➤ **paletta di Coggiola**, a rare ham.

pesca peach (*Prunus persica vulgaris*). A native of China, the fruit was introduced to the Mediterranean from Persia, and is now extensively cultivated in Italy, one of its major producer countries. A great many varieties exist, which may be subdivided into three large families: common peaches, nectarines, protected in Emilia-Romagna by the PGI seal (➤ **pesca e nettarina di Romagna**) and clingstones (➤ **percoca**). Thanks to the great number of varieties, many early- or late-harvesting, peaches are available in Italy from May to October. The Italian Ministry of Agriculture's database of native and/or traditional food products lists the following: *percoca giallona di Siano, percoca col pizzo, percoca puteolana, percoca terzarola, pesca belella di Melito, pesca bianca napoletana* (Campania); *pesca bella di Cesena* (Emilia-Romagna); *pesca iris rosso, pesca isontina, pesca triestina* (Friuli-Venezia Giulia); *pesca birindella* (Liguria); *pesca del Cuneese, pesca di Baldissero, pesca di Borgo d'Ale, pesca di Canale,* pesca di Volpedo (Piedmont); ➤ **pesca tardiva di Leonforte** (Sicily); *pesca alberta, cotogna del poggio, cotogna di Rosano, cotogna toscana, diga, limone, maglia rosa, michelini, mora di Dolfo, passerina, regina di Londa, trionfo peloso, peschetti di vigna di Candia* (Tuscany); *pesca bianca di Venezia, pesca di Povegliano, pesca di Verona, pesca nettarina* (Veneto). In confectionery and baking, peaches are used to make jams, cakes, tarts and tartlets, in homes they are used fresh to make desserts (➤ **pesche ripiene**, ➤ **matsafam**) and also preserves (➤ **persicata**).

pesca e nettarina di Romagna PGI peach varieties cultivated in the provinces of Ferrara, Bologna, Forlì-Cesena and Ravenna. Emilia-Romagna.

pescatora, alla term used to describe pasta or seafood dishes that make use of seafood (mollusks and crustaceans) cooked in tomato sauce.

pesce (1) fish. In *colloquial* Italian the term includes the full gamut of seafood, including mollusks, crustaceans and more besides. Fish has always been part of the human diet. The Greeks were certainly eating fish at the time of Hippocrates (4th century BC) and the Romans fermented the heads, bones and skin to *garum*, one of the most popular condiments in their cuisine. From the 4th century, when the Church imposed 100-150 days of "abstinence from the eating of meat," fish acquired a "penitential" connotation that lasted for at least a thousand years. Fresh sea fish, prevalent in the Roman era was supplanted by freshwater fish—sturgeon, trout, pike, tench, lampern, crayfish—not to mention easily preserved sea fish, salted or dried, available even a long distance away from the sea (➤ **baccalà**, ➤ **stoccafisso**). Hence the advent and rise of the canning industry, particularly in The Netherlands. Fresh fish, seasonal, expensive and local (as the extraordinary variety of its regional and dialect names testifies) was restricted to lagoons and seaside fishing villages. In Italia, it was only in Venice and Sicily that fish had a leading role in traditional gastronomy. Its popular success is a recent phenomenon that dates from the post-World War II years, when refrigeration and transport systems were developed and the dietary concept of slimming, with the consequent search for low-fat foods (not that all fish is lean), began to catch on. The growth in demand combined with the deterioration of sea, river and lake systems has triggered a worrying decline in fish stocks, hence the urgent need to protect threatened species and others besides in the mating season and in the larval phase, more sustainable fishing techniques and a greater recourse to eco-compatible fish farming.

pesce (2) cut of beef roughly equivalent to end cut round. Also known as ➤ **gallinella** or ➤ **campanello**.

pesce angelo common name for ➤ **squadro**, angel shark.

pesce azzurro literally "blue fish." The name refers to different varieties of generally small fish (anchovy, mackerel sardine, garfish, shad, sand eel, needlefish, scabbard fish, horse mackerel etc.), which have in common a green-blue back and silvery-white sides and belly. Most varieties are relatively abundant, hence cheap, but are also perishable and have to be cooked or preserved (in oil, salted, processed into paste, marinated) as quickly as possible. The *pesce azzurro del delta del Po* (Veneto) is listed in the Italian Ministry of Agriculture's database of native and/or traditional food products.

pesce balestra smooth hammerhead shark (*Sphyrna zygaena*). Common off the southern Italian coastline, where it is cooked in the same ways as tuna (➤ **tonno**). Common and regional names: ➤ **pesce martello**, ➤ **pesce porco**, ➤ **pesce stampella**.

pesce bandiera another name for ➤ **pesce sciabola**, silver scabbard fish.

pesce briaco Tuscan name for ➤ **capone ubriaco**, streaked gurnard.

pesce capone aka **pesce cappone** Lazio dialect terms for ➤ **scorfano nero**, black scorpion fish.

pesce castagna pomfret (*Brama raii*). Albe-

it of meager commercial value, a fish that is excellent boiled, broiled, braised and fried. Common and regional names: ➤ **carraginu**, ➤ **fatula**, **ociada bastarda**, ➤ **saracu impiriali**.

pesce cetra regional term for ➤ **sampietro**, John Dory.

pesce chitarra guitar fish (*Rhinobatos rhinobatus*). A shark common in the Mediterranean whose meat is cooked in the same way as that of the skate ➤ **razza**. Common and regional names: ➤ **pesce violino**, ➤ **tamburrino**.

pesce colombo another name for ➤ **aquila di mare**, eagle ray, traditionally fished off Friuli-Venezia Giulia, where it is known in dialect as ➤ **matàn**.

pesce cordela dialect term for ➤ **cepola**, red band fish.

pesce di lago in carpione marinated lake fish. Bleak and freshwater sardines coated in flour, fried and marinated in a mixture of onions, garlic, celery, carrots, thyme, cloves, salt, pepper, vinegar, wine and parsley. Typical of the areas round the lakes in the provinces of Como e Lecco. Lombardy.

pesce fiamma another name for ➤ **pesce sciabola**, scabbard fish.

pesce fritto in salsa fried freshwater fish (catfish and the like) marinated in a sauce of extra virgin olive oil, vinegar (or vinegar and white wine), garlic and, more rarely, onion, and parsley. A recipe typical of the province of Mantua. Lombardy.

pesce gallo regional term for ➤ **sampietro**, John Dory.

pesce gatto catfish. Freshwater fish of the Siluriformes order with a flattened head and eight barbels, imported from North America at the turn of the 19th and 20th centuries. Mainly carnivorous, it lives at river mouths and ponds and is also farmed. It has few bones and is hence easy to fillet. It is cooked fried (it is an ingredient in → **frittura di pesce del Po**), marinated, in risottos and in stews (→ **barbon in tecia**).

pesce gatto in ajoon fried catfish covered with a sauce of garlic cloves cooked in vinegar and preserved in hermetically sealed glass jars. A recipe typical of the province of Cremona that can also be applied to other freshwater fish. Lombardy.

pesce gatto in umido stewed catfish. The fish, filleted or whole, is first fried, then turned in a skillet with tomato sauce flavored with finely minced onion (or garlic) and celery (or parsley), sometimes with a dash of vinegar or white wine. In Emilia, the fish is served with toasted polenta.

pesce lama another name for → **pesce sciabola**, scabbard fish.

pesce lucerna stargazer (*Uranoscopus scaber*). A member of the Trachinidae family with firm and delicate flesh. It may be boiled or stewed and is one of the fishes most used to flavor soups and stews in the northern Adriatic regions (→ **brodetti dell'alto Adriatico**). Not to be confused with → **luserna**, tub gurnard. Common and regional names: → **boca in cao**, → **bocca in cava**, → **bocca in cielo**, → **buccuni**, → **cac**, → **chiachia**, → **cozzolo**, → **lucerna**, → **mesoro**, → **pesce prete**, → **prete**, → **toti**.

pesce lupo a synonym of → **spigola**, sea bream, and a word used in the Marche to refer to → **nasello**, hake.

pesce martello another name for → **pesce balestra**, smooth hammerhead shark

pesce morgano regional name for → **melù**, blue whiting.

pesce natalizio Christmas version of the → **agnello pasquale** Easter cake, made with the same ingredients and following the same procedures. Puglia.

pesce persico aka **perca** aka **persico reale** a member of the Percidae and one of the most prized freshwater fish for its fine, firm flesh. Its presence in the Po Valley and Veneto has been documented for centuries and it is now also to be found in central and southern Italy. Perch is best enjoyed fried or stewed. The flesh may also be used to stuff **crespelle** or → **tortelli**, while the breaded fried fillets are often served with risotto. The Italian Ministry of Agriculture's database of native and/or traditional food products lists *persico reale del Trasimeno* (Umbria), which is used locally in → **carbonaretti sui sarmenti**.

pesce persico fritto fried perch. A recipe typical of the Italian lakes, from Garda to Trasimeno, consisting simply of perch fillets coated in flour and plunged into oil. In the Lake Garda version, the fillets are dipped first in beaten egg, then in a mixture of breadcrumbs and flour, then fried in butter until golden.

pesce persico in padella fillets of perch coated in flour, fried in butter until golden, doused with white wine and simmered in a fumet made with the fish's heads, bones and skin, and acidulated with lemon juice. Veneto.

pesce pilota pilot fish. A sea fish of the Carangidae family, similar to amberfish (→ **ricciola**) and cooked in the same way. It owes its name to the fact that it often places itself in front of sharks, turtles and ships as if it were guiding them. Common and regional names: → **fanfolo**, → **infanfolo**, → **'nfanfulo**, → **pisci d'ummra**.

pesce porco southern Italian name for → **pesce balestra**, smooth hammerhead shark.

pesce prete name used in Friuli and Veneto for → **nasello**, hake; elsewhere for → **pesce lucerna**, stargazer.

pesce ragno weever (*Trachinus araneus*). A member of the Trachinidae family like the greater weever: ➤ **tracina** (➤ **varagno**, ➤ **dragone**). Both burrow in sand in shallow waters near the coast, and have tasty flesh, excellent for stewing or broiling. Known on the northern Adriatic coast as ➤ **ragno pagano**.

pesce rospo central Italian name for ➤ **rana pescatrice**, monkfish.

pesce sciabola scabbard fish (*Lepidopus caudatus*), Similar to swordfish (➤ **pesce spada**), it is fished in the spring, fall and winter when it comes close to the coast. Its meat is excellent cut into pieces and fried or stewed. It is listed under Calabria in the Italian Ministry of Agriculture's database of native and/or traditional food products. Common and regional names: ➤ **pesce bandiera**, ➤ **pesce fiamma**, ➤ **pesce lama**, ➤ **pesce spatola**, ➤ **pesce vela**.

pesce secco di Monte Isola e del lago d'Iseo a preserving technique developed at Monte Isola on Lake Iseo that has been used by local fishermen for at least a thousand years. It consists of cleaning fish and leaving them to dry out in the sun for a whole day. The fish are then washed and hung in racks for a week or more, after which they are transferred to glass jars and covered with extra virgin olive oil. They are ready for the table after a few months. The fish used are bleak (➤ **alborella**), rudd (➤) and freshwater sardinese (➤ **sardena** aka ➤ **agone**). Lombardy.

pesce spada swordfish (*Xiphias gladius*). Large elongated predatory fish with a characteristic long, flat bill. It lives in the deep and can reach 12 feet in length. It is fished from April to September, especially off Calabria and Sicily. Its meat, sold in slices or "steaks," is tasty yet delicate, less fatty than tuna's and, sliced finely, may be eaten raw. The most prized part is the belly (*ventresca*). A traditional Sicilian recipe is ➤ **braciolette di spada**.

pesce spada alla bagnarese a specialty of Bagnara Calabra, in the province of Reggio Calabria. Slices of swordfish flavored with olive oil, capers, lemon juice, oregano and parsley, cooked in a bain-marie. Tropea red onions and sweet peppers may also be added. Calabria.

pesce spatola another name for ➤ **pesce sciabola**, scabbard fish.

pesce stampella regional term for ➤ **pesce balestra**, smooth hammerhead shark.

pesce vela regional term for ➤ **pesce sciabola**, scabbard fish.

pesce violino regional term for ➤ **pesce chitarra**, guitar fish.

pescestocco southern Italian word for ➤ **stoccafisso**, stockfish.

pesche all'alchermes traditional dainty cakes, typical of Emilia-Romagna and Marche, thus named because they look like peaches (*pesca/pesche* in Italian). Two half-spheres of soft risen pastry are scooped out and filled with chocolate cream or confectioner's custard. They are then joined together to form a "peach," bathed with alkermes (➤ **alchermes**) and dusted with refined sugar. The cake is a tradition in a village in the province of Ascoli Piceno (*pesche di Acquaviva*). In Tuscany they make a similar confection, but smaller and with a filling of confectioner's custard only. In the postwar years, they used to use walnut husks as molds and fit a peach stone into the custard to heighten the resemblance with the fruit itself. Emilia-Romagna, Marche, Tuscany.

pesche di Acquaviva a local version of ➤ **pesche all'alchermes**, a type of cake.

pesche di vigna "vine peach," a very sweet,

floury peach variety, thus named because the trees used to be planted between vine rows. Piedmont.

pesche ripiene stuffed peaches, Peaches sliced in half, flesh scooped out, stuffed with their own flesh mixed with cocoa, ground amaretti cookies, eggs and sugar, and baked in the oven. Created in bourgeois homes at the end of the 19th century, the recipe has now become a classic summer dessert (a similar recipe exists in the province of Ferrara, in Emilia-Romagna, where the stuffing consists of bread soaked in milk, crushed almonds, peach flesh, sugar and egg). Piedmont.

pesche tardive di Leonforte the peach orchards of Leonforte, in the province of Enna, clash with the citrus groves that characterize the landscape in this part of Sicily. Leonforte peaches ripen in September and October and even as late as November. They are wrapped in paper bags to protect them from the wind and from parasites, and are harvested only when perfectly ripe. Since they are protected inside the bags, they ripen late and take on a bright yellow color with red streaks. Their firm, beautifully scented yellow flesh is sweet with a distinctive, slightly caramelized flavor. A Slow Food presidium is seeking to use this prime quality fruit to relaunch the economy of the local area. Sicily.

peschine all'alchermes another name for ➤ **pesche all'alchermes**.

peschiole a preserve of tiny peaches from the first pruning of the tree, when the stone is still soft. Cooked in acidulated water and preserved in glass jars, they are crisp and crunchy with a tangy flavor. A homemade specialty, they are served with aperitifs or included as an ingredient in a number of dishes. Campania.

pesci de muntagna "mountain fish." The white ribs of Swiss chard boiled, breaded and fried. The name refers to the fact that they look like fish, which were not always available as an ingredient in inland peasant cooking. Typical of the western Riviera. Liguria.

pescio cappon Ligurian term for ➤ **scorfano rosso**, red scorpion fish.

pescutelle dialect name for ➤ **biscotto cegliese**, a type of almond cookie

pess còj aka **pess 'd còj** literally "cabbage fishes." Savoy cabbage leaves rolled and stuffed, like ➤ **caponet**, with ingredients such as ground meat, salami, sausage, rice, cheese and vegetables, or simply breaded and fried. Piedmont.

pess in ajon freshwater fish, fried covered with crushed garlic (*ajon*) and parsley plus a dash of vinegar and a few bay leaves. Preserved in this way, the fish can be kept for a few days. In the province of Piacenza and down the Po, the dish is made with fish from the river itself. Emilia-Romagna.

pessate sotto sisam bleak (➤ **alborella**) fried and preserved in vinegar. Typical of the area round Lake Ledro. Trentino-Alto Adige.

pessit small freshwater fish (generally bleak, ➤ **alborelle**, and freshwater sardines, ➤ **agoni**, coated with flour, fried and served with polenta. Sometimes the fried fish are mixed with onion, celery and carrots and splashed with vinegar, which is then allowed to evaporate. In this case the recipes changes name to *pessit in conscia*. Again the dish is served with polenta. Lombardy.

pestadice a snack cum nibble of roasted corn kernels, sweetened with sugar and crushed. Typical of the Carnia area. Friuli-Venezia Giulia.

pestare (of cookery) to grind or pound a food (spices, aromatic herbs, dried fruit) in a mortar, or another recipient, with a pestle.

pestarei another name for ➤ **patugoi**, soft polenta.

pestàt di Fagagna a Slow Food presidium-sponsored ancient cured meat made in homes and by a few pork butchers. Lardo from pigs raised in semi-wild conditions on small local farms is ground and mixed with minced carrots, celery, onion, sage, rosemary, garlic and parsley, and seasoned with salt and pepper. The mixture is cased in a natural intestine and put to mature. It is ready for the table after a few weeks, but is at its best after a year. In either case, it is not eaten raw but lightly fried and used to flavor vegetable soups, ➤ **broàde** (fermented turnips) and meat stews. A specialty of the province of Udine, Friuli.

pestata another name for ➤ **lardo pesto**, crushed lardo.

pestazzuole another name for ➤ **orecchiette**, a type of pasta.

pesto genovese pasta sauce made with basil (➤ **basilico genovese**) pine kernels, garlic, Parmigiano and Pecorino Sardo, olive oil and salt. According to tradition, all the ingredients should be pounded together in a mortar. Many versions exist, 60 or so of which in the province of Genoa alone. One such is the so-called *pesto d'inverno*, winter pesto, made with walnuts, cheese curd, parsley and chard in the months in which fresh basil is not available. Liguria.

pesto pantesco sauce made by pounding garlic, basil and mint, stirring in skinned, chopped tomatoes and emulsifying the resulting mixture with oil, salt, chili and oregano. Served with pasta or fish or spread on toasted bread. Typical of the island of Pantelleria (province of Trapani). Sicily.

pesto trapanese sauce usually served with ➤ **busiate**, a type of pasta. Made by crushing together garlic, basil, almonds, grated Pecorino, tomatoes, salt, and pepper, and binding the mixture with extra virgin olive oil. Sicily.

péstöm Brescia dialect word for ➤ **pistume**.

pet 'd nòna flour, eggs and sugar molded into balls and fried. Typical of the Alpine valleys of the province of Cuneo. Piedmont.

peta a large, round, squat ➤ **pitina**, a cured meat, weighing up to two pounds. A specialty of the village of Andreis, in the province of Pordenone. Friuli-Venezia Giulia.

pete aka **torta rustica** baked cake made with a mixture of wheat flour and cornflour, polenta, milk and sugar. In the past, the main ingredient was the solid residue from the preparation of melted butter clarified with flour, and the cake was cooked in the hearth wrapped in Savoy cabbage leaves, like ➤ **buiadnik** and ➤ **pan zal**. Typical of the Carnia and Valcellina areas of the province of Udine. Friuli-Venezia Giulia.

petit four literally "small oven" in French. In French and international confectionery the term refers to dainty little cakes with assorted fillings. In Italy (particularly in Piedmont and Sardinia), it means small cookies and pastries made with almond paste, egg whites and sugar decorated with candied cherries, almonds, hazelnuts and so on.

petorai pears baked in the oven, with or without wine. A specialty of Trieste. Friuli-Venezia Giulia.

petrafennula aka **petramennula** very hard nougat (➤ **torrone**). Almonds and sugared almond chips bound with honey, cinnamon and strips of orange and citron zest. Sicily.

petroselino regional term for ➤ **prezzemolo**, flat-leaved parsley.

pettine (1) comb-like utensil used to make pastas such as ➤ **garganelli al pettine**.

pettine (2) another name for ➤ **canestrello**, a type of mollusk.

pettl' e fasul fresh pasta (similar to ➤ **fettuccine**) with beans. A popular dish in the province of Latina. Lazio

petto breast. Referred to veal, lamb, chicken, turkey and so on.

petto d'oca "goose breast." Cured meat consisting of two goose breasts pressed together and wrapped in the skin of the same bird, previously cured with salt, pepper and natural aromas. After maturing for a few days, it is aged for 40. The above is the method used in Mortara, in the province of Pavia. In the province of Udine, they smoke the goose breasts over a fire of beech and oak branches, juniper berries and bay leaves. Lombardy, Friuli-Venezia Giulia.

petto di vitello alla fornara breast of veal massaged with finely minced garlic and rosemary, and roast in the oven with white wine and diced potatoes. A classic Roman roast. Lazio.

petto ripieno breast of veal sewed into a pouch and stuffed with a mixture of bread soaked in milk, sausage meat and aromatic herbs, browned in oil with pacnetta and finished in water and wine. Friuli-Venezia Giulia.

pettola (1) aka **pettula** aka **pittula** fried leavened savory pasty stuffed with mashed potatoes, salt cod, anchovies, cauliflower, raisins, broccoli, pine kernels, onions, olives and tomatoes. Traditionally made at Christmas in the Salento peninsula (province of Lecce). A sweet version, coated in honey or dusted with sugar or with ➤ **vincotto** in the filling, is typical of the Carnival period. Puglia, Basilicata.

pettola (2) a type of homemade pasta typical of Caserta. Campania.

petuccia a variation on the ➤ **pitina** of the Val Cellina, in the province of Udine, aromatized with wild fennel and juniper berries.

petza Sardinian dialect word for "meat."

petza a cassola meat stew, reminiscent of ➤ **ghisadu**, to which beans, peas and other vegetables are sometimes added. Sardinia.

petza arrustida meat slowly spit-roast over a fire. Sometimes whole animals (suckling pigs, baby lambs, kids, sheep, goats, calves, chickens, thrushes) are cooked in this way. Sardinia.

petza imbinada meat marinated overnight in local wine with garlic, laurel, juniper, rosemary, thyme and oregano, browned in olive oil with onions, and finished off in the marinade liquid. A specialty of the Montiferru area, in the west of the island. Sardinia.

petza in brou beef, lamb or, more rarely, pork boiled with herbs, potatoes and cauliflower. A classic holiday treat. Sardinia.

pevarassa aka **poverassa** Veneto terms for ➤ **vongola commune**, clam.

pevarini tangy dry biscuits made with flour, yeast, treacle, sugar, honey, pepper and other spices such as cinnamon, nutmeg, ginger and cloves. A specialty of the provinces of Padua and Venice. Veneto.

peverada an ancient Veneto sauce made with chicken livers, salami (➤ **soppressa**), desalted anchovies, vinegar and plenty of pepper, served with game, guinea fowl and roast duck. In Lombardy the same name is used for a fiery sauce (with pepper and chili) served with boiled meats, a close relative of the French **poivrade**. Veneto, Lombardy.

peverino regional term for ➤ **serpillo**, wild thyme.

peverone Lombard term for → **peperoncino**, chili; Veneto term for → **pepe**, pepper.

pevium aka **pevrum** dialect terms for → **peperoncino**, chili.

pezzata in the Marche, a mutton stew cooked in a pot with aromatic herbs (pennyroyal in particular) and sprinkled with grated Pecorino. In Abruzzo and Molise, baby lamb stuffed with aromas, olive, capers, anchovies, capers, pickled peppers and grated cheese cooked in white wine.

Pezzata nera, razza black or brown and white spotted dairy cattle breed typical of the Val d'Aosta.

Pezzata rossa, razza red and white spotted dairy cattle breed, possibly of northern European origin, which has lived in the Val d'Aosta since the 5th century.

pezzente della montagna materana Slow Food presidium-supported ancient cured meat, produced today by only one pork butcher. Pork from local pigs ground and cured with powdered sweet and hot pepper (→ **peperone di Senise**), wild fennel, garlic and sea salt. After two weeks, it is used to make → **sugo rosso**, otherwise it is aged for at least 20 days. Basilicata.

pezzentelle mixed parts of the pig (jowl, snout, ear) preserved in salt. Desalted, they are an ingredient of → **minestra maritata**, mixed meat and vegetable soup. In some areas of the region, **pezzentelle** are cased as a cured meat and the name is sometimes used as a synonym of → **annoglia** salami. Campania.

pezzetti horsemeat stew. Typical of the province of Lecce, an area in which horsemeat is traditionally consumed a lot. A simplified version of → **pignata di cavallo**. Puglia.

pezzo duro (1) ice cream containing candied fruits. Sicily.

pezzo duro (2) layered brick-shaped semi-freddo. Typical of the area round Locri (Reggio Calabria), traditionally made with vanilla, chocolate and hazelnut flavors. Calabria.

pezzogna term used in some southern regions for → **pagello**, sea bream.

Piacentino cheese aromatized with peppercorns and saffron. It is matured for 30 days but can be aged for much longer. Typical of Enna, Sicily.

piacentinu in foglie di limone pieces of grilled → **Piacentino** cheese wrapped in lemon leaves. Sicily.

piada aka **piadina** disk-shaped flatbread, originally made with unleavened dough, cooked on a hot-plate (though in the village of Montetiffi, in the province of Forlì-Cesena they make it on refractory terra cotta). Known as *piè* in dialect, it is eaten with ham, lardo, fresh sausage, soft cheese (→ **squaquarone** or → **raviggiolo**), chard or wild greens. A classic street food (→ **cibo di strada**) at the seaside, where it is sold at characteristic kiosks. Emilia-Romagna.

piada dei morti sweet flatbread made with almonds, walnuts, pine kernels and red wine for All Saints' Day in November. Emilia-Romagna.

piadone con l'uva flatbread baked in the oven made with a dough dotted with grapes. Typical of the Rimini area. Emilia-Romagna.

piantaggine, ribwort plantain (*Plantago lanceolata*, *P. major* and *P. media*). Wild herbaceous plants whose leaves and flowers are gathered in the Alps, in Liguria and in Tuscany and cooked in vegetable soups. Common and regional names: → **erba dei cinque nervi**, → **lingua di cane**, → **orecchie d'asino**, → **tirafilo**.

piastra, alla cooked on a hot-plate.

piattello another name for → **costolina**, beaked hawksbeard.

piatto maggese rural snack of diced → **spalla contadina pisana**, a cured meat, with fresh fava beans and Pecorino. Typical of the province of Pisa. Tuscany.

piava snail-shaped bread rolls typical of the province of Padua. Veneto.

Piave cheese produced with heat-treated, raw milk. Used to be made at community dairies, now industrially. Veneto.

pibiri moriscu dialect term for → **peperoncino**, chili.

picaia aka **picaja** dialect name for brisket, in Parma and Bologna it also means oven-roast veal or a stuffed veal pouch similar to → **tasto piacentino**. Emilia-Romagna

piccagge broad egg pasta ribbons. Made with wholemeal flour, *piccagge avvantaggiate*; made with chestnut flour, *piccagge matte*. Liguria.

piccasorcio regional term for → **pungitopo**, butcher's broom.

piccata aka **piccatina** slices of veal coated in flour, lightly fried in butter, cooked with lemon juice, Marsala, mushrooms or tomato and garnished with minced flat-leaved parsley. A dish typical of Milan. In Italian culinary terminology, the term has come to mean → **scaloppina**, escalope or cutlet (in Lazio they use the term *frittura piccata*). Lombardy.

picchettare another word for → **lardare**, to lard.

picchiante ancient stew of offal (calf's lungs and heart) and vegetables. Tuscany.

picchiapò, alla term used in Rome for a dish similar to → **lesso rifatto**. Boiled beef flavored with onion, tomatoes and capers. Lazio.

picchierelli large fresh handmade spaghetti similar to → **pici**, → **umbricelli** and → **stringozzi**. Umbria.

piccillato another name for → **cuzzupa**, an Easter cake.

piccillatu pì causi di mulliche du pè bread made with the residues from the preparation of → **pè** and filled with olives and other ingredients. Sicily.

piccione pigeon. Name commonly attributed to domestic breeds deriving from the *Columba livia* species, which live in numerous flocks in large cities and are notably smaller than the → **colombaccio**, wood pigeon. Bred for their exceptional sense of orientation (homing pigeons), for competition purposes (racing pigeons) and for their meat.

piccione allo spiedo Veneto pigeon recipe (→ **torresano**).

piccione in umido Veneto pigeon recipe (→ **torresano**).

piccione ripieno stuffed pigeon. Oven-roasted pigeon stuffed with sausage meat, the bird's giblets, breadcrumbs, Parmigiano, parsley, garlic and egg, and served with the filtered pan juices. Tuscany, Umbria.

piccioni alla bresciana pigeons stuffed with their own giblets and minced almonds, and roast in the oven. Lombardy.

piccioni alla perugina young pigeons cooked in white wine vinegar in a pot sealed with parchment. Umbria.

piccioni arrosto pigeons roast in the oven and served with the filtered cooking juices. Tuscany.

piccoli frutti "small fruits," a synonym of → **frutti del sottobosco**, woodland fruits.

pichi another name for → **umbricelli**, a type of pasta.

pici aka **pinci** thick fresh flour and water spaghetti typical of the province of Siena, but also common in the province of Grosseto and in Umbria. Tuscany, Umbria.

piconi another name for → **calcione**, sweet fried raviolo.

pìcula ad cavàl a stew of ground horsemeat meat, traditionally served for breakfast in the old osterias of Piacenza on market day. Emilia-Romagna.

piè dialect term for → **piada**, a flatbread.

piè d'asino small member of the mussel family (*Glycimeris orbicularis, G. violascens*) known in southern Italy as *cozza 'e schiave* or *cozza scarpara*.

piè di pellicano pelican's foot (*Aporrhais pesplecani*). Marine gastropod mollusk popular mainly in the Marche region in recipes reminiscent of those used for the common snail (→ **lumaca**). In one they are cooked in tomato sauce and served as an antipasto with toasted bread or as a condiment for pasta. Common and regional names: → **crocetta**, → **crucelle**, → **garàgol**.

piede di bue ox's trotter. The trotter is boiled for hours in salted water, allowed to cool, dressed with olice, oil, salt, minced garlic and parsley, and a dash of vinegar, then left to rest for one day. Sardinia.

piedino trotter. Pigs' and calves' trotters are used to make gelatin (→ **gelatina**) and eaten boiled and served with oil and vinegar. Other recipes include → **batsoà** (Piedmont), → **zampetti in umido** (Tuscany), → **zampa alla parmigiana** (Emilia-Romagna). Pig's trotters are used to make → **zampone**. Lambs' and kids' trotters are only used in Sardinia.

piedini di agnello meat from a lamb's trotter boiled in salted water, browned in oil, onion, garlic and parsley and finished with chopped ripe tomatoes. Sardinia.

piedini di maiale con cavolo pig's trotters and cabbage. The trotters are flamed and scraped, split lengthwise and immersed in boiling water with celery, carrot, onion and bay leaf for three hours. Shredded white cabbage leaves are boiled in a separate pan. A tablespoonful of flour is toasted in lardo and the trotters are add-ed to it. The drained cabbage is then transferred to the pan and the mixture is seasoned with salt and pepper. The dish is served piping hot covered with grated → **cren**, horseradish. Friuli-Venezia Giulia.

pieni large oval gnocchi made with boiled shredded chard, breadcrumbs, grated grana, ricotta, eggs and flour. Cooked in boiling water, they are served with melted butter. A specialty of the village of Cerignale in the Val Trebbia (province of Piacenza). Emilia-Romagna.

piennolo another word for → **pomodorino al piennolo**, cherry tomato.

pierrade mixed meat and vegetables cooked directly at the table on a heated granite slab (→ **alla pietra**) and accompanied by sauces. A relatively recent usage. Val d'Aosta, Piedmont.

pietra, alla method of cooking on a red-hot slab.

pigna southern Lazio Easter cake. In Formia (Latina) it is a baked ring-shaped braid made of eggs, flour, melted butter, sugar, milk and yeast, with a hard-boiled egg at the center. In Arpino (Frosinone) the cake is a sort of panettone dotted with raisins, candied fruits, vanilla, cinnamon and anise, glazed with sugar icing.

pignata (aka **pignato**) earthenware pot. As in the case of → **tiano**, → **tiella**, → **taeddha**, → **rote**, → **ruoto**, it refers by extension also to the dish cooked in it: → **pignata di pecora** (Calabria), → **pignata di cavallo** (Puglia).

pignata di cavallo (aka **carne di cavallo alla pignata**) a whole piece of horsemeat is cooked slowly with water, garlic, chopped onion, mixed herbs, chopped ripe tomatoes, tomato paste chili and peppercorns. The meat is then cut into pieces and returned to the now reduced sauce. A traditional, more complex version of ➤ **pezzetti**. Puglia.

pignata di pecora chunks of mutton stewed in a ➤ **pignata** with vegetables. A specialty of Matera (Basilicata).

pignattaccia baked layered casserole of potatoes and cheaper cuts of beef (head, tail, tongue etc.). Typical of the Tuscia area. Lazio.

pignatto grasso another name for ➤ **minestra maritata**, a soup.

pignoccata aka **pignolata** cake similar to ➤ **cicerchiata**. Balls of dough fried in oil, piled into a pine cone-shape (*pigna* means pine cone) bound together with honey or (in Messina) with lemon or chocolate icing. Sicily.

pignolini aka **pignoletti** tiny picarel (➤ **zerri**) eaten fried or marinated in ➤ **carpione**.

pigo large-headed chub (*Rutilus pigo*). Freshwater fish often used to make pâtés, though its fillets are also dried. The variety typical of Lake Como (Lombardy) is in the Italian Minstry of Agriculture's database of native and/or traditional food products.

pilacca preserve of fried chili peppers. Puglia.

pilaf boiled rice served as a side dish with meat, fish or vegetables. Probably of Persian origin, common in the Middle East and India. A Sardinian relative of the dish is ➤ **pilau**.

pilafi another word for ➤ **pilau**.

pilargiu Sardinian word for ➤ **grancevola** spider crab.

pilau chopped goat meat browned in olive oil with garlic, thyme, bay leaf, myrtle and rosemary, bound with egg yolk and lemon juice lemon, mixed with boiled rice (➤ **pilaf**), and served as a side dish with roast kid. In some modern versions, rice is replaced by balls of durum wheat, water and saffron. Sardinia.

pillas aka **pillus** sheets of pasta baked in the oven with goat and chicken sauce. Sardinia.

pillonca Nuoro dialect for ➤ **pane carasau** a type of bread (Sardinia).

pillottare to baste meat roasting on a spit.

pillotto aka **pilotto** a large paper-straw funnel lined with a slice of lardo. The funnel is placed over roasting meats and an edge of the paper is set on fire. The heat from the flame causes the lardo to melt and drip on the meat, thus basting it constantly. Umbria.

pimento della Giamaica another word for ➤ **quattro spezie**, allspice.

pimpinella common name for ➤ **salvastrella**, small burnet.

pinacchiotto regional term for ➤ **pinaiolo** mushrooms.

pinaiolo name of two Boletus mushrooms: *Boletus luteus* and *Boletus granulatus*. Used in sauces to dress pasta and risottos. Common names: ➤ **pinacchiotto**, ➤ **pinino**, ➤ **pinarello**.

pinarello common name for ➤ **pinaiolo** mushrooms.

pinci another name for ➤ **pici**, a type of pasta.

pincinelle in Colonna, in the province of Rome, fresh bucatini; in the Marche a synonym of ➤ **pingiarelle**, small gnocchi.

pindl soft bread made from a mixture or rye and fine wholemeal wheat flour with the shape of three flat rolls joined together. Typical of the Val d'Ultimo, in the province of Bolzano. Trentino-Alto Adige.

pindulis an old specialty typical of the Canal del Ferro and Val Canale areas. Mutton or goat meat is cut into slices, which are cured for four to five days with salt, pepper, rosemary, bay leaves and garlic. The meat is then smoked for five to seven days over a fire of juniper berries, rosemary and bay leaves, and aged for 30-35 days. Friuli.

pingiada stew made with equal amounts of goat meat, wild boar, beef and mutton. Plus a couple of pigeons, flavored with onion, celery and parsley. The stew takes its name from the pan in which it is cooked. Sardinia.

pingiarelle aka **pincinelle** aka **penciarelle** small spindle- or olive-shaped gnocchi made with bread dough. Marche.

pinguino chocolate-coated ice cream bar on a stick. Invented by the Turin ice cream parlor Pepino in 1937.

pinino another name for ➤ **pinaiolo** mushrooms.

pinoccate small cake of toaste pine kernels amalgamated with caramelized sugar and served on ostias. Typical at Christmas in Assisi, Perugia and Gubbio. Similar cakes made of meringue, almonds and sugar are traditional at Christmas in Offida (Ascoli Piceno). Umbria, Marche.

pinoeti dialect term for ➤ **pignolini**, tiny picarel.

pinolata sandwich cake filled with confectioner's custard and pine kernels. Tuscany.

pinolate baked ostias filled with egg whites, sugar and pine kernels. Typical of the Chianti area. Tuscany.

pinoli alla ricotta small potato and chard gnocchi typical of the province of Pavia. Lombardy.

pinolo pine kernel. Much used in confectionery (➤ **pinoccate**, ➤ **pinolata**) but also in the kitchen, especially in Liguria. The Italian Ministry of Agriculture's database of native and/or traditional food products lists *pinoli del litorale laziale* (Lazio) and *pinoli del Parco di Migliarino San Rossore* (Tuscany).

pinos fried semolina and egg fingers, shaped like tiny pine kernels and coated in honey. Sardinia.

pinza ancient sweet or focaccia common, with variations, all over northeast Italy. In Trieste and Gorizia, the same word refers to an Easter cake. Veneto, Trentino-Alto Adige, Friuli-Venezia Giulia.

pinza a la munara aka **munaro** an oil bread once baked by millers on the Po, today served in restaurants with cured meats. Typical of the Polesine area, Veneto.

pinza de lat cake made by baking a mixture of day-old bread, flour, milk, eggs, sugar, raisins, cinnamon and lemon zest. Sometimes topped with sliced (➤ **pinza de peri**) or with sliced apples (➤ **pinza de pomi**). Trentino-Alto Adige.

pinza de patate oven-baked risen flour and potato dough. A specialty of the Mocheni, a small linguistic minority in the Valle del Fersina. Trentino-Alto Adige.

pinza de peri, **pinza de pomi** varieties of ➤ **pinza de lat**, a cake.

pinza dei cuchi cake of day-old bread, sugar, eggs, cocoa, raisins and pine kernels, flavored with cinnamon cloves. Baked in the Polesine area to celebrate the arrival of spring. Veneto.

pinza montanara pastry tart (originally baked at Christmas, now all year round) filled with jam, almonds, walnuts, hazelnuts, cocoa, raisins, dried figs, butter and lemon zest. The recipe is registered at the Bologna Chamber of Commerce. Emilia-Romagna.

pinza mula pumpkin and sweet potato (➤ **batata**) purée aromatized with raisins. Typical of the Polesine area. Veneto.

pinzimonio condiment of extra virgin olive oil, salt and pepper into which raw vegetables are dipped. In Piedmont it is called ➤ **bagné 'nt l'euli** and in the south ➤ **cazzimperio**.

pinzin Ferrara name for ➤ **crescentina fritta**, fried pastry.

piode irregular potato and dough squares. Lombardy.

pioggia, a "like rain." Expression to describe the steady, gradual pouring of a powder (flour, cocoa, semolina and the like) into a liquid (broth, milk and the like).

piopparello another name for → **pioppino**, black poplar mushroom.

pioppino black poplar mushroom (*Agrocybe aegerita*, *A. cylindracea*). Spring and fall mushroom variety. Usually stewed, used in sauces or preserved in oil.

pipare to simmer. Term used in Veneto and Lombardy.

piparelli crisp, crumbly, spicy fruit buns with the appearance of slices of salami, typical of the provinces of Reggio Calabria and Messina. Calabria, Sicilia.

pipasener flatbread, once common in the provinces of Mantua, Cremona and Brescia, made with the the same ingredients as → **chisola**, with the addition of chocolate chips or raisins. Traditionally made on January 17 for the feast of Sant'Antonio Abate. The name derives from the fact that it was cooked in the fireplce in hot ash (*cenere* in Italian, *sener* in dialect). Lombardy.

pipazzu Calabrian term for → **peperoncino**, chili.

pipe curved, hollow commercial durum wheat dried pasta. Another name for = **lumache**.

pipeto mixture of Savoy cabbage, garlic, butter, Grana Padano and nutmeg used as a stuffing for fowl or cooked as a frittata. Typical of Cremona. Lombardy.

pipi Calabrian term for → **peperone**, sweet pepper. Peppers fried with potatoes are *pipi friuti*, and a chili pepper is *pipi vruscente*.

pipi addenti aka **pipi russi** Sicilian terms for → **peperoncino**, chili.

pippias de zuccuru another name for → **pistoccheddos tostaos**, Sardinian cookies.

Pireddas name used for → **Casizolu** in southern Sardinia.

pirichittos aka **pirikitos** round iced cakes of Spanish origin. Sardinia.

pirlìin sweet buns made with wheat flour, milk, lard and sugar. Traditional in the province of Cremona. Lombardy.

pisantuni Sicilian dialect word for → **tambarello**, frigate tuna.

pisarei e fasò small gnocchi of grated day-old bread turned in a sauce of beans, sausage (or lardo and pork rind), tomato and garden herbs. A classic first course of the province of Piacenza, a way of using up old bread. The same recipe extends to the areas of Voghera, in the province of Pavia, and Tortona, in the province of Alessandria, where the pasta is known as → **pisaren**. Emilia-Romagna, Lombardy, Piedmont.

pisaren an other name for → **pisarei e fasò**, a pasta dish.

pischeddu another name for → **Murutzulu** cheese.

pisci a collettu soup of dried fava beans, aromatized with garlic and mint and served hot with a drizzle of extra virgin olive oil. A recipe typical of Cagliari. Sardinia.

pisci d'ummra in Italian *pesce d'ombra*, literally "shadow fish." Sicilian dialect name for → **pesce pilota**, pilot fish.

pisci palu Calabrian and Sicilian term for → **molva**, ling.

pisci rè Marsala term for → **frittura di paranza**, mixed fried fish. Sicily.

pisci scabecciau fish coated in flour, fried and preserved in a marinade of extra virgin olive oil, garlic and tomato. Sardinia.

pisciacane regional name for → **tarassaco**, dandelion.

pisciadela aka **piscialandrea** another name for → **sardenaira**, Ligurian pizza.

piscialetto aka **piascialletto** common regional names for ➛ **tarassaco**, dandelion.

pisciarà another name for ➛ **sardenaira**, Ligurian pizza.

pisciarada potato pie typical of the western Riviera. Liguria.

piscicapuni Sicilian dialect word for ➛ **lampuga**, dolphin fish.

piscirova aka **piscirovu** a sort of omelet of eggs, parsley and Pecorino. The dialect name means "fish made with eggs" and refers to the appearance of the dish. Sicily.

pisellata spring pea soup typical of the province of Macerata. Marche.

pisello pea (*Pisum sativum*). Cultivated varieties are subdivided into podding peas and mangetouts whose pod is edible too. The Italian Ministry of Agriculture's database of native and/or traditional food products lists: *piselli cornetti* (Campania); *pisello di Lavagna, nero di L'Ago* (Liguria); *pisello di Casalborgone* (Piedmont); *nano di Zollino, riccio di Sannicola* (Puglia); *pisello a mezza frasca aretino, pisello a tutta frasca aretino, mugellano* (Tuscany); *bisi de Lumignan, biso di Peseggia, pisello di Borso del Grappa* (Veneto). In the kitchen, the legume is used in soups and pasta sauces (➛ **bazzoffia**, ➛ **lepudrida**, ➛ **menestra de bisi spacai**, ➛ **pisellata**, ➛ **risi e bisi**, ➛ **zavardella**, ➛ **zuppa di piselli**) and as a side dish or complement (➛ **carciofi coi piselli**; ➛ **piselli al prosciutto**, ➛ **piselli con lo zafferano**, ➛ **vignarola**).

piselli al prosciutto classico Roman side dish of sweet fresh peas, lettuce and prosciutto. Lazio.

piselli alla fiorentina popular side dish of fresh peas gently stewed with chopped pancetta (or prosciutto), garlic and minced parsley. Tuscany.

piselli con lo zafferano side dish of fresh peas gently stewed with onion in olive oil with the addition of saffron diluted in hot water. Sardinia.

pisì 'n rosa in carpione fried bleak (➛ **alborelle**) marinated in a warm mixture of vinegar, white wine, finely sliced onion, bay leaf and peppercorns. Lombardy.

pissarella dialect term for ➛ **ioseride**, perennial hyoseris.

pista o salata in rural areas the term refers to all the various operations carried out after the killing of the pig to cure the meat. Marche.

pista 'd gras mixture of finely chopped lardo, garlic and parsley, eaten spread on bread or used as a base for other dishes. Typical of the province of Piacenza. Emilia-Romagna.

pistaada another word for ➛ **gras pistà**, finely minced lard.

pistacchio pistachio (*Pistacia vera*). Tree of the Anacardiaceae of Middle Eastern origin, introduced to the West by the Arabs. In Italy it is cultivated only in Sicily, ➛ **pistacchio di Bronte** accounting for 80% of the island's production.

pistacchio di Bronte bright green, intensely perfumed pistachio variety that grows only on the lava soil of Bronte, in the province of Catania. Unable to withstand competition from inferior quality, cheaper nuts from Iran, Turkey and America, it is protected by a Slow Food presidium. A large part of production goes into cured meats (➛ **mortadella**), the rest to the confectionery and ice cream industries. In Sicily, Bronte pistachios are used to make cakes, nougats and cakes. Sicily.

pistacoppi Macerata and Pesaro dialect name for ➛ **piccione**, pigeon (derived from *coppi*, roof tiles, where pigeons often sit). A traditional recipe is *pistacoppi ripieno*, pigeon stuffed with ground beef, breadcrumbs, eggs, grated lemon zest, cinnamon, and nutmeg with the addition, in the winter, of chestnuts. Marche.

pistiddos large round tarts (six inches in diameter), typical of Nuoro and surrounds. Water, honey and/or ➤ **sapa**, citrus fruit zest, and cinnamon are boiled for a couple of hours to a jam-like consistency. The mixture is divided into portions and left to cool. The individual portions are then enclosed between pastry dough disks and baked in the oven. The resulting tarts are cut into slices and served. In the Barbagia area, the same name, **pistiddos**, refers to fancily shaped tarts ("S"s, hearts, circles, "8"s) filled with honey and/or ➤ **sapa** and often hazelnuts (➤ **caschettas**). Sardinia.

pistilli another word for ➤ **pastiddri**, dried chestuts.

pistinco another name for ➤ **frustingo**, a Christmas cake.

pisto napoletano mixture of spices (cloves, powdered vanilla, cinnamon, confectioner's sugar, noce nutmeg and pepper) used mainly in confectionery. Campania.

pistoccheddos de cappa another name for ➤ **pistoccheddos tostaos**, Sardinian cookies.

pistoccheddos grussos another name for ➤ **gallettinas**, Sardinian cookies.

pistoccheddos tostaos aka **pistoccheddos de Serrenti** simple baked vanilla cookies traditionally shaped into dolls, small hands, animals and so on, glazed with icing (➤ **ghiaccia**) and decorated with confetti sugar (➤ **traggera** (Sardinia).

pistoccos incappausos another name for ➤ **pistoccheddos tostaos**, Sardinian cookies.

pistoccu variation on ➤ **fresa (1)**, a type of rusk. Normally eaten dressed with tomato, basil, garlic, oregano and piquant cheese. Sardinia.

pistoccus another name for ➤ **savoiardi** sponge finger produced in Sardinia.

pistofatru traditional cake made by cooking durum wheat flour in ➤ **vincotto**, cooked grape must, and adding cocoa and powdered cinnamon, and allowing the mixture to cool. Cut into lozenge shapes, it is served dusted with refined sugar. Typical of the province of Lecce. Puglia.

pistringo another name for ➤ **frustingo**, Christmas cake.

pistum (1) Veneto word for the mixture for fresh cured meats.

pistum (2) spicy raisin dumplings boiled in meat broth and served as a first course. Friuli-Venezia Giulia.

pistume a mixture of salami and sausage meat used to dress pasta or rice. Alternatively it can be rolled into a ball and barbecued. In the province of Mantua it features in ➤ **risotto alla pilota**. Lombardy.

pita e curnitt boiled chicken served cold, sometimes in aspic, with runner beans. Typical of the Swiss Cantone Ticino.

pitaggiu girgintanu soup of artichokes, carrots, peas, fava beans and, on special occasions, meatballs. The name derives from the French *potage*. A specialty of Agrigento. Sicily.

pite "full sack" in dialect. The name of an apple cake enriched with walnuts and raisins. Typical of the Carnia area. Friuli-Venezia Giulia.

piticelle aka **pitticelle di rosamarina** fritters made with the fiery fish relish ➤ **rosamarina**. Calabria.

pitina rare smoked cured meat made with roe deer venison and mutton or goat meat (chamois used to be used) typical of the Val Tramontina and relaunched by a Slow Food presidium. Friuli-Venezia Giulia.

pitta risen flatbread made in various shapes and filled with offal (➤ **morzeddu**) and countless other combinations of ingredients. Calabria.

pitta 'mpigliata an ancient recipe for spicy

fruit loaves formed into different shapes and presented on disks of puff pastry. Calabria.

pitta 'nchiusa another word for ➤ **pitta 'mpigliata**.

pitta chicculiata risen bread dough ➤ **pitta** filled with tomato sauce, tuna, capers, anchovies and olives. Calabria.

pitta minata a by-product of baking made by vigorously mixing leftover bread dough. Typical of San Giovanni in Fiore (Cosenza). Calabria.

pittapie another word for ➤ **nepitelle**, sweet ravioli.

pittinicchi Sicilian term for pork chops.

pittule another name for ➤ **pettole**, pastries.

pizacra aka **pizzacra** aka **pizzarda** dialect terms for ➤ **beccaccia**, woodcock.

pizz' e ffojie another name for ➤ **pizza e minestra**, a soup.

pizz'onta a bread dough fritter. Abruzzo.

pizza arguably the Italian word and food best known worldwide. In reality, **pizza** is a generic term in central and southern Italy with different nuances of meaning. The word, ancient in origin, refers to a usually round sweet or savory flatbread made with wheat or other flours. In regional spelling and pronunciation, it has been corrupted over the centuries, but it is still easily recognizable in variants such as ➤ **pinza** (Veneto) and ➤ **pitta** (Calabria). In the 19th century, thanks mainly to the entrpreneurship of Neapolitan *pizzaiuoli*, the ➤ **pizza napoletana** asserted itself over all the other regional versions.

pizza di patate aka **pitta di patate** a sort of baked ➤ **gattò** made by spreading a layer of mashed potatoes with a mixture of onion, tomato, olives, capers and anchovies and covering with another layer of potatoes. Puglia.

pizza al formaggio aka **pizza di Pasqua** a sort of cheese pie (with many variations) eaten all over central Italy on Easter Monday, accompanied by hard-boiled eggs and cured meats.

pizza alla Campofranco Neapolitan flatbread sliced horizontally, filled with tomato sauce, mozzarella, grated Parmigiano and diced ham, and topped with more sauce and grated cheese. According to tradition, it was the Prince of Campofranco, lieutenant of the Kingdom of the Two Sicilies, who brought the recipe to the city, hence its name. Campania.

pizza bianca common name for ➤ **crescia maceratese**. The same name is used in the north for plain focaccia.

pizza bianca di Roma large flatbread made with all-purpose flour, sea salt, brewer's yeast, olive oil and malt. Lazio.

pizza chiena a flatbread filled with cheese (Parmigiano and Provolone), eggs and salami, traditionally baked at Easter. Campania.

pizza cioncia fried flour and water batter. Typical of Frosinone, Lazio.

pizza con ciccioli e uvetta bread dough softened with olive oil, topped with pork scratchings (➤ **ciccioli**) and sultanas, shaped into a ring, and baked in the oven. Calabria.

pizza con cotenna e ciccioli pizza pie made with bread dough and filled with pork scratchings (➤ **ciccioli**) and pork rind. Basilicata.

pizza con i tanni pie filled with broccoli rabe. Typical of the Ciociaria area, in the province of Frosinone. Lazio.

pizza de turco con cicoria baked cornflour pizza sliced in half and filled with boiled chicory. Typical of Frosinone, Lazio.

pizza della venuta flatbread made with wheat flour, eggs, sultanas, extra virgin olive oil, salt and grated Pecorino. Traditionally baked on the night of December 9 when, according to legend, angels on their way to the sanctuary of Loreto flew over Umbria (*la venuta* means "the coming"). Umbria.

pizza di farina gialla cornflour flatbread that used to be baked in the burning embers of the fireplace. In Orvieto (Terni), they make the dough by mixing the flour with salted boiling water aromatized with sage, celery, rosemary and cloves, then adding extra virgin olive oil, raisins and pine kernels. Umbria.

pizza di granone another name for ➤ **polenta in tortiera**, cornflour with broccoli rabe.

pizza di Maiyu) baked bread dough stuffed with pork scratchings (➤ **ciccioli**), mozzarella or Provola, ricotta, salami and eggs or with roasted tomatoes. A specialty of Ardore (Reggio Calabria). Calabria.

pizza di Pasqua sweet or savory "pizza," baked in a mold, that looks more like a panettone. Made all over Lazio, especially in the Tuscia area in the province of Viterbo. A close relative of ➤ **crescia di Pasqua** (Marche) and ➤ **pizza al formaggio** (Umbria). Lazio.

pizza di polenta a mixture of ➤ **Ricotta Romana** diluted in water, refined sugar, cornflour, cinnamon and raisins, is spooned into the bottom of a cake tin and scattered with pine kernels, dotted with butter or lard, and baked in the oven. In the south of the region, the same name is used for a savory flatbread filled with chicory or broccoli. Lazio.

pizza di ricotta aka **pizza dolce** shortcrust pastry tart filled with confectioner's custard mixed with milk, ricotta and candied fruit or almonds. Campania.

pizza di san Martino long pastry roll, baked in the oven and stuffed with anchovies. A specialty of the Sannio area, in the province of Benevento. Campania.

pizza di scarola traditional Christmas flatbread made with bread dough and topped with boiled escarole finished in oil and garlic, chili, Gaeta olives, capers, raisins, pine kernels and anchovy fillets. Campania.

pizza doce (aka **pizza teramana**) layers of sponge caked soaked in liqueur (alkermes or maraschino) filled with egg custard, coated with meringue and baked to golden in the oven. Abruzzo.

pizza dolce ring-shaped cake made by amalgamating flour, sugar, butter, extra virgin olive oil, milk, eggs, grated lemon zest and yeast, baked in the oven and dusted with confectioner's sugar. At Easter, Vin Santo, Marsala or cinnamon-flavored = **rosolio** are added to the mixture (➤ **torta dolce di Pasqua**) Umbria.

pizza e minestra rustic soup of potatoes and cultivated and wild greens flavored with garlic, oil and chili, into which cornflour flatbread is broken. Also known, in dialect, as *pizz' e ffojie*. Molise.

pizza figliata aka **pizza fogliata** pastry typical of the commune of Pignataro, in the province of Caserta. A thin sheet of puff pastry aromatized with white wine, coated in honey and filled with honey, walnuts, hazelnuts, almonds, spices (vanilla and cinnamon) and pieces of citron. Baked for the feast of the patron saint, San Vito, on September 16. Campania.

pizza frella long, soft bread loaf typical of Cori (Latina). Lazio.

pizza grassa aka **pizzetto chieno** wholemeal pastry pie filled with sausage (➤ **soperzata di Rivello**), sliced hard-boiled eggs, scrambled eggs and grated Pecorino. A specialty of Potenza. Basilicata.

pizza napoletana since 2004 protected by the European Union's GTS (guaranteed traditional specialty) recognition. The traditional version is regulated by precise standards. The twice-risen dough must be made by kneading soft wheat flour with drinking water and brewer's yeast. The disk must be rolled out by hand and have a thickness at the center of no more than a quarter of an inch and a border (*cornicione*) no higher than an inch or so. The topping must consist of crushed skinned or fresh tomatoes, sea salt and extra virgin olive oil, and the pizza must be baked in a wood oven until the *cornicione* is golden brown. The protocol also recognizes two richer versions: ➤ **pizza napoletana margherita** and ➤ **pizza napoletana marinara**.

pizza napoletana margherita classic variant of ➤ **pizza napoletana**, dedicated to the late 19th century queen of Italy for whom it is named. According to the production protocol, the pizza must be topped with crushed skinned or fresh tomatoes, ➤ **Fior di latte** cheese from the southern Apennines and salt, and garnished with basil leaves. A so-called *extra* version replaces Fior di latte with ➤ **Mozzarella di bufala campana**. Campania.

pizza napoletana marinara the traditional version consists of a classic ➤ **pizza napoletana**, with the addition of slices of garlic and oregano, though another (which strays outside the production protocol) also comprises capers and anchovies.

pizza perugina risen flatbread, first topped with Grana cheese, fresh Pecorino and diced prosciutto, then baked in the oven. Served as an antipasto.

pizza ripiena two disks of wholemeal dough filled with onion, anchovies and raisins, and baked in the oven. A specialty of Potenza. Basilicata.

pizza ripiena casarinola bread dough stuffed with ricotta, mortadella and thin slices of ➤ **Caciocavallo** and ➤ **Fior di latte**, and baked in the oven. Campania.

pizza rustica sweet shortcrust pastry pie filled with ricotta, eggs, prosciutto, cheese (mozzarella, Provola and grated Parmigiano), sausage, salami and black pepper, brushed with beaten eggs. Many versions exist, one in particular, *tasca pasquale* (shortcrust pastry, eggs, ➤ **soppressata**, cheese and sugar) traditionally made at Easter in Campania. Abruzzo, Campania, Puglia.

pizza sfoglia another name for ➤ **sfogliata pugliese**, a savory pastry spiral.

pizza tarantina "pizza" made from a dough of flour, mashed potatoes, yeast and salt. Topped with slices of mozzarella, tomato, oregano, salt and oil. Puglia.

pizza teramana another name for ➤ **pizza doce**, a type of cake.

pizzaiola, alla term to describe a cooking technique in which meat, fresh fish, salt cod and eggplants, for example, are stewed with tomatoes, oregano and garlic. Now common nationwide, it originated in Campania.

pizzata bread made from a dough of cornflour, sourdough, water and salt, wrapped in cabbage leaves and baked in the oven. Common on the southern Ionian coast. Calabria.

pizzatolo "feminine" version of ➤ **varone**, a ring-shaped cookie, longer in shape and with one egg in the middle.

pizzelle another name for ➤ **ferratelle**, sweet wafers.

pizzelle alla napoletana balls of fried batter, served as an antipasto as they are or filled with prosciutto, salami, Provola, vegetables or anchovies. Campania.

pizziato crisp long beer bread loaf (➤ **pane a birra**) with random gashes on the surface. Sicily.

pizzica-lingua regional term for ➤ **cren**, horseradish.

pizzicannelli large cinnamon-scented chocolate cookies glazed with a chocolate icing. The name derives from ➤ **cannella**, cinnamon. Basilicata.

pizzicata a ring-shaped variation on ➤ **pignoccata**, decorated with small cubes of candied citron. Sicily.

pizzicati aka **pizziconi** aka **pizzicotti** small fresh flour and water gnocchi. In the province of Rieti, they substitute bran flakes for flour. Lazio.

pizzo irregularly-shaped bread loaf similar to ➤ **pane purecasciu** with the addition of black olives. Typical of the province of Lecce. Puglia.

pizzocheri short buckwheat tagliatelle which originated in the vllage of Teglio (Sondrio), cooked with potatoes, Savoy cabbage (in summer, chards), mixed with cheese (➤ **Latteria**) and served with garlic butter and sage. A classic meal-in-one typical of the Valtellina, in the province of Sondrio. Lombardy.

pizzocorno regional term for ➤ **raperonzolo**, rampion.

pizzodos savory version of ➤ **seadas**, sweet ravioli. A simple flour and water pasta dough stuffed with fresh cheese, sometimes flavored with mint leaves. Popular in the Barbagia area. Sardinia.

pizzola fried pizza sprinkled with salt or sugar. A specialty of Terni. Umbria.

pizzuoccolo a flatter version of ➤ **pane di Rivello**. Basilicata. **platessa** plaice (*Pleuronectes platessa*). A flatfish similar to sole (➤ **sogliola**), which lives in the Atlantic. In Italy it is mostly imported from northern Europe and sold in frozen fillets.

pleskavica flat meatball (pork, onion, onion, parsley) cooked on the grill. Typical of areas on the border with Slovenia. Friuli-Venezia Giulia.

pociacche large ➤ **orecchiette**, a type of pasta.

pocio (1) Veneto term for sauce or gravy.

pocio (2) Piedmontese term for ➤ **nespola**, medlar.

pocio de vedel Veneto term for meat sauce.

Podolica gray-coated cattle breed probably introduced to Italy in Roman times, or by the Huns. By the 5th century AD it was common all over the peninsula, from Istria to Calabria. Bulls have half moon-shaped horns, cows lyre-shaped. It is raised for its sapid, mineral salt-rich meat and aromatic milk, most of which is used to make cheese. The Gargano Podilica is a Slow Food presidium. Puglia.

poina aka **puina** northeastern Italian terms for ➤ **ricotta**.

pola northern dialect term for ➤ **beccaccia**, woodcock.

polastro de la batidura roast chicken served with lightly blanched vegetables (tomatoes, yellow, read and green peppers, onions). A dish typical of the Polesine area, in the province of Rovigo. Veneto.

polastro de la menanda roast chicken served on a bed of onions. A dish typical of the Polesine area, in the province of Rovigo. Veneto

polastro imbotìo Veneto term for stuffed chicken (➤ **pollo ripieno**).

polastro in tecia in Veneto, chicken stewed with onion, carrot celery, cloves, cinnamon, white wine and tomato sauce. In Friuli-Venezia Giulia, chicken stewed in an earthenware pot with herbs and spices. Veneto, Friuli-Venezia Giulia

pold a runny polenta served either with milk or cream, or with meat sauce. Typical of Milan. Lombardy.

polenta a blend or porridge of water and ground cereals or legumes. Polenta is wrongly believed to be made only with cornflour. It actually existed long before corn came to Europe from America. In ancient Rome, *puls*, crushed buckwheat or fava beans boiled in water, was a daily staple for legionaries and plebeians. The same ingredients, together with barley, millet and emmer, mixed with oil and onion or honey, continued to nourish the less well-off for centuries. Corn began to play a leading role from the 18th century, when polenta as we know it today imposed itself as the main and often only dish in the diet of peasants, especially in northern Italy. Today it is no longer eaten as a subsistence food but as an accompaniment to other ingredients: meat stews, cured meats, cheese and so on.

polenta accomodata polenta mixed with cheese (➤ **polenta concia**).

polenta al latte slices of polenta topped with mountain dairy cheese, covered with milk, dotted with knobs of butter, sprinkled with pepper and slow-cooked on a low heat. A dish typical of the mountain valleys of the province of Cuneo. Piedmont.

polenta alla varesotta vegetable soup thickened with polenta flour, allowed to cool and set and cut into slices. Typical of the province of Varese. Lombardy.

polenta bianca polenta made with white flour (➤ **mais biancoperla**). Veneto, Friuli-Venezia Giulia.

polenta brustolà day-old polenta cut into slices and grilled. Served with slivers of cheese. Veneto.

polenta carbonara aka **polenta carbonera** wet cornflour polenta into which other ingredients (butter, cheese, sausage, sometimes chestnuts and beans) are mixed. Trentino-Alto Adige, Veneto.

polenta comodà another name for ➤ **polenta concia**.

polenta con la salvia polenta flavored with onion, sage, parsley, mushrooms and anchovies, allowed to cool and set, coated in flour and fried in oil with sage leaves. Typical of the provinces of Como and Lecco. Lombardy.

polenta con la zucca soft polenta mixed with pumpkin flesh and served with cold milk. Friuli-Venezia Giulia.

polenta con le ciammotte polenta covered with a sauce of snails, tomato, garlic, pennyroyal and mint and sprinkled with grated Pecorino. Lazio.

polenta concia aka **polenta conscia** aka **polenta cuncia** aka **polenta cunscia** polenta mixed with cheese and other dairy products: butter, Fontina, Toma, Montasio and so on. Combinations vary according to area.

polenta d'Ivrea a cake of very finely ground cornflour (➤ **fumetto (2)**), potato flour, butter, egg yolks, sugar and lemon zest glazed with an icing of honey and orange juice. A creation of the Strobbia brothers, confectioners in Ivrea (Turin), in 1922. Piedmont.

polenta di castagne thick chestnut polenta typical of the Apennines (registered as "traditional" in Emilia-Romagna). In the mountains of the province of Cuneo, it is eaten wet with milk or, the day after, sliced and fried in butter.

polenta di farro buckwheat polenta. A typical "poor" dish of central Italy.

polenta di Marengo cornflour and almond cake glazed with icing and sprinkled with minced almonds. Recipe created in 1933 by a pastry chef in Alessandria, who dedicated it to Napoleon's famous victory in his second Italian campaign. Piedmont.

polenta di Ovada cake of cornflour, almonds, amaretti cookies, eggs, butter and sugar. Typical of the province of Alessandria. Piedmont.

polenta di patate polenta of boiled potatoes and buckwheat flour with a purée-like consistency. Typical of Emilia-Romagna, but also of the northeastern Italian regions.

polenta dolce baked cake of cornflour, milk, egg yolks, amaretti cookies, butter, confectioner's sugar and cinnamon. Typical of Crema, in the province of Cremona. Lombardy.

polenta e ciccioli, in dialect aka **pulêinta e grasèi** polenta with pork scratchings (➤ **ciccioli**) and onions. Emilia-Romagna.

polenta e merluzzo polenta with fried salt cod flavored with parsley, spinach or chard and garlic. Piedmont.

polenta e osei (1) polenta served with roasted song birds (thrushes, sparrows, ortolan buntings, larks) and their cooking juices. Typical of the provinces of Bergamo, Brescia and Vicenza. Lombardy, Veneto.

polenta e osei (2) chocolate- and orange-flavored sponge cake coated with yellow-dyed almond paste and decorated with dainty almond paste birds coated with cocoa powder. Lombardy.

polenta e porri slices of polenta layered with cheese and a sauce of leeks and anchovies, and baked in the oven. Piedmont.

polenta grassa another name for ➤ **polenta concia**.

polenta in tortiera aka **pizza di granone** cornflour polenta mixed with broccoli rabe (➤ **friarielli**) and sausage meat and browned in the oven. Campania.

polenta incassata another name in Romagna for ➤ **polenta pasticciata**.

polenta incatenata rich polenta, cooked in broth with beans, potatoes, and "black cabbage" (➤ **cavolo nero**). Served soft with grated Parmigiano or Pecorino and extra-virgin olive oil. Liguria. Tuscany.

polenta infasolà aka **polenta infavà** polenta cooked with beans or fava beans. Cooked on November 2, All Souls' Day, in the Polesine ara and the province of Padua. Veneto.

polenta macafana polenta with wild chicory and cheese (➤ **Spressa**), flavored with onion, grated ➤ **Trentingrana** cheese and pepper. Trentino-Alto Adige.

polenta mata name used in the mountains of the province of Cuneo for potato polenta (➤ **polenta di patate**). Piedmont.

polenta mugna polenta made with a mixture of buckwheat flour and others. Typical of the Valtellina. Lombardy.

polenta nera buckwheat flour polenta, common in all northern mountain areas.

polenta nera con bagna bianca polenta of buckwheat and wheat flour and potatoes served with buttered leeks. A specialty of the mountains of the province of Cuneo. Piedmont.

polenta onta day-old polenta cut into slices and fried in butter and oil. Veneto.

polenta pasticciata in Emilia-Romagna, they bake polenta as they do pasta. In Piacenza, slices of day-old polenta are layered with meat sauce and a generous sprinkling of grated Grana or Pecorino. In Reggio Emilia and Ferrara, they add mushrooms and sausage meat. In Romagna, they call similar recipes and speak of ➤ **polenta incassata**. Likewise in Veneto, where they layer slices of polenta with a sauce of chicken giblets, tomatoes and mushrooms, and in Friuli-Venezia Giulia, where polenta is alternated with stewed lamb, pork, chicken and pigeon, sausage and ham or tomato sauce. In Lombardy the sauce is made with ground meat, sausage, dried mushrooms, tomato and generous amounts of grated Parmigiano-Reggiano.

polenta pasticciata con i cicoli name used for ➤ **migliaccio campano**, cornflour polenta, in the area round Nola, in the province of Naples.

polenta rifatta aka **polenta carbonara** day-old cornflour polenta cut into slices and baked in the oven with ➤ **guanciale**

(cheek bacon) and grated Pecorino. A specialty of Gubbio. Umbria.

polenta sarda a meal-in-one of layers of polenta dressed with tomato and sausage sauce sprinkled generously with grated Pecorino, and baked in the oven. Sardinia.

polenta smalzada buckwheat polenta baked in the oven with anchovy fillets and grated Pecorino. Trentino-Alto Adige.

polenta taragna buckwheat polenta mixed with cheese, preferably ➤ **Bitto**, and served with sausage (➤ **luganega lombarda**). Lombardy.

polenta unta aka **polenta vuncia** polenta layered with grated Parmigiano-Reggiano and butter aromatized with garlic or onion and sage. Lombardy.

polente brusade slices of polenta turned in a skillet with lardo and sage. Friuli-Venezia Giulia.

polente cuinzade diced day-old polenta with mature cheese or smoked ricotta smothered with melted butter. Friuli-Venezia Giulia.

polente frite diced cold polenta fried in butter and sprinkled with sugar and cinnamon. Once given to children for breakfast or as a snack between meals. Friuli-Venezia Giulia.

polentina astigiana soft, sponge-like cake dotted with sultana, soaked with maraschino and topped with minced almonds. Created in the late 1920s, a popular treat in Asti and environs. Piedmont.

polentina di Cittadella leavened cake made with a mixture of flour, potato flour, sugar and eggs, dusted with vanilla sugar. A specialty of Cittadella, in the province of Padua. Veneto.

polentini aka **polentine** shortcrust pastry cookies made with a paste of wheat and cornflour and lemon zest. A specialty of Reggio. Emilia-Romagna.

polentone polenta flavored with grape must and slow-cooked unfermented wine must (➤ **sapa**). Marche.

pollame poultry. Farmyard birds: namely, chickens, ducks, geese, turkeys and guinea fowl.

pollanca another word for ➤ **pollo**, chicken.

pollastra, **pollastro** other words for ➤ **pollo**, chicken.

pollin con el pien roast turkey stuffed with a mixture of the bird's chopped liver and heart, lardo, ➤ **luganega** sausage, eggs, apples, chestnuts, prunes, nutmeg and brandy. Typical Milanese Christmas dish. Lombardy.

pollina alla lodigiana turkey hen of about three months, barded with lardo, prosciutto, garlic, salt and pepper, rubbed with butter, wrapped in greaseproof paper, and roast on the spit. Typical of the city of Lodi. Lombardy.

pollo chicken. Gastronomically speaking, chicken—which arrived in Greece from India via Persia, and was already being farmed by the Romans—began to be appreciated in Europe in the 17th and 18th centuries. In the second half of the last century, battery farming made chicken affordable for every pocket, but undermined the meat's quality and gastronomic versatility. Today laudable attempts are being made to return to free-range breeding. The methods for cooking chicken are countless, as are the local variations thereof. The Italian Ministry of Agriculture's database of native and/or traditional food products lists the following varieties: *razza gigante nera d'Italia* (Liguria), *pollo combattente di corte padovana, rustichello della Pedemontana* (Veneto), *i polli delle razze fidentina e romagnola* (Emilia-Romagna) and ➤ **pollo del Valdarno** (Tuscany).

pollo al mattone a young chicken flavored

with rosemary and garlic, flattened with an earthenware tile and cooked in a pot or roat in the oven. Tuscany

pollo alla cacciatora chicken pieces stewed in tomato with herbs. A dish common, with countless regional variations all over Italy.

pollo alla diavola a chicken slit down the middle and pounded flat, flavored with salt and extra virgin olive oil, barbecued and sprinkled with ground pepper and chili. A recipe typical of Florence, but also common elsewhere. Tuscany.

pollo alla Marengo chicken jointed, browned in oil and finished in tomato sauce, accompanied with mushrooms, crayfish and fried eggs on toast. Anecdotes abound about the origin of this odd dish. Most suggest it was assembled either by Napoleon's personal chef or by a local cook for the great man himself on the eve of the Battle of Marengo, near Alessandria. The recipe is now an international classic, but it has never taken root locally. Piedmont.

pollo alla 'ncip 'nciap chicken (though guinea fowl or rabbit may also be used) jointed and cooked with tomato, garlic, white wine and aromatic herbs. The name of the recipe, common in the Piceno area, may be an onomatopeic reference to the sizzling of the meat as it browns in the pan prior to being stewed. Marche.

pollo alla padovana Padua version of ➤ **pollo in fricassea**, fricasséed chicken.

pollo alla potentina chicken stewed in white wine with tomatoes basil, parsley and chili. Basilicata.

pollo alla romana chicken with tomatoes and sweet peppers. Lazio.

pollo arrosto roast chicken.

pollo con i funghi chicken stewed with mushrooms, rosemary and marjoram. Veneto.

pollo del Valdarno a breed of hen. The cock is tall with white feathers and a red crest. It grows slowly and its meat is excellent. The hens are smaller and lay tasty eggs with big yolks. The breed is raised in the upper Valdarno in the provinces of Arezzo and Florence, and is protected by a Slow Food presidium. Tuscany.

pollo fritto alla carsolina quartered chicken marinated in lemon juice, then fried in butter. A specialty of the Carso area in the province of Trieste. Friuli-Venezia Giulia.

pollo grillettato alla romana chicken stew with chopped ham, parsley, garlic, marjoram, white wine and tomatoes. Lazio.

pollo in fricassea fricasséed chicken. Pieces of chicken coated in flour browned with herbs, bathed with white wine and finished off with broth. Eggs beaten with lemon juice, salt and pepper are incorporated off the heat. Veneto.

pollo ripieno stuffed chicken. Many versions exist. In Veneto and Trentino, they bone the chicken, stuff it with a mixture of giblets, bread, cheese, eggs, walnuts, pine kernels, salt, pepper, and nutmeg, and boil it. In Umbria, the stuffing consists of giblets, prosciutto, grated Pecorino, bread, lemon zest, garlic and eggs, and the chicken is roasted in the oven.

polmonaria common lungwort (*Pulmonaria officinalis*). A wild herbaceous plant gathered mainly in central Italy, where it is fried (like sage or borage) and its flowers are added to salads. Common and regional names: ➤ **borrana selvatica**, ➤ **erba macchiata**, ➤ **milzera**, ➤ **salvia di Gerusalemme**.

polmonata another name for ➤ **salsiccia di polmone**, an offal sausage.

polmone lung. Lungs are full of connective tissue and are thus used little in the kitchen, where they have to be cooked polpa di maiale sott'olio

longer than other offal. Lamb's and kid's lungs are always used in combination with other offal (→ **coratella**), whereas calf's lung and, to a lesser extent, pig's lung are the principal ingredient in some recipes (eg, → **picchiante toscano**). Also known as → **frittura bianca**.

polpa di maiale sott'olio pork preserved in oil. An ancient artisan preparation, typical of the upper Maremma, of the hills of Albegna and Montemerano, in the province of Grosseto. The pork used comes from the shoulder of the pig and chops left from other cured meats. It is salted and cooked in oil with salt, pepper, garlic, rosemary and sage. It is then preserved in oil in glass jars and can be kept for up to 12 months. Tuscany.

polpetta (pl. **polpette**) meatballs or patties. Normally made round or spindle-shaped and stewed with or without tomato or fried. Meatballs (→ **polpette di carne**) used to be made at home to use up leftovers from the roast, but are now made with prime quality meat.

polpette di alici fish cakes made with chopped anchovies, eggs, cheese, garlic, parsley and fresh breadcrumbs. They may be served fried or turned in a skillet with crushed cherry tomatoes. Campania.

polpette di carne meatballs. In Emilia-Romagna, made of ground beef and pork, sausage and/or mortadella, grated Parmigiano, and egg, stewed with tomato and herbs (sometimes after prior frying). In Veneto, the beef is ground raw with breadcrumbs, onion, garlic, parsley, salt, pepper, and cinnamon, rolled into small balls, coated in flour, and fried in lard or olio. In Trieste and its province, meatballs are made of ground veal and pork, fried, then finished in the pan with red wine.

polpette di carne lombarde rolls of veal or pork stuffed with ground meat, pancetta, eggs, garlic, parsley, Parmigiano-Reggiano and breadcrumbs, stewed with tomato and served with potato purée or polenta. In the province of Milan, they are stuck on skewers, alternated with chunks of ham and sage leaves and cooked in the pan. Lombardy.

polpette di cavedano balls of baked chub, milk, parsley, garlic, eggs, cheese and breadcrumbs fried in oil and sprinkled with white wine. Typical of Lake Garda. Lombardy, Trentino, Veneto.

polpette di fagioli patties of boiled bean purée, eggs, parsley and breadcrumbs fried in oil. Trentino-Alto Adige.

polpette di lavarello balls of chub flesh coated in flour, fried in oil and finished off with finely sliced leeks, white wine, diced tomato and basil. Lombardy, Trentino, Veneto.

polpette di mussillo oblong salt cod and olive fritters finished in a skillet with tomatoes, capers and olives. Campania.

polpette di pane round fritters made of day-old bread soaked in milk, egg, grated Pecorino, parsley and salt. Served in tomato sauce. Puglia.

polpette di Pelliccia meatballs traditionally made with leftover boiled and roast beef, eggs, herbs and mashed potatoes. Now Pecorino, minced garlic and parsley, lemon zest and nutmeg are also added. A Florentine family dish. Tuscany.

polpette di verza Savoy cabbage leaves covered with mixture of ground beef or pork (sometimes with the leftovers from a roast), sausage, salami, grated Grana Padano, bread soaked in milk, eggs, and parsley, rolled up and secured with cocktail sticks, coated in flour, browned in oil with onion and pancetta, and finished off in dry white wine and meat broth.

Recipe typical of the province of Milan. Lombardy.

polpetti affogati alla civitavecchiese small octopuses lightly fried in a → **soffritto** of extra virgin olive oil, garlic and parsley, bathed with white wine and gently stewed. Lazio.

polpettone meat loaf. A family dish subject to many variations.

polpettone di manzo the Tuscan meat loaf recipe consists of ground beef amalgamated with chopped, eggs, grated Parmigiano salt and pepper, and rolled in breadcrumbs, The loaf is browned in oil, then stewed in tomato with porcini mushrooms. It is served sliced with its sauce. In Emilia-Romagna, the ground meat is mixed with Parmigiano, breadcrumbs, ground lardo, eggs, spices, lemon juice and milk. The loaf (sometimes with a hard-boiled egg in the middle) is first browned on a high heat, then baked in the oven on a base of onions softened in butter. It can be eaten hot or cold.

polpettone di pollo chicken loaf. A Roman recipe of Jewish origin. A loaf of finely ground chicken breast and leg mixed with eggs, breadcrumbs, cinnamon, salt and pepper, browned in oil, then stewed with chopped carrots and artichokes. Lazio.

polpettone di tacchino turkey loaf. A recipe probably of Jewish origin. Loaf of ground turkey mixed with eggs, bread soaked in milk, grated Parmigiano, salt, pepper, nutmeg and thick béchamel sauce. It is either boiled wrapped in canvas or breaded, fried and finished with white wine. Ferrara.

polpettone fritto fried meat loaf. Ground veal, ham, eggs, pepper, cloves and cinnamon, shaped into a "sausage" and fried in oil (in the past in lard). Friuli-Venezia Giulia.

polpettone genovese a vegetable loaf made of mashed potatoes flavored with onions and herbs, eggs and cheese, and, according to season, runner beans, zucchini, peas and artichokes, baked in the oven. Liguria.

polpo octopus (*Octopus vulgaris*). Most Italian octopus recipes are aromatized stews which exploit the water released by the mollusk in the pan.

polpi alla luciana octopus cooked in a covered pot with fresh tomato, oil, garlic, parsley and black pepper, without the addition of water. Named for the fishing neighborhood of Santa Lucia, in Naples, where fishermen used to slowly boil freshly caught octopus, cut them into pieces and serve them in bowls with their cooking broth flavored with oil and chili. Campania.

polpi cotti nella loro acqua medium-sized octopus slow-cooked on a bed of sliced onion, parsley and cherry tomatoes without the addition of water. A specialty of Bari. Puglia.

polpi in galera small octopus cut into pieces, stewed with olive oil, garlic and minced parsley, and seasoned with salt and pepper. Tuscany.

polpo alla pignata octopus cut into pieces and cooked in an earthenware pot (→ **pignata**) with onion, tomato and parsley. Puglia.

polpo asinisco Neapolitan word for → **moscardino** *bianco*, curled octopus.

polpo di sabbia another word for → **moscardino** *bianco*, curled octopus.

polpo e patate octopus and potatoes. The two ingredients are boiled separately, cut into pieces, mixed together and dressed like a salad with oil, lemon juice and minced parsley and garlic. Liguria.

polpo muschiato another name for → **moscardino muschiato**, musky octopus.

polpo sott'aceto pickled octopus. Boiled octopus, allowed to cool, cut it pieces and preserved in glass jars with vinegar, garlic and mint leaves. Puglia.

poltricce simple country snack cum dessert consisting of small bread dough focaccias spread with honey and jam. Umbria.

pom e pasta pasta and potatoes mixed with melted cheese and fried onions. Typical of the Swiss Cantone Ticino.

pomino rosso regional term for ➤ **corbezzolo**, strawberry tree, arbutus.

pomodoro tomato (*Lycopersicum esculentum*). A native of the Andes, the tomato was brought to Europe by the explorers of the Americas, but only found fortune in the kitchen in the 19th century. It was then that it began to be processed industrially into sauces and conserves, an activity in which the Turinese Francesco Cirio was a pioneer. Cultivated varieties are subdivided into: tomatoes for industrial use, salad tomatoes, tomatoes for home storage and sun-dried tomatoes.

pomodori arrostiti roasted tomatoes. Whole tomatoes barbecued, squashed, dressed with salt, pepper and extra virgin olive oil served on fresh bread. Calabria.

pomodori ripieni a crudo stuffed tomatoes. Summer antipasto made in various regions in various ways. In Piedmont and Tuscany, the flesh is scooped out of the tomatoes, which are stuffed with minced tuna, capers, garlic, parsley, mayonnaise, olive oil and salt.

pomodori ripieni al forno baked stuffed tomatoes. A dish common everywhere with different stuffings. In Umbria and the southern regions they might use a mixture of dried breadcrumbs, oil, aromatic herbs and garlic with eggs to bind it, or boiled rice and herbs (in Lazio minced pennyroyal and parsley). In northern Piedmont they use beaten eggs and grated cheese, in Trentino mixed ground meats. In Calabria, finally, they stuff tomatoes with short pasta dressed with oil, minced parsley and mint.

pomodorino a ciliegia cherry tomato (➤ **pomodorino al piennolo**).

pomodorino al piennolo aka **piennoli** aka **spongilli** "pendulum" tomatoes, so-called because they are hung in bunches. These tiny tomatoes, each weighing less than an ounce, can be distinguished from the famous Pachino tomato by the two grooves down their sides and the point at one end, known as a *pizzo*. The skin is thick and the flesh firm, compact, dried by the strong sun of the Vesuvius, where the tomato grows. Both flavor and aroma become more intense with time.

pomodoro da conserva conserve tomatoes. All the varieties used for conserves: canned, passatas, concentrates and juices. Varieties used for canning include the Slow Food presidium-sponsored ➤ **tomato sanmarzano dell'Agro sarnese-nocerino**, so-called *seccagni*, full of flavor since they are cultivated without irrigation, and certain cherry tomatoes. Round, scented tomatoes are used for juices and concentrates. The Italian Ministry of Agriculture's database of native and/or traditional food products lists: *pomodoro a pera* (Abruzzo); *pomodorino corbarino, pomodorino vesuviano* (Campania); *pomodoro corno di toro* (Lazio); *piatta di Bernezzo* (Piedmont); *pomodorino di Manduria* (Puglia); *pomodoro seccagno pizzutello di Paceco* (Sicily); *pomodoro costoluto fiorentino da conserva, quarantino, stella* (Tuscany); *pomodoro del Cavallino* (Veneto). In the kitchen, tomato passata, canned tomatoes, chopped tomatoes and tomato concentrate are used in countless recipes. The most common pasta sauce is ⮞ **salsa di pomodoro**, and canned skinned tomatoes are envisaged by the protocol that regulates ⮞ **pizza napoletana**.

pomodoro da mensa salad tomatoes. Among the most common varieties are ⮞ **pomodoro di Pachino**, *cuore di bue* aka *bovaiolo* (or beefsteak tomato), *tondo liscio*, *costoluto*, *marmade* and other varieties of cherry tomatoes. The Italian Ministry of Agriculture's database of native and/or traditional food products lists: *pomodoro a pera* (Abruzzo); *pomodoro di Belmonte* (Calabria); *pomodorino corbarino, vesuviano, pomodoro di Sorrento* (Campania); *corno di toro, scatolone di Bolsena, spagnoletta del golfo di Gaeta e di Formia* (Lazio); *cuore di bue* (Liguria); *costoluto di Cambiano, costoluto di Chivasso, piatta di Bernezzo* (Piedmont); *pomodorino di Manduria* (Puglia); *pomodoro di Vittoria, pomodorino di Licata* (Sicily); *pomodoro canestrino di Lucca, cuore di bue* (aka *bovaiolo*), *pomodoro fragola di Albiano Minacciano, grinzoso sanminiatese, marmande, pendentino, pisanello, stella* (Tuscany); *pomodoro* del *Cavallino* (Veneto).

pomodoro da serbo tomato for home storage. The category comprises some small, round or oval, yellow to red varieties, often in bunches, mostly grown in central and southern Italy. They can be eaten fresh or sun-dried and stored in appropriate conditions until the next harvest. The Italian Ministry of Agriculture's database of native and/or traditional food products lists: *pomodoro spuniello* or ⮞ **pomodorino al piennolo** (Campania); *pomodori gialli invernali* (Molise); *pomodoro da serbo giallo* (Puglia); *pomodoro pallino da serbo, ciliegino toscano, pomodorino da inverno pendolino* (Tuscany); *tamatica de appiccai* (Sardinia). Another variety, ⮞

pomodoro fiaschetto di Torre Guaceto, is protected by a Slow Food presidium. The flesh of these tomatoes is used to dress fish, pizzas, sauces, pasta and meat.

pomodoro di Pachino PGI tomato (*pomodoro ciliegino, costoluto, tondo liscio* and *pomodoro a grappolo* varieties cultivated round Pachino and Portopalo di Capo di Passero (Siracusa), in other communes of the same province, in the province of Ragusa. Sicily.

pomodoro fiaschetto di Torre Guaceto small, sweet rare cultivar grown organically in the nature reserve of Torre Guaceto and round Carovigno in the province of Brindisi. A Slow Food presidium is reviving production of the tomato. Puglia

pomodoro sanmarzano a tomato that had not been cultivated for years but is now being sown again with seeds of the father ecotype owned by the Campania regional authority and kept at the Cirio research centre. Granted PDO status as *pomodoro sanmarzano dell'Agro sarnesenocerino*, it is protected by a Slow Food presidium and a consortium. It is grown in the provinces of Naples and Salerno. Campania.

pomodoro seccagno a type of conserve tomato ⮞ **pomodoro da conserva**.

pomodoro secco sun-dried tomato. One of the traditional ways to preserve tomatoes is to slice them in two, season them with salt and dry them in the sun until they are totally dehydrated. Sun-dried tomatoes are commercialized as they are or washed in vinegar and preserved in oil, flavored with chili and aromatic herbs. They are eaten as an antipasto, often with cured meats or used to strengthen conserves.

pompelmo grapefruit (*Citrus paradisi*). A citrus fruit that came to Italy relatively recently from India via the United States, and is now grown in traditional citrus-growing areas (Sicily, Calabria, Liguria). It is eaten fresh or used to make juices. Creative chefs sometimes use it in antipastos and salads and with crustaceans.

pompìa Persian lime (*Citrus latifolia*). A yellow citrus fruit with a thick skin. Typical of Siniscola and the coastal plain of the Baronia area in the province of Nuoro, where it has grown for over two centuries. The peel is used to make liqueurs, while the white part is steeped in honey and simmered for hours (*pompìa intrea*). It may be filled with minced almonds (*pompìa prena*) or used to make ➤ **aranzada** and other local cakes and pastries. It is protected by Slow Food presidium. Sardinia.

ponce alla livornese aka **torpedine** aka **bomba** popular traditional drink consisting of espresso coffee, sugar, rum and lemon zest served hot in a large, short glass. Typical of Livorno. Tuscany.

ponce alla romana sorbet of spumante, orange and lemon juice, egg whites whisked to a peak, confectioner's sugar and rum. Lazio.

poncio dark liqueur made by macerating citrus fruit zest and spices in alcohol with caramelized sugar. Made in Campobasso with the same recipe since 1840. The name was Italianized from the English "punch" during Fascism, when the use of foreign words was banned. A second version exists aromatized with coffee. Molise

poncrè fruit cake with raisins, pine kernels and candied fruits created in the early 20th century as an alternative to the ➤ **pandolce** of Genoa. Its soft consistency is reminiscent of that of plum cake. Typical of Lerici, in the province of La Spezia. Liguria.

poolish semi-liquid leavening blend of water, yeast and flour. Created in France in the early 20th century by a group of Viennese bakers.

popcorn traditionally eaten in northeast Italy, where dialect names include: ➤ **galiti**, ➤ **moneghete**, ➤ **pestadice**, ➤ **sioris**.

poperati another name for ➤ **prupate**, ring-shape cookies.

popizze another name for ➤ **pettole**, pastries.

poppa another name for ➤ **mammella**, a cured meat.

poppe di monaca aka **sospiri** (literally "nun's beasts" or "sighs") classic meringues (➤ **meringhe**) often prepared and served with ➤ **africani**, cakes. A specialty of Impruneta, in the province of Florence. Tuscany.

porbaccittu baked salt cod served with a sauce of olive oil, parsley and pepper. A specialty of Castelfidardo, in the province of Ancona. Marche.

porcacchia dialect term for ➤ **porcellana**, little hogweed.

porceddhuzzi leccesi the Puglia version of Campania's ➤ **struffoli**. Dimpled balls made with a mixture of flour, eggs, oil, white wine and orange zest and juice fried in boiling oil, smothered in warm honey, arranged in a serving dish and covered with cinnamon, candied fruits, pine kernels or other decorations (colored sugared almonds, flakes of chocolate etc). Traditionally served at Christmas.

porcellana little hogweed (*Portulaca oleracea*). A wild herbaceous plant to be found on fallow land and at the roadside. In central Italy its fleshy leaves are eaten raw in salads (➤ **misticanza**), elsewhere they are pickled in vinegar or tossed in a skillet with garlic and anchovies. Common and regional names: ➤ **barzellana**, erba grassa, → erba dei porci, → porcacchia, → portulacca, → sportellacchia.

porcellitto aglio forno term used in the province of Latina (Lazio) for roast suckling pig.

porcello aka **porco** other words for → **maiale**, pig.

porcetto aka **porchetto** other names for → **porcheddu**, roast suckling pig.

porcheddu suckling pig roast on a spit or in the oven, flavored as it cooks with drops of lardo and salt. Excellent hot or cold. In the latter case, it is wrapped in myrtle leaves as it cools (**porcheddu ammurtau**). Sardinia.

porchetta roast pork. An ancient recipe of Umbrian origin, but now also common in Lazio and Abruzzo. A whole young lean pig is skinned, gutted and boned. It is then rubbed inside with salt, ground pepper and minced garlic and wild fennel. The innards are washed, blanched, cut into pieces and put back into the pig, which is sewn up and slowly roasted for four to five hours. In Ariccia, in the province of Rome, they use a boned, gutted sow, its shoulders and legs removed, flavor it inside with salt, black pepper, garlic, rosemary and spices, and tie it up securely before roasting it on a spit. In Abruzzo too the principal flavorings are garlic and rosemary; the version cooked in Campli, in the province of Teramo, is especially good. In Marche they sometimes sprinkle white wine or cooked wine must (→ **vincotto**) over the pig before it goes into the oven.

porchetta, in way of cooking meat, normally that of small farm animals, using a technique similar to that for → **porchetta**. In the Marche and Abruzzo regions, the expression has a broader yet precise meaning: meat, fish, sea and earth snails, goose, rabbit and even eggs are said to be in porchetta when they are cooked flavored with wild fennel.

porcina aka **porzina** name of a cut of pork from the neck or shoulder. By extension the name used to refer generically to → **bollito misto alla triestina**. A specialty of Trieste. Fruli-Venezia Giulia.

porcinello name for mushrooms of the Leccinum genus. The most common are *L. scabrum* (synon. *Boletus scaber*) and *L. auraticum* (synon. *Boletus rufus*). Both are suitable for frying and stewing, but not for grilling. Common and dialect names: → **porcinello rosso**, → **porcinello grigio**, → **gambetta rossa**, → **crava rossa**, → **gambetta grisa**, → **crava grisa**, → **cravetta**.

porcinello grigio aka **porcinello rosso** other names for → **porcinello** mushroom.

porcino porcini mushroom. A common name for four similar types of mushrooms all members of the Boletus family: *Boletus edulis*, *B. aereus*, *B. reticulatus* aka *B. aestivalis*, and *B. pinophilus*, all to be found growing under tall trees (oak, beech, chestnut). Highly prized, they can be eaten raw or cooked, on their own (→ **cappelle di porcini in frasca**, → **porcini fritti**, → **porcini ripieni**) or mixed with other foods. They are excellent also dried, preserved in oil and pickled in vinegar. The → **fungo di Borgotaro** of the Val di Taro, in the province of Parma has received PGI status. Common names: → **porcino estivo**, → **porcino reticolato** (*B. aestivalis*); → **porcino nero**, → bronzino (*B. aereus*); → **porcino rosso** (*B. pinophilus*). Dialect names: → **bolé**, → **bolé dij fò**, → **carej**, → **caplet**, → **porsin**.

porcini fritti porcini deep-fried in oil either as they are or dipped in egg and breaded.

porcini ripieni stuffed porcini mushrooms. The caps are stuffed with various ingredients which change from region to region. In Liguria they use oregano, marjoram, breadcrumbs, grated Parmigiano and eggs; in Friuli-Venezia Giulia breadcrumbs, grated cheese, parsley, garlic and oil; in Tuscany (in the province of Lucca) ground meat and the chopped flesh of the mushroom itself; in Emilia-Romagna egg, meat sauce and breadcrumbs; in Piedmont egg yolks, Grana cheese and basil mixed with the minced stalks lightly fried with calf's brains.

porcino bianco another name for ➤ **basilisco**, white ferula mushroom.

porcospino literally "porcupine." A dessert of sponge fingers or sponge cake soaked in coffee, coated with cream into which toasted almonds are stuck to look like the animal's quills. Emilia-Romagna.

porraccio wild leek, elephant leek (*Allium ampeloprasum, A. triquetrum*). Herbaceous plants with a long yellowish-skinned bulb. The bulbs and soots are used in central Italy (especially in Tuscany) to flavor soups, frittatas and salads. Common and regional names: ➤ **garlic delle vigne**, ➤ **garlic triangolare**, ➤ **porradello**, ➤ **porro selvatico**.

porradello ➤ **porraccio**, wild leek.

porrettaccio ➤ **lampascione**, grape hyacinth bulb.

porro leek (*Allium porrum*). Generally produced and marketed in the fall. Prized varieties are *porro del Polesine* (Veneto), *porro lungo di Carmagnola* (Piedmont) and *porro di Cervere* (Piedmont). The latter is celebrated in the village of Cervere in the province of Cuneo with an annual festival. Leeks appear in many regional dishes. They are particularly prominent in the so-called *cucina bianca*, or "white cooking" (the other staples of which are butter, milk, cream, chestnuts and pasta without eggs or tomato) of the mountain valleys of the province of Cuneo: ➤ **po-**

lenta e porri, ➤ **polenta nera con bagna bianca**, ➤ **tagliatelle al latte**.

porro selvatico another name for ➤ **porraccio**, wild leek.

porro sottile another name for ➤ **erba cipollina**, chives.

porsin dialect term for ➤ **porcino**, porcini mushroom.

portafoglio, a literally "wallet-style." An expression to describe a food (eg, a slice of meat or a pancake) turned over and filled with a other ingredients.

portulacca common name for ➤ **porcellana**, little hogweed.

porzelo Veneto dialect word for ➤ **maiale**, pig.

posciandra another name for ➤ **casoeûla**, a Milanese stew.

potacchio, in term to describe a way of stewing meat, fish or mollusks (chiefly monkfish, snails, chicken and rabbit) in white wine with garlic, chili and aromatics. Marche.

potassolo regional name for ➤ **melù**, blue whiting.

potia aka **poutia** aka **poutie** a creamy polenta of mixed corn, buckwheat or rye and wheat flours cooked in water and milk and served piping hot with grated cheese. Typical of the mountain valleys of Pinerolo, in the province of Turin, and of the province of Cuneo. Piedmont.

potiza aka **putiza** aka **putizza** baked pastry roll (the Slovenian term *potica* means "rolled") filled with dried and candied fruit, raisins, grated chocolate and rum, similar to ➤ **gubana**, but rolled in the same dough as the ➤ **pinza** Easter cake of Trieste. In the city's cake shops, **potiza** is to be found only at Easter, but on the Carso plateau it is made, with variations, on all holidays. Friuli-Venezia Giulia.

poutine Ligurian term for newborn sardines (➤ **novellame di pesce**, fish fry).

poveraccia term used in Romagna, Marche and Abruzzo for ➤ **vongola commune**, clam.

povesen simple cake of Bohemian origin, similar to ➤ **schnitte**, but with white wine instead of milk. Typical of Trieste. Friuli-Venezia Giulia.

povronin Piedmontese term for ➤ **peperoncino**, chili.

pralina praline. Originally a toasted almond coated with caramelized sugar, now a filled chocolate.

pratahapla a frittata of roughly mashed potatoes and Toma cheese cooked in a skillet with butter and onions, then browned in the oven. A dish traditionally made by the Walsers, a Germanic people who settled in the Ossola and Monte Rosa areas centuries ago. Typical of the Val Formazza. Piedmont.

prataiolo name for several wild and cultivated mushrooms of the Psalliota (synon. *Agaricus*) genus, including champignon (*A. biosporus*). Eaten raw, fried or stewed or used as a garnish.. Another common name is ➤ **cappellaccio**.

pratesi ➤ **biscottini alla mandorla**, almond cookies.

pratolina common name for ➤ **margheritina dei prati**, English daisy.

prattu de cassa stew of game, potatoes and onions, flavored with wild herbs and cooked in a special pot. Sardinia.

prazzida strong flour pastry, similar to a shortbread, filled with tomatoes and/or eggplant and potatoes and sausage. Sardinia.

preboggion aka **prebuggion** mixture of mostly spontaneous herbs the composition of which varies according to place and season. The most common are: borage, dandelion, chard, wild chicory, rampion, nettle, hyoseris, white cabbage, field sowthistle and common brighteyes.

Used to make fillings (➤ **pansoti**, a type of stuffed pasta), pies and soups. Also eaten boiled, dressed with oil and served with potatoes. Typical of the province of Genoa. Liguria.

prebugiun peasant dish of potatoes and ➤ **cavolo nero**. Typical of the village of Ne, in the province of Genoa. Liguria.

prescinsoea (aka **prescinseua**) name given in the Genoa area to sour full-cream milk curd, an important ingredient in pasta and pie fillings. Liguria.

presnitz very thin spiral pastry roll filled with dried fruit, sugar and rum. Its shape is supposed to represent the crown of thorns placed on Christ's head. A typical Triestine Easter cake, it is a close relative of ➤ **potiza** and ➤ **gubana**. Friuli-Venezia Giulia.

pressatura pressing. A technique used mainly for uncooked hard cheeses. Pressure is applied for a period of one to 24 hours to expel whey before a sturdy outer rind forms.

prete (1) cured meat made with the pig's shin and shoulder cured with salt, juniper berries, cinnamon and pepper, and typically served with parsley sauce. A specialty of Colorno and the southern part of the province of Parma. Emilia-Romagna.

prete (2) Tuscan name for ➤ **pesce lucerna**, stargazer.

prete (3) a Piedmontese specialty ➤ **previ (1)**.

pretzel another name for ➤ **bretzel**, a savory cookie.

previ (1) "priest." A roll of pork rind used to flavor soups and stews (➤ **tofeja canavesana**). Piedmont.

previ (2) aka **fratti** rolls of lettuce or cabbage filled with a mixture of eggs, Parmigiano, marjoram, peas and other vegetables, cooked in a sauce of tomato, sausage and peas. Liguria.

prezzemolo parsley (*Petroselinum sativum* synon. *P. hortense* e and *P. crispum*). In Italy mostly flat-leaved parsley is used in cooking, the curly variety being reserved largely for decorative purposes. Minced fresh flat-leaved parsley is frequently sprinkled on fish, meat, eggs, condiments and foods preserved in oil. Parsley is also a component of *bouquets garnis* (➤ **mazzetto aromatico**), of most types of ➤ **battuto** and of sauces (➤ **salsa verde**, ➤ **bagnet piemontese**). Common and regional names: ➤ **apio**, ➤ **petroselino**.

prezzemolo cinese regional term for ➤ **coriandolo**, coriander.

primavera cowslip (*Primula veris*). Spontaneous herbaceous plant typical of the Alps and Apennines, where it grows in grassy areas on the edge of woodland. Traditionally used in soups (➤ **minestrella**), now enjoying revival thanks to the contemporary boom in natural diets. Common and regional names: ➤ **pan del lupo**, ➤ **primula selvatica**, ➤ **trombetta**.

primula selvatica common name for ➤ **primavera**, cowslip.

princisgras another name for ➤ **vincisgrassi**, type of lasagne.

prisintuni Sicilian term for ➤ **tambarello**, frigate tuna.

pro 'heddu Sardinian word for ➤ **porcheddu**, roast suckling pig.

probusto a sausage which used to be made only with beef, but is now made with pork (with the exception of one butcher's shop in Rovereto). Flavored with salt, pepper, paprika, ppimento and mace, it can be eaten boiled or broiled. Typical of the Vallagarina, in the province of Trento. Trentino-Alto Adige.

profezeni slices of day-old bread spread with calf's brains browned with onion and parsley, joined into sandwiches, dipped in milk and flour batter and fried in boiling oil. Typical of the province of Trento. Trentino-Alto Adige.

prosciutta castelnovese cured meat made from the legs of mostly Emilian heavy pigs, created in 1980 by Mirco Bertini in Castelnegg Magra (La Spezia) and recognized as a traditional product in 2000. Liguria

prosciuttino d'oca ham made from the legs of local geese. A specialty of the Lomellina area. Lombardy.

prosciutto ham. Though the legs of other animals (wild boar, red deer, chamois, goat, goose, turkey) can be processed into ham, prosciutto normally refers to pigs. The words *presuctu*, *presutium* and *presciutto*, deriving from Latin terms for "dry" or"dried," appear in documents of the 13th and 14th centuries, but the making and consumption of ham goes back to antiquity. Romans called ham made with pork leg *perna* and that made with the shoulder *petaso*, both words of Greek origin, and Cato and others wrote detailed treatises on the topic. There are two fundamental typologies: *crudo*, raw or cured, and *cotto*, cooked, baked or boiled. The following raw hams have been granted PDO status: ➤ **prosciutto di Modena**, *prosciutto di Parma* (Emilia-Romagna), *prosciutto di San Daniele* (Friuli-Venezia Giulia), *prosciutto di Carpegna*, *prosciutto toscano* (Tuscany), *jambon de Bosses* (Val d'Aosta), **prosciutto veneto berico-euganeo** (Veneto). Another, ➤ **prosciutto di Norcia** (Umbria), has PGI status. Slow Food presidia promote ➤ **prosciutto bazzone**, ➤ **prosciutto del Casentino** (Tuscany) and *paletta di Coggiola* (Piedmont), made with top shoulder.

prosciutto al forno ham flavored with garlic, rosemary, bay leaves, pepper and lemon juice and baked in the oven. Bathed with white wine and brandy halfway through the cooking process, it is served sliced with the thickened pan juices. Dish typical of the Modena and Reggio areas but now also made in other parts of the region. Emilia-Romagna.

prosciutto alla brace di Saint-Oyen aka **jambon à la braise de Saint-Oyen** boiled, lightly smoked ham coated with chopped aromatic herbs and roast over a wood fire. Typical of the Great St Bernard. Val d'Aosta.

prosciutto arrosto di Canale legs of locally bred pigs boned, salted and massaged with a secret mixture of aromatic herbs. Wrapped in calf's caul, it is baked in the oven for four to seven hours. Typical of the province of Cuneo. Piedmont.

prosciutto bazzone ham made in the Valle del Serchio and Garfagnana area, in the province of Lucca, with meat from local pigs. A Slow Food presidium has brought together producers to monitor the entire production chain. Tuscany

prosciutto crudo d'oca raw goose ham of Jewish origin produced in southern Friuli since the 15th century. Friuli.

prosciutto dei Monti Nebrodi characteristically square ham made with meat from pigs that live in the wild, especially those of the local breed, → **suino nero dei Nebrodi**, cured with a mixture of salt, wild fennel, garlic, oregano and vinegar. Sicily.

prosciutto del Casentino a Slow Food presidium-sponsored ham made from the meat of hybrids of the Cinta Senese or Mora Romagnola pig breeds with Large White and Landrace. The pig whose meat was originally used is now extinct. The ham may be lightly smoked before aging for a minimum of 12 months. Tuscany.

prosciutto del Fortore an increasingly rare ham made from the legs of Large White, Landrace and, sometimes, Nero Caser-

tano pigs. Produced in the province of Benevento, Campania.

prosciutto della Val d'Ossola ham made with meat from mountain-raised pigs smoked over fires of beech wood, juniper berries and vegetable essences. Piedmont.

prosciutto della Val Vigezzo ham made with meat from mountin-raised pigs cured with salt, pepper, cinnamon, nutmeg, cloves, rosemary and bay leaves. Piedmont.

prosciutto di Bassiano ham produced in the village of the same name in the Apennine foothills with meat from pigs weighing at least 70 pounds. Lazio.

prosciutto di Bosses aka **jambon de Bosses** other names for → **Valle d'Aosta jambon de Bosses**.

prosciutto di Carpegna crudo PDO ham produced in the town of the same name since the 15th century. Made from the rear legs of pigs of at least ten months of age born and raised in the Marche, Emilia-Romagna and Lombardy. Marche.

prosciutto di cinghiale wild boar ham typical of San Gimignano (Siena). Tuscany.

prosciutto di Cormons the leg of an Italian-raised pig is massaged by hand and left to rest for four to five days. It is then massaged again, salted and rested for as many days as its kilos of weight. It is then washed, put under a press for 48 hours and lightly smoked over a wood fire. Halfway through the aging process, which lasts for about a year, the ham is trimmed and coated with a mixture of suet and spices. Typical of Cormons in the province of Gorizia. Friuli-Venezia Giulia.

prosciutto di Desulo a ham produced in limited quantities in winter in on the western slopes of the Gennargentu mountain range, in the province of Nuoro. The leg (sometimes the shoulder) of a pig raised in the wild is steeped in a brine of salt, vinegar, garlic and pepper for a period that varies according to its weight. After air-drying for a few weeks, it is aged for a few months in a heated room, then for at least a year in a cellar. Sardinia.

prosciutto di Faeto typical regional ham made from the meat of local pigs raised using traditional methods. Legs are salted in wood tubs, pressed down with heavy stones, cleaned with water and vinegar, massaged and dried in cool, airy rooms. Faeto, in the province of Foggia, is the highest village in the region and (partly thanks to the nearby river Celone, which creates the right humidity) the ideal place for the aging of the hams, which proceeds for at least 12 months. Puglia.

prosciutto di Modena a raw PDO ham produced in some communes in the provinces of Modena, Bologna and Reggio Emilia with legs from white pigs of at least nine months of age from farms in Piedmont, Lombardy, Veneto, Emilia-Romagna, Tuscany, Umbria, Marche, Lazio, Abruzzo and Molise. After being salted twice, hams rest for two months before being washed, dried and aged for a year. Emilia-Romagna.

prosciutto di Norcia raw PGI ham produced in the communes of Cascia, Monteleone di Spoleto, Norcia, Poggiodomo and Preci, in the province of Perugia, with the legs of heavy adult crossbred white pigs. Trimmed to a pear-shape, they are cured in two different ways. At an industrial level, the hams are rubbed twice in the course of 20-25 days with sea salt and pepper, then aged for a year. Artisan hams are cured with kitchen salt for 20-25 days, washed with warm water, rubbed with pepper and hung for 50 days, during which time they are lightly smoked. Aging lasts for 22 months. Umbria.

prosciutto di Parma PDO raw ham made in the province of Parma from the legs of → **Large White**, → **Landrace** or → **Duroc** pigs weighing at least 70 pounds, raised and butchered from their ninth month in Piedmont, Lombardy, Veneto, Emilia-Romagna, Tuscany, Umbria, Marche, Lazio, Abruzzo amd Molise. Trimmed of muscle, rind and fat for 24% of its weight, the leg is salted twice, the skin with damp salt, the lean pork with dry salt. After seven days, it is rubbed lightly with salt and left to rest for two to three weeks. After another 60 to 90 days it is washed, dried, hung and beaten into a roundish shape. It is aged for ten to twelve months. After inspection by the local producers' consortium it is branded with the seal of guarantee: "corona ducale a 5 punte" (five-pointed ducal crown).

prosciutto di Pietraroja ham made in the village of the same name, in the province of Benevento, since the 18th century from pigs' legs cured with sea salt for 20 days. It is aged in old stone cellars for 12 to 20 months. Campania.

prosciutto di Praga Prague ham. Cooked ham which came into being in the Czech capital over 150 years ago. It disappeared from butchers' shops in Prague long ago, but it continues to be very common throughout the province of Trieste. It is usually on the bone and lightly smoked over a fire of fir shavings. It is cooked on a low heat inside special cauldrons. Friuli-Venezia Giulia.

prosciutto di Saint-Marcel aka **jambon de Saint-Marcel** raw ham aromatized with mountain herbs, aged in the small village of Saint-Marcel. Val d'Aosta.

prosciutto di San Daniele PDO raw ham produced exclusively in the Friulian town of the same name (in the province of Udine) with legs from pigs raised on farms in Friuli, Veneto, Lombardy, Piedmont, Emilia-Romagna, Piedmont, Tuscany, Umbria, Marche, Lazio and Abruzzo. The leg, trotter included, is cured with salt, trimmed, massaged and pressed into a classic violin shape. It is put to mature in special resting chambers before aging for at least 12 months. Friuli-Venezia Giulia.

prosciutto di Sauris ham made in the village of the same name, in the province of Udine, from the legs of Italian pig breeds raised locally. After being salted repeatedly over a period of two months, the ham is smoked for a month over a fire of wood from local resinous trees. It is then aged for a year. Friuli-Venezia Giulia.

prosciutto in crosta di pane ham *en croûte*. A 19th-century recipe still popular in the pork restaurants (➤ **buffet**) of Trieste. A small Prague ham (➤ **prosciutto di Praga**) is wrapped in a thin sheet of bread dough, sprinkled with peppercorns and bay leaves and baked in the oven. Friuli-Venezia Giulia.

prosciutto lucano an artisan ham made in the Apennines with legs from pigs raised locally on natural feed. After being repeatedly salted, it is aged for 14-18 months. It is sold both on the bone and, more rarely, boned. Basilicata.

prosciutto toscano raw PDO ham made with the legs of heavy pigs raised and butchered in Lombardy, Emilia-Romagna, Tuscany, Umbria, Marche and Lazio. After trimming, it is cured with salt, pepper and natural aromas. After being washed in warm water, it is put to age for ten to 12 months. Tuscany.

prosciutto veneto berico-euganeo raw PDO ham produced in some villages in the provinces of Vicenza, Padua and Verona from the legs of adult pigs raised on Italian farms. Made with or without the trotter, it is semi-pressed, trimmed and treated with sea salt. After maturing for two months, it is washed in warm water, dried and put to age for ten months. Veneto.

Provatura (1) stretched curd buffalo's milk cheese, halfway between mozzarella and Provola. Eaten as it is or fried or as an ingredient in numerous recipes (eg, ➤ **crostini alla provatura**). Lazio.

Provatura (2) synonym of ➤ **Provola**, a cheese.

Provola soft stretched curd central-southern Italian cheese usually made with cow's milk.

Provola affumicata stretched curd cow's milk cheese smoked over burning straw. In the Cilento area, a version is made with raw buffalo's cheese. Campania.

provola dei Nebrodi egg-shaped stretched curd raw cow's milk cheese produced in the Nebrodi mountains (Messina). Promoted by a Slow Food presidium. Sicily.

provola delle Madonie flat egg-shaped stretched curd cow's milk cheese produced in the province of Palermo. A Slow Food presidium promotes the best artisan versions and the Madonie regional park in which they are made. Sicily.

Provolone stretched curd cheese which originated in southern Italy but is now also common in the north. According to aging, it may be sweet or strong, semi-hard or hard.

Provolone del monaco di razza agerolese headless raw cow's milk Caciocavallo produced in the Monti Lattari, on the Sorrentine peninsula (Naples). A Slow Food presidium supports producers who use the milk of the local Agerolese cow breed. Campania.

Provolone valpadana the production of this PDO cow's cheese, which originated in southern Italy, began to spread to the Po Valley in the 19th century. Now it is made in Lombardy, Trentino, Veneto and Emilia-Romagna.

prugna plum. A summer fruit with countless varieties which may be subdivided into two main groups: Euro-Asiatic (*Prunus domestica*), green or purple-blue, medium-small, round or oblong, available from the middle of June to September, and Sino-Japanese (*P. simonii*), golden yellow, red, black, medium-large, generally round, ripe in June. The major producer regions are Campania and Emilia-Romagna. The Italian Ministry of Agriculture's database of native and/or traditional food products lists: *susina botta a muro, marmulegna, pappacona, pazza, scarrafona, turcona, prugna coglipiecuri* (Campania); *susina di Vignola, vaca zebeo* (Emilia-Romagna); *susine balle d'ase, fiaschette di Levanto, susina collo storto, massina* (Liguria); *santa clara del Saluzzese, susina della collina torinese* (Piedmont); *susina sanacore,* ➤ *susine bianche di Monreale* (Sicily); *susina di Dro* (Trentino); *susina gialla di Lio Piccolo* (Veneto). Besides being eaten raw, plums appear fresh in home baking (➤ **torta di prugne,** ➤ **torta di ramassin**), dried and in jams. They are also used in savory dishes (➤ **zuppa di baccalà in agrodolce,** ➤ **gnocchi di susine**).

prugnola sloe (*Prunus spinosa*). Wild plum used to make infusions and liqueurs (eg, in Emilia-Romagna, *bargnolino*). **prugnolo** mousseron mushroom (*Lyophillum georgii, Calocybe gambosa, Tricholoma georgii*). Much prized and much used in the kitchen in sauce, soups and stews. Common and dialect names: ➤ **spinarolo,** ➤ **spignolo,** ➤ **maggengo,** ➤ **maggi-**

olino, ➤ **fungo di san Giorgio,** ➤ **sangiorgino,** ➤ **musciarone,** ➤ **masìn,** ➤ **misciarulu,** ➤ **fungo de la saeta**.

prupate sweet, spicy baked ring-shaped cookies traditionally served at weddings and at Carnival. Typical of the Gargano peninsula, in the province of Foggia.

prustinenga a fricassée of lamb's offal (liver, lung, sweetbreads, kidneys, heart, spleen) flavored with Marsala and spiced with cinnamon and cloves. A Waldensian specialty served at wedding lunches. Piedmont.

puccellato rare rustic Easter bread loaf typical of the province of Benevento. Campania).

puccia a flat bread loaf (70% rye flour and 30% soft flour aromatized with cumin seeds, wild fennel and *zigoinr,* a local wild oregano) produced in the mountains of the province of Belluno. It is eaten filled with cured meats and heated. Veneto.

puccia all'ampa another name for ➤ **puccia pugliese (2)**.

puccia cu l'aulìe another name for ➤ **puccia pugliese (1)**.

puccia delle Langhe very soft polenta of cornflour and wheat flour mixed with beans and Savoy cabbage or with stewed pork. Typical of the Langhe hills, in the province of Asti. Piedmont.

puccia pugliese (1) round, soft flatbread whose dough includes black olives. In dialect known as ➤ **puccia cu l'aulìe** aka **uliata** Typical of the provinces of Lecce and Brindisi.

puccia pugliese (2) leavened durum wheat flour focaccia which is cut in half and filled with pickles and ricotta in Novoli, in the province of Lecce, where it is made on the patron saint's day. Elsewhere it may be filled with sausage, strong salami, anchovies, cheese or mixed onions, tomatoes and olives. **Puccia** is to the inhabitants of the Salentine peninsula (Lecce, Brindisi, Taranto) what pizza is to Neapolitans. Puglia.

pucciatidd sweet ➤ **taralli** (ring cookies) made with flour, eggs, oil and salt kneaded to a dough, shaped into rings, boiled in water, browned in the oven, and iced. At Easter they are made into the shape of horses and coated with confetti sugar. In this case they are called ➤ **cavaddistr**. Puglia.

püces aka **püces sotides** soft rye and wheat bread, typical of the Ladin Dolomiti. Trentino-Alto Adige.

puddica pizza topped with onions, tomato, garlic cloves, salt, extra virgin olive oil and oregano. In Bari, it is served with raw seafood. Puglia

puddighinus a prenu chicken stuffed with a chopped mixture of the bird's intestine and giblets, breadcrumbs, hard-boiled eggs, cream, sun-dried tomatoes, salt and pepper, and baked in the oven. Sardinia.

puledro pony. A horse of one to two years of age.

pulegio aka **puleggio** pennyroyal (*Mentha pulegium*). Used in the kitchen, especially in Lazio, to flavor lamb, eggs and frittatas, snails and vegetables (eg, ➤ **carciofi alla romana**). Common and regional names: ➤ **menta strisciante**, ➤ **mentastro**, ➤ **mentuccia**.

pulezze dialect term for ➤ **cime di rapa**, broccoli rabe.

puligioni aka **pulingioni** typical round ravioli stuffed with ricotta, eggs, parsley, salt, sugar and, sometimes, orange zest, served with tomato sauce and grated Pecorino or stewed mutton. Sardinia.

pulljata a now almost extinct ➤ **acquasale** consisting of boiling water flavored with calamint, salt and chili served in bowls with day-old bread. Basilicata.

pulupitt aka **purpitt** meatballs (horsemeat or pork) in tomato sauce, traditionally served with ➤ **orecchiette**, a type of pasta. Puglia.

pumidorata stew of *pomodori agroni* (not quite ripe tomatoes), with other vegetables and herbs into which eggs are scrambled. Typical of Livorno, Tuscany.

puncerle half moon pastries filled with jam or toasted poppy seeds and fried in boiling oil. Typical of the Ladin Dolomites. Trentino-Alto Adige.

pungiporci aka **pungiratto** regional terms for ➤ **pungitopo**, butcher's broom.

pungitopo butcher's broom (*Ruscus aculeatus*). Small evergreen shrubs whose young spring shoots used in the kitchen and preserved in oil. Common and regional names: ➤ **asparago bastardo**, ➤ **brusco**, ➤ **piccasorcio**, ➤ **pungiporci**, ➤ **pungiratto**, ➤ **rusco**, ➤ **scoparina**, ➤ **spinafrutici**.

punta di coltello, in term used to describe the technique of hand-chopping cured meats, sausage and so on.

punta di culatta another term for ➤ **codone**, tenderloin.

punta di petto ripiena ➤ **picaia**, brisket.

punta di petto another term for brisket.

puntarelle the long crisp white leaves of winter endive, typical of the Roman countryside, served in salad and dressed with a sauce of anchovy, garlic, extra virgin olive oil, salt and vinegar. Lazio.

puntine di maiale pork chops.

punto, a synonym of ➤ **sangue, al**, rare.

puoto pandolce doll-shaped cake, traditionally Santa Lucia's gift to children. Veneto.

pupazza frascatana long, often very long, cookie made in the form of a woman with three breasts. Possibly a symbol of abundance (Frascati wine spurts from the extra breast), possibly a baker's joke. Typical of Frascati (Rome). Lazio.

pupazzelle 'a cumposta small red round peppers harvested in September, covered with salt, garlic, vinegar and water, and eaten in December. Basilicata.

pupe 'd monia dialect name for ➤ **pampavia**, a cookie.

pupu cu l'ovu Easter bread made in different shapes: people, animals, objects and so on. Sicily.

purcidd fried sweet Christmas pastries. Puglia.

purcit Friulian term for ➤ **maiale**, pig. A suckling pig is known as a *varul*.

purè aka **purea** purée.

purè di fave e cicoria another name for ➤ **'ncapriata**, fava bean purée and wild chicory.

purè di lenticchie lentil purée, served on fried or toasted bread or on its own as a first course. Umbria.

purpetielle affucate stew of octopus, ripe tomatoes and chili cooked in a pot sealed with straw paper. Campania.

purpo all'insalata Campania term for octopus salad.

purpu de sicco Palermo term for ➤ **moscardino** *bianco*, curled octopus.

purpuzza sausage meat. Sardinia.

putana cake typical of Vicenza, similar to ➤ **pinza**, traditionally made for Epiphany. Veneto.

putìca eatery typical of the province of Catanzaro, where ➤ **pitta** bread is served with ➤ **morzello** (offal). Calabria.

puticiana another name for ➤ **barbotta**, a sort of focaccia.

putizza ➤ **potiza**, a type of pastry.

putt another word for ➤ **pold**, runny polenta.

puttanesca, alla pasta sauce, invented relatively recently on the island of Ischia (Naples), made with tomatoes, garlic, extra virgin olive oil, capers, black olives, oregano, parsley and chili. Campania.

puzzone di Moena raw milk cow's cheese made with milk from two milkings. Typical and Predazzo e Moena (Trento), where it used to be called Nostrano or, in Ladin, *spretz tzaorì*. A Slow Food presidium protects the version branded with an "M," made exclusively with mountain dairy milk. Trentino-Alto Adige.

pzzetto chieno term used in Basilicata for ➤ **pizza grassa**, a savory pie.

qQ

quadaro aka **quadaru** fish stew, typical of Crotone, named for the copper pot in which it is made. Mixed fish cooked with olive oil, garlic, aromatic herbs, tomatoes, peppers, parsley and chili. The single fish and the broth are served separately. Calabria.

quadrettini another name for ➤ **quadrucci**, type of pasta.

quadrucci aka **quadrettini** small pasta squares usually cooked and served in broth.

quadrucci e ceci egg pasta squares served with boiled chickpeas, rosemary, pancetta (optional) and chopped skinned tomatoes. Umbria.

quadrucci e piselli Roman soup made of peas cooked with chopped lardo or guanciale (cheek bacon), aromatics and tomato paste. The mixture is transferred to a pot of broth to which the ➤ **quadrucci** are then added. Lazio.

quagghiaridde sheep's tripe stuffed with sheep's offal, Scamorza cheese, salami, and eggs, then baked in the oven. Eaten sliced with a side dish of rocket or boiled chicory. Traditional dish of the shepherds of Andria, in the province of Bari. Puglia.

quaglia (pl. **quaglie**) quail (*Coturnix coturnix*). Bird of passage, now mostly farmed. Its delicate aromatic meat (especially that of wild birds) is excellent roasted or broiled, and its eggs are tasty too.

quaglie aka **melanzane a quaglia** literally "quails." Eggplants deep-fried in oil until golden brown. So named because, fried in this way, the vegetables resemble the birds. Typical Palermo street food (➤ **cibo di strada**). Sicily

quaglie con il riso quails and rice. Quails barded with lardo or pancetta, browned in butter and herbs, stewed in wine or broth, and served on a bed of white rice. Recipe common in Piedmont, but more popular still in Veneto.

quaglie in foglie di vite quails in vine leaves. The bird is cleaned, wrapped first in a slice of lardo, then in a vine leaf, browned in oil, and cooked in wine or broth. Friuli-Venezia Giulia

quaglie ripiene quails boned, stuffed with slices of speck and boiled Savoy cabbage leaves, first sautéed, then roast in the oven. Served with a wine must reduction and apple sauce. Trentino-Alto Adige.

quajëtte "little quails" in Piedmontese dialect. Name given to rolled slices of veal stuffed with ground veal, eggs, grated cheese and herbs, and pan-fried with our without tomato salsa. Piedmont.

qualiceddu Sicilian dialect term for ➤ **cavolicello**, Mediterranean cabbage.

quaquare ring-shaped cookies made of flour, eggs, butter, sugar and lemon zest. A specialty of Genola, in the province of Cuneo, where the name means "May bug" in the local dialect. Traditionally baked in a communal oven in May on the days in leading up to the festival of the village's patron saint, San Marziano. Nowadays a few artisan bakeries turn out the cookies all year round. Piedmont.

quaresimali alphabet cookies baked, with many variations, during Lent all over central and southern Italy (Tuscany, Sicily, Campania, Puglia). In Tuscany, the traditional paste (flour, honey, caramelized sugar and egg whites) is enriched with egg yolks and cocoa in lieu of caramel. Almonds and hazelnuts may also be added. In Sicily the paste is made of toasted chopped almonds, chopped candied orange zest, sugar, egg whites, flour, ammonium carbonate, cinnamon and nutmeg, cut into strips, sometimes brushed with gum Arabic and coated with chopped pistachio nuts. In Campania, they follow a similar recipe, but sometimes replace almonds with pine kernels or hazelnuts. In Puglia, instead, the cookie is soft, made of sponge cake, almonds, sugar, egg whites and orange zest. For the Genoa version, ➤ **marzapani quaresimali**.

quartiretto boned breast of kid stuffed with spinach, eggs, and cheese, and roast in the oven. Typical of the Val Vermenagna, in the province of Cuneo. Piedmont.

Quartirolo lombardo PDO cheese made with whole or part-skimmed cow's from two or more milkings. The most prized version is *Quartirolo di monte*, produced in mountain dairies in the fall.

quarto quarter. Butcher's term for each of the two parts, front and rear into which a ➤ **mezzena**, half carcass, is divided.

quattro spezie (1) allspice (*Pimenta officinalis*), also known as Jamaica pepper or myrtle pepper. Has an intense perfume, redolent of nutmeg, pepper, cloves, cinnamon and ginger. Used to flavor stews.

quattro spezie (2) "four spices." Commercial mixed spices usually comprising nutmeg, cloves, pepper, and powdered cinnamon.

quecciulo Puglia dialect term for ➤ **murice**, murex, rock snail.

quenelle French term Italianized as ➤ **chenella**.

questeme Taranto dialect term for ➤ **novellame di pesce**, fry.

quiche Lorraine savory flan (the name derives from the German *Kuchen*). A brisée pastry case filled with a mixture of eggs, cream and smoked bacon cut into strips. Popular in Italy, sometimes with the addition of mushrooms and cheese.

quinto quarto fifth quarter. Butcher's term to refer to all the bits of an animal not comprised in the four quarters (two front, two rear) into which a carcass is normally cut. Ie, offal (➤ **frattaglie**), head, muzzle or snout, cheeks, brains, spinal marrow, tail and hooves or trotters.

rR

rabarbaro alpino common name for ➤ **lapazio**, munk's rhubarb.

rabarbaro rhubarb (*Rheum palmatum*). Plant native to northwest China. Cultivated in Europe, used in herbal medicine and to make digestive drinks and aperitifs. The stalks (or sticks) are used to make preserves, jellies, sorbets and syrups.

rabaton large elongated gnocchi made with field greens (such as nettles, hops, and dandelions), chard or spinach, ricotta or curd, Parmigiano and eggs. Boiled briefly in broth, baked in the oven with butter, milk, cheese, sage or rosemary. The dialect name is *ruzzolati*, "coated in flour before cooking." The recipe is said to have been created by the shepherds of Fraschetta, a low-lying area in the province of Alessandria. Piedmont.

raclette dish named for the cheese of the Swiss Vallese canton, common today in Italy, especially in mountain eateries. Half a form of cheese (Raclette, or even ➤ **Fontina**, or a non-mature mountain ➤ **Toma**, is heated and, as it melts, is gradually transferred to a dish (the French verb *racler* means "to scrape" or "to scratch"), and served with boiled potatoes and pickles.

radiatori literally "radiators." Short dried cylindrical durum wheat pasta served with simple tomato and vegetable sauces .

radic dal glaz dialect term for ➤ **radicchio di monte**, alpine blue sowthistle.

radic de l'ors dialect term for ➤ **radicchio di monte**, alpine blue sowthistle.

radic di mont dialect term for ➤ **radicchio di monte**, alpine blue sowthistle.

radicchiella beaked hawksbeard (*Crepis vesicaria*), a herb that grows spontaneously in fields and meadows. Its very bitter leaves are eaten raw or cooked, usually mixed with other species. The name also applies to another 40 or so *Crepis* species including *C. aurea*, golden hawksbeard, which is limited to Alpine and Apennine areas. Common and regional names: ➤ **cicorietta amara**, ➤ **cicoria**, ➤ **cicoriella**, **grugno**, ➤ **maroglia**.

radicchio the name for several varieties of the ➤ **cicoria** (chicory or endive) family with clusters of long red or red and white striped leaves. The best known cultivars are named after places in the Veneto region, where there is a long tradition of cultivation: ➤ **radicchio rosso di Treviso**, also known as ➤ **spadone trevigiano**, ➤ **rosso di Chioggia** and ➤ **radicchio variegato di Castelfranco**. The Italian Ministry of Agriculture's database of native and/or traditional food products lists the following varieties: *radicchio canarino, rosa di Gorizia* (Friuli-Venezia Giulia); *radicchia di Lucca* (Tuscany); *radicchio bianco fior di Maserà, bianco variegato di Lusia, rosso di Chioggia, rosso di Verona, variegato bianco di Bassano, radicio verdon da cortel* (Veneto). Radicchio is best enjoyed cooked in risottos or grilled or sautéed as a side dish for meats: ➤ **radicio fumegà**, ➤ **radicchio in saor**, ➤ **radicchio e lardo**.

radicchio di campo depending on the region, another word for ➤ **cicoria selvatica**, wild chicory, ➤ **dente di leone**, bristly hawkit, ➤ **tarassaco**, dandelion.

radicchio di monte blue sow thistle (*Cicer-*

bita alpina synon. *Mulgedium alpinum*). Spontaneous member of the daisy family common throughout the Alps, but picked and cooked in Friuli-Venezia Giulia and Trentino-Alto Adige. The young shoots, to be found in springtime in alpine turf, pastureland and snow patches, are broiled, boiled or sautéed, then preserved in oil or pickled. In the Carnic Alps, where picking is regulated, the plant is promoted by a Slow Food presidium. Local names: ➤ **radic di mont**, ➤ **radic dal glaz**, ➤ **radic de l'ors**.

radicchio di prato another name for ➤ **tarassaco**, dandelion.

radicchio e fagioli radicchio and beans, a recipe that comes in two versions: i) raw radicchio cut into strips and fresh boiled beans served with diced lardo or prosciutto; ii) grilled radicchio with a bean purée dip flavored with pepper and vinegar. Veneto.

radicchio e lardo radicchio cut into strips and served with lightly fried diced lardo, vinegar, salt and pepper. Veneto.

radicchio fritto sliced heads of radicchio coated in flour or dipped in batter and fried in oil until golden brown. Veneto.

radicchio in saor broiled radicchio marinated in onion softened in oil, vinegar or white wine, raisins, pine kernels and lemon and orange zest (➤ **saor**). Veneto.

radicchio marinato heads of radicchio either parboiled and macerated for 10-12 hours in water flavored with lemon juice, juniper berries, pepper and sugar or, according to an alternative recipe, parboiled in water and vinegar with bay leaves and juniper berries and marinated in extra virgin olive oil for 24 hours. Veneto.

radicchio peloso regional term for ➤ **aspraggine**, bristly oxtongue.

radicchio rosso di Treviso PGI red radicchio (late and early varieties) cultivated in the provinces of Treviso, Padua and Venice. The early variety is harvested in June and July, the late in early September. Both stand out for their crispness and distinctive flavor. Today the vegetable is fried, grilled and used as an ingredient in risottos, but more traditional recipes still survive: eg, ➤ **radicio fumegà**, ➤ **radicchio in saor**, ➤ **radicchio marinato**. Veneto.

radicchio selvatico regional term for ➤ **ioseride**, tree of death.

radicchio variegato di Castelfranco PGI radicchio cultivated in some communes in the provinces of Treviso, Padua and Venice. The leaves are cream in color with bright red streaks, their flavor is delicate and slightly bitter, Thanks to their crispness, they are best enjoyed raw. Veneto.

radice dolce "sweet root." Regional term for ➤ **scorzonera**, black salsify.

radicetta regional term for ➤ **cicoria selvatica**, wild cicory.

radici literally "roots." Term normally used in Piedmont for the roots of black salsify (➤ **scorzonera**) or salsify (➤**scorzobianca**), but also of chicory (➤ **cicoria**). In Veneto, the term also refers to various types of wild radicchio (➤ **radici de camp**) such as ➤ **dente di leone**, bristly hawkbit.

radici de camp Veneto term for ➤ **dente di leone**, bristly hawkbit.

radici e fasoi peasant dish of borlotti beans (➤ **borlotto**) roughly mashed and mixed with wild greens such as dandelion leaves and bristly hawkbit. Veneto.

radicio fumegà leaves of various varieties of radicchio lightly cooked with onion and diced smoked pancetta. Veneto.

rafanastro common and regional term for ➤ **rapastrello** wild radish.

rafanata baked frittata made with grated

horseradish (➤ **cren**), mashed potatoes, eggs and fresh breadcrumbs. At Carnival time, the same mixture is formed into balls, which are coated in flour and fried. Basilicata.

rafano an alternative name for ➤ **cren**), horseradish.

rafano orientale another name for ➤ **cren**, horseradish.

raffioli aka **raffiuoli** small cakes made of flour, eggs and honey, baked in the oven, brushed with apricot jam and glaced with sugar icing. In a richer version, *raffioli a cassata*, the cakes are joined together, sandwich-style, with a filling of ricotta cream, chocolate shavings, sugar and candied citron, garnished with a piece of pistachio paste (or orange zest) and glazed with sugar icing. Campania.

raffreddare to cool.

rafioi another name for ➤ **rofioi**, a type of ravioli.

ragno name for a type of ➤ **stoccafisso**, stockfish.

ragno pagano regional term for ➤ **pesce ragno**, weever.

ragù meat sauce for pasta or other first courses (polenta, pasta timbales) slowly cooked with various herbs and, often, tomato. The word derives from the French *ragoût* (meat, fish, or vegetables cut into pieces and stewed). In Italy there are two main schools of **ragù**: one made of ground or finely chopped meat (the prototype of ➤**ragù alla bolognese**), the other obtained by slowly cooking a whole piece of meat (➤ **ragù napoletano** and other southern versions). In colloquial Italian the term **ragù** is synonymous with ➤ **sugo di carne**, meat sauce, in some areas.

ragù all'ennese ground pork softened in red wine and cooked slowly with tomato purée diluted in water, cinnamon, piec-

es of dark chocolate and sugar. Probably of noble origin, it is served with homemade pasta, though in the old days it was the classic accompaniment for ➤ **sciabbò**, curly lasagne. Typical of Enna as the name suggests. Sicily.

ragù alla bolognese the recipe for the classic Bologna meat sauce was registered at the city's Chamber of Commerce in 1982. The "official" ingredients are: ground beef, pancetta, white or red wine, beef broth, tomato sauce or purée, milk, onion, carrot and celery. The aromatics are finely chopped and gently cooked, then the meat is added, together with the wine, tomato, salt and pepper. The sauce is left to simmer for a couple of hours with the occasional addition of milk. It is finished with the addition of full cream from the top of the milk. Emilia-Romagna.

ragù alla potentina a pork or beef roll, flavored internally with garlic, parsley, and pancetta is browned in oil or lardo, then slowly cooked first in white wine then in tomato. Sauce served with all the typical regional pastas with a sprinkling of grated Pecorino. Basilicata.

ragù calabrese lean veal and pork, veal or pork rib and various cured meats (capocollo, pancetta, and so on), chopped and slowly cooked in wine and tomato with onion, garlic, chili, parsley, salt and pepper. Sauce served with ➤ **maccaruni 'i casa** and ➤ **cannaruozzoli**, egg pasta squares. Calabria.

ragù di brasciole beef rolls (➤ **brasciola**) stuffed with herbs, lardo or sausage, Pecorino and, depending on the recipe, sliced hard-boiled eggs, browned in chopped lardo, garlic and parsley, bathed with red wine, covered with tomato sauce, and left to simmer. Sauce served with all the typical regional pastas with a sprinkling of grated Pecorino or Caciori-cotta. Puglia.

ragù di carne e piselli meat and pea sauce. Ground beef cooked with herbs, toma-to sauce (or skinned tomatoes), and fresh peas. Popular with long egg pasta. (In Romagna they make a similar sauce with sausage and peas to accompany ➤ **grami-gna**, short egg pasta). Umbria.

ragù di coniglio rabbit sauce. Popular in many regions, suitable for both long and short pasta. In Umbria, chopped rabbit meat and pancetta and crumbled sausage are browned in a pot with finely sliced aromatics and herbs (onion, carrot, gar-lic, and bay leaf), then cooked in white wine and broth. In Piedmont, they sim-ply combine the browned rabbit meat with tomato sauce. See also ➤ **sughi di carne alla Toscana,** Tuscan meat sauces.

ragù di rigaglie chicken giblet sauce. Chick-en giblets browned with onion (in some recipes also with aromatics), bathed with white wine, left to simmer, and finished with tomato passata or crushed skinned tomatoes. Similar recipes are to be found in Umbria, Romagna and Piedmont (➤ **sugo di fegatini,** chicken liver sauce). In some areas—Veneto, for example—they leave out the tomato (➤ **bigoli coi rovinassi**).

ragù di stridoli bladder campion sauce. Bladder campion shoots, finely chopped and cooked briefly with chopped pancet-ta, garlic, and onion, sometimes with the addition of tomato. The herb (known lo-cally as ➤ **stridoli,** in Italian as ➤ **silene rigonfia**) is especially popular in Romag-na. Emilia-Romagna.

ragù di verzino salami sauce. Cooked in the same way as a normal northern Italian ➤ **ragù,** but using crumbled sausage instead of ground meat. A sauce typical of the town of Crema. Lombardy.

ragù napoletano the Neapolitan take on ➤ **ragù,** in which whole pieces of meat are left to simmer in some form of sauce. In-gredients vary not only from area to area, but also from neighborhood to neighbor-hood, from family to family. They nor-mally include some of the following: lean beef or pork, pork ribs, beef rolls stuffed with garlic, Pecorino Romano, parsley, salt, and pepper, plenty of chopped on-ion, red wine, and tomato puree diluted in warm water. The sauce is used to ac-company pasta, while the meat is eaten separately as a second course (➤ **geno-vese**). Campania.

ragusa Abruzzo and Marche word for ➤ **mu-rice,** murex or rock snail.

Ragusano PDO cheese produced in the provinces of Ragusa and Siracusa. It is shaped into a parallelepiped using wood-en tools. May be eaten fresh but best af-ter an aging for eight to 24 months. A Slow Food presidium protects artisan **Ragusano** made according to tradition-al methods from the raw, full-cream milk of the Modicana cattle breed in the semi-wild state. Sicily.

ramaiolo aka **romaiolo** ladle used to stir, skim and pour soups. The word is not commonly used today, but may still be heard in Tuscany.

ramassin del Monviso Valle Bronda in this small valley a few miles from Saluzzo, in the province of Cuneo, are cultivated beautifully sweet small damson plums (in dialect *darmassin* or *ramassin*). The mi-croclimate and altitude (just over 1,500 feet) ensure excellent harvests, but the plums are very delicate and need to reach markets and be eaten within two days of picking. A Slow Food presidium is seek-ing to prolong their availability by mar-keting them also in the form of tradition-al jams, liqueurs and preserves. In the area between Cuneo and Saluzzo, ➤ **torta di ramassin**, damson cake, is popular. Piedmont.

rambasici aka **rambasicci** a recipe of Slav origin in which Savoy cabbage leaves are stuffed with a mixture of ground pork and beef, sausage, eggs, cheese and paprika, and stewed with or without tomato. Typical of the provinces of Trieste and Gorizia. Friuli-Venezia Giulia.

ramerino Tuscan word for ➤ **rosmarino**, rosemary.

rametti di nocciole half-moon cookies baked at Easter and Christmas. The paste is made by mixing durum wheat flour, bicarbonate of soda dissolved in warm water, sugar, toasted chopped hazelnuts and cinnamon. When the cookies swell and turn red in color, they are removed from the oven, allowed to cool and glazed with white icing. A specialty of Messina. Sicily.

ramiccia very thin egg fettuccine usually served with lamb sauce. A specialty of Percile in the province of Rome. Lazio.

ramolaccio common name for ➤ **rapastrello**, wild radish.

ramoraccia Lazio term for ➤ **rapastrello**, wild radish.

rampùssoli Veneto term for ➤**raperonzolo**, rampion.

rana, frog. Amphibian with tender, delicate flesh. Can be found in Italy, especially in the north, in two species: the edible frog (*Rana esculenta*) and the common frog (*Rana temporaria*). In the past, frogs, eaten since the late Middle Ages, were considered a food for the poor, caught freely and very common, especially in rice-growing areas, but today those on sale are mostly imported. Traditional regional cuisines are rich in frog recipes: from ➤ **risotto al guazzetto** (➤ **rane in guazzetto**) to ➤ **zuppa di rane**.

rana pescatrice monkfish (*Lophius piscatorius*). A fish that can sometimes grow to six feet in length and over 100 pounds in weight. It is usually sold, skinned and decapitated (the head is used to make broths and gelatin), for the flesh of the tail (➤ **coda di rospo**), which is firm, delicate in flavor and without bones. It may be broiled, baked, stewed, or boiled in a ➤ **court-bouillon** and served with olive oil and lemon juice. The tripe and liver are considered great culinary delicacies. Common and regional names: ➤ **boldrò**, ➤ **budegasso**, ➤ **bùdego**, ➤ **coda di rospo**, ➤ **diavolo di mare**, ➤ **giuranna di mari**, ➤ **magu**, ➤ **pesce rospo**.

rana pescatrice all'otrantina pieces of monkfish fried and finished off with tomatoes, oregano and parsley. Served on slices of toasted bread. A recipe typical of Otranto, in the province of Lecce. Puglia.

rancetto sauce made of chopped onions, diced pancetta and chopped skinned onions, perfumed with marjoram and pepper, and sprinkled with a generous handful of grated Pecorino. Served with long pasta, spaghetti for example. Bar for the addition of the marjoram, the sauce is a close relative of ➤ **amatriciana**. Umbria.

rancio 'e funno aka **rancio fellone** Campania terms (the first in dialect) for ➤ **grancevola**, spider crab.

randorche word used in the province of Ascoli Piceno for ➤ **mais**, corn or maize. A popular local soup is, or at least used to be, made with sweetcorn, potatoes, onion, zucchini, peppers, broth and chili. Marche.

rane embragade frogs fried in batter. Frogs, gutted, skinned, decapitated, are marinated in water and vinegar for an hour or thereabouts. After drying, the legs are crossed over, dipped in a batter of water,

rane fritte

white wine (or grappa), flour, egg yolks and egg whites whisked to a peak, and fried in boiling oil. Trentino-Alto Adige.

rane fritte fried frogs. Frogs, skinned and gutted, marinated in white wine aromatized with garlic, parsley, salt, pepper and nutmeg, coated in flour and fried in boiling oil. Emilia-Romagna.

rane in guazzetto stewed frogs, a traditional northern Italian dish. In Pavia (Lombardy), the frogs, cleaned and gutted, are lightly floured and cooked in a pot with oil and pepper, or with butter and leeks, then covered with a sauce of ripe tomatoes and finely minced flat-leaved parsley. In the province of Vercelli (Piedmont), a sauce of finely minced aromatics and fresh tomato is prepared first and the frogs added afterwards. In Emilia, stewed frogs are served with polenta, but also with risottos and short pasta.

ranfele 'e funnale Campania dialect term for ➤ **scampo**, scampi.

rapa turnip (*Brassica campestris* var. *rapa*). Many varieties exist, all cultivated for their roots, some also for their leaves or tops. Turnips are most common in the north of Italy thanks to their resistance to cold and frost. The province of Cuneo, in Piedmont, is a prolific producer, and some ecotypes grown on the border with Liguria are highly prized: *rape di Nasino* and ➤ **rapa di Caprauna**). In the kitchen, turnips are stewed, baked and puréed, and served as a side dish with pork and sausage (➤ **rape al lardo**), or on their own. Typical of northeast Italy are ➤ **rape agrodolci**. They also figure in soups (➤ **rapata lombarda**) and in cured meats (➤ **ciuiga del Banale**, ➤ **luganeghette di passola**). One of the most famous turnip-based culinary preparations in Italy is ➤ **broàde** aka **brovàde**, in which they are layered in tubs with pomace. The subspecies brocco-

li rabe (➤ **cime di rapa**) is popular mainly in central and southern regions.

rapa di Caprauna Caprauna is a small village in the upper Val Tanaro, in the province of Cuneo, with a population of a few hundred inhabitants and excellent turnips. In the past, turnips were a staple in the diet of people living in the Piedmontese Alps, but were eventually supplanted by the potato. Once harvested, the Caprauna turnip, with its sweet, unusually pale yellow flesh, does not keep well and is best left underground until ripe, in the fall and winter months. A Slow Food presidium is seeking to protect its cultivation in an area (Caprauna itself and the nearby commune of Alto) at risk of depopulation. Piedmont.

rapa rossa common name for ➤ **barbabietola**, beetroot.

rapanello selvatico another name for ➤ **rapastrello**, wild radish.

rapastello another name for ➤ **rapastrello**, wild radish.

rapastrello wild radish (*Raphanus raphanistrum*). Wild herbaceous plant common all over Italy, and eaten mostly in the central regions, Marche and Lazio in particular, with pasta or tossed with garlic and chili. Common and regional names: ➤ **gedule**, ➤ **gramolaccio**, ➤ **rafanastro**, ➤ **rafano**, ➤ **ramolaccio**, ➤ **rapanello selvatico**, ➤ **rapastello**, ➤ **rati**.

rapata rice and turnip soup. Rice and tender young turnips boiled in meat broth with finely chopped lard, garlic and flat-leaved parsley, and served with a sprinkling of grated Parmigiano and more parsley. Lombardy.

rape 'nfucate side dish of broccoli rabe (➤ **cime di rapa**), oil, garlic and chili. Puglia.

rape agrodolci boiled beetroot dressed with sugar, vinegar and grated horseradish (➤ **cren**). Trentino-Alto Adige.

464

rape e ciccioli side dish of broccoli rabe (➤ **cime di rapa**, known locally as ➤ **rapini**) boiled and turned with pork scratchings (➤ **ciccioli**) and ripe tomatoes. Tuscany.

rape e patate turnips and potatoes. Traditional side dish in which the two vegetables are diced and cooked with lard, garlic, cumin, and sausage or smoked pork ribs. Friuli-Venezia Giulia.

rape e riso turnip and rice soup. Turnips sautéed in butter with garlic and onion and covered with broth in which the rice is subsequently cooked. Soup typical of the valleys of the province of Cuneo. Piedmont.

raperonzolo rampion (*Campanula rapunculus*). Root vegetable that grows wild on moorland and in woods. The roots have a mild nutty flavor and are popular, especially in central Italy, cooked in broth or raw in salads. An important ingredient in vegetable and herb mixtures, such as ➤ **cucina** or ➤ **preboggion**. Also used in Emilia-Romagna and Veneto. Common and regional names: ➤ **campanula selvatica**, ➤ **pizzocorno**, ➤ **rampùssoli**, ➤ **raponzolo**.

rapini Tuscan term for ➤ **cime di rapa**, broccoli rabe.

raponzolo regional term for ➤ **raperonzolo**, rampion.

rapprendersi (of a food) to set, to solidify.

rasagnolo regional term for ➤ **matterello**, rolling pin.

rascatieddi aka **rascatielli** type of pasta similar to ➤ **cavatelli**, made from a dough of durum wheat meal, mashed potatoes and salt. Calabria.

Raschera square PDO cheese made in the province of Cuneo with cow's milk and the occasional addition of ewe's and/or goat's milk. It is aged for 20 days to three months and is denominated *Raschera d'Alpeggio* (ie, mountain dairy cheese), if it is produced at an altitude in excess of 2,700 feet. Piedmont.

raschietta aka **grisëtta** a crisp version of the ➤ **biova** bread roll named for the tool (*raschia*) used to break up the dough. Typical of the Canavese district, northwest of Turin. Piedmont.

Rasco smoked cheese, now very rare, once made with milk from cattle grazing in the summer pastures of the Sila plateau. Calabria.

rasnici aka **raznici** roast skewers of veal, pork, chicken, sausages, onion and peppers. A dish of Dalmatian origin. Friuli-Venezia Giulia.

raspadura aka **raspatura** snack of wafer-thin slivers of local Grana locale (preferably ➤ **Tipico Lodigiano**) eaten on their own or with cured meats. A specialty of the province of Lodi. Lombardy.

rassodare (of a food) to solidify or to set.

rasumà Emilian version of the Lombard ➤ **rosumada**. A specialty of the province of Piacenza, the drink is made with eggs beaten with sugar, to which red wine is added. To make a thirst-quenching beverage, water and lemon juice are added. Emilia-Romagna.

ratafià aka **ratafia** aka **rattaffia** a liqueur popular in the 18th and 19th centuries, especially in Piedmont, Val d'Aosta and France, where it is still produced industrially and at home. The drink is made by infusing in alcohol fresh fruit juice (black cherry, sour cherry, apricot, orange, redcurrant, plum, walnut, lemon and broom), boiled and sweetened with sugar. The resulting liqueur is dark in color and mildly alcoholic with a sweet, fruity flavor.

ratatoia aka **ratatuia** a close relative of the Provencal ratatouille. Mixed fresh vegetables (zucchini, peppers, carrots, onions, eggplants etc.) diced and stewed with tomato. Piedmont.

rati Friuli word for ➤ **rapastrello**, wild radish

ratta an alternative name for ➤ **omento**, omentum.

rava term used in some northern Italian dialects for ➤ **rapa**, turnip.

ravanello radish (*Raphanus sativus*). A member of the Brassicaceae family, cultivated for its globular red root, the white flesh of which is crisp in texture and pungent in flavor. The principal Italian producer regions are Lazio, Campania, Sardinia, Emilia-Romagna and Puglia. Two varieties with long roots (one in Piedmont, the other in Sardinia) are listed in the Italian Ministry of Agriculture's database of native and/or traditional food products. Radish is gathered from spring until the late fall and is eaten mostly fresh, either finely sliced and dressed with oil and salt, or as a component of ➤ **pinzimonio**.

rave dolze turnips stewed with pancetta lightly caramelized with sugar. A side dish of Bohemian origin. A recipe now typical of Trieste. Friuli- Venezia Giulia.

ravieu ravioli typical of Genoa. Slightly different from other north Italian ravioli insofar as the stuffing includes lean veal but also offal (udder, bone marrow, brain and sweetbreads), borage and escarole. The shape is quadrangular, the pasta is made of flour and water with only a few eggs and the classic accompaniment is beef sauce (➤ **tocco**). Liguria.

ravieu di Gavi ravioli (or rather ➤ **agnolotti**) typical of the area of the province of Alessandria that borders with Liguria. The ingredients for the stuffing include beef neck, pork sausage meat, borge and marjoram. The ravioli are served with meat sauce (➤ **tocco**) or splashed with red wine or *a culo nudo*, literally "bare-assed," sprinkled with generous amounts of grated Parmigiano without mixing so that one side of the pasta stays "natural." Liguria.

Raviggiolo regional term for a fresh cheese equivalent to ➤ **Giuncata**.

Raviggiolo dell'Appennino Toscoromagnolo an old, now relatively hard to find fresh cheese, produced in a number of valleys in the Romagna Apennines with raw cow's milk, without milling the curd, but merely draining it and salting it on the surface. Today a few cheesemakers in the Foreste Casentinesi, national park continue to use raw milk, but this cheese can be kept for no more than four days, it is only found from October to March. Buttery in texture, Raviggiolo, protected by a Slow Food Presidium, has a soft, white body and a delicate, almost sweet flavor. On the Tuscan side of the Apennines, and elsewhere in Tuscany, they make ewe's milk ➤ **Raviggiolo di pecora**. Emilia-Romagna.

Raviggiolo di pecora fresh pasteurized ewe's milk cheese to be eaten within two days of production. Tuscany.

raviole another word for ➤ **ravioli**.

raviole di san Giuseppe half-moon short-crust pastries filled with jam, traditionally baked all over Emilia for the saint's day. In Bologna instead they fill them with ➤ **mostarda bolognese**, Emilia-Romagna.

ravioles spindle-shaped gnocchi made with potatoes and fresh ➤ **Toma**, usually served with melted butter and grated cheese. A typical dish of the Provencal valleys of the province of Cuneo, traditionally made on festive occasions, in particular for the Bajo di Sampeyre, a festival held every four years to celebrate the chasing of the Saracens from the area in the Middle Ages. Piedmont.

ravioli (1) (sing. **raviolo**, aka **rabiola**, **raffiolo**, **raviggiolo**, **ravanolo**) egg pasta filled with ingredients which differ all over Italy by season and region (variations on the theme include ➤ **agnolotti**, ➤ **pansoti**, ➤ **cappelletti**, ➤ **tortellini**, ➤ **casonsei**, ➤ **tortelli di zucca**, ➤ **culurgiones**, ➤ **cauzuni**).

ravioli (2) in regional cuisines today, the term defines specific recipes: eg, ➤ **ravieu**, Ligurian ravioli. In southern Piedmont, the word is synonymous with ➤ **agnolotti**.

ravioli (3) on account of similarity of shape, the word also refers to a number of sweet cakes and pastries.

ravioli al papavero pasta squares stuffed with poppy seeds (➤ **papavero (2)**) crushed and boiled in milk, sugar and honey, fried in boiling oil. Trentino-Alto Adige.

ravioli alla napoletana fresh egg pasta half-moons stuffed with mozzarella, ricotta, prosciutto, Parmigiano and flat-leaved parsley, served with tomato or meat sauce. Campania.

ravioli alla potentina large fresh pasta squares stuffed with ricotta, prosciutto, eggs and flat-leaved parsley. Generally served with meat sauce and grated salted ricotta. Basilicata.

ravioli alla vernantina large egg pasta ➤ **tortelli** stuffed with mashed potatoes, leeks softened in butter, eggs and nutmeg, served with melted butter. A specialty of Vernante, in the province of Cuneo. Piedmont.

ravioli calabresi round or square ravioli stuffed with a mixture of Provola, ➤ **soppressata di Calabria**, hard-boiled eggs and black pepper. Calabria.

ravioli di patate ravioli made with a dough of flour and mashed potatoes, similar to potato gnocchi but firmer, stuffed with a mixture of ricotta, spinach and nutmeg and served with Parmigiano-Reggia-

no and melted butter. Typical of the Val Pusteria. Trentino-Alto Adige.

ravioli di rane square egg ravioli stuffed with boned frogs and perch, eggs, grated Grana Padano and herbs, and boiled in frog broth. Traditionally made at Lent. Lombardy.

ravioli dolci sweet ravioli stuffed with ricotta, refined sugar and lemon. Sardinia..

ravioli genovesi another name for ➤ **ravieu**.

ravioli gnudi alla fiorentina the term *gnudi* refers to the lack of a pasta casing. The mixture is made with boiled spinach amalgamated with eggs, ricotta, wheat flour, grated Parmigiano, salt, pepper and nutmeg. It is shaped into rectangles, which are boiled in salted water and served with melted butter. Tuscany.

ravioli panteschi ravioli stuffed with ricotta and mint, typical of the island of Pantelleria (province of Trapani). Sicily.

ravioli pusteresi another name for ➤ **türteln**, large round ravioli.

raviolini di carne in brodo small ravioli stuffed with roast beef, chicken or turkey, cheese and eggs, cooked in meat broth and served with grated cheese, often with a dash of red wine. In some places, the stuffing is supplemented with other ingredients such as boiled cow's udder, prosciutto or salami, gravy from the roast, cinnamon, nutmeg, garlic and flat-leaved parsley. Lombardy.

razza skate. The name applies to a number of members of the Rajidae family. The varieties used in the kitchen are the spotted *razza quattrocchi* (*Raja miraletus*), *razza stellata* (*R. asterias*), thornback ray (*R. clavata*) and white ray (*R. alba*). The *quattrocchi* (*u cchialine*) *del Molise* is listed in the Ministry of Agriculture's database of native and/or traditional food products. All rays live on sandy, muddy sea beds and are usually sold skinned and cut into slices. They are boiled and served cold with a sauce of garlic and vinegar (a simplified variation on ➤ **burrida sarda**), or cooked in a sweet and sour sauce or with peppers, or used as an ingredient in soups. It is also the principal ingredient in the Lazio classic ➤ **pasta e broccoli in brodo di arzilla**.

reale aka **sottospalla** a cut of beef, that covers the first three to four vertebrae of an adult bovine, roughly equivalent to third cut cover ribs.

Reblec aka **Réblèque** small artisan cream cheese made with the surface portion of the curd from cow's milk. It is eaten within two or three days of production. Val d'Aosta.

Rebruchon another name for ➤ **Formaggio a crosta rossa**, a Piedmontese cheese.

recchie de prevete aka **recchietedde** Puglia dialect term for ➤ **orecchiette**, a type of pasta.

rece de lievaro "hare's ears." Veneto name for ➤ **piantaggine**, ribwort plantain.

refrigerare to refrigerate.

regina di San Daniele filleted trout (➤ **trota**), dry-salted and cold- or hot-smoked. A specialty of San Daniele del Friuli (Udine).

reginella Sicilian name for ➤ **sesamo**, sesame.

reginelle (1) another name for ➤ **reginette**, a type of dried pasta

reginelle (2) another name in Sicily for ➤ **biscotti regina**, a type of cookie.

reginette commercial durum wheat pasta ribbons with curly edges. Very popular in the south, they are served with rich meat and game sauces. Other names: ➤ **fettuccelle ricce**, ➤ **reginelle**.

reginette co-e euve soup similar to ➤ **stracciatella (1)** (Emilia, Tuscany). Small pasta cooked in meat broth with the addition of eggs beaten with marjoram and grated Parmigiano. Typical of the province of Genoa. Liguria.

reginette di Omegna almond and chocolate cookies produced for the last 70 years or so in Omegna, on Lake Orta, in the province of Novara. Piedmont.

remesciùn a sort of savory pie made with cornflour, onion, potatoes, grated Parmigiano, sausage or lardo and pancetta. Typical of the inland part of the province of Genoa. Liguria.

Renaz a new type of tangy cheese, created in 1983, made with whole and part-skimmed cow's milk and aged for at least three months. Produced in Livinallongo, in the province of Belluno. Veneto.

Rendena, razza a cow breed with a brown or red-brown coat, created in the early 19th century by crossing local animals with others from Switzerland. About 7,000 head still live in the province of Trento and some areas of Veneto. Trentino-Alto Adige, Veneto.

rene another word for ➤ **rognone**, kidney.

renga Veneto word for ➤ **aringa**, herring.

renghe aka **rati** popular dish, traditional at Lent, composed of preserved herring (*renga*) and grated wild radish (*rati*). Friuli.

rentròcele, lu Abruzzo term for a special rolling pin (➤ **matterello**) used to make ➤ **maccheroni a lu rentròcele**.

repouta conserve of vegetables (chard, Savoy cabbage, turnip), which are poached and kept in hermetically sealed glass jars with salt and aromas. Val d'Aosta.

resca aka **resta** traditional Easter bread in the Lake Como area, now virtually extinct. Made with wheat flour, brewer's yeast, eggs, sugar, honey, butter, candied fruits, raisins and grated lemon zest. The loaf is oblong in shape with a fish pattern on the top (*resca* means fish bone) and an olive branch inserted lengthwise into its crust. Lombardy.

resta (1) braided string of onions or garlic, normally hung in a dry, cool place to keep.

resta (2) regional term for fish bone.

resta (3) another name for ➤ **resca**, a traditional Lombard cake.

rete caul. Term used in gastronomy for the omentum (➤ **omento**), a large fold of peritoneum that extends from one abdominal wall to another. In the kitchen pig's caul (and, less frequently, lamb's) is used to wrap foods, such as offal and lean meat, liver (➤ **fegatelli**) and rabbit, to protect them from a direct contact with heat and keep them soft.

reticolo reticulum. The second and smallest of the four components of the stomachs in ruminants (➤ **trippa**), where the food is subdivided into cud and regurgitated into the mouth. Also known as ➤ **cuffia** or ➤ **nido d'ape** (honeycomb) and, regionally, as ➤ **ciapa**, ➤ **bonetto**, ➤ **beretta**.

revölt a mixture of runner beans (*curnitt* in dialect), cornflour, butter and salt. A specialty of the Val Morobbia, in the Swiss Italian Cantone Ticino.

rezdora aka **arzdora** farmer's wife. The dialect term refers, in Emilia-Romagna, to the farmer's wife as a housewife cum governess cum cook, the woman of the house who manage its food resources from pantry to stove.

rianata durum wheat pizza topped with finely minced garlic, slivers of ➤ **Primosale** cheese, pieces of anchovy, chopped ripe tomatoes, salt, grated Pecorino, olive oil and a generous sprinkling of oregano. A specialty of Trapani. Sicily.

Riavulillo small smoked ➤ **Scamorza** typical of Vico Equense, in the province of Naples. When the cheese is being modeled into its distinctive shape, a filling of black olives and chili is put into the stretched curd. Eaten as it is or lightly grilled. Campania.

ribes redcurrant or blackcurrant. *Ribes comune*, redcurrant (*Ribes rubrum*), is widely cultivated in Italy and also grows wild in mountain areas. *Ribes di monte*, blackcurrant (*R. nigrum*), also known in Italian as *cassis* and *ribes nero*, grows wild in the mountains. Redcurrants are eaten fresh or used in baking and confectionery as an ingredient in ice creams and syrups. Blackcurrants are used exclusively to make syrups and liqueurs, especially ➤ **ratafià** and, in France, cassis.

ribollita abbreviated name for ➤ **minestra di pane per la ribollita**, a Tuscan bread soup.

riccetti di Gesù Bambino another name for ➤**caranciuli**, Christmas cookies.

riccetto regional term for ➤ **grespigno**, field sowthistle.

ricci di donna another name for ➤ **scialatielli**, a type of pasta.

riccia aka **ricciolino** other names for ➤ **abomaso**, abomasum.

ricciarelli aromatic cookies made with chopped almonds, sugar, honey, grated lemon zest, bicarbonate of soda and egg whites. Shaped into lozenges and dusted with confectioner's sugar, they are left to rest for a few hours before being baked in the oven. The cookie is of ancient origin (records of it date from the 15th century) and, judging by the shape (reminiscent of a sultan's slippers) and ingredients (common in Arab confectionery) it may come from the East. In a variant, *ricciarelli rozzi*, the paste is covered with dark chocolate. A specialty of Siena. Tuscany.

riccio di mare sea urchin (*Paracentrotus lividus*). Fished in the late winter and early spring, when the edible parts are at their fattest and tastiest. Sea urchins are generally eaten raw with a drop of lemon. Lightly cooked they are an ingredient in frittatas and pasta sauces. In the southern regions, seaside kiosks, stalls and trattorias sell fresh sea urchins ready-opened.

ricciòla amberjack (*Seriola dumerili*). A marine fish of the Carangidae family with firm, delicately flavored white flesh. Cut into slices, it is excellent baked, broiled, barbecued or cooked in a ➤ **court-bouillon**. It may also be marinated and combined with herbs and vegetables, especially basil. In central and northern Italy, it is called ➤ **leccia** aka **leccia bastarda**, but elsewhere the name *leccia* (*Lichia amia*) refers to the leer fish, whose flesh is also firm but less delicate. In the Marche and Puglia, the amberjack is called ➤ **ombrina boccadoro**.

ricciòla in boreto flavored with oil and garlic and cooked with white wine, vinegar and water. Served with the deglazed cooking juices, a sprinkling of parsley and toasted polenta. Veneto, Friuli-Venezia Giulia.

ricciolina a variant of ➤ **baùle**, a bread roll, reminiscent of ➤ **coppietta ferrarese**.

ricola dialect word for ➤ **rucola selvatica**, perennial wallrocket.

ricotta the name, from the Latin *recoctus*, refers to leftover whey from the day's cheesemaking that has been recooked. It is eaten fresh, after salting, or matured for 15 to 30 days. If it is smoked, it can be aged for a week to a month. Ricotta is to be had all over Italy and is also extensively used in the kitchen in sweet and savory recipes. One regional product, ➤ **Ricotta Romana**, has received PDO recognition.

Ricotta affumicata di Mammola characteristic mushroom-shaped goat's milk whey ricotta produced in Mammola, in the province of Reggio Calabria. Continuing an ancient tradition, it is made on a number of family-run farms. It is smoked for about 24 hours. Calabria.

Ricotta al fumo di ginepro typical of the Abruzzo national park, this ricotta is made with organic ewe's milk whey. It is matured for seven days, then smoked for 24 hours and offers characteristic balsamic aromas. Abruzzo.

ricotta alla fuscella very fresh ricotta drained in cone-shaped baskets.

Ricotta ascquante aka **scante** aka **schiante** dialect names for ➤ **Ricotta forte**.

ricotta briaca literally "drunken ricotta." A simple dessert of fresh ricotta, sugar, coffee powder and Vin Santo. The ingredients are worked to a soft cream. The preparation is reminiscent of the Lazio sweet snack ➤ **budino di ricotta**. Tuscany.

Ricotta forte, in dialect aka **Ricotta ascquante** (**scante**, **schiante**) ricotta made from leftover fresh goat's, ewe's and cow's milk whey allowed to acidify for a few days then transferred to earthenware pitchers, where it is washed every two or three days for three or four months. It is subsequently kept for a year or so in smaller recipients. The type made in the province of Brindisi is particularly prized. Puglia.

ricotta fritta antipasto consisting of firm, well-dried ricotta cut into slices, which are coated in flour, dipped in beaten eggs and fried in extra virgin olive oil or lard. A specialty of Gubbio, in the province of Perugia. Umbria.

Ricotta infornata ricotta produced with cow's, ewe's and goat's milk whey, baked in stone ovens for 30 minutes. After a day, it is ready to eat, but may also be aged for grating. Sicily.

Ricotta marzotica tangy ewe's milk whey ricotta produced in the spring (*marzo* means March in Italian, hence the name).

Eaten after a months' aging, by which time it has gathered a light mold. Puglia.

Ricotta mustia ewe's milk whey ricotta typical of the province of Sassari. It is drained overnight, salted and smoked for five to six hours over a fire of aromatic herbs. Sardinia.

Ricotta Romana a PDO ricotta that dates from ancient Rome. It is produced mainly in the Agro romano countryside from November to June with milk from Sarda, Siciliana and Comisana sheep fed on pasture grass and a small amount of forage. White, compact and slightly lumpy, it has a sweetish milky taste and is sold in cone-shapes that can weigh up to one pound. Lazio.

ricotta salaprisa Sicilian term for semi-mature ricotta.

ridurre to reduce. To concentrate a liquid, usually a sauce or gravy.

riduzione a reduction.

riebl buckwheat (➤ **grano saraceno**) and milk fritters fried in lard. Trentino-Alto Adige.

rifatto Tuscan term for a food finished off, turned or tossed in a skillet with butter and oil before serving (➤ **ripassare**).

rifreddo in historical menus the term refers to a cooked dish served cold, between the main meat course and the dessert (the great 19th century Italian gastronome Pellegrino Artusi lists galantines, and liver and game pâtés among others). Today it is only ever heard, though rarely, in Emilia-Romagna and Tuscany.

rigaglie giblets. The innards of poultry and game birds. They comprise the liver, the heart, the stomach, the testicles, egg embryos, crests and wattle. Trimmed and cleaned, they are used as ingredients in many traditional regional dishes (from ➤ **cibreo** in Tuscany to ➤ **finanziera** in Piedmont) and in sauces (➤

ragù di rigaglie) to serve with pastas and risottos.

rigano dialect term for ➤ **origano**, oregano.

rigatino flat, pressed pancetta: streaked with lean meat, cured with salt, pepper and spices and hung to age. Tuscany.

rigatino finocchiato a variant of ➤ **rigatino**, prepared from September to May in San Miniato, in the province of Pisa. The bacon is trimmed, salted and aromatized with garlic, pepper, wild fennel and saltpeter and aged for ten days. It is then rolled up, the aromatized part facing inwards, secured with string and put to age in a cellar for another 60 to 120 days. Tuscany.

rigatoncini another type of ➤ **rigatoni**, a type of dried pasta.

rigatoni ridged, tubular commercial durum wheat pasta. Served with sauce or baked in the oven. Other names: ➤ **bombardoni**, ➤ **maniche rigate**, ➤ **rigatoncini**.

rigatoni alla pastora rigatoni served with ricotta (sometimes smoked), Pecorino, black pepper and sausage. Calabria.

rigatoni alla toranese rigatoni served with strips of lardo, softened with onion and grated Pecorino. A specialty of Torano Castello (Cosenza). Calabria.

rigatoni con la pajata a Roman classic. Rigatoni first sprinkled with grated Pecorino Romano, then tossed in a sauce made with ➤ **pajata**, minced ham fat, spices (nutmeg and cloves), salt, pepper, white wine and tomato passata. Lazio.

rigatoni con sugo di maiale rigatoni served with pork sautéed in butter with cinnamon, powdered cloves and eggs beaten with grated cheese (➤ **Latteria** or smoked ricotta). Friuli-Venezia Giulia.

rigatoni imbottiti a baked crustless timbale (➤ **timballo**) of rigatoni stuffed with a mixture of mortadella, Provolone, mozzarella and ground meat lightly fried in oil, layered with tomato sauce, onion and aromatic herbs. Puglia.

rigojanci aka **rigojancsi** other names for ➤ **torta rigojanci**, a type of cake.

rinvenire to revive, to rehydrate, to soften a dried food (raisins, dried figs, for example) by soaking in water, liqueur or wine.

riondela Piedmontese term for ➤ **malva**, mallow.

ripario another word for ➤ **granchio marino commune**, crab.

ripassare to finish, turn or toss cooked food, usually vegetables, in a skillet with oil or butter. The technique is common in traditional recipes (eg, ➤ **cavoli strascinati**) and sometimes involves the addition of aromas and spices (often garlic and chili) and the use of sauces, gravies or pan juices (➤ **fagioli rifatti**), in which case it extends to pasta too (➤ **bucatini con i broccoli arriminati**, ➤ **penne strascicate**).

ripieni aka **verdure ripiene** baked stuffed vegetables (onion, pepper, zucchini, zucchini flowers, eggplant). The filling consists of the flesh of the vegetables themselves, boiled green beans and potatoes, amalgamated with eggs, breadcrumbs, oil and marjoram. Liguria.

ripieno filling or stuffing. A mixture of diverse ingredients used to fill or stuff a food: eg, vegetables, a fowl, pasta (➤ **pasta ripiena**), cakes and pastries etc. The most common ingredients are eggs, which often serve as a binding agent (➤ **legare**), cheeses, cured meats, vegetables, raw or cooked ground meats and, in the case of cakes or pastries, custards, jams and marmalades, chocolate and dried fruit. A **ripieno** differs from a ➤ **farcia** (*farce*) on account of its coarser texture.

riposare to rest.

ris e còj rice and Savoy cabbage soup. First the cabbage leaves are sautèed with lar-

do, pork rind, or pancetta, then cooked in broth, to which the rice is subsequently added. Piedmont.

ris e corada soup of boiled calf's lung (➤ **corada**), pancetta, leeks, sage, parsley and grated Parmigiano-Reggiano. Lombardy.

ris e erborin rice and parsley cooked in beef broth and finished with butter and grated Grana Padana. Specialty of Milan. Lombardy.

ris e malastre soup of rice thickened with mashed potatoes and colored with wild pansy petals. Specialty of Biella. Piedmont.

ris e riondele spring soup of rice cooked in water (or milk) with herbs, potatoes and mallow (➤ **malva**, in dialect ➤ **riondele**), and garnished with butter. A specialty of the province of Biella. Piedmont.

ris e spargitt a soup of rice and asparagus flavored with butter and grated Grana. A specialty of the Milan area. Lombardy.

ris e versi dialect name for ➤ **riso e verze**, rice and cabbage soup.

riscaldare to heat.

risela Piedmontese dialect term for ➤ **omento**, omentum.

riservare to reserve, to set aside.

risi (aka **risini**) commercial dried egg pasta in the shape of small grains of rice.

risi a la canarola rice cooked in a stew with ➤ **cotechino**, boiling sausage, and beans, herbs and tomato. Recipe typical, in the old days, of the rush cutters of the River Adige. Veneto.

risi al brusiolo rice cooked in a sauce of cuttlefish and tomato. The name derives from *brusa*, the Veneto dialect word for the grill on which freshly caught cuttlefish used to be cooked. Veneto.

risi co' la luganega originally rice and sausage soup, today a risotto with crumbled ➤ **luganega trevisana** browned in onion and lubricated with white wine. Typical of the Marca Trevigiana area (province of Treviso), the dish is now common throughout Veneto and Friuli-Venezia Giulia.

risi e bisato rice with eel. The fish, gutted, skinned, and cut into small pieces, is browned in oil with garlic, parsley and bay leaf. The rice is then added and the dish is finished off like a risotto with the addition of the occasional ladleful of broth. A traditional Christmas Eve recipe. Veneto.

risi e bisi thick pea soup with rice (*bisi* is the Veneto word for "peas"). The peas (particularly suitable those of Borso del Grappa, in the province of Treviso) are cooked in broth over a base of softened pancetta, onion and parsley. The soup is finished off with a knob of butter and grated Parmigiano-Reggiano. It is likely that at one time the pea pods, poached in salted boiling water and puréed, were also added to the pot. Traditional dish for the banquet of the Doge of Venice on the feast of San Marco (April 25). Veneto.

risi e figadini thick soup of chicken livers and gizzards. Veneto.

risi e suca dialect term for ➤ **riso e zucca**, rice and pumpkin.

risi e tripe another term for ➤ **sopa de tripe**, tripe soup.

risi in cavroman rice with stewed mutton. Recipe of oriental origin, for centuries part of the Venetian tradition. The mutton (from an animal castrated at birth) is cut into pieces and browned in oil or butter with chopped onion, to which skinned tomatoes and cinnamon are added. When the meat is almost cooked, rice is poured into the pan along with the occasional ladleful of boiling broth, risotto-style. Veneto.

risichelle another name for ➤ **ciambelle al vino bianco**, ring-shaped cookies.

risimoglie Calabrian term for ➤ **ciccioli** or ➤ **curcùci**.

risini another name for ➤ **risi**, a type of pasta.

riso rice (*Oryza sativa*). A cereal that has long been a food staple, especially in Asia. The Oryza species numbers many varieties, which can be grouped into three subspecies: *indica, japonica* and *javanica*. The hybrids traditionally cultivated in Italy (where rice, known by the Romans only as a medicinal plant, was spread and cultivated as a source of nutrition by the Arabs and achieved economic importance thanks to the reclamation of agricultural land by monks and the irrigation work carried out by the Sforzas in the duchy of Milan) belong to the *japonica* subspecies, whose short relatively soft grains release starch easily and are thus suitable for the preparation of risottos (➤ **risotto**). The main varieties of rice cultivated in Italy are classed by Italian legislation into four groups: *comune* aka *originario, semifino, fino* and *superfino*. The members of the first (such as *balilla* and *ambra*) have small, round, pearl grains; members of the second (*rosa marchetti, padano, vialone nano, venere*) have medium-long round grains; members of the third (*ribe, santandrea*) have tapered or semi-tapered grains; members of the fourth (*arborio, baldo, roma, carnaroli, thaibonnet*) have long and very long grains. *Comune* varieties are generally used for soups and cakes; *semifino* varieties for soups, ➤ **timballo** and ➤ **supplì**; *fino* varieties for fillings, ➤ **sartù** and ➤ **bomba**; *superfino* for risottos. In Italy, Europe's leading rice producing country, rice fields are mainly situated along the eastern tributaries of the Po (Dora Baltea, Sesia, Agogna, Ticino, Mincio), between the province of Verona and the

Polesine area, and in the Po delta. The largest rice-growing areas are the provinces of Pavia, Vercelli and Novara. The ➤ **riso di baraggia** variety grown on relatively unfertile ground in the provinces of Biella and Vercelli (Piedmont) has received PDO recognition, and ➤ **riso vialone nano** (Veneto) is PGI. The Italian Ministry of Agriculture's database of native and/or traditional food products lists *risi della valle del Po* and *santandrea* (Piedmont), *riso lombardo* (Lombardy), ➤ **riso di Grumolo delle Abbadesse** (Vicenza), *riso del Delta* (Veneto) and rice produced and processed in Sardinia.

riso alla lombarda rice boiled and finished with butter, egg yolks and grated Parmigiano-Reggiano. Lombardy.

riso alla valtellinese rice boiled with shredded Savoy cabbage, mixed with boiled beans and served with melted butter flavored with sage leaves and grated Parmigiano-Reggiano. Lombardy.

riso arrosto along with ➤ **riso in cagnone** (also to be found in other regions), one of Genoa cuisine's few risottos. It is made by cooking rice in meat sauce aromatized with onion and flat-leaved parsley softened in butter, with the addition of ground cow's udder and veal. As an unusual finishing touch, the risotto is baked in the oven with grated Grana cheese. Liguria.

riso con il preboggion a dish halfway between a soup and a risotto, typical of the inland part of the province of Genoa. It is made with mixed wild greens (➤ **preboggion**) and with the addition, at he end of the cooking process, of ➤ **pesto genovese**. Liguria.

riso con pesce canterano a risotto consisting of rice cooked separately and covered with a sauce made with eels from the Valli del Po and frogs, once common in the rivers in the southern part of the province of Bologna and along the river Reno, aromatic vegetables, white wine, bay leaves and tomato. Emilia-Romagna.

riso di baraggia PDO rice of different varieties (*arborio, baldo, balilla, carnaroli, santandrea, loto, gladio*) grown in the provinces of Biella and Vercelli. Piedmont.

riso di Grumolo delle Abbadesse *vialone nano* cultivar introduced to the small Veneto plainland commune of Grumolo delle Abbadesse (province of Vicenza) by the Benedictine monks of San Pietro di Vicenza, and grown there since the 16th century. Its tiny grains swell as they cook and absorb condiments and sauces well. They provide the ideal base for ➤ **risi e bisi** and soft risottos (with chicken livers, eel, scampi or cuttlefish). A Slow Food presidium supports farmers who continue to grow the rice, even though it has a lower yield than other varieties. Veneto.

riso e castagne rice and chestnut soup. Thick, creamy soup, made with milk, dried chestnuts and rice garnished with butter. Val d'Aosta.

riso e cavolo sul lampredotto rice, cabbage and tripe soup. To a ➤ **soffritto** of aromatic vegetables are added shredded "black" and Savoy cabbage, tomato concentrate, puréed boiled beans, broth and chopped tripe (➤ **lampredotto (1)**). The rice is cooked directly in the soup, which is perfumed with thyme. A classic Florentine winter dish. Tuscany.

riso e latte a traditional soup popular in northern Italy and considered especially suitable for young children and the elderly. It is made by boiling rice with a pinch of salt, sometimes with a potato, to a semi-thick consistency and creaming it with butter. In the mountain valleys of the province of Cuneo (Piedmont), the rice is cooked in milk with the addition of wheat flour to form a cream (the dish is called ➤ **riso in prigione**, "rice in prison"). In Piacenza (Emilia-Romagna), they add a piece of cinnamon to the rice and cream it with butter and grated Grana or, alternatively, a little sugar. On the Lombard plain, they sometimes flavor the dish with pumpkin or chestnuts.

riso e rape alla milanese another name for ➤ **rapata**, rice and turnip soup.

riso e verza con costine rice and Savoy cabbage leaves cooked in broth with the addition of pork ribs. A traditional winter dish in the province of Piacenza. Emilia-Romagna.

riso e verze, in dialect aka **ris e versi** risotto made with meat broth flavored with tomatoes lightly fried in butter and garlic and shredded Savoy cabbage, finished with butter and sprinkled with grated Parmigiano-Reggiano. Lombardy, Piedmont.

riso e verze matte rice cooked in a broth of pig's bones flavored with shredded Savoy cabbage leaves, sausage meat (➤ **pistume**) and red wine. A Cremona recipe typical of the period of the killing of the pig. Lombardy.

riso e zucca rice with pumpkin. Rice boiled with pumpkin, drained and dressed with butter and a generous sprinkling of grated Parmigiano-Reggiano. In some areas, the pumpkin is pre-baked in the oven and only then added to the cooked rice. In the provinces of Mantua and Cremona, the pumpkin is sautéed in oil with chopped onion prior to the addition of beef broth and, subsequently, the rice. The resulting dish resembles a risotto, as does the Veneto recipe ➤ **risi e suca** (which, when cooked with a high proportion of pumpkin to rice is called ➤ **sucarisi**).

riso in cagnone the name, whose etymology is uncertain, refers to a number of different rice dishes. In Biella (Piedmont), rice is boiled in broth and served with butter and pieces of cheese (➤ **Macagn** in particular). In Lombardy, it is cooked in water and served with grated Grana and butter, flavored with garlic and sage. In Liguria, where rice dishes are rare, most of them borrowed from Piedmont, the rice is cooked al dente and finished in the pan with meat and sausage, butter, and sauce In Veneto, the name is given to rice dressed with butter and sage. Piedmont, Lombardy, Veneto, Liguria.

riso in prigione literally "rice in prison." Another name for ➤ **riso e latte**, rice and milk soup.

riso in tortiera boiled rice is mixed with a generous amount of ➤ **ragù**, meat sauce. Half the amount is spooned into a pie tin and topped with fried meatballs, sliced hard-boiled eggs and mozzarella, Pecorino and more ragù. The rest of the rice is added and topped with more fried meatballs, sliced hard-boiled eggs and mozzarella, Pecorino and even more ragù, then drizzled with extra virgin olive oil and sprinkled with grated Pecorino and breadcrumbs. The tin is then put into the oven to bake. Calabria.

riso verde "green rice." In Lombardy, a thick spring soup, reminiscent of ➤ **risi e bisi** (Veneto), of rice, peas cooked with pancetta, flat-leaved parsley, garlic, onion and a generous amount of grated Parmigiano-Reggiano. In Piedmont (province of Asti), a dish halfway between a risotto and a thick soup made with rice toasted in a base of wild spring herbs (poppy, nettle, borage, hops etc.) finished with the addition of broth. Lombardy, Piedmont.

riso vialone nano veronese PGI vialone nano rice cultivated in numerous communes of the province of Verona. Veneto.

risòle fried Carnival pastries (➤ **cenci**) filled with jam. Typical of the mountain valleys of the province of Cuneo. Piedmont.

risotto first course of *fino, superfino* (*roma, arborio, carnaroli, baldo*) or *semifino* (*vialone nano*) rice "toasted" on a base of aromatic herbs softened in butter and/or oil, and cooked with the addition, a ladelful at a time, of hot broth until the liquid has been completely absorbed and the rice has taken on a creamy consistency. The dish is of Piedmontese-Lombard origin, but is now made in virtually every region of Italy with all sorts of additions and variations.

risot cui croz dialect name for ➤ **risotto con le rane**, frog risotto.

risot menà rice "toasted" in olive oil with onions, finished with fish or vegetable broth, creamed with butter and grated Grana Padano, and garnished with deep-fried pond shrimp (➤ **saltarèl**) or, as an alternative, eel, catfish, tench and so on. A recipe typical of the province of Mantua. Lombardy.

risoto a la ciosota another name for ➤ **risoto de gô**, goby risotto.

risoto a la sbiraglia rice with pieces of chicken and, sometimes, ground veal. The meat is browned in a ➤ **soffritto** of oil, butter and herbs, bathed with white wine and cooked on a low heat in a pan covered with a lid. After about half an hour, rice is added to the pan and cooked through with the occasional addition of broth made with the chicken carcass and aromatic vegetables. A recipe typical of the province of Treviso.

risoto al tagio aka **risoto al tajo** a risotto made with two main ingredients: eels and crayfish, for example. Veneto.

risoto co le secole soft risotto with pieces of meat (➤ **secole**) onion, celery, carrot, oil and butter. Veneto.

risoto coi bruscandoli rice "toasted" in oil and butter with onion, cooked with the addition of meat broth and flavored with hops shoots (➤ **luppolo**). Veneto.

risoto coi caparossoli risotto with clams, cooked in a low, broad pan (*casso*) with fish broth and the mollusks' cooking liquid, sprinkled with chopped flat-leaved parsley and creamed with butter. Veneto.

risoto coi rovinassi a dish prepared in various areas of Veneto (Treviso, Padua, Rovigo) with rice and chicken giblets (liver, heart, stomach) cooked in the chicken's broth, sometimes aromatized with cinnamon, cloves and black pepper.

risoto col pastin another name for ➤ **risoto col tastasal**.

risoto col pessin de fosso risotto made with small fish from rice fields. Veneto.

risoto col tastasal risotto made with vialone nano rice, sausage meat, butter, onion and rosemary and sprinkled with grated Grana. A very popular dish in Verona. Veneto.

risoto de gô risotto with gobies. Rice "toasted" in oil with garlic and cooked with the gradual addition of a filtered ➤ **court-bouillon** of lagoon gobies (➤ **ghiozzo**). A specialty of Chioggia, in the province of Venice. Veneto.

risott coi borlòtt rice with beans. A risotto of rice "toasted" in olive oil and butter with onion and lardo or pancetta, red wine and borlotti beans (➤ **borlotto**). Served with butter and a generous amount of Parmigiano-Reggiano. Lombardy.

risott de Natal cunt l'inguila risotto with eel. Pieces of eel, skin on, are cooked in butter with bay leaves. Rice is added to the pan and cooks in the fish's fat. A traditional Christmas recipe. Lombardy

risott rustì rice cooked in vegetable broth and red wine to which borlotti beans

(➤ **borlotto**) are added. The finished risotto is creamed with butter and sprinkled with grated Parmigiano-Reggiano. Lombardy.

risotto al Barbera rice "toasted" in butter, bathed with Barbera red wine and finished with beef broth. A specialty of the Monferrato hills in the province of Asti (in other parts of the region they use other red wines). Piedmont.

risotto al colombaccio risotto made with pieces of wood pigeon (➤**colombaccio**), olive oil, white wine, onion, flat-leaved parsley and broth. Tuscany.

risotto al salto a risotto made with rice left over from the preparation of ➤ **risotto alla milanese**. Rice is spooned over melted butter and pressed down with the back of a wooden spoon until it develops a crisp "crust." It is then flipped over like a frittata and fried until golden on the other side. The resulting "cake" is served sprinkled with Parmigiano-Reggiano. In more recent versions, mushrooms, stewed snails and frogs (➤ **rane in guazzetto**) are added to the rice. Lombardy.

risotto alla campagnola rice, sausage, pork rind, tomatoes and beans. Typical of the province of Lodi. Lombardy.

risotto alla certosina rice, freshwater crayfish, frogs, perch or sole fillets, peas, mushrooms, tomatoes, dry white wine, olive oil and herbs. A risotto said to have been invented by the monks of the Charterhouse of Pavia. Lombardy.

risotto alla fiorentina the rice is toasted in chopped onion and butter, bathed with wine and, once the alcohol has evaporated, mixed with meat sauce, peas and broth. When it is cooked, it is blended with butter and Parmigiano. Tuscany.

risotto alla milanese the rice is toasted in a base of butter, beef marrow and meat gravy and, sometimes, chopped onion, and cooked adding beef or mixed beef and chicken broth and saffron (some people stir it in a few minutes before the rice is cooked, others at the end). The risotto is served with grated cheese (➤ **Granone Lodigiano**, ➤ **Grana Padano** or ➤ **Parmigiano-Reggiano**) and butter, which melt with the heat of the rice to create the characteristic creamy ➤ **onda**. Lombardy.

risotto alla parmigiana rice cooked in a base of onions softened in butter and meat broth. More butter and grated Parmigiano are incorporated during or at the end of the cooking process. A similar dish, known as *risotto bianco*, is made in Lombardy and Piedmont with the addition of truffles, mushrooms, chicken giblets or kidneys (and sometimes bone marrow). Emilia-Romagna, Piedmont, Lombardy.

risotto alla piemontese name applied to risotto recipes which have the following ingredients in common: ground veal, chopped sausage, chicken giblets, red wine and crushed skinned tomatoes. Typical of the province of Asti and the Langhe hills, in the province of Cuneo. Piedmont.

risotto alla pilota risotto named for the workers responsible for the *pilatura*, or husking, of the rice, a tiring job that used to be carried out by hand. The rice is boiled in water and served with ➤ **salamelle mantovane** or sausage meat (➤ **pistum**), or pond shrimp (➤ **saltarèl**), loach, frogs and fried small freshwater fish. The rice can also be served with pieces larger fish fried or boiled (in which case it is cooked in the fish broth). Lombardy.

risotto alla pitocca risotto made with chicken livers and scraps browned in olive oil with onion. Similar to the Venetian ➤

risoto a la sbiraglia, and typical of the province of Brescia. Lombardy.

risotto alla veneziana risotto, aromatized with cinnamon, of mollusks and crustaceans (clams, scallops, scampi and so on) which is given an unusual flavor by the subsequent addition of spider crab's liver. Veneto.

risotto col puntel risotto similar to ➤ **risotto alla pilota**, but which replaces ➤ **salamelle mantovane** with the juices from grilled or fried pork ribs or chops. It is spooned over the meat itself which acts as a support (*puntel*). Typical of Mantua and surrounds. Lombardy.

risotto con fagioli rice and beans. Orginally, like ➤ **risi a la canarola**, a soup of rice in bean broth. Today dried borlotti beans (➤ **borlotto**) are boiled with aromatic vegetables and a piece of pork rind, and added to rice "toasted" in oil. The cooking continues with the occasional addition of bean broth. This method is typical of the Polesine area (Veneto; but a variant exists in Friuli-Venezia Giulia in which the pork rind is replaced by sliced boiling sausage ➤ **muset**). Veneto, Friuli-Venezia Giulia.

risotto con filetti di pesce persico plain boiled rice covered with perch fillets fried in butter. Typical of the Brianza and lake areas. Lombardy.

risotto con i carciofi rice with artichoke. Wedges of artichoke are slow-cooked in minced prosciutto, flat-leaved parsley and butter. Rice is then added to the mixture and cooked with the gradual addition of meat broth. The finished dish is creamed with butter and sprinkled with grated Parmigiano and minced flat-leaved parsley. Tuscany.

risotto con i codini di maiale rice with pig's tails. A now rare dish typical of the provinces of Cremona, Mantua and Piacenza. It used to be made after the killing of the pig with the tails (or other perishable parts of the animal) parboiled and finished off in chopped prosciutto, garlic, onion, white wine and tomatoes. Lombardy, Emilia-Romagna.

risotto con la fonduta risotto made with chicken broth and served with pieces of boiled chicken covered with cheese fondue (➤ **Fonduta**). A recipe of bourgeois origin, also known as *riso con la gallina*. Piedmont.

risotto con la tinca rice with tench. A recipe found, with variants, all over the north of Italy. The fish, poached in water and vinegar, is normally filleted, and the head and bones are used to make the broth to cook the rice with. In Lombardy, they make a plain risotto with minced garlic and flat-leaved parsley and the tench broth. They then cover the rice with the fried fillets of tench (catfish, ➤ **pesce gatto**, may also be used) and garnish it with more flat-leaved parsley. In the Lake Garda area, in the province of Verona (Veneto), they boil the tench and turn it in lightly fried onion with a sprinkling of ground pepper and powdered cinnamon, sometimes adding tomato concentrate diluted in water. They then add the rice and cook it with the gradual addition of the tench broth. In the past in the houses of fisherfolk on Lake Garda, the risotto was served with the fish's innards cooked with chard.

risotto con la trota rice with trout. The trout is boiled in water aromatized with garlic, laurel leaves, wild fennel and mixed spices, then filleted, minced and turned in butter. White wine is poured over the fish, and when it has evaporated, the rice is added and cooked with the addition of the trout broth, a ladleful at a time. Veneto.

risotto con le allodole plain risotto creamed with butter and grated Parmigiano-Reggiano served with sky larks (or quails) wrapped in slices of lean pancetta, browned in butter with onions and finished with white wine and broth. Lombardy.

risotto con le folaghe rice with coot. A dish of the Po delta that makes use of a waterfowl, the coot (➤ **folaga**), now somewhat forgotten in the kitchen. The birds are skinned, cut into pieces and marinated or parboiled. They are then added to a ➤ **soffritto** of celery, carrot and shallot, bathed with white wine and, when this has evaporated, covered with tomato sauce. The rice is cooked in a separate pan with butter and broth. When ready, it is creamed with more butter, sprinkled with Parmigiano-Reggiano and served with some of the coot sauce. The rest of the sauce is served in a boat so that diners can help themselves. Emilia-Romagna, Veneto.

risotto con le rane rice with frogs. A dish typical of the rice-growing areas of northern Italy. The frogs' legs are normally boned and cooked, sometimes previously parboiled, with or without tomato, while the other parts of the bodies are crushed and used to make the broth to cook the rice with. The cooked frog meat may be added to the rice during the cooking process or at the end. In the provinces of Vercelli and Novara (Piedmont), they lightly fry the legs with herbs and add them to the rice, "toasted" in butter, splashed with white wine and cooked with the frog broth. In Lombardy there are many variations on the recipe. In the province of Milan, they boil the frogs in water aromatized with herbs and vegetables, finish them in butter with onion or shallot, then add them

to the rice cooked in their broth. In the province of Mantua, they serve frog meat cooked in tomato and spices to garnish ➤ **risotto alla pilota**. In the provinces of Pavia and Reggio Emilia (Emilia-Romagna) and in some parts of Veneto, they brown the frogs in lightly fried celery and onion, and add the hot broth and rice to obtain a sort of thick soup. In Friuli, **risot cui croz** consists of rice "toasted" in butter with finely minced onion, then bathed with white wine and frog broth. When it is ready, it is topped with frogs' legs cooked in butter with garlic, flat-leaved parsley and broth. Of the non-rice-growing regions, only Tuscany has a frog risotto (*risotto dei granocchiai*).

risotto con lo sclopit rice with bladder campion (➤ **silene rigonfia**). A very popular regional spring dish. The tips of the plant are softened in butter and oil with minced onion. The rice is added, bathed with white wine and, when this has evaporated, finished with broth. The risotto is served creamed with butter and sprinkled with grated Parmigiano and minced flat-leaved parsley. Friuli-Venezia Giulia.

risotto con radicchio risotto with strips of radicchio cooked in oil with onion and red wine. Veneto.

risotto con seppie e bietole rice with cuttlefish and chard. Cuttlefish, cleaned and cut into pieces and cooked with the chard flavored with onion and garlic. The cuttlefish's ink and the rice are then added to the pan and the mixture is first bathed with wine and, when this has evaporated, finished with fish broth. The risotto is served garnished with minced flat-leaved parsley. Tuscany.

risotto dei granocchiai another name for ➤ **risotto con le rane**, frog risotto.

risotto di anguilla eel risotto. Rice cooked in a broth made with eel carcasses, together with cooked puréed eel meat. The dish is aromatized with nutmeg and lemon zest and sprinkled with grated Parmigiano. A recipe typical of the Po delta, in the province of Ferrara. Emilia-Romagna.

risotto e trigoi rice with water chesnuts. The water chestnuts, *trigoi* in local dialect (➤ **castagna d'acqua**) are simmered for at least four hours, then turned in butter with onion and partly squashed with a fork. The resulting mixture is used to top a plain risotto (In another version, pancetta and tomato are added but tend to overpower the delicate aroma of the water chestnuts). This recipe has always been rare and is now virtually extinct due to pollution in the lakes round Mantua, whence it originated. Lombardy.

risotto mar piccolo a risotto with mussels named for the Mar Piccolo, or small sea, which part of the city of Taranto overlooks. Puglia.

risotto monzese risotto flavoured with the crumbled meat of a ➤ **luganega lombarda**, fried in butter with onion and sprinkled with grated Grana Padano. Typical of Monza and the Brianza area. Lombardy.

risotto nero "black" risotttos, made with variations, in many coastal regions, from Veneto to Tuscany, where they prepare a sauce by cutting cuttlefish into pieces, cooking them in olive oil with onion and garlic, splashing them with white wine and, when this has evaporated, flavoring with tomato sauce. When the sauce is ready, rice is added together with hot water (or ➤ **fumetto**) and the cuttlefish ink.

risotto trippato rice and tripe. The tripe is boiled and diced and turned in a ➤ **soffritto** of onion, garlic and olive oil. The rice is then added to the pot and bathed occasionally with the tripe broth until cooked al dente. The risotto is served with a generous sprinkling of grated Parmigiano and minced flat-leaved parsley. Tuscany.

risulèn o ricciolini variously shaped baked Carnival pastries made with wheat flour, yeast, sugar, white wine and ➤ **sassolino** liqueur. The same mixture is also used to make a cake. Typical of the province of Mantua and the lower Po Valley. Lombardy.

risulimiti like ➤ **curcùci**, a Calabrian term for ➤ **ciccioli**, pork scratchings.

ritortelli d'ova alle mele dessert of thin pancakes filled with a mixture of apples stewed with butter and sugar, crushed cookies, rum, cream, cinnamon and apricot jam, rolled up, dusted with sugar and baked in the oven for a few minutes. Tuscany.

roastbeef in Italian the term is used to refer to cuts of meat from the back of a bovine and a particular way of spit-or oven-roasting beef so that the crust is browned, but the meat stays pink inside. Served sliced with its deglazed juices, it often appears on restaurant menus with the French transcription *rosbif* or, especially in Tuscany, as *rosbiffe*.

roastbeef alla toscana beef sirloin boned and trimmed, flavored with minced garlic and rosemary, salt and pepper, seared in a pan, then briefly roast in the oven (the meat should be pink inside). Served sliced with an emulsion of extra virgin olive oil and the meat juices. In Tuscan they pronounce and write the name as *rosbiffe*.

roba cotta a dish now virtually extinct, very similar to ➤ **carnacotta** (Campania). It derives from the old habit of using pork offal to make tasty stews and selling them on street corners on impromptu "plates." In Umbria fig lives were used for the purpose. The dish itself consists of pig's head, intestines, trotters, tripe and tail cooked in a skillet with lardo, onion, marjoram, garlic, wild fennel and spices. Umbria.

robatà a crisper, less friable Cuneo variation on the ➤ **grissino stirato** breadstick, made by manually rolling strips of dough until they reach a length of about twelve inches. Piedmont.

robinia botanical name for ➤ **acacia**, acacia.

Robiola a fresh cheese of cow's, ewe's, goat's or variably mixed milks to be found principally in Piedmont and Lombardy. The name derives either from the village of Robbio, in the province of Pavia, where this type of cheese has been made since time immemorial, or from the Latin *ruber*, red, and its derivative, *rubeola*, a reference to the color the rind sometimes assumes on aging.

Robiola d'Alba cheese produced nowadays mostly with cow's milk in the province of Cuneo. It has a firm body that breaks cleanly when cut. Piedmont.

Robiola del bec goat's milk produced in October and November, when the nannies are in heat and produce very fat milk. Made round Acqui Terme, in the province of Alessandria, and in the same areas as ➤ **Robiola di Roccaverano**. Piedmont.

Robiola di Ceva generally homemade cow's milk cheese of the upper Val Tanaro, in the province of Cuneo. Coagulation takes place at relatively low temperatures, and the cheese matures for about 20 days, after which the rind will have a light bloom of white mold. Piedmont.

Robiola di Cocconato flat, soft white cheese with no rind and a mild, slightly acidulous flavor. Typical of the village of the same name, in the province of Asti. Piedmont.

Robiola di Mondovì another name for ➤ **Robiola di Ceva**.

Robiola di Roccaverano Italy's most historic goat's milk cheese, produced in the hills in the provinces of Asti and Alessandria. Though the PDO protocol envisages the use of as much as 85% cow's milk, the classic Slow Food presidium-sponsored version is made exclusively with raw goat's milk. The traditional technique varies little from one cheesemaker to another, but the differences between cheeses are significant. The flowers, herbs and bacterial flora of pastures and byres are transferred to the cheese, making it possible to draw a "cru map" for Robiola, almost as if it were a wine. Piedmont.

Roccaverano another name for ➤ **Robiola di Roccaverano**.

rocchini In some areas, such as the province of Arezzo and the Valdarno, the name refers to cylindrical celery fritters or patties. Celery stalks are sliced, boiled, squeezed dry, chopped finely and mixed with egg (in some recipes with meat sauce), coated in flour and fried. The fritters are served as side dish with stewed duck or chicken. According to an alternative Valdarno recipe, once fried, they are baked in the oven, covered with duck or hare sauce and liberally sprinkled with grated cheese. Tuscany.

rocciata a pastry traditionally baked during the Christmas holidays and on All Saints' Day. Remiscent of a strudel, it may have been brought to Umbria by people fleeing from central Europe following the dissolution of the Carolingian Empire. Now available all year round, it is made from a dough of wheat flour, eggs, extra virgin olive oil, sugar and white wine (or anise liqueur or rosolio) and rolled into a thin sheet.This is covered with diced fresh fruit, minced walnuts and pine kernels, sugar, cocoa and cinnamon, rolled up and formed into a horsehoe-shape.

After baking in the oven, it is sprinkled with alkermes, dusted with confectioner's sugar and, sometimes, decorated with confetti sugar (*sesimanti*). Umbria.

roccocò ring-shaped cookies made from a paste of wheat flour, chopped almonds and candied orange zest, perfumed with vanilla powder, cinnamon and ➤ **pisto napoletano** (mixed spices), and brushed with beaten eggs before being baked in the oven. Campania.

rodoleti de persuto slices of prosciutto wrapped round pickled gherkins. Eaten as a savory with aperitifs (➤ **cicheti**). Friuli- Venezia Giulia.

rofioi aka **rufioi (1)** large wheat and rye flour square ravioli, stuffed with cabbage or chard or spinach, smoked cheese, salt and pepper (in the Mocheni and Rendena valleys also with day-old bread, cheese, eggs and sultanas), boiled and served as a first course with melted butter, sage and Grana cheese or with veal sauce. A traditional mountain dish for important occasions. Trentino-Alto Adige.

rofioi (2) sweet ➤ **tortelli**, made from a dough of flour, sugar, butter, eggs and white wine, generally triangular and fried in oil or lard. The stuffing varies; in the Soave area (Verona) and the province of Vicenza, it is often made of jam (preferably, sour cherry plum or blackberry), dried fruit, honey or ➤ **mostarda**; in the southern part of the province of Verona and in the Polesine area, in the province of Rovigo, it is made of grated twice-baked bread, milk and sugar, with candied fruit, raisins and anise or chopped almonds, chocolate and rum. Veneto.

rognonata (1) term used in the province of Chieti (Abruzzo) for loin of lamb. In central and southern Italy, saddle of lamb or kid (➤ **sella**) includes the kidneys (➤ **rognone**).

rognonata (2) in the north of Italy, a transversal cut of loin of veal (➤ **lombata**), including one of the kidneys, boned, secured with string and roast in the oven.

rognone kidney. The main organ in an animal's urinary apparatus, the shape and size of which varies from species to species. Bovine kidneys are subdivided into numerous lobes; lambs' and kids' kidneys are bean-shaped; pigs' kidneys are smooth and egg-shaped; horses' kidneys, finally, are heart-shaped on the right and bean-shaped on the left. The most prized kidney in the kitchen is the calf's, while those of lamb or kid are used as ingredients in recipes such as ➤ **rognonata (1)** or ➤ **coratella**. Like all offal, kidneys should be eaten very fresh and cooked briefly.

rognone alla cacciatora calf's kidney, blanched and cut into slices, which are sautéed in oil with minced garlic and onion. Fresh mushrooms (porcini or honey) are added to the pan and the mixture is bathed with white wine or Marsala. Once this has evaporated, equal quantities of tomato sauce and meat gravy are added. The kidneys are served with their sauce, if need be thickened with a little flour. Trentino-Alto Adige, Veneto.

rognone in padella in Friuli-Venezia Giulia, kidney marinated in water and vinegar, sliced, coated with flour and cooked in butter with sage and paprika. In Trentino-Alto Adige, sliced kidney browned in butter with onion, bathed with vinegar, finished off with meat gravy and served garnished with minced flat-leaved parsley. Friuli-Venezia Giulia, Trentino-Alto Adige.

rognone in umido stewed kidney. The kidney is sliced very thinly and seared in a skillet to release its bitter internal fluids. After draining, it is cooked in white wine with chopped skinned tomatoes, and served sprinkled with finely minced flat-leaved parsley. Lazio.

rolata aka **rollata** regional terms for ➤ **rollè**, stuffed roll of veal.

rollè aka **rolata** aka **rollata** from the French **rouleau** (roll). The term refers to a sufed roll of meat, a dish typical of home cooking. It is prepared with a large slice of veal (or a flattened breast of chicken or other poultry or boned rabbit), spread with herbs or prosciutto and pancetta, frittata, vegetables or other ingredients, and rolled up. The resulting meat roll is baked in the oven and served in slices.

rombo turbot (*Psetta maxima*). A flatfish like sole (➤ **sogliola**) but larger. A fish so highly prized for its firm, white delicate flesh that it is nicknamed the "pheasant of the sea." It can be broiled or cooked in a ➤ **court-bouillon**, or skinned, boned and baked in the oven, whole or filleted, with potatoes and artichokes. The fillets are also excellent dressed with lemon juice, pepper and tarragon. The head and bones can be used to make a good fumet (**fumetto** ➤(1)) as a base for sauces and soups. Many varieties exist, one of which, the smaller *rombo liscio* or *rombetto* (known on the Adriatic as ➤ **soaso** or ➤ **suaso**, brill in English), is much used as an ingredient in fish soups and stews (➤ **brodetto**). **romice** botanical name for ➤ **lapazio**, monk's rhubarb.

ronditt (aka **runditt**) very flat scones made of flour (traditionally buckwheat), water and salt dough toasted on a hot plate and spread with butter. Typical of the Ossola valleys. Piedmont.

ronseggio Ligurian term for ➤ **murice**, murex or rock snail.

rosa cut of beef roughly equivalent to first cut round (➤ **fesa interna**).

rosa canina dog rose (*Rosa canina*). Bushy shrub with prickly branches, crenellated oval leaves and pinkish-white flowers, common in scrubland all over Italy, from the sea to the mountains. The most important part of the plant for culinary purposes is the hip, which is used to make delicious jams and preserves. Common and regional names: ➤ **rosa di macchia**, ➤ **rosa selvatica**.

rosa di Gorizia winter ➤ **radicchio** with crisp red or yellow-green leaves. Venezia Giulia.

rosa di macchia common name for ➤ **rosa canina**, dog rose.

rosa di Parma fillet of veal (or horse o pork) flattened and covered with slivers of Parmigiano and slices of prosciutto, rolled up and cooked in a reduction of wine and Marsala. Served in slices. Emilia-Romagna.

rosa selvatica another name for ➤ **rosa canina**, dog rose.

rosada aka **rosade** a custard of eggs, milk, sugar, grappa and, sometimes, crushed almonds, cooked in a bain-marie and cooled in the refrigerator. Veneto, Friuli-Venezia Giulia.

rosamarina fiery relish made with anchovy or sardine fry (➤ **novellame di pesce**), salt, wild fennel, red chili and powdered sweet chili. The mixture is put to macerate in brine in a cool place for a few days, then well stirred. It is then drained and transferred to earthenware jars (➤ **cugnitti**) and covered with olive oil. The relish may be spread on toasted bread or served with pasta. A delicacy of the province of Cosenza. Calabria.

rosas de mendula literally "almond roses." Pastry petals made with wheat flour, eggs, lard, sugar, wine (generally Malvasia), a splash of alkermes and a drop of cochineal. A little ball made of a mixture of peeled, chopped almonds and vanilla sugar is placed at the center and the pastry is brushed with alkermes and cochineal before baking. Sardinia.

rosata cake of almonds, grated lemon zest, vanilla and eggs. The mixture is spooned into a tin lined with ostias and baked in the oven at a moderate temperature. Puglia.

rosbif French spelling of ➤ **roastbeef**.

roscani all'anconetana oppositeleaf Russian thistle (see ➤ **barba di frate**) boiled, allowed to cool and served as a salad, dressed with an emulsion of oil, vinegar, pennyroyal and garlic. Typical of Ancona but popular throughout the region. Marche.

roscano (pl. **roscani**) Marche regional term for ➤ **barba di frate**, oppositeleaf Russian thistle.

roscioletti Marche term for newborn mullet. See ➤ **novellame di pesce**, fry.

roscioli aka **roscioletti** Marche and Abruzzo terms for red mullet (➤ **triglia**), a very popular fish in local gastronomic traditions. It is cooked simply, roast, stewed or in soups, or lightly marinated (without too much vinegar, which would overpower its delicate flavor). In an old, now rare, recipe from L'Aquila, mullet are lightly stewed with saffron and other ingredients. Marche, Abruzzo.

rose fritte "fried roses." A very thin sheet of egg dough, supplemented with cream and white wine, is cut into disks of varying sizes, which are shaped into petals and joined together into flowers. The "roses" are fried in lard and at the center of each is placed a candied cherry or a tiny ball of jam. Trentino-Alto Adige.

rosetta name used in other regions for equivalents of the the Milanese bread roll ➤ **michetta**. It is very popular in Venice and Verona (Veneto), where it seems to have arrived during the Austrian oc-

cupation. In Trieste (Venezia-Giulia), it is often sprinkled with sesame or poppy seeds.

rosmarino rosemary (Rosmarinus officinalis). Evergreen shrub with bright green needle-like leaves. It grows wild in coastal areas and is cultivated virtually everywhere in three main varieties: *prostratus, aureus, roseus*). In the kitchen it is noted for its versatility. Its fresh leaves are crushed in *battuti* (➤ **battuto**), its flowers in salads and risottos, and whole sprigs are used in *bouquets garnis* (➤ *mazzetto odoroso*). It is also used to aromatize oils and to flavor roasts, broils, stews and savory and sweet flatbreads. Also known, in Tuscany, as ➤ **ramerino**.

rosola common name for ➤ **papavero**, poppy.

rosolaccio common name for ➤ **papavero (1)** poppy.

rosolare to brown. To sear the outer surface of meat to seal in the juices, sometimes using a cooking fat such as oil or butter.

rosolina regional term for ➤ **papavero (1)**, poppy.

rosolio alcoholic infusion created in the 15th century for therapeutic purposes. Rose petals macerated in pure alcohol with water and honey. Thanks to its sweetness and low alcohol content, the liqueur subsequently found fortune outside Italy. Especially in France and Holland, where it became popular as a drink with desserts, occasioning the production of special cups and glasses. Today it has lost favor, though it is still produced in Piedmont.

rossal baby red mullet, fished exclusively in September, coated in flour, fried and finished off in a sauce of fresh tomatoes. Emilia-Romagna

rossella dorata another name for ➤ **russola**, russula mushroom.

rossetto (pl. **rossetti**) transparent goby (*Aphia minuta*). Tiny fish of the Gobidae family, which even when fully grown rarely exceed an inch or so in length. Eaten boiled and dressed with oil, lemon juice, garlic and flat-leaved parsley, or in fritters and molds.

Rossini, alla a term attached to a number of dishes prepared for the great composer by cooks and gastronomes, usually comprising "rich" ingredients of French cuisine, such as fillet steak, game, black truffle and foie gras. The most famous such creations are tournedos, cannelloni and poached eggs.

rosso di Chioggia a variety of ➤ **radicchio**.

rosso di Treviso a variety of ➤ **radicchio**.

rosso di Verona a variety of ➤ **radicchio**.

rosticciana lean pork ribs broiled, roast in the oven with potatoes, or cooked in the pan with oil, garlic and herbs. Tuscany.

rosticciata another name for ➤ **gröstl**, a beef dish.

rostìe Ligurian term for ➤ **caldarroste**, roast chestnuts.

rostin negàa minute steaks coated in flour, browned in butter with pancetta and herbs, and finished with white wine and broth. Often served with potato purée or ➤ **risotto alla milanese**. Lombardy.

rosumada (1) (aka **rossumata**) thick restorative drink made of beaten eggs with sugar and red wine. The wine is sometimes replaced by cold water or milk and the egg whites, whisked to a peak, may also be folded in. Lombardy.

rosumada (2) beaten eggs poured into boiling beef broth diluted with red wine. Trentino-Alto Adige.

rote aka **ruoto** terms which, in Puglia and Campania respectively, mean a round baking tin whose name, as in the case of ➤ **tiana**, ➤ **tiella**, ➤ **taeddha**, ➤ **pignata** or ➤ **pignato**, is, by extension, also used for the dish that is cooked in it (eg, ➤ **ruoto di patate**).

rotolo ripieno a sheet of egg pasta dough rolled and stuffed with a mixture of cheese, spinach, chicken giblets, sausage, ground veal and chopped liver. The roll is wrapped in canvas, boiled, cut into slices and baked in the oven dotted with butter and sprinkled with Parmigiano. Emilia-Romagna.

rottura della cagliata cutting the curd. In cheesemaking, the mechanical operation of breaking the curd in order to promote the separation and expulsion of the whey. The curd is cut with a special knife (*spino* or *lira*). Initially, the soft curd is cut into large pieces. The operation is then repeated until the granules are of the dimensions required. The lumps for fresh, soft cheeses are walnut- or hazelnut-sized, corn kernel-sized for uncooked pressed cheeses and the size of a grain of rice for cooked hard cheeses.

roux a blend of butter and flour generally used to bind white sauces.

roveja field pea (*Pisum arvense*). A small wild legume with a dark brown, reddish or dark green skin, which has been grown for centuries, first records dating back to 1545. Grown on the high slopes of the Monti Sibillini, it used to be, along with lentils, one of the staples of the local population. Though it has almost disappeared from the table, it is highly nutritious and an excellent ingredient in soups or on toasted bread. Ground into flour, it can be used to make a type of polenta (➤ **farecchiata**), which is traditionally served with anchovies. Typical of the Valnerina, in the province of Perugia, the pea is promoted by a Slow Food presidium. Umbria.

rovelline fried breaded minute steaks finished in a skillet with butter, crushed skinned tomatoes, salt, pepper, caper and lemon juice. Normally served with puréed potatoes. A specialty of Lucca. Tuscany.

roventini aka **migliaccini** (➤ **migliaccio (2)**) flat "puddings" of pig's blood, vegetable broth, flour, pepper, cinnamon, nutmeg, rosemary and lemon zest, fried and sprinkled with grated Parmigiano. A traditional dish, now almost extinct but not quite, typical of the province of Florence. Tuscany.

rovinassi Veneto term for ➤ **rigaglie**, chicken giblets.

rrashkatjel a sort of long egg *fusillo* (➤ **fusilli**), made by wrapping the pasta dough round a needle. Typical of ➤ **Arbëreshë** cooking. Calabria.

'rrustelle Abruzzo term for ➤ **arrosticini**, spit-roast lamb or mutton skewers.

'rrusti e mancia another dialect term for ➤ **arrusti e mancia**, barbecued meat or fish.

ruccul a focaccia topped with oil, garlic, oregano and chili. Basilicata.

ruchetta common name both for ➤ **rucola domestica**, rocket or arugula, and for ➤ **rucola selvatica**, perennial wallrocket.

rucola domestica rocket or arugula (*Eruca sativa*). Its aromatic, pungent leaves are used in salads mixed with tomatoes and peppers and so on, in sauces, on carpaccios (often combined with slivers of Grana cheese) and to aromatize soft cheeses.

rucola selvatica perennial wallrocket (*Diplotaxis tenuifolia*). Spontaneous or naturalized herbaceous plant used mostly in central and southern Italy. More delicate than cultivated rocket, it is eaten raw in salad but also cooked with pasta, turned with garlic and chili. In Puglia it is also used to make ➤ **pancotto** (➤ **pancotto con rucola e patate**). Common and regional names: ➤ **erba rugo**, ➤ **ricola**, ➤ **ruchetta**, ➤ **rughetta**.

rufioi aka **rufioli** alternative names for ➤ **rofioi**, large ravioli.

rughetta common name both for ➤ **rucola domestica**, rocket or arugula, and for ➤ **rucola selvatica**, perennial wallrocket.

rumine rumen. The first and largest of the four compartments that compose a ruminant's stomach (➤ **trippa**). A large sac that takes up tree quarters of the animal's abdominal cavity, its function is to collect newly ingested food. Regional names: ➤ **croce** aka **crocetta**, ➤ **pancia**, ➤ **trippa liscia**.

ruonco 'e funnale Campania term for ➤ **molva**, ling.

ruote "wheels." Durum wheat pasta of varying size whose shape is reminiscent of that of a cartwheel. Served either in broth or with tomato and meat sauces. Other names: ➤ **rotelle**, ➤ **rotelline**.

ruoto di patate layered bake of thin wedges of potato and finely sliced onions covered with slices or ripe tomato and sprinkled with olive oil, salt and aromatic herbs. The dish takes its name from the baking tin (➤ **rote** aka **ruoto**). A specialty of Naples. Campania.

ruscetti Ligurian term for transparent goby (➤ **rossetto**).

rusco regional term for ➤ **pungitopo**, butcher's broom.

russilidda Sicilian term for newborn larval sand eels or red mullet (➤ **novellame di pesce**, fry).

russola russula mushrooms. The name, derived from the Latin name for the genus, Russula, refers to various types of edible mushroom with with rounded, convex caps, often irregular edges. The flesh, white and compact, is delicate but tasty. Such mushrooms are good baked with garlic and flat-leaved parsley, or fried with other varieties. The species most used in the kitchen differ one from another for the color of their caps, which ranges from fire-red to orange (*Russola aurea*), greenish (*R. virescens*), from lilac to bluish violet and cyclamen (*R. cyanoxantha*), from greenish lilac to reddish brown (*R. vesca*). The most common names are: ➤ **colombina dorata**, ➤ **rossella dorata** (*R. aurea*); ➤ **verdone**, ➤ **colombina verde**, ➤ **ginevrina** (*R. virescens*); ➤ **brunello** (*R. vesca* and *R. cyanoxantha*).

rust dialect term for ➤ **pungitopo**, butcher's broom.

rustico (pl. **rustici**) small puff pastry pizza pie, similar to a vol-au-vent, filled with béchamel sauce, mozzarella and tomato, on sale in bakeries and bars. A specialty of the Salento peninsula (provinces of Lecce and Brindisi). The same name is also given to bread dough focaccias filled with sweet red onions and ➤ **Ricotta forte**. Puglia.

rustida another name in Lombardy for ➤ **rustisciada**, pork stew with onions.

rustida romagnola mixed fish (mainly sardines, anchovies, mackerel and baby cuttlefish on skewer, broiled on a grill, ➤ **gardela**). Emilia-Romagna.

rustisana stewed peppers or (➤ **friggione**). Recipe typical of the province of Piacenza. Emilia-Romagna.

rustisciada pork stew with onions, traditionally served with polenta. Piedmont, Lombardy.

SS

saba aka **sapa** ancient condiment made from slowly cooked, unfermented ➤ **mosto**, wine must, sometimes with the addition of lemon zest, cinnamon and cloves. The resulting sweet concentrate (used in the last century as a sugar substitute) is preserved in glass bottles. Common throughout Italy, it is still prepared in homes in Romagna (as the base for ➤ **savor**), in Sardinia, in Puglia, in Calabria (where it is known as ➤ **vincotto**), and in the central and southern Marche. Used to flavor and garnish traditional cookies and cakes, such as ➤ **pani 'e saba** and ➤ **sabadoni**, and today also as a condiment for savory dishes.

sabadoni sweet tortelloni filled with ➤ **saba**, cooked wine must, puréed beans, dried chestnuts, puréed pumpkin, quince, candied fruit, figs, pine kernels, jam, honey, raisins, and breadcrumbs. The tortelloni may be either baked, broiled, fried or boiled, then left to macerate in more wine must before serving. Emilia-Romagna.

sabbiosa cake with a soft but grainy texture made of flour, yeast, butter, sugar, and eggs. Once baked, it is dusted with confectioner's sugar. Typical of the province of Verona. Veneto.

Sachertorte chocolate cake spread with a thin layer of apricot jam, invented by the confectioners of the Sacher hotel in Vienna and popular all over the world since the 19th century. The name is protected by a registered trademark.

sacòcia breast of veal cut and shaped like a pouch or pocket (*sacòcia* in dialect), stuffed with ground veal, carrots, peas, eggs, and cheese, boiled and served cold in slices. A typically spring dish, it is traditionally served with salads of mixed leaves. A specialty of the Langhe and Monferrato districts. Piedmont.

sacripante rectangular sandwich cake, created in the 19th-century, consisting of three layers of sponge soaked in orange liqueur, filled with vanilla and chocolate cream, and coated with dark chocolate. Liguria.

sacripantina sandwich cake consisting of layers of sponge filled with egg, butter and liqueur cream. The domed surface is topped with very fine sponge crumbs. Created on the Riviera di Ponente (western Liguria) in the 19th century, it has since enjoyed popularity elsewhere. Liguria.

sagne one of the most popular pastas in the Abruzzo region. Made from durum wheat and water dough cut into broad rectangular strips and served with meat or fish sauces or in legume soups. Abruzzo.

sagne alla furese fresh lasagne served with a sauce of onion, sausage, mushrooms, green beans, tomato and grated Pecorino. Puglia.

sagne chine or **lasagne imbottite**, similar to ➤ **lasagna napoletana**. Layers of pasta, dressed when half-cooked with fried pork balls and roast boneless chops, hard-boiled eggs, mozzarella, Pecorino, Scamorza, and, when in season, mushrooms, artichokes, and peas. A recipe for special occasions. Calabria

sagne co' gliu baccalà fettuccine served with a sauce of salt cod, tomato, onion and celery. A specialty of Pisoniano, in the province of Rome. Lazio.

sagne 'ncannulate or sagne torte spiral-shaped homemade durum wheat and water pasta pasta served with mainly mixed meat sauces. Puglia, Lazio.

saiggicciott Abruzzo dialect term for ➤ salsicciotto frentano, a cured pork sausage.

saìn Friulian term for ➤ strutto, lard.

saittì Marche dialect term for ➤ peperoncino, chili.

salacca aka saracca commercial names for salted or smoked ➤ cheppia, Mediterranean shad.

salagione salting. A method of preserving fish (➤ salatura).

salam 'd turgia cured meat made with coarsely ground beef and pork fat. The mixture is cured with salt, spices, and peppercorns, and pushed into a calf's intestine. After a week's maturation in chambers (paiole), it ages for 15 to 30 days. Eaten raw or cooked. Typical of the Valli di Lanzo area. Piedmont.

salam d'la doja ancient salami of the lower Valsesia, in the provinces of Vercelli and Novara. Made from a chopped mixture of pork leg, head meat and leg trimmings, lardo or pancetta fat, cured with salt, pepper, garlic and Barbera red wine, based in a bullock's or calf's small intestine, and aged for three to 12 months covered in lard inside a doja, a large earthenware jar. Piedmont.

salam da cos slightly garlicky, spicy salami made with lean leg pork (➤ salame cremonese all'aglio). Lombardy.

salama da sugo aka salamina refined cured meat with a spicy, almost exotic flavor, made from different cuts of pork and small quantities of pig's tongue and liver flavored with salt, pepper, and red wine,

sometimes also cinnamon and cloves. It ages from six to 24 months, after which time it is boiled for six to eight hours in a linen sack hanging from a stick. Served with potato or pumpkin purée. Promoted by a Slow Food presidium. A great specialty of Ferrara. Emilia-Romagna.

salame (pl. salami) salami. Long cylindrical cured meat made with a mixture of ground lean and fat meat (usually pork), cured with herbs and cased in intestines. Aged according to factors such as type of meat mixture, thickness of the intestine and size (➤ salume, cured meat).

salame abruzzese salami made from a coarse mixture of lean and fat cuts of pork, cured with salt, pepper, salt, herbs and spices. Pressed into a natural pig's intestine, it is cylindrical in shape, and can weigh up to a couple of pounds. Commercial salamis are aged for 25-40 days, artisan salamis for 100-180 days. Abruzzo

salame affumicato di Carnia salami made with the same mixture as ➤ salsiccia affumicata di Carnia but cased in a larger intestine, smoked for 72-96 hours, and aged for about three weeks. Friuli-Venezia Giulia.

salame all'aceto fresh cured meat sliced, fried in butter and sprinkled with vinegar. Served with wet or grilled polenta or with sautéed potatoes. Friuli-Venezia Giulia.

salame aquila flat, slightly curved salami made by grinding lean and fat pork cured with salt, pepper and white wine. It is cased in an intestine and secured with string. After drying for 48-72 hours, it is pressed between wood boards or metal nets for four or five days, then aged for a month. Typical of L'Aquila but now common all over the region. Abruzzo.

salame bastardo a pork and beef salami cured with salt dissolved in red wine, peppercorns and powdered pepper. Tuscany.

salame bellunese salami once made with pork and horsemeat, today with a mixture of pork and beef (a rare horsemeat version still survives in the area round Agordo, in the Dolomites). The meat mixture, traditionally very finely grained and rather fatty, is pressed into intestines with a diameter of four inches, secured at ten- to twelve-inch intervals. Typical of the province of Belluno. Veneto.

salame brianza PDO pork salami made in the Brianza area with meat from pigs raised in Lombardy, Emilia-Romagna and Piedmont. According to size, it is aged for two weeks to five months. Lombardy.

salame casalin a salami made with coarsely ground pork produced, with variations, in the northern and southern parts of the province of Mantua. Lombardy.

salame chianino salami made with pork fillet and loin, typical of the province of Arezzo. Tuscany.

salame con lingua pork salami including whole or diced pig's tongue marinated with cloves, cinnamon, juniper berries, mace and bay leaves. Aged for two months, it is traditionally boiled and eaten on August 15, the feast of the Assumption. A specialty of the province of Mantua. Lombardy.

salame cotto (1) boiled salami made with coarsely ground cheaper cuts of pork cured with red wine, pepper, cinnamon, mint, savory and cloves. In Cavour (Turin), a rare version is made with Savoy cabbage in the mixture. Piedmont, Liguria.

salame cotto (2) boiling sausage served warm as an antipasto or hot with polenta as a main course. Typical of the province of Piacenza, Emilia-Romagna.

salame cotto di Viterbo rare salami, already popular in Roman times, made with finely ground pork cured with aromatic herbs. Lazio.

salame cremona PGI salami, said to date from the 13th century, produced in Lombardy, Emilia-Romagna, Piedmont and Veneto, with meat and fat from the large White, Landrace, Duroc breeds and hybrids thereof. Cured with salt, spices, peppercorns and crushed garlic, sometimes with the addition of white or red wine and sugar. Pressed into a natural intestine, the salami ages for at least five weeks. Lombardy.

salame cremonese all'aglio salami made with a mixture of coarsely ground lean pork, lardo and pork fat cured with salt, peppercorns, white or red wine and crushed garlic (sometimes filtered in the wine). Aged in an intestine for four to 12 months. A specialty of Cremona. Lombardy.

salame crudo raw salami. Produced with coarsely ground lean pork cured with an infusion of garlic, nutmeg and cloves, peppercorns and red wine. Piedmont.

salame d'asino donkey salami. Typical of the province of Novara, but common elsewhere in Piedmont. Made of select, finely ground donkey meat (nowadays mixed on occasion with beef) and pork fat, cured with salt, ground pepper and peppercorns, garlic, nutmeg and Barbera red wine, and pressed into a cow's intestine. After three to four days of maturation, it is aged for anything from two weeks to five months. A limited quantity of donkey salami is also produced in the province of Vicenza from the meat of the Furlana breed mixed with pancetta or lardo. In some places, the meat is macerated in red wine, cured with nutmeg, pepper and cinnamon, matured for a week, and aged for two-three months. Piedmont/Veneto.

salame d'oca di Mortara PGI salami of the Jewish tradition. A mixture of equal parts of the lean meat of geese bred and butchered in Piedmont, Lombardy, Trentino-Alto Adige, Veneto, Friuli-Venezia Giulia, Emilia-Romagna, and lean pork and pancetta. Cured with sea salt, pepper, herbs and spices, nitrites and nitrates, it is pressed into the skin of the bird's neck, back or belly, tied up with string and wrapped in a cloth. After resting for up to three days, the salami is boiled in water for an hour and served. Lombardy.

salame d'oca ecumenico raw variation of ➤ salame d'oca di Mortara, goose salami of Jewish origin. The name "ecumenical" refers to the fact that the salami can be eaten by Christians, Jews and Muslima. Lombardy.

salame d'oca friulano salami made with a mixture of coarsely ground meat from a goose's legs and wings and pork shoulder cured in salt, garlic macerated in vinegar, cloves, peppercorns and, sometimes, fennel seeds. Cased in the goose's neck or a pig's intestine, it is matured or smoked briefly and aged for one to six months. Eaten exclusively raw. Friuli.

salame d'oca giudeo artisan pure goose salami traditionally produced by the Jewish community (a rabbi is required to affix a seal of guaranteed purity). The coarsely ground or chopped breast meat and fat of a Romagnola goose cured with salt, pepper, and wine. The mixture is then pressed into the goose's neck, which is hung to dry for a few days. The salami is aged for one to five months to be ready for the Pesach holiday, the Jewish Easter. Friuli.

salame del papa another name for ➤ salame dolce).

salame del re a roll of sponge cake aromatized with grated lemon zest and filled with chocolate cream and confectioner's custard. Traditionally made for christenings. Umbria.

salame delle valli tortonesi a coarse-grained pork salami cured with sea salt, black peppercorns, powdered black pepper and an infusion of fresh garlic and red wine. Cased in a natural intestine, it is aged for three to 18 months. A Slow Food presidium is working to recover the old aging rooms. Piedmont.

salame di Agerola a salami produced in the village of the same name, in the province of Naples, with every cut of pork, bar lardo and innards, from traditionally raised pigs. Lightly smoked with chestnut, beech, oak branches bay leaves and rosemary, it is aged for three to four months. Campania.

salame di bue now rare ox meat salami sold cooked or raw, produced in the upper Po Valley, in the provinces of Cuneo and Turin. Piedmont.

salame di bue garfagnino salami made with the beef of the native Garfagnina cow breed mixed with pork. Typical of the Garfagnana area and the Valle del Serchio. Tuscany.

salame di capra spicy salami made with lean goat meat mixed with pork fat. Typical of the Val d'Ossola. Piedmont.

salame di castagne "chestnut salami." A dessert typical of mountain areas, consisting of a roll of sweet leavened pastry filled with boiled chestnuts perfumed with vanilla, dusted with sugar and baked in the oven. Piedmont.

salame di cavallo now rare salami made with ground prime horsemeat and roughly chopped pancetta. Typical of the provinces of Asti and Novara. A similar salami is also made in the provinces of Padua, Rovigo, Venice and Treviso simply cured with salt, pepper and, sometimes, garlic. Piedmont, Veneto.

salame di Chiaramonte Gulfi salami produced in the village of the same name in the province of Ragusa with trimmings of lean pork and fat from pigs raised in the wild. Sicily.

salame di cinghiale wild boar salami typical of the province of Siena. Tuscany.

salame di cioccolato another name for ➤ **salame dolce**.

salame di Fabriano ancient salami made from October to March with a mixture of coarsely ground leg and shoulder pork and diced lardo. The salamis are hung up to dry in strings of two in front of a fire, but without smoking. A Slow Food presidium promotes the product, typical of Fabriano, in the province of Ancona. Marche.

salame di Felino a salami of finely ground prime pork, ham and pancetta trimmings produced for at least two centuries in the town of the same name and the hills of the province of Parma. Emilia-Romagna.

salame di Mugnano fist-shaped smoked salami made in the village of the same name in the province of Avellino with coarsely ground pork shoulder, ham and pork fat. Campania.

salame di patate salami made with a mixture of mashed potatoes and pork flavored with garlic, nutmeg, cinnamon and cloves. After 24 hours it can be eaten fried or baked in the oven. Aged for seven to 20 days, it can be eaten raw. An ancient peasant specialty produced from October to March in the Canavese area north of Turin and the province of Biella. Piedmont.

salame di pecora salami made with mutton flavored with chili and crushed juniper berries. A specialty of the province of

Macerata and the Abruzzo national park. In Abruzzo, they add lardo and pancetta to the mixture, and smoke the salami with juniper and oak. The salami may also be preserved in oil aromatized with cumin or dill. Marche, Abruzzo.

salame di rape another name for ➤ **luganeghette di passola**, a cured meat.

salame di San Marco another name for ➤ **fellata (2)**, a cured meat.

salame di Sant'Angelo di Brolo salami produced in the village of the same name in the province of Messina with meat from naturally raised local pigs raised with natural techniques. Recently granted PGI status. Sicily.

salame di Sant'Olcese salami produced since the early 19th century in the village of the same name in the province of Genoa. The mixture consists of equal amounts of Piemontese and Bruna Alpina beef and pork and fat from heavy pigs. Cased in natural intestines, it is smoked for a few days and aged for no longer than three months. Liguria.

salame di Varzi coarse-grained PDO salami made from the fresh pork of pigs raised in the Lomellina district or in the provinces of Alessandria and Piacenza. According to size, it ages for anything from 45 days to six months and more. Piedmont, Lombardy, Emilia-Romagna.

salame dolce "salami"-shaped dessert made by mixing softened butter, sugar, sweet and bitter cocoa, egg yolks, crushed dry cookies and a drop of liqueur, refrigerated and cut into slices. It is made all over Piedmont, Veneto and Emilia-Romagna, and ingredients vary from place to place. Names include: ➤ **dolce salame,** ➤ **salame di cioccolato,** ➤ **salame del papa,** ➤ **salame moro**. In Tuscany, ➤ **gattò aretino** and ➤ **tronco** are close relatives.

salame fiorettino salame, typical of the

Apennines in the province of Reggio Emilia, named for the way in which it is tied up, which makes it look like a little flower (*fiorettino*). Made with a mixture of coarsely ground prime cuts of pork and diced lardo, it is cured with salt, cinnamon, cloves, nutmeg, pepper and a infusion of crushed garlic in white wine. Emilia-Romagna.

salame friulano salami produced throughout the region from a mixture of coarsely ground pork leg, fillet, chop, lardo and belly cuttings, cured with salt, pepper and, sometimes, crushed garlic, and macerated on red and white wine. Cased in a natural intestine, it is aged for at least two months. Friuli.

salame gentile salami named for the part of the intestine in which it is cased (➤ **budello gentile**, large intestine). The lean part of the mixture is made of prime pork and the cure consists of salt, whole or crushed peppercorns, crushed garlic and wine. Aged for three months, it is a specialty of Parma, where it has been made since the 13ᵗʰ century. Emilia-Romagna

salame lardellato salami of pork loin and shoulder ground and mixed with diced lardo, cured with sea salt, powdered black pepper and peppercorns, and cased and pressed in the large intestine. After brief smoking, the salami is aged for at least two months. Marche.

salame milano salami produced almost exclusively at industrial level in the province of Milan and the Brianza area. Ground lean beef and pork and pork fat are cured with salt, pepper, natural aromas, white wine, spices and, sometimes, crushed or macerated garlic. In Codogno, in the province of Lodi, they sometimes add a small amount of pig's blood. Cased in a natural intestine, the salami is ready for the table after 10-15 days, whereas artisan versions are aged for three to six months. Lombardy.

salame moro Venetian name for ➤ **salame dolce**, a dessert.

salame napoli a salami made with finely ground veal and coarsely ground pork, now produced in limited quantities. Campania.

salame pappone another name for ➤ **buffa**, a rare Sicilian salami.

salame piacentino PDO salami made with meat from pigs on farms in Emilia-Romagna and Lombardy authorized for the production of ➤ **prosciutto di Parma**. Emilia-Romagna.

salame prosciuttato di Ghivizzano salami made with cuts of pork normally used to make ham, and in the past reserved for important occasions. Produced in the Valle del Serchio and the Garfagnana area (Lucca). Tuscany.

salame toscano pork salami produced all over the region. Tuscany.

salamella small cured meat made of ground pork and/or beef. Broiled or barbecued, it is popular in a number of Italian regions.

salamella di fegato another name for ➤ **fegatino (2)**, a cured meat.

salamella di Mantova traditional salami made of finely ground pork scraps cured with salt, ground pepper, crushed garlic, and wine. The mixture is pushed into a natural intestine with a diameter of a couple of inches and twisted into small "sausages" of three to four inches in length. Eaten within a fortnight of production. A specialty of Mantua. Lombardy.

salamella di tratturo an Abruzzo name for ➤ **salame di pecora**.

salamina an alternative name for ➤ **salama da sugo**.

salamino cotto di Siena an ancient boiled salami now produced by only a few Sienese pork butchers. Boned pork shoulder, lean beef, pancetta and diced pork fat are cured with salt, pepper and garlic. The mixture is cased in a natural calf's intestine and tied up with string. The salami is aged for a few days, then boiled in water and eaten fresh. Tuscany.

salamino italiano alla cacciatora small salami produced virtually all over Italy. Those made in Piedmont, Lombardy, Veneto, Friuli, Emilia-Romagna, Tuscany, Umbria, Marche, Lazio, Abruzzo, and Molise have PDO recognition. The name was invented in the 19th century, and refers to the fact that hunters enjoyed the salami for breakfast (*cacciatore* means "hunter" in Italian). The mixture consists of pork, pork fat, salt, pepper, garlic, wine, sugar, milk or caseinate, sodium and potassium nitrate, and ascorbic acid may be added. Pressed into a natural or artificial intestine, it is aged for a few weeks.

salamoia, in method of pickling and preserving fish, olives and some cuts of pork in a concentrated salt and water solution.

salamoia bolognese a blend of sea salt and finely minced rosemary, sage and garlic.

salamora di Belvedere an aromatic oil made in the fall in Belvedere Ostrense (Ancona) by macerating the green parts of wild fennel, orange zest and garlic clove in new oil.

salatino (pl. **salatini**) a small savory nibble made with puff pastry in various shapes with various flavorings (cheese, anchovy fillets, olives, peppers, sausage and so on). Served with aperitifs.

salatura salting. An ancient method of preserving foods based on the antiseptic properties of salt and its capacity to absorb humidity. Foods may be dry-salt-ed, steeped in brine (➤ **salamoia**) or first dry-salted, then steeped in brine.

salaturu mixed sweet peppers, pressed olives, green tomatoes and eggplants flavored with wild fennel and chili and preserved in an earthenware jar. Calabria.

sale salt.

sale, al term to describe the baking of meat and large fish in a salt crust.

sale marino artigianale di Cervia artisan sea salt. The salt pans of Cervia, in the province of Cesena-Forlì have been exploited since Roman times. The small Camillone pan still produces salt with trditional methods and is protected by a Slow Food presidium. Emilia-Romagna.

sale marino artigianale di Trapani artisan sea salt. The salt pans of Trapani, Paceco and Marsala are protected by a Slow Food presidium. The salt, produced by evaporating sea water is collected by hand and piled up in pyramids in natural tanks dug into the ground. Sicily.

salicornia aka **asparago di mare** samphire (*Salicornia europaea/fruticosa/ veneta*). A genus of about 30 species of wild plants that grow in brackish water. On the Puglia coast they preserve the fleshy leaves in oil (➤ **savezudde sott'ogghie**). Elsewhere, the culinary potential is only now beginning to be realized.

Salignon aka **Salignoun** aka **Sargnun** tangy, lightly smoked cow's milk ricotta aromatized with salt and paprika. It comes from the Germanic dairy tradition of the Walser people who have lived in the valleys of the Monte Rosa, on the border between Val d'Aosta and Piedmont, since the Middle Ages. Val d'Aosta, Piedmont.

salimbecco soup of day-old bread smothered with bean broth. Today the dish is enriched with whole beans, extra virgin olive oil and ground black pepper. Tuscany.

salmerino char. A much prized member of the salmon family. Two species live in the north of Italy: the Arctic char (*Salvelinus alpinus*) and the smaller brook char (*Salmerino fontinalis*). The second is also farmed ➤ **salmerino del Corno alle Scale**). Smaller char can be cooked like trout (➤ **trota**), larger ones lik salmon (➤ **salmone**).

salmerino del Corno alle Scale brook char farmed in spring water on natural feed in a small park in the Apennines, in the province of Bologna. Protected by a Slow Food presidium. Emilia-Romagna.

salmerino in carpione fillets of char coated in flour, fried in oil and marinated in a boiling mixture of vinegar, aromatic white wine, water, oil, sliced onion, capers, bay leaf and pepper. Trentino-Alto Adige.

salmì, in technique, common in parts of northern and central Italy, for stewing meat, usually game, by cooking in wine (sometimes with the addition of broth), usually after marinating (➤ **marinatura**). The cooking gravy is then puréed and served as a sauce.

salmis French term from which the Italian ➤ **salmì** derives.

salmistrare to corn. Ancient preservation technique, originally used for fish, now for meat, especially tongue, whereby the food is salted and steeped in brine.

salmistrino rare preserve made of small air-dried eels. A specialty of Comacchio (Ravenna) Emilia-Romagna.

salmone salmon (*Salmo salar*). Fish of great gastronomic prestige for its soft, firm flesh. Sold fresh, canned or smoked.

salmoriglio sauce of oil, warm water, lemon juice, garlic, salt, pepper, minced parsley and fresh oregano typical of the south of Italy (especially Sicily and Calabria), generally served with roast fish.

salmuerie preserving liquid of salt, milk and high-fat cream, capable, if made properly, of keeping for centuries. Friuli-Venezia Giulia.

salosso regional term for ➤ **consolida maggiore**, common comfrey.

salòt brioche dough roll filled with apricot jam, candied citron and sultanas. Traditionally baked for the Epiphany. Typical of Bra (Cuneo). Piedmont.

salsa a la sangeuannidde aka **sangiovannino** sauce of tomato, anchovies, black olives, capers, garlic, parsley, chili and extra virgin olive oil served with various types of long pasta. Typical of Bari, Puglia.

salsa agrodolce alla parmigiana a sauce of oil, parsley, garlic, tomato, sugar and aromatic vinegar served with boiled meats. Typical of the province of Parma, but now common throughout the region. Emilia-Romagna.

salsa agrodolce di fegato di coniglio sauce made by crushing rabbit's liver, salted anchovies, crumbly savory biscuits, onion, celery, lemon zest and cloves and simmering the mixture in oil, water, vinegar and sugar. Served with roast or stewed rabbit. Trentino-Alto Adige.

salsa al limone lemon sauce. Lemon juice boiled with a mixture of melted butter, Malvasia wine, raisins, pepper, cinnamon and nutmeg. A sauce served with game. Friuli-Venezia Giulia.

salsa all'acciuga anchovy sauce served with boiled or roast meats. Veneto, Friuli-Venezia Giulia.

salsa allemande allemande sauce. A sauce based on velouté (➤ **vellutata**) but thickened with egg yolks and butter. One of the basic sauces (➤ **salse base**) of French cuisine. Also known as sauce parisienne.

salsa bastarda butter sauce served with fish and vegetables.

salsa bercy French sauce made with shallots, white wine and cream served with boiled crustaceans and fish.

salsa bernese French herb sauce (tarragon, chervil, peppercorns) served with broiled red meats.

salsa calabra sauce made of onion, garlic, lard, tomato, basil, chili and prosciutto. Served with pasta and boiled meats. Calabria.

salsa demi-glace one of the French basic sauces (➤ **salse base**) made by reducing sauce espagnole (➤ **salsa spagnola**) with the addition of meat stock and wine (usually Madeira).

salsa di cipolle onions roasted in the oven, sliced and cooked in butter with breadcrumbs, vinegar, bay leaves, cloves, capers and broth, pushed through a sieve and served hot or warm. Trentino-Alto Adige.

salsa di corniole cornelian cherry sauce served with boiled meats. Marche, Lombardy.

salsa di cren horseradish sauce served with boiled or roast beef and pork.

salsa di dragoncello tarragon sauce served with boiled meats and fish. A specialty of Siena. Tuscany.

salsa di noci crushed walnut sauce flavored with marjoram, traditionally served with ➤ **pansoti**, a type of pasta. Liguria.

salsa di pomodoro tomato sauce. One of the French mother sauces (➤ **salse madri**), fundamental for the preparation of others. Many variations exist, but the main ingredients are skinned tomatoes, oil, garlic and minced garlic.

salsa di senape mustard sauce served with boiled meats, especially pork. Friuli-Venezia Giulia,

salsa genovese cold sauce for fish made by blending crushed pistachio nuts and pine kernels with béchamel sauce, egg yolks, oil, lemon juice and herbs. Liguria.

salsa olandese hollandaise sauce.

salsa parigina another name for ➤ see **salsa allemande**, allemande sauce.

salsa ravigotta sauce ravigote. Versatile emulsion of oil, vinegar, salt, pepper and finely minced capers, onion, parsley and chives.

salsa san Bernardo sweet and sour sauce made by amalgamating breadcrumbs, chopped toasted almonds, desalted anchovies, sugar, bitter cocoa, water and vinegar in a bain-marie to a smooth, creamy consistency. Said to have originated in the island's monasteries and convents, it is served with boiled vegetables and meat and ➤ **caponata**. Sicily.

salsa spagnola sauce espagnole. One of the ➤ **salse madri** from which many others derive. The preparation is long and laborious and consists of blending meat stock, roux, carrots, onions, chopped ham and tomato paste, filtering the resulting sauce and further reducing it.

salsa suprême French sauce made by blending velouté (➤ **salsa vellutata**) with chicken and mushroom stock, cream and butter.

salsa tartara tartare sauce. Cold sauce made by mixing hard-boiled egg yolks, salt, white pepper, oil, mustard and finely chopped chives.

salsa tredura sauce of Medieval origin made by mixing eggs, ginger, saffron, bay leaves, Pecrino cheese and honey. Typical of the province of Viterbo, it is served with roast red meats. Lazio.

salsa vellutata aka **salsa bianca** velouté. One of the French mother sauces (➤ **salse madri**). A blend of roux, veal stock and flour. An alternative version is made with fish fumet in lieu of stock.

salsa verde "green sauce." Common in many Italian regions, especially those with a tradition of ➤ **bollito misto**, mixed boiled meats, for which it is a classic accompaniment. Most recipes consist of blending a generous amount of minced parsley with garlic, chopped hard-boiled egg yolks, fresh breadcrumbs soaked in vinegar, salt, pepper and oil. In Emilia -Romagna (*sälsa ad savur*, typical of the province of Piacenza), in Tuscany and in Piedmont (➤ **bagnet verd**), they add capers and anchovy fillets. In Bologna, finally, they add chopped pickled onions and, sometimes, pine kernels and a boiled potato as a thickener.

salsare to sauce, to cover a dish with sauce.

salsarella regional term for ➤ **acetosa**, sorrel.

salse base basic sauces. French cuisine recognizes three basic sauces: ➤ **salsa demiglace**, which derives directly from sauce espagnole (➤ **salsa spagnola**), allemande sauce (➤ **salsa allemande**) and suprême sauce ➤ (**salsa supreme**). The latter two derive from velouté (➤ **salsa vellutata**).

salse madri mother sauces. French cuisine recognizes four mother sources from which all other warm sauces derive.

salsefica common name for ➤ **barba di becco**, salsify.

salsiccia sausage. In Italy, usually made with pork, variously flavored, eaten fresh and cooked or aged and raw.

salsiccia affumicata di Carnia smoked pork sausage typical of the Carnia area, in the province of Udine. Friuli-Venezia Giulia.

salsiccia alla Barbera pork sausage browned in oil with herbs and finished off with Barbra red wine. Piedmont.

salisccia cragno a smoked beef and pork sausage of Slovenian origin, typical of Trieste. Its name is the Italianization of Krainer, the region which it comes from. Served hot with mustard and grated horseradish. Friuli-Venezia Giulia

salsiccia di Bra unique sausage of finely ground veal cured with sea salt, white pepper, nutmeg, cinnamon and mace, sometimes enriched with garlic, fennel, leeks, cheese (Parmigiano, mature Robiola or Toma), and wine, is pressed into a small ram's intestine. Eaten fresh raw, or, more rarely, broiled. Bra. Piedmont.

salsiccia di Calabria PDO sausage produced with pork from pigs born and/or raised in the region cured with spices and herbs, pressed into a pig's intestine, weaved into a characteristic chain shape, left to rest for a few hours, and aged for at least 30 days.

salsiccia di Cancellara one of the most popular varieties of ➤ **lucanica** sausage. Cheap cuts of pork from locally raised pigs are hand-ground and cured with salt, fennel seeds and lard mixed with chili. The mixture is cased in natural intestines in strings of sausages each about 12 inches long. The sausages are matured for a few days and aged for a month or so, though reserved in oil or lard, they can be kept for up to a year. Produced in winter in the town of Cancellara, in the province of Potenza. Basilicata.

salsiccia di castrato very fine-grained sausage made from a mixture of castrated lamb (➤ **castrato**), beef and, sometimes, pork (one only lamb was used), salt, ground pepper, a few spices, a little crushed garlic and lamb broth. Cased and linked in rings (*sercòi*), the sausage is boiled in water and eaten immediately. Produced from July to October in the Valcamonica, in the province of Brescia. Lombardy.

salsiccia di Castro dei Volsci pork sausage flavored with orange zest produced in the village of the same name in the province of Frosinone. May be eaten fresh or preserved in oil. Lazio.

salsiccia di cinghiale wild boar sausage sometimes flavored with Chianti. Tuscany.

salsiccia di fegato liver sausage. Ancient sausage made with pig's liver flavored with wild fennel, pepper and orange zest. May be eaten fresh grilled or broiled or, aged for a month, raw. It may also be preserved in oil. Lazio, Abruzzo, Molise.

salsiccia di Lecce veal and pork sausage cured with salt, pepper and white wine. Puglia.

salsiccia di Mola di Bari extremely rare pork and veal sausage. The cure may include garlic and mozzarella, or grated cheese, or stewed mushrooms. Puglia.

salsiccia di Monte San Biagio lightly smoked linked sausage made with all the lean parts of the pig, cheek bacon (➤ **guanciale**), lardo, and pancetta cured with chili, red pepper, coriander, sea salt and Moscato di Terracina. Aged in old shepherds' huts, it may be preserved in suet or extra virgin olive oil. Typical of the province of Latina, Lazio.

salsiccia di patate ancient salami made with mashed potatoes and boiled pig's tripe and raw tongue. Eaten cooked. Marche.

salsiccia di pecora mutton sausage, a variation on ➤ **salame di pecora**. Marche, Abruzzo.

salsiccia di polmone lung sausage. Produced all over the region with mixed offal (lung, spleen, blood, heart, liver, kidneys). Unsuitable for aging, it is either eaten raw or used as an ingredient in numerous recipes (A similar sausage exists in Puglia flavored with garlic). Campania.

salsiccia lucana another name for ➤ lucanica.

salsiccia (1) rare cured meat still to be found in hilly and mountain areas. The mixture is made of pig's offal and blood and flavored with salt, pepper, garlic,

nutmeg and orange zest. Usually eaten barbecued. Marche.

salsiccia (2) another name for ➤ **ciavàr**, a type of sausage.

salsiccia pasqualora ancient fiery pork sausage, typical of the provinces of Trapani and Enna but made all over the island. Traditionally made at Easter, hence its name (*Pasqua* means Easter). Linked on strings or palm leaf strips. Eaten raw or barbecued. Eaten raw or barbecued. Sicily.

salsiccia rossa di Castelpoto pork sausage made in the village of the same name in the province of Benevento. Campania.

salsiccia stagionata di Minervino Murge sausage made with hand-diced prosciutto and pork shoulder and belly. In the past it was preserved in terra cotta jars with suet. Typical of the province of Bari. Puglia.

salsicciotto di Guilmi sausage made with hand-chopped lean pork loin, aged in fat or oil or fat for five months. A veritable symbol of the region. Abruzzo.

salsicciotto di Pennapiedimonte pork sausage, typical of the village of the same name in the province of Chieti, covered with a batter of pork fat, salt, ground black pepper, thyme, juniper berries, rosemary, bay leaves, chives, chili, fennel and sage.

salsicciotto frentano handmade pork sausage aged in glass jars with olive oil or lard. Produced since the 16th century, it is typical of the Valle del Sangro and the Aventino area. Abruzzo.

salsola botanical name for ➤ **barba di frate**, oppositeleaf Russian thistle.

saltare to sauté.

saltarèl aka **saltarei**, in standard Italian aka **saltarelli** pond shrimp (*Palaemonetes antennarius*). Tiny shrimp (➤ **gamberetto**), excellent fried and in sauces. Common in Lombardy and Veneto.

Saltarello fresh ➤ **Latteria** cheese attacked in the late spring by cheese flies. During three months of maturation in cellars, it turns into a very strong creamy paste crawling with white worms. Produced for self-consumption in Socchieve (Udine) and other villages in the Carnia area. Friuli-Venezia Giulia.

saltasö dialect term for ➤ **gale**, fried pastries.

saltimbocca alla romana thin slices of veal spread with ham and sage, secured with cocktail sticks and gently fried. Lazio.

saltzstanghel long bread roll made with the same dough as ➤ **bretzel** and scattered with salt and cumin seeds. Trentino-Alto Adige.

salume cured meat. Italian cured meats can be divided into two categories: those made with whole body parts, generally of pigs but not only, such as prosciutto, coppa, pancetta and culatello, and those made with ground meat, mainly pork but not only, preserved with salt and aromatized with spices, such as mortadella, sausage, salami, zampone and so on. Pigs have lived in the Mediterranean since the 3rd millennium BC, and their meat has always been a staple in the peasant diet. It was the need to preserve the meat that led to the development of drying, smoking and salting techniques. In northern Italy, where they began to be bred on farms in the 12th century, pigs tended to be fatter than those of the center and south, where they continued to be raised in the wild. In the days of sharecropping, peasant families were allowed only one pig a year, so learned to exploit every part of the animal, blood included. Italy is the European country with the most PDO and PGI cured meats, respectively 20 and nine. Most native Italian pig breeds are now extinct, but attempts have recently been made to recover some of them (➤ **Cinta Senese**, ➤ **Mora Romagnola**).

Salva cow's milk cheese produced in much the same way as ➤ **Quartirolo** in the Franciacorta area (Brescia) and some communes in the provinces of Bergamo and Cremona. Lombardy.

salvastrella small burnet (*Sanguisorba minor*). Aromatic herb whose cucumber-flavored leaves are used in central Italy in mixed salads (➤ **misticanze**). Common and regional names: ➤ **erba spezia**, ➤ **erba stella**, ➤ **meloncello**, ➤ **pimpinella**.

salvia sage (*Salvia officinalis*). Grows wild in the Mediterranean and its ornamental and aromatic varieties are cultivated all over Italy. It is used to perfume butter to serve with pasta and to flavor a number of meat dishes. Broad-leaved varieties are fried in batter and served with aperitifs. Common and regional names: **erba sacra**, **erba savia**.

salvia di Gerusalemme regional name for ➤ **polmonaria**, common lungwort.

salvia fritta sage leaves dipped in batter and deep-fried in olive oil, in Tuscany flavored with anchovy. Often an ingredient in ➤ **fritto misto alla toscana**.

salviade aka **surîs** ("little mice"). Sage leaves dipped in a creamy sweet batter, fried in lard or butter and dusted with confectioner's sugar. Friuli-Venezia Giulia.

sambuca liqueur of the ➤ **anicione** (aniseed) family. Produced mainly in the provinces of Roma and Viterbo (Lazio), but also, with variations, in other regions. Made with the aromatic oils of dill, star anise and ➤ **fiori di sambuco** (elderflowers), hence its name. Used to flavor cocktails and confectionery and to lace coffee.

sambuco elder (*Sambucus nigra*). Shrub common on fallow ground up to an altitude of 4,000 feet. Its flowers are fried in batter and its drupes used to make jams and syrups.

sambudello typical of the Romagna Apennines, a variation on the ➤ **sanbudello casentinese** sausage. Emilia-Romagna.

sammartina shortcrust pastry tart filled with walnuts, almonds, raisins and cooked wine must, and covered with colored confetti sugar. Calabria.

sammartinelli another name for ➤ **biscotti di san Martino**.

sampietro John Dory (*Zeus faber*). Sea fish with tasty white flesh. Cooked in the same way as sole (➤ **sogliola**) and turbot (➤ **rombo**) and in soups. Common and regional names: **pesce cetra, pesce gallo**.

San sté recently invented name for an ancient cow's milk cheese produced at the dairy in Val d'Aveto, in the province of Genoa. Liguria.

sanapo dialect term for ➤ **senape selvatica**, wild mustard.

sanato in Piedmont and Veneto, a calf whose weaning is delayed by supplementing its diet with pasta and eggs to produce pale, tender tasty veal. In intensive breeding, the word means a calf fed not on its mother's milk but on regenerated powdered milk.

sanbudello casentinese small pork offal sausage made in the Casentino area. Eaten grilled or raw after a few weeks' aging. Tuscany.

sanc brugnì name given to the ➤ **brigaldo** blood sausage on the Brescia side of Lake Garda. Lombardy.

sancelli pudding of pig's blood, ricotta, walnuts grated Pecorino and breadcrumbs, usually served warm. A sweet version with chocolate, dried fruit and spices is made with lamb's or kid's blood. Sicily.

sancrao aka **sancrò** Piedmontese version of sauerkraut (➤ **crauti**), typical of the Mon-ferrato hills, flavored with anchovies. Piedmont.

sandomenico a variation on the ➤ **ministeriale**, a filled chocolate medallion.

sandra another name for ➤ **lucioperca**, zander or pike-perch.

sangiorgino regional term ➤ **prugnolo**, mousseron mushroom.

sangue blood. Though its use is now legally restricted, pig's blood in particular is an ingredient in both savory and sweet recipes: ➤ **boudin, biroldo, buristo, mallegato, marzapane (2)**, ➤ **sanguinaccio**.

sangue, al (of roast meat and steaks) rare.

sanguetto an old rural recipe in which the innards of fowl are pressed together with the birds' blood and cooked in oil with garlic, rosemary, sage, chili and tomatoes. Umbria.

sanguin Ligurian dialect word for **sanguinello**, saffron milk-cap mushroom.

sanguinaccio blood sausage or pudding. Name used for various savory and sweet recipes made with filtered (usually pig's) blood. In the north, the term generally refers to cured meats (➤ **biroldo**, ➤ **boudin**, ➤ **brigaldo**, ➤ **brôd, brusto**, ➤ **buristo senese**, ➤ **mallegato**, ➤ **marzapane (2)**, ➤ **mustardela delle valli valdesi**), in the south to thick, creamy "puddings," flavored with sugar, chocolate, dried fruit and spices. In some regions, such as Emilia-Romagna, Marche and Abruzzo) the term ➤ **migliaccio** is used more frequently.

sanguinello (pl. **sanguinelli**) saffron milkcap (*Lactarius deliciosus*). Mushroom with a characteristic red-orange cap which, when cut, releases a milky fluid. Eaten since antiquity, it is normally fried or sautéed, often accompanied by strong sauces and spices. In Liguria, it is also stuffed (➤ **sanguinelli ripieni al forno**). Common and dialect names: ➤ **lattaiolo**,

→ **pennecciola**, → **fungo del sangue**, → **agarico delizioso**, → **lapacendro buono**, → **sanguin**, → **trun**, → **tarun russ.**

sanguinelli ripieni saffron milk-cap mushroom stuffed with a mixture of their own chopped stalks, bread soaked in milk, egg, oil, grated grana, and, sometimes, → **bruzzu**, fermented sheep's milk ricotta, placed on a bed of sliced potatoes, and baked in the oven. Liguria.

sangusu Sicilian dialect term for → **tambarello**, frigate tuna.

sansa residues (skins, flesh, and stones) from the pressing of olives.

santarosa another name for → **sfogliatelle**, a cake.

santoreggia summer savory (*Satureja hortensis*). A cultivated aromatic herb used fresh or dried with fish and legumes. Common and regional names: → **erba cerea**, → **erba pepe**, → **peperna**, → **timo dritto**.

sanvigilini small baked cakes named for San Vigilio, a resort on Lake Garda (Verona). Veneto.

saor (aka **savor**) traditional marinade for vegetables, fish, and meat made with onions softened in oil, wine, and vinegar. In Venice, they also add pine kernels, raisins and, sometimes, lemon zest and candied fruit, for a sweet and sour effect. The fish, meat or vegetables are fried and layered in an earthenware pot with the onions and their hot cooking liquid. The pot is then covered and left in a cool place for two days. This type of marinade is particularly suitable for sardines, anchovies, shad, mackerel and the like, and vegetables such as pumpkin, eggplant, and radicchio. Veneto.

saorina sauce made with cooked wine must, used as a filling for tortelli and cakes and as an accompaniment to boiled meats. Diluted with water in summer, it becomes a refreshing drink. Lombardy.

saossa d'avije sauce of honey (*avija* means "bee" in dialect), crushed walnuts and powdered mustard, served with boiled meats. Piedmont.

saoucesse aka **saouseusse** sausage of beef, lardo and spices, which used to be preserved in lard. Val d'Aosta.

sapa another word for → **saba**, cooked wine must.

sapa di fichi d'India confection obtained by slowly boiling prickly pear pulp and juice, filtering through a jute canvas to eliminate the seeds, and further cooking with the addition of orange zest and wild fennel. When the juice is reduced by about a fifth, it is left to cool and stored in glass bottles. Used to flavor traditional cakes. Sardinia.

sapajean a sort of → **zabaglione** made with eggs, vintage red wine, sugar and lemon juice. Served with shortcrust pastries and dried cookies. A specialty of Milan. Lombardy.

sapienze another name for the central and southern Italian Christmas cookies → **susamielli** and → **sciuscelle (2)**.

saponina common name for → **valeriana rossa**, red valerian.

saporiglio another name for → **suffritte**, an offal dish.

saporita a commercial blend of mixed spices made by the Bertolini. Much used in home cooking until the 1970s to flavor roasts and stews.

saraca ara cinnara herring cooked in hot ash. Calabria.

saracca another name for → **salacca**, Mediterranean shad.

saraco dialect term for → **sarago**, bream.

saracu impiriali Sicilian term for → **pesce castagna**, pomfret.

saraghina another name for → **papalina) (1)**, brisling, a small fish.

sarago bream (*Diplodus sargus*, *D. vulgaris*).

A sea fish of the Sparidae cooked in the same ways as sea bream (→ **orata**), especially broiled and baked. Smaller specimens go into soups. Common and regional names: → **saraco**, → **sargo**, → **sparo**.

sarago bastardo regional term for → **tanuta**, black sea bream.

saras another name for → **seirass**, Piedmontese ricotta.

saras del fen ricotta made with cow's, ewe's and goat's milk whey, matured in hay for no longer than four months. Piedmont.

sarda sardine (*Sardina pilchardus sardina*). A member of the → **pesce azzurro** category of sea fish. Known as **sarda**, → **sardela** or → **sardella** when prepared fresh, → **sardina** when preserved in oil. Cooked in the same ways as anchovy (→ **acciuga**).

sarda papalina another name for → **papalina**, brisling, a small fish.

Sarda, razza native island sheep breed (→ **agnello di Sardegna** is recognized as PGI), now common also on the mainland. Mainly reared for its milk. Sardinia.

sarde a beccafico sardines slit open, boned and decapitated and stuffed with combinations of ingredients such as breadcrumbs, raisins, capers, pine kernels and so on, rolled up and baked or fried. The word *beccafico* means garden warbler and the rolls are so named because they supposedly resemble the bird. Sicily.

sarde alla cetrarese aka **sarde alla maniera di Cetraro** sardines baked with olive oil and oregano. Cetraro is a town in the province of Cosenza. Calabria.

sarde alla napoletana baked sardines with tomato, basil and oil. Campania.

sarde allinguate sardines slit open, coated in flour and fried. Sicily.

sarde farcite sardines stuffed with egg, grated Pecorino and minced parsley and garlic, dipped in egg and flour, and fried. A specialty of Bari. Puglia.

sarde in saor fried sardines preserved in → **saor**, a marinade. Veneto.

sarde incinte in agrodolce boned sardines marinated in vinegar, stuffed with garlic, parsley, pine kernels, breadcrumbs and raisins softened in orange juice, sprinkled with oil and lemon juice, and baked in the oven. Veneto.

sarde ripiene stuffed sardines. A common dish made in different variations and with different names all round the Italian coast.

sardela Veneto term for → **acciuga**, anchovy, and → **sarda**, sardine.

sardele col pien sardines stuffed with breadcrumbs, grated cheese, parsley and garlic, and baked in the oven. Veneto, Friuli-Venezia Giulia.

sardele in sesame sardines marinated in a mixture of herbs and spices. Friuli-Venezia Giulia.

sardella (1) a spreadable paste of newborn sardines, red pepper and wild fennel. Calabria.

sardella (2) another name for → **sarda**, sardine and, in Veneto, for → **agone**, freshwater sardine.

sardena Veneto term for → **agone**, freshwater sardine.

sardenaira baked Ligurian pizza, a close relative of the *pissaladière* of Provence, topped with tomato, onion, sardines, olives, garlic, oil and oregano. Other names: → **pisciadela**, → **pisciarà**, → **piscialandrea**, → **pizzalandrea**, → **machettera**, → **machetusa**). Liguria.

sardene en consa freshwater sardines put in brine, sun-dried and preserved in glass jars with extra virgin oil, garlic and bay leaves. Typical of the Lake Garda area (Verona). Veneto.

sardina another word for → **sarda**, sardine.

Sardo Modicana hardy red cow breed with black horns, protected by a Slow Food presidium. Created in the late 19th century from a cross between local Podolica cows and Modicana bulls from Ragusa in Sicily. The cattle live in the wild in the Montiferru area, in the province of Oristano, and yield excellent milk and meat. Sardinia.

sardòn term used in Veneto and Friuli-Venezia Giulia for ► **acciuga**, anchovy.

sardone term used in Romagna for ► **acciuga**, anchovy.

sardoni all'agro anchovies baked in the oven with oil, capers and lemon juice. Venezia Giulia.

sardoni in savor fried anchovies preserved in a marinade of oil, vinegar and onion (► **saor**). Friuli-Venezia Giulia.

sardoni in tegame anchovies fried in olive oil olive, garlic, vinegar and parsely. Emilia-Romagna.

Sargnon mixture of fermented cheeses, similar to ► **Bross**. A Biella delicacy. Piedmont.

sargo dialect name for ► **sarago**, bream.

sarignà potatoes arranged over slices of lard, covered with water and cooked until the latter is absorbed. A specialty of the Valsusa (Turin). Piedmont.

Sarner semi-hard cow's milk cheese produced in the Val Sarentino. Trentino-Alto Adige.

sarset Piedmontese term for ► **valerianella**, common cornsalad.

sartizzu another name for ► **cannaca**, a cured meat.

sartù a sumptuous rice timbale filled with chicken livers, peas, mushrooms, sausages, tiny meatballs, breadcrumbs, mozzarella and eggs, and often covered with meat sauce (► **ragù alla napoletana**). One of the great creations of the *monzù*, the head chefs in aristocratic Neapolitan households in the 18th and 19th centuries. A simpler version exists called *sartù al-*

la morconese, in which the rice is flavored with butter and Parmigiano, then filled with layers of mozzarella, fried zucchini and grated Parmigiano. A specialty of Naples. Campania.

sarzegna Veneto name for ► **alzavola**, teal.

sarzenta another name for ► **bonissima** cake.

sasaka aka **sassaka** an old woodman's snack of lardo and bacon ground to a paste with onion and spread on rye bread. Today the paste is commercialized in jars and tubes and served as an antipasto. A specialty of the Val Canale. Friuli.

sasanidd dialect name for ► **cingoli**, pastries.

saschitedda word used in Buscemi (Siracusa) for ► **nucatili**, pastries.

sassefica regional term for ► **barba di becco**, salsify.

sassolino spirit distilled from star anise, a specialty of the town of Sassuolo (province of Modena), and common throughout Emilia. The original recipe envisaged a large amount of sugar and a low alcohol content, hence the drink's fame as a lady's tipple. Today it is used mainly to flavor traditional cakes and pastries, and as a digestif, sometimes accompanied by a glass of white wine. Production is protected by the trademark of the Modena Chamber of Commerce. Emilia-Romagna.

Saticulano another name for ► **Cacioforte** cheese.

sattizzu another name for ► **cannaca**, a cured meat.

saùc a variation on ► **muset**, a boiling sausage. Typical of the province of Pordenone. Friuli.

saucciciott Abruzzo dialect term for ► **salsicciotto frentano**, a cured meat.

Sauerbraten beef bathed with vinegar and slow-roasted with onions. Trentino-Alto Adige.

sauerkraut → **crauti**.

Sauersuppe a soup of tripe, onion, toasted flour, lemon zest and vinegar, served with a dash of more vinegar or red wine. Trentino-Alto Adige.

sauru cu l'agghiata horse mackerel (→ **suro**) fried in oil and garnished with mint leaves and garlic cloves fried in the same oil. Sicily.

savezudde sott'ogghie dialect name for → **salicornia sott'olio**, boiled samphire preserved in jars with garlic, mint and oil. Puglia.

savoiardi light, friable sponge fingers, probably of Piedmontese origin but now produced, industrially and domestically, all over Italy. They appear in similar recipes in Piedmont, Sicily and Sardinia in particular. In Sicily they are often larger than normal and in Fonni (Sardinia), they are known as *pistoccus*. Savoiardi can be eaten on their own or with custard, hot chocolate or dessert wine. They are also an ingredient in desserts such as → **charlotte**, → **tiramisù**, → **zuppa inglese** and → **zuccotto**.

savor a relish made of unfermented grape must, fresh seasonal fruit (quince, pears, figs, apricots and so on) and chopped dried and candied fruit, served with bread, polenta, boiled meats and cheese and also used to flavor cakes and ice creams. A specialty of Romagna, where it is known as → **savour**, it is also made, with variations, in Emilia and Lombardy.

savore sauce made with minced almonds mixed with garlic, parsley, fresh breadcrumbs and grape juice (though many variations exist), and served with boiled meat. Tuscany.

savoret preserve made with cooked grape must, honey and sugar. Lombardy.

savôrs diced mixed vegetables preserved in glass jars. Friuli-Venezia Giulia.

savour Romagna dialect name for → **savor**, a relish.

savurett a fruit relish, typical of Reggio Emilia, similar to → **savor**. Used to stuff → **tortellini dolci**. Emilia-Romagna.

sazizza fiery aged sausage flavored with chili and fennel seeds. Calabria.

sbattere to beat. To mix food vigorously to introduce air, thereby making it lighter and fluffier, using a wooden spoon, whisk or electric mixer.

sbianchire synonym of → **sbollentare**, to blanche.

sbira a stew of tripe, herbs, dried mushrooms, pine kernels and meat sauce, served with toasted bread, chopped potatoes and hot broth. Liguria.

sbirraglia, alla term associated with a number of "poor" dishes (→ **risoto a la sbiraglia**, → **sbira**). In Italian the slang word **sbirro** corresponds to the English "cop." The expression may derive from the fact that "cops" once confiscated food supplies and forced people to get by on leftovers.

sbollentare to blanche. To boil briefly: to soften certain food items (eg, vegetables); to harden others (eg, offal such as brains); to remove fat from others (eg, certain cuts of pork; to make others (eg, tomatoes or peppers) easier to skin or peel; to set or fix certain colors. The verb is a synonym of → **sbianchire** and → **scottare**.

sbombata a traditional peasant pasta casserole cum pie. A crust of dough made with plain flour and eggs (*sbombata*) filled with large egg pasta squares layered with a sauce of goose, chicken giblets and grated Pecorino cheese, then baked in the oven. Umbria.

sbreghette twice-baked version of → **pan co l'ua**, a raisin bread typical of Chioggia, in the province of Venice. Veneto.

sbriciolona another name for ➤ **finocchiona**, a cured meat.

sbrisolina aka **sbrisolona, sbrisolosa** three names (used respectively in Piacenza, Mantua and Cremona) for a traditional dry cake that tends to "fall into crumbs" (*sbriciolarsi* in Italian, hence the names). Recipes vary from city to city, but the main ingredients are wheat flour, cornflour, eggs, butter, lard, grated lemon zest and white wine. The cake is usually served with ➤ **zabaglione**, ➤ **crema di mascarpone** and ➤ **caulat** or with a glass of sweet white wine. Lombardy, Emilia-Romagna.

sbrofadei ➤ **brofadei**, a type of pasta.

sbroscia a soup of fish from Lake Bolsena (Viterbo). In the past the lake water was apparently used too. Lazio.

sbucciare to peel.

sburrita di baccalà stew of salt cod, garlic, thyme, calamint and chili, served on toasted bread. A specialty of Elba which probably dates from the Spanish occupation of the island. Tuscany.

scabeccio, a Ligurian term for ➤ **scapece, a,** marinating technique.

scacciata aka **scaccia** aka **scaccetta** a rectangular flatbread filled with ingredients such as anchovies, ham, olives, onions, tomatoes, sausage, cauliflower and Pecorino cheese. Typical of Catania. Sicily.

Scacione pasteurized cows' milk cheese, once made with goat's milk, hence the alternative name ➤ **Caprone** (*capra* means goat). Ready to eat within an hour and a half of production, it is used in salads and on pizzas, or deep-fried in batter. Lazio.

scafata traditional fresh fava bean soup common in the Viterbo area and similar to other regional soups, such as ➤ **bagiana umbra.** Its other ingredients are chopped ham fat, garlic, mint, pancetta,

onions, lettuce, tomatoes and pork rind. It is served with slices of country bread and, in the Maremma area, wedges of artichoke. The name comes from the dialect word *scafa*, meaning fava bean. In Montefiascone, the same dish is known as *baggianata*, meaning something of little value, an allusion to the fact that it used to be made with leftovers and garden vegetables. Lazio.

scagliozze ➤ **scagliuozzi**, fried polenta.

scagliuozzi typical Neapolitan street food (➤ **cibo di strada**), now served as an antipasto. Day-old polenta sliced and fried in oil and filled with ➤ **Provolone** cheese (in Puglia, similar fritters are called *scagliozze*). Campania.

scalcione pizza cut in half and filled with greens flavored with anchovy. Traditionally prepared on Easter Friday. Puglia.

scaldatelle (1) small fried pastries (= **zeppole**) coated in chestnut flower honey or sugar. Campania.

scaldatelle (2) ring-shaped pastries (➤ **taralli**) made of unleavened dough, plunged into boiling water, aromatized with wild fennel, then baked in the oven. Known as **scaldatelli** in Puglia and as **cancelle** in the province of Matera. Calabria, Puglia, Basilicata.

scaldatelli Puglia word for ➤ **scaldatelle (2)**, ring-shaped pastries.

scaledde spiral-shaped fried Christmas pastries, made by twisting the dough round sticks, smothered with julep (➤ **giulebbe**) or honey. Calabria.

scaletta spiral-shaped ➤ **pane a birra**, "beer bread," sprinkled with sesame seeds (➤ **sesamo**). Obtained by twisting a dough cylinder four times over. Sicily.

scalfo cut of beef that comprises top of sirloin and flank.

scaliddre aka **scalille** other names for ➤ **scaledde**, Christmas pastries.

scalinata in bollito beef boiled with onion, carrots, celery and cherry tomatoes. The meat is served sliced with vegetables preserved in oil. The broth is used to cook ➤ **frascarelli**, a type of pasta. Umbria.

scalmarita aka **scalmerita** names used in the Upper Tiber Valley for ➤ **capocollo umbro**, a cured meat. Umbria.

scalogno shallot (*Allium ascalonicum*). The Italian Ministry of Agriculture's database of native and/or traditional varieties lists: *scalogno nostrale toscano* (Tuscany) and ➤ **scalogno di Romagna** (Emilia-Romagna). Traditionally more used in France, the shallot is beginning to catch on in Italy, especially in new, creative recipes.

scalogno di Romagna PGI shallot cultivated in the provinces of Ravenna, Forlì and Bologna since the early 20th century. Emilia-Romagna.

scaloppa word for a round or oval slice of meat or fish, derived from the French *escalope*.

scaloppina round or oval slice of lean veal, pork or turkey coated in flour and lightly fried with lemon juice, Marsala, butter and sage.

scamerita aka **scammarita** Tuscan and Lazio terms for ➤ **capocollo**, a cured meat.

scàmmaro the opposite of ➤ **càmmaro**. Namely a sauce without meat (anchovy, garlic, capers, Gaeta olives) used to dress long pasta. Leftover pasta may be made into a ➤ **frittata di scàmmaro**. Campania.

scamone a cut of beef roughly equivalent to hip sirloin.

Scamorza spherical, stretched curd, pasteurized cow's milk cheese with a prominent of vestigial head. Produced all over the south of Italy.

Scamorza in carrozza a variation on ➤ **mozzarella in carrozza**, a toasted sandwich.

scampo scampi (*Nephrops norvegicus*). Med-

iteranean lobster-like crustacean fished in spring and fall. Cooked like other crustaceans. Common and regional names: ➤ **arganello**, ➤ **astracio**, ➤ **lempitu di fangu**, ➤ **ranfele 'e funnale**.

scanata (1) large bread loaf typical of the Pollino national park. Basilicata.

scanata (2) name used in Foggia for a large durum wheat and potato bread loaf. Puglia.

scandela Lombard term for ➤ **orzo**, barley.

scannature d'abbacchio coagulated lamb's blood cooked with tomato and white wine. A recipe typical of the province of Viterbo. Lazio.

scapece, a technique used to preserve fish or vegetables by frying them and covering them with a marinade of vinegar and aromatics and herbs. The name is of Spanish origin (*escabeche*). Similar to ➤ **carpione** and ➤ **saor**, the technique has many regional variations. The term **scapece** is used all over southern Italy, whereas in Liguria the technique is referred to as ➤ **scabeccio**.

scapece abruzzese regional version of the ➤ **scapece** marinade made with vinegar and saffron stigmas. Abruzzo.

scapece gallipolino regional version of the ➤ **scapece** marinade made with vinegar and saffron stigmas. Typical of Gallipoli (Lecce). Puglia.

scapice anchovies marinated in ➤ **scapece**. Basilicata.

scapicollata a ➤ **capocollo**, cured meat, typical of Viterbo. Lazio.

scarafuagli a Calabrian term for ➤ **ciccioli**, pork scratchings.

scaramella cut of beef roughly equivalent to plate (➤ **biancostato**).

scaramella al forno roast veal with garlic and herbs. Piedmont.

scarcella another name for ➤ **cuddhura**, Easter bread.

scardiccione another name for ➤ **cardo asinine**, milkthistle or ➤ **cardogna**, common goldenthistle.

scardola common rudd (*Scardinius erythrophthalmus*), a freshwater fish common all over Italy, usually eaten filleted and fried.

scarola escarole (➤ **indivia**).

scarola 'mbuttunata stuffed escarole. Side-dish or meal-in-one of escarole leaves boiled until tender, opened and filled with a mixture of breadcrumbs, capers, raisins, pine kernels, Gaeta olives, and chopped anchovy fillets, and baked in the oven coated with breadcrumbs or fried in extra virgin olive oil with cloves of garlic. Campania.

scarpacc large ravioli stuffed with herbs and cheese. A winter dish typical of the province of Brescia. Lombardy.

scarpariello simple pasta sauce of cherry tomatoes, grated Parmigiano and basil leaves. Campania.

scarpazza (1) spinach (or chard or cardoon) pie. Lombardy

scarpazza (2) another name for ➤ **torta d'erbi**, a vegetable pie.

scarpazzoun another name for ➤ **erbazzone**, a vegetable pie.

scarpena negra aka **scarpena rossa** Venezia Giulia terms for ➤ **scorfano nero**, **scorfano rosso**, black and red scorpion fish.

scarpetta Puglia term for ➤ **seppia**, squid.

scarpinocc local meatless variant of ➤ **casonsei de la Bergamasca**, a stuffed pasta. Lombardy.

scarponi di melanzane eggplant stuffed with its own flesh, garlic, anchovies cheese, breadcrumbs and basil. Campania.

scarsellina common name for ➤ **borsa del pastore**, shepherd's purse.

scartagghiate dialect term for ➤ **cartellate**, fried pastries.

scattiata pasta sauce of stewed peppers and tomatoes. Puglia.

Scaudatu aka **Scauratu** delicate cream cheese now virtually extinct. Sicily.

scauratello tuna cooked with eggplant and pennyroyal. Sicily.

scazzuoppoli small fried pasta squares served with tomato and basil. Campania.

schenal de porzel Veneto term for ➤ **lombo di maiale**, pork loin.

scherpada aka **stirpada** vegetable pie. Liguria.

schia aka **schila** red Mediterranean shrimp (➤ **gambero**). Typical of the Venice lagoon and listed in the Italian Ministry of Agriculture's database of native and/or traditional food products. Eaten fried or sautéed with garlic and parsley. Veneto.

schiaccia briaca round Christmas fruit loaf typical of the island of Elba (Livorno). Tuscany.

schiaccia maremmana savory or sweet flatbread. Tuscany.

schiaccia pala another name for ➤ **schiaccia maremmana**, a flatbread.

schiacciata a larger, richer version of ➤ **schiacciatina mantovana**, a flatbread. Lombardy.

schiacciata alla campigliese another name for ➤ **campigliese**, a cake.

schiacciata alla fiorentina twice-leavened fruit loaf traditionally baked on *il giorno del Berlingaccio* (Maundy Thursday). Tuscany.

schiacciata con l'uva simple rosemary-flavored loaf dotted with grapes, traditionally made during the wine harvest. Tuscany.

schiacciata con la cipolla twice-leavend flatbread topped with sage and onion. Umbria.

schiacciatina simple square-shaped flatbread, typical of the province of Mantua. Lombardy.

---

schiaffettoni large hollow → **maccheroni** stuffed with meat and served with tomato sauce. Calabria.

schiaffoni southern term for → **ziti** or → **paccheri**, types of pasta.

schiappagrotti regional term for → **ioseride**, perennial hyoseris.

schienali bovine bone marrow.

schinco de porco/ schinco de vedel northeastern dialect terms for pig's/calf's shin.

schinella Pesaro variation on → **lonza marchigiana**, a cured meat, with juniper berries, thyme, savory and rosemary added to the mixture.

Schinkenfleckernl egg pasta lozenges of Austrian origin, baked in the oven with a mixture of butter, egg yolk, egg whites whisked to a peak and diced ham. Trentino-Alto Adige.

schioppetti regional term for → **silene rigonfia**, bladder campion.

schirifizu Sicilian word for → **canocchia**, mantis shrimp.

schissoeula shortbread, also known as → **chisola**, with pork scratchings and raisins. Lombardy.

schiuma di mare (1) Puglia neologism for an antipasto of raw anchovies dressed with oil, lemon juice and pepper.

schiuma di mare (2) another word for → **novellame di pesce**, fish fry.

schiumare to skim.

schiumini aka **spumini** Emilia names for small meringues (→ **meringa**).

Schiz saltless raw cow's milk cheese produced in the province of Belluno. Also known as → **Tosella**. Veneto.

schizoto flatbread of flour, lard and sugar. Typical of the province of Padua. Veneto.

Schlickkrapten egg ravioli of Austro-German origin stuffed with ham, cheese, ricotta and eggs. Cooked in broth. Friuli-Venezia Giulia.

Schlutzer aka **Schlutzkrapfen** half-moon rye flour Tyrolese ravioli stuffed with spinach, ricotta and herbs. Trentino-Alto Adige.

Schmarrn another name for → **Kaiserschmarrn**, a sweet omelet.

Schmorbraten beef marinated in wine and herbs and slow-cooked in the marinade liquid with the addition of tomatoes. Trentino-Alto Adige.

schnitte slices of day-old bread softened in sugared milk aromatized with vanilla or lemon zest, breaded, fried in oil and dusted with confectioners' sugar and powdered cinnamon. Friuli-Venezia Giulia.

Schopsernes lamb stew with potatoes and cabbage. Trentino-Alto Adige.

Schüttelbrot crisp rye bread flavored with fennel seeds. Trentino-Alto Adige.

Schwarzer weggen wholemeal bread loaf. Trentino-Alto Adige.

Schweinestelze another name for → **stinco di maiale affumicato**, smoked shin of pork. Trentino-Alto Adige.

sciabbò ancient broad curly lasagne. The name is a Sicilianization of the French *jabot*, "a lace bib." Produced commercially today as → **lasagne ricce** or *sciablò* or *sciabò*. Sicily.

scialatielli fresh durum wheat pasta typical of central and southern Italy.

s-ciancon Piedmontese term for → **maltagliati**, a type of pasta.

s-ciancui con rape di Caprauna pasta (→ **maltagliati**) with a sauce of turnips (→ **rape di Caprauna**), potatoes, mushrooms, walnuts and cream. Typical of the Val Pennavaire (Cuneo). Piedmont.

sciaschitedda word used for → **nucatili**, a type of pastry, in Buscemi (Siracusa). Sicily.

sciatt buckwheat fritters filled with cheese. Typical of the Valtellina, in the province of Sondrio. Lombardy.

scieddu traditional rural vegetable soup supplemented with pork rind and tiny patties of egg, cheese, parsley and breadcrumbs. Campania.

scigulada mustard-flavored onion sauce served with boiled meat. Typical of the province of Como. Lombardy.

scigulett e peverun sott'aceto pickled onions and peppers. Typical of the province of Milan. Lombardy.

scilatelli aka **sciliatelli** aka **scivatiddi** local dialect terms for ➤ **scialatielli**, a type of pasta.

Scimudin soft fat cheese produced in the Valtellina, in the province of Sondrio. Lombardy.

scimut semi-fat mountain cheese, typical of the Valmalenco, in the province of Sondrio. Lombardy.

sciogliere to dissolve, to melt.

s'ciopeti aka **s'ciupet** northern dialect terms for ➤ **silene rigonfia**, bladder campion.

sciouette dainty flower-shaped colored cakes baked to a secret recipe in the Augustine monastery of Varese Ligure (La Spezia). Liguria.

sciroppato term used to describe fruit preserved in a sugar and water syrup.

sciroppo di rose rose syrup. Perfumed rose petals infused in boiling water, sugar, lemon zest and vanilla. Typical of the province of Genoa. Liguria.

sciscùla dialect term for ➤ **giuggiola**, jujube.

sciumette dialect word for a dessert similar to the French *îles flottantes*. Liguria.

Sciungata soft cream cheese. Calabria.

sciurilli zucchini flours coated in batter and deep-fried in boiling oil. Campania.

sciuscelle small baked and iced Christmas buns, typical of Formia and Gaeta. Lazio, Campania.

sciuscello aka **sciusceddu** soup of French origin prepared in Puglia (broth with tiny balls of eggs, cheese, breadcrumbs, garlic and parsley) at Christmas and in Sicily (broth with meatballs) at Easter. Puglia, Sicily.

Sciusciello vegetable broth thickened to a cream with the addition of beaten egg and served on slices of toast. Typical of the Cilento area, in the province of Salerno. Campania.

sclopit Friulian term for ➤ **silene rigonfia**, bladder campion.

scoglio, allo term used mainly in restaurants to describe dishes (usually pastas or soups) involving mollusks or crustaceans.

scoglio troncato regional term for ➤ **murice**, murex or rock shell.

scognariente Puglia word for ➤ **tellina**, tellin or wedge shell clam.

scolino common name for ➤ **cardogna**, common or spotted goldenthistle.

conciglio word used in Tuscany for ➤ **murice**, murex or rock shell.

scoparina regional term for ➤ **pungitopo**, butcher's broom.

scopeton aka **renga**, Veneto term for ➤ **aringa**, herring.

scoppularicchi Siracusa term for baby cuttlefish (➤ **seppia**).

scorfano scorpion fish. Used in the kitchen are **scorfano rosso** red scorpion fish (*Scorpaena scrofa*) and **scorfano nero** black scorpion fish (*Scorpaena porcus*), both with firm, tasty flesh. Excellent in soups, stews and sauces. Common and regional names: (red scorpion fish) ➤ **cappone**, ➤ **cipuddazza**, ➤ **pescio cappon**, ➤ **scarpena rossa**; (black scorpion fish) ➤ **pesce capone**, ➤ **scarpena negra**, ➤ **scrofanu niuro** per scorfano nero.

scorzobianca (aka **scorzabianca**) common name for a variety of ➤ **barba di becco**, salsify.

scorzone (1) variety of ➤ **tartufo**, truffle.

scorzone (2) another name for ➤ **budello gentile**, large intestine.

scorzonera black salsify (*Scorzonera hispanica*). A plant native to and widespread in central and southern Europe. Its root is eaten fried, stewed and boiled, especially in Liguria. The Italian Ministry of Agriculture's database of native and/or traditional food products lists the following varieties: *barba massese* (Tuscany), *radice di Chiavari* (Liguria) and *scorzonera di Castellazzo Bormida* (Piedmont).

scottadito Roman name for a lamb cutlet or chop. Lazio.

scottare synonym of ➤ **sbollentare**, to blanche, to boil briefly, to poach.

scottiglia stew of mixed meats (lamb, kid, wild boar, goose, turkey, chicken) typical of the Maremma and Casentino areas. Tuscany.

scottona a young cow or heifer.

scriccioli Tuscan term for ➤ **ciccioli**, pork scratchings.

scrippelle Abruzzo term for ➤ **crespelle**, crêpes or pancakes.

scrippelle 'mbusse traditional soup made of ➤ **crespelle** rolled up, sprinkled with grated Pecorino and covered with chicken broth. Abruzzo.

scroccadenti Italianization of ➤ **straca dent**, a type of cake.

scroccafusi small Carnival cakes flavored with anise liqueur (➤ **mistrà**), fried and covered with honey or baked and soaked in alkermes or rum. Marche.

scrofa sow.

scrucchijata aka **scrucchiata** dialect name for a jam made with grapes, often of the Montepulciano d'Abruzzo variety. Abruzzo.

scucuzzu tiny handmade couscous-like pasta balls cooked in broth or ➤ **minestrone alla genovese**. Liguria.

scuete frante ricotta (*scuete* in dialect) aromatized with salt and pepper and aged for a couple of months, after which it turns into a tangy cream. Friuli-Venezia Giulia.

scuete fumade smoked cow's milk whey ricotta (*scuete*). Friuli-Venezia Giulia.

scuma di patati potato soufflé (eggs, butter, grated Pecorino, Provola, ➤ **soppressata**, parsley), typical of Catanzaro. Calabria.

scurdijata another name for ➤ **'ncapriata**, fava bean purée with wild chicory.

scuriazno dialect term for ➤ **cepola**, red band fish.

scutturniate ➤ **ciambelle scottolate**, sweet ring-shaped cookies.

sdramel aka **sdramelòt** baguette-like variation on ➤ **bechi-panzalini** bread with oil in the dough. Trentino-Alto Adige.

seadas large sweet half-moon or round ravioli filled with cream cheese, deep-fried and covered with arbutus or chestnut honey. A specialty of Oliena, in the province of Nuoro, but popular all over the island. Sardinia.

sebadas Cagliari name for ➤ **seadas**, sweet ravioli. Sardinia.

sebos abausos Provencal for ➤ **cipolle ripiene**, stuffed onions.

seccia Campania dialect term for ➤ **seppia**, cuttlefish.

sechili dialect term for ➤ **bietola selvatica**, wild chard.

secoe aka **secole** pieces of meat extracted from the interstices of the ribs of cows, used to flavor risottos. Veneto.

sedani straight, tubular commercial durum wheat pasta with a smooth or ridged surface. Other names: ➤ **diavoletti**, ➤ **fagiolini**, ➤ **sedanini**.

sedani di Trevi ripieni celery stalks stuffed with sausage meat, ground beef, eggs, parsley, marjoram and thyme, dipped in flour and beaten eggs, fried in olive oil, covered with meat or tomato sauce, sprinkled with grated Parmigiano and browned in the oven. Umbria.

sedani ripieni alla pratese "sandwiches" of fried celery stalks filled with a cooked mixture of ground veal and chicken livers, covered with meat sauce and browned in the oven. A specialty of Prato. Tuscany.

sedanini a smaller version of ➤ **sedani**, a type of pasta.

sedano celery (*Apium graveolens*). The *dulce* variety is used as an aromatic with carrot and onion, eaten raw (➤ **pinzimonio**) and an ingredient in regional recipes such as ➤ **sedani ripieni alla pratese**. The *scalinum* variety, with more leaves and thinner stalks, is used to make soups (➤ **minestra di accio e baccalà**, ➤ **selinka**, ➤ **zuppa di accia**). The Italian Ministry of Agriculture's data base of native and/or traditional food products lists: *sedano di Alluvioni Cambiò, sedano dorato astigiano* (Piedmont); *costolino di Montevarchi* (Tuscany); *sedano rapa della Val di Gresta* (Trentino); *sedano di Rubbio, sedano verde di Chioggia, sedano rapa di Ronco dell'Adige* (Veneto); ➤ **sedano nero di Trevi** (Umbria).

sedano d'acqua European marshwort (➤ **gurgulestro**).

sedano di monte lovage (*Levisticum officinale*). Wild aromatic herb whose roots, shoots and seed are used mainly in Piedmont, Lombardy and Liguria to flavor sauces, liqueurs, cookies, soups, stuffings, salads and fish. Common and regional names: ➤ **appio montano**, ➤ **levistico**, ➤ **ligustico**.

sedano nero di Trevi tall, aromatic Slow Food-protected celery grown along the Clitumnus, near Trevi in the province of Perugia. Traditionally sowed on Good Friday, it is eaten stuffed, in molds or raw (➤ **pinzimonio**). Umbria.

sedano rapa aka **sedano di Verona** (*Apium graveoleons* var. *rapaceum*). The round edible root is popular largely in northeast Italy.

segala aka **segale** tall cereal which originated in Asia Minor, extensively cultivated in central and northern Europe. In Italy, especially in Trentino-Alto Adige and Val d'Aosta, its flour is used to make bread, grissini, cookies, cakes and pastries.

segalino soft, crisp rye bread flavored with fennel seeds. Trentino-Alto Adige.

segrigeula aka **segrigiola** a variety of savory (➤ **santoreggia**) that grows in the Tremezzina area, on the shores of Lake Como. Lombardy.

Seirass cone-shaped cow's or ewe's milk whey ricotta. Piedmont.

Seitenspeck smoked cured meat made of boned pork rubbed repeatedly with salt, pepper, bay leaf, juniper berries, garlic and pimento. Trentino-Alto Adige.

Selchkarre smoked cured meat made of pork aromatized with garlic, juniper berries, pepper, mace and pimento. Trentino-Alto Adige.

selinka slow-cooked soup of celery (*selin* in Slovenian), potatoes and beans served with pieces of white polenta. Typical of the Carso area, in the province of Gorizia. Friuli-Venezia Giulia.

sella saddle. Name of a cut of meat applied to lamb and veal, but also to other animals, such as rabbit and roe deer.

selvaggina game. The term applies to both animals and birds.

semelle round glossy bread roll typical of Florence. Often used by the city's tripe vendors to make ➤ **panino al lampredotto**. Tuscany.

sementino regional term for ➤ **chiodino**, honey armillary mushroom.

semi e legumi tostati toasted seeds and legumes. In northern and central Italy, "nibbles" such as peanuts and salted pumpkin seeds. In the south, toasted chickpeas and fava bans, pistachio nuts etc.

Semicotto caprino ewe's and goat's milk cheese typical of the provinces of Nuoro and Cagliari. Sardinia.

semifreddo soft ice or frozen mousse, less cold than ice-cream, made of custard, whipped cream and, often, egg whites whisked to a firm peak with concentrated sugar and water syrup.

Semigrasso d'alpe aka **Livigno** a semi-cooked cheese typical of the Valtellina. Made with cow's milk, sometimes with the addition of goat's. Lombardy.

semola bran or meal. The main product of the grinding and processing of durum wheat. Used mostly to make pasta and, in the south of Italy, some kinds of bread.

semolino semolina. An ingredient in numerous recipes, both savory and sweet: ➤ **minestra alla viterbese**, ➤ **minestra al sacco**, ➤ **minestra imperiale**, ➤ **gnocchi alla romana**, ➤ **gnocchi di semolino**, ➤ **budino di semolino**, ➤ **budino di puina**, ➤ **panvinesco**. Fried semolina (➤ **frittura dolce**) is one of the main ingredients of ➤ **fritto misto alla piemontese**.

semolino fritto Piedmontese term for ➤ **frittura dolce**, fried semolina.

senape mustard. Its most important use in Italy is in the preparation of ➤ **mostarda**.

senape selvatica wild mustard. The name refers to a number of spontaneous plants—black mustard (*Brassica nigra*), white mustard (*Sinapsis alba*), charlock (*Sinapsis arvensis*), hairy mustard (*Sinapsis pubescens*), shortpod mustard (*Hirschfeldia incana*)—all with yellow flowers, a pungent aroma and a bitterish flavor. All are specific to southern Italy, where they eat the leaves and tops sautéed in oil with garlic and chili, often to dress pasta. The main dialect words are: ➤ **amareddu**, ➤ **cimaredda**, ➤ **mazzaredda**, ➤ **sinapa**, ➤ **sanapo**.

seneppia aka **sgnepa** aka **snepa** dialect terms for ➤ **beccaccino**, common snipe.

sepa Veneto term for **seppia**, cuttlefish.

sepoline da burcelo small cuttlefish, fished in the Venice lagoon in midsummer. Eaten either coated in flour and fried or steamed (➤ **cassopipa**) and served with white polenta. Veneto.

seppia cuttlefish (*Sepia officinalis*). Small baby cuttlefish can be eaten raw or fried. Larger specimens have to be boned and cleaned before being broiled, fried, stewed, baked or stuffed. Common and regional names: ➤ **seccia**, ➤ **sepa**, ➤ **sepia**, ➤ **scarpetta**.

seppie a zemin Ligurian dialect name for ➤ **seppie in inzimino**, cuttlefish with chard.

seppie al nero cuttlefish stewed with tomatoes and finished with its ink, diluted in warm water. Served with soft or grilled polenta. Some of the sauce may be used to dress pasta. Veneto.

seppie alla veneziana another name for ➤ **seppie al nero**.

seppie con le patate a stew of cuttlefish with potatoes. A recipe typical of the Gargano peninsula, in the province of Foggia. Puglia.

seppie in inzimino cuttlefish stewed with herbs and tomatoes with the addition of chard and/or spinach. Liguria, Tuscany.

seppie ripiene stuffed cuttlefish. A popular recipe all round the Italian coast. Stuffings vary according to locality.

seppietta aka **seppiola** dwarf bobtail squid (*Sepiola rondeletii*). Cooked in the same way as cuttlefish (➤ **seppia**).

seppioline di rezzella small cuttlefish caught with a net. Lazio.

Sérac aka **Séras** aka **Ceré** ricotta made from cow's, ewe's and goat's milk whey. Val d'Aosta.

serpe serpent-shaped shortcrust pastry tart filled with dried and candied fruit. Typical of the provinces of Ascoli Piceno and Macerata. Marche.

serpentaria another name for ➤ **dragoncello**, tarragon.

serpentone another name for ➤ **torciglione**, a cake.

serpillo wild thyme (*Thymus serpyllum*). Herb used mostly in the southern Apennines and Tuscany to flavor vegetable soups, meat (rabbit and lamb), snails and vegetables. Common and regional names: ➤ **pepolino**, ➤ **peverino**, ➤ **timo peparello**, ➤ **timo selvatico**, ➤ **timo serpillo**.

servelade lightly smoked short, thick ➤ **würstel** sausage wrapped in a natural intestine. Trentino-Alto Adige, Friuli-Venezia Giulia.

sesam aka **sesame** mixture of herbs and spices in which sardines, anchovies and similar fish are marinated. Friuli-Venezia Giulia.

sesamielli another word for ➤ **susamielli**, Christmas cookies.

sesamo sesame (*Sesamum indicum*). Sesame seeds are widely used in the south of Italy, especially Sicily, to flavor and decorate bread and as an ingredient in cookies (➤ **biscotti regina**), nougats and brittles (➤ **cubbaita**, ➤ **giuggiulena**). Common and regional names: ➤ **cimino**, ➤ **giuggiulena**, ➤ **reginella**.

seupa a la ueca oven-baked soup of pearl barley and vegetables with rye flour and Fontina. Val d'Aosta.

seupa de gri soup of pearl barley (*gri* in the patois of the valley) slow-cooked with aromatic vegetables, pancetta and pork ribs. Val d'Aosta.

seupa paisanne layers of bread and Fontina and Toma cheese covered with meat broth and baked in the oven. Val d'Aosta.

seupa vapellenentse aka **seupa valpellinentze** layers of day-old bread, Savoy cabbage previously softened in lardo and slices of Fontina cheese covered with meat broth and baked in the oven. Typical of the Valpelline. Val d'Aosta.

seupetta cogneintze layers of risotto with Fontina cheese and day-old bread (or croutons fried in butter), flavored with a pinch of cinnamon, and baked in the oven. A delicacy of Cogne. Val d'Aosta.

seviero, 'n old Neapolitan term for "sweet and sour," still used for certain recipes (eg, *cinghiale 'n seviero*, sweet and sour wild boar). Campania.

sfarinati flour or meal.

sfars another name for ➤ **farsò**, sweet fritters.

sfigghiata aka **sfiggiata** Sicilian terms for newborn anchovies or sardines (➤ **novellame di pesce**, fish fry).

sfilacci shredded dried horsemeat, dressed with extra virgin olive oil. Veneto.

sfilacci di Padova another name for ➤ **carne sfilata**, smoked horsemeat.

sfilettare to fillet.

sfinci di san Giuseppe sweet fritters coated with a ricotta cream mixed with pieces of candied fruit and chocolate, and garnished with strips of candied orange, powdered sugar and minced pistachio nuts. A Palermo delicacy. Sicily.

sfincione a soft durum wheat flatbread topped with tomatoes, anchovies, onion, Caciocavallo, salt, pepper and olive oil. A traditional Palermo street food, perhaps invented by the nuns in the monastery of San Vito. Sicily.

sfizi "caprices." Word used in Naples and the rest of the region for tasty treats such as fried ➤ **panzarotti** and small ➤ **zeppole**, small pizzas and ➤ **mozzarella in carrozza**. Campania.

sfogeti in saor small soles coated in flour, fried and marinated in ➤ **saor**. Fishermen of the parish of Santa Marta used to eat them during the feast of their patron saint at the end of July. Veneto.

sfogio or **sfogia** Veneto terms for ➤ **sogliola**, sole.

sfoglia (1) sheet of pasta dough usually made of flour, salt and water, sometimes with eggs.

sfoglia (2) abbreviation of ➤ **pasta sfoglia**, puff pastry.

sfogliata aka **pizza sfoglia** rectangles of bread dough spread with oil and wild fennel flowers, closed and rolled into a spiral, baked in the oven and served hot or cold. Puglia.

sfogliatelle light, crisp snail-shaped pastries, probably created in convents, with a filling of semolina, ricotta, eggs, sugar, candied fruits and spices (vanilla and cinnamon). Other variations exist with other names (eg, *santarosa*, *aragostelle*), Campania.

sfogliatine di Villafranca, in dialect aka **sfoiadine** small ring-shaped cakes created by a confectioner in Villafranca di Verona in the late 18th century. Veneto.

sfoglina a housewife skilled at rolling out the dough for pasta (➤ **sfoglia**).

sfoglio shortcrust pastry tart filled with a mixture of egg whites whisked to a peak, grated ➤ **Tuma** cheese, sugar, grated lemon zest, chocolate and candied lime. Probably created in a convent, the most ancient and famous cake in the Madonie area. Sicily.

sfogliola Tuscan term for ➤ **sogliola**, sole.

sfoiada puff pastry filled with custard and dusted with confectioner's sugar. Friuli-Venezia Giulia.

sfoiade large buckwheat tagliatelle. Trentino-Alto Adige.

sfoiadini aka **sfojadini** disks of puff pastry baked one on top of another. Veneto.

sformare to turn out (eg, from a mold).

sformato a mixture of beaten eggs and often béchamel sauce blended with a food, generally a vegetable, cooked in the oven and turned out (➤ **sformare**).

sformato di baccalà alla certosina mold of salt cod layered with mushroom sauce, potato purée and other vegetables. Lombardy.

sformato di bucce di piselli ancient mold made with pea pods. Tuscany.

sformato di pipeto mold made with minced cabbage stuffing (➤ **pipeto**), béchamel sauce, eggs, grated Parmigiano. Typical of Crema, in the province of Cremona.

sformato di sedano mold of julienned celery (➤ **sedano nero di Trevi**). Umbria.

sformato di spinaci spinach mold flavored with nutmeg. A Florentine recipe. Tuscany.

sformato di zucca pumpkin mold. A specialty of the northeastern regions.

sfrappe aka **sfrappole** regional names for fried pastries similar to ➤ **cenci**.

sfratto dei Goym cylindrical pastry filled with minced walnuts, honey, orange zest, aniseed and nutmeg. A recipe of the Jewish community in Pitigliano and Sorano (Grosseto), protected by a Slow Food presidium. Tuscany.

sfregolini pastry fingers dotted with raisins and pine kernels. Typical of the Polesine area. Veneto.

sfregolota abbreviated name for ➤ **torta de fregoloti**, a type of cake.

sfricone tomato soup flavored with garlic and chili. A specialty of Bisceglie (Bari). Puglia.

sfricugliata di cicerchie soup of puréed grass peas with diced potatoes and pickled peppers. Campania.

sfrionza pork stew with potatoes and pickled red peppers. Campania.

sfrizzoli aka **sfriccioli** southern and central Italian term for ➤ **ciccioli**, pork scratchings.

sfumare to bathe a cooking food with a liquid (water, broth, wine, vinegar, liqueur) and allow this to evaporate.

sgabei strips of bread dough fried in oil and eaten with cured meats and cheese. Typical of the Val di Magra (La Spezia). Liguria.

sgamirru Sicilian term for ➤ **tambarello**, frigate tuna.

sgavaioni Lazio term for fishes for soup.

sgnapa Veneto term for grappa.

sgombro mackerel (*Scomber scombrus*). Sea fish of the Scombridae family. Found in the Mediterranean in large shoals, it migrates to deeper water in the winter. A fatty fish best cooked grilled or stewed. Also suitable for canning.

sgombri all'aceto boiled mackerel fillets marinated in vinegar. A Bari delicacy. Puglia.

sgombri allardiati broiled mackerel finished off with tomatoes and almonds. Sicily.

sgombro bastardo another name for ➤ **suro**, horse mackerel.

sgranare (of peas, beans etc) to pod.

sgrassare to remove fat or grease.

sgriscioli Marche term for ➤ **ciccioli**, pork scratchings.

sgrizoi dialect term for ➤ **silene rigonfia**, bladder campion.

sgroppino sorbet made by whipping lemon ice cream with vodka and prosecco. A traditional digestif. Veneto.

sguazet aka **sguazeto** Veneto terms for stew (➤ **guazzetto**).

sguazet di frattaglie calf's offal stew. Trentino-Alto Adige.

sguazeto a la bechera ("butcher's stew"). Calf's offal stew with aromatic herbs. Veneto.

sguazzabarbuz soup of ➤ **maltagliati** and beans. Typical of the province of Ferrara. Emilia-Romagna.

sgusciare to shell, to shuck.

shtridhëlat large spaghetti typical of Italy's Albanian communities (➤ **Arbëreshë**). Calabria.

siccioli dialect term for ➤ **ciccioli**, pork scratchings.

siero whey. The liquid by-product of cheesemaking used to make ➤ **ricotta**, in the confectionery industry as a powder or concentrate and as an animal feed.

sievoli in savor fried gray mullet marinated in onion, oil and vinegar. Friuli-Venezia Giulia.

sigarette another name for ➤ **tubetti**, a type of pasta.

signora di Conca Casale knobbly, irregular, coarse-textured raw pork salami, flavored with fennel seeds and cinnamon. Produced in the winter in the village of the same name in the province of Isernia. Promoted by a Slow Food presidium. Molise.

signorina regional term for ➤ **cepola**, red band fish.

silene rigonfia bladder campion (*Silene vulgaris*). Spontaneous herb with a net-veined bladder and pale green fleshy leaves, picked and eaten especially in northern and central Italy. The young florets are eaten boiled and buttered, in omelets, in risottos, stuffings (➤ **tortelli**, ➤ **piadina**) and soups. In Romagna, where the herb is particularly popular, it is used as an ingredient for a sauce: ➤ **ragù di stridoli**. Common and regional names: ➤ **bubbolini**, ➤ **carletti**, ➤ **cavoli della comare**, ➤ **erba del cucco**, ➤ **erba striscia**, ➤ **schioppetti**, ➤ **stridoli**, ➤ **strigoli**, ➤ **tagliatelle della Madonna**.

silene rossa red catchfly (*Silene dioica*). Mountain herb whose shoots are gathered in Friuli and Veneto and cooked in soups, pasta fillings and frittatas. Common and regional names: ➤ **gittone**, ➤ **licnide**, ➤ **orecchie di lepre**.

Silter cow's milk cheese of the Valcamonica. Lombardy.

simbua fritta porridge of durum wheat meal (*simbua*), onion, parsley, sausage, ➤ **mustela** cured meat and lard. At Villanovaforru, in the province of Medio Campidano area, a festival is held to celebrate the dish every year in September. Sardinia.

simenza aka **semenza** other terms for ➤ **semi e legumi tostati**, toasted seeds and legumes.

simmuledda alla foggiana buckwheat polenta cooked with potatoes and wild fennel, served sliced topped with grated cheese. Puglia.

sinapa dialect term for ➤ **senape selvatica**, wild mustard.

sinipi a cross between chicory and asparagus, typical of Cagnano Varano on the Gargano peninsula, in the province of Foggia. Puglia.

sioris chicchi popcorn dusted with sugar. Friuli-Venezia Giulia.

siras another name for ➤ **seirass**, Piedmontese ricotta.

sisam bleak (➤ **alborella**) dried, stewed with onion and marinated in its own cooking liquid. A recipe which dates from the 14th century, typical of Lake Garda. Lombardy, Trentino-Alto Adige, Veneto.

sise delle monache three-pointed sponge buns filled with confectioner's custard and dusted with confectioner's sugar. Typical of Guardiagrele (Chieti). Abruzzo.

sissole Veneto term for ➤ **ciccioli**, pork scratchings.

sivé another spelling of ➤ **civé**.

sivone Puglia word for ➤ **grespigno**, field sowthistle.

sizzigorros snails in tomato sauce. Sardinia.

skilà known as "shepherds' soup." A broth of potatoes, onion, leek and celery served with rye bread and pieces of mountain cheese. Val d'Aosta, Piedmont.

slikrofi herb and potato tortellini of Slovenian origin. Friuli-Venezia Giulia.

slinzega scraps of beef or horsemeat from the production of ➤ **bresaola della Valtellina** cured with salt, ground pepper, cinnamon, nutmeg, sugar, minced bay leaf, crushed juniper berries and garlic, red wine, chili and fennel. Typical of the province of Sondrio. Lombardy.

smacafam Carnival pastry of buckwheat flour mixed with broth and ➤ **lucanica trentina** sausage. A sweet version exists similar to ➤ **macafame**. Trentino-Alto Adige.

smegiassa aka **smegiazza** rustic fruit loaf made of crumbs of day-old polenta mixed with milk, eggs, treacle, raisins, pine kernels and, sometimes, pieces of pumpkin. Traditionally baked in the Polesine area, in the province of Rovigo, and in the province of Padua on Christmas Eve. Veneto.

smorm de pan Trentino equivalent of ➤ **Kaiserschmarren**. A sweet fritter of day-old bread, eggs, sugar, raisins and lemon zest fried in butter and dusted with confectioner's sugar. Trentino-Alto Adige.

snocciolare (of olives, cherries, plums etc) to pit, to stone.

soaso aka **suaso** word used on the Adriatic from Venice to Abruzzo for ➤ **rombo liscio** aka **rombetto**. Turbot.

sobbollire to simmer.

soça casserole of salted beef boiled with Savoy cabbage, potatoes and leeks and baked in the oven dotted with butter and Fontina cheese. Val d'Aosta.

Soela aka **Sola** mixed milk mountain cheese produced in the Val Tanaro, in the province of Cuneo. So named because of its shape, reminiscent of the sole (*suola* in Italian) of a shoe. Piedmont.

soffiato alla trentina sandwich cake, typical of the province of Trento, with an egg custard filling, glazed with egg whites whisked to a peak. Trentino-Alto Adige.

soffione common name for ➤ **tarassaco**, dandelion.

soffriggere to lightly cook in fat without actually frying.

soffritto (1) mixture of chopped aromatics (onion, carrot, and herbs (➤ **battuto**), sometimes with the addition of lardo or pancetta, gently cooked in oil or butter as the foundation for countless, soups, sauces, and other dishes.

soffritto (2) Neapolitan pig's offal specialty (➤ **suffritte**).

sogliola sole (**Solea vulgaris**). Flatfish cooked, whole, filleted or sliced, *à la meunière*, grilled, fried, baked, steam or boiled in a ➤ **court-bouillon**. Common and regional names: ➤ **lengua**, ➤ **sfogia**, ➤ **sfogio**, ➤ **sfogliola**.

soglioletta pelosa in Abruzzo name for ➤ **linguattola**, spotted flounder.

solada aka **solata** rosemary and garlic fritters typical of Reggio Emilia. Emilia-Romagna.

sòma d'aj slice of bread spread with garlic, oil and salt. Piedmont.

sommommoli aka **sommomoli** sweet rice fritters cooked in Florence for the feast of San Giuseppe. In Prato they make them at Carnival time. Tuscany.

sonchi field sowthistle (➤**grespigno**, in Puglia known as *sivone* or *sonco*, in dialect as *zangune*), blanched and turned in extra virgin olive oil with pancetta, cherry tomatoes, salt and chili. Puglia.

soncino common name for ➤ **valerianella**, common cornsalad.

sones apple fritters. Typical of the Valle di Fassa and Valle di Fiemme. Trentino-Alto Adige.

songino common name for ➤ **valerianella**, common cornsalad.

sopa coada baked layered casserole of bread fried in butter and stewed pigeon. One of the great delicacies of Treviso. Veneto.

sopa de pevarasse clams stewed with tomatoes, white wine and herbs (basil, parsley, oregano). Friuli-Venezia Giulia.

sopa de tripe tripe soup. Fresh tripe (➤ **omaso**, omasum, plus ➤ **abomaso**, abomasums) marinated in wine and herbs, boiled, diced, flavored with a lightly cooked mixture of parsley and aromatics, covered with beef broth and left to simmer. Seasoned with pepper, the soup is served with croutons in deep bowls. This traditional dish used to be served for breakfast in winter in the osterias of Treviso. In some areas tomato is added to the dish, in others it is spiced with cinnamon and nutmeg. In the provinces of Venice, Padua, and Rovigo, they add rice to the soup (➤ **risi e trippa**). Veneto.

sope di cjaval the name means "horsemeat soup," but the dish is actually a mush of day-old bread and scrambled eggs covered with warm spicy wine sweetened with sugar. The mixture was believed to restore the vigor to exhausted horses, and was given as a reconstituent to women after childbirth. It was also traditionally served on the day of Pentacost. Friuli-Venezia Giulia.

soperzata di Rivello fillet and leg muscle and a little fat from naturally raised pigs, hand-chopped into tiny pieces and cured with salt and peppercorns. Cased in a pig's intestine, the mixture is pressed for 24 hours, then matured for 40 days, during which time it is lightly smoked. A rare artisan cured meat made for at least three centuries in Rivello, a town to the south of Potenza. Basilicata.

sopprassata another name for ➤ **soppressata** Toscana.

soppressa di costa a type of ➤ **soppressa**

friulana in which pork rib is included in the mixture. Friuli-Venezia Giulia.

soppressa friulana a type of ➤ **salame friulano** made from a fattier mixture and larger in size. Can age for up to two years. Friuli-Venezia Giulia.

soppressata della Presila mountain cured meat made from the pork of home-raised and home-butchered pigs. Hand-ground, the meat is cured with salt and a sauce of peppers typical of the village of Pizzo Calabro. Cased in a pig's intestine, it is smoked for ten days over oak, chestnut, turkey oak and beech fires, then aged for four to ten months. Calabria.

soppressata di Calabria coarse-grained cured meat made all over the region with pork from local pigs. Calabria.

soppressata di Decollatura another name for ➤ **soppressata della Presila**.

soppressata di Gioi one of the oldest cured meats in Campania, records of which date from 1835. Protected by a Slow Food presidium, it is made with smoked prime pork and encloses a stick of lardo. Campania.

soppressata di Martina Franca cured meat made with coarsely chopped pork leg and shoulder flavored with salt, pepper and white or cooked wine. Typical of the province of Taranto, Puglia.

soppressata di Ricigliano e San Gregorio Magno cured meat produced in the two villages of the same name in the province of Salerno with finely ground ham and pork fillet. Campania. **soppressata molisana** cured meat made with ground pork loin and 2-3% fat cured with salt and pepper and, in some localities, fennel seeds (A similar meat is made in Abruzzo with the addition of shoulder, leg and belly pork). Molise.

soppressata toscana large cured meat made all over Tuscany from October to March with boned pig's head, pork rind and tongue. Tuscany.

sopranno colt. A horse of two to three years of age.

Sopravvissana sheep breed created in Macerata (Marche) in the 18th century by crossing Vissana ewes with Merino rams. It is produced mainly for its meat in Marche, Umbria, Tuscany, Lazio, Abruzzo, Molise and Puglia.

sopressa aka **soppressa** aka **soppressata** names (the first used in Veneto, the second two in central and southern Italy) for pressed salami-like cured meats made by grinding lean pork of different cuts and pork fat in different proportions.

sopressa di Asiago cured meat made with coarsely ground prime pork on the plateau of Asiago e dei Sette Comuni and in the villages of Lugo, Caltrano and Calvene, in the province of Vicenza. Veneto.

sopressa di cavallo a version of ➤ **salame di cavallo**, horsemeat salami, with a lower percentage of fat. Veneto.

sopressa investia another name for ➤ **ossocòlo**, a cured meat.

sopressa vicentina PDO cured meat made in the Valli del Pasubio, in the province of Vicenza, with pork from local pigs. Veneto.

sopressata di cavallo cured meat made with prime horsemeat and pork belly flavored overnight with Marsala. Veneto.

Söra another name for ➤ **Soela**, a cheese.

sorba service tree (*Sorbus domestica*). Service berries are used to make jams and cider, or split in half and dried.

sorbetto sorbet. Water ice made with fruit juice or purée, sometimes also with dry or sweet wines.

sorbir d'agnoli a summer *amuse-bouche* of ➤ **angoli** in broth served in a cup.

sorcha stew of diced summer vegetables (runner beans, zucchini, onions, potatoes and so on) with pieces of lardo, aromatic herbs and clarified butter. Typical of the Mont Blanc and Great St. Bernard areas. Val d'Aosta.

sorello Ligurian term for ➤ **suro**, horse mackerel.

sorra another word for ➤ **ventresca**, the meat from a fish's abdomen.

sospiri Italianization of ➤ **suspiros**, cakes.

sospiri di monaca "nun's sighs." In Sicily, small meringues; in Calabria, small cassatas. Sicily, Calabria.

Sot la trape cheese (➤ **Latteria** or ➤ **Caciotta**) steeped for four to ten days in unfermented grape must and pomace, then aged for a month. Typical of the Carnia area. Friuli-Venezia Giulia.

soté di vongole clams sautéed in oil, garlic, white wine and minced parsley. The name is an Italianization of the French. Campania.

sott'aceto pickled in vinegar.

sott'olio preserved in oil.

sottile spesso another word for ➤ **pancia** (1), a cut of beef roughly equivalent to plate.

sotto spirito method of preserving fresh or dried fruit either with alcohol diluted with a sugar and water syrup or with a spirit such as grappa, vodka, cognac or Armagnac.

sottofesa cut of beef roughly equivalent to socket.

sottofiletto another word for ➤ **costata**, rib steak.

sottospalla another word for ➤ **reale**, third cut cover ribs.

sottovuoto vacuum-packed.

soufflé soufflé. Baked dish consisting of a purée or sauce thickened with egg yolks into which stiffly whisked egg whites have been folded.

soupe grasse soup of crushed day-old rye bread cooked in broth with butter and

bits of ➤ Toma cheese, to which onions flavored with nutmeg and juniper berries are added. A specialty of the Valle di Susa and other Alpine valleys. Piedmont.

spaccatelle short curved commercial durum wheat pasta of Sicilian origin. Aka ➤ **gramignoni**.

spaccatina soft oblong bread roll with a slash in the top crust. Veneto, Trentino-Alto Adige.

spada rossa regional term for ➤ **cepola**, red band fish

spadone Treviso variety of ➤ **radicchio**.

spaghetti spaghetti. Long commercial or artisan pasta the name of which means "small strings." The first mentions of spaghetti date from the 1820s and 1830s, hence long after ➤ **maccheroni** and ➤ **vermicelli**, but today the word, like pizza, has become an international symbol of Italy and its cooking. At the time of the Italian marine republics, dried pasta was already being shipped all over the Mediterranean. It was produced mainly in Sicily, Liguria, and, later, the Kingdom of Naples, where in 1579 the guild of Vermicellari, pasta makers, broke away from that of bakers to manage grain supplies autonomously. From the 17th century *maccheroni di Napoli* was considered, along with *pasta di Genova*, the finest pasta in Europe. Dried pasta making is also documented in Puglia, Sardinia and Rome from the Middle Ages. By the 20th century spaghetti had become the common food of all Italians, at home and abroad.

spaghetti aglio e olio spaghetti tossed with lightly fried garlic flavored with ground black pepper and garnished with minced parsley. This popular dish probably originated in Campania but is also common in Lazio, Puglia, Calabria and Sicily, especially with the addition of chili.

spaghetti al pesce gatto spaghetti with catfish and tomato.

spaghetti alla carlofortina spaghetti with fresh tuna, typical of the island of Carloforte (Carbonia-Iglesias). Sardinia.

spaghetti alla colatura di alici spaghetti with anchovy extract (➤ **colatura di alici di Cetara**). Campania.

spaghetti alla nursina aka **spaghetti alla norcina** spaghetti with anchovies and black truffle. Without the anchovies, the dish is known as *spaghetti alla spoletina*.

spaghetti alla puverielle "poor man's spaghetti." Spaghetti with a fried egg on top. Typical of Naples. Campania.

spaghetti alla zappatora Foggia version of ➤ **spaghetti aglio e olio**, with the addition of chili.

spaghetti di Maratea spaghetti cooked al dente, tossed with fresh tomato, garlic and oil, and covered in a pot in a bain-marie for ten minutes before serving. Typical of the province of Potenza. Basilicata.

spaghettini thin spaghetti. Commercial durum wheat pasta, very popular in the south of Italy. Other names: ➤ **mezzi vermicelli**, ➤ **vermicellini**.

spaghettoni large spaghetti. Commercial durum wheat pasta of central Italian origin. Other names: ➤ **vermicelloni**, ➤ **filatelli**.

spagnolin Piedmontese term for ➤ **peperoncino**, chili.

spalla generic name for ham from the front leg of the pig.

spalla contadina pisana cured meat made with pork shoulder cured with sea salt, vinegar, fresh garlic, chili and pepper. Typical of the province of Pisa. Tuscany.

spalla cotta della Lunigiana cured meat made with pork shoulder. It is produced in December and February, these days almost exclusively on a domestic level. Typical of Massa-Carrara, Tuscany.

spalla cotta di San Secondo cured meat typical of the provinces of Parma (Emilia) and Cremona (Lombardy) made with pork shoulder on the bone, sometimes smoked. Emilia-Romagna, Lombardy.

spalla cruda cured meat made with pork shoulder, boned or on the bone. Very sweet in flavor, it has an aroma of chestnut with a note of pepper. Protected by a Slow Food presidium. Produced in the province of Parma. Emilia-Romagna.

spalletta common name for ➤ **spalla** in the Marche. Cured meat made with pork shoulder, boned or on the bone, cured with sea salt and washed with white wine. Marche.

spanocchia Campania regional term for ➤ **canocchia**, mantis shrimp.

sparacalaci Trapani term for newborn red mullet (➤ **novellame di pesce**, fish fry).

sparacane aka **sparacogne** regional terms for ➤ **asparago pungente**, wild asparagus.

sparacelli Sicilian term for ➤ **broccolo ramoso**, broccoli.

sparagnella regional term for ➤ **asparago pungente** wild asparagus.

sparaso aka **sparg** aka **sparz** northern Italian dialect words for ➤ **asparago**, asparagus.

sparnocchia Livorno term for ➤ **canocchia**, mantis shrimp.

sparo regional term for ➤ **sarago**, bream.

spatatata soup of potatoes, tomatoes, eggs and pennyroyal. Typical of the province of Viterbo. Lazio.

Spätzle aka **Spätzli** small dumplings of Germanic origin, made with a special grater. Served in broth or as a side dish with game. Trentino-Alto Adige.

speck d'oca unrolled variation on smoked goose breast (➤ **petto d'oca**). Friuli.

speck dell'Alto Adige PGI cured meat known since the 13th century with other names (it was christened speck in the 18th century). A boned pig's leg is steeped for two weeks in a dry brine of salt, pepper, pimento, garlic, juniper berries and sugar, then smoked for two to three weeks and aged for 20 to 24. Trentino-Alto Adige.

spellare ➤ to peel

spelta another word for ➤ **farro**, emmer.

spennare to pluck (➤ **spiumare**).

speo Venetian term for **spiedo**, spit.

speronara term used in Puglia for ➤ **acciuga**, anchovy.

spezie spices. Substances extracted from aromatic plants, most of which native to the Far East. Much used in the past, they have now been largely supplanted by milder aromatic herbs. Nonetheless they, especially chili and pepper, appear frequently in regional Italian recipes, in marinades and in cures for meats. Cloves, juniper berries and cinnamon are also popular.

spezzatino small chunks of veal, beef, lamb, pork or other meats stewed with or without tomato, with vegetables such as potatoes and peas.

spezzatino di capriolo roe deer venison stew with celery, potatoes, onions, carrots and tomatoes. Umbria.

spezzatino di cinghiale wild boar stew with aromatic herbs and olives. A specialty of the province of Nuoro. Sardinia.

spezzatino di manzo beef stew with tomato and red wine. Tuscany.

spezzatino stew made with cubed beef marinated in dry white wine and flavored with sage and rosemary. Friuli-Venezia Giulia.

spianada round flat durum wheat bread. Once baked, the loaves are rubbed on the surface with a damp hand (a technique know as *imbriadau*) and returned to the oven for a few minutes. This gives them a glossy sheen. Sardinia.

spianata Modena version of ➤ **gnocco ingrassato**, in which prosciutto is replaced by ➤ **ciccioli**, pork scratchings. Emilia-Romagna.

spianata di Ozieri flatbread made from a durum wheat dough, pressed with the fingertips into disks vaguely reminiscent of old 33 rpms. These are baked for six to seven hours in the summer, for ten to 12 in the winter. Typical of the Logudoro area. Sardinia.

spianatoio regional term for **matterello**, rolling pin.

spicatielli scoppiettati mixed fried vegetables, including the shoots of wild field greens or broccoli rabe (➤ **cime di rapa**), eggplants and other seasonal vegetables, all cut into pieces and dipped in batter. Campania.

spicchitedda variously shaped baked fruit buns typical of the Aeolian Islands (Messina). Each is decorated with half an almond and the favorite shape is a wheel. Sicily.

spiedini di anguilla e pane spit-roast chunks of eel, marinated in lemon juice, alternated with pieces of bread. Calabria.

spiedino a skewer. By extension the term also means a dish made by roasting, broiling or frying a food on a skewer. Sometimes a sprig of fennel is used in lieu of the skewer itself.

spiedo bresciano song birds impaled on a skewer alternated with sage leaves and slow-roasted for four or five hours. In the countryside outside Brescia, they may also add pieces of pork chop and liver, duck, chicken, rabbit, pork roll, potato and so on. The meats are served with their own cooking juices and polenta. Typical of the province of Brescia. Lombardy.

spiensa aka **spienza** Veneto dialect word for ➤ **milza**, spleen. Calf's spleen, boiled and sliced is one of the traditional ➤ **cicheti**, savory snacks.

spigatelli regional term for ➤ **cime di rapa**, broccoli rabe.

spighitta, a term to describe the wheat ear motif on the edge of handmade ➤ **culurjones**, Sardinian savory or sweet ravioli.

spignolo regional term for ➤ **prugnolo**, mousseron mushroom.

spigo (aka **spighetto**) common name for ➤ **lavanda**, lavender.

spigola sea bass (*Dicentrarchus labrax, Morone labrax*). Fish much prized for its firm, tasty but delicate flesh and versatility in the kitchen. Wild sea bream are hard to come by, most specimens coming from farms. The fish farmed in the Po delta are listed in the Italian Ministry of Agriculture's database of native and/or traditional food products. Sea bream are also farmed extensively in Puglia. The fish may be eaten raw, *carpaccio*-style, baked in a salt crust, *en papillote*, or boiled in a ➤ **court-bouillon**. Common and regional names: ➤ **branzino**, ➤ **lupu de mari**, ➤ **pesce lupo**, ➤ **spina**, ➤ **spinola**.

spina aka **spinola** central and southern Italian word for ➤ **spigola**, gilthead bream.

spina bianca regional term for ➤ **cardo asinino**, milk thistle.

spinaci alla romana boiled spinach finished in a skillet with butter, garlic, raisins and pine kernels. Lazio.

spinacino (1) another word for ➤ **fiocco**, brisket.

spinacino (2) a ➤ **rollè**, a roll of veal stuffed with ground veal, cured meats, day-old bead soaked in milk, grated Parmigiano-Reggiano, baten eggs and herbs. Lombardy.

spinacio (pl. **spinaci**) spinach (*Spinaci oleracea*). In Italy, cultivated mostly in Lazio and Tuscany and, albeit a winter vegetable, now available all year round. It is eat-en raw in salads, or steamed, boiled and stewed. Recipes in which spinach plays a part include: ➤ **zuppa pasqualina**, ➤ **scarpazza**; ➤ **lasagne alla bolognese**, ➤ **ravioli gnudi alla fiorentina**, ➤ **strangolapreti trentini**, ➤ **malfatti**, ➤ **crespelle alla fiorentina**, ➤ **tortelli maremmani**, ➤ **casunziei**, ➤ **cajincì**, ➤ **rofioi**.

spinacio selvatico aka **spinacio di montagna** common name for ➤ **buon enrico**, good King Henry.

spinacione common name for ➤ **atreplice**, rare variety of cultivated spinach.

spinafrutici dialect term for ➤ **pungitopo**, butcher's broom.

spinare to bone (a fish).

spinarolo (1) spiny dogfish (*Squalus acanthias e lo S. fernandinus*) shark often confused with smooth hound (➤ **palombo**) and cooked in the same ways.

spinarolo (2) common name for ➤ **prugnolo**, mousseron mushroom.

spingituro the habit of accompanying pasta dishes with raw vegetables (usually celery, fennel, cucumber and so on) to refresh the palate. Puglia.

spinu pork chops cooked in oil with garlic, parsley, bay leaves, dry white wine and black olives. Sardinia.

spisuculöch literally "hand-snapped." A potato soup to which irregularly shaped egg pasta, milk and mature ➤ **Spressa** cheese are added. Typical of the Val Rendena, in the province of Trento. Trentino-Alto Adige.

spiumare to pluck (poultry or fowl).

splinsiugni d'Uò "little nips of Ovada." Small ➤ **amaretti** cookies shaped by nipping the paste with three fingers. Ovada is a town in the province of Alessandria. Piedmont.

spogna term used in Campania for "ear of corn."

spoia lorda small ravioli stuffed with fresh

cheese, nutmeg and lemon zest, and cooked in broth. Emilia-Romagna.

spollichini dialect term for new ➤ **cannellino** beans, in season from May to October. Campania.

spolverare aka **spolverizzare** to sprinkle, to dust, to scatter (lightly and evenly).

sponcion aka **spuncione** aka **spuncioto** snack or nibble (➤ **cicheti**). Veneto, Friuli-Venezia Giulia.

spongada Brescia name for ➤ **spongata**, a cake.

spongata shortcrust pastry tart of ancient, maybe Jewish, origin filled with honey, walnuts, almonds, pine kernels, raisins and, in some cases, ➤ **mostarda di frutta** or jam. Created in the province of Reggio-Emilia, but now baked with variations in other regions. Emilia-Romagna, Lombardy, Liguria.

spongillo another name for ➤ **pomodorino al piennolo**, a type of tomato.

sponzala aka **sponsale** aka **spunzali** ➤ Puglia words for "leek" (➤ **porro**).

sporcamusi puff pastry cakes filled with warm confectioner's custard and liberally dusted with confectioner's sugar which, if you blow on it, "dirties your face," which is the meaning of the Italian name. A specialty of Lecce. Puglia.

sporchia regional term for ➤ **succiamele delle fave**, bean broomrape.

sportella typical ring-shaped cake on the island of Elba, traditionally exchanged between fiancés at Easter, and still baked locally. Tuscany.

sportellacchia regional term for ➤ **porcellana**, little hogweed.

sposatella pastry shaped like a girl with her hands on her hips, decorated with confetti sugar and with grains of pepper for eyes. Traditionally baked in Capena (Rome) for the feast of San Marco Evangelista (April 25). Lazio.

spratto synonym of ➤ **papalina**, brisling, a small fish.

sprelle Emilia-Romagna word for fried pastries similar to ➤ **cenci**.

spremere to squeeze (a fruit).

Spress another name for ➤ **Mezzapasta** cheese.

Spressa delle Giudicarie ancient low-fat PDO part-skimmed cow's milk cheese made in the mountain dairies of the Valli Giudicarie, Chiese, Rendena and Ledro, in the province of Trento. Trentino-Alto Adige

sprinzuli southern Italian term for ➤ **ciccioli**, pork scratchings.

sproccolati long skewers of sun-dried figs stuffed with wild fennel seeds, often sold on the streets at Christmas. Campania.

spugnola morel. A mushroom of the Morchella genus, which comprises three species. Much prized, more in France than Italy, and eaten both fresh (in pasta sauces for example) and dried.

spullecarielli dialect word for ➤ **spollichini**, new cannelloni beans (➤ **cannellino**).

spuma di gota di maiale di San Miniato cured pig's cheek produced in the lower Valdarno from September to May according to a recipe that dates from 1920. After five months' aging, it is finely chopped to a creamy consistency and spread on toast as an antipasto. Tuscany.

spuma di mortadella a mousse of finely chopped ➤ **mortadella classica di Bologna**, fresh ricotta, grated Parmigiano and cream, served on toast as an antipasto. The recipe is registered at the Bologna Chamber of Commerce. Emilia-Romagna.

spumette di nocciole another name for ➤ **sospiri di monaca**, meringues.

spumiglie meringues aromatized with vanilla, chocolate, coffee and pistachio. Veneto.

spumini aka **spumette** small meringues perfumed with lemon zest and cinnamon. Marche.

spumone in Naples a now rare hard ice cream filled with a light foam dotted with pieces of candied fruit, chocolate and toasted almonds. In Lecce, a coupe of layered ice cream of different flavors (chocolate, pistachio, hazelnut etc.). Campania, Puglia.

spunciacurente name given in Liguria to the tiny *Sepia elegans* cuttlefish. Excellent fried or stewed with garlic and tomato. Liguria.

spungarda name used in Crema (Lombardy) for ➤ **spongata**, a cake.

spungata name used in Sarzana (Liguria) for ➤ **spongata**, a cake.

spuntature con la polenta pork spare ribs and sausage stewed with tomato and served with polenta. Lazio.

squadro angel shark (*Squatina squatina*). Member of the shark family whose much prized meat is cooked in the same way as that of the smooth hound (➤ **palombo**) and the skate (➤ **razza**). Common and regional names: ➤ **squadrolino pellenera**, ➤ **pesce angelo**.

squadrolino pellenera regional term for ➤ **squadro**, angel shark.

squamare to scale, to remove scales from (a fish).

Squaquarone pasteurized cow's milk cheese made with liquid rennet. Cream white in color, soft and sweet, it is eaten spread on focaccia or ➤ **piadina**. Other spellings: **Squacquarone**, **Squacquerone**, **Squaquerone**.

s'scios o s'cioss Veneto dialect names for snails (*Helix pomatia* and *H. aspersa*).

stagghiodde dialect name for ➤ **orecchiette**, a type of pasta.

Stagionato de Vaise ancient semi-cooked organic cow's milk cheese of the Val di

Vara (La Spezia). Liguria.

stagionatura aging or maturing (of cheese and cured meats).

stakanje patate mashed potatoes, runner beans (*tegoline*) and radicchio served with a ➤ **soffritto** of onion, lardo and vinegar. Friuli-Venezia Giulia.

stanghèc local term for ➤ **tortelli cremaschi**. Lombardy.

starna a type of ➤ **pernice**, partridge.

stecchi now rare skewers of mixed meats, mushrooms and artichokes, covered with a mixture of the same ingredients pounded in a mortar, breaded and fried. Liguria.

stecchi fritti alla petroniana skewers of fried chicken livers, and sweetbreads, alternated with diced Gruyère cheese, black truffle and tongue, smothered in béchamel sauce, coated in flour, eggs and breadcrumbs, and fried in oil. The recipe is registered at the Bologna Chamber of Commerce. Emilia-Romagna.

stelina Bergamo word for ➤ **michetta, a bread roll,**

stelle alla cannella Italian name for ➤ **Zimtsterne**, star-shaped Christmas cookies.

stelline aka **stele** commercial egg pasta shaped like small stars with a hole in the middle. Available in two sizes, both cooked in broth.

Stelvio PDO whole or part-skimmed cow's milk cheese produced in the province of Bolzano. Trentino-Alto Adige.

stenderello regional term for ➤ **matterello**, rolling pin.

stentenielli another word for ➤ **abbuoti**, baby lamb's intestines.

sterz cornflour browned in butter and mixed with milk or milky coffee. Friuli-Venezia Giulia.

Sterzing aka **Sterzinger** tangy semi-fat cow's milk cheese produced at Vipiteno-Sterzing (Bolzano). Trentino-Alto Adige.

stiaccia briaca another name for ➤ schiaccia briaca, round Christmas fruit loaf.

Stiacciata term used in Umbria and Tuscany for a focaccia, usually savory.

stiacciata di Pasqua aniseed-flavored sweet Easter flatbread. Tuscany.

stigghiola aka stigliola classico barbecued bundles of calf's or, less traditionally, sheep's offal secured inside knotted intestines. A typical western Sicilian street food (➤ cibo di strada).

Stilfser another name for ➤ Stelvio cheese.

stinchett another name for ➤ ronditt, scones.

stinchetti white marzipan cakes shaped like bones, baked for All Saints' Day and at Christmas. Umbria.

stinco cut of veal (front shank) and pork (shin).

stinco di maiale affumicato smoked shin of pork. Cured meat typical of Trentino-Alto Adige and Friuli-Venezia Giulia.

stirato abbreviated name for ➤ grissino stirato, a breadstick.

stirpada another name for ➤ scherpada, vegetable pie.

stoccafisso stockfish. Wind-dried cod, the most prized variety of which is called ragno, for the name of the Norwegian selector Ragnar. Usually sold ready-soaked in slices (dehydrating it at home is a long and laborious process).

stoccafisso accomodato pieces of soaked, boned stockfish stewed with tomato, olives, pine kernels and potatoes. A great delicacy in Genoa. Liguria.

stoccafisso all'acquese stockfish stewed in white wine with anchovies, garlic, olives, pine kernels, potatoes. Typical of Acqui Terme, in the province of Alessandria. Piedmont.

stoccafisso all'anconetana pieces of stockfish stewed in white wine with anchovies celery, carrot, onion, chili, herbs, tomatoes and black olives. A specialty of Ancona, a port that boasts a long history of trade with the Baltic. In other areas of the region, they may add prunes or marjoram to the dish. Marche.

stoccafisso alla badalucchese stockfish simmered in broth and oil with a mixture of minced dried mushrooms, anchovies, pine kernels, walnuts, hazelnuts, amaretti cookies and herbs. Typical of Badalucco, in the province of Imperia. Liguria.

stoccafisso alla certosina pieces of stockfish simmered in oil and lemon juice and seasoned with salt and pepper. Lombardy.

stoccafisso alla livornese crumbled stockfish flesh stewed in red and white wine with celery, tomato sauce, basil, cherry tomatoes and lemon zest. A specialty of Livorno. Tuscany.

stoccafisso alla perasca chopped stockfish stewed with onion, dried mushrooms, anchovies, tomato, pine kernels and minced parsley. Typical of Borgo Peri, in the province of Imperia. Liguria.

stocche e bacilli codfish and dried fava beans boiled, mixed and dressed with an emulsion of oil, lemon juice and crushed garlic. Liguria.

stocco slang for ➤ stoccafisso, stockfish, in some southern regions, and also in Liguria.

stocco a fungitello chopped stockfish boiled, coated in flour and browned in lard with crushed garlic, tomatoes, salt and pepper. Campania.

stocco alla calabrese chopped stockfish cooked in tomato sauce flavored with onion and parsley, potatoes, basil and olives. Calabria.

stocco alla mammolese stew of stockfish potatoes and dried peppers. A great delicacy in the village of Mammola (Reggio Calabria). Calabria.

stocco alla mulinara chunks of stockfish dipped in flour, fried in boiling oil and finished with onions, parsley, olives and capers. Calabria.

stocco con le amareii pieces of stockfish softened in oil and garlic and mixed with broccoli rabe (*amareii*) that has been boiled separately. Calabria.

stoccopesce aka **stoccofissu** Sicilian terms for ➤ **molva**, ling

Stollen spicy Chrismas cake of Bavarian origin. Trentino-Alto Adige.

stomatico spicy square baked cookies typical of Reggio Calabria. Calabria.

stopeta salt cod marinated for a few days in oil, chili, thyme and sliced onions, then served on slices of toasted bread. A specialty of La Spezia. Liguria

stoppione regional term for ➤ **cardo asinino**, milk thistle.

storione sturgeon. The variety farmed most successfully in Italy is the white sturgeon (*Acipenser transmontanus*), the most prized is the beluga (*A. huso*). The fish's delicate white flesh is sold fresh and smoked, generally in slices. These are cooked in a ➤ **court-bouillon** and served with mayonnaise, broiled or fried. The sturgeon's roe is used to make caviar.

storti strips of egg and flour pasta, fried and curled in a sieve or a ladle. They are served warm or cold. Friuli-Venezia Giulia.

stortina veronese sotto lardo small salami made from locally-raised pigs preserved in lardo. Veneto.

stozze almond cookies, similar to ➤ **quaresimali** but larger, typical of the Vulture area. Basilicata.

straboi aka **straboli** aka **strauben** other names for ➤ **fortaes**, fritters.

straca dent aka **straccadeint** hard "tooth grinding" almond and honey cookies. Emilia-Romagna.

straccaganasse lozenge-shaped honey and oil cakes typical of Viterbo. Lazio.

straccetti (1) small strips of beef or veal dipped in flour and briefly fried in oil. Lazio.

straccetti (2) artisan egg pasta cut like irregular lasagne.

Stracchino fresh, butter raw milk cow's cheese produced mainly in Lombardy.

stracchino gelato aka **lattemiele in cassetta** rectangular or tower-shaped ice cream made of layers of whipped cream (➤ **lattemiele** in Emilia), each with a different flavoring: minced toasted almonds, ground coffee, vanilla, zabaglione, grated chocolate and so on. A specialty of Piacenza. Emilia-Romagna.

stracci regional name for fried pastries similar to ➤ **cenci**.

stracci di Antrodoco egg and flour fritters filled with ground meat, mozzarella, Pecorino, tomato and parsley covered with tomato sauce and Pecorino, and baked in the oven. Specialty of Antrodoco in the province of Rieti. Lazio.

Stracciata stretched curd raw cow's milk cheese. Molise.

stracciatella (1) meat broth into which eggs are beaten. Lazio.

stracciatella (2) ice cream of cream, milk and flaked chocolate invented by the Bergamo confectioner Enrico Panattoni in 1962.

stracciavocc' Abruzzo dialect name for ➤ **canocchia**, mantis shrimp.

strachitund blue cheese made with milk from Bruno Alpina cows. Typical of the Val Taleggio. Lombardy.

straciamuus literally "splash in the face." Bean soup with fresh pasta, usually fettuccine. Typical of the provinces of Cremona and Mantua. Lombardy.

stracotto term applied, mostly in the north of Italy, to the slow braising of beef, veal, pork, donkey or horsemeat (➤ **brasato**).

stracotto alla piacentina beef stuck with lardo and garlic, first browned in chopped onion, pancetta and garlic (chopped lardo, carrot, celery and parsley may also be added), then slow cooked in a covered pan in wine, tomato sauce and broth or hot water. Served with polenta or potato purée, the stew is also used to make the filling for ➤ **anolini** and ➤ **mes mànag da frà**. A recipe typical of the province of Piacenza. In Bobbio, also in the province of Piacenza, they make a spicier version, adding bay leaf, cloves and nutmeg, and using the sauce to dress ➤ **maccheroni bobbiesi**. Emilia-Romagna.

stracotto di asinina loin of donkey braised in wine, tomato concentrate and aromatic vegetables, and served with polenta. Emilia-Romagna.

stracotto di lingua calf tongue first boiled and cured with salt, cinnamon, cloes and garlic, then slowly braised in broth with vegetables. Emilia-Romagna.

stracotto toscano beef braised with ripe tomatoes and red wine. The rich sauce can also be served with pasta. Tuscany.

straeca tenderized horsemeat steak. Veneto.

strafritto chicken giblet sauce used to dress tagliatelle. Typical of the Langhe and Monferrato hills. Piedmont.

strangoiapreve Piedmontese term for ➤ **strozzapreti**, a type of pasta.

strangolapreti fritti small flour, egg and lemon zest dumplings fried in oil, dried and dusted with confectioner's sugar. Basilicata.

strangolapreti meridionali "priest stranglers." Small hollow gnocchi similar to ➤ **cavatelli**, made with variations in name and form all over the south of Italy.

strangozzi another name for ➤ **stringozzi**,

stranguglapreviti aka **strangulapreuti** aka **strangulaprievete** dialect terms common in Calabria, Basilicata and Campania for

➤ **strangolapreti meridionali**, types of pasta.

strangulet Calabrian term to describe ➤ **Arbëreshë**, or Albanian, potato gnocchi.

strapazzare to scramble

strapazzato scrambled (eg, *uova strapazzate*, scrambled eggs). **strappatelli** roughly torn homemade flour and water pasta. Lazio.

strascenate Puglia dialect term for ➤ **orecchiette**, a type of pasta

strascinare to finish, turn or toss cooked food. A central and southern Italian term (➤ **ripassare**).

strascinati southern term for homemade pasta shapes made by pulling or drawn small cylinders of dough over the baking board or over special grooved boards using a a blunt knife, a special iron or applying pressure with the fingers. Two classic examples of this kind of pasta are ➤ **orecchiette** and ➤ **cavatelli**.

strascinati chiusi Puglia dialect term for ➤ **cavatelli**.

strascinati con la menta pasta served with a condiment of oil, lardo, garlic, fresh mint and chili (sometimes with the addition of ➤ **peperoni cruschi**). Basilicata.

strascinati cu lu 'ntruppc strascinati served with a sauce of veal, pork, sausage, onion and Pecorino, traditionally served on important occasions. Basilicata.

strascinati ricotta e sausage strascinati with sausage, ricotta, parsley and Pecorino. Basilicata.

strazzate typical almond cakes. Basilicata.

stria thin flatbread served with cured meats. Emilia-Romagna, Veneto, Lombardy.

stricasale, a dialect term used to describe various foodstuffs (tomatoes, octopus, snails etc.), boiled or raw, rubbed (*stricati*) in salt. Sicily.

stricc' in carpion Small Po bleak (*stricc*) fried and preserved (➤ **carpione**) in oil, garlic, onion or spring onions (*bavaron* in dialect) and vinegar. Traditional recipe of the Po area of the province of Piacenza. Emilia-Romagna.

stricchetti aka **strichetti** aka **strichet** very thin butterfly-shaped egg pasta flavored with Parmigiano and nutmeg.

strichetti spherical almond cakes baked in the oven and served on ostias. Umbria.

stridoli common name for ➤ **silene rigonfia**, bladder campion. **strigoli (1)** another name for ➤ **stridoli** (➤ **silene rigonfia**, bladder campion).

strigoli (2) spiral-shaped fresh homemade pasta. Veneto, Trentino-Alto Adige.

strinare to singe (to remove any remaining feathers after plucking fowl).

stringozzi aka **strangozzi** long fresh flour and water (sometimes egg) pasta typical of the area between Spoleto and Foligno, in the province of Perugia. Umbria.

strinù pork sausage eaten broiled or boiled. A specialty of the Valcamonica, Lombardy.

stripiddi barley meal flatbread. Sardinia.

striscia word used in Piedmont and Lombardy for ➤ **lasca**, roach.

strolghino ancient curved pork salami produced in limited amounts in the province of Parma. Emilia-Romagna.

stroncatura coarse durum wheat and carob flour pasta. Calabria.

stroscia crumbly cake flavored with vermouth. Typical of Imperia.

strozzapreti "priest chokers." Irregular matchstick-shaped homemade flour and water pasta. Sometimes the name is mixed up with that of ➤ **strangolapreti**, "priest stranglers." Both seem to evoke the greed of clergymen and popular anticlericalism. Emilia-Romagna.

strucchi aka **struki** aka **struklji** fried puff pastry bundles with the same filling as ➤ **gubana**. Friuli-Venezia Giulia.

struccolo aka **strucolo pastry roll of Slovenian origin filled with apples, apricots,** sugar, breadcrumbs, butter, pine kernels, lemon zest, cinnamon and grappa. Friuli-Venezia Giulia.

struccolo salato aka **strucolo salato** boiled potato and flour pastry roll stuffed with meat sauce and vegetables or spinach or chard. Friuli-Venezia Giulia.

Strudel German name (meaning "vortex") for a Hungarian pastry very popular in Austria and, with many local variations, in bordering Italian regions. Thin leaves of pastry dough, filled with fruit, nuts or savory mixtures, which are rolled and baked. Trentino-Alto Adige, Friuli-Venezia Giulia.

struffoli ancient Neapolitan cake consisting of tiny deep-fried pastries coated in honey and grated orange zest, then hand-shaped into a pyramid, which may be decorated with confetti or confectioner's sugar. Campania.

strufoli fried Carnival dumplings flavored with liqueur and coated with honey or dusted with confectioner's sugar, made in numerous regions with as many variations.

struki aka **struklji** other names for ➤ **strucchi**, a type of cake.

strunzi d'ancilu Sicilian term for ➤ **biscotti regina**, a type of cookie.

strutto lard. Natural or refined pork fat.

struzza long pointed bread loaves with oblique slashes on the top. Friuli-Venezia Giulia.

stuarz creamy mixture of eggs, flour, sugar and lemon zest, sprinkled with minced almonds, baked in the oven, then cut into strips and shaped into spirals. Friuli-Venezia Giulia.

stuezzi small almond cookies usually eaten dunked in warm grape must ➤ **vincotto**. Puglia.

stufadin di castrato lamb stew cooked in an earthenware pot with vegetables and dried mushrooms. Veneto.

stufare to stew.

stufatino slow-cooked beef stew popular in Rome. Lazio.

stufato a stew.

stufato a rolò slices of beef, lightly floured, seasoned with salt, pepper, and nutmeg, covered with lightly fried mushrooms, ham, and garlic, and cooked in butter, oil, and chopped onions, with the addition of meat broth and tomato purée. Recipe typical of Ferrara. Emilia-Romagna.

stufato all'alessandrina beef stew. Chunks of beef browned in oil, butter, and chopped mixed herbs, then cooked in hot spiced wine. The stew is the chief ingredient for the filling and condiment of the pasta dish → **agnolotti alessandrini**. The recipe is typical of the plains round Alessandria, but is similar to others in the nearby province of Piacenza. Piedmont.

stufato di asino stew of donkey meat previously marinated in red wine, served with soft polenta. Typical of the provinces of Asti and Novara. Piedmont.

stufato di fagioli bean stew with wild fennel and Savoy cabbage. A specialty of the Gallura area. Sardinia.

stufato di fave fresh fava beans stewed in an earthenware pot with aromatics and pancetta. Tuscany.

stufato piccante di alici anchovies stewed with onion, parsley, oregano, chili and ripe cherry tomatoes. Served on toasted bread or with pasta. A specialty of Diamante (Cosenza). Calabria.

stufatura ripening. The stage of cheesemaking that comprises storing the cheese in a warm, humid room for a few hours to complete the fermentation process.

stuzzichino a snack or savory nibble.

suacia aka **cianchetta** scaldfish (*Arnoglossus laterna*). Fish similar to sole (→ **sogliola**) and cooked in the same ways. Younger specimens are coated in flour and fried. Marche.

subiachini small lozenge-shaped almond cookies baked in a tin lined with ostias or confectioner's sugar, glazed with icing (→ **ghiaccia reale**), and decorated with a gold thread. A specialty of Subiaco, in the province of Rome. Lazio.

subioti Veneto version of → **maccheroni al (con il) ferretto**.

subrich potato croquettes served as an antipasto. Piedmont.

suc aka **sugolo** dessert made with red wine grapes, pushed through a sieve and thickened over a heat with wheat flour. Lombardy.

sucamele hand-drawn strong flour, sourdough and water maccheroni which used to be served in Sicily with honey and cinnamon, a custom of Arab origin. In the province of Lecce, they are served with pork sauce. Sicily, Puglia.

sucarisi another name for → **riso e zucca**, rice with pumpkin.

succiamele delle fave bean broomrape (*Orobanche crenata*). Parasite of fava bean and other legume roots. Its appearance is that of a fleshy turion, and it is cooked like asparagus in central and southern Italy. Common and regional names: → **orobanca**, → **sporchia**.

suenne Puglia term for → **grancevola**, spider crab.

suffritte (aka **zuppa di soffritto**) Neapolitan word for → **soffritto (2)**, also known as → **tosciano** or → **saporiglio**. Pig's offal (lung, spleen, heart, and trachea), lightly fried in lard with tomato purée, flavored with bay leaf, rosemary, abundant chili, and red wine, and served with slices of toasted bread. Campania.

sufrit aka **suffrit** custard obtained by thickening a mixture of flour fried to golden in butter, milk, water, grape must or Marsala and sugar on a heat. Typical of the Carnia area. Friuli.

sugali another term for ➤ **sughi di mosto**, wine must sauces.

sugamele regional term for ➤ **acetosella**, sorrel.

sugaro Tuscan term for ➤ **suro**, horse mackerel.

sugeli small flour and water boiled with potatoes and served with fermented cheese. A specialty of the Valle Vermenagna (Cuneo). Piedmont.

sugherello regional name for ➤ **suro**, horse mackerel.

sughetti another name for ➤ **sughi di mosto**, must sauces and desserts.

sughi di carne alla toscana Tuscan meat sauces. The principal ingredient of a good ➤ **ragù** (meat sauce) in any region is time. In the Tuscan version, ground beef, beef fat and chicken livers are browned in a mixture of chopped onion, celery, carrot, parsley, rosemary e basil, and lubricated with red wine. Tomato passata, chili, nutmeg, salt and pepper are then added, and the sauce is left to simmer gently for at least three hours. Games sauces (wild boar, rabbit, and hare) are made following the same technique, with the addition of bay leaves to the aromatic mixture. Sauces made from the innards of chicken, ➤ **nana** (➤ **anatra**, duck), ➤ **ocio** (➤ **oca**, goose), or sheep, follow the same procedure. Goose sauces are flavored with thyme, bay leaf and orange zest. Tuscany.

sughi di mosto must sauces and desserts. In

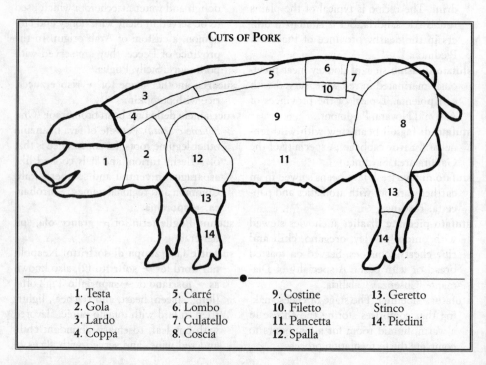

CUTS OF PORK

1. Testa	5. Carré	9. Costine	13. Geretto
2. Gola	6. Lombo	10. Filetto	Stinco
3. Lardo	7. Culatello	11. Pancetta	14. Piedini
4. Coppa	8. Coscia	12. Spalla	

Emilia (Bologna, Modena and Ferrara) and Lombardy the post-harvest tradition continues of cooking white and red grape must and binding it with flour to make sauces and desserts.

sugna suet. In southern Italy, a synonym of ➤ **strutto**, lard.

sugo (1) juice.

sugo (2) gravy or jus.

sugo (3) pasta sauce (➤ **ragù**).

sugo all'anguilla eel sauce, served with egg pasta.

sugo di arrosto meat gravy. Traditional condiment for ➤ **agnolotti** made from the pan juices of the meats used to make the pasta filling, though in restaurants today it often consists merely of a spoonful of ➤ **fondo bruno**, gravy. Piedmont.

sugo di castrato castrated lamb sauce (➤ **castrato**), popular throughout central and southern Italy. Particularly good with ➤ **stringozzi** or gnocchi.

sugo di cinghiale wild boar sauce (➤ **sughi di carne alla toscana**). Tuscany.

sugo di coniglio rabbit sauce (➤ **sughi di carne alla toscana**). Tuscany.

sugo di fegatini chicken liver sauce, served with ➤ **tajarin**. Piedmont.

sugo di interiora di pollo chicken giblet sauce (➤ **sughi di carne alla toscana**).

sugo di lepre hare sauce, flavored with cloves and cinnamon and thickened with the animal's blood (➤ **sughi di carne alla toscana**).

sugo di ocio goose sauce (➤ **sughi di carne alla toscana**).

sugo di papera duck sauce, served with tagliatelle and gnocchi. Marche.

sugo di pecora mutton sauce (➤ **sughi di carne alla toscana**).

sugo di pesce di lago pasta sauce of mixed freshwater fish (perch, eel, tench, trout etc.). Lombardy.

sugo finto literally "pretend sauce." Ironic term used in central Italy for meatless vegetable sauces.

sugoli homemade grape juice jam. Typical of the province of Padua. Veneto.

sugolo another name for ➤ **suc o sugolo**, red grape dessert.

suina mora romagnola pig breed once on the verge of extinction, now protected by a Slow Food presidium. The Mora Romagnolo is ideal for breeding in the open and produces soft, tasty pork, perfect for the production of cured meats, salami and hams. Emilia-Romagna.

suino pig. Perhaps domesticated for the first time in China in the 4th millennium BC, the pig was always the main source of protein for Italian peasants, who learned to exploit every part of the animal. In recent times, intensive Italian pig breeding has replaced many native breeds (Emiliana, Lombarda, Macchiaiola, Romagnola, Perugina, Casertana etc.) with imported ones (eg, ➤ **Large White** and ➤ **Landrace**). For more historical and gastronomic references: ➤ **maiale**.

suino nero calabrese possibly of Spanish descent, the Nero Calabrese pig used to be common all over the region, but is now on the verge of extinction. Calabria.

suino nero dei Nebrodi a pig breed that lives virtually in the wild in the Nebrodi mountains, it looks and behaves like a wild boar. Its meat is excellent but, given the small scale of breeding and processing companies, has a limited market. A Slow Food presidium is seeking to save the breed and promote its fresh pork and cured meats (including ➤ **salame di Sant'Angelo di Brolo**). Sicily.

suino pesante heavy pig. Pigs slaughtered when they have reached a weight of 320-350 pounds, usually at the age of nine to ten months. Their meat is highly suitable for processing, hence constitutes the raw material for the curing industry. The only parts of the animal for direct consumption are the dorsal and lumbar vertebrae, from which chops are cut. Such pigs usually belong to imported prolific, high-yield breeds, such as the ➤ **Large White** and the ➤ **Landrace**.

sulla French honeysuckle (*Hedysarium coronarium*). Melliferous herb, common in the south of Italy.

supa 'd còi baked cabbage soup with cheese typical of the mountain valleys of the Canavese area, north of Turin. Piedmont.

supa barbëtta layered soup of day-old bread, cabbage and cheese covered with chicken broth. A specialty of the Waldensian valleys of the province of Turin. Piedmont.

supa de tridarini homemade pasta "crumbs" grated from a solid dough of eggs, breadcrumbs, Parmigiano-Reggiano and nutmeg (*tridarini*), cooked in broth. Lombardy.

supa dj marghé soup of milk, ➤ Toma and other mountain cheese. Typical of the Valsusa. Piedmont.

supa mitonà soup of slices of day-old bread rubbed with garlic and simmered in meat broth. Traditional dish in the Cuneo mountains and the province of Asti. Piedmont.

supa rostida Ladin equivalent of ➤ **brö brüsà**. A cream made by blending flour toasted in lard with water or broth and flavoring it with chives and cumin seeds. Typical of the Ladin valleys in northeast Italy. Trentino-Alto Adige, Friuli-Venezia Giulia.

suppa cuatta aka **suppa quatta** aka **zuppa gallurese** aka **zuppa sarda** baked soup of slices of farmhouse bread layered with fresh cheese and herbs, covered with mutton broth. Sardinia.

supplì al telefono another name for ➤ **supplì alla romana**.

supplì alla romana orange-sized balls of boiled rice, stuffed with diced mozzarella, dipped in beaten eggs, in breadcrumbs and deep-fried. Lazio.

surbìa Piedmontese term for the addition of a glass of red wine, usually Barbera, to a soup.

surgitti aka **suricitti** Marche words for gnocchi.

suri sottovento horse mackerel covered with a sauce of peppers, tomatoes and vinegar. A dish served cold. Marche.

surîs another name for ➤ **salviade**, sweet sage leaves.

suro horse mackerel (*Trachurus trachurus*). A sea fish with firm, tasty flesh. Very good grilled, baked and fried. Common and regional names: ➤ **sauro**, ➤ **sauru**, ➤ **sgombro bastardo**, ➤ **sorello**, ➤ **sugaro**, ➤ **sugherello**.

surra southern Italian term for ➤ **ventresca**, fish's abdomen.

susamielli "S"-shaped Christmas cookies. Lazio, Campania.

suscìa bean soup thickened with flour and aromatized with herbs. Friuli-Venezia Giulia.

susianella rare offal and herb cured meat of the province of Viterbo, inspired by an ancient Etruscan recipe. Lazio.

susina word used colloquially as a synonym of ➤ **prugna**, plum, though the fruit is really a specific Prunus (*P. domestica*).

susine bianche di Monreale white plums typical of the province of Palermo, once on the verge of extinction, now protected by a Slow Food presidium. Sicily.

suspiros "sighs." Baked çakes typical of Ozieri, in the province of Sassari. Sardinia.

susumelle flat, oval Christmas fruit cookies coated with chocolate or glazed with icing and decorated with chocolate curlicues. Typical of the provinces di Crotone and Vibo Valentia. Calabria.

sutta e supra pork chops cooked in white wine. Sicily

suvet soft polenta scented with mountain herbs. Typical of the Canavese area, northwest of Turin. Piedmont.

suzu Sicilian term for ➤ **gelatina di maiale**.

svizzera Italian name for hamburger.

tT

tabbaccò southern Marche dialect term for ➤ **totano**, squid.

tacchino (pl. **tacchini**) turkey (*Meleagris gallopavo*). Probably of Mexican origin, the only farmyard animal to come to Europe from the Americas (the synonyms ➤ **gallo d'India** and ➤ **dindo** derive from "West Indies" not India.). Most turkeys today are productive hybrids selected above all in the United States, and can reach a weight of seven to eight pounds in just five to six months. The best meat comes from smaller birds, especially young hens. Like ➤ **cappone**, capon, turkey is eaten mostly at Christmas (➤ **tacchino ripieno**) and in some all-year-round regional recipes (➤ **tacchino alla canzanese**, ➤ **tacchino alla storiona**). The Italian Ministry of Agriculure's database of native and/or traditional food products includes the following ecotypes: *tacchino ermellinato di Rovigo, tacchino comune bronzato* (Veneto), *galnacc bronzato rustic* aka *dindo bronzato rustico* (Marche).

tacchino alla canzanese recipe typical of Canzano, in the province of Teramo, where turkey is popular. In nearby Nereto, they cook the bird *in porchetta* (➤ **porchetta**), in Canzano they bone it and flavor it with herbs, then bake it slowly in the oven with the bones and water. After skimming, it is allowed to cool in its own gelatin. Abruzzo.

tacchino alla storiona the cavity of the turkey is flavored with herbs, boiled, allowed to cool and boned. It is then covered with the gelatin from its own broth and garnished with pine kernels and pistachio nuts. The same recipe can be used with ➤ **cappone**, capon. Liguria.

tacchino ripieno stuffed turkey. A Christmas favorite throughout the north of Italy. In Lombardy they prefer to use a turkey hen, stuffing it with ground veal, pancetta, apples, pears, chestnuts, walnuts and, in recent recipes, prunes and brandy. In Friuli the stuffing consists of boiled chestnuts, bread soaked in milk, eggs, white wine, the bird's liver fried with onion and sausage and chopped rosemary and sage.

taccola (pl. **taccole**) aka **pisello mangiattutto** mangetout. Common in the Marche, where it is harvested from April to June. Eaten stewed with tomato and onion or boiled.

tacconcelli, **tacconelle** another name for ➤ **tacconi (1)**.

tacconi (1) fresh square or lozenge-shaped pasta common in central Italy (➤ **maltagliati**). Other common names: **taccozze**, **tacconelle**, **tacconcelli**. Popular in the Abruzzo region, where they serve it with sauces of fish, mutton (➤ **castrato**) or lamb, with peas or beans. In Abruzzo they make the pasta with durum wheat and water, whereas in the Marche, where the common name is **taccù**, they add cornflour to the mix. The name could derive from *tacco*, heel, or from *tacca*, patch. In some regions, such as Tuscany, they sometimes make **tacconi** with eggs: ➤ **tacconi sul conigliolo**.

tacconi (2) sweet half-moon ravioli filled with ricotta, usually fried but also boiled in water. Specialty of Viterbo. Lazio.

tacconi sul conigliolo egg tacconi with rabbit. The rabbit is jointed and marinated in red wine, spices and herbs, and cooked with chopped aromatic herbs, pancetta, bay leaves and wine. The meat is then boned and the mixture passed through a mincer. The resulting sauce is spread in layers over the boiled egg pasta and sprinkled with grated Parmigiano. Tuscany.

taccozze, taccù Marche names for → **tacconi (1)**, type of pasta.

tacoi Venetian name for → **patugoi**, soft polenta.

tacui fresh pasta made with chestnut and wheat flour. Traditionally served with a → **pesto** of garlic, basil, marjoram, walnuts, Parmigiano and oil. Liguria.

tacula now rare specialty of the provinces of Cagliari and Nuoro. Thrushes boiled, transferred to a canvas bag containing myrtle leaves, and served cold. Sardinia.

taeddha aka **taieddha** aka **taeddhra** words used in southern Italian dialects, especially in Puglia, for **teglia da forno**, baking tin. Like → **tiana**, **tiella**, **pignata** or **pignato**, **rote** or **ruoto**, it also refers, by extension, to the dish baked in it. In the Salento area, the dish consists of a layered bake or casserole (similar to → **tiella barese**) of zucchini, potatoes, onions, rice and mussels covered with the liquid from the mollusks, oil, parsley and, sometimes, tomato.

taeddhra another word for → **taeddha**, baking tin.

tafelspitz sliced boiled beef served with potatoes sautéed in butter and onion and sprinkled with grated → **cren**, horseradish. Dish typical of the Sudtirolo area. Trentino-Alto Adige.

taganu di Aragona rare Easter baked casserole of rigatoni layered with beaten

eggs, saffron, salt, pepper, parsley, grated Pecorino and → **Tuma** cheese. In an older version, bread was used instead of pasta. In some recipes, pork sauce is added. Sicily.

tagghiarine aka **tagghiarini** central and southern Italian words for → **tagliolini**, a type of pasta.

tagliati di mezzani another name for → **tubetti**, a type of pasta.

tagliancozzi Trapani dialect term for → **quaresimali** Lent cookies.

tagliare to cut.

tagliarelli another name for → **tagliatelle**, type of pasta.

tagliata tender top of sirloin broiled or fried and flavored with olive oil, salt, pepper and herbs.

tagliatelle fresh pasta ribbons. Originally made simply with flour and water, now mostly made with the addition of eggs. The best known tagliatelle are those from Bologna (→ **tagliatelle alla bolognese**). Other versions, of varying lengths and thicknesses, include: → **bardele** in Lombardy, rye flour → **tajadele smalzade** in Trentino, → **fettuccine** in Lazio. In southern Italy, the terms → **curiuli**, → **làgane**, and → **tria** are also used. Other names: **fettuccelle**, **fettucce romane**, **tagliarelli**.

tagliatelle al milk soup of snapped tagliatelle cooked in water and milk with fried leeks. A dish typical of the mountain valleys of the province of Cuneo. Piedmont.

tagliatelle alla bolognese egg tagliatelle (four eggs per four ounces of flour) served with → **ragù alla bolognese** and a sprinkling of grated Parmigiano-Reggiano. Emilia-Romagna.

tagliatelle col papavero egg and flour tagliatelle served with butter flavored with poppy seeds and ground black pepper. In one variation, almonds are added and the pasta is sprinkled with sugar before serving. Friuli-Venezia Giulia.

tagliatelle con la trota Tagliatelle with tomato sauce flavored with onion, celery, carrot and filleted young trout. Trentino-Alto Adige.

tagliatelle con salsiccia, fegatini, funghi e tartufo nero tagliatelle with sausage, chicken livers, mushrooms and black truffle. A sauce that brings together four of the region's most representative ingredients. Umbria.

tagliatelle della Madonna regional term for ➤ **silene rigonfia**, bladder campion.

tagliatelle di fromentin wheat and buckwheat flour tagliatelle boiled with potatoes and chard (or other greens) and served with pieces of Toma cheese and grated Parmigiano. Traditional dish of Valloriate and Bagni di Vinadio, in the province of Cuneo. Piedmont.

taglierini another name for ➤ **tagliolini**, a type of pasta.

taglierini nei fagioli taglierini with beans. Egg pasta "drowned" in a thick sauce of beans, diced potatoes, pork rind, rosemary, aromatics, salt, pepper and chili. Tuscany.

taglietelle nervate another name for ➤ **mafalde**, a type of pasta.

tagliolini very fine pasta ribbons (➤ **tagliatelle**) made of flour and eggs, occasionally with the addition of water. Regional versions and names abound: ➤ **tajarin** in Piedmont, ➤ **paparele** in Veneto, ➤ **bazot** in Emilia-Romagna, ➤ **fini-fini** in Lazio, ➤ **taglierini**, ➤ **tajarille**, ➤ **tajulì**, ➤ **tagghiarine**, ➤ **tagghiarini** throughout central and southern Italy. Condiments vary according to local traditions and customs. This type of pasta is also used to make ➤ **torta di tagliatelle**.

tagliolini dell'Ascensione egg tagliolini cooked in milk flavored with sugar and cinnamon.

tagliolini freddi "cold" tagliolini, cooked on Friday and dressed with pepper and oil, then served cold on Saturday. A Jewish dish from Ancona. Marche.

tagliolini in brodo con gli inciampi egg tagliolini cooked in meat broth with chicken livers. Once a dish for major occasions, cooked for important guests. Tuscany.

tagliolini in brodo di osso di prosciutto egg tagliolini cooked in broth made with a ham shank and aromatics. Umbria.

taieddha synonym of ➤ **taeddha**, baking tin.

tajadele smalzade wheat and rye flour tagliatelle served with beef gravy, cream and cheese. Trentino.

tajarille e fasciule short rectangular flour and water pasta served with beans, tomato, onion and chili. Typical of Pescara. Abruzzo.

tajarin fresh thin tagliatelle made with an abundant use of egg yolks. Served with butter and sage, gravy from the roast, in summer tomato and basil. Especially in the Langhe hills, in the province of Cuneo, the classic accompaniment is chicken liver sauce (➤ **sugo di fegatini**). Piedmont.

tajulì pilusi coarse ➤ **quadrucci** (*pelosi* means "hairy"), traditionally served with lardo and onion, in spring with fava beans. Marche.

tajut Friulian term for the Italian *taglio* or *taglietto*, which means "cut." It is used in slang to refer to a glass of wine and, by extension, an aperitif. The equivalent of ➤ **ombra** in Venice.

Taleggio washed-rind, soft, raw or pasteurized cow's milk cheese with a sweet, buttery flavor. Produced throughout Lombardy and, elsewhere, in the provinces of Treviso and Novara. Especially prized are cheeses aged in the natural grottoes of the Valsassina (province of Como). Lombardy, Piedmont, Veneto.

talegua Ligurian term for ➤ **grattalingua**, common brighteyes.

talli shoots or sprouts. In southern Italy, the word refers specifically to the tender stalks and leaves of the zucchini plant, used to make soups and dress pasta. A classic Sicilian recipe is ➤ **pasta con i tenerumi**.

tamarindo tamarind (*Tamarindus indica*). Tropical plant whose pods contain seeds with a sharp but pleasant taste. In Italy, tamarind syrup is used to make refreshing drinks and granitas.

tamaro black bryony (*Tamus communis*). A climbing plant with heart-shaped leaves and shiny bright red berries that grows in ditches and hedgerows. Though the berries and roots are poisonous, the tips are eaten (boiled preserved in oil, in frittatas and in soups) in the provinces of Marcerata and Pesaro and in the Tuscia area of Lazio, where they are known as ➤ **abbojeli**. Common and regional names: ➤ **cerasiola**, ➤ **tanno**, ➤ **tanoni**, ➤ **uva tamina**, ➤ **vite nera**, ➤ **viticella**.

tambarello frigate tuna (*Auxis thazard*). Common throughout the Mediterranean and comparable to the ➤ **sgombro**, mackerel in appearance, habits, and culinary uses (its flesh is eaten fresh or preserved). Common and regional nomes: ➤ **biso**, ➤ **pisantuni**, ➤ **prisintuni**, ➤ **sangusu**, ➤ **sgamirru**, ➤ **tombarello**, ➤ **tunnacchiu**.

tamburrino regional name for ➤ **pesce chitarra**, common guitar fish.

tamplun fritters of chestnut flour, yeast, soaked bread crumbs, raisins, dried figs, lemon juice and aniseed, sprinkled with refined sugar. Typical of the Polesine district, but also to be found in the province

of Ferrara. Veneto, Emilia-Romagna.

tanaceto common name for ➤ **partenio**, feverfew.

tani dialect term for ➤ **pungitopo**, butcher's broom.

tanni dialect term for ➤ **cime di rapa**, broccoli rabe.

tanno aka **tanoni** regional terms for ➤ **tamaro**, black bryony.

tanuta black seabream (*Spondyliosoma cantharus*). Relatively unknown sea fish with tasty white flesh that can be cooked in the same way as that of sea bream (➤ **orata**). Common and regional names: ➤ **cantarella**, ➤ **cantaro**, ➤ **sarago** ➤ **bastardo**.

tapioca starchy substance extracted from the roots of the manioc, a tropical plant native to Brazil. Used in lieu of flour in the preparation of baby foods and as a binding agent in sauces and gravies.

tappada Cagliari term for ➤ **monzetta**, earth snail.

tapulon donkey meat stew typical of Borgomanero (Novara). Piedmont.

tarallo (pl. **taralli**), **taralluccio** (pl. **tarallucci**) twice-baked friable ring-shaped biscuit typical of southern Italy. Born as an alternative to bread, now commonly eaten as a snack. **Taralli** may be savory or sweet, leavened or unleavened, baked directly or pre-scalded in boiling water. In Campania, they are often flavored with wild fennel seeds: in the province of Benevento they are braided; in the province of Naples, the dough is enriched with suet and pepper and the biscuits are decorated with lightly toasted unpeeled almonds; in the province of Avellino they are boiled when half-leavened; in the province of Caserta they make ➤ **auciati**, small **taralli** with aromatic doughs. In Puglia **taralli** come in all shapes and sizes, changing name, depending on whether they contain yeast or pre-boiled (➤ **scaldatelle**, or *cancelle* in some areas of Basilicata). Also are boiled before baking are ➤ **ciambelle scottolate**, sweet ring-shaped cookies typical of Lazio. Other sweet versions are made in Sicily (flavored with wine, aniseed and lemon), in Abruzzo (➤ **tarallucci lessi**), in Puglia (➤ **occhi di santa Lucia**, ➤ **pucciatidd**), most of them served spread with or dipped in ➤ **naspro**, icing.

tarallucci lessi ring-shaped cookies made at Lent. Flour, eggs, aniseed, sugar and oil kneaded to a dough, shaped into rings, boiled in water, drained, dried on a cloth, then baked for 15 minutes. Typical of the province of Teramo. Abruzzo.

tarantello the prized upper belly of the tuna (➤ **tonno**), comercialized preserved in oil.

tarantula Sicilian term for ➤ **grancevola**, spider crab.

tarassaco dandelion (*Taraxacum officinale*). The leaves are gathered, especially in northern and central Italy, where they are used in salads (➤ **misticanza**), frittatas and risottos or boiled and dressed. Common and regional names: ➤ **dente di leone**, ➤ **dente di cane**, ➤ **girasole selvatico**, ➤ **insalata matta**, ➤ **piscialetto**, ➤ **pisciacane**, ➤ **radicchio di prato**, ➤ **radicchio di campo**, ➤ **soffione**.

tarese Valdarno large flat pancetta cured with a mixture of powdered pepper, orange zest and spices. Now made only by one producer in San Giovanni Valdarno (Arezzo), it is protected by a Slow Food presidium.

taroncioli balls of fried ➤ **Tuma**. Sicily.

tarozz another word for ➤ **maüsc**, a vegetable dish.

tarta d'Ols, in Italian aka **torta di Oulx**. "Cake" made by pouring eggs, milk, sugar and lemon zest over slices bread. Typical of the Valsusa (Turin). Piedmont.

tartaruga (tortoise) variation on the Milanese bread roll ➤ **michetta** with a checked pattern on the top.

tartelletta round tart of shortcrust, brisée or puff pastry filled with fresh fruit, fruit preserved in syrup, cream, chocolate etc.

tartifla a la sarinera another name for ➤ **sarignà**, a potato dish.

tartina canapé. A thin slice of plain or toasted bread garnished with the most varied and imaginative ingredients. Served as an *amuse-buche* or appetizer.

tartra aka **tartrà** savory mold of milk, onions or leeks, butter, eggs, Parmigiano and herbs (bay leaf, sage and rosemary) cooked in a bain-marie. Typical of the Langhe and Monferrato hills, Piedmont.

tartufare to flavor or garnish a dish with white or black truffle.

tartufata cake of cream and confectioner's custard garnished at the base with crushed hazelnuts, coated with slivers of chocolate and dusted with confectioner's sugar. Specialty of Vercelli, but now famous everywhere. Piedmont.

tartufo (pl. **tartufi**) truffle. A fungus that develops underground in a symbiotic relationships with certain trees. The truffles known in Italy are the white (or Alba for the name of the chief city in the Langhe area where they grow) and the black (or Périgord or Norcia). The first have much more flavor and are eaten raw in wafer-thin slices with ➤ **fonduta**, ➤ **tajarin**, risottos, raw beef and eggs. The prized white truffle (*Tuber magnatum Pico*), known in Piedmont as *trifola*, is found from October to December under limes, poplars and willows. Besides the Langhe, it is also found in the central Apennines and Istria. The black truffle (*T. melanosporum*) is common in symbiosis with oaks, poplars and hazels in the south of France, northeast Spain and in

Italy, especially in Umbria and Tuscany. The Italian Ministry of Agriculture's database of native and/or traditional food products lists: *tartufi d'Abruzzo; tartufo di Liguria; tartufo nero di Lombardia; tartufo bianchetto (marzuolo) della Toscana; tartufo bianco di Emilia-Romagna, Molise, Marche, Piemonte, Toscana e Umbria; tartufo dei Monti Lepini, tatufo della montagna Veronese, nero dei Berici* (Veneto); *nero di Fragno* (Emilia-Romagna); *bianco di Campoli Appennino, nero di Cervara e Saracinesco* (Lazio); *nero di Colliano e Bagnoli Irpino* (Campania); *tartufo nero estivo di Marche, Emilia-Romagna e Toscana; tartufo nero pregiato di Marche, Toscana e Umbria; tartufo nero uncinato della Toscana.*

tartufo delle Madonie another name for the ➤ **basilisco**, white ferula mushroom.

tartufo di canna regional term for ➤ **topinambur**, Jerusalem artichoke.

tartufo di mare another name for ➤ **vongola**, clam.

tartufo di Pizzo hazelnut and chocolate ice-cream coated with cocoa. A specialty of Pizzo, in the province of Catanzaro. Calabria.

tartufo dolce (1) truffle. A praline made of chocolate and other ingredients (liqueur, chopped walnuts, butter) shaped into small irregular spheres reminiscent of the fungus of the same name, left in the refrigerator to set, and coated in cocoa.

tartufo dolce (2) semispherical semifreddo of vanilla ice-cream coated in chocolate.

tartufolo Campania term for ➤ **tartufo di mare** (➤ **vongola**, clam).

tarun russ Lombard dialect term for ➤ **sanguinello**, saffron milk-cap mushroom.

tasca pasquale another name for ➤ **pizza rustica**.

tascone another name for a cow's caecum intestine.

tastasal mixture of ground spiced pork, a synonym of ➤ **pastin** (Veneto) and ➤ **pistume** (Lombardy). Lombardy, Veneto.

tasto aka **tasca** belly or breast of veal opened like a pouch and stuffed with a mixture of chard, eggs and Parmigiano. Emilia-Romagna.

tatin French apple tart popular in Italy, where the word is often used to refer to any upside-down cake.

tatù cube-shaped or spherical almond cookies glazed with chocolate. Sicily.

tecia name used in Veneto and Trieste for an earthenware pot in which various foods are cooked.

tegamaccio soup of lake fish (eel, perch, pike, tench) served on toasted bread. Umbria.

tegamino di cozze mussels cooked with vinegar, oil and lemon juice sprinkled with breadcrumbs. Campania.

tegole literally "tiles." Convex wafers made from a mixture of chopped hazelnuts and almonds, flour, sugar and beaten egg whites. A relatively recent recipe. Val d'Aosta.

tegoline in tecia green beans stewed in broth with lardo, onion, garlic and cinnamon. Veneto.

tellina tellin or wedge shell clam (*Donax trunculus*). Small edible marine bivalve mollusk with an almost triangular shell. Lives on sandy sea beds and is almost always eaten cooked. Sometimes the word refers to ➤ **vongola**, clam. Common and regional names: ➤ **arsella**, ➤ **cozzola**, ➤ **fasiola**, ➤ **scognariente**, ➤ **tunninola**, ➤ **ziga**.

temolo grayling (*Thymallus thymallus*) rare freshwater fish of the Timallidae family, which owes its name to the scent of thyme (*timo* in Italian) characteristic of its delicate flesh. It cannot be farmed and lives only in cold clean river water. A healthy population still inhabits the area of the confluence between the rivers Pellice and Po near Carignano, in the province of Turin. Piedmont.

temolo alle nocciole fillets of grayling spread with butter mixed with small pieces of anchovy, sprinkled with finely chopped toasted hazelnuts, scented with sage leaves and baked in the oven. Piedmont.

tempestine commercial irregularly-shaped egg pasta cubes. Usually cooked in broth. Other names: ➤ **grattata**, ➤ **grattoni**.

tempia temple. Gastronomic term for head meat, especially that of the pig (➤ **ceci con la tempia di maiale**).

tenca col pien stuffed tench. The fish is stuffed with a mixture of fresh breadcrumbs, tuna, garlic, parsley and, sometimes, anchovies, capers, egg, grated cheese and aromatic herbs, then fried in oil flavored with sage leaves or broiled. Veneto.

Tendaio ancient, uncooked, pressed curd cow's milk cheese. Produced from November to April by a single craft dairy in Castiglione di Garfagnana, in the province of Lucca. Aged for 60 days. Tuscany.

tenerina "tender" sponge cake made of flour, eggs and sugar. Typical of Ferrara. Emilia-Romagna.

terracrepolo regional term for ➤ **grattalingua**, common brighteyes.

terrina terrine.

terzaluru cylindrical earthenware recipient with a lid known as a ➤ **timpagnu**. Used to store foodstuffs such as ➤ **mustica**, ➤ **sardella**, ➤ **gelatina di maiale**. Calabria.

testa di cinghiale alla castagnana wild boar's head boiled, cleaned, boned, marinated in water, vinegar and aromatic herbs, cut into symmetrical pieces, flavored with chopped spices and herbs, secured with string and simmered in water with oil, onion and more aromatic herbs. The pan juices are then filtered and poured over the meat. A dish typical of Castagneto Carducci (province of Livorno), where the recipe was revived in the 19th Century by a cook called Tavernello. Tuscany.

testa di moro "Moor's head." Italian name for ➤ **Mohrenkopfe**, chestnut cake.

testa di turco "Turk's head." Strips of pastry fried and wound into a turban shape. Sicily.

testa in cassetta cured meat typical of the area inland from Genoa. Shoulder and head pork cure with spices and pressed in special square molds lined with caul. Liguria.

testa in cassetta di Gavi cured meat of head pork, pig's tongue and cow's heart, produced in winter in the Val Lemme and Gavi areas (Alessandria). A Slow Food presidium supports pork butchers who still use the original recipe. Piedmont.

testarelle di abbacchio in teglia baked baby lamb's brains and tongue flavored with garlic, parsley and lemon. Lazio.

testaroli traditional specialty of the Lunigiana area on the border between Liguria and Tuscany. Disks made with a batter of flour, warm water and salt cooked in a ➤ **testo**, or griddle pan, and served with ➤ **pesto genovese** or, more traditionally, Parmigiano or Pecorino with finely chopped parsley and extra virgin olive oil. Liguria, Tuscany.

testarolo artigianale pontremolese soft, light disks handmade with a batter of flour, warm water and salt, cooked in the traditional wrought iron ➤ **testo**, griddle pan. A Slow Food presidium supports producers who follow traditional techniques and use the flour of the native wheat *ventitré* cultivar. Massa-Carrara, Tuscany.

testicciola roast lamb's head roast in the oven with herbs. A dish traditionally made at Easter. Umbria.

testicoli testicles. Bull's testicles are known as ➤ **granelli**. Cockerel's testicles are considered giblets (➤ **rigaglie**).

testina in gastronomic language, the heads of calves, pigs, lambs and kids.

testina all'agro boiled boned head veal served cold dressed with onion, vinegar and oil (Trentino-Alto Adige), or warm marinated with wine, vinegar, garlic and herbs (Umbria).

testina di vitello al sugo boiled bone head veal cut into pieces and flavored with tomato sauce, sage, parsley and lemon zest. Sicily.

testina e lingua al brusco diced calf's head and tongue served cold with a warm sauce of oil, vinegar, anchovies, peppers and capers. Piedmont.

testina in dolzegarbo boned boiled head veal served with a sauce of butter, onion, breadcrumbs, vinegar and sugar. Veneto.

testina in salsa verde pieces of boiled head veal served with a sauce of minced aromatic vegetables, garlic, parsley and pickles. Piedmont.

testo griddle pan. Pan with low edges or a disk made of terra cotta, stone, wrought iron or clay used for cooking batters and flatbreads, such as ➤ **piada**, ➤ **piadina**, ➤ **tigella**, ➤ **crescentina**, ➤ **necci**, ➤ **testaroli**, ➤ **torta al testo**, ➤ **crescia**, ➤ **ciaccia**). Names, shapes and cooking techniques vary from place to place.

Testun cheese produced in the valleys of the province of Cuneo with 100% ewe's milk or ewe's milk mixed with small quantities of cow's milk. It ages for two months to a year in cellars or caves. Piedmont.

tetette another name for ➤ **teutenne**, a cured meat.

teteun aka **tetin** cured meat made from cow's udders pressed with salt and spices, dried, and boiled. Val d'Aosta.

teutenne ancient, rare cured meat made of fresh cow's udders layered in a ➤ **doil** with bay leaves, rosemary, sage, juniper berries, spices and salt.

tiana aka **tiano** aka **tianello** words used in southern dialects for an earthenware pot that, by extension, also refers to the food cooked in it. Eg, in Calabria, **tiana** is a kid stew with potatoes and peas.

tibuia aka **torta degli ebrei** pie of puff pastry layered with slivers of Parmigiano. A specialty of Finale Emilia, in the province of Modena, where it is said to have been brought by a family of Jews converted to Christianity. Emilia-Romagna.

tiella word used in southern dialect for a tin or copper baking tin that, by extension, also refers to the food cooked in it. Eg, in Puglia ➤ **tiella barese**.

tiella barese aka **tiella di riso, patate e cozze** baked casserole consisting of layers of sliced onions and potatoes, mussels, rice fresh tomato and Pecorino. Puglia.

tiella di baccalà e patate baked casserole consisting of layers of fried salt cod, sliced potatoes, minced garlic, parsley and onions and halved cherry tomatoes. A specialty of the province of Foggia. Puglia.

tiella di cardoncelli baked casserole consisting of layers of onion, potatoes, king oyster mushrooms (➤ **cardoncello**). Puglia.

tiella di Gaeta baked "sandwich" consisting of two round leavened focaccias filled with anchovies, tomatoes, Gaeta olives, garlic, parsley oil and chili or other ingredients, including seafood. Lazio.

tiella di verdure baked casserole of peppers, eggplants, potatoes and tomatoes. Puglia.

tigella a sort of round earthenware griddle or hot plate (➤ **testo**) used to cook ➤ **crescentina**. By extension, the word has come to refer to the flatbread itself. The utensil and the flatbread are both typical of the Apennines in the province of Modena. Today metal plates, known as *tigelliere*, with room to cook more than one flatbread at once, have taken over. Emilia-Romagna.

tighe sott'aceto sweet green peppers left to wither, pressed into glass jars, salted and covered with vinegar. Stored for at least a month, they are excellent with -> **Salva**, cow's milk cheese. Typical of Crema (Cremona), where they call the peppers *tighe* in local dialect, though variations on the theme exist all over Italy. Lombardy.

tiliccas another name for -> **caschettas**, Sardinian pastries.

timbala apple, pear, peach and amaretti tart typical of Cigliano, in the province of Vercelli. Piedmont.

timballo timbale. A large cup-shaped earthenware or metal mold and, by extension, the dishes prepared in it. Such dishes normally involve rice or pasta cased inside a shortcrust or brisée pastry crust and mixed with a ragù and/or other ingredients. Regional examples include: -> **bomba di riso**, -> **lasagna napoletana**, -> **pasta china**, -> **pasticcio di maccheroni**, -> **sartù**, -> **timpàno di maccheroni**.

timballo Bonifacio VIII a timbale without a crust, which is replaced by large slices of prosciutto, and a filling of egg fettuccine with a sauce of meatballs, chicken giblets, mushrooms and tomato sauce. A specialty of Anagni (Frosinone) in honor of Pope Boniface VIII, who was struck in the face there by an agent of the King of France. Lazio.

timballo di anellini layered casserole of -> **anellini**, meat sauce, fried eggplant, ham and peas. A dish for festive occasions typical of Palermo. Sicily.

timballo di cicorielle layered casserole of wild field chicory (-> **cicorielle**) mozzarella, mortadella, hard-boiled eggs and grated Pecorino. Puglia.

timballo di maccheroni alla chitarra another name for -> **timballo di scrippelle**.

timballo di martin sec a shortcrust pastry pie filled with -> **martin sec** pears cooked in wine and flavored with cloves. Piedmont.

timballo di piccione a timbale of a thin shortcrust or brisée pastry crust filled with rigatoni or fettuccine tossed in pigeon stew. A specialty of Mantua and Cremona. Lombardy.

timballo di riso a baked mold of rice mixed with chicken livers and hearts, tomato sauce, onion, and broth. A specialty of Rome. Lazio.

timballo di scrippelle baked layers of small pancakes (-> **scrippelle**) filled with a nest of maccheroni alla chitarra tossed in a sauce of lamb, Parmigiano, meatballs, Scamorza and hard-boiled eggs. Abruzzo.

timo thyme. The generic name for 20 or so herbs of the Thymus genus. Garden thyme (*Thymus vulgaris*) is cultivated to be used fresh or dried. Some varieties are specific to the south and the islands, while serpillo thyme is found both wild and cultivated. All varieties go well with fish, meat and legumes.

timo dritto regional term for -> **santoreggia**, summer savory.

timo peparello regional term for -> **serpillo**, wild thyme.

timo serpillo aka **timo selvatico** -> **serpillo**, wild thyme.

timpagnu wooden lid used to seal earthenware jars hermetically. Calabria.

timpàno di maccheroni a timbale (-> **timballo**) of sweet shortcrust pastry filled with pasta (-> **perciatelli**) mixed with a sauce of fried pork meatballs, mushrooms, peas and onion, layered with chicken giblets, pigeon mozzarella and hard-boiled eggs. This is the classic recipe, but many other exist, some without the pastry. Campania.

tinca tench. A freshwater fish, a relative of the carp, the barbel and the chub. Eaten fried, stewed, stuffed and baked, broiled, marinated (➤ **carpione, in**) or as an ingredient in soups and risottos. The Italian Ministry of Agriculture's database of native and/or traditional foodproducts lists *tinca del Trasimeno* (Umbria), and ➤ **tinca gobba dorata del pianalto di Poirino** (Piedmont) has PDO recognition.

tinca a cappone tench stuffed with Parmigiano-Reggiano, breadcrumbs, garlic, parsley, garlic, cinnamon and cloves, and baked in the oven with olive oil and bay leaves. A specialty of Clusane di Iseo (Brescia). Lombardy.

tinca al forno baked tench. Tench baked in the oven flavored with oil, lemon juice, minced parsley, garlic and oregano and breadcrumbs. Typical of Lake Trasimeno. Umbria.

tinca alla lariana pieces of tench cooked in white wine with peas, mushrooms and sage. Typical of Lake Como. Lombardy.

tinca fritta all'aceto fried tench covered with a marinade of the filtered frying oil, finely sliced onions, vinegar, wine, pine kernels and raisins. Friuli-Venezia Giulia.

tinca gobba dorata del pianalto di Poirino the "golden hunchback" tench has been farmed for centuries in the ponds of an area between the provinces of Turin, Cuneo and Asti. Soft and tasty, the fish features extensively in the local cooking (fried or in ➤ **carpione**). It has PDO recognition and is protected by a Slow Food presidium. Piedmont.

tinca in carpione fried tench preserved in a marinade of oil, sliced onions, bay leaves, sage, peppercorns and a blend of vinegar and white wine. A specialty of the low-lying part of the Monferrato area, in the province of Asti. Piedmont.

tinca in guazzetto tinch parboiled in salted water aromatized with herbs, transferred to a ➤ **soffritto** of garlic, onion, celery, carrot and rosemary, bathed with white wine and stewed, with or without the addition of tomato. Served as a second course, and the sauce is also used to make ➤ **risotto con la tinca**. Typical of Lake Garda (Verona). Veneto.

Tipico Lodigiano raw cow's milk cheese, the modern version of the extinct Granone Lodigiano. Lombardy.

tirà a baked fruit loaf typical of the provinces of Asti and Alessandria, Piedmont.

tirafilo regional term for ➤ **piantaggine**, ribwort plantain.

tiramisù popular dessert of sponge fingers (➤ **savoiardi**) soaked in coffee, layered with ➤ **mascarpone** cream, whisked egg yolks and sugar, and dusted with cocoa. It was invented by a confectioner in Treviso in the second half of the 20th century as *tiramesu* and is mentioned in the recipe books of local Jewish families as *crema di mascarpone*. Veneto.

tire small crisp foccaccia disks filled with sausage and turned over. A traditional specialty of Altare and Cairo Montenotte in the province of Savona. Liguria.

tirot a variation on ➤ **schiacciata mantovana** with a generous amount of sliced onion in the dough. Lombardy.

tirtlan another name for ➤ **türteln**, round ravioli.

tisichelle hard ring-shaped cookies flavored with fennel seeds and red wine. Umbria.

titola a braided Easter cake with a red-dyed hard-boiled egg at either end. A specialty of Trieste. Friuli-Venezia Giulia.

toast in Italian the term means a toasted

sandwich, normally filled with boiled ham and cheese.

toc'/tocj de patatis aka **toc'/tocj de cartufules** potato purée flavored with milk, butter, garlic and cinnamon. Friuli-Venezia Giulia.

toc'/tocj de purcit toc' the Friuli variant of ➤ **tocio**. In this case, not just a sauce but a pork stew. Friuli-Venezia Giulia.

toc'/tocj di vores "women workers' lunch." A cream of milk, cheese, ricotta, butter and flour used to flavor toasted polenta, so named because it was the version of ➤ **toc' in braide** reserved for women. Friuli-Venezia Giulia.

toc'/tocj in braide literally "sauce of the farm." Very soft polenta and melted cheese, originally a snack farm workers ate in the fields, now served with meat sauce, sausage, asparagus, mushrooms or truffle. Friuli-Venezia Giulia.

tocco, in dialect aka **tucco** words originally for meat sauce, now applied to sauces in general (eg, *tocco di funghi*, in dialect *tucco de funzi*, mushroom sauce). Liguria.

tocio generic northeast Italian word for sauce, invariably involving tomatoes. The terms *in tocio* and *al tocio* mean "stewed," and the verb *tociar* means to mop up sauce with bread.

tòdaru Sicilian term for ➤ **totano**, European flying squid.

tofeja thick bean and pork rind soup cooked in a pot of the same name made with the typical local Castellamonte terra cotta. A specialty of the Canavese area northwest of Turin. Piedmont. **tofettine** another name for ➤ **conchiglie**, a type of pasta.

tognaque cabbage soup with cheese and spices. A specialty of the Canavese area northwest of Turin. Piedmont.

toma generic name for fat or semi-fat, fresh or semi-mature cheeses produced in Piedmont, Val d'Aosta and Liguria.

Toma brusca aka **Toma 'd la cajà** other names for ➤ **Toma del lait brusch**.

Toma del bot a cow's milk cheese aged for three months. Typical of the Valle Stura, Piedmont.

Toma del lait brusch cow's milk cheese made by mixing the naturally acidified milk of the evening milking (*brusch*) with that of the morning after. Typical of the Valli di Susa, Sangone and Lanzo valleys. Piedmont.

Toma della Valsesia whole raw cow's milk cheese produced in the valley of the same name. Piedmont.

Toma di Balme cow's milk cheese typical of the village of Balme (Turin). Piedmont.

Toma di Elva another name for ➤ **Caso di Elva**.

Toma di Gressoney semi-fat raw cow's milk cheese produced in the valley of the same name. Val d'Aosta.

Toma di Lanzo cheese produced in the valley of the same name, similar to ➤ **Toma Piemontese**, but with a more irregular shape. Piedmont.

Toma Piemontese PDO cheese made virtually all over the region with whole or skimmed cow's milk. Piedmont.

tomasina di ricotta a round flatbread made from a durum wheat dough covered with diced fresh ➤ **Ragusano** cheese, pieces of sausage and wedges of hard-boiled egg, rolled up, brushed with beaten egg and baked. A specialty of Modica (Ragusa). Sicily.

tomaxelle slices of veal stuffed with a mixture of lean ground veal, calf's udder, dried mushrooms, pine kernels, eggs, Parmigiano, marjoram and garlic, cooked in the pan with beef sauce. Liguria.

tombarello another name for ➤ **tambarello**, frigate tuna.

Tombea cow's milk cheese produced

in the commune of Magasa (Brescia). Lombardy.

Tome di pecora brigasca two types of cheese produced in mountain dairies in the province of Imperia on the border with France: Sora, made with ewe's milk, and Toma made with mixed ewe's and goat's milk. A Slow Food presidium promotes the Toma and the native Brigasaca sheep whose milk it is made from. Liguria.

Tomino small fresh cylindrical ewe's and cow's milk cheese. Piedmont.

Tomino di Talucco fresh goat's milk cheese of the Val Chisone. Piedmont.

Tomino elettrico fresh goat's or ewe's milk cheese dressed with garlic, pepper, chili and oil. Piedmont.

tonco Trentino term for sauce or gravy.

tonco de boia condiment for polenta made with smoked sausages browned in butter and simmered in a little of the polenta itself diluted with milk. Trentino-Alto Adige.

tonco de patate a thick mixture of potatoes, onions, sage, bay leaves, water and tomato conserve. Trentino-Alto Adige.

tonco de pontesel fluid stew of mixed meats (beef, veal and pork) and broth, served with polenta. Trentino-Alto Adige.

tonnarelli regional term for square maccheroni similar to → **maccheroni alla chitarra** (Abruzzo). Lazio.

tonnetto name used to refer to two different fishes, each often marketed as → **tonno** (tuna): striped-bellied bonito (*Euthynnus pelamis*) and little tunny (*E. alletteratus*).

tonnina (1), in dialect aka **tunnina** Sicilian terms for the meat of the tuna fish.

tonnina (2) in the province of Trapani (and also in Sardinia and Orbetello in Tuscany), tuna fillets or belly (→ **ventresca**) preserved in salt.

tonno tuna. The most common varieties of the fish in Italian are longfin tuna (*Thunnus alalunga*), and bluefin tuna (*T. thinnus*). Their tasty, fatty meat is sold fresh in slices, which can be broiled, stewed with vegetables and breaded and fried, or frozen and canned (the quality of the latter depending on the species and oil used). The most prized parts, → **ventresca** and → **tarantello**, come from the belly. The Italian Ministry of Agriculture's database of native and/or traditional products lists *tonno di tonnara della Sicilia*.

tonno alla portoscusese tuna stewed in red wine. Typical of Portoscuso (Carbonia-Iglesias). Sardinia.

tonno ammuttunatu slices of tuna stuck with mature Caciocavallo and stewed in tomato with peas and pennyroyal. Sicily.

tonno bonita → **tonnetto**.

tonno briaco alla livornese tuna cooked in red wine with onion. A specialty of Livorno. Tuscany.

tonno di coniglio shredded rabbit meat preserved in oil with garlic and sage. Typical of the Langhe and Monferrato areas. Piedmont.

tonno tonnina → **tonnetto**.

topinabò Piedmontese dialect word for → **topinambur**, Jerusalem artichoke.

topinambur Jerusalem artichoke (*Heliantuhus tuberosus*). The tuber is eaten cooked (in purées, pies and gratins) and raw, finely sliced and dressed with oil and lemon. In Piedmont it is a classic component of → **bagna caoda**. Common and regional names: → **patata selvatica**, → **tartufo di canna**, → **fior di sole**.

topini aka **ravioli di marroni** sweet ravioli with a chestnut filling. Emilia-Romagna.

topini di patate Tuscan term for potato gnocchi.

toponin round bread roll with a friable crust. Typical of the province of Cuneo. Piedmont.

torcetti dry ring-shaped cookies made of flour, yeast, water, sugar and butter. Typical of Saint-Vincent, though similar cookies are also to be found in Piedmont and some regions of central Italy. Val d'Aosta.

torciglione (1) long braided bread loaf, popular in the provinces of Palermo and Trapani. A member of the beer bread (➤ **pane a birra**) family. Sicily.

torciglione (2) aka **serpentone** snake-like pastry roll filled with fresh and dried fruits bound with Vin Santo, with two cherries or coffee beans for the eyes and an almond for the mouth. Typical of the Lake Trasimeno area.

torciolo Lazio term for a cow's pancreas.

torcionata slow-cooked almond, flour, butter and sugar brittle. Typical of the Monferrato hills south of Casale, in the province of Alessandria. Piedmont.

torcoletti al formaggio small pastries flavored with sweet Pecorino. Umbria.

torcolo di san Costanzo a soft fruit cake baked on January 29 in Perugia to celebrate the feast of the city's patron saint. Umbria.

tordelli stuffed half-moon-shaped pasta typical of Lucca. Tuscany.

tordo thrush. In Italy thrushes are traditionally roast on skewers with other small birds. Their meat is at its best in the fall, when they feed on grapes, olives and berries.

tordi al forno thrushes roasted in the oven wrapped in slices of pancetta. Veneto.

tordi con l'uva thrushes wrapped in pancetta and cooked with grapes and chicken livers. Tuscany.

tordi finti literally "fake thrushes." Slices of pork covered with sage, chicken livers, anchovies, juniper berries and pancetta, rolled up and fried.

tordi in salmì spit-roast thrushes finished in a sauce flavored with juniper berries and Marsala. Tuscany.

tordi matti stuffed veal rolls stuck on skewers (like headless, hence "mad" thrushes) and barbecued or baked. A specialty of Spoleto (Perugia). The same name is used for horsemeat rolls in Zagarolo (Roma). Umbria, Lazio.

Törggelen a traditional celebration of the end of the grape harvest in which new wine and roast chestnuts are offered to all-comers. Trentino-Alto Adige.

toro bull.

torresano pigeon raised, according to an old Veneto tradition, especially in the towns of Breganze and Torreglia, in the province of Vicenza, in roosts on medieval towers and belfries. *Torresano allo spiedo* is the characteristic dish of Breganze: spit-roasted pigeon brushed with an emulsion of oil, crushed juniper berries and laurel leaves, salt and pepper, barded with slices of lardo, and spit-roast. "Tower pigeons" are also stewed with tomato and served with polenta. Veneto.

torrese name used in Torre del Greco, in the province of Naples, for ➤ **pane cafone**, a type of bread.

torricella turret shell (*Turritella communis*). Cone-shaped gastropod common in the Venice lagoons and Romagna coast. Common and regional names: ➤ **caragol longo**, ➤ **cornetto**.

torroncino (1) vanilla ice cream with nougat chips. A classic Italian flavor.

torroncino (2) small, rectangular ➤ **torrone**, nougat candy, usually wrapped in paper.

torrone nougat. Traditionally brittle confection made from a syrup of cooked honey and sugar mixed with almonds, egg whites whisked to a peak and vanilla. It may be of Arab origin, but seems to have been codified in Italian gastronomy by a Cremonese cook in 1441, on the occasion of Bianca Maria Visconti's marriage to Francesco Sforza. Once associated with Christmas, torrone is now available all year round, from north to south, in countless varieties: with almonds, with hazelnuts, with pistachio nuts, with chocolate, with candied fruit and so on. Crushed torrone is also used by confectioners to cover and decorate ice creams and desserts.

torrone gelato a rectangular soft nougat dotted with chopped candied fruits and toasted almonds. Calabria.

torta cake, torte, pie.

torta 900 (novecento) round chocolate sandwich cake filled with a delicate chocolate cream and dusted with confectioner's sugar. On sale exclusively at the Balla cake shop in Ivrea, where it is baked to a secret recipe invented by Ottavio Bertinotti in the late 19th century. Piedmont.

torta al formaggio baked cake made with grated fresh Pecorino and flavored with saffron. Sardinia.

torta al testo similar to the ➤ **piadina romagnola**, and also known as ➤ **panaro**, ➤ **crescia**, ➤ **ciaccia**. A sort of round flatbread made of flour, salt, extra virgin olive oil or lard and bicarbonate of soda. After rising a little, the disks are cooked on a ➤ **testo**, or griddle pan, and pricked with the prongs of a fork. Served hot with cured meats and cold cuts. In some places milk, eggs, grated Pecorino, butter, and pepper are added to the dough. Umbria.

torta Barozzi soft flat cake made of eggs, cocoa, coffee, dark chocolate, sugar, butter, powdered vanilla, rum, almonds, and toasted peanuts. Created at the start of the 20th century by the Vignola pastry chef Eugenio Gollini, and dedicated to the architect Jacopo Barozzi, nicknamed *il Vignola*, also from the town (province of Modena). Emilia-Romagna.

torta beca baked cake made of day-old bread (*beca* is an Italianization of the German *Bechen*, a long bread loaf) and milk. In the old days flavored only with grappa, now enriched with flour, yeast, sugar, eggs, oil, powdered vanilla and raisins. Also known as *torta dei poveri*, "cake of the poor." Trentino-Alto Adige.

torta co' becchi shortcrust pastry tart filled with buttered chard, parsley, bread soaked in milk, cinnamon, pepper, nutmeg, liqueur, grated Parmigiano and Pecorino, eggs, a pinch of sugar, pine kernels and raisins. Like ➤ **torta co' bischeri**, the tart is topped with crisscrossed strips of pastry, know as *becchi*, meaning lace. Specialty of Lucca and Garfagnana. Tuscany.

torta co' bischeri shortcrust pastry tart filled with boiled rice, chocolate, cocoa, raisins, candied fruit, pine kernels, beaten eggs, sugar and spices (cinnamon, coriander, cloves). Topped with crisscrossed strips of pastry, know as *bischeri*. Typical of the Pisa area, recorded since the 11th century and traditionally baked for the Feast of the Ascension. Tuscany.

torta con i ciccioli pie with pork scratchings. Sometimes the meat residues from the fusion of pork or goose fat (➤ **ciccioli**, pork scratchings) feature in sweet pies. In the area round Crema, in Lombardy, they make one with goose or pork scratchings, apples and sugar. In the northeast of Italy, ➤ **torta di frize** is a sort of shortcrust pasty tart in which chopped pork scratchings, milk and yeast are added to the dough. Lombardy, Friuli-Venezia Giulia.

torta con le erbe focaccia filled with chard (or, in season, ➤ **borragine**, borage), salt, eggs, onions, milk, extra virgin olive oil and Grana Padano and topped with taggiasca olives. A specialty of the province of Imperia. Liguria.

torta d' ris doza simple rice cake (rice, milk, sugar, eggs, grated lemon zest) flavored with aniseed liqueur Typical of the province of La Spezia. Liguria.

torta d'erbi savory pie with chard, typical of Pontremoli, in the province of Massa-Carrara. Tuscany.

torta de erbe sweet baked cake flavored with wild herbs such as nettle and hops shoots, wild spinach, dandelion, rhubarb and so on. Trentino-Alto Adige.

torta de fregoloti ancient friable cake of flour sugar and butter made with or without almonds, sometimes flavored with grappa, cinnamon and lemon zest. Best enjoyed with a glass of Vin Santo. Typical of the province of Trento. Trentino-Alto Adige.

torta de paparele layered cake of cooked tagliatelle (*paparele*), minced almonds, sugar and lemon zest, finished with a sprinkling of lemon juice. Typical of Verona. Veneto.

torta degli Addobbi cake or rice cooked in milk aromatized with lemon zest and vanilla sugar, mixed with eggs, caramelized sugar, minced almonds, amaretti, candied citron, cloves and bitter almond liqueur. A specialty of Bologna, typical of a religious festival, the Festa degli Addobbi (Feast of Decorations), in which houses throughout the city are decorated with flags and banners. The recipe is registered at the Bologna Chamber of Commerce. Emilia-Romagna.

torta degli ebrei another name for ➤ **tibuia**.

torta dei cinque minuti non-leavened almond cake whose mixture has to be kneaded in five minutes. Emilia-Romagna.

torta dei Tetti baked pastry filled with a mixture of pears (➤ **pera madernassa**) cooked in Barbera, amaretti, almonds, cocoa, sugar and rum. A specialty of Borgata Tetti di Dronero (Cuneo), Piedmont.

torta della Vallera baked almond cake typical of Borgata Vallera di Caraglio (Cuneo). Piedmont.

torta delle rose ingenious buttery pastry which, as it leavens, develops into the shape of a bunch of roses. A specialty of Valeggio sul Mincio, in the province of Mantua. Lombardy.

torta di asparagi savory baked asparagus pie. A sweet version also exists in which the asparagus is boiled with sugar, eggs, ricotta and mascarpone. Veneto.

torta di bosine a pie of tiny burbots (➤ **bosine**), mixed with Parmigiano-Reggiano and spices. A specialty of Lake Iseo. Lombardy.

torta di briciole a friable shortcrust pastry cake (➤ **sbrisolona**). Typical of Reggio Emilia. Emilia-Romagna.

torta di carote sweet carrot cake with almonds. Trentino-Alto Adige. Veneto.

torta di castagne chestnut cake. A baked cake common all over Italy with variations. Made with fresh chestnuts, dried chestnuts or chestnut flour.

torta di ceci another name for ➤ **cecina**, chickpea focaccia.

torta di flour gialla e bianca simple cake made with a mixture of cornflour and wheat flour, egg yolks, sugar, butter and white wine. Lombardy.

torta di fave a sort of spring frittata made with new fava beans, eggs and breadcrumbs. Served as an antipasto. Sardinia.

torta di fichi fresh fig tart. A specialty of the village of Albarola di Vigolzone (Piacenza), where it is made with a local fig variety. Emilia-Romagna.

torta di fioretto another name for ➤ **fioret**, a sweet flatbread.

torta di frize a type of ➤ **torta con i ciccioli**, pie with pork scratchings.

torta di grano saraceno leavened cake of

buckwheat flour with apples and hazelnuts, known in German-speaking areas as *Buchweizentorte*. Trentino-Alto Adige.

torta di latte con le mele Italian name for ➤ **pinza de pomi**.

torta di limoni lemon tart. A disk of shortcrust pastry topped with a soft cream of eggs, sugar, butter and lemon juice and zest. Campania.

torta di mais in graticola savory cornflour pastry served with cured meats or field greens. Marche.

torta di mandorle almond tart. In Varzì (Pavia), it is made with a mixture of cornflour, sugar, eggs, grated lemon zest and minced almonds, but many other versions exist with different names and combinations of ingredients. **torta di marroni** chestnut tart. A specialty of Marradi, in the province of Florence. A puff pastry tart filled with a mixture of puréed boiled chestnuts (➤ **marrone del Mugello**), sugar, alkermes, rum, vanilla, beaten eggs and milk. Tuscany.

torta di melanzane e cioccolato eggplant and chocolate tart. Campania.

torta di mele apple cake. Many different recipes exist, especially in the north of Italy, which can be classed into three main types: with the apples included in the cake mixture, with the apples sliced over the mixture, or with the apples sliced under the mixture as in a *tarte tatin*.

torta di nocciole hazelnut cake. A specialty of southern Piedmont made with a mixture of minced hazelnuts, milk, eggs and sugar. The cake is typical especially of the Langhe area, in the province of Cuneo, where the local hazelnut variety (➤ **nocciola del Piemonte**) is used. Today it is served as a dessert with warm ➤ **zabaglione**. Piedmont.

torta di noci walnut cake. The basic ingredients are flour, sugar, butter, eggs, grated lemon zest and finely minced walnuts, but recipes vary all over the north of Italy.

torta di Ormea savory pie filled with chard, rice and butter and sprinkled with sugar. Traditionally eaten on Easter Monday. Typical of the Val Tanaro, in the province of Cuneo. Piemont.

torta di Orvieto a soft fruit loaf typical of the city of the same name in the province of Terni. Umbria.

torta di pane di segale rye bread cake. Made with finely ground rye bread, minced almonds, egg whites whisked to a peak, sugar and lemon juice. An old recipe typical of Ptredazzo, in the province of Trento. Trentino-Alto Adige.

torta di pane e cacao bread and cocoa cake. A way of using of leftover stale bread, which is soaked in milk, amalgamated with whole eggs, butter, refined and vanilla sugar and cocoa. The resulting mixture is dotted with raisins and pine kernels and baked in the oven. Trentino-Alto Adige.

torta di pane e latte a mixture of day-old bread, milk, eggs, sugar, chopped walnuts, raisins and grappa or sweet liqueur baked in the oven. Typical of the Valle Vigezzo. Piedmont.

torta di papavero a cake, made without flour, of poppy seeds (➤ **papavero (2)**), sugar, eggs, yeast, cinnamon and poppy seeds. A delicacy in the Sudtirolo area. Trentino- Alto Adige.

torta di Pasqua al formaggio another name for ➤ **pizza al formaggio**.

torta di patate potato pie. A common dish throughout the Italian Alps and Apennines. Additions to the basic potato filling include grated Grana, leeks, lardo and gravy from the roast (Romagna). In Piedmont, the pastry crust is sometimes eliminated and the potatoes are layered with cabbage, leeks, pumpkins, cheese and so on in dishes more similar to baked casseroles than pies as such.

torta di pere pear cake. Sometimes the pears are part of the cake mixture, sometimes they form the filling for a pie with a pastry crust.

torta di ramassin damson pie. A sort of timbale of layers of puff pastry alternated with small local damsons. A delicacy in Saluzzo, in the province of Cuneo. Piedmont.

torta di ricotta ricotta tart. Shortcrust pastry filled with a filling of ricotta sugar, eggs, orange juice, grated lemon zest, sultanas and rum. Friuli-Venezia Giulia.

torta di riso carrarina baked dessert consisting of layers of rice and a cream made with eggs, sugar, grated lemon zest, liqueur, vanilla and milk. Typical of Massa-Carrara, it was traditionally made at Christmas and Easter. Tuscany.

torta di riso salata a baked mixture of parboiled, rice, eggs, milk, salt, pepper, nutmeg, butter and breadcrumbs. Typical of the Lunigiana area in the province of Massa-Carrara. Tuscany.

torta di san Pietro risen baked cake of rye flour and butter, filled with a purée of potatoes, fava beans and boiled dried chestnuts. Typical of the Val Susa, in the province of Turin. Piedmont.

torta di sangue blood pudding. A specialty born of the ritual annual killing of the pig that has now virtually disappeared. It is made with a mixture of onions, cheese, breadcrumbs, walnuts, pig's blood, milk and nutmeg, which is heated in the oven to set.

torta di tagliatelle aka **torta ricciolina** cake made with very fine egg taglioline arranged over a shortcrust pastry disk with a mixture of candied fruits (lime and orange), almonds, amaretti (optional), liqueur (➤ **sassolino**), sugar and butter,

dusted with vanilla sugar and melted butter and baked in the oven. The recipe is registered at the Bologna Chamber of Commerce. Lombardy, Emilia-Romagna.

torta di Vigolo a baked tart filled with chocolate cream, Typical of Vigolo Marchese (Piacenza). Emilia-Romagna.

torta di zucca a baked pumpkin purée mixed with eggs, sugar, crushed amaretti cookies, cocoa, sultanas, liqueur and vanilla or lemon zest. A specialty of Reggio Emila. Emilia-Romagna.

torta Dobos six disks of dough (flour, sugar, eggs, lemon zest), baked separately in the oven, alternated with layers of confectioner's custard mixed with ➤ **gianduia** paste, butter, egg whites whisked to a peak, caramelized sugar and cocoa, iced with hot caramel and coated round the sides with chopped toasted almonds or hazelnuts. Created in 1885 by the Hungarian businessman and restaurateur Jozef Dobos. Friuli-Venezia Giulia.

torta dolce di granturco sweet cornflour cake. Round and relatively tall, made of cornflour, butter, sugar, and almonds, midway between ➤ **amor polenta** and ➤ **sbrisolona**. Typical of the Lower Po Valley. Lombardy.

torta dolce di Pasqua aka **pizza dolce di Pasqua** a twice-leavened panettone-like Easter cake baked in a wood oven. Umbria.

torta dolce di patate sweet potato cake with almonds. A traditional specialty of Reggio Emilia. Emilia-Romagna.

torta Donizetti a ➤ **ciambella** flavored with candied apricot and pineapple dedicated to the Bergamo-born composer Gaetano Donizetti. Lombardy.

torta dura grattugiata a hard, friable cake, like ➤ **sbrisolona**, flavored with ➤ **sassolino** liqueur. Typical of Reggio Emilia. Emilia-Romagna.

torta **Fiat** two almond pastry disks filled with dark chocolate and amaretti cookies. Created by a confectioner in Reggio Emilia to mark the debut of Fiat's Balilla model. Emilia-Romagna.

torta **fina di Vignolo** flat baked cake of flour, crushed dry cookies, minced hazelnuts, egg yolks and sugar. Typical of Vignolo (Cuneo) where it is made to celebrate the patron saint. Piedmont.

torta **fregolotta** ➤ **fregolotta**.

torta **fritta** name used in Parma for ➤ **crescentina fritta**.

torta **garfagnina dolce** baked cake of butter, flour, sugar, anise seeds or liqueur, leavening agent and grated lemon zest. Typical of the province of Lucca. Tuscany.

torta **gianduia** a mixture of crushed caramelized hazelnuts, flour, potato flour, eggs, butter, sugar and melted dark chocolate is baked, allowed to cool, and cut into two. The two parts are soaked in liqueur, filled with whipped cream and chocolate, and coated with fruit jelly and chocolate. Piedmont.

torta **greca** "Greek cake." Soft cake consisting of a puff pastry base, turned up at the edges to create a curly effect, coated with a mixture of eggs, sugar, crushed sweet and bitter almonds, flour, yeast and butter, and decorated, prior to baking, with whole almonds and confectioner's sugar. Popular in Mantua, where it is to be found in most cake and confectionery shops. In Venice it is the traditional cake of the Castello neighborhood, which used to be inhabited mainly by Albanians and Greeks. Lombardy, Veneto.

torta **nera** "black cake." Consists of a shortcrust pastry shell filled with a mixture of chopped almonds and walnuts, chocolate or cocoa and sugar. The pastry or the filling is generally flavored with aniseed liqueur. A specialty of Reggio and Parma. Emilia-Romagna.

torta **nicolotta** ➤ **nicolotta**.

torta **Ortigara** baked tart made of wheat and almond flour, yeast, eggs, butter and sugar, decorated with almond slices. Created in Asiago (province of Vicenza) at the start of the 20th century, it was named Ortigara in memory of the victims of the battle fought on the mountain at the start of World War I. Veneto.

torta **paradiso** "Paradise cake." Butter is creamed with sugar to form a very soft mousse, to which egg yolks, sugar, lemon juice, flour and potato flour is in equal (small) amounts. The mixture is baked in the oven and dusted with confectioner's sugar. Served with tea or dunked in wine at the end of a meal. A symbol of Pavia, where it was invented in 1878 by pastry chef Enrico Vigoni. Lombardy.

torta **pasqualina** savory puff pastry pie filled with chard (another version is also made with artichokes), ricotta (or, better still, ➤ **prescinsoea**), eggs and aromatic herbs, including borage. Cavities are pressed into the filling to contain shelled eggs, which are then covered by numerous very fine layers of puff pastry (according to tradition 33, like the years of Jesus Christ. Liguria.

torta **pasticciotto** classic full round cake version of ➤ **pasticciotto**. Puglia.

torta **pazientina** another name for ➤ **pazientina**, cake typical of Padua.

torta **ricciolina** another name for ➤ **torta di tagliatelle**, tagliatelle cake.

torta **rigojanci** square or heart-shaped sponge cake spread with a mixture of cream, cocoa and sugar, and covered with dark chocolate. Specialty of Trieste but of Hungarian origin, named for the gypsy musician Rigó Jancis, said to have created it at the start of the 20th century.

Friuli-Venezia Giulia.

torta rustica savory puff pastry pie filled
with a mixture of prosciutto, mozzarella, ricotta, Caciocavallo, and eggs. Puglia.

torta sabbiosa another name for ➤
sabbiosa.

torta Sacher Italian name for ➤ **sachertorte**.

torta simona rather liquid mixture of milk,
eggs, flour, sugar and cinnamon (or nutmeg), baked in the oven, stirred when
half-baked. The name of the recipe
could be a tribute to the mythical medieval Donna Simona, an exquisite cook.
Trentino.

torta sul panaro another name for ➤ **torta
al testo**. Thus named for the local word
for "griddle pan" (➤ **testo**, griddle pan).
Marche, Umbria.

uU

u cchialine Molise term for ➤ **razza** *quattrocchi*, brown skate.

uardi e fasui traditional popular barley and bean soup with the addition of aromatics, potatoes and chopped lardo. In some variations, a ham shank is also added. Friuli-Venezia Giulia.

uberlekke dish of mixed boiled meats (beef, pork and mutton), typical of the Walser tradition in the Monte Rosa, Valle di Gressoney, and Valsesia areas. Val d'Aosta, Piedmont.

uccelli scappati aka **uccelletti scappati** aka **uccellini scappati** in northeast Italy and parts of Lombardy diced veal alternated with bay leaves on skewers resembling headless (*scapaa* or *scapai* in dialect) birds. In other regions (Emilia-Romagna, Lazio, Tuscany), veal or pork rolls stuffed with pancetta and sage leaves and fried. In Tuscany and Lazio, known as ➤ **tordi finti**, **tordi matti**.

uccuna Sicilian term for ➤ **lumaca di mare**, winkle.

ueca abbreviated name for ➤ **seupa a la ueca**, barley soup.

ues di muart Friulian term for ➤ **oss de mord** baked sponge fingers.

uliata another name for ➤ **puccia pugliese** (1), a type of flatbread.

umbricelli long fresh spaghetti-like flour and water pasta. The name evokes *lombrichi*, or earth worms. Very popular in Umbria, where local names include ➤ **pici**, ➤ **pichi**, ➤ **bringoli**, and ➤ **umbrichelli**. In Lazio the slightly spindle-shaped **lombrichi** (aka **lombrichelli**) are also very similar to **umbricelli**. Common

condiments are ➤ **battuto**, tomato sauce, and sausage and mushroom sauce.

umbrichelli another name for ➤ **umbricelli**, type of pasta.

umido, in term used to describe a stewed dish (➤ **brasato**, **stufato**, ➤ **stracotto**, ➤ **civé**, ➤ **salmì**, ➤ **ragù napoletano** , ➤ **spezzatino**).

umido di cipolle e alborelle secche onion and dried bleak casserole. The onions are finely chopped and baked in the oven with tomato passata and dried bleak (➤ **alborelle**), typical of the western shore of Lake Garda. Lombardy.

ungere to grease (with butter, lard, or oil).

uomini nudi al testo Romagna name (*uomini nudi* means "naked men") for ➤ **rossetti**, tiny fish, briefly cooked in a ➤ **testo**, griddle pan, then sprinkled with salt and pepper. Emilia-Romagna.

uovo (pl. **uova**) egg. *Uovo alla coque*, soft-boiled egg. *Uovo bazzotto*, coddled egg. *Uovo* all'occhio di bue aka *uovo fritto* aka *uovo al burro*, fried egg. *Uovo sodo*, hard-boiled egg. *Uovo in camicia*, poached egg. *Uovo strapazzato*, scrambled egg.

uova al cirighet aka **uova al cirighit** eggs fried in butter and covered with a sauce of oil, vinegar, chopped parsley, garlic, chili and anchovies, left to stand for a few hours and served cold. Piedmont, Lombardy.

uova al funghetto coddled eggs cut in half, sprinkled with minced flat-leaved parsley and mixed with stewed mushrooms. In dialect, *ûs in fonghet*. Friuli-Venezia Giulia.

uova al pomodoro eggs fried with the addition of ripe tomatoes and garnished with basil. A traditional peasant dish typical of the Chianti area. Tuscany.

uova alla monacella hard-boiled eggs are cut in half and their yolks removed. The yolks are chopped and mixed with cocoa powder, sugar, cinnamon and beaten egg yolks. The mixture is used to fill the whites, which are then joined together, dipped in a mixture of cinnamon-flavored cocoa powder and whites whisked to a peak, then fried. A recipe typical of Castrovillari, in the province of Cosenza. Calabria.

uova alla monachina hard-boiled eggs are cut in half and their yolks removed. The yolks are amalgamated with béchamel sauce, grated Parmigiano and nutmeg. The mixture is piled onto each half white to simulate whole eggs, then breaded and deep-fried. Campania.

uova alla provatura diced ➤ **Provatura** cheese melted in a frying pan with butter. Eggs are then added, fried, seasoned with salt and sprinkled with Parmigiano. Lazio.

uova e funghi eggs and mushrooms. Fresh mixed mushrooms sautéed in oil and butter with chopped onion and a splash of grappa, to which eggs and milk are then added and scrambled. Trentino-Alto Adige.

uova e lumache eggs and snails. Boiled, shelled snails cooked in olive oil, garlic, parsley and white wine. When the snails are well cooked, eggs are added and scrambled. Veneto.

uova in bagna del diavolo another name for ➤ **bagna del diavolo.**

uova in trippa small frittatas sliced very finely to look like strips of tripe, and then prepared like tripe. In Lazio they use parsley, fresh Roman mint and grated Pecorino to flavor the dish. Other regional variations on the theme are ➤

busecca matta in Lombardy and ➤ **frittatine trippate** in some of the central Italian regions.

uova ripiene stuffed eggs. Hard-boiled egg whites cut in half and filled with a mixture of the yolks chopped together with anchovies preserved in oil and softened butter. Friuli-Venezia Giulia and Piedmont.

uov'a sciusciellu soup of onions, sliced sausage, Grana rind and skinned cherry tomatoes plus a poached egg poured over day-old sliced bread. Campania.

uovo di mare type of seafood (➤ **frutti di mare**).

urgiada another name for ➤ **oriada (1)**, barley soup.

Ur-Paarl rare traditional version of ➤ **Paarl**, made from a dough of rye and buckwheat flour, sourdough, fennel seeds, cumin and blue fenugreek (➤ **trigonella cerulea**). The bread is shaped like a flattened figure "8," made by combining two round loaves, hence its name, (*Paarl* means "couple"). The recipe was probably invented by Benedictine monks at the Monte Maria monastery in Burgusio, who baked the bread regularly until a few years ago. Typical of the province of Bolzano and protected by a Slow Food presidium. Trentino-Alto Adige.

urrania Sicilian term for ➤ **borragine**, borage.

urticions Friulian term for ➤ **luppolo**, hops.

urtuti another word for ➤ **ertuti**, legume stew.

ussari "hussars." Round shortcrust cookies with a jam-filled "dimple." Friuli-Venezia Giulia.

uva grapes (*Vitis vinifer*) a huge variety of grapes is grown in Italy both for wine-making and for eating after a meal as a dessert. Two of the finest table grapes, both Sicilian and both PGI, are: ➤ **uva**

da tavola di Canicattì and → uva da tavola di Mazzarrone (Sicily). The Italian Ministry of Agriculture's database of native/and or traditional food products also lists the following varieties: *uva di Tollo e Ortona* (Abruzzo); *catalanesca, cornicella* (Campania); *antiche varietà piacentine* (Emilia-Romagna); *pizzutello da Tivoli* (Lazio); *uva fragola di Borgo d'Ale* (Piedmont); *uva da tavola pugliese* (Puglia); *colombana di Peccioli* (Tuscany). Recipes, both savory and sweet, in which grapes are ingredients include: → **tordi con l'uva**, → **fegatini di pollo con l'uva**, → **sòma d'aj**, and → **schiacciata con l'uva**. The use of raisins (→ **uva passa**) is also widespread, and in many regions grape must (→ **mosto**) is a popular ingredient.

uva da tavola di Canicattì large, yellowish, aromatic PGI table grape cultivated in the provinces of Agrigento and Caltanisetta. Sicilia.

uva da tavola di Mazzarrone sweet white, red and black PGI table grape cultivated on the border between the provinces of Catania and Ragusa. Sicily.

uva passa (aka **uvetta**) raisins. Sugary grapes with few seeds dried in the sun or wind. The main varieties are: *uva sultanina* (*Vitis vinifera sativa* var. *sultanina Bianca*), cultivated in Italy the most common and the smallest; *uva di Corinto, uva di Smirne, uva di Malaga*, all larger, imported from the Middle East and Spain; *zibibbo*, cultivated in Sicily, especially on Pantelleria. Raisins are much used in Italian confectionery, often together with pine kernels.

uva spina gooseberry (*Ribes grossularia*). Not as popular in Italy as in Britain and France, but cultivated nonetheless in the province of Turin (Piedmont).

uva tamina regional term for → **tamaro**, black bryony.

uvetta an alternative word for → **uva passa**, raisins.

vV

vacca, cow that has already given birth or is beyond the sixth month of pregnancy. Legally, a member of the ➤ **bovino adulto**, adult bovine, category.

vacca bianca modenese white Modenese cow, also known as the Val Padana (Po Valley) cow, bred mainly for milk, though the quality of its meat is also excellent. It has a white coat with a black muzzle and hooves, and black-tipped horns. Its milk is ideal for the production of ➤ **Parmigiano-Reggiano**. A Slow Food presidium promotes a cheese made exclusively from its milk as well as its meat. Emilia-Romagna.

vacca rossa reggiana Reggiana red cow, used for milk, meat and labor. This is the breed whose milk, rich in protein, calcium and phosphor, ➤ **Parmigiano-Reggiano** cheese was first made with. After World War II, mechanization and the introduction of more productive dairy breeds, such as the Friesian, almost caused its extinction. Emilia-Romagna.

vaccalà Marche dialect word for ➤ **baccalà** (especially in the area between Fermo and Macerata).

vaccaredde aka **vaccareddi** Catania term for ➤ **babbaluci**, snails.

vaccarelle di san Biagio large rectangular cookies made of flour, sugar, powdered vanilla, oil and fennel seeds. Traditionally served with a glass of sweet wine. Basilicata.

vacuonza concave, flatter version of ➤ **muffoletta**, a bread roll. Typical of San Giuseppe Jato (province of Palermo). Sicily.

vairone stroemling (*Leuciscus souffia*). Cyprinid fish that inhabits river systems in northern and central Italy. Cooked like ➤ **cavedano**, chub.

Valcasotto rare raw, mainly cow's milk cheese of the Valle Tanaro, in the province of Cuneo. Ages at least 10-20 days. Piedmont.

valeriana rossa red valerian (*Centranthus ruber*). Spontaneous plant with reddish leaves and corymbs that grows by the roadside and on walls. Especially in Liguria, northwest Tuscany, Marche and Umbria, the leaves are used as an ingredient in vegetable soups (in Liguria, ➤ **gattafin**. Common and regional names: ➤ **camarezza**, ➤ **fava grassa**, ➤ **fisti**, ➤ **saponina**.

valerianella common cornsalad (*Valerianella locusta*, var. *olitoria*), small spontaneous plant, intensively cultivated nowadays and even sold in supermarkets. Traditionally popular in the regions of northern and central Italy, it is a classic ingredient of mixed salads and is widely used in restaurants as a garnish. Common and regional names: ➤ **ardielut**, ➤ **dolcetta**, ➤ **gallinella**, ➤ **gallinetta**, ➤ **lattughella**, ➤ **lattughino**, ➤ **sarset**, ➤ **soncino**, ➤ **songino**.

valigini (1) rolled ➤ **cavolo verza**. Savoy cabbage, leaves stuffed with chicken, potatoes, garlic, parsley, breadcrumbs, and Parmigiano-Reggiano, and cooked in tomato sauce flavored with onion. A specialty of the province of Mantua, usually served as an antipasto. Lombardy.

valigini (2) rolls (➤ **involtini**) of pork stuffed with mortadella, egg, Parmigiano, garlic and parsley, and cooked in tomato sauce. A specialty of Reggio Emilia. Emilia-Romagna.

Valle d'Aosta fromadzo PDO cheese made with skimmed cow's milk from two milkings, to which 10% goat's milk may be added. It is legally permitted to aromatize it with the seeds or other parts of aromatic plants. It is aged for three to 12 months. Val d'Aosta.

Valle d'Aosta jambon de Bosses PDO ham produced for centuries in the village of Saint-Rhemy-en-Bosses. Made from the rear legs of pigs bred locally and in Piedmont, Lombardy, Veneto and Emilia-Romagna. Dry-cured with a mixture of sea salt, minced garlic, sage, rosemary and local berries, it ages for at least 12 months. Val d'Aosta.

Valle d'Aosta lard d'Arnad PDO cured meat dating from the 16th century, made using fat from the shoulders and backs of pigs bred locally and at farms in Piedmont, Lombardy, Veneto and Emilia-Romagna. The fat is cured for three months in a ➤ **doil**, a special container, layered with sea salt and a brine of water boiled with garlic, bay leaves, rosemary, sage, cloves, cinnamon, juniper, nutmeg and achillea, an Alpine herb. For longer cures (three to 12 months) white wine is added. The meat is sold in pieces with the skin on one side. Val d'Aosta.

Valtellina casera PDO cheese made with the milk of the Bruno Alpina cow from two or more milkings. Forms are wheel-shaped with a yellow rind and a compact body with numerous "eyes." Produced in the province of Sondrio, it is aged for at least two months. Lombardy.

vaniglia vanilla (*Vanilla planifolia*). A native of Central America and cultivated in many tropical countries, has long been prized in the kitchen for its seed pods which fermented and dried, release a beautifully penetrating aroma. The brown pods (*stecche*) are sold whole and are used not only in confectionery, but also in the cures of certain meats (➤ **cotechino alla vaniglia**). Today, pods are often replaced in households by powdered vanilla (➤ **vaniglina**) and the use of vanilla sugar is common in households.

vaniglina (aka **vanillina**) aromatic component of ➤ **vaniglia**, vanilla. Produced chemically it fails to match the intensity and fragrance of the original. Diluted with alcohol or warm water, it is used in confectionery.

vapore, al "steamed."

varàcola Marche term for ➤ **razza**, skate.

varagno another name for ➤ **pesce ragno**, weever.

variegato di Castelfranco variety of ➤ **radicchio**.

variegato di Lusia variety of ➤ **radicchio**.

varone savory ring-shaped pastry made of all-purpose or cake flour. Strips of dough are interwoven by hand and fresh eggs are placed in the gaps before baking. A traditional Easter specialty in the province of Potenza. Basilicata.

vartis Piedmontese dialect word for ➤ **luppolo**, hops.

varva di san Binidittu "beard of St Benedict." Another name for ➤ **pasta a ventu**, a type of cake.

vastedda generic Sicilian word for large round durum wheat bread loaves. Especially good is the one made in Enna, baked in a wood oven.

Vastedda del Belice the only stretched curd ewe's milk cheese, produced in the Valle del Belice, in the provinces of Trapani, Agrigento and Palermo with milk from one or two milkings. Round and flat in shape, it is eaten within three days of production. The name derives from the Sicilian dialect word *vasta*, *guasta* in standard Italian meaning "spoiled." This is because the cheesemakers of the Valle del Belice created the cheese to recycle defective ewe's milk cheese by stretching it at high temperatures. A Slow Food presidium is seeking to rationalize production, conservation and transport systems. Sicily.

vavaluci Sicilian dialect word for → **babbaluci**, snails.

vecchiarelle another word for → **anime beate**, ring-shaped cakes.

vecchioni regional name for → **viette**, dried chestnuts.

vecia col caval pist a stew of peppers, tomatoes, runner beans and potatoes served with breaded, fried horsemeat patties. The dialect term *vecia* (*vecchia* in Italian), meaning "old," alludes to the use of leftovers (ie, day-old boiled meat transformed into meatballs), whereas *pist* (*pesto* in Italian) means ground or crushed, and refers to the use of ground meat, in this case horsemeat, traditionally popular all over the province of Parma. Emilia-Romagna.

vedel impanà minute steak breaded and fried in butter. A typical everyday family dish. Trentino-Alto Adige, Veneto, Friuli-Venezia Giulia.

vellutata *velouté*. Name of a → **salsa madre**, one of the basic sauces of international cuisine, but also a word used to describe a creamy soup of one or more vegetables, sometimes thickened with cream, and usually served with croutons.

ventresca (1) the meat from the abdomen of a fish, usually tuna, preserved in oil. Considered a delicacy on account of its soft texture and delicate flavor.

ventresca (2) in central Italy, a synonym of pancetta, but also used to refer to fresh belly pork.

ventriceddi aka **ventricelle** southern Italian term for fish innards, also known as *trippette*.

ventriceddi 'i stoccu chini fish innards (→ **ventriceddi**) cleaned, stretched, coated with a mixture of breadcrumbs, Parmigiano-Reggiano, egg chopped olives, capers and parsley, rolled up, secured with string, and cooked in tomato sauce. Eaten as they are or used to accompany → **maccaruni 'i casa**, → **perciatelli**, and other homemade pastas. Traditionally cooked and served on Christmas Eve in Calabria's Greek communities. Calabria.

ventricina alla paparolica di Montemitro a cured meat of **guanciale** (cheek bacon), lean pancetta and trimmings of pork shoulder coarsely ground with the addition of a generous amount of pork fat and lard, cured with salt, abundant paprika and fennel seeds. Pressed into a natural intestine and shaped into a ball, it is aged for a few months. A specialty of the village of Montemitro, in the province of Campobasso, where ancient Croatian is still spoken (*paparolica* is the local dialect word for "paprika").

ventricina del Teramano cured meat produced in the Monti della Laga and Gran Sasso areas with ham and pig's head trimmings, pancetta and pork suet. The mixture is cured with salt, ground white and black pepper, chili, garlic, fennel seeds, rosemary and orange zest, and cased in a pig's bladder or stomach, or preserved in glass jars. Dried for a week in rooms in which fires are burning, and usually aged for three months. Abruzzo.

ventricina del Vastese pork leg, loin and shoulder cut into small pieces and cured with salt, powdered sweet pepper, pepper and wild fennel. The mixture is pressed into a pig's bladder to form a ball of one to two kilos in weight, which is secured by hand and hung to dry in a room in which a fire is burning. The meat is aged for seven to eight months. After 90 days, surface mold is removed and the form is covered with lard. Specialty of the province of Chieti. Abruzzo.

verbena odorosa common name for ➤ **cedrina**, lemon verbena.

verdesca squaloideo blue shark (*Prionace glauca*). Relatively common in the Mediterranean, its meat is not highly prized and is generally used in soups and stews (➤ **brodo alla sciabicota**).

verdone regional term for ➤ **russola**, russula mushroom.

verdura 'ssetata boiled wild chicory or chard covered with tomato sauce and slices of fresh pancetta, sprinkled with dried breadcrumbs and grated Pecorino and baked in the oven. Puglia

verdure ripiene alla ligure stuffed vegetables Ligurian-style: ➤ **ripieni**.

vermicelli very thin spaghetti. In reality, the term is also used, especially in Campania, to mean spaghetti.

vermicelli alla calabrese vermicelli served with sweet green peppers and chopped pancetta, lightly fried in olive oil and garlic, and sprinkled with a generous amount of grated Pecorino.

vermicelli alla sammartinese vermicelli with crumbled dried chilis, lightly fried in oil and garlic, and sprinkled with a generous amount of grated Pecorino. A specialty of San Martino di Finita, in the province of Cosenza. Calabria.

vermicelli con le cozziche spaghetti (called vermicelli in Naples) dressed with the liquid from freshly opened mussels, oil and garlic, and garnished with chopped parsley. Campania.

vermicelli con marrozze vermicelli served with a sauce of snails (known locally as ➤ **marrozze** or ➤ **monacelle**), tomato, garlic, parsley and pepper. Calabria.

vermicelli cu' 'o pesce fujuto vermicelli served with cherry tomatoes (➤ **pomodorini al piennolo**), garlic and roughly torn basil. The ironic name means that the sauce was meant to include fish but it has "escaped." Campania.

vermicellini an alternative name for ➤ **spaghettini**.

vermicelloni an alternative name for ➤ **spaghettoni**.

vermut aka **vermouth** a fortified or "special" wine of Piedmontese origin whose name derives from the German *Wermut*, wormwood, one of its main ingredients. According to Italian law, the "special wine" category comprises spumantes and liqueur, passito and aromatized wines. The industrial production of vermouth began in Turin in the second half of the 18th century with a range of wines with a Moscato d'Asti base. In the 20th century, production developed and diversified and today vermouth is made with about 30 aromatic herbs, fruit and spices, including wormwood, rhubarb, gentian, quinine, pomegranate, cardamom, elderberry, ginger and vanilla. The ingredients are blended in large barrels and left to rest for four to six months before being pasteurized and bottled. Vermouth is drunk on its own or mixed in cocktails. It is also used in the kitchen to flavor cakes and pastries.

veròle Lazio term for roast chestnuts.

verruch Puglia dialect name for ➤ **cavolo rapa**, kohlrabi. Eaten raw, finely sliced and dressed with oil and vinegar.

verza another word for ➤ **cavolo verza**, Savoy cabbage.

verza ripiena stuffed cabbage. The tougher outer leaves and the heart a removed from a Savoy cabbage, which is then filled with a stuffing, reassembled, secured with kitchen string and cooked.

Stuffings and cooking methods vary from region to region. In Veneto the stuffing consists of grated cheese and bread, chopped fresh salami and beaten egg and the cabbage is first turned in oil and butter with chopped onions, then finished in a little water. In Friuli, the cabbage leaves are spread with a mixture of sausage meat and bread, soaked in water and squeezed dry, tied into bundles, coated with flour and cooked in tomato sauce. In Liguria they make ➤ **gaggette pinn-e**, in Piedmont ➤ **cavolo ripieno**.

verzata fluid soup with Savoy cabbage, garlic, parsley and butter, served with toasted day-old bread and cheese. Lombardy.

verze e luganeghe Savoy cabbage leaves softened in lard, blanched in broth and finished with chopped sausage and dry white wine. Veneto.

verze imbracate side dish of shredded Savoy cabbage (➤ **cavolo verza**) sautéed in chopped onion and finished with a drop of vinegar and crumbled ➤ **salamella di Mantova**. Lombardy.

verze sofegae strips of Savoy cabbage softened in a ➤ **soffritto** of oil, goose fat, onion and garlic, then "suffocated" (*sofegae*) in a covered pan on a low heat for at least two hours before being finished with a few tablespoons of vinegar. A Venetian recipe of Jewish origin. Artichokes, eggplants and zucchini are prepared in the same way. Veneto.

verzi farsiti another name for ➤ **nosecc**, stuffed Savoy cabbage. **verzolini** Savoy cabbage leaves stuffed with a mixture of day-old bread soaked in milk, Parmigiano, dried breadcrumbs and eggs, cooked in an onion and tomato sauce. The dish is typical of the provinces of Piacenza and Parma, and is traditionally cooked on Christmas Eve in Borgotaro (Parma). Similar recipes are to be found all over

northern Italy (➤ **caponet**, ➤ **capuc**, ➤ **nosecc**). Emilia-Romagna.

verzotti another name for ➤ **polpette di verza**, cabbage patties.

verzulì Lombard term for ➤ **silene rigonfia**, bladder campion.

vescica (1) bladder. In the kitchen, pigs' bladders are steeped in cold salted and acidulated water, dried and used to case lard and cured meats. They are also used to boil meats, especially poultry (for the technique, ➤ **cappone alla canavera**)

vescica (2) rare and ancient cured meat. A pig's bladder is blown up like a balloon, first dried, then steeped in warm water to keep it elastic. It is filled with pieces of sausage and ➤ **soppressata** scorched in liquid lard, topped up with more lard and secured with string. It is steeped again in water, then dried. At this point it can be eaten immediately or aged for two to five months. The pieces of sausage are also used as ingredients in other local dishes, and the bladder itself, once empty, used to be fried and eaten. Basilicata.

vettaioli the small walnut-sized fruits of late melons or water melons. Blanched in vinegar, they are preserved in oil or pickled in vinegar and eaten during the winter, on their own or with boiled meats. Tuscany.

Vezzena mountain cheese produced on the plateau of Lavarone, Vezzena and Folgaria (province of Trento) with raw cow's milk from two milkings (part-skimmed milk from the evening and whole milk drawn the morning after). The cheese is at its best after aging for 12 to 18 months, during which time the rinds are cleaned and brushed with linseed oil. A Slow Food presidium protects cheese produced in summer with mountain dairy milk marked with an "M" (for ➤ **malga**) on the rind. Trentino-Alto Adige.

viandon polenta cooked in milk, dressed with butter and Fontina, and served with rye bread croutons. Typical of the Valtournanche. Val d'Aosta.

viccilli di patate sweet fritters made with a mixture of eggs, mashed potatoes, milk, butter, grated lemon zest, yeast and sugar, shaped into small balls, which are fried in olive oil and dusted with a blend of sugar and powdered cinnamon. Campania.

viccillo ring-shaped risen pastry filled with hard-boiled eggs, salami and mozzarella. A specialty of Salerno, reminiscent of ➤ **casatiello** and ➤ **currupa**. Campania.

viette aka **vecchioni** aka **castagne del prete** dried unpeeled chestnuts. Sometimes, after drying, chestnuts are baked in the oven, in which case they are called *castagne biscotti*, *bischeuit* in Piedmontese dialect, and are eaten boiled and peeled.

vignarola a vegetable stew of peas, spring onions, fava beans, pancetta, artichoke and garlic, cooked separately then mixed, flavored with pennyroyal, olive oil and wine, and garnished with finely minced parsley. Lazio.

vilana cake of day-old bread soaked in milk, flour, eggs, sliced apples, raisins and candied lime zest. Typical of the Polesine area, in the province of Rovigo. Veneto.

vin brulé mulled wine. Restorative drink of hot full-bodied red wine flavored with cloves, cinnamon and lemon and/or orange zest. Traditional especially in the north of Italy, where it is also an ingredient in a cured meat, ➤ **mortadella di fegato di Novara**.

vinaigrette condiment made by blending oil, vinegar, and salt.

vincisgrassi broad ribbons of pasta made of flour, eggs, butter, olive oil and ➤ **Vin Santo**, boiled, layered in a baking tin with béchamel sauce, a sauce made of chicken livers and, according to local usage, sweetbreads, calf's brain, ground beef or lamb, mushrooms, grated Parmigiano and knobs of butter, and baked in the oven. The cities of Macerata and Ancona contend the merit of the dish's invention. It may be named for the Austrian general Windisch Grätz, who fought for Napoleon's troops near the latter city in the 1799. On the other hand, the volume *Il cuoco maceratese* (1779) already cites a sauce for a dish called *princisgras*. Marche.

vincotto traditional confection of ancient origin made from fresh grape must slowly cooked until reduced by a third. Brownish in color with red or purple highlights, sweet in flavor, thick in consistency. An ingredient of ➤ **biscotto cegliese**, ➤ **cingoli**, ➤ **ficarelli**, ➤ **fichi imbottiti**, ➤ **gigi**, ➤ **grano dolce**, ➤ **'ntreme de vicchie**, ➤ **panvinesco**, ➤ **paparotta**, ➤ **pistofatru**, ➤ **spicchitedde**, ➤ **stuezzi**, while ➤ **cartellate** are dipped in it. Produced and consumed mostly in Puglia, in the southern-central Marche (especially in the village of Loro Piceno), in Basilicata, Calabria (where fig syrup, ➤ **cotto di fichi**, is also used as an alternative) and, to some degree, in Sicily. In Emilia-Romagna and Sardinia, it is referred to as ➤ **saba** or ➤ **sapa**. Today **vincotto** is also used to accompany cheese and meat.

vino wine. In Italian regional cooking, wine is a fundamental ingredient in marinades (➤ **salmì**, ➤ **civé**) and in many a ➤ **court-bouillon**, and is used to stew and braise meats (red for ➤ **brasato**, ➤ **stufato**, ➤ **stracotto** and game, mostly white with fish and white meats), to cook risottos and to flavor innumerable cakes and pastries.

vino cotto another name for ➤ **vincotto**, cooked grape must.

vino di visciole aka **visciolato** and **visner** wild cherry wine. In areas of the province of Pesaro, wild cherries are macerated in wine, to which sugar is added, hence a new fermentation. In the area round Jesino, the cherries are dried in the sun, then macerated with sugar to form a syrup which, during the wine harvest, is added to the fermenting grape must. The resulting beverage has a sweet, delicate flavor with a bitterish aftertaste. One of a long Marche tradition of fruit-flavored wines, it is served with local cakes and pastries or as an after-dinner drink. Marche.

Vin Santo aka **vinsanto** dessert wine made from trebbiano or malvasia grapes. Its name ("holy wine") probably derives from the fact that it used to be used as a Communion wine. Traditionally drunk with ➤ **biscottini alla mandorla.**

vinschgauer struzn bread typical of the Val Venosta, in the province of Bolzano, with a characteristic horseshoe shape. Baked from a dough of rye flour (60%), soft wheat flour (40%) and water, with the addition of figs, sultanas, salt, aniseed, cumin and fenugreek. Trentino-Alto Adige.

viola di san Giuseppe regional term for ➤ **violetta**, violet.

violetta violet (*Viola odorata* and *V. mirabilis*). Violets are gathered in Piedmont, Friuli and Tuscany, where their flowers and leaves are eaten in salads and soups. In confectionery, the flowers are also candied; the delicacy is produced in limited quantities by a company in the province of Cuneo (Piedmont). In the Marche, violets are used to aromatize a cardoon preserve. Common and regional names: ➤ **mammola**, ➤ **viola di san Giuseppe**, ➤ **zoppina.**

violino di capra della Valchiavenna rare old violin-shaped ham made from goat leg and shoulder of a goat. The most flavorsome "violins" are the ones aged the longest and naturally. A Slow Food presidium supports a version made using traditional techniques with the meat from animals raised in the wild in the province of Sondrio. Lombardy.

violino di pecora sheep's ham produced in the winter in the area between the villages of Baiso and Carpineti, so named on account of its violin-like shape. Two days after the killing of the sheep, the leg is salted and cured for ten to 12 days. Washed with water and vinegar, it is dried and hung for a week. It is then rubbed with pig fat, pepper and salt, and aged for a month. Reggio-Emilia

viriola Sicilian term for ➤ **donzella (1)**, Mediterranean rainbow wrasse.

virni Campanian term for ➤ **prugnolo**, St George's mushroom.

virtù rich soup of fresh and dry legumes, chopped seasonal vegetables, pieces of pork, mixed pasta shapes, and aromatic herbs. The pride of Teramo cooking, it is celebrated with ritual devotion on May 1, the day that marks the end of the winter, its purpose being partly to clear out the winter pantry and partly to herald new spring herbs and vegetables. The name of the dish, literally "virtue," derives from the fact that is said to have been first cooked by seven "virtuous" damsels with seven ingredients, but now a vast variety of versions exist and the number of ingredients has multiplied. Abruzzo

viscidu another word for ➤ **frue,** fresh sheep's or goat's curd.

visciola sour or morello cherry (*Prunus cerasus*, var. *austera*). Wild cherry widely used in central Italy to make syrups and liqueurs (➤ **vino di visciole**).

visciolato (aka **visner**) ➤ **vino di visciole**, wild cherry wine

vitabbia, vitacchia central Italian dialect words for ➤ **vitalba** (*Clematis vitalba*) old man's beard or traveler's joy. A spontaneous woody climber, abundant in hedgerows and damp thickets all over Italy. The shoots are gathered and used exclusively in soups, omelets, and risottos. Especially popular in central Italy, Marche and Umbria, in particular. Common and regional names: ➤ **viticello**, ➤ **vitabbia**, ➤ **vitacchia**.

vite vine (*Vitis vinifera*). In Trentino, Friuli and Lombardy, vine leaves are used in numerous recipes such as ➤ **capuc**, ➤ **quaglie in foglie di vite** and ➤ **cappelle di porcini in frasca**.

vite nera common name for ➤ **tamaro**, black bryony.

vitel tonné boiled veal, served cold with a sauce of finely chopped tuna preserved in oil, capers and desalted anchovies bound with mayonnaise. Piedmont.

vitella al tonno ➤ **vitel tonné**.

vitello calf.

vitello al latte veal in milk. A single piece of veal coated with minced garlic, browned in butter, bathed with vinegar, covered with milk and cooked in the pan with the lid on. Tuscany.

vitello all'uccelletto a version of ➤ **straccetti di vitello (1)**. Very thin slices of veal, shredded with the hands, turned in a skillet with oil, butter and bay leaves, and bathed with white wine. Liguria.

vitello della coscia a particular Piedmontese calf (➤ **bovina piemontese, razza**).

vitello ripieno breast of veal cut into a pouch shape and stuffed with a mixture of prosciutto, fresh breadcrumbs, egg yolks, butter and parsley, and baked in the oven. Friuli-Venezia Giulia.

vitello scappato quartered potatoes and tomato purée. The ironic name means "the bird that got away." Friuli-Venezia Giulia:

vitello tonnato Italianization of ➤ see **vitel tonné**.

vitello trifolato alla bolognese slices of veal cooked in a skillet with butter, oil, salt and pepper, layered in a casserole dish with slices of boiled potatoes, raw ham cut into strips and topped with knobs of butter and slivers of Parmigiano. After baking in the oven, the dish is garnished with white truffle shavings. The recipe has been registered at the Bologna Chamber of Commerce. Emilia-Romagna.

vitellone a calf slaughtered between eight and ten months of age.

vitellone bianco dell'Appennino centrale in 1998 this PGI denomination was granted to Chianina, Marchigiana and Romagnola cattle of twelve to 24 months of age raised in the following provinces: Bologna, Ravenna, Forlì-Cesena, Rimini, Pesaro e Urbino, Ancona, Macerata, Ascoli Piceno, Teramo, Pescara, Chieti, L'Aquila, Campobasso, Isernia, Benevento, Avellino, Frosinone, Rieti, Viterbo, Terni, Perugia, Grosseto, Siena, Arezzo, Firenze, Prato, Livorno, Pisa.

viticci in insalata vine tendrils cooked in water and vinegar and dressed with extra virgin olive oil, garlic, mint and salt. Puglia.

viticella regional term for ➤ **tamaro**, black bryony.

viticello regional term for ➤ **vitalba**, old man's beard.

vivaroli Pavia term for ➤ **malfatti**.

voccolotti Marche term for ➤ **rigatoni**.

Vollkornpaarl a variation on ➤ **Paarl** baked from a dough of wholemeal rye flour (60%) wheat flour (40%), water, salt, yeast, linseed, sunflower seeds, wild fennel seeds, corn flakes, cumin, and fenugreek. Trentino-Alto Adige.

volterrano Tuscan name for ➤ **imbutino**, common funnel mushroom.

vongola common clam. Many varieties of clam exist. They are mostly eaten cooked and used in risottos, soups and spaghetti sauces. The Italian Ministry of Agricultures' database of native and/or traditional food products lists: *vongola comune del Molise* (Molise) and *vongola verace del Polesine* (Veneto).

vongole alla napoletana clams stewed with oil, parsley, tomatoes and pepper. Campania.

vopa dialect term for ➤ **boga**, bogue.

Vorderkas washed rind cow's milk cheese produced in the Val Senales in the province of Bolzano. Trentino-Alto Adige.

Vorschlag German word for flour from the first grinding, and by extension another name for ➤ **segalino**, rye bread.

vota e svota a variation on ➤ **muffoletta**, an oblong bread loaf baked in a wood oven. Typical of Partinico (Palermo), Sicily.

vrocculu Sicilian dialect word for ➤ **cavolfiore**, cauliflower.

vuccuni ➤ **buccuni**.

vulp patties made by spreading a mixture of salami meat, red wine, salt and spices on washed and dried Savoy cabbage leaves. Each leaf is closed into a bundle, wrapped in ovenproof paper and baked for 20 minutes. Typical of the Lomellina area. Lombardy.

vurrania Sicilian dialect word for ➤ **borragine**, borage.

wxy WXY

wafer a very thin confection of British origin, often sandwiched together in two or more layers and filled with vanilla or chocolate cream. Popular in Italy as a snack for children or to garnish or (in conical or cylindrical form) contain ice cream or other creamy desserts.

waracke spicy mixture of pancetta and lardo, similar to ➤ **sasaka**. Friuli-Venezia Giulia.

Weinsuppe creamy soup made by gently blending concentrated meat broth, white wine (preferably Terlano-Terlaner), egg yolks, cream and cinnamon on a low heat. Served with diced bread fried in butter and cinnamon. Trentino-Alto Adige.

Wienerschnitzel breaded veal cutlet (➤ **cotoletta alla Viennese**).

würstel sausage of German origin, now produced all over the world. Made of finely ground salted and spiced pork or mixed pork and beef and subsequently smoked. Prepared boiled or broiled, in Alto Adige and Friuli, served with mustard and/or horseradish (➤ **cren**, it is often combined with sauerkraut (➤ **crauti**) or boiled potatoes. **Würstel** is the Austrian spelling, whereas *wurst* and *weisswurst* (literally "white meat") refer respectively to the typical German version and a version made with veal and pancetta.

xaeti aka **zaeti** aka **zaleti** round or lozenge-shaped cookies made with polenta flour (hence the name, from the Venetian dialect word for *giallo*, yellow) mixed with wheat flour, butter, sugar, raisins, pine kernels and lemon zest. Veneto, Trentino-Alto Adige, Friuli-Venezia Giulia.

yogurt fermented milk, the result of the combined action of *Streptocossus thermophilus* and *Lactobacillus bulgaricus*, available in a whole range of industrial products. Similar artisan products are the Sardinian ➤ **gioddu**, made with sheep's milk, and the Ligurian ➤ **prescinsoea**.

zZ

zabaglione (aka **zabaione**) frothy cream made by cooking in a bain-marie eggs well beaten with sugar and diluted with an alcoholic element, traditionally dry Marsala secco, but also Madeira, ➤ **Vin Santo**, Porto, or Malaga. In Piedmont, a lighter **zabaglione** is made with Moscato, in other regions rum or other liqueurs are used to reinforce the Marsala. In Piedmont it is served as a warm dessert with ➤ **paste di meliga**, corn cookies, but it is also excellent cold. According to the tradition of Montalcino, in the province of Siena (Tuscany), **zabaglione** is flavored with nutmeg and vanilla, sweetened with honey as opposed to sugar, and strengthened with strong red wine and alkermes. **Zabaglione** is a versatile ingredient in a whole range of confections, from sandwich cakes to ice-creams. The cream may derive from certain popular north Italian restorative drinks made of eggs, sugar, and wine. Examples include ➤ **rosumada**, ➤ **rasumà**, ➤ **arsomà**.

zabbina mixture of warm ricotta and whey eaten with black bread. Traditional shepherds' breakfast. Sicily.

zaeti (aka **zaleti**) other words for ➤ **xaeti**, type of cookie.

zafaran crusch dialect name for ➤ **peperoni crusch**, sun-dried red peppers.

zafarani a rusceddra (aka **zafarani a ruscella** and **zafarani cruschi**) fried sun-dried peppers. Calabria.

zafferano saffron (*Crocus sativus*). Herbaceous plant of which some varieties grow wild, while others are cultivated, especially in Abruzzo, Tuscany, Sardinia and Umbria, where the stigmas of the crocus are gathered by hand. The Italian MInistry of Agriculture's database of native and/or traditional food products lists: ➤ **zafferano dell'Aquila** (Abruzzo); ➤ **zafferano di San Gavino Monreale** (Sardinia); *zafferano aretino, zafferano delle Colline fiorentine* (*zima di Firenze*), *zafferano di Maremma*, ➤ **zafferano di San Gimignano** (Tuscany); *zafferano di Cascia* (Umbria). Besides in the celebrated ➤ *risotto alla milanese*, saffron also appears in traditional dishes such as ➤ **trippa allo zafferano di Montalcino**, ➤ **scapece abruzzese** and ➤ **scapece gallipolino**, in Sardinian specialties such as ➤ **anzelottos**, ➤ **malloreddos**, ➤ **pardulas** and ➤ **zippulas**, in ewe's cheeses such as ➤ **Piacentino**, in breads such as ➤ **panina gialla aretina**, and in cakes and pastries such as ➤ **pangiallo**.

zafferano dell'Aquila DPO saffron grown in ten or so communes in the province of L'Aquila, where it has provided an important source of income for centuries. The plants are cultivated an altitude of 1,000 to 3,000 feet in an area on the plateau of Navelli. In regional gastronomy, its use (especially in risottos and pasta dishes and with cheese and fish) has increased in recent years. Traditionally, it is also used in the preserving technique known as ➤ **scapece**. Abruzzo.

zafferano di San Gavino Monreale saffron grown in and a round the village of the same name in the province of Cagliari, and promoted by a Slow Food presidium.

Every operation (from sowing to gathering to drying) is performed by hand. Every hectare cultivated produces from ten to 100 kilos of dried saffron, which is bright red in color with a very intense aroma and a strong taste. Sardinia.

zafferano di San Gimignano DPO saffron produced in and around San Gimignano, in the province of Siena. Records show that it was exported to markets in Pisa and Genoa as early as the Middle Ages. Its dark red stigmas have a strong aroma and a bitterish taste. Tuscany.

zalett dialect name for ➤ **gialletti**, cookies.

zambudello old name for ➤ **salamella di Mantova**, a type of sausage.

zammù Palermo dialect name (possibly of Arab origin, perhaps a corruption of ➤ **sambuca**) for a spirit distilled from ➤ **anice stellato**, star anise, thirst-quenching and digestive mixed with cold water. As far back as the 18th century it was a common custom to buy the drink from water sellers in the streets. In the 19th century, a local company patented the secret recipe, which it still produces today.

zampa aka **zampetto** aka **zampino** words used in central Italy for ➤ **piedino**, trotter.

zampa alla parmigiana aka **burrata** boned calf's trotter cut into strips, boiled with herbs, and stewed with vegetables and tomato sauce, with the addition of broth or water, if necessary. Served piping hot with a generous sprinkling of grated Parmigiano and freshly ground black pepper. A traditional dish of Florence and the Chianti area. Tuscany.

zampa di vacca (cow's hoof) regional term for ➤ **arca di Noè**, Noah's ark clam.

zampa di vitello fritta fried calf's trotter. Trotters boiled, sliced, marinated in salt, pepper, parsley, and lemon juice, drained, dipped in a batter of water,

flour, salt, oil and beaten egg, and fried in boiling oil. Friuli-Venezia Giulia.

zampanella a thicker version of the ➤ **borlengo** wafer, typical of the Bologna and Modena Apennines. Emilia-Romagna.

zampetti in umido stewed pig's trotters. The trotters are boiled, then stewed in a mixture of onion, celery, carrot, bay leaves, garlic, sage, and crushed skinned tomatoes with boiled borlotti beans. Umbria, Lazio.

zampi (aka **zampetti**) pig's trotters cooked in boiling salted water for three hours, drained and left to cool, cut lengthwise, and dressed with an aromatic mixture of sea salt, pepper, garlic, chili, rosemary, oil, and vinegar. A traditional recipe of the Castelli Romani area. Lazio.

zampina a mixture of meats dressed with tomato, basil and Pecorino, pressed into lambs' or kids' intestines, wrapped into a spiral and barbecued. Specialty of the province of Bari. Puglia.

zampitti long thin sausages made from scraps of veal, pork and lamb flavored with salt and chili. They are eaten roast or stewed. Puglia.

zampone alla modenese one of the symbols of Emilian cooking. A ➤ **zampone Modena** is steeped in cold water for ten hours, pricked all over with a large needle and nicked at the base. It is then simmered for three to four hours and served in slices with buttered spinach, stewed beans and lentils and puréed potatoes. In Modena they also accompany it with zabaglione made with balsamic vinegar (➤ **aceto balsamico tradizionale**). Emilia-Romagna.

zampone Modena PGI cured meat born in the city of the same name in 1511, today produced in the provinces di Modena, Ferrara, Ravenna, Rimini, Forlì-Cesena, Bologna, Reggio Emilia, Parma, Piacenza, Cremona, Lodi, Pavia, Milan, Varese, Como, Lecco, Bergamo, Brescia, Mantua, Verona and Rovigo. Pork muscle, fat and rind are ground and seasoned with salt and pepper, wine, water, natural flavorings, wine, aromatic spices and herbs. The mixture is cased in the boned hind trotter of a pig. Once dried it can be sold fresh or cooked. Lombardy, Veneto, Emilia-Romagna.

zanchetta aka **zanchettone** names used on the Adriatic coast for ➤ **linguattola**, spotted flounder.

zangone Puglia term for ➤ **grespigno**, field sowthistle.

zanzarele Veneto term for ➤ **stracciatella (1)**, meat broth with eggs.

zanzarella regional term for ➤ **acetosella**, wood sorrel

zarche regional term for ➤ **bietola selvatica**, wild chard.

zassaka another word for ➤ **sasaka**, an old woodmen's snack.

zastoch mixed vegetables (potatoes, pumpkin, beans) boiled and fried with lardo and onions. Friuli-Venezia Giulia.

zavardella a soup whose composition varies according to season, it used to be made with leftover vegetables. It consists of boiled beans, chickpeas, runner beans and field greens, chopped potatoes, peppers and eggplants (in season peas or artichokes might also be added). When the soup is almost ready, roughly torn pieces of toasted bread are addded. It is served hot or warm with a drizzle of extra virgin oil. Lazio.

zavata another word for ➤ **sfoiada**, cream pastry.

zazzicchia pork sausage flavored with chili and orange zest. Usually served broiled. Lazio.

zebinata baked vegetable casserole. Agrigento. Sicily.

Zelten rich ➤ **pandolce** made of bread dough or a dough of flour (traditionally rye flour), yeast, milk, eggs, butter, and sugar, to which chopped dried figs, dates, raisins, walnuts, almonds, pine kernels and candied orange zest, sugar and grappa or brandy are added. Worked into a round or rectangular (or, in Alto Adige, oval) shape, it is topped with walnuts and/or almonds, brushed with honey and baked. Before serving, it is decorated with candied cherries and other fruits. Originally baked at Christmas. Trentino-Alto Adige.

zembi d'arzillo ravioli filled with fish (mullet, scorpion fish, cappone, all rock fish with a smell of algae, *arzillo* in dialetto), escarole, borage, and aromatic herbs. Served with a sauce made with a broth from the heads and bones of the fish and tomato. A specialty of Genoa. Liguria.

zemin Ligurian dialect name for ➤ **zimino**, a stew or soup which includes spinach or chard among the ingredients. The word refers both to the type of preparation (➤ **seppie a zemin**, the equivalent of the Tuscan ➤ **seppie in inzimino**) and to the recipe that requires it (➤ **zemin di ceci**, a soup in which boiled chickpeas are used to flavor a base of lightly fried onion and parsley, dried mushrooms, tomatoes and chopped chard, sprinkled with grated grana. Liguria.

zemin di ceci ➤ **zemin**.

zenzero (1) ginger (*Zingiber officinalis*). Root of the plant of the same name, a native of Asia. Sold fresh or dried, whole, in pieces or powdered. It is not widely used in Italian cooking, save in confectionery (candied), in a few old sauces (➤ **salsa tredura**) and in contemporary creative cooking.

zenzero (2) term used in Tuscany for ➤ **peperoncino**, chili.

zeppole sweet ring-shaped fritters common

throughout southern Italy and the islands. Traditionally made during the Carnival period with wheat flour, sugar and a variety of ingredients depending on locality. In Naples, they cook wheat flour in water and wine and shape the dough into rings, which they fry and dust with sugar and cinnamon. In another version, ➤ scauratielli, typical of inland areas, they are coated with a syrup of honey, sugar, cinnamon and vanilla, and scattered with ➤ diavulilli (➤ diavolina, confetti sugar). On the Sorrentina peninsula, they are sometimes aromatized with anise liqueur and decorated with grapes in alcohol and citrus fruit zest, in which case they are called ➤ zeppule vullute (boiled).

zeppole di rossetti fritters of the tiny transparent goby (➤ rossetti), mixed with grated Parmigiano and Pecorino, fresh breadcrumbs soaked in fumet (➤ fumetto (1)) and squeezed dry. The mixture is shaped into small balls, which are first left to set in the refrigerator, then fried in olive oil. Campania.

zeppole di san Giuseppe beignets shaped into rings, fried and dusted with confectioner's sugar. The hollowed center is filled with confectioner's custard and decorated with dollops of cherry jam. A relatively recent recipe made in Campania for the saint's feast day. Very similar are the zeppole of the Salentine peninsula (Puglia), the only difference being that eggs are added to the mixure and the beignets are fried twice, first in hot oil, then in boiling oil (a technique that causes them to swell up more). They are served filled with confectioner's custard, garnished with a syruped almond and dusted with confectioner's sugar.

zeppule vullute ➤ zeppole.

zeppulelle small ➤ zeppole made of ➤ pasta cresciuta.

zeraria cold dish of boiled veal and ham (head and trotters included) first cooled, then sliced and covered with their own broth, which solidifies into jelly. The meat is served on lemon leaves and the jelly is flavored with saffron. A traditional specialty of Imperia. Liguria.

zerlo aka zero aka zerolo regional terms for ➤ zerro, pickarel.

zerro pickarel (Centrocanthus cirrus). A fish common in Italian waters whose rather bony flesh is much enjoyed in some regions, such as Liguria and Puglia. The smallest specimens can be preserved in salt and covered with olive oil and vinegar. The zerlo di Noli (Liguria) is included in the Italian Ministry of Agriculture's database of native and/or traditional food products.

zerri sotto pesto pickarel dipped in flour and fried, then transferrd to a bowl with peppercorns and finely minced garlic and chili. Covered with vinegar, they are left to rest for half a day before serving. Specialty of Livorno. Tuscany. Livorno, Toscana.

zest candied orange zest, a specialty of Carignano (Turin), Piedmont.

zibba Sardinian term for ➤ salicornia, samphire.

zichi ladu another name for ➤ spianada, a type of bread.

Ziegel in Italian aka Mattone. A washed rind cheese made with raw milk from Pinzgauer cows. Trentino-Alto Adige.

ziga Tuscan term for ➤ tellina, tellin or wedge shell clam.

zigarella regional term for ➤ cepola, red band fish.

zigari sweet fingers made with crumbled cookies, flour, eggs, sugar, and cinnamon, dipped in beaten egg and baked in the oven. Friuli-Venezia Giulia.

Ziger aka Zigerkäse rare cow's milk cheese aromatized with chives, salt and pepper.

Typical of the Val Pusteria Valle Isarco. Veneto.

ziminada aka **zimino** other words for → **trattalia**, an offal dish.

zimino the term may derive from the Arab *samin* (fat), *samana* (to grease) or *cimino* (a corruption of → **cumino**, cumin). Today it refers to stews or soups which include spinach or chard among the ingredients. Common with fish (cuttlefish and salt cod), legumes (chickpeas and beans) and meat, especially offal (→ **lampredotto**, tripe), especially popular in Tuscany (→ **inzimino**) and Liguria (→ **zemin**).

Zimtsterne spicy, star-shaped cookies traditionally hung on the Christmas tree. Trentino-Alto Adige.

Zincarlin della Val di Muggio uncooked cheese made with cow's milk and small additions of goat's milk, aromatized with black pepper and salt. A Slow Food presidium protects a version aged for at least a month and a half inside earthenware pitchers (*ole*). Produced on the border between Lombardy and the Swiss Cantone Ticino.

zingara slices of pork flavored with a sauce of peppers, pickled onions, capers and parsley. A specialty of Reggio Emilia. Emilia-Romagna.

zinurra wild artichokes with oil, pepper and parsely. If eggs are scrambled into the mixture, the name becomes *zinurra ca' trimma*. Calabria.

zippulas Carnival fritters flavored with orange, grappa and saffron. Sardinia.

zireno part of a cow's intestine, eaten roasted or boiled.

zite allardiate pasta served with onion, lard, tomato and a generous sprinkling of Percorino cheese and ground black pepper.

ziti aka **zite** very long hollow commercial durum wheat pasta, usually snapped into two or more parts before cooking. Best enjoyed with rich sauces or baked with strong cheeses. Other names: → **candele**, → **schiaffoni**, → **zitoni**.

ziti tagliati → **penne**.

zitoncini alla Campolattaro pasta (→ **ziti**) served with a thick sauce of crushed anchovies and tuna belly (→ **ventresca**). Campania.

zitoni → **ziti**.

zizola Veneto term for → **giuggiola**, jujube.

zlicnijaki soft pumpkin dumplings of Slovenian origin. Friuli.

zoccolo a layer of rice, polenta or purée that serves as a base or bed for another food.

zonclada aka **zonglada** shortcrust pastry tart filled with a mixture of ricotta and dried fruits. A recipe of medieval origin typical of Treviso. Veneto.

zonzella another name for → **ficattola**, a small fried focaccia.

zoppina regional term for → **violetta** violet.

zotolo Veneto and Friuli word for → **seppietta**, dward bobtail squid.

zucca pumpkin. Of the many varieties cultivated in Italy, the two most cultivated are *Cucurbita moschata* and *C. maxima*. Every part of the pumpkin is edible, from the flowers to the flesh to the seeds, toasted and salted and known as → **bruscolini** or → **brustolini**, In the south, even the skin is cut into thin slices and marinated. The Italian Ministry of Agriculture's database of native and/or traditional food products lists: *zucca lunga di Napoli e napoletana* (Campania); *zucca di Rocchetta Cengio* (Liguria); *zucca mantovana e altre della Lombardia* (Lombardy); *zucca di Castellazzo Bormida* (Piedmont); *zucca da semi toscana, zucca lardaia* (Tuscany); *marina di Chioggia, santa bellunese* (Veneto). The pumpkin is extremely versatile in the kitchen, where it can be fried (→ **zucca fritta**, → **zucca in tegame**), baked or marinated (→ **zucca gialla all'agrodolce**,→

zucca alla veneta. Pastas stuffed with pumpkin include ➤ **cappellacci ferraresi,** ➤ **tortelli di zucca,** and pumpkin flesh is mixed into the dough of ➤ **gnocchi di zucca** and ➤ **pane di zucca.** It appears in risottos and soups (➤ **minestra di zucca,** ➤ **riso e zucca**) and also cakes and confectionery (➤ **torta di zucca,** ➤ **frittelle di zucca,** ➤ **pan zal,** ➤ **zuccata**). Its flowers, finally, are stuffed and fried like those of zucchini.

zucca alla veneta la zucca, fried pumpkin slices layered with basil leaves and marinated in warm vinegar flavored with garlic, salt and pepper.

zucca fritta pumpkin slices boiled in milk, breaded and fried in butter. Lombardy.

zucca gialla all'agrodolce fried pumpkin slices marinated in a mixture of vinegar, sugar and the frying oil aromatized with crushed garlic and mint. Sicily.

zucca in tegame diced pumpkin flesh stewed with onion until creamy. Veneto.

zucca ripiena pumpkin stuffed with ground meat, eggs, breadcrumbs, Pecorino, garlic and parsley. Calabria.

zucca secca dehydrated pumpkin revived in warm water and fried. Sicily, Campania.

zuccarini similar to ➤ **savoiardi** sponge fingers but sprinkled with refined sugar. Typical of Nicosia, in the province of Enna. Sicily.

zuccata common name for candied pumpkin, used in Sicilian confectionery as an ingredient or as a decoration.

zuccherare to sugar or to sweeten.

zuccherini iced anise cookies typical of the Valle del Bisenzio (Tuscany), where they are baked for weddings and eaten dunked in Vin Santo, milk or coffee. A similar recipe with minced almonds in the paste and anise liqueur in the icing is made in the province of Modena (Emilia-Romagna).

zuccherini di Bettona small round cakes dotted with raisins, pine kernels, anise seeds and candied fruit typical of the town of the same name in the province of Perugia. Umbria.

zucchero sugar.

zucchero d'orzo a hard sugar candy aromatized with orange blossom water, mint or lemon.

zucchetta another name for ➤ **bondeana,** cow's or pig's intestine.

zucchina aka **zucchino** zuccchini (*Cucurbita pepo*). A member of the same family as the water melon and the cucumber. Besides the flesh, the bright yellow flowers are also edible. The Italian Ministry of Agriculture's database of native and/ or traditional food products lists: *zucchina con il fiore* (Lazio); *alberello di Sarzana, genovese, trombetta* (Liguria); *zucchina di Borgo d'Ale* (Piedmont); *lunga fiorentina, mora pisana, sarzanese, tonda fiorentina* (Tuscany); *zucchino di Misilmeri* (Sicily). Young zucchini may be eaten raw, finely sliced in salads, preserved in oil, stuffed (➤ **zucchine ripiene**), grilled, fried, baked (➤ **zucchine alla velletrana**), marinated (➤ **carpionata,** ➤ **saor**), stewed (➤ **zucchine alla poverella**), or used as an ingredient in pies, molds, soups and first courses (➤ **parmigiana di zucchine,** ➤ **frittata di zucchine,** ➤ **zuppa di zucchine,** ➤ **minestra alla viterbese**). The flowers can be used to make frittatas, or stuffed and fried (➤ **sciurilli**).

zucchine a cassola zucchini cut into matchsticks and cooked with oil, onion, parsley, basil and, in some cases, tomato sauce. Sardinia.

zucchine a scapece fried zucchini with Roman mint marinated with vinegar and water boiled with garlic cloves and a few spoonfuls of the frying oil. Campania.

zucchine al funghetto ➤ **zucchine trifolate**.

zucchine alla poverella zucchini cut into rounds, fried until golden and served with minced mint and parsley and a dash of vinegar. Puglia.

zucchine alla velletrana zucchini sliced into rounds, dipped in flour and baked in the oven with rosemary and garlic. Lazio.

zucchine ripiene zucchini stuffed with a mixture of their own minced flesh, ground meat, eggs, Parmigiano and breadcrumbs cooked in tomato sauce and served with meatballs. Emilia-Romagna.

zucchine ripiene alla lodigiana zucchni stuffed with a sweet and sour mixture of their own minced flesh, onions, bèchamel sauce, cream, mascarpone, grated cheese, sultanas, crushed amaretti cookies, eggs, salt, pepper and nutmeg. Lombardy.

zucchine trifolate zucchini cut into thin rounds, fried in oil and garlic until golden and aromatized with minced calamint or parsley. Tuscany.

zuccotto said to be one of the first Italian semifreddi. A dessert consisting of a domed sponge cake casing, soaked in liqueur, with a creamy chocolate-flavored ricotta filling dotted with candied fruit, almonds and hazelnuts. Today the ricotta is sometimes replaced by confectioner's custard.

zuf a sort of soft polenta of wheat flour, milk and water seasoned with salt and dotted with generous amounts of butter (sometimes boiled pumpkin flesh is also added). Friuli-Venezia Giulia.

zuffritto ➤ **suffritte**.

zuppa soup. The Italian word originally referred to a soup or broth poured over a slice of day-old bread or toast bread, but the meaning now also comprises *minestra in brodo*, a broth in which rice or pasta are cooked, or a broth in which other sliced or diced ingredients such as meat or vegetables or fish are cooked.

züpa cundida dry rye bread softened with hot water or broth to which pieces of cheese and onions are added. Lombardy.

zuppa ai funghi cardoncelli soup of beans, pork rind, king oyster mushrooms (➤ **cardoncello**) and bread. Basilicata.

zuppa al vino ➤ **Weinsuppe**.

zuppa alla marinara aka **zuppa alla napoletana** fish soup with fresh tomatoes, flavored with parsley and garlic and served over toasted bread. Campania.

zuppa alla pavese hot broth poured over toasted bread with a freshly shelled egg on top. When the yolk sets, the soup is sprinkled with Parmigiano-Reggiano and served. A dish said to have been invented by a peasant woman to feed a hungry Francois I, King of France, during the Battle of Pavia. Lombardy.

zuppa con il cavolo nero a soup of "black cabbage" (➤ **cavolo nero**) typical of Lake Trasimeno. Umbria.

zuppa corsa "Corsican" fish soup, made along the coast from Massa to Piombino, in which the fish flesh is liquidized and served with a *rouille* of red peppers, boiled potato, fish livers and fumet (➤ **fumetto**) and julienned Gruyère cheese. Tuscany.

zuppa dei prati mixed meadow flowers and herbs (primulas, violets, campion, good KIng Henry, shepherd's purse, wild cardoon, mountain oregano and so on) cooked in meat broth thickened with eggs. An old recipe from Parre (Bergamo). Lombardy.

zuppa dei trappetari soup of boiled fava beans, cherry tomatoes and chicory or broccoli. Typical of the Gargano peninsula (Foggia). Puglia.

zuppa del monaco Christmas Eve soup of chicory cooked in chicken broth. Basilicata.

zuppa del Tarlati a sort of chicken velouté said by some to be of French origin, imported during the period in which Tarlati, the Ghibelline bishop of Arezzo had a stormy relationship with the Pope in Avignon. The people of Arezzo claim it as their own. Tuscany.

zuppa di accia/accio (1) celery soup with toasted bread, sliced hard-boiled eggs, diced Caciocavallo and sausage. Basilicata, Calabria.

zuppa di accia/accio (2) salad of shredded boiled beef and celery. Calabria.

zuppa di aglietti garlic soup thickened with beaten eggs. Campania.

zuppa di agnello lamb's offal cooked in broth. An old specialty of the province of Grosseto. Tuscany.

zuppa di ajucche baked soup of spiked rampion leaves (➤ ajucca), boiled in a broth of pork ribs and pig's trotters, layered with day-old bread, sausage, Parmigiano-Reggiano and cheese. Typical of the Canavese area. Piedmont.

zuppa di amarene a dessert of sour cherries cooked in red wine aromatized with sugar, cinnamon, cloves and lemon zest and sugar poured over thin slices of bread. Lombardy.

zuppa di anguille alla comacchiese eel soup with vegetables, a recipe typical of Comacchio (Ravenna). Emilia-Romagna.

zuppa di arselle soup of clams, garlic and parsley. Sardinia.

zuppa di asparagi asparagus soup. Veneto.

zuppa di baccalà e cavoletti soup of salt cod and "black cabbage" (➤ cavolo nero). Lazio.

zuppa di baccalà sweet and sour soup of salt cod, dried figs, sweet peppers, walnuts prunes, raisins and boiled cauliflower. Campania.

zuppa di boldrò/bùdego soup of monkfish (➤ rana pescatrice in Italian, boldrò or bùdego in dialect) with tomatoes and dried mushrooms. Liguria.

zuppa di broccolo fiolaro soup with the broccolo fiolaro, a broccoli ecotype grown in Creazzo (Vicenza). Veneto.

zuppa di cacigni e fagioli soup of beans and field sowthistle (➤ grespigno in Italian,➤ cascign in dialect), a herb that is particularly popular in the region. Abruzzo.

zuppa di cappone small "dumplings" of fresh breadcrumbs, eggs, minced prosciutto, nutmeg, salt and bone marrow. Cooked and served in capon broth. Lazio.

zuppa di carciofi e patate seasonal soup of artichokes and potatoes. Umbria.

zuppa di carni e rigaglie a soup of finely chopped beaf and chicken giblets, bone marrow, vegetables and tomato paste poured over bread and sprinkled with grated Grana Padano cheese. Veneto.

zuppa di castagne e ceci classic Christmas Eve soup of chestnuts and chickpeas, Umbria.

zuppa di cavoli alla canavesana baked soup of Savoy cabbage leaves layered with slices of day-old bread and cheese. Typical of the Canavese area. Piedmont.

zuppa di ceci chickpea soup, usually flavored with garlic, sage and rosemary, though combinations vary. Tuscany.

zuppa di cetrioli cold soup of cucumbers and ripe tomatoes. Trentino-Alto Adige.

zuppa di cicale soup of mantis shrimps and tomato. Typical of the province of Livorno. Tuscany.

zuppa di cicerchie al tartufo a velouté of grass peas, bacon, rosemary, parsley, chili potatoes and tomatoes, served with egg pasta quadrucci. Umbria.

zuppa di cicoria alla napoletana soup of chicory in pork broth with sausage (➤ cervellatine). Campania.

zuppa di cipolle onion soup. Common, with variations, all over Italy, in the central regions also known as ➤ **cipollata**.

zuppa di cocchi soup made with Caesar mushrooms (➤ **ovoli** in Italian, *cocchi* in dialect), fresh tomatoes and broth, thickened with beaten eggs. Typical of the northern Maremma area. Tuscany.

zuppa di cozziche soup of mussels with garlic and ripe tomatoes. Campania.

zuppa di crauti soup of sauerkraut and polenta flavored with cumin seeds. Trentino-Alto Adige.

zuppa di farro soup of emmer (➤ **farro**) and vegetables. Umbria.

zuppa di farro e cavolo emmer (➤ **farro**) and cabbage soup. Umbria.

zuppa di fave velouté of fava beans. A soup common all over southern Italy.

zuppa di fegato liver soup. Ground calf's liver browned in butter, placed on slices of bread and covered with boiling meat broth garnished with chopped chives. The same soup is sometimes made with chopped spleen instead of liver. Trentino-Alto Adige.

zuppa di fegato e polmoni pork offal soup with tomatoes and raisins.

zuppa di finocchi baked soup of boiled wild fennel layered with slices of fried bread and cheese. Sardinia.

zuppa di fosso an old, now rare soup of snails, frogs, eels, crabs and chard made in the area round Castagneto, in the province of Livorno. Tuscany.

zuppa di funghi mushroom soup. Made in a variety of ways, with a variety of names and a variety of mushrooms all over Italy.

zuppa di indivia baked soup of boiled endive flavored with ground beef layered with toasted day-old bread and Pecorino. Sardinia.

zuppa di lenticchie a soup of lentils, tomatoes, celery, chard and potatoes served with toasted ➤ **fregola**. Sardinia.

zuppa di lumache soup of snails with peas and cream. Typical of the Val Venosta, Trentino-Alto Adige.

zuppa di lupini in compagnia soup of lupins (➤ **lupino**) land mixed vegetables, broth, shredded pork and diced Caciocavallo cheese. Campania.

zuppa di mandorle a baked dessert of fried bread covered with a cream of almonds, milk, sugar and spices. Val d'Aosta.

zuppa di milza meat broth with meatballs made with calf's spleen, eggs, breadcrumbs and marjoram. Veneto.

zuppa di muscoli soup of mussels, tomato, onion and garlic. Liguria.

zuppa di orzo e sedano barley and celery soup. Umbria.

zuppa di pane e pomodori soup of day-old bread and tomatoes, flavored with basil, locally known as ➤ **pancotto**. Umbria.

zuppa di patate potato soup. Various recipes exist, in some of which (in Tuscany in particular) the potatoes are puréed to a cream.

zuppa di pesce fish soup. Made in various ways all round the Italian coast.

zuppa di pesce alla lariana aka **zuppa di pesce alla tremezzina** soup of lake fish (perch, el, pike, trout and so on) typical of Tremezzo (Como). Lombardy.

zuppa di pesce azzurro soup of fish made with so-called ➤ **pesce azzurro**: garfish, mackerel, horse mackerel and so forth. Tuscany.

zuppa di pollo chicken soup. A specialty of Treviso. Veneto.

zuppa di poveracce soup of clams (*poveracce* in dialect) with parsley and cherry tomatoes. Emilia-Romagna.

zuppa di radicchio soup of red radicchio cooked in beef or chicken broth. Veneto.

zuppa di rane soup of boned frogs with aromatic vegetables. Typical of Imola, in the province of Bologna. Emilia-Romagna.

zuppa di ricotta slices of day-old bread soaked in salted boiling water covered with melted butter and dusted with grated smoked ricotta. Friuli-Venezia Giulia.

zuppa di ripieni vegetables (pumpkins, zucchini, eggplants, tomatoes, peppers, potatoes) stuffed with ground veal, eggs, breadcrumbs, Pecorino, garlic and parsley and stewed in tomato sauce. Calabria.

zuppa di santa Lucia a thick soup of beans, wheat berries, herbs and peppers (➤ **papaccella**) prepared on the eve of the saint's day. Campania.

zuppa di sarde a mixture of finely minced fried sardines, garlic, parsley and red pepper sprinkled with parsley and oregano and served on toast.

zuppa di scarole e spollichini escarole and bean soup. Liquid soup of fresh ➤ **canellino** beans and escarole with the addition of chili, guanciale, skinned tomatoes, and garlic, poured over toasted bread. In Naples they prepare a thicker version by adding pork rind, salami and ham bones to the bean broth. Campania.

zuppa di soffritto➤ **suffritte.**

zuppa di telline a stew of wedge shell clams, garlic and tomatoes. Lazio.

zuppa di tozzetti dessert typical of the Viterbo countryside of cookies (➤ **tozzetti**) covered with a chocolate cream and decorated with confetti sugar. Lazio.

zuppa di trippe a soup of tripe, tomatoes and vegetables flavored with nutmeg. Piedmont.

zuppa di vino a soup of meat broth, white wine (preferably Terlano), egg whites and cream flavored with cinnamon. Trentino-Alto Adige.

zuppa di vongole soup of clams, garlic, parsley and tomatoes. Campania.

zuppa di zucca pumpkin soup. A velouté served with slices of toasted bread or, in some cases, rice. Veneto, Friuli-Venezia Giulia.

zuppa di zucchine zucchini soup thickened with beaten eggs and garnished with minced basil and parsley. Campania.

zuppa frantoiana puréed beans with mixed vegetables (variable according to season) poured over slices of bread and drizzled liberally with extra virgin olive oil.

zuppa imperiale squares of a flatbread made from a dough of semolina, eggs, Parmigiano, salt, nutmeg and butter, cooked in meat broth. Emilia-Romagna.

zuppa inglese literally "English soup." Normally translated as trifle, but actually a dessert of sponge cake or fingers layered with confectioner's custard and chocolate cream.

zuppa lombarda bean soup with garlic served on toast rubbed with garlic. Tuscany.

zuppa pasqualina an elaborate soup of chicken and lamb broth with spinach, chicken livers and the shredded meat from the broth served over thin slices of day-old bread. Typical of Siena, Tuscany.

zuppa sarda ➤ **suppa cuatta.**

zuppa volterrana soup of bean broth, vegetables and pork rind. Typical of Volterra (Pisa). Tuscany.

zuppetta di alici anchovy soup. Campania.

zuppetta di latte e ricotta runny polenta topped with smoked ricotta. Friuli.

zuppetta di semolino a cream of semolina, water and milk. Friuli- Venezia Giulia.

zuppino a hearty soup of ➤ **cotechino,** pork rind, Savoy cabbage and other vegetables. Lombardy.

zurrette spring dish of lamb's stomach filled with the animal's blood mixed with pieces of fried lard, bread and slightly acid fresh cheese.